Commentary on the First Geneva Convention

Convention (I) for the Amelioration of the Condition of the Wounded and Sick in Armed Forces in the Field

The application and interpretation of the four Geneva Conventions of 1949 and their two Additional Protocols of 1977 have developed significantly in the sixty years since the International Committee of the Red Cross (ICRC) first published its Commentaries on these important humanitarian treaties. To promote a better understanding of, and respect for, this body of law, the ICRC commissioned a comprehensive update of its original Commentaries, of which this is the first volume.

The First Convention is a foundational text of international humanitarian law. It contains the essential rules on the protection of the wounded and sick, those assigned to their care, and the red cross and red crescent emblems. This article-by-article Commentary takes into account developments in the law and practice to provide up-to-date interpretations of the Convention. The new Commentary has been reviewed by humanitarian-law practitioners and academics from around the world. It is an essential tool for anyone working or studying within this field.

INTERNATIONAL COMMITTEE OF THE RED CROSS

COMMENTARY ON THE FIRST GENEVA CONVENTION

Convention (I) for the Amelioration of the Condition of the Wounded and Sick in Armed Forces in the Field

EDITORIAL COMMITTEE
Knut Dörmann, Liesbeth Lijnzaad, Marco Sassòli and
Philip Spoerri

PROJECT TEAM
Jean-Marie Henckaerts, Head of Project
Lindsey Cameron, Bruno Demeyere, Eve La Haye,
Iris Müller and Heike Niebergall-Lackner

CAMBRIDGE
UNIVERSITY PRESS

CAMBRIDGE
UNIVERSITY PRESS

University Printing House, Cambridge CB2 8BS, United Kingdom

One Liberty Plaza, 20th Floor, New York, NY 10006, USA

477 Williamstown Road, Port Melbourne, VIC 3207, Australia

4843/24, 2nd Floor, Ansari Road, Daryaganj, Delhi – 110002, India

79 Anson Road, #06–04/06, Singapore 079906

Cambridge University Press is part of the University of Cambridge.

It furthers the University's mission by disseminating knowledge in the pursuit of education, learning and research at the highest international levels of excellence.

www.cambridge.org
Information on this title: www.cambridge.org/9781107170100

First published 2016

Printed in the United Kingdom by TJ International Ltd. Padstow Cornwall

A catalogue record for this publication is available from the British Library.

ISBN 978-1-107-17010-0 Hardback
ISBN 978-1-316-62123-3 Paperback

CONTENTS

Contents ix

Contents

FOREWORD BY PETER MAURER
President of the International Committee of the Red Cross

When the original Commentary on the First Geneva Convention was written in 1952, the horrors of the Second World War were still fresh in people's memory, but so was the humanitarian spirit that prevailed at the 1949 Diplomatic Conference and that made the adoption of the Geneva Conventions possible. More than 60 years later, we find ourselves confronted with a similar contradiction.

On the one hand, we are witnessing an increasing fragmentation and complexity in today's armed conflicts, which are often characterized by disregard for the law. The misery they engender – the suffering of children, the despair of families trapped in sieges or forced from their homes, the abuse of the wounded and sick – is brought daily to our attention through different media channels. On the other hand, the community of States has agreed on a stronger and more comprehensive normative legal framework than ever before. We know that the values that found expression in the Geneva Conventions have become an essential part of our common heritage of humanity, as growing numbers of people around the world share a moral and legal conviction in them.

These contradicting realities challenge us to act: to react to the suffering and violations of the law, and to prevent them from occurring in the first place.

In these efforts, it is part of the ICRC's role and mandate to work towards a common understanding of international humanitarian law through engagement with all stakeholders, including political and religious leaders, key opinion and policymakers, academic circles, the judiciary and, last but not least, weapon bearers.

With this updated Commentary on the First Geneva Convention, the ICRC presents a new tool for practitioners and scholars, as part of our joint endeavour to close the gap between the law as it stands and the law as it is applied on the ground.

We know that the first editions of the Commentaries on the four Geneva Conventions have been useful for military and civilian practitioners as well as for judges and academics. A lot of time has passed since the first editions were published, and we have gained a great deal of experience in applying and interpreting the Conventions in contexts very different from those that led to their adoption. This is why, five years ago, the ICRC committed itself to the monumental task of updating all the existing Commentaries and of preparing new guidance on the basis of a variety of sources, including interpretations by States and courts over the past decades. With the publication of the first instalment, the Commentary on the First Convention, we have reached the first milestone.

The ICRC is in a unique position to oversee the updating of the Commentaries. The organization combines the perspectives of law and operations, and the updated Commentaries benefit from the input of colleagues representing these aspects of our work. Equally importantly, the updated Commentary was opened to unprecedented external input from a global network of scholars and practitioners, who drafted commentaries on specific articles of the Convention, reviewed all the drafts and gave advice. The final text is thus the result of a collaborative process.

The new Commentary provides guidance on and contextualization of the Convention's rules. It presents the ICRC's interpretation of the law, but it also indicates the main diverging views and issues requiring further discussion and clarification. The ICRC will duly take this updated Commentary into account in its daily work, while being aware that practice and interpretations may evolve over time.

The ICRC expresses its gratitude to the experts who gave freely of their time and expertise, in particular the external contributors and peer reviewers. It also thanks the members of the Editorial Committee, the project team and other staff members who brought the updated Commentary to fruition.

In presenting this volume to the States party to the Geneva Conventions, to National Red Cross and Red Crescent Societies and other humanitarian organizations, to judges and scholars and to other interested parties, the ICRC sincerely hopes that this Commentary, along with others to come in the years ahead, will clarify the meaning and significance of the Geneva Conventions and help to ensure greater protection for war victims.

ACKNOWLEDGEMENTS

This Commentary would not have been possible without the involvement of numerous persons, and the ICRC expresses its gratitude to all of them. We apologize to anyone whose name may have been inadvertently omitted.

Editorial Committee

The Editorial Committee supervised the drafting and reviewed all drafts prior to the peer-review process and again prior to publication. It consisted of two ICRC staff members: Philip Spoerri, ICRC Permanent Observer to the United Nations in New York and Director of International Law and Cooperation from 2006 until 2014, and Knut Dörmann, Chief Legal Officer and Head of the Legal Division, as well as two external members, Liesbeth Lijnzaad, Legal Adviser of the Ministry of Foreign Affairs of the Netherlands and Professor of the Practice of International Law at the University of Maastricht, and Marco Sassòli, Professor of International Law at the University of Geneva and Associate Professor of International Law at the University of Quebec in Montreal.

ICRC project team

The ICRC project team was composed of Jean-Marie Henckaerts, who, as head of project, was responsible for the project's overall coordination and final harmonization, as well as Lindsey Cameron, Bruno Demeyere, Eve La Haye, Iris Müller and Heike Niebergall-Lackner, legal advisers in the ICRC Legal Division.

The project team organized, coordinated and supervised the research, drafting and review of this Commentary throughout the various stages. In addition, it conducted most of the research for the Commentary. Its members contributed numerous drafts, revised, edited and harmonized all drafts, and integrated the peer-review feedback, in consultation with the authors.

Reading Committee

The Reading Committee consisted of the external contributors, in addition to the project team. It reviewed the drafts to ensure the cross-subject coherence and overall consistency of the Commentary. It comprised:

- François Bugnion, Member of the ICRC Assembly
- Dana Constantin, academic coordinator of the Berlin Potsdam Research Group 'The International Rule of Law – Rise or Decline?', Humboldt University, Berlin (until May 2016)
- Prof. Geoffrey S. Corn, Professor of Law, South Texas Law School, Houston; Lieutenant Colonel (ret.), US Army
- Helen Durham, Director of International Humanitarian Law, Australian Red Cross (2007–2014) and currently Director of Law and Policy, ICRC
- Prof. Robin Geiss, Chair of International Law and Security, University of Glasgow
- Prof. Jann K. Kleffner, Professor of International Law and Head of the International Law Centre, Swedish Defence University, Stockholm
- Michael Meyer, Head of International Law, British Red Cross
- Stephan Michel, Head of Treaty Section, Swiss Federal Department of Foreign Affairs, Directorate of International Law
- Claude Schenker, Deputy Head of Treaty Section, Swiss Federal Department of Foreign Affairs, Directorate of International Law
- Prof. Sandesh Sivakumaran, Professor of Public International Law, University of Nottingham
- Sylvain Vité, Lecturer at Bilkent University, Ankara (2013–2015) and currently Legal Adviser, ICRC.

In addition, Professors Wolff Heintschel von Heinegg of Europa-Universität Viadrina (Viadrina European University), Frankfurt (Oder), Bruce Oswald of Melbourne Law School, Gary Solis of Georgetown Law School and Sean Watts of Creighton University Law School provided comments on select commentaries, and Professor Georg Nolte of Humboldt University Berlin kindly reviewed the Introduction.

Peer-review group

The drafts were submitted to a large and geographically representative group of peer reviewers, who, between September 2014 and February 2015, reviewed the drafts and provided comments in their personal capacity. The feedback from the peer-review group has been important to completing the drafting process.

The peer-review process would not have been possible without the assistance of ICRC legal advisers in delegations around the world.

The peer-review group consisted of the following persons:

Algeria

Prof. Kamel Filali, Professor of International Law at the University of Constantine; Member of the African Union Commission on International Law; former Vice-President of the UN Committee on the Rights of the Child.

Argentina

Dr Jose Alejandro Consigli, Rector of FASTA University of Córdoba; former Invited Professor of International Humanitarian Law at the Naval War College and the Superior War College of the Army of Argentina.

Armenia

Dr Vladimir Vardanyan, Head of the Legal Advisory Service, Constitutional Court of the Republic of Armenia; Lecturer, European and International Law Department, Yerevan State University.

Australia

Prof. Rob MacLaughlin, Associate Professor, Australian National University College of Law, Canberra.

Richard Rowe PSM, former Senior Legal Adviser, Department of Foreign Affairs and Trade, Australia; Adjunct Professor, Australian National University College of Law, Canberra.

Azerbaijan

Dr Latif Hüseynov, Professor of Public International Law, Baku State University; former Member of the European Committee for the Prevention of Torture; Director of the Department for Constitutional Law, Secretariat of the Milli Mejilis (Parliament) of the Republic of Azerbaijan.

Belarus

Dr Andrey L. Kozik, Secretary-General of the International Law and Arbitration Association (Belarus); Member of the Belarus National Commission on the Implementation of International Humanitarian Law.

Belgium

Prof. Eric David, Professor Emeritus, Université Libre de Bruxelles; Member of the International Humanitarian Fact-Finding Commission.

Bolivia

Prof. Elizabeth Santalla Vargas, Consultant, Professor and Researcher specializing in international law, international criminal law, humanitarian law and human rights law; Rapporteur for the Oxford International Organizations Project conducted by the Manchester International Law Centre.

Brazil

Tarciso Dal Maso Jardim, Member of the National Commission of International Humanitarian Law of Brazil; Legal Adviser of the Senate of Brazil; Adviser to the President of the Supreme Court of Brazil.

Canada

Major-General Blaise Cathcart, Judge Advocate General of the Canadian Armed Forces.

Chile

Ambassador Hernán Salinas Burgos, Professor of International Law and Head of the Department of International Law, Pontificia Universidad Católica de Chile (Pontifical Catholic University of Chile); Member of the Inter-American Juridical Committee of the Organization of American States; former Member of the International Humanitarian Fact-Finding Commission and former President of the National Commission of International Humanitarian Law of Chile.

China

Senior Colonel (ret.) Xiao Fengcheng, Professor of Law at China University of Political Science and Law, Beijing; former Member of the Bureau of Legislative Affairs of the Central Military Commission.

Dr Ling Yan, Professor of International Law, Faculty of International Law, China University of Political Science and Law, Beijing.

Colombia

Prof. Alejandro Ramelli Arteaga, Professor at the Universidad Externado de Colombia; Magistrado Auxiliar de la Corte Constitucional de Colombia (Assistant Magistrate of the Constitutional Court of Colombia).

Brigadier General del Aire (Air Force Brigadier General) Juan Carlos Gómez Ramírez, Jefe de la Jefatura Jurídica y Derechos Humanos de la Fuerza Aérea Colombiana (Head of the Legal and Human Rights Office of the Colombian Air Force).

Côte d'Ivoire

Prof. Djedjro Francisco Meledje, Professeur titulaire de droit public et de science politique, Université de Cocody (Full Professor of Public Law and Political Science, University of Cocody).

Croatia

Prof. Davorin Lapas, Faculty of Law, University of Zagreb.

Democratic Republic of the Congo

Prof. Gérard Balanda Mikuin Leliel, Professor at the Université de Kinshasa, Faculté de Droit and Université Protestante au Congo (Professor at the University of Kinshasa, Faculty of Law, and Congo Protestant University); President, Commission permanente de réforme du droit congolais (President of the Standing Committee on Congolese Law Reform); former President of the Supreme Court (until 1998).

Egypt

Prof. Ahmed Abou El Wafa, Professor of International Law, Faculty of Law, Cairo University.

France

Eric Darré, médecin général, inspecteur du service de santé des armées, Ministère français de la Défense (Major General MD, Inspector of the French Military Medical Services, French Ministry of Defence).

Prof. Emmanuel Decaux, Professor at Université Panthéon-Assas Paris II; Member of the UN Committee on Enforced Disappearances and former Chair (2012–2015).

Georgia

Tamar Tomashvili, Assistant Professor of Law, Free University of Tbilisi, Faculty of Law.

Germany

Dr Dieter Fleck, former Director of International Agreements and Policy, German Ministry of Defence.

Greece

Ambassador Stelios Perrakis, Professor at Panteion University, Athens; Permanent Representative of Greece to the Council of Europe; Member of the International Humanitarian Fact-Finding Commission; Director of the European Centre of Research and Training on Human Rights and Humanitarian Action, with the assistance of Maria-Daniella Marouda, Assistant Professor at Panteion University and Deputy Director of the European Centre of Research and Training on Human Rights and Humanitarian Action.

India

Prof. V. S. Mani, Pro Vice-Chancellor and Director, School of Law, Jaipur National University and former President of the Asian Society of International Law (2011–2013).

Prof. Sanoj Rajan, Dean of Ansal University School of Law, Gurgaon.

Indonesia

Prof. Romli Atmasasmita, Universitas Padjadaran Bandung and former Director General of Legal Administrative Affairs, and once of Legislation, of the Ministry of Law and Human Rights, with the assistance of Dr Trihoni Nalesti Dewi, Lecturer, Universitas Katholik Sugiyapranata of Semarang, Dr Fadillah Agus, former Legal Adviser, ICRC Jakarta Delegation, and now working as a consultant, and Rina Rusman, Legal Adviser, ICRC Jakarta Delegation.

Iran

Prof. Djamchid Momtaz, Professor of Public International Law, University of Tehran; former Member and President of the UN International Law Commission.

Israel

Prof. Eyal Benvenisti, Tel Aviv University Faculty of Law; Whewell Professor of International Law at the University of Cambridge.

Italy

Prof. Paolo Benvenuti, Università degli Studi Roma Tre, Dipartimento di Giurisprudenza (Roma Tre University, Department of Jurisprudence).

Kenya

Brigadier Titus Githiora, retired from the Judge Advocate General's Department of the Kenya Defence Force; former ICRC Armed and Security Forces Delegate and currently teaching international humanitarian law at the Kenya School of Governance.

Korea (Republic of)

Judge Seon Ki Park, Judge at the United Nations Mechanism for International Criminal Tribunals; Partner, Daedong Law & Notary Firm; former ad litem Judge at the International Criminal Tribunal for Rwanda; former General Counsel of the Ministry of National Defence.

Kuwait

Dr Rashid Hamed Al Anezi, Professor of International Law, Faculty of Law, Kuwait University.

Lebanon

Dr Karim El Mufti, Professor of International Law and Director of the Legal Clinic at Université La Sagesse, Beirut.

Mexico

Mariana Salazar, Director for International Humanitarian Law in the Ministry of Foreign Affairs and Technical Secretary of the National Committee on International Humanitarian Law.

Morocco

Prof. Mohamed Al Bazaz, Professor of International Law, Faculty of Law, Meknes University.

Nepal

Prof. Geeta Pathak Sangroula, Executive Director, Kathmandu School of Law.

Niger

Dr Oumarou Narey, Faculté de Droit de l'Université Abdou Moumouni de Niamey (Faculty of Law, Abdou Moumouni University, Niamey); Conseiller à la Cour Constitutionnelle du Niger (Judge of the Constitutional Court of Niger).

Nigeria

Prof. Boniface Obina Okere, Emeritus Professor of Law at the Enugu Campus of the University of Nigeria; Member of the African Union Commission on International Law.

Pakistan

Prof. Sikander Shah, Professor at the Lahore University of Management Sciences; former Legal Adviser, Ministry of Foreign Affairs.

Peru

Prof. Elizabeth Salmon Garate, Professor of International Law at Pontificia Universidad Católica de Perú (Pontifical Catholic University of Peru).

Philippines

Prof. Raul Pangalangan, University of the Philippines Law School, Manila.

Prof. Harry Roque, University of the Philippines Law School, Manila.

Russian Federation

Judge Bakhtiyar R. Tuzmukhamedov, former Judge in the Appeals Chamber of the International Criminal Tribunals for Rwanda and for the former Yugoslavia; Professor of International Law.

Serbia

Prof. Marko Milanovic, Associate Professor at the University of Nottingham School of Law; Vice-President of the European Society of International Law.

South Africa

Prof. Garth Abraham, Chief Executive Officer of St Augustine's College of South Africa; former Professor, Faculty of Law, University of Witwatersrand.

Colonel André Retief, Senior Staff Officer: Law of Armed Conflict, Education, Training and Development, South African National Defence Forces.

Sri Lanka

Dr Rohan Perera, Permanent Representative of Sri Lanka to the United Nations in New York; former Legal Adviser, Ministry of Foreign Affairs; former Member of the UN International Law Commission (2007–2011).

Sweden

Cecilia Tengroth, Senior Legal Adviser, Swedish Red Cross.

Kristina Lindvall, Legal Adviser, Swedish Red Cross.

Thailand

Prof. Vitit Muntarbhorn, Professor of International Law, Chulalongkorn University, Bangkok.

Turkey

Prof. Emre Öktem, Galatasaray University, Istanbul; Member of the Editorial Board of the International Review of the Red Cross, with the assistance of Mehmet Uzun.

United Kingdom

Colonel (ret.) Charles H. B. Garraway, Member and former Vice-President, International Humanitarian Fact-Finding Commission; Fellow at the Human Rights Centre, University of Essex.

Ukraine

Prof. Mykola Gnatovsky, Professor of International Law, Taras Shevchenko National University, Kyiv; President, European Committee for the Prevention of Torture.

United States of America

Colonel (ret.) Richard Jackson, Special Assistant to the Army Judge Advocate General for Law of War Matters.

Professor Michael Schmitt, Director of the Stockton Center for the Study of International Law at the United States Naval War College and Professor of Public International Law at the University of Exeter.

International and Other Organizations

United Nations: Stephen Mathias, Assistant Secretary-General for Legal Affairs, with the assistance of Luke Mhlaba, Principal Legal Officer; Katarina Grenfell and Keiichiro Okimoto, Legal Officers.

International Federation of Red Cross and Red Crescent Societies: Mathias Schmale, former Under-Secretary-General (until 2015).

Human Rights Watch: James Ross, Legal and Policy Director.

ICRC staff

Numerous ICRC staff provided feedback, advice and support, without which this Commentary could not have been completed.

Several lawyers in the ICRC Legal Division reviewed drafts and provided useful feedback: Alexander Breitegger (the wounded and sick, medical personnel and transports), Cordula Droege (common Article 3), Tristan Ferraro (common Articles 1 and 3), Gloria Gaggioli (common Article 3), Laurent Gisel (common Article 3), Sarah McCosker (Articles 38–39), Jose Serralvo (common Article 1) and Jelena Pejic (common Article 3 and Articles 13–14).

In addition, this project benefited from the advice of other members of the ICRC Legal Division, as well as lawyers in delegations who gave freely of their time. The same applies to ICRC delegates to armed forces, in particular Raoul Forster, Andrew Carswell, Pete Evans and Can Akdogan.

Numerous other colleagues reviewed drafts related to their field of expertise and gave valuable feedback: Katya Gisin and Sophie Barbey (recording and forwarding of information, prescriptions regarding the dead); Morris Tidball-Binz, Shuala Martin Drawdy and Oran Finegan (prescriptions regarding the dead); Massimo Marelli (data protection); Dr Paul Bouvier (the wounded and sick); Cristina Pellandini and Antoine Bouvier (penal sanctions, dissemination and final provisions); Richard Desgagné and Anne-Marie La Rosa (penal sanctions); Audrey Palama (role of non-State armed groups); Ximena Londoño, Coline Rapneau and Maria Teresa Garrido (protection of women, sexual violence); Thomas de Saint Maurice and Pascal Daudin (right of humanitarian initiative); Claire de Feu (humanitarian principles); Raffaella Diana, Mariya Nikolova, Etienne Kuster and François Sénéchaud (dissemination and detailed execution). Stéphane Hankins and Antoine Bouvier reviewed all commentaries in relation to the protection of the emblem, as well as the auxiliary role of National Societies (Articles 26–27), and provided insightful comments. Leslie Leach and Sue Featherstone provided invaluable assistance in gathering practice on the use of the emblem.

The project team received invaluable research support from the following persons who were at the time legal trainees in the ICRC Legal Division:

Nicole Anderson, Audrey Baëté, Tracey Begley, Marcela Giraldo, Andrea Harrison, Öykü Irmakkesen, Yvette Issar, Claudia Maritano, Jérôme Massé, Anna Leshchinskaya, Ximena Londoño, Rochus Peyer, Vanessa Pooudomsak, Tilman Rodenhäuser, Jose Serralvo, Helena Sunnegardh, Nele Verlinden, Oliver Waters and Cornelius Wiesener.

Particular mention should be made of Michèle Hou, Sonia Crenn and Ismaël Raboud of the ICRC Library who provided unstinting support for the research. Fabrizio Bensi, Jean-Michel Diez and Daniel Palmieri of the ICRC Archives did the same with respect to the archival research, together with Maya Rombaldi Revaz, Isabelle Nikles and Nicole Ducraux.

The administrative support provided by Catherine Délice and Mélanie Schweizer is also gratefully acknowledged.

Numerous other persons provided support and advice and the ICRC would like to thank them, in particular the legal advisers of National Societies.

English-language editors

Christina Grisewood and Susan Wald undertook the monumental task of editing the Commentary.

Online and print versions

The online version was developed by Valéry Blanc and Florent Isselin, who benefited from the advice and support of Sandra Manzi.

The print production was organized by Sarah Fleming and Christina Grisewood at the ICRC and Finola O'Sullivan and Emma Collison at Cambridge University Press.

ABBREVIATIONS

AU	African Union
DRC	Democratic Republic of the Congo
ECCC	Extraordinary Chambers in the Courts of Cambodia
EU	European Union
ICC	International Criminal Court
ICJ	International Court of Justice
ICJ Reports	International Court of Justice, Reports of Judgments, Advisory Opinions and Orders
ICRC	International Committee of the Red Cross
ICTR	International Criminal Tribunal for Rwanda
ICTY	International Criminal Tribunal for the former Yugoslavia
IHL	International humanitarian law
IHFFC	International Humanitarian Fact-Finding Commission
ILA	International Law Association
ILC	International Law Commission
IMT	International Military Tribunal
LOAC	Law of armed conflict
NATO	North Atlantic Treaty Organisation
OAS	Organization of American States
OAU	Organization of African Unity (now African Union)
PCIJ	Permanent Court of International Justice
UN	United Nations
UNESCO	United Nations Education, Scientific and Cultural Organization
UNHCR	United Nations High Commissioner for Refugees
UNICEF	United Nations Children's Emergency Fund
UDFR	Union des forces démocratiques pour le rassemblement
USSR	Union of Soviet Socialist Republics
UK	United Kingdom of Great Britain and Northern Ireland
US	United States of America

INTRODUCTION

Contents

A. The ICRC project to update the Commentaries

1. Background and scope of the project

1 The 1949 Geneva Conventions and their 1977 Additional Protocols constitute the foundation of international humanitarian law today. They contain the
essential rules of humanitarian law protecting civilians, persons who are *hors
de combat* and medical and religious personnel, as well as a range of protected
objects such as civilian objects and medical units and transports. At the time
of writing, the Geneva Conventions have been universally ratified or adhered
to. Furthermore, a large majority of countries, more than five out of every six,
are party to the 1977 Additional Protocols.[1]

2 Upon the adoption of the Conventions in 1949, a group of ICRC lawyers
who had been involved in the drafting and negotiation of the Conventions set
out to write a detailed commentary on each of their provisions. This led to
the publication between 1952 and 1960 of a Commentary on each of the four
Conventions, under the general editorship of Jean Pictet.[2] Similarly, when the
Additional Protocols were adopted in 1977, ICRC lawyers involved in their
negotiation set out to write a commentary on both Protocols. These were published in 1986–1987.[3]

3 Over the years, these six ICRC Commentaries have come to be recognized as
well-respected and authoritative interpretations of the Conventions and their
1977 Additional Protocols, essential for the understanding and application of
the law.[4]

4 The original Commentaries were based primarily on the negotiating history
of these treaties, as observed at first hand by the authors, and on prior practice.
In this respect, they retain their historic value. They often contain a detailed
comparison with previous conventions, e.g. a comparison between the 1949

---

[1] For a continuous update, see the websites of the ICRC (http://www.icrc.org/ihl) and the depositary (https://www.fdfa.admin.ch/depositary).

[2] Geneva Convention I: commentary by Jean S. Pictet, with contributions by Frédéric Siordet,
Claude Pilloud, Jean-Pierre Schoenholzer, René-Jean Wilhelm and Oscar M. Uhler, published in
1952 (French original and English). Geneva Convention II: commentary by Jean S. Pictet, with
the co-operation of Rear-Admiral M.W. Mouton (Netherlands), with contributions by Frédéric
Siordet, Claude Pilloud, Jean-Pierre Schoenholzer, René-Jean Wilhelm and Oscar M. Uhler, published in 1959 in French and in 1960 in English. Geneva Convention III: commentary by Jean
de Preux, with contributions by Frédéric Siordet, Claude Pilloud, Henri Coursier, René-Jean
Wilhelm, Oscar M. Uhler and Jean-Pierre Schoenholzer, published in 1958 in French and in 1960
in English. Geneva Convention IV: commentary by Oscar M. Uhler and Henri Coursier, with
Frédéric Siordet, Claude Pilloud, Roger Boppe, René-Jean Wilhelm and Jean-Pierre Schoenholzer,
published in 1956 in French and in 1958 in English.

[3] Additional Protocol I (and Annex I): commentary by Claude Pilloud, Jean de Preux, Yves Sandoz,
Bruno Zimmermann, Philippe Eberlin, Hans-Peter Gasser and Claude F. Wenger. Additional Protocol II: commentary by Sylvie S. Junod. Both commentaries were prepared under the editorship
of Yves Sandoz, Christophe Swinarski and Bruno Zimmermann and published in French in 1986
and in English in 1987.

[4] See e.g. W. Hays Parks, 'Pictet's Commentaries', in Christophe Swinarski (ed.), *Studies and
Essays on International Humanitarian Law and Red Cross Principles in Honour of Jean Pictet*,
ICRC/Martinus Nijhoff Publishers, The Hague, 1984, pp. 495–497.

Conventions and the 1929 Geneva Conventions on the Wounded and Sick and on Prisoners of War.

5   However, with the passage of time and the development of practice, a genuine need was felt to update the Commentaries. The ICRC therefore decided to embark upon an ambitious project to achieve that purpose. This update seeks to reflect the practice that has developed in applying and interpreting the Conventions and Protocols during the decades since their adoption, while preserving those elements of the original Commentaries that are still relevant. The objective is to ensure that the new editions reflect contemporary practice and legal interpretation. Therefore, the new editions are more detailed as they have the benefit of more than 60 years of application of the Conventions – 40 years in the case of the 1977 Additional Protocols – and their interpretation by States, courts and scholars. The new Commentaries reflect the ICRC's current interpretations of the law, where they exist. They also indicate the main diverging views where these have been identified.

6   The update preserves the format of the original Commentaries, that is to say an article-by-article analysis of each of the provisions of the Conventions and Protocols. The commentaries on the common articles in the First Convention have been drafted to cover the four Conventions. They will be adapted to the specific context of a Convention where this is particularly relevant, for example to provide a definition of 'shipwrecked' in the context of the Second Convention.

7   The present volume is the first instalment in a series of six updated Commentaries. A commentary on Additional Protocol III that was published in 2007 is not being updated as part of this project.[5]

2. *The ICRC's role in the interpretation of the Conventions and Protocols*

8   The ICRC mandated the writing of the original Commentaries pursuant to its role as guardian and promoter of humanitarian law. The same is true for the current updated edition. This role is recognized in the Statutes of the International Red Cross and Red Crescent Movement, in particular the ICRC's role 'to work for the understanding and dissemination of knowledge of international humanitarian law applicable in armed conflicts and to prepare any development thereof'.[6] But it also follows from its role 'to undertake the tasks incumbent upon it under the Geneva Conventions' and 'to work for the faithful

---

[5] Jean-François Quéguiner, 'Commentary on the Protocol additional to the Geneva Conventions of 12 August 1949, and relating to the Adoption of an Additional Distinctive Emblem (Protocol III)', *International Review of the Red Cross*, Vol. 89, No. 865, March 2007, pp. 175–207.

[6] Statutes of the International Red Cross and Red Crescent Movement (1986), Article 5(2)(g). On the ICRC's role in the interpretation of international humanitarian law, see also François Bugnion, *The International Committee of the Red Cross and the Protection of War Victims*, ICRC/Macmillan, Oxford, 2003, pp. 914–922.

application of international humanitarian law applicable in armed conflicts and to take cognizance of any complaints based on alleged breaches of that law'.[7] In many cases, these tasks require the ICRC to interpret the humanitarian law treaties underlying this mandate. Hence, the interpretation of humanitarian law is at the heart of the organization's daily work across its operations.

9   A wide variety of other actors also interpret the Conventions and Protocols, in particular States (through government lawyers in ministries, military commanders, staff officers and lawyers, advocates before courts), national and international courts and tribunals, arbitral tribunals, international organizations, components of the Red Cross and Red Crescent Movement, and non-governmental organizations and academics. Where relevant, the interpretations given by these actors have been taken into account in this Commentary, in particular interpretations by States and decisions of courts and tribunals which are among the most important sources of interpretative guidance.

10   In addition, what sets the updated Commentaries mandated by the ICRC apart from other academic commentaries is that the contributors were able to draw on research in the ICRC archives, while respecting their confidential nature, to assess the application and interpretation of the Conventions and Protocols since their adoption.

B. Drafting process

11 The research and coordination for this Commentary has been carried out by an ICRC project team. Together with a group of external contributors and some additional ICRC staff lawyers, they drafted this Commentary. All draft commentaries were submitted for review to the group of contributors, the Reading Committee.

12   At the same time, many drafts were also submitted for review to other ICRC staff, including staff working in the field of integration and promotion of the law, policy, cooperation within the Red Cross and Red Crescent Movement, protection and assistance. For specific issues, additional consultations with governmental, military and National Red Cross or Red Crescent Society lawyers took place.

13   The draft commentaries were subsequently submitted to an Editorial Committee comprising senior ICRC and external humanitarian law experts for review. Based on the Committee's comments, new drafts were prepared and submitted to a comprehensive process of peer review by a wide selection of 60 scholars and practitioners from around the world involved in the study and implementation of humanitarian law. Based on the feedback from the peer

---

[7] Statutes of the International Red Cross and Red Crescent Movement (1986), Article 5(2)(c).

review, the project team prepared a final draft for approval by the Editorial Committee. The final text is thus the result of a collaborative process.[8]

14 These various steps of consultation and review sought to ensure that the updated Commentary, being written more than 60 years after the initial 1952 Commentary, reflects current practice as accurately as possible and provides up-to-date legal interpretations based on the latest practice, case law, academic commentary and ICRC experience. Details on the treaties, other documents, military manuals, national legislation, national and international case-law referred to can be found in the corresponding tables at the end of this volume.

15 The updated Commentary has been drafted to serve a wide audience including, in particular, practitioners of international humanitarian law such as military commanders, staff officers and lawyers, judges and lawyers at national and international courts and tribunals, the ICRC and other components of the Red Cross and Red Crescent Movement, NGO staff, as well as academics and scholars.

C. Methodology

1. Introduction

16 The updated Commentary applies the methodology for treaty interpretation as set out in the 1969 Vienna Convention on the Law of Treaties, in particular Articles 31–33.[9] Even though that Convention was adopted 20 years after the Geneva Conventions, these rules are generally considered to reflect customary international law.[10]

17 The text below addresses how the methodology has been applied to the interpretation of the Conventions, in particular the First Convention.

18 Pursuant to Article 31 of the Vienna Convention on the Law of Treaties, a treaty must be interpreted 'in good faith in accordance with the ordinary meaning to be given to the terms of the treaty in their context and in the light of its object and purpose'. Although this rule of interpretation has different

---

[8] For details concerning the persons involved in the research, drafting and review, see the Acknowledgements.

[9] What follows is only a summary of the issues raised by these articles. For a more detailed commentary on these provisions, see Aust, pp. 205–226; Gardiner, 2015; Sinclair, pp. 114–158; and the sections on Articles 31–32 in Corten/Klein, Dörr/Schmalenbach, and Villiger.

[10] See e.g. ICJ, *Kasikili/Sedudu Island case*, Judgment, 1999, paras 18–20; *Application of the Genocide Convention case*, Merits, Judgment, 2007, para. 160; ILC, Subsequent agreements and subsequent practice in relation to the interpretation of treaties, Conclusion 1.1 (provisionally adopted), *Report of the International Law Commission on the work of its sixty-fifth session*, UN Doc. A/68/10, 2013, p. 11.

elements, which are examined under separate headings below, the interpretation itself must combine all the elements.[11]

19   The obligation to interpret the terms of a treaty in good faith flows from the general obligation to respect treaty obligations in good faith, known under the Latin maxim as *pacta sunt servanda* ('agreements must be honoured').[12]

2. Ordinary meaning of the terms

20   The ordinary meaning of most of the terms in the Conventions can easily be ascertained. They tend to be written in plain language and provide significant details in the provisions themselves (see e.g. many of the detailed provisions of the Third Convention).

21   In order to achieve their objectives, the Conventions were drafted in such a way that they should easily be understood by soldiers and their commanders, as well as by civilians. The Conventions provide for their study to be included in programmes of military instruction,[13] and for the Third Convention to be posted in its entirety in prisoner-of-war camps, 'in the prisoners' own language, at places where all may read [it]'.[14] The purpose is for prisoners of war to be able to read the Convention and to be made fully aware of their rights under the Convention during their internment. Similarly the Conventions foresee a role for the civilian population, for example in the search for and collection of the wounded and sick, and hence it is important that civilians be able to understand the (plain) text of the Conventions. Furthermore, civilians are protected under the Fourth Convention, which makes it all the more relevant that they be able to fully understand this treaty.

22   However, as practice in the application and interpretation of the Conventions over the past six decades have shown, the meaning of the Conventions' terms is not always clear or may give rise to a need for further interpretation. Where necessary, this Commentary determines the ordinary meaning of terms with reference to authoritative, standard English dictionaries such as the *Concise Oxford English Dictionary*, or legal dictionaries such as *Black's Law Dictionary*.

23   Although the updated Commentary has been drafted in English, the authors have consistently consulted and compared the French version of the

---

[11] See ILC, *Yearbook of the International Law Commission*, Vol. II, 1966, p. 220, paras 9–10; 'Subsequent agreements and subsequent practice in relation to the interpretation of treaties, Conclusion 1.5 provisionally adopted', *Report of the International Law Commission on the work of its sixty-fifth session*, UN Doc. A/68/10, 2013, p. 11; Gardiner, 2015, pp. 31–32; and Aust, p. 208.

[12] Vienna Convention on the Law of Treaties (1969), Article 26. For more details, see Gardiner, 2015, pp. 167–181.

[13] First Convention, Article 47; Second Convention, Article 48; Third Convention, Article 127; and Fourth Convention, Article 144.

[14] Third Convention, Article 41. Similarly, the Fourth Convention needs to be posted inside camps for civilian internees; see Fourth Convention, Article 99.

Convention, which is equally authentic.[15] Where divergences between the two versions appear to exist, the Commentary proposes an interpretation which reconciles both versions.[16] To ascertain the meaning of the terms in the French version of the Convention, the authors consulted authoritative, standard French dictionaries, such as *Le Petit Robert* or *Le Petit Larousse*.

3. Context

24   Pursuant to Article 31(1) of the Vienna Convention on the Law of Treaties, in order to determine the ordinary meaning to be given to the terms of the treaty those terms have be placed 'in their context'. According to Article 31(2), the context to be considered for treaty interpretation comprises not only the text of treaty, but also its preamble and annexes.

25   The First Convention has two annexes: the first is a draft agreement relating to hospital zones and localities and the second is a model identity card for medical and religious personnel attached to the armed forces. These annexes are referred to where relevant in the context of a particular provision.[17] The commentaries on the annexes themselves have not been updated, as this was not considered of sufficient practical relevance.

26   The context also comprises the structure of the Conventions, their titles, the chapter headings and the text of the other articles. The Final Act and the annexed 11 resolutions adopted by the 1949 Diplomatic Conference of Geneva are also considered part of the context for the purposes of interpretation of these respective treaties.[18]

27   In the case of the Conventions, the marginal titles are neither part of the text nor of the context because these were established after the Diplomatic Conference by the depositary, the Swiss Federal Council. This was done for ease of reference, as the articles of the Conventions have no titles, unlike the articles of the Protocols.[19] The marginal titles of some articles have been slightly adapted in the present Commentary to better identify their subject matter.

4. Object and purpose

28   Strictly speaking the object of a treaty may be said to refer to the rights and obligations stipulated by the treaty,[20] while the purpose refers to the aim which

---

[15] See First Convention, Article 55, and Vienna Convention on the Law of Treaties (1969), Article 33.
[16] For further details, see the commentary on Article 55, section B.2.
[17] See the commentaries on Articles 23 and 28.
[18] See Aust, p. 211; Gardiner, 2015, p. 86; Sinclair, p. 129; and Villiger, p. 430.
[19] See Marginal Headings (or Titles of Articles) Established by the Swiss Federal Political Department, *Final Record of the Diplomatic Conference of Geneva of 1949*, Vol. I, Part III.
[20] Reuter, p. 186, para. 283; see also Buffard/Zemanek, pp. 331–332.

is to be achieved by the treaty provisions.[21] However, the terms 'object and purpose' are used as 'a combined whole'.[22] Thus, a treaty's object and purpose is said to refer to its 'raison d'être',[23] its 'fundamental core',[24] or 'its essential content'.[25]

29   Consideration in good faith of the object and purpose will ensure the effectiveness of the treaty's terms:

> When a treaty is open to two interpretations one of which does and the other does not enable the treaty to have appropriate effects, good faith and the objects and purposes of the treaty demand that the former interpretation be adopted.[26]

As can be seen from this quote, and as recognized by the International Court of Justice, a treaty may have several objects and purposes.[27] A usual place to look for the object and purpose of a treaty is its preamble.[28] In the case of the Geneva Conventions, the preambles are very short and provide only limited guidance, contrary to the Additional Protocols which have more substantial preambles.[29] However, beyond the preambles, the whole text of the Conventions, including the titles and annexes, has to be taken into account in ascertaining their object and purpose.[30]

30   On this basis, it can be ascertained that the overall object and purpose of the First Convention is to ensure respect for and protection of the wounded and sick, as well as the dead, in international armed conflict. The other provisions in the Convention are geared towards this purpose, for example the rules on the search for and collection of the wounded and sick and of the dead. In addition, the rules that require respect for and protection of medical and religious

---

[21] Buffard/Zemanek, pp. 331–332.

[22] Villiger, p. 427, with further references; Gardiner, 2015, pp. 212–213 ('a composite item'); David S. Jonas and Thomas N. Saunders, 'The Object and Purpose of a Treaty: Three Interpretive Methods', *Vanderbilt Journal of Transnational Law*, Vol. 43, No. 3, May 2010, pp. 565–609, at 578 ('a unitary concept').

[23] ICJ, *Reservations to the Genocide Convention*, Advisory Opinion, 1951, para. 23.

[24] Alain Pellet, 'Article 19. Formulation of reservations', in Corten/Klein, pp. 405–488, at 450–451.

[25] David S. Jonas and Thomas N. Saunders, 'The Object and Purpose of a Treaty: Three Interpretive Methods', *Vanderbilt Journal of Transnational Law*, Vol. 43, No. 3, May 2010, pp. 565–609, at 576.

[26] ILC, *Yearbook of the International Law Commission*, Vol. II, 1966, p. 219, para. 6. See also ICJ, *Territorial Dispute case (Libya v. Chad)*, Judgment, 1994, para. 51: in international law, *effet utile* is regarded as 'one of the fundamental principles of interpretation of treaties'.

[27] ICJ, *Morocco case*, Judgment, 1952, p. 196; see also Villiger, p. 427, para. 11; Mark E. Villiger, *Customary International Law and Treaties*, Martinus Nijhoff Publishers, Dordrecht, 1985, pp. 321–322; Gardiner, 2015, p. 214 ('sometimes there seems no particularity in distinguishing between the object and purpose of the treaty and the purpose of particular provisions'); Sinclair, p. 130; and Fitzmaurice, p. 228. But see Jan Klabbers, 'Some Problems Regarding the Object and Purpose of Treaties', *Finnish Yearbook of International Law*, Vol. 8, 1997, pp. 138–160, at 152–153 (potential problems of admitting arguments based on object and purpose of individual provisions).

[28] ICJ, *Morocco case*, Judgment, 1952, p. 196; see also Fitzmaurice, p. 228, and Sinclair, pp. 125–126.

[29] For more details, see the commentary on the Preamble.

[30] See Gardiner, 2015, p. 213; Fitzmaurice, p. 228; and Buffard/Zemanek, p. 332.

personnel, units and transports and the distinctive emblems all serve the purpose of protecting and caring for the wounded and sick. Lastly, a number of other provisions are intended to ensure respect for the Convention through its promotion, implementation and enforcement.

31   Common Article 3 provides the First Convention, and indeed all four Conventions, with another object and purpose, as it serves to protect persons not or no longer participating in hostilities in situations of non-international armed conflict.

32   The balance between humanitarian considerations, on the one hand, and military necessity, on the other, is a hallmark of international humanitarian law. This balance is reflected in the text of the Conventions adopted by the Diplomatic Conference of 1949.

5. Additional elements of interpretation

33   Pursuant to Article 31(3) of the Vienna Convention on the Law of Treaties, together with the context, the interpretation provided in the Commentary also has to take into account:

(a) any subsequent agreement between the Parties regarding the interpretation of the treaty or the application of its provisions;

(b) any subsequent practice in the application of the treaty which establishes the agreement of the Parties regarding its interpretation;

(c) any relevant rules of international law applicable in the relations between the Parties.

Items (b) and (c) are particularly important considerations when interpreting the Geneva Conventions. It is important to ascertain the subsequent practice in the application of the Conventions which has accumulated over the decades since their adoption.

34   Subsequent practice that does not fulfil the criteria of this provision, i.e. to establish the agreement of the Parties regarding the interpretation of a treaty, may still be relevant as a supplementary means of interpretation under Article 32.[31] This consists of conduct by one or more Parties in the application of the treaty after its conclusion.[32] The weight of such practice may depend on its clarity and specificity, as well as its repetition.[33] The six decades since the adoption of the Geneva Conventions have seen the development of

---

[31] ILC, Subsequent agreements and subsequent practice in relation to the interpretation of treaties, Conclusion 1.4 provisionally adopted, *Report of the International Law Commission on the work of its sixty-fifth session*, UN Doc. A/68/10, 2013, p. 11.

[32] *Ibid.* Conclusion 4.3 provisionally adopted, p. 12.

[33] ILC, Subsequent agreements and subsequent practice in relation to the interpretation of treaties, Conclusion 8.3 provisionally adopted, *Report of the International Law Commission on the work of its sixty-fifth session*, UN Doc. A/69/10, 2014, p. 169.

significant practice in their application, which is particularly useful in this respect.

35   Other relevant rules of international law include customary humanitarian law and the three Additional Protocols, as well as other relevant treaties of international law, including international criminal law and human rights law where applicable.[34] The latter bodies of law were still in their infancy when the Geneva Conventions were adopted in 1949 but have grown significantly since then. As stated by the International Court of Justice: '[A]n international instrument has to be interpreted and applied within the framework of the entire legal system prevailing at the time of the interpretation.'[35]

a. International criminal law

36   With respect to international criminal law, for example, the growing body of case law from the various international criminal courts and tribunals, as well as national courts, illustrates the way in which identical or similar concepts and obligations of international humanitarian law have been applied and interpreted for the purpose of assessing individual criminal responsibility. To the extent that this is relevant for the interpretation of the Conventions, this has been examined.

37   For example, the 1979 International Convention against the Taking of Hostages has become a starting point for the interpretation of the notion of the taking of hostages. This is also borne out by subsequent practice, e.g. in the form of the war crime of hostage-taking in the 1998 ICC Statute, the definition in the 2002 ICC Elements of Crimes, and case law.[36]

38   That said, it is important to underscore that the humanitarian treaty obligation may be broader than the criminalized parts of it in a rule contained in an instrument of international criminal law. The humanitarian treaty obligation exists independently of the rule of international criminal law on which the case law is founded. The content of the obligation may therefore not be identical in both bodies of law and differences are pointed out wherever they exist.

---

[34] It should be noted that treaties, other than the Conventions themselves, that are referred to in the Commentaries are used on the understanding that they apply only if all the conditions relating to their geographic, temporal and personal scope of application are fulfilled. In addition, they apply only to States that have ratified or acceded to them, unless and to the extent they reflect customary international law.

[35] ICJ, *Namibia case*, Advisory Opinion, 1971, para. 53. For further details, see also ILC, Conclusions of the work of the Study Group on Fragmentation of International Law: Difficulties arising from the diversification and expansion of international law, reproduced in *Report of the International Law Commission on the work of its fifty-eighth session*, UN Doc. A/61/10, 2006, Chapter XII, para. 251, subparagraphs (17)–(23), pp. 413–415.

[36] For details, see the commentary on common Article 3, section G.3.

b. International human rights law

39 With respect to the relationship between humanitarian law and human rights law, it is generally recognized that human rights law applicable in situations of armed conflict complements the protection afforded by humanitarian law because the two bodies of law share a common value of protecting human life and dignity.[37] The relationship between these bodies of law is, however, complex and still subject to further clarification and evolution. It is also highly contextual and therefore the interaction between the two bodies of law depends on the issue at hand. The Commentaries do not purport to set forth a general theory of the relationship applicable to all possible interactions between every rule of the Conventions and human rights law. It will address the relationship on a case-by-case basis, based on the premise of the complementary nature of both bodies of law.

40 Therefore, human rights law has been referred to where relevant in order to interpret shared concepts (e.g. cruel, inhuman and degrading treatment). This does not mean that human rights law and interpretations can be transposed mechanically to humanitarian law provisions and differences have been pointed out where relevant. For example, the definition of torture is set forth in the 1984 Convention against Torture, although ICTY case law and the ICC Elements of Crimes have interpreted this notion to be wider in humanitarian law than in the Convention against Torture.[38]

41 Human rights law, while retaining its separate existence and scope of application, may also be relevant where the application of the Conventions may be affected by international human rights obligations. For example, the commentary on common Article 3 (and on Articles 100–101 of the Third Convention and Article 68 of the Fourth Convention) which anticipates the possibility of the use of the death penalty, would be incomplete without a reference to international treaties aiming to abolish the death penalty.[39] These references are not so much a matter of interpreting the obligations in the Conventions through human rights law, but of mentioning parallel obligations in order to provide a complete overview of the relevant international legal rules.

---

[37] See e.g. ICJ, *Legality of the Threat or Use of Nuclear Weapons*, Advisory Opinion, 1996, para. 25; *Legal Consequences of the Construction of a Wall in the Occupied Palestinian Territory*, Advisory Opinion, 2004, para. 106; and *Armed Activities on the Territory of the Congo case*, Judgment, 2005, paras 215–220. See also ICRC, *Handbook on International Rules Governing Military Operations*, ICRC, Geneva, 2013, p. 67; Cordula Droege, 'The Interplay between International Humanitarian Law and International Human Rights Law in Situations of Armed Conflict', *Israel Law Review*, Vol. 40, No. 2, Summer 2007, pp. 310–355; and Cordula Droege, 'Elective affinities? Human rights and humanitarian law', *International Review of the Red Cross*, Vol. 90, No. 871, September 2008, pp. 501–548.

[38] For details, see the commentaries on Article 3, section G.2, and Article 50, section D.2.a.

[39] See European Convention on Human Rights (1983), Protocol 6; Second Optional Protocol to the International Covenant on Civil and Political Rights (1989); and Protocol to the American Convention on Human Rights to Abolish the Death Penalty (1990).

c. *The Additional Protocols*

42 A special issue is the relationship between the Geneva Conventions of 1949 and the Additional Protocols of 1977 and 2005. The original Commentaries on the Conventions were drafted prior to the adoption of the Additional Protocols. The updated Commentaries aim to provide the clearest picture of the content of the obligations set forth in each article of the Conventions, in the light of the obligations for States that are party to the Additional Protocols.

43   Therefore, the updated Commentaries indicate, where relevant, the legal impact of relevant Protocol rules on the interpretation of the Conventions. The commentary on the Additional Protocols will indicate in detail how a Protocol rule has altered, supplemented and/or reinforced a related rule in the Conventions. For example, the impact of the definitions of medical personnel, units and transports in Article 8(k) of Additional Protocol I will be mentioned briefly in the commentaries on the relevant provisions in the First Convention, while the commentary on Article 8 of the Protocol itself will discuss these definitions in more detail.

d. *Customary international humanitarian law*

44 Another issue is the relationship between treaty law and customary humanitarian law. The Geneva Conventions have been ratified by 196 States and are generally considered to be part of customary law.[40] Nevertheless, references have been made to relevant rules of customary international humanitarian law as identified by international courts or other bodies, or from the ICRC study on the subject, in situating a provision of the Conventions in the general context of international law.

45   However, the updated Commentaries do not seek to determine for each provision whether it amounts to customary law, because this is beyond their scope and, as noted, the Conventions are generally considered to be customary. Therefore, the absence of a reference to the customary status of a provision should not be interpreted as meaning that that provision is not part of customary international law; the issue was simply not examined as part of updating the Commentaries.

6. *Special meaning of terms*

46 According to Article 31(4) of the Vienna Convention on the Law of Treaties, 'a special meaning shall be given to a term if it is established that the Parties so intended'. With respect to the First Convention, this rule is relevant, for

---

[40] See e.g. ICJ, *Legality of the Threat or Use of Nuclear Weapons*, Advisory Opinion, 1996, paras 79 and 82; Eritrea-Ethiopia Claims Commission, *Prisoners of War, Eritrea's Claim*, Partial Award, 2003, para. 40; and *Prisoners of War, Ethiopia's Claim*, Partial Award, 2003, para. 31.

example, to the definition of the wounded and sick, which is both narrower and wider than the ordinary meaning of these words.[41]

7. *Preparatory work*

47 Lastly, according to Article 32 of the Vienna Convention on the Law of Treaties, 'recourse may be had' to the treaty's preparatory work and the circumstances of its conclusion in order to confirm the meaning resulting from the application of the general rule of interpretation, or to determine the meaning when the application of the general rule leaves the meaning ambiguous or obscure or leads to a result which is manifestly absurd or unreasonable.

48 The formulation 'recourse may be had' gives the impression that recourse to the preparatory work is optional. In practice, however, most academic commentaries on treaties examine the preparatory work as a matter of standard research, and do not use it only in cases where the meaning is ambiguous or obscure or leads to a result which is manifestly absurd or unreasonable.[42]

49 Indeed, it seems logical for a thorough examination of all the issues to look at the preparatory work even if the general rule of interpretation yields a satisfactory result. It also helps the commentator to understand 'the terms of the treaty in their context' which is a requirement under the general rule (see Article 31(1) and (2) of the Vienna Convention on the Law of Treaties). Recourse to the preparatory work is particularly important when no recent practice on a topic can be found, such as for Articles 33 and 34 of the First Convention dealing with the fate of buildings and material of medical units of the armed forces and aid societies after they fall into enemy hands.

---

[41] See the commentary on Article 12, section D.2.

[42] See e.g. Corten/Klein; Dörr/Schmalenbach; Villiger; Jiří Toman, *The Protection of Cultural Property in the Event of Armed Conflict: Commentary on the Convention for the Protection of Cultural Property in the Event of Armed Conflict and its Protocol*, Dartmouth/UNESCO, Aldershot, 1996; Stuart Maslen (ed.), *Commentaries on Arms Control Treaties, Volume I: The Convention on the Prohibition of the Use, Stockpiling, Production, and Transfer of Anti-Personnel Mines and on their Destruction*, Oxford University Press, 2004; Manfred Nowak, *U.N. Covenant on Civil and Political Rights: CCPR Commentary*, 2nd revised edition, N.P. Engel, Kehl am Rhein, 2005; Manfred Nowak and Elizabeth McArthur (eds), *The United Nations Convention Against Torture: A Commentary*, Oxford University Press, 2008; Jiří Toman, *Commentary on the Second Protocol to the Hague Convention of 1954 for the Protection of Cultural Property in the Event of Armed Conflict*, UNESCO Publishing, Paris, 2009; William A. Schabas, *The International Criminal Court: A Commentary on the Rome Statute*, Oxford University Press, 2010; Gro Nystuen and Stuart Casey-Maslen (eds), *The Convention on Cluster Munitions: A Commentary*, Oxford University Press, 2010; Andreas Zimmermann, Jonas Dörschner and Felix Machts (eds), *The 1951 Convention Relating to the Status of Refugees and its 1967 Protocol: A Commentary*, Oxford University Press, 2011; Bruno Simma, Daniel-Erasmus Khan, Georg Nolte and Andreas Paulus (eds), *The Charter of the United Nations: A Commentary*, 3rd edition, Oxford University Press, 2012; Christian J. Tams, Lars Berster and Björn Schiffbauer, *Convention on the Prevention and Punishment of the Crime of Genocide: A Commentary*, Beck/Hart/Nomos, Oxford, 2014; Andrew Clapham, Paola Gaeta and Marco Sassòli (eds), *The 1949 Geneva Conventions: A Commentary*, Oxford University Press, 2015; and Otto Triffterer and Kai Ambos (eds), *The Rome Statute of the International Criminal Court: A Commentary*, 3rd edition, Hart Publishing, Oxford, 2016.

50   The preparatory work that has been examined in this Commentary is listed in the corresponding table at the end of this volume.

8. Absence of practice and desuetude

51 Certain provisions of the Convention do not seem to have been applied extensively in the past six decades. However, the absence of practice in the application of a provision does not, in and of itself, lead to the falling into desuetude of such a provision. Desuetude means that a treaty rule is no longer applicable or has been modified, a conclusion that should not be reached lightly. It is subject to stringent conditions and requires the agreement, at least tacit, of the Parties or the emergence of an inconsistent rule of customary international law.[43]

52   Examples of provisions in the First Convention with no or only limited practice include:

– Articles 8 and 10 on Protecting Powers and their substitutes, which have rarely been used since 1949;
– Articles 11 and 52 on the conciliation and enquiry procedure, which have not been relied upon as such in recent conflicts;
– Article 26 on personnel of National Red Cross and Red Crescent Societies placed at the disposal of army medical services. This has rarely been done since 1949. Article 34 on the property of these Societies also has not been used in practice.
– Articles 27, 32 and 43 dealing with medical units belonging to aid societies of neutral countries and their staff have not been put into practice since 1949.
– Articles 28, 30 and 31 on the retention of medical and religious personnel have rarely been an issue in recent armed conflicts.

Yet these provisions continue to exist as valid treaty rules and must be applied where their conditions for application are fulfilled.

D. Structure of the Commentaries

53 Each commentary presents the text of the provision in question. For multiple-paragraph articles, the paragraph numbers have been added for ease of reference. Following the text of the provision, reservations and declarations as at the time of publication are listed.

---

[43] Jan Wouters and Sten Verhoeven, 'Desuetudo', version of November 2008, in Rüdiger Wolfrum (ed.), *Max Planck Encyclopedia of Public International Law*, Oxford University Press, http://opil.ouplaw.com/home/EPIL, paras 10–11. For example, the current application of Article 38 of the First Convention on the use of the distinctive emblems may be considered a rule that has been modified by a subsequent rule of customary international law, as well as by the tacit agreement of the High Contracting Parties. For further details, see the commentary on Article 38.

54 The commentary itself is preceded by a table of contents which serves as an outline of the issues addressed. It allows the reader to navigate easily within a commentary and to identify quickly which parts of a commentary may be most relevant. Each commentary is structured in a similar way:

55 *Introduction*: The introduction serves as an executive summary of the commentary. It highlights the main issues covered and allows for a quick overview of what a given provision deals with. Further details can be found in the discussion section. In some cases the introduction is merged with the next section on historical background.

56 *Historical background*: This part highlights the main phases in the development of a specific provision, rather than seeking to give an exhaustive overview of the entire drafting history. The length of this part depends on the relevance of the historical background for the current understanding of the provision and the amount of change and development over time for a specific provision. The footnotes in this part guide the reader to the necessary details.

57 Those elements of the drafting history that have a direct impact on the interpretation of a particular aspect of a provision are included in the discussion section.

58 For multiple-paragraph articles, such as common Article 3, this section focuses on the general historical background of the provision rather than on that of each paragraph. The historical background of a specific paragraph may then be set out in a separate section, or elements of it may be interwoven with the introduction or with the discussion of the paragraph.

59 *Discussion*: This part forms the core of each commentary. For single-paragraph articles this part may be divided into thematic sections. For multiple-paragraph articles, it is divided by paragraph and may have additional thematic subsections. The commentary outlines and explains the content of the provision. As noted, the commentary follows the rules on interpretation set out in the Vienna Convention on the Law of Treaties. The precise content of the discussion section depends on the article under scrutiny, but in general the aims of this section include:

- providing an interpretation of the ordinary meaning of the text in the light of its context and the object and purpose;
- setting out the practice in implementing a provision where this helps to clarify its scope and content;
- analytically describing any interpretations of the article by international courts and tribunals;
- indicating areas where the exact requirements of a rule are subject to debate;
- setting forth the broad outlines, including references, of the most authoritative academic doctrine on the issue focusing on the main fault lines among diverging opinions;

- indicating the ICRC position, if any, in relation to how the article should be interpreted and applied and the rationale for this position;
- providing key elements for implementing the obligation from a practical perspective, both humanitarian and military;
- describing briefly, where relevant, how the application in practice of a provision may affect women, men, girls and boys differently; and
- indicating briefly, where relevant, whether a violation of a provision entails the individual criminal responsibility of the author under international law.

60   *Select bibliography*: When specific literature on the provision is available, a select bibliography is appended to the commentary. This includes the specific works cited, as well as further reading. Treaties, other documents, military manuals, national legislation, national and international case-law referred to are referenced in the tables at the end of this volume.

E. The First Geneva Convention

1. Introduction

61   The Geneva Convention for the Amelioration of the Condition of the Wounded and Sick in Armed Forces in the Field is the first of four Conventions adopted by the Diplomatic Conference of Geneva of 1949.

62   The decision to revise the two 1929 Conventions and to establish a fuller legal framework for the protection of victims of armed conflict was prompted by the violence of the Second World War, which was unprecedented in its scope and in the suffering it caused among both combatants and the civilian population. While improvements of the protection afforded by international humanitarian law had been under discussion well before the outbreak of the Second World War, the experiences of that war persuaded the governments participating in the Diplomatic Conference to fill some of the gaps in conventional international humanitarian law that the Second World War had exposed.

63   Over 65 years later, the four Geneva Conventions of 1949 continue to constitute the bedrock of international humanitarian law, and are among the most important treaties governing the protection of victims of armed conflict. These victims include the wounded and sick, the shipwrecked, prisoners of war, civilian internees and civilians living under the control of an enemy State, under occupation or in the territory of an adverse Party, including specific categories of persons, such as women, children and displaced people. As such, the Conventions contain the essential rules protecting persons who are not, or no longer, taking a direct part in hostilities.

64   The 1949 Conventions rapidly gained broad acceptance by States and, without exception, have always been ratified by them as a set. The four Conventions

entered into force on 21 October 1950 after the first two ratifications.[44] They were ratified by another 74 States in the 1950s and obtained a further 48 ratifications in the 1960s. The ratifications steadily increased in the 1970s and 1980s. A wave of 26 new ratifications occurred in the early 1990s, resulting in particular from the break-up of the Soviet Union, Czechoslovakia and the former Yugoslavia. With the last few ratifications since the year 2000, the applicability of the Geneva Conventions has become universal, with 196 States Parties at the time of writing.[45] Furthermore, they are generally considered to be part of customary law.[46] The universal ratification of the four Geneva Conventions and the customary-law character of their rules are important testimony to the commonly shared conviction that wars must have limits.

2. Historical background

65   The origin of the First Convention is inseparable from the history of the ICRC and its original founders. At the end of his book *A Memory of Solferino*, published in October 1862, Henry Dunant had expressed a twofold wish – first, that each country should in peacetime set up a relief society that would aid the army medical service in times of war; and, second, that States should ratify by convention a solemn principle which would give international recognition to such societies to assist the medical service of the armed forces during armed conflict. Red Cross and Red Crescent Societies continue to translate the first of these aspirations into reality. It was the second aspiration, however, that led to the conclusion of the very first Geneva Convention, the 1864 Convention for the Amelioration of the Condition of the Wounded in Armies in the Field. The adoption of that treaty in such a short time was achieved in large part due to the vision and determination of the ICRC's founders.

66   The 1864 Convention consisted of only 10 articles, but it laid a foundation that has never since been shaken. It embodied the principle that members of the armed forces who are *hors de combat* because they are wounded or sick, and without means of defence, must be protected and cared for regardless of their nationality. As a corollary, and in the exclusive interest of the wounded, it added that ambulances and military hospitals, as well as the medical personnel, were to be protected against hostile acts. The distinctive emblem of a red cross on a white ground was chosen as the visible sign of this protection.

---

[44] Switzerland and Yugoslavia were the first two countries to ratify the Geneva Conventions, on 31 March and 21 April 1950, respectively; see 'Les Conventions de Genève du 12 août 1949 entrent dans le droit positif', *Revue internationale de la Croix-Rouge et Bulletin international des Sociétés de la Croix-Rouge*, Vol. 32, No. 378, June 1950, p. 448. On the entry into force of the First Convention, see also the commentary on Article 58.

[45] For the current status of ratification and the dates of ratification or accession by States Parties, see https://www.icrc.org/ihl or https://www.fdfa.admin.ch/depositary.

[46] See e.g. ICJ, *Legality of the Threat or Use of Nuclear Weapons*, Advisory Opinion, 1996, paras 79 and 82.

67   The importance of the codification of the principle that the wounded and sick
of the armed forces must be protected and cared for without distinction cannot
be overemphasized. It was the starting point for unceasing efforts by governments, the ICRC and National Societies to revise and improve the protection
afforded to victims in times of war. While this protection was initially extended
only to the wounded and sick in the armed forces and did not cover civilians, it
developed into the comprehensive body of international humanitarian treaty
law that today governs the protection of all victims of armed conflict.

68   As early as 1868, a Diplomatic Conference met to discuss the adaptation of
the 1864 Convention to warfare at sea, but the additional articles produced at
this Conference were never ratified.

69   The Diplomatic Conference of 1906 adopted a new and expanded Convention on the Wounded and Sick, increasing the number of articles to 33. The
1906 Geneva Convention added the notion of 'respect for the wounded and
sick' to the general obligation to collect and care for mentioned in the 1864
Convention, and included new provisions concerning the burial of the dead
and the transmission of information regarding their identity.

70   In 1929, a new Convention was adopted which, based on the experience of
the First World War, expanded upon the earlier provisions. The most significant
changes were the abolition of the *clausula si omnes*, according to which the
Convention was applicable only if all the belligerents in a conflict were party
to the Convention; the addition of the clauses recognizing the introduction
of medical aircraft; the extension of the use of the emblem to the peacetime
activities of National Societies; and the requirement to repress violations of
the Convention.

71   As noted above, the revisions that followed 20 years later were heavily influenced by the experience of the Second World War. A choice had to be made
between developing more detailed rules covering all possible eventualities, or
formulating general principles sufficiently flexible to be adapted to the existing
circumstances in each country. In the end, the Diplomatic Conference agreed
on a compromise that involved detailed provisions and included certain general and inviolable principles. It is these principles that today give the Geneva
Conventions their specific legal characteristics. They ensure that protection
under the Convention is absolute and that the Conventions' reach extends
beyond the inter-State level to ultimate beneficiaries who cannot renounce
the rights secured to them.[47] While the possibility was left open for special
agreements along the lines indicated by the model agreements and regulations
annexed to the Conventions, these agreements cannot lower the level of protection provided by the Conventions. For the first time, the Conventions explicitly provide that the States Parties undertake to respect and ensure respect
for the Conventions. The interests protected by the Conventions are of such

---

[47] See common Article 7 (Article 8 in the Fourth Convention). See also Abi-Saab, pp. 267–268.

fundamental importance that every State Party has a legal interest in their observance. The proper functioning of the system of protection provided by the Conventions demands that States Parties not only apply the provisions themselves, but also do everything reasonably in their power to ensure that the provisions are respected universally. The Conventions thus create obligations *erga omnes partes*, i.e. obligations towards all of the other High Contracting Parties.[48]

72   To get to these results, several expert conferences were convened in Geneva, where preparatory material gathered by the ICRC and first drafts were centralized and discussed. The most important were the Preliminary Conference of National Red Cross Societies in 1946 and the Conference of Government Experts in 1947. The drafts prepared by these Conferences were presented to the 1948 International Conference of the Red Cross in Stockholm, where further amendments were adopted.

73   The Stockholm Drafts served as the basis for negotiation at the Diplomatic Conference, which, convened by the Swiss Federal Council as depositary of the 1929 Conventions, met in Geneva from 21 April to 12 August 1949. Fifty-nine States were officially represented by delegations with full powers to discuss the texts; four States sent observers. The Conference immediately set up four main committees, which sat simultaneously and considered (1) the revision of the First Geneva Convention and the drafting of the Second Geneva Convention, which adapts the First Convention to sea warfare; (2) the revision of the Geneva Convention on Prisoners of War; (3) the drafting of a completely new convention that for the first time addressed the protection of civilians; and (4) the provisions common to all four Conventions.

74   Besides numerous working groups,[49] a Coordination Committee and a Drafting Committee, which edited the text for uniformity and consistency, were formed towards the end of the Conference.

75   The discussions and results obtained in these different committees and working groups are reflected in the commentaries on the individual articles, usually in the historical background sections, and thus need not be summarized here. Nevertheless, it merits mentioning that the records of the Diplomatic

---

[48] See ICJ, *Legal Consequences of the Construction of a Wall in the Occupied Palestinian Territory*, Advisory Opinion, 2004, para. 157 ('In the Court's view, these rules [of humanitarian law applicable in armed conflict] incorporate obligations which are essentially of an *erga omnes* character.'); ICTY, *Kupreškić* Trial Judgment, 2000, para. 519 ('[N]orms of international humanitarian law do not pose synallagmatic obligations, i.e. obligations of a State vis-à-vis another State. Rather ... they lay down obligations towards the international community as a whole ... '); and Pictet (ed.), *Commentary on the First Geneva Convention*, ICRC, 1952, p. 25 ('It is not an engagement concluded on a basis of reciprocity, binding each party to the contract only in so far as the other party observes its obligations. It is rather a series of unilateral engagements solemnly contracted before the world as represented by the other Contracting Parties.'). See also the commentary on common Article 1 and Abi-Saab, p. 270.

[49] While the French text of the preparatory work refers to 'groupes de travail', these groups are referred to as 'Working Parties' in the English version.

Conference, which are published,[50] as well as the reports from individual participants, testify to the plenipotentiaries' unstinting work for almost four months. They reflect a remarkable humanitarian spirit and a willingness to cooperate that, despite divergent opinions, prevailed throughout the Diplomatic Conference.

3. Content of the First Geneva Convention

76 The basic principle underlying all four Conventions is respect for the life and dignity of the individual, even – or especially – in situations of armed conflict. Those who suffer during armed conflict must be aided, protected and cared for. They must in all circumstances be treated humanely, without any adverse distinction founded on race, colour, religion or faith, sex, birth, wealth or any other similar criteria.

77 This principle is the basis for the specific rules found in the First Convention with regard to wounded and sick members of the armed forces, which above all contain the central obligation for the Parties to respect and protect them in all circumstances, treat them humanely and care for them without any adverse distinction. The wounded and sick members of the armed forces must be searched for and collected, and protected against pillage and ill-treatment.

78 Closely related to this obligation are the provisions related to the dead. These demand that the dead be searched for and protected from despoliation, that they be given an honourable burial and that their graves be respected. Measures must be taken to record information that can assist in the identification of the wounded, sick or dead, so that information about their fate can be forwarded to the Power on which they depend and, ultimately, to their families. Burial of the dead must be preceded by a careful examination with a view to establishing identity, and their graves must be properly marked and their location recorded.

79 As an essential condition for the wounded and sick to be collected and cared for, the First Convention affords protection to military medical personnel, material and transports, as well as to the buildings which shelter them. This protection applies both on the battlefield and when they are in enemy hands. The First Convention also stipulates certain circumstances under which such protection may be lost. These clearly defined and limited circumstances, however, only add weight to the fundamental obligation that military medical and religious personnel and facilities, including, under certain circumstances, auxiliary personnel, may not be attacked and must be respected and protected by the Parties to the conflict.

80 As a means of improving the protection of wounded and sick soldiers and members of the armed forces' medical service, the First Convention confirms

---

[50] See *Final Record of the Diplomatic Conference of Geneva of 1949*, 4 volumes, Volume I, Volume II-A, Volume II-B, Volume III, Federal Political Department, Berne, 1950.

the red cross or red crescent on a white ground as the distinctive emblem to be used by the medical service of a country's armed forces.[51] The distinctive emblem indicates that its bearers enjoy specific protection from attack, harm, or other interference with their tasks. The medical service of the armed forces is considered to be the primary user of the emblems. At the same time, the Convention confirms that National Red Cross and Red Crescent Societies may use the red cross or red crescent emblem to indicate their connection to the International Red Cross and Red Crescent Movement, without implying protection under the Geneva Conventions or any intention to invoke them. The First Convention requires the Parties to respect and ensure respect for and control of the use of the emblems and to prevent their misuse at all times.

81   Given that the majority of today's armed conflicts are of a non-international character, common Article 3, which applies to such conflicts, has become one of the key provisions of international humanitarian law and has gained an importance that was probably not foreseen by the drafters in 1949. Common Article 3 was the first treaty provision to specifically address non-international armed conflict. It is, in many respects, a mini-convention within the Convention,[52] and the fundamental character of its provisions has been recognized as a reflection of 'elementary considerations of humanity' and as a 'minimum yardstick' binding in all armed conflicts.[53] Common Article 3 has been supplemented in a number of important areas by Additional Protocol II and by the continuous development of customary international law in this area.

82   Lastly, the First Convention contains a comprehensive set of provisions on the suppression of abuses and penal sanctions, aimed at ensuring respect for the First Convention and increasing the protection it provides. These provisions were completely new in 1949, and similar provisions were incorporated in all four Conventions. Article 49 obliges States Parties to enact legislation providing effective penal sanctions, and to either prosecute or extradite, regardless of their nationality, alleged offenders who are suspected of having committed one of the grave breaches listed in Article 50.

4. Structure

83 The First Convention starts with the common provisions which are practically identical in all four Conventions. These common provisions contained in Chapter I deal with the obligation to respect and to ensure respect for the Conventions, and set out the Conventions' scope of application. They also provide for the conclusion of special agreements between the Parties, prohibiting

---

[51] The red lion and sun emblem, which is also mentioned in Article 38 of the First Convention, has not been used by any State since 1980.
[52] See *Final Record of the Diplomatic Conference of Geneva of 1949*, Vol. II-B, pp. 35, 98 and 326.
[53] See ICJ, *Military and Paramilitary Activities in and against Nicaragua case*, Merits, Judgment, 1986, paras 218–219.

those that might waive or lower the level of protection afforded in the Convention, and they confirm the inalienability of the rights of protected persons. They outline the role foreseen for the Protecting Powers or their substitutes, and provide for a conciliation procedure between Parties. They also enshrine the right of the ICRC and other impartial humanitarian organizations to offer their humanitarian activities for the protection of the wounded and sick to the Parties to an international armed conflict. As mentioned above, common Article 3 is a convention in miniature that sets out, for the first time in treaty law, rules on non-international armed conflict.

84   Provisions common to the four Conventions are also found at the end of the First Convention, notably those on dissemination, translations, reprisals and penal sanctions, and the final provisions, which define the procedure for signature, ratification and entry into force of the Convention, and for accession to it.

85   The common provisions in Chapter I are followed by Chapter II, which represents the core of the Convention, as it contains the rules regarding the protection of the wounded and sick of the armed forces. Article 12 contains a list of prohibited acts, which include attempts upon life, torture, and wilfully leaving the wounded and sick without medical assistance and care. Article 12 is complemented by Article 15, which imposes on the Parties certain core obligations vis-à-vis the wounded and sick, including the obligation to search for them and to collect and remove them from the danger zone. While Article 13 enumerates the categories of persons entitled to protection under the Convention when they are wounded or sick, Article 14 makes it clear that the military wounded and sick who fall into enemy hands are prisoners of war and, as such, enjoy the protection of both the First and the Third Conventions. The information to be given about wounded captives and the duties in respect of the dead are defined in Articles 16 and 17.

86   Chapter III deals with the protection of medical units and establishments and provides for the creation of safety zones and localities.

87   Chapter IV addresses the legal status of military medical and religious personnel and requires that they be respected and protected on the battlefield. In principle, when they have fallen into enemy hands, they must be returned to the Party to the conflict to which they belong. However, the First Convention provides that they may, in certain circumstances, be retained to care for prisoners of war. Their special status and the conditions for the return of those not required for the care of wounded and sick prisoners of war have been carefully defined in Articles 28, 30 and 31. In Articles 26, 27 and 30, the chapter also addresses the role and protection of the staff of national aid societies when they are acting as auxiliaries to the medical service of their own or of another State's armed forces.

88   Chapter V consists of two articles only. Article 33 regulates the protection of mobile medical units and of fixed medical establishments of the armed forces

when they fall into enemy hands. Article 34 provides that the property of aid societies must be regarded as private property and may never be taken as booty of war or confiscated.

89 Similar provision is made in Chapter VI for the protection of transport vehicles and medical aircraft. Additionally, Article 37 of the First Convention authorizes medical aircraft, in certain circumstances, to fly over neutral countries.

90 Chapter VII contains the provisions relating to the use and protection of the distinctive emblem of the red cross or red crescent. This chapter reaffirms the protective functions of the distinctive emblem and clarifies the parameters of its use. Additional provisions on preventing and punishing misuses of the emblem can be found in Chapter IX.

91 Chapter VIII deals with the execution of the Convention and with its dissemination as an essential condition for its effective application and an important element in creating an environment conducive to lawful behaviour. This chapter also contains a provision stipulating an absolute prohibition on belligerent reprisals against the wounded, the sick, and personnel, buildings and equipment protected by the Convention. It is through this absolute prohibition that persons protected under the First Convention on all sides of an armed conflict are safeguarded from the risk of rapid and disastrous deterioration in the treatment provided to them because of belligerent Parties responding to offences by taking identical or similar action.

92 The First Convention ends with Chapter IX, which contains articles relating to the repression of abuses and infractions, and with a final section containing the final provisions.

93 Since its adoption in 1949, the First Convention has been supplemented in a number of important areas by Additional Protocol I and by the continuous development of customary international law in this area. Among other things, Additional Protocol I no longer distinguishes between the military and civilian wounded and sick, but affords protection to all wounded and sick persons. This, as well as other additions and clarifications, are addressed in greater detail in the commentary on Additional Protocol I.

5. Contemporary relevance and challenges

94 The First Convention is as relevant today as it was at the time of its adoption. The fundamental values of humanity and dignity on which all the Geneva Conventions are based are timeless. Warfare is changing and new weapon systems are being developed, but there remains one distressing constant: armed conflicts continue to be characterized by scores of people in urgent need of medical care and by the destruction of health infrastructure and the large-scale displacement of civilians. Enhancing the protection of medical personnel and resources, thereby facilitating the effective performance of medical duties and

ensuring that victims of armed conflict can be assisted and protected, thus continues to be a key challenge.

95   The First Convention has proven to be crucial for ensuring the care and protection of the wounded and sick of the armed forces, and has had a profound influence on the development of national military policies and procedures and on resource allocation, training and implementation. On the basis of the Convention's rules, the ICRC calls upon States to abide by certain standards of treatment of the wounded and sick in times of armed conflict; and these rules, among others, enable the ICRC to carry out its humanitarian mission in the field and to offer humanitarian activities during armed conflict.

96   While the positive effects of the Geneva Conventions are not easy to quantify, this does not mean that they do not exist: ICRC delegates present in armed conflicts around the world witness them time and again. Indeed, the millions of individuals who have been harmed by armed conflict, but who have survived with their dignity intact, are perhaps the greatest testament to the humanitarian influence of the Conventions. The distinctive emblems of the red cross and the red crescent have enhanced the protection of innumerable hospitals, medical units and personnel, as well as countless wounded and sick persons. These emblems, which derive their protective value from the First Convention, are known throughout the world.

97   Despite the specific protective regime set up by the First Convention and its successes, the protection of the wounded and sick continues to face challenges. A number of armed forces and many armed groups do not employ distinct medical personnel at all, and in some cases medical personnel, transports and units choose not to identify themselves with the emblem. Contemporary armed conflicts have also been characterized by widespread interference with, and threats and attacks against, medical personnel, facilities and transports. These failures to respect the Convention significantly affect the ability of the wounded and sick to obtain medical care and undermine the efforts to mitigate suffering. The Health Care in Danger project[54] of the International Red Cross and Red Crescent Movement – aimed at making the delivery of health care safer both in armed conflict and in other emergencies – has collected incidents in various countries in which the wounded and sick, as well as medical personnel and objects, have been directly attacked or otherwise harmed in the conduct of hostilities.[55] Medical facilities and transports have also been used for

---

[54] Health Care in Danger is an ICRC-led project of the International Red Cross and Red Crescent Movement scheduled to run from 2012 to 2017 and aimed at improving the efficiency and delivery of effective and impartial health care in armed conflict and other emergencies by mobilizing experts to develop practical measures that can be implemented in the field by decision-makers, humanitarian organizations and health professionals. For further information, see http://healthcareindanger.org/hcid-project/.

[55] See e.g. ICRC, *Health Care in Danger: Violent Incidents Affecting the Delivery of Health Care, January 2012 to December 2014*, ICRC, Geneva, 2015.

military purposes: for launching attacks, storing and transporting weapons, or establishing military command and control centres. These incidents all too often constitute deliberate violations of unequivocal rules. They might not only lead to a loss of protection under the First Convention, but also undermine the trust in the purely medical character of medical facilities and transports and, as such, put all of them at risk of attack by the opposing Party. This in turn may impede efforts to collect and care for the wounded and sick.

98   It must be stressed that the fundamental challenges posed by such incidents are not due to the inadequacy of the rules of humanitarian law. The rules contained in the First Convention can only be effective, however, if they are respected and properly implemented by the belligerents. Without neglecting the possibility of and need for specific improvements in the law, the ICRC is therefore convinced that the key to increasing the care and protection of the wounded and sick of the armed forces during armed conflict is respect for and better implementation of the existing rules.

99   Since the adoption of the 1864 Convention, this body of law has been continually refined. In order to fully appreciate the significance of the First Geneva Convention more than 65 years after its adoption, it must not be viewed in isolation, but in conjunction with the other three Conventions, as well as the Additional Protocols and the large body of customary international humanitarian law that exists today. Taken together, these rules represent the principal legal regime intended to alleviate human suffering during war.

Select bibliography

Abi-Saab, Georges, 'The specificities of humanitarian law', in Christophe Swinarski (ed.), *Studies and Essays on International Humanitarian Law and Red Cross Principles in Honour of Jean Pictet*, ICRC/Martinus Nijhoff Publishers, The Hague, 1984, pp. 265–280.

Aust, Anthony, *Modern Treaty Law and Practice*, 3rd edition, Cambridge University Press, 2013, pp. 205–226.

Buffard, Isabelle and Zemanek, Karl, 'The "Object and Purpose" of a Treaty: An Enigma?', *Austrian Review of International & European Law*, Vol. 3, 1998, pp. 311–343.

Corten, Olivier and Klein, Pierre (eds), *The Vienna Conventions on the Law of Treaties: A Commentary*, Oxford University Press, 2011.

Dörr, Oliver and Schmalenbach, Kirsten (eds), *Vienna Convention on the Law of Treaties: A Commentary*, Springer, Berlin, 2012.

Fitzmaurice, Gerald, 'The Law and Procedure of the International Court of Justice 1951–4: Treaty Interpretation and Other Treaty Points, *British Yearbook of International Law*, Vol. 33, 1957, pp. 203–293.

Gardiner, Richard K., 'The Vienna Convention Rules on Treaty Interpretation', in Duncan B. Hollis, *The Oxford Guide to Treaties*, 2012, pp. 475–506.

– *Treaty Interpretation*, 2nd edition, Oxford University Press, 2015.

Reuter, Paul, *Introduction to the Law of Treaties*, 2nd edition, Graduate Institute of International Studies, Geneva, 1995.

Sinclair, Ian, *The Vienna Convention on the Law of Treaties*, 2nd edition, Manchester University Press, 1984.

Villiger, Mark E., *Commentary on the 1969 Vienna Convention on the Law of Treaties*, Martinus Nijhoff Publishers, Leiden, 2009.

PREAMBLE

❖ Text of the Preamble

The undersigned Plenipotentiaries of the Governments represented at the Diplomatic Conference held at Geneva from April 21 to August 12, 1949, for the purpose of revising the Geneva Convention for the Relief of the Wounded and Sick in Armies in the Field of July 27, 1929, have agreed as follows:

❖ Reservations or declarations

None

Contents

A. Introduction

100 The Preamble to the First Convention is very brief. It consists merely of an introductory formula that links the title of the Convention with its operative parts, but does not state, as is usual with preambles, the motivations behind the operative text. Apart from a reference to the governments represented at the 1949 Diplomatic Conference, it notes only that the Conference's purpose was to revise the 1929 Geneva Convention on the Wounded and Sick. A commentary on this rather perfunctory text might therefore seem unnecessary. However, the Conference discussed several more detailed draft preambles. While these were ultimately not adopted, important elements of them have found expression in the dispositive provisions of the Geneva Conventions, justifying a discussion here of this introductory sentence and its historical background.

101 Comparable introductory sentences were adopted as preambles to the Second, Third and Fourth Geneva Conventions.[1] In contrast, the operative texts

---

[1] For details, see the commentaries on the preambles to the Second, Third and Fourth Conventions.

of the 1977 Additional Protocols are preceded by more detailed preambles elaborating on the background, object and purpose of these instruments.[2]

B. Historical background

102 With the exception of the 1864 Geneva Convention, the conventions preceding the 1949 Geneva Conventions contained more elaborate preambles. These not only listed the States concerned and specified the preceding conventions that were revised or adapted by the respective new convention, but they also briefly set out the motivation underlying the adoption of the new convention. For example, the preamble to the 1929 Geneva Convention on the Wounded and Sick stated:

> Being equally animated by the desire to lessen, so far as lies in their power, the evils inseparable from war and desiring, for this purpose, to perfect and complete the provisions agreed to at Geneva on 22 August 1864, and 6 July 1906, for the amelioration of the condition of the wounded and sick in armies in the field, ... [3]

103   The drafts submitted by the ICRC to the International Conference of the Red Cross in Stockholm in 1948, convened for the revision of the 1929 Geneva Conventions on the Wounded and Sick and on Prisoners of War, for the revision of the 1907 Hague Convention (X) and for the creation of a new convention on the protection of civilians in time of war, contained no preambles, as the ICRC preferred to leave the task of drawing these up to the subsequent Diplomatic Conference.[4]

104   At the French delegation's suggestion, however, the Stockholm Conference adopted a draft preamble for the new civilians convention,[5] prompting the

---

[2] For details, see the commentaries on the preambles to Additional Protocols I and II.

[3] See, similarly, the preambles to the 1899 Hague Convention (III), the 1906 Geneva Convention, the 1907 Hague Convention (X) and the 1929 Geneva Convention on Prisoners of War. The preamble to the 1906 Geneva Convention noted: 'Being equally animated by the desire to lessen the inherent evils of warfare as far as is within their power, and wishing for this purpose to improve and supplement the provisions agreed upon at Geneva on 22 August 1864, ...'. In the authentic French version of the 1906 and 1929 Geneva Conventions, the preambles note in identical terms: 'également animés du désir de diminuer, autant qu'il dépend d'eux, les maux inséparables de la guerre...'.

[4] Since preambles are not part of the dispositive treaty text, it is said that ideally they are negotiated only after the main treaty text has been determined; see Aust, p. 368, and Pazarci, p. 2, para. 1.

[5] This draft preamble stated:

> The High Contracting Parties, conscious of their obligation to come to an agreement in order to protect civilian populations from the horrors of war, undertake to respect the principles of human rights which constitute the safeguard of civilisation and, in particular, to apply, at any time and in all places, the rules given hereunder:
> (1) Individuals shall be protected against any violence to their life and limb.
> (2) The taking of hostages is prohibited.
> (3) Executions may be carried out only if prior judgment has been passed by a regularly constituted court, furnished with the judicial safeguards that civilised peoples recognize to be indispensable.
> (4) Torture of any kind is strictly prohibited.
> These rules, which constitute the basis of universal human law, shall be respected without prejudice to the special stipulations provided for in the present Convention in favour of protected persons.

> See *Draft Conventions adopted by the 1948 Stockholm Conference*, p. 113.

ICRC to suggest the following preamble for inclusion in all four draft conventions, setting forth 'the main principle underlying all the humanitarian Conventions':

Respect for the personality and dignity of human beings constitutes a universal principle which is binding even in the absence of any contractual undertaking.

Such a principle demands that, in time of war, all those not actively engaged in the hostilities and all those placed *hors de combat* by reason of sickness, wounds, capture, or any other circumstance, shall be given due respect and have protection from the effects of war, and that those among them who are in suffering shall be succoured and tended without distinction of race, nationality, religious belief, political opinion or any other quality.

The High Contracting Parties solemnly affirm their intention to adhere to this principle. They will ensure its application, by the terms of the present Convention, to the wounded and sick of armed forces in the field, and pledge themselves to respect, and at all times to ensure respect for, the said Convention.[6]

105   The 1949 Diplomatic Conference addressed the question of preambles in the three committees established to discuss the four draft conventions.[7] Within these committees, this question was intensely debated. While there was no fundamental objection to the inclusion of preambles in the four Conventions or to the proposed drafts, agreement on their precise content proved difficult to achieve. In particular, the Holy See's proposal 'that there should be some reference to the Deity in each Preamble' gave rise to debate.[8] Other proposals underlined the importance of a reference to the prohibition and punishment by States Parties of certain violations of the Conventions.[9]

106   Ultimately, considering it preferable to have no preamble rather than a preamble on which unanimous agreement could not be reached,[10] the three committees decided against the adoption of any of the proposed preambles.[11]

---

[6] *ICRC Remarks and Proposals on the 1948 Stockholm Draft*, pp. 8, 26 and 36. For the draft new civilians convention, the ICRC also suggested an additional alternative text; see *ibid.* pp. 66–67.

[7] See *Final Record of the Diplomatic Conference of Geneva of 1949*, Vol. II-A, p. 33. Committee I was tasked with the discussion of the draft revised 1929 Geneva Convention on the Wounded and Sick and of the draft revised 1907 Hague Convention (X), Committee II with the discussion of the draft revised 1929 Geneva Convention on Prisoners of War, and Committee III with the discussion of the draft new convention on the protection of civilians in time of war.

[8] See *Final Record of the Diplomatic Conference of Geneva of 1949*, Vol. II-A, pp. 112–114.

[9] See *ibid.* p. 165.

[10] During the debate, for example, the ICRC had 'ventured to recommend that the Preamble to be adopted should be an element of union, embod[y]ing at least the one principle upon which all could agree – that of respect for suffering humanity. The purpose of the Conference was to agree upon the provisions in the humanitarian conventions, and not upon the philosophical or metaphysical motives which inspired them and which might be different for different nations'; see *ibid.* p. 166.

[11] First Committee III and then Committee II decided not to adopt preambles; see *ibid.* pp. 691–697, 777–782, 807 and 813 (Committee III) and pp. 322–323, 366–367, 393–398 and 561 (Committee II). In view of this, Committee I also decided against the inclusion of a preamble in the two draft conventions it had been mandated to discuss; see *ibid.* pp. 181–182. Previously, Committee I had adopted a draft preamble text elaborated by the Working Party set up for that purpose; see *ibid.* pp. 164–168.

107   As a result, no substantive preambles to the four 1949 Geneva Conventions were adopted. Important elements of the drafts that had been discussed at the Diplomatic Conference, however, found entry in the operative parts of the Conventions, in particular the fundamental obligation of humane treatment in common Article 3 governing non-international armed conflicts.[12]

108   If the imperative of humane treatment applies as a minimum in non-international armed conflicts, that minimum must *a fortiori* also be applicable in international armed conflicts, even though it was not repeated in the Convention's preamble. It thus represents a guiding principle common to all the Geneva Conventions.

C. Discussion

109 Although not a prerequisite under international law, treaties are often introduced by a preamble. They note the States or State representatives that took part in the conclusion of the treaty or refer, more generally, to the States party to the treaty; and traditionally, they also set out the motivations for the adoption of the treaty.[13] While preambles are not part of the operative clauses of a treaty,[14] they are part of a treaty's context and can thus be consulted for guidance on its interpretation, in particular as they may give an indication of a treaty's object and purpose.[15]

110   The introductory sentence adopted as the preamble to the First Convention is very brief. Apart from a reference to the 'undersigned Plenipotentiaries of the Governments represented at the Diplomatic Conference held at Geneva from April 21 to August 12, 1949', it notes only that the Conference was held 'for the purpose of revising the Geneva Convention for the Relief of the Wounded and Sick in Armies in the Field of July 27, 1929'.

111   The relationship between the First Convention and the 1929 Convention referred to in the preamble and other previous conventions is elaborated in Article 59, which provides that the First Convention 'replaces' these earlier conventions 'in relations between the High Contracting Parties'.[16]

112   The preamble provides no further reasons for the adoption of the 1949 First Convention, rendering it of limited use in determining the Convention's object and purpose. One may, however, deduce its object and purpose by considering the preambles of the Conventions that preceded it in 1906 and 1929.[17] Thus, the object and purpose of the 1949 First Geneva Convention would also be to

---

[12] For details, see the commentary on common Article 3, section B.
[13] See Aust, pp. 366–367; Mbengue, para. 1; and Pazarci, p. 3, paras 5–6.
[14] For a discussion, see Mbengue, paras 11–14.
[15] On the interpretative function of preambles, see Vienna Convention on the Law of Treaties (1969), Article 31(1)–(2); Gardiner, pp. 192, 194 (fn. 162) and 196–197; and Mbengue, paras 3–5.
[16] See the commentary on Article 59, para. 3199.
[17] Geneva Convention (1906) and Geneva Convention on the Wounded and Sick (1929). As noted earlier, the 1864 Geneva Convention contained no preamble.

'lessen, so far as lies in [the power of States], the evils inseparable from war',[18] by providing legal rules for the amelioration of the condition of the wounded and sick in armed forces in the field.

Select bibliography

Aust, Anthony, *Modern Treaty Law and Practice*, 3rd edition, Cambridge University Press, 2013.

Gardiner, Richard K., *Treaty Interpretation*, Oxford University Press, 2008, pp. 192–197.

Kovacs, Peter, 'Article 7. Full powers', in Olivier Corten and Pierre Klein (eds), *The Vienna Conventions on the Law of Treaties: A Commentary*, Vol. I, Oxford University Press, 2011, pp. 126–144.

Mbengue, Makane Moïse, 'Preamble', in Rüdiger Wolfrum (ed.), version of September 2006, *Max Planck Encyclopedia of Public International Law*, Oxford University Press, http://www.mpepil.com.

Pazarci, Hüseyin, 'Preamble', in Olivier Corten and Pierre Klein (eds), *The Vienna Conventions on the Law of Treaties: A Commentary*, Vol. I, Oxford University Press, 2011, pp. 1–11.

Salmon, Jean, 'Representatives of States in International Relations', version of August 2007, in Rüdiger Wolfrum (ed.), *Max Planck Encyclopedia of Public International Law*, Oxford University Press, http://www.mpepil.com.

---

[18] See Geneva Convention on the Wounded and Sick (1929), Preamble; see also section B of this commentary.

CHAPTER I

GENERAL PROVISIONS

113 The 1949 Geneva Conventions contain certain provisions of a general character and others which are more limited in their application. In the 1929 Geneva Convention on the Wounded and Sick, as in the earlier Conventions, these two kinds of provisions were intermingled. But when it was proposed to revise the Conventions, it was thought necessary to arrange the provisions methodically. Accordingly, the ICRC placed at the beginning of each of the four draft conventions the principal provisions of a general character, in particular those which enunciated fundamental principles to be repeated in the four conventions. This more logical arrangement had the advantage of preparing the way for the combination of the four conventions in a single instrument, which was contemplated at the time.[1] The suggested arrangement was adopted by the 1948 International Conference of the Red Cross in Stockholm, and later by the Diplomatic Conference.

114 Most of the articles in the present chapter are accordingly to be found in identical, or slightly modified, form in the three other Conventions. As a result, the commentaries on these provisions are also largely identical, except with regard to their specific application in the context of a particular Convention.

115 The articles in this chapter have come to be known as the 'common articles' of the Geneva Conventions. They are, first and foremost:

– common Article 1, on the obligation to respect and ensure respect for the Convention;
– common Article 2, setting out the scope of application of the Convention in respect of international armed conflict and occupation; and
– common Article 3, concerning non-international armed conflict.

116 Articles 4 and 5 are also included in this chapter although they are not common as such: Article 4 deals with the application of the Convention by neutral Powers, and Article 5 with the duration of application of the Convention.[2]

---

[1] See *Report of the Conference of Government Experts of 1947*, p. 332, and *Draft Conventions submitted to the 1948 Stockholm Conference*, p. 4.

[2] In the Second Convention, Article 4 deals with the field of application of the Convention, whereas Article 5 deals with the application of the Convention by neutral Powers. In the Third Convention, Article 4 sets out the list of persons entitled to prisoner-of-war status or treatment, and Article 5 regulates the beginning and end of application of the Convention. In the Fourth

Because the Fourth Convention has an additional separate provision in Article 6, from this article onwards the common articles have the same numbering in the first three Conventions, with the corresponding article in the Fourth Convention being one digit higher. Therefore, the remaining articles in this chapter are:

– common Article 6 (Article 7 in the Fourth Convention), dealing with the special agreements that the High Contracting Parties may conclude;
– common Article 7 (Article 8 in the Fourth Convention), containing the principle of non-renunciation of rights;
– common Article 8 (Article 9 in the Fourth Convention), regulating the role of the Protecting Powers;
– common Article 9 (Article 10 in the Fourth Convention), dealing with the activities of the ICRC or other impartial humanitarian organizations;
– common Article 10 (Article 11 in the Fourth Convention), on appointing a substitute for the Protecting Powers; and
– common Article 11 (Article 12 in the Fourth Convention), setting out the conciliation procedure under the Conventions.

117   There are also common articles at the end of the Convention, in particular in Chapter VIII (Execution of the Convention) and Chapter IX (Repression of abuses and infractions), as well as the final provisions. For more details, see the introductions to those chapters.

Convention, Article 4 defines the persons protected by the Convention, and Article 5 sets out some very limited derogations from the rights and privileges afforded under the Convention.

RESPECT FOR THE CONVENTION

❖ Text of the provision

The High Contracting Parties undertake to respect and to ensure respect for the present Convention in all circumstances.

❖ Reservations or declarations

None

Contents

A. Introduction

118 In the very first article of each of the four 1949 Geneva Conventions, the High
Contracting Parties 'undertake to respect and to ensure respect for the present
Convention in all circumstances'. This clause attests to the special character
of the Conventions, a great many of whose rules give expression to 'elementary
considerations of humanity'.[1] The High Contracting Parties therefore deemed
it appropriate to explicitly reiterate the general principle that the Conventions
are binding upon its Parties, which have 'to respect' them. Moreover, the High
Contracting Parties commit themselves to do everything reasonably in their
power 'to ensure respect' for the Conventions. The phrase 'to respect and to
ensure respect' applies first and foremost to the High Contracting Parties themselves, their armed forces, other persons and groups acting on their behalf, and
their populations as a whole.

119   In addition, the High Contracting Parties undertake, whether or not they are
themselves party to an armed conflict, to ensure respect for the Conventions by
other High Contracting Parties and non-State Parties to an armed conflict. The
interests protected by the Conventions are of such fundamental importance
to the human person that every High Contracting Party has a legal interest in
their observance, wherever a conflict may take place and whoever its victims
may be.[2] Moreover, the proper functioning of the system of protection provided
by the Conventions demands that States Parties not only apply the provisions
themselves, but also do everything reasonably in their power to ensure that the
provisions are respected universally. The Conventions thus create obligations
erga omnes partes, i.e. obligations towards all of the other High Contracting
Parties.[3]

---

[1] ICJ, *Military and Paramilitary Activities in and against Nicaragua case*, Merits, Judgment, 1986,
para. 218, with regard to common Article 3 ('they are rules which, in the Court's opinion, reflect
what the Court in 1949 called "elementary considerations of humanity"'); *Legality of the Threat
or Use of Nuclear Weapons*, Advisory Opinion, 1996, para. 79: 'It is undoubtedly because a great
many rules of humanitarian law applicable in armed conflict are so fundamental to the respect of
the human person and "elementary considerations of humanity" ... that the Hague and Geneva
Conventions have enjoyed a broad accession.'

[2] Similar considerations apply, for example, to the 1948 Genocide Convention, in which 'the contracting States do not have any interests of their own; they merely have, one and all, a common
interest, namely, the accomplishment of those high purposes which are the *raison d'être* of the
convention'; ICJ, *Reservations to the Genocide Convention*, Advisory Opinion, 1951, p. 23.

[3] See ICJ, *Legal Consequences of the Construction of a Wall in the Occupied Palestinian Territory*, Advisory Opinion, 2004, para. 157 ('In the Court's view, these rules [of humanitarian
law applicable in armed conflict] incorporate obligations which are essentially of an *erga omnes*
character.'); ICTY, *Kupreškić* Trial Judgment, 2000, para. 519 ('norms of international humanitarian law do not pose synallagmatic obligations, i.e. obligations of a State *vis-à-vis* another
State. Rather ... they lay down obligations towards the international community as a whole');
and Pictet (ed.), *Commentary on the First Geneva Convention*, ICRC, 1952, p. 25 ('It is not an
engagement concluded on a basis of reciprocity, binding each party to the contract only in so far
as the other party observes its obligations. It is rather a series of unilateral engagements solemnly
contracted before the world as represented by the other Contracting Parties.').

120   The interpretation of common Article 1, and in particular the expression 'ensure respect', has raised a variety of questions over the last decades. In general, two approaches have been taken. One approach advocates that under Article 1 States have undertaken to adopt all measures necessary to ensure respect for the Conventions only by their organs and private individuals within their own jurisdictions. The other, reflecting the prevailing view today and supported by the ICRC, is that Article 1 requires in addition that States ensure respect for the Conventions by other States and non-State Parties. This view was already expressed in Pictet's 1952 Commentary.[4] Developments in customary international law have since confirmed this view.[5]

121   Common Article 1 is not a mere stylistic clause but is invested with imperative force and counts among the means available to ensure compliance with the Conventions. By committing themselves to 'respect and ensure respect' for the Conventions, States have also recognized the importance of adopting all reasonable measures to prevent violations from happening in the first place.

B. Historical background

122 The 1864 and 1906 Geneva Conventions did not contain a provision similar to common Article 1. Even so, the first element of common Article 1 ('to respect') and that of ensuring respect by one's own armed forces was already implicit in the 1864 Convention, which stated: 'The implementing of the present Convention shall be arranged by the Commanders-in-Chief of the belligerent armies following the instructions of their respective Governments and in accordance with the general principles set forth in this Convention.'[6] The provision, phrased in similar terms, was reproduced in the 1906 Geneva Convention and the 1907 Hague Convention (X).[7]

123   The principle of *pacta sunt servanda* ('agreements must be honoured'), complemented by the words 'in all circumstances', was for the first time expressly spelled out in the two Geneva Conventions of 1929: 'The provisions of the present Convention shall be respected by the High Contracting Parties in all circumstances.'[8] In the original draft, this phrase was linked to the obligation to apply the Conventions in relation to other Contracting Parties, even if not all belligerents were party to the Conventions. In the course of the drafting

---

[4] Pictet (ed.), *Commentary on the First Geneva Convention*, 1952, p. 26 (while the English version of the Commentary uses the verb 'should endeavour', the French original, by the use of the verb 'doivent' ('must'), is clear that it was seen as an obligation).

[5] See ICJ, *Military and Paramilitary Activities in and against Nicaragua case*, Merits, Judgment, 1986, para. 220, and ICRC Study on Customary International Humanitarian Law (2005), Rule 144.

[6] Geneva Convention (1864), Article 8.

[7] Geneva Convention (1906), Article 25; Hague Convention (X) (1907), Article 19.

[8] Geneva Convention on the Wounded and Sick (1929), Article 25, first paragraph; Geneva Convention on Prisoners of War (1929), Article 82, first paragraph.

process, however, these obligations were separated into two different paragraphs, whereby the obligation to respect the Convention in all circumstances
acquired an independent meaning.[9]

124   In 1948, in the drafts submitted to the International Conference of the Red
Cross in Stockholm, the obligation to respect the Conventions in all circumstances was moved to its present, prominent position in Article 1 of the four
Conventions and the element of 'ensure respect' was added in order to 'stress
that if the system of protection of the Convention is to be effective, the High
Contracting Parties cannot confine themselves to implementing the Convention' but 'must also do everything in their power to ensure that the humanitarian principles on which the Convention is founded shall be universally
applied'.[10] Article 1 of the draft conventions thus read: 'The High Contracting
Parties undertake, in the name of their peoples, to respect, and to ensure respect
for the present Convention in all circumstances.'[11] The same text, apart from
the phrase 'in the name of their peoples', which had been removed by the Stockholm Conference,[12] was proposed to the Diplomatic Conference the following
year and adopted without much discussion, after only a handful of delegations
had commented on the provision.[13]

C. Scope of application

1. Rules applicable in international and non-international armed conflict

125   The High Contracting Parties undertake to respect and to ensure respect for
'the present Convention' in all circumstances. This wording covers not only
the provisions applicable to international armed conflict, including occupation,
as defined by common Article 2, but also those applicable to non-international
armed conflict under common Article 3, which forms part of 'the present Convention'. Thus, the High Contracting Parties must also ensure respect for the
rules applicable in non-international armed conflict, including by non-State
armed groups (for details on the extent of this obligation, see sections E.2
and E.3).[14] This interpretation corresponds with the fundamental nature of

---

[9] The obligation to ensure respect in all circumstances became the first paragraph of Article 25
   of the 1929 Geneva Convention on the Wounded and Sick, and the obligation to apply the
   Conventions in relation to other Contracting Parties, even if not all belligerents are party to
   the Conventions, became the second paragraph. Article 82 of the 1929 Geneva Convention
   on Prisoners of War was similarly worded. For a detailed overview of the drafting history, see
   Kalshoven, pp. 6–10.

[10] *Draft Conventions submitted to the 1948 Stockholm Conference*, p. 5.

[11] *Ibid.* pp. 4, 34, 51 and 153 for the four draft conventions, respectively.

[12] *Draft Conventions adopted by the 1948 Stockholm Conference*, pp. 9, 31, 51 and 114.

[13] *Final Record of the Diplomatic Conference of Geneva of 1949*, Vol. II-B, p. 53 (statements by
   France, Italy, Norway and the United States). See also the remarks made on other occasions by
   the delegates of Monaco (p. 79) and France (p. 84).

[14] See ICJ, *Military and Paramilitary Activities in and against Nicaragua case*, Merits, Judgment,
   1986, para. 220.

common Article 3, which has been qualified by the International Court of Justice as a 'minimum yardstick' in the event of any armed conflict.[15]

126   In addition, according to the ICRC study on customary international humanitarian law, the obligation to respect and ensure respect is not limited to the Geneva Conventions but to the entire body of international humanitarian law binding upon a particular State.[16]

2. Rules applicable in armed conflict and in peacetime

127   The obligation to respect and to ensure respect for the Conventions is not limited, however, to armed conflict, but applies equally in peacetime. Otherwise, the obligation could have been addressed to the 'Parties to the conflict' rather than to the 'High Contracting Parties' more generally. During the discussions at the 1929 Diplomatic Conference, this implication was specifically alluded to in response to concerns raised by China that the original wording of the draft article proposed by the ICRC – 'in case of war' – did not take into account those provisions of the Convention that were applicable in peacetime.[17]

128   Thus, the obligations to respect and to ensure respect also cover those provisions of the Conventions that expressly apply already in peacetime. These rules are also alluded to in common Article 2(1) ('In addition to the provisions which shall be implemented in peacetime').[18]

129   The broad temporal scope of application is also reflected in the phrase 'in all circumstances', which has been interpreted to mean both during armed conflict and in peacetime.[19]

D. Addressees of common Article 1

130   This section sets out which actors are bound by the obligations to respect and to ensure respect for the Conventions. For further details on the content of these obligations, see section E.

---

[15] *Ibid.* para. 218.
[16] ICRC Study on Customary International Humanitarian Law (2005), Rule 139.
[17] *Proceedings of the Geneva Diplomatic Conference of 1929*, pp. 329–330.
[18] For further details, see the commentary on common Article 2, section C. Sceptical Focarelli, p. 159.
[19] See Des Gouttes, *Commentaire de la Convention de Genève de 1929 sur les blessés et malades*, ICRC, 1930, p. 186: 'On a voulu signaler ici que la Convention doit s'appliquer en toutes circonstances – ce que ne disait pas celle de 1906 – en temps de paix comme en temps de guerre, quant aux dispositions qui se trouvent appliquables dans l'un comme dans l'autre cas. On a insisté sur son caractère d'obligation générale.' ('The desire here was to make it clear that the Convention must be applied in all circumstances – something that was not specified in the 1906 Convention – both in time of peace and in time of war, with respect to the provisions that are applicable in either of these situations. The emphasis was to be on the general character of the obligation.')

1. High Contracting Parties

131   Common Article 1 is addressed to the 'High Contracting Parties'. Contrary to some other provisions in the Convention, it is not addressed to the 'Parties to the conflict'. Hence, it does not cover non-State armed groups which are party to a non-international armed conflict.

132   Nevertheless, it follows from common Article 3, which is binding on all Parties to a conflict, that non-State armed groups are obliged to 'respect' the guarantees contained therein.[20] Furthermore, such groups have to 'ensure respect' for common Article 3 by their members and by individuals or groups acting on their behalf.[21] This follows from the requirement for armed groups to be organized and to have a responsible command which must ensure respect for humanitarian law. It is also part of customary international law.[22]

2. High Contracting Parties engaged in multinational operations

133   Questions on the application of common Article 1 may arise where the High Contracting Parties engage in multinational operations, i.e. operations conducted by the forces of two or more States under the auspices of an international organization, a permanent alliance or an ad hoc coalition. Examples include operations carried out under the umbrella of the United Nations or a regional organization.

134   Such operations may take a variety of forms, differing in the extent to which States retain authority over their forces. In practice, however, troop-contributing countries never transfer full 'command' to the State or international organization leading an operation but only 'operational control' or sometimes 'operational command'.[23] In addition, States almost always retain disciplinary control and criminal jurisdiction over their national contingents.

135   This may raise questions about the extent to which the conduct of these contingents is still attributable to the High Contracting Parties and thus about which subject(s) of international law may be held responsible for their conduct. This is a question of international law on the responsibility of States and

---

[20] For more details on the binding nature of common Article 3 on all Parties to the conflict, see the commentary on that article, section D.1.

[21] See also the commentary on common Article 3, section M.5.a, and Liesbeth Zegveld, *The Accountability of Armed Opposition Groups in International Law*, Cambridge University Press, 2002, pp. 92–93. For some tools, see e.g. ICRC, *Increasing Respect for International Humanitarian Law in Non-International Armed Conflicts*, ICRC, Geneva, 2008, and Sandesh Sivakumaran, 'Implementing humanitarian norms through non-State armed groups', in Heike Krieger (ed.), *Inducing Compliance with International Humanitarian Law: Lessons from the African Great Lakes Region*, Cambridge University Press, 2015, pp. 125–146.

[22] See ICRC Study on Customary International Humanitarian Law (2005), Rule 139, and Henckaerts/Doswald-Beck, commentary on Rule 139, pp. 497–498.

[23] For a definition of these terms, see Terry D. Gill and Dieter Fleck (eds), *The Handbook of the International Law of Military Operations*, Oxford University Press, 2010, pp. 631 and 638.

of international organizations that is independent of common Article 1.[24] Irrespective of attribution, the High Contracting Parties remain bound to respect and to ensure respect for the Conventions during multinational operations.

136 The fact of participating in a multinational operation does not release the High Contracting Parties from their obligations under common Article 1. To the extent that they always retain some authority over their national contingents, the High Contracting Parties must continue to ensure respect for the Conventions by these contingents. They may fulfil this obligation, in particular, by ensuring that their troops are adequately trained, equipped and instructed;[25] by exercising the disciplinary and criminal powers remaining to them; by attempting to ensure their coalition partners desist in potentially unlawful conduct; and, ultimately, by opting out of specific operations if there is an expectation that these operations may violate the Conventions.[26]

137 As a result, the High Contracting Parties remain bound to ensure respect for the Conventions; they may not evade their obligations by placing their contingents at the disposal of an international organization, a permanent alliance or an ad hoc coalition.[27] Following this logic, they should make their transfer of command and control conditional on adequate guarantees of compliance with the Conventions by these contingents.[28]

3. International organizations

138 In addition to the troop-contributing countries themselves, an international organization which exercises command and control over national contingents or which has mandated the recourse to armed force by its Member States is also obliged to respect and to ensure respect for the Conventions by these forces.

---

[24] See Draft Articles on State Responsibility (2001), Articles 4–5 and 8, and Draft Articles on the Responsibility of International Organizations (2011), Articles 6–7.

[25] See e.g. 20th International Conference of the Red Cross, Vienna, 1965, Res. XXV, Application of the Geneva Conventions by the United Nations Emergency Forces, para. 2 (recommending, following a reference to common Article 1 in the preamble, that 'the Governments of countries making contingents available to the United Nations give their troops – in view of the paramount importance of the question – adequate instruction in the Geneva Conventions before they leave their country of origin as well as orders to comply with these Conventions').

[26] For further details on the negative and positive aspects of the obligation to ensure respect for the Conventions by other Parties to a conflict, see section E.3.

[27] Draft Articles on the Responsibility of International Organizations (2011), Article 61. See also Naert, p. 510.

[28] See e.g. 20th International Conference of the Red Cross, Vienna, 1965, Res. XXV, Application of the Geneva Conventions by the United Nations Emergency Forces, para. 1 (recommending that 'appropriate arrangements be made to ensure that armed forces placed at the disposal of the United Nations observe the provisions of the Geneva Conventions'). Naert, p. 511, considers that common Article 1 may 'reinforce a State's obligations not to endow international organizations with powers without adequate guarantees'. See also Zwanenburg, p. 108 ('Arguably, a state's transfer of powers over part of its armed forces to an international organization without adequate guarantees that the organization will respect humanitarian law breaches such an obligation.').

139   International organizations are – in the current state of international law – not directly or formally bound by the Conventions because only States may become 'High Contracting Parties'. However, it is now widely agreed that, as subjects of international law, they are bound by customary international humanitarian law,[29] and thus also by the obligations to respect and to ensure respect for that body of law.[30]

140   To the extent that an international organization exercises command and control in respect of an operation, it is obliged to respect and to ensure respect for humanitarian law by the national contingents placed at its disposal in essentially the same way as States must respect and ensure respect for the Conventions by their armed forces. For example, the United Nations systematically provides training in humanitarian law for the personnel of its military contingents, both at the start and in the course of their deployment.[31]

141   The applicability of humanitarian law to UN forces has been affirmed by the 1999 UN Secretary-General's Bulletin, which was promulgated 'for the purpose of setting out fundamental principles and rules of international humanitarian law applicable to United Nations forces conducting operations under United Nations command and control' and may be seen as a means to respect and to ensure respect for humanitarian law.[32] In addition, status-of-forces agreements (SOFAs) concluded between the United Nations and a State hosting a UN peace operation typically require the United Nations to ensure that its operation is conducted 'with full respect for the principles and rules of the international conventions applicable to the conduct of military personnel', including 'the four Geneva Conventions of 12 August 1949 and their Additional Protocols of 8 June 1977 and the UNESCO Convention of 14 May 1954 for the Protection of Cultural Property in the Event of Armed Conflict', and place a corresponding duty on the host State to treat at all times the military personnel of the operation with full respect for such principles and rules.[33]

---

[29] See ICJ, *Reparation for Injuries Suffered in the Service of the United Nations*, Advisory Opinion, 1949, p. 179; *Interpretation of the Agreement of 25 March 1951 between the WHO and Egypt*, Advisory Opinion, 1980, para. 37; and *Legality of the Use by a State of Nuclear Weapons in Armed Conflict (WHO)*, Advisory Opinion, 1996, para. 25, holding that 'international organizations...do not, unlike States, possess a general competence. International organizations are governed by the "principle of speciality", that is to say, they are invested by the States which create them with powers'. For a discussion of the implications of this principle for the applicability of humanitarian law to international organizations, see Kolb/Porretto/Vité, pp. 121–143; Naert, pp. 533–534; Shraga, 1998, p. 77; and Engdahl, p. 519.

[30] See ICJ, *Legal Consequences of the Construction of a Wall in the Occupied Palestinian Territory*, Advisory Opinion, 2004, para. 160; ICTY, *Tadić* Decision on the Defence Motion for Interlocutory Appeal on Jurisdiction, 1995, para. 93; see also Boisson de Chazournes/Condorelli, 2000, p. 70; Boisson de Chazournes/Condorelli, 2006, pp. 15–16; and Engdahl, p. 517.

[31] See e.g. Agreement between the UN and the AU and the Government of Sudan concerning the Status of the AU/UN Hybrid Operation in Darfur (2008).

[32] UN Secretary-General's Bulletin (1999), Preamble.

[33] See e.g. The Status of Forces Agreement between the United Nations and the Government of Republic of South Sudan concerning the United Nations Mission in South Sudan (UNMISS), Juba, 8 August 2011, paras 6(a) and (b). While such provisions are not included in the 'Model status-of-forces agreement for peace-keeping operations' as prepared by the UN Secretary-General at the request of the General Assembly (UN Doc. A/45/594, 9 October 1990), they have

142   At the same time, and even absent any such exercise of command and control, international organizations, whether or not they are themselves party to the conflict, are also obliged under customary international law to ensure respect by others.[34] This is particularly the case where the organization has mandated the use of armed force in the first place,[35] or engages in operations in support of other Parties to the conflict.[36]

E. The obligations flowing from common Article 1

1. The obligations to respect and to ensure respect by the armed forces and other persons or groups whose conduct is attributable to the High Contracting Parties

143   The duty to respect the Geneva Conventions reaffirms the general principle of the law of treaties *'pacta sunt servanda'* as codified in Article 26 of the 1969 Vienna Convention on the Law of Treaties: 'Every treaty in force is binding upon the parties to it and must be performed by them in good faith.'

144   Acts or omissions which amount to breaches of the Conventions entail the international responsibility of a High Contracting Party, provided those acts or omissions are attributable to that Party according to the rules on State responsibility. This concerns not only the conduct of State organs as defined by the internal law of the State but also that of other persons or groups acting on its behalf, such as volunteer and militia forces within the meaning of Article 4(A)(2) of the Third Convention, other armed groups under the requisite control of the State, and in certain cases private military and security companies whose services are contracted by the State.[37] As far as this principle

---

been included in relevant SOFAs since the UN concluded such an agreement with Rwanda in respect of the UN Assistance Mission in Rwanda (UNAMIR) on 5 November 1993, United Nations *Treaty Series*, Vol. 1748, 1993, pp. 3–28.

34 See Shraga, 1998, p. 71, and David, para. 3.13. The obligation to ensure respect by others was alluded to by the ICJ in its 2004 Advisory Opinion on the *Legal Consequences of the Construction of a Wall in the Occupied Palestinian Territory*, para. 160, specifically with regard to the UN, which it addresses last, in three paragraphs (paras 158–160) dealing with the obligations to respect and to ensure respect for humanitarian law: 'Finally, the Court is of the view that the United Nations, and especially the General Assembly and the Security Council, should consider what further action is required to bring to an end the illegal situation resulting from the construction of the wall and the associated régime, taking due account of the present Advisory Opinion.'

35 See Shraga, 1998, pp. 71–72, and Kolb/Porretto/Vité, pp. 153–154 and 332–333.

36 See Human rights due diligence policy on United Nations support to non-United Nations security forces, UN Doc. A/67/775–S/2013/110, 5 March 2013. For a practical example, see e.g. UN Security Council, Res. 1906, 23 December 2009, para. 22: *'Reiterates...* that the support of MONUC [United Nations Organization Stabilization Mission in the Democratic Republic of the Congo (DRC)] to FARDC [Armed Forces of the DRC]-led military operations against foreign and Congolese armed groups is strictly conditioned on FARDC's compliance with international humanitarian, human rights and refugee law and on an effective joint planning of these operations.'

37 On private military and security companies contracted by a State, see Montreux Document on Private Military and Security Companies (2008), Part I, para. 7.

is concerned, common Article 1 does not add anything new to what is already provided for by general international law.

145   The novelty of the provision lies in the addition of the duty to 'ensure respect', which must be done 'in all circumstances'. This sets a clear standard, as 'ensuring' means 'to make certain that something will occur or be so' or inversely 'make sure that (a problem) does not occur'.[38] States are thus required to take appropriate measures to prevent violations from happening in the first place.[39] Accordingly, the High Contracting Parties must – starting in peacetime – take all measures necessary to ensure respect for the Conventions.[40] Respecting the Conventions in case of an armed conflict regularly presupposes that preparations have been made in advance.[41]

146   In principle, the High Contracting Parties have some latitude in choosing the measures by which to ensure respect for the Conventions, as long as these are adequate to achieve the desired result. Their margin of choice is limited, however, especially in cases where the Conventions oblige the High Contracting Parties to take specific measures. The Conventions contain a number of provisions designed to ensure their implementation by the High Contracting Parties:

- *Instruction within armed forces*: The High Contracting Parties are required to disseminate the Conventions as widely as possible in their respective countries and, in particular, to include the study thereof in their programmes of military instruction.[42]
- *Rules of application*: The High Contracting Parties are required to communicate to one another official translations of the Conventions, as well as laws and regulations they may adopt to ensure their application.[43]
- *Suppression of breaches*: The High Contracting Parties are required to search for, prosecute or extradite alleged perpetrators of grave breaches 'regardless of their nationality' and to enact any necessary legislation in this respect. They are further required to suppress all other breaches of the Conventions.[44]

---

[38] *Concise Oxford English Dictionary*, 12th edition, Oxford University Press, 2011, p. 475.

[39] See also Basic Principles and Guidelines on the Right to a Remedy and Reparation for Victims of Gross Violations of International Human Rights Law and Serious Violations of IHL (2005), para. 3(a).

[40] See also common Article 2(1) ('In addition to the provisions which shall be implemented in peacetime'); First Convention, Article 45; and Second Convention, Article 46. See also Additional Protocol I, Article 80.

[41] On preparatory measures, see the commentary on common Article 2, section C.

[42] First Convention, Article 47; Second Convention, Article 48; Third Convention, Article 127; Fourth Convention, Article 144. These provisions are supplemented by Additional Protocol I, Article 83; Additional Protocol II, Article 19; and Additional Protocol III, Article 7.

[43] First Convention, Article 48; Second Convention, Article 49; Third Convention, Article 128; Fourth Convention, Article 145. These provisions are supplemented by Additional Protocol I, Article 84.

[44] First Convention, Article 49; Second Convention, Article 50; Third Convention, Article 129; Fourth Convention, Article 146. These provisions are supplemented by Additional Protocol I, Article 85.

– *Abuses of the emblem*: The High Contracting Parties are required, if their legislation is not already adequate, to take measures necessary for the prevention and repression, at all times, of abuses of the emblem.[45]

147   The Conventions propose several other measures by which the High Contracting Parties may ensure respect, notably appointing a Protecting Power or a substitute,[46] and using the enquiry procedure provided for in the Conventions.[47]

148   In addition, a number of measures can be seen as implicit in the Conventions or are considered part of customary international law and should therefore be adopted by States as means to fulfil their obligations to respect and to ensure respect for the Conventions. These include, in particular, giving orders and instructions to subordinate personnel to ensure respect for the Conventions and supervising their implementation,[48] and making legal advisers available to the armed forces when necessary.[49]

149   States party to a non-international armed conflict may ensure respect for their obligations under common Article 3 through essentially the same measures. Common Article 3(3) specifically requires the Parties to the conflict to endeavour to conclude special agreements in order to bring into force all or parts of the other provisions of the Conventions.

2. The obligation to ensure respect by the whole population over which a High Contracting Party exercises authority

150   The duty to ensure respect covers not only the armed forces and other persons or groups acting on behalf of the High Contracting Parties but extends to the whole of the population over which they exercise authority, i.e. also to private

---

[45] First Convention, Article 54; Second Convention, Article 45. These provisions are supplemented by Additional Protocol I, Article 18, and Additional Protocol III, Article 6.

[46] First Convention, Articles 8 and 10; Second Convention, Articles 8 and 10; Third Convention, Articles 8 and 10; Fourth Convention, Articles 9 and 11.

[47] First Convention, Article 52; Second Convention, Article 53; Third Convention, Article 132; Fourth Convention, Article 149. These provisions are supplemented by the creation of the International Humanitarian Fact-Finding Commission pursuant to Additional Protocol I, Article 90.

[48] See Pictet (ed.), *Commentary on the First Geneva Convention*, ICRC, 1952, p. 26 ('It would not, for example, be enough for a State to give orders or directives to a few civilian or military authorities, leaving it to them to arrange as they pleased for the details of their execution. It is for the State to supervise their execution.'); Sandoz/Swinarski/Zimmermann (eds), *Commentary on the Additional Protocols*, ICRC, 1987, para. 41 ('[T]he duty to respect implies that of ensuring respect by civilian and military authorities, the members of the armed forces, and in general, by the population as a whole. This means not only that preparatory measures must be taken to permit the implementation of the Protocol, but also that such implementation should be supervised. In this respect, the phrase "to ensure respect" essentially anticipates the measures for execution and supervision laid down in Article 80 ("Measures for execution").') See also Additional Protocol I, Article 80(2).

[49] See Additional Protocol I, Article 82, and ICRC Study on Customary International Humanitarian Law (2005), Rule 141.

persons whose conduct is not attributable to the State.[50] This constitutes a general duty of due diligence to prevent and repress breaches of the Conventions by private persons over which a State exercises authority, including persons in occupied territory.[51] This is an obligation of means, whose content depends on the specific circumstances, in particular the foreseeability of the violations and the State's knowledge thereof, the gravity of the breach, the means reasonably available to the State and the degree of influence it exercises over the private persons.[52]

151   In addition, a number of provisions in the Conventions expressly require the High Contracting Parties to take measures to ensure respect for the Conventions by private persons:

– *Dissemination among the civilian population*: The High Contracting Parties undertake to include the study of the Conventions, if possible, in their programmes of civil instruction, so that the principles thereof may become known to the entire population.[53]
– *Suppression of breaches*: The High Contracting Parties are required to search for, prosecute or extradite alleged perpetrators of grave breaches 'regardless of their nationality' and to suppress all other breaches of the Conventions. This includes breaches committed by private persons.[54]

152   Several other provisions oblige the High Contracting Parties more generally to *protect* specific persons or objects, which includes their protection against acts of private persons. These provisions cover some of the following areas:

– *Wounded, sick and shipwrecked*: The First and Second Conventions require that the wounded, sick and shipwrecked be respected and protected in all

---

[50] *Final Record of the Diplomatic Conference of Geneva of 1949*, Vol. II-B, p. 53 (Norway, United States) ('ensure respect of the Conventions by the population as a whole'). See also Inter-American Court of Human Rights, *Mapiripán Massacre case*, Judgment, 2005, para. 114.

[51] See Koivurova, para. 32; Sassòli, pp. 411–412; and Ryngaert/Van de Meulebroucke, pp. 462–463.

[52] On the standard of due diligence, see ICJ, *Application of the Genocide Convention case*, Merits, Judgment, 2007, paras 430–431. See also Pisillo-Mazzeschi, p. 45, and Ryngaert/Van de Meulebroucke, p. 463. For an interpretation of the due diligence standard in the context of human rights law, see European Court of Human Rights, *Osman v. UK*, Judgment, 1998, paras 115–116; Inter-American Court of Human Rights, *Velásquez Rodríguez case*, Judgment, 1988, paras 172–175; *Pueblo Bello Massacre case*, Judgment, 2006, paras 123–141; UN Human Rights Committee, *General Comment No. 31, The Nature of the General Legal Obligation Imposed on States Parties to the Covenant*, UN Doc. CCPR/C/21/Rev.1/Add. 13, 26 May 2004, para. 8; African Commission on Human and Peoples' Rights, *Association of Victims of Post Electoral Violence & INTERIGHTS v. Cameroon*, Decision, 2009, paras 89–92.

[53] First Convention, Article 47; Second Convention, Article 48; Third Convention, Article 127; Fourth Convention, Article 144. These provisions are supplemented by Additional Protocol I, Article 83(1).

[54] First Convention, Article 49; Second Convention, Article 50; Third Convention, Article 129; Fourth Convention, Article 146. These provisions are supplemented by Additional Protocol I, Article 85.

circumstances.[55] The First Convention, in particular, enjoins the civilian population to respect the wounded and sick and to abstain from offering them violence.[56] Furthermore, the First and Second Conventions explicitly state the duty to protect the wounded, sick and shipwrecked against pillage and ill-treatment.[57]

– *Medical units and establishments, medical and religious personnel, medical transports*: The First and Second Conventions provide for the respect and protection of fixed establishments and mobile medical units of the medical service, medical and religious personnel, medical transports, and hospital ships and their crews.[58]

– *The dead*: The First and Second Conventions set out the duty to prevent the dead from being despoiled. This includes acts of despoliation committed by the civilian population.[59]

– *Prisoners of war*: The Third Convention provides for the duty to protect prisoners of war at all times, particularly against acts of violence or intimidation and against insults and public curiosity.[60]

– *Civilian wounded and sick, the infirm, expectant mothers*: The Fourth Convention requires that the wounded and sick, as well as the infirm and expectant mothers, be given particular protection and respect. This includes protection from any violence, harassment or other improper acts by the civilian population.[61]

– *Civilian hospitals and their staff*: The Fourth Convention provides for the protection of civilian hospitals and their staff, as well as the transportation of wounded and sick civilians, the infirm and maternity cases.[62]

– *Protected persons*: The Fourth Convention provides for the duty to respect protected persons, and especially to protect them against all acts of violence or threats thereof and against insults and public curiosity.[63]

– *Women*: The Fourth Convention provides for the duty to protect women against any attack on their honour, in particular against rape, enforced prostitution, or any form of indecent assault.[64]

---

[55] First Convention, Article 12(1); Second Convention, Article 12(1). These provisions are supplemented by Additional Protocol I, Article 10, and Additional Protocol II, Article 7.

[56] First Convention, Article 18(2). This provision is supplemented by Additional Protocol I, Article 17(1).

[57] First Convention, Article 15(1); Second Convention, Article 18(1).

[58] First Convention, Articles 19(1), 24, 25, 26 and 35(1); Second Convention, Articles 22(1), 24, 25, 27, 36 and 37(1). These provisions are supplemented by Additional Protocol I, Article 12 (medical units) and Articles 21–31 (medical transportation).

[59] First Convention, Article 15(1); Second Convention, Article 18(1). These provisions are supplemented by Additional Protocol I, Article 34.

[60] Third Convention, Article 13(2).   [61] Fourth Convention, Article 16.

[62] Fourth Convention, Articles 18(1), 20(1), 21 and 22. These provisions are supplemented by Additional Protocol I, Article 12 (medical units), Article 15 (civilian medical personnel) and Articles 21–31 (medical transportation).

[63] Fourth Convention, Article 27(1).

[64] Fourth Convention, Article 27(2). This provision is supplemented by Additional Protocol I, Article 76(1).

3. The obligation to ensure respect by others

153 The obligation to ensure respect also has an external dimension related to ensuring respect for the Conventions by others that are Party to a conflict. Accordingly, States, whether neutral, allied or enemy, must do everything reasonably in their power to ensure respect for the Conventions by others that are Party to a conflict.

154   This duty to ensure respect by others comprises both a negative and a positive obligation. Under the negative obligation, High Contracting Parties may neither encourage, nor aid or assist in violations of the Conventions by Parties to a conflict. Under the positive obligation, they must do everything reasonably in their power to prevent and bring such violations to an end. This external dimension of the obligation to ensure respect for the Conventions goes beyond the principle of *pacta sunt servanda*.

155   Common Article 1 does not spell out whose respect for the Conventions must be ensured, and it has been argued that the drafters only intended to impose a duty on States to ensure respect by their peoples.[65] The statements made by the delegates of Norway and the United States during the Diplomatic Conference leading to the adoption of the Conventions indicate that they understood the phrase 'to ensure respect' essentially as an undertaking by States to ensure respect of the Conventions by their populations as a whole.[66] The drafters did, however, agree upon a very broad formulation. Taking into consideration the overwhelming humanitarian importance of the Geneva Conventions and the timing of their drafting – shortly after the end of the Second World War – this broad formulation accommodates the external dimension of the obligation to ensure respect for the Conventions. In statements prior to the 1948 Stockholm Conference and during the Diplomatic Conference of 1949, the ICRC made clear that in its view common Article 1 meant that the Contracting Parties 'should do all in their power to see that the basic humanitarian principles of the Conventions were universally applied'.[67]

156   Subsequent practice has confirmed the existence of an obligation to ensure respect by others under common Article 1. The obligation was expressly acknowledged by the Teheran Conference on Human Rights in 1968,[68] and

---

[65] See Kalshoven, p. 28.

[66] *Final Record of the Diplomatic Conference of Geneva of 1949*, Vol. II-B, p. 53 (Norway and United States).

[67] *Ibid.* For the original statement, see *Draft Conventions submitted to the 1948 Stockholm Conference*, p. 5: 'The ICRC believes it necessary to stress that if the system of protection of the Convention is to be effective, the High Contracting Parties cannot confine themselves to implementing the Convention. They must also do everything in their power to ensure that the humanitarian principles on which the Convention is founded shall be universally applied.'

[68] International Conference on Human Rights, Teheran, 1968, Res. XXIII, Human Rights in Armed Conflict, Preamble.

subsequently referred to by the UN General Assembly.[69] It was in full knowledge of these developments that the clause was reaffirmed in Article 1(1) of Additional Protocol I,[70] and later in Article 38(1) of the 1989 Convention on the Rights of the Child and Article 1(1) of the 2005 Additional Protocol III. The 2013 Arms Trade Treaty, which subjects arms transfer decisions to respect for humanitarian law by the recipient, refers explicitly to the obligations to respect and to ensure respect.[71] The obligation to ensure respect by others was explicitly endorsed by the International Court of Justice,[72] the UN Security Council,[73] the International Conference of the Red Cross and Red Crescent,[74] and the High Contracting Parties meeting in other fora.[75] The ICRC has taken a number of steps, confidentially or publicly, to encourage States, even those not party to a conflict, to use their influence or offer their cooperation to ensure respect for the Conventions.[76]

---

[69] UN General Assembly, Res. 2851 (XXVI), Report of the Special Committee to Investigate Israeli Practices Affecting the Human Rights of the Population of the Occupied Territories, 20 December 1971, Preamble and para. 9.

[70] See e.g. ICRC, Questionnaire concerning measures intended to reinforce the implementation of the Geneva Conventions of August 12, 1949, Geneva, 1973, p. 19; Levrat, p. 269; and Sandoz/Swinarski/Zimmermann (eds), *Commentary on the Additional Protocols*, ICRC, 1987, para. 44. But see Kalshoven, p. 52, who considers that 'the (incontestable) reiteration and (merely technical) reaffirmation of the text of common Article 1 in Protocol I cannot seriously be claimed to express anything like a full understanding and wish of that Conference with respect to the text they were simply repeating verbatim'.

[71] Arms Trade Treaty (2013), Preamble, 5th paragraph of the 'Principles'.

[72] ICJ, *Military and Paramilitary Activities in and against Nicaragua case*, Merits, Judgment, 1986, para. 220; *Legal Consequences of the Construction of a Wall in the Occupied Palestinian Territory*, Advisory Opinion, 2004, paras 158–159; and *Armed Activities on the Territory of the Congo case*, Judgment, 2005, paras 211 and 345.

[73] UN Security Council, Res. 681, 20 December 1990, para. 5.

[74] 25th International Conference of the Red Cross, Geneva, 1986, Res. I, Respect for international humanitarian law in armed conflicts and action by the ICRC for persons protected by the Geneva Conventions, para. 5; 26th International Conference of the Red Cross and Red Crescent, Geneva, 1995, Res. I, International humanitarian law: From law to action. Report on the follow-up to the International Conference for the Protection of War Victims, para. 2, and Res. II, Protection of the civilian population in period of armed conflict, para. A(a); 27th International Conference of the Red Cross and Red Crescent, Geneva, 1999, Adoption of the Declaration and the Plan of Action, Res. I, Final goal 1.1, para. 1; 28th International Conference of the Red Cross and Red Crescent, Geneva, 2003, Res. I, Adoption of the Declaration and Agenda for Humanitarian Action, Final Goal 2.3; and 30th International Conference of the Red Cross and Red Crescent, Geneva, 2007, Res. 3, Reaffirmation and implementation of international humanitarian law: Preserving human life and dignity in armed conflict, para. 2.

[75] See e.g. International Conference for the Protection of War Victims, Geneva, 1993, Final Declaration, Part II, para. 11; Conference of High Contracting Parties to the Fourth Geneva Convention, Geneva, 5 December 2001, Declaration, para. 4; and Conference of High Contracting Parties to the Fourth Geneva Convention, Geneva, 17 December 2014, Declaration, para. 4.

[76] See e.g. ICRC, News Release 03/63, Israel and the occupied and autonomous Palestinian territories: Deliberate attacks on civilians must stop, 10 September 2003; News Release 82/07, Myanmar: ICRC denounces major and repeated violations of international humanitarian law, 29 June 2007; News Release 95/8, Rwanda: ICRC sounds alarm on appalling prison conditions, 31 March 1995; Conflict in Southern Africa, ICRC Appeal, 19 March 1979, reproduced in *International Review of the Red Cross*, Vol. 19, No. 209, April 1979, pp. 85–90, at 89; Conflict between Iraq and Iran, ICRC Appeal, 11 May 1983, reproduced in *International Review of the Red Cross*, Vol. 23, No. 235, August 1983, pp. 220–222, at 222; Conflict between Iraq and Iran, Second ICRC Appeal, 15 February 1984, reproduced in *International Review of the Red Cross*, Vol. 24,

157   As mentioned, the duty to ensure respect by others comprises both negative and positive obligations:

a. Negative obligations

158 Pursuant to common Article 1, the High Contracting Parties have certain negative obligations, which means they must abstain from certain conduct. In particular, they may neither encourage, nor aid or assist in violations of the Conventions.[77] It would be contradictory if common Article 1 obliged the High Contracting Parties to 'respect and to ensure respect' by their own armed forces while allowing them to contribute to violations by other Parties to a conflict. Accordingly, the International Court of Justice recognized in 1986 the negative obligation 'not to encourage persons or groups engaged in the conflict in Nicaragua to act in violation of the provisions of Article 3 common to the four 1949 Geneva Conventions'.[78] This obligation 'not to encourage' has also been expressly acknowledged by the High Contracting Parties themselves.[79]

159   In addition, under general international law States are responsible for knowingly aiding or assisting another State in the commission of an internationally wrongful act.[80] According to the ILC, this requires that 'the relevant State organ *intended*, by the aid or assistance given, to facilitate the occurrence of the wrongful conduct' (emphasis added).[81] The subjective element of 'intent' is unnecessary, however, for the purposes of common Article 1. In line with the rationale laid out in the preceding paragraph, common Article 1 does not tolerate that a State would knowingly contribute to violations of the Conventions by a Party to a conflict, whatever its intentions may be.

160   Common Article 1 and the rules on State responsibility thus operate at different levels. The obligation to ensure respect for the Conventions is an autonomous primary obligation that imposes more stringent conditions than those required for the secondary rules on State responsibility for aiding or assisting. What is at stake is more than aid or assistance to violations of the rules of international law but concerns aid or assistance to violations of rules

---

No. 239, April 1984, pp. 113–115, at 115; and ICRC appeal for a humanitarian mobilization, reproduced in *International Review of the Red Cross*, Vol. 25, No. 244, October 1985, pp. 30–34, at 33.

[77] On the corresponding customary duty to ensure respect, see ICRC Study on Customary International Humanitarian Law (2005), Rule 144 ('States may not encourage violations of international humanitarian law by parties to an armed conflict.').

[78] ICJ, *Military and Paramilitary Activities in and against Nicaragua case*, Merits, Judgment, 1986, para. 220.

[79] 30th International Conference of the Red Cross and Red Crescent, Geneva, 2007, Res. 3, Reaffirmation and implementation of international humanitarian law: Preserving human life and dignity in armed conflict, para. 2.

[80] See Draft Articles on State Responsibility (2001), Article 16.

[81] *Ibid.* commentary on Article 16, para. 5. See also para. 9 with regard to human rights abuses. For a critique of the reference to 'intent' in this context, see Boivin, pp. 471–472, with further references.

whose observance the High Contracting Parties have specifically undertaken to respect and ensure respect for.[82] Financial, material or other support in the knowledge that such support will be used to commit violations of humanitarian law would therefore violate common Article 1, even though it may not amount to aiding or assisting in the commission of a wrongful act by the receiving States for the purposes of State responsibility.

161   In the event of multinational operations, common Article 1 thus requires High Contracting Parties to opt out of a specific operation if there is an expectation, based on facts or knowledge of past patterns, that it would violate the Conventions, as this would constitute aiding or assisting violations.

162   An illustration of a negative obligation can be made in the context of arms transfers. Common Article 1 requires High Contracting Parties to refrain from transferring weapons if there is an expectation, based on facts or knowledge of past patterns, that such weapons would be used to violate the Conventions.[83]

163   Lastly, under general international law, there are additional negative obligations, namely not to recognize as lawful a situation created by a serious breach of peremptory norms of international law and not to render aid or assistance in maintaining such a situation.[84] These obligations are relevant for the Geneva Conventions inasmuch as they embody norms from which no derogation is permitted.[85] In its 2004 Advisory Opinion in the *Wall* case, the International Court of Justice seems to have linked the same obligations with Article 1 of

---

[82] See also in the context of arms transfers, Sassòli, p. 413, who considers that once a State knows that the receiving State systematically commits violations of humanitarian law with certain weapons, 'ongoing assistance is necessarily given with a view to facilitating further violations. Such a strict standard may not be that of the ILC in its Commentary, but it is supported by the special obligation, under international humanitarian law, of the third State not only *not* to assist in violations, but also to "ensure respect" for the rules of international humanitarian law by all other States. A State providing assistance, knowing that the latter is used for violations, is certainly not complying with that specific obligation.' See also Brehm, pp. 385–386.

[83] This would require an appropriate assessment prior to any arms transfer. See Dörmann/Serralvo, pp. 732–735; Daniel Thürer, *International Humanitarian Law: Theory, Practice, Context*, The Hague Academy of International Law, 2011, p. 223; and ICRC, *Arms Transfer Decisions: Applying International Humanitarian Law Criteria*, ICRC, Geneva, May 2007.

[84] See Draft Articles on State Responsibility (2001), Article 41(2).

[85] See ICJ, *Legality of the Threat or Use of Nuclear Weapons*, Advisory Opinion, 1996, para. 79 ('a great many rules of humanitarian law applicable in armed conflict...constitute intransgressible principles of international customary law'); *Legal Consequences of the Construction of a Wall in the Occupied Palestinian Territory*, Advisory Opinion, 2004, para. 157; Draft Articles on State Responsibility (2001), commentary on Article 40, para. 5 ('the basic rules of international humanitarian law applicable in armed conflict' are part of peremptory norms of international law); ILC, Conclusions of the work of the Study Group on the Fragmentation of International Law: Difficulties arising from the diversification and expansion of international law, reproduced in *Report of the International Law Commission on the work of its fifty-eighth session*, UN Doc. A/61/10, 2006, Chapter XII, para. 251, subparagraph (33), p. 182 ('The most frequently cited examples of *jus cogens* norms are...basic rules of international humanitarian law applicable in armed conflict'); and ICTY, *Kupreškić* Trial Judgment, 2000, para. 520 ('most norms of international humanitarian law, in particular those prohibiting war crimes, crimes against humanity and genocide, are also peremptory norms of international law or *jus cogens*, i.e. of a non-derogable and overriding character').

the Fourth Convention.[86] These obligations can be seen, moreover, as a corollary of the duty neither to encourage nor to aid or assist in the *commission* of violations of the Conventions.

b. Positive obligations

164 The High Contracting Parties also have positive obligations under common Article 1, which means they must take proactive steps to bring violations of the Conventions to an end and to bring an erring Party to a conflict back to an attitude of respect for the Conventions, in particular by using their influence on that Party.[87] This obligation is not limited to stopping ongoing violations but includes an obligation to prevent violations when there is a foreseeable risk that they will be committed and to prevent further violations in case they have already occurred.[88]

165 States remain in principle free to choose between different possible measures, as long as those adopted are considered adequate to ensure respect. The duty to ensure respect is to be carried out with due diligence. As noted above, its content depends on the specific circumstances, including the gravity of the breach, the means reasonably available to the State, and the degree of influence it exercises over those responsible for the breach. Unlike the negative obligation described above, it is an obligation of means, i.e. the High Contracting Parties are not responsible for a possible failure of their efforts as long as they have done everything reasonably in their power to bring the violations to an end.[89]

---

[86] See ICJ, *Legal Consequences of the Construction of a Wall in the Occupied Palestinian Territory*, Advisory Opinion, 2004, paras 158–159. See also Tom Moerenhout, 'The Obligation to Withhold from Trading in Order Not to Recognize and Assist Settlements and their Economic Activity in Occupied Territories', *Journal of International Humanitarian Law Studies*, Vol. 3, 2012, pp. 344–385.

[87] See 30th International Conference of the Red Cross and Red Crescent, Geneva, 2007, Res. 3, Reaffirmation and implementation of international humanitarian law: Preserving human life and dignity in armed conflict, para. 2. See also ICRC, 'Action by the International Committee of the Red Cross in the event of violations of international humanitarian law or of other fundamental rules protecting persons in situations of violence', A 1308, 16 February 2005, reproduced in *International Review of the Red Cross*, Vol. 87, No. 858, June 2005, pp. 393–400, at 396: 'Moreover, it is generally recognized that common Article 1 requires States that are not party to an armed conflict to strive to *ensure respect* for the law by taking every possible measure to put an end to violations of the law by a party to a conflict, in particular by using their influence on that party.' On the corresponding customary duty to ensure respect, see ICRC Study on Customary International Humanitarian Law (2005), Rule 144 ('[States] must exert their influence, to the degree possible, to stop violations of international humanitarian law.'). More cautious, Gasser, p. 32: 'In conclusion, it can be argued that a third-party State has at least an obligation to examine a situation involving a breach of humanitarian law by a belligerent and to consider in good faith whether action should be taken.'

[88] See 30th International Conference of the Red Cross and Red Crescent, Geneva, 2007, Res. 3, Reaffirmation and implementation of international humanitarian law: Preserving human life and dignity in armed conflict, para. 2; Dörmann/Serralvo, pp. 728–732; Geiss, 2015a, p. 117; Devillard, pp. 96–97; Gasser, pp. 31–32; and Levrat, p. 277.

[89] See also ICJ, *Application of the Genocide Convention case*, Merits, Judgment, 2007, para. 430. See also ICRC Study on Customary International Humanitarian Law (2005), Rule 144 ('to the

166   A similar due diligence obligation exists under Article 1 of the 1948 Genocide Convention, according to which '[t]he Contracting Parties confirm that genocide, whether committed in time of peace or in time of war, is a crime under international law which they undertake to prevent and to punish'. In the *Genocide Convention* case, the International Court of Justice held:

> [T]he obligation in question [to prevent genocide] is one of conduct and not one of result, in the sense that a State cannot be under an obligation to succeed, whatever the circumstances, in preventing the commission of genocide: the obligation of States parties is rather to employ all means reasonably available to them, so as to prevent genocide so far as possible. A State does not incur responsibility simply because the desired result is not achieved; responsibility is however incurred if the State manifestly failed to take all measures to prevent genocide which were within its power, and which might have contributed to preventing the genocide. In this area the notion of 'due diligence', which calls for an assessment *in concreto*, is of critical importance.[90]

As for the applicable standard of due diligence, the Court considered:

> Various parameters operate when assessing whether a State has duly discharged the obligation concerned. The first, which varies greatly from one State to another, is clearly the capacity to influence effectively the action of persons likely to commit or already committing, genocide. This capacity itself depends, among other things, on the geographical distance of the State concerned from the scene of the events, and on the strength of the political links, as well as links of all other kinds, between the authorities of that State and the main actors in the events.[91]

167   The duty to ensure respect for the Geneva Conventions is particularly strong in the case of a partner in a joint operation, even more so as this case is closely related to the negative duty neither to encourage nor to aid or assist in violations of the Conventions. The fact, for example, that a High Contracting Party participates in the financing, equipping, arming or training of the armed forces of a Party to a conflict, or even plans, carries out and debriefs operations jointly with such forces, places it in a unique position to influence the behaviour of those forces, and thus to ensure respect for the Conventions.

168   In the case of the transfer of detainees to a co-belligerent, non-belligerent or neutral State, the High Contracting Parties should, even absent specific provisions dealing with post-transfer responsibilities (see e.g. Article 12(3) of the

---

degree possible'); ICRC, 'Action by the International Committee of the Red Cross in the event of violations of international humanitarian law or of other fundamental rules protecting persons in situations of violence', A 1308, 16 February 2005, reproduced in *International Review of the Red Cross*, Vol. 87, No. 858, June 2005, pp. 393–400, at 396 ('taking every possible measure'); Condorelli/Boisson de Chazournes, p. 24 ('agir par tout moyen approprié'); Boisson de Chazournes/Condorelli, 2000, p. 69 ('take all possible steps'); Pfanner, p. 305 ('act by all appropriate means'); Bothe/Partsch/Solf, p. 43 ('any lawful means at their disposal in their international relations'); Benvenuti, p. 29 ('any lawful means at their disposal'); Azzam, p. 69 ('use all legal means at their disposal'); and Sandoz, p. 167 ('dans la mesure de ses possibilités').

[90] ICJ, *Application of the Genocide Convention case*, Merits, Judgment, 2007, para. 430.
[91] *Ibid.*

Third Convention), monitor the fate of those transferred and, if necessary, exercise their influence in order to ensure observance of the Conventions by the receiving State.[92]

169   Some have expressed doubts as to the legal nature of the positive component of the duty to ensure respect by others because the content of the obligation is not clearly defined and its concretization to a large extent left to the High Contracting Parties.[93]

170   The fact that common Article 1 is part of an international treaty, however, means that it is not a loose pledge but a commitment vested with legal force. This was affirmed by the International Court of Justice in the *Nicaragua* case where the Court considered that the clause reflected a legal obligation.[94] The term 'undertake' used in common Article 1 also underlines the High Contracting Parties' commitment to ensure respect by others. In its ordinary meaning to 'undertake' means to 'formally guarantee, pledge or promise'.[95] The International Court of Justice held that the term is 'not merely hortatory or purposive'.[96]

171   In 1973, the existence of such a positive duty was expressly acknowledged by a number of States in response to a questionnaire sent out by the ICRC.[97] Since then, the UN Security Council,[98] the UN General Assembly,[99] the UN

---

[92] See e.g. Colassis, pp. 467–468:

> Transferring States, in particular, have greater means to ensure respect in contexts where they have a strong diplomatic and military presence in the receiving State, as is the case with the United States in Iraq. They can engage in a dialogue on the treatment of detainees and undertake other measures, such as post-transfer follow-up or capacity building at the different levels of the chain of custody, to ensure that the receiving State abides by its obligations.

> See also the commentary on common Article 3, section G.7, as well as Article 12 of the Third Convention and Article 45 of the Fourth Convention.

[93] See Kalshoven, pp. 59–61 ('a moral incentive'); ICJ, *Legal Consequences of the Construction of a Wall in the Occupied Palestinian Territory*, Separate Opinion of Judge Kooijmans, 2004, paras 46–50 ('I fail to see what kind of positive action, resulting from this obligation, may be expected from individual States, apart from diplomatic démarches.'); Focarelli, p. 125 ('a mere recommendation') and pp. 170–171 ('an unspecified recommendatory meaning'); Frutig; and Kolb, p. 518 ('une *faculté* d'intervenir . . . mais . . . pas l'existence d'une *obligation* en toutes circonstances' ('the *power* to act . . . but . . . not an *obligation* to do so in all circumstances')).

[94] ICJ, *Military and Paramilitary Activities in and against Nicaragua case*, Merits, Judgment, 1986, para. 220.

[95] *Concise Oxford English Dictionary*, 12th edition, Oxford University Press, 2011, p. 1573.

[96] On the meaning of the term 'undertake' in Article 1 of the 1948 Genocide Convention, see ICJ, *Application of the Genocide Convention case*, Merits, Judgment, 2007, para. 162 ('It is not merely hortatory or purposive. The undertaking is unqualified . . . ; and is not to be read merely as an introduction to later express references to [other obligations].').

[97] ICRC, Questionnaire concerning measures intended to reinforce the implementation of the Geneva Conventions of August 12, 1949, Geneva, 1973, answers to question 2 by the Federal Republic of Germany (p. 20), Belgium (p. 21), Republic of Korea (p. 23), United States (pp. 24–25) and United Kingdom (p. 30). The same view was expressed by Pakistan during the Diplomatic Conference: 'Article 1 common to the four Geneva Conventions of 1949 and article 70 of draft Protocol I implied that, if a Party failed to carry out its obligations, the other Contracting Parties were bound to endeavour to bring it back to an attitude of respect for its engagements.' *Official Records of the Diplomatic Conference of Geneva of 1974–1977*, Vol. VIII, p. 185, para. 3.

[98] UN Security Council, Res. 681, 20 December 1990, para. 5.

[99] UN General Assembly, Res. 43/21, The uprising (*intifadah*) of the Palestinian people, 3 November 1988, para. 5.

Secretary-General,[100] the Parliamentary Assembly of the Council of Europe,[101] and the High Contracting Parties themselves[102] have expressly referred to a positive obligation to ensure respect. On this basis, the ICRC has called upon States to actively ensure compliance by other High Contracting Parties.[103] In 2004, the International Court of Justice concluded from Article 1 of the Fourth Convention 'that every State party to that Convention, whether or not it is a party to a specific conflict, is under an obligation to ensure that the requirements of the instruments in question are complied with'.[104]

172   Certainly, the precise content of this positive obligation is difficult to determine in the abstract, yet this difficulty is not sufficient in itself to deny the existence of such an obligation. Common Article 1 is a living provision which must be interpreted in the overall context of the Conventions and, where applicable, the Protocols, and the international legal order as a whole. Its content will be further concretized and operationalized in the decades ahead.

173   Accordingly, there is a positive legal duty to ensure respect for the Conventions, and this is widely supported by experts and scholars.[105] It is in this sense that the corresponding customary duty to ensure respect for humanitarian law has been understood.[106]

---

[100] UN Secretary-General, *Report on the situation in the territories occupied by Israel submitted in accordance with the UN Security Council Resolution 605 (1987)*, UN Doc. S/19443, 21 January 1988, para. 27.

[101] Council of Europe, Parliamentary Assembly, 39th Ordinary Session, Res. 881 (1987) on the activities of the International Committee of the Red Cross (ICRC) (1984–86), 1 July 1987, para. 21, see also para. 23(iii).

[102] See e.g. International Conference for the Protection of War Victims, Geneva, 1993, Final Declaration, Part II, para. 11, and 30th International Conference of the Red Cross and Red Crescent, Geneva, 2007, Res. 3, Reaffirmation and implementation of international humanitarian law: Preserving human life and dignity in armed conflict, para. 2.

[103] See e.g. ICRC, Letter dated 18 October 1989 from the ICRC Director of Principles, Law and Relations within the Movement to two UK Members of Parliament, reproduced in Labour Middle East Council and Conservative Middle East Council (eds), *Towards a Strategy for the Enforcement of Human Rights in the Israeli Occupied West Bank and Gaza, A Working Symposium*, London, 25 July 1989, pp. vii–viii; ICRC Statement, The Balkan conflict and respect for international humanitarian law, 26 April 1999, reproduced in *International Review of the Red Cross*, Vol. 81, No. 834, June 1999, pp. 408–411, at 411; and ICRC, News Release 82/07, Myanmar: ICRC denounces major and repeated violations of international humanitarian law, 29 June 2007. See generally ICRC, 'Action by the International Committee of the Red Cross in the event of violations of international humanitarian law or of other fundamental rules protecting persons in situations of violence', A 1308, 16 February 2005, reproduced in *International Review of the Red Cross*, Vol. 87, No. 858, June 2005, pp. 393–400, at 396.

[104] ICJ, *Legal Consequences of the Construction of a Wall in the Occupied Palestinian Territory*, Advisory Opinion, 2004, para. 158; see also para. 159.

[105] See Sassòli/Bouvier/Quintin, pp. 368–369; Bothe/Partsch/Solf, p. 43; Kessler, 2001b, pp. 504–507; David, para. 3.13; Levrat, pp. 267 and 276–279; Benvenuti, p. 29; Azzam, p. 68; Condorelli/Boisson de Chazournes, p. 24; Boisson de Chazournes/Condorelli, 2000, p. 69; Brehm, pp. 374–375; Sachariew, p. 184; Palwankar, p. 9; Sandoz, p. 167; Gasser, p. 32; Vöneky, para. 1432, pp. 696–697; Niyungeko, p. 127; Pfanner, pp. 304–305; Obradović, pp. 487–488; Fleck, p. 182; Zwanenburg, p. 108; and Dörmann/Serralvo. Five regional expert consultations on improving compliance with humanitarian law in 2003 also showed general agreement that this was a legal obligation; see ICRC, *International Humanitarian Law and the Challenges of Contemporary Armed Conflict*, Report prepared for the 28th International Conference of the Red Cross and Red Crescent, Geneva, 2003, p. 22.

[106] See ICRC Study on Customary International Humanitarian Law (2005), Rule 144.

c. Limits of permissible action

174   Common Article 1 does not provide a ground to deviate from applicable rules of international law.[107] Most notably, it does not by itself justify a State or group of States to engage in a 'threat or use of force' contrary to Article 2(4) of the UN Charter. Only the rules of international law on the resort to armed force (*jus ad bellum*) determine the legality of any threat or use of force, even where such force is meant to put an end to serious violations of the Conventions.

175   The obligation to ensure respect does not authorize derogations from the safeguards of the Conventions themselves as this would directly contravene the duty to respect their provisions 'in all circumstances'. Such derogations are only allowed to the extent that they constitute lawful reprisals.[108]

176   Furthermore, the fact that the law of neutrality requires neutral Powers to treat all Parties to an international armed conflict on a non-discriminatory basis does not absolve these Powers of their obligation to ensure respect under common Article 1. Conversely, common Article 1 does not provide a ground for violating the law of neutrality.[109]

177   The principle of non-intervention is not as such an impediment to the taking of measures by third States pursuant to common Article 1. It follows from the *erga omnes partes* nature of the obligations under the Conventions that violations of their provisions by a High Contracting Party should not be seen as the exclusive internal affair of that Party, even if the violations took place in the context of a non-international armed conflict.[110]

178   Lastly, common Article 1 does not establish any primacy of collective measures over individual measures.[111] Hence, in case of violations of the

---

[107]   See ICJ, *Legal Consequences of the Construction of a Wall in the Occupied Palestinian Territory*, Advisory Opinion, 2004, para. 159 ('while respecting the United Nations Charter and international law'); Additional Protocol I, Article 89 ('in conformity with the United Nations Charter'); and 30th International Conference of the Red Cross and Red Crescent, Geneva, 2007, Res. 3, Reaffirmation and implementation of international humanitarian law: Preserving human life and dignity in armed conflict, para. 2 ('in accordance with international law'). See also, with respect to the obligation to prevent genocide, ICJ, *Application of the Genocide Convention case*, Merits, Judgment, 2007, para. 430 ('every State may only act within the limits permitted by international law').

[108]   For the prohibitions of reprisals, see First Convention, Article 46; Second Convention, Article 47; Third Convention, Article 13(3); and Fourth Convention, Article 33(3). See also Additional Protocol I, Articles 20, 51(6), 52(1), 53(c), 54(4), 55(2) and 56(4).

[109]   On the scope of application of the law of neutrality, see the commentary on Article 4.

[110]   See e.g. ICTY, *Kupreškić* Trial Judgment, 2000, para. 519, with regard to the *erga omnes* nature of most obligations imposed by rules of humanitarian law ('each and every member of the international community has a "legal interest" in their observance and consequently a legal entitlement to demand respect for such obligations'). See also Draft Articles on State Responsibility (2001), Article 48, and ICRC, *International Humanitarian Law and the Challenges of Contemporary Armed Conflict*, Report prepared by the ICRC for the 28th International Conference of the Red Cross and Red Crescent, Geneva, 2003, p. 49 ('action taken pursuant to common Article 1 should not be understood as an illegal interference in the internal affairs of another State').

[111]   The same is the case for the duty to prevent genocide pursuant to Article 1 of the 1948 Genocide Convention; see ICJ, *Application of the Genocide Convention case*, Merits, Judgment, 2007, para. 427. But see Sachariew, p. 193, who expresses a general preference for collective measures.

Conventions, each of the High Contracting Parties is entitled to resort individually to appropriate measures in order to put an end to the violations.[112] Accordingly, Article 48(1)(b) of the 2001 Draft Articles on State Responsibility considers that any State is entitled to invoke the responsibility of a State in breach of *erga omnes* obligations. In practice, States do individually denounce violations of humanitarian law or resort to coercive measures in order to prevent or bring violations to an end.[113] However, the particular gravity of certain violations of the Conventions may call for collective measures, particularly within the framework of the United Nations.[114] This option is specifically provided for in Article 89 of Additional Protocol I, whereby '[i]n situations of serious violations of the Conventions or of this Protocol, the High Contracting Parties undertake to act, jointly or individually, in co-operation with the United Nations and in conformity with the United Nations Charter'.

179   The obligations under common Article 1 and under Article 89 of Additional Protocol I exist independently of any other concept, such as 'the responsibility to protect populations from genocide, war crimes, ethnic cleansing and crimes against humanity' recognized by the UN General Assembly and the UN Security Council.[115]

d. Overview of possible measures

180 Conceptually, it is possible to distinguish between individual and collective measures to ensure respect by others.[116]

181   Individual measures include:

- addressing questions of compliance within the context of a diplomatic dialogue;
- exerting diplomatic pressure by means of confidential protests or public denunciations;
- conditioning joint operations on a coalition partner's compliance with its obligations under the Conventions and/or planning operations jointly in order to prevent such violations;[117]

---

[112] See 30th International Conference of the Red Cross and Red Crescent, Geneva, 2007, Res. 3, Reaffirmation and implementation of international humanitarian law: Preserving human life and dignity in armed conflict, para. 2.

[113] See the examples cited by Palwankar, p. 16.

[114] Under general international law, there is at least a tendency towards a duty to cooperate; see Draft Articles on State Responsibility (2001), Article 41(1): 'States shall cooperate to bring to an end through lawful means any serious breach within the meaning of article 40.'

[115] UN General Assembly, Res. 60/1, 2005 World Summit Outcome, 24 October 2005, paras 138–139, and UN Security Council, Res. 1674, 28 April 2006, para. 4. For a discussion of the related concept of 'humanitarian intervention' and humanitarian law, see Ryniker.

[116] For an overview of measures, a number of which have been integrated into the following list, see Palwankar, pp. 12–24 (who distinguishes between measures to exert diplomatic pressure, coercive measures that States may take themselves, and measures taken in cooperation with international organizations, among others).

[117] See e.g. Human rights due diligence policy on United Nations support to non-United Nations security forces, UN Doc. A/67/775–S/2013/110, 5 March 2013. In the context of MONUC, see

– intervening directly with commanders in case of violations, for example an imminent unlawful attack against civilians, by a coalition partner;

– offering legal assistance to the Parties to the conflict and/or supporting assistance provided by others, such as instruction or training;

– acting as a Protecting Power in accordance with common Article 8 (Article 9 in the Fourth Convention) or a substitute in accordance with common Article 10 (Article 11 in the Fourth Convention);

– lending good offices to settle a disagreement on the application or interpretation of the Conventions in accordance with Article 11;

– agreeing to set up an enquiry procedure concerning an alleged violation of the Convention in accordance with Article 52;

– referring, where applicable, a situation to the International Humanitarian Fact-Finding Commission;[118]

– requesting a meeting of the High Contracting Parties;[119]

– applying measures of retorsion, such as the halting of ongoing negotiations or refusing to ratify agreements already signed, the non-renewal of trade privileges, and the reduction or suspension of voluntary public aid;

– adopting lawful countermeasures such as arms embargoes, trade and financial restrictions, flight bans and the reduction or suspension of aid and cooperation agreements;

– conditioning, limiting or refusing arms transfers;[120]

---

e.g. UN Security Council, Res. 1906, 23 December 2009, para. 22; for further measures, see *ibid.* para. 9 ('Joint Protection Teams, Early Warning Centres, [and] communications liaisons with local villages').

[118] Additional Protocol I, Article 90(2)(a) and (d). See also Pfanner, p. 286:

> In principle, the International Fact-Finding Commission can undertake an enquiry only if all the parties concerned have given their consent, but there is nothing to prevent a third state from requesting an enquiry by the Commission into a grave breach or serious violation of humanitarian law committed by a party to conflict, provided that the party concerned has also recognized the Commission's competence. This possibility arises out of the obligation to 'ensure respect for' the law of armed conflict.

[119] Three conferences of the High Contracting Parties to the Fourth Convention have, with express reference to common Article 1, so far been convened to enforce that Convention in the occupied Palestinian territory: the first on 15 July 1999 (as recommended, among others, by UN General Assembly, Res. ES-10/6, Illegal Israeli actions in Occupied East Jerusalem and the rest of the Occupied Palestinian Territory, 9 February 1999, para. 6); the second on 5 December 2001 (following UN General Assembly, Res. ES-10/7, Illegal Israeli actions in Occupied East Jerusalem and the rest of the Occupied Palestinian Territory, 20 October 2000, para. 10); and the third on 17 December 2014 (as recommended by UN General Assembly, Res. 64/10, Follow-up to the report of the United Nations Fact-Finding Mission on the Gaza Conflict, 5 November 2009, para. 5). See also UN Security Council, Res. 681, 20 December 1990, para. 6.

[120] See e.g. 31st International Conference of the Red Cross and Red Crescent, Geneva, 2011, Res. 2, Annex 1: Action Plan for Implementing International Humanitarian Law, Objective 5: Arms transfers; 30th International Conference of the Red Cross and Red Crescent, Geneva, 2007, Res. 3, Reaffirmation and implementation of international humanitarian law: Preserving human life and dignity in armed conflict; 28th International Conference of the Red Cross and Red Crescent, Geneva, 2003, Agenda for Humanitarian Action, Final goal 2(3); and Updated EU Guidelines on Compliance with International Humanitarian Law (2009), para. 16(i). See also Dörmann/Serralvo, p. 734; Boivin, pp. 475–479; Fleck, pp. 182–183; and Brehm, pp. 375–377.

– referring the issue to a competent international organization, e.g. the UN Security Council or General Assembly;[121]
– referring, where possible, a specific issue to the International Court of Justice or another body for the settlement of disputes;[122]
– resorting to penal measures to repress violations of humanitarian law;[123] and
– supporting national and international efforts to bring suspected perpetrators of serious violations of international humanitarian law to justice.[124]

182   Many of these measures, as well as more general measures designed to clarify the law or improve compliance with the Conventions, may equally be taken collectively by a group of States[125] or within the framework of an international organization.[126] A particular role in ensuring compliance with the Conventions falls upon the United Nations, a role that in 1977 was expressly recognized in Article 89 of Additional Protocol I. The United Nations has increasingly become active in this respect and has engaged in a variety of activities ranging from the condemnation of specific violations and the deployment of fact-finding missions to the adoption of sanctions under Chapter VII of the 1945 UN Charter and the deployment of peace operations with a mandate to protect civilians.[127]

183   As regards measures the High Contracting Parties may adopt vis-à-vis States party to a non-international armed conflict, reference can be made to essentially the same measures available in the context of international armed conflict. In practice, States and international organizations regularly denounce violations of common Article 3, including by non-State armed groups, and adopt economic and other non-military sanctions.[128]

The 2013 Arms Trade Treaty requires States Parties to consider respect for humanitarian law by the recipients of proposed arms transfers (Articles 6–7).
[121] See UN Charter (1945), Article 35(1).
[122] See e.g. ICJ, *Armed Activities on the Territory of the Congo case*, Judgment, 2005, Separate Opinion of Judge Simma, para. 34:

> Thus, regardless of whether the maltreated individuals were Ugandans or not, Uganda had the right – indeed the duty – to raise the violations of international humanitarian law committed against the private persons at the airport. The implementation of a State party's international legal duty to ensure respect by another State party for the obligations arising under humanitarian treaties by way of raising it before the International Court of Justice is certainly one of the most constructive avenues in this regard.

[123] See e.g. ICTY, *Tadić* Decision on the Defence Motion on Jurisdiction, 1995, para. 71 ('The requirement in common Article 1 that all Contracting Parties must respect and ensure respect for the Conventions may entail resort to penal measures.')
[124] See also Additional Protocol I, Article 88, on mutual assistance in criminal matters.
[125] See e.g. Montreux Document on Private Military and Security Companies (2008).
[126] See e.g. the list of means of action contained in the 2009 Updated EU Guidelines on Compliance with International Humanitarian Law, para. 16, setting out the operational tools for the EU and its institutions and bodies to promote compliance with humanitarian law.
[127] For further details, see the commentary on Article 89 of Additional Protocol I.
[128] See generally Updated EU Guidelines on Compliance with International Humanitarian Law (2009), para. 2: 'These Guidelines are in line with the *commitment* of the EU and its Member States to IHL, and aim to address compliance with IHL by third States, and, as appropriate, non-State actors operating in third States' (emphasis added). Specific examples include the

F. The phrase 'in all circumstances'

184 Lastly, the High Contracting Parties have undertaken to respect and to ensure respect for the Conventions 'in all circumstances'. This phrase was originally linked to the abolishment of the so-called *si omnes* clause,[129] a provision contained, among others, in the 1906 Geneva Convention and in the 1907 Hague Conventions to the effect that the Conventions were only applicable if all of the belligerents in a given conflict were party to it.[130] In 1929, the drafters felt that the participation of a State not party to the Conventions in a conflict should no longer affect the binding nature of the Conventions on those belligerents who were party to the Conventions. As noted earlier, in the course of the drafting process the obligation to ensure respect in all circumstances and the obligation to apply the Conventions in relation to other Contracting Parties, even if not all belligerents are party to the Conventions, were separated into two different paragraphs, whereby the former acquired an independent meaning.[131] The

sanctions adopted by the UN Security Council against: UNITA (e.g. UN Security Council, Res. 864, 15 September 1993, section B, para. 19); Liberia, including non-State actors (e.g. UN Security Council, Res. 1521, 22 December 2003, section B, paras 2 and 4); foreign and Congolese armed groups and militias operating in the Democratic Republic of the Congo (e.g. UN Security Council, Res. 1493, 28 July 2003, para. 20); Côte d'Ivoire (e.g. UN Security Council, Res. 1572, 15 November 2004, paras 7, 9 and 11); and non-governmental entities and individuals operating in Darfur (e.g. UN Security Council, Res. 1556, 30 July 2004, paras 7 and 8). For an overview of the issue of enforcing compliance by non-State Parties, see Kessler, 2001a, pp. 219–234.

[129] It was in an amendment to draft article 24 of the 1929 Geneva Convention on the Wounded and Sick, submitted by the UK delegate, that the obligation to respect the Convention in all circumstances made its first appearance:

> Les dispositions de la présente Convention doivent être respectées par les Hautes Parties Contractantes en toutes circonstances, sauf le cas où une Puissance belligérante ne serait pas partie à cette dernière. En ce cas, les dispositions de la Convention ne seront pas applicables entre ce belligérant et ses adversaires, mais devront néanmoins être respectées dans les rapports entre les belligérants parties à la Convention.
>
> (The High Contracting Parties shall respect the provisions of the present Convention in all circumstances, except where a belligerent Power is not party to the Convention. In that case, the provisions of the Convention shall not apply between this belligerent and its adversaries, but must nonetheless be respected in relations between the belligerents who are Parties to the Convention.)

> *Actes de la conférence diplomatique de Genève de 1929*, p. 322.

[130] Geneva Convention (1906), Article 24: 'The provisions of the present Convention are obligatory only on the Contracting Powers, in case of war between two or more of them. The said provisions shall cease to be obligatory if one of the belligerent Powers should not be signatory to the Convention.' See also St Petersburg Declaration (1868), ninth paragraph; Hague Convention (IV) (1907), Article 2; Hague Convention (V) (1907), Article 20; Hague Convention (VI) (1907), Article 6; Hague Convention (VII) (1907), Article 7; Hague Convention (VIII) (1907), Article 7; Hague Convention (IX) (1907), Article 8; Hague Convention (X) (1907), Article 18; Hague Convention (XI) (1907), Article 9; Hague Convention (XII) (1907), Article 51, first paragraph; Hague Convention (XIII) (1907), Article 28; Hague Declaration (XIV) (1907), third paragraph; and London Declaration concerning the Laws of Naval War (1909), Article 66.

[131] The obligation to ensure respect in all circumstances became the first paragraph of Article 25 of the 1929 Geneva Convention on the Wounded and Sick, and the obligation to apply the Conventions in relation to other Contracting Parties, even if not all belligerents are party to the Conventions, became the second paragraph of Article 25: 'If, in time of war, a belligerent is not a party to the Convention, its provisions shall, nevertheless, be binding as between all the belligerents who are parties thereto.' The same is the case for the 1929 Geneva Convention

latter is now explicitly provided for in common Article 2(3), namely that even where not all Parties to an armed conflict are party to the Conventions, those who are party remain bound by the Conventions in their mutual relations.[132]

185 Furthermore, as mentioned above (para. 129), the words 'in all circumstances' indicate that the obligations to respect and to ensure respect apply both during armed conflict and in peacetime, depending on the obligation in question. The fact that certain provisions of the Conventions must already be implemented in peacetime is clearly alluded to in common Article 2(1) ('In addition to the provisions which shall be implemented in peacetime').[133]

186 The undertaking to respect and to ensure respect 'in all circumstances' also reaffirms the strict separation of *jus ad bellum* and *jus in bello* as one of the basic safeguards for compliance with the Conventions. In other words, the application of the Conventions does not depend on the legal justification for the conflict under the *jus ad bellum*. As soon as one of the conditions of application for which common Article 2 or 3 provides is present, no State bound by the Conventions can offer any valid pretext, legal or other, for not respecting the Conventions in their entirety and in regard to all whom they protect. Whether an armed conflict is 'just' or 'unjust', whether it is a war of aggression or of resistance to aggression, the Conventions' guarantees are in no way affected.[134] Accordingly, self-defence against an armed attack (see Article 51 of the UN Charter) does not preclude the wrongfulness of violations of the Conventions,[135] nor does the fact that the High Contracting Parties are acting on the basis of a UN Security Council mandate.

187 Furthermore, a military, economic, geographical or other factual inequality of the Parties to the conflict does not affect their obligations under the Conventions; the Conventions must be observed regardless of actual capacity. A differential application based on means available is possible for provisions that reflect an obligation of means.[136] Obligations that impose a minimum may also be applied in a differential manner above that minimum.[137]

---

on Prisoners of War, Article 82. For a detailed overview of the drafting history, see Kalshoven, pp. 6–10, and Dörmann/Serralvo, pp. 712–716.

[132] For more details, see the commentary on common Article 2, section F.1. This is independent of the fact that all States remain bound by customary international law.

[133] For more details, see the commentary on common Article 2, section C.

[134] This principle has been expressly reaffirmed in Additional Protocol I, Preamble, para. 5. But see Kalshoven, p. 48: 'The need to include this language effectively defeats the argument that common Article 1 once and for all had settled these issues.'

[135] See Draft Articles on State Responsibility (2001), commentary on Article 21, para. 3, according to which the Geneva Conventions and Additional Protocol I 'apply equally to all the parties in an international armed conflict', with reference to ICJ, *Legality of the Threat or Use of Nuclear Weapons*, Advisory Opinion, 1996, para. 79 ('intransgressible principles of international customary law').

[136] See e.g. First Convention, Article 15(1); Second Convention, Article 18(1); Third Convention, Article 76(1); and Fourth Convention, Article 76(1).

[137] See e.g. the rules on the provision for the basic needs of persons deprived of their liberty (food, water, clothing, shelter and medical attention) contained in Articles 25–32 of the Third Convention and Articles 76, 85, 87 and 89–92 of the Fourth Convention. In its Partial Award on

188   The words 'in all circumstances' moreover support the non-reciprocal nature of the Conventions, which bind each High Contracting Party regardless of whether the other Parties observe their obligations.[138] This principle is expressly acknowledged in Article 60(5) of the 1969 Vienna Convention on the Law of Treaties, which excludes the termination or suspension of the operation of a treaty as a consequence of its material breach with regard to 'provisions relating to the protection of the human person contained in treaties of a humanitarian character, in particular to provisions prohibiting any form of reprisals against persons protected by such treaties'.

189   On the other hand, respect 'in all circumstances' does not seem to imply, by itself, an absolute prohibition on reprisals beyond those prohibitions specifically provided for in the Conventions,[139] although there is support for such reasoning in the case law of the ICTY.[140] That was also the situation under customary international law as assessed in 2005.[141]

190   The phrase 'in all circumstances' would, however, seem to exclude to a large extent recourse to the so-called 'circumstances precluding wrongfulness' recognized under the general law of State responsibility in order to justify violations of the Conventions.[142] The 2001 Draft Articles on State Responsibility enumerate six circumstances that, if shown to exist, preclude the wrongfulness of an act that would otherwise constitute a breach of a State's international obligations. Those circumstances are: (a) consent; (b) self-defence; (c) countermeasures; (d) *force majeure*; (e) distress; and (f) necessity.[143] As far as violations of the Conventions are concerned, consent may not serve as a justification, as may be inferred from the prohibition on absolving oneself or any other High Contracting Party of any liability incurred in respect of breaches of

Eritrea's claim concerning prisoners of war, the Eritrea-Ethiopia Claims Commission observed that Eritrea and Ethiopia could not, at least at present, be required to have the same standards for medical treatment as developed countries. However, scarcity of finances and infrastructure could not excuse a failure to grant the minimum standard of medical care required by humanitarian law (*Prisoners of War, Eritrea's Claim*, Partial Award, 2003, para. 138).

[138] See 30th International Conference of the Red Cross and Red Crescent, Geneva, 2007, Res. 3, Reaffirmation and implementation of international humanitarian law: Preserving human life and dignity in armed conflict, Preamble ('*recalling* that the obligation to respect international humanitarian law binds all parties to an armed conflict, and *emphasizing* that this obligation is not based on reciprocity'), and ICTY, *Kupreškić* Trial Judgment, 2000, para. 517. On the customary character of this principle, see ICRC Study on Customary International Humanitarian Law (2005), Rule 140. On the 1929 Convention, see Condorelli/Boisson de Chazournes, p. 19.

[139] See First Convention, Article 46; Second Convention, Article 47; Third Convention, Article 13(3); and Fourth Convention, Article 33(3). See also Additional Protocol I, Articles 20, 51(6), 52(1), 53(c), 54(4), 55(2) and 56(4).

[140] See ICTY, *Martić* Rule 61 Decision, 1996, para. 15.

[141] According to Henckaerts/Doswald-Beck, p. 523, 'it is difficult to conclude that there has yet crystallized a customary rule specifically prohibiting reprisals against civilians during the conduct of hostilities'.

[142] See also Vöneky, para. 1402 (violations of the Geneva Conventions, Additional Protocol I and customary law are not lawful 'because of recourse to certain circumstances precluding wrongfulness, as for instance self-defence, consent of the victim state, a state of necessity, and so on').

[143] Draft Articles on State Responsibility (2001), Articles 20–25 respectively.

the Conventions.[144] The same idea is expressed in the provision that protected persons may not renounce the rights secured to them by the Conventions.[145] Recourse to the circumstance of national self-defence against an armed attack in order to justify violations of the Conventions is excluded, as previously discussed, by the strict separation of *jus in bello* and *jus ad bellum*.[146] In addition, it is generally agreed that military necessity, subject to provisions that specifically provide for exceptions,[147] may not justify violations of the Conventions as military necessity has already been taken into account in the formulation of their provisions.[148] Similar considerations apply to distress.[149]

191   In respect of countermeasures in response to an internationally wrongful act other than a violation of the rules of humanitarian law, the Draft Articles expressly provide that these shall not affect 'obligations of a humanitarian character prohibiting reprisals'.[150] Given that, as previously observed, not even self-defence against unlawful attacks may justify violations of the Conventions – and the Protocols where applicable – one may, however, wonder whether this exception should not have been formulated more broadly to cover generally all 'obligations of a humanitarian character', regardless of whether these fall under the prohibition of reprisals.[151] Lastly, Article 26 of the Draft Articles stipulates that none of the six circumstances may preclude the wrongfulness of violations of peremptory norms of international law, which the ILC itself understood to cover also the basic rules of humanitarian law.[152]

Select bibliography

Azzam, Fateh, 'The Duty of Third States to Implement and Enforce International Humanitarian Law', *Nordic Journal of International Law*, Vol. 66, No. 1, 1997, pp. 55–75.
Benvenuti, Paolo, 'Ensuring Observance of International Humanitarian Law: Function, Extent and Limits of the Obligations of Third States to Ensure Respect of

---

[144] See First Convention, Article 51; Second Convention, Article 52; Third Convention, Article 131; and Fourth Convention, Article 148.

[145] See common Article 7 (Article 8 of the Fourth Convention).

[146] See also Draft Articles on State Responsibility (2001), commentary on Article 21, para. 3: 'As to obligations under international humanitarian law and in relation to non-derogable human rights provisions, self-defence does not preclude the wrongfulness of conduct.'

[147] See e.g. First Convention, Articles 8(3), 33(2) and 34(2); Second Convention, Articles 8(3) and 28; Third Convention, Article 126(2); and Fourth Convention, Articles 27(4), 42, 53, 55(3), 78(1), 108(2) and 143(3).

[148] On the issue of 'military necessity', see Draft Articles on State Responsibility (2001), commentary on Article 25, para. 21, which considers that 'while considerations akin to those underlying article 25 may have a role, they are taken into account in the context of the formulation and interpretation of the primary obligations'; see also ICJ, *Legal Consequences of the Construction of a Wall in the Occupied Palestinian Territory*, Advisory Opinion, 2004, para. 140.

[149] Sassòli, p. 417.   [150] Draft Articles on State Responsibility (2001), Article 50(1)(c).

[151] Sassòli, pp. 425–426.

[152] Draft Articles on State Responsibility (2001), commentary on Article 40, para. 5. For an overview of the different circumstances precluding wrongfulness, see Sassòli, pp. 413–417.

IHL', *Yearbook of the International Institute of Humanitarian Law*, 1989–90, pp. 27–55.

Boisson de Chazournes, Laurence and Condorelli, Luigi, 'Common Article 1 of the Geneva Conventions revisited: Protecting collective interests', *International Review of the Red Cross*, Vol. 82, No. 837, March 2000, pp. 67–87.

– 'De la "responsabilité de protéger", ou d'une nouvelle parure pour une notion déjà bien établie', *Revue générale de droit international public*, Vol. 110, No. 1, 2006, pp. 11–18.

Boivin, Alexandra, 'Complicity and beyond: International law and the transfer of small arms and light weapons', *International Review of the Red Cross*, Vol. 87, No. 859, September 2005, pp. 467–496.

Bothe, Michael, Partsch, Karl Josef and Solf, Waldemar A. *New Rules for Victims of Armed Conflicts: Commentary on the Two 1977 Protocols Additional to the Geneva Conventions of 1949*, Martinus Nijhoff Publishers, The Hague, 1982, pp. 43–44.

Brehm, Maya, 'The Arms Trade and States' Duty to Ensure Respect for Humanitarian and Human Rights Law', *Journal of Conflict and Security Law*, Vol. 12, No. 3, 2007, pp. 359–387.

Colassis, Laurent, 'The Role of the International Committee of the Red Cross in Stability Operations', in Raul A. 'Pete' Pedrozo (ed.), *The War in Iraq: A Legal Analysis*, International Law Studies, U.S. Naval War College, Vol. 86, 2010, pp. 457–476.

Condorelli, Luigi and Boisson de Chazournes, Laurence, 'Quelques remarques à propos de l'obligation des Etats de "respecter et faire respecter" le droit international humanitaire "en toutes circonstances"', in Christophe Swinarski (ed.), *Etudes et essais sur le droit humanitaire et sur les principes de la Croix-Rouge en l'honneur de Jean Pictet*, ICRC/Martinus Nijhoff Publishers, The Hague, 1984, pp. 17–35.

David, Eric, *Principes de droit des conflits armés*, 5th edition, Bruylant, Brussels, 2012, paras 3.11–3.20.

Devillard, Alexandre, 'L'obligation de faire respecter le droit international humanitaire: l'article 1 commun aux Conventions de Genève et à leur premier Protocole additionnel, fondement d'un droit international humanitaire de coopération?', *Revue québécoise de droit international*, Vol. 20, No. 2, 2007, pp. 75–129.

Dörmann, Knut, and Serralvo, Jose, 'Common Article 1 to the Geneva Conventions and the obligation to prevent international humanitarian law violations', *International Review of the Red Cross*, Vol. 96, No. 895–896, December 2014, pp. 707–736.

Engdahl, Ola, 'Compliance with International Humanitarian Law in Multinational Peace Operations', *Nordic Journal of International Law*, Vol. 78, No. 4, 2009, pp. 513–526.

Fleck, Dieter, 'International Accountability for Violations of the Ius in Bello: The Impact of the ICRC Study on Customary International Humanitarian Law', *Journal of Conflict and Security Law*, Vol. 11, No. 2, 2006, pp. 179–199.

Focarelli, Carlo, 'Common Article 1 of the 1949 Geneva Conventions: A Soap Bubble?', *European Journal of International Law*, Vol. 21, No. 1, 2010, pp. 125–171.

Frutig, Andreas, *Die Pflicht von Drittstaaten zur Durchsetzung des humanitären Völkerrechts nach Art. 1 der Genfer Konventionen von 1949*, Helbing Lichtenhahn Verlag, Basel, 2009.

Gasser, Hans-Peter, 'Ensuring Respect for the Geneva Conventions and Protocols: The Role of Third States and the United Nations', in Hazel Fox and Michael A. Meyer (eds), *Armed Conflict and the New Law, Vol. II: Effecting Compliance*, The British Institute of International and Comparative Law, London, 1993, pp. 15–49.

Geiss, Robin, 'The Obligation to Respect and to Ensure Respect for the Conventions', in Andrew Clapham, Paola Gaeta and Marco Sassòli (eds), *The 1949 Geneva Conventions: A Commentary*, Oxford University Press, 2015, pp. 111–134. (2015a)

– 'Common Article 1 of the Geneva Conventions: scope and content of the obligation to 'ensure respect' – 'narrow but deep' or 'wide and shallow'?', in Heike Krieger (ed.), *Inducing Compliance with International Humanitarian Law: Lessons from the African Great Lakes Region*, Cambridge University Press, 2015, pp. 417–441. (2015b)

Happold, Matthew, 'Comment – obligations of States contributing to UN peacekeeping missions under Common Article 1 of the Geneva Conventions', in Heike Krieger (ed.), *Inducing Compliance with International Humanitarian Law: Lessons from the African Great Lakes Region*, Cambridge University Press, 2015, pp. 382–398.

Henckaerts, Jean-Marie and Doswald-Beck, Louise, *Customary International Humanitarian Law, Volume I: Rules*, ICRC/Cambridge University Press, 2005, available at https://www.icrc.org/customary-ihl/eng/docs/v1.

Kalshoven, Frits, 'The Undertaking to Respect and Ensure Respect in All Circumstances: From Tiny Seed to Ripening Fruit', *Yearbook of International Humanitarian Law*, Vol. 2, 1999, pp. 3–61.

Kessler, Birgit, *Die Durchsetzung der Genfer Abkommen von 1949 in nicht-internationalen bewaffneten Konflikten auf Grundlage ihres gemeinsamen Art. 1*, Duncker & Humblot, Berlin, 2001. (2001a)

– 'The duty to "ensure respect" under common Article 1 of the Geneva Conventions: its implications on international and non-international armed conflicts', *German Yearbook of International Law*, Vol. 44, 2001, pp. 498–516. (2001b)

Koivurova, Timo, 'Due Diligence', version of February 2010, in Rüdiger Wolfrum (ed.), *Max Planck Encyclopedia of Public International Law*, Oxford University Press, http://www.mpepil.com.

Kolb, Robert, 'Commentaires iconoclastes sur l'obligation de faire respecter le droit international humanitaire selon l'article 1 commun des Conventions de Genève de 1949', *Revue belge de droit international*, Vol. 46, No. 2, 2013, pp. 513–520.

Kolb, Robert, Porretto, Gabriele and Vité, Sylvain, *L'application du droit international humanitaire et des droits de l'homme aux organisations internationales: Forces de paix et administrations civiles transitoires*, Bruylant, Brussels, 2005.

Levrat, Nicolas, 'Les conséquences de l'engagement pris par les Hautes Parties contractantes de "faire respecter" les Conventions humanitaires', in Frits Kalshoven and Yves Sandoz (eds), *Mise en œuvre du droit international humanitaire*, Martinus Nijhoff Publishers, Dordrecht, 1989, pp. 263–296.

Momtaz, Djamchid, 'L'engagement des Etats à "faire respecter" le droit international humanitaire par les parties aux conflits armés', in *Actes du Colloque de Bruges, Améliorer le respect du Droit International Humanitaire*, 11–12 septembre 2003, Collegium No. 30, Summer 2004, pp. 27–34.

– 'Les défis des conflits armés asymétriques et identitaires au droit international humanitaire', in Michael J. Matheson and Djamchid Momtaz (eds), *Les règles et institutions du droit international humanitaire à l'épreuve des conflits armés récents*, Martinus Nijhoff Publishers, Leiden, 2010, pp. 3–137, at 70–101.

Moulier, Isabelle, 'L'obligation de "faire respecter" le droit international humanitaire', in Michael J. Matheson and Djamchid Momtaz (eds), *Les règles et institutions du droit international humanitaire à l'épreuve des conflits armés récents*, Martinus Nijhoff Publishers, Leiden, 2010, pp. 725–783.

Naert, Frederik, *International Law Aspects of the EU's Security and Defence Policy, with a Particular Focus on the Law of Armed Conflict and Human Rights*, Intersentia, Antwerp, 2010.

Niyungeko, Gérard, 'The implementation of international humanitarian law and the principle of State sovereignty', *International Review of the Red Cross*, Vol. 31, No. 281, April 1991, pp. 105–133.

Obradović, Konstantin, 'Que faire face aux violations du droit humanitaire? Quelques réflexions sur le rôle possible du CICR', in Christophe Swinarski (ed.), *Etudes et essais sur le droit international humanitaire et sur les principes de la Croix-Rouge en l'honneur de Jean Pictet*, ICRC/Martinus Nijhoff Publishers, The Hague, 1984, pp. 483–494.

Palwankar, Umesh, 'Measures available to States for fulfilling their obligation to ensure respect for international humanitarian law', *International Review of the Red Cross*, Vol. 34, No. 298, February 1994, pp. 9–25.

Pfanner, Toni, 'Various mechanisms and approaches for implementing international humanitarian law and protecting and assisting war victims', *International Review of the Red Cross*, Vol. 91, No. 874, June 2009, pp. 279–328.

Pisillo-Mazzeschi, Riccardo, 'The Due Diligence Rule and the Nature of the International Responsibility of States', *German Yearbook of International Law*, Vol. 35, 1992, pp. 9–51.

Ryngaert, Cedric and Van de Meulebroucke, Anneleen, 'Enhancing and Enforcing Compliance with International Humanitarian Law by Non-State Armed Groups: an Inquiry into some Mechanisms', *Journal of Conflict and Security Law*, Vol. 16, No. 3, 2011, pp. 443–472.

Ryniker, Anne, 'The ICRC's position on "humanitarian intervention"', *International Review of the Red Cross*, Vol. 83, No. 842, June 2001, pp. 527–532.

Sachariew, Kamen, 'States' entitlement to take action to enforce international humanitarian law', *International Review of the Red Cross*, Vol. 29, No. 270, June 1989, pp. 177–195.

Sandoz, Yves, 'Appel du C.I.C.R. dans le cadre du conflit entre l'Irak et l'Iran', *Annuaire français de droit international*, Vol. 29, No. 1, 1983, pp. 161–173.

Sassòli, Marco, 'State responsibility for violations of international humanitarian law', *International Review of the Red Cross*, Vol. 84, No. 846, June 2002, pp. 401–434.

Sassòli, Marco, Bouvier, Antoine A. and Quintin, Anne, *How Does Law Protect in War?*, Vol. I, 3rd edition, ICRC, Geneva, 2011, pp. 368–372.

Shraga, Daphna, 'The United Nations as an Actor Bound by International Humanitarian Law', *International Peacekeeping*, Vol. 5, No. 2, 1998, pp. 64–81.

– 'The Secretary-General's Bulletin on the Observance by United Nations Forces of International Humanitarian Law: A Decade Later', *Israel Yearbook on Human Rights*, Vol. 39, 2009, pp. 357–377.

Tonkin, Hannah, 'Common Article 1: A Minimum Yardstick for Regulating Private Military and Security Companies', *Leiden Journal of International Law*, Vol. 22, No. 4, December 2009, pp. 779–799.

Vöneky, Silja, 'Implementation and Enforcement of International Humanitarian Law', in Dieter Fleck (ed.), *The Handbook of International Humanitarian Law*, 3rd edition, Oxford University Press, 2013, pp. 647–700.

Zwanenburg, Marten, *Accountability of Peace Support Operations*, Martinus Nijhoff Publishers, Leiden, 2005.

Zych, Tomasz, 'The Scope of the Obligation to Respect and to Ensure Respect for International Humanitarian Law', *Windsor Yearbook of Access to Justice*, Vol. 27, No. 2, 2009, pp. 251–270.

ARTICLE 2

APPLICATION OF THE CONVENTION

❖ Text of the provision*

(1) In addition to the provisions which shall be implemented in peacetime, the present Convention shall apply to all cases of declared war or of any other armed conflict which may arise between two or more of the High Contracting Parties, even if the state of war is not recognized by one of them.

(2) The Convention shall also apply to all cases of partial or total occupation of the territory of a High Contracting Party, even if the said occupation meets with no armed resistance.

(3) Although one of the Powers in conflict may not be a party to the present Convention, the Powers who are parties thereto shall remain bound by it in their mutual relations. They shall furthermore be bound by the Convention in relation to the said Power, if the latter accepts and applies the provisions thereof.

❖ Reservations or declarations

None

Contents

* Paragraph numbers have been added for ease of reference.

A. Introduction

192 This provision is a central pillar of the Geneva Conventions as it establishes the circumstances and conditions under which the Conventions apply.[1] Article 2, common to the four Geneva Conventions, constituted a major step forward when adopted in 1949 as it addressed a lacuna in earlier international humanitarian law instruments. Indeed, neither the 1899 and 1907 Hague Conventions nor the 1864, 1906 and 1929 Geneva Conventions specified under what conditions their application would be triggered. In the absence of any explicit indication, it was generally understood that these instruments applied only during a declared war, with recognition by the belligerents that a state of war existed between them.

193 Article 2(1) broadens the Geneva Conventions' scope of application by introducing the notion of 'armed conflict', thereby making their application less dependent on the formalism attached to the notion of 'declared war'. In addition, Article 2(2) specifies that the Geneva Conventions apply to all kinds of foreign military occupation, even if such occupation does not meet with armed opposition during or after the invasion. In this regard, paragraph 2 complements paragraph 1 of Article 2, which covers situations of occupation resulting from hostilities between States. Article 2 – along with common Article 3 – contributes to establishing a distinction between international and

---

[1] With the exception of common Article 3, which regulates non-international armed conflict. For more details, see the commentary on that article, in particular section C.

non-international armed conflict, a dichotomy confirmed over time by humanitarian law treaties adopted after the Geneva Conventions.

194   Common Article 2 plays a fundamental role in the humanitarian law archi-
tecture, even though non-international armed conflicts are now the most
prevalent form of armed conflicts. Indeed, armed conflicts between States continue to arise, and Article 2 remains pertinent notwithstanding the UN Charter
banning the resort to armed force between States as a means to settle their
differences.[2] Given the political and emotional dimensions attached to the
notion of war or armed conflict, States are frequently reluctant to admit that
they are engaged in one. This renders Article 2(1) all the more relevant in so
far as it clearly indicates that the Geneva Conventions and humanitarian law
more generally apply based on objective criteria.

195   Article 2(3) confirms the abandonment of the *si omnes* clause,[3] which had
previously been an obstacle to the effective application of humanitarian law
to inter-State armed violence. It also allows a non-party State the possibility of
applying the Geneva Conventions through express acceptance, which might be
relevant when newly created States become involved in armed conflict before
having ratified these instruments.

196   Common Article 2 also plays a role in determining the scope of application
of Additional Protocol I.[4]

B. Historical background

197 The 1864, 1906 and 1929 Geneva Conventions did not contain a specific provision setting out their scope of application. In the 1930s, it became apparent that it would be useful to indicate precisely to which situations the 1929
Geneva Conventions on the Wounded and Sick and on Prisoners of War would
apply, as some provisions in those Conventions referred to 'time of war' or similar expressions, which, if interpreted narrowly, might be understood to mean
only cases of declared war.[5] At the same time, especially in the light of the

---

[2] Except in situations of self-defence and when authorized by the UN Security Council; see UN
Charter (1945), Articles 51 and 42, respectively.

[3] The *si omnes* clause found in early law-of-war treaties provided that if one Party to a conflict
was not party to the instrument, no Parties were bound by the instrument. See, for instance,
Article 2 of the 1907 Hague Convention (IV), which provides: 'The provisions contained in the
Regulations referred to in Article 1, as well as in the present Convention, do not apply except
between Contracting powers, and then only if all the belligerents are parties to the Convention.'
A similar provision can be found in Article 24 of the 1906 Geneva Convention.

[4] Article 1(3) of Additional Protocol I provides: 'This Protocol, which supplements the Geneva
Conventions of 12 August 1949 for the protection of war victims, shall apply in the situations
referred to in Article 2 common to those Conventions.'

[5] See e.g. Articles 24, 25 and 29 of the 1929 Geneva Convention on the Wounded and Sick. Article 37 of the same Convention refers to a 'state of war'. The 1929 Geneva Convention on Prisoners of War refers to 'the extreme event of a war' (Preamble), 'time of war' (Article 82) and 'state
of war' (Article 95). Reacting to these concerns, the 15th International Conference of the Red

Spanish Civil War, it became apparent that armed conflicts did not necessarily occur only between States and that the 1929 Conventions did not apply to 'civil wars'.[6] In addition, the experience of the Second World War brought to light the need to apply the Conventions to all situations of military occupation. The draft of common Article 2 that was approved by the International Conference of the Red Cross in Stockholm in 1948 and debated at the Diplomatic Conference of 1949 was designed to address all of these concerns.[7]

198   The aspects of the draft article specifying that the Conventions applied to all situations of armed conflict between States, including belligerent occupation, were uncontroversial and passed without debate.[8] The first three paragraphs of the article that was debated were almost identical to common Article 2 as it stands today. The element of draft article 2 that proved to be controversial was the proposed application in the fourth paragraph of the original text of Article 2 of the whole of the Conventions to non-international armed conflicts; that provision was modified and eventually became common Article 3.[9]

C. Paragraph 1: Applicability of the Conventions in peacetime

199 The first clause of common Article 2 serves as an important reminder that, although the Geneva Conventions become fully applicable in situations of armed conflict, States Parties have obligations already in peacetime. In particular, States must adopt and implement legislation to institute penal sanctions

---

Cross in Tokyo in 1934 adopted a resolution expressing the wish that the 1929 Conventions be applicable by analogy in case of armed conflict occurring between States even when war had not been declared. See *Revue internationale de la Croix-Rouge et Bulletin international des Sociétés de la Croix-Rouge*, Vol. 16, No. 191, November 1934, p. 899. See also *Report of the Preliminary Conference of National Societies of 1946*, pp. 14–15, and *Report of the Conference of Government Experts of 1947*, pp. 8, 102 and 272. See also fn. 29 of this commentary.

[6] ICRC, *Report on the Interpretation, Revision and Extension of the Geneva Convention of July 27, 1929*, Report prepared for the 16th International Conference of the Red Cross, London, 1938, pp. 7–8.

[7] Draft article 2 of the *Draft Conventions adopted by the 1948 Stockholm Conference* provided that:

In addition to the stipulations which shall be implemented in peace time, the present Convention shall apply to all cases of declared war or of any other armed conflict which may arise between two or more of the High Contracting Parties, even if the state of war is not recognized by one of them.

The Convention shall also apply to all cases of partial or total occupation of the territory of a High Contracting Party, even if the said occupation meets with no armed resistance.

If one of the Powers in conflict is not party to the present Convention, the Powers who are party thereto shall, notwithstanding be bound by it in their mutual relations.

In all cases of armed conflict not of an international character which may occur in the territory of one or more of the High Contracting Parties, each of the adversaries shall be bound to implement the provisions of the present Convention. The Convention shall be applicable in these circumstances, whatever the legal status of the Parties to the conflict and without prejudice thereto.

[8] *Final Record of the Diplomatic Conference of 1949*, Vol. II-B, p. 128.

[9] For further details, see the commentary on common Article 3, paras 372–383.

for grave breaches and take measures to suppress other violations of the Conventions; they must adopt and implement legislation to prevent misuse and abuse of the emblems; and they must train their armed forces to know and be able to comply with the Conventions and spread knowledge of them as widely as possible among the civilian population.[10] As training and education are usually most effective in one's own language, States should also translate the Conventions (and indeed all humanitarian law instruments) into the national language(s).[11]

200   Further obligations in the Conventions may best be implemented during armed conflicts if preparatory steps are taken already in peacetime to execute them. In relation to the First Convention, this includes technical tasks such as stamping and distributing armbands to military medical personnel and marking medical units and establishments, but also extends to more complex obligations such as ensuring that a sufficient number of medical personnel are properly trained, equipped and prepared to provide medical services.[12] States may also wish to establish hospital zones during peacetime.[13] Moreover, as the obligation to disseminate the Conventions underlines, training all members of the armed forces in all of their operations to respect the wounded and sick and medical personnel, units and transports is a crucial peacetime task.[14]

---

[10] See Article 49 of the First Convention, Article 50 of the Second Convention, Article 129 of the Third Convention and Article 146 of the Fourth Convention (legislation on grave breaches and suppression of other violations); and Article 47 of the First Convention, Article 48 of the Second Convention, Article 127 of the Third Convention and Article 144 of the Fourth Convention (dissemination). See also Article 54 of the First Convention (prevention of misuse of the emblem).

[11] Article 48 of the First Convention, Article 49 of the Second Convention, Article 128 of the Third Convention and Article 145 of the Fourth Convention require States to communicate official translations of the Conventions to one another.

[12] See Articles 12 and 40–43. For specific obligations related to each Convention, see the commentary on common Article 2 in each of them.

[13] Article 23.

[14] In addition, States have obligations that continue to apply after an armed conflict is over (Article 6(4) of the Fourth Convention) or that must also apply after the conflict in order to be meaningful and effective (e.g. Articles 16 and 17 of the First Convention). The National Information Bureau referred to under Article 122 of the Third Convention (and its equivalent in Article 136 of the Fourth Convention), among others, must continue to function after a conflict. In addition to the obligations in the Geneva Conventions, States party to Additional Protocol I have specific peacetime obligations. These include training qualified personnel to facilitate the application of the Geneva Conventions and their Additional Protocols and ensuring the availability of legal advisers to advise military commanders when necessary (Articles 6(1) and 82 of Additional Protocol I, respectively). Other humanitarian law treaties also impose obligations in peacetime to ensure the effectiveness of the protection they provide during armed conflict. For example, the 1954 Hague Convention for the Protection of Cultural Property requires States Parties to prepare in time of peace for the safeguarding of cultural property (Article 3); to adapt their military regulations or instructions to ensure respect for the Convention (Article 7(1)); and to plan for or establish, within the armed forces, services or specialist personnel whose purpose is to secure respect for cultural property and to cooperate with the civilian authorities responsible for safeguarding it (Article 7(2)), among others).

D. Paragraph 1: Declared war or any other armed conflict between High Contracting Parties

201   Article 2(1) encompasses the concepts of 'declared war' and 'armed conflict'. Both trigger the application of the Geneva Conventions but cover different legal realities, the latter being more flexible and objective than the former. However, they are complementary, may even overlap, and cover a larger spectrum of belligerent relationships than was the case in the law prior to the 1949 Geneva Conventions.

202   The rationale of Article 2(1) is to extend the scope of application of the Geneva Conventions so that their provisions come into force even when hostilities between States do not result from a formal declaration of war. In this way, Article 2(1) serves the humanitarian purpose of the Geneva Conventions by minimizing the possibility for States to evade their obligations under humanitarian law simply by not declaring war or refusing to acknowledge the existence of an armed conflict.[15]

1. The concept of declared war

203   The concept of declared war in the Geneva Conventions corresponds to the concept of war as reflected in Article 2 of the 1899 Hague Convention (II), as well as in the preamble to the 1907 Hague Convention (III) relative to the opening of hostilities. The notion of declared war is more limited than that of armed conflict in Article 2(1) in so far as it is imbued with formalism and subjectivity. If the Geneva Conventions hinged only on the formal notion of war, their application would be contingent on the formal recognition (or creation) of a state of war by one of the belligerents through the issuance of a declaration of war. A declaration of war, which is unilateral in nature, triggers a state of war regardless of the position and behaviour of the addressee(s).[16] This notion is reiterated in Article 2(1), which confirms that a state of war exists even if not recognized by one of the belligerents.

204   Under the traditional theory of declared war, the mere fact that States are engaged in armed violence is insufficient to displace the law of peace and trigger the applicability of humanitarian law. Therefore, declared war in its legal meaning starts with a declaration of war,[17] which is interpreted as the only expression of the States' belligerent intent.

---

[15] For instance, by labelling their actions operations short of war or military operations other than war or by considering that they are just law-enforcement operations to which humanitarian law does not apply.

[16] Dinstein, 2011, p. 30.

[17] See Hague Convention (III) (1907), Article 1: 'The contracting Powers recognize that hostilities between themselves must not commence without previous and explicit warning, in the form either of a declaration of war, giving reasons, or of an ultimatum with conditional declaration of war.'

205   The significance of a declaration of war was specified in 2005 by the Eritrea-Ethiopia Claims Commission, which stated that 'the essence of a declaration of war is an explicit affirmation of the existence of a state of war between belligerents'.[18] A declaration of war should be understood as 'a unilateral and formal announcement, issued by the constitutionally competent authority of a State, setting the exact point at which war begins with a designated enemy'.[19] Declared war will therefore mark the transition from the application of the law of peace to the law of war. It will also bring about other legal consequences, such as the application of the law of neutrality,[20] the potential disruption of diplomatic relations between belligerents,[21] and the application of international prize law.[22]

206   The Geneva Conventions become automatically applicable even when a declaration of war is not followed by armed confrontations between the declaring State and its designated opponent(s).[23] Indeed, the declaration of war does not need to be underpinned by hostile actions against the enemy to make humanitarian law applicable.[24] Therefore, a State which confines itself to a declaration of war but does not participate in the fighting has to apply the Geneva Conventions. This also highlights the complementarity between the notion of declared war and the notion of armed conflict as the latter would need to be substantiated by hostile actions for humanitarian law to govern the conduct of those involved in the armed conflict within the meaning of Article 2(1).

207   Since the entry into force of the Geneva Conventions, States have rarely declared war. The adoption of the UN Charter in 1945 and the institution of a *jus ad bellum* regime rendering wars of aggression unlawful have resulted in a significant decrease in the practice of States declaring war on one another. However, this does not necessarily mean that the notion of declared war has

---

[18] Eritrea-Ethiopia Claims Commission, *Jus Ad Bellum, Ethiopia's Claims*, Partial Award, 2005, para. 17.

[19] Dinstein, 2011, p. 30.

[20] The law of neutrality applies when a declaration of war has been issued and the related state of war recognized and also applies when an international armed conflict within the meaning of Article 2(1) of the Geneva Conventions has come into existence. See Michael Bothe, 'The Law of Neutrality', in Dieter Fleck (ed.), *The Handbook of International Humanitarian Law*, 3rd edition, Oxford University Press, 2013, pp. 549–580, at 549; Wolff Heintschel von Heinegg, '"Benevolent" Third States in International Armed Conflicts: The Myth of the Irrelevance of the Law of Neutrality', in Michael N. Schmitt and Jelena Pejic (eds), *International Law and Armed Conflict: Exploring the Faultlines. Essays in Honour of Yoram Dinstein*, Martinus Nijhoff Publishers, Leiden, 2007, pp. 543–568; Dietrich Schindler, 'Transformations in the Law of Neutrality since 1945', in Astrid J.M. Delissen and Gerard J. Tanja (eds), *Humanitarian Law of Armed Conflict: Challenges Ahead, Essays in Honour of Frits Kalshoven*, Martinus Nijhoff Publishers, Dordrecht, 1991, pp. 367–386; and Wolff Heintschel von Heinegg, 'Wider die Mär vom Tode des Neutralitätsrechts', in Horst Fischer (ed.), *Crisis Management and Humanitarian Protection: Festschrift für Dieter Fleck*, Berliner Wissenschafts-Verlag, 2004, pp. 221–241.

[21] Greenwood, 1987, pp. 283–306.

[22] Wolff Heintschel von Heinegg, 'The Current State of International Prize Law', in Harry H.G. Post (ed.), *International Economic Law and Armed Conflict*, Martinus Nijhoff Publishers, Dordrecht, 1994, pp. 5–50.

[23] Milanovic/Hadzi-Vidanovic, p. 268; Greenwood, 2008, p. 43.

[24] For instance, in the Second World War most Latin American States declared war against the Axis Powers but did not participate in any hostilities; see Schindler, p. 132.

fallen into desuetude. Even if academic writers have claimed that the concept of war has disappeared,[25] the possibility for a State to issue a declaration of war cannot be discarded.[26] It would therefore be premature to conclude the demise of the concept of declared war, even if its progressive decline cannot be ignored.[27]

208   Maintaining the notion of declared war also serves a humanitarian purpose in so far as it makes it possible – even if States have not yet engaged in open hostilities – for enemy nationals who find themselves in the territory of the opposing Party to benefit from the protection conferred by humanitarian law should they be exposed to the adverse effects of a declaration of war and its correlative bellicose rhetoric and atmosphere. In such a case, States would have to treat civilians on their territories who are nationals of the opposing State in accordance with the Fourth Convention. The application of the Conventions in case of declared war would thus prove useful from a protection perspective and would fit with their humanitarian objectives.[28]

209   In the absence of a more objective definition of the conditions triggering the application of humanitarian law, the sole reliance on the concept of declared war and its correlative subjectivity could thwart the humanitarian objectives of the Geneva Conventions.[29] Consequently, in 1949 it was felt that there was a pressing need to dispense with the subjectivity and formalism attached to the notion of declared war and to ensure that the applicability of humanitarian law would mainly be premised on objective and factual criteria. Against this background, the Geneva Conventions introduced the fact-based concept of armed conflict, i.e. defined in its material rather than legal sense, in order to supplement the notion of declared war. Through this semantic shift, the drafters of the Geneva Conventions moved away from conditioning the applicability of

---

[25] See Kolb, 2009, p. 161; Partsch, p. 252; and Marco Sassòli, 'La "guerre contre le terrorisme", le droit international humanitaire et le statut de prisonnier de guerre', *Annuaire canadien de droit international*, Vol. 39, 2001, pp. 211–252, at 215. It is also noteworthy that the ICTY in *Tadić* defined international armed conflict without any reference to 'war' (*Tadić* Decision on the Defence Motion for Interlocutory Appeal on Jurisdiction, 1995, para. 70).

[26] International Law Association, Committee on the Use of Force, *Final Report on the Meaning of Armed Conflict in International Law*, The Hague Conference, 2010, pp. 7–8. See also Greenwood, 1987, p. 294: 'State practice suggest[s] that many States still regard the creation of a state of war as a possibility and thus, presumably, accept that war continues to exist as a legal institution.'

[27] Dinstein, 2011, p. 32.

[28] The application of the Geneva Conventions of 1949 in such circumstances is without prejudice to the parallel application of human rights law, whose applicable protections may complement those afforded by humanitarian law.

[29] The only thing that a State would have to do to avoid the strictures of the Geneva Conventions if the Conventions applied only to 'declared wars' would be to deny the existence of a state of war in the legal sense (owing to a lack of a declaration of war), even if armed confrontations take place. The most notorious example of this was the Sino-Japanese conflict that broke out in 1931, when China and Japan refused to recognize that a state of war existed between them despite their involvement in intensive military operations, the occupation of Manchuria and the high level of casualties (Voelckel, p. 10). Such a situation would result in legal uncertainty: if humanitarian law does not regulate such situations, what would be the applicable legal framework? In that case, those affected by the hostilities would be bereft of appropriate legal protection.

the Geneva Conventions solely on the legal concept of war. The applicability of humanitarian law would thenceforth be not only related to the declared will of States but would also depend on objective and factual criteria stemming from the notion of armed conflict introduced in Article 2(1), making it applicable as soon as a State undertakes hostile military action(s) against another State.

2. The concept of armed conflict

210   As stated above, before the 1949 Geneva Conventions the rule prevailed that the laws of war were only applicable if there was a legal state of war between two or more States. Article 2(1) overcame this rigid rule by establishing that, besides declared war, the Geneva Conventions would also be applicable if a state of war was not recognized.[30] Since 1907, experience has shown that many armed conflicts, displaying all the characteristics of a war, may arise without being preceded by any of the formalities laid down in the 1907 Hague Convention (III).[31] It follows from Article 2(1) that the factual existence of an armed conflict suffices for humanitarian law to apply.[32] In addition, the notion of armed conflict under Article 2(1) includes the case of occupation resulting from hostilities or declared war.[33] Therefore, the main added value of the notion of armed conflict is to base the application of the Geneva Conventions on objective and factual criteria.

211   Indeed, Article 2(1) underlines the pre-eminence of the factual existence of armed conflict over the formal status of war. Therefore, the determination of the existence of an armed conflict within the meaning of Article 2(1) must be based solely on the prevailing facts demonstrating the *de facto* existence of hostilities between the belligerents, even without a declaration of war.

212   This view, besides being widely held by academic writers,[34] is also reflected in recent international decisions and in certain military manuals. Indeed, the ICTY and the ICTR have confirmed that the applicability of humanitarian law should be determined according to the prevailing circumstances instead of the

---

[30] Dietrich Schindler, 'The Different Types of Armed Conflicts according to the Geneva Conventions and Protocols', *Collected Courses of the Hague Academy of International Law*, Vol. 163, 1979, pp. 117–164, at 131.

[31] Hague Convention (III) (1907), Article 1.

[32] International Law Association, Committee on the Use of Force, *Final Report on the Meaning of Armed Conflict in International Law*, The Hague Conference, 2010, p. 2.

[33] For a detailed analysis of the notion of occupation, see section E.

[34] See e.g. David, p. 120; Robert Kolb and Richard Hyde, *An Introduction to the International Law of Armed Conflicts*, 3rd edition, Hart Publishing, Oxford, 2008, pp. 75–76; Kleffner, pp. 47–48; Geoffrey S. Corn *et al.* (eds), *The Law of Armed Conflict: An Operational Approach*, Wolters Kluwer Law & Business, New York, 2012, pp. 72 and 80; Gabriele Porretto and Sylvain Vité, 'The application of international humanitarian law and human rights to international organisations', *Research Papers Series No. 1*, Centre Universitaire de Droit International Humanitaire, 2006, p. 32; and Shraga, 2008, p. 94. See also International Law Association, Committee on the Use of Force, *Final Report on the Meaning of Armed Conflict in International Law*, The Hague Conference, 2010, p. 33: 'The *de jure* state or situation of armed conflict depends on the presence of actual and observable facts, in other words, objective criteria.'

subjective views of the Parties to the conflict.[35] For instance, the ICTY Trial Chamber stated in *Boškoski and Tarčulovski* that 'the question of whether there was an armed conflict at the relevant time is a factual determination to be made by the Trial Chamber upon hearing and reviewing the evidence admitted at trial'.[36] In a similar vein, the ICTR underlined in *Akayesu* that '[i]f the application of international humanitarian law depended solely on the discretionary judgment of the parties to the conflict, in most cases there would be a tendency for the conflict to be minimized by the parties thereto'.[37]

213   In this regard, one cannot discard the possibility that some States might be tempted to deny the existence of an armed conflict even if facts on the ground prove otherwise. Even if none of the Parties recognizes the existence of a state of war or of an armed conflict, humanitarian law would still apply provided that an armed conflict is in fact in existence. How States characterize the armed confrontation does not affect the application of the Geneva Conventions if the situation evidences that the State concerned is effectively involved in hostile armed actions against another State. The fact that a State does not, for political or other reasons, explicitly refer to the existence of an armed conflict within the meaning of Article 2(1) in a particular situation does not prevent it from being legally classified as such. The UN Security Council has also, in a resolution for example, stated its own classification of a situation under humanitarian law.[38] The applicability of the Geneva Conventions is independent of official pronouncements in order to avoid cases in which States could deny the protection of the Conventions.[39]

---

[35] Even if most of these cases dealt with the determination of the existence of a non-international armed conflict, international tribunals' analyses are also relevant for situations of international armed conflict. Most of these decisions relied on the definition of armed conflict given in the ICTY's 1995 *Tadić* decision, which encompasses both international and non-international armed conflicts. In *Lubanga* and *Bemba*, the ICC Trial Chamber used the test established by the ICTY in *Tadić* in order to determine the existence of an armed conflict. ICC, *Lubanga* Trial Judgment, 2012, paras 531–538, and *Bemba* Trial Judgment, 2016, para. 128. The ICC therefore admits implicitly that the existence of an armed conflict is to be determined based on the facts at the time.

[36] ICTY, *Boškoski and Tarčulovski* Trial Judgment, 2008, para. 174.

[37] ICTR, *Akayesu* Trial Judgment, 1998, para. 603. See also ICTY, *Milutinović* Trial Judgment, 2009, para. 125: 'The existence of an armed conflict does not depend upon the views of the parties to the conflict.' In the same vein, see *Blaškić* Trial Judgment, 2000, para. 82: 'Whatever the case, the parties to the conflict may not agree between themselves to change the nature of the conflict, which is established by the facts whose interpretation, where applicable, falls to the Judge.' See also United Kingdom, *Manual of the Law of Armed Conflict*, 2004, para. 3.2.3.

[38] Based on Article 103 of the 1945 UN Charter, it could be argued that a determination by the UN Security Council invoking Chapter VII would be binding. While this may have merit, such a conclusion would be doubtful if it would lead to ending or modifying obligations which are of a *ius cogens* nature. See e.g. Robert Kolb, *Peremptory International Law: Jus Cogens*, Hart Publishing, Oxford, 2015, pp. 119–121; Marco Sassòli, 'Legislation and Maintenance of Public Order and Civil Life by Occupying Powers', *European Journal of International Law*, Vol. 16, No. 4, 2005, pp. 661–694, at 680–682 and 684.

[39] See ICRC, *International Humanitarian Law and the Challenges of Contemporary Armed Conflicts*, Report prepared for the 31st International Conference of the Red Cross and Red Crescent, Geneva, 2011, p. 8, and Vité, 2009, p. 72.

214   It should be noted that there is no central authority under international law to identify or classify a situation as an armed conflict. States and Parties to a conflict need to determine the legal framework applicable to the conduct of their military operations. For its part, the ICRC makes an independent determination of the facts and systematically classifies situations for the purposes of its work. It is a task inherent in the role that the ICRC is expected to exercise under the Geneva Conventions, as set forth in the Statutes of the International Red Cross and Red Crescent Movement.[40] Other actors such as the United Nations and regional organizations may also need to classify situations for their work, and international and national courts and tribunals need to do so for the purposes of exercising their jurisdiction. In all cases, the classification must be made in good faith, based on the facts and the relevant criteria under humanitarian law.[41]

215   A determination based on the prevailing facts should also conform to – and help preserve – the strict separation of *jus in bello* from *jus ad bellum*.[42] Indeed, by virtue of this distinction, the determination of the existence of an armed conflict and the related applicability of international humanitarian law depend

---

[40] Statutes of the International Red Cross and Red Crescent Movement (1986), Article 5.

[41] As international law is a self-applied system, it is possible that different actors will have different views of the same facts. In any case, it is the facts that determine whether a situation constitutes an international armed conflict, a non-international armed conflict or not an armed conflict at all.

[42] Besides treaty law (common Article 1 and the preamble to Additional Protocol I), international and domestic tribunals, numerous academic writers and many military manuals confirm the validity and relevance not only of the strict separation between *jus in bello* and *jus ad bellum* but also of its corollary, the principle of equality of belligerents before humanitarian law. In particular, the judgment by the US Military Tribunal at Nuremberg in the *Hostages case* in 1948 forms a landmark decision in relation to the strict separation between *jus ad bellum* and *jus in bello*. Other judgments concerning war crimes perpetrated during the Second World War have followed the same approach and confirmed the importance of maintaining the strict separation (see Okimoto, p. 17, and Orakhelashvili, pp. 167–170). Following the path of this consistent case law, academic writers have been overwhelmingly supportive of the strict separation and have confirmed that the legal status of the belligerents under *jus ad bellum* should not affect the applicability or the application of humanitarian law: see e.g. Hersch Lauterpacht, *Oppenheim's International Law*, 6th edition, Longman's, Green and Co., London, 1940, pp. 174–175; Charles Rousseau, *Le droit des conflits armés*, Pedone, Paris, 1983, pp. 24–26; Myres S. McDougal and Florentino P. Feliciano, *The International Law of War: Transnational Coercion and World Public Order*, New Haven Press, 1994, pp. 530–542; Yoram Dinstein, *War, Aggression and Self-Defence*, 5th edition, Cambridge University Press, 2011, pp. 167–175; Leslie C. Green, *The Contemporary Law of Armed Conflict*, 2nd edition, Manchester University Press, 2000, pp. 18–19; Christopher Greenwood, 'International Humanitarian Law (Laws of War): Revised Report for the Centennial Commemoration of the First Hague Peace Conference 1899', in Frits Kalshoven (ed.), *The Centennial of the First International Peace Conference: Reports and Conclusions*, Kluwer, The Hague, 2000, pp. 173–192; François Bugnion, 'Guerre juste, guerre d'agression et droit international humanitaire', *Revue internationale de la Croix-Rouge*, Vol. 84, No. 847, September 2002, pp. 523–546; Okimoto; Sassòli, 2007, pp. 241–264; Christopher Greenwood, 'The relationship between *jus ad bellum* and *jus in bello*', *Review of International Studies*, Vol. 9, No. 4, 1983, pp. 221–234; Ryan Goodman, 'Controlling the recourse to war by modifying *jus in bello*', *Yearbook of International Humanitarian Law*, Vol. 12, 2009, pp. 53–84; and Jasmine Moussa, 'Can *jus ad bellum* override *jus in bello*? Reaffirming the separation of the two bodies of law', *International Review of the Red Cross*, Vol. 90, No. 872, December 2008, pp. 963–990.

only on the circumstances prevailing on the ground and not on whether the use of force against another State is permitted under the UN Charter. Whether a State uses force in accordance with its right of self-defence, because it has been authorized to do so by a UN Security Council mandate, or in violation of the prohibition on the use of force does not affect the determination of the existence of an international armed conflict. The mandate and the actual or perceived legitimacy of a State to resort to armed force are issues which fall within the province of *jus ad bellum*, and have no effect on the applicability of international humanitarian law to a specific situation involving two or more High Contracting Parties.

216 The very object and purpose of international humanitarian law – to protect those who are not or no longer taking part in the hostilities during armed conflict – would be defeated were the application of that body of law made dependent on the lawfulness of the conflict under *jus ad bellum*. To conclude that humanitarian law does not apply or applies differently to a belligerent that is waging an armed conflict that it deems 'just' or 'legitimate' would arbitrarily deprive the victims of that conflict of the protections due to them. It would also open the door for Parties to armed conflicts to deny their legal obligations under humanitarian law by branding the enemy's use of force as unlawful or by emphasizing their international legitimacy. Humanitarian law ignores such distinctions and applies equally to all States involved in the conflict.

a. The constitutive elements of the definition of armed conflict

217 Article 2(1) speaks merely of 'any other armed conflict which may arise between two or more of the High Contracting Parties'. While it defines the Parties to an international armed conflict, it does not provide a definition of armed conflict. The main purpose of introducing the notion of armed conflict in Article 2(1) was to provide an objective standard to be assessed on the basis of the prevailing facts.

218 State practice, case law and academic literature have developed the legal contours of the notion of armed conflict and provided insight into how Article 2(1) should be interpreted. Armed conflicts in the sense of Article 2(1) are those which oppose High Contracting Parties (i.e. States) and occur when one or more States have recourse to armed force against another State, regardless of the reasons for or the intensity of the confrontation.[43] In *Tadić*, the ICTY stated that 'an armed conflict exists whenever there is a resort to armed force between States'.[44] This definition has since been adopted by other international bodies

---

[43] ICRC, 'How is the term "armed conflict" defined in international humanitarian law?', Opinion Paper, March 2008, p. 1. The 1958 Commentary on the Fourth Geneva Convention also played an important role in clarifying the notion of 'armed conflict': see Pictet (ed.), *Commentary on the Fourth Geneva Convention*, Geneva, 1958, pp. 20–21.

[44] ICTY, *Tadić* Decision on the Defence Motion for Interlocutory Appeal on Jurisdiction, 1995, para. 70.

and is generally considered as the contemporary reference for any interpretation of the notion of armed conflict under humanitarian law.

219   All the foregoing shows that the notion of armed conflict under Article 2(1) requires the hostile resort to armed force involving two or more States.[45]

i. The legal status of the belligerents: 'between two or more of the High Contracting Parties'

220 By virtue of common Article 2(1), the 1949 Geneva Conventions apply to 'all cases of . . . armed conflict which may arise between two or more of the *High Contracting Parties*, even if the state of war is not recognized by one of them' (emphasis added). The expression 'High Contracting Parties' refers to the States for which these instruments are in force.[46] The situations referred to in Article 2(1) are therefore limited to armed conflicts between opposing States.[47]

221   Under Article 2(1), the identity of the actors involved in the hostilities – States – will therefore define the international character of the armed conflict.[48] In this regard, statehood remains the baseline against which the existence of an armed conflict under Article 2(1) will be measured.

222   When dealing with the notion of armed conflict contained in Article 2(1), the 1958 Commentary on the Fourth Geneva Convention refers to '[a]ny difference arising *between* two States and leading to the *intervention of members of the*

---

[45] ICRC, 'How is the term "armed conflict" defined in international humanitarian law?', Opinion Paper, March 2008, p. 1.

[46] The expression 'High Contracting Parties' as used in the Conventions must be understood in the sense given by Article 2(1)(g) of the 1969 Vienna Convention on the Law of Treaties to the word 'party', namely 'a State which has consented to be bound by the treaty and for which the treaty is in force'. See Kritsiotis, p. 275: 'The transposition of "States" instead of "High Contracting Parties" as the actors who enter the legal relationship that is called an "international armed conflict" is, of course, a necessary move for the [ICTY] Appeals Chamber to have made in defining the concept of an international armed conflict from the perspective of custom given the intrinsically conventional idiom of *High Contracting Parties*.'

[47] Contemporary armed conflicts show that, besides States, international organizations such as the UN or NATO can be involved in armed conflict. See ICRC, *International Humanitarian Law and the Challenges of Contemporary Armed Conflicts*, Report prepared for the 31st International Conference of the Red Cross and Red Crescent, Geneva, 2011, pp. 30–33, and Ferraro, 2012a. However, the Geneva Conventions do not as such apply to international organizations. International organizations cannot be signatories of the Geneva Conventions and thus cannot become High Contracting Parties, but they are bound by customary international humanitarian law.

[48] In its efforts post-9/11 to eradicate the threat from al-Qaeda, the US Government qualified the situation as an international armed conflict even though one Party was not a State (see *Hamdan case*, Government Brief on the Merits, 2006.) Following the US Supreme Court's decision in *Hamdan* that common Article 3 applies to that situation, the US Government has considered it to be a transnational non-international armed conflict. See United States, Supreme Court, *Hamdan case*, Judgment, 2006, pp. 629–631; John B. Bellinger, 'Prisoners in War: Contemporary Challenges to the Geneva Conventions', lecture at the University of Oxford, 10 December 2007, reported in *American Journal of International Law*, Vol. 102, pp. 367–370. See also Marko Milanovic, 'Lessons for human rights and humanitarian law in the war on terror: comparing *Hamdan* and the Israeli *Targeted Killings* case', *International Review of the Red Cross*, Vol. 89, No. 866, June 2007, pp. 373–393.

armed forces' (emphasis added).[49] However, this would mean that for an armed conflict to exist in the sense of Article 2(1), the simultaneous involvement of at least two opposing States through their armed forces is required. That interpretation is too narrow.

223 Such a position would in fact exclude from the scope of armed conflict the unilateral use of force by one State against another. This reading of Article 2(1) would be at odds with the object and purpose of the Geneva Conventions, which is to regulate any kind of use of armed force involving two or more States. An armed conflict can arise when one State unilaterally uses armed force against another State even if the latter does not or cannot respond by military means. The unilateral use of armed force presupposes a plurality of actors and still reflects an armed confrontation involving two or more States, the attacking State and the State(s) subject to the attack, therefore satisfying the requirement of Article 2(1). The fact that a State resorts to armed force against another suffices to qualify the situation as an armed conflict within the meaning of the Geneva Conventions. In this perspective, the declaration, establishment and enforcement of an effective naval or air blockade, as an 'act of war', may suffice to initiate an international armed conflict to which humanitarian law would also apply.[50] In a similar vein, an unconsented-to invasion or deployment of a State's armed forces on the territory of another State – even if it does not meet with armed resistance – could constitute a unilateral and hostile use of armed force by one State against another, meeting the conditions for an international armed conflict under Article 2(1).[51]

224 Similarly, the use of armed force not directed against the enemy's armed forces but only against the enemy's territory, its civilian population and/or civilian objects, including (but not limited to) infrastructure, constitutes an international armed conflict for the purposes of Article 2(1). Under humanitarian law, the existence of an international armed conflict does not require that the persons and/or objects targeted necessarily be part of the executive authority, nor is it conditioned on the attack only being directed against the government in place.[52] International armed conflicts are fought between States. The

---

[49] Pictet (ed.), *Commentary on the Fourth Geneva Convention*, ICRC, 1958, p. 20. In a similar vein, Pictet defined international armed conflict as 'any opposition between two states involving the intervention of their armed forces and the existence of victims'; see Jean S. Pictet, *Humanitarian Law and the Protection of War Victims*, Henry Dunant Institute, Geneva, 1975, p. 52. The ICTY in *Tadić* uses almost the same formula and affirms that 'armed conflict exists whenever there is resort to armed force *between* States' (emphasis added); *Tadić* Decision on the Defence Motion for Interlocutory Appeal on Jurisdiction, 1995, para. 70. See also Kritsiotis, p. 274.

[50] Wolff Heintschel von Heinegg, 'Naval Blockade', in Michael N. Schmitt (ed.), *International Law Across the Spectrum of Conflict: Essays in Honour of Professor L.C. Green on the Occasion of his Eightieth Birthday*, International Law Studies, U.S. Naval War College, Vol. 75, 2000, pp. 203–230, at 204.

[51] This would be the case when such unilateral military action is not the result of mistakes or *ultra vires* actions (see paras 236–244).

[52] Akande, p. 75.

government is only one of the constitutive elements of the State, while the territory and the population are the other constitutive elements. Therefore, any attack directed against the territory, population, or the military or civilian infrastructure constitutes a resort to armed force against the State to which this territory, population or infrastructure belongs.[53]

225   The existence of an international armed conflict presupposes the involvement of the armed forces of at least one of the opposing States.[54] Indeed, armed conflict presumes the deployment of military means in order to overcome the enemy or force it into submission, to eradicate the threat it represents or to force it to change its course of action. When classic means and methods of warfare – such as the deployment of troops on the enemy's territory, the use of artillery or the resort to jetfighters or combat helicopters – come into play, it is uncontroversial that they amount to an armed confrontation between States and that the application of the Geneva Conventions is triggered.

226   However, one should not discard outright the possibility that armed conflict within the meaning of Article 2(1) may come into existence even if the armed confrontation does not involve military personnel but rather non-military State agencies such as paramilitary forces, border guards or coast guards.[55] Any of those could well be engaged in armed violence displaying the same characteristics as that involving State armed forces.

227   In the naval context, under international law applicable at sea, States may, in certain circumstances, lawfully use force against a vessel owned or operated by another State, or registered therein. This may be the case, for example, when coast guards, suspecting a violation of their State's fisheries legislation, attempt to board such a vessel but meet with resistance. The use of force in the course of this and other types of maritime law enforcement operations is regulated by legal notions akin to those regulating the use of force under human rights law.[56]

---

[53] See paras 236–244.

[54] See Milanovic/Hadzi-Vidanovic, p. 274; Schindler, p. 131; and David, p. 122.

[55] It has sometimes been argued that because the use of force between States during minor and/or sporadic armed clashes involved non-military agencies, such a situation should not be read as an international armed conflict and would not be governed by humanitarian law. See Arimatsu, p. 77.

[56] Examples of relevant cases setting out the legal framework include: ICJ, *Fisheries Jurisdiction case (Spain v. Canada)*, Jurisdiction of the Court, Judgment, 1998, para. 84; International Tribunal for the Law of the Sea (ITLOS), *The M/V 'Saiga' (No. 2) case, Saint Vincent and the Grenadines v. Guinea*, Judgment, 1 July 1999, paras 155–159 (see also the last paragraph of the Separate Opinion of Judge Anderson); and Arbitral Tribunal constituted Pursuant to Article 287, and in accordance with Annex VII, of the United Nations Convention on the Law of the Sea, *In the Matter of an Arbitration between Guyana and Suriname*, Award of the Arbitral Tribunal, Registry: The Permanent Court of Arbitration, The Hague, 17 September 2007, para. 445. See further *Claim of the British Ship 'I'm Alone' v. United States*, Joint Interim Report of the Commissioners, 30 June 1933, in *American Journal of International Law*, Vol. 29, 1936, pp. 326–331, and 'Investigation of certain incidents affecting the British Trawler *Red Crusader*', Report of 23 March 1962 of the Commission of Enquiry established by the Government of the United Kingdom of Great Britain and Northern Ireland and the Government of the Kingdom of Denmark on 15 November 1961, *International Law Reports*, 1962, Vol. 35, p. 485. For academic literature, see Efthymios Papastavridis, *The Interception of Vessels on the High Seas*,

In principle, such measures do not constitute an international armed conflict between the States affiliated with the vessels, in particular where the force is exercised against a private vessel. It cannot be excluded, however, that the use of force at sea is motivated by something other than a State's authority to enforce a regulatory regime applicable at sea. Depending on the circumstances, such a situation may qualify as an international armed conflict.

228   The question of 'who' is involved in the armed opposition between States should not significantly affect the classification of the situation as an international armed conflict. When a State resorts to means and methods of warfare against another State, that situation qualifies as an international armed conflict, irrespective of the organ within that State that has resorted to such means and methods.

229   Even if armed conflicts under Article 2(1) generally imply the deployment and involvement of military means, there might be situations in which the use of force by other State officials or persons qualified as 'agents' of a State would suffice. However, only the use of force by the *de jure* or *de facto* organs of a State, but not by private persons, will constitute an armed conflict.[57] The ICC Pre-trial Chamber followed a similar reasoning in *Bemba*, concluding that 'an international armed conflict exists in case of armed hostilities between States through their respective armed forces or *other actors acting on behalf of the State*' (emphasis added).[58]

230   These positions emphasize that non-military State agencies, even if not formally integrated into the armed forces, can be at the origin of an armed conflict provided they qualify as an organ of the State concerned. To limit the existence of an international armed conflict to the involvement on both sides of their armed forces as defined in their domestic law would allow States to bypass the application of humanitarian law by using non-military agencies or other surrogates not officially considered members of the armed forces. Such an interpretation of Article 2(1) would lead to a result which is manifestly unreasonable as it would defeat the protective goal of the Geneva Conventions.

231   One of the recurrent problems in determining the existence of an international armed conflict is whether one of the Parties thereto claiming statehood is

Hart Publishing, Oxford, 2014, pp. 68–72; Douglas Guilfoyle, *Shipping Interdiction and the Law of the Sea*, Cambridge University Press, 2009, pp. 271–272; Patricia Jimenez Kwast, 'Maritime Law Enforcement and the Use of Force: Reflections on the Categorisation of Forcible Action at Sea in Light of the *Guyana/Suriname* Award, *Journal of Conflict and Security Law*, Vol. 13, No. 1, 2008, pp. 49–91; Natalie Klein, *Maritime Security and the Law of the Sea*, Oxford University Press, 2001, pp. 62–146; Ivan Shearer, 'The Development of International Law with Respect to the Law Enforcement Roles of Navies and Coast Guards in Peacetime', *International Law Studies*, Vol. 71, 1998, pp. 429–453; and Anna van Zwanenberg, 'Interference with Ships on the High Seas', *International and Comparative Law Quarterly*, Vol. 10, No. 4, 1961, pp. 785–817.

[57] Greenwood, 2008, p. 48.

[58] ICC, *Bemba* Decision on the Confirmation of Charges, 2009, para. 223. This approach was also applied at trial; see *Bemba* Trial Judgment, 2016, paras 654–656. For a more detailed analysis of the situation in which international armed conflict is determined on the basis of a State's control over non-State armed groups located in the territory of its enemy, see paras 265–273.

effectively a State as defined under international law. This issue can be encountered notably at the occasion of a secessionist project or the disintegration of a
State as a consequence of a non-international armed conflict.[59] In this regard,
it is possible that what started as a non-international armed conflict becomes
international if the secessionist entity is successful in becoming a State by fulfilling the criteria for statehood under international law. The statehood of the
belligerents, which determines the nature of the armed conflict as an international armed conflict, is ascertained by objective criteria under international
law, which carry their own complexities.[60] The fact that one of the Parties
does not recognize the other as a State is irrelevant.

232   In a similar vein, the legal status of the belligerents also raises some problems
in relation to a State's representation. While it is clear that international armed
conflicts are fought between States, the question of who gets to represent those
States may be a thorny issue.[61] The determination of which entity is the government of a State matters because a number of international law issues turn on
that question, in particular the nature of an armed conflict involving the government of that State. Indeed, answering this question may have some impact
on the classification of the armed conflict at its very beginning or on its reclas-
sification over time if the government changes as a result of a transitional/
political process or a military victory of a non-State armed group.[62]

---

[59] For instance, the ICTY had to identify whether Croatia had become a State in order to determine
whether the conflict in the former Yugoslavia was an international armed conflict. See ICTY,
Slobodan Milošević Decision on Motion for Judgment of Acquittal, 2004, paras 85–93.

[60] See Montevideo Convention on the Rights and Duties of States (1933), Article 1 ('The state
as a person of international law should possess the following qualifications: a) a permanent
population; b) a defined territory; c) government; and d) capacity to enter into relations with the
other states').

[61] Milanovic/Hadzi-Vidanovic, p. 279.

[62] See e.g. Letter from the ICRC legal adviser to the UK House of Commons (Select Committee
on International Development), 20 December 2002:

> In response to the questions raised, I would nevertheless like to seize this opportunity to
> inform the International Development Committee on the ICRC's legal qualification of the
> conflict in Afghanistan and some implications thereof.
>
> It may be recalled in particular that the ICRC regarded the four Geneva Conventions of 12
> August 1949 as being fully applicable to the armed conflict which commenced in Afghanistan
> on 7 October 2001. The ICRC had therefore qualified this conflict as an international armed
> conflict.
>
> Following the convening of the Loya Jirga in Kabul in June 2002 and the subsequent estab-
> lishment of an Afghan transitional government on 19 June 2002 which not only received
> unanimous recognition by the entire community of States but could also claim broad-based
> recognition within Afghanistan through the Loya Jirga process the ICRC has changed its ini-
> tial qualification as follows: The ICRC no longer views the ongoing military operations in
> Afghanistan directed against suspected Taliban or other armed groups as an international
> armed conflict.
>
> Hostilities conducted by United States and allied forces against groups such as the Taliban
> and al-Qaeda in Afghanistan after 19 June 2002 are therefore governed by the rules applicable
> to situations of non-international armed conflict, since the military operations in question
> are being carried out with the consent of the government of a recognized sovereign State, the
> Islamic State of Afghanistan.

233　However, the fact that an incumbent government has been defeated does not in itself divest the armed conflict of its initial international character, nor does the establishment of a puppet government by the victorious belligerent. The only possible way the nature of the armed conflict could change as a result of the defeat of the former government is to ascertain that the new government is effective and consents to the presence or military operations of foreign forces in its territory, unless, however, it is instituted by an Occupying Power.[63]

234　Under international law, the key condition for the existence of a government is its effectiveness, that is, its ability to exercise effectively functions usually assigned to a government within the confines of a State's territory, including the maintenance of law and order.[64] Effectiveness is the ability to exert State functions internally and externally, i.e. in relations with other States.[65]

235　The problem might also come from a divided State, where there are competing claims to be the government of a State. Such a situation existed in Afghanistan in 2001, in Côte d'Ivoire in 2010–11 and in Libya in 2011. In this regard, it does not matter that a government failed to gain recognition by the international community at large. The very fact that the said government is effective and in control of most of the territory of the State concerned means that it is the *de facto* government and its actions have to be treated as the actions of the State it represents with all the consequences this entails for determining the existence of an international armed conflict.[66]

ii. Intensity of the armed confrontation

236　For international armed conflict, there is no requirement that the use of armed force between the Parties reach a certain level of intensity before it can be said that an armed conflict exists. Article 2(1) itself contains no mention of any

---

[63] See Fourth Convention, Article 47. In situations in which, during an occupation, a local government emerges 'with a good deal of authority and credibility, and accepted as being a representative body', its consent could potentially change the nature of the armed conflict. See ICRC, *Occupation and Other Forms of Administration of Foreign Territory*, p. 29.

[64] Hersch Lauterpacht, 'Recognition of Governments: I', *Columbia Law Review*, Vol. 45, 1945, pp. 815–864, especially at 825–830; Malcolm N. Shaw, *International Law*, 5th edition, Cambridge University Press, 2003, pp. 376–382.

[65] This factor is considered by some to be a legitimacy factor. For further discussion, see Jean d'Aspremont, 'Legitimacy of Governments in the Age of Democracy', *New York University Journal of International Law and Politics*, Vol. 38, 2006, pp. 877–917; see also Hersch Lauterpacht, 'Recognition of Governments: I', *Columbia Law Review*, Vol. 45, 1945, pp. 815–864, especially at 830–833, and Malcolm N. Shaw, *International Law*, 5th edition, Cambridge University Press, 2003, 379.

[66] Dinstein, 2004, p. 888. See also Christopher Greenwood, 'International law and the "war against terrorism"', *International Affairs*, Vol. 78, No. 2, April 2002, pp. 301–317, at 312–313. The issue of State representation will also have some importance in relation to the situation in which a third State intervenes in the territory of another one. In this case, the applicability of humanitarian law and the correlative determination of the nature of the armed conflict will revolve around the notion of consent. In this regard, the identity of the consenter and its ability to give consent will be crucial elements to take into consideration. See paras 257–263.

threshold for the intensity or duration of hostilities. Indeed, in the frequently cited 1958 commentary on common Article 2, Pictet stated:

> Any difference arising between two States and leading to the intervention of armed forces is an armed conflict within the meaning of Article 2, even if one of the Parties denies the existence of a state of war. It makes no difference how long the conflict lasts, or how much slaughter takes place. The respect due to the human person as such is not measured by the number of victims.[67]

Furthermore, it makes no difference 'how numerous are the participating forces; it suffices for the armed forces of one Power to have captured adversaries falling within the scope of Article 4' of the Third Convention.[68] This view remains pertinent today.

2.37   Even minor skirmishes between the armed forces, be they land, air or naval forces, would spark an international armed conflict and lead to the applicability of humanitarian law.[69] Any unconsented-to military operations by one State in the territory of another State should be interpreted as an armed interference in the latter's sphere of sovereignty and thus may be an international armed conflict under Article 2(1).

2.38   In the decades since the adoption of the Conventions, there has been practice and doctrine in support of this interpretation. Some States, for example, have considered that an international armed conflict triggering the application of the Geneva Conventions had come into existence after the capture of just one member of their armed forces.[70] The lack of a requirement of a certain level of intensity has also been endorsed by international tribunals, with, for example, the ICTY holding that 'the existence of armed force between States is sufficient of itself to trigger the application of international humanitarian law'.[71] This view is also shared by a significant number of academic experts.[72]

2.39   There are compelling protection reasons for not linking the existence of an international armed conflict to a specific level of violence. This approach corresponds with the overriding purpose of the Geneva Conventions, which is

---

[67] Pictet (ed.), *Commentary on the Fourth Geneva Convention*, ICRC, 1958, pp. 20–21.

[68] Pictet (ed.), *Commentary on the Third Geneva Convention*, ICRC, 1960, p. 23.

[69] The Office of the Prosecutor of the ICC used the same low threshold approach, notably in relation to a naval incident that occurred in 2010 in the Yellow Sea; see *Situation in the Republic of Korea: Article 5 Report*, June 2014, paras 45–46.

[70] *Digest of United States Practice in International Law (1981–1988)*, Vol. III, 1993, p. 3456. See also Sassòli, 2008, p. 94, and Berman, p. 39.

[71] ICTY, *Delalić* Trial Judgment, 1998, para. 184 (see also para. 208); *Tadić* Decision on the Defence Motion for Interlocutory Appeal on Jurisdiction, 1995, para. 70; ICC, *Lubanga* Decision on the Confirmation of Charges, 2007, para. 207. The Special Court for Sierra Leone used the definition of international armed conflict proposed by the ICTY in *Tadić*; see SCSL, *Taylor* Trial Judgment, 2012, paras 563–566.

[72] See Hans-Peter Gasser, 'International humanitarian law: An introduction', in Hans Haug (ed.), *Humanity for All: The International Red Cross and Red Crescent Movement*, Henry Dunant Institute, Geneva, 1993, pp. 510–511; David, p. 122; Kolb, 2003, p. 73; Milanovic/Hadzi-Vidanovic, p. 274; Kritsiotis, pp. 278–279; Clapham, pp. 13–16. Schmitt, 2012b, pp. 459–461; and Grignon, p. 75, fn. 255.

to ensure the maximum protection of those whom these instruments aim to protect.[73] For example, under the Third Convention, if members of the armed forces of a State in dispute with another fall into enemy hands, they are eligible for prisoner-of-war status regardless of whether there is full-fledged fighting between the two States. Prisoner-of-war status and treatment are well defined under the Geneva Conventions, including the fact that a prisoner of war may not be prosecuted by the detaining State for lawful acts of war. In the absence of a classification of a situation as an armed conflict, detained military personnel would not enjoy equivalent legal protection under the domestic law of the detaining State, even when supplemented by international human rights law.[74]

240   This approach also permits the application of humanitarian law to the opening phase of the hostilities, thereby avoiding the uncertainty surrounding the period during which one would try to observe whether a given threshold of intensity has been reached.[75]

241   It is important, however, to rule out the possibility of including in the scope of application of humanitarian law situations that are the result of a mistake or of individual *ultra vires* acts, which – even if they might entail the international responsibility of the State to which the individual who committed the acts belongs – are not endorsed by the State concerned. Such acts would not amount to armed conflict.[76] The existence of an international armed conflict is determined by the occurrence of hostilities against the population, armed forces or territory of another State, carried out by State agents acting in an official capacity and under instructions or by other persons specifically instructed to carry out such hostilities by State agents or organs, and not done in error.[77] When a situation objectively shows for example that a State is effectively involved in military operations or any other hostile actions against another State, neutralizing enemy military personnel or assets, hampering its military operations or using/controlling its territory, it is an armed conflict. The existence of an armed conflict must be deduced from the facts.

242   It must be acknowledged, however, that some consider that hostilities must reach a certain level of intensity to qualify as an armed conflict under Article 2(1).[78] Isolated or sporadic inter-State use of armed force is sometimes

---

[73] Arimatsu, p. 76.

[74] ICRC, *International Humanitarian Law and the Challenges of Contemporary Armed Conflicts*, Report prepared for the 31st International Conference of the Red Cross and Red Crescent, Geneva, 2011, p. 7.

[75] See also the commentary on common Article 3, paras 422–437.

[76] Berman considers, however, that a low threshold approach takes no account of accidents (pp. 39–40).

[77] See e.g. Vité, p. 72; Kritsiotis, p. 262; David, p. 122; Françoise J. Hampson, 'The relationship between international humanitarian law and human rights law from the perspective of a human rights treaty body', *International Review of the Red Cross*, Vol. 90, No. 871, September 2008, pp. 549–572, at 553; Nils Melzer, *Targeted Killing in International Law*, Oxford University Press, 2008, at 250; and Ferraro, 2012b, p. 19.

[78] International Law Association, Committee on the Use of Force, *Final Report on the Meaning of Armed Conflict in International Law*, The Hague Conference, 2010, pp. 32–33.

described as a 'border incursion', 'naval incident', 'clash' or other kind of 'armed provocation', leading some to suggest that such situations would not qualify as international armed conflicts because of their short duration or the low intensity of the violence involved.[79]

243   Indeed, States might not publicly acknowledge such situations as armed conflicts and may describe them simply as 'incidents'. They may also choose not to respond with violence to an attack against their military personnel or populations, or on their soil. Nevertheless, given that humanitarian law applies based on the facts, the fact that a State publicly uses a term other than 'armed conflict' to describe a situation involving hostilities with another State is not in itself determinative of the classification of that situation as an armed conflict. Moreover, once States start using force against one another, humanitarian law provides a recognized framework to protect all those who are affected. If minor clashes between States are not considered to be an international armed conflict or if the very beginning of hostilities is not regulated by humanitarian law, one would have to identify an alternative in terms of the applicable law. Human rights law and domestic law do not seem to be equipped to deal fully with inter-State violence. For its part, the *jus ad bellum* provides a general framework on the lawfulness of the recourse to the use of force but contains only very general rules on the way force may be used.[80] Once force is actually being used by one State against another, humanitarian law provides detailed rules that are well tailored to inter-State armed confrontations. It is therefore logical and in conformity with the humanitarian purpose of the Conventions that there be no requirement of a specific level of intensity of violence to trigger an international armed conflict.

244   Lastly, it should be recalled that the application of the Conventions does not necessarily involve the intervention of cumbersome machinery. It all depends on the circumstances. In the case of the First Convention, for example, if only one person is wounded as a result of the conflict, the Convention will have been applied as soon as that person has been collected and tended to, the provisions of Article 12 observed, and his or her identity notified to the Power on which he or she depends.

b. Specific issues in relation to the notion of international armed conflict

i. Armed conflict involving multinational forces

245 No provision of international humanitarian law precludes States or an international organization sending multinational forces[81] from becoming Parties to

---

[79] *Ibid.* pp. 32–33; Greenwood, 2008, p. 48. See also Marouda, pp. 393–400.

[80] See Article 51 of the 1945 UN Charter, in combination with the requirements of necessity and proportionality.

[81] The term 'multinational forces' used in this section describes the armed forces put by troop-contributing countries at the disposal of a peace operation. There is no clear-cut definition of

an armed conflict if the classic conditions for applicability of humanitarian law are met. By virtue of the strict separation between *jus in bello* and *jus ad bellum* addressed above, the applicability of humanitarian law to multinational forces, just as to any other actors, depends only on the circumstances on the ground, regardless of any international mandate given by the UN Security Council and of the designation given to the Parties potentially opposing them. This determination will be based on the fulfilment of specific legal conditions stemming from the relevant norms of humanitarian law, i.e. common Article 2(1) for international armed conflict and common Article 3 for non-international armed conflict.[82] The mandate and the legitimacy of a mission entrusted to multinational forces fall within the province of *jus ad bellum* and have no effect on the applicability of humanitarian law to their actions.

246   Some have argued, however, that there is or should be a higher threshold of violence for the applicability of humanitarian law governing international armed conflict when multinational forces under UN command and control are involved in military action on the basis of a UN Security Council mandate.[83] This view does not challenge the applicability of humanitarian law as a whole, but suggests that the conditions triggering its applicability are different when multinational forces under UN command and control are involved.[84] Less frequently, it has also been contended that when multinational forces were operating under a UN mandate, but not under UN command and control, the States contributing troops to the operation were not involved in an international armed conflict in so far as the military operations had the sole aim of protecting civilians and re-establishing international peace and security.[85]

247   However, nothing in the Geneva Conventions implies that conditions for their applicability differ when multinational forces – including those under UN

peace operations in international law. The terms 'peace operations', 'peace-support operations', 'peacekeeping operations' and 'peace-enforcement operations' do not appear in the UN Charter. They may be interpreted in various ways and are sometimes used interchangeably. In general, the term 'peace operations' covers both peacekeeping and peace-enforcement operations conducted by international organizations, regional organizations or coalitions of States acting on behalf of the international community pursuant to a UN Security Council resolution adopted under Chapter VI, VII or VIII of the 1945 UN Charter. The considerations contained in this section would, in principle, also be applicable to multinational forces operating outside a mandate assigned by the international community, for instance when military operations are conducted on the basis of self-defence.

[82] For a discussion, see the commentary on common Article 3, paras 411–413.

[83] See Shraga, 2008; Berman, p. 41; Christopher Greenwood, 'International Humanitarian Law and United Nations Military Operations', *Yearbook of International Humanitarian Law*, Vol. 1, 1998, pp. 3–34, at 24; and International Law Association, Committee on the Use of Force, *Final Report on the Meaning of Armed Conflict in International Law*, The Hague Conference, 2010, p. 17. For an overview of the discussion, see Ferraro, 2013, pp. 580–583.

[84] Shraga, 2008, pp. 359–360.

[85] This argument was raised in the context of 'Operation Unified Protector', conducted in 2011 by NATO forces in Libya. Engdahl, p. 259, referring to a statement of the Norwegian prime minister according to which Norway could not be considered a Party to the international armed conflict while participating in the NATO operations in Libya because it was executing a mission assigned by the UN.

command and control – are involved in an armed conflict. Under existing law, the criteria for determining the existence of an armed conflict involving multinational forces are the same as those used for more 'classic' forms of armed conflict.[86] Requiring a higher intensity of hostilities to reach the threshold of armed conflict involving multinational armed forces is neither supported by general practice nor confirmed by *opinio juris*.[87] Therefore, a determination as to whether multinational forces are involved in an international or non-international armed conflict, or not involved in an armed conflict at all, should conform to the usual interpretation of common Articles 2 and 3, also when acting on the basis of a mandate of the UN Security Council.[88]

248   Once multinational forces have become involved in an international armed conflict, it is important to identify who among the participants in a multinational operation should be considered a Party to the conflict. Depending on the circumstances, the Party or Parties to the conflict may be the troop-contributing countries, the international organization under whose command and control the multinational forces operate, or both.

249   When multinational operations are conducted by States not subject to the command and control of an international organization, the individual States participating in military operations against another State(s) should be considered as Parties to the international armed conflict.

250   The situation is more complex when it comes to multinational operations conducted under the command and control of an international organization. International organizations involved in such operations generally share one characteristic, which is that they do not have armed forces of their own. In order to carry out such operations, they must rely on member States to place armed forces at their disposal. States that place troops at the disposal of an international organization always retain some form of authority and control over their own armed forces, such that, even when a State's armed forces operate on behalf of an international organization, they simultaneously act as an organ of their State. Therefore, the dual status of armed forces involved in multinational operations conducted under the command and control of an international organization – as organs of both the troop-contributing country and the international organization – complicates the determination of who should be considered a Party to the armed conflict.

---

[86] ICRC, *International Humanitarian Law and the Challenges of Contemporary Armed Conflicts*, Report prepared for the 32nd International Conference of the Red Cross and Red Crescent, Geneva, 2015, pp. 21–23. Kolb/Porretto/Vité, pp. 180–181; see also references in fn. 88. But see Marten Zwanenburg, *Accountability of Peace Support Operations*, Martinus Nijhoff Publishers, Leiden, 2005, p. 207.

[87] Ferraro, 2013, p. 582.

[88] Ola Engdahl, 'The Status of Peace Operation Personnel under International Humanitarian Law', *Yearbook of International Humanitarian Law*, Vol. 11, 2008, pp. 109–138, at 118; Garth J. Cartledge, 'Legal Restraints on Military Personnel Deployed on Peacekeeping Operations', in Helen Durham and Timothy L.H. McCormack (eds), *The Changing Face of Conflict and the Efficacy of International Humanitarian Law*, Martinus Nijhoff Publishers, The Hague, 1999, pp. 125–130.

251   One way to determine which is the Party to a conflict in such situations may be to identify the entity to which the conduct may be attributed according to the rules of international law.[89] Under the rules on attribution of conduct developed for the responsibility of international organizations and States, the notion of control over the conduct in question is key.[90] Thus, if this approach were to be adopted, it would mean that determining which entity is a Party – or which entities are Parties – to an armed conflict requires an examination of the level of control the international organization exercises over the troops put at its disposal.

252   This may be a difficult enterprise as there is no 'one-size-fits-all' approach concerning the command and control arrangements and the corresponding levels of authority in force in multinational operations. Command and control arrangements vary from one operation to another and from one international organization to another.[91] In this regard, a case-by-case approach is required in order to determine which entity has effective or overall control over the military operations and therefore who should be considered a Party to the international armed conflict.[92] In some cases, both the international organization and some or all of the States contributing troops to the operation may be Parties to the armed conflict.[93]

---

[89] Zwanenburg, 2012b, pp. 23–28.

[90] See Draft Articles on the Responsibility of International Organizations (2011), paras 77–88. See also Tom Dannenbaum, 'Translating the Standard of Effective Control into a System of Effective Accountability: How Liability Should be Apportioned for Violations of Human Rights by Member State Troop Contingents Serving as United Nations Peacekeepers', *Harvard International Law Journal*, Vol. 51, No. 1, 2010 pp. 113–192, and Christopher Leck, 'International Responsibility in United Nations Peacekeeping Operations: Command and Control Arrangements and the Attribution of Conduct', *Melbourne Journal of International Law*, Vol. 10, No. 1, 2009, pp. 346–364. For States, see also paras 265–273.

[91] Terry D. Gill, 'Legal Aspects of the Transfer of Authority in UN Peace Operations', *Netherlands Yearbook of International Law*, Vol. 42, 2011, pp. 37–68; Blaise Cathcart, 'Command and control in military operations', in Terry D. Gill and Dieter Fleck (eds) *The Handbook of the International Law of Military Operations*, Oxford University Press, 2010, pp. 235–244.

[92] For a discussion of these issues, see Engdahl, pp. 233–271; Zwanenburg, 2012b, pp. 23–28; and Ferraro, 2013, pp. 588–595. It may happen that troop-contributing countries are so closely associated with the command and control structure of the international organization that it is almost impossible to discern whether it is the international organization itself or the troop-contributing countries that have overall or effective control over military operations. In such situations, operations should usually be attributed to the international organization and the troop-contributing countries simultaneously. The logical legal consequence of this in terms of humanitarian law is that both should be considered Parties to the armed conflict; see ICRC, *International Humanitarian Law and the Challenges of Contemporary Armed Conflicts*, Report prepared for the 32nd International Conference of the Red Cross and Red Crescent, Geneva, 2015, pp. 23–24.

[93] It has come to be accepted that such organizations are bound by customary international law. See ICJ, *Reparation for Injuries Suffered in the Service of the United Nations*, Advisory Opinion, 1949, p. 179; *Interpretation of the Agreement of 25 March 1951 between the WHO and Egypt*, Advisory Opinion, 1980, para. 37; and *Legality of the Use by a State of Nuclear Weapons in Armed Conflict (WHO)*, Advisory Opinion, 1996, para. 25. See also commentary on common Article 3, section D.1.c.

ii. International armed conflict triggered by cyber operations

253 Technological advances, in particular the exponential increase in States' cyber capabilities and their potential impact on the civilian population and infrastructure as well as on the military capabilities of an enemy State, pose important questions in relation to the applicability of humanitarian law. More specifically, it is important to determine whether cyber operations can bring an international armed conflict into existence.

254 When cyber activities are carried out by one State against another in conjunction with and in support of more classic military operations, there is no doubt that such a situation would amount to an international armed conflict.[94] However, the situation appears less clear when cyber operations are the only means by which hostile actions are undertaken by a State. The question is even more complex when such operations remain isolated acts. Could they be considered as a 'resort to armed force' between States as a constitutive element of the notion of armed conflict?

255 It is generally accepted that cyber operations having similar effects to classic kinetic operations would amount to an international armed conflict.[95] Indeed, if these operations result in the destruction of civilian or military assets or cause the death or injury of soldiers or civilians, there would be no reason to treat the situation differently from equivalent attacks conducted through more traditional means and methods of warfare.

256 However, cyber operations do not always and necessarily have such effects. Without physically destroying or damaging military or civilian infrastructure, cyber attacks might also disrupt their operation. Could these still be considered as a resort to armed force under Article 2(1)? Would the low intensity approach still be appropriate for hostile actions carried out only through cyber operations? Would the threshold of harm tolerated by States affected by cyber operations be different depending on the military or civilian nature of the 'targeted' object? For the time being, these questions are left open and the law is uncertain on the subject. Therefore, it remains to be seen if and under what conditions States will treat such cyber operations as armed force amounting to armed conflict under humanitarian law in future operations.[96]

---

[94] See Tallinn Manual on the International Law Applicable to Cyber Warfare (2013), Rule 22.

[95] See Schmitt, 2012a, p. 251; Knut Dörmann, *Applicability of the Additional Protocols to Computer Network Attacks*, ICRC, 2004, p. 3; Heather Harrison Dinniss, *Cyber Warfare and the Laws of War*, Cambridge University Press, 2012, p. 131; Nils Melzer, *Cyberwarfare and International Law*, UNIDIR Resources Paper, 2011, p. 24; and Tallinn Manual on the International Law Applicable to Cyber Warfare (2013), Rule 23, para. 15. See, however, *Report of the Group of Governmental Experts on Developments in the Field of Information and Telecommunications in the Context of International Security*, UN Doc. A/68/98, 24 June 2013, para. 16.

[96] Cordula Droege, 'Get off my cloud: cyber warfare, international humanitarian law, and the protection of civilians', *International Review of the Red Cross*, Vol. 94, No. 886, June 2012, pp. 545–549.

iii. The relevance of consent to the existence of an international armed
conflict

257 Contemporary armed conflicts show that increasingly States carry out military operations in the territory of another State. These interventions are often
directed against non-State armed groups and form part of the military support provided to the local government within the framework of a pre-existing
non-international armed conflict. In other cases, the intervention against such
groups might be part of a non-international armed conflict taking place on the
territory of another State and to which that State is not party. Third States may
also intervene in a pre-existing non-international armed conflict by supporting
and even exerting some form of control over the armed groups fighting the territorial government.[97]

258 All these forms of extraterritorial intervention pose the question of the influence of the third State's military actions on the classification of the situation
for the purposes of humanitarian law. In some cases, these situations may constitute an international armed conflict in the sense of Article 2(1).

259 First of all, it should be specified that not every use of armed force in the territory of another State, including its territorial waters and airspace, creates a
belligerent relationship with the territorial State and would therefore not necessarily be classified as an international armed conflict. Indeed, a State might
consent to the use of force in its own territory by a foreign State; it might even
call for such an intervention, for instance to respond to the threat emanating
from a non-State armed group fighting the government or operating against
other States from its territory. In such cases, the existence of consent would
clearly rule out the classification of the intervention as an international armed
conflict, provided the intervention stays within the limits posited by the consenting State and that the consent is not withdrawn.

260 The presence or absence of consent is essential for delineating the applicable legal framework between the two States as it affects the determination of
the international or non-international character of the armed conflict involving those States.[98] Should the third State's intervention be carried out without
the consent of the territorial State, it would amount to an international armed
conflict between the intervening State and the territorial State.[99]

– Armed intervention in the territory of another State

261 In some cases, the intervening State may claim that the violence is not directed
against the government or the State's infrastructure but, for instance, only at

---

[97] For a more detailed review of these different scenarios, see Vité, pp. 69–94.

[98] Fleck, p. 608: 'Given that a use of force by one State on the territory of another, without the
consent of the latter, is a use of force by the foreign State against the territorial State, a situation
of armed conflict between the two automatically arises.'

[99] This is without prejudice to the question of any effect consent may have in regard to the *jus ad
bellum*.

another Party it is fighting within the framework of a transnational, cross-border or spillover non-international armed conflict. Even in such cases, however, that intervention constitutes an unconsented-to armed intrusion into the territorial State's sphere of sovereignty, amounting to an international armed conflict within the meaning of common Article 2(1).[100] This position was implicitly confirmed by the International Court of Justice in *Armed Activities on the Territory of the Congo*, in which the Court applied the law governing international armed conflict to the military actions undertaken by Uganda in the Democratic Republic of the Congo (DRC) outside the parts of the DRC it occupied. According to the International Court of Justice, the conflict was international in nature even though Uganda claimed to have troops in the DRC primarily to fight non-State armed groups and not the DRC armed forces.[101] This does not exclude the existence of a parallel non-international armed conflict between the intervening State and the armed group.

262   Some consider that in situations in which a State attacks exclusively members of a non-State armed group or its property on the territory of another State, no parallel international armed conflict arises between the territorial State and the State fighting the armed group.[102] While that view is consequential in some respects, it is useful to recall that the population and public property of the territorial State may also be present in areas where the armed group is present and some group members may also be residents or citizens of the territorial State, such that attacks against the armed group will concomitantly affect the local population and the State's infrastructure. For these reasons and others, it better corresponds to the factual reality to conclude that an international armed conflict arises between the territorial State and the intervening State when force is used on the former's territory without its consent.

263   Where a territorial State consents to the actions of an intervening State, thereby removing the existence of a parallel international armed conflict, the consent given must have been previously expressed or established (explicitly

---

[100] Akande, pp. 74–75. For a discussion of the question of non-international armed conflict not of a purely internal character, see the commentary on common Article 3, section C.3.c.

[101] ICJ, *Armed Activities on the Territory of the Congo case*, Judgment, 2005, paras 108, 146 and 208ff. For a similar position, see UN Commission of Inquiry on Lebanon, *Report of the Commission of Enquiry on Lebanon pursuant to Human Rights Council resolution S-2/1*, UN Doc. A/HRC/3/2, 23 November 2006, paras 50–62, recognizing that an international armed conflict took place in 2006 between Israel and Lebanon even if the hostilities only involved Hezbollah and Israeli armed forces.

[102] See Noam Lubell, *Extraterritorial Use of Force against Non-State Actors*, Oxford University Press, 2010, pp. 92–134; Djemila Carron, *L'acte déclencheur d'un conflit armé international*, Thèse de doctorat, Université de Genève, 2015, pp. 402–425; Andreas Paulus and Mindia Vashakmadze, 'Asymmetrical war and the notion of armed conflict – a tentative conceptualization', *International Review of the Red Cross*, Vol. 91, No. 873, March 2009, pp. 95–125, at 111–119; and Claus Kreß, 'Some Reflections on the International Legal Framework Governing Transnational Armed Conflicts', *Journal of Conflict and Security Law*, Vol. 15, No. 2, 2010, pp. 245–274, at 255–277.

or tacitly).[103] It must be valid, i.e. given by an authority authorized to do so on behalf of the State, and given without any coercion from the intervening State.[104] However, the existence of such consent might be very difficult to establish for a number of reasons. States often do not publicize their consensual agreements. Moreover, the intervention of a third State might not give rise to any protest from the territorial State, may prompt contradictory statements by its authorities, or trigger symbolic protests aimed at satisfying its own constituency. If the absence of protest is a strong indicator of the existence of – at least – tacit consent, the two other situations remain very complex and sensitive. However, if the territorial State has explicitly protested against the intervention and this protest has been made by authorities that are entitled to give or withdraw the consent, it should be presumed that the consent did not exist in the first place or has been withdrawn, triggering the application of humanitarian law to the relationship between the territorial State and the intervening State.

– Presence of armed forces in another State providing support to a non-State armed group

264 States sometimes intervene via their armed forces on the territory of another State in support of one or more non-State armed groups in their fight against the local government. The nature of such support may vary but has frequently taken the form of direct involvement of that State's armed forces alongside the armed group(s). In such a situation – and besides the fact that a non-international armed conflict exists between the local government and the armed group(s) – the nature of the armed confrontation between the intervening State and the territorial State is international. Indeed, the third State forcibly intervenes in the territory of another State through military means used against the territorial State. All the conditions for the existence of an armed conflict under Article 2(1) are met and the Geneva Conventions in their entirety will govern the belligerent relationship between the intervening State and the territorial State (while simultaneously the law applicable to non-international armed conflict will govern the conflict between the territorial State and the armed group(s)).[105]

---

[103] ILC, 'Report of the 53rd session', *Yearbook of the International Law Commission*, Vol. II, Part Two, 2001, p. 73. See also Antonio Cassese, *International Law*, 2nd edition, Oxford University Press, 2005, pp. 370–371.

[104] Draft Articles on State Responsibility (2001), commentary on Article 20, p. 73. For a more detailed discussion of the notion of consent in the context of armed conflict, see ICRC, *Occupation and Other Forms of Administration of Foreign Territory*, pp. 20–23.

[105] See Vité, pp. 85–87. Some consider that where a foreign State has intervened in an ongoing non-international armed conflict, the entire conflict becomes international, but this view has not been accepted by practice or in case law. See e.g. David, pp. 167–178. See also George H. Aldrich, 'The Laws of War on Land', *American Journal of International Law*, Vol. 94, No. 1, 2000, pp. 42–63, especially at 62–63.

iv. State control over a non-State armed group and international armed
conflict

265 In some situations, the support provided by the outside State to the non-State
armed group(s) is tantamount to a form of control. Such control may be exercised in addition to or in lieu of the physical presence of a State's armed forces
in the territory of the other State. This scenario has been addressed by international tribunals, which have accepted that a situation takes on an international
dimension when another State intervenes in a pre-existing non-international
armed conflict through the exercise of a particular level of control over one or
more of the armed groups that were party to the conflict.

266   In such a situation, there will no longer be parallel non-international
and international armed conflicts, but only an international armed conflict
between the intervening State and the territorial State, even though one of
them makes use of a non-State armed group.[106] This was the case in the 1990s
in the conflict in the former Yugoslavia, where, according to the ICTY's findings, the Governments of Croatia and Serbia exercised overall control over certain armed groups fighting in the non-international armed conflicts in Bosnia
and Herzegovina and in Croatia. This kind of control highlights the relationship of subordination between the armed group(s) and the intervening State,
which, depending on its degree, might turn a pre-existing non-international
armed conflict into a purely international one.

267   In order to determine the existence of a relationship of subordination, one
needs to prove that the armed group is indeed acting on behalf of the intervening State. This means that the actions of the armed group need to be
linked to the intervening State so as to be legally considered as actions of
the latter. Because there is no specific test under humanitarian law for determining whether an armed group's forces 'belong' to a third State,[107] one has
to look to general rules of international law, which help to determine when
and under which conditions private persons (including members of non-State
armed groups) can be considered to act on behalf of a third State. International
law regulating State responsibility suggests some suitable solutions.

268   As under international law regulating State responsibility, the issue at stake
for the classification of the conflict is whether the actions carried out by individuals or a group of individuals can be linked to the bearer of the international
obligations (i.e. the intervening State). This means that the test that is used
to identify the relationship between a group of individuals and a State for the

---

[106] However, it can be envisaged that an international armed conflict is triggered in the absence
of a prior non-international armed conflict if a State engages in military operations against
another State using an armed group over which it has the requisite control. In such a situation,
the armed clashes would immediately and solely be governed by the law of international armed
conflict.

[107] Only Article 4(A)(2) of the Third Convention refers to such a relationship of subordination but
describes it in a factual way and does not necessarily require the exercise of control over the
group.

purposes of the classification of a conflict under humanitarian law should be the same as the one used to attribute an action carried out by private individuals (or a group of private individuals) to a State under international law of State responsibility.[108] The question of 'attribution' plays a major role in defining an armed conflict as international since, by virtue of this operation, the actions of the armed group can be considered as actions of the intervening State[109] and the relationship of subordination can be established.

269   The level of control by the foreign State over the non-State armed group necessary to render an armed conflict international in such a way is debated.[110] The International Law Commission[111] and some international tribunals (ICC, ICTY),[112] as well as academic writers,[113] have recognized that the notion of control is central to the question of attribution of the actions of a non-State armed group to a State. However, the international tribunals seised of the issue initially interpreted the notion of control in a non-uniform way. Subsequently, the different tests suggested by the courts, notably the ones on effective control and overall control, have fostered a doctrinal debate. Without delving too much into the details of the legal analysis of the notion of control in identifying the humanitarian law rules applicable to a given situation, it is necessary to emphasize that international jurisprudence – and doctrine – has long hesitated between the more restrictive options of complete dependence and control or 'effective control' adopted by the International Court of Justice for the purposes of State responsibility in decisions in 2007[114] and 1986[115] and the broader notion of 'overall control' suggested by the ICTY.[116] The notion of effective control requires that the non-State armed group that is subjected to control

---

[108] Zwanenburg, 2012b, p. 26. See also Marina Spinedi, 'On the Non-Attribution of the Bosnian Serbs' Conduct to Serbia', *Journal of International Criminal Justice*, Vol. 5, No. 4, 2007, pp. 829–838, at 832–833. Note that the ICJ appears to indicate that the tests need not be the same for the attribution of conduct and the classification of a conflict; see ICJ, *Application of the Genocide Convention case*, Merits, Judgment, 2007, paras 404–405.

[109] ICTY, *Tadić* Appeal Judgment, 1999, para. 104.

[110] For an overview of the debate, see e.g. Akande, pp. 57–62 and 63–64.

[111] Draft Articles on State Responsibility (2001), commentary on Article 8, pp. 110–112.

[112] ICC, *Lubanga* Decision on the Confirmation of the Charges, 2007, and Trial Judgment, 2012, para. 541; ICTY, *Tadić* Appeal Judgment, 1999. The European Court of Human Rights has been asked by the Parties in cases before it to apply the attribution test to find jurisdiction; in a number of judgments the Court asserts that it uses a distinct test. See e.g. *Chiragov and others v. Armenia*, Grand Chamber, Judgment, 2015, para. 169; see also Partly Dissenting Opinion of Judge Ziemele, paras 6–12, and Dissenting Opinion of Judge Gyuluman, paras 49–95. See also *Al-Skeini and others v. UK*, Judgment, 2011, paras 130–142; *Catan and others v. Moldova and Russia*, Grand Chamber, Judgment, 2012, paras 106–107; *Jaloud v. The Netherlands*, Judgment, 2014; *Loizidou v. Turkey*, Judgment, 1996; and *Cyprus v. Turkey*, Judgment, 2001.

[113] Milanovic, pp. 553–604; Cassese, pp. 649–668; Talmon, p. 496.

[114] ICJ, *Application of the Genocide Convention case*, Merits, Judgment, 2007, paras 392–393.

[115] ICJ, *Military and Paramilitary Activities in and against Nicaragua case*, Merits, Judgment, 1986, para. 115.

[116] This hesitation is reflected in the ILC's commentaries on the 2001 Draft Articles on State Responsibility. The ILC, while discussing the notion of control in the framework of the commentary on Article 8, does not choose between effective control and overall control, and simply states that '[i]n any event it is a matter for appreciation in each case whether particular

be not only equipped and/or financed and its actions supervised by the intervening Power, but also receives specific instructions from that Power, or that
the intervening Power controls the specific operation in which the violation
occurs.[117] Conversely, in 1999 in *Tadić* the ICTY affirmed:

> In order to attribute the acts of a military or paramilitary group to a State, it must be
> proved that the State wields overall control over the group, not only by equipping
> and financing the group, but also by coordinating or helping in the general planning
> of its military activity. Only then can the State be held internationally accountable
> for any misconduct of the group. However, it is not necessary that, in addition, the
> State should also issue, either to the head or to members of the group, instructions
> for the commission of specific acts contrary to international law.[118]

The ICTY has therefore rejected the application of the effective control criterion for the purposes of classifying an armed conflict in the case of a military
or paramilitary group and opted for the condition of 'overall control'.[119]

270   While the International Court of Justice does not accept the use of the 'overall control' test as articulated by the ICTY for the purpose of attribution of
conduct to a State, the most recent decisions of international tribunals display
a clear tendency to apply the overall control test for the purposes of classifying a conflict. Of course, the ICTY was a precursor in this context since it was
under its auspices that the concept of overall control was first developed.[120]
This approach was then followed by the ICC in the *Lubanga* case. In 2007, the
ICC Pre-Trial Chamber stated that 'where a State *does not intervene directly*
on the territory of another State through its own troops, the overall control
test will be used to determine whether armed forces are acting on behalf of

---

conduct was or was not carried out under the control of a State, to such an extent that the
conduct controlled should be attributed to it' (p. 48).

[117] ICJ, *Military and Paramilitary Activities in and against Nicaragua case*, Merits, Judgment,
1986, para. 115.

[118] ICTY, *Tadić* Appeal Judgment, 1999, para. 131. In this sense, the notion of overall control does
not refer simply to the monitoring or controlling activity but also requires the exercise of a form
of authority over another entity. It is clear that the notion of 'authority' to which reference is
made is more general and global than the notion of 'power to give instructions', and the former
is therefore much more similar to a 'direction and coordination' Power.

[119] However, the ICTY has also acknowledged that where the controlling State is not the territorial
State, 'more extensive and compelling evidence is required to show that the state is genuinely
in control of the units and groups', meaning that the State's involvement in the planning and
coordination of military operations might be more difficult to demonstrate (*Tadić* Appeal Judgment, 1999, paras 138–140). The Tribunal also noted that a different approach is taken when
individuals or groups are *not* organized into military structures (*ibid*. paras 132–137).

[120] The decision of the ICTY Appeals Chamber in the *Tadić* case has often captured the attention of
commentators, but in reality the concept of overall control was already developed beforehand
in the *Aleksovski* Trial Judgment in 1999. Indeed, in that judgment, Judges Vohrah and Nieto-
Navia concluded in their joint opinions on the applicability of Article 2 of the 1993 ICTY
Statute, para. 27:

> [T]he Prosecution failed to discharge its burden of proving that, during the time-period and
> in the place of the indictment, the HVO [Croatian Defence Council] was in fact acting under
> the overall control of the HV [Army of the Republic of Croatia] in carrying out the armed
> conflict against Bosnia and Herzegovina. The majority of the Trial Chamber finds that the
> HVO was not a *de facto* agent of Croatia . . . Therefore, the Prosecution has failed to establish
> the internationality of the conflict.

the first State'.[121] In its 2012 judgment in the same case, the Trial Chamber agreed with this analysis.[122] Lastly, the International Court of Justice in 2007 expressly indicated that the notion of overall control could be used to determine the legal classification of a situation under humanitarian law.[123]

271 In order to classify a situation under humanitarian law when there is a close relationship, if not a relationship of subordination, between a non-State armed group and a third State, the overall control test is appropriate because the notion of overall control better reflects the real relationship between the armed group and the third State, including for the purpose of attribution. It implies that the armed group may be subordinate to the State even if there are no specific instructions given for every act of belligerency. Additionally, recourse to the overall control test enables the assessment of the level of control over the *de facto* entity or non-State armed group as a whole, and thus allows for the attribution of several actions to the third State.[124] Relying on the effective control test, on the other hand, might require reclassifying the conflict with every operation, which would be unworkable. Furthermore, the test that is used must avoid a situation where some acts are governed by the law of international armed conflict but cannot be attributed to a State.

272 This position is not at present uniformly accepted. The International Court of Justice conceives that the overall control test can be used to classify conflicts whereas the effective control standard remains the test for attribution of conduct to a State, without clarifying how the two tests could work together.[125] A minority of academic commentators have questioned the use of the overall control test.[126]

---

[121] ICC, *Lubanga* Decision on the Confirmation of the Charges, 2007, para. 211.

[122] ICC, *Lubanga* Trial Judgment, 2012, para. 541:

> As regards the necessary degree of control of another State over an armed group acting on its behalf, the Trial Chamber has concluded that the 'overall control' test is the correct approach. This will determine whether an armed conflict not of an international character may have become internationalised due to the involvement of armed forces acting on behalf of another State.

See also *Bemba* Trial Judgment, 2016, para. 130.

[123] ICJ, *Application of the Genocide Convention case*, Merits, Judgment, 2007, para. 404. The wording used by the ICJ is: 'Insofar as the "overall control" test is employed to determine whether or not an armed conflict is international . . . , it may well be that the test is applicable and suitable.'

[124] In opposition, effective control linked to every single operation is almost impossible to prove because it requires a level of proof that will unlikely be reached. *A fortiori*, the attribution test based on 'total control and dependence' used by the ICJ in 2007 in the *Application of the Genocide Convention case* and in 1986 in *Military and Paramilitary Activities in and against Nicaragua case* in order to determine the State's responsibility for any internationally wrongful act makes the test for attribution even stricter. See Ascencio, pp. 290–292, and Jörn Griebel and Milan Plücken, 'New Developments regarding the Rules of Attribution? The International Court of Justice's Decision in *Bosnia* v. *Serbia*', *Leiden Journal of International Law*, Vol. 21, No. 3, 2008, pp. 601–622.

[125] ICJ, *Application of the Genocide Convention case*, Merits, Judgment, 2007, paras 404–407.

[126] For an analysis of these views, see e.g. Milanovic, 2006, pp. 553–604; Milanovic, 2007, pp. 669–694; Talmon, pp. 493–517; Akande, pp. 57–62; Katherine Del Mar, 'The Requirement of "Belonging" under International Humanitarian Law', *European Journal of International Law*, Vol. 21, No. 1, 2010, pp. 105–124; and Theodor Meron, 'Classification of Armed Conflict in

273   In the view of the ICRC, the consequences of the notion of overall control will be decisive in so far as the non-State armed group then becomes subordinated to the intervening State. The members of the armed group become the equivalent of 'agents' of the intervening State under international law. This means that the intervening State becomes a Party to the existing conflict in lieu of the armed group and that the conflict has become entirely international in nature. The notion of overall control might prevent the intervening Power from hiding behind the proxy's veil in order to avoid its obligations and international responsibilities under humanitarian law. It also makes it possible to challenge the third State's claim that the actions were in fact those of actors who could not be considered as officials or persons acting on its behalf and therefore that it could not itself be considered as a Party to the conflict.[127]

c. The end of international armed conflict

274   Assessing the end of an armed conflict in the sense of Article 2(1) may be a very difficult enterprise. This is mainly due to the silence of the Geneva Conventions on this question but also to State practice, which indicates that States resort less and less to the conclusion of peace treaties.[128]

275   According to the traditional doctrinal approach, a war is ended by the conclusion of a peace treaty or by any other clear indication (e.g. a declaration) on the part of the belligerents that they regard the state of war to be terminated. This position supports the argument that once a state of war (in the traditional legal sense) has come into being, the fact that active hostilities and military operations cease 'is not in itself sufficient to terminate the state of war'.[129] Accordingly, any other agreements, be they in the form of a ceasefire or a truce, a cessation of hostilities or an armistice, were considered as temporary and as suspending, not terminating, hostilities.[130] The common characteristic of these agreements is that they do not alter the fact that there is still an international armed conflict under way and, in general, fall short of peace. Nevertheless, all of them are meant to temporarily suspend hostilities and can be seen as a step towards a definitive termination of the armed conflict.[131]

276   Nowadays, international armed conflicts rarely end with the conclusion of a peace treaty but are often characterized by unstable ceasefires, a slow and progressive decrease in intensity, or the intervention of peacekeepers. In some

---

the former Yugoslavia: *Nicaragua's Fallout'*, *American Journal of International Law*, Vol. 92, No. 2, April 1998, pp. 236–243.

[127] Cassese, p. 656. See also ICTY, *Tadić* Appeal Judgment, 1999, para. 117.

[128] The Conventions do, however, contain a number of provisions related to the duration of their application. See e.g. First Convention, Article 5, and Fourth Convention, Article 6; see also Additional Protocol I, Article 3.

[129] Kleffner, p. 62; Dinstein, 2004, pp. 889–890.   [130] Dinstein, 2004, pp. 889–890.

[131] Shields Delessert, p. 97. In terms of substance, it is probably the armistice agreement that goes the furthest by implicitly including the intention of the belligerents to begin making preparations for the termination of a war; see Greenwood, 2008, p. 58.

cases, there remains a strong possibility that hostilities will resume.[132] With this trend, the distinction between agreements aimed at suspending hostilities and peace treaties has become blurred. In any case, the determination that an international armed conflict has ended is based not on the existence of a peace agreement, but rather on an appreciation of the facts on the ground.

277   In this regard, evidence that there has been a 'general close of military operations' is the only objective criterion to determine that an international armed conflict has ended in a general, definitive and effective way.[133] Hostilities must end with a degree of stability and permanence for the international armed conflict to be considered terminated.[134] The ICTY confirmed in *Gotovina* that the general close of military operations constituted the crux of the determination of the end of an international armed conflict:[135]

> Once the law of armed conflict has become applicable, one should not lightly conclude that its applicability ceases. Otherwise, the participants in an armed conflict may find themselves in a revolving door between applicability and non-applicability, leading to a considerable degree of legal uncertainty and confusion. The Trial Chamber will therefore consider whether at any point during the Indictment period the international armed conflict had found a sufficiently general, definitive and effective termination so as to end the applicability of the law of armed conflict. It will consider in particular whether there was a general close of military operations.[136]

278   This notion of general close of military operations was interpreted in the 1958 Commentary on the Fourth Convention as the 'final end of all fighting between all those concerned'.[137] Later, in the 1987 Commentary on Additional Protocol I, it was argued that the expression 'general close of military operations' was something more than the mere cessation of active hostilities since military operations of a belligerent nature do not necessarily imply armed violence and can continue despite the absence of hostilities.[138] The general close of military operations would include not only the end of active hostilities but also the end of military movements of a bellicose nature, including those that reform, reorganize, or reconstitute, so that the likelihood of the resumption of hostilities can reasonably be discarded.

279   Since 'military operations' are defined as 'the movements, manoeuvres and actions of any sort, carried out by the armed forces with a view to combat',[139] the fact of redeploying troops along the border to build up military capacity

---

[132] Sassòli/Bouvier/Quintin, pp. 134–135.
[133] The argument is further supported by Article 6(2) of the Fourth Convention, which states that the Convention ceases to apply 'after the general close of military operations'. See also Greenwood, 2008, p. 72: the 'cessation of active hostilities should be enough to terminate the armed conflict'.
[134] *Ibid.* p. 88.   [135] ICTY, *Gotovina* Trial Judgment, 2011, para. 1697.   [136] *Ibid.* para. 1694.
[137] Pictet (ed.), *Commentary on the Fourth Geneva Convention*, ICRC, 1958, p. 62.
[138] Sandoz/Swinarski/Zimmermann (eds), *Commentary on the Additional Protocols*, ICRC, 1987, para. 153.
[139] *Ibid.* para. 152.

or mobilizing or deploying troops for defensive or offensive purposes should be regarded as military measures with a view to combat. Even in the absence of active hostilities, such military operations having a continuing nexus with the international armed conflict will justify maintaining the classification of the situation as an international armed conflict. The overall picture emanating from this situation is one that objectively speaks of an armed conflict that has not ended in a general, definitive and effective way.

280   Thus, when belligerent States are no longer involved in hostilities but, for instance, maintain troops on alert, mobilize reservists or undertake military movements on their borders, the absence of ongoing hostilities will generally be a lull or a temporary suspension of armed clashes rather than a stable ceasefire or armistice that can be interpreted as the first stage towards an impending state of peace. Military operations short of active hostilities pitting one belligerent against another would still justify *per se* the continued existence of an international armed conflict provided one can reasonably consider that the hostilities between the opposing States are likely to resume in the near future owing to their ongoing military movements. In such circumstances, it cannot be concluded that there has been a general close of military operations.

281   In a similar vein to the 'general close of military operations' test, it has been suggested that the assessment of the end of an armed conflict revolves around one basic general principle, namely that 'the application of IHL will cease once the conditions that triggered its application in the first place no longer exist'.[140] The application of this principle would mean that armed conflict within the meaning of Article 2(1) would end when the belligerent States are no longer involved in armed confrontation. This would be clear in situations where, for instance, the armed conflict was triggered by and consisted solely of the mere capture of soldiers or sporadic and temporary military incursions in the enemy State's territory. In these cases, the release of the soldiers or the cessation of the military incursions would suffice to put an end to the situation of armed conflict. However, the determination of the end of an armed conflict might be more complex in contexts where the armed conflict resulted from a more classic armed confrontation, i.e. open hostilities between two or more States' armed forces. The general principle thus articulated should thus be read in line with the factors providing evidence of a general close of military operations as indicated above.

282   The consideration that armed conflict is neither a technical nor a legal concept but rather a recognition of the fact of hostilities supports the conclusion that agreements less formal than peace treaties can indicate the end of an

---

[140] Milanovic, 2013, pp. 86–87. However, this author also specified rightly that this general principle might be subject to exceptions.

armed conflict. Any of the agreements mentioned above that fall short of peace treaties might nonetheless have the effect of permanently terminating hostilities. That said, a suspension of hostilities, a ceasefire, an armistice or even a peace treaty does not constitute the end of an international armed conflict if the facts on the ground show otherwise.[141] Rather, an agreement is only a piece of evidence that, coupled with other elements, might reveal a certain intention of the belligerents to end the armed conflict definitively. The 'labelling' of an agreement is therefore irrelevant; it is rather the *de facto* situation that results from an agreement that defines its real meaning and its ability objectively to put an end to the armed conflict.[142] Therefore, ceasefire agreements or any such instruments leading to or coinciding with a *de facto* general close of military operations might indicate the point at which the armed conflict will be considered to have ended.

283   Accordingly, the end of an armed conflict, like its beginning, must be determined on the basis of factual and objective criteria.[143] What counts is that the armed confrontation between the belligerent States has ceased to such an extent that the situation can reasonably be interpreted as a general close of military operations.

284   The end of an armed conflict does not mean that humanitarian law will cease to apply entirely. Some provisions continue to apply after the end of armed conflict. Examples include Article 5 of the First Convention, Article 5(1) of the Third Convention, Article 6(4) of the Fourth Convention and Article 3(b) of Additional Protocol I, which provides:

[T]he application of the Conventions and of this Protocol shall cease, in the territory of Parties to the conflict, on the general close of military operations and, in the case of occupied territories, on the termination of the occupation, except, in either circumstance, for those persons whose final release, repatriation or re-establishment takes place thereafter. These persons shall continue to benefit from

---

[141] In this respect, the ICTY, in *Boškoski and Tarčulovski* Trial Judgment, 2008, para. 293, rightly stated:

> The temporal applicability of the laws and customs of war was described by the Appeals Chamber in the case of internal armed conflicts as lasting until a peaceful settlement is achieved. This finding is not to be understood as limiting the jurisdiction of the Tribunal to crimes committed until a peace agreement between the parties was achieved; rather, if armed violence continues even after such agreement is reached, an armed conflict may still exist and the laws and customs of war remain applicable.

> While that case dealt with non-international armed conflict, it is submitted here that this view can be perfectly transposed to international armed conflict as it exactly reflects the rationale of Article 2(1) and its objective to assess the applicability of humanitarian law solely on the basis of the prevailing facts. See also Venturini, p. 57.

[142] Shields Delessert, pp. 97–100.

[143] With its decision in *Gotovina*, the ICTY appears also to have identified a more fact-based test than the one postulated in *Tadić* 'until a general conclusion of peace is reached', which also risked introducing an undesirable degree of formalism.

the relevant provisions of the Conventions and of this Protocol until their final release, repatriation or re-establishment.

E. Paragraph 2: Applicability of the Conventions in case of occupation

1. Occupation meeting with no armed resistance

285   Article 2(2) is the first provision of the Geneva Conventions expressly referring to the notion of occupation. However, occupation is already implied by common Article 2(1), which covers occupation occurring during or as a result of hostilities in the context of declared war or armed conflict.[144] However, for editorial reasons, all issues related to occupation are addressed in this section of the commentary.

286   Article 2(2) was inserted to ensure that the law of occupation applies even when the occupation is not resisted. It aims to address cases of occupation established without hostilities and fills a gap left by Article 2(1). The historical origin of Article 2(2) is based on the experience of the Second World War and in particular the occupation of Denmark by Nazi Germany in 1940. On that occasion, Denmark decided not to resist the occupation owing to the overwhelming superiority of the German troops. In addition, prior to the adoption of the 1949 Geneva Conventions, the International Military Tribunal for Germany considered Bohemia and Moravia as occupied territories even though they fell under Germany's effective control without any armed resistance.[145] Article 2(2) thus introduced in treaty law a scenario that was already acknowledged by academics and tribunals and was not a legal novelty when adopted.[146]

287   Article 2(2) is thus complementary to Article 2(1) and ensures that the law of occupation applies to all types of occupation.

288   The fact that an occupation does not meet with armed resistance does not preclude it from being hostile. The hostile nature of an occupation derives from the unconsented-to invasion or presence of a State's armed forces in the territory of another State.[147] Military occupation is by definition an asymmetric relationship: the existence of an occupation implies that foreign forces are imposing their authority over the local government by military or other coercive means. The imposition of such authority by military means does not necessitate open hostilities. It can be obtained by the mere show of force. A real or perceived military superiority might induce the local government to refrain

---

[144] See *Final Record of the Diplomatic Conference of Geneva of 1949*, Vol. II-B, pp. 331–339. See also Pictet (ed.) *Commentary on the Fourth Geneva Convention*, ICRC, 1958, pp. 18–22.

[145] International Military Tribunal for Germany, *Case of the Major War Criminals*, Judgment, 1946, pp. 220–222.

[146] Arnold D. McNair and Arthur D. Watts, *The Legal Effects of War*, Cambridge University Press, 1966, p. 423.

[147] This may also be in the case if, for instance, a State's armed forces stay in the territory of another State once the latter has withdrawn its consent to their presence. See e.g. Roberts 2005, pp. 43–44; Dörmann/Colassis, pp. 309–311. See also para. 289.

from opposing militarily the deployment of foreign troops on its territory. A lack of military opposition by the local sovereign should not be interpreted as a form of consent to the foreign forces' presence in its territory precluding the application of the law of occupation, but rather a decision made under duress.[148] In this context, the foreign forces' presence clearly results from military coercion and is to be qualified as hostile, providing evidence of the belligerent character of the occupation.

289   The fact that the occupation does not meet with armed resistance does not mean that the Occupying Power is 'accepted' by the local population and that the latter does not require legal protection. Whenever civilians and civilian property find themselves under the military and administrative control of a belligerent enemy, including during occupation without hostilities, there is a risk of arbitrariness and abuse. Therefore, the rationale for the application of humanitarian law still exists when occupation is established without armed resistance. The fact that part of the local population may welcome the foreign forces has no impact on the classification of the situation as an occupation.

290   It should be specified that multinational forces operating under UN command and control in accordance with a UN Security Council resolution and with the consent of the host State would not be considered as occupying forces.[149] In such cases, the basis for the lack of armed resistance to the force lies in the State's clearly communicated consent for the presence and operations of the multinational force. However, in a situation in which such a multinational force remains in a State and continues to operate in the absence of the consent of the host State, or when it is deployed without such consent, that force (or the States contributing troops to it) may meet the criteria for occupation, no matter the legal basis of their mandate.[150]

291   The existence of an occupation within the meaning of humanitarian law prompts the application of the four Geneva Conventions in their entirety. It triggers in particular the application of Part III, Section III of the Fourth Convention ('Occupied Territories') and other norms governing occupation set forth in other treaties such as the 1907 Hague Regulations and Additional Protocol I, for Parties thereto.[151]

---

[148] A clear distinction should be made between the absence of opposition to foreign troops' deployment in the territory of another State and formal consent given by the local sovereign, the former not necessarily implying the latter.

[149] See Roberts, 1984, pp. 289–91; Dinstein, 2009, p. 37; Kolb/Vité, pp. 102–103; and Michael Kelly, *Restoring and Maintaining Order in Complex Peace Operations*, Martinus Nijhoff Publishers, 1999, pp. 167–181. See also section E.4.e.

[150] Most consider this possibility as existing in the case of what is commonly known as an 'enforcement operation' or 'peace enforcement'. See Alexandre Faite, 'Multinational Forces Acting Pursuant to a Mandate of the United Nations: Specific Issues on the Applicability of International Humanitarian Law', *International Peacekeeping*, Vol. 11, No. 1, 2007, pp. 143–157, especially at 150–151; Shraga, 1998, pp. 64–81, especially at 68–70; Kolb/Vité, pp. 99–105; and Dinstein, 2009, p. 37. See also Benvenisti, pp. 62–66.

[151] See Hague Regulations (1907), Articles 42 to 56, and Additional Protocol I, notably Articles 14, 15, 63 and 69.

2. The definition of the concept of occupation

292 The law of occupation, more particularly the provisions contained in Part III, Section III of the Fourth Convention, constitutes the most detailed and protective set of norms afforded by humanitarian law to 'protected persons' as defined under Article 4 of that Convention. Therefore, it is essential to delineate with precision the notion of occupation as, in so far as the armed conflict leading to the occupation has not already done so, it will trigger the application of the law of occupation and also the relevant provisions of the First, Second and Third Conventions, as well as Additional Protocol I, for Parties thereto.

293   This delineation is not easy owing to a number of potentially complicating factors, such as a continuation of hostilities, the continued exercise of a degree of authority by the local government, or the invading Party's refusal to assume the obligations stemming from the exercise of its authority over a foreign territory.

294   The determination of the existence of an occupation is rendered even more complex by the absence in the Geneva Conventions of a definition of occupation. Instead, the notion of occupation has only been sketched out by Article 42 of the 1907 Hague Regulations, which reads: 'Territory is considered occupied when it is actually placed under the authority of the hostile army. The occupation extends only to the territory where such authority has been established and can be exercised.' Subsequent treaties, including the Geneva Conventions, have not altered this definition.

295   As discussed above, the notion of occupation in Article 2(2) specifically includes occupation that has encountered no armed resistance. However, beyond the addition ensuring that such scenarios are covered, nothing in the preparatory work indicates that the drafters of the Conventions intended to change the widely accepted definition of occupation contained in Article 42 of the Hague Regulations; they only wanted to clarify its content.[152]

296   Since common Article 2 explicitly recognizes the application of these instruments to all cases of occupation but fails to define the notion of occupation, one can logically conclude that the applicability of the relevant norms of the Conventions is predicated on the definition of occupation laid down in Article 42 of the Hague Regulations. This is also suggested by Article 154 of the Fourth Convention governing the relationship between this instrument and the 1907 Hague Conventions.[153] As stipulated in that article, the Fourth Convention is supplementary to the Hague Regulations. In other words, the Fourth

---

[152] See *Final Record of the Diplomatic Conference of Geneva of 1949*, Vol. II-A, pp. 650, 672, 675–676, 728 and 811. See also ICJ, *Legal Consequences of the Construction of a Wall in the Occupied Palestinian Territory*, Advisory Opinion, 2004, paras 78 and 89; ICTY, *Naletilić and Martinović* Trial Judgment, 2003, para. 215; and Dinstein, 2009, pp. 6–7. See also Kolb/Vité, pp. 70–71.

[153] For further details, see the commentary on Article 154 of the Fourth Convention.

Convention builds on the Hague Regulations but does not replace them for the purposes of defining the notion of occupation.

297   The law of occupation is thus a normative construction essentially made up of the Hague Regulations, the Fourth Convention and, when applicable, Additional Protocol I.[154]

298   This interpretation of the concept of occupation is confirmed by the International Court of Justice and the ICTY, which have described Article 42 of the Hague Regulations as the exclusive standard for determining the existence of an occupation under humanitarian law.[155]

299   Therefore, as the concept of occupation as used in the Geneva Conventions is not distinct from that used in the Hague Regulations, the conditions for determining whether an occupation exists are based on Article 42 of the Hague Regulations.[156]

300   As mentioned in the commentary on common Article 2(1), the existence of an occupation as a type of international armed conflict must be determined solely on the basis of the prevailing facts. A determination based on the prevailing facts conforms with the strict separation of *jus in bello* and *jus ad bellum* and has been endorsed by the US Military Tribunal at Nuremberg which stated that 'whether an invasion has developed into an occupation is a question of fact'.[157] Considering the notion of occupation to be the same in the 1907 Hague Regulations and the 1949 Geneva Conventions does not mean that

---

[154]   It has been argued that two distinct definitions of occupation exist, one drawing on the Hague Regulations and the other on the Fourth Geneva Convention. See Pictet (ed.), *Commentary on the Fourth Geneva Convention*, ICRC, 1958, p. 60; Sassòli, 2012, pp. 42–50; Akande, pp. 44–48; and Koutroulis, pp. 719–728. However, in the absence of any express definition of occupation under the Fourth Convention and given the operation of its Article 154, the assertion that the Geneva Conventions provide a distinct definition of occupation is not unanimously accepted (see Zwanenburg, 2012a, pp. 30–36, and Ferraro, 2012b, pp. 136–139).

[155]   The ICTY has used the definition of occupation contained in the Hague Regulations in various decisions in order to determine whether an occupation existed within the meaning of the Fourth Convention. Relying on Article 154 of the Convention, it decided that:

   [W]hile Geneva Convention IV constitutes a further codification of the rights and duties of the occupying power, it has not abrogated the Hague Regulations on the matter. Thus, in the absence of a definition of 'occupation' in the Geneva Conventions, the Chamber refers to the Hague Regulations and the definition provided therein, bearing in mind the customary nature of the Regulations.

   Naletilić and Martinović Trial Judgment, 2003, para. 215. The Trial Chamber then quoted Article 42 of the Hague Regulations and specified that it endorsed this definition (para. 216). In its 2004 Advisory Opinion in *Legal Consequences of the Construction of a Wall in the Occupied Palestinian Territory* and in its 2005 Judgment in *Armed Activities on the Territory of the Congo case*, the ICJ relied exclusively on Article 42 of the Hague Regulations to determine whether an occupation existed in the territories in question and whether the law of occupation applied in those situations.

[156]   For a further discussion, see the commentary on Article 6 of the Fourth Convention. See also United Kingdom, *Military Manual*, 1958, p. 141, para. 501; United States, *Field Manual*, 1956, p. 138, para. 352(b); and ICTY, *Naletilić and Martinović* Trial Judgment, 2003, paras 221–222.

[157]   United States, Military Tribunal at Nuremberg, *Hostages case*, Judgment, 1948. The same approach has been reaffirmed in ICJ, *Armed Activities on the Territory of the Congo case*, Judgment, 2005, para. 173, and ICTY, *Naletilić and Martinović* Trial Judgment, 2003, para. 211.

certain rules of the law of occupation cannot be applicable during the invasion phase. Some norms of the law of occupation may well apply during the invasion phase.

3. *The constitutive elements of occupation*

301 In order to identify the elements constituting the notion of occupation, one must first examine the concept of effective control, which is at the heart of the notion of occupation and has long been associated with it. The phrase 'effective control' is very often used in relation to occupation; however, neither the Geneva Conventions nor the 1907 Hague Regulations contain any reference to it. 'Effective control' reflects a notion developed over time in the legal discourse pertaining to occupation to describe the circumstances and conditions for determining the existence of a state of occupation.[158]

302   It is self-evident that occupation implies some degree of control by hostile troops over all or parts of a foreign territory in lieu of the territorial sovereign. However, under humanitarian law, it is the effectiveness of that control that sets off the application of the law of occupation. Indeed, only effective control will allow the foreign troops to apply the law of occupation. In this regard, 'effective control' is an essential concept as it substantiates and specifies the notion of 'authority' lying at the heart of the definition of occupation contained in Article 42 of the Hague Regulations. Accordingly, effective control is the main characteristic of occupation as there cannot be occupation of a territory without effective control exercised over it by hostile foreign forces. However, effective control does not require the exercise of full authority over the territory; instead, the mere capacity to exercise such authority would suffice. Military occupation can be said to exist despite the presence of resistance to it

---

[158] The notion of 'effective control' in relation to occupation is distinct from the notion of effective control in the law on State responsibility. The choice of the word 'effective', which is commonly associated with the notion of control in order to define the nature of the foreign forces' ascendancy over the territory in question, reflects the analogy made between occupation and blockade during the negotiations related to the 1874 Brussels Declaration. During the drafting of the Declaration, the delegates, almost without exception, pointed out the similarities between occupation and blockade: both had to be effective to be said to exist for the purposes of the law of armed conflict. See Marten Zwanenburg, 'The law of occupation revisited: the beginning of an occupation', *Yearbook of International Humanitarian Law*, Vol. 10, 2007, pp. 99–130 at 102; Shane Darcy and John Reynolds, 'An Enduring Occupation: The Status of the Gaza Strip from the Perspective of International Humanitarian Law', *Journal of Conflict and Security Law*, Vol. 15, No. 2, 2010, pp. 211–243, at 218–220; Thomas J. Lawrence, *The Principles of International Law*, 6th edition, Macmillan & Co., London, 1917, pp. 435–436; and James M. Spaight, *War Rights on Land*, Macmillan & Co., London, 1911, pp. 328–329. It was argued that, just as blockades are not recognized unless they are effective, the existence of occupations, too, must be decided on the basis of effective control. In this regard, a consensus emerged among the delegates indicating that, in fact, an occupation would come into existence only to the extent to which the foreign army could exercise a certain degree of control over the territory in question. See Doris A. Graber, *The Development of the Law of Belligerent Occupation 1863–1914: A Historical Survey*, Columbia University Press, New York, 1949.

and can be said to exist even when some part of the territory in question is temporarily controlled by resistance forces.[159]

303   Even if the Geneva Conventions do not contain any definition of occupation, the 1907 Hague Regulations and their preparatory work, academic literature, military manuals and judicial decisions demonstrate the pre-eminence accorded to three elements in the occupation equation, namely the unconsented-to presence of foreign forces, the foreign forces' ability to exercise authority over the territory concerned in lieu of the local sovereign, and the related inability of the latter to exert its authority over the territory. All together, these elements constitute the so-called 'effective control test' used to determine whether a situation qualifies as an occupation for the purposes of humanitarian law. These three elements are also the only ones that – cumulatively – reflect the tension of interests between the local government, the Occupying Power and the local population, which is characteristic of a situation of belligerent occupation.[160]

304   On this basis, the following three cumulative conditions need to be met in order to establish a state of occupation within the meaning of humanitarian law:[161]

– the armed forces of a State are physically present in a foreign territory without the consent of the effective local government in place at the time of the invasion;
– the effective local government in place at the time of the invasion has been or can be rendered substantially or completely incapable of exerting its powers by virtue of the foreign forces' unconsented-to presence;
– the foreign forces are in a position to exercise authority over the territory concerned (or parts thereof) in lieu of the local government.[162]

---

[159]   United States, Military Tribunal at Nuremberg, *Hostages case*, Judgment, 1948, pp. 55–59. The UK military manual stipulates:

> The fact that some of the inhabitants are in a state of rebellion, or that guerrillas or resistance fighters have occasional successes, does not render the occupation at an end. Even a temporarily successful rebellion in part of the area under occupation does not necessarily terminate the occupation so long as the occupying power takes steps to deal with the rebellion and re-establish its authority or the area in question is surrounded and cut off.

> *Manual of the Law of Armed Conflict*, 2004, para. 11.7.1. However, if foreign armed forces are required to engage in significant combat operations to recapture the area in question from forces of the local armed resistance, that part of the territory cannot be considered to be occupied until the foreign forces have managed to re-establish effective control over it. See also United States, *Law of War Manual*, 2015, p. 746. See also ICRC, *Occupation and Other Forms of Administration of Foreign Territory*, pp. 16–26, and Dinstein, 2009, pp. 42–45 and Roberts, 2005, p. 34.

[160]   See also ICRC, *Occupation and Other Forms of Administration of Foreign Territory*, pp. 16–26.

[161]   For a detailed analysis of the constitutive elements of the notion of occupation, see Ferraro, 2012b, pp. 133–163; Sassòli, 2015; Dinstein, 2009, pp. 31–45; and Benvenisti, 2012, pp. 43–51. See also ICRC, *Occupation and Other Forms of Administration of Foreign Territory*, pp. 16–35.

[162]   While occupation law assumes that the Occupying Power will bear all responsibility in occupied territory as the result of the enforcement of its military domination, it also allows a vertical sharing of authority. The Occupying Power may determine – in accordance with

305   The end of an occupation may also be difficult to assess from a legal perspective. Progressive phasing out, partial withdrawal, retention of certain responsibilities over areas previously occupied, the maintenance of a military presence on the basis of consent that is open to question, or the evolution since the Hague Regulations of the means of exercising control: all of these issues can complicate the legal classification of a given situation and raise numerous questions about when an occupation may be said to have ended.[163]

306   In principle, the effective control test applies equally for establishing the beginning and the end of an occupation. In fact, the criteria for establishing the end of occupation are generally the same as those used to determine its beginning,[164] but in reverse.[165] Therefore, the physical presence of foreign forces, their ability to enforce authority over the territory concerned in lieu of the existing local governmental authority, and the continued absence of the local government's consent to the foreign forces' presence, cumulatively, should be scrutinized when assessing if an occupation has been terminated. If any of these conditions ceases to exist, the occupation can be considered to have ended.

307   However, in some specific and exceptional cases – in particular when foreign forces withdraw from occupied territory (or parts thereof) while retaining key elements of authority or other important governmental functions that are typical of those usually taken on by an Occupying Power – the law of occupation

humanitarian law – to what degree it exercises its powers of administration and which powers it leaves in the hands of the occupied authority. Such a situation does not affect the factual existence of effective control exerted by the Occupying Power over the occupied territory. See Ferraro, 2012b, pp. 148–150, and ICRC, *Occupation and Other Forms of Administration of Foreign Territory*, p. 20. See also Israel, Supreme Court sitting as High Court of Justice, *Tzemel case*, Judgment, 1983, pp. 373–374.

[163] Occupation may also end after a treaty of peace in which the restored sovereign may choose to cede title over the occupied territory to the Occupying Power insofar as such cession complies with the requirements of Article 52 of the 1969 Vienna Convention on the Law of Treaties.

[164] Shraga has argued that Article 6(3) of the Fourth Convention created a new definition of the end of occupation, one that changed the criterion from effective control to the exercise of functions of government; see Daphna Shraga, 'Military Occupation and UN Transitional Administrations – the Analogy and its Limitations', in Marcelo G. Kohen (ed.), *Promoting Justice, Human Rights and Conflict Resolution through International Law: Liber Amicorum Lucius Caflisch*, Martinus Nijhoff, Leiden, 2007, pp. 479–498, at 480–481. However, it is submitted that this position is premised on a misinterpretation of Article 6(3). This provision was never intended to provide a criterion for assessing the beginning and end of occupation, but only to regulate the end or the extent of the Fourth Convention's applicability on the basis that occupation would still continue. Article 42 of the 1907 Hague Regulations and Article 6(3) of the Fourth Convention are two distinct provisions pertaining to different specific material circumstances. Therefore, Article 6(3) cannot be used as a provision of reference for determining the end of occupation. See Ferraro, 2012b, p. 149.

[165] Yuval Shany, 'Faraway, So Close: The Legal Status of Gaza after Israel's Disengagement', *Yearbook of International Humanitarian Law*, Vol. 8, 2005, pp. 369–383, at 378. The identical nature of the tests for determining the beginning and the end of an occupation can be deduced from the legal literature and military manuals, as these do not distinguish between the criteria to be used for assessing the beginning or the end of an occupation, implying that the test is the same for both. See Kolb/Vité, p. 150.

might continue to apply within the territorial and functional limits of those competences.[166]

308   Indeed, although the foreign forces are not physically present in the territory concerned, the authority they retain may still amount to effective control for the purposes of the law of occupation and entail the continued application of the relevant provisions.[167]

309   Today, the continued exercise of effective control from outside a previously occupied territory cannot be discarded. Indeed, it may be argued that technological and military developments have made it possible to assert effective control over all or parts of a foreign territory without a continuous military presence in the area concerned. In such situations, it is important to take into account the extent of authority retained by the foreign forces rather than focusing exclusively on the means by which it is actually exercised. One should also recognize that, in these circumstances, any geographical contiguity existing between the belligerent States might play a key role in facilitating the remote exercise of effective control, for instance by permitting an Occupying Power that has relocated its troops outside the territory to make its authority felt within reasonable time.

310   This functional approach to occupation would thus be used as the relevant test for determining the extent to which obligations under the law of occupation remain incumbent on hostile foreign forces that are phasing out or suddenly withdrawing from an occupied territory while retaining a certain authority over it. This test applies to the extent that the foreign forces still exercise within all or part of the territory governmental functions acquired when the occupation was undoubtedly established and ongoing.

311   This approach also permits a more precise delineation of the legal framework applicable to situations where it is difficult to determine with certainty if the occupation has ended or not. This is all the more important in so far as the law of occupation does not expressly address the question of the legal obligations applicable during unilateral withdrawal from an occupied territory. The silence on this issue is notably due to the fact that occupation usually ends by force, by agreement, or by a unilateral withdrawal often followed by a related empowerment of the local government. In most of the cases, the foreign forces leaving the occupied territory do not continue – at least not without the consent of the local government – to exercise important functions there.

312   The continued application of the relevant provisions of the law of occupation is indeed particularly important in that it is specifically equipped to deal with

---

[166] ICRC, *Occupation and Other Forms of Administration of Foreign Territory*, pp. 31–33; Ferraro, 2012b, p. 157.

[167] The relevant provisions will depend on the nature of the competences retained. It is therefore not possible in the abstract to identify specific norms except the overarching Article 43 of the 1907 Hague Regulations.

and regulate the sharing of authority – and the related assignment of responsibilities – between belligerent States.

313   A contrary position, which would not allow for the application of certain
relevant provisions of the law of occupation in such specific situations, could
encourage Occupying Powers to withdraw their troops from all or parts of the
occupied territory while retaining some important functions remotely exerted
in order to evade the duties imposed by humanitarian law.[168] Such an approach
would ultimately leave the local population bereft of legal protection and would
run counter to the object and purpose of the law of occupation.

4. Specific issues in relation to the notion of occupation

a. Territorial scope of occupation

314 The second sentence of Article 42 of the 1907 Hague Regulations indicates
that the territorial extent of an occupation is commensurate with the capacity
of the occupant to establish and project its authority over that territory, suggesting that some parts of the invaded territory might be beyond the occupant's
effective control and therefore not considered as being occupied.

315   Common Article 2(2) confirms this approach in so far as it expressly refers to
the notion of partial occupation. Together with Article 42 of the Hague Regulations, it rejects the idea that a territory is either fully occupied or not occupied
at all. Such an approach would not take into account the variety of possible situations. Even though it is well accepted that a whole State could be occupied,
Article 2(2) clarifies that occupation can be limited to parts of it. Nevertheless,
neither Article 42 of the Hague Regulations nor common Article 2(2) indicates
the precise delimitation of the geographical boundaries of an occupation. Under
humanitarian law, nothing precludes even very small places (such as villages or
small islands) from being occupied.[169] However, identifying the exact boundaries of the occupied territory in the case of partial occupation might prove
complicated.[170]

316   This difficulty arises because under the law of occupation, the notion of effective control does not require that the foreign forces inhabit every square metre
of the occupied territory. Indeed, effective control can be exerted by positioning

---

[168] Yuval Shany, 'Faraway, So Close: The Legal Status of Gaza after Israel's Disengagement', *Yearbook of International Humanitarian Law*, Vol. 8, 2005, pp. 369–383, at 380–383. See also Israel,
Supreme Court sitting as High Court of Justice, *Bassiouni case*, Judgment, 2008, para. 12. But
compare e.g. Dinstein, pp. 276–280, Michael Bothe, Cutting off electricity and water supply for
the Gaza Strip: Limits under international law, preliminary expert opinion commissioned by
Diakonia, 18 July 2014, p. 2, and ICC, Office of the Prosecutor, Situation on Registered Vessels
of Comoros, Greece and Cambodia, Article 53(1) Report, 6 November 2014, para. 16.

[169] ICRC, *Occupation and Other Forms of Administration of Foreign Territory*, p. 24.

[170] See, for example, the difficulty encountered by the ICJ in 2005 in setting the territorial limits
of the Ugandan occupation of parts of the Democratic Republic of the Congo (*Armed Activities
on the Territory of the Congo case*, Judgment, 2005, paras 167–180).

troops in strategic positions in the occupied territory, provided it is possible to dispatch these troops, within a reasonable period of time, to make the occupant's authority felt throughout the area in question.[171] This situation can arise when parts of a territory have already fallen under the foreign forces' effective control while others are still subject to open hostilities, or when foreign forces' available resources are scarce in relation to the size of the enemy territory. The territorial limits of an occupation may also be difficult to determine when the occupying forces phase out from the occupied territory while maintaining effective control over specific areas.

317   Thus, the territorial dimension of an occupation may vary depending on the circumstances.[172]

b. Temporal scope of occupation

318 The question of whether the law requires a minimum period of time in order to ascertain that an occupation is effectively established has not been addressed in detail.

319   It has been argued that a certain amount of time is necessary in order to distinguish the invasion phase from an occupation. According to this approach, occupation implies some degree of stability and requires some time before considering that the contested area has been solidly seized by the foreign forces and the local sovereign has been rendered substantially or completely incapable of exerting its powers by virtue of the foreign forces' unconsented-to presence.[173] In this regard, some experts have argued that effective control should be enforced for a certain amount of time before considering that a territory is occupied for the purposes of humanitarian law and that the Occupying Power is in a position to assume its responsibilities under the law of occupation.[174]

320   However, the law of occupation does not set specific time limits for occupation and, in fact, is silent on the subject of minimum duration.[175] An occupation can be very short, lasting, for example, for only a few weeks or a few days.[176] The transition between the invasion phase and occupation can be very quick, in particular when the invading forces do not meet with armed resistance and have sufficient resources to be swiftly in a position to exert authority over the territory concerned.

---

[171] See United States, *Field Manual*, 1956, p. 139.   [172] Dinstein, 2009, pp. 45–47.

[173] ICRC, *Occupation and Other Forms of Administration of Foreign Territory*, pp. 38–40.

[174] *Ibid*. p. 24.

[175] Dinstein, 2009, p. 39: '[T]here is no hard and fast rule as to the maximal length of time of a raid and a minimal duration of belligerent occupation.'

[176] The Eritrea-Ethiopia Claims Commission has endorsed this position: '[W]here combat is not occurring in an area controlled for just a few days by the armed forces of a hostile Power, the Commission believes that the legal rules applicable to occupied territory should apply'; *Central Front, Eritrea's Claim*, Partial Award, 2004, para. 57.

321 Under the law of occupation, the notion of effective control does not require that the occupant be able to meet all the responsibilities assigned to it in order to determine that an occupation has come into existence. Rather, it allows for a gradual application of the law of occupation over time.

322 The law of occupation comprises both negative and positive obligations. Negative obligations, such as the prohibition on deporting protected persons outside the occupied territory, apply immediately, whereas positive obligations, the vast majority of them being obligations of means, would take effect over time according to the level of control exerted, the constraints prevailing in the initial phases of the occupation, and the resources available to the foreign forces. In a very short occupation, for example, the occupant is expected to provide the population with basic necessities such as water and food and not to deport protected persons, but it cannot be expected to set up a workable education or health system if it was not in place before the occupation or had collapsed as a result of the occupation. On the other hand, it would be required to allow existing systems to continue to function. In other words, duties incumbent on an Occupying Power are commensurate with the duration of the occupation. If the occupation lasts, more and more responsibilities fall on the Occupying Power.[177]

c. Occupation of territories whose international status is unclear

323 It has been argued that Part III, Section III of the Fourth Convention relating to occupied territories would only apply within the boundaries of a 'State' as defined by international law. Accordingly, only territory over which the sovereignty of a State has been effectively established could be considered as occupied territory.[178]

324 However, this argument goes against the spirit of the law of occupation and has been widely rejected by case law[179] and legal literature.[180] Indeed, the unclear status of a territory does not prevent the applicability of the rules of the Fourth Convention, including those relating to occupied territory. For the

---

[177] ICRC, *Occupation and Other Forms of Administration of Foreign Territory*, pp. 18 and 24–26.

[178] This position finds its basis in the fact that Section III of the 1907 Hague Regulations is entitled 'Military authority over the territory of the hostile *state*' (emphasis added) and that common Article 2(2) refers to the territory of a 'High Contracting Party', a phrase that has been interpreted as designating a well-established State. According to this approach, the territory belonging to an entity not yet meeting the legal criteria of a State would not come within the ambit of the term 'High Contracting Party' mentioned in common Article 2(2). See Meir Shamgar, 'Legal concepts and problems of the Israeli military government: The initial stage', in Meir Shamgar (ed.), *Military Government in the Territories Administered by Israel 1967–1980: The Legal Aspects*, Vol. I, Harry Sacher Institute for Legislative Research and Comparative Law, Jerusalem, 1982, pp. 31–43, and 'The observance of international law in the administered territories', *Israel Yearbook on Human Rights*, 1971, pp. 262–277.

[179] For example, ICJ, *Legal Consequences of the Construction of a Wall in the Occupied Palestinian Territory*, Advisory Opinion, 2004, para. 95.

[180] See Greenwood, 1992, pp. 243–244; Roberts, 1984, p. 283; Benvenisti, p. 4; Kolb/Vité, pp. 81–85; Dinstein, 2009, pp. 20–25; Bothe, p. 794; and Gasser/Dörmann, pp. 270–271.

Fourth Convention to apply, it is sufficient that the State whose armed forces have established effective control over the territory was not itself the rightful sovereign of the place when the conflict broke out or when the invasion meeting no armed resistance took place. Occupation exists as soon as a territory is under the effective control of a State that is not the recognized sovereign of the territory. It does not matter who the territory was taken from. The occupied population may not be denied the protection afforded to it because of disputes between belligerents regarding sovereignty over the territory concerned.[181]

325   This interpretation – according to which the term 'occupation' is meant to cover cases in which a State occupies territories with a controversial international status – is reflected in recent international decisions. As stated by the International Court of Justice in its Advisory Opinion in 2004:

> The object of the second paragraph of Article 2 is not to restrict the scope of application of the [Fourth Geneva] Convention, as defined by the first paragraph, by excluding therefrom territories not falling under the sovereignty of one of the contracting parties. It is directed simply to making it clear that, even if occupation effected during the conflict met no armed resistance, the Convention is still applicable.[182]

326   The Eritrea-Ethiopia Claims Commission took the same approach in 2004, stating:

> The Hague Regulations considered occupied territory to be territory of a hostile State actually placed under the authority of a hostile army, and the 1949 Geneva Convention Relative to the Protection of Civilian[s] ... applies to 'all cases of partial or total occupation of the territory of a High Contracting Party.' However, neither text suggests that only territory the title to which is clear and uncontested can be occupied territory.[183]

327   Any other interpretation would lead to a result that is unreasonable as the applicability of the law of occupation would depend on the invading State's subjective considerations. It would suffice for that State to invoke the controversial international status of the territory in question in order to deny that the areas in question are occupied territory and thus evade its responsibilities under the law of occupation.

d. Occupation by proxy

328 In the context of 'classic' occupation, armed forces of the occupying State are physically present in the occupied territory. However, situations such as the one that prevailed in the former Yugoslavia in the 1990s have shown that

---

[181] Eritrea-Ethiopia Claims Commission, *Central Front, Ethiopia's Claim*, Partial Award, 2004, para. 28.
[182] ICJ, *Legal Consequences of the Construction of a Wall in the Occupied Palestinian Territory*, Advisory Opinion, 2004, para. 95.
[183] Eritrea-Ethiopia Claims Commission, *Central Front, Ethiopia's Claim*, Partial Award, 2004, para. 29.

States, even without deploying their own armed forces (as defined under their domestic law) on the ground, might be acting in the territory of another State through armed groups operating on their behalf.

329   As noted above, occupation is established when forces exercise effective control over territory. Under humanitarian law, effective control over all or parts of a foreign territory may be exercised through surrogate armed forces as long as they are subject to the overall control of the foreign State.[184] Thus, a State could be considered as an Occupying Power when it exercises overall control over *de facto* local authorities or other local organized groups that are themselves in effective control of all or part of a territory.

330   The existence and relevance of this theory is corroborated by various decisions of international tribunals. In *Tadić*, for example, the ICTY decided that 'the relationship of de facto organs or agents to the foreign Power includes those circumstances in which the foreign Power "occupies" or operates in certain territory solely through the acts of local de facto organs or agents'.[185] In *Armed Activities on the Territory of the Congo*, the International Court of Justice examined whether Uganda exerted control over Congolese armed groups. The Court seemed to accept the possibility of an occupation being conducted through indirect effective control, but on the basis of the State exercising effective control over the armed group or groups in question.[186]

331   The notion of indirect effective control has scarcely been addressed in the legal literature or in military manuals. It is submitted that the criterion requiring the military presence of hostile foreign troops is fulfilled when indirect effective control is ascertained. The overall control exerted over local entities themselves having effective control over the areas in question turns the individuals belonging to those entities into 'agents' or 'auxiliaries' of the foreign State. Such control exerted over these local entities reflects a real and effective link between the group of persons exercising the effective control and the foreign State operating through those surrogates.[187]

---

[184] See paras 265–273 on overall control over an entity or an armed group. The question of overall control over the group or entity is distinct from the question of whether that group or entity exercises effective control over the territory.

[185] ICTY, *Tadić* Trial Judgment, 1997, para. 584. The ICTY confirmed this interpretation in *Blaškić*, stating:

> In these enclaves, Croatia played the role of occupying Power through the overall control it exercised over the HVO [Croatian Defence Council], the support it lent it and the close ties it maintained with it. Thus, by using the same reasoning which applies to establish the international nature of the conflict, the overall control exercised by Croatia over the HVO means that at the time of its destruction, the property of the Bosnian Muslims was under the control of Croatia and was in occupied territory.

> *Blaškić* Trial Judgment, 2000, para. 149.

[186] ICJ, *Armed Activities on the Territory of the Congo case*, Judgment, 2005, paras 160 and 177.

[187] The question of indirect effective control is addressed in the UK military manual:

> In some cases, occupying troops have operated indirectly through an existing or newly appointed indigenous government...In such cases, despite certain differences from the classic form of military occupation, the law relating to military occupation is likely to be

332   The theory of indirect effective control is important in so far as it prevents a legal vacuum arising as a result of a State making use of local surrogates to evade its responsibilities under the law of occupation.

e. Occupation by multinational forces[188]

333   For a long time, the applicability of the law of occupation to multinational forces, notably those under UN command and control, was rejected. It was argued that their special status under international law based on a specific mandate conferred by the UN Security Council, the altruistic nature of their actions, and the perceived absence of antagonism between them and the local population were in contradiction with the concept of military occupation.[189]

334   However, the first argument mixes *jus ad bellum* and *jus in bello* and the reasoning disregards the fact that the applicability of the law of occupation is determined on the basis of the prevailing facts and the fulfilment of the criteria derived from Article 42 of the Hague Regulations, regardless of the mandate assigned to multinational forces.[190]

335   As per other forms of armed conflict, there is nothing in humanitarian law that would prevent the classification of multinational forces as an Occupying Power when the conditions for occupation are met.[191] The mandate assigned to multinational forces by the international community in no way shields them from the operation of the law of occupation and from qualifying as an Occupying Power, in the same way as it would not do so for other actors. When a multinational force operating under UN command and control is implementing a mandate adopted by the UN Security Council under Chapter VI of the UN Charter, however, it is unlikely that such a multinational force will meet the criteria to be an Occupying Power.

336   Recent features of some multinational operations – in particular when multinational forces are deployed without the consent of the host State or in a country experiencing a breakdown of governmental authority and State

---

applicable. Legal obligations, policy considerations, and external diplomatic pressures may all point to this conclusion.

Manual of the Law of Armed Conflict, 2004, para. 11.3.1.

[188] For a definition of multinational forces for the purposes of this commentary, see fn. 81.

[189] Shraga, 1998, pp. 69–70.

[190] ICRC, *Occupation and Other Forms of Administration of Foreign Territory*, pp. 33–34. For a detailed analysis of this issue, see Tristan Ferraro, 'The applicability of the law of occupation to peace forces', in Gian Luca Beruto (ed.), *International Humanitarian Law, Human Rights and Peace Operations*, Proceedings of the 31st Round Table on Current Problems of International Humanitarian Law, International Institute of Humanitarian Law, San Remo, 2008, pp. 133–156.

[191] See Roberts, 1984, pp. 289–291; Christopher Greenwood, 'International Humanitarian Law and United Nations Military Operations', *Yearbook of International Humanitarian Law*, Vol. 1, 1998, pp. 3–34, at 28; Marco Sassòli, 'Legislation and Maintenance of Public Order and Civil Life by Occupying Powers', *European Journal of International Law*, Vol. 16, No. 4, 2005, pp. 661–694, at 689–690; and Kolb/Porretto/Vité, p. 218.

infrastructure – further point to the relevance of the law of occupation as a legal framework in such situations and to the necessity to determine when and how this branch of humanitarian law applies to multinational forces.

337   The classic conditions for determining a state of occupation apply equally to multinational forces; however, the main difficulty lies in determining which among the participants in a multinational operation enforcing effective control over a territory should be considered Occupying Powers for the purposes of humanitarian law. For multinational forces under the command and control of an international organization, the international organization, in principle, should be considered to be the Occupying Power.[192]

338   This determination is particularly difficult with respect to an occupation run by a multinational force led by States.[193] The States participating in such multinational forces may be assigned different tasks within the operation. There are two options for determining which States participating in a multinational force that is exercising effective control over a territory can be classified as Occupying Powers. The first option consists of assessing the legal criteria for occupation for each troop-contributing State separately. In such situations, humanitarian law would require that to qualify as an Occupying Power, each State contributing to the multinational force needs to have troops deployed on the ground without the consent of the local governmental authority and be in a position to exert authority, in lieu of the displaced local government, over those parts of the occupied territory to which it is assigned.

339   The second option is a so-called 'functional approach'.[194] Pursuant to this approach, in addition to the States that individually fulfil the criteria of the effective control test, other States contributing to the multinational force that perform functions and tasks that would typically be carried out by an Occupying Power, and for which the law of occupation would be relevant, should also be classified as Occupying Powers. Accordingly, the actions of these contributing States and the functions assigned to them would turn them into Occupying Powers.

340   Despite the relevance of the functional approach, in practice it could be difficult to differentiate the legal status of the various States contributing to a multinational force occupying a country, taking into account the wide range of activities they carry out. Nevertheless, performing tasks under the command or instruction of the 'uncontested' Occupying Powers would tend to confer the status of Occupying Power on those cooperating with these Occupying Powers,

---

[192] Kolb/Vité, pp. 99–105. See also Benvenisti, p. 63 (with further references); Dinstein, 2009, p. 37. While some continue to distinguish between 'peacekeeping' and 'peace enforcement' when it comes to the possibility of a UN commanded and controlled force as an Occupying Power due to the usual circumstances of the deployment of such forces, it is appropriate to rely on the facts of the situation and not the name given to the operation to draw a conclusion.

[193] See paras 248–252.

[194] This approach was used by the ICRC in relation to the occupation of Iraq in 2003; see Dörmann/Colassis, pp. 302–304; ICRC, *Occupation and Other Forms of Administration of Foreign Territory*, pp. 34–35; and Ferraro, 2012b, pp. 160–162.

particularly when such tasks are essential to the fulfilment of the administrative responsibilities stemming from the law of occupation.[195]

341   In addition, one should also recognize that the evolution of the Occupying Power's rights and duties vis-à-vis the occupied territory, and the acknowledged role of full-fledged administrator – as supposed by Article 43 of the Hague Regulations and Article 64 of the Fourth Convention – make it difficult to distinguish between core tasks assigned to an occupier (such as enforcing law and order) and other less emblematic tasks, since all of these tasks would fall under the competence of the occupier. Thus, a presumption seems to exist that those States participating in a multinational force exercising effective control over a foreign territory should be considered as occupying forces if they assume functions that would normally be among those of an Occupying Power. This presumption is rebuttable, however, for instance when a contributing State relinquishes operational command or control over its troops to another State participating in the multinational force.

F. Paragraph 3: Applicability of the Conventions when a Party to the conflict is not a Party to the Conventions

342 Common Article 2(3) deals with situations in which not all States that are Parties to a conflict are Parties to the Conventions. At the time of writing, the Geneva Conventions enjoy universal ratification, meaning that such situations should rarely arise. However, the potential formation of new States (no matter how infrequently that may occur) means that there may be a lapse between statehood and ratification of the Conventions, such that these provisions may become relevant.

343   An identical provision exists in Article 96(2) of Additional Protocol I.

1. First sentence: Abolition of the si omnes clause

344 The first sentence of Article 2(3) states that '[a]lthough one of the Powers in conflict may not be a party to the present Convention, the Powers who are parties thereto shall remain bound by it in their mutual relations'. This sentence must be read in the context of Article 2 as a whole, which stipulates that the Conventions apply to a conflict between two or more High Contracting Parties. Thus, in a conflict between only two States, where one is not party to the Conventions (unless it 'accepts and applies' the Conventions, as it may do according to the second sentence of paragraph 3), the Conventions do not apply *de jure* to that conflict, although the substantive obligations will nonetheless be binding on the Parties to the extent they reflect customary international law.

345   Today, it may appear obvious and unnecessary to state that if there are three Parties to a conflict but only two of the opposing States are party to the Geneva

---

[195] See Roberts, 2005, p. 33, and Lijnzaad, p. 298.

Conventions, the Conventions nevertheless apply between those two Parties. However, this was not always the case. In fact, according to a provision in the 1906 Geneva Convention, as well as in the 1899 and 1907 Hague Conventions, *all* Parties to a conflict had to be Parties to the Conventions in order for the Conventions to apply.[196] This was known as the *si omnes* clause. When the 1906 Convention was revised in 1929, the abolition of the *si omnes* clause was put on the agenda in the light of the experience of the First World War.[197] After the discussion of various proposals, a provision almost identical to that in Article 2(3) was adopted in 1929.[198] It was maintained without debate in 1949.

346   The provision also has a particular relevance for States that participate in multinational operations – no matter whether their command structure is integrated or not – as co-belligerents or partners of a State that is not party to the Geneva Conventions (or Additional Protocol I). In such a situation, States party to the Conventions remain bound by their obligations in relation to all other States that are equally bound by these treaties.

2. *Second sentence:* De facto *application of the Conventions by a State not Party*

347   During the Second World War, some of the States that were Parties to the conflict were not Parties to the 1929 Geneva Convention on Prisoners of War, which gravely undermined the protection of prisoners of war.[199] In this respect, there is an important difference between humanitarian law treaties and human

---

[196] See Hague Convention (II) (1899), Article 2:

> The provisions contained in the Regulations mentioned in Article 1 are only binding on the Contracting Powers, in case of war between two or more of them.
>   These provisions shall cease to be binding from the time when, in a war between Contracting Powers, a non-Contracting Power joins one of the belligerents.

> See also Article 2 of the 1907 Hague Convention (IV): 'The provisions contained in the Regulations referred to in Article 1, as well as in the present Convention, do not apply except between Contracting powers, and then only if all the belligerents are parties to the Convention.'

[197] During the First World War, strictly speaking the 1906 Geneva Convention was never in force for the Parties to the conflict as Montenegro was not a Party to the Convention; however, it was applied and invoked by virtually all of the States involved in the conflict; see Paul Des Gouttes, 'De l'applicabilité des Conventions de La Haye de 1889 et de 1907, ainsi que de celles de Genève de 1864 et de 1906', *Revue internationale de La Croix-Rouge et Bulletin international des Sociétés de la Croix-Rouge*, Vol. 1, No. 1, 1919, pp. 3–10. While most States continued to invoke the Conventions and considered them applicable, one, the United States, did not consider itself bound by the 1906 Convention owing to the operation of Article 24 (*si omnes* clause). Consequently, Germany refused to return captured US medical personnel. However, the United States apparently later changed its position. See Des Gouttes, *Commentaire de la Convention de Genève de 1929 sur les blessés et malades*, ICRC, 1930, p. 188, fn. 2. The Hague Conventions were in force until 1917, at which point several States not party to those Conventions joined the conflict.

[198] Geneva Convention on the Wounded and Sick (1929), Article 25(2): 'If, in time of war, a belligerent is not a party to the Convention, its provisions shall, nevertheless, be binding as between all the belligerents who are parties thereto.'

[199] See Bugnion, pp. 169–170 and 176–194. This particular problem did not arise for the application of the 1929 Geneva Convention on the Wounded and Sick as it enjoyed more universal ratification than its counterpart on prisoners of war.

rights law treaties: when one Party to a conflict is not bound by the Geneva Conventions, the State in conflict with that Party is not bound in relation to that State either, even when it is a Party to the Conventions, whereas human rights law treaties bind the States party to them at all times.[200] The second sentence of paragraph 3 was introduced in order to provide a remedy for such situations.

348 Various potential formulations of this provision were discussed during the Diplomatic Conference of 1949, including the possibility of requesting a Party to a conflict to accept to be bound by the Convention and providing a period of time to acquiesce to such a request, as well as the more pragmatic *de facto* approach ultimately chosen.[201]

349 The preparatory work indicates that States did not want to make a State Party's obligations solely contingent on another State's formal declaration of acceptance. Consequently, a State acting in a way that shows that it accepts and applies the Conventions is sufficient for both Parties to be fully subject to the obligations set out in the Conventions.[202] This has occurred on a number of occasions, for example during the Suez crisis in 1956.[203] Conversely, if a State that is not party to the Conventions explicitly refuses to accept that it is bound by them, Article 2(3) cannot operate to bring the Conventions into force for either Party.[204]

350 The importance of the *de facto* application of the Conventions is reduced in practice today because the Geneva Conventions have been universally ratified and, in addition, their provisions are generally considered part of customary international law.[205]

Select bibliography

Akande, Dapo, 'Classification of Armed Conflicts: Relevant Legal Concepts', in Elizabeth Wilmshurst (ed.), *International Law and the Classification of Conflicts*, Oxford University Press, 2012, pp. 32–79.

Arimatsu, Louise, 'Beginning of IHL Application: Overview and Challenges', in *Scope of Application of International Humanitarian Law*, Proceedings of the 13th Bruges Colloquium, 18–19 October 2012, College of Europe/ICRC, Collegium No. 43, Autumn 2013, pp. 71–82.

---

[200] However, in such a case, both Parties would still be bound by their customary obligations.
[201] *Final Record of the Diplomatic Conference of 1949*, Vol. II-B, pp. 53–55, and Vol. III, pp. 27–28.
[202] *Ibid.* Vol. II-B, pp. 53–55.
[203] Jean S. Pictet, *Humanitarian Law and the Protection of War Victims*, A.W. Sijthoff, Leiden, 1975, p. 52. The authorities of Bangladesh expressed their intention to respect the Geneva Conventions during the conflict between India and Pakistan in 1971; see 'Activités extérieures', *Revue internationale de la Croix-Rouge*, Vol. 54, No. 637, January 1972, pp. 20–29, at 20.
[204] In the conflict between Ethiopia and Eritrea, Eritrea did not accept the Geneva Conventions and did not accept that it was bound by them. See Eritrea-Ethiopia Claims Commission, *Prisoners of War, Ethiopia's Claim*, Partial Award, 2003, paras 24–28.
[205] See e.g. ICJ, *Legality of the Threat or Use of Nuclear Weapons*, Advisory Opinion, 1996, paras 79 and 82; Eritrea-Ethiopia Claims Commission, *Prisoners of War, Eritrea's Claim*, Partial Award, 2003, para. 40; and *Prisoners of War, Ethiopia's Claim*, Partial Award, 2003, para. 31.

Ascencio, Hervé, 'La responsabilité selon la Cour internationale de Justice dans l'affaire du génocide bosniaque', *Revue générale de droit international public*, Vol. 111, No. 2, 2007, pp. 285–304.

Benvenisti, Eyal, *The International Law of Occupation*, Princetown University Press, 1993.

Berman, Paul, 'When Does Violence Cross the Armed Conflict Threshold: Current Dilemmas', in *Scope of Application of International Humanitarian Law*, Proceedings of the 13th Bruges Colloquium, 18–19 October 2012, College of Europe/ICRC, Collegium No. 43, Autumn 2013, pp. 33–42.

Bothe, Michael, 'Belligerent Occupation', *Encyclopedia of Public International Law*, Vol. 4, North-Holland Publishing Company, Amsterdam, 1982, pp. 64–66.

Cassese, Antonio, 'The *Nicaragua* and *Tadić* Tests Revisited in Light of the ICJ Judgment on Genocide in Bosnia', *European Journal of International Law*, Vol. 18, No. 4, 2007, pp. 649–668.

Clapham, Andrew, 'The Concept of International Armed Conflict', in Andrew Clapham, Paola Gaeta and Marco Sassòli (eds), *The 1949 Geneva Conventions: A Commentary*, Oxford University Press, 2015, pp. 3–26.

David, Eric, *Principes de droit des conflits armés*, 5th edition, Bruylant, Brussels, 2012.

Dinstein, Yoram, 'Comments on War', *Harvard Journal of Law and Public Policy*, Vol. 27, No. 3, Summer 2004, pp. 877–892.

– *The International Law of Belligerent Occupation*, Cambridge University Press, 2009.

– *War, Aggression and Self-Defence*, 5th edition, Cambridge University Press, 2011.

Dörmann, Knut and Colassis, Laurent, 'International Humanitarian Law in the Iraq Conflict', *German Yearbook of International Law*, Vol. 47, 2004, pp. 293–342.

Engdahl, Ola, 'Multinational peace operations forces involved in armed conflict: who are the parties?', in Kjetil Mujezinović Larsen, Camilla Guldahl Cooper and Gro Nystuen (eds), *Searching for a 'Principle of Humanity' in International Humanitarian Law*, Cambridge University Press, 2012, pp. 233–271.

Ferraro, Tristan, 'IHL applicability to international organisations involved in peace operations', in *International Organisations' Involvement in Peace Operations: Applicable Legal Framework and the Issue of Responsibility*, Proceedings of the 12th Bruges Colloquium, 20–21 October 2011, College of Europe/ICRC, Collegium No. 42, Autumn 2012, pp. 15–22. (2012a)

– 'Determining the beginning and end of an occupation under international humanitarian law', *International Review of the Red Cross*, Vol. 94, No. 885, March 2012, pp. 133–163. (2012b)

– 'The applicability and application of international humanitarian law to multinational forces', *International Review of the Red Cross*, Vol. 95, No. 891, December 2013, pp. 561–612.

Fleck, Dieter, 'The Law of Non-international Armed Conflict', in Dieter Fleck (ed.), *The Handbook of International Humanitarian Law*, 3rd edition, Oxford University Press, 2013, pp. 581–610.

Gasser, Hans-Peter and Dörmann, Knut, 'Protection of the Civilian Population', in Dieter Fleck (ed.), *The Handbook of International Humanitarian Law*, 3rd edition, Oxford University Press, 2013, pp. 231–320.

Greenwood, Christopher, 'The Concept of War in Modern International Law', *International and Comparative Law Quarterly*, Vol. 36, No. 2, April 1987, pp. 283–306.

– 'The Administration of Occupied Territory in International Law', in Emma Playfair (ed.), *International Law and the Administration of Occupied Territories*, Clarendon Press, Oxford, 1992, pp. 241–266.

– 'Scope of Application of Humanitarian Law', in Dieter Fleck (ed.), *The Handbook of International Humanitarian Law*, 2nd edition, Oxford University Press, 2008, pp. 45–78.

Grignon, Julia, *L'applicabilité temporelle du droit international humanitaire*, Schulthess, Geneva, 2014.

ICRC, *Occupation and Other Forms of Administration of Foreign Territory*, Report of expert meeting edited and prepared by Tristan Ferraro, ICRC, Geneva, March 2012.

Kleffner, Jann K., 'Scope of Application of International Humanitarian Law', in Dieter Fleck (ed.), *The Handbook of International Humanitarian Law*, 3rd edition, Oxford University Press, 2013, pp. 43–78.

Kolb, Robert, *Ius in bello : Le droit international des conflits armés*, Précis, Helbing and Lichtenhahn, Basel, 2003.

– *Ius in bello : Le droit international des conflits armés*, Précis, 2nd edition, Helbing and Lichtenhahn, Basel, 2009.

Kolb, Robert, Porretto, Gabriele and Vité, Sylvain, *L'application du droit international humanitaire et des droits de l'homme aux organisations internationales: Forces de paix et administrations civiles transitoires*, Bruylant, Brussels, 2005.

Kolb, Robert and Vité, Sylvain, *Le droit de l'occupation militaire : Perspectives historiques et enjeux juridiques actuels*, Bruylant, Brussels, 2009.

Koutroulis, Vaios, 'L'affaire des Activités armées sur le territoire du Congo (Congo c. Ouganda) : une lecture restrictive du droit de l'occupation?', *Revue belge de droit international*, Vol. 39, No. 2, 2006, pp. 703–741.

Kritsiotis, Dino, 'The Tremors of *Tadić*', *Israel Law Review*, Vol. 43, 2010, pp. 262–300.

Lijnzaad, Liesbeth, 'How Not to Be an Occupying Power: Some Reflections on UN Security Council Resolution 1483 and the Contemporary Law of Occupation', in Liesbeth Lijnzaad, Johanna van Sambeek and Bahia Tahzib-Lie (eds), *Making the Voice of Humanity Heard*, Martinus Nijhoff Publishers, Leiden, 2004, pp. 291–305.

Lubell, Noam, 'What does IHL regulate and is the current armed conflict classification adequate?', in *Scope of Application of International Humanitarian Law*, Proceedings of the 13th Bruges Colloquium, 18–19 October 2012, College of Europe/ICRC, Collegium No. 43, Autumn 2013, pp. 17–24.

Marouda, Maria-Daniella, 'Application of international humanitarian law in contemporary armed conflicts: Is it 'simply' a question of facts?', in Stelios Perrakis and Maria-Daniella Marouda (eds), *Armed Conflicts and International Humanitarian Law 150 Years after Solferino: Acquis and Prospects*, Bruylant, Brussels, 2009, pp. 201–244.

Milanovic, Marko, 'State Responsibility for Genocide', *European Journal of International Law*, Vol. 17, No. 3, 2006, pp. 553–604.

– 'State Responsibility for Genocide: A Follow-Up', *European Journal of International Law*, Vol. 18, No. 4, 2007, pp. 669–694.

– 'End of IHL Application: Overview and challenges', in *Scope of Application of International Humanitarian Law*, Proceedings of the 13th Bruges Colloquium, 18–19 October 2012, College of Europe/ICRC, Collegium No. 43, Autumn 2013, pp. 83–94.

Milanovic, Marko and Hadzi-Vidanovic, Vidan, 'A taxonomy of armed conflict', in Nigel D. White and Christian Henderson (eds), *Research Handbook on International Conflict and Security Law: Jus ad Bellum, Jus in Bello and Jus post Bellum*, Edward Elgar, Cheltenham, 2013, pp. 256–314.

Okimoto, Keiichiro, *The Distinction and Relationship between Jus ad Bellum and Jus in Bello*, Hart Publishing, Oxford, 2011.

Orakhelashvili, Alexander, 'Overlap and Convergence: The Interaction between Jus ad Bellum and Jus in Bello', *Journal of Conflict and Security Law*, Vol. 12, No. 2, 2007, pp. 157–196.

Partsch, Karl Josef, 'Armed conflict', in Rudolf Bernhardt (ed.), *Encyclopedia of Public International Law*, Vol. I, North-Holland Publishing Company, Amsterdam, 1992, p. 252.

Roberts, Adam, 'What Is a Military Occupation?', *British Yearbook of International Law*, Vol. 55, No. 1, 1984, pp. 249–305.

– 'The End of Occupation: Iraq 2004', *International and Comparative Law Quarterly*, Vol. 54, No. 1, January 2005, pp. 27–48.

Sassòli, Marco, 'Jus ad Bellum and Jus in Bello, The Separation between the Legality of the Use of Force and Humanitarian Rules to be Respected in Warfare: Crucial or Outdated?', in Michael N. Schmitt and Jelena Pejic (eds), *International Law and Armed Conflict: Exploring the Faultlines, Essays in Honour of Yoram Dinstein*, Martinus Nijhoff Publishers, Leiden, 2007, pp. 241–264.

– 'International humanitarian law and peace operations, scope of application ratione materiae', in Gian Luca Beruto (ed.), *International Humanitarian Law, Human Rights and Peace Operations*, Proceedings of the 31st Round Table on Current Problems of International Humanitarian Law, 4–6 September 2008, International Institute of Humanitarian Law, San Remo, 2008, pp. 100–106.

– 'A plea in defence of Pictet and the inhabitants of territories under invasion: the case for the applicability of the Fourth Geneva Convention during the invasion phase', *International Review of the Red Cross*, Vol. 94, No. 885, March 2012, pp. 42–50.

– 'The Concept and the Beginning of Occupation', in Andrew Clapham, Paola Gaeta and Marco Sassòli (eds), *The 1949 Geneva Conventions: A Commentary*, Oxford University Press, 2015, pp. 1389–1419.

Sassòli, Marco, Bouvier, Antoine and Quintin, Anne, *How Does Law Protect in War?* Vol. I, 3rd edition, ICRC, Geneva, 2011, p. 122.

Schindler, Dietrich, 'The Different Types of Armed Conflicts According to the Geneva Conventions and Protocols', *Recueil des cours de l'Académie de droit international de La Haye*, Vol. 163, 1979, pp. 117–164.

Schmitt, Michael N., 'Classification of cyber conflict', *Journal of Conflict and Security Law*, Vol. 17, No. 2, 2012, pp. 245–260. (2012a)

– 'Classification in Future Conflict', in Elizabeth Wilmshurst (ed.), *International Law and the Classification of Conflicts*, Oxford University Press, 2012, pp. 455–477. (2012b)

Shields Delessert, Christiane, *Release and Repatriation of Prisoners of War at the End of Active Hostilities: A Study of Article 118, Paragraph 1 of the 3rd Geneva*

Convention Relative to the Treatment of Prisoners of War, Schulthess Polygraphischer Verlag, Zurich, 1977.

Shraga, Daphna, 'The United Nations as an Actor Bound by International Humanitarian Law', *International Peacekeeping*, Vol. 5, No. 2, 1998, pp. 64–81.

– 'The applicability of international humanitarian law to peace operations, from rejection to acceptance', in Gian Luca Beruto (ed.), *International Humanitarian Law, Human Rights and Peace Operations*, Proceedings of the 31st Round Table on Current Problems of International Humanitarian Law, 4–6 September 2008, International Institute of Humanitarian Law, San Remo, 2008, pp. 90–99.

– 'The Secretary General's Bulletin on the Observance by United Nations Forces of International Humanitarian Law: A Decade Later', *Israel Yearbook on Human Rights*, Vol. 39, 2009, pp. 357–377.

Talmon, Stefan, 'The Responsibility of Outside Powers for Acts of Secessionist Entities', *International and Comparative Law Quarterly*, Vol. 58, No. 3, July 2009, pp. 493–517.

Venturini, Gabriella, 'The Temporal Scope of Application of the Conventions', in Andrew Clapham, Paola Gaeta and Marco Sassòli (eds), *The 1949 Geneva Conventions: A Commentary*, Oxford University Press, 2015, pp. 51–66.

Vité, Sylvain, 'Typology of armed conflicts in international humanitarian law: legal concepts and actual situations', *International Review of the Red Cross*, Vol. 91, No. 873, March 2009, pp. 69–94.

Voelckel, Michel, 'Faut-il encore déclarer la guerre?', *Annuaire français de droit international*, Vol. 37, 1991, pp. 7–24.

Zwanenburg, Marten, 'Is the law of occupation applicable to the invasion phase? Challenging the Pictet theory', *International Review of the Red Cross*, Vol. 94, No. 885, March 2012, pp. 30–36. (2012a)

– 'International organisations vs. troops contributing countries: Which should be considered as the party to an armed conflict during peace operations?', *International Organisations' Involvement in Peace Operations: Applicable Legal Framework and the Issue of Responsibility*, Proceedings of the 12th Bruges Colloquium, 20–21 October 2011, College of Europe/ICRC, Collegium No. 42, Autumn 2012, pp. 23–28. (2012b)

ARTICLE 3

CONFLICTS NOT OF AN INTERNATIONAL CHARACTER

❖ Text of the provision*

1. In the case of armed conflict not of an international character occurring in the territory of one of the High Contracting Parties, each Party to the conflict shall be bound to apply, as a minimum, the following provisions:

   (1) Persons taking no active part in the hostilities, including members of armed forces who have laid down their arms and those placed *hors de combat* by sickness, wounds, detention, or any other cause, shall in all circumstances be treated humanely, without any adverse distinction founded on race, colour, religion or faith, sex, birth or wealth, or any other similar criteria.

   To this end, the following acts are and shall remain prohibited at any time and in any place whatsoever with respect to the above-mentioned persons:
   (a) violence to life and person, in particular murder of all kinds, mutilation, cruel treatment and torture;
   (b) taking of hostages;
   (c) outrages upon personal dignity, in particular humiliating and degrading treatment;
   (d) the passing of sentences and the carrying out of executions without previous judgment pronounced by a regularly constituted court, affording all the judicial guarantees which are recognized as indispensable by civilized peoples.
   (2) The wounded and sick shall be collected and cared for.

2. An impartial humanitarian body, such as the International Committee of the Red Cross, may offer its services to the Parties to the conflict.
3. The Parties to the conflict should further endeavour to bring into force, by means of special agreements, all or part of the other provisions of the present Convention.
4. The application of the preceding provisions shall not affect the legal status of the Parties to the conflict.

❖ Reservations or declarations
None[1]

---

* Paragraph numbers have been added for ease of reference.
[1] When signing the Geneva Conventions in 1949, Argentina entered the following reservation to common Article 3 (see United Nations *Treaty Series*, Vol. 75, 1950, p. 422):

126

Contents

> ...I shall, therefore, sign the four Conventions in the name of my Government and subject to ratification, with the reservation that Article 3, common to all four Conventions, shall be the only Article, to the exclusion of all others, which shall be applicable in the case of armed conflicts not of an international character.

However, the reservation was not formally confirmed upon Argentina's ratification of the Geneva Conventions in 1956 (see United Nations *Treaty Series*, Vol. 251, 1956, pp. 372–375).

Portugal entered the following reservation upon signature of the four Geneva Conventions in 1949 (see United Nations *Treaty Series*, Vol. 75, 1950, p. 446):

> As there is no actual definition of what is meant by a conflict not of an international character, and as, in case this term is intended to refer solely to civil war, it is not clearly laid down at what moment an armed rebellion within a country should be considered as having become a civil war, Portugal reserves the right not to apply the provisions of Article 3, in so far as they may be contrary to the provisions of Portuguese law, in all territories subject to her sovereignty in any part of the world.

The reservation was withdrawn upon Portugal's ratification of the Geneva Conventions in 1961; see United Nations *Treaty Series*, Vol. 394, 1961, p. 258.

A. Introduction

351 Among the many important advances in international humanitarian law wrought by the adoption of the 1949 Geneva Conventions, Article 3 stands out in particular. With its inclusion, States agreed for the first time on regulating, in an international treaty framework, what they described as 'armed conflict not of an international character'.[2] Common Article 3 represented one of the first provisions of international law that dealt with what was at the time

---

[2] Unless otherwise specified, armed conflicts as regulated by Article 3 will generally be referred to as 'non-international armed conflicts'; what that term comprises is discussed in section C.

considered by States as being exclusively their domestic affair. The provision is common to the four Geneva Conventions.[3]

352 Subsequent decades have proven the importance of this article. While international armed conflicts still occur, the vast majority of recent armed conflicts have been non-international in character and have generated a level of suffering that is no less than that encountered in international armed conflicts.[4]

353 Since 1949, the law of non-international armed conflict has developed considerably. States have adopted additional treaty law regulating non-international armed conflict, in particular Additional Protocol II of 1977 and a number of other instruments that apply in non-international armed conflicts.[5] In addition, the ICRC's study on customary international humanitarian law has identified a number of customary rules applicable in non-international armed conflict.[6]

354 Despite these developments, common Article 3 remains the core provision of humanitarian treaty law for the regulation of non-international armed conflicts. As part of the universally ratified 1949 Geneva Conventions, it is the only provision that is binding worldwide and governs all non-international armed conflicts. In comparison, Additional Protocol II is not universally ratified and its scope of application is more limited, without, however, modifying common Article 3's existing conditions of application.[7]

355 Compared with the number and detail of the provisions governing international armed conflict in the Geneva Conventions, common Article 3 is brief and formulated in general terms.

356 The quality of common Article 3 as a 'Convention in miniature' for conflicts of a non-international character was already noted during the 1949 Diplomatic

---

[3] The text of 'common' Article 3 is identical in the four Geneva Conventions, except for in the Second Convention, which refers to the 'wounded, sick and shipwrecked' as opposed to just the 'wounded and sick' as referred to in the First, Third and Fourth Conventions.

[4] For various assessments from the perspective of international humanitarian law and other disciplines, see e.g. Stuart Casey-Maslen (ed.), *The War Report: Armed Conflict in 2013*, Oxford University Press, 2014, pp. 26–32 and 35–233, and Lotta Themnér and Peter Wallensteen, 'Patterns of organized violence, 2002–11', *SIPRI Yearbook 2013*, Oxford University Press, 2013, pp. 41–60.

[5] See e.g. Hague Convention for the Protection of Cultural Property (1954), Article 19; Amended Protocol II to the Convention on Certain Conventional Weapons (1996), Article 1(3); Anti-Personnel Mine Ban Convention (1997); Second Protocol to the Hague Convention for the Protection of Cultural Property (1999), Article 22; Optional Protocol on the Involvement of Children in Armed Conflict (2000); Amendment to Article 1 of the 1980 Convention on Certain Conventional Weapons (2001) (extending the application of the Convention and its Protocols to non-international armed conflict); and Convention on Cluster Munitions (2008).

[6] Jean-Marie Henckaerts and Louise Doswald-Beck (eds), *Customary International Humanitarian Law, Volume I: Rules* and *Volume 2: Practice*, ICRC/Cambridge University Press, 2005, available at https://www.icrc.org/customary-ihl/eng/docs/v1. The study was prepared by the ICRC following Recommendation II of the 1995 Meeting of the Intergovernmental Group of Experts for the Protection of War Victims, which was endorsed by Resolution 1 of the 26th International Conference of the Red Cross and Red Crescent, Geneva, 1995.

[7] For the current status of the Geneva Conventions and Additional Protocols, see https://www.icrc.org/ihl. For a comparison between the scope of application of common Article 3 and that of Additional Protocol II, see section C.2 of this commentary, as well as the commentaries on Articles 1 and 2 of Additional Protocol II.

Conference.[8] Since then, the fundamental character of its provisions has been recognized as a 'minimum yardstick', binding in all armed conflicts, and as a reflection of 'elementary considerations of humanity'.[9]

B. Historical background

357 Non-international armed conflicts were not a new phenomenon when, in 1949, they were first regulated by common Article 3, as violence of either an international or a non-international character has long marred and formed human history.[10]

358   Nevertheless, the first Geneva Convention – the 1864 Geneva Convention for the Amelioration of the Condition of the Wounded in Armies in the Field – dealt exclusively with armed conflict between States, more precisely with 'war',[11] as did its subsequent revisions and the treaties successively adopted on related issues of humanitarian concern.[12] This reflected the understanding that the initiation and waging of war was an exercise of sovereign power, a prerogative held by States, suitable for regulation by international law. In contrast, violence that was unsupported by such prerogative was regarded as unsuitable for such regulation.[13] Treating it as 'war' and subjecting it to international law would have unduly elevated the status of those exercising such violence.[14]

359   This does not mean, however, that before the adoption of common Article 3 in 1949 there was no awareness of the need to regulate certain aspects of violence involving non-State armed groups.[15] The 1928 Convention on Duties and Rights of States in the Event of Civil Strife, for example, stipulated rules for States Parties in the event of civil strife in another contracting State.[16]

---

[8] See *Final Record of the Diplomatic Conference of Geneva of 1949*, Vol. II-B, p. 326. At the time, this expression was used to point out the brevity and self-contained character of the draft ultimately adopted as common Article 3, in distinction to other approaches considered at the Diplomatic Conference that would have made certain provisions of the Geneva Conventions as such applicable in non-international armed conflicts. See also section B.

[9] See ICJ, *Military and Paramilitary Activities in and against Nicaragua case*, Merits, Judgment, 1986, paras 218–219.

[10] For a detailed discussion of situations of violence perceived as of an international or a non-international character over the centuries and across cultures, see Neff.

[11] For details of the notion of 'war' under international law, see the commentary on common Article 2, section D.

[12] See Hague Convention (III) (1899); Geneva Convention (1906); Hague Convention (X) (1907); Geneva Convention on the Wounded and Sick (1929); and Geneva Convention on Prisoners of War (1929). See also St Petersburg Declaration (1868) and Hague Regulations (1899) and (1907).

[13] See e.g. Moir, p. 3, and Sivakumaran, 2012, p. 9.

[14] See e.g. Milanovic/Hadzi-Vidanovic, pp. 261–262, and Sivakumaran, 2012, p. 9.

[15] See e.g. the work of Emer de Vattel, *The Law of Nations, Or, Principles of the Law of Nature, Applied to the Conduct and Affairs of Nations and Sovereigns*, Slatkine Reprints – Henry Dunant Institute, Geneva, 1983, Book III, Chapter XVIII, paras 287–296 (calling for both sides in a civil war to observe the established laws of war to avoid civil wars escalating into barbarism).

[16] See also the two resolutions adopted by the *Institut de Droit International* at its session in Neuchâtel in 1900: Resolution I, Règlement sur la responsabilité des Etats à raison des dommages soufferts par des étrangers en cas d'émeute, d'insurrection ou de guerre civile; and

Furthermore, States experiencing internal armed violence occasionally entered into ad hoc agreements with non-State Parties,[17] or issued unilateral instructions to their armed forces, a notable example of which is the 1863 Lieber Code.[18]

360 In addition, in the course of the nineteenth century, the concept of the recognition of belligerency developed.[19] Acknowledging that some non-State Parties had the factual capability of waging 'war' of a scale that could affect the interests of third States, even though they lacked the legal capacity to do so,[20] the recognition of belligerency made it possible to apply certain rules of international law governing inter-State 'war' – namely the law of neutrality between belligerent and neutral States, and the laws and customs of war between belligerent States – in certain armed conflicts involving non-State Parties.[21] Provided that the armed conflict fulfilled certain conditions,[22] third States were therefore considered to be permitted (or even required according to some authors)[23] to recognize the non-State Party to the conflict as a 'belligerent', triggering the application of the law of neutrality.[24]

361 However, recognition of belligerency by third States had no legal consequence for relations between the Parties to the conflict. It neither brought the international laws and customs of war into effect between them, nor created a legal obligation for the State Party to the conflict to recognize its internal opponent as a belligerent.[25] The State Party to the conflict was free to recognize its

---

Resolution II, Droits et devoirs des Puissances étrangères, au cas de mouvement insurrectionnel, envers les gouvernements établis et reconnus qui sont aux prises avec l'insurrection.

[17] For examples, see Sivakumaran, 2012, pp. 25–28.

[18] The 1863 Lieber Code laid down the rules to be respected by the forces of the Union during the American Civil War.

[19] On this concept, see e.g. Milanovic/Hadzi-Vidanovic, pp. 263–264; Moir, pp. 4–18; and Sivakumaran, 2012, pp. 9–20.

[20] See e.g. Oppenheim, pp. 92–93.

[21] See Milanovic/Hadzi-Vidanovic, p. 262, with reference to Neff, p. 251, noting the desire to make neutrality law applicable as the decisive factor for the development of the concept of the recognition of belligerency.

[22] See e.g. Oppenheim, p. 93, para. 76:

It is a customary rule of the Law of Nations that any State may recognise insurgents as a belligerent Power, provided (1) they are in possession of a certain part of the territory of the legitimate Government; (2) they have set up a Government of their own; and (3) they conduct their armed contention with the legitimate Government according to the laws and usages of war.

See also Institut de Droit International, Resolution II, Droits et devoirs des Puissances étrangères, au cas de mouvement insurrectionnel, envers les gouvernements établis et reconnus qui sont aux prises avec l'insurrection, adopted at its Neuchâtel Session, 1900, Article 8. See further Lauterpacht, 1947, pp. 175–176, and 1952, pp. 249–250, with additional considerations.

[23] See Lauterpacht, 1947, pp. 175–176, and 1952, pp. 249–250. However, that was not a generally held view.

[24] See Oppenheim, p. 69, and Lauterpacht, 1952, p. 209. With respect to the State Party to the armed conflict, it was 'believed that the lawful Government is in any case entitled to assert belligerent status and the resulting belligerent rights'; see Lauterpacht, 1952, p. 249, fn. 4, with further references.

[25] See e.g. Oppenheim, pp. 69 and 366. See also Lauterpacht, 1947, pp. 246–247, with further considerations, and 1952, pp. 251 and 209–210.

opponent as a belligerent or not; only if it chose to do so did international law become applicable, making the conflict subject to the international laws and customs of war.[26] Once the conflict was over, however, the fact that it had recognized the insurgents as belligerents was not seen as preventing a victorious State Party from treating them as traitors and applying its criminal law to them, as the character of a belligerent Power gained through recognition was lost by the defeat.[27] In practice, with some exceptions,[28] States were reluctant to make use of the instrument of recognition of belligerency, disinclined as they were to admit to the existence within their borders of a situation justifying and requiring the application of international law and to raise the status of an internal opponent. Moreover, third States often did not want to affront other States by recognizing their internal opponents as belligerents and preferred not to subject themselves to the limitations of neutrality law.[29]

362   Initially, the ICRC was also hesitant to consider non-international armed conflicts a matter of international humanitarian concern.[30] However, in the light of experience on the ground, the need for and suitability of rules similar to those laid down in the 1864 Geneva Convention in situations of non-international armed conflict became evident to the ICRC.[31] In 1912, two reports by individual National Red Cross Societies addressing the role of the Red Cross in situations of 'civil war' and 'insurrection' were presented to the 9th International Conference of the Red Cross,[32] but strong resistance

---

[26] In addition, the State Party to the armed conflict became bound to respect the law of neutrality vis-à-vis third States, whereas third States were not bound by the law of neutrality in consequence of the State Party's recognition of the non-State Party as belligerent, nor were third States obligated to recognize the non-State Party as belligerent because the State Party had done so; see e.g. Oppenheim, pp. 69 and 366, and Lauterpacht, 1947, pp. 246–247, with further considerations. See also Sivakumaran, 2012, pp. 15–16, with further references.

[27] See Oppenheim, pp. 69–70, and Milanovic/Hadzi-Vidanovic, p. 264. See also Lieber Code (1863), Article 154: 'Treating, in the field, the rebellious enemy according to the law and usages of war has never prevented the legitimate government from trying the leaders of the rebellion or chief rebels for high treason, and from treating them accordingly, unless they are included in a general amnesty.'

[28] An example often discussed is the recognition of the Confederation as belligerent during the American Civil War; see Milanovic/Hadzi-Vidanovic, p. 264, and Sivakumaran, 2012, pp. 17–19.

[29] See Milanovic/Hadzi-Vidanovic, p. 264, and Duculesco, p. 126.

[30] The minutes of the second meeting of the ICRC's founding body on 17 March 1863, the sub-committee established by the Geneva Public Welfare Society to study the implementation of the suggestions made by Henry Dunant in his book, *A Memory of Solferino*, noted:

> The Committee agreed, first and foremost, that, in its opinion, no action should be contemplated during civil wars, and that the Committees should concern themselves only with European wars. After a few years' experience, the welfare scheme, once universally adopted and established, could of course be extended in various ways, but for the moment we should confine ourselves to the question of large-scale conflicts between European Powers.

Reproduced in *Revue internationale de la Croix-Rouge et Bulletin international des Sociétés de la Croix-Rouge*, Supplement, Vol. II, No. 3, March 1949, p. 130.

[31] See Moynier, p. 304, and Ador/Moynier, pp. 168–169.

[32] The American Red Cross submitted a report on 'Le rôle de la Croix-Rouge en cas de guerre civile ou d'insurrection', and the Cuban Red Cross on 'Mesures à prendre par la Croix-Rouge dans un pays en état d'insurrection permettant à cette institution d'accomplir ses fonctions

from States prevented them from being opened to detailed discussion and vote.[33]

363 At the 10th International Conference of the Red Cross in 1921, however, a resolution was adopted addressing humanitarian concerns, *inter alia*, during situations of 'civil war'.[34] While not a binding instrument, the resolution affirmed the right and duty of the Red Cross to afford relief in case of civil war and social and revolutionary disturbances. It recognized that all victims of civil war or of such disturbances are, without any exception whatsoever, entitled to relief, in conformity with the general principles of the Red Cross.[35]

364 The important step taken in the 1921 resolution was reaffirmed in 1938 when, during the Spanish Civil War, the 16th International Conference of the Red Cross adopted a further resolution requesting the ICRC, 'making use of its practical experience, to continue the general study of the problems raised by civil war as regards the Red Cross, and to submit the result of its study to the next International Red Cross Conference'.[36]

365 The Second World War prevented the International Conference of the Red Cross from taking place as planned in 1942. After the end of the war and against the background of the experiences of the Spanish Civil War and the Greek Civil War, the ICRC gave renewed thought to the humanitarian issues arising in non-international armed conflict as part of its work on a revision of the 1929 Geneva Conventions and the 1907 Hague Convention (X) and on the drafting of a new convention relating to the protection of civilian persons in time of war.

366 In 1946, the ICRC convened a 'Preliminary Conference of National Red Cross Societies for the study of the Conventions and of various Problems relative to the Red Cross'. With respect to a revision of the 1929 Geneva Convention on the Wounded and Sick, the ICRC proposed that 'in case of Civil War within the frontiers of a State the adversaries should be invited to declare their readiness to apply the principles of the Convention, subject to reciprocity being observed'.[37]

367 The Preliminary Conference chose a more direct approach by replacing the condition of reciprocal application contained in the ICRC draft by an assumption of application. It suggested inserting at the beginning of the Convention

---

entre les deux belligérants sans manquer à la neutralité'; see American Red Cross, *Neuvième Conférence Internationale de la Croix-Rouge tenue à Washington du 7 au 17 Mai 1912, Compte Rendu*, Washington, 1912, pp. 45–49.

[33] See *ibid.* pp. 45 and 199–208. For example, one State delegation noted that each direct or indirect offer of services of Red Cross Societies to 'insurgents or revolutionaries' could only be seen as an 'unfriendly act'.

[34] 10th International Conference of the Red Cross, Geneva, 1921, Resolution XIV, Guerre Civile, reproduced in *Dixième conférence internationale de la Croix-Rouge tenue à Genève du 30 mars au 7 avril 1921. Compte rendu*, Imprimerie Albert Renaud, Geneva, 1921, pp. 217–218.

[35] *Ibid.* section entitled 'Résolutions', paras 4–6.

[36] 16th International Conference of the Red Cross, London, 1938, Resolution XIV, Role and Activity of the Red Cross in Time of Civil War, reproduced in *Sixteenth International Red Cross Conference, London, June 1938, Report*, p. 104.

[37] *Report of the Preliminary Conference of National Societies of 1946*, p. 15.

an article defining its scope of application which included the following paragraph:

In the case of armed conflict within the borders of a State, the Convention shall also be applied by each of the adverse parties, unless one of them announces expressly its intention to the contrary.[38]

368   The Preliminary Conference was guided by the consideration that 'no State or insurgent body would venture to proclaim, in the face of world opinion, its intention of disregarding the laws of humanity, whose value and essential character are universally recognized'.[39] As regards the 1929 Geneva Convention on Prisoners of War, the Preliminary Conference considered that 'the provisions embodied in the Convention . . . must be applied . . . , in principle, in case of civil war'.[40]

369   These proposals were discussed at the 1947 Conference of Government Experts. With respect to the revision of the 1929 Geneva Conventions and the drafting of a new civilians convention, the participants agreed on a provision that again included a condition of reciprocal application:

In case of civil war, in any part of the home or colonial territory of a Contracting Party, the principles of the Convention shall be equally applied by the said Party, subject to the adverse Party also conforming thereto.[41]

370   In preparation for the 17th International Conference of the Red Cross in Stockholm in 1948, the ICRC subsequently drew up the following wording for a draft article 2(4) to be inserted in each of the future revised or new conventions:

In all cases of armed conflict which are not of an international character, especially cases of civil war, colonial conflicts, or wars of religion, which may occur in the territory of one or more of the High Contracting Parties, the implementing of the principles of the present Convention shall be obligatory on each of the adversaries. The application of the Convention in these circumstances shall in nowise depend on the legal status of the parties to the conflict and shall have no effect on that status.[42]

---

[38] *Ibid.*   [39] *Ibid.*

[40] *Ibid.* p. 70. Furthermore, with respect to specific Red Cross problems, the Preliminary Conference 'desire[d] to see embodied in the Convention . . . the following activities: . . . in case of civil war, the Red Cross shall be authorized to extend its care to all wounded, without distinction of the party to which they may belong'; *ibid.* p. 105.

[41] *Report of the Conference of Government Experts of 1947*, p. 8 (text adopted for the revision of the convention on the wounded and sick). The paragraph had slightly differing, but substantively identical, wording for the revision of the prisoner-of-war convention and the new convention on the protection of civilians; see also pp. 103 and 271. The reinsertion of the formulation 'principles of the Convention' (contained in the 1946 ICRC proposal but replaced by 'the Convention' in the text adopted by the 1946 Preliminary Conference) followed the suggestion of one delegation; see *Minutes of the Conference of Government Experts of 1947*, Vol. II-1, Commission I, pp. 5–6. Insofar as the text adopted by the Conference of Government Experts reverts to the term 'civil war' (whereas the 1946 Preliminary Conference had adopted the term 'armed conflict'), see *Report of the Conference of Government Experts of 1947*, pp. 9 and 270.

[42] *Draft Conventions submitted to the 1948 Stockholm Conference*, pp. 5, 34–35, 52, 153 and 222.

371 The exclusion of the condition of reciprocal application in the ICRC's draft was based on its consideration that it might 'render this stipulation valueless, as one Party could always allege that its adversary disregarded some specific clause of the Convention'. The explicit clarifications regarding the legal status of the Parties to the conflict took up on a recommendation made by a delegation during the 1947 Conference of Government Experts.[43]

372 On that basis, the Stockholm Conference adopted the following draft article 2(4) for the revision of the 1929 Geneva Convention on the Wounded and Sick and of the 1907 Hague Convention (X):

In all cases of armed conflict not of an international character which may occur in the territory of one or more of the High Contracting Parties, each of the adversaries shall be bound to implement the provisions of the present Conventions. The Convention shall be applicable in these circumstances, whatever the legal status of the Parties to the conflict and without prejudice thereto.[44]

373 With respect to the revision of the 1929 Geneva Convention on Prisoners of War and to a new convention on the protection of civilians, the Stockholm Conference included the condition of reciprocal application:

In all cases of armed conflict not of an international character which may occur in the territory of one or more of the High Contracting Parties, each of the Parties to the conflict shall be bound to implement the provisions of the present Convention, subject to the adverse party likewise acting in obedience thereto. The Convention shall be applicable in these circumstances, whatever the legal status of the Parties to the conflict and without prejudice thereto.[45]

The inclusion of a condition of reciprocal application in the draft conventions on prisoners of war and civilians resulted from the prevailing view that, while the humanitarian character of the conventions on the wounded, sick and shipwrecked supported an application of their provisions in non-international armed conflicts even without reciprocity, the same was not true for all of the provisions of the prisoner-of-war and new civilians conventions, such as, in particular, the provisions on Protecting Powers.[46] The deletion of the examples of armed conflicts not of an international character contained in the ICRC draft

---

[43] *Ibid.* p. 6.
[44] See *Draft Conventions adopted by the 1948 Stockholm Conference*, pp. 10 and 32. The change from 'principles of the present Convention' to 'provisions of the present Convention' represented a harmonization of the English and French texts. The original French text of the ICRC proposal submitted to the Stockholm Conference had used the term 'dispositions de la présente Convention', which had been incorrectly translated as 'principles'. See *Minutes of the Legal Commission at the 1948 Stockholm Conference*, p. 46.
[45] See *ibid.* pp. 51–52 and 114, emphasis omitted.
[46] See *Minutes of the Legal Commission at the 1948 Stockholm Conference*, pp. 48–57 and 64. For a summary of all of the arguments of delegations in favour of including the condition of reciprocal application in these Conventions, see *ICRC Remarks and Proposals on the 1948 Stockholm Draft*, pp. 37–38.

('especially cases of civil war, colonial conflicts, or wars of religion') was ultimately guided by the view that too much detail risked weakening the provision
because it was impossible to foresee all future circumstances and because the
armed conflict character of a situation was independent of its motives.[47]

374   In early 1949, in preparation for the Diplomatic Conference to be held in
Geneva later that year, the ICRC circulated to States a number of comments
and suggestions on the draft conventions. With respect to Article 2(4) of the
draft revised 1929 Geneva Convention on Prisoners of War and the draft new
civilians convention, the ICRC underlined its belief that 'it would be preferable
to delete the words "subject to the adverse party likewise acting in obedience
thereto"' also in these conventions.[48]

375   During the Diplomatic Conference, as had already become apparent during
the debates leading up to it, the regulation of 'armed conflicts not of an international character' proved to be one of the most difficult issues on the table.

376   States' divergent positions became evident during the first reading of draft
article 2 in the Joint Committee.[49] While some disapproved of the inclusion of
any provision governing non-international armed conflicts in the new Conventions, others were in favour of regulating all non-international armed conflicts.
Some agreed that there should be some regulation, but preferred to limit such
regulation to strictly defined situations.[50]

377   A Special Committee was formed and tasked with finding a compromise
formula. After agreeing on the fundamental question that non-international
armed conflicts should be addressed in the new conventions in one way or
another, the Special Committee focused its work on the following two options:

1. Applying the entire Conventions to specific cases of non-international
   armed conflict only; or
2. Applying only certain provisions of the Conventions to all non-international
   armed conflicts.[51]

---

[47] See *Minutes of the Legal Commission at the 1948 Stockholm Conference*, pp. 36–45 and 64.
[48] See *ICRC Remarks and Proposals on the 1948 Stockholm Draft*, pp. 36–38 and 68, *inter alia*,
noting at 38:

> The ICRC wish to stress, as they have so far done in their comments on the Draft Conven-
> tions, and as one National Red Cross Society has recently remarked, that if the reciprocity
> clause is inserted in this Paragraph, the application of the Convention in the event of civil
> war may be completely stultified. One of the parties to the conflict could always assert, as
> would be all too easy in a war of this nature, that the adversary was not observing such and
> such a provision of the Convention.

[49] See *Final Record of the Diplomatic Conference of Geneva of 1949*, Vol. II-B, pp. 9–15. The
Joint Committee united the three committees established by the Conference to discuss, respectively: the draft wounded and sick and draft maritime conventions; the draft prisoner-of-war
convention; and the draft new civilians convention. The Joint Committee was tasked with the
discussion of the articles common to these drafts.
[50] See *Final Record of the Diplomatic Conference of Geneva of 1949*, Vol. II-B, pp. 16 and 26.
[51] See *ibid.* p. 122, further noting that '[t]hese two ways did not exclude each other, and the possibility of solving the problem in different ways in the four Conventions increased the number
of solutions to be envisaged'. See also, subsequently, p. 76.

378   To study these options, the Special Committee set up a 'Working Party'.[52] The first draft proposed by the Working Party foresaw the application of the whole of the Conventions to non-international armed conflict, with the exception of the provisions on Protecting Powers, in strictly defined circumstances; lacking those, only the 'underlying humanitarian principles' of the Conventions would be generally applicable.[53] However, this proposal did not find favour with either the supporters or the opponents of the regulation of non-international armed conflict.[54]

379   Based on the feedback received, the Working Party submitted a second draft, with separate versions for, on the one hand, the revisions of the two 1929 Geneva Conventions and the 1907 Hague Convention (X)[55] and, on the other hand, the new convention for the protection of civilian persons in time of armed conflict.[56]

380   These drafts again prompted several proposals for amendments,[57] among them one by the French delegation that abandoned the approach of a full application of the Conventions in strictly circumscribed situations of non-international armed conflict, with other non-international armed conflicts generally subject only to the 'underlying humanitarian principles' of the Conventions. Instead, the French draft, referring to the provisions of the draft preamble to the civilians convention,[58] pointed to a limited, but distinct set of humanitarian norms to be applied in all situations of non-international armed conflict.[59]

---

[52] See *ibid.* pp. 45 and 122.   [53] See *ibid.* pp. 46–47 and 124, Annex A.

[54] See *ibid.* pp. 47–50. The ICRC representative noted, *inter alia*, with respect to the draft, that '[i]n his view, the text drawn up by the Working Party could never have been applied in any recent case of civil war. It therefore did not represent a progress with regard to the present situation' (*ibid.* pp. 47–48).

[55] See *ibid.* pp. 76–77 and 125, Annex B.   [56] See *ibid.* pp. 76–77 and 125, Annex C.

[57] See *ibid.* pp. 77–79 and 122–123. The seventh report of the Special Committee to the Joint Committee summarized delegations' responses to the second draft text as follows:

> The main objections to the second Draft of the Working Party were that the sub-division of non-international conflicts into two categories would raise interminable discussions at the beginning of each civil, colonial, or other war as to whether it belonged to one or the other category; no juri[s]diction had been provided for to determine whether the conditions for full application of the Conventions had been met in a specific case; that in reality such a decision was left to the discretion of the *de jure* government; and that the conditions in question would very seldom be fulfilled (*ibid.* p. 123).

[58] An option also suggested by the Italian delegation during the early discussions in the Joint Committee and in the Special Committee before the setting up of the first Working Group; see *ibid.* pp. 13 and 40.

[59] For the text of the French proposal, see *ibid.* p. 123. The draft preamble to which the French proposal referred had first been developed for the draft civilians convention by the 1948 Stockholm Conference; see *Draft Conventions adopted by the 1948 Stockholm Conference*, p. 113. The ICRC had subsequently proposed a similar preamble text for inclusion in all four Conventions; see *ICRC Remarks and Proposals on the 1948 Stockholm Draft*, pp. 8, 26, 36 and 67 (with an additional alternative text for the civilians convention). Ultimately, the Diplomatic Conference decided not to adopt substantive preambles for the four Geneva Conventions; however, the essence of the draft preambles found its entry in common Article 3. For details, see the commentary on the Preamble, section B.

381   On that basis, a second Working Party was set up to study the French proposal,[60] reporting back to the Special Committee with a draft text for inclusion in all four Conventions which laid the ground for the text finally adopted.[61]

382   While voting took place on a considerable number of proposals for amendments during its meeting,[62] the Special Committee succeeded in referring a text to the Joint Committee that almost completely foreshadowed the wording that would ultimately be adopted as common Article 3.[63] Further drafts were considered by the Joint Committee, including one submitted by the USSR delegation which called for the application of the provisions of the Geneva Conventions, in so far as they served a fundamentally humanitarian purpose, in all non-international armed conflicts.[64] In the end, the text that had been referred to the Joint Committee by the Special Committee found a majority of votes and was ultimately adopted as a new draft article 2A and submitted to the Plenary Assembly.[65]

383   In the final vote in the Plenary Assembly, draft article 2A was adopted by 34 votes to 12 with 1 abstention.[66] In the sequence of articles altogether adopted, draft article 2A was given its ultimate position as Article 3 common to the four Geneva Conventions.[67]

C. Paragraph 1: Scope of application of common Article 3

1. Introduction

384   Common Article 3 does not provide a detailed definition of its scope of application, nor does it contain a list of criteria for identifying the situations in which it is meant to apply. It merely stipulates that '[i]n the case of armed conflict not of an international character occurring in the territory of one of the High Contracting Parties', certain provisions must be respected by the Parties to the conflict.

385   The ostensible simplicity of its formulation is the result of common Article 3's negotiating history.[68] Positions at the 1949 Diplomatic Conference ranged from opposition to any limitation being imposed by international law on States' right to respond to armed violence within their sovereign spheres to a strong resolve to subject non-international armed conflicts to the regime of the Geneva Conventions to the greatest extent possible. A compromise had to be found. Faced with a choice between limiting the situations regulated to a circumscribed subset of non-international armed conflicts and restricting the

---

[60] See *Final Record of the Diplomatic Conference of Geneva of 1949*, Vol. II-B, p. 79.
[61] See *ibid.* pp. 82–83 and 125–126.   [62] See *ibid.* pp. 83–84, 90, 91 and 93–95.
[63] See *ibid.* pp. 101 and 126, Annex E.   [64] See *ibid.* pp. 97–98 and 127.
[65] See *ibid.* pp. 34–35 and 36–37.   [66] See *ibid.* p. 339.
[67] See *ibid.* Vol. I, pp. 383–385.   [68] For details, see section B.

number of rules binding in non-international armed conflicts while ensuring that they would be applicable to a broad range of situations, States ultimately chose the latter, while leaving the door open for special agreements to be concluded allowing for the application of more of the Conventions' rules.[69]

386   Nonetheless, the wording agreed upon does not resolve the persistent question of the scope of application of common Article 3. The intentional lack of detail on this point may have facilitated States' adoption of common Article 3. However, clarity as to its scope of application is important, as whether or not a given situation is an 'armed conflict not of an international character' entails significant consequences. In this respect, it is useful to note that the qualification of 'internal disturbances and tensions, such as riots, isolated and sporadic acts of violence and other acts of a similar nature' in Article 1 of Additional Protocol II as 'not being armed conflicts' is also considered accurate for common Article 3.[70]

387   A situation of violence that crosses the threshold of an 'armed conflict not of an international character' is a situation in which organized Parties confront one another with violence of a certain degree of intensity. It is a determination made based on the facts.

388   If a situation of violence amounts to a non-international armed conflict, the applicability of common Article 3 and other provisions of humanitarian law applicable in non-international armed conflict ensures that the Parties to that conflict are under an international legal obligation to grant certain fundamental protections to the victims of the conflict and to respect the rules on the conduct of hostilities.[71] Importantly, humanitarian law binds all Parties to the conflict, State and non-State alike.[72] The application of common Article 3 and other provisions of humanitarian law developed precisely to address the realities of non-international armed conflict can therefore make a vital difference to the survival, well-being and dignity of the victims of a conflict.

389   While common Article 3 contains rules that serve to limit or prohibit harm in non-international armed conflict, it does not in itself provide rules governing the conduct of hostilities. However, when common Article 3 is applicable, it is understood that other rules of humanitarian law of non-international armed conflict, including those regarding the conduct of hostilities, also apply.

---

[69] *Final Record of the Diplomatic Conference of Geneva of 1949*, Vol. II-B, pp. 122–123; see also pp. 46–50, 76–79 and 122–125.

[70] See Bothe/Partsch/Solf, p. 719, noting for Article 1(2) of Additional Protocol II that the 'passage ["as not being armed conflicts"] should not be interpreted as an attempt to change the sense of common Art. 3, whose "existing conditions of application" are not modified by Art. 1 of Protocol II'.

[71] In addition to common Article 3, other humanitarian law treaties may also become applicable in a non-international armed conflict, in particular Additional Protocol II. For details, see the commentary on Article 1 of Additional Protocol II and section C.2 of this commentary. Furthermore, rules of customary international law applicable to non-international armed conflict will need to be respected; for an assessment, see Henckaerts/Doswald-Beck.

[72] For details on the binding force of common Article 3, see section D.1.

Thus, while there may be no apparent need to discern possible limits to the scope of application of common Article 3, it is important that the rules applicable in armed conflicts apply only in the situations for which they were created.[73]

390   The existence of a situation that has crossed the threshold of an 'armed conflict not of an international character occurring in the territory of one of the High Contracting Parties' must therefore be neither lightly asserted nor denied. Humanitarian law standards must be applied only in the situation – armed conflict – for which they were intended and developed, carefully balancing considerations of military necessity and humanity.

391   Apart from the question of whether a situation of violence has crossed the threshold of a non-international armed conflict, the assessment of the scope of application of common Article 3 serves a further purpose: it confirms the distinction between international and non-international armed conflict. There are still important elements of humanitarian law governing international armed conflicts that have no counterpart in the law applicable to non-international armed conflicts, despite the considerable development of conventional and customary international humanitarian law applicable to non-international armed conflicts since 1949. In particular, humanitarian law governing non-international armed conflicts does not provide for prisoner-of-war status and contains no equivalent to the occupation law regime. The distinction between international and non-international armed conflict is therefore of continuing relevance.

392   It should be noted that there is no central authority under international law to identify or classify a situation as an armed conflict. States and Parties to a conflict need to determine the legal framework applicable to the conduct of their military operations. For its part, the ICRC makes an independent determination of the facts and systematically classifies situations for the purposes of its work. It is a task inherent in the role that the ICRC is expected to exercise under the Geneva Conventions, as set forth in the Statutes of the International Red Cross and Red Crescent Movement.[74] Other actors such as the United Nations and regional organizations may also need to classify situations for their work, and international and national courts and tribunals need to do so for the purposes of exercising their jurisdiction. In all cases, the classification must be made in good faith, based on the facts and the relevant criteria under humanitarian law.[75]

---

[73] For details on the geographic and temporal scope of application of common Article 3, see sections C.3 and C.4.

[74] Statutes of the International Red Cross and Red Crescent Movement (1986), Article 5.

[75] As international law is a self-applied system, it is possible that different actors can have different views of the same facts. In any case, it is the facts that determine whether a situation constitutes an international armed conflict, a non-international armed conflict, or is not an armed conflict at all.

2. 'In the case of armed conflict not of an international character'

a. The Parties to a non-international armed conflict

i. General

393 Common Article 3 is based on a negative description: it is applicable in the case of armed conflicts 'not of an international character'. Armed conflicts 'not of an international character' are armed conflicts where at least one Party is not a State. This reading is supported by the context of common Article 3: it comes after common Article 2, which applies to armed conflicts between States, i.e. international armed conflicts. The field of application of common Article 3 distinguishes itself from inter-State armed conflicts covered by common Article 2.[76] Accordingly, armed conflicts not of an international character are first of all armed conflicts which oppose the government of a State Party and one or more non-State Parties.[77] This was the type of non-international armed conflict that dominated discussions during the negotiation of common Article 3.[78]

394 In addition, it is widely accepted that non-international armed conflicts in the sense of common Article 3 also comprise armed conflicts in which no State Party is involved, i.e. armed conflicts exclusively opposing non-State armed groups.[79] It should be noted, however, that Additional Protocol II does not apply to such conflicts.[80] However, this does not modify the scope of application of common Article 3.[81] With the adoption of the ICC Statute in 1998, States

---

[76] See e.g. Australia, *Manual of the Law of Armed Conflict*, 2006, para. 3.8: 'A non-international armed conflict is distinct from an international armed conflict because of the legal status of the entities opposing each other; the parties to the conflict are not sovereign states, but the Government of a single state in conflict with one or more armed forces within its territory.' See also United States, Supreme Court, *Hamdan case*, Judgment, 2006, p. 67: 'The term "conflict not of an international character" is used here in contradistinction to a conflict between nations. So much is demonstrated by the "fundamental logic [of] the Convention's provisions on its application."' But see Israel, Supreme Court, *Public Committee against Torture in Israel case*, Judgment, 2006, para. 18, defining armed conflicts of an international character as follows: 'This law [international law regarding international armed conflict] applies in any case of an armed conflict of international character – in other words, one that crosses the borders of the state.'

[77] See e.g. ICTY, *Tadić* Decision on the Defence Motion for Interlocutory Appeal on Jurisdiction, 1995, para. 70. See also Gasser, p. 555.

[78] For details, see section B.

[79] See e.g. ICTY, *Tadić* Decision on the Defence Motion for Interlocutory Appeal on Jurisdiction, 1995, para. 70. See also Gasser, p. 555: 'Another case [of non-international armed conflict] is the crumbling of all government authority in the country, as a result of which various groups fight each other in the struggle for power.'

[80] According to Article 1(1) of Additional Protocol II, the Protocol applies to armed conflicts 'which take place in the territory of a High Contracting Party between its armed forces and dissident armed forces or other organized armed groups'; for details, see the commentary on that article.

[81] According to Article 1(1) of Additional Protocol II, the Protocol 'develops and supplements' common Article 3 'without modifying its existing conditions of application'. For the same reason, the requirement in Article 1(1) of Additional Protocol II that the non-State Party to the conflict exercise territorial control only applies to Additional Protocol II and not to common Article 3. For common Article 3, territorial control may be one factual indicator that the organization of a non-State armed group has reached the level of a Party to a non-international armed conflict, but it is not an independent precondition of its applicability; for details, see section C.2.b.

reaffirmed that they considered that fighting which occurs only between different armed groups and not involving a State can also amount to a non-international armed conflict.[82]

ii. Specific cases

395 The understanding that non-international armed conflicts in the sense of common Article 3 are armed conflicts involving opponents of which at least one is not a State will usually allow an easy distinction between international and non-international armed conflict. However, situations may arise where this is less obvious.

396   International humanitarian treaty law itself addresses certain cases. According to Article 1(4) of Additional Protocol I, international armed conflicts in the sense of common Article 2 of the Geneva Conventions also

include armed conflicts in which peoples are fighting against colonial domination and alien occupation and against racist régimes in the exercise of their right of self-determination, as enshrined in the Charter of the United Nations and the Declaration on Principles of International Law concerning Friendly Relations and Co-operation among States in accordance with the Charter of the United Nations.

397   For States party to the Protocol, humanitarian law governing international armed conflicts thus applies to such conflicts.[83]

398   Situations in which the international or non-international character of an armed conflict may not be obvious are those in which a State is engaged in a conflict against an entity whose statehood is uncertain. Depending on whether that entity is a State, the conflict will be international or non-international, making either the law of international or non-international armed conflict applicable.[84] Common Article 3 or humanitarian law more generally does not give an answer on whether an entity is a State under international law; it is the rules of general international law that set out the relevant criteria.[85] The

---

[82] Article 8(2)(d) of the 1998 ICC Statute, determining the scope of application of Article 8(2)(c), does not introduce a limitation to non-international armed conflicts involving at least one State, even though it otherwise makes use of notions developed in Additional Protocol II. Furthermore, according to Article 8(2)(f) of the Statute, Article 8(2)(e) explicitly applies to 'armed conflicts that take place in the territory of a State when there is protracted armed conflict between governmental authorities and organized armed groups or between such groups'.

[83] See Additional Protocol I, Article 96(3). For details, see the commentaries on Articles 1(4) and 96 of Additional Protocol I.

[84] Provided, in the latter case that the non-international armed conflict threshold has been reached; for details, see section C.2.b.

[85] On statehood under international law, see e.g. James R. Crawford, 'State', version of January 2011, in Rüdiger Wolfrum (ed.), *Max Planck Encyclopedia of Public International Law*, Oxford University Press, http://opil.ouplaw.com/home/EPIL, as well as, for a detailed analysis, James R. Crawford, *The Creation of States in International Law*, 2nd edition, Oxford University Press, 2006. The general, 'classical' criteria for statehood, based on effectiveness, were formulated in Article 1 of the 1933 Montevideo Convention on the Rights and Duties of States: 'The state as a person of international law should possess the following qualifications: (a) a permanent population; (b) a defined territory; (c) government; and (d) capacity to enter into relations with the other States.' See also the commentary on common Article 2, para. 231. For the role of

question of whether or not and when opponents were States arose, for example, during the conflicts in the former Yugoslavia in the early 1990s leading to the independence of Croatia and Bosnia and Herzegovina.[86] This and other situations have also served to illustrate that an armed conflict can change from a non-international to an international armed conflict, and vice versa.

399   Furthermore, when a State is party to a conflict against an entity which may or may not be the *government* of another State, it may also be unclear whether the conflict is of an international or a non-international character. Unlike in the situation above, here it is not the statehood that is uncertain. The question is rather whether or not the first State's opponent is the government of that second State. Humanitarian law does not provide guidance in deciding whether an entity is the government of a State; instead, this assessment is made according to the rules of general international law. Under international law, the key condition for the existence of a government is its effectiveness, that is, its ability to exercise effectively the functions usually assigned to a government within the confines of a State's territory, including the maintenance of law and order.[87] Put another way, effectiveness is the ability to exercise State functions both internally and externally, i.e. in relation to other States. If the entity in question is the government, the armed conflict is international, opposing two States, represented by their respective governments. If it is not the government, the conflict is non-international, provided, of course, that the threshold for non-international armed conflict has been reached.[88]

400   This question arose, for example, in connection with the military operation in Afghanistan launched by the US-led coalition of NATO States in October 2001. Based on the above considerations, the ICRC classified the initial phase as an international armed conflict between the US-led coalition and the Taliban regime in Afghanistan, which controlled at the time almost 90% of the Afghan territory. Following the establishment of a new Afghan Government in June 2002 through a *loya jirga* (grand assembly), the ICRC reclassified the situation as a non-international armed conflict between, on the one hand, the

---

the depositary in this respect, see the commentaries on Article 60, section C.1, and Article 62, section C.2.

[86] ICTY, *Slobodan Milošević* Decision on Motion for Judgment of Acquittal, 2004, paras 87–115; *Delalić* Trial Judgment, 1998, paras 96–108 and 211–214; *Tadić* Decision on the Defence Motion for Interlocutory Appeal on Jurisdiction, 1995, para. 72.

[87] See Hersch Lauterpacht, 'Recognition of Governments: I', *Columbia Law Review*, Vol. 45, 1945, pp. 815–864, especially at 825–830, and Malcolm N. Shaw, *International Law*, 5th edition, Cambridge University Press, 2003, pp. 376–382. See also Siegfried Magiera, 'Governments', version of September 2007, in Rüdiger Wolfrum (ed.), *Max Planck Encyclopedia of Public International Law*, Oxford University Press, http://opil.ouplaw.com/home/EPIL, paras 14 and 17. See also Article 4(A)(3) of the Third Convention, from which it can be inferred that the non-recognition by a Detaining Power of a government or authority does not influence the international character of an armed conflict; for details, see the commentary on that article.

[88] And provided that the entity does not belong to another State. See section C.2.b for details on the threshold of non-international armed conflict.

new Afghan Government supported by the coalition States and, on the other hand, the Taliban and other non-State armed groups.[89]

401   Some States involved classified the conflict differently, however, ranging from an international armed conflict initially,[90] to a stability operation, possibly including a peacekeeping mission, that may not always have been recognized as an armed conflict (be it international or non-international).[91]

iii. Involvement of one or more foreign States in a non-international armed conflict

402   The classification of an armed conflict as international or non-international can also be complicated when one or more foreign States joins a non-international armed conflict. A foreign State might join a conflict and fight on the governmental side of the State party to the conflict or on the side of the non-State armed group. In the case of the involvement of several foreign States, it is also conceivable that one or more would fight in support of the government, while one or more others would fight in support of the non-State armed group.

403   In view of the potential complexity of such scenarios, it has been suggested that any military involvement (i.e. fighting in support of a Party) by a foreign State in a non-international armed conflict internationalizes the conflict as a whole, making humanitarian law governing international armed conflict applicable in relations between all the opposing Parties.[92] Such an approach was also suggested by the ICRC to the 1971 Conference of Government Experts, but was rejected.[93]

---

[89] See e.g. ICRC, *International Humanitarian Law and the Challenges of Contemporary Armed Conflicts*, 2007, p. 7, and *International Humanitarian Law and the Challenges of Contemporary Armed Conflicts*, 2011, p. 10.

[90] United States, Memorandum on Humane Treatment of Taliban and al Qaeda Detainees, The White House, Washington, 7 February 2002, classifying the conflict as an international armed conflict.

[91] Germany, Federal Prosecutor General at the Federal Court of Justice, *Fuel Tankers case*, Decision to Terminate Proceedings, 2010, pp. 33–36. See also Nina M. Serafino, *Peacekeeping and Related Stability Operations: Issues of U.S. Military Involvement*, Congressional Research Service Report, updated 24 January 2007; Constantine D. Mortopoulos, 'Note: Could ISAF be a PSO? Theoretical Extensions, Practical Problematic and the Notion of Neutrality', *Journal of Conflict and Security Law*, 2010, Vol. 15, No. 3, pp. 573–587; and Françoise J. Hampson, 'Afghanistan 2001–2010', in Elizabeth Wilmshurst (ed.), *International Law and the Classification of Conflicts*, Oxford University Press, 2012, pp. 242–279.

[92] See e.g. UN Security Council, *Interim Report of the Commission of Experts Established Pursuant to Security Council Resolution 780 (1992)*, UN Doc S/25274, 10 February 1993, Annex 1, para. 45, suggesting the application of humanitarian law governing international armed conflict to 'the entirety of the armed conflicts in the territory of the former Yugoslavia'. See also David, p. 178: 'En résumé, le principe du fractionnement du conflit est théoriquement admissible mais difficile à mettre en pratique et parfois susceptible de mener à des incohérences. Nous sommes donc favorable à l'internationalisation générale du conflit en cas d'intervention étrangère.' ('In sum, it is theoretically -possible to split the conflict [into internal and international components], but it would be difficult to put into practice and may lead to inconsistencies. Thus, in the case of foreign intervention, it is preferable to deem it a general internationalization of the conflict.')

[93] The proposal read: 'When, in case of non-international armed conflict, one or the other Party, or both, benefits from the assistance of operational armed forces afforded by a third State, the

404   Instead, a differentiated approach has become widely accepted, distinguishing between whether an outside State fights in support of the State Party to the
conflict or in support of the armed group.[94] In the first case, the armed conflict will retain its non-international character, because it continues to oppose
a non-State armed group and the State authorities. In the second case, the original armed conflict between the non-State armed group and the State Party
also remains non-international in character (unless the intervening State exercises a certain degree of control over the armed group).[95] At the same time, in
the second case a parallel international armed conflict between the intervening foreign State and the State party to the original armed conflict also arises,
because in that instance two States are opposed. Lastly, where several foreign
States intervene on either side of the original non-international armed conflict,
the international or non-international character of each bilateral conflict relationship will depend on whether the opposing Parties only consist of States or
involve non-State armed groups. This approach is today also followed by the
ICRC.[96]

405   While legally precise, it has been pointed out that the differentiated approach
is sometimes not easily applied in practice.[97] For example, in the scenario of
parallel non-international and international armed conflicts arising following
the intervention of a foreign State in support of the non-State armed group that
is party to the original armed conflict, different legal regimes apply to persons
deprived of their liberty by either the non-State armed group or the intervening
State. Depending on the status of those persons, the intervening State is under
the obligation to treat them in line with the Third or Fourth Geneva Convention, whereas the non-State armed group is bound only by the law governing
non-international armed conflict.

iv. Control by an intervening foreign State over a non-State armed group that
is party to the conflict

406 A particular case occurs when a foreign State not only joins but in fact controls
a non-State armed group in its armed conflict against a State's armed forces.
In such a situation, there will not be parallel non-international and international armed conflicts, but only an international armed conflict between the

---

Parties to the conflict shall apply the whole of the international humanitarian law applicable in
international armed conflicts'; *Report of the Conference of Government Experts of 1971*, p. 50.
Among the reasons noted by the experts to reject the proposal was that it would encourage
non-international armed groups to seek support from foreign States; see *ibid.* pp. 51–52.

[94] The differentiated approach has been implicitly reaffirmed by the ICJ, *Military and Paramilitary
Activities in and against Nicaragua case*, Merits, Judgment, 1986, para. 219. See also Akande,
pp. 57 and 62–64; Schindler, p. 150; and *Sanremo Manual on the Law of Non-International
Armed Conflict* (2006), commentary on Section 1.1.1.

[95] See paras 406–410.

[96] See ICRC, *International Humanitarian Law and the Challenges of Contemporary Armed Conflicts*, 2011, p. 10, and for multinational forces intervening within the framework of an international organization, p. 31.

[97] See e.g. Schindler, p. 150; Vité, p. 86; and, generally, Stewart.

intervening State and the territorial State, even though one of them is acting through a non-State armed group. The level of control by the foreign State over the non-State armed group necessary to render an armed conflict international in such a way is debated.[98]

407   In 1999, in *Tadić*, the ICTY Appeals Chamber looked to the international law of State responsibility for guidance on this question.[99] In its 1986 *Nicaragua* decision, the International Court of Justice had identified certain levels of control for the attribution of non-State activity to a foreign State for the purposes of State responsibility: complete dependence of a non-State armed group on a foreign State for the attribution to the State of any act of the non-State armed group; or effective control of specific operations for the attribution to the State of acts committed in the course of such operations.[100] Against that background, the ICTY developed a test of 'overall control' of a State over a non-State armed group, as best suited both for the classification of conflicts as international or non-international and for the purposes of attribution of State responsibility.[101] According to this test, what is required to create an international armed conflict and to make acts of a non-State armed group attributable to a State is a degree of control that goes 'beyond the mere financing and equipping' of the armed group by the intervening State, 'involving also participation in the planning and supervision of military operations', but not requiring 'that such control should extend to the issuance of specific orders or instructions relating to single military actions'.[102]

408   In its 2007 decision in the *Application of the Genocide Convention case*, the International Court of Justice noted that'[i]nsofar as the "overall control" test is employed to determine whether or not an armed conflict is international, ... it may well be that the test is applicable and suitable'. The International Court of Justice does not accept, however, the 'overall control' test for the attribution of wrongful acts to a State.[103]

409   In order to classify a situation under humanitarian law involving a close relationship, if not a relationship of subordination, between a non-State armed group and a third State, the overall control test is appropriate because the notion

---

[98] For an overview of the debate, see e.g. Akande, pp. 57–62 and 63–64.

[99] See ICTY, *Tadić* Appeal Judgment, 1999, paras 88–114.

[100] See ICJ, *Military and Paramilitary Activities in and against Nicaragua case*, Merits, Judgment, 1986, paras 110–116.

[101] See ICTY, *Tadić* Appeal Judgment, 1999, paras 115–145.

[102] *Ibid.* para. 145. See in this sense also ICC, *Lubanga* Decision on the Confirmation of Charges, 2007, paras 210–211, and Trial Judgment, 2012, para. 541. It has been questioned whether for the purpose of conflict classification an argumentation starting from the secondary-law level of attribution under State responsibility law is appropriate, or whether a solution on the primary-law level of international humanitarian law itself should have been found. For a discussion, see Cassese, 2007, and Milanovic, 2006 and 2007a.

[103] See ICJ, *Application of the Genocide Convention case*, Merits, Judgment, 2007, paras 404–407. For a detailed discussion of the suggested control tests and an assessment in particular of their practicability for the classification of a situation as an international or non-international armed conflict, see the commentary on common Article 2, paras 265–273.

of overall control better reflects the real relationship between the armed group and the third State, including for the purpose of attribution. It implies that the armed group may be subordinate to the State even if there are no specific instructions given for every act of belligerency. Additionally, recourse to the overall control test enables the assessment of the level of control over the *de facto* entity or non-State armed group as a whole and thus allows for the attribution of several actions to the third State.[104] Relying on the effective control test, on the other hand, might require reclassifying the conflict with every operation, which would be unworkable. Furthermore, the test that is used must avoid a situation where some acts are governed by the law of international armed conflict but cannot be attributed to a State.

410   This position is not at present uniformly accepted. The International Court of Justice has determined that the overall control test can be used to classify a conflict but that the effective control standard remains the test for attribution of conduct to a State, without clarifying how the two tests would work together.[105]

v. Multinational forces in non-international armed conflict

411 No provision of international humanitarian law precludes States or an international organization sending multinational forces[106] from becoming Parties to an armed conflict if the classic conditions for the applicability of that law are met.[107] The applicability of humanitarian law to multinational forces, just as to any other actors, depends only on the circumstances on the ground, regardless of the international mandate assigned to those forces by the UN Security Council or of the designation given to the Parties potentially opposed to them.

---

[104] In opposition, effective control linked to every single operation is almost impossible to prove because it requires a level of proof that will unlikely be reached. *A fortiori*, the attribution test based on 'total control and dependence' used by the ICJ in 2007 in *Application of the Genocide Convention* and in 1986 in *Military and Paramilitary Activities in and against Nicaragua case* in order to determine the State's responsibility for any internationally wrongful act makes the test for attribution even stricter. See Hervé Ascencio, 'La responsabilité selon la Cour internationale de Justice dans l'affaire du génocide bosniaque', *Revue générale de droit international public*, Vol. 111, No. 2, 2007, pp. 285–304, at 290–292, and Jörn Griebel and Milan Plücken, 'New Developments regarding the Rules of Attribution? The International Court of Justice's Decision in *Bosnia v. Serbia*', *Leiden Journal of International Law*, Vol. 21, No. 3, 2008, pp. 601–622.

[105] ICJ, *Application of the Genocide Convention case*, Merits, Judgment, 2007, paras 404–407.

[106] The term 'multinational forces' is used in this section to describe the armed forces put by troop-contributing countries at the disposal of a peace operation. There is no clear-cut definition of peace operations in international law. The terms 'peace operations', 'peace-support operations', 'peacekeeping operations' and 'peace-enforcement operations' do not appear in the 1945 UN Charter. They may be interpreted in various ways and are sometimes used interchangeably. In general, the term 'peace operations' covers both peacekeeping and peace-enforcement operations conducted by international organizations, regional organizations or coalitions of States acting on behalf of the international community pursuant to a UN Security Council resolution adopted under Chapters VI, VII or VIII of the UN Charter.

[107] This is without prejudice to the distinct question whether it is the international organization as a whole or a subsidiary body of the organization that is a Party to the conflict.

This determination will be based on the fulfilment of specific legal conditions stemming from the relevant norms of humanitarian law, i.e. common Article 3 in the case of a non-international armed conflict.

412   Thus, no matter how such forces are labelled or constituted, be it as peace-keeping forces acting pursuant to a UN Security Council resolution, or as multinational forces operating with or without a mandate from the UN Security Council, if in fact the forces are engaged in collective hostilities meeting the threshold for a non-international armed conflict against one or more armed groups, the international organization sending the multinational force or the States comprising it can become a Party/Parties to that conflict.[108]

413   Given the international background of multinational forces, it has been suggested that any conflict in which such forces engage in activities equivalent to those of a Party to the conflict is an international armed conflict, no matter whether the multinational forces fight against the State or a non-State armed group.[109] However, one may ask whether such an automatic internationalization of the conflict is appropriate, in particular when the intervening forces only become engaged in hostilities against non-State armed groups.[110] According to another view, shared by the ICRC,[111] the assessment of the international or non-international character of an armed conflict in which multinational forces become engaged follows the same differentiated approach as for interventions by individual foreign States.[112] Accordingly, the international or non-international character of the armed conflict is determined by the State or non-State character of the opposing Parties. Therefore, only when multinational forces become engaged in an armed conflict against a State will that specific conflict be of an international character, without influencing the characterization of that State's original parallel armed conflict with a non-State armed group as non-international. When, in contrast, multinational forces fight in support of a State Party against a non-State armed group, the relations between

---

[108] For a discussion of who is the Party to the conflict (e.g. the international organization or the States contributing troops to the force), see the commentary on common Article 2, paras 245–252. See also Ferraro, 2013b, pp. 588–595 and ICRC, *International Humanitarian Law and the Challenges of Contemporary Armed Conflicts*, 2015, pp. 21–26.

[109] See e.g. Shraga, 1998, p. 73, and David, pp. 178–186.

[110] For a discussion, see Ferraro, 2013b, pp. 596–599.

[111] See ICRC, *International Humanitarian Law and the Challenges of Contemporary Armed Conflicts*, 2011, p. 31.

[112] See e.g. Pejic, 2007, p. 94; Ferraro, 2013b, pp. 536–539; Marten Zwanenburg, *Accountability of Peace Support Operations*, Martinus Nijhoff Publishers, Leiden, 2005, pp. 185–193; Ola Engdahl, 'The Status of Peace Operation Personnel under International Humanitarian Law', *Yearbook of International Humanitarian Law*, Vol. 11, 2008, pp. 109–138; Françoise J. Hampson, 'Afghanistan 2001–2010', in Elizabeth Wilmshurst (ed.), *International Law and the Classification of Conflicts*, Oxford University Press, 2012, pp. 242–279; and Robert Kolb, Gabriele Porretto and Sylvain Vité, *L'application du droit international humanitaire et des droits de l'homme aux organisations internationales: Forces de paix et administrations civiles transitoires*, Bruylant, Brussels, 2005.

the opposing Parties will be governed by the law of non-international armed conflict.[113]

b. The threshold of non-international armed conflict

i. Introduction

414 Armed violence between non-State actors and government authorities or between several non-State actors is not an unusual phenomenon. It is part of the role of the State to control violence within its borders, maintaining and restoring law and order, if necessary by exercising the monopoly of the legitimate use of force entrusted to it for that purpose.[114] Domestic law and international law, especially international and regional human rights law, as applicable, provide the framework within which a State may exercise this right.

415 In situations of violence between non-State armed groups and government authorities or between several non-State armed groups, the fundamental question is at what point such violence becomes a non-international armed conflict subject to humanitarian law.

416 The threshold for non-international armed conflicts is different to that for international armed conflicts. For international armed conflicts, any 'resort to armed force between States' is sufficient to make humanitarian law immediately applicable between them.[115] However, a situation of violence that cannot be characterized as an international armed conflict owing to the non-State character of one of the Parties is not necessarily a non-international armed conflict. The different thresholds for non-international and international armed conflict is a consequence of the fact that States may have a greater tendency to guard against regulation of their domestic affairs by international law than against regulation of their external relations with other sovereign States. This was certainly the case at the time of the adoption of common Article 3.[116]

[113] The differentiated approach in the case of intervention of multinational forces has also found the support of States party to the Geneva Conventions; see e.g. Germany, Federal Prosecutor General at the Federal Court of Justice, *Fuel Tankers case*, Decision to Terminate Proceedings, 2010, p. 34:

> The NATO-led international troops of ISAF are in Afghanistan at the behest and sufferance of the Afghan Government; this means that the relevant territorial state has consented to the ISAF deployment in a manner valid under international law. Thus, notwithstanding the involvement of international troops, the conflict must be classified as "non-international" in nature under international law because ISAF is fighting on behalf of the government authorities of Afghanistan.

[114] Max Weber, 'Politik als Beruf', speech at Munich University, 1919, in *Gesammelte Politische Schriften*, Munich, 1921, pp. 396–450.

[115] See ICTY, *Tadić* Decision on the Defence Motion for Interlocutory Appeal on Jurisdiction, 1995, para. 70. For a detailed discussion, see the commentary on common Article 2, paras 236–244.

[116] For a detailed discussion and further references, see e.g. Milanovic/Hadzi-Vidanovic, pp. 269–272. At the Stockholm Conference in 1948, some States criticized the draft (according to which the whole of the Conventions would be applicable in non-international armed conflicts) out of

417   Pictet's 1952 Commentary on the First Geneva Convention, referring to the absence of a definition of the term 'armed conflict not of an international character', stated:

> [M]any of the delegations feared that it might be taken to cover any act committed by force of arms – any form of anarchy, rebellion, or even plain banditry. For example, if a handful of individuals were to rise in rebellion against the State and attack a police station, would that suffice to bring into being an armed conflict within the meaning of the Article?[117]

These concerns relating to sovereignty help to explain the higher threshold for the applicability of humanitarian law in non-international armed conflict than in international armed conflict.

418   It should be noted, however, that when negotiating and adopting Additional Protocol II in 1977, States established a relatively narrow scope of application specific to Additional Protocol II, without altering the scope of application of common Article 3.[118]

419   The Commentaries on the Geneva Conventions published by the ICRC under the general editorship of Jean Pictet between 1952 and 1960 listed a number of 'convenient criteria' for assessing the applicability of common Article 3.[119] As these Commentaries noted, the 'convenient criteria' were drawn

a concern that 'it would cover in advance all forms of insurrection, rebellion, anarchy, and the break-up of States, and even plain brigandage'; Pictet (ed.), *Commentary on the First Geneva Convention*, ICRC, 1952, p. 43. States were especially concerned about the possible implications that would flow from the recognition of any legal status for non-State Parties arising under humanitarian law.

[117] Pictet (ed.), *Commentary on the First Geneva Convention*, ICRC, 1952, p. 49.

[118] Additional Protocol II, Article 1. See also para. 394 of this commentary and Cullen, pp. 88–101 for an overview of the drafting history of Additional Protocol II.

[119] See Pictet (ed.), *Commentary on the First Geneva Convention*, ICRC, 1952, pp. 49–50:
   (1) That the Party in revolt against the *de jure* Government possesses an organized military force, an authority responsible for its acts, acting within a determinate territory and having the means of respecting and ensuring respect for the Convention.
   (2) That the legal Government is obliged to have recourse to the regular military forces against insurgents organized as military and in possession of a part of the national territory.
   (3) (a) That the *de jure* Government has recognized the insurgents as belligerents; or
       (b) that it has claimed for itself the rights of a belligerent; or
       (c) that it has accorded the insurgents recognition as belligerents for the purposes only of the present Convention; or
       (d) that the dispute has been admitted to the agenda of the Security Council or the General Assembly of the United Nations as being a threat to international peace, a breach of the peace, or an act of aggression.
   (4) (a) That the insurgents have an organization purporting to have the characteristics of a State.
       (b) That the insurgent civil authority exercises *de facto* authority over persons within a determinate territory.
       (c) That the armed forces act under the direction of the organized civil authority and are prepared to observe the ordinary laws of war.
       (d) That the insurgent civil authority agrees to be bound by the provisions of the Convention.
   See further Pictet (ed.), *Commentary on the Third Geneva Convention*, ICRC, 1960, pp. 35–36, and *Commentary on the Fourth Geneva Convention*, ICRC, 1958, pp. 35–36. These criteria were not reproduced in the Commentary on the Second Convention.

from 'the various amendments discussed' during the 1949 Diplomatic Conference, considering that 'these different conditions, although in no way obligatory, constitute convenient criteria', which 'are useful as means of distinguishing a genuine armed conflict from a mere act of banditry or an unorganized and
short-lived insurrection'.[120]

420　These 'convenient criteria' are merely indicative, however.[121] They stem
from proposals for amendments submitted during the 1949 Diplomatic Conference at a time when the full application of the Geneva Conventions to non-
international armed conflict, and not merely the application of some minimum provisions contained in common Article 3 as ultimately adopted, was
still being discussed. Thus, States suggested the listed criteria for the purpose of limiting the scope of application of the future common Article 3 in
view of the highly detailed and demanding duties that would fall on all Parties if the whole of the Conventions were to apply to non-international armed
conflicts.[122] Since common Article 3 as finally adopted abandoned the idea of
a full application of the Geneva Conventions to non-international armed conflicts, in exchange for a wide scope of application, not all of these criteria are
fully adapted to common Article 3.[123] Nonetheless, if met, the 'convenient
criteria' may certainly indicate the existence of a non-international armed
conflict.

421　Over time, of the criteria enumerated in the Pictet Commentaries, two are
now widely acknowledged as being the most relevant in assessing the existence of a non-international armed conflict: that the violence needs to have
reached a certain intensity and that it must be between at least two organized
Parties/armed groups. The existence of a non-international armed conflict thus
needs to be assessed according to these specific criteria.

ii. Organization of the Parties to the conflict and intensity of the conflict

422　The wording of common Article 3 gives some rudimentary guidance on its
threshold of application: what is required is an 'armed' 'conflict' not of an
international character, in which 'Part[ies] to the conflict' are involved. This
indicates that for common Article 3 to apply, a situation of violence must
have reached a certain level of intensity, characterized by recourse to arms

---

[120] *Ibid.*　　[121] See e.g. ICTY, *Boškoski and Tarčulovski* Trial Judgment, 2008, para. 176.

[122] Thus, the criteria reflect elements of the traditional concept of belligerency, such as the necessity of recognition by the State concerned, or demand State-like features on the side of the
non-State armed group, including an express declaration of submission to the binding force of
the Geneva Conventions.

[123] For example, if the criterion of the recognition of the insurgent Party as a belligerent were met,
that would mean that the whole of the laws of armed conflict, and not only common Article 3,
would be applicable – which would make common Article 3 superfluous. It is acknowledged,
however, that the original Pictet commentary advocated for common Article 3 to be applied
'as widely as possible'; see Pictet (ed.), *Commentary on the First Geneva Convention*, ICRC,
1952, p. 50.

by non-State armed groups that are capable of being Parties to an armed conflict.[124]

423   The ICRC has expressed its understanding of non-international armed conflict, which is based on practice and developments in international case-law, as follows:

> Non-international armed conflicts are *protracted armed confrontations* occurring between governmental armed forces and the forces of one or more armed groups, or between such groups arising on the territory of a State [party to the Geneva Conventions]. The armed confrontation must reach a *minimum level of intensity* and the parties involved in the conflict must show a *minimum of organisation*.[125]

424   The definition of a non-international armed conflict as 'protracted armed violence between governmental authorities and organized armed groups or between such groups', as well as the determining criteria of 'intensity' and 'organization', have been extensively reflected in the practice of other institutions.[126] They have also found expression in the practice of States party to the Geneva Conventions.[127]

425   These criteria were identified as early as 1962, when a Commission of Experts convened by the ICRC to study the question of humanitarian aid to victims of internal armed conflicts assessed the question of the threshold of applicability of common Article 3.[128] Furthermore, in 1979, one authority,

---

[124] It may be noted that the term hostilities 'refers to the (collective) resort by the parties to the conflict to means and methods of injuring the enemy'. ICRC, *Interpretive Guidance*, p. 43.

[125] ICRC, *How is the Term 'Armed Conflict' Defined in International Humanitarian Law?*, Opinion Paper, March 2008, p. 5. The leading case for this understanding is ICTY, *Tadić* Decision on the Defence Motion for Interlocutory Appeal on Jurisdiction, 1995, para. 70, and Trial Judgment, 1997, para. 562.

[126] See e.g. SCSL, *Sesay* Trial Judgment, 2009, para. 95, and ICC, *Bemba* Decision on the Confirmation of Charges, 2009, para. 231, and Trial Judgment, 2016, para. 128. For further examples, see Sivakumaran, 2012, p. 166.

[127] See e.g. Canada, *Use of Force for CF Operations*, 2008, para. 104.6; Colombia, *Operational Law Manual*, 2009, Chapter II; Netherlands, *Military Manual*, 2005, para. 1006; Peru, *IHL Manual*, 2004, Chapter 9, Glossary of Terms; and United Kingdom, *Manual of the Law of Armed Conflict*, 2004, p. 29. See also Colombia, Constitutional Court, *Constitutional Case No. C-291/07*, Judgment, 2007, pp. 49–52; and Germany, Federal Prosecutor General at the Federal Court of Justice, *Fuel Tankers case*, Decision to Terminate Proceedings, 2010, p. 34.

[128] Invited to consider, *inter alia*, the question in 'which cases . . . article 3 common to the four Geneva Conventions of August 12, 1949 [is] legally applicable', the Commission noted the following:

> [P]ractice observed enabled the Commission to define the types of situation entering the field of application of article 3. . . . It must be a question of an internal 'armed' conflict which gives rise to 'hostilities'. . . .
>
>   In the Commission's opinion, the existence of an armed conflict, within the meaning of article 3, cannot be denied if the hostile action, directed against a legal government, is of a collective character and consists of a minimum amount of organization. In this respect and without these circumstances being necessarily cumulative, one should take into account such factors as the length of the conflict, the number and framework of the rebel groups, their installation or action on a part of the territory, the degree of insecurity, the existence of victims, the methods employed by the legal government to re-establish order, etc.

reaffirming a certain intensity of the hostilities and organization of the Parties as guiding elements, observed:

> Practice has set up the following criteria to delimit non-international armed conflicts from internal disturbances. In the first place, the hostilities have to be conducted by force of arms and exhibit such intensity that, as a rule, the government is compelled to employ its armed forces against the insurgents instead of mere police forces. Secondly, as to the insurgents, the hostilities are meant to be of a collective character, that is, they have to be carried out not only by single groups. In addition, the insurgents have to exhibit a minimum amount of organization. Their armed forces should be under a responsible command and be capable of meeting minimal humanitarian requirements.[129]

426   In the 1990s, rulings by the ICTY and the ICTR made an important contribution to the clarification of the definition or constitutive criteria of non-international armed conflict. In order to be able to exercise their jurisdiction over grave breaches and other war crimes, the Tribunals had to establish whether the situations in which crimes had allegedly been committed constituted armed conflicts and, if so, whether they were of an international or a non-international character.[130]

427   In its decision on jurisdiction in *Tadić* in 1995, the ICTY Appeals Chamber found that the threshold of a non-international armed conflict is crossed 'whenever there is . . . protracted armed violence between governmental authorities and organized armed groups or between such groups within a State'.[131] In its trial judgment in the same case in 1997, the ICTY further developed this approach by holding that the 'test applied by the Appeals Chamber . . . focuses on two aspects of a conflict . . . the intensity of the conflict and the organization of the parties to the conflict'.[132] These conclusions were subsequently

---

ICRC, 'Humanitarian aid to the victims of internal conflicts. Meeting of a Commission of Experts in Geneva, 25–30 October 1962, Report', *International Review of the Red Cross*, Vol. 3, No. 23, February 1963, pp. 79–91, at 82–83.

[129] See Schindler, pp. 146–147.

[130] See ICTY Statute (1993), Articles 2 and 3, and ICTR Statute (1994), Article 3.

[131] ICTY, *Tadić* Decision on the Defence Motion for Interlocutory Appeal on Jurisdiction, 1995, para. 70.

[132] See ICTY, *Tadić* Trial Judgment, 1997, para. 562:

> (a) *Protracted armed violence between governmental forces and organized armed groups*
> 562. The test applied by the Appeals Chamber to the existence of an armed conflict for the purposes of the rules contained in Common Article 3 focuses on two aspects of a conflict; *the intensity of the conflict* and *the organization of the parties to the conflict*. In an armed conflict of an internal or mixed character, these closely related criteria are used solely for the purpose, as a minimum, of distinguishing an armed conflict from banditry, unorganized and short-lived insurrections, or terrorist activities, which are not subject to international humanitarian law. Factors relevant to this determination are addressed in the Commentary to Geneva Convention for the Amelioration of the Condition of the Wounded and Sick in Armed Forces in the Field, Convention I ('*Commentary*, Geneva Convention I'). [Emphasis added.]

reaffirmed in the case law of the ICTY, the ICTR and the ICC.[133] As noted by the ICTY and the ICTR, 'the determination of the intensity of a conflict and the organisation of the parties are factual matters which need to be decided in light of the particular evidence and on a case-by-case basis'.[134]

428   The approach developed in international criminal jurisprudence is congruent with the ICRC's understanding of the concept of 'armed conflict not of an international character' under common Article 3. The jurisprudence of the international tribunals provides further elements helpful in understanding the content of these criteria.

429   First, with regard to the 'organization' criterion, State armed forces are presumed to be organized. In order for a non-State armed group to be sufficiently organized to become a Party to a non-international armed conflict, it must possess organized armed forces. Such forces 'have to be under a certain command structure and have the capacity to sustain military operations'.[135] In addition, '[w]hile the group does not need to have the level of organisation of state armed forces, it must possess a certain level of hierarchy and discipline and the ability to implement the basic obligations of IHL'.[136]

430   In order to assess the requisite level of organization of non-State armed groups, the ICTY identified certain indicative factors, while specifying that none of them is, in itself, essential to whether the criterion is met:

> Such indicative factors include the existence of a command structure and disciplinary rules and mechanisms within the group; the existence of a headquarters; the fact that the group controls a certain territory; the ability of the group to gain access to weapons, other military equipment, recruits and military training; its ability to plan, coordinate and carry out military operations, including troop movements and logistics; its ability to define a unified military strategy and use military tactics; and its ability to speak with one voice and negotiate and conclude agreements such as cease-fire or peace accords.[137]

431   Second, the requisite degree of intensity may be met 'when hostilities are of a collective character or when the government is obliged to use military force against the insurgents, instead of mere police forces'.[138] In this light, it is

---

[133] See e.g. ICTY, *Limaj* Trial Judgment, 2005, para. 84, and *Boškoski and Tarčulovski* Trial Judgment, 2008, para. 175. See also e.g. ICTR, *Akayesu* Trial Judgment, 1998, paras 619–620, and *Rutaganda* Trial Judgment, 1999, paras 91–92.

[134] See ICTY, *Limaj* Trial Judgment, 2005, para. 84. See also *Boškoski and Tarčulovski* Trial Judgment, 2008, para. 175, and ICTR, *Rutaganda* Trial Judgment, 1999, para. 92.

[135] ICRC, *How is the Term 'Armed Conflict' Defined in International Humanitarian Law?*, Opinion Paper, 2008, p. 3.

[136] Droege, 2012, p. 550. See also ICRC, *International Humanitarian Law and the Challenges of Contemporary Armed Conflicts*, 2003, p. 19.

[137] ICTY, *Haradinaj* Trial Judgment, 2008, para. 60. See further ICTY, *Boškoski and Tarčulovski* Trial Judgment, 2008, paras 199–203, and *Limaj* Trial Judgment, 2005, paras 94–134. Some of these elements have also been applied by the ICC; see *Lubanga* Trial Judgment, 2012, para. 537, *Katanga* Trial Judgment, 2014, para. 1186, and *Bemba* Trial Judgment, 2016, paras 134–136.

[138] ICRC, *How is the Term 'Armed Conflict' Defined in International Humanitarian Law?*, Opinion Paper, 2008, p. 3.

understood that Article 1(2) of Additional Protocol II, which provides that the 'Protocol shall not apply to situations of internal disturbances and tensions, such as riots, isolated and sporadic acts of violence and other acts of a similar nature, as not being armed conflicts', also defines the lower threshold of common Article 3.[139] This understanding has been confirmed by State practice in that, for other treaties applicable to non-international armed conflict, States have chosen to refer to a combination of common Article 3 and Article 1(2) of Additional Protocol II.[140]

432   The ICTY has developed a number of 'indicative factors' that can be used to assess the intensity of the violence, including:

the seriousness of attacks and whether there has been an increase in armed clashes, the spread of clashes over territory and over a period of time, any increase in the number of government forces and mobilisation and the distribution of weapons among both parties to the conflict, as well as whether the conflict has attracted the attention of the United Nations Security Council, and whether any resolutions on the matter have been passed. Trial Chambers have also taken into account in this respect the number of civilians forced to flee from the combat zones; the type of weapons used, in particular the use of heavy weapons, and other military equipment, such as tanks and other heavy vehicles; the blocking or besieging of towns and the heavy shelling of these towns; the extent of destruction and the number of casualties caused by shelling or fighting; the quantity of troops and units deployed; existence and change of front lines between the parties; the occupation of territory, and towns and villages; the deployment of government forces to the crisis area; the closure of roads; cease fire orders and agreements, and the attempt of representatives from international organisations to broker and enforce cease fire agreements.[141]

433   As underlined by the Tribunals, the above indicators of intensity and organization are only examples, which can, but need not, all be present in a particular

---

[139] See Bothe/Partsch/Solf, p. 719, noting for Article 1(2) of Additional Protocol II that the 'passage ["as not being armed conflicts"] should not be interpreted as an attempt to change the sense of common Art. 3, whose "existing conditions of application" are not modified by Art. 1 of Protocol II'. See also e.g. Abi-Saab, p. 147, noting that Article 1(2) of Additional Protocol II is, in fact, of more importance to common Article 3 than to Additional Protocol II; for more details, see the commentary on Article 1 of Additional Protocol II.
  See also, for descriptions of 'internal disturbances' and 'tensions', ICRC, 'The ICRC, the League and the Report on the re-appraisal of the Role of the Red Cross (III): Protection and assistance in situations not covered by international humanitarian law, Comments by the ICRC', *International Review of the Red Cross*, Vol. 18, No. 205, August 1978, pp. 210–214. See also Sandoz/Swinarski/Zimmermann (eds), *Commentary on the Additional Protocols*, ICRC, 1987, paras 4475–4476.

[140] See e.g. ICC Statute (1998), Article 8(2)(c)–(d); Second Protocol to the Hague Convention for the Protection of Cultural Property (1999), Article 22(1)–(2); and Amendment to Article 1 of the 1980 Convention on Certain Conventional Weapons (2001), Article 1(2).

[141] See ICTY, *Boškoski and Tarčulovski* Trial Judgment, 2008, para. 177, footnotes with references to ICTY case law deleted. See further *Haradinaj* Trial Judgment, 2008, paras 49 and 90–99, and *Limaj* Trial Judgment, 2005, paras 90 and 135–170. Some of these elements have also been applied by the ICC; see *Lubanga* Trial Judgment, 2012, para. 538; *Katanga* Trial Judgment, 2014, para. 1187; and *Bemba* Trial Judgment, 2016, paras 137–141.

case in order to conclude that the criteria of intensity and organization are fulfilled in a particular situation.

434   In any case, the criteria of intensity and organization must be present cumulatively in order for a situation of violence to reach the threshold of a non-international armed conflict. Depending on the circumstances, however, it may be possible to draw some conclusions from one criterion for the other. For example, the existence of highly intense armed confrontations between State authorities and non-State armed groups, or between several non-State armed groups, may indicate that these groups have reached the level of organization required of a Party to a non-international armed conflict.

435   In sum, the intensity of the conflict and the level of organization of the opponents, assessed on the basis of a comprehensive reading of various factual indicators, are the crucial markers of such situations. The fact that these two criteria have been referred to from soon after the adoption of common Article 3, and have been reaffirmed and fleshed out over the years, confirms their decisiveness for determining the threshold of application of common Article 3. That said, there are some situations in which the interpretation of these criteria is particularly difficult.

436   In this light, it should be noted that, much like in relation to international armed conflicts, technological developments raise the question of whether and at what point cyber operations can amount to a non-international armed conflict.[142] In order to determine the existence of a non-international armed conflict involving cyber operations, the same criteria apply as with regard to kinetic violence.[143] If the requirements of sufficient organization and intensity are met in situations that involve or are exclusively based on cyber operations, such situations fall under the scope of common Article 3.

437   Particular challenges arise when applying the established classification criteria to cyber operations. First, a non-State armed group that is sufficiently organized to be a Party to a conventional non-international armed conflict would be sufficiently organized to be Party to a conflict that includes or is solely based on cyber operations. However, for a group that only organizes online it may be difficult – yet arguably not impossible[144] – to determine whether it meets the threshold of organization required to become a Party to a non-international armed conflict.[145] Second, if cyber operations 'have the same violent consequences as kinetic operations, for instance if they were used to open the

---

[142] See the commentary on common Article 2, paras 253–256.
[143] See Tallinn Manual on the International Law Applicable to Cyber Warfare (2013), Rule 23, and Droege, 2012, pp. 549–550.
[144] Tallinn Manual on the International Law Applicable to Cyber Warfare (2013), Rule 23, para. 13.
[145] See Droege, 2012, p. 550. For stronger opposition to the idea that 'a decentralized virtual group' may qualify as a Party to a non-international armed conflict, see Robin Geiss, 'Cyber Warfare: Implications for Non-international Armed Conflicts', International Law Studies, U.S. Naval War College, Vol. 89, 2013, pp. 627–645, at 637.

floodgates of dams, or to cause aircraft or trains to collide',[146] they may reach a sufficient degree of intensity to amount to a non-international armed conflict. In contrast, certain cyber operations may not have a similar impact to that of kinetic attacks but be limited to blocking internet functions, exploiting networks, or stealing, deleting or destroying data. If cyber operations consist exclusively of the latter kind of acts, the intensity of violence as required under humanitarian law is unlikely to be reached.[147]

iii. Duration as an independent criterion?

438　The use of the term '*protracted* armed violence' in some definitions raises the question of whether the duration of hostilities between governmental authorities and non-State armed groups or between such groups constitutes an independent, additional criterion to determine the existence of a non-international armed conflict.

439　　The duration of hostilities is particularly suited to an assessment after the fact, for example during judicial proceedings. From the perspective of the practical application of humanitarian law, an independent requirement of duration could, in contrast, lead to a situation of uncertainty regarding the applicability of humanitarian law during the initial phase of fighting among those expected to respect the law, or to a belated application in situations where its regulatory force was in fact already required at an earlier moment.

440　　The duration of hostilities is thus appropriately considered to be an element of the assessment of the intensity of the armed confrontations. Depending on the circumstances, hostilities of only a brief duration may still reach the intensity level of a non-international armed conflict if, in a particular case, there are other indicators of hostilities of a sufficient intensity to require and justify such an assessment.[148]

---

[146] Droege, 2012, p. 551.

[147] It remains to be seen how State practice on classifying cyber operations as non-international armed conflicts will develop. Some commentators accept that in the light of 'ever more destructive and disruptive cyber operations and societies becoming deeply dependent on the cyber infrastructure, State practice accompanied by *opinio juris* can be expected to result in a lowering of the current threshold'; Michael N. Schmitt, 'Classification of Cyber Conflict', *Journal of Conflict and Security Law*, Vol. 17, No. 2, 2012, pp. 245–260, at 260.

[148] See e.g. Sivakumaran, 2012, pp. 167–168. In 1997, in the *Tablada case*, the Inter-American Commission on Human Rights, generally applying the criteria of intensity and organization, came to the conclusion that an attack by 42 armed persons against an army barracks, leading to combat lasting about 30 hours, had crossed the threshold of a non-international armed conflict; see *Case 11.137 (Argentina)*, Report, 1997, paras 154–156. But see Germany, Federal Prosecutor General at the Federal Court of Justice, *Fuel Tankers case*, Decision to Terminate Proceedings, 2010, pp. 34–35:

> As regards the time component of an armed conflict, the Code of Crimes Against International Law (VStGB) stipulates that the fighting must have a certain duration. . . . This does not mean that military operations must be carried out without interruption. On the other hand, the hostilities carried out with armed force must usually last significantly longer than hours or days (however, also see the Inter-American Commission on Human Rights, Report no. 55/97 Case no. 11.137 in Argentina, in which an attack on a military barracks lasting only two days was classified as an 'armed conflict' due to its unusual intensity).

441   In this respect, the ICTY, clarifying its understanding of duration as one of the indicators of the intensity of the armed confrontations, noted:

> The criterion of protracted armed violence has therefore been interprcted in practice, including by the *Tadić* Trial Chamber itself, as referring more to the intensity of the armed violence than to its duration. Trial Chambers have relied on indicative factors relevant for assessing the 'intensity' criterion, none of which are, in themselves, essential to establish that the criterion is satisfied. These indicative factors include the number, duration and intensity of individual confrontations; ... [149]

442   However, the ICTY also noted that the duration of armed confrontations should not be overlooked when assessing whether hostilities have reached the level of intensity of a non-international armed conflict:

> [C]are is needed not to lose sight of the requirement for protracted armed violence in the case of [a]n internal armed conflict, when assessing the intensity of the conflict. The criteria are closely related. They are factual matters which ought to be determined in light of the particular evidence available and on a case-by-case basis.[150]

443   The negotiation and adoption in 1998 of the ICC Statute offered States a new opportunity to address the question of the definition or constitutive criteria of a non-international armed conflict – including the question of how protracted the armed confrontations have to be. States adopted one war crime provision reflecting common Article 3, Article 8(2)(c) of the ICC Statute, and one war crime provision listing other serious violations of the laws of war, Article 8(2)(e) of the Statute. With respect to Article 8(2)(c), States restated the scope of application of common Article 3, adding only the clarifying exclusion of internal disturbances and tensions found in Article 1(2) of Additional Protocol II.[151] The scope of application adopted by States for the list of other war crimes under Article 8(2)(e) is contained in Article 8(2)(f) and reads:

> [It] applies to armed conflicts not of an international character and thus does not apply to situations of internal disturbances and tensions, such as riots, isolated and sporadic acts of violence or other acts of a similar nature. It applies to armed conflicts that take place in the territory of a State when there is *protracted armed conflict* between governmental authorities and organized armed groups or between such groups. [Emphasis added.]

444   After the adoption of the ICC Statute, a question was raised whether this provision created a distinct type of non-international armed conflict.[152] Some

---

[149] ICTY, *Haradinaj* Trial Judgment, 2008, para. 49. See, in contrast, an early ICTY judgment, which noted that 'in order to distinguish from cases of civil unrest or terrorist activities, the emphasis is on the protracted extent of the armed violence and the extent of organisation of the parties involved'; see *Delalić* Trial Judgment, 1998, para. 184.
[150] ICTY, *Boškoski and Tarčulovski* Trial Judgment, 2008, para. 175.
[151] See ICC Statute (1998), Article 8(2)(d).
[152] For an overview of the various views, see Vité, pp. 80–83, with further references, and Cullen, pp. 174–185.

interpreted the reference to 'protracted armed conflict' as creating a new, intermediary type of non-international armed conflict, situated between common Article 3 and Additional Protocol II.[153] Others believed that Article 8(2)(f) of the ICC Statute did not envisage a new form of non-international armed conflict as the use of the term 'protracted armed conflict' had served the purpose of preventing the inclusion of the restrictive criteria of Additional Protocol II in the ICC Statute, offering States a compromise formula inspired by the ICTY case law.[154] The first ICC judgments do not endorse the existence of two distinct types of non-international armed conflict under Article 8(2)(c) and (e) of the ICC Statute.[155] To establish the existence of a non-international armed conflict, the Prosecutor has had to prove that armed groups show a sufficient degree of organization to enable them to carry out protracted armed confrontations.[156] These Trial Chambers clearly rejected the requirements for an armed group to have control over part of the territory or to be under responsible command borrowed from Article 1(1) of Additional Protocol II, as applicable under Article 8(2)(e) of the ICC Statute.[157] Furthermore, as Article 8(2)(f) specifies that the violence must not be sporadic or isolated, Trial Chambers have considered the intensity of the armed conflict.[158] In appraising the intensity of a conflict, the ICC has used factors similar to those used by the ICTY Trial Chambers, clearly showing that the intensity of the armed hostilities and the organized character of the armed groups are the two criteria necessarily defining any armed conflict of a non-international character.

iv. Participation of additional armed forces in a pre-existing non-international armed conflict

445 As stated above, multinational or foreign armed forces can become a Party to an armed conflict, whether collectively or as individual States, when they are taking part in a peace operation.[159] When it comes to peace operations in which a non-international armed conflict is occurring, the ICRC is of the view that it is not always necessary to assess whether, on their own, the actions of multinational forces meet the level of intensity required for the existence of a new non-international armed conflict in order for them to become Parties to that conflict. This may be the case, for instance, in situations in which there is a non-international armed conflict between the government of a State and a

---

[153] See e.g. Sassòli/Bouvier/Quintin, Vol. I, p. 123; Condorelli, pp. 112–113; and Bothe, 2002, p. 423.

[154] See e.g. von Hebel/Robinson, pp. 119–120; Meron, 2000, p. 260; and Fleck, p. 588.

[155] See ICC, *Lubanga* Trial Judgment, 2012, paras 534–538, and *Katanga* Trial Judgment, 2014, paras 1183–1187.

[156] See ICC, *Lubanga* Trial Judgment, 2012, para. 536; *Katanga* Trial Judgment, 2014, para. 1185; and *Bemba* Trial Judgment, 2016, paras 134–136.

[157] See ICC, *Lubanga* Trial Judgment, 2012, para. 536; *Katanga* Trial Judgment, 2014, para. 1186; and *Bemba* Trial Judgment, 2016, para. 136.

[158] See, in particular, ICC, *Lubanga* Trial Judgment, 2012, para. 538; *Katanga* Trial Judgment, 2014, para. 1187; and *Bemba* Trial Judgment, 2016, paras 138–140.

[159] See paras 411–413 of this commentary.

non-State armed group and in which foreign forces support the government. Or, it may be the case when multinational forces are already involved in a non-international armed conflict against a non-State armed group and additional foreign forces provide support to the multinational forces. A third scenario might see multinational forces engaged in a non-international armed conflict, with some national contingents providing support short of involvement in the collective conduct of hostilities. In the latter two cases, depending on the function(s) they fulfil, the States sending such forces may also become parties to the non-international armed conflict. This is because that criterion has already been met by the existence of the non-international armed conflict in which they are participating.[160]

446   It is important to emphasize that such an approach to determining who is a Party to a non-international armed conflict complements, but does not replace, the determination of the applicability of humanitarian law on the basis of the criteria of the organization of the Parties and the intensity of the hostilities. Furthermore, not all actions/forms of participation/forms of support would mean that multinational forces would become Parties to a pre-existing non-international armed conflict. The decisive element would be the contribution such forces make to the collective conduct of hostilities. Only activities that have a direct impact on the *opposing* Party's ability to carry out military operations would turn multinational forces into a Party to a pre-existing non-international armed conflict. In contrast, activities such as those that enable the Party that benefits from the participation of the multinational forces to build up its military capacity/capabilities would not lead to the same result. Some concerns about this approach have nevertheless been expressed.[161]

v. Specific purpose as an additional criterion?

447   Another question that may arise is whether, apart from the intensity of the conflict and the organization of the armed group(s), additional criteria come into play in determining whether a situation of violence amounts to a non-international armed conflict, and not merely a case of common criminality, even if it is intense and well organized.

448   In particular, political purpose has been noted as a typical characteristic of non-international armed conflict.[162] The inclusion of certain purposes as a

---

[160] For a description of this approach, see Ferraro, 2013b, especially pp. 583–587.

[161] See the remarks by Marten Zwanenburg and Mona Khalil, in 'Peace Forces at War: Implications Under International Humanitarian Law', in *Proceedings of the 108th Annual Meeting of the American Society of International Law*, April 7–12, 2014, pp. 149–163.

[162] See e.g. Gasser, p. 555:

Non-international armed conflicts are armed confrontations that take place within the territory of a State, that is between the government on the one hand and armed insurgent groups on the other hand. The members of such groups – whether described as insurgents, rebels, revolutionaries, secessionists, freedom fighters, terrorists, or by similar names – *are fighting*

necessary element of non-international armed conflict was discussed during the negotiation of common Article 3. However, States did not adopt the proposals to that effect.[163]

449   Over the years, the purpose of engaging in acts of violence has been explicitly rejected as a criterion for establishing whether or not a situation amounts to a non-international armed conflict. As held by the ICTY,

the determination of the existence of an armed conflict is based solely on two criteria: the intensity of the conflict and organisation of the parties, the purpose of the armed forces to engage in acts of violence or also achieve some further objective is, therefore, irrelevant.[164]

450   It should also be considered that introducing political motivation as a prerequisite for non-international armed conflict could open the door to a variety of other motivation-based reasons for denying the existence of such armed conflicts.[165] Furthermore, in practice it can be difficult to identify the motivations of a non-State armed group. What counts as a political objective, for example, might be controversial; non-political and political motives may co-exist; and non-political activities may in fact be instrumental in achieving ultimately political ends.[166]

> to take over the reins of power, or to obtain greater autonomy within the State, or in order to secede and create their own State.... Another case is the crumbling of all government authority in the country, as a result of which various groups fight each other in the *struggle for power*. [Emphasis added.]

[163] The draft that ultimately became common Article 3 submitted to the International Conference of the Red Cross in Stockholm in 1948 gave specific examples of 'cases of armed conflict which are not of an international character', namely 'cases of civil war, colonial conflicts, or wars of religion'. However, these examples were rejected by the Stockholm Conference, following discussions during which the view prevailed that too much detail risked weakening the provision, as it was impossible to foresee all future circumstances and as the character of a situation is independent of its motives. During the 1949 Diplomatic Conference, the Danish delegation suggested 'to add a criterion to the conditions of application, [specifying] that the word "political armed conflict" should be inserted. This would differentiate between cases of a judicial character and those of a political character'. However, the French delegation responded that it 'did not consider that the adjective "political" was appropriate, because the conflict might be of a religious character or have aspects pertaining to common law. The French Government was prepared to apply the principles contained in the text of the second Working Party, even to bandits'; see *Final Record of the Diplomatic Conference of Geneva of 1949*, Vol. II-B, p. 99. The Danish proposal was not pursued.

[164] See ICTY, *Limaj* Trial Judgment, 2005, para. 170. See also Germany, Federal Prosecutor General at the Federal Court of Justice, *Fuel Tankers case*, Decision to Terminate Proceedings, 2010, p. 33: 'For purposes of classifying armed conflicts involving non-state actors, the political orientation or other motivations of the parties involved are legally irrelevant, as is the manner in which they describe themselves and their actions.' See also Germany, Federal Prosecutor General, *Targeted Killing in Pakistan case*, Decision to Terminate Proceedings, 2013, pp. 741–742.

[165] See ICRC, *International Humanitarian Law and the Challenges of Contemporary Armed Conflicts*, 2011, p. 11.

[166] See e.g. Vité, p. 78, and ICRC, *International Humanitarian Law and the Challenges of Contemporary Armed Conflicts*, 2011, p. 11.

451   In the view of the ICRC, the question of whether a situation of violence amounts to a non-international armed conflict should therefore be answered solely by reliance on the criteria of intensity and organization.[167]

3. Geographical scope of application

a. Introduction

452 Once the existence of a non-international armed conflict has been established based on the character of the Parties involved, as well as on the intensity of the conflict and the organization of the Parties, common Article 3 is applicable. There is some debate, however, as to the geographical scope of application of humanitarian law governing non-international armed conflict as described by common Article 3.

453   Furthermore, when hostilities cross the boundaries of a single State, the question arises as to whether the geographic location of actions affects the classification of the situation as a non-international armed conflict.

454   Owing to developments in practice, these questions have gained considerable prominence, in particular with respect to questions on the use of force. They are, at the time of writing, the subject of ongoing discussion.[168]

b. 'Internal' non-international armed conflicts

455 Traditionally, non-international armed conflicts have predominantly been understood as conflicts occurring within the confines of a single State, in the sense of an 'internal' armed conflict.[169] The applicability of common Article 3 and humanitarian law governing non-international armed conflict more generally to these 'internal' non-international armed conflicts is not controversial.

456   However, the question has arisen as to whether humanitarian law applies in the whole of the territory of the State concerned or only in areas where hostilities are occurring. In areas of a State where hostilities are few and far

---

[167] See ICRC, *International Humanitarian Law and the Challenges of Contemporary Armed Conflicts*, 2011, pp. 11–12. See also Akande, p. 52, with further references, and Moir, 2015, pp. 408–409.

[168] See e.g. Akande; Anderson; Arimatsu; Bartels, 2012; Bianchi, pp. 10–11; Blank; Corn/Jensen; Corn, 2013; Ferraro, 2013a; Koh, pp. 218–220; Kreß; Milanovic/Hadzi-Vidanovic; Pejic, 2011; Radin; Sassòli, 2006; Schmitt; Schöndorf; Sivakumaran, 2012, pp. 228–235 and 250–252; and Vité. See also ILA Committee on the Use of Force, *Final Report on the Meaning of Armed Conflict in International Law* (ILA, *Report of the Seventy-Fourth Conference*, The Hague, 2010), and ILA Study Group on the Conduct of Hostilities (ongoing).

[169] This was the interpretation provided in the Pictet Commentaries: 'conflicts…which…take place within the confines of a single country'; see Pictet (ed.), *Commentary on the Fourth Geneva Convention*, ICRC, 1958, p. 36 (see also *Commentary on the Second Geneva Convention*, 1960, ICRC, p. 33, and *Commentary on the Third Geneva Convention*, ICRC, 1960, p. 37. This statement was not made in the commentary on the First Convention.) See also Gasser, p. 555; *Sanremo Manual on the Law of Non-International Armed Conflict* (2006), para. 1.1.1; and Milanovic, 2007b, pp. 379–393.

between or even non-existent it may seem questionable whether humanitarian law applies. There is concern that humanitarian law, and especially the rules on the conduct of hostilities, should not apply in regions where hostilities are not taking place, even in a State in which an armed conflict is occurring. In the more peaceful regions of such a State, the State's criminal law and law enforcement regimes, within the boundaries set by the applicable international and regional human rights law, may provide a sufficient legal framework.[170]

457   The wording of common Article 3, however, indicates that, once a non-international armed conflict has come into existence, the article applies in the whole of the territory of the State concerned: 'the following acts are and shall remain prohibited at any time and *in any place whatsoever*' (emphasis added).

458   In 1995, in *Tadić*, the ICTY noted the following:

> 67. ... the temporal and geographical scope of both internal and international armed conflicts extends beyond the exact time and place of hostilities. ...
>
> ...
>
> 69. ... beneficiaries of common Article 3 of the Geneva Conventions are those taking no active part (or no longer taking active part) in the hostilities. This indicates that the rules contained in Article 3 also apply outside the narrow geographical context of the actual theatre of combat operations. ...
>
> 70. ... international humanitarian law continues to apply in the whole territory of the warring States or, in the case of internal conflicts, the whole territory under the control of a party, whether or not actual combat takes place there.[171]

459   Once the threshold of a non-international armed conflict has been crossed in a State, the applicability of common Article 3 and other humanitarian law provisions governing non-international armed conflict can therefore generally be seen as extending to the whole of the territory of the State concerned.[172]

460   However, the applicability of humanitarian law in the whole of the territory of a State party to the conflict does not mean that all acts within that territory therefore fall necessarily under the humanitarian law regime. As noted by the ICTY, a particular act must be 'closely related to the hostilities occurring in other parts of the territories controlled by the parties to the conflict' for that act to be committed in the context of the armed conflict

---

[170] Even where humanitarian law applies, a State's domestic law continues to apply, in addition to international human rights law, to the extent that a State has not made a derogation.

[171] ICTY, *Tadić* Decision on the Defence Motion for Interlocutory Appeal on Jurisdiction, 1995, paras 67–70. See further *Delalić* Trial Judgment, 1998, para. 185, and ICTR, *Akayesu* Trial Judgment, 1998, para. 636.

[172] See e.g. Germany, Federal Prosecutor General at the Federal Court of Justice, *Fuel Tankers case*, Decision to Terminate Proceedings, 2010, p. 36: '[T]he the basic objectives of international humanitarian law and the practical impossibility of differentiating in this context tend to support the conclusion that, in principle, a subject of international law such as Afghanistan – including its allies – cannot be involved in a non-international armed conflict except as a territorial whole.' See further David, pp. 261–262, and Kleffner, 2013b, p. 59. For the purposes of humanitarian law, a State's territory includes not only its land surface but also rivers and landlocked lakes, the territorial sea, and the national airspace above this territory.

and for humanitarian law to apply.[173] The applicability of humanitarian law to a specific act therefore requires a certain nexus between that act and the non-international armed conflict. Acts that have no such connection to the conflict generally remain regulated exclusively by domestic criminal and law enforcement regimes, within the boundaries set by applicable international and regional human rights law.[174]

461   Furthermore, if a specific act carried out or taking effect in more peaceful areas of a State could – in line with the considerations addressed above – generally fall under the scope of application of humanitarian law, questions regarding the applicable legal standards in a particular scenario might still arise. It may also need to be determined whether, in a given case, a specific use of force is necessarily governed by conduct of hostilities law or whether it is governed by the law enforcement regime based on human rights law.[175]

462   These issues are the subject of some discussion.[176] In situations of actual hostilities, the use of armed force against lawful targets by the parties to the armed conflict is governed by the humanitarian law rules on the conduct of hostilities.[177] The situation is less clear, however, with regard to the use of force against isolated individuals who would normally be considered lawful targets, under international humanitarian law but who are located in regions under the State's firm and stable control, where no hostilities are taking place and it is not reasonably foreseeable that the adversary could readily receive reinforcement.

463   The law is not yet settled on this issue. However, a number of different legal readings have been advanced, which can be loosely grouped into four approaches. According to one view, the humanitarian law rules on the conduct of hostilities will govern the situation described above, without restraints other than those found in specific rules of humanitarian law.[178] According to the

---

[173] See ICTY, *Tadić* Decision on the Defence Motion for Interlocutory Appeal on Jurisdiction, 1995, para. 70. This interpretation has been followed by the ICC; see ICC, *Katanga* Trial Judgment, 2014, para. 1176, and *Bemba* Trial Judgment, 2016, paras 142–144.

[174] See e.g. ICRC, *The Use of Force in Armed Conflicts*, p. 5: 'In order to be covered by IHL, the use of force must take place in an armed conflict situation and must have a nexus with the armed conflict.' From the perspective of international criminal law, see further e.g. ICTR, *Akayesu* Trial Judgment, 1998, para. 636, and ICTY, *Kunarac* Appeal Judgment, 2002, paras 58–59. This might also include emergency laws.

[175] For a detailed discussion, with further references, see ICRC, *The Use of Force in Armed Conflicts*, pp. 13–23, addressing the example of the use of force against legitimate targets during armed conflict.

[176] See expert meetings on the notion of direct participation in hostilities under humanitarian law and on the use of force in armed conflicts. For details, see ICRC, *Interpretive Guidance* and *The Use of Force in Armed Conflicts*.

[177] The question of who or what is a lawful target is a separate issue. For details, see the commentary on Article 13 of Additional Protocol II. For persons, the position of the ICRC is set out in *Interpretive Guidance*.

[178] Under this view, while the principles of military necessity and humanity inform the entire body of humanitarian law, they do not create obligations above and beyond specific rules of humanitarian law. See e.g. W. Hays Parks, 'Part IX of the ICRC "Direct Participation in

second view, the use of force in that scenario is be governed by Recommendation IX of the ICRC's Interpretive Guidance on the Notion of Direct Participation in Hostilities under International Humanitarian Law.[179] That Recommendation in conjunction with its commentary states that in the more peaceful areas of a State, the 'kind and degree of force which is permissible against persons not entitled to protection against direct attack must not exceed what is actually necessary to accomplish a legitimate military purpose in the prevailing circumstances'.[180] Yet another view holds that the applicable legal framework for each situation will need to be determined on a case-by-case basis, weighing all of the circumstances.[181] Lastly, there is the view that in such circumstances, the use of force would be governed by the rules on law enforcement based on human rights law.[182]

464   It may be observed that the application of any of the last three approaches may be likely to lead to similar results in practice.

c. Non-international armed conflict not confined to the territory of one State

465 As noted above, traditionally non-international armed conflicts have predominantly been understood as armed conflicts against or between non-State armed groups within the confines of a State, in the sense of an 'internal' armed

---

Hostilities" Study: No Mandate, No Expertise, and Legally Incorrect', *N.Y.U. Journal of International Law and Politics*, Vol. 42, 2009–2010, pp. 769–830.

[179]   In 2009, the ICRC published the *Interpretive Guidance on the Notion of Direct Participation in Hostilities under International Humanitarian Law*, which addressed the use of force from the perspective of humanitarian law only, without prejudice to other bodies of law – particularly human rights law – that may concurrently be applicable in a given situation.

[180]   The full text of Recommendation IX reads:

> In addition to the restraints imposed by international humanitarian law on specific means and methods of warfare, and without prejudice to further restrictions that may arise under other applicable branches of international law, the kind and degree of force which is permissible against persons not entitled to protection against direct attack must not exceed what is actually necessary to accomplish a legitimate military purpose in the prevailing circumstances.

> Under this view, the fundamental principles of military necessity and humanity reduce the sum total of permissible military action from that which humanitarian law does not expressly prohibit to that which is actually necessary for the accomplishment of a legitimate military purpose in the prevailing circumstances; ICRC, *Interpretive Guidance*, pp. 77–82. It is acknowledged that, at the time of writing, this interpretation is not universally shared. See e.g. 'Forum: The ICRC Interpretive Guidance on the Notion of Direct Participation in Hostilities Under International Humanitarian Law', *New York University Journal of International Law and Politics*, Vol. 42, No. 3, 2010, pp. 637–916.

[181]   Marco Sassòli and Laura Olson, 'The relationship between international humanitarian and human rights law where it matters: admissible killing and internment of fighters in non-international armed conflicts', *International Review of the Red Cross*, Vol. 90, No. 871, September 2008, pp. 599–627, at 603–605. See also ICRC, *The Use of Force in Armed Conflicts*, pp. 20–21.

[182]   Charles Garraway, 'Armed Conflict and Law Enforcement: Is There a Legal Divide?, in Mariëlle Matthee, Brigit Toebes and Marcel Brus (eds), *Armed Conflict and International Law: In Search of the Human Face, Liber Amicorum in Memory of Avril McDonald*, Asser Press, The Hague, 2013, pp. 259–283, at 282.

conflict.[183] However, that raises the question of whether the limitation to the territory of one State is a requirement for a non-international armed conflict in the sense of common Article 3.

466   At first sight, the wording of common Article 3 requires such a limitation: not only does it speak of armed conflicts 'not of an international character',[184] but it also requires armed conflicts to occur 'in the territory of one of the High Contracting Parties'. One reading of this phrase could be that the conflict must occur in the territory of precisely 'one' of the High Contracting Parties, thereby limiting the application of common Article 3 to 'internal' armed conflicts. However, another reading could put the emphasis on the fact that the conflict must occur in the territory of one of the 'High Contracting Parties', thereby merely excluding conflicts which occur on the territory of a State not party to the Geneva Conventions.[185] Common Article 2 likewise contains a reference to the States party to the Geneva Conventions. Viewed in this context, the reference to 'High Contracting Parties' in both articles may have been included to avoid any misunderstanding to the effect that the 1949 Geneva Conventions would create new obligations for States not party to them.

467   The object and purpose of common Article 3 supports its applicability in non-international armed conflict reaching beyond the territory of one State. Given that its aim is to provide persons not or no longer actively participating in hostilities with certain minimum protections during intense armed confrontations between States and non-State armed groups or between such groups, it is logical that those same protections would apply when such violence spans the territory of more than one State.[186]

468   It is true, however, that when common Article 3 is applicable, other rules, especially those on the conduct of hostilities, with different restraints on the way force may be used compared to peacetime law, may also apply. It must be recalled that it is not the applicability of common Article 3 to a situation that makes other rules of humanitarian law governing non-international armed conflicts applicable. Rather, it is the existence of a non-international armed conflict which makes common Article 3 and other humanitarian law provisions applicable.[187] Viewed in this light, it may be consistent with the purpose of common Article 3 for it to apply to non-international armed conflicts that are not confined to the territory of a single State.

---

[183] See para. 455 of this commentary.

[184] Which can, but not necessarily must, be understood primarily as a reference to the State or non-State character of the Parties to a potential non-international armed conflict; see section C.2.b.

[185] See, in this sense, e.g. Sassòli, 2006, p. 9. Viewed in this context, the reference to 'High Contracting Parties' in both articles may have been included to avoid any misunderstanding to the effect that the 1949 Geneva Conventions would create new obligations for States not party to them.

[186] See, in this sense, e.g. Sassòli, 2006, p. 9.

[187] In this respect, it must be recalled that common Article 3 does not define non-international armed conflict; it merely indicates those armed conflicts to which it applies.

469   In so far as the above analysis leaves doubt as to whether common Article 3 is limited to internal armed conflicts,[188] the drafting history of the article can be consulted for clarification. At one point, States considered a draft which referred to armed conflicts 'which may occur in the territory of one *or more* of the High Contracting Parties' (emphasis added).[189] For unspecified reasons, the additional phrase 'or more' was not adopted by the 1949 Diplomatic Conference, such that no conclusion can be drawn from its absence for the interpretation of common Article 3.[190] In the 1940s, it seems that States predominantly had the regulation of internal armed conflicts in mind. The protection of their domestic affairs against comprehensive regulation by international law was one of their main concerns and motivators for limiting the substantive provisions applicable to non-international armed conflicts.[191] However, if the wording of common Article 3 'meant that conflicts opposing states and organized armed groups and spreading over the territory of several states were not "non-international armed conflicts", there would be a gap in protection, which could not be explained by states' concerns about their sovereignty'.[192]

470   In sum, while the text and drafting history are somewhat ambiguous, the object and purpose of common Article 3 suggests that it applies in non-international armed conflicts that cross borders.

471   At the time of writing, there is some evidence of practice by States party to the Geneva Conventions that supports the view that non-international armed conflicts may occur across State borders in certain, limited circumstances.[193]

472   Non-international armed conflicts with an extraterritorial aspect have been described variously as 'cross-border' conflicts, 'spillover' conflicts and 'transnational armed conflicts'. Other terms, such as 'extraterritorial non-international

---

[188] State practice is examined below, paras 473–478.

[189] See *Draft Conventions submitted to the 1948 Stockholm Conference* and *Draft Conventions adopted by the 1948 Stockholm Conference*, p. 10; see also section B.

[190] For a detailed history, see Katja Schöberl, 'The Geographical Scope of Application of the Conventions', in Andrew Clapham, Paola Gaeta and Marco Sassòli (eds), *The 1949 Geneva Conventions: A Commentary*, Oxford University Press, 2015, pp. 67–83, at 79–82.

[191] See e.g. *Final Record of the Diplomatic Conference of Geneva of 1949*, Vol. II-B, pp. 10–15; see also section B.

[192] Marco Sassòli, 'Transnational Armed Groups and International Humanitarian Law' *HPCR Occasional Paper Series*, Winter 2006, p. 9.

[193] See United States, Supreme Court, *Hamdan case*, Judgment, 2006, pp. 66–67. Germany's Military Manual notes that a non-international armed conflict is a confrontation that is 'normally' carried out within the territory of a State; while emphasizing the typically internal character of non-international armed conflict, this wording also seems to allow for situations where this is not the case; see *Military Manual*, 2013, p. 186, para. 1301. See also Netherlands, Advisory Committee on Issues of Public International Law, *Advisory Report on Armed Drones*, Advisory Report No. 23, The Hague, July 2013, p. 3 ('In non-international armed conflicts between one or more states and one or more organised armed groups, or between such groups, in principle IHL applies only to the territory of the state where the conflict is taking place.'), and United States, *Law of War Manual*, 2015, section 3.3.1: '[T]wo non-State armed groups warring against one another or States warring against non-State armed groups may be described as "non-international armed conflict," even if international borders are crossed in the fighting.'

armed conflicts' have also been used.[194] These are not legal categories or terms, but they may be useful for descriptive purposes.

473   One type of armed conflict not confined to the borders of a single State that States appear to have accepted as 'non-international' in practice occurs when a State fighting an armed group on its territory is joined by one or more other States. Although such a conflict may occur within the territory of one State, other States use force extraterritorially, i.e. outside their own territory, as Parties to the conflict. In such cases, the conflict remains non-international in nature.[195] The question of the extent of the applicability of common Article 3 and humanitarian law more generally has become pertinent in such situations, particularly where the territory of that State is sub-divided into areas of responsibility of the various intervening foreign States, with some areas experiencing more intense fighting than others. In such situations, humanitarian law applies in the same manner in regard to all participating States as in a purely 'internal' non-international armed conflict as outlined above.[196] Further questions have arisen in respect to whether international law also applies on the 'home' territory of States party to such conflicts.[197] At the time of writing, there is insufficient identifiable State practice on its applicability in the territory of the home State.

474   Second, an existing non-international armed conflict may spill over from the territory of the State in which it began into the territory of a neighbouring State not party to the conflict.[198] These are sometimes called 'spillover'

---

[194] See Vité, p. 89.

[195] See paras 402–405 of this commentary. This is without prejudice to whether a separate international armed conflict exists between the territorial government and the States concerned; for details see the commentary on common Article 2, paras 257–264.

[196] The conflict in Afghanistan after 2002 is widely considered to be an example of a non-international armed conflict in which a number of States participate extraterritorially.

[197] See e.g. Schmitt, pp. 10–11.

[198] See Germany, Federal Prosecutor General at the Federal Court of Justice, *Targeted Killing in Pakistan case*, Decision to Terminate Proceedings, 2013, p. 742: 'the Afghan Taliban's use of the FATA region as a haven and staging area has evidently caused the Afghan conflict to "spill over" onto this particular part of Pakistan's national territory.' See also p. 723:

> At the time of the drone strike [4 October 2010], there existed at least two separate non-international armed conflicts. One was between the government of Pakistan and non-State armed groups operating in the FATAs (including Al Qaeda). Another one was between the Afghan Taliban and affiliated groups and the government of Afghanistan, as supported by ISAF forces, a conflict which spilled over into the territory of Pakistan.

> Netherlands, Advisory Committee on Issues of Public International Law, *Advisory Report on Armed Drones*, Advisory Report No. 23, The Hague, July 2013, p. 3: 'The applicability of IHL may be extended if the conflict spills over into another state in cases where some or all of the armed forces of one of the warring parties move into the territory of another – usually neighbouring – state and continue hostilities from there.' Further examples of conflicts which have been considered to spill over into the territory of another State are given in Milanovic, 2015, paras 52, 56 and 58 (citing spillovers from the Democratic Republic of the Congo into neighbouring countries; incursions of Ogaden militias from Ethiopia and Al-Shebab militias from Somalia into Kenya; Kurds into Turkey and Iran; and by Colombian armed forces and the Revolutionary Armed Forces of Colombia (FARC) into Ecuador. Melzer, pp. 259–260, cites, among others, Sudan giving consent to Uganda to conduct operations on its territory against

non-international armed conflicts, although this is only a descriptive term and not a legal term of art. Assuming, for the purpose of this analysis, that the second State consents to the use of its territory by the State party to the conflict, thereby precluding the existence of an international armed conflict between the two States, the question arises as to whether the relations between the first State and the non-State party to the conflict continue to be regulated by humanitarian law governing non-international armed conflicts when the Parties are operating in the territory of the second, neighbouring State.[199] This could be the case if the armed violence between them, on the territory of the second State, in itself meets the criteria of a non-international armed conflict, i.e. intensity and organization. But where this is not the case, and when only occasional or sporadic acts of hostilities take place there, one may wonder whether this occasional 'spillover' can be linked to the existing non-international armed conflict in the first State, as a mere continuation of that conflict.[200] In such cases, State practice seems to indicate that the crossing of an international border does not change the non-international character of the armed conflict.[201] The examples of State practice in relation to 'spillover' conflicts all relate to situations in which the conflict has spilled over from one territory into a neighbouring or adjacent territory.

475   The existence of such situations also seems to be acknowledged in the 1994 ICTR Statute, which describes the jurisdiction of the Tribunal as extending to the prosecution of 'Persons Responsible for Genocide and Other Serious Violations of International Humanitarian Law Committed in the Territory of Rwanda and Rwandan Citizens responsible for genocide and other such violations *committed in the territory of neighbouring States*' (emphasis added).[202]

---

the Lord's Resistance Army; South African operations in Botswana, Mozambique and Zimbabwe against the African National Congress; and the spillover of the Vietnam conflict into Cambodia.

[199] This question may also arise when the second State does not give its consent. In that case an international and a non-international armed conflict may exist concurrently.

[200] As the ICTY has noted, individual acts that are 'closely related' to confrontations carried out in other parts of the territory of a State can be linked to that non-international armed conflict; see *Tadić* Decision on the Defence Motion for Interlocutory Appeal on Jurisdiction, 1995, para. 70. It has been suggested that the same consideration could apply in spillover situations; see Milanovic/Hadzi-Vidanovic, pp. 290–291.

[201] See the practice listed in fn. 198. See also ICRC, *International Humanitarian Law and the Challenges of Contemporary Armed Conflicts*, 2011, pp. 9–10, noting:

> [I]t is submitted that the relations between parties whose conflict has spilled over remain at a minimum governed by Common Article 3 and customary IHL [international humanitarian law]. This position is based on the understanding that the spill over of a NIAC [non-international armed conflict] into adjacent territory cannot have the effect of absolving the parties of their IHL obligations simply because an international border has been crossed. The ensuing legal vacuum would deprive of protection both civilians possibly affected by the fighting, as well as persons who fall into enemy hands.

[202] ICTR Statute (1994), Title and Preamble. But see ICTR, *Musema* Trial Judgment, 2000, para. 248: 'The expression "armed conflicts" introduces a material criterion:... Within these

476   Questions remain, however, as to how far into a neighbouring country an existing non-international armed conflict can be seen as 'spilling over'. Put another way, it is not yet clear whether humanitarian law would be applicable throughout the territory of the State into which the conflict has spilled over (as in the case of classic 'internal' armed conflicts), or whether its application is more limited.[203] As long as the State into whose territory the conflict has spilled does not become a Party to the conflict, there is reason to doubt that it applies throughout its whole territory.[204] Practice has not yet established a clear rule, although different legal theories have been put forward.[205] In addition, the question arises as to whether, depending on geographical circumstances or technical abilities, the 'spilling over' of an existing non-international armed conflict is limited to neighbouring countries. This last scenario will be addressed below.

477   A third scenario of a non-international armed conflict not limited to the territory of one State is that of armed confrontations, meeting the requisite intensity threshold, between a State and a non-State armed group which operates from the territory of a second, neighbouring State.[206] The armed confrontations could also be between two organized non-State armed groups. In such a scenario, the confrontations are of a 'cross border' nature. If the non-State armed group acts on behalf of the second State, an international armed conflict may exist because in that case the confrontation would in fact be between two States.[207] However, if the non-State armed group does not act on behalf of the second State, it is conceivable that the confrontation between the first State and the non-State armed group should be regarded as a non-international armed conflict.[208] In such a situation, an international armed conflict between the first and the second State could also occur if the second State does not consent to the operations of the first State in its territory.[209] Thus, there may be a non-international armed conflict, in parallel to an international armed conflict between the States concerned.

---

limits, non-international armed conflicts are situations in which hostilities break out between armed forces or organized armed groups *within the territory of a single State*' (emphasis added).

[203] Schöberl, p. 82; Lubell/Derejko, p. 78.

[204] ICTY, *Tadić* Decision on the Defence Motion for Interlocutory Appeal on Jurisdiction, 1995, para. 70 (humanitarian law applies to the whole of the territory under the control of one of the Parties).

[205] For example, limiting the applicability of humanitarian law only to people, places and objects with a nexus to the armed conflict. See e.g. Milanovic/Hadzi-Vidanovic, pp. 307–308; Lubell/Derejko, pp. 75–76; ICRC, *International Humanitarian Law and the Challenges of Contemporary Armed Conflicts*, 2015, p. 15, fn. 13.

[206] For discussions, see e.g. the literature noted in fn. 168.

[207] See paras 406–410 and the commentary on common Article 2, paras 265–273.

[208] See, in this respect, ICRC, *International Humanitarian Law and the Challenges of Contemporary Armed Conflicts*, 2011, p. 10, noting: 'Such a scenario was hardly imaginable when Common Article 3 was drafted and yet it is submitted that this Article, as well as customary IHL, were the appropriate legal framework for that parallel track, in addition to the application of the law of IAC [international armed conflict] between the two states.'

[209] For details, see the commentary on common Article 2, paras 257–264.

478   Lastly, the question arises as to whether geographical considerations could play a minimal role with respect to non-international armed conflicts.[210] For example, the question has arisen whether a non-international armed conflict between a non-State armed group and a State could exist, with or without having an anchor in a particular State as the primary or key theatre of hostilities. There are two possible scenarios. The first is the situation of an extended spillover conflict described above. In this scenario, the intensity and organization are sufficient for a conflict to arise and be classified as such in the primary theatre of hostilities and the only question remaining is how far the spillover may stretch. A second scenario considers the possibility of a conflict arising solely on the basis of the actions of a non-State armed group but where hostilities and the members of the armed group are in geographically disparate locations. In that scenario, the main question is whether it is possible to assess far-flung hostilities as a whole so as to conclude that there is one armed conflict between a non-State armed group and a State. Thus, while not abandoning the criteria of organization and intensity required for a non-international armed conflict to exist, this approach would accept that acts that may seem sporadic or isolated within the confines of each State in which they occur may be considered cumulatively as amounting to a non-international armed conflict.

479   The assumption of such a global or transnational non-international armed conflict could make humanitarian law applicable in the territory of a State not involved in the confrontation between the Parties to such a conflict, where otherwise domestic law, including criminal law and law enforcement rules on the use of force, within the boundaries of applicable human rights law, would apply exclusively.

480   This scenario raises important protection concerns. It would mean, for example, that when a Party to such a global or transnational non-international armed conflict attacks an individual fighter of the opposing Party in the territory of another State not involved in the conflict, the population of that State could be subject to the application of humanitarian law standards on the use of force. Under humanitarian law, for example, only attacks on military targets which may be expected to cause incidental loss of civilian life that would be excessive in relation to the concrete and direct military advantage anticipated would be unlawful. This would mean that, depending on the circumstances, a certain amount of 'collateral damage' among the civilian population of a State not involved in the confrontation between the Parties to the global or transnational non-international armed conflict might not be unlawful. This would considerably diminish the protection of this population under international law.

481   However, as indicated above, even if humanitarian law were to be considered applicable in such a scenario, it would not necessarily mean that all actions in such a case were governed by that law.[211]

---

[210] For discussions, see e.g. the literature noted in fn. 168.
[211] See paras 460–463 of this commentary.

482   In addition, the practice of States party to the Geneva Conventions in support of a global or transnational non-international armed conflicts remains isolated.[212] The ICRC has thus expressed the view that the existence of an armed conflict or the relationship of a particular military operation to an existing armed conflict has to be assessed on a case-by-case basis.[213]

4. Temporal scope of application

a. Introduction

483   Common Article 3 applies to armed conflicts not of an international character that are 'occurring' in the territory of one of the High Contracting Parties. No guidance is given in common Article 3 on when such an armed conflict is to be regarded as 'occurring'. Unlike the Geneva Conventions in their application to international armed conflicts,[214] or indeed Additional Protocol I[215] and Additional Protocol II,[216] common Article 3 contains no specific provision whatsoever on its temporal scope of application.

b. The beginning of a non-international armed conflict

484   With respect to the beginning of the applicability of common Article 3, no specific provision is necessary: common Article 3 becomes applicable as soon as a non-international armed conflict comes into existence, in line with the

---

[212] See e.g. United States, Remarks by President Obama at the National Defense University, 23 May 2013: 'Under domestic law, and international law, the United States is at war with al Qaeda, the Taliban, and their associated forces.' See also e.g. US Department of Justice, Office of Legal Counsel, Memorandum for the Attorney General Re: Applicability of Federal Criminal Laws and the Constitution to Contemplated Lethal Operations Against Shaykh Anwar al-Aulaqi, 16 July 2010, released publicly on 23 June 2014, p. 24: '...would make the DoD [Department of Defense] operation in Yemen part of the non-international armed conflict with al-Qaida'. Compare also United States, Supreme Court, *Hamdan case*, Judgment, 2006, pp. 66–67. For the question of whether the US Supreme Court considered the non-international armed conflict it affirmed in that decision to be of a global character, see e.g. Milanovic, 2007b, pp. 378–379, with further references. But see Germany, Federal Prosecutor General at the Federal Court of Justice, *Targeted Killing in Pakistan case*, Decision to Terminate Proceedings, 2013, p. 745, according to which 'a determination that an armed conflict exists will be valid only where it is made with respect to a specific territorial extent and duration of time'.

[213] See ICRC, *International Humanitarian Law and the Challenges of Contemporary Armed Conflicts*, 2011, p. 10, and, for the specific context of multinational forces intervening within the framework of an international organization, pp. 10–11.

[214] See First Convention, Article 5; Third Convention, Article 5(1); and Fourth Convention, Article 6.

[215] See Additional Protocol I, Article 3.

[216] See Additional Protocol II, Article 2(2):

> At the end of the armed conflict, all the persons who have been deprived of their liberty or whose liberty has been restricted for reasons related to such conflict, as well as those deprived of their liberty or whose liberty is restricted after the conflict for the same reasons, shall enjoy the protection of Articles 5 and 6 until the end of such deprivation or restriction of liberty.

analysis in the sections above, i.e. as soon as the criteria of intensity and organization are fulfilled in a situation of violence between a State and a non-State armed group or between two or more non-State armed groups.

c. The end of a non-international armed conflict

485 As with the beginning of a non-international armed conflict, determining when a conflict ends has important consequences. Therefore, as with the initial existence of a non-international armed conflict, its end must be neither lightly asserted nor denied: just as humanitarian law is not to be applied to a situation of violence that has not crossed the threshold of a non-international armed conflict, it must also not be applied to situations that no longer constitute a non-international armed conflict.

486 The ICTY has held that '[i]nternational humanitarian law applies from the initiation of [a non-international armed conflict] and extends beyond the cessation of hostilities until . . . in the case of internal conflicts, a peaceful settlement is achieved'.[217] This approach has subsequently been affirmed in international case law and restated in other national and international sources.[218]

487 It is necessary to rely on the facts when assessing whether a non-international armed conflict has come to an end, or, in other words, a 'peaceful settlement' has been reached.[219] This approach not only reflects the purely fact-based assessment of the beginning of a non-international armed conflict,[220] but is also in line with modern humanitarian law more generally, for whose applicability formal requirements are not decisive.[221]

488 An assessment of the facts to determine whether a non-international armed conflict has come to an end should take into account the following:

489 First, a non-international armed conflict can cease by the mere fact that one of the Parties ceases to exist. A complete military defeat of one of the Parties,

---

[217] ICTY, *Tadić* Decision on the Defence Motion for Interlocutory Appeal on Jurisdiction, 1995, para. 70.

[218] See e.g. ICTY, *Haradinaj* Trial Judgment, 2008, para. 100; ICTR, *Akayesu* Trial Judgment, 1998, para. 619; *Rutaganda* Trial Judgment, 1999, para. 92; and ICC, *Lubanga* Trial Judgment, 2012, paras 533 and 548. It has also been reflected in State practice; see e.g. United Kingdom, *Manual of the Law of Armed Conflict*, 2004, para. 15.3.1; Council of the European Union, Independent International Fact-Finding Mission on the Conflict in Georgia, *Report*, Vol. II, 2009, pp. 299–300; Colombia, Constitutional Court, *Constitutional Case No. C-291-07*, Judgment, 2007, para. 1.2.1. For a discussion of the notion of 'peaceful settlement', see e.g. Jean-François Quéguiner, 'Dix ans après la création du Tribunal pénal international pour l'ex-Yougoslavie: évaluation de l'apport de sa jurisprudence au droit international humanitaire', *Revue internationale de la Croix-Rouge*, Vol. 85, No. 850, June 2003, pp. 271–311, at 282–283.

[219] See ICTY, *Boškoski and Tarčulovski* Trial Judgment, 2008, para. 293. See e.g. David, pp. 267–268, generally for the end of application of humanitarian law where there are no specific provisions. See also Kolb/Hyde, p. 102, for both international and non-international armed conflicts, as well as Sivakumaran, 2012, pp. 253–254.

[220] See section C.2.

[221] See the inclusion in common Article 2 of the concept of 'other armed conflict' in addition to the traditional formal concept of 'declared war'. For details, see the commentary on common Article 2, paras 201–202.

the demobilization of a non-State Party, or any other dissolution of a Party means that the armed conflict has come to an end, even if there are isolated or sporadic acts of violence by remnants of the dissolved Party. When, however, a Party has suffered a lesser degree of defeat and is in some disarray, it may still regroup, even over a lengthy period of time, and carry on the hostilities. This may especially be the case where a non-State armed group controls territory or continues to recruit, train and arm forces. In such cases, it is not possible to conclude that the Party has ceased to exist.

490   Second, armed confrontations sometimes continue well beyond the conclusion or unilateral pronouncement of a formal act such as a ceasefire, armistice or peace agreement. Relying solely on the existence of such agreements to determine the end of a non-international armed conflict could therefore lead to a premature end of the applicability of humanitarian law in situations when in fact a conflict continues.[222] Conversely, armed confrontations may also dissipate without any ceasefire, armistice or peace agreement ever being concluded, or before the conclusion of such an agreement. Thus, while the existence of such agreements may be taken into account when assessing all of the facts, they are neither necessary nor sufficient on their own to bring about the termination of the application of humanitarian law.

491   Third, a lasting cessation of armed confrontations without real risk of resumption will undoubtedly constitute the end of a non-international armed conflict as it would equate to a peaceful settlement of the conflict, even without the conclusion or unilateral pronouncement of a formal act such as a ceasefire, armistice or peace agreement.

492   Fourth, a temporary lull in the armed confrontations must not be taken as automatically ending the non-international armed conflict. The intensity of a conflict might 'oscillate',[223] but, without more, periods of calm while the Parties to the conflict continue to exist are not sufficient to conclude that a conflict has come to an end. It is impossible to state in the abstract how much time without armed confrontations needs to pass to be able conclude with an acceptable degree of certainty that the situation has stabilized and equates to a peaceful settlement. A Party may, for instance, decide to temporarily suspend hostilities, or the historical pattern of the conflict may be an alternation between cessation and resumption of armed confrontations. In such cases, it is not yet possible to conclude that a situation has stabilized, and a longer period of observation will be necessary. In the meantime, humanitarian law will continue to apply.

---

[222] See e.g. ICTY, *Boškoski and Tarčulovski* Trial Judgment, 2008, para. 293. See also the practical application, in para. 294: '[T]he temporal scope of the armed conflict covered and extended beyond 12 August and the Ohrid Framework Agreement of 13 August to at least the end of that month.'

[223] ICTY, *Haradinaj* Trial Judgment, 2008, para. 100.

493   The classification of a conflict must not be a 'revolving door between applicability and non-applicability' of humanitarian law, as this can 'lead[] to a considerable degree of legal uncertainty and confusion'.[224] An assessment based on the factual circumstances therefore needs to take into account the often fluctuating nature of conflicts to avoid prematurely concluding that a non-international armed conflict has come to an end.

494   In this regard, it is not possible to conclude that a non-international armed conflict has ended solely on the grounds that the armed confrontations between the Parties have fallen below the intensity required for a conflict to exist in the first place.[225] However, the lasting absence of armed confrontations between the original Parties to the conflict may indicate – depending on the prevailing facts – the end of that non-international armed conflict, even though there might still be minor isolated or sporadic acts of violence.

495   Examples of elements that may indicate that a situation has sufficiently stabilized to consider that a non-international armed conflict has ended include: the effective implementation of a peace agreement or ceasefire; declarations by the Parties, not contradicted by the facts on the ground, that they definitely renounce all violence; the dismantling of government special units created for the conflict; the implementation of disarmament, demobilization and/or reintegration programmes; the increasing duration of the period without hostilities; and the lifting of a state of emergency or other restrictive measures.

496   A determination as to whether a situation has stabilized to such a degree and for such a time to constitute a 'peaceful settlement' of the conflict can thus only be made via a full appraisal of all the available facts. Obviously, such predictions can never be made with absolute certainty. It is not a perfect science. In this light, in the view of the ICRC, it is preferable not to be too hasty and thereby risk a 'revolving door' classification of a conflict which might lead to legal uncertainty and confusion.

d. Continuing application of common Article 3 after the end of a non-international armed conflict

497   The question arises as to whether, despite the end of a non-international armed conflict, there are certain aspects of common Article 3 that, if necessary, may continue to apply after the end of the non-international armed conflict. Common Article 3 contains no indications in this respect.

---

[224] ICTY, *Gotovina* Trial Judgment, 2011, para. 1694.

[225] For a discussion, see Marko Milanovic, 'End of application of international humanitarian law', *International Review of the Red Cross*, Vol. 96, No. 893, March 2014, pp. 163–188, at 178–181. See also Bartels, 2014, pp. 303 and 309, and Grignon, pp. 270–275, who emphasizes a global end of armed conflict, comparable to the notion of general close of military operations in international armed conflicts, as decisive for the end of a non-international armed conflict. For a similar view in the context of multinational operations, see Ferraro, 2013, p. 607, and Sivakumaran, 2012, pp. 253–254. See also Kolb/Hyde, p. 102, and Sassòli/Bouvier/Quintin, Vol. I, p. 135, paraphrasing ICTY, *Haradinaj* Trial Judgment, 2008, para. 100.

498   However, as early as 1962, the Commission of Experts convened by the ICRC to study the question of humanitarian aid to victims of internal conflicts noted:

The Commission also examined the extent of the application of article 3 in the past. The settling of an internal conflict, dependent on article 3, does not put an end, by itself and of full right, to the application of that article, whatever the form or the conditions of this settlement may be, whether the legal government re-establishes order itself, whether it disappears in favour of a government formed by its adversaries, or whether it concludes an agreement with the other party. The Commission pointed out that the obligations described in article 3 should be respected 'in all circumstances... at all times and in all places'. The Commission therefore considers that *the provisions of article 3 remain applicable to situations arising from the conflict and to the participants in that conflict*.[226] [Emphasis added.]

499   In 1977, States adopted the following provision in the context of Additional Protocol II:

At the end of the armed conflict, all the persons who have been deprived of their liberty or whose liberty has been restricted for reasons related to such conflict, as well as those deprived of their liberty or whose liberty is restricted after the conflict for the same reasons, shall enjoy the protection of Articles 5 and 6 until the end of such deprivation or restriction of liberty.[227]

500   The guarantees of common Article 3 – binding State and non-State Parties alike – can be of vital importance for the victims of a non-international armed conflict even after the conflict as such has come to an end.

501   Persons protected under common Article 3, even after the end of a non-international armed conflict, continue to benefit from the article's protection as long as, in consequence of the armed conflict, they are in a situation for which common Article 3 provides protection. Thus, for example, persons who have been detained in connection with the conflict should, after the end of the conflict, continue to be treated humanely, including not being subjected to torture or cruel treatment or being denied a fair trial.[228]

---

[226] See ICRC, "Humanitarian aid to the victims of internal conflicts. Meeting of a Commission of Experts in Geneva, 25–30 October 1962, Report', *International Review of the Red Cross*, Vol. 3, No. 23, February 1963, pp. 79–91, at 83. See also Sassòli/Bouvier/Quintin, Vol. I, p. 136, and David, p. 265.

[227] Additional Protocol II, Article 2(2). Articles 5 and 6 of the Protocol provide protections for persons deprived of their liberty for reasons related to the armed conflict and during penal prosecutions. For details, see the commentaries on Articles 1, 5 and 6 of Additional Protocol II. For international armed conflict, compare also Article 5 of the First Convention, Article 5(1) of the Third Convention and Article 6(3) of the Fourth Convention, as well as Article 3(b) of Additional Protocol I.

[228] Article 2(2) of Additional Protocol II does not limit the continuing protection of its Articles 5 and 6 after the end of the conflict to deprivations or restrictions of liberty for reasons related to the conflict *during* the conflict, but grants it also for deprivations or restrictions of liberty for reasons related to the conflict *after* the conflict. Parties to a non-international armed conflict in the sense of common Article 3 that has come to an end may also want to consider granting such broad continuing protections under common Article 3.

502   In so far as the return to the normal domestic and international legal framework after the end of a non-international armed conflict would provide persons
protected under common Article 3 with more favourable protections than common Article 3, such protections must, of course, be applied.[229]

D. Paragraph 1: Binding force of common Article 3

1. 'each Party to the conflict shall be bound to apply'

a. General

503 Once a non-international armed conflict in the sense of common Article 3 has
come into existence, common Article 3 categorically states that 'each Party to
the conflict shall be bound to apply' the fundamental provisions of the article.

504   This simple but unequivocal provision is an important achievement. As soon
as common Article 3 applies, the obligation to respect its provisions is automatic and absolute for State and non-State Parties to the conflict alike. That
obligation is not only independent of an express acceptance of common Article 3 by the non-State Party, but also of whether an opposing Party in practice adheres to the provisions of common Article 3.[230] Furthermore, common
Article 3 is based on the principle of equality of the Parties to the conflict.
It grants the same rights and imposes the same obligations on both the State
and the non-State Party, all of which are of a purely humanitarian character.[231]
This does not, however, imply combatant immunity for members of non-State
armed groups as this concept is not as such applicable in non-international
armed conflicts.

b. Binding force of common Article 3 on non-State armed groups

505 Non-State armed groups are not 'High Contracting Parties' to the Geneva Conventions. In 1949, States decided that non-State entities could not become party
to the Geneva Conventions. Nevertheless, it is today accepted that common
Article 3 is binding on non-State armed groups, both as treaty and customary
law.[232]

506   The wording of common Article 3, which differentiates between 'High Contracting Parties' and Parties to the conflict, clearly supports this: 'In the case
of armed conflict not of an international character occurring in the territory of

---

[229] See e.g. David, p. 268.   [230] See also section F.1.c.
[231] Sandoz/Swinarski/Zimmermann (eds), *Commentary on the Additional Protocols*, ICRC, 1987,
para. 4442. See also Sivakumaran, 2012, pp. 242–244; Bugnion, 2003b, p. 167; and Christopher
Greenwood, 'The relationship between *ius ad bellum* and *ius in bello*', *Review of International
Studies*, Vol. 9, No. 4, 1983, pp. 221–234, at 221.
[232] For the customary law status of common Article 3, see e.g. ICJ, *Military and Paramilitary
Activities in and against Nicaragua case*, Merits, Judgment, 1986, paras 218–219; ICTY, *Tadić
Decision on the Defence Motion on Jurisdiction*, 1995, para. 98; *Naletilić and Martinović* Trial
Judgment, 2003, para. 228; and ICTR, *Akayesu* Trial Judgment, 1998, paras 608–609.

one of the *High Contracting Parties, each Party to the conflict* shall be bound to apply ...' (emphasis added). During the negotiation of common Article 3, an amendment proposing a reference to the High Contracting Parties also in the second part of the sentence was rejected.[233]

507   The exact mechanism by which common Article 3 becomes binding on an entity that is not a High Contracting Party to the Geneva Conventions is the subject of debate.[234] Explanations include: that an entity claiming to be representing a State or parts of it, in particular by exercising effective sovereignty over it, enters into the international obligations of that State;[235] that following the ratification of the Geneva Conventions by a State, common Article 3 becomes part of domestic law and therefore binds all individuals under the State's jurisdiction, including members of a non-State armed group;[236] that common Article 3 and other humanitarian law treaties intended to bind non-State Parties to non-international armed conflicts are international treaty provisions lawfully creating obligations for third parties, similar to how treaties can, under certain circumstances,[237] create obligations for States not party to them;[238] that when a State ratifies a treaty, it does so on behalf of all individuals under its jurisdiction, who can therefore become the addressees of direct rights and obligations under international law;[239] that it 'derives from the fundamental nature of the rules [common Article 3] contains and from their recognition by the entire international community as being the absolute minimum needed to safeguard vital humanitarian interests';[240] and that non-State armed groups can also consent to be bound by common Article 3, for example through the issuance of a unilateral declaration or special agreement between Parties to an armed conflict.[241]

---

[233] See *Final Record of the Diplomatic Conference of Geneva of 1949*, Vol. II-B, p. 90, with a response by the ICRC; see further pp. 93–94 and 99–100.

[234] For an overview, see Sivakumaran, 2012, pp. 238–242, and 2015, pp. 415–431; Kleffner, 2011; Moir, pp. 52–58; Murray, pp. 101–131; and Dinstein, 2014, pp. 63–73.

[235] See e.g. Pictet (ed.), *Commentary on the First Geneva Convention*, ICRC, 1952, pp. 51–52; *Commentary on the Second Geneva Convention*, ICRC, 1960, p. 34; *Commentary on the Third Geneva Convention*, ICRC, 1960, pp. 37–38; *Commentary on the Fourth Geneva Convention*, ICRC, 1958, p. 37; Elder, p. 55; Schindler, p. 151; and Sivakumaran, 2015, pp. 422–423.

[236] This is often referred to as the doctrine of legislative jurisdiction. See e.g. Pictet (ed.), *Commentary on the Second Geneva Convention*, ICRC, 1960, p. 34; Sandoz/Swinarski/Zimmermann (eds), *Commentary on the Additional Protocols*, ICRC, 1987, para. 4444; Sivakumaran, 2015, pp. 418–419; Dinstein, p. 70; and Elder, p. 55. See also *Final Record of the Diplomatic Conference of Geneva of 1949*, Vol. II-B, p. 94 (statement by Greece).

[237] See Vienna Convention on the Law of Treaties (1969), Articles 34–36.

[238] See Cassese, 1981, pp. 423–429, and Sivakumaran, 2015, pp. 419–420.

[239] See Sivakumaran, 2015, pp. 417–418; Antonio Cassese, 'La guerre civile et le droit international', *Revue générale de droit international public*, Vol. 90, 1986, pp. 553–578, at 567; Dinstein, p. 66; and Schindler, p. 151.

[240] See Bugnion, p. 336, who also argues that the binding nature of common Article 3 'derives from international custom, the laws of humanity and the dictates of public conscience'. On this point, see also Sivakumaran, 2015, p. 424.

[241] See Sivakumaran, 2015, pp. 420–422, and Dinstein, pp. 70–71.

508   A variety of these legal theories have been advanced to explain how non-State armed groups are bound by common Article 3, but it is undisputed that the substantive provisions of common Article 3 bind all such armed groups when they are party to an armed conflict.

c. Binding force of common Article 3 on multinational forces

509 As noted earlier,[242] multinational forces can engage in activities that would make States or international organizations sending them a Party to a non-international armed conflict, whether in execution of their mandate or owing to factual developments. A distinction can be made between multinational operations conducted by a coalition of States not subject to the command and control of an international organization, on the one hand, and multinational operations conducted under the command and control of the United Nations or other international organizations, on the other hand.

510   In situations where multinational operations are conducted by a coalition of States not subject to the command and control of an international organization, the individual States participating in the multinational forces become Parties to the conflict.[243] Depending on whether the multinational forces become engaged against a State or a non-State Party, the law governing either international or non-international armed conflict is binding on the troop-contributing States. In the latter case, common Article 3 will be binding on those States' forces.

511   In situations where the organization within whose framework the multinational operation is carried out exercises command and control over such forces, it can become a Party to the armed conflict.[244] Since international organizations deploying multinational forces are not States and thus generally cannot become a Party to the Geneva Conventions or other humanitarian law treaties, these treaties are not as such binding on them. However, status-of-forces agreements (SOFAs) concluded between the United Nations and States hosting UN peace operations typically require the United Nations to ensure that its operation is conducted with 'full respect for the principles and rules of the international conventions applicable to the conduct of military personnel'.[245] With respect to forces under UN command and control,

---

[242] See paras 411–413, as well as the commentary on common Article 2, paras 245–252.

[243] For more details, see paras 411–413 of this commentary.

[244] It is also possible that in some circumstances, both the international organization and the States contributing troops are considered Parties to the armed conflict. For more details on this issue, see paras 411–413; the commentary on common Article 2, paras 245–252, and Ferraro, 2013, pp. 588–595.

[245] See e.g. The Status of Forces Agreement between the United Nations and the Government of the Republic of South Sudan concerning the United Nations Mission in South Sudan (UNMISS), Juba, 8 August 2011, paras 6(a) and (b). While such provisions are not included in the 'Model status-of-forces agreement for peace-keeping operations' as prepared by the UN Secretary-General at the request of the General Assembly (UN Doc. A/45/594, 9 October 1990),

the applicability of certain 'fundamental principles and rules of international humanitarian law' to multinational forces has also been explicitly affirmed by the UN Secretary-General.[246]

512   Furthermore, it has come to be accepted that such organizations are bound by customary international law.[247] The International Court of Justice has stated that international organizations, including the United Nations, are subjects of international law and are bound by any obligations incumbent upon them under general rules of international law.[248]

513   In addition, as troop-contributing States do not normally relinquish all control over their forces to the organization deploying multinational forces, many States consider that these forces remain bound by their own State's humanitarian law obligations.[249]

2. 'as a minimum, the following provisions'

514   All Parties to a non-international armed conflict are bound to comply with the 'minimum' provisions listed in common Article 3. These fundamental obligations are automatically applicable in any non-international armed conflict as soon as it has come into existence.

515   As noted by common Article 3 itself, these provisions are only 'minimum' provisions.

---

they have been included in relevant SOFAs since the UN concluded such an agreement with Rwanda in respect of the UN Assistance Mission in Rwanda (UNAMIR) on 5 November 1993, United Nations *Treaty Series*, Vol. 1748, 1993, pp. 3–28.

[246] See e.g. the 1999 UN Secretary-General's Bulletin, which does not distinguish between international and non-international armed conflict.

[247] See ICJ, *Reparation for Injuries Suffered in the Service of the United Nations*, Advisory Opinion, 1949, p. 179; *Interpretation of the Agreement of 25 March 1951 between the WHO and Egypt*, Advisory Opinion, 1980, para. 37; and *Legality of the Use by a State of Nuclear Weapons in Armed Conflict (WHO)*, Advisory Opinion, 1996, para. 25.

[248] In *Legality of the Use by a State of Nuclear Weapons in Armed Conflict (WHO)*, Advisory Opinion, 1996, para. 25, the ICJ stated:

[I]nternational organizations...do not, unlike States, possess a general competence. International organizations are governed by the 'principle of speciality', that is to say, they are invested by the States which create them with powers...The powers conferred on international organizations are normally subject of an express statement in their constituent instruments.

For a discussion of the implications of this principle for the applicability of humanitarian law to international organizations, see Kolb/Porretto/Vité, pp. 121–143; Naert, pp. 533–534; Shraga, 1998, p. 77; and Engdahl, p. 519.

[249] See Section 2 of the 1999 UN Secretary-General's Bulletin, which states that '[t]he present provisions do not...replace the national laws by which military personnel remain bound throughout the operation'. See also e.g. Netherlands, *Military Manual*, 2005, para. 1231 ('Naturally, the various countries participating in such an operation under the UN flag are bound by the customary law, treaties and conventions which they have signed and ratified.'), and Germany, *Military Manual*, 2013, para. 1405 ('Whether a UN mandate was issued or not does not affect the question of the applicability of LOAC [law of armed conflict]. Instead, the norms of international humanitarian law are directly applicable if they apply to the sending states in question and if there is an armed conflict in the country of deployment').

516   While the States adopting common Article 3 in 1949 could not find agreement on making more or all provisions of the Geneva Conventions automatically applicable in non-international armed conflict,[250] they were nevertheless aware that the application of additional and more detailed rules might be desirable in such conflicts. They therefore agreed on the inclusion of paragraph 3 of common Article 3, according to which the 'Parties to the conflict should further endeavour to bring into force, by means of special agreements, all or part of the other provisions' of the Geneva Conventions.[251]

517   In addition to the fundamental obligations under common Article 3 and the option of special agreements, Parties to non-international armed conflict may also be bound by other humanitarian law treaties.[252] Furthermore, they are bound by customary humanitarian law applicable to non-international armed conflict as well as by obligations under international human rights law, within its scope of application. The question of whether and to what extent human rights law applies to non-State armed groups is not settled. At a minimum, it seems accepted that armed groups that exercise territorial control and fulfil government-like functions thereby incur responsibilities under human rights law.[253]

E. Subparagraph (1): Persons protected

1. Introduction

518 Subparagraph (1) covers all '[p]ersons taking no active part in the hostilities, including members of armed forces who have laid down their arms and those placed *hors de combat* by sickness, wounds, detention, or any other cause'. The article does not expand on these notions and this part of the article did not give rise to much discussion at the 1949 Diplomatic Conference. The protection afforded under this subparagraph requires that the person be in the power of a Party to the conflict (see section E.4).[254]

---

[250] For more details, see section B.   [251] For details, see section K.

[252] In particular, by Additional Protocol II, depending on ratification, and provided that a particular non-international armed conflict fulfils the criteria for the applicability of that Protocol. For details, see the commentary on Additional Protocol II. See also the examples of other treaties noted in fn. 5 of this commentary.

[253] For an overview of the practice and debate on this issue, see e.g. Sivakumaran, 2012, pp. 95–99; Jean-Marie Henckaerts and Cornelius Wiesener, 'Human rights obligations of non-state armed groups: a possible contribution from customary international law?', in Robert Kolb and Gloria Gaggioli (eds), *Research Handbook on Human Rights and Humanitarian Law*, Edward Elgar, Cheltenham, 2013, pp. 146–169; Andrew Clapham, 'Focusing on Armed Non-State Actors', in Andrew Clapham and Paola Gaeta (eds), *The Oxford Handbook of International Law in Armed Conflict*, Oxford University Press, 2014, pp. 766–810, at 786–802; and Konstantinos Mastorodimos, *Armed Non-State Actors in International Humanitarian and Human Rights Law: Foundation and Framework of Obligations, and Rules on Accountability*, Ashgate, Farnham, 2016.

[254] For the persons protected by subparagraph (2) on the wounded and sick, see section I.4.

519   The protection of persons not or no longer participating in hostilities is at the heart of humanitarian law. The persons protected by common Article 3 are accordingly described by way of explicit delimitations: 'persons taking *no* active part in the hostilities, including members of armed forces who have *laid down* their arms and those placed *hors de combat* by sickness, wounds, detention, or any other cause' (emphasis added). Parties to a non-international armed conflict are under the categorical obligation to treat these persons humanely, in all circumstances and without any adverse distinction.

520   Nevertheless, outside common Article 3, humanitarian law contains a number of provisions that benefit persons during the time they are actively participating in hostilities. These include the general prohibition on the use of means or methods of warfare that are of a nature to cause superfluous injury or unnecessary suffering, and prohibitions on specific means and methods of warfare.[255]

2. Persons taking no active part in the hostilities

521   Common Article 3 protects '[p]ersons taking no active part in the hostilities'. These are first and foremost the civilian population, which typically does not take an active part in the hostilities.[256] Thus, civilians benefit from the protection of common Article 3, except for such time as they take an active part in hostilities. They are protected when and as soon as they cease doing so, including when they are 'placed *hors de combat* by sickness, wounds, detention, or any other cause'.[257] The civilian population also includes former members of armed forces who have been demobilized or disengaged.[258]

522   Second, persons taking no active part in the hostilities include non-combatant members of the armed forces, namely medical and religious personnel. As they must be exclusively assigned to medical and religious duties, they typically do not take an active part in hostilities.[259]

---

[255] These rules have been found to apply in non-international armed conflict as a matter of customary international law; see ICRC Study on Customary International Humanitarian Law (2005), in particular Rules 46, 64–65, 70, 72–74, 77–80 and 85–86.

[256] See also ICC Elements of Crimes (2002), elements common to all crimes under Article 8(2)(c) of the 1998 ICC Statute (describing persons protected by common Article 3 of the Geneva Conventions as: 'such person or persons were either *hors de combat*, or were civilians, medical personnel, or religious personnel taking no active part in the hostilities').

[257] For details on persons *hors de combat*, see section E.3.b. That the considerations on persons *hors de combat* apply to civilians who take an active part in hostilities follows from the link between 'those placed *hors de combat*' to 'persons taking no active part in the hostilities'. The French version is clearer as it repeats the term 'persons' ('Les personnes qui ne participent pas directement aux hostilités, y compris...les personnes qui ont été mises hors de combat...'). See also Kleffner, 2015, pp. 442–443.

[258] On disengagement from non-State armed groups, see ICRC, *Interpretive Guidance*, pp. 72–73.

[259] See also ICC Elements of Crimes (2002), elements common to all crimes under Article 8(2)(c) of the 1998 ICC Statute (describing persons protected by common Article 3 as: 'such person or persons were either *hors de combat*, or were civilians, medical personnel, or religious personnel taking no active part in the hostilities').

523 Third, as spelled out in common Article 3, persons taking no active part in hostilities include 'members of armed forces who have laid down their arms and those placed *hors de combat*'. This category is further discussed in section E.3.

524 The notion of active participation in hostilities is not defined in common Article 3, nor is it contained in any other provision of the 1949 Geneva Conventions or earlier treaties.[260] However, the differentiation between persons actively participating in hostilities and persons not or no longer doing so is a key feature of humanitarian law.

525 The notion of participation in hostilities is contained in the 1977 Additional Protocols, which provide that civilians enjoy protection against dangers arising from military operations 'unless and for such time as they take a direct part in hostilities'.[261] It has become widely accepted that 'active' participation in hostilities in common Article 3 and 'direct' participation in hostilities in the Additional Protocols refer to the same concept.[262]

526 The purpose of the reference to direct participation in hostilities in the Protocols is to determine when a civilian becomes a lawful target under humanitarian law during the conduct of hostilities. The scope and application of the notion of direct participation in hostilities is the subject of debate in the framework of the rules on the conduct of hostilities.[263]

527 Whichever view on the notion of direct participation in hostilities a Party to the conflict adopts for the purposes of its targeting decisions, as soon as a person ceases to take an active part in hostilities, for example when falling into the hands of the enemy, that person comes under the protective scope of common Article 3 and must be treated humanely.

528 Thus, any form of ill-treatment – such as torture or cruel, humiliating or degrading treatment – can never be justified because a person may have actively

---

[260] But see Article 15 of the Fourth Convention, providing for the possibility of Parties to an international armed conflict to establish neutralized zones for sheltering, *inter alia*, 'civilian persons who take no part in hostilities, and who, while they reside in the zones, perform no work of a military character'.

[261] See Additional Protocol I, Article 51(3), and Additional Protocol II, Article 13(3). See also ICRC Study on Customary International Humanitarian Law (2005), Rule 6.

[262] See e.g. ICTR, *Akayesu* Trial Judgment, 1998, para. 629, and ICRC, *Interpretive Guidance*, p. 43. The equally authentic French version of common Article 3 refers to 'personnes qui ne participent pas *directement* aux hostilités' (emphasis added).

[263] For the purpose of the principle of distinction in the conduct of hostilities, the ICRC has provided recommendations on the interpretation of the notion of direct participation in hostilities; see ICRC, *Interpretive Guidance*. For a discussion of this publication, see e.g. Michael N. Schmitt, 'The Interpretive Guidance on the Notion of Direct Participation in Hostilities: A Critical Analysis', *Harvard National Security Journal*, Vol. 1, 2010, pp. 5–44; *Report of the Special Rapporteur on Extra-Judicial, Summary or Arbitrary Executions, Philip Alston, Addendum: Study on targeted killings*, UN Doc. A/HRC/14/24/Add.6, 28 May 2010, pp. 19–21; and 'Forum: The ICRC Interpretive Guidance on the Notion of Direct Participation in Hostilities Under International Humanitarian Law', *New York University Journal of International Law and Politics*, Vol. 42, No. 3, 2010, pp. 637–916. For further details, see the commentaries on Article 51 of Additional Protocol I and Article 13 of Additional Protocol II.

participated in hostilities in the past. There is no place for retribution under humanitarian law.

3. Members of armed forces who have laid down their arms and those placed hors de combat

a. Members of armed forces

529   The term 'members of armed forces' is not defined in either common Article 3 or in the Geneva Conventions more generally.[264]

530   In the context of common Article 3, the term 'armed forces' refers to the armed forces of both the State and non-State Parties to the conflict. This is implied by the wording of common Article 3, which provides that 'each Party to the conflict' must afford protection to 'persons taking no active part in the hostilities, including members of armed forces'.[265] Furthermore, common Article 3 does not refer to 'the' armed forces, which could suggest State armed forces alone, but rather to 'armed forces'.[266] Lastly, common Article 3 is built on a balance of obligations between all Parties to the conflict and requires that members of both State armed forces and non-State armed groups be treated humanely as soon as they lay down their arms or are otherwise placed *hors de combat*.[267]

531   The requirement of humane treatment does not, however, imply combatant immunity for members of non-State armed groups as this concept is not as such applicable in non-international armed conflict. Such persons may be prosecuted under domestic law for their participation in hostilities, including for acts that are not unlawful under humanitarian law. The last paragraph of common Article 3 confirms that the application of this article does not affect the legal status of the Parties to the conflict.

532   State armed forces first of all consist of a State's regular armed forces. However, the notion of State armed forces also includes other organized armed groups or units that are under a command responsible to the State Party to the non-international armed conflict.[268]

---

[264] It was only in 1977 that a definition of armed forces was included in humanitarian treaty law with respect to international armed conflict; see Additional Protocol I, Article 43.

[265] See also ICRC, *Interpretive Guidance*, p. 28.

[266] See also the equally authentic French version of common Article 3, referring to 'les membres *de* forces armées' and not 'les membres *des* forces armées' (emphasis added).

[267] See also Sassòli, 2006, p. 977.

[268] This can include entities that may not fall under the definition of the armed forces under domestic law, but that are either formally incorporated into them or factually assume the functions of regular armed forces, such as a national guard, customs, police or any other similar forces. See e.g. Sandoz/Swinarski/Zimmermann (eds), *Commentary on the Additional Protocols*, ICRC, 1987, para. 4462; ICRC, *Interpretive Guidance*, pp. 30–31; and Sivakumaran, 2012, p. 180.

533   State armed forces traditionally consist of personnel with a combatant function and personnel with a non-combatant function, namely medical and religious personnel. As mentioned above, medical and religious personnel typically do not take an active part in hostilities and, while adhering to their non-combatant role, fall under the protective scope of common Article 3.[269]

534   For their part, non-State Parties to a non-international armed conflict do not have armed forces in the sense established under domestic law.[270] However, the existence of a non-international armed conflict requires the involvement of fighting forces on behalf of the non-State Party to the conflict that are capable of engaging in sustained armed violence, which requires a certain level of organization.[271] Such organized armed groups constitute the 'armed forces' of a non-State Party to the conflict in the sense of common Article 3.[272]

b. *Laying down arms or being placed* hors de combat

535   Common Article 3 refers to 'members of armed forces who have laid down their arms' separately from 'those placed *hors de combat* by sickness, wounds, detention, or any other cause'. What distinguishes members of armed forces 'who have laid down their arms' from 'those placed *hors de combat* by sickness, wounds, detention, or any other cause' is that the cessation of their involvement in the conflict is not the consequence of external factors that are out of their control, but involves a decision on their part to surrender.[273] The result of that decision, however, is the same as if they had been placed *hors de combat* by external factors: they are no longer engaged in the conflict. The individual laying down of arms grants protection under common Article 3; it is not required that the armed forces as a whole do so.[274]

---

[269] See para. 522 of this commentary.

[270] Even though, occasionally, they may include dissident armed forces of a State; see Additional Protocol II, Article 1(1).

[271] See section C.2.b.

[272] See ICRC, *International humanitarian law and the challenges of contemporary armed conflict*, 2011, p. 43; ICRC, *Interpretive Guidance*, pp. 27–36; and the commentaries on Articles 1(1) and 13 of Additional Protocol II.

[273] During the 1949 Diplomatic Conference, the formulation ultimately adopted, 'who have laid down their arms', was preferred over the proposed formulation 'and those who surrender'; see *Final Record of the Diplomatic Conference of Geneva of 1949*, Vol. II-B, pp. 84, 90 and 100.

[274] In the equally authentic French version of common Article 3, the phrase 'members of armed forces who have laid down their arms' ('les membres de forces armées qui ont déposé les armes') can be understood as either referring to individual members of armed forces laying down their arms or as requiring armed forces as a whole to have laid down their arms in order for their members to benefit from the protections of common Article 3. However, the discussions at the 1949 Diplomatic Conference make clear that it was the first reading which was intended. The adoption of the English version in the present form, using 'who have laid down their arms', whereby 'who' can only relate to persons, was deliberate. A proposal to replace 'who' by 'which', 'to indicate that the armed forces as a whole must lay down their arms', was rejected. See *Final Record of the Diplomatic Conference of Geneva of 1949*, Vol. II-B, p. 100.

536   The notion of *hors de combat* is not defined in common Article 3 or the Geneva Conventions more generally.

537   For the purpose of the conduct of hostilities, however, the effect and requirements of being '*hors de combat*' are defined in Additional Protocol I:

1. A person who is recognized or who, in the circumstances, should be recognized to be *hors de combat* shall not be made the object of attack.
2. A person is *hors de combat* if:
   (a) he is in the power of an adverse Party;
   (b) he clearly expresses an intention to surrender; or
   (c) he has been rendered unconscious or is otherwise incapacitated by wounds or sickness, and therefore is incapable of defending himself; provided that in any of these cases he abstains from any hostile act and does not attempt to escape.[275]

   This rule is part of customary law applicable in non-international armed conflict.[276]

538   The final part of this definition ('provided that in any of these cases he abstains from any hostile act and does not attempt to escape') explains why a person *hors de combat* must no longer be attacked. When a person abstains from hostile acts and does not attempt to escape, there is no longer a reason to harm that person. These conditions would therefore also seem relevant for common Article 3, determining from what moment a member of armed forces (or a civilian who is taking an active part in hostilities) is to be regarded as placed *hors de combat* and therefore protected under common Article 3.

539   In particular, persons who are *hors de combat* by clearly expressing an intention to surrender are laying 'down their arms' in the sense of common Article 3 and come within the protective scope of the article.[277] Common Article 3 then notes the following other factors potentially rendering a person *hors de combat*: 'sickness, wounds, detention, or any other cause'. Sickness and wounds are typical incidences for members of armed forces during non-international armed conflict, as is detention, resorted to by both State and non-State Parties to the conflict.[278] Other causes of being *hors de combat* could, for example, be shipwreck, parachuting from an aircraft in distress, or falling or otherwise

---

[275] Additional Protocol I, Article 41.

[276] ICRC Study on Customary International Humanitarian Law (2005), Rule 47.

[277] Persons who have been demobilized or disengaged can also be said to 'have laid down their arms', but when this has occurred before falling into the power of the enemy, they come under the protective scope of common Article 3 when falling into the power of the enemy because they are at that moment 'taking no active part in the hostilities'; see also para. 521.

[278] At the Diplomatic Conference, the term 'detention' in common Article 3 was preferred over the term 'captivity'. One delegation expressed the view that captivity 'implied the status of a prisoner of war and was incompatible with the idea of civil war' and suggested therefore the use of the term 'detention', while another delegation saw 'no difficulty in the use of the word "captivity" which meant "taking into custody" either by police or by opposing troops'; see

being in the power of a Party to the conflict – for example at a checkpoint – even if the situation may not yet be regarded as amounting to detention. The addition of 'any other cause' indicates that the notion of 'hors de combat' in common Article 3 should not be interpreted in a narrow sense.[279]

4. Common Article 3 and the conduct of hostilities

540   Common Article 3 does not address the conduct of hostilities. The substantive protections in common Article 3 themselves, for example the prohibitions on torture and hostage-taking, envision a certain level of control over the persons concerned: they are in the power of a Party to the conflict. This includes civilians living in areas under the control of a Party to the conflict but not with respect to actions by Parties governed by the rules on the conduct of hostilities. This reading finds support in the preparatory work for the Geneva Conventions and in military manuals and case law.[280] It is also supported in academic literature.[281]

541   The only protection that has given rise to doubt in this regard is the prohibition of murder which has been found in some cases to apply to unlawful attacks in the conduct of hostilities.[282] Some authors support the view that common

---

Final Record of the Diplomatic Conference of Geneva of 1949, Vol. II-B, pp. 94 and 100. On detention outside a criminal process, see section H.

[279] This was also the understanding of the drafters of the 2002 ICC Elements of Crimes; see Dörmann, p. 389.

[280] See e.g. *Final Record of the Diplomatic Conference of Geneva of 1949*, Vol. II-B, pp. 407–410 (statements by the United States, Canada, Mexico, France and Switzerland on the meaning of 'in the hands of' in Article 32 of the Fourth Convention, a provision which is explicitly compared to common Article 3 in those discussions); United Kingdom, *Manual of the Law of Armed Conflict*, 2004, p. 215; and Inter-American Commission on Human Rights, *Case 11.137 (Argentina)*, Report, 1997, para. 176 (civilians 'are covered by Common Article 3's safeguards when they are captured by or otherwise subjected to the power of an adverse party').

[281] See Meron, 1991, p. 84; Pejic, 2011, pp. 203, 205–206 and 219 (common Article 3 protects persons in the 'power' of or 'captured'; deals with the 'protection of persons in enemy hands'); Melzer, 2008, p. 216 (with respect to the prohibition of murder); Yukata Arai-Takahashi, *The Law of Occupation: Continuity and Change of International Humanitarian Law, and its Interaction with International Human Rights Law*, Martinus Nijhoff Publishers, Leiden, 2009, p. 299 (common Article 3 applies to persons 'captured in armed conflict'; murder can only be committed in the law and order, rather than the hostilities, context); Knuckey, p. 456 (with respect to the prohibition of murder); and Dinstein, p. 134.

[282] ICTY, *Strugar* Trial Judgment, 2005, dealing with an artillery attack against the old town of Dubrovnik inhabited by persons not taking an active part in hostilities. The Court found that the charges of the war crimes of murder and cruel treatment, as well as of attacks on civilians, were fulfilled; see paras 234–240, 260–261 and 277–283, with references to earlier case law. Compare further ICC, *Katanga* Trial Judgment, 2014, paras 856–879. See also Inter-American Commission on Human Rights, *Third Report on the Human Rights Situation in Colombia*, 26 February 1999, para. 41; Human Rights Council, *Report of the International Commission of Inquiry to investigate all alleged violations of international human rights law in the Libyan Arab Jamahiriya*, UN Doc. A/HRC/17/44, 12 January 2012, para. 146; and UN, *Report of the Secretary-General's Panel of Experts on Accountability in Sri Lanka*, 31 March 2011, paras 193, 206 and 242.

Article 3 contains some regulation of the conduct of hostilities.[283] If this were the case, the prohibition of murder would have to be interpreted in the light of the specific rules on the conduct of hostilities, in particular the rules on distinction, proportionality and precautions. A taking of life in compliance with the rules on the conduct of hostilities would not amount to murder under common Article 3.

542   In the view of the ICRC, it follows from the context of the 1949 Geneva Conventions in which common Article 3 is placed, however, that it was not intended to govern the conduct of hostilities.[284] Common Article 3 as ultimately adopted evolved from drafts proposing the application of the principles of the Geneva Conventions – or of the provisions of the Conventions as such – to non-international armed conflict. The primary concern of the Conventions is the protection of the victims of international armed conflicts in the power of a Party to the conflict, but not the regulation of the conduct of hostilities as such. The same should therefore apply for common Article 3, which was adopted to extend the essence of the Conventions to non-international armed conflicts.[285]

543   That hostilities may lead to the death or injury of persons who are taking no active part in hostilities is a reality of non-international armed conflict, be it because such persons are unlawfully made the target of attacks or because they become incidental victims of attacks. However, common Article 3 is not suited to assessing the lawfulness of the conduct of hostilities, which is governed by specific rules of humanitarian law. For non-international armed conflict, these rules can be found in Additional Protocol II and customary international law.[286]

5. *The applicability of common Article 3 to all civilians and to a Party's own armed forces*

544 While many provisions of the Conventions, in particular the Third and Fourth Conventions, are limited to protection when in the power of the enemy,[287]

---

[283] See e.g. Bond, p. 348; William H. Boothby, *The Law of Targeting*, Oxford University Press, 2012, p. 433; Cassese, p. 107; and Rogers, p. 301. For a more intermediate position, see Bothe/Partsch/Solf, p. 667, fn. 1.

[284] This was also the understanding in 1977 during the drafting of what became Article 13 of Additional Protocol II, which prohibits attacks against the civilian population and civilians not taking a direct part in hostilities; see *Official Records of the Diplomatic Conference of Geneva of 1974–1977*, Vol. XV, p. 363: '[T]he only general international law with respect to non-international armed conflicts is Article 3 common to the four Geneva Conventions of 1949, which contains no provision pertinent to the subject-matter of this article of Protocol II.' See also Sandoz/Swinarski/Zimmermann (eds), *Commentary on the Additional Protocols*, ICRC, 1987, paras 4365 and 4776; Draper, 1965, pp. 84–85 (the Geneva Conventions 'adopted the solution of eschewing any direct attempt to legislate for the conduct of hostilities...the prohibitions relate to treatment outside of combat'); ICRC, *Interpretive Guidance*, p. 28; Pejic, 2011, p. 219; Gasser, p. 478; Meron, 1991, p. 84; Watkin, p. 271, with fn. 31; Zegveld, pp. 82–84; and Abresch, p. 748, with fn. 22.

[285] For details, see section B.

[286] See, in particular, Additional Protocol II, Articles 13–17, and ICRC Study on Customary International Humanitarian Law (2005), Rules 1–2, 5–21, 42–48 and 53–54.

[287] See Third Convention, Article 4, and Fourth Convention, Article 4.

some provisions are not so limited. In the First Convention, this is notably the case for the provision setting out the central protections of the Convention: Article 12.[288]

545   The wording of common Article 3 indicates that it applies to all persons taking no active part in the hostilities, 'without any adverse distinction'.[289] It contains no limitation requiring a person taking no active part in hostilities to be in the power of the *enemy* in order to be protected under the article.

546   It is logical that civilians should enjoy the protection of common Article 3 regardless of whose power they are in. In practice, it is often impossible in non-international armed conflict to determine whether members of the general population not actively participating in hostilities are affiliated with one or other Party to the conflict. Unlike usually in international armed conflict,[290] objective criteria such as nationality cannot be resorted to.[291] Limiting protection under common Article 3 to persons affiliated or perceived to be affiliated with the opposing Party is therefore difficult to reconcile with the protective purpose of common Article 3.

547   Another issue is whether armed forces of a Party to the conflict benefit from the application of common Article 3 by their own Party.[292] Examples would include members of armed forces who are tried for alleged crimes – such as war crimes or ordinary crimes in the context of the armed conflict – by their own Party and members of armed forces who are sexually or otherwise abused by their own Party.[293] The fact that the trial is undertaken or the abuse committed by their own Party should not be a ground to deny such persons the protection of common Article 3. This is supported by the fundamental character of common Article 3 which has been recognized as a 'minimum yardstick' in all armed conflicts and as a reflection of 'elementary considerations of humanity'.[294]

548   In many cases, of course, recourse to common Article 3 may not be necessary to make a Party to a conflict treat its own armed forces humanely, be it because a Party to a conflict will feel under a natural obligation to do so, because it will do so out of self-interest, or because, at least in the case of a State Party, domestic law and international human rights law require treatment at least equivalent to that of humane treatment in the sense of common Article 3.

---

[288] See the commentary on Article 12, paras 1337, 1368 and 1370.
[289] On the prohibition of adverse distinction, see section F.2.
[290] For details, see the commentary on Article 4 of the Fourth Convention.
[291] For a discussion of nationality as a prohibited criterion for adverse distinction under common Article 3, see section F.2.b.
[292] For a detailed discussion, see Kleffner, 2013c, and Sivakumaran, 2012, pp. 246–249.
[293] See ICC, *Ntaganda* Decision on the Confirmation of Charges, 2014, paras 76–82, confirming charges of rape and sexual slavery of child soldiers as war crimes allegedly committed against them by their own Party to the conflict; see also *Katanga* Decision on the Confirmation of Charges, 2008, para. 248, noting that the use of child soldiers in hostilities 'can be committed by a perpetrator against individuals in his own party to the conflict'. But see SCSL, *Sesay* Trial Judgment, 2009, paras 1451–1457, holding that 'the law of armed conflict does not protect members of armed groups from acts of violence directed against them by their own forces'.
[294] See ICJ, *Military and Paramilitary Activities in and against Nicaragua case*, Merits, Judgment, 1986, paras 218–219.

549   Nevertheless, in so far as a specific situation has a nexus to a non-international armed conflict, as in the examples given above, all Parties to the conflict should, as a minimum, grant humane treatment to their own armed forces based on common Article 3.

F. Subparagraph (1): Fundamental obligations under common Article 3

1. The obligation of humane treatment

a. Introduction

550   The obligation of humane treatment is the cornerstone of the protections conferred by common Article 3. It is expressed in few words, but is nonetheless fundamental. From it derive the specific prohibitions under common Article 3(1), subparagraph (1), and it serves to ensure that all persons not or no longer participating in hostilities are treated humanely by both State and non-State Parties to non-international armed conflicts.

551   Jean Pictet wrote in 1958 that the principle of humane treatment 'is in truth the leitmotiv of the four Geneva Conventions'.[295] For international armed conflict, the principle of humane treatment has been codified in the 1899 and 1907 Hague Regulations, the successive Geneva Conventions and Additional Protocol I.[296] For non-international armed conflict, however, it was codified for the first time in common Article 3 and was subsequently reaffirmed in Additional Protocol II.[297]

b. Humane treatment

552   Humane treatment of persons protected under common Article 3 is not merely a recommendation or a moral appeal. As evident from the use of the word 'shall', it is an obligation of the Parties to the conflict under international law.

---

[295] Pictet (ed.), *Commentary on the Fourth Geneva Convention*, ICRC, 1958, p. 204.

[296] See Hague Regulations (1899) and (1907), Article 4; Geneva Convention on the Wounded and Sick (1929), Article 1; and Geneva Convention on Prisoners of War (1929), Article 2. Today, see, in particular, First Convention, Article 12; Second Convention, Article 12; Third Convention, Article 13; Fourth Convention, Article 27; and Additional Protocol I, Articles 10 and 75.

[297] Formal rules to this effect date back to the Lieber Code, which was promulgated in the context of a non-international armed conflict, the American Civil War; see Lieber Code (1863), Articles 4 and 76. See also Brussels Declaration (1874), Article 23. Article 73 of the Lieber Code is a notable illustration of the distinctive importance attributed to humane treatment: 'All officers, when captured, must surrender their side arms to the captor. They may be restored to the prisoner in marked cases, by the commander, to signalize admiration of his distinguished bravery or *approbation of his humane treatment of prisoners before his capture*' (emphasis added). See Article 4 of Additional Protocol II, the first provision of Part II of the Protocol, which is entitled 'Humane treatment'. According to Article 5(1) and (3) of Additional Protocol II, the imperative of humane treatment also applies to persons 'deprived of their liberty for reasons related to the armed conflict, whether they are interned or detained', and to persons 'whose liberty has been restricted in any way whatsoever for reasons related to the armed conflict'.

553   Despite this, the precise meaning of 'humane treatment' is not defined either in common Article 3 or in any other provision of humanitarian treaty law. However, this is not a defect of these provisions. The meaning of humane treatment is context specific and has to be considered in the concrete circumstances of each case, taking into account both objective and subjective elements, such as the environment, the physical and mental condition of the person, as well as his or her age, social, cultural, religious or political background and past experiences. In addition, there is a growing acknowledgement that women, men, girls and boys are affected by armed conflict in different ways. Sensitivity to the individual's inherent status, capacities and needs, including how these differ among men and women due to social, economic, cultural and political structures in society, contributes to the understanding of humane treatment under common Article 3.[298]

554   Including a comprehensive definition of humane treatment in common Article 3 would have created a framework that risked being too narrow and inflexible, and as such incapable of ensuring humane treatment in situations where unforeseen or particular circumstances, such as climatic conditions, cultural sensitivities or individual needs, have to be taken into account. At the same time, giving no guidance at all on the meaning of humane treatment could have left Parties to an armed conflict with too much latitude, leading to interpretations incompatible with the objectives of this fundamental rule.[299] The approach chosen for common Article 3 was to make the imperative of humane treatment its central axis, while illustrating it with examples of prohibited acts. Accordingly, common Article 3 categorically requires that persons not or no longer taking an active part in hostilities be treated humanely in all circumstances, adding that 'to this end' violence to life and person, taking of hostages, outrages upon personal dignity and the passing of sentences without a fair trial 'are and shall remain prohibited at any time and in any place'.

555   The formulation 'to this end' makes clear that the obligation of humane treatment is the substantive core of common Article 3. Humane treatment has a meaning of its own, beyond the prohibitions listed. These prohibitions

---

[298] For more information on the differing impacts of armed conflict, see e.g. Lindsey, 2001, or Lindsey/Coomaraswamy/Gardam, 2005, or parallel information in UN Security Council, *Report of the Secretary-General on women, peace and security*, UN Doc. S/2002/1154, 16 October 2002. Both women and men need to be actively involved in the planning and implementation of activities carried out for their benefit. It is therefore important to include the perspectives of men and women of different ages and backgrounds in the identification and assessment of these issues. For guidance, see e.g. Cecilia Tengroth and Kristina Lindvall, *IHL and gender – Swedish experiences*, Swedish Red Cross and Swedish Ministry for Foreign Affairs, Stockholm, 2015, Recommendations, and chapter 6, Checklist – a gender perspective in the application of IHL.

[299] See e.g. ICTY, *Aleksovski* Trial Judgment, 1999, para. 49; see also Elder, p. 61, and Sivakumaran, 2012, pp. 257–258.

are merely specific examples of conduct that is indisputably in violation of the humane treatment obligation.[300]

556   In accordance with the ordinary meaning of the word 'humane', what is called for is treatment that is 'compassionate or benevolent'[301] towards the persons protected under common Article 3. This is more directly reflected in the French version of the text in which the obligation is formulated as requiring that persons protected under common Article 3 'are treated with humanity' ('traitées avec humanité').

557   State practice has called for treatment that respects a person's inherent dignity as a human being.[302] The same understanding of humane treatment is also reflected in international case law.[303] Persons protected under common Article 3 must never be treated as less than fellow human beings and their inherent human dignity must be upheld and protected.

558   Furthermore, the ways States have elaborated on the obligation of humane treatment in their military manuals, codes of conduct and policy documents give further indications of what the obligation entails, in particular with regard to persons deprived of their liberty. These documents not only list practices incompatible with the notion of humane treatment, but provide examples of what the requirement of humane treatment entails. Such examples include treatment with all due regard to the person's sex,[304] respect for convictions and religious practices,[305] provision of adequate food and drinking water[306] as

---

[300] This approach was reaffirmed in Article 4(1)–(2) of Additional Protocol II. See also Sivakumaran, 2012, pp. 257–258.

[301] *Concise Oxford English Dictionary*, 12th edition, Oxford University Press, 2011, p. 693, adding 'inflicting the minimum of pain' as another element.

[302] See e.g. Colombia, *Constitutional Case No. C-291/07*, Judgment, 2007, section III-D-5: 'La garantía general de trato humano provee el principio guía general subyacente a las convenciones de Ginebra, en el sentido de que su objeto mismo es la tarea humanitaria de proteger al individuo en tanto persona, salvaguardando los derechos que de allí se derivan.' ('The general guarantee of humane treatment provides the overall guiding principle behind the Geneva Conventions, in the sense that the object itself is the humanitarian task of protecting the individual as a person, safeguarding the rights derived from it.') See also United States, *Naval Handbook*, 2007, paras 11.1–11.2: 'Humane Treatment . . . All detainees shall: . . . f. Be respected as human beings.'

[303] See e.g. ICTY, *Aleksovski* Trial Judgment, 1999, para. 49.

[304] See e.g. Australia, *Manual of the Law of Armed Conflict*, 2006, paras 9.48 and 9.49; Canada, *Code of Conduct*, 2007, p. 2–9, para. 5; Djibouti, *Manual on International Humanitarian Law*, 2004, p. 23; Turkey, *LOAC Manual*, 2001, p. 49; and Sri Lanka, *Military Manual*, 2003, para. 1603.

[305] See e.g. Australia, *Manual of the Law of Armed Conflict*, 2006, para. 9.58; Chad, *IHL Manual*, 1996, p. 28 (version before Chad ratified Additional Protocol II); Nepal, *Army Handbook*, 2011, p. 6; Sri Lanka, *Military Manual*, 2003, para. 1222; Turkey, *LOAC Manual*, 2001, p. 158; United Kingdom, *Joint Doctrine Captured Persons*, 2015, p. 2–5; and United States, *Naval Handbook*, 2007, para. 11.2.

[306] See e.g. Chad, *IHL Manual*, 1996, p. 28; Sri Lanka, *Military Manual*, 2003, para. 1221; Turkey, *LOAC Manual*, 2001, p. 158; United Kingdom, *Joint Doctrine Captured Persons*, 2015, p. 2–4; and United States, *Naval Handbook*, 2007, para. 11.2.

well as clothing,[307] safeguards for health and hygiene,[308] provision of suitable medical care,[309] protection from violence and against the dangers of the armed conflict,[310] and appropriate contacts with the outside world.[311]

c. In all circumstances

559   According to common Article 3, the obligation of humane treatment applies 'in all circumstances', a formula that also appears in other provisions of humanitarian treaty law.[312]

560   The formula emphasizes that the obligation of humane treatment is absolute and knows no exceptions. No circumstances justify deviating from the obligation.[313] Even though, as pointed out above, the implementation of the obligation, for example the provision of adequate food or medical care, might differ depending on the specific circumstances of the armed conflict,[314] the treatment provided to a person protected under common Article 3 must never

---

[307] See e.g. United Kingdom, *Joint Doctrine Captured Persons*, 2015, p. 2–5, and United States, *Naval Handbook*, 2007, para. 11.2.

[308] See e.g. Chad, *IHL Manual*, 1996, p. 28; Sri Lanka, *Military Manual*, 2003, para. 1228; Turkey *LOAC Manual*, 2001, p. 158; and United Kingdom, *Joint Doctrine Captured Persons*, 2015, p. 2–4.

[309] See e.g. Canada, *Prisoner of War Handling Manual*, 2004, p. 1B-4; Chad, *IHL Manual*, 1996, p. 28; Sri Lanka, *Military Manual*, 2003, para. 1228; Turkey, *LOAC Manual*, 2001, pp. 159–160; United Kingdom, *Joint Doctrine Captured Persons*, 2015, p. 2–5: and United States, *Naval Handbook*, 2007, para. 11.2.

[310] See e.g. Chad, *IHL Manual*, 1996, p. 28; Sri Lanka, *Military Manual*, 2003, para. 1228; and Turkey, *LOAC Manual*, 2001, p. 158.

[311] See e.g. Chad, *IHL Manual*, 1996, p. 28; Nepal, *Army Handbook*, 2011, p. 3; Sri Lanka, *Military Manual*, 2003, para. 1228; Turkey, *LOAC Manual*, 2001, pp. 159–160; United Kingdom, *Joint Doctrine Captured Persons*, 2015, p. 2–5; and United States, Department of Defense (DoD), *DoD Detainee Program*, Directive No. 2310.01E, 19 August 2014, section 3(b)(1) 'Policy'. See also Copenhagen Process: Principles and Guidelines (2012), paras 2, 9 and 10.

[312] With reference to the treatment, respect and protection of specific categories of persons 'in all circumstances', see e.g. First Convention, Articles 12 and 24; Second Convention, Article 12; Third Convention, Article 14; Fourth Convention, Article 27; Additional Protocol I, Articles 10(2) and 75(1); and Additional Protocol II, Articles 4(1) and 7(2). The formula also appears in common Article 1 of the Geneva Conventions and Article 1(1) of Additional Protocol I, obligating the High Contracting Parties to respect and to ensure respect for the Conventions or the Protocol 'in all circumstances'. In the context of the conduct of hostilities, an obligation to observe the rules ensuring the protection of civilians against the dangers arising from military operations 'in all circumstances' is contained in Article 51(1) of Additional Protocol I and Article 13 of Additional Protocol II.

[313] See e.g. United States, *Manual on Detainee Operations*, 2014, with respect to detained persons, p. I-1: 'Inhumane treatment of detainees is prohibited by the Uniform Code of Military Justice, domestic and international law, and DOD [Department of Defense] policy. *Accordingly, there is no exception to or deviation from this humane treatment requirement*' (emphasis added). See also United States, *Naval Handbook*, 2007, paras 11.1–11.2.

[314] See e.g. Côte d'Ivoire, *Teaching Manual*, 2007, Book IV, p. 14; United Kingdom, *Joint Doctrine Captured Persons*, 2015, pp. 2–5 and 2–8; and United States, *Naval Handbook*, 2007, para. 11.1. See also Elder, p. 60.

be less than humane, as the minimum standard of treatment to be accorded to all fellow human beings.[315]

561   The phrase 'in all circumstances' has also been read as a confirmation that military necessity may not be invoked as an argument against fulfilling the obligation of humane treatment under common Article 3.[316] Some provisions of humanitarian law explicitly incorporate considerations of military necessity, balancing them against the demands of humanity. Where a provision does not do so, it must be presumed that the balance between military necessity and humanity has already been incorporated into the rule and thus military necessity may not be invoked to justify non-compliance with it.[317] The obligation of humane treatment in common Article 3 is not subject to any explicit qualification based on military necessity. Military necessity arguments therefore do not justify acts or omissions inconsistent with the requirement of humane treatment.

562   The phrase 'in all circumstances' also reinforces the non-reciprocal nature of humanitarian law, including common Article 3. A Party to an armed conflict is bound by its humanitarian law obligations irrespective of the conduct of an opposing Party. The non-observance of its obligations by one Party to an armed conflict does not relieve another Party of its obligations.[318] Such an understanding is supported by the drafting history of common Article 3. As discussed in Section B, early drafts of this article required reciprocity in order for humanitarian law to be applicable between the Parties to a non-international armed conflict.[319] However, the reciprocity requirement was dropped from

---

[315] See e.g. ICTY, *Aleksovski* Trial Judgment, 1999, paras 168, 173 and 18, and in the context of international armed conflict, Eritrea-Ethiopia Claims Commission, *Prisoners of War, Eritrea's Claim*, Partial Award, 2003, paras 58, 65, 68 and 138.

[316] See Kleffner, 2013a, pp. 326–327, commenting on 'in all circumstances' in Article 12 of the First Convention.

[317] In the words of the US Military Tribunal at Nuremberg in the *Hostages case*, Judgment, 1948, pp. 66–67, '[m]ilitary necessity or expediency do not justify a violation of positive rules'. See further Kalshoven/Zegveld, pp. 32–33 and 84; O'Connell, pp. 36–38; and Rogers, pp. 7–10.

[318] See Condorelli/Boisson de Chazournes, p. 19; Moir, p. 60; and Sandoz/Swinarski/Zimmermann (eds), *Commentary on the Additional Protocols*, ICRC, 1987, paras 49–51, commenting on 'in all circumstances' in Article 1 of Additional Protocol I. See also ICTY, *Kupreškić* Trial Judgment, 2000, para. 517:

[T]he *tu quoque* argument is flawed in principle. It envisages humanitarian law as based upon a narrow bilateral exchange of rights and obligations. Instead, the bulk of this body of law lays down absolute obligations, namely obligations that are unconditional or in other words not based on reciprocity.

See in this respect also Article 60(5) of the 1969 Vienna Convention on the Law of Treaties, which precludes States from suspending or terminating for material breach any treaty provision 'relating to the protection of the human person contained in treaties of a humanitarian character, in particular to provisions prohibiting any form of reprisals against persons protected by such treaties'.

[319] See e.g. draft article 2(4) of the draft convention relative to the treatment of prisoners of war, adopted by the 17th International Conference of the Red Cross in Stockholm in 1948 and used as the basis for negotiations at the 1949 Diplomatic Conference:

the text and the opposite was expressed through the 'in all circumstances' formula.

563   In the context of non-international armed conflict, international law contains no rules on the resort to force in the sense of *jus ad bellum*. The phrase 'in all circumstances' reaffirms that the lawfulness of one's own resort to force or the unlawfulness of an opponent's use of force do not justify violations of the law governing the way in which such use of force is conducted.[320] While the national laws of a State usually prohibit violent acts against governmental authorities or between persons on its territory, States generally have a right to use force in order to restore domestic public security, law and order.[321] Irrespective of this right, once a situation of violence reaches the threshold of a non-international armed conflict, all Parties to that conflict must comply with their obligations under humanitarian treaty and customary law. Whether or not a State or a non-State Party to a non-international armed conflict has a right to engage in that conflict under domestic law is of no relevance to its obligations under humanitarian law. Humanitarian law applicable to non-international armed conflict was developed precisely to regulate such situations of violence, in particular to protect all persons not or no longer actively participating in hostilities. If the applicability of humanitarian law was dependent on the lawfulness or unlawfulness of a resort to force, humanitarian law could not fulfil this purpose.[322]

564   Lastly, it is important to point out that 'in all circumstances' is not to be understood as meaning that common Article 3, as a treaty law provision, applies in all armed conflicts, i.e. in international and non-international armed conflicts alike. Such a reading would be inconsistent with the specific scope of application of common Article 3, which is limited to non-international armed conflict. Nevertheless, the fundamental rules of humanitarian law set forth in common Article 3 are today recognized as a 'minimum yardstick' that is binding in all armed conflicts as a reflection of 'elementary considerations of humanity'.[323] In addition, however, there are more detailed rules of treaty law

---

In all cases of armed conflict not of an international character which may occur in the territory of one or more of the High Contracting Parties, each of the *Parties to the conflict* shall be bound to implement the provisions of the present Convention, *subject to the adverse party likewise acting in obedience thereto*. The Convention shall be applicable in these circumstances, whatever the legal status of the Parties to the conflict and without prejudice thereto.

   Draft Conventions adopted by the 1948 Stockholm Conference, pp. 51–52. For more details, see section B.

[320] See Bugnion, p. 173, with reference to the 'in all circumstances' formula in common Article 1.
[321] For more details, see Bugnion, pp. 169–170. For an overview of the debate on whether Article 51 of the 1945 UN Charter also includes a right of States to use force in self-defence against non-State actors operating from the territory of another State, see Tams.
[322] For more details, see Bugnion, pp. 186 and 197, and Sassòli/Bouvier/Quintin, pp. 114–121.
[323] ICJ, *Military and Paramilitary Activities in and against Nicaragua case*, Merits, Judgment, 1986, paras 218–219.

that prescribe humane treatment of persons comparable in their vulnerability to those protected under common Article 3 during international armed conflict.[324]

2. The prohibition of adverse distinction

a. Introduction

565 The persons protected under common Article 3(1), subparagraph (1), are in all circumstances to be treated humanely 'without any adverse distinction founded on race, colour, religion or faith, sex, birth or wealth, or any other similar criteria'.

566 This obligation is reaffirmed by Additional Protocol II.[325]

567 The insistence that certain rules of humanitarian law be applied without distinction can be traced back to the origins of the codification of humanitarian law applicable to international armed conflict.[326] Article 4 of the 1929 Geneva Convention on Prisoners of War formulated the considerations that are at the basis of the prohibition of adverse distinction in humanitarian law: 'Differences of treatment between prisoners are permissible only if such differences are based on the military rank, the state of physical or mental health, the professional abilities, or the sex of those who benefit from them.' As such, differentiation in treatment is not prohibited *per se* and may even be required under humanitarian law. The clause in common Article 3 reflects this approach. Any form of differentiation that is not justified by substantively different situations and needs is prohibited.[327]

---

[324] For the imperative of humane treatment of the wounded, sick and shipwrecked, see Article 12(2) of the First and Second Conventions; for prisoners of war, see Article 13(1) of the Third Convention; for civilian protected persons, see Article 27(1) of the Fourth Convention; and for persons who are in the power of a Party to the conflict and who do not benefit from more favourable treatment under the Geneva Conventions or under Additional Protocol I, see Article 75(1) of Additional Protocol I.

[325] Article 2(1) of Additional Protocol II in fact extends the prohibition of adverse distinction to the application of the Protocol as a whole. With respect to humane treatment 'without any adverse distinction' of persons not or no longer taking a direct part in hostilities, see Article 4(1) of Additional Protocol II. For more details, see the commentaries on Articles 2 and 4 of Additional Protocol II.

[326] See Geneva Convention (1864), Article 6; Geneva Convention (1906), Article 1; Hague Convention (X) (1907), Article 11; and Geneva Convention on the Wounded and Sick (1929), Article 1. For more details, see the commentary on Article 12, section F.1.c.

[327] For international armed conflict, the prohibition of adverse distinction is laid down for the wounded, sick and shipwrecked in Article 12 of the First and Second Conventions and in Article 9 of Additional Protocol I; for prisoners of war, in Article 16 of the Third Convention; for the whole of the populations of countries in conflict, in Article 13 of the Fourth Convention; for protected persons, in Article 27 of the Fourth Convention; and for persons who are in the power of a Party to the conflict and who do not benefit from more favourable treatment under the Geneva Conventions or under Additional Protocol I, in Article 75 of the Protocol.

b. Adverse distinction

568 Common Article 3 requires humane treatment 'without any adverse distinction'. This phrase reinforces the absolute character of the obligation of humane treatment under common Article 3.

569 Common Article 3 lists 'race, colour, religion or faith, sex, birth or wealth' as prohibited grounds for adverse distinction among protected persons. As is evident from the addition of the concluding phrase 'or any other similar criteria', this list is not exhaustive but only illustrative. Adverse distinction founded on other grounds, such as age, state of health, level of education or family connections of a person protected under common Article 3 would therefore equally be prohibited.

570 Further prohibited grounds for adverse distinction were explicitly added in Article 2(1) of Additional Protocol II: language, political or other opinion, and national or social origin, again accompanied by the concluding phrase 'or any other similar criteria'.[328] These grounds, too, would constitute 'other similar' adverse criteria prohibited under common Article 3.

571 Unlike other provisions of humanitarian law,[329] common Article 3 does not list 'nationality' as a prohibited criterion.[330] This might be seen as merely a reflection of the consideration that in non-international armed conflict questions of nationality arise less frequently than in international armed conflict. However, this is not necessarily the case; persons of varying nationalities may well be involved in or affected by a non-international armed conflict. While recognizing this, the Working Party preparing the draft of the final text of common Article 3 at the 1949 Diplomatic Conference nevertheless decided not to include nationality as a criterion, given that it might be perfectly legal for a government to treat insurgents who are its own nationals differently in an adverse sense from foreigners taking part in a civil war. The latter might be looked on as being guilty of a worse offence than nationals of the country

---

[328] See Additional Protocol II, Article 2(1). These criteria are very similar to those in Article 2(1) of the 1966 International Covenant on Civil and Political Rights: 'race, colour, sex, language, religion, political or other opinion, national or social origin, property, birth or other status'. For an explanation of these criteria, see e.g. Nowak, pp. 47–57. For prohibited adverse distinction criteria listed for international armed conflict, First Convention, Article 12; Second Convention, Article 12; Third Convention, Article 16; Fourth Convention, Article 27(3); and Additional Protocol I, Articles 9(1) and 75(1).

[329] For international armed conflict, see First and Second Conventions, Article 12, and Third Convention, Article 16.

[330] Article 2(1) of Additional Protocol II, like Articles 9(1) and 75(1) of Additional Protocol I and Article 2(1) of the 1966 International Covenant on Civil and Political Rights, refers to 'national origin', thereby introducing a nationality-related concept, albeit not nationality as such; see e.g. Sivakumaran, 2012, p. 259. In the context of the International Covenant, however, national origin has been interpreted as overlapping with the criteria of race, colour and ethnic origin, rather than as referring to nationality as such, with nationality falling under 'other status'; for an overview of the discussion, see e.g. Nowak, pp. 54–55, with further references.

concerned or, conversely, they might be treated less severely or merely subject to deportation.[331]

572   Not including 'nationality' in the list validly takes into account the right of States to impose sanctions under domestic law on persons engaging in a non-international armed conflict. That, however, has no bearing on common Article 3's imperative of humane treatment without any adverse distinction. Common Article 3 is strictly humanitarian in character. It does not limit a State's right to suppress a non-international armed conflict or to penalize involvement in such a conflict. It is focused exclusively on ensuring that every person not or no longer actively participating in the hostilities is treated humanely. In the domestic judicial assessment of a non-international armed conflict, nationality may be regarded as an aggravating or extenuating circumstance, but it cannot be regarded as affecting in any way the humanitarian law obligation of humane treatment. To subject foreign nationals in a non-international armed conflict to inhumane treatment is incompatible with common Article 3.[332] While, for the reasons described above, the 1949 Diplomatic Conference did not list nationality as a prohibited criterion, it must therefore be understood as falling within the concept of 'other similar criteria' under common Article 3.[333]

573   In order to be fully effective, the prohibition of 'any adverse distinction' under common Article 3 must be understood to comprise not only measures that single out certain persons protected under common Article 3 for adverse treatment, but also seemingly neutral measures that have the effect of adversely affecting certain persons. For persons falling within the protective scope of common Article 3, it makes no difference whether they are directly selected for inhumane treatment, or whether their inhumane treatment is the indirect

---

[331] See *Final Record of the Diplomatic Conference of Geneva of 1949*, Vol. II-B, p. 94.

[332] Similar considerations apply to 'political or other opinion', explicitly listed in Article 2(1) of Additional Protocol II as a prohibited ground for adverse distinction and subsumable under common Article 3's prohibition of adverse distinction on 'any other similar criteria'. The 'political or other opinion' of a person protected under common Article 3, leading for example to active participation in a non-international armed conflict or allegiance with one of the Parties to the conflict, may be of consequence under domestic law. It is, however, of no relevance for the absolute obligation of the Parties to the conflict under common Article 3 to treat that person humanely. Unlike nationality, the question of political or other opinion was not specifically discussed at the 1949 Diplomatic Conference.

[333] In not listing nationality as a prohibited criterion, common Article 3 is similar to Article 27(3) of the Fourth Convention prohibiting adverse distinction against protected persons. Considering that the applicability of certain provisions of the Fourth Convention in fact depend on a person's nationality, the 1949 Diplomatic Conference omitted nationality from the list of criteria in Article 27(3): 'the word "nationality" had been omitted in Article 25 [ultimately adopted as Article 27] because internment or measures restricting personal liberty were applied to enemy aliens precisely on grounds of nationality'; see *Final Record of the Diplomatic Conference of Geneva of 1949*, Volume II-A, p. 641. However, as in the case of common Article 3, the absolute obligation of humane treatment contained in Article 27(1) of the Fourth Convention exists independently of these considerations. For more details, see the commentary on Article 27 of the Fourth Convention.

consequence of general policies.[334] When adopting general policies, a Party to a non-international armed conflict will therefore need to take into account the potential consequences of these policies on all persons protected under common Article 3 who are affected by them.

c. Non-adverse distinction

574 As indicated above, common Article 3, like other provisions of humanitarian law, does not prohibit distinctions as such.

575 It does not prohibit non-adverse distinctions, i.e. distinctions that are justified by the substantively different situations and needs of persons protected under common Article 3.

576 This allows for differentiated treatment that in fact serves the purpose of realizing a person's humane treatment. While the legal obligation of humane treatment under common Article 3 is absolute; the ways to achieve such treatment must be adapted to a person's specific needs.[335] Humane treatment accorded to one person is not necessarily sufficient to constitute humane treatment for another person. Therefore, common Article 3 does not prohibit differentiated treatment that is actually necessary in order to achieve humane treatment.[336]

577 Common Article 3 does not specifically mention possible grounds that justify differential treatment among the persons it protects. Such grounds can, however, be found in many other provisions of humanitarian law. In particular, a person's state of health, age or sex is traditionally recognized as justifying, and in fact requiring, differential treatment.[337] In order to ensure survival, for example, the gravity of a person's wounds or illness may necessitate prioritization of that person's medical treatment over the treatment of other, less severely

---

[334] An example of the latter would be the distribution of standardized food rations to persons deprived of their liberty, which, while generally of adequate nutritional value, might be inadequate or culturally intolerable for some.

[335] In the context of international human rights law, this is commonly referred to as the concept of substantial rather than formal equality. In *Thlimmenos v. Greece*, the European Court of Human Rights held with regard to Article 14 of the 1950 European Convention on Human Rights that '[t]he right not to be discriminated against in the enjoyment of the rights guaranteed under the Convention is also violated when States without an objective and reasonable justification fail to treat differently persons whose situations are significantly different' (Judgment, 2000, para. 44).

[336] See e.g. Pejic, 2001, p. 186.

[337] See, for non-international armed conflict, Article 4(3) of Additional Protocol II: 'Children shall be provided with the care and aid they require.' For international armed conflict, see e.g. First and Second Conventions, Article 12(3)–(4); Third Convention, Article 16; Fourth Convention, Article 27(2)–(3); and Additional Protocol I, Articles 76 and 77–78. See also the provisions regulating the pronouncement and execution of the death penalty on persons under the age of 18, pregnant women, and mothers of dependent infants/young children: Additional Protocol II, Article 6(4); Fourth Convention, Article 68(4); and Additional Protocol I, Articles 77(5) and 76(3). See also Rona/McGuire, p. 195.

injured or ill persons.[338] The age of a person deprived of liberty may require appropriate treatment, for example in terms of the kind of food or medical care provided; and pregnant or nursing women in detention may similarly require tailored nourishment and medical care or adjustments in the organization and equipment of their accommodation.

578   Grounds for non-adverse distinction could also be found in an awareness of how the social, economic, cultural or political context in a society forms roles or patterns with specific statuses, needs and capacities that differ among men and women of different ages and backgrounds. Taking such considerations into account is no violation of the prohibition of adverse distinction, but rather contributes to the realization of humane treatment of all persons protected under common Article 3.[339]

579   A Party to a non-international armed conflict can always choose to grant treatment above the standard of humane treatment. There exists, however, no legal obligation in this respect in common Article 3.

580   In any event, treatment above the standard of humane treatment that is accorded to some persons must under no circumstances lead to less than humane treatment of all other persons protected under common Article 3(1), subparagraph (1).

G. Subparagraph (1): Acts prohibited under common Article 3

1. Introduction

581   This subparagraph is introduced by the sentence '[t]o this end, the following acts are and shall remain prohibited at any time and in any place whatsoever with respect to the above-mentioned persons'. The first words of this sentence – '[t]o this end' – reaffirm that the prohibitions set out in this subparagraph aim at ensuring the humane treatment of all persons falling within its protective scope.

582   In addition, the words 'are and shall remain prohibited' reaffirm that the prohibitions are absolute and admit no exception.

583   The phrase 'at any time and in any place whatsoever' refers to the geographical and temporal scope of application of common Article 3.[340] The reference to 'the above-mentioned persons' refers to the persons protected by this subparagraph.[341]

---

[338] For more details, see section I.6.

[339] In permitting and in fact requiring distinction that is not adverse but favourable to the persons concerned, so that they fully benefit from humane treatment, humanitarian law is not dissimilar to human rights law in its approach to non-discrimination; see e.g. UN Human Rights Committee, *General Comment No. 18: Non-discrimination*, 10 November 1989, paras 7–8 and 13.

[340] For details, see sections C.3 and C.4.   [341] For details, see section E.

2. *Violence to life and person, in particular murder of all kinds, mutilation, cruel treatment and torture*

a. *Violence to life and person*

i. Introduction

584 Violence to life and person is listed first among the acts specifically prohibited in common Article 3. The prominent position given to this prohibition underlines its fundamental importance in ensuring humane treatment.

585 Common Article 3 protects persons not or no longer participating in hostilities.[342] It is therefore evident why the article outlaws violence to their lives and persons. Such violence has no bearing on the enemy's military operations or capacities. There is no military need to violate their persons.[343] The gratuitous taking of human life or violation of a person's physical or mental well-being is irreconcilable with the imperative of humane treatment that is at the basis of common Article 3.

586 The prohibition of violence to life and person is reaffirmed in Article 4(2)(a) of Additional Protocol II.

587 Common Article 3 illustrates the prohibition of violence to life and person by listing '*in particular* murder of all kinds, mutilation, cruel treatment and torture' (emphasis added) as being prohibited. This means that acts omitted from the list of specific examples can still fall under the more general prohibition. An act that, for example, does not amount to torture or cruel treatment can still be prohibited as an act of violence to person.

588 International and regional human rights treaties, within their respective fields of application, require respect for the right to life[344] and the right to integrity of the person.[345] In general, these instruments exclude these rights from derogation in time of public emergency.[346]

---

[342] For details, see section E.

[343] As succinctly formulated in the preamble to the 1868 St Petersburg Declaration, albeit in the context of international armed conflict, 'the only legitimate object which States should endeavour to accomplish during war is to weaken the military forces of the enemy; ... for this purpose it is sufficient to disable the greatest possible number of men'.

[344] See e.g. International Covenant on Civil and Political Rights (1966), Article 6; European Convention on Human Rights (1950) Article 2; American Convention on Human Rights (1969), Article 4; and African Charter on Human and Peoples' Rights (1981), Article 4.

[345] Some human rights instruments explicitly protect the right to integrity of the person, while other instruments only address it in the form of the more specific prohibitions of torture or cruel, inhuman or degrading treatment or punishment. See International Covenant on Civil and Political Rights (1966), Article 7; European Convention on Human Rights (1950), Article 3; American Convention on Human Rights (1969), Article 5; and African Charter on Human and Peoples' Rights (1981), Article 4.

[346] See e.g. International Covenant on Civil and Political Rights (1966), Article 4; European Convention on Human Rights (1950), Article 15; and American Convention on Human Rights (1969), Article 27. Note, however, that according to Article 15(2) of the European Convention, derogations from the right to life are not prohibited 'in respect of deaths resulting from lawful acts of war'; compare also, in this context, Article 2(2)(c) of the European Convention. The 1981 African Charter on Human and Peoples' Rights contains no derogation clause.

ii. Protected values: life and person

589 The first value protected by the prohibition of violence to life and person is human life. This prohibition underlines the all-encompassing importance of respect for the lives of persons benefiting from the protection of common Article 3. Where not even their lives are respected, the provision's ultimate purpose, humane treatment, is unattainable.[347]

590   The second value protected by this prohibition is the human 'person'. In the English text, common Article 3 does not indicate whether this comprises only the integrity of the physical person or also a person's mental integrity. In the equally authentic French version, the wording is more specific ('atteintes portées à la vie et à l'intégrité corporelle'), suggesting that a person's mental integrity is excluded from the protective scope of the prohibition of violence to person in common Article 3. Article 4(2) of Additional Protocol II expressly proscribes 'violence to the ... health and *physical or mental* well-being of persons' (emphasis added). On the one hand, this could be read as a clarification that violence to person also includes violence to a person's mental integrity or, on the other hand, it can be seen as an indication that violence to mental integrity was intentionally excluded from common Article 3's prohibition of violence to person.[348] Today, however, it is widely accepted that the prohibition of torture and cruel treatment under common Article 3 – specific examples of the prohibition of violence to person – includes acts detrimental to the mental integrity of the person.[349]

iii. Prohibited behaviour: violence to life and person

591 Common Article 3 prohibits 'violence' to the lives and persons of the individuals coming under its protection; it does not define the meaning of 'violence'.

592   The prohibition of violence to life and person evidently covers violence that results in the death or injury of a person protected under common Article 3. The transgression of the prohibition of violence to life and person is not however contingent on whether death of the victim takes place. In many instances, an act of violence to life that does not lead to the death of the victim will, at least, lead to some bodily or mental harm, thereby falling under the prohibition of violence to person.

593   Considering the purpose of the prohibition of violence to life and person – to ensure humane treatment of persons not or no longer actively participating in hostilities – the prohibition must also be understood as comprising omissions under certain circumstances. For example, letting persons under one's

---

[347] See Nowak, p. 121, with further references, noting in the context of international human rights law: 'The right to life has properly been characterized as the supreme human right, ... since without effective guarantee of this right, all other rights of the human being would be devoid of meaning.'

[348] See Sandoz/Swinarski/Zimmermann, para. 4532, as well as Zimmermann/Geiss, para. 888.

[349] For details, see sections G.2.d and G.2.e.

responsibility starve to death by failing to provide food, or letting such persons die or continue to suffer from wounds or sickness by failing to provide medical care, while having the possibility to do so, is irreconcilable with the requirement of humane treatment.[350]

594 As is manifest from the acknowledgment of 'executions' in subparagraph (1)(d), common Article 3 does not prohibit the death penalty against persons falling within its protective scope. However, it does require that a death sentence be passed and an execution carried out only following a 'previous judgment pronounced by a regularly constituted court, affording all the judicial guarantees which are recognized as indispensable by civilized peoples'.[351] A death sentence or execution not respecting these strict requirements would not only be in violation of subparagraph (1)(d), but would also constitute unlawful violence to life within the meaning of subparagraph (1)(a).[352]

595 Common Article 3 does not contain a specific prohibition on corporal punishment. Such an explicit prohibition is, however, included in Article 4(2)(a) of Additional Protocol II, which prohibits 'violence to the life, health and physical or mental well-being of persons, in particular murder as well as *cruel treatment such as* torture, mutilation or *any form of corporal punishment*' (emphasis added). This could be read as an indication that corporal punishment required an explicit prohibition in Additional Protocol II and is not prohibited under common Article 3.[353] Common Article 3 does, however, contain the specific prohibition of cruel treatment, the category under which Article 4(2)(a) of Additional Protocol II mentions corporal punishment as an example. In addition, provided that it fulfils the specific requirements of, for example, mutilation or torture, corporal punishment would also be prohibited through these prohibitions contained in common Article 3.[354]

---

[350] On the issue of omission, see the commentary on Article 50, para 2954.

[351] For more details, see section G.5.

[352] From the perspective of international armed conflict, see Dörmann, 2003, pp. 40–41, noting, as regards the war crime of 'wilful killing' under Article 8(2)(a)(i) of the 1998 ICC Statute, that the following behaviours have been held to constitute war crimes: '[K]illing in the absence of a (fair) trial.... The decision for and execution of an unlawful death penalty, which means contrary especially to Arts. 100–2, 107 GC III [Third Geneva Convention] with respect to prisoners of war, and Arts. 68, 71, 74, 75 GC IV [Fourth Geneva Convention] with respect to civilians,... also constitute cases of wilful killing.'

[353] The drafting history of Article 4 of Additional Protocol II might support this conclusion: unlike other parts of Article 4(2)(a) of the Protocol, the inclusion of the reference to corporal punishment gave rise to debate at the 1974–1977 Diplomatic Conference, with some delegations preferring a prohibition of 'any form of bodily harm', arguing that corporal punishment would include imprisonment and noting that corporal punishment was 'a means of punishment recognized in many national legislations'; see, in particular, *Official Records of the Diplomatic Conference of Geneva of 1974–1977*, Vol. VIII, pp. 421–429, paras 5 and 12, and Vol. X, pp. 49–50, paras 146–147, and pp. 103–104.

[354] In the context of international armed conflict, an explicit prohibition of corporal punishment of protected persons was already included in Article 46 of the 1929 Geneva Convention on Prisoners of War, and subsequently in Article 87 of the Third Convention, Article 32 of the Fourth Convention and Article 75(2)(a)(iii) of Additional Protocol I.

b. Murder

596   The first specific example of 'violence to life and person' listed in common Article 3 is 'murder of all kinds'. The prohibition of murder is reaffirmed in Article 4(2)(a) of Additional Protocol II. It is also part of customary international law.[355]

597   Neither common Article 3 nor other provisions of humanitarian law define 'murder'. It has been stated that '[m]urder is a crime that is clearly understood and well defined in the national law of every State. This prohibited act does not require any further explanation.'[356] However, conceptions of the notion of murder vary in national laws, influenced by national criminal-law tradition.[357] It is therefore useful to note that common Article 3 prohibits murder 'of all kinds'. This indicates that the prohibition of murder in common Article 3 is not to be interpreted narrowly.

598   Violations of common Article 3, including 'murder' of persons not or no longer actively participating in hostilities, have consistently been prosecuted under Article 3 of the 1993 ICTY Statute (Violations of the laws or customs of war).[358] According to the ICTY, 'there can be no line drawn between "wilful killing" and "murder" which affects their content',[359] the only difference being that 'under Article 3 of the Statute the offence need not have been directed against a "protected person" but against a person "taking no active part in the hostilities"'.[360] This approach was reaffirmed in the 2002 ICC Elements of Crimes, which, for the war crimes of 'wilful killing' in international armed conflict and 'murder' in non-international armed conflict, adopted substantively identical elements of crimes, except for the victims of the crimes.[361] International case law on 'wilful killing' can therefore be consulted for the meaning of 'murder' and vice versa.[362]

599   Based on the above, the following elements of the prohibition of 'murder' under common Article 3 can be identified:

– It is prohibited to kill, or cause the death of, a person protected under common Article 3(1).[363]

---

[355] ICRC Study on Customary International Humanitarian Law (2005), Rule 89.
[356] See ILC Draft Code of Crimes against the Peace and Security of Mankind (1996), p. 48, commenting on 'murder' as a crime against humanity.
[357] For an overview of some systems, see e.g. Horder.
[358] See e.g. ICTY, *Mucić* Trial Judgment, 1998, para. 316.   [359] *Ibid.* para. 422.
[360] ICTY, *Kordić and Čerkez* Trial Judgment, 2001, para. 233.
[361] See ICC Elements of Crimes (2002), Article 8(2)(a)(i) and (c)(i).
[362] For more details, see the commentary on Article 50, section D.1.
[363] See e.g. ICTY, *Mucić* Trial Judgment, 1998, para. 424; *Jelisić* Trial Judgment, 1999, para. 35; *Blaškić* Trial Judgment, 2000, para. 153; *Kordić and Čerkez* Appeal Judgment, 2004, paras 36–37; *Blagojević and Jokić* Trial Judgment, 2005, para. 556; *Limaj* Trial Judgment, 2005, para. 241; *Krajišnik* Trial Judgment, 2006, para. 715; *Mrkšić* Trial Judgment, 2007, para. 486; *Dragomir Milošević* Appeal Judgment, 2009, para. 108; *Milutinović* Trial Judgment, 2009, paras 137–138; *Gotovina* Trial Judgment, 2011, para. 1725; *Đorđević* Trial Judgment, 2011, para. 1708; *Perišić* Trial Judgment, 2011, para. 102; ICTR, *Ndindiliyimana* Trial Judgment, 2011, para. 2143; *Nyiramasuhuko* Trial Judgment, 2011, para. 6165; *Nizeyimana* Trial Judgment, 2012, para. 1552;

– Prohibited as 'murder' is the intentional killing or causing of death of such persons, as well as the reckless killing or causing of their death. Death that is purely accidental or an unforeseeable consequence of a person's negligent act or omission does not fall under the prohibition of 'murder'.[364] In many situations, such as deprivation of liberty, persons protected under common Article 3 are under the complete control of a Party to a conflict and are therefore dependent on that Party for their survival. The creation or tolerance of unhealthful conditions of detention might therefore be regarded as a reckless or intentional act or omission.[365]

– Both acts and omissions are prohibited.[366] For instance, the failure to provide persons protected by common Article 3 who are under one's responsibility with sufficient food or medical care, while having the possibility to do so, leading to their death by starvation, can also fall under the prohibition of murder under common Article 3.[367]

600　　The concept of murder in common Article 3 does not, however, apply to killing during the conduct of hostilities.[368] The legality of such killing has to be assessed on the basis of the specific rules on the conduct of hostilities, in particular the rules on distinction, proportionality and precautions.

SCSL, *Brima* Trial Judgment, 2007, paras 688–690; *Fofana and Kondewa* Trial Judgment, 2007, para. 146; *Sesay* Trial Judgment, 2009, para. 142; *Taylor* Trial Judgment, 2012, paras 412–413; and ICC, *Bemba* Trial Judgment, 2016, paras 91–97. For more details, see the commentary on Article 50, section D.1.

[364] See e.g. ICTY, *Mucić* Trial Judgment, 1998, paras 437 and 439; *Blaškić* Trial Judgment, 2000, para. 153; *Kordić and Čerkez* Trial Judgment, 2001, para. 229; *Naletilić and Martinović* Trial Judgment, 2003, para. 248; *Stakić* Trial Judgment, 2003, para. 587; *Brđanin* Trial Judgment, 2004, para. 386; and *Kordić and Čerkez* Appeal Judgment, 2004, para. 36. See also Dörmann, 2016, p. 329–331, commenting on Article 8(2)(a)(i) of the 1998 ICC Statute. For more details, see the commentary on Article 50, section D.1.b.

[365] See Dörmann, 2003, p. 43, referring, *inter alia*, to United Kingdom, Military Court at Brunswick, *Gerike case* (also known as *The Velpke Children's Home case*), 1946, pp. 76–81, in which several defendants charged with committing a war crime were found guilty, 'in that they at Velpke, Germany, between the months of May and December, 1944, in violation of the laws and usages of war, were concerned in the killing by wilful neglect of a number of children, Polish Nationals'.

[366] This is independent of the question of whether the violation of the prohibition will lead to international criminal responsibility. Individual criminal responsibility for omission has been recognized by international courts and tribunals. See e.g. ICTY, *Mucić* Trial Judgment, 1998, para. 424; *Blaškić* Trial Judgment, 2000, para. 153; *Kordić and Čerkez* Trial Judgment, 2001, para. 229; *Blagojević and Jokić* Trial Judgment, 2005, para. 556; *Limaj* Trial Judgment, 2005, para. 241; *Krajišnik* Trial Judgment, 2006, para. 715; *Mrkšić* Trial Judgment, 2007, para. 486; *Dragomir Milošević* Appeal Judgment, 2009, para. 108; *Milutinović* Trial Judgment, 2009, paras 137–138; *Đorđević* Trial Judgment, 2011, para. 1708; *Gotovina* Trial Judgment, 2011, para. 1725; *Perišić* Trial Judgment, 2011, para. 102; ICTR, *Nyiramasuhuko* Trial Judgment, 2011, para. 6165; *Nizeyimana* Trial Judgment, 2012, para. 1552; SCSL, *Brima* Trial Judgment, 2007, paras 688–690; *Fofana and Kondewa* Trial Judgment, 2007, para. 146; *Sesay* Trial Judgment, 2009, para. 142; and *Taylor* Trial Judgment, 2012, paras 412–413.

[367] See the commentary on the grave breach of 'wilful killing' in Article 50, section D.1. The ECCC found an accused guilty of the grave breach of wilful killing as detainees died 'as the result of omissions known to be likely to lead to death and as a consequence of the conditions of detention imposed upon them'; see *Kaing* Trial Judgment, 2010, para. 437.

[368] For more details, see section E.4. See also Knuckey, pp. 452–456.

c. Mutilation

601 The second specific example of prohibited 'violence to life and person' is mutilation. This prohibition is a long-standing rule of humanitarian law.[369] It is
also included in other provisions of the Third and Fourth Conventions and
reaffirmed in the 1977 Additional Protocols.[370] The prohibition is now part of
customary international law.[371] There is no indication in law or derived from
practice that the term 'mutilation' has a different meaning in international and
non-international armed conflict.[372]

i. Definition of mutilation

602 Mutilation is not specifically defined in the Geneva Conventions or the Additional Protocols. The Conventions and Protocols use both the terms 'physical
mutilation' and 'mutilation'.[373] In its ordinary meaning, to 'mutilate' is defined
as to 'injure or damage severely, typically so as to disfigure'.[374] The term mutilation thus refers to an act of physical violence. Hence, the terms 'mutilation' and
'physical mutilation' must be understood to have synonymous meanings.[375]

603 The ICC Elements of Crimes provides that mutilation consists 'in particular'
of 'permanently disfiguring the person or persons' or 'permanently disabling or
removing an organ or appendage'.[376] This definition is followed in the case law
of the Special Court for Sierra Leone.[377] There does not, however, seem to exist
at present any national or international case law to further interpret the terms
'mutilation', 'permanent disfigurement' or 'disabling or removal' as used in the
Elements of Crimes.

604 The term 'permanent' injury used in the Elements of Crimes should be
understood in its ordinary meaning as 'lasting or remaining unchanged indefinitely, or intended to be so; not temporary'.[378] This implies that it would not
be necessary for the injury to last forever.[379]

---

[369] See e.g. Lieber Code (1863), Articles 16 and 44 (prohibiting maiming) and 56 (prohibiting
mutilation).
[370] See Third Convention, Article 13(1); Fourth Convention, Article 32; Additional Protocol I,
Articles 11(2)(a) and 75(2)(a)(iv); and Additional Protocol II, Article 4(2)(a).
[371] ICRC Study on Customary International Humanitarian Law (2005), Rule 92.
[372] See Dörmann, 2003, pp. 231 and 484.
[373] The Conventions and Protocols use the term 'mutilation', the exception being Article 13(1) of
the Third Convention and Article 11(2)(a) of Additional Protocol I, which use the term 'physical
mutilation(s)'.
[374] *Concise Oxford English Dictionary*, 12th edition, Oxford University Press, 2011, p. 945.
[375] See Dörmann, 2012, pp. 230 and 397, and Zimmermann, pp. 489–490.
[376] ICC Elements of Crimes (2002), Article 8(2)(b)(x)-1, (c)(i)-2 and (e)(xi)-1. For a commentary on
these elements, see Dörmann, 2012, pp. 229–233, 396–397 and 482–484. See also La Haye, 2001,
pp. 164–166 and 208–209.
[377] See SCSL, *Brima* Trial Judgment, 2007, para. 724, and *Sesay* Trial Judgment, 2009, para. 180,
and Appeal Judgment, 2009, para. 1198.
[378] *Concise Oxford English Dictionary*, 12th edition, Oxford University Press, 2011, p. 1068.
[379] See also United States, *Manual for Military Commissions*, 2010, Part IV, para. 5(14)(c), which
considers the offence of mutilation to be complete 'even though there is a possibility that the

605 The term 'disfiguring' used in the Elements of Crimes should also be understood in its ordinary meaning as spoiling someone's appearance.[380] To 'spoil', in turn, requires a certain degree of severity.[381]

606 Practices documented in contemporary armed conflicts illustrate conduct that qualifies as mutilation. These include such acts as amputating hands or feet,[382] cutting off other body parts,[383] mutilation of sexual organs,[384] or carving someone's body.[385] Other examples cited include taking out a person's eye, knocking out teeth, injuring internal organs or scarring a face with acid.[386]

ii. Exception

607 Mutilation may be justified only on strict medical grounds, namely if it is conducive to improving the state of health of the person concerned, such as the amputation of a gangrenous limb. Although this exception is not explicitly stated in common Article 3, any other interpretation would be inconsistent with the article's object and purpose, as it would conflict with the obligation to care for the wounded and sick. This conclusion is reinforced by reference to the Third Convention and Additional Protocol I, which explicitly spell out this exception.[387]

---

victim may eventually recover the use of the member or organ, or that the disfigurement may be cured by surgery'.

[380] See *Concise Oxford English Dictionary*, 12th edition, Oxford University Press, 2011, p. 410 (to 'disfigure' is defined as to 'spoil the appearance of').

[381] See *ibid.* p. 1395 ('spoil' is defined as 'diminish or destroy the value or quality of'). See SCSL, *Sesay* Trial Judgment, 2009, para. 179 ('mutilation is a particularly egregious form of prohibited violence'); ICTR, *Kayishema and Ruzindana* Trial Judgment, 1999, para. 108 (mutilation amounts to 'serious bodily harm'), and Appeal Judgment, 2001, para. 361 (some types of harm are more severe than others, for instance mutilation); *Akayesu* Trial Judgment, 1998, paras 706–707 (mutilation inflicts 'serious' bodily harm); and Canada, Superior Court, Criminal Division, Province of Québec, *Munyaneza case*, Judgment, 2009, para. 88 (mutilation is recognized as an act 'causing serious physical harm'). See also United States, *Manual for Military Commissions*, 2010, Part IV, para. 5(14)(c):

A disfigurement need not mutilate any entire member to come within the article, or be of any particular type, but must be such as to impair perceptibly and materially the victim's comeliness. The disfigurement, diminishment of vigor, or destruction or disablement of any member or organ must be a serious injury of a substantially permanent nature.

[382] See e.g. SCSL, *Koroma* Indictment, 2003, para. 31.

[383] See e.g. ICTR, *Kajelijeli* Trial Judgment, 2003, paras 935–936, and Human Rights Watch, *Shattered Lives: Sexual Violence during the Rwandan Genocide and its Aftermath*, September 1996.

[384] See e.g. ICTR, *Bagosora* Trial Judgment, 2008, para. 2266; *Kajelijeli* Trial Judgment, 2003, paras 935–936; and ICTY, *Tadić* Trial Judgment, 1997, paras 45 and 237; UN Commission on Human Rights, *Report of the Special Rapporteur on violence against women, its causes and consequences on her mission to Colombia (1–7 November 2001)*, UN Doc. E/CN.4/2002/83/Add.3, para. 42; and Human Rights Watch, *Shattered Lives: Sexual Violence during the Rwandan Genocide and its Aftermath*, September 1996.

[385] See e.g. SCSL, *Koroma* Indictment, 2003, para. 31.

[386] See United States, *Manual for Military Commissions*, 2010, Part IV, para. 5(14)(c).

[387] See Third Convention, Article 13(1), and Additional Protocol I, Article 11(1)–(2).

608   The ICC Elements of Crimes, for the elements adopted for the war crime of mutilation, also provides for the exception when the conduct is 'justified by the medical, dental or hospital treatment of the person or persons concerned [or] carried out in such person's or persons' interests'.[388] The exception is confirmed in the case law of the Special Court for Sierra Lcone.[389]

609   This is the only exception. Consent may never justify an act of mutilation. This is stated explicitly in Article 11(2) of Additional Protocol I. It is also reflected in the ICC Elements of Crimes, which specifies that the consent of the victim is not a defence.[390]

610   Furthermore, persons protected by common Article 3 may not be subjected to mutilation as part of a punishment under domestic law, as this exception is not foreseen in common Article 3 or in humanitarian law in general.

iii. Mutilation of dead bodies

611   The prohibition of mutilation in common Article 3 applies only to the living and does not extend to the mutilation of corpses. The protection from *permanent* disfigurement or loss of an organ or appendage necessarily presupposes that the victim is a living human being at the time of the prohibited act. Hence, the object and purpose of the prohibition of mutilation in common Article 3 does not relate to the dead. The mutilation of dead bodies is, however, prohibited under common Article 3 as it constitutes an outrage upon personal dignity.[391] It is also a distinct prohibition under customary international law.[392]

d. Cruel treatment

i. Introduction

612   Cruel treatment is the third specific example of prohibited violence to life and person. This prohibition is a long-standing rule of humanitarian law.[393] It is also included in other provisions of the Third and Fourth Conventions and reaffirmed in Additional Protocol II.[394] The prohibition is now part of customary international law.[395] International and regional human rights treaties, within their respective fields of application, list the prohibition of cruel treatment as non-derogable.[396]

---

[388] ICC Elements of Crimes (2002), Article 8(2)(c)(i)-2, Element 2. See also La Haye, 2001, p. 209.
[389] See SCSL, *Brima* Trial Judgment, 2007, para. 725, and *Sesay* Trial Judgment, 2009, para. 181.
[390] See ICC Elements of Crimes (2002), fn. 46 pertaining to Article 8(2)(b)(x)-1, Element 3, and fn. 69 pertaining to Article 8(2)(e)(xi)-1, Element 3. The omission of this footnote in relation to Article 8(2)(c)(i) might be 'a drafting error', according to Dörmann, 2003, p. 396.
[391] See section G.4.
[392] See ICRC Study on Customary International Humanitarian Law (2005), Rule 113.
[393] See e.g. Lieber Code (1863), Article 16; see also Articles 11 and 56.
[394] See Third Convention, Article 87; Fourth Convention, Article 118; and Additional Protocol II, Article 4(2)(a).
[395] See ICRC Study on Customary International Humanitarian Law (2005), Rule 90.
[396] See International Covenant on Civil and Political Rights (1966), Article 7; European Convention on Human Rights (1950), Article 3; American Convention on Human Rights (1969), Article 5(2); and African Charter on Human and Peoples' Rights (1981), Article 5.

613   In addition to cruel treatment, common Article 3 prohibits torture and outrages upon personal dignity – all of these terms are sometimes referred to as
various forms of 'ill-treatment'. These prohibitions are similar but not identical, and are addressed separately below in the order in which they appear in
common Article 3.

614   The distinction between the terms 'cruel treatment', 'torture' and 'outrages'
is of no consequence, however, in terms of their prohibition, and the textual
ordering in no way suggests an ascending or descending scale of prohibitory
effect. Common Article 3 absolutely prohibits all these forms of ill-treatment
in all circumstances of non-international armed conflict.[397] No grounds, be
they political, economic, cultural or religious, can justify any form of prohibited treatment; nor can such treatment be justified on the grounds of national
security, including fighting terrorism or insurgency. Authorizing torture or
other forms of ill-treatment based on prevailing circumstances is contrary to
the absolute nature of the prohibitions, dilutes the prohibitory effect of common Article 3, and increases the risk of subsequent violations. Indeed, this is
a proverbial door that must remain locked; use of these forms of ill-treatment
in any circumstances tends to induce the search for justifications to engage in
prohibited conduct, making the escalation of these practices almost unavoidable (the so-called 'slippery slope' argument). It may also undermine respect for
common Article 3 among the Parties to the conflict, as it may signal to them
that these prohibitions are qualified, while they are absolute under common
Article 3 (see also the phrase 'the following acts are and shall remain prohibited at any time and in any place whatsoever').

ii. Definition of cruel treatment

615 The Geneva Conventions and Additional Protocols do not define cruel
treatment.[398]

616   The ICTY concluded that the prohibition of cruel treatment in common Article 3 'is a means to an end, the end being that of ensuring that persons taking no
active part in the hostilities shall in all circumstances be treated humanely'.[399]
As a result, the ICTY defined cruel treatment as:

---

[397] Similarly, international human rights law absolutely prohibits all forms of ill-treatment; this
prohibition also applies in situations of emergency, such as war or the threat of war. See International Covenant on Civil and Political Rights (1966), Article 4; European Convention on
Human Rights (1950), Article 15; American Convention on Human Rights (1969), Article 27;
and Convention against Torture (1984), Article 2(2).

[398] Human rights instruments also do not define cruel treatment, although a link is established
in two instruments between the prohibition of cruel treatment and respect for the inherent dignity of the human person. See American Convention on Human Rights (1969), Article 5(2) ('All persons deprived of their liberty shall be treated with respect for the inherent
dignity of the human person'), and African Charter on Human and Peoples' Rights (1981), Article 5 ('Every individual shall have the right to respect for the dignity inherent in a human
being.').

[399] ICTY, *Tadić* Trial Judgment, 1997, para. 723.

treatment which causes serious mental or physical suffering or constitutes a serious attack upon human dignity, which is equivalent to the offence of inhuman treatment in the framework of the grave breaches provisions of the Geneva Conventions.[400]

617   Hence, the Tribunal does not differentiate between 'cruel treatment' as prohibited in common Article 3 and 'inhuman treatment' as a grave breach of the Geneva Conventions.[401] The ICC Elements of Crimes follows the same approach.[402] Thus the terms 'cruel' and 'inhuman' treatment can be used interchangeably. For more details on 'inhuman treatment' as a grave breach in international armed conflict, see the commentary on Article 50, section D.3.

618   To qualify as cruel (or inhuman) treatment, an act must cause physical or mental suffering of a serious nature. Unlike for torture, no specific purpose is required for cruel treatment. As far as the seriousness of the mental or physical suffering is concerned, the ICTY considers that 'whether particular conduct amounts to cruel treatment is a question of fact to be determined on a case by case basis'.[403] This interpretation mirrors that of human rights bodies and texts.[404]

619   In order to assess the seriousness of the suffering, the individual circumstances of each case have to be considered, both the objective elements related to the severity of the harm and the subjective elements related to the condition of the victim. Cruel treatment frequently does not take the form of an isolated act. It can be committed in one single act, but can also result from a combination or accumulation of several acts which, taken individually may not amount to cruel treatment.[405] According to the ICTY, these include 'the

---

[400] ICTY, *Delalić* Trial Judgment, 1998, para. 551. See also *Naletilić and Martinović* Trial Judgment, 2003, para. 246; *Kordić and Čerkez* Trial Judgment, 2001, para. 256; *Blaškić* Trial Judgment, 2000, paras 154–155; *Limaj* Trial Judgment, 2005, para. 231; *Orić* Trial Judgment, 2006, para. 351; *Haradinaj* Trial Judgment, 2008, para. 126; *Mrkšić* Trial Judgment, 2007, para. 514; *Lukić and Lukić* Trial Judgment, 2009, para. 957; and *Tolimir* Trial Judgment, 2012, para. 853. The ICRC policy on torture and cruel, inhuman or degrading treatment inflicted on persons deprived of their liberty of 9 June 2011 follows the same definition; see *International Review of the Red Cross*, Vol. 93, No. 882, June 2011, pp. 547–562, fn. 1.

[401] See ICTY, *Delalić* Trial Judgment, 1998, paras 550–552 ('cruel treatment is treatment that is inhuman'); see also *Kordić and Čerkez* Trial Judgment, 2001, para. 265, and *Blaškić* Trial Judgment, 2000, para. 186.

[402] See ICC Elements of Crimes (2002), Article 8(2)(a)(ii)-2 (War crime of inhuman treatment) and (c)(i)-3 (War crime of cruel treatment). The elements of crimes for the war crime of cruel treatment read in part: '1. The perpetrator inflicted severe physical or mental pain or suffering upon one or more persons.' For a commentary, see Dörmann, 2003, pp. 398–401; see also pp. 63–70 (inhuman treatment).

[403] ICTY, *Limaj* Trial Judgment, 2005, para. 232, confirmed in *Orić* Trial Judgment, 2006, para. 352; *Mrkšić* Trial Judgment, 2007, para. 517; *Lukić and Lukić* Trial Judgment, 2009, para. 957; and *Tolimir* Trial Judgment, 2012, para. 854.

[404] For more details, see Droege, 2007, pp. 521–522, and Doswald-Beck, 2011, pp. 196–199.

[405] See European Court of Human Rights, *Dougoz* v. *Greece*, Judgment, 2001, para. 46; *Iovchev* v. *Bulgaria*, Judgment, 2006, para. 137; and UN Committee against Torture, *Consideration of reports submitted by States parties under Article 19 of the Convention: Israel*, UN Doc. A/52/44, 10 September 1997, para. 257.

nature of the act or omission, the context in which it occurs, its duration and/or repetition, the physical, mental and moral effects of the act on the victim and the personal circumstances of the victim, including age, sex and health'.[406] The suffering caused by the cruel treatment does not need to be lasting, as long as it is 'real and serious'.[407] But the fact that a treatment has long-term effects may be relevant to establishing the seriousness of the act.[408]

620   Specific acts that have been considered cruel by the ICTY include the lack of adequate medical attention,[409] inhumane living conditions in a detention centre,[410] beatings,[411] attempted murder,[412] the use of detainees to dig trenches at the front under dangerous circumstances,[413] and the use of human shields.[414]

621   Examples of cruel treatment gleaned from the practice of human rights bodies and standards include: certain methods of punishment, especially corporal punishment,[415] certain methods of execution,[416] the imposition of the death penalty after an unfair trial,[417] involuntary sterilization,[418] gender-based

---

[406] ICTY, *Krnojelac* Trial Judgment, 2002, para. 131; see also *Hadžihasanović* Trial Judgment, 2006, para. 33; *Orić* Trial Judgment, 2006, para. 352; *Martić* Trial Judgment, 2007, para. 80; *Delić* Trial Judgment, 2008, para. 51; *Lukić and Lukić* Trial Judgment, 2009, para. 957; and *Tolimir* Trial Judgment, 2012, para. 854. Not all of the judgments listed mention the full list of factors to be taken into account.

[407] ICTY, *Krnojelac* Trial Judgment, 2002, para. 131. See also *Martić* Trial Judgment, 2007, para. 80, and *Lukić and Lukić* Trial Judgment, 2009, para. 957.

[408] See ICTY, *Vasiljević* Trial Judgment, 2002, para. 235.

[409] See ICTY, *Mrkšić* Trial Judgment, 2007, para. 517; see also Inter-American Court of Human Rights, *Tibi case*, Judgment, 2004, para. 157, and European Court of Human Rights, *Koval* v. *Ukraine*, Judgment, 2006, para. 82.

[410] See ICTY, *Delalić* Trial Judgment, 1998, paras 554–558 and 1112–1119, confirmed in *Orić* Trial Judgment, 2006, para. 352. See also *Hadžihasanović* Trial Judgment, 2006, para. 35. For conditions of detention, see Droege, 2007, pp. 535–541, and Doswald-Beck, 2011, pp. 205–214.

[411] See ICTY, *Jelisić* Trial Judgment, 1999, paras 42–45, confirmed in *Orić* Trial Judgment, 2006, para. 352; see also *Hadžihasanović* Trial Judgment, 2006, para. 35.

[412] See ICTY, *Vasiljević* Trial Judgment, 2002, para. 239, confirmed in *Orić* Trial Judgment, 2006, para. 352.

[413] See ICTY, *Blaškić* Trial Judgment, 2000, para. 713, confirmed in *Orić* Trial Judgment, 2006, para. 352.

[414] See ICTY, *Blaškić* Trial Judgment, 2000 para. 716, confirmed in *Orić* Trial Judgment, 2006, para. 352.

[415] International humanitarian law absolutely prohibits the use of corporal punishment. See Third Convention, Articles 87(3), 89 and 108; Fourth Convention, Articles 32 and 118–119; Additional Protocol I, Article 74; and Additional Protocol II, Article 4. See also UN Human Rights Committee, *Osbourne* v. *Jamaica*, Views, 2000, para. 9.1; Inter-American Court of Human Rights, *Caesar* v. *Trinidad and Tobago*, Judgment, 2005, paras 67–89; and African Commission on Human and Peoples' Rights, *Doebbler* v. *Sudan*, Decision, 2003, paras 42–44.

[416] See UN Committee against Torture, *Consideration of reports submitted by States Parties under Article 19 of the Convention: United States of America*, UN Doc. CAT/C/USA/CO/2, 25 July 2006, para. 31.

[417] See European Court of Human Rights, *Öcalan* v. *Turkey*, Judgment, 2005, paras 168–175, and UN Committee against Torture, *Consideration of reports submitted by States Parties under Article 19 of the Convention: Guatemala*, UN Doc. CAT/C/GTM/CO/4, 25 July 2006, para. 22.

[418] See UN Committee against Torture, *Consideration of reports submitted by States Parties under Article 19 of the Convention: Peru*, UN Doc. CAT/C/PER/CO/4, 25 July 2006, para. 23.

humiliation such as shackling women detainees during childbirth,[419] and the use of electroshock devices to restrain persons in custody.[420] Such acts would also amount to violations under common Article 3.

622   As indicated by the definition of cruel treatment, the suffering need not be physical. Mental suffering in itself can be of such a serious nature as to qualify as cruel treatment.[421] This understanding of cruel treatment also derives from the inseparable link between the prohibition of cruel treatment and the absolute requirement of humane treatment, which is not confined to preserving a person's physical integrity. For instance, serving as a human shield may inflict such mental suffering as to constitute cruel treatment.[422] Other examples from ICTY decisions include threats to life,[423] being forced to bury a fellow detainee,[424] and random beating of and shooting at prisoners.[425] Human rights bodies have found the following instances of mental suffering to constitute cruel treatment: threats of torture,[426] witnessing others being ill-treated,[427] raped[428] or executed.[429]

623   In this respect, it is important to note that the element of 'serious attack on human dignity' was not included in the definition of cruel treatment in the ICC Elements of Crimes.[430] This element, established in ICTY decisions and maintained consistently, was left out by the Preparatory Commission that developed the Elements of Crimes because it considered that attacks on human dignity would be covered by the war crime of 'outrages upon personal dignity'.[431]

---

[419] See UN Committee against Torture, *Consideration of reports submitted by States Parties under Article 19 of the Convention: United States of America*, UN Doc. CAT/C/USA/CO/2, 25 July 2006, para. 33.

[420] See *ibid.* para. 35.

[421] See e.g. ICTY, *Naletilić and Martinović* Trial Judgment, 2003, para. 369; Inter-American Court of Human Rights, *Loayza Tamayo* v. *Peru*, Judgment, 1997, para. 57; European Court of Human Rights, *Ireland* v. *UK*, Judgment, 1978, para. 167; and UN Committee against Torture, *Consideration of reports submitted by States Parties under Article 19 of the Convention: United States of America*, UN Doc. CAT/C/USA/CO/2, 25 July 2006, para. 13.

[422] See ICTY, *Blaškić* Trial Judgment, 2000, para. 716, confirmed in *Orić* Trial Judgment, 2006, para. 352.

[423] See ICTY, *Limaj* Trial Judgment, 2005, para. 655.   [424] See *ibid.* paras 313 and 657.

[425] See ICTY, *Naletilić and Martinović* Trial Judgment, 2003, para. 394.

[426] See Inter-American Court of Human Rights, *Villagrán Morales and others* v. *Guatemala*, Judgment, 1999, para. 165; *'Juvenile Reeducation Institute'* v. *Paraguay*, Judgment, 2004, para. 167; and Inter-American Commission on Human Rights, *Case 11.710 (Colombia)*, Report, 2001, para. 34. For a finding that a threat of torture does not necessarily constitute cruel treatment, see European Court of Human Rights, *Hüsniye Tekin* v. *Turkey*, Judgment, 2005, para. 48.

[427] See Inter-American Court of Human Rights, *Caesar* v. *Trinidad and Tobago*, Judgment, 2005, para. 78.

[428] See Inter-American Commission on Human Rights, *Case 11.565 (Mexico)*, Report, 2000, para. 53.

[429] See Inter-American Commission on Human Rights, *Case 11.520 (Mexico)*, Report, 1998, para. 76.

[430] See ICC Elements of Crimes (2002), Article 8(2)(c)(i)-3.

[431] See Dörmann, 2003, pp. 63–64.

e. Torture

i. Introduction

624 Torture is the last specific example of prohibited violence to life and person provided in common Article 3. This prohibition is a long-standing rule of humanitarian law.[432] It is included also in other provisions of the four Geneva Conventions and reaffirmed in the 1977 Additional Protocols.[433] The prohibition is now considered part of customary international law.[434] International and regional human rights treaties, within their respective fields of application, list the prohibition of torture as non-derogable.[435] There is no indication in law or derived from practice that the term 'torture' has a different meaning in international and non-international armed conflict.[436]

625 The French version of common Article 3 prohibits 'tortures et supplices', while the English text prohibits 'torture'. The use of the word 'supplices' in French does not, however, create any additional types of prohibited treatment that would not be covered by the term 'torture'.[437]

ii. Definition of torture

626 The Geneva Conventions and Additional Protocols do not define torture. The first definition in international treaty law is contained in Article 1(1) of the 1984 Convention against Torture. This definition includes the requirement that torture be committed 'by or at the instigation of or with the consent or acquiescence of a public official or other person acting in an official capacity'. However, humanitarian law does not require an official involvement in the act of torture (see para. 645).

627 Thus, the ICTY defines torture for the purposes of humanitarian law as the intentional infliction, by act or omission, of severe pain or suffering, whether physical or mental, for such purposes as to obtain information or a confession, to punish, intimidate or coerce the victim or a third person, or to discriminate, on any ground, against the victim or a third person.[438]

---

[432] See e.g. Lieber Code (1863), Article 16.

[433] In addition to common Article 3, the prohibition of torture is included in Article 12 of the First Convention; Article 12 of the Second Convention; Articles 17 and 87 of the Third Convention; Article 32 of the Fourth Convention; Article 75(2)(a)(ii) of Additional Protocol I; and Article 4(2)(a) of Additional Protocol II.

[434] See ICRC Study on Customary International Humanitarian Law (2005), Rule 90.

[435] See International Covenant on Civil and Political Rights (1966), Article 7; European Convention on Human Rights (1950), Article 3; American Convention on Human Rights (1969), Article 5(2); and the African Charter on Human and Peoples' Rights (1981), Article 5. See also the specific anti-torture conventions: the Convention against Torture (1984) and the Inter-American Convention against Torture (1985).

[436] See Dörmann, 2003, p. 401.

[437] *Le Grand Robert & Collins français-anglais*, 2008, translates 'supplice' as 'form of torture, torture'.

[438] The ICTY initially listed the purposes in a closed list: see *Kunarac* Trial Judgment, 2001, para. 497. At the time, the Trial Chamber was satisfied that these purposes had become part of customary international law and it did not need to look into other possible purposes for the

628   Accordingly, the difference between torture and cruel treatment is that for torture there is a higher threshold of pain or suffering, which must be 'severe' rather than 'serious', and the infliction of pain or suffering must be the result of a specific purpose or motivation.

– Severe pain or suffering

629   The threshold of pain or suffering required by the ICTY for torture is higher than that for cruel treatment: 'severe' rather than 'serious'. The ICC Elements of Crimes, on the other hand, requires 'severe' physical or mental pain or suffering for both torture and cruel treatment.[439] They only differentiate between the two based on the purpose of the treatment. This was the result of a compromise, and departed from the case law of the ICTY.[440]

630   Some authors have challenged the need to establish a hierarchy of suffering for cruel treatment and torture.[441] For them, the only element distinguishing torture from cruel treatment should be the specific purpose required for torture. An argument in favour of this doctrine is that it is difficult to define the threshold of intensity between serious suffering and severe suffering. It is also somewhat absurd to think of treatment more severe than 'cruel'.[442]

631   The wording of the different treaties leaves the question open.[443] Article 16 of the Convention against Torture speaks of 'acts of cruel, inhuman or degrading treatment or punishment which do not *amount* to torture' (emphasis added), which could imply a higher intensity of suffering for torture than for cruel, inhuman or degrading treatment. However, it could also mean that the specific purpose required for torture constitutes the aggravating element, and it seems that the question was left open during the drafting of that Convention.[444]

632   Even after the adoption of the ICC Elements of Crimes, the ICTY has continued to apply a differentiated threshold of pain or suffering to distinguish between torture and cruel treatment.[445] The European Court of Human Rights

---

particular case on trial; see *ibid.* para. 485. The ICTY subsequently recognized that the list of purposes was not exclusive: see e.g. *Brđanin* Trial Judgment, 2004, para. 487; *Limaj* Trial Judgment, 2005, para. 235; and *Mrkšić* Trial Judgment, 2007, para. 513.

[439] See ICC Elements of Crimes (2002), Article 8(2)(c)(i)-3 (War crime of cruel treatment) and (c)(i)-4 (War crime of torture).

[440] See Dörmann, 2003, p. 63.

[441] See Evans; Rodley, 2002; and Nowak, 2005, p. 678, and 2006, p. 822. See also Nowak/McArthur, pp. 74 and 558, referring to the European Commission of Human Rights, *Greek case*, Report, 1969, p. 186 ('the word "torture" is often used to describe inhuman treatment, which has a purpose … and it is generally an aggravated form of inhuman treatment'), as confirmed by ICTY, *Delalić* Trial Judgment, 1998, para. 442. See also Rodley/Pollard, pp. 123–124.

[442] See Evans, pp. 33–49, especially at 49.

[443] See, in particular, International Covenant on Civil and Political Rights (1966), Article 7; European Convention on Human Rights (1950), Article 3; American Convention on Human Rights (1969), Article 5(2); and African Charter on Human and Peoples' Rights (1981), Article 5.

[444] Burgers/Danelius, p. 150, refer only to the purpose as a distinctive feature; see also the account in Rodley, 2002.

[445] See ICTY, *Delalić* Trial Judgment, 1998, para. 468; *Kvočka* Trial Judgment, 2001, para. 142; *Krnojelac* Trial Judgment, 2002, paras 180–181; *Brđanin* Trial Judgment, 2004, para. 483; *Martić* Trial Judgment, 2007, paras 75 and 80; *Haradinaj* Trial Judgment, 2008, paras 126–127; *Haradinaj* Retrial Judgment, 2012, para. 422; and *Limaj* Trial Judgment, 2005, paras 231 and 235.

also requires a higher threshold of pain, in which the purpose of its infliction is a relevant factor,[446] and sometimes a determining one.[447] The Inter-American Commission and Court, like the ICTY, require a higher intensity of pain for torture than for cruel, inhuman or degrading treatment, as well as a purpose.[448] The ICRC also works on the basis of a different threshold of pain.[449] The UN Human Rights Committee, on the other hand, does not attempt to distinguish between the two.[450]

633   The main consequence of using the sole criterion of purpose to distinguish between torture and cruel treatment is that, in situations in which cruel treatment is inflicted for a specific purpose, it automatically amounts to torture. Considering the very wide definition of 'purpose', which includes such broad intentions as to intimidate or to coerce,[451] this would leave only an extremely narrow margin for cruel treatment between torture and outrages upon personal dignity. As pointed out above, case law has hitherto not discarded the intensity of suffering as an element distinguishing torture from cruel treatment, but it is not excluded that this may change in the future, especially if the ICC follows the clear wording of the Elements of Crimes. But if it does so, this should not be at the cost of raising the threshold of severity required for treatment to be deemed cruel.

634   To assess the severity of pain or suffering, the individual circumstances of each case have to be considered, both the objective elements related to the severity of the harm and the subjective elements related to the condition of the victim.[452] This assessment must therefore consider a number of factual elements, such as the environment, duration, isolation, physical or mental condition of the victim, cultural beliefs and sensitivity, gender, age, social, cultural, religious or political background, or past experiences.[453]

For an example of cruel treatment not deemed severe enough to amount to torture, see ICTY, *Naletilić and Martinović* Trial Judgment, 2003, para. 369.

[446] See European Court of Human Rights, *Ireland v. UK*, Judgment, 1978, para. 167; *Aksoy v. Turkey*, Judgment, 1996, para. 64; *Selmouni v. France*, Judgment, 1999, paras 96–105; *Salman v. Turkey*, Merits, Judgment, 2000, para. 114; European Commission of Human Rights, *Corsacov v. Moldova*, Judgment, 2006, para. 63; and *Menesheva v. Russia*, Judgment, 2006, para. 60.

[447] See European Commission of Human Rights, *Kismir v. Turkey*, Judgment, 2005, paras 129–132.

[448] See Inter-American Court of Human Rights, *Caesar v. Trinidad and Tobago*, Judgment, 2005, paras 50, 68 and 87.

[449] See the ICRC policy on torture and cruel, inhuman or degrading treatment inflicted on persons deprived of their liberty of 9 June 2011, reproduced in *International Review of the Red Cross*, Vol. 93, No. 882, June 2011, pp. 547–562, fn. 1.

[450] The UN Human Rights Committee, in its General Comment No. 20 on Article 7 of the International Covenant on Civil and Political Rights, refers to the 'nature, purpose and severity' of the treatment (*General Comment No. 20, Article 7 (Prohibition of torture, or other cruel, inhuman or degrading treatment or punishment)*, 10 March 1992, para. 4); Rodley, 2002, points out that it is impossible to infer any general criteria from the Committee's early case law.

[451] See ICTY, *Kvočka* Appeal Judgment, 2005, para. 140, and ICTR, *Akayesu* Trial Judgment, 1998, para. 682.

[452] See ICTY, *Kvočka* Trial Judgment, 2001, para. 143, and *Brđanin* Trial Judgment, 2004, para. 483.

[453] See ICTY, *Mrkšić* Trial Judgment, 2007, para. 514; *Krnojelac* Trial Judgment, 2002, para. 182; *Limaj* Trial Judgment, 2005, para. 237; *Haradinaj* Retrial Judgment, 2012, para. 417; *Naletilić*

635   Specific factors include 'the nature and context of the infliction of pain',[454] 'the premeditation and institutionalisation of the ill-treatment', 'the physical condition of the victim', 'the manner and method used' and 'the position of inferiority of the victim'.[455] As with all forms of ill-treatment, 'in certain circumstances the suffering can be exacerbated by social and cultural conditions and it should take into account the specific social, cultural and religious background of the victims when assessing the severity of the alleged conduct'.[456]

636   Like cruel treatment, torture frequently does not take the form of an isolated act. It can be committed in one single act, but can also result from a combination or accumulation of several acts which, taken individually, may not amount to torture. The duration, repetition and variety of forms of mistreatment should therefore be assessed as a whole.[457] However, 'no rigid durational requirement is built into the definition' of torture.[458] It does not need to cause a permanent injury.[459] As a result, 'evidence of the suffering need not even be visible after the commission of the crime'.[460]

637   Some acts meet the threshold of severity *per se*, as they necessarily imply severe pain or suffering.[461] This is the case, in particular, for rape.[462] In this respect, the ICTY has stated:

Some acts, like rape, appear by definition to meet the severity threshold. Like torture, rape is a violation of personal dignity and is used for such purposes as intimidation, degradation, humiliation and discrimination, punishment, control or

---

and Martinović Appeal Judgment, 2006, para. 300; *Brđanin* Trial Judgment, 2004, paras 483–484; *Kvočka* Trial Judgment, 2001, para. 143; and *Martić* Trial Judgment, 2007, para. 75.

[454] ICTY, *Krnojelac* Trial Judgment, 2002, para. 182, confirmed by ICTY, *Mrkšić* Trial Judgment, 2007, para. 514. See also *Limaj* Trial Judgment, 2005, para. 237; *Haradinaj* Retrial Judgment, 2012, para. 417; and *Martić* Trial Judgment, 2007, para. 75 (only mentioning 'nature').

[455] ICTY, *Krnojelac* Trial Judgment, 2002, para. 182. See also *Mrkšić* Trial Judgment, 2007, para. 514; *Limaj* Trial Judgment, 2005, para. 237; *Haradinaj* Retrial Judgment, 2012 para. 417; *Naletilić and Martinović* Appeal Judgment, 2006, para. 300; *Brđanin* Trial Judgment, 2004, para. 484; and *Martić* Trial Judgment, 2007, para. 75.

[456] ICTY, *Limaj* Trial Judgment, 2005, para. 237.

[457] See ICTY, *Krnojelac* Trial Judgment, 2002, para. 182, and *Limaj* Trial Judgment, 2005, para. 237.

[458] ICTY, *Naletilić and Martinović* Appeal Judgment, 2006, para. 300.

[459] See ICTY, *Kvočka* Trial Judgment, 2001, paras 148–149; *Brđanin* Trial Judgment, 2004, para. 484; *Limaj* Trial Judgment, 2005, para. 236; *Mrkšić* Trial Judgment, 2007, para. 514; and *Haradinaj* Retrial Judgment, 2012, para. 417. See also *Brđanin* Appeal Judgment, 2007, para. 249 ('physical torture can include acts inflicting physical pain or suffering less severe than "extreme pain or suffering" or "pain . . . equivalent in intensity to the pain accompanying serious physical injury, such as organ failure, impairment of bodily function, or even death').

[460] ICTY, *Brđanin* Trial Judgment, 2004, para. 484; see also *Kunarac* Appeal Judgment, 2002, para. 150, and *Stanišić and Župljanin* Trial Judgment, 2013, para. 48.

[461] See ICTY, *Naletilić and Martinović* Appeal Judgment, 2006, para. 299, and *Brđanin* Appeal Judgment, 2007, para. 251.

[462] See ICTY, *Delalić* Trial Judgment, 1998, paras 495–497; *Kunarac* Appeal Judgment, 2002, para. 151; ICTR, *Akayesu* Trial Judgment, 1998, para. 682; European Court of Human Rights, *Aydin* v. *Turkey*, Judgment, 1997, paras 82–86; UN Committee against Torture, *T.A.* v. *Sweden*, Decisions, 2005, paras 2.4 and 7.3; and Inter-American Commission on Human Rights, *Case 10.970 (Peru)*, Report, 1996, p. 185. See also UN Commission on Human Rights, *Torture and other cruel, inhuman or degrading treatment or punishment, Report by the UN Special Rapporteur on Torture*, UN Doc. E/CN.4/1986/15, 19 February 1986, para. 119.

destruction of a person. Severe pain or suffering, as required by the definition of the crime of torture, can be said to be established once rape has been proved, since the act of rape necessarily implies such pain or suffering.[463]

638   Other examples of torture gleaned from international decisions include electric shocks,[464] burning,[465] knee spread,[466] kneeling on sharp instruments,[467] suffocation by or under water,[468] burying alive,[469] suspension,[470] flogging and severe beatings,[471] especially beatings on the soles of the feet,[472] mock executions,[473] mock burials,[474] threats to shoot or kill,[475] exposure of detainees under interrogation to severe cold for extended periods,[476] beating followed by detention for three days where food and water and the possibility to use a lavatory are denied,[477] a combination of restraining in very painful conditions, hooding under special conditions, sounding of loud music for prolonged periods, threats, including death threats, violent shaking and using cold air to chill.[478]

---

[463] ICTY, *Brđanin* Trial Judgment, 2004, para. 485. See also *Stanišić and Župljanin* Trial Judgment, 2013, para. 48.

[464] See International Military Tribunal for the Far East, *Case of the Major War Criminals*, Judgment, 1948, in Röling/Rüter, pp. 406–407; UN Human Rights Committee, *Rodríguez* v. *Uruguay*, Views, 1994, paras 2.1 and 12.1; *Tshitenge Muteba* v. *Zaire*, Views, 1984, paras 8.2 and 12; European Court of Human Rights, *Çakici* v. *Turkey*, Judgment, 1999, para. 93; and UN Committee against Torture, *Consideration of reports submitted by States Parties under Article 19 of the Convention: Switzerland*, UN Doc. CAT/C/CR/34/CHE, 21 June 2005, para. 4(b)(i).

[465] See International Military Tribunal for the Far East, *Case of the Major War Criminals*, Judgment, 1948, in Röling/Rüter, p. 407.

[466] See *ibid.*   [467] See *ibid.*

[468] See *ibid.* p. 406 (the so-called 'water treatment'); see also UN Human Rights Committee, *Rodríguez* v. *Uruguay*, Views, 1994, paras 2.1 and 12.1.

[469] See UN Human Rights Committee, *Eduardo Bleier* v. *Uruguay*, Views, 1980, paras 2.3 and 12.

[470] See International Military Tribunal for the Far East, *Case of the Major War Criminals*, Judgment, 1948, in Röling/Rüter, pp. 406–407 (sometimes combined with flogging); European Court of Human Rights, *Aksoy* v. *Turkey*, Judgment, 1996, para. 64; and UN Human Rights Committee, *Torres Ramírez* v. *Uruguay*, Views, 1980, para. 2.

[471] See International Military Tribunal for the Far East, *Case of the Major War Criminals*, Judgment, 1948, in Röling/Rüter, p. 408, and European Court of Human Rights, *Selmouni* v. *France*, Judgment, 1999, para. 101.

[472] See European Court of Human Rights, *Aksoy* v. *Turkey*, Judgment, 1996, para. 64.

[473] See International Military Tribunal for the Far East, *Case of the Major War Criminals*, Judgment, 1948, in Röling/Rüter, p. 408; European Commission of Human Rights, *Greek case*, Report, 1969, p. 500; and UN Human Rights Committee, *Tshitenge Muteba* v. *Zaire*, Views, 1984, pp. 182–188, paras 8.2 and 12.

[474] See Inter-American Commission on Human Rights, *Case 7823 (Bolivia)*, Resolution, 1982, p. 42.

[475] See European Commission of Human Rights, *Greek case*, Report, 1969, p. 500.

[476] See UN Committee against Torture, *Report on Mexico produced by the Committee under Article 20 of the Convention, and reply of the Government of Mexico*, UN Doc. CAT/C/75, 26 May 2003, para. 165.

[477] See UN Committee against Torture, *Danilo Dimitrijević* v. *Serbia and Montenegro*, Decisions, 2005, paras 2.1, 2.2, 7.1 and 7.2.

[478] See UN Committee against Torture, *Consideration of reports submitted by States Parties under Article 19 of the Convention: Israel*, UN Doc. A/52/44, 10 September 1997, paras 253–260.

639   Mental pain and suffering on its own can be severe enough to amount to torture.[479] The Third Geneva Convention and Additional Protocol I explicitly spell out that both physical and mental torture are prohibited.[480] Psychological methods of torture as well as the psychological effects of torture can cause suffering as severe as physical torture and its physical effects.[481] The ICTY has considered that being forced to watch severe mistreatment inflicted on a relative,[482] or being forced to watch serious sexual attacks inflicted on an acquaintance, was torture for the coerced observer.[483] It has held likewise with regard to threats of death causing severe mental suffering, and falsely informing the victim that his father had been killed,[484] or obliging victims to collect the dead bodies of other members of their ethnic group, in particular those of their neighbours and friends.[485]

– Specific purpose

640   A constitutive element of torture is that it is committed for a specific purpose or motive. The Convention against Torture gives the following examples: (a) obtaining information or a confession, (b) punishing, intimidating or coercing the victim or a third person, and (c) discriminating, on any ground, against the victim or a third person.[486] The ICTY considers these purposes to be part of customary international law.[487]

641   These purposes are illustrative in nature, and do not constitute an exhaustive list. This is confirmed by the wording of Article 1 of the Convention against Torture, which speaks of 'such purposes as'.[488] The non-exhaustive list set out in the Convention against Torture is also reflected in the ICC Elements of Crimes.[489] The ICTY also considers the list non-exhaustive.[490]

642   In practice, this leads to an extremely wide meaning of improper purpose. Indeed, 'intimidating or coercing [the victim] or a third person' and 'reason

---

[479]   See ICTY, *Kvočka* Trial Judgment, 2001, para. 149; see also *Limaj* Trial Judgment, 2005, para. 236; *Haradinaj* Retrial Judgment, 2012, para. 417; and *Mrkšić* Trial Judgment, 2007, para. 514.

[480]   See Third Convention, Article 17, and Additional Protocol I, Article 75(2)(a)(ii).

[481]   See Inter-American Court of Human Rights, *Maritza Urrutia v. Guatemala*, Judgment, 2003, para. 93. For more details on this subject, see Reyes.

[482]   See ICTY, *Kvočka* Trial Judgment, 2001, para. 149.

[483]   See ICTY, *Furundžija* Trial Judgment, 1998, para. 267.

[484]   See ICTY, *Naletilić and Martinović* Trial Judgment, 2003, paras 294–295.

[485]   See ICTY, *Brđanin* Trial Judgment, 2004, para. 511.

[486]   See Convention against Torture (1984), Article 1.

[487]   See ICTY, *Kunarac* Trial Judgment, 2001, para. 485. In this case, the Tribunal did not have to address whether other purposes were included under customary international law. See also *Krnojelac* Trial Judgment, 2002, para. 185.

[488]   See also ICTY, *Delalić* Trial Judgment, 1998, para. 470, and ICTR, *Musema* Trial Judgment, 2000, para. 285.

[489]   See ICC Elements of Crimes (2002), Article 8(2)(a)(ii) and (c)(i): 'The perpetrator inflicted the pain or suffering for such purposes as: obtaining information or a confession, punishment, intimidation or coercion or for any reason based on discrimination of any kind.'

[490]   See e.g. ICTY, *Brđanin* Trial Judgment, 2004, para. 487; *Limaj* Trial Judgment, 2005, para. 235; and *Mrkšić* Trial Judgment, 2007, para. 513.

based on discrimination of any kind' are such broad notions that most deliberate acts causing severe suffering to a specific person, especially in detention, will be caused for one of these purposes or a purpose very similar to this one. The purpose cannot, however, be of any sort, but must have 'something in common with the purposes expressly listed'.[491] Hence, the ICTY considered that 'humiliation', which it considered to be close to the notion of intimidation, was also one of the possible purposes of torture.[492]

643　As a result, the ICTY affirmed that these purposes would be present in the case of rape during interrogation of a detainee: 'Rape is resorted to either by the interrogator himself or by other persons associated with the interrogation of a detainee, as a means of punishing, intimidating, coercing or humiliating the victim, or obtaining information, or a confession, from the victim or a third person.'[493]

644　The ICTY has also determined that a prohibited purpose 'need be neither the sole nor the main purpose of inflicting the severe pain or suffering' for it to support a finding of torture.[494]

– Official involvement

645 The definition of torture under humanitarian law does not require an official involvement in the act. The 1984 Convention against Torture, on the other hand, provides that the pain or suffering must be 'inflicted by or at the instigation of or with the consent or acquiescence of a public official or other person acting in an official capacity'.[495] In its early decisions, the ICTY determined that this definition was part of customary international law applicable in armed conflict.[496] Subsequently, however, the Tribunal concluded that the definition of torture under humanitarian law did not comprise the same elements. In particular, 'the presence of a state official or of any other authority-wielding person in the torture process' was not considered necessary for the offence to be regarded as torture under humanitarian law.[497] This reasoning corresponds to

---

[491]　Burger/Danelius, p. 118.

[492]　See ICTY, *Furundžija* Trial Judgment, 1998, para. 162. See also *Naletilić and Martinović* Trial Judgment, 2003, para. 337.

[493]　ICTY, *Furundžija* Trial Judgment, 1998, para. 163.

[494]　ICTY, *Kvočka* Trial Judgment, 2001, para. 153. See also *Delalić* Trial Judgment, 1998, para. 470; *Krnojelac* Trial Judgment, 2002, para. 184; *Kunarac* Trial Judgment, 2001, para. 486, and Appeal Judgment, 2002, para. 155; *Haradinaj* Trial Judgment, 2008, para. 128, and Retrial Judgment, 2012, para. 418; *Limaj* Trial Judgment, 2005, para. 239; *Martić* Trial Judgment, 2007, para. 77; *Mrkšić* Trial Judgment, 2007, para. 515; *Brđanin* Trial Judgment, 2004, para. 487; and *Kunarac* Trial Judgment, 2001, para. 486, and Appeal Judgment, 2002, para. 155.

[495]　Convention against Torture (1984), Article 1.

[496]　See ICTY, *Delalić* Trial Judgment, 1998, para. 459, and *Furundžija* Trial Judgment, 1998, para. 162, and Appeal Judgment, 2000, para. 111.

[497]　ICTY, *Kunarac* Trial Judgment, 2001, para. 496, confirmed in Appeal Judgment, 2002, para. 148. See also *Simić* Trial Judgment, 2003, para. 82; *Brđanin* Trial Judgment, 2004, para. 488; *Kvočka* Appeal Judgment, 2005, para. 284; *Limaj* Trial Judgment, 2005, para. 240; *Mrkšić* Trial Judgment, 2007, para. 514; *Haradinaj* Retrial Judgment, 2012, para. 419; and *Stanišić and Župljanin* Trial Judgment, 2013, para. 49.

the scope of application of common Article 3, which prohibits torture not only when committed by State armed forces, but also when committed by non-State armed groups.

3. Taking of hostages

a. Introduction

646   Up through the Second World War, the taking of hostages was still considered lawful, albeit under very strict conditions.[498] However, in response to hostage-related abuses during the Second World War, the 1949 Geneva Conventions completely outlawed this practice.[499] The two Additional Protocols reaffirmed this categorical prohibition.[500] The prohibition is now part of customary international law.[501]

b. Definition of hostage-taking

647   The Geneva Conventions and Additional Protocols do not define hostage-taking. In a different legal context, the 1979 International Convention against the Taking of Hostages defines hostage-taking as the seizure or detention of a person (the hostage), accompanied by the threat to kill, to injure or to continue to detain that person in order to compel a third party to do or to abstain from doing any act as an explicit or implicit condition for his or her release.[502]

648   This definition provided the basis for the elements of the war crime of hostage-taking in the 1998 ICC Statute, but with the addition of the catch-all formulation that the person was seized, detained 'or otherwise held hostage'.[503] On this basis, the SCSL Appeals Chamber concluded that 'the precise means by which the individual falls into the hands of the perpetrator is not the defining characteristic of the offence'.[504]

---

[498] See United States, Military Court at Nuremberg, *Hostages case*, Judgment, 1948, pp. 1249–1251.

[499] For more details on the history of the prohibition of hostage-taking, see the commentary on Article 34 of the Fourth Convention.

[500] Additional Protocol I, Article 75(2)(c); Additional Protocol II, Article 4(2)(c).

[501] ICRC Study on Customary International Humanitarian Law (2005), Rule 96.

[502] International Convention against the Taking of Hostages (1979), Article 1.

[503] Article 8(2)(a)(viii) of the 2002 ICC Elements of Crimes, concerning the war crime of taking hostages, reads in part:
 1. The perpetrator seized, detained or otherwise held hostage one or more persons.
 2. The perpetrator threatened to kill, injure or continue to detain such person or persons.
 3. The perpetrator intended to compel a State, an international organization, a natural or legal person or a group of persons to act or refrain from acting as an explicit or implicit condition for the safety or the release of such person or persons.
 4. Such person or persons were protected under one or more of the Geneva Conventions of 1949 [i.e. they were either *hors de combat*, or were civilians, medical personnel or religious personnel taking no active part in the hostilities].
 For a commentary on these elements, see Dörmann, 2003, pp. 406–407; see also pp. 124–127.

[504] SCSL, *Sesay* Appeal Judgment, 2009, para. 598.

649   The broad definition set forth in the ICC Elements of Crimes is also valid for the underlying prohibition of hostage-taking contained both in common Article 3 and in Article 34 of the Fourth Convention. Indeed, the group of experts who drafted the Elements of Crimes was of the view that there can be no difference between hostage-taking in international armed conflict and hostage-taking in non-international armed conflict.[505]

650   Accordingly, for the purpose of common Article 3, hostage-taking can be defined as the seizure, detention or otherwise holding of a person (the hostage) accompanied by the threat to kill, injure or continue to detain that person in order to compel a third party to do or to abstain from doing any act as an explicit or implicit condition for the release, safety or well-being of the hostage.

651   Today, hostages are often taken to exact a ransom, to obtain prisoner exchanges or to recover 'war taxes'.[506] Such practices are sometimes referred to as kidnapping or abduction, but the different labels do not affect the legal qualification.[507] Provided all the requisite conditions are met, these practices constitute hostage-taking and are prohibited under common Article 3.

i. The hostage

652   The prohibition of hostage-taking in common Article 3 applies to all persons falling within the protective scope of the article.[508] In *Sesay*, the SCSL Trial Chamber held that 'the person or persons held hostage must not be taking a direct part in the hostilities at the time of the alleged violation'.[509] In the Trial Chamber's opinion, 'the term "hostage" must be interpreted in its broadest sense'.[510] In this instance, the accused were charged with the abduction of several hundred members of the UN Mission in Sierra Leone peacekeeping forces and with using them as hostages.[511]

653   Hostages are often persons – such as civilians posing no security threat – who are captured and detained unlawfully. However, unlawful detention is not a precondition for hostage-taking. Persons whose detention may be lawful, such as in the case of civilians posing a security threat, could nevertheless be used as hostages, which would then qualify the situation as hostage-taking. The

---

[505] Dörmann, 2003, p. 406.

[506] For examples of current practice, see Herrmann/Palmieri, pp. 142–145, and Sivakumaran, 2012, pp. 269–271.

[507] For a definition of kidnapping, see ECOSOC, Res. 2002/16, International cooperation in the prevention, combating and elimination of kidnapping and in providing assistance for the victims, 24 July 2002, para. 1 ('unlawfully detaining a person or persons against their will for the purpose of demanding for their liberation an illicit gain or any other economic gain or other material benefit, or in order to oblige someone to do or not to do something'). Abduction is not defined in international law. In its ordinary meaning it refers to taking someone away illegally by force or deception; see *Concise Oxford English Dictionary*, 12th edition, Oxford University Press, 2011, p. 2.

[508] For more details, see section E.   [509] SCSL, *Sesay* Trial Judgment, 2009, para. 241.

[510] *Ibid.* with reference to Pictet (ed.), *Commentary on the Fourth Geneva Convention*, ICRC, 1958, Article 34, p. 230, cited with approval by ICTY, *Blaškić* Trial Judgment, 2000, para. 187.

[511] SCSL, *Sesay* Corrected Amended Consolidated Indictment, 2006, Count 18.

requisite intent to take hostages need not be present at the outset of a detention; it can develop during the detention.[512] This was confirmed by the SCSL
Appeals Chamber in 2009:

> As a matter of law, the requisite intent [for hostage-taking] may be present at the
> moment the individual is first detained or may be formed at some time thereafter
> while the persons were held. In the former instance, the offence is complete at
> the time of the initial detention (assuming all the other elements of the crime are
> satisfied); in the latter, the situation is transformed into the offence of hostage-
> taking the moment the intent crystallises (again, assuming the other elements of
> the crime are satisfied).[513]

654   This is significant because earlier ICTY decisions seemed to indicate that
unlawful deprivation of liberty was part of the definition of hostage-taking.[514]
However, these decisions can also be interpreted for the proposition that the
deprivation of liberty was unlawful *because* it was hostage-taking. Perhaps
more importantly, the ICTY did not examine the same question as the SCSL,
i.e. whether an initial detention not carried out for the purpose of hostage-
taking can become hostage-taking if the unlawful purpose arises at some time
thereafter.

ii. Threats made to the hostage

655   As defined above, hostage-taking involves threats to kill, injure or continue to
detain the hostage. Threats to injure hostages cover threats to both their physical and their mental well-being. This interpretation follows from the prohibition of violence to both the physical and the mental well-being of detainees.[515]
Thus, the ICTY held that '[t]he additional element that must be proved to establish the crime of unlawfully taking civilians hostage is the issuance of a conditional threat in respect of the physical and mental well-being of civilians'.[516]

656   The threat made must itself be unlawful under humanitarian law. A threat
to continue the detention of a person, therefore, would not always amount to
hostage-taking. For example, as part of the negotiation of a prisoner exchange,

---

[512] See also Sivakumaran, 2010a, p. 1033, and 2012, p. 269.
[513] SCSL, *Sesay* Appeal Judgment, 2009, para. 597.
[514] See ICTY, *Blaškić* Trial Judgment, 2000, paras 158 ('civilian hostages are persons unlawfully
deprived of their freedom, often arbitrarily and sometimes under threat of death. However, as
asserted by the Defence, detention may be lawful in some circumstances, *inter alia* to protect civilians or when security reasons so impel.') and 187 ('The definition of hostages must be
understood as being similar to that of civilians taken as hostages within the meaning of grave
breaches under Article 2 of the [1993 ICTY] Statute, that is – persons unlawfully deprived of
their freedom, often wantonly and sometimes under threat of death.'); and *Kordić and Čerkez*
Trial Judgment, 2001, para. 314 ('an individual commits the offence of taking civilians as
hostages when he threatens to subject civilians, who are unlawfully detained, to inhuman
treatment or death as a means of achieving the fulfilment of a condition').
[515] See section G.2.a. and Additional Protocol II, Article 4(2)(a). It is furthermore consistent with
the fact that threats of such behaviour are also unlawful; see Additional Protocol II, Article 4(2)(h).
[516] ICTY, *Kordić and Čerkez* Trial Judgment, 2001, para. 313.

it would not violate the prohibition of hostage-taking to threaten to continue to detain someone whose release is not legally required. It would, however, be unlawful to make such a threat if the detention would be arbitrary.[517] The mere fact of detention of a combatant by a non-State armed group cannot be seen as hostage-taking under common Article 3.

iii. Intent to compel a third party

657 Hostage-taking is done 'in order to compel' a third party. Hence, a conditional threat must be issued that is 'intended as a coercive measure to achieve the fulfilment of a condition'.[518] As indicated in the definition of hostage-taking, the threat may be explicit or implicit.[519]

658   In *Sesay*, the SCSL Trial Chamber held that the 'offence of hostage taking requires the threat to be communicated to a third party, with the intent of compelling the third party to act or refrain from acting as a condition for the safety or release of the captives'.[520] In this case, the Trial Chamber found that the accused had repeatedly threatened captured peacekeepers,[521] but it found no evidence that the threat had been communicated to a third party, nor evidence of an implicit threat that the peacekeepers would be harmed or the communication of an implicit condition for the safety or release of the peacekeepers.[522] However, the SCSL Appeals Chamber considered that '[i]t does not follow from a requirement that the threat be made with an intention to coerce that the threat be communicated to the third party' and concluded that '[i]t suffices that the threat be communicated to the detained individual'.[523]

iv. Purpose of hostage-taking

659 As reflected in the definition, hostage-taking is carried out in order to compel a third party to do or to abstain from doing 'any act', which is a very broad notion. The ICTY stated that hostage-taking is carried out 'to obtain a concession or gain an advantage', which is equally broad.[524]

660   In *Sesay*, for example, the accused, members of the Revolutionary United Front (RUF), had detained peacekeeping forces who, after the capture of the RUF leader, were used as hostages in order to compel his release.[525]

---

[517] On the customary prohibition of arbitrary detention, see Henckaerts/Doswald-Beck, Rule 99 and its commentary, pp. 344–352.

[518] ICTY, *Kordić and Čerkez* Trial Judgment, 2001, para. 313; SCSL, *Sesay* Trial Judgment, 2009, para. 243, and Appeal Judgment, 2009, para. 583.

[519] See SCSL, *Sesay* Trial Judgment, 2009, para. 1964.

[520] *Ibid.*   [521] *Ibid.* para. 1963.   [522] *Ibid.* paras 1965–1968.

[523] SCSL, *Sesay* Appeal Judgment, 2009, paras 582–583.

[524] ICTY, *Blaškić* Trial Judgment, 2000, para. 158; see also para. 187 ('to be characterised as hostages the detainees must have been used to obtain some advantage or to ensure that a belligerent, other person or other group of persons enter into some undertaking'); *Blaškić* Appeal Judgment, 2004, para. 639 ('the use of a threat concerning detainees so as to obtain a concession or gain an advantage'); *Kordić and Čerkez* Trial Judgment, 2001, para. 319.

[525] SCSL, *Sesay* Appeal Judgment, 2009, paras 596–601.

661   Other purposes of hostage-taking may include rendering areas or military objectives immune from military operations by using captive civilians as human shields.[526] In such instances, hostage-taking may also violate the prohibition of cruel treatment or the prohibition of collective punishments.[527] However, the analysis of each specific violation has to be carried out separately.

662   Hostage-taking is prohibited irrespective of the conduct that the hostage-taker seeks to impose. Thus, hostage-taking is not lawful even when it is aimed at compelling a third party to cease an unlawful conduct. Violations of common Article 3 are not a legitimate way to ensure respect for humanitarian law.[528]

4. Outrages upon personal dignity, in particular humiliating and degrading treatment

a. Introduction

663   The prohibition of outrages upon personal dignity first appeared in common Article 3. It was reaffirmed in the Additional Protocols and is today considered part of customary international law.[529] International and regional human rights treaties, within their respective fields of application, list the prohibition of 'inhuman and degrading treatment' as non-derogable.[530] As noted above, the term 'outrages upon personal dignity' can relate to cruel treatment and torture, but also has its own characteristics.

b. Definition of outrages upon personal dignity

664   The Geneva Conventions and Additional Protocols do not define the term 'outrages upon personal dignity'. The ICTY requires that 'the accused intentionally committed or participated in an act or omission which would be generally considered to cause serious humiliation, degradation or otherwise be a serious attack on human dignity'.[531] It has held that this assessment should not be

---

[526] See also Gasser/Dörmann, para. 535(3).

[527] For the qualification of the use of 'human shields' as cruel treatment, see paras 620 and 622. For the prohibition of collective punishments, see Additional Protocol II, Article 4(2)(b); see also ICRC Study on Customary International Humanitarian Law (2005), Rule 103.

[528] On the concept of belligerent reprisals in non-international armed conflicts, see section M.6.

[529] Additional Protocol I, Article 75(2)(b); Additional Protocol II, Article 4(2)(e); ICRC Study on Customary International Humanitarian Law (2005), Rule 90.

[530] International Covenant on Civil and Political Rights (1966), Article 7; European Convention on Human Rights (1950), Article 3; American Convention on Human Rights (1969), Article 5(2); African Charter on Human and Peoples' Rights (1981), Article 5. See also Convention against Torture (1984); Inter-American Convention against Torture (1985); and European Convention for the Prevention of Torture (1987).

[531] ICTY, *Kunarac* Trial Judgment, 2001, para. 514, and Appeal Judgment, 2002, paras 161 and 163. See also *Haradinaj* Trial Judgment, 2008, para. 132 (using 'severe' instead of 'serious'); ICTR, *Bagosora* Trial Judgment, 2008, para. 2250; *Renzaho* Trial Judgment, 2009, para. 809; *Nyiramasuhuko* Trial Judgment, 2011, para. 6178; SCSL, *Taylor* Trial Judgment, 2012, para. 431; *Sesay* Trial Judgment, 2009, para. 175; and *Brima* Trial Judgment, 2007, para. 716.

based only on subjective criteria related to the sensitivity of the victim, but also on objective criteria related to the gravity of the act.[532] Concerning the gravity of the act, the Tribunal held that the humiliation of the victim must be so intense that any reasonable person would be outraged.[533]

665   Like cruel treatment and torture, outrages upon personal dignity frequently do not take the form of an isolated act. The offence can be committed in one single act but can also result from a combination or accumulation of several acts which, taken individually, might not amount to an outrage upon person dignity. According to the ICTY:

[T]he seriousness of an act and its consequences may arise either from the nature of the act *per se* or from the repetition of an act or from a combination of different acts which, taken individually, would not constitute a crime within the meaning of Article 3 of the [1993 ICTY] Statute. The form, severity and duration of the violence, the intensity and duration of the physical or mental suffering, shall serve as a basis for assessing whether crimes were committed.[534]

666   While the humiliation and degradation must be 'real and serious', it need not be lasting.[535] No prohibited purposes such as those which characterize the crime of torture are required.[536]

667   The ICC Elements of Crimes defines the material elements of outrages upon personal dignity as an act in which '[t]he perpetrator humiliated, degraded or otherwise violated the dignity of one or more persons' and '[t]he severity of the humiliation, degradation or other violation was of such degree as to be generally recognized as an outrage upon personal dignity'.[537] While this definition is tautological, it gives the indication that the violation does not require severe mental or physical pain (as torture does), but that it has to be significant in order to be distinguished from a mere insult.[538] This also follows from the ordinary meaning of the term 'outrage'.[539]

668   According to the ICC Elements of Crimes, the prohibition of outrages upon personal dignity, in particular humiliating and degrading treatment, includes those committed against dead persons.[540] This clarification is important

---

[532] See ICTY, *Aleksovski* Trial Judgment, 1999, para. 56, and *Kunarac* Trial Judgment, 2001, para. 504, and Appeal Judgment, 2002, paras 162–163.

[533] *Ibid.*   [534] ICTY, *Aleksovski* Trial Judgment, 1999, para. 57.

[535] See ICTY, *Kunarac* Trial Judgment, 2001, para. 501, and *Kvočka* Trial Judgment, 2001, para. 168. See also SCSL, *Sesay* Trial Judgment, 2009, para. 176.

[536] ICTY, *Kvočka* Trial Judgment, 2001, para. 226.

[537] ICC Elements of Crimes (2002), Article 8(2)(c)(ii).

[538] For a view that the prohibition under international humanitarian law is wider than the prohibition under international criminal law, see Sivakumaran, 2012, p. 264.

[539] *Concise Oxford English Dictionary*, 12th edition, Oxford University Press, 2011, p. 1017 ('an extremely strong reaction of anger or indignation; violate or infringe (a law or principle) flagrantly').

[540] ICC Elements of Crimes (2002), Article 8(2)(c)(ii), fn. 57. See also UN Human Rights Council, Advisory Committee, Fourth Session, 25–29 January 2010, *Study on best practices on the issue of missing persons*, UN Doc. A/HRC/AC/4/CRP.2/Rev.1, 25 January 2010, paras 66–71, and ICTY, *Tadić* Trial Judgment, 1997, para. 748.

because recent armed conflicts show that it is not unusual, even today, for human remains to be treated in a degrading and humiliating manner. The ICTR and the ICTY, for example, have documented the mutilation of dead bodies.[541]

669   The ICC Elements of Crimes further specifies that the victim need not personally be aware of the humiliation.[542] The last point was made in order to cover the deliberate humiliation of unconscious persons or persons with mental disabilities. The Elements of Crimes also notes that relevant aspects of the cultural background of the person need to be taken into account, thereby covering treatment that is, for example, humiliating to someone of a particular nationality, culture or religion, while not necessarily to others.[543]

670   None of the international criminal tribunals have attempted to distinguish between 'humiliating' and 'degrading' treatment. While common Article 3 uses both terms in juxtaposition, suggesting that they could refer to different concepts, their ordinary meaning is nearly identical.[544] The question of whether there could conceivably be any treatment amounting to outrages upon personal dignity that would be humiliating but not degrading (or vice versa) is ultimately irrelevant since both acts are prohibited by common Article 3. The same could be said of 'outrages upon personal dignity' in relation to the two other concepts. Despite the use of 'in particular' in the provision, it is hard to conceive of 'outrages' which would not be humiliating or degrading.

671   The question also arises of whether the physical or mental suffering must attain a higher threshold in order to constitute cruel treatment. The fact that the grave breaches provisions criminalize inhuman (or cruel) treatment but not outrages upon personal dignity might suggest so. That said, the ICTY's definitions of cruel or inhuman treatment and of outrages upon personal dignity overlap, since both definitions include the phrase 'serious attacks on human dignity'. Indeed, the two notions do necessarily overlap to a certain extent. Depending on the circumstances, treatment which is considered degrading or humiliating could turn into cruel treatment if repeated over a certain period of time or if committed against a person in a particularly vulnerable situation. Degrading or humiliating treatment could also qualify as torture if committed for a specific purpose and causing severe pain or suffering.

672   Specific acts that have been considered as degrading treatment by international criminal tribunals include: forced public nudity;[545] rape and sexual violence;[546] 'sexual slavery, including the abduction of women and girls as

---

[541] See ICTR, *Niyitegeka* Trial Judgment, 2003, para. 303, and ICTY, *Delalić* Trial Judgment, 1998, para. 849. Other examples of outrages upon personal dignity include taking body parts as trophies and exposing a corpse to public display and denigration.

[542] ICC Elements of Crimes (2002), Article 8(2)(c)(ii), fn. 57.   [543] *Ibid.*

[544] The *Concise Oxford English Dictionary*, 12th edition, Oxford University Press, 2011, p. 377, defines degrading as 'causing a loss of self-respect; humiliating'.

[545] ICTY, *Kunarac* Trial Judgment, 2001, paras 766–774.

[546] ICTY, *Furundžija* Trial Judgment, 1998, paras 270–275; ICTR, *Ndindiliyimana* Trial Judgment, 2011, para. 2158.

"bush wives", a conjugal form of sexual slavery';[547] the use of detainees as human shields or trench diggers;[548] inappropriate conditions of confinement; being forced to perform subservient acts; being forced to relieve bodily functions in one's clothing; or enduring the constant fear of being subjected to physical, mental or sexual violence.[549]

673   Examples of degrading treatment gleaned from decisions of human rights bodies include: treatment or punishment of an individual if it 'grossly humiliates him before others or drives him to act against his will or conscience';[550] not allowing a prisoner to change his or her soiled clothes;[551] and cutting off a person's hair or beard as punishment.[552]

5. Requirement of a regularly constituted court affording all the indispensable judicial guarantees

a. Introduction

674 Common Article 3 prohibits 'the passing of sentences and the carrying out of executions without previous judgment pronounced by a regularly constituted court, affording all the judicial guarantees which are recognized as indispensable by civilized peoples'. This provision was fleshed out in Additional Protocol II and is part of customary international law.[553]

675   This provision prohibits 'summary' justice or trial by any tribunal that fails to qualify as fair and regular. It does not, however, provide immunity from trial for any offence; it does not prevent a person suspected of an offence from being arrested, prosecuted, sentenced and punished according to the law.

676   Common Article 3 refers to 'the passing of sentences and the carrying out of executions'. 'Sentence' is defined as a '[t]he judgement that a court formally pronounces after finding a criminal defendant guilty; the punishment imposed on a criminal wrongdoer'.[554] This means that the guarantee of a fair trial in common Article 3 applies to the prosecution and punishment of persons charged with a penal offence.

677   As regards the 'carrying out of executions', which is not prohibited by common Article 3, other treaties may have an impact for States Parties. First, Additional Protocol II limits the right to impose and carry out the death penalty on persons who were under the age of 18 years at the time they committed the

---

[547] SCSL, *Taylor* Trial Judgment, 2012, para. 432.
[548] ICTY, *Aleksovski* Trial Judgment, 1999, para. 229.
[549] ICTY, *Kvočka* Trial Judgment, 2001, para. 173.
[550] European Commission of Human Rights, *Greek case*, Report, 1969, p. 186.
[551] European Court of Human Rights, *Hurtado* v. *Switzerland*, Judgment, 1994, para. 12.
[552] European Court of Human Rights, *Yankov* v. *Bulgaria*, Judgment, 2003, paras 114 and 121.
[553] Additional Protocol II, Article 6(2); ICRC Study on Customary International Humanitarian Law (2005), Rule 100. See also Additional Protocol I, Article 75.
[554] Bryan A. Garner (ed.), *Black's Law Dictionary*, 10th edition, Thomson Reuters, 2014, pp. 1569–1570.

offence and on pregnant women and mothers of young children, respectively.[555] Humanitarian law does not prohibit the imposition of death sentences or the carrying out of a death sentence against other persons. However, it sets out strict rules in respect of international armed conflicts for the procedure under which a death sentence can be pronounced and carried out.[556] In addition, several treaties prohibit the death penalty altogether for States Parties.[557] Many countries have abolished the death penalty, even for military offences.[558]

b. Regularly constituted courts

678   The requirement that a court be regularly constituted was replaced in Article 6(2) of Additional Protocol II by the requirement that a court offer 'the essential guarantees of independence and impartiality'. This formula was taken from Article 84 of the Third Convention. It focuses more on the capacity of the court to conduct a fair trial than on how it is established. This takes into account the reality of non-international armed conflict (see also paras 692–693). The ICC Elements of Crimes also defines a 'regularly constituted' court as one that affords 'the essential guarantees of independence and impartiality'.[559] According to these texts, the requirements of independence and impartiality are the touchstones for interpreting the meaning of this term.

679   The 1966 International Covenant on Civil and Political Rights and other human rights treaties provide for the right to a fair trial. These treaties specify that for a trial to be fair it must be conducted by a court that is 'independent' and 'impartial'.[560] Human rights bodies have stated that the

---

[555] Additional Protocol II, Article 6(4). For international armed conflict, see Article 68(4) of the Fourth Convention and Articles 76(3) and 77(5) of Additional Protocol I.

[556] See Third Convention, Articles 100–101 and 107, and Fourth Convention, Articles 68, 71 and 74–75.

[557] Second Optional Protocol to the International Covenant on Civil and Political Rights (1989); Protocol to the American Convention on Human Rights to Abolish the Death Penalty (1990); and Protocols 6 (1983) and 13 (2002) to the European Convention on Human Rights.

[558] Article 2(1) of the 1989 Second Optional Protocol to the International Covenant on Civil and Political Rights allows States to enter a reservation to the Protocol which 'provides for the application of the death penalty in time of war pursuant to a conviction for a most serious crime of a military nature committed during wartime'. Eight reservations were entered to this article, of which three were withdrawn and five are still in force. The 1990 Protocol to the American Convention on Human Rights to Abolish the Death Penalty allows for similar reservations. Two States entered reservations in this respect, both of which are still in force. For more information on the death penalty, see e.g. Hans Nelen and Jacques Claessen (eds), *Beyond the Death Penalty: Reflections on Punishment*, Intersentia, Cambridge, 2012; Austin Sarat and Jürgen Martschukat (eds), *Is the Death Penalty Dying? European and American Perspectives*, Cambridge University Press, 2011; William A. Schabas, *The Abolition of the Death Penalty in International Law*, 3rd edition, Cambridge University Press, 2002, and 'The Right to Life', in Andrew Clapham and Paola Gaeta (eds), *The Oxford Handbook of International Law in Armed Conflict*, Oxford University Press, 2014, pp. 365–385; and Elizabeth Wicks, *The Right to Life and Conflicting Interests*, Oxford University Press, 2010.

[559] ICC Elements of Crimes (2002), Article 8(2)(c)(iv).

[560] International Covenant on Civil and Political Rights (1966), Article 14(1); Convention on the Rights of the Child (1989), Article 40(2)(b); European Convention on Human Rights (1950), Article 6(1); American Convention on Human Rights (1969), Article 8(1); and African Charter on Human and Peoples' Rights (1981), Articles 7 and 26.

fundamental principles of fair trial and the requirement that courts be independent and impartial can never be dispensed with.[561] The interpretation given to these terms by these bodies is also relevant in the context of common Article 3, at least for courts operated by State authorities.

680   For a court to be independent, it must be able to perform its functions without interference from any other branch of government, especially the executive.[562] Therefore, the judges must have guarantees of security of tenure.[563] The requirement of independence does not necessarily preclude the court from being composed of persons from the executive branch of government, for example members of the armed forces, so long as procedures are in place to ensure they perform their judicial functions independently and impartially.

681   The requirement of impartiality has two aspects, one subjective and one objective. First, in order to be impartial, the judges composing the court must not allow their judgement to be influenced by personal bias or prejudice, nor harbour preconceptions about the matter before them, nor act in ways that improperly promote the interests of one side.[564] Second, the court must be impartial from an objective viewpoint, i.e. it must appear to a reasonable observer to be impartial.[565] These two aspects of the

---

[561]   See UN Human Rights Committee, *General Comment No. 29, States of Emergency (Article 4)*, UN Doc. CCPR/C/21/Rev.1/Add.11, 31 August 2001, paras 11 and 16; African Commission on Human and Peoples' Rights, *Civil Liberties Organisation and others* v. *Nigeria*, Decision, 2001, para. 27; Inter-American Commission on Human Rights, *Report on Terrorism and Human Rights*, OAS Doc. OEA/Ser.L/V/II.116 Doc. 5 rev. 1 corr., 22 October 2002, paras 245–247; and Inter-American Court of Human Rights, *Judicial Guarantees case*, Advisory Opinion, 1987, paras 29–30.

[562]   See e.g. African Commission on Human and Peoples' Rights, *Centre for Free Speech* v. *Nigeria*, Decision, 1999, paras 15–16; European Court of Human Rights, *Belilos case*, Judgment, 1988, para. 64; *Findlay* v. *UK*, Judgment, 1997, paras 73–77; and UN Human Rights Committee, *Bahamonde* v. *Equatorial Guinea*, Views, 1993, para. 9.4.

[563]   For more details, see UN Human Rights Committee, *General Comment No. 32, Article 14: Right to equality before courts and tribunals and to a fair trial*, UN Doc. CCPR/C/GC/32, 23 August 2007, para. 19, and Basic Principles on the Independence of the Judiciary (1985). The Inter-American Commission on Human Rights underlined the need for freedom from interference from the executive and for judges' security of tenure; see Inter-American Commission on Human Rights, *Annual Report 1992–1993*, OAS Doc. OEA/Ser.L/V/II.83 doc. 14, 12 March 1993, p. 207, and *Case 11.006 (Peru)*, Report, 1995, section VI(2)(a). See also Canada, Supreme Court, *Ell case*, Judgment, 2003, paras 18–32, and United States, Supreme Court, *Hamdan case*, Judgment, 2006, p. 632.

[564]   UN Human Rights Committee, *General Comment No. 32, Article 14: Right to equality before courts and tribunals and to a fair trial*, UN Doc. CCPR/C/GC/32, 23 August 2007, para. 21; *Karttunen* v. *Finland*, Views, 1992, para. 7.2; and European Court of Human Rights, *Incal* v. *Turkey*, Judgment, 1998, para. 65. See also Australia, Military Court at Rabaul, *Ohashi case*, Judgment, 1946.

[565]   See UN Human Rights Committee, *General Comment No. 32, Article 14: Right to equality before courts and tribunals and to a fair trial*, UN Doc. CCPR/C/GC/32, 23 August 2007, para. 21; see also African Commission on Human and Peoples' Rights, *Constitutional Rights Project* v. *Nigeria*, Decision, 1995, para. 8; *Malawi African Association and others* v. *Mauritania*, Decision, 2000, para. 98; European Court of Human Rights, *Piersack* v. *Belgium*, Judgment, 1982, paras 28–34; *De Cubber case*, Judgment, 1984, paras 24–26; *Findlay* v. *UK*, Judgment, 1997, para. 73; and Inter-American Commission on Human Rights, *Case 10.970 (Peru)*, Report, 1996, section V(B)(3)(c).

requirement of impartiality have also been applied by the ICTY and the ICTR.[566]

682   The requirements of independence of the judiciary, in particular from the executive, and of subjective and objective impartiality apply equally to civilian, military and special security courts. The trial of civilians by military or special security courts should be exceptional and take place under conditions which genuinely afford the full guarantees of fair trial as required by common Article 3.[567]

c. Judicial guarantees which are indispensable

683   There was some debate at the 1949 Diplomatic Conference as to whether to include a list of guarantees in common Article 3 or whether to make reference to the rest of the Conventions and the guarantees contained therein. A proposal to refer to the judicial guarantees of the Conventions, including Article 105 of the Third Convention, was not retained.[568] In the end, the wording 'judicial guarantees which are recognized as indispensable by civilized peoples' was adopted without listing any specific guarantees. The delegates did not, however, leave the interpretation entirely open since the sentence provides that the guarantees must be 'recognized as indispensable by civilized peoples'. The formulation 'recognized as indispensable by civilized peoples' was replaced in the ICC Elements of Crimes with 'generally recognized as indispensable under international law',[569] and this is how it should be interpreted nowadays.

684   While common Article 3 does not list specific judicial guarantees, Article 6 of Additional Protocol II does, and the requirement of fair trial in common Article 3 today has to be interpreted in the light of these provisions and their customary equivalent.[570] As follows from the phrase 'in particular' in Article 6, this list is not exhaustive but spells out the minimum guarantees of fair trial

---

[566] See e.g. ICTY, *Furundžija* Appeal Judgment, 2000, paras 189–191; *Mucić* Appeal Judgment, 2001, paras 682–684; and *Galić* Appeal Judgment, 2006, paras 37–41; ICTR, *Akayesu* Appeal Judgment, 2001, paras 203–207; *Rutaganda* Appeal Judgment, 2003, paras 39–41; and *Nahimana* Appeal Judgment, 2007, paras 47–50.

[567] UN Human Rights Committee, *General Comment No. 32, Article 14: Right to equality before courts and tribunals and to a fair trial*, UN Doc. CCPR/C/GC/32, 23 August 2007, para. 22. In a number of cases such courts were found to fall short. See e.g. UN Human Rights Committee, *Espinoza de Polay* v. *Peru*, Views, 1997, para. 8; African Commission on Human and Peoples' Rights, *Constitutional Rights Project* v. *Nigeria*, Decision, 1995, para. 8; *Civil Liberties Organisation and others* v. *Nigeria*, Decision, 2001, paras 25, 27 and 43–44; European Court of Human Rights, *Findlay* v. *UK*, Judgment, 1997, paras 73–77; *Çiraklar* v. *Turkey*, Judgment, 1998, para. 38; *Mehdi Zana* v. *Turkey*, Judgment, 2001, paras 22–23; *Şahiner* v. *Turkey*, Judgment, 2001, paras 45–47; Inter-American Commission on Human Rights, *Case 11.084 (Peru)*, Report, 1994, section V(3); and Inter-American Court of Human Rights, *Castillo Petruzzi and others* v. *Peru*, Judgment, 1999, paras 132–133. For more details, see Doswald-Beck, 2011, pp. 337–344.

[568] *Final Record of the Diplomatic Conference of Geneva of 1949*, Vol. II-B, pp. 83–84.

[569] ICC Elements of Crimes (2002), Article 8(2)(c)(iv).

[570] See also Sandoz/Swinarski/Zimmermann (eds), *Commentary on the Additional Protocols*, ICRC, 1987, para. 4597.

that are generally recognized as indispensable under international law today.[571] The judicial guarantees listed in Article 6 of Additional Protocol II are considered customary today.[572]

685   Thus, judicial guarantees that are generally recognized as indispensable today include, as a minimum:

- the obligation to inform the accused without delay of the nature and cause of the offence alleged;[573]
- the requirement that an accused have the necessary rights and means of defence;[574]
- the right not to be convicted of an offence except on the basis of individual penal responsibility;[575]
- the principle of *nullum crimen, nulla poena sine lege* ('no crime or punishment without a law') and the prohibition of a heavier penalty than that provided for at the time of the offence;[576]
- the right to be presumed innocent;[577]
- the right to be tried in one's own presence;[578]
- the right not to be compelled to testify against oneself or to confess guilt;[579]

---

[571] This list is supported by various human rights law instruments. See, in particular, International Covenant on Civil and Political Rights (1966), Article 14; European Convention on Human Rights (1950), Article 6; American Convention on Human Rights (1969), Article 8; and African Charter on Human and Peoples' Rights (1981), Article 7.

[572] See ICRC, Customary International Humanitarian Law, practice relating to Rule 100, available at https://www.icrc.org/customary-ihl/eng/docs/v2_rul.

[573] Additional Protocol II, Article 6(2)(a). See also Additional Protocol I, Article 75(4)(a); International Covenant on Civil and Political Rights (1966), Article 14(3)(a); European Convention on Human Rights (1950), Article 6(3)(a); and American Convention on Human Rights (1969), Article 8(2)(b).

[574] Additional Protocol II, Article 6(2)(a). See also Additional Protocol I, Article 75(4)(a); International Covenant on Civil and Political Rights (1966), Article 14(3); European Convention on Human Rights (1950), Article 6(3); American Convention on Human Rights (1969), Article 8(2); and African Charter on Human and Peoples' Rights (1981), Article 7(c).

[575] Additional Protocol II, Article 6(2)(b). See also Additional Protocol I, Article 75(4)(b).

[576] Additional Protocol II, Article 6(2)(c). See also Additional Protocol I, Article 75(4)(c); International Covenant on Civil and Political Rights (1966), Article 15; European Convention on Human Rights (1950), Article 7; American Convention on Human Rights (1969), Article 9; and African Charter on Human and Peoples' Rights (1981), Article 7(2).

[577] Additional Protocol II, Article 6(2)(d). See also Additional Protocol I, Article 75(4)(d); International Covenant on Civil and Political Rights (1966), Article 14(2); European Convention on Human Rights (1950), Article 6(2); American Convention on Human Rights (1969), Article 8(2); and African Charter on Human and Peoples' Rights (1981), Article 7(1)(b).

[578] Additional Protocol II, Article 6(2)(e). See also Additional Protocol I, Article 75(4)(e), and International Covenant on Civil and Political Rights (1966), Article 14(3)(d). On the issue of trial *in absentia*, see the commentary on Article 49, para. 2871.

[579] Additional Protocol II, Article 6(2)(f). See also Additional Protocol I, Article 75(4)(f); International Covenant on Civil and Political Rights (1966), Article 143)(g); and American Convention on Human Rights (1969), Article 8(2)(g) and (3). This right is not explicitly stipulated in the 1950 European Convention on Human Rights, but it has been interpreted by the European Court of Human Rights as one of the elements of fair trial under Article 6(1); see e.g. *Pishchalnikov* v. *Russia*, Judgment, 2009, para. 71.

– the right to be advised of one's judicial and other remedies and of the time limits within which they may be exercised.[580]

For more details on these judicial guarantees, see the commentary on Article 6 of Additional Protocol II.

686   A similar list is provided in Article 75 of Additional Protocol I, which has also been found to be relevant in this context.[581] Both lists were inspired by the 1966 International Covenant on Civil and Political Rights.[582] Article 75 lists three additional guarantees:

– the right to present and examine witnesses;[583]
– the right to have the judgment pronounced publicly;[584]
– the right not to be prosecuted or punished more than once by the same Party for the same act or on the same charge (*non bis in idem*).[585]

687   The first two of these additional guarantees were not included in Additional Protocol II in response to the wish of some delegates to keep the list as short as possible.[586] Arguably, however, they should apply in non-international armed conflict to the extent that they are essential to a fair trial and they appear in the main human rights instruments. The third guarantee, the principle of *non*

---

[580]   Additional Protocol II, Article 6(3). See also Additional Protocol I, Article 75(4)(j). Human rights instruments guarantee a right to appeal; see International Covenant on Civil and Political Rights (1966), Article 14(5); Convention on the Rights of the Child (1989), Article 40(2)(b)(v); American Convention on Human Rights (1969), Article 8(2)(h); African Charter on Human and Peoples' Rights (1981), Article 7(1)(a); and Protocol 7 to the European Convention on Human Rights (1984), Article 2(1). 'The influence of human rights law on this issue is such that it can be argued that the right of appeal proper – and not only the right to be informed whether appeal is available – has become a basic component of fair trial rights in the context of armed conflict' (Henckaerts/Doswald-Beck, commentary on Rule 100, pp. 369–370).

[581]   See e.g. United States, Supreme Court, *Hamdan case*, Judgment, 2006, pp. 632–634. (The Court looked to Article 75 of Additional Protocol I, noting that even though the United States had not ratified the Protocol, the US government did not have a problem with Article 75, and Article 75 lays out many of the minimum requirements. Furthermore, the United States is a party to the 1966 International Covenant on Civil and Political Rights, which contains many of these same fair trial requirements. The Court determined that the military commissions violated the basic principles that an accused must have access to the evidence against him and must be present at the trial.) See also Sandoz/Swinarski/Zimmermann (eds), *Commentary on the Additional Protocols*, ICRC, 1987, para. 3084, and ICRC, *International Humanitarian Law and the Challenges of Contemporary Armed Conflicts*, 2011, p. 16.

[582]   On the relevance of the International Covenant on Civil and Political Rights, see e.g. United Kingdom, *Manual of the Law of Armed Conflict*, 2004, para. 15.30.5, and United States, Supreme Court, *Hamdan case*, Judgment, 2006, pp. 632–634.

[583]   Additional Protocol I, Article 75(4)(g). See also International Covenant on Civil and Political Rights (1966), Article 14(3)(e); European Convention on Human Rights (1950), Article 6(3)(d); and American Convention on Human Rights (1969), Article 8(2)(f).

[584]   Additional Protocol I, Article 75(4)(i). See also International Covenant on Civil and Political Rights (1966), Article 14(1); European Convention on Human Rights (1950), Article 6(1); and American Convention on Human Rights (1969), Article 8(5).

[585]   See Third Convention, Article 86; Fourth Convention, Article 117(3); and Additional Protocol I, Article 75(4)(h). See also International Covenant on Civil and Political Rights (1966), Article 14(7); Protocol 7 to the European Convention on Human Rights (1984), Article 4; and American Convention on Human Rights (1969), Article 8(4).

[586]   Bothe/Partsch/Solf, p. 745.

bis in idem, was not included because 'this principle could not apply between the courts of the government and the courts of the rebels'.[587] It may thus be argued, *a contrario*, that it should apply as a prohibition on double jeopardy of prosecution or punishment by the same Party, in the same manner as this principle is formulated in Article 75 of Additional Protocol I. A second trial by the same Party for the same act or on the same charge, after a final judgment acquitting or convicting the person concerned, should be deemed unfair.

688   As already noted, the lists in both Additional Protocols are illustrative and not limitative. Their cumulative effect is to ensure the accused receives a fair trial. Each right should be applied in such a way that a fair trial is guaranteed. Human rights instruments furthermore include the right to be tried 'without undue delay' or 'within a reasonable time'.[588] This principle is also set forth in Article 103 of the Third Convention but not in Article 6 of Additional Protocol II or in Article 75 of Additional Protocol I. However, undue delay could also taint a trial in the context of a non-international armed conflict and should thus be taken into account to assess the fairness of such a trial.

d. Courts convened by non-State armed groups

689   In practice, non-State armed groups are known to have convened courts, in particular to try their own members for criminal offences related to the armed conflict.[589] Although the establishment of such courts may raise issues of legitimacy, trial by such means may constitute an alternative to summary justice and a way for armed groups to maintain 'law and order' and to ensure respect for humanitarian law.[590] Armed groups are frequently called upon to ensure respect for humanitarian law, for example by the UN Security Council.[591]

690   The application of the doctrine of command responsibility to non-international armed conflict bolsters this assessment.[592] According to this doctrine, commanders of armed groups would be criminally responsible if they knew, or had reason to know, that their subordinates committed war crimes and did not take all necessary and reasonable measures in their power to punish the persons responsible.[593] The ICC considered the availability of a judicial system through which a commander of a non-State armed group could have

---

[587] *Ibid.*

[588] International Covenant on Civil and Political Rights (1966), Article 14(3)(c); European Convention on Human Rights (1950), Article 6(1); American Convention on Human Rights (1969), Article 8(1); African Charter on Human and Peoples' Rights, Article 7(1)(d).

[589] See examples of practice provided by Sivakumaran, 2009, pp. 490–495, and 2012, pp. 550–555; Somer, pp. 678–682; and Willms, pp. 22–24.

[590] Sivakumaran, 2009, pp. 490 and 497, and 2012, p. 550.

[591] See e.g. UN Security Council, Res. 1479 (2003) on Côte d'Ivoire, para. 8; Res. 1509 (2003) on Liberia, para. 10; Res. 1962 (2010) on Côte d'Ivoire, para. 9; Res. 1933 (2010) on Côte d'Ivoire, para. 13; Res. 2041 (2012) on Afghanistan, para. 32; and Res. 2139 (2014) on Syria, para. 3.

[592] Sivakumaran, 2009, p. 497, and 2012, p. 557; Sassòli, 2010, p. 35; Somer, p. 685.

[593] ICRC Study on Customary International Humanitarian Law (2005), Rule 152.

punished war crimes as an important element in the application of this doctrine in practice.[594]

691   These courts, even if not recognized as legitimate by the State, are subject to the requirement of fair trial in common Article 3. This follows from paragraph 1 of common Article 3, which reads 'each Party to the conflict shall be bound to apply'.

692   Common Article 3 requires 'a regularly constituted court'. If this would refer exclusively to State courts constituted according to domestic law, non-State armed groups would not be able to comply with this requirement. The application of this rule in common Article 3 to 'each Party to the conflict' would then be without effect. Therefore, to give effect to this provision, it may be argued that courts are regularly constituted as long as they are constituted in accordance with the 'laws' of the armed group.[595] Alternatively, armed groups could continue to operate existing courts applying existing legislation.

693   This difficulty in interpreting common Article 3 was recognized at the 1974–77 Diplomatic Conference. As a result, the requirement of a regularly constituted court was replaced in Additional Protocol II with the requirement of a court 'offering the essential guarantees of independence and impartiality'. The formula in Protocol II was taken from Article 84 of the Third Convention and did not meet any opposition from the Conference delegates.[596]

694   No trial should be held, whether by State authorities or by non-State armed groups, if these guarantees cannot be provided. Whether an armed group can hold trials providing these guarantees is a question of fact and needs to be determined on a case-by-case basis.[597] If a fair trial cannot be provided, other forms of detention may be considered, in particular internment for security reasons (see section H). In such a case, the prohibition of arbitrary detention must be respected.[598]

695   The above analysis is offered for the purposes of assessing an armed group's compliance with the requirements of common Article 3. Nothing in the article

---

[594] ICC, *Bemba* Decision on the Confirmation of Charges, 2009, para. 501, and Trial Judgment, 2016, paras 205–209.

[595] See Bond, p. 372; Sivakumaran, 2009, pp. 499–500, and 2012, p. 306; Somer, pp. 687–689; and Willms, p. 6. The UK *Manual on the Law of Armed Conflict*, 2004, notes that 'the use of the bare word "law" [in Article 6(2)(c) of Additional Protocol II] . . . could also be wide enough to cover "laws" passed by an insurgent authority' (para. 15.42, fn. 94). According to Bothe/Partsch/Solf, p. 746, '[t]here is no basis for the concept that the rebels are prevented from changing the legal order existing in the territory where they exercise factual power'. The European Court of Human Rights has held that '[i]n certain circumstances, a court belonging to the judicial system of an entity not recognised under international law may be regarded as a tribunal "established by law" provided that it forms part of a judicial system operating on a "constitutional and legal basis" reflecting a judicial tradition compatible with the Convention, in order to enable individuals to enjoy the Convention guarantees' (*Ilaşcu and others* v. *Moldova and Russia*, Judgment, 2004, para. 460).

[596] Sandoz/Swinarski/Zimmermann (eds), *Commentary on the Additional Protocols*, ICRC, 1987, para. 4600.

[597] See generally Sivakumaran, 2009; Somer; and Willms.

[598] ICRC Study on Customary International Humanitarian Law (2005), Rule 99.

implies that a State must recognize or give legal effect to the results of a trial or other judicial proceeding conducted by a non-State Party to the conflict. This is consistent with the final paragraph of common Article 3 with respect to the legal status of such Parties.

6. Sexual violence

a. Introduction

696 While common Article 3 does not explicitly prohibit sexual violence, it does so implicitly because it establishes an obligation of humane treatment and prohibits violence to life and person, including mutilation, cruel treatment, torture and outrages upon personal dignity.

697   The term 'sexual violence' is used to describe any act of a sexual nature committed against any person under circumstances which are coercive.[599] Coercive circumstances include force, threat of force, or coercion caused, for example, by fear of violence, duress, detention, psychological oppression or abuse of power.[600] Also included are situations where the perpetrator takes advantage of a coercive environment or a person's incapacity to give genuine consent.[601] The force, threat of force or coercion can be directed against either the victim or another person.[602] Sexual violence also comprises acts of a sexual nature a person is caused to engage in by the circumstances described above.[603]

698   Sexual violence encompasses acts such as rape, enforced prostitution,[604] indecent assault,[605] sexual slavery, forced pregnancy and enforced sterilization.[606] Other examples gleaned from decisions of international criminal tribunals include forced public nudity,[607] sexual harassment, such as

---

[599] See ICTR, *Akayesu* Trial Judgment, 1998, para. 688. For an overview of this concept in armed conflicts, see e.g. Durham; Gardam/Jarvis; Haeri/Puechguirbal; Brammertz/Jarvis; and Viseur Sellers/Rosenthal.

[600] See ICC Elements of Crimes (2002), Article 8(2)(e)(vi)-6; see also Articles 7(1)(g)-6 and 8(2)(b)(xxii)-6, and WHO, *World report on violence and health*, Geneva, 2002, pp. 149–181.

[601] The ICC Elements of Crimes notes in footnotes to the war crime of rape, which also applies to the war crime of sexual violence: 'It is understood that a person may be incapable of giving genuine consent if affected by natural, induced or age-related incapacity.'

[602] See ICC Elements of Crimes (2002) Article 8(2)(e)(vi)-6.

[603] *Ibid.* See also ICTY, *Delalić* Trial Judgment, 1998, para. 1066.

[604] See Additional Protocol II, Article (4)(2)(e). See also Fourth Convention, Article 27, and Additional Protocol I, Article 75(2)(b). Rape and enforced prostitution are listed as war crimes in Article 8(2)(e)(vi) of the 1998 ICC Statute, in Article 4(e) of the 1994 ICTR Statute, in Section 6(1)(e)(vi) of UNTAET Regulation No. 2000/15 and in Article 3(e) of the 2002 SCSL Statute.

[605] See Additional Protocol II, Article (4)(2)(e). See also Fourth Convention, Article 27, and Additional Protocol I, Article 75(2)(b). Indecent assault is listed as a war crime in Article 4(e) of the 1994 ICTR Statute and Article 3(e) of the 2002 SCSL Statute.

[606] Sexual slavery, forced pregnancy and enforced sterilization are listed as war crimes in Article 8(2)(e)(vi) of the 1998 ICC Statute and Section 6(1)(e)(vi) of UNTAET Regulation No. 2000/15.

[607] ICTR, *Akayesu* Trial Judgment, 1998, para. 688. See also ICTY, *Kunarac* Trial Judgment, 2001, paras 766–774.

forced stripping,[608] and mutilation of sexual organs.[609] Sexual violence has also been considered to include acts such as forced marriage, forced inspections for virginity, sexual exploitation, such as obtaining sexual services in return for food or protection, forced abortions,[610] and trafficking for sexual exploitation.[611]

699   As explained below, the case law and statutes of international criminal tribunals show that sexual violence can amount to one or more prohibited acts listed in common Article 3. Often such acts will not fall into only one of the categories of prohibited acts under common Article 3 but may constitute, for example, both 'violence to life and person' and 'outrages upon personal dignity'. In addition, sexual violence may occur as a succession of prohibited acts, for example rape being accompanied by murder or forced public nudity.[612]

700   Article 27(2) of the Fourth Convention provides specifically for the protection of women against rape, enforced prostitution and indecent assault.[613] Today, however, the prohibition of sexual violence is recognized to encompass violence not only against women and girls, but any person, including men and boys.[614] Both Article (4)(2)(e) of Additional Protocol II and Article 75(2)(b) of Additional Protocol I prohibit acts of sexual violence regardless of the sex of the victim.[615] The same is true under customary international law.[616] The statutes of international criminal courts and tribunals also define crimes of sexual violence in gender-neutral terms.[617] While the majority of victims of sexual violence in armed conflict are women and girls, men and boys are also frequently victims of sexual violence, in particular when held in detention facilities.[618]

---

[608] ICTR, *Akayesu* Trial Judgment, 1998, para. 693. See also Bastick/Grimm/Kunz, p. 19.

[609] See ICTR, *Bagosora* Trial Judgment, 2008, para. 976.

[610] For all these examples, see Bastick/Grimm/Kunz, p. 19; WHO, *World report on violence and health*, Geneva, 2002, p. 149 and WHO, *Guidelines for medico-legal care for victims of sexual violence*, Geneva, 2003, p. 7.

[611] Trafficking for sexual exploitation will often come within the definition of enforced prostitution but may involve, for example, the sexual exploitation of persons for pornography. See Inter-Agency Standing Committee, *Guidelines for Integrating Gender-based Violence Interventions in Humanitarian Action*, p. 6. See also Protocol on Trafficking in Persons (2000), Article 3.

[612] See e.g. ICTR, *Bagosora* Trial Judgment, 2008, para. 933.

[613] See also Additional Protocol I, Article 76(1).

[614] With the exception of forced pregnancy, forced abortion and forced inspection of virginity, which, by their nature, can only be committed against women and girls.

[615] Sandoz/Swinarski/Zimmermann (eds), *Commentary on the Additional Protocols*, ICRC, 1987, para. 3049.

[616] Henckaerts/Doswald-Beck, commentary on Rule 93, p. 327.

[617] See ICTR Statute (1994), Article 4(e); ICC Statute (1998), Article 8(2)(e)(vi); UNTAET Regulation No. 2000/15, Section 6(1)(e)(vi); and SCSL Statute (2002), Article 3(e).

[618] See Lindsey, p. 29; Solangon/Patel, pp. 417–442; and Sivakumaran, 2010b.

b. The prohibition of sexual violence under common Article 3

i. Sexual violence and the requirement of humane treatment

701 Sexual violence is prohibited by common Article 3 as it amounts to a violation of the obligation of humane treatment of persons taking no active part in hostilities. Rape, enforced prostitution and indecent assault are listed as examples of treatment that is considered inhumane in Article 27 of the Fourth Convention. Therefore, these acts should also be considered inhumane in the context of common Article 3.[619]

ii. Sexual violence and the prohibition of violence to life and person, in particular mutilation, cruel treatment and torture

702 Sexual violence will often fall within the prohibition of 'violence to life and person' and has been found to amount to torture, mutilation or cruel treatment.

703   The ICTY and the ICTR have held that rape and some other forms of sexual violence may constitute torture. Both Tribunals, as well as some human rights bodies, found rape *per se* to meet the threshold of severity for torture, as it necessarily implies severe pain and suffering.[620] For example, in *Kunarac*, the ICTY Appeals Chamber held that '[s]exual violence necessarily gives rise to severe pain or suffering, whether physical or mental, and in this way justifies its characterisation as an act of torture'.[621] The ICTY also considered that being forced to watch sexual attacks on an acquaintance was torture for the forced observer.[622]

704   Acts of sexual violence have also been held to amount to mutilation and cruel or inhuman treatment. In *Prlić*, the ICTY Trial Chamber held that 'any sexual violence inflicted on the physical and moral integrity of a person by means of threat, intimidation or force, in such a way as to degrade or humiliate the victim, may constitute inhuman treatment'.[623] Involuntary sterilization has

---

[619] In the context of crimes against humanity, inhumane acts have been found to include sexual violence; see e.g. ICTR, *Muvunyi* Trial Judgment, 2006, para. 528; *Kamuhanda* Trial Judgment, 2004, para. 710; and SCSL, *Brima* Appeal Judgment, 2008, para. 184.

[620] See ICTY, *Brđanin* Trial Judgment, 2004, para. 485; *Stanišić and Župljanin* Trial Judgment, 2013, para. 48; *Delalić* Trial Judgment, 1998, para. 495; *Kunarac* Appeal Judgment, 2002, para. 151; and ICTR, *Akayesu* Trial Judgment, 1998, para. 682. For examples taken from human rights law, see European Court of Human Rights, *Aydin* v. *Turkey*, Judgment, 1997, paras 82–86; UN Committee against Torture, *T.A.* v. *Sweden*, Decisions, 2005, paras 2.4 and 7.3; Inter-American Commission on Human Rights, *Case 10.970 (Peru)*, Report, 1996, p. 185; and *Report of the Special Rapporteur on Torture*, UN Doc. E/CN.4/1986/15, 19 February 1986, para. 119.

[621] ICTY, *Kunarac* Appeal Judgment, 2002, para. 150.

[622] ICTY, *Furundžija* Trial Judgment, 1998, para. 267. See also *Kvočka* Trial Judgment, 2001, para. 149. The Inter-American Commission on Human Rights found that being forced to witness others being raped amounted to cruel treatment; see *Case 11.565 (Mexico)*, Report, 1999, para. 53.

[623] ICTY, *Prlić* Trial Judgment, 2013, para. 116. There is no difference between the notion of 'inhuman treatment' committed in an international armed conflict and the notion of 'cruel treatment' prohibited under common Article 3; see the commentary on Article 50, para. 2982.

been found to amount to cruel treatment.[624] An example of mutilation in the context of sexual violence is the mutilation of sexual organs.[625]

iii. Sexual violence and the prohibition of outrages upon personal dignity

705 The prohibition of 'outrages upon personal dignity' contained in common Article 3 covers acts of sexual violence. This understanding has been confirmed by the subsequent inclusion of some acts of sexual violence as outrages upon personal dignity in Article (4)(2)(e) of Additional Protocol II and in the statutes of international criminal tribunals. Article (4)(2)(e) of Additional Protocol II explicitly lists 'rape, enforced prostitution and any form of indecent assault' as outrages upon personal dignity.[626] The ICTR and SCSL Statutes also list rape, enforced prostitution and any form of indecent assault as outrages upon personal dignity under common Article 3.[627]

706 International tribunals have held on numerous occasions that sexual violence falls under the category of outrages upon personal dignity, including humiliating and degrading treatment. Examples of sexual violence held to be degrading or humiliating treatment include rape,[628] forced public nudity,[629] sexual slavery, including the abduction of women and girls as 'bush wives', a conjugal form of sexual slavery,[630] sexual assault,[631] or enduring the constant fear of being subjected to physical, mental or sexual violence.[632] In *Bagosora*, the ICTR Trial Chamber found the accused guilty of outrages upon personal dignity for rape as a violation of common Article 3 and of Additional Protocol II.[633]

707 Lastly, it is also important to note that some acts of sexual violence have been recognized to amount to distinct war crimes in international and non-international armed conflicts and included as such in the ICC Statute.[634]

---

[624] UN Committee against Torture, *Consideration of reports submitted by States Parties under Article 19 of the Convention: Peru*, UN Doc. CAT/C/PER/CO/4, 25 July 2006, para. 23.

[625] See e.g. ICTR, *Bagosora* Trial Judgment, 2008, para. 2266; *Kajelijeli* Trial Judgment, 2003, paras 935–936; ICTY, *Tadić* Trial Judgment, 1997, paras 45 and 237; UN Commission on Human Rights, *Report of the Special Rapporteur on violence against women, its causes and consequences*, UN Doc. E/CN.4/2002/83/Add.3, 11 March 2002, para. 42; and Human Rights Watch, *Shattered Lives: Sexual Violence during the Rwandan Genocide and its Aftermath*, New York, September 1996.

[626] This wording in Additional Protocol II was taken directly from Article 27 of the Fourth Convention. See *Official Records of the Diplomatic Conference of Geneva of 1974–1977*, Report to Committee I on the proceedings of Working Group B, p. 104.

[627] See ICTR Statute (1994), Article 4(e), and SCSL Statute (2002), Article 3(e).

[628] ICTY, *Furundžija* Trial Judgment, 1998, paras 270–275; ICTR, *Ndindiliyimana* Trial Judgment, 2011, para. 2158.

[629] ICTY, *Kunarac* Trial Judgment, 2001, paras 766–774.

[630] SCSL, *Taylor* Trial Judgment, 2012, para. 432.

[631] ICTY, *Furundžija* Trial Judgment, 1998, para. 272.

[632] ICTY, *Kvočka* Trial Judgment, 2001, para. 173.

[633] ICTR, *Bagosora* Trial Judgment, 2008, para. 2254.

[634] ICC Statute (1998), Article 8(2)(e)(vi)1–6: war crimes of rape, sexual slavery, enforced prostitution, forced pregnancy, enforced sterilization and any other form of sexual violence constituting a serious violation of common Article 3. For the first conviction by the ICC for the war

7. Non-refoulement *under common Article 3*

708 Because of the fundamental rights it protects, common Article 3 should be understood as also prohibiting Parties to the conflict from transferring persons in their power to another authority when those persons would be in danger of suffering a violation of those fundamental rights upon transfer. The prohibition on such transfer is commonly known as '*non-refoulement*'.

709   The principle of *non-refoulement*, in its traditional sense, prohibits the transfer of a person from one State to another in any manner whatsoever if there are substantial grounds for believing that the person would be in danger of suffering the violation of certain fundamental rights in the jurisdiction of that State. This is especially recognized in respect of torture or cruel, inhuman or degrading treatment or punishment, arbitrary deprivation of life (including as the result of a death sentence pronounced without the fundamental guarantees of fair trial), or persecution on account of race, religion, nationality, membership of a particular social group or political opinion. The principle of *non-refoulement* is expressed, with some variation in scope, in a number of international legal instruments, including in humanitarian law, refugee law, human rights law, and some extradition treaties.[635] It is also, in its core, a principle of customary international law.[636]

710   Common Article 3 does not contain an explicit prohibition of *refoulement*. However, in the ICRC's view, the categorical prohibitions in common Article 3 would also prohibit a transfer of persons to places or authorities where there are substantial grounds for believing that they will be in danger of being subjected to violence to life and person, such as murder or torture and other forms of

---

crime of rape, see *Bemba* Trial Judgment, 2016, paras 98– 112 and 631–638. See also UNTAET Regulation No. 2000/15, Section 6(1)(e)(vi).

[635] The Third Convention prohibits States Parties from transferring prisoners of war to States that are not willing and able to apply the Third Convention (Article 12) and requires that '[n]o sick or injured prisoner of war . . . may be repatriated against his will during hostilities' (Article 109(3)); the Fourth Convention prohibits the transfer of protected persons to States that are not willing and able to apply the Fourth Convention and stipulates that '[i]n no circumstances shall a protected person be transferred to a country where he or she may have reason to fear persecution for his or her political opinions or religious beliefs' (Article 45). Other treaties that specifically prohibit *refoulement* include: Refugee Convention (1951), Article 33; OAU Convention Governing Refugee Problems in Africa (1969), Article II(3); Convention against Torture (1984), Article 3; Convention on Enforced Disappearance (2006), Article 16(1); American Convention on Human Rights (1969), Article 22(8); Inter-American Convention against Torture (1985), Article 13(4); and EU Charter of Fundamental Rights (2000), Article 19(2). See also Bangkok Principles on Status and Treatment of Refugees (2001), Article III(1). This commentary does not deal with a State's obligations not to *refoule* en masse persons seeking to enter its territory when fleeing a situation of armed conflict.

[636] UNHCR, 'The Principle of Non-Refoulement as a Norm of Customary International Law. Response to the Questions Posed to UNHCR by the Federal Constitutional Court of the Federal Republic of Germany in Cases 2 BvR 1938/93, 2 BvR 1953/93, 2 BvR 1954/93', 31 January 1994; UNHCR, 'Advisory Opinion on the Extraterritorial Application of *Non-Refoulement* Obligations under the 1951 Convention relating to the Status of Refugees and its 1967 Protocol', 26 January 2007, paras 15 and 21. See also Lauterpacht/Bethlehem, pp. 87–177, and Hathaway, pp. 503–536.

ill-treatment.[637] While the arguments in favour of reading a *non-refoulement* obligation into humanitarian law applicable in non-international armed conflict have been said to be 'extremely tenuous',[638] some government experts have, in contrast, noted that such an obligation 'is already implicit in existing IHL'.[639] Indeed, in the same way that the Geneva Conventions prohibit circumvention of the protection owed to protected persons in international armed conflict by transfer to a non-compliant High Contracting Party,[640] humanitarian law applicable in non-international armed conflict should not be circumvented by transferring persons to another Party to the conflict, or to another State or international organization not party to the conflict.[641] Arguably, this would be true for all of the fundamental guarantees in common Article 3, including humane treatment, as well as the prohibition of hostage-taking and of the passing of sentences without affording all judicial guarantees.[642] For the last case, however – and considering also the more restrictive interpretation in human rights jurisprudence – the prohibition of *non-refoulement* would probably be confined at most to trials which are manifestly unfair.[643]

711   To a certain extent, this logic is also enshrined in Article 5(4) of Additional Protocol II, which requires authorities who decide to release a person to take 'necessary measures to ensure their safety'. It is also a principle that was invoked, and put into practice, in relation to the return of prisoners of war in accordance with Article 118 of the Third Convention, even though the text of that article does not explicitly refer to *non-refoulement*.[644] Last but not

---

[637] See Gisel.

[638] Françoise J. Hampson, 'The Scope of the Obligation Not to Return Fighters under the Law of Armed Conflict', in David James Cantor and Jean-François Durieux (eds), *Refuge from Inhumanity? War Refugees and International Humanitarian Law*, Brill Nijhoff, Leiden, 2014, pp. 373–385, at 385.

[639] ICRC, *Strengthening International Humanitarian Law Protecting Persons Deprived of Their Liberty, Synthesis Report from Regional Consultations of Government Experts*, ICRC, Geneva, November 2013, p. 23.

[640] See especially Third Convention, Article 12; Fourth Convention, Article 45; and common Article 1 of the four Geneva Conventions.

[641] During ICRC expert consultations, '[m]any experts agreed that common Article 3 would at least prohibit a party to a NIAC [non-international armed conflict] from circumventing the Article's rules by deliberately transferring a detainee to another party that would violate them'. ICRC, *Strengthening International Humanitarian Law Protecting Persons Deprived of Their Liberty, Synthesis Report from Regional Consultations of Government Experts*, ICRC, Geneva, November 2013, p. 23. See also ICTY, *Mrkšić* Appeal Judgment, 2009, paras 70–71.

[642] See Copenhagen Process: Principles and Guidelines (2012), Commentary, para. 15.4 ('In transfer situations, it is important to ensure that the detainee who is to be transferred is not subject to a real risk of violations that breach international law obligations concerning humane treatment and due process').

[643] European Court of Human Rights, *Mamatkulov and Askarov* v. *Turkey*, Judgment, 2005, para. 90; UN Human Rights Committee, *Yin Fong* v. *Australia*, Views, 2009, para. 9.7.

[644] Pictet (ed.), *Commentary on the Third Geneva Convention*, ICRC, 1960, pp. 547–548:

> No exception may be made to this rule [that the Detaining Power must repatriate prisoners of war without delay after the cessation of active hostilities] unless there are serious reasons for fearing that a prisoner of war who is himself opposed to being repatriated may, after his repatriation, be the subject of unjust measures affecting his life or liberty, especially on

least, common Article 1 of the Geneva Conventions contains the obligation to 'ensure respect' for the Conventions.[645] If a Party to the conflict transfers a detainee to another authority, under the custody of which the detainee would be in danger of being subjected to a violation of his or her fundamental rights enshrined in common Article 3, that Party to the conflict would not have done all it could to ensure respect for common Article 3.[646]

712   The interpretation that common Article 3 would prohibit *refoulement* is reinforced by the fact that the absolute prohibition of torture, cruel treatment or outrages upon personal dignity in common Article 3 should be interpreted 'in light of the parallel provisions in human rights law'.[647] Indeed, the logic for common Article 3 is the same: if the absolute prohibitions in human rights law mean that authorities must not only refrain from subjecting persons to such treatment but also from transferring them to places where they will be subjected to such treatment, there is no reason why it should not be the same under humanitarian law.[648] Furthermore, *non-refoulement* has also been found in international jurisprudence and by the UN Human Rights Committee to constitute an integral component of the protection of certain rights – in particular the right not to be subjected to torture, cruel, inhuman or degrading treatment, or arbitrary deprivation of life – even when not set down as a separate provision.[649]

grounds of race, social class, religion or political views, and that consequently repatriation would be contrary to the general principles of international law for the protection of the human being. Each case must be examined individually.

See also ICRC, *Annual Report 1987*, ICRC, Geneva, 1988, p. 77; ICRC, *Annual Report 1991*, ICRC, Geneva, 1992, pp. 111–112; ICRC, *Annual Report 1992*, ICRC, Geneva, 1993, pp. 141–142; ICRC, *Annual Report 2000*, ICRC, Geneva, 2001, p. 201. See further Alain Aeschlimann, 'Protection of detainees: ICRC action behind bars', *International Review of the Red Cross*, Vol. 87, No. 857, March 2005, pp. 83–122, at 104–105; and Meron, 2000, pp. 253–256.

[645] ICRC, *Strengthening International Humanitarian Law Protecting Persons Deprived of Their Liberty, Synthesis Report from Regional Consultations of Government Experts*, ICRC, Geneva, November 2013, p. 24 (which recalls that some experts regarded transfer obligations 'as part of a State's obligations under common Article 1 to take appropriate measures to ensure that other States respect IHL'); Horowitz, pp. 50–51. Reuven (Ruvi) Ziegler develops this argument for the transfer of detainees by non-belligerent States to States party to a non-international armed conflict in 'Non-Refoulement between "Common Article 1" and "Common Article 3"', in David James Cantor and Jean-François Durieux (eds), *Refuge from Inhumanity? War Refugees and International Humanitarian Law*, Brill Nijhoff, Leiden, 2014, pp. 386–408.

[646] See Gisel, pp. 118–120.

[647] Droege, 2008, p. 675. See also Bellinger/Padmanabhan, p. 236, and Horowitz, p. 57.

[648] Droege, 2008, p. 675. See also Sanderson, pp. 798–799, and Byers.

[649] On torture, cruel, inhuman or degrading treatment, see paras 613–614. On Article 7 of the 1966 International Covenant on Civil and Political Rights, see UN Human Rights Committee, *General Comment No. 20, Article 7 (Prohibition of Torture, or Other Cruel, Inhuman or Degrading Treatment or Punishment)*, 10 March 1992, para. 9, and *General Comment No. 31, The Nature of the General Legal Obligation Imposed on States Parties to the Covenant*, UN Doc. CCPR/C/21/Rev.1/Add. 13, 26 May 2004, para. 12, and case law. On Article 3 of the 1950 European Convention on Human Rights, see European Court of Human Rights, *Soering* v. *UK*, Judgment, 1989, paras 88–91; *Chahal* v. *UK*, Judgment, 1996, para. 74; and *El Masri* v. *the former Yugoslav Republic of Macedonia*, Judgment, 2012, para. 212. Transfers that may trigger a chain of *refoulements* are also prohibited: see *Hirsi Jamaa and others* v. *Italy*, Judgment, 2012,

713   In terms of who is bound by the prohibition of *refoulement*, the logic of common Article 3 requires that not only States, but also non-State Parties to non-
international armed conflicts abide by it. The trigger for the *non-refoulement*
principle is the transfer of control of the non-State Party to the control of
another (State or non-State) authority. For instance, common Article 3 would
prohibit a non-State Party to the conflict from returning a person to territory
controlled by an adversary or to an allied non-State Party if there was a risk that
the person would be ill-treated in that territory or at the hands of that group,
respectively.

714   Where foreign troops or authorities find themselves detaining or exercising
authority and control over persons, the principle of *non-refoulement* will apply
to any transfer of an individual by such authorities to the territory or control
of another State (often the host State) or international organization.[650] If the
foreign troops are under the command and control of an international organization, the prohibition of *refoulement* flows from customary law, which is binding on international organizations, and from the continued applicability of the
humanitarian and human rights law obligations of States contributing troops
to international organizations, even when these are operating abroad.[651] Some
States involved in transfers by their forces abroad have however not accepted
the application of the principle of *non-refoulement* in these situations.[652] This
position has been criticized by human rights bodies.[653] In the ICRC's view, the

paras 146–147, among others. The European Court of Human Rights has also held that States
party to the Convention that have ratified its Protocol 13 of 2002 prohibiting the death penalty
may also not return persons to States in which they risk facing the death penalty, regardless
of the fairness of the trial: see *Al-Saadoon and Mufdhi* v. *UK*, Judgment, 2010, paras 115–120
and 137. See also UN Committee on the Rights of the Child, *General Comment No. 6 (2005),
Treatment of unaccompanied and separated children outside their country of origin*, para. 28,
which provides that in view of the high risk of irreparable harm involving fundamental human
rights, including the right to life, States should not return children 'where there is a real risk
of underage recruitment, including recruitment not only as a combatant but also to provide
sexual services for the military or where there is a real risk of direct or indirect participation
in hostilities, either as a combatant or through carrying out other military duties'.

[650] Droege, 2008, pp. 683–687. See also UN Department of Peacekeeping Operations, *Interim Standard Operating Procedures: Detention in United Nations Peace Operations*, 24 January 2010,
para. 80.

[651] UN Human Rights Committee, *General Comment No. 31, The Nature of the General Legal
Obligation Imposed on States Parties to the Covenant*, UN Doc. CCPR/C/21/Rev.1/Add. 13,
26 May 2004, para. 10; *Concluding observations: Belgium*, UN Doc. CCPR/CO/81/BEL, 12
August 2004, para. 6; *Comments by the Government of Germany to the Concluding Observa-
tions*, UN Doc. CCPR/CO/80/DEU/Add.1, 5 January 2005; *Concluding observations: Poland*,
UN Doc. CCPR/CO/82/POL, 2 December 2004, para. 3; *Consideration of periodic reports:
Italy*, UN Doc. CCPR/C/SR.1680, 24 September 1998, para. 22; *Consideration of periodic
reports: Belgium*, UN Doc. CCPR/C/SR.1707, 27 October 1998, para. 22; and *Consideration
of periodic reports: Canada*, UN Doc. CCPR/C/SR.1738, 7 March 1999, paras 29 and 32–33.
See also UN Secretary-General's Bulletin (1999), Section 2. The human rights obligations of
the host State may also apply; see UN Human Rights Committee, *Concluding observations:
Kosovo (Republic of Serbia)*, UN Doc. CCPR/C/UNK/CO/1, 14 August 2006.

[652] See Gillard, pp. 712–715, and Bellinger/Padmanabhan, p. 237.

[653] See European Court of Human Rights, *Al-Saadoon and Mufdhi* v. *UK*, Judgment, 2010,
para. 143; Committee against Torture, *Conclusions and Recommendations: United Kingdom*

principle of *non-refoulement* applies irrespective of the crossing of a border. What matters for the purposes of the *non-refoulement* principle under common Article 3 is a transfer of control over a person.[654]

715   It follows from the prohibition of *refoulement* that a Party to the conflict that is planning to return or transfer a person to the control of another authority must assess carefully and in good faith whether there are substantial grounds for believing that the person would be subjected to torture, other forms of ill-treatment, arbitrary deprivation of life or persecution after transfer. If there are substantial grounds to believe so, the person must not be transferred unless measures are taken that effectively remove such risk. The assessment should cover the policies and practices of the receiving authorities and the personal circumstances and subjective fears of the individual detainee,[655] based on interviews with the detainee, the Detaining Power's own knowledge of the receiving authority's detention practices, and information from independent sources.[656]

716   In recent non-international armed conflicts, some States and international organizations have agreed upon and put in place various forms of post-transfer monitoring.[657] In most cases, the duration of the monitoring was meant to be commensurate with the period during which it had been assessed that the detainee would be in danger of being subjected to unlawful treatment. These post-transfer monitoring mechanisms notably granted the transferring authority access to the transferred detainees, so that it could monitor their

---

of *Great Britain and Northern Ireland – Dependent Territories*, UN Doc. CAT/C/CR/33/3, 10 December 2004, para. 5(e); UN Human Rights Committee, *Concluding observations: United States of America*, UN doc. CCPR/C/USA/CO/3/Rev.1, 18 December 2006, para. 16.

[654] While no treaty explicitly stipulates as much, this interpretation is consistent with the object and purpose of the prohibition against *refoulement*. In view of the Copenhagen Principles' focus on international military operations, its paragraph 15 primarily addresses transfer without border crossing, which is confirmed by the reference to 'host State' in its commentary; see Copenhagen Process: Principles and Guidelines (2012), para. 15(2). Some participants in the ICRC expert consultations also 'felt that any existing non refoulement obligation would prevail over any request by a host State to transfer', while other noted on the contrary that it might be difficult to justify it in some circumstances; see ICRC, *Strengthening International Humanitarian Law Protecting Persons Deprived of Their Liberty, Synthesis Report from Regional Consultations of Government Experts*, ICRC, Geneva, November 2013, p. 33. See the references in fn. 652 above.

[655] ICRC, *Meeting of all States on Strengthening Humanitarian Law Protecting Persons Deprived of their Liberty: Chair's Conclusion*, 27–29 April 2015, p. 12.

[656] ICRC, *Strengthening International Humanitarian Law Protecting Persons Deprived of Their Liberty, Synthesis Report from Regional Consultations of Government Experts*, ICRC, Geneva, November 2013, p. 25. While some experts suggested that circumstances could limit the need for individualized assessments, such need had been identified long ago with regard to the transfer of prisoners of war despite the absence of an express provision; (Pictet (ed.), *Commentary on the Third Geneva Convention*, ICRC, 1960, p. 547. See also Droege, 2008, pp. 679–680; Gillard, pp. 731–738; and Gisel, pp. 125–127. For a partially different view, see Horowitz, p. 64.

[657] During the ICRC consultations, '[s]ome [State experts] considered [post-transfer monitoring] a legal obligation, while others considered it solely as a good practice'; ICRC, *Strengthening International Humanitarian Law Protecting Persons Deprived of Their Liberty, Synthesis Report from Regional Consultations of Government Experts*, ICRC, Geneva, November 2013, p. 26. For examples of agreements putting in place post-transfer monitoring mechanisms, see Gisel, pp. 128–130, text in relation to fns 60–78.

welfare and base future transfer decisions on the findings, in some cases leading to the suspension of transfers.[658] The States and international organizations concerned also carried out various forms of capacity building with regard to detention operations, including detainee treatment. If effective, such measures would also correspond to States' duty to ensure respect as provided for in common Article 1.

H. Detention outside a criminal process

717 Detention is a regular occurrence in both international and non-international armed conflicts and is practised by State and non-State Parties alike.[659] For detention in relation to a criminal process, common Article 3 imposes the obligation of fair trial (see section G.5).

718   This section deals with detention outside a criminal process, also known as internment. The term 'internment' refers to detention for security reasons in situations of armed conflict, i.e. the non-criminal detention of a person based on the serious threat that his or her activity poses to the security of the detaining authority in relation to an armed conflict.[660]

719   In international armed conflicts, the Third and Fourth Convention regulate such detention in considerable detail.[661] In non-international armed conflicts, neither common Article 3 nor Additional Protocol II contain a similar framework for internment.[662] It is a requirement under customary international law, however, that any detention must not be arbitrary.[663] Therefore, certain

---

[658] See Horowitz, pp. 57 and 61–64; *U.S. Monitoring of Detainee Transfers in Afghanistan: International Standards and Lessons from the UK & Canada*, Human Rights Institute, Columbia Law School, December 2010; and United Kingdom, High Court of Justice, *R (on the application of Maya Evans) v. Secretary of State for Defence*, Judgment, 2010, paras 287–327.

[659] See e.g. 32nd International Conference of the Red Cross and Red Crescent, Geneva, 2015, Res. 1, Strengthening international humanitarian law protecting persons deprived of their liberty, Preamble, para. 1 ('*mindful* that deprivation of liberty is an ordinary and expected occurrence in armed conflict . . .'); and Copenhagen Process: Principles and Guidelines (2012), Preamble, para. III ('Participants recognised that detention is a necessary, lawful and legitimate means of achieving the objectives of international military operations.'). See also ICRC, *International Humanitarian Law and the challenges of contemporary armed conflicts*, 2011, p. 17; and Dörmann, p. 349.

[660] Not every deprivation of liberty incidental to the conduct of military operations – for example, stops at checkpoints or restrictions on movement during searches – will amount to internment. But when deprivation of liberty reaches a certain temporal threshold, or is motivated by a decision to detain an individual on account of the serious security threat he or she poses, the risk of arbitrariness must be mitigated by clarity on the grounds for internment and the required procedures.

[661] See, in particular, Third Convention, Article 21, and Fourth Convention, Articles 42 and 78.

[662] Article 5 of Additional Protocol II deals with the treatment of 'persons deprived of their liberty for reasons related to the armed conflict, whether they are interned or detained', but does not regulate the grounds and procedures for such deprivation of liberty.

[663] ICRC Study on Customary International Humanitarian Law (2005), Rule 99. See also Copenhagen Process: Principles and Guidelines (2012), commentary, para. 4.4:

   As an important component of lawfulness detentions must not be arbitrary. For the purposes of *The Copenhagen Process Principles and Guidelines* the term 'arbitrary' refers to the need

grounds and procedure for such detention must be provided. However, the exact content of those grounds and procedure are unsettled under international law today.

720   The lack of sufficient rules in humanitarian law applicable in non-international armed conflict has become a legal and protection issue. Common Article 3 refers to detention in general, but only to indicate that persons in detention are entitled to its protection. The article is silent, however, on the grounds and procedural safeguards for persons interned in non-international armed conflict, even though, as mentioned, internment is practised by both States and non-State armed groups. Additional Protocol II explicitly mentions internment, thus confirming that it is a form of deprivation of liberty inherent to non-international armed conflict, but likewise does not refer to the grounds for internment or the procedural rights.

721   The ICRC has relied on 'imperative reasons of security' as the minimum legal standard that should inform internment decisions in non-international armed conflict. This standard was chosen because it emphasizes the exceptional nature of internment and is already in wide use if States resort to non-criminal detention for security reasons. It seems also to be appropriate in non-international armed conflict with an extraterritorial element, in which a foreign force, or forces, are detaining non-nationals in the territory of a host State, as the wording is based on the internment standard applicable in occupied territories under the Fourth Convention.[664] It also reflects a basic feature of humanitarian law, which is the need to strike a balance between the considerations of humanity, on the one hand, and of military necessity, on the other.

722   In an effort to address the uncertainty resulting from the silence of humanitarian treaty law on the procedure for deprivation of liberty in non-international armed conflict, in 2005 the ICRC issued institutional guidelines entitled 'Procedural principles and safeguards for internment/administrative detention in armed conflict and other situations of violence'.[665] The guidelines are based on law and policy and are meant to be implemented in a manner that takes into account the specific circumstances at hand. The ICRC has used the

to ensure that each detention continues to be legally justified, so that it can be demonstrated that the detention remains reasonable and lawful in all the circumstances. Justifying detention requires that the decision to detain is based in law on valid reasons that are reasonable and necessary in light of all the circumstances. Furthermore, detention cannot be a collective punishment. Detention therefore must serve a lawful and continuingly legitimate objective, such as a security objective or criminal justice.

[664] See Fourth Convention, Article 78.

[665] See ICRC, 'Procedural principles and safeguards for internment/administrative detention in armed conflict and other situations of violence', 2007. These guidelines address internment/administrative detention, which they define as 'deprivation of liberty of a person that has been initiated/ordered by the executive branch ... without criminal charges being brought against the internee/administrative detainee'. They do not address pre-trial detention of a person held on criminal charges and they do not address the internment of prisoners of war in international armed conflict, for which there exists a separate legal framework under the Third Convention.

guidelines in its operational dialogue with States, international and regional forces, and other actors.

723   As regards the review process to determine the lawfulness of internment, the 12 specific guidelines provide that a person must, among other things, be informed promptly, in a language he or she understands, of the reasons for internment. An internee likewise has the right to challenge, with the least possible delay, the lawfulness of his or her detention.[666] The review of lawfulness of internment must be carried out by an independent and impartial body.[667] It should be noted that, in practice, mounting an effective challenge will presuppose the fulfilment of several procedural and practical steps, including: i) providing internees with sufficient evidence supporting the allegations against them; ii) ensuring that procedures are in place to enable internees to seek and obtain additional evidence; and iii) making sure that internees understand the various stages of the internment review process and the process as a whole. Where internment review is administrative rather than judicial in nature, ensuring the requisite independence and impartiality of the review body will require particular attention. Assistance of counsel should be provided whenever feasible, but other means of ensuring expert legal assistance may be considered as well.

724   The guidelines also provide for the right to periodical review of the lawfulness of continued internment. Periodical review obliges the detaining authority to ascertain whether the detainee continues to pose an imperative threat to security and to order release if that is not the case. The safeguards that apply to initial review are also to be applied at periodical review.

725   At the time of writing, however, the question of which standards and safeguards are required in non-international armed conflict to prevent arbitrariness is still subject to debate and needs further clarification, in part linked to unresolved issues on the interplay between international humanitarian law and international human rights law.[668]

---

[666] For the legal sources and rationale for the formulation of this principle, see Pejic, pp. 385–386.
[667] For the legal sources and rationale for the formulation of this principle, see *ibid.* pp. 386–387.
[668] These issues, among others, were discussed during a consultation process on strengthening legal protection for victims of armed conflicts, facilitated by the ICRC based on Resolution 1 of the 31st International Conference of the Red Cross and Red Crescent, Geneva, 2011. See e.g. *Strengthening International Humanitarian Law Protecting Persons Deprived of Their Liberty, Synthesis Report from Regional Consultations of Government Experts*, ICRC, Geneva, November 2013, pp. 10–11; *Strengthening international humanitarian law protecting persons deprived of their liberty, Concluding Report*, Document prepared by the ICRC for the 32nd International Conference of the Red Cross and Red Crescent, June 2015, pp. 12 and 20–21; 32nd International Conference of the Red Cross and Red Crescent, Res. 2, Strengthening compliance with international humanitarian law, para. 8; and Copenhagen Process: Principles and Guidelines (2012), Preamble, para. IV ('Participants recalled and reiterated the relevant obligations of States, international organisations, non-State actors and individuals under applicable international law, recognizing in particular the challenges of agreeing upon a precise description of the interaction between international human rights law and international humanitarian law.').

726   In a non-international armed conflict occurring in the territory of a State between State armed forces and one or more non-State armed groups, domestic law, informed by the State's human rights obligations, and humanitarian law, constitutes the legal framework for the possible internment by States of persons whose activity is deemed to pose a serious security threat.

727   The question of whether humanitarian law provides inherent authority or power to detain is, however, still subject to debate.[669] This issue has led to controversy particularly in non-international armed conflicts with an extraterritorial element, i.e. those in which the armed forces of one or more State, or of an international or regional organization, fight alongside the armed forces of a host State, in its territory, against one or more non-State armed groups.

728   One view is that a legal basis for deprivation of liberty in non-international armed conflict has to be explicit, as is the case in the Third and Fourth Conventions for international armed conflict.[670] Another view, shared by the ICRC, is that both customary and international humanitarian treaty law contain an inherent power to detain in non-international armed conflict.[671] However, additional authority related to the grounds and procedure for deprivation of liberty in non-international armed conflict must in all cases be provided, in keeping with the principle of legality.[672]

I. Subparagraph (2): Collection and care of the wounded and sick

1. Introduction

729 Common Article 3 extends specific legal protection to the wounded and sick on land (as well as to the shipwrecked by virtue of Article 3 of the Second Convention) in times of non-international armed conflict. It contains two core obligations in this regard: the wounded and sick must be a) collected and b) cared for. Although concise, when interpreted in conjunction with the other obligations and protections in common Article 3, it provides the foundation for comprehensive protection of the wounded and sick in non-international armed conflicts.

---

[669] See e.g. 'Expert meeting on procedural safeguards for security detention in non-international armed conflict, Chatham House and International Committee of the Red Cross, London, 22–23 September 2008', *International Review of the Red Cross*, Vol. 91, No. 876, December 2009, pp. 859–881.

[670] See e.g. United Kingdom, England and Wales High Court, *Serdar Mohammed and others* v. *Ministry of Defence*, Judgment, 2014, paras 239–294; and England and Wales Court of Appeal, Appeal Judgment, 2015, paras 164–253.

[671] See 32nd International Conference of the Red Cross and Red Crescent, Geneva, 2015, Res. 1, Strengthening international humanitarian law protecting persons deprived of their liberty, Preamble, para. 1; ICRC, *Internment in Armed Conflict: Basic Rules and Challenges*, Opinion Paper, November 2014, p. 7; and Jann K. Kleffner, 'Operational Detention and The Treatment of Detainees', in Terry D. Gill and Dieter Fleck (eds), *The Handbook of the International Law of Military Operations*, 2nd edition, Oxford University Press, 2015, para. 26.03.

[672] See ICRC, *Internment in Armed Conflict: Basic Rules and Challenges*, Opinion Paper, November 2014, p. 8.

730   In non-international armed conflicts, the indirect effects of armed conflict on public health can 'constitute a far greater health threat to the people affected than violent injury'.[673] Armed conflict can impede access to health-care facilities and medicines, whether for acute or chronic conditions; it can also favour the spread of infectious disease, contribute to malnutrition, hamper the effective implementation of preventive medicine, such as vaccination campaigns, and disrupt maternal and paediatric care.[674]

731   Collecting and caring for the wounded and sick necessarily implies respecting and protecting them. This also follows from the general obligation in sub-paragraph (1) to treat them humanely, with the explicit prohibition of certain acts. Therefore, an obligation to respect and protect the wounded and sick has been recognized *de facto* since the adoption of the 1949 Geneva Conventions.[675] Moreover, the obligations to collect and to care also necessarily imply respecting and protecting medical personnel, facilities and transports.[676] This is because the respect and protection of medical personnel, facilities and transports is essential for the effective fulfilment of the obligations to collect and to care for the wounded and sick.

732   Additional Protocol II contains more detailed provisions related to the wounded and sick, notably explicit protections for medical personnel, facilities and transports.[677] The protections set down therein are considered implicit in the basic obligations to collect and to care for the wounded and sick: as they are essential to the implementation of those obligations, they are inseparable from them.[678] Nevertheless, it was thought useful to spell them out in Protocol II. These rules are also generally considered to be part of customary international law.[679] The Conventions contain similar obligations for international armed conflicts.[680]

2. Historical background

733   The obligations to collect and to care for the wounded and sick have been part of the legal regime protecting the wounded and sick since its inception

---

[673] Müller, p. 213.
[674] *Ibid.*; ICRC, *Health Care in Danger: A Sixteen Country Study*, ICRC, Geneva, 2011, p. 3.
[675] Pictet (ed.), *Commentary on the First Geneva Convention*, ICRC, 1952, p. 57.
[676] *Report of the Conference of Government Experts of 1971*, Vol. VII, pp. 30–31.
[677] See Additional Protocol II, Articles 7–12.
[678] The preparatory work for Additional Protocol II shows that the protection of medical personnel, facilities and transports was already considered implicit in common Article 3. See *Report of the Conference of Government Experts of 1971*, Vol. V, pp. 53–55. See also Sandoz/Swinarski/Zimmermann (eds), *Commentary on the Additional Protocols*, ICRC, 1987, para. 4634.
[679] See ICRC Study on Customary International Humanitarian Law (2005), Rules 25, 26, 28, 29, 30, 59, 109, 110 and 111.
[680] See First Convention, Articles 12 and 15; Second Convention, Articles 12 and 18; and Fourth Convention, Article 16.

in 1864. This is only logical given that Henry Dunant's proposal for an international convention to ameliorate the condition of wounded and sick soldiers was inspired by the appalling conditions he witnessed on the battlefield of Solferino, where some 40,000 fallen Austrian, French and Italian soldiers lay unattended.[681] The provision was expanded upon in the 1906, 1929 and 1949 Geneva Conventions.[682] However, the basic principles that the wounded, sick and shipwrecked may not be attacked and must not be left to suffer without medical care have remained constant.

734   In 1949, the obligations to collect and to care for the wounded and sick were extended to civilians by the Fourth Convention, as well as to non-international armed conflicts by common Article 3.

3. Discussion

a. Addressees of the obligations

735 The obligations to collect and to care for the wounded and sick apply to each Party to the conflict, whether State or non-State. This follows also from common Article 3(1), which reads that 'each Party to the conflict shall be bound to apply'. It is worth noting that the codes of conduct of a number of armed groups reflect their understanding that they are bound by the obligations to respect and to protect, as well as to collect and to care for the wounded and sick.[683] Moreover, most military manuals make no distinction

---

[681] Dunant, p. 126.

[682] Geneva Convention (1864), Article 6; Geneva Convention (1906), Articles 1 and 3; Geneva Convention on the Wounded and Sick (1929), Article 3. In 1899, the principles of the 1864 Geneva Convention were adapted to maritime warfare and to wounded, sick and shipwrecked soldiers at sea by virtue of the Hague Convention (III). In 1907, the Hague Convention (X) superseded the Hague Convention (III) adapting to maritime warfare the principles of the 1906 Geneva Convention (see Article 25). For more details about the historical background, see the commentaries on Article 12 of the First and Second Conventions, section B.

[683] See e.g. Ejército de Liberación Nacional (ELN), Colombia, Our Principles on Military Doctrine, 1996, Principle 2 ('[The ELN] will give humanitarian treatment to enemies who have surrendered or been wounded in combat and will respect their dignity and provide them with the aid necessary for their condition.); Moro Islamic Liberation Front/Bangsamoro Islamic Armed Forces, Philippines, General Order No. 2 (An order amending Articles 34 and 36 of the code of conduct of the Bangsamoro Islamic Armed Forces and for other purposes), 2006, Article 34(4) ('Wounded enemy combatants – Never betray or be treacherous or vindictive. Do not mutilate....(Al-Hadith)) and (6) ('Prisoners of war or captives – Be kind at all times to captives or prisoners of war. Collect and care for wounded combatants. (Al Insan: 5:9)'); Transitional National Council (TNC) Libya, Guidelines on the Law of Armed Conflict, 2011, p. 3, Rules on the treatment of detainees ('Give immediate medical treatment/first aid to anyone who needs it. There is a duty to search for, collect, and aid the injured and wounded from the battlefield of both sides. The dead must also be collected, treated with respect, and buried'); and Fuerzas Armadas Revolucionarias de Colombia-Ejército del Pueblo (FARC-EP), Colombia, Beligerancia, Suplemento, 2000, p. 13 ('Las FARC-EP tienen como norma de obligado cumplimiento respetar la vida, suministrar auxilio médico, alimentación y un trato humanitario y digno a los prisioneros de guerra vencidos en combate.' ('FARC-EP abides by rules which oblige it to respect the lives of prisoners of war defeated in combat, to provide them with food and medical care and to treat them humanely and with dignity.')); all available at http://theirwords.org/.

in regard to the protection of the wounded and sick based on the nature of a conflict.[684]

b. Scope of application

i. Categories of persons covered

736 This subparagraph applies to the wounded and sick, whether members of armed forces or civilians. The obligations to collect and to care for are owed equally to the wounded and sick of a Party's own armed forces as to those of the enemy armed forces, as well as to wounded and sick civilians. As a minimum, persons who are wounded or sick as a result of the armed conflict, for example owing to military operations or explosive remnants of war, as well as persons whose medical condition or access to treatment is affected by the conflict, must be considered as falling within the scope of protection of the wounded and sick in common Article 3. A person's medical condition or access to treatment may be said to be affected by the conflict when, for example, a medical facility on which their treatment depends has been destroyed, when they do not have access to medical personnel or facilities on which they depend owing to the conflict, or where they do not have access to medicines vital for their ongoing treatment for reasons related to the conflict.

ii. The wounded and sick

737 The Geneva Conventions in general and common Article 3 in particular do not specify when a person is legally considered to be 'wounded' or 'sick'. Starting from the ordinary meaning of the words, a person would normally be considered wounded or sick if that person is suffering from either a wound or a sickness. The wording is sufficiently open to accommodate a wide range of more or less severe medical conditions, be they physical or mental. It is widely accepted, and also reflected in the definition contained in Article 8(a) of Additional Protocol I, that in order to qualify as wounded or sick for the purposes of humanitarian law, a person must cumulatively fulfil two criteria: first, the person must be in need of medical assistance or care; and second, the person must refrain from any act of hostility.[685]

738   The definition contained in Article 8(a) of Additional Protocol I reflects a contemporary understanding of the terms 'wounded' and 'sick', which provides a useful touchstone for understanding the scope of the obligations in common Article 3. It would be illogical to apply one definition of 'wounded' or 'sick' in international armed conflicts and another in non-international armed conflicts; therefore, it seems appropriate to use the definition in Article 8(a) of

---

[684] See ICRC, Customary International Humanitarian Law, practice relating to Rules 109 and 110, available at https://www.icrc.org/customary-ihl/eng/docs/v2_rul.
[685] Kleffner, 2013a, pp. 324–325.

Additional Protocol I for the purposes of common Article 3.[686] Moreover, similar definitions to those in Article 8(a) and (b) of Additional Protocol I had been foreseen for inclusion also in Additional Protocol II.[687] The decision ultimately not to include them in the final text of Protocol II was prompted by the desire to shorten the text more generally. However, the definitions as such and their applicability in non-international armed conflicts were not disputed.[688]

739   The status of being wounded or sick is thus based both on a person's medical condition and on his or her conduct. The humanitarian law definitions of 'wounded' and 'sick' are both broader and narrower than the ordinary meaning of these words.[689] They are broader because they encompass a range of medical conditions in addition to the injuries or disease that would not render a person wounded or sick in the colloquial sense of these terms. At the same time, they are narrower because abstention from any act of hostility is part of the humanitarian law requirement for being wounded or sick.

740   It is useful to recall that for legal purposes (as opposed to medical purposes and the determination of the appropriate medical treatment), it makes no difference whether a person is 'wounded' or 'sick' in the colloquial sense of the words; these terms also cover all other persons in need of immediate medical treatment.

741   For legal purposes, the decisive criterion, in addition to refraining from any act of hostility, is whether a person is in need of medical assistance or care. It is this particular need, and the specific vulnerability that comes with it, to which the legal regime protecting the wounded and sick aims to respond. Indeed, such a reading is also in line with the wording of the first sentence of Article 8(a) of Additional Protocol I, which does not specify any degree of severity of wounds or sickness, but rather refers to persons 'in need of medical assistance or care', and by way of example enumerates a range of conditions. Therefore, as far as the relevant medical condition is concerned, the terms 'wounded' and 'sick' are to be interpreted broadly to apply to anyone who is in need of medical assistance or care without any qualitative requirements as to the severity of the medical condition. Nor is a distinction made between an acute illness and a chronic illness; the only relevant factor is the need for medical assistance or care.[690] It follows that victims of sexual violence or other crimes may also fall within

---

[686] See also Bothe/Partsch/Solf, pp. 655–656, and Sandoz/Swinarski/Zimmermann (eds), *Commentary on the Additional Protocols*, ICRC, 1987, para. 4631.

[687] *Official Records of the Diplomatic Conference of Geneva of 1974–1977*, Vol. IV, p. 40, Article 11(a). Article 3 of the Second Convention also mentions shipwrecked persons as needing to be collected and cared for.

[688] *Official Records of the Diplomatic Conference of Geneva of 1974–1977*, Vol. IV, pp. 39–43, and Vol. XII, pp. 259–272. See Sandoz/Swinarski/Zimmermann (eds), *Commentary on the Additional Protocols*, ICRC, 1987, para. 4631, and Sivakumaran, 2012, p. 190.

[689] Sivakumaran, 2012, p. 274.

[690] Article 8(a) of Additional Protocol I refers to a need for medical care based on any 'physical or mental disorder or disability'. The fact that a person is 'wounded or sick' under common Article 3 is without prejudice to the fact that the person may simultaneously qualify as a

the definition of 'wounded and sick', as persons who may need medical care. Mental or psychological conditions, including post-traumatic stress disorder, also qualify, provided they require medical assistance or care.

742   The second sentence of Article 8(a) of Additional Protocol I also makes it clear that 'wounded and sick' covers 'maternity cases, new-born babies and *other persons . . . such as* the infirm or expectant mothers' (emphasis added), as they may be in immediate need of medical assistance or care. All of these cases are merely examples; the decisive criterion is always whether a person is in need of medical assistance or care.

743   It is also irrelevant whether the need for care arises from a medical condition that pre-dates the conflict or is linked to, even if not caused by, the conflict.[691] The definition is 'not restricted to those conflict-affected individuals who are wounded or sick for reasons related to the armed conflict, but covers all persons in need of immediate medical treatment'.[692]

744   In addition to the required medical condition, a person must also refrain from any act of hostility in order to qualify as 'wounded' or 'sick' in the legal sense. Thus, contrary to the colloquial understanding of the terms, a person who continues to engage in hostilities does not qualify as wounded or sick in the legal sense, no matter how severe the person's medical condition may be. For most civilians, this requirement will usually be met. This condition for qualifying as wounded or sick is therefore particularly relevant for fighters,[693] even if it is a general criterion.

745   Fighters who are wounded or sick but who continue to carry out normal roles in their armed forces may be considered to engage in hostile acts. Thus, for example, a fighter who has a minor medical condition or who is recovering from a battle wound, but who nevertheless continues to drive an ammunition truck or clean weapons, does not enjoy the protection accorded to the wounded and sick. Nonetheless, that person should receive any necessary medical care from his or her own armed forces. If, however, a fighter is being treated in a first-aid clinic or hospital for, say, pneumonia or wounds requiring medical care or supervision, and is not engaging in any hostile act, he or she may not be attacked and must be protected. In practice, attacking Parties may primarily be able to distinguish such wounded or sick fighters from their able-bodied comrades by the fact that they are receiving treatment in a medical facility.

---

person with a disability under the 2006 Convention on the Rights of Persons with Disabilities, where that Convention applies.

[691] During armed conflicts, many deaths are caused by preventable and treatable illnesses that go untreated for reasons related to the conflict. This was the case in the Democratic Republic of the Congo, for example. See ECOSOC, *Consideration of Reports Submitted by States Parties under Articles 16 and 17 of the International Covenant on Civil and Political Rights, Concluding observations: DRC*, UN Doc. E/C.12/COD/CO/4, 16 December 2009, para. 34.

[692] Müller, p. 205. See also para. 736 of this commentary.

[693] In this commentary, the term 'fighter' refers to members of the armed forces of non-State armed groups as well as to combatant members of State armed forces.

Such persons are entitled to the medical care required by their condition. This may be harder to determine during close combat, but factors such as being located in what appears to be a casualty collection point, not carrying arms, or being incapable of movement without the aid of other comrades all suggest the fighter is no longer engaging in any hostile act.

746 During hostilities, when a fighter is wounded in battle, there may be a moment when an attacker must cease the attack on that person and begin to respect and protect him or her. Under combat conditions, in the very moment that a fighter is injured, it may be extremely difficult to determine with any degree of certainty whether that person is wounded or sick in the legal sense, and in particular whether he or she is refraining from any hostile acts. In the context of ongoing hostilities, a fighter's condition may change within seconds from being a lawful target to a wounded person – and therefore a protected person. In such situations, considering the short timeframe in which the initial assessment has to be made, the focus may primarily be on whether there are visible signs that a person has been wounded and thereafter refrains from any act of hostility.

747 The relevant criterion is whether a reasonable fighter under the given circumstances would consider the person in question to abstain from hostile acts. For example, a fighter who was engaged in combat and who has just suffered a bullet wound to the lower leg may still be holding a gun. Even on the basis of a relatively light wound such as this, the fighter may cease all acts of hostility. The attacking force must be alert to a possible renunciation of hostilities by an injured fighter and adapt its attack accordingly. In such situations, the authority to continue to engage the fighter is contingent on a good faith assessment of whether the person is wounded and refrains from any act of hostility. The visible absence of all hostile acts on the part of a wounded or sick fighter should put an end to all acts of hostility against that person. In some cases, however, it may be difficult to determine on the battlefield whether a wounded person is refraining from any hostile act.

748 A person who continues to fight, even if he or she is severely wounded, will not qualify as wounded in the legal sense. There is no obligation to abstain from attacking a person who is wounded or sick in the colloquial sense and who continues to engage in hostilities. Parties to the conflict may provide guidance to their armed forces to help them assess such situations by issuing an internal document such as 'rules of engagement', which must comply with humanitarian law.

749 As stated above, the wounded and sick must be respected and protected. This notion is at the heart of common Article 3 and reinforced by the express terms of Article 7 of Additional Protocol II.[694] In this context, the obligation to respect the wounded and sick entails, as a minimum, that they be spared from attack

---

[694] *Official Records of the Diplomatic Conference of Geneva of 1974–1977*, Vol. XI, pp. 209–210.

and must not be murdered or ill-treated. In addition, they must be protected, meaning that all Parties have an obligation to come to their defence to try to stop or prevent harm to them, be it from third parties, from the effects of ongoing hostilities or from other sources. For example, the obligation to protect may entail that measures be taken to facilitate the work of medical personnel, including steps to facilitate the passage of medical supplies.[695]

c. The obligation to collect the wounded and sick

750 Parties to the conflict are obliged to collect the wounded and sick. Consistent with the humanitarian objectives of common Article 3 and humanitarian law more generally, the word 'collect' must be interpreted broadly and includes an obligation to search for the wounded and sick and to evacuate them to a more secure location.[696] Should this not be done, many would be left behind in the area of hostilities, contrary to the object and purpose of this subparagraph. The aim of the provision is to remove the wounded and sick from the immediate danger zone and to enable them to receive the necessary medical treatment as rapidly as possible and under better and more secure conditions. Searching for and collecting the wounded and sick would be meaningless if there were no corresponding obligation to evacuate them to a more secure location. Under customary international law, the obligation of evacuation exists alongside the obligations of search and collection.[697]

751 The obligation to collect the wounded and sick, as well as the obligations to search for and to evacuate them, are obligations of conduct. As such, they are to be exercised with due diligence. Due diligence is a relative standard, and the precise content of what is required depends on the circumstances.[698] Thus, in each case it needs to be determined when it is reasonable to commence search, collection and evacuation activities and with what means and measures.

752 The obligation to collect the wounded and sick is a continuous obligation, i.e. it applies for the duration of the non-international armed conflict. Article 8 of Additional Protocol II requires Parties to take all possible measures to search for, collect and protect the wounded, sick and shipwrecked 'whenever circumstances permit'. The same requirement exists under customary international

---

[695] ICRC, *Safeguarding the Provision of Health Care: Operational Practices and Relevant International Humanitarian Law Concerning Armed Groups*, ICRC, Geneva, 2015, p. 23.

[696] Similar obligations exist for international armed conflicts in Article 15 of the First Convention and Article 16 of the Fourth Convention.

[697] ICRC Study on Customary International Humanitarian Law (2005), Rule 109.

[698] Riccardo Pisillo-Mazzeschi, 'The Due Diligence Rule and the Nature of the International Responsibility of States', *German Yearbook of International Law*, Vol. 35, 1992, pp. 9–51, at 44; Timo Koivurova, 'Due Diligence', version of February 2010, in Rüdiger Wolfrum (ed.), *Max Planck Encyclopedia of Public International Law*, Oxford University Press, 2011, http://opil.ouplaw.com/home/EPIL.

law.[699] Whenever there is an indication that wounded and sick persons may be in the area, and provided that circumstances permit, search, collection and evacuation activities must begin. It is evident that, particularly after an engagement, there is a high likelihood that wounded and sick persons will be present. Although 'particularly after an engagement' is not mentioned in common Article 3, it is mentioned in Article 8 of Additional Protocol II.[700] It can be inferred that unless there are clear indications to the contrary, a good faith application of common Article 3 requires search, collection and evacuation activities after every engagement.

753   Common Article 3 does not require that search, collection and evacuation activities put lives at risk. Inadequate security conditions may, for example, prevent such activities taking place for a time.[701] Thus, the obligation does not require that search, collection and evacuation activities necessarily take place during an ongoing engagement. Nevertheless, there may be exceptions. For example, if during an engagement on the ground it becomes apparent that there are wounded persons in the area and a Party to the conflict has the possibility to collect and evacuate them by air, or by any other means, without great risk to its personnel, a good faith application of the rule would require it to do so. Similarly, if significant resources in terms of personnel and equipment are available, their deployment is required according to what is reasonable. Conversely, if resources are scarce, the Convention does not require Parties to do the impossible, but they must do what is feasible under the given circumstances, taking into account all available resources.

754   Given that quick medical treatment is often life-saving, it is crucial that the wounded and sick are searched for and collected as soon as possible.[702] Hence, it is inherent in the obligation that search and rescue activities must begin as soon as circumstances permit. Parties are strongly encouraged to conclude special agreements allowing for a pause in fighting in order to carry out such activities.[703]

755   Although it is clear that Parties to a non-international armed conflict are responsible for searching for and collecting the wounded and sick, common Article 3 does not specify who it is that has actually to carry out these activities. The typical scenario envisaged in the article involves search, collection and evacuation activities by the Party or Parties to the conflict that have been involved in the engagement that has resulted in wounded persons. In a

---

[699] ICRC Study on Customary International Humanitarian Law (2005), Rule 109. See also Mali, *Army Service Regulations*, 1979, Article 36; Morocco, *Disciplinary Regulations*, 1974, Article 25(4); and Netherlands, *Military Handbook*, 2003, p. 7–44.

[700] It is also implied in Article 15 of the First Convention.

[701] In this regard, for example, Canada's *Code of Conduct*, 2007, p. 2–12, para. 3, states that '[i]t is understood however that this obligation only comes into play once the area has been secured'.

[702] Atul Gawande, 'Casualties of War – Military Care for the Wounded from Iraq and Afghanistan', *The New England Journal of Medicine*, Vol. 351, 2004, pp. 2471–2475.

[703] For more details, see section K.

multi-Party conflict, however, it may also mean that a Party that was not involved in a particular engagement needs to assist in the search for and collection of the wounded and sick.

756   If the resources of a Party to the conflict are not sufficient to carry out search, collection and evacuation activities, in order to meet its obligations under common Article 3 that Party may call upon civilians or humanitarian organizations to assist in these efforts.[704] Similarly, when the medical needs of the wounded and sick go beyond what a Party to the conflict is able to provide, that Party should seek to evacuate them to a place where more extensive medical facilities are available. If a Party is not able to search for, collect or evacuate the wounded and sick itself, it needs to provide all the relevant information to enable others to carry out these tasks safely. Parties should thus facilitate the safe and efficient passage of medical collection and evacuation transports and personnel and any other necessary equipment, and provide transport routes and times that do not subject the personnel or transports to the risk of mined areas or other obstacles.[705] For example, Parties should take measures to protect humanitarian workers from the effects of mines and other explosive remnants of war. Specific treaty obligations exist under the Protocols to the Convention on Certain Conventional Weapons.

757   The obligations to collect and to care for the wounded and sick entail a corollary obligation on opposing Parties to permit evacuations and transport to medical facilities to take place as rapidly as possible. To implement these obligations, for example, procedures at checkpoints are required to allow for the quickest possible collection, evacuation and care of the wounded and sick and to avoid the unnecessary delay of medical transports. Security checks would have to be carried out as quickly as possible. Even short delays, such as those lasting less than an hour, can be fatal.[706] When a Party deems it necessary to arrest or detain a wounded or sick person who is being transported to a medical facility, it must balance any security measures against the patient's medical condition. In any case, such security measures may not impede access to necessary and adequate medical care and a Party that proceeds to an arrest must ensure the continuous medical treatment of the person arrested and detained. Likewise, if a person transporting the wounded and sick or providing aid is arrested or detained, the transport of the wounded or sick persons to medical facilities or the provision of the necessary care during transport would nevertheless have to be ensured.

---

[704] Henckaerts/Doswald-Beck, commentary on Rule 109, p. 398. See also First Convention, Article 18.

[705] For States party to 1996 Amended Protocol II to the Convention on Certain Conventional Weapons, each Party to the conflict must respect the relevant obligations in Article 12 of that Protocol (see in particular Article 12(2)–(5)), and for States party to 2003 Protocol V to the Convention on Certain Conventional Weapons, each Party to the conflict must respect the relevant obligations in Article 6 of that Protocol.

[706] ICRC, *Health Care in Danger: Violent Incidents Affecting the Delivery of Health Care*, p. 8.

758   In a similar vein, Parties transporting the wounded and sick of the adversary to medical facilities are required to do so as quickly as possible, and in any case may not intentionally prolong the journey for any purposes that are not warranted by the medical condition of the wounded or sick persons during transit.

759   If a Party is unable or unwilling to evacuate the wounded or sick, authorization for impartial humanitarian organizations to do so should be liberally granted and must in no circumstance be withheld arbitrarily.[707] Practice shows that the ICRC in particular has frequently engaged in the evacuation of the wounded and sick.[708]

760   Although common Article 3 does not mention an obligation to collect the dead, Article 8 of Additional Protocol II includes obligations to search for the dead, to prevent their being despoiled and to dispose of them decently. Similar obligations exist under customary international law.[709] Under customary international law, Parties to the conflict must also take all feasible steps to identify deceased persons and, whenever possible, return the bodies to the families for proper burial, cremation or funeral rites.[710] This can only be done if the dead are searched for and collected. In practice, the dead may be searched for and collected at the same time as the wounded and sick, although different procedures may need to be followed.[711] That said, priority must be given to the wounded and sick so that they receive proper and timely treatment.

d. The obligation to care for the wounded and sick

761 The obligation to care for the wounded and sick requires that the Parties to the conflict take active steps to ameliorate the medical condition of the wounded and sick. Like the other obligations in common Article 3, this obligation applies equally to State and non-State Parties. Some non-State armed groups have the capacity to provide sophisticated medical care, while others have more rudimentary capacities. In any case, non-State armed groups must endeavour to develop their capacities to provide treatment to the best of their abilities and

---

[707] For more details, see section J.

[708] For example, during the clashes in Budapest in 1956 (*International Review of the Red Cross*, Vol. 38, No. 456, December 1956, p. 720); during the civil war in the Dominican Republic in 1961 (*International Review of the Red Cross*, Vol. 47, No. 558, June 1965, p. 283); during the civil war in Lebanon in 1976 and 1981 (*International Review of the Red Cross*, Vol. 58, No. 692, August 1976, pp. 477–478, and ICRC, *Annual Report 1981*, ICRC, Geneva, 1982, pp. 52–53); and during the civil war in Chad in 1979 (*International Review of the Red Cross*, Vol. 61, No. 716, April 1979, pp. 95–96). See also ICRC, Communication to the Press No. 96/25, Russian Federation/Chechnya: ICRC calls on all parties to observe truce, 10 August 1996.

[709] ICRC Study on Customary International Humanitarian Law (2005), Rules 112–116.

[710] *Ibid.* Rules 114, 115, 116 and supporting practice, available at https://www.icrc.org/customary-ihl/eng/docs/v2_rul.

[711] For example, ambulances should not be used to collect the dead. See also ICRC, *Management of Dead Bodies after Disasters*, pp. 7–8. Searching for and recording the dead also helps to prevent the deceased from becoming missing.

should be permitted to do so. Like State Parties, they should ensure that their forces are trained in first aid. Likewise, they may have recourse, if necessary, to medical aid provided by impartial humanitarian organizations.

762   The obligation to care for the wounded and sick is an obligation of means. Its exact content depends on the specific circumstances of each case.[712] Evidently, a person who is severely wounded will require greater medical care than a person with minor injuries;[713] a Party that has significant medical supplies at its disposal will be required to do more than a Party that only has limited means;[714] and if medical doctors are present, higher standards of medical care can be expected than in circumstances where there are only fighters with more limited training.[715] Notably, the corresponding provision in Additional Protocol II and customary law require medical care to be provided 'to the fullest extent practicable and with the least possible delay'.[716] In terms of substance, the same kind and quality of medical care is owed under the Geneva Conventions, Additional Protocol II and customary international law.

763   First aid is essential and often life-saving. Nevertheless, given that it may have to be administered on the battlefield after or possibly even during an engagement, it is clear that common Article 3 does not require the same standard of treatment as that required under more secure conditions once the wounded and sick have been transferred to a medical unit. While medical care in accordance with the highest medical standards is the most desirable, common Article 3 requires only what can reasonably be expected under the given circumstances, taking into consideration factors such as the security conditions and the available resources.

764   With respect to the kind and quality of medical care that is owed by virtue of common Article 3, the basic rule is that the wounded and sick must receive the medical care required by their condition. Albeit not explicitly mentioned in this article, this is generally accepted and explicitly provided for in Additional Protocol II and corresponds to customary law.[717] General guidance regarding the applicable standards of professional medical conduct may be derived from universally applicable, general stipulations and instruments adopted by the World Medical Association (WMA).[718] These standards may change over time

---

[712] ICJ, *Application of the Genocide Convention case*, Merits, Judgment, 2007, para. 430.

[713] Even in the case of fatal wounds, due diligence requires they be treated, notably to address pain and distress; see United States, *Law of War Deskbook*, 2010, p. 51.

[714] See e.g. Lindsey, p. 112: 'Especially in armed conflicts, the necessary resources for providing safe blood donations may be limited.'

[715] Eritrea-Ethiopia Claims Commission, *Prisoners of War, Ethiopia's claim*, Partial Award, 2003, paras 57 and 69–70.

[716] Additional Protocol II, Article 7(2), and ICRC Study on Customary International Humanitarian Law (2005), Rule 110.

[717] *Ibid.*

[718] Instruments concerning medical ethics in times of armed conflict, especially: the World Medical Association's Regulations in Times of Armed Conflict (adopted by the 10th World Medical Assembly, Havana, Cuba, October 1956, as amended or revised in 1957, 1983, 2004, 2006

and there may be differences from country to country. However, as far as the standard of medical care is concerned, the obligation requires the kind of treatment that would be administered by a medical practitioner under the given circumstances and in view of the person's medical condition.[719]

765   In all cases, care must be provided in accordance with medical ethics.[720] This requires that care be dictated exclusively by the principles of triage.[721] Thus, it would be a violation of the obligation to care for the wounded and sick for any Party to insist, for example, that lightly wounded fighters be given priority over civilians or others in urgent need of medical care. Indeed, no grounds for discrimination in treatment are permitted other than medical ones.[722]

766   Women, men, boys and girls of different ages and backgrounds can have different medical needs, be exposed to different risks hindering equal care, or face different social stigma connected to being wounded or sick. It is thus important to include the perspectives of women and men from different ages and backgrounds in needs assessments relating to medical care, taking into account possible limitations such as physical access, security, financial constraints and socio-cultural constraints, as well as possible solutions.[723]

767   Lastly, medical care in the strict sense, i.e. exclusively medical treatment of a wound or disease in and of itself, is not sufficient to ameliorate the condition of a wounded or sick person. Indeed, it would be meaningless to provide medical care if adequate food, clothing, shelter and hygiene were not provided alongside. This is especially the case when severely wounded persons are being treated over a longer period of time. In light of its object and purpose, the obligation to care for the wounded and sick in common Article 3 should be interpreted broadly, to pertain not only to medical care but also, at a minimum, to the

---

and 2012); Rules Governing the Care of Sick and Wounded, Particularly in Time of Conflict (adopted by the 10th World Medical Assembly, Havana, Cuba, October 1956, edited and amended in 1957 and 1983); Standards of Professional Conduct regarding the Hippocratic Oath and its modern version, the Declaration of Geneva, and its supplementary International Code of Medical Ethics (adopted by the 3rd WMA General Assembly, London, England, October 1949, as amended in 1968, 1983 and 2006). See also ICRC, *Health Care in Danger: The Responsibilities of Health-Care Personnel Working in Armed Conflicts and Other Emergencies*, ICRC, Geneva, 2012, pp. 55–62.

[719] There are many studies on the type of equipment and techniques that medical practitioners should use and on the procedures they should follow; see e.g. ICRC, *War Surgery*.

[720] Bothe/Partsch/Solf, p. 108, para. 2.3. See also the explicit reference to medical ethics in Article 16(1)–(2) of Additional Protocol I.

[721] For the principles of triage, see ICRC, *First Aid in Armed Conflicts and Other Situations of Violence*, p. 116.

[722] See Additional Protocol II, Article 7(2), and ICRC Study on Customary International Humanitarian Law (2005), Rule 110.

[723] See Charlotte Lindsey-Curtet, Florence Tercier Holst-Roness and Letitia Anderson, *Addressing the Needs of Women Affected by Armed Conflict: An ICRC Guidance Document*, ICRC, Geneva, 2004, p. 76. When planning for and providing care, therefore, it is essential to be sensitive to how social, cultural, economic and political structures create roles or patterns that, in turn, may carry a specific status as well as generate needs and capacities that differ among men and women. Understanding the impact of gender and other diversities on the opportunities people have and their interactions with others will contribute to more effective protection and respect in caring for the wounded and sick.

provision of food, clothing, shelter and hygiene, which help to ameliorate the condition of the wounded and sick. In any event, depriving the wounded and sick of such essentials would also in most circumstances amount to inhuman treatment in violation of the general obligation imposed by common Article 3.[724] Caring for the sick may also entail taking preventive measures to ensure the basic health of the population, including vaccinating people against infectious diseases.

e. Obligations implicit in collecting and caring for the wounded and sick

768   In order to protect the wounded and sick, those searching, collecting and caring for them, as well as their transports and equipment, also need to be protected. It is thus implicit in common Article 3 that medical personnel must be respected and protected, as it is understood that 'the protection of medical personnel is a subsidiary form of protection granted to ensure that the wounded and sick receive medical care'.[725] This protection is recognized as a part of customary international law governing non-international armed conflicts and is codified in Article 9 of Additional Protocol II.[726] It also results from subparagraph (1) of common Article 3 as medical personnel who do not participate directly in hostilities are protected under this provision. The act of administering health care to a member of a non-State armed group may not be interpreted as supporting the group's cause, nor may it be construed as engaging in a hostile act. Thus, medical personnel may not be punished for the mere fact of providing treatment or care for wounded and sick persons in accordance with medical ethics.[727] Harassing or punishing medical personnel for such acts would constitute a violation of the obligation to care for the wounded and sick as it impedes the provision of care.

769   Likewise, medical units and transports may not be attacked, including when they are being used to transport wounded fighters.[728] If they are used to commit

---

[724] For more details, see section F.1.

[725] *Official Records of the Diplomatic Conference of Geneva of 1974–1977*, Vol. XI, pp. 209–210. See also the commentary on Article 24 and Henckaerts/Doswald-Beck, commentary on Rule 25, p. 80.

[726] For the definition that was proposed during the Diplomatic Conference, see *Official Records of the Diplomatic Conference of Geneva of 1974–1977*, Vol. XIII, p. 304. See also Henckaerts/Doswald-Beck, commentary on Rule 25, pp. 81–83, affirmed by Breau, pp. 177–178.

[727] See also Additional Protocol II, Article 10(1), and ICRC Study on Customary International Humanitarian Law (2005), Rule 26.

[728] The ICC lists as war crimes in non-international armed conflicts the intentional attack against 'buildings, material, medical units and transport, and personnel using the distinctive emblems of the Geneva Conventions in conformity with international law' and against 'hospitals and places where the sick and wounded are collected, provided they are not military objectives'; see ICC Statute (1998), Article 8(2)(e)(ii) and (iv). See also Dörmann, 2003, p. 462. It may be noted that the Commission of Inquiry on Syria found that '[a]ttacks on medical personnel and facilities violate common article 3 of the Geneva Conventions and customary international humanitarian law and amount to war crimes'; see Human Rights Council, *Commission of Inquiry Report on Syria*, 13 August 2014, UN Doc. A/HRC/27/60, para. 111.

acts of hostility, such as transporting weapons or able-bodied fighters, they lose their protection from attack. Thus, Parties to the conflict must take all feasible precautions to protect medical units, facilities and transports from the dangers arising from military operations. This would include avoiding using them in ways that may lead to their loss of protection against attack in order to ensure that they can continue to collect and care for the wounded and sick. If such units have lost their protection against attack, Parties to the conflict must give a warning and may proceed with an attack only if that warning has gone unheeded after a reasonable time limit, as recognized by Article 11(2) of Additional Protocol II.[729] What constitutes a reasonable time limit will vary according to the circumstances; however it must be long enough either to allow the unlawful acts to be stopped or for the wounded and sick, as well as medical personnel, who are present within the unit, to be removed to a safe place. The warning also allows the medical facility to reply to an unfounded accusation. However, the setting of a time limit may be entirely dispensed with if the misuse places the attacking forces in immediate danger to their lives, in which case they may respond in self-defence. This may occur, for example, when a medical transport is approaching a checkpoint while firing on those guarding the checkpoint.[730]

770   These implicit obligations also mean, for instance, that medical facilities or transports needed or used for providing medical care must not be pillaged or destroyed. The pillaging of medical facilities impedes the provision of care for wounded and sick persons, and thus would violate this subparagraph. This is the case even when pillaging of such facilities is driven by a need for medical supplies by a Party to the conflict. Parties may therefore need to take measures to ensure that medical facilities and transports are not looted or pillaged by others.

771   In addition, armed entry into medical facilities in order to carry out search operations can severely disrupt the provision of medical care. Military search operations in medical facilities must therefore be an exceptional measure and should be carried out in a manner that minimizes any negative impact on the provision of care. If a person is arrested, continuing care must be ensured. To avoid loss of protection from attack on medical facilities or transports, Parties must not take actions that lead to such a loss. Actions that lead to loss of protection include, for example, storing weapons in hospitals (with the exception of weapons belonging to the wounded and sick being treated in the hospital held temporarily during their care) or using ambulances for the transport of able-bodied forces, weapons or ammunition.

---

[729] See also ICRC Study on Customary International Humanitarian Law (2005), Rules 28 and 29 and commentary (Henckaerts/Doswald-Beck, pp. 91–102); *Sanremo Manual on the Law of Non-International Armed Conflict* (2006), section 4.2.1; United States, *Law of War Manual*, 2015, p. 1045; Breau, pp. 177–178; and Kleffner, 2013a, p. 338.

[730] Kleffner, 2013a, p. 338.

772   Furthermore, it is helpful if those caring for the wounded and sick and their facilities are identifiable so that they will not be attacked. Marking medical facilities, under proper authorization and control, such as with a red cross, red crescent, or red crystal emblem can make it easier for the opposing Party and the public to identify such facilities and enhance access to medical care.

773   Common Article 3 is silent with respect to the use of the distinctive emblems in non-international armed conflicts. However, Article 12 of Additional Protocol II sets down the conditions for lawful use of the emblems for protective purposes in non-international armed conflicts:

> Under the direction of the competent authority concerned, the distinctive emblem of the red cross, red crescent or red lion and sun on a white ground shall be displayed by medical and religious personnel and medical units, and on medical transports. It shall be respected in all circumstances. It shall not be used improperly.

774   During the negotiations leading to the adoption of Article 12, there was no objection to the notion that the medical personnel of non-State armed groups may display the emblem on the same footing as that permitted for States.[731] This means that the leadership of the group must be in a position to authorize and control the use of the emblem. The improper use of the distinctive emblems of the Geneva Conventions is prohibited under customary international law.[732] Improper use means any use of the emblems for a purpose other than those for which they were intended.[733] Moreover, the protective emblem must be in its pure form. That is, it must contain only the red cross, red crescent or red crystal on a white background, devoid of any additional markings or wording.[734]

775   Practice known to the ICRC shows that the medical personnel of some non-State armed groups do wear an armband with a red cross or red crescent emblem, while many others do not. Parties may also wish to make the presence of medical facilities known by communicating the GPS coordinates of medical facilities to other Parties.

776   Whether or not State armed forces or non-State armed groups choose to display the emblem, it is imperative that they respect its use by their adversaries in order to ensure that the wounded and sick may be collected and cared for. In this light, it must be underscored that, as is the case in international armed conflicts, if medical personnel carry light weapons exclusively for self-defence or for the defence of wounded or sick persons in their care, it does not entail a loss

---

[731] *Official Records of the Diplomatic Conference of Geneva of 1974–1977*, Vol. XI, pp. 427–431.
[732] ICRC Study on Customary International Humanitarian Law (2005), Rule 59.
[733] Henckaerts/Doswald-Beck, commentary on Rule 59, p. 209.
[734] In practice, for protective purposes the ICRC uses its 'roundel' (a red cross enclosed in two concentric circles between which are written the words 'COMITE INTERNATIONAL GENEVE'), and this is widely accepted. This practice applies only to the ICRC, however. See ICRC, *Study on the Use of the Emblems: Operational and Commercial and Other Non-operational Issues*, ICRC, Geneva, 2011, pp. 156–157.

of protection from attack.[735] Thus, the fact that medical personnel are carrying such weapons for such purposes does not excuse the Parties to a conflict from the obligation to respect – and not attack – such medical personnel. That said, in order to maintain their protection, medical personnel may not commit acts harmful to the enemy.[736]

777   In some non-international armed conflicts, an alternative emblem to the red cross or red crescent has been adopted in order to designate personnel and facilities providing health care uniquely to the civilian population. This is the case, for example, for the Misión Médica in Colombia.[737] In any case, even if health facilities or transports are not marked with an emblem or identified by other means indicating protection, as soon as they are known, they must be respected and protected.[738]

778   Lastly, Parties to the conflict may also create zones, using special agreements, as provided for in common Article 3(3), in which the wounded and sick may be cared for.[739] They must be created with the consent of all Parties and must be demilitarized. Such zones have been established in a number of non-international armed conflicts.[740] It is important to recall that, in any case, the wounded and sick and any medical personnel providing treatment in such zones are protected owing to their being wounded or sick or to their role as medical personnel; protection is not contingent on the creation of the zone itself. Moreover, persons outside such zones remain protected according to the general rules of humanitarian law. Thus, even if such zones are not created, the wounded and sick and medical personnel and facilities, as well as civilians who are not directly participating in hostilities, must be respected and protected. Directing an attack against such a zone is prohibited.[741]

J. Paragraph 2: Offer of services by an impartial humanitarian body such as the ICRC

1. Introduction

779 Common Article 3(2) grants impartial humanitarian bodies the right to offer their services to the Parties to a non-international armed conflict. The

---

[735] See Article 22.
[736] For a discussion of the notion of acts harmful to the enemy committed by medical personnel, see the commentary on Article 24, section F; see also the commentary on Article 21, section C.1, in relation to medical units.
[737] See Colombia, Ministry of Health and Social Protection, *Manual de Misión Médica*, Bogotá, 2013, Resolución 4481 de 2012, pp. 11–12.
[738] See also Annex I to Additional Protocol I, Article 1(2).
[739] See also ICRC Study on Customary International Humanitarian Law (2005), Rules 35 and 36.
[740] These include, for example, the conflicts in Cambodia, Chad, Cyprus, Lebanon, Nicaragua and Sri Lanka. See Henckaerts/Doswald-Beck, commentary on Rule 35, p. 120, fn. 6.
[741] See ICRC Study on Customary International Humanitarian Law (2005), Rule 35.

International Committee of the Red Cross (ICRC) is explicitly mentioned as an example of an entity entitled to rely on this provision. This right can be exercised vis-à-vis all Parties to a conflict, including non-State Parties.

780   Other humanitarian law provisions dealing with this subject qualify the way in which this right is to be exercised: in order to undertake the proposed activities, an impartial humanitarian organization needs to have consent. Since 1949, international law has developed to the point where the consent may not be arbitrarily withheld by any of the Parties to a non-international armed conflict (see section J.6.b).

781   Through the adoption of both this paragraph and other related provisions, the High Contracting Parties have recognized that the right to offer services, be it in international or non-international armed conflict, merits a firm footing in international law.[742] This broad legal foundation is unsurprising, and merely reflects the axiom that, irrespective of its legal characterization, every armed conflict generates humanitarian needs. Regardless of the legal qualification of the armed conflict, therefore, States have recognized that, as a matter of international law, the ICRC and other impartial humanitarian bodies will most likely have a role to play in meeting those needs.

782   The willingness and ability of impartial humanitarian bodies to respond to the humanitarian needs of persons affected by a non-international armed conflict do not detract from the fact that, as a matter of international law, the primary responsibility for meeting those needs lies with the Parties to the conflict. The activities of impartial humanitarian bodies should only complement, where necessary, the efforts of that Party in this regard. This is also why impartial humanitarian organizations are under no legal obligation to offer their services, as is clear from the wording 'may offer' in common Article 3(2); they can do so at their discretion.

783   For their part, National Red Cross and Red Crescent Societies (hereinafter 'National Societies') nevertheless have a duty to consider seriously any request by their own public authorities to carry out humanitarian activities falling within their mandate, provided these activities can be implemented in accordance with the Fundamental Principles of the International Red Cross and Red Crescent Movement (hereinafter 'the Movement'). This duty stems from their special status and unique auxiliary role to their own public authorities in the humanitarian field – a status articulated in the Movement's Statutes.[743] The Fundamental Principles are listed in the preamble to the Statutes, adopted by the International Conference of the Red Cross and Red Crescent, which brings together the States party to the 1949 Geneva Conventions, as

---

[742] Other related provisions are common Article 9 (Article 10 of the Fourth Convention) for international armed conflicts, and Article 18 of Additional Protocol II for non-international armed conflicts.

[743] Statutes of the International Red Cross and Red Crescent Movement (1986), Article 4(3).

well as the components of the Movement, and can therefore be considered authoritative.[744]

784   The right to offer services, which is also sometimes referred to as the 'right of humanitarian initiative', is not to be confused with the so-called 'right of humanitarian intervention' nor with the 'responsibility to protect' (R2P), two distinct concepts which have engendered much debate, for example as to whether international law permits measures such as the threat or the use of force when motivated by humanitarian considerations.[745] Similarly, the analysis of common Article 3(2) remains without prejudice to the UN Security Council's entitlement to act, on the basis of the 1945 UN Charter and in line with the effect of its decisions under international law, as it deems fit with regard to humanitarian activities. These issues are regulated by international law in general and the law on the use of force (*jus ad bellum*) in particular. Thus, they have to be kept separate from the subject of humanitarian activities carried out within the framework of common Article 3(2).

2. Historical background

785 Practical examples of humanitarian activities undertaken in the context of a non-international armed conflict predate the adoption of common Article 3.[746] Indeed, prior to 1949 no general treaty provision as such regulated non-international armed conflicts.[747] As a corollary, no treaty law regulated the conditions under which humanitarian activities could be proposed, and implemented, in non-international armed conflicts. Initially, however, the absence of an international legal framework on the matter proved to be no obstacle for both the ICRC (founded in 1863) and National Societies (founded thereafter) to deploy activities in several such conflicts. Over time, however, the need for a treaty-based normative framework to clarify some basic questions became increasingly apparent: notably, were humanitarian organizations entitled, as a matter of treaty law, to offer their services in the context of a non-international armed conflict?

786   With this in mind, the 10th International Conference of the Red Cross in 1921 adopted a resolution on the normative framework applicable to the ICRC

---

[744] The Fundamental Principles were first proclaimed by the 20th International Conference of the Red Cross in Vienna in 1965. They were then integrated into the preamble to the Statutes of the International Red Cross and Red Crescent Movement, adopted by the 25th International Conference of the Red Cross in 1986 and amended in 1995 and 2006.

[745] Vaughan Lowe and Antonios Tzanakopoulos, 'Humanitarian Intervention', version of May 2011, in Rüdiger Wolfrum (ed.), *Max Planck Encyclopedia of Public International Law*, Oxford University Press, para. 2, http://opil.ouplaw.com/home/EPIL.

[746] For details, see Bugnion, 2003a, pp. 244–296, Chapter IX, The International Committee of the Red Cross and Internal Conflicts (1863–1945).

[747] See also section A.

and National Societies.[748] Until 1949, this resolution remained the principal instrument governing the right to offer services.[749]

787   No trace of what eventually became common Article 3(2) can be found in the drafting stages leading up to the 1949 Diplomatic Conference. During the Conference, the first Working Party used a different formulation with regard to the right to offer services: the possibility for an impartial humanitarian body, such as the ICRC, to offer its services to a Party to a non-international armed conflict was preconditioned on the absence of an agreement between the Parties on the designation and functioning of Protecting Powers.[750] In the First Draft, the activities of the impartial humanitarian body were thus to be those conferred by the Geneva Conventions on the Protecting Powers.[751] The second Working Party, however, dropped the reference to the absence of Protecting Powers in both of its drafts and instead foresaw the possibility for an impartial humanitarian body, such as the ICRC, to offer its services simply 'to the Parties to the conflict'.[752]

3. Impartial humanitarian bodies

a. General

788   Only an 'impartial humanitarian body' is entitled to offer its services in the sense of this provision, and with the legal consequences attached thereto. As is the case with the substantively identical notion of 'impartial humanitarian organization' used in common Article 9 dealing with the right to offer services in international armed conflict, this concept is not defined in the Geneva Conventions. The equally authentic French version of the Geneva Conventions uses the term 'organisme humanitaire impartial' in both common Article 3(2) and common Article 9, thus reinforcing the conclusion that 'impartial humanitarian body' and 'impartial humanitarian organization' can be considered substantively identical notions.

789   When these words were inserted in the text of common Article 3, the High Contracting Parties primarily had the ICRC and the National Societies in mind as examples they were familiar with. Since 1949, the number and diversity of

---

[748] 10th International Conference of the Red Cross, Geneva, 1921, Resolution XIV, Principles and Rules for Red Cross Disaster Relief, Principle I; see Bugnion, 2003a, pp. 260–262. An unsuccessful attempt had already been made to have a resolution adopted on the subject at the 9th International Conference of the Red Cross in Washington in 1912; see Bugnion, 2003a, pp. 248–250.

[749] See Bugnion, 2003a, pp. 263–286. Of note from this period is a draft resolution proposed by the ICRC at the 16th International Conference of the Red Cross in London in 1938. This resolution, which would have provided a more solid legal foundation for the ICRC to act in the case of non-international armed conflict, while solidifying its role in the case of 'civil war', fell short of comprehensively clarifying the legal framework on this topic; see *ibid.* pp. 283–286.

[750] *Final Record of the Diplomatic Conference of Geneva of 1949*, Vol. II-B, p. 122.

[751] *Ibid.* p. 124.   [752] *Ibid.* pp. 125–126.

organizations that consider themselves to be impartial humanitarian organizations in the sense of common Article 3, and which are recognized as such by Parties to an armed conflict, have grown significantly to include both certain non-governmental and intergovernmental organizations.

790   For an organization to qualify as a 'humanitarian organization', there is no requirement that the scope of its activities be limited to humanitarian activities.[753] Thus, an organization that focused solely on development activities prior to the outbreak of the armed conflict may subsequently become, for the purposes of common Article 3, a humanitarian organization, without prejudice to the possibility of the organization concurrently pursuing activities of a different nature elsewhere.

791   Common Article 3 requires that the entity wishing to offer its services be an impartial humanitarian 'body'. Thus, a loose association of individuals, while their activities may alleviate human suffering, would not qualify on the basis of this provision. Nor would a private person wishing to engage in charitable activities. A minimum structure is required for the 'body' to be able to function as a humanitarian organization. In addition, at all times the organization ought to be capable of complying with professional standards for humanitarian activities.[754] Otherwise, in practice there is a risk that the authorities to whom the offer of services is made may doubt the impartial and humanitarian nature of the organization.

792   Humanitarian organizations require financial means in order to sustain their staff and operations and to purchase the necessary goods and services. Therefore, the fact that money is involved can by no means be considered as depriving the organization or its activities of their 'humanitarian' character. Further, provided the organization continues to act as an impartial humanitarian organization, nothing precludes it from maintaining a relationship with an economic actor such as a private or a State-owned company. Examples of such relationships include: when economic actors with the capacities to deliver humanitarian services, such as a commercial aviation company used for the transport of relief goods, sell their services to impartial humanitarian organizations at a profit; or when economic actors provide their services to impartial humanitarian organizations for free, for example as part of a corporate social responsibility programme.

793   While there are a wide variety of instances in which economic actors can be involved in humanitarian activities, even when they provide free services

---

[753] For an analysis of which activities qualify as 'humanitarian activities', see section J.4.c.

[754] See e.g. ICRC, *Professional Standards for Protection Work Carried Out by Humanitarian and Human Rights Actors in Armed Conflict and Other Situations of Violence*, 2nd edition, ICRC, Geneva, 2013. These standards, adopted through an ICRC-led consultation process, reflect shared thinking and common agreement among humanitarian and human rights agencies (UN agencies, components of the Movement, and non-governmental organizations). The ICRC is of the view that the standards of protection that an agency provides should not fall below those set out in this document.

within the framework of a particular humanitarian activity, their otherwise profit-making profile precludes them from qualifying as an impartial humanitarian organization in their own right. Other examples of the involvement of economic actors in humanitarian activities include: receiving payment from another actor (such as the armed forces) for delivering humanitarian services; and delivering humanitarian services directly themselves, i.e. without having a relationship with an impartial humanitarian organization. Thus, economic actors may not invoke the right to offer services in the sense of common Article 3 since they do not qualify as impartial humanitarian organizations.

794   The Geneva Conventions require a humanitarian organization wishing to offer its services on the basis of common Article 3 to be 'impartial'. Impartiality refers to the attitude to be adopted vis-à-vis the persons affected by the armed conflict when planning and implementing the proposed humanitarian activities. As one of the Movement's Fundamental Principles, 'impartiality' is the requirement not to make any 'discrimination as to nationality, race, religious beliefs, class or political opinions' or any other similar criteria.[755] Further, the Fundamental Principle of impartiality, which has been endorsed by the International Court of Justice,[756] requires the components of the Movement to 'endeavou[r] to relieve the suffering of individuals, being guided solely by their needs, and to give priority to the most urgent cases of distress'.[757] As a matter of good practice, this definition is followed not only by the components of the Movement, but also by actors outside the Movement.

795   For an organization to qualify as an 'impartial humanitarian body', it does not suffice for it to claim unilaterally that it qualifies as such: it needs to operate impartially at all times. In operational reality, it matters that the authorities to whom an offer of services is made perceive the organization to be both impartial and humanitarian in nature, and that they trust that the organization will behave accordingly.

796   The principle of impartiality applies at both the planning and the implementation stages of any humanitarian activity: only the needs of the persons affected by the conflict may inspire the proposals, priorities and decisions of humanitarian organizations when determining which activities to undertake

---

[755] While the words 'any other similar criteria' do not appear in common Article 9, they do in other provisions of the Geneva Conventions. See e.g. Article 12(2) of the First Convention.

[756] ICJ, *Military and Paramilitary Activities in and against Nicaragua case*, Merits, Judgment, 1986, para. 242.

[757] See also The Sphere Project, *Sphere Handbook: Humanitarian Charter and Minimum Standards in Humanitarian Response*, 3rd edition, 2011, para. 6, which states:

> [Humanitarian] assistance must be provided according to the principle of impartiality, which requires that it be provided solely on the basis of need and in proportion to need. This reflects the wider principle of non-discrimination: that no one should be discriminated against on any grounds of status, including age, gender, race, colour, ethnicity, sexual orientation, language, religion, disability, health status, political or other opinion, national or social origin.

and where and how to implement them (for example, who receives medical assistance first).

797   For an organization to qualify as an impartial humanitarian body in the sense of common Article 3, there is no requirement as to where it has its headquarters, which may be outside the territory of the State in which a non-international armed conflict occurs.

798   The concept of impartiality is distinct from neutrality. Even though, in reality, neutrality is often essential as an attitude in order to be able to work impartially, common Article 3 does not require organizations wishing to qualify on the basis of this provision to be 'neutral'. In the context of humanitarian activities, 'neutrality' refers to the attitude to be adopted towards the Parties to the armed conflict. Neutrality is also one of the Movement's Fundamental Principles, described as follows: 'In order to continue to enjoy the confidence of all, the Movement may not take sides in hostilities or engage at any time in controversies of a political, racial, religious or ideological nature.'

799   It should be noted that, whilst humanitarian activities may also be performed by actors which do not qualify as impartial humanitarian organizations, and such activities may alleviate human suffering, they are nevertheless not covered by common Article 3(2) nor by the principles guiding the conduct of impartial humanitarian bodies.

b. The International Committee of the Red Cross

800 Common Article 3 mentions the ICRC as an example ('such as') of an organization that qualifies as an impartial humanitarian body.

801   The ICRC is the only organization identified by name both in common Article 3(2) and in common Article 9 regarding the right to offer services. For the drafters of the Conventions, the ICRC epitomizes an impartial humanitarian body. Conversely, by virtue of it being an example of an impartial humanitarian organization, States having conferred on the ICRC the right to offer its services have signalled that this explicit mention is contingent upon the ICRC operating at all times as an impartial humanitarian organization.

802   In the 1949 Geneva Conventions and their 1977 Additional Protocol I, there are a considerable number of provisions in which the High Contracting Parties have explicitly granted the ICRC the right to offer to perform specific humanitarian activities when it comes to international armed conflict.[758] As far as treaty law applicable to non-international armed conflict is concerned, however, only common Article 3 explicitly mentions the ICRC without linking it to specific activities. In parallel, the Movement's Statutes provide a legal basis

---

[758] For more details, see the commentary on Article 9, para. 1132.

for the ICRC to offer its services in these types of conflicts, among other types of situation.[759]

4. The offer of services

803   On the basis of common Article 3, the High Contracting Parties explicitly recognize that impartial humanitarian organizations are entitled, without being obliged, to offer any services which they deem pertinent to meet the humanitarian needs engendered by an armed conflict. Such an offer may be unconditionally made, regardless of any prior approach or request from one or more of the Parties to the conflict concerned, and regardless of any other factor which would restrain these organizations' entitlement to offer their services.

804   When an offer of services is made, it may be regarded neither as an unfriendly act nor as an unlawful interference in a State's domestic affairs in general or in the conflict in particular.[760] Nor may it be regarded as recognition of or support to a Party to the conflict. Therefore, an offer of services and its implementation may not be prohibited or criminalized, by virtue of legislative or other regulatory acts. Nothing precludes a Party to the non-international armed conflict from inviting the ICRC or other impartial humanitarian organizations to undertake certain humanitarian activities. However, as a matter of international law, these organizations are not obliged to accept such a request; it is at their discretion to decide whether or not to respond positively in any particular context.[761] When making an offer of services to one Party to a non-international armed conflict, there is no requirement in common Article 3 to make an equivalent offer to the other Party or Parties to the conflict.

805   An offer of services by the ICRC or another impartial humanitarian organization has no bearing on the international legal status of the entity to which the offer is made. As is clear from common Article 3(4), the fact that an offer of services is made to a non-State Party to the armed conflict has no impact on that Party's legal status. Likewise, an offer of services may not be interpreted as endorsement of the reasons for which the entity is engaged in an armed conflict.

806   In order for the treaty-based right to offer services to be effective, the authorities representing a Party to a non-international armed conflict should make sure that those in charge of making the decision in this regard are available to receive it.

---

[759] See Statutes of the International Red Cross and Red Crescent Movement (1986), Article 5(2)(c)–(d) and (3). For details on the origin of these Statutes, see para. 783.

[760] See ICJ, *Military and Paramilitary Activities in and against Nicaragua case*, Merits, Judgment, 1986, para. 242: 'There can be no doubt that the provision of strictly humanitarian aid to persons or forces in another country, whatever their political affiliations or objectives, cannot be regarded as unlawful intervention, or as in any other way contrary to international law.'

[761] As to the special status of National Societies in this regard, see para. 783.

5. The services offered

a. Humanitarian activities

807 Common Article 3 states concisely that, in the case of a non-international armed conflict, an impartial humanitarian body may offer 'its services'. The notion of services is not defined in common Article 3 and no examples are provided.

808 Common Article 9, the provision enshrining the right to offer services applicable in international armed conflict, allows the ICRC or another impartial humanitarian organization to offer to undertake 'humanitarian activities' for the 'protection' and 'relief' (a term which can be used interchangeably with the term 'assistance') of certain categories of persons.

809 The humanitarian needs engendered by an armed conflict are likely to be very much the same regardless of the conflict's legal qualification. Thus, absent any indication to the contrary, the term 'services' in common Article 3 should be interpreted broadly, i.e. as encompassing all types of humanitarian activities required to meet the needs of all persons affected by the armed conflict. The nature of the armed conflict should not have any impact on the humanitarian activities that can be offered, be they protection or relief/assistance activities.

810 Arguably, humanitarian protection and humanitarian assistance activities both have the same objective, i.e. to safeguard the life and dignity of the persons affected by the armed conflict. Therefore, in practice, they should be seen neither as separate, nor as mutually exclusive: assisting the persons affected by an armed conflict also protects them, and vice versa. Thus, activities of 'humanitarian protection' may simultaneously qualify as activities of 'humanitarian relief'. Therefore, it would go against the purpose of common Article 3 for a Party to the conflict to allow one type of activity (for example, humanitarian relief) while refusing its consent, as a matter of principle, for the other (in this example, humanitarian protection).

811 An indication of what qualifies as 'humanitarian' can be found in the definition of the Fundamental Principle of 'humanity'. This principle, which has also been endorsed by the International Court of Justice,[762] is the first of the seven Fundamental Principles of the Movement.[763] From the definition, it can be inferred that humanitarian activities are all activities that 'prevent and alleviate human suffering wherever it may be found', and the purpose of which is to 'protect life and health and to ensure respect for the human being'.[764] The use of the term 'life' in this definition is without prejudice to the fact that

---

[762] ICJ, *Military and Paramilitary Activities in and against Nicaragua case*, Merits, Judgment, 1986, para. 242.

[763] For further information about the origin and status of the Fundamental Principles, see para. 783.

[764] A further discussion of the principle of 'humanity' and related terms can be found in Jean S. Pictet, 'Commentary on the Fundamental Principles of the Red Cross (I)', *International Review of the Red Cross*, Vol. 19, No. 210, June 1979, pp. 130–149.

humanitarian activities may also be undertaken for the benefit of dead persons, for example when it comes to handling human remains with dignity.[765]

812   Accordingly, in the context of an armed conflict, humanitarian activities are those that seek to preserve the life, security, dignity and physical and mental well-being of persons affected by the conflict, or that seek to restore that well-being if it has been infringed upon. These activities must be concerned with human beings as such. Thus, as also informed by the requirement of impartiality, humanitarian activities and the way in which they are implemented must not be affected by any political or military consideration, or by any consideration related to the person's past behaviour, including behaviour that is potentially punishable on the basis of criminal or other disciplinary norms. Humanitarian activities seek to save human life, integrity and dignity with no other motive than to accomplish this objective. Lastly, those offering to undertake humanitarian activities focus solely on the needs of the persons affected by the conflict.

813   Besides the above general considerations, the High Contracting Parties have not specified which activities may in their eyes qualify as humanitarian activities. This is not surprising given that it would be difficult to anticipate the humanitarian needs that might arise as a result of a particular armed conflict; moreover, as the nature of armed conflicts may change, so may the humanitarian needs they engender, and hence also the services that may be offered on the basis of common Article 3. It is also impossible to generically define, especially when an armed conflict lasts for several years or even decades, which activities in a particular context are of a nature to safeguard the life, security, dignity and physical and mental well-being of the persons affected.

b. Protection

814   In its ordinary meaning, to 'protect' means to 'keep safe from harm or injury'.[766] For its part, humanitarian law has as one of its core objectives to 'protect' people in situations of armed conflict against abuses of power by the Parties to the conflict.

815   Common Article 3(2) provides no guidance on which activities impartial humanitarian organizations may deploy to ensure that the Parties to a non-international armed conflict 'protect' people by complying with the applicable legal framework. Even among impartial humanitarian organizations themselves there are differing views on what constitutes protection activities. For

---

[765] Another definition of the term 'humanitarian' is included in the *Sphere Handbook: Humanitarian Charter and Minimum Standards in Humanitarian Response*, which defines the 'humanitarian imperative' as the imperative to undertake action 'to prevent or alleviate human suffering arising out of disaster or conflict'. See also, *Code of Conduct for the International Red Cross and Red Crescent Movement and Non-Governmental Organisations (NGOs) in Disaster Relief*, 1994, p. 3: 'The humanitarian imperative comes first.'

[766] *Concise Oxford English Dictionary*, 12th edition, Oxford University Press, 2011, p. 1153.

the ICRC and the Inter-Agency Standing Committee,[767] the concept of 'protection' encompasses all activities aimed at ensuring full respect for the rights of the individual in accordance with the letter and spirit of the relevant bodies of law, including international humanitarian law, international human rights and refugee law.[768]

816   Accordingly, in the context of humanitarian law, 'protection activities' refer to all activities that seek to ensure that the authorities and other relevant actors fulfil their obligations to uphold the rights of individuals.[769] Protection activities include those that seek to put an end to or prevent the (re)occurrence of violations of humanitarian law (for example by making representations to the authorities or by making the law better known), and those which seek to ensure that the authorities cease or put a stop to any violations of the norms applicable to them.

817   When pursuing its protection activities in the context of a non-international armed conflict, the ICRC aims to ensure that the applicable rules of humanitarian law and, where relevant, of other applicable law are observed or implemented by all Parties to the conflict. Such activities may include visits to persons deprived of their liberty and engaging in an informed, confidential dialogue with the authorities on their obligations under humanitarian law.[770] More generally, the ICRC may propose to undertake any activity which it deems necessary for the monitoring of the implementation of humanitarian law rules and other legal frameworks which may be relevant.

818   Beyond the Geneva Conventions, the term 'protection' has come to mean different things to different actors, and not all such activities fall within the scope of common Article 3. In practice, this complicates the conceptual analysis. For example, when a military actor such as a unit participating in a UN-authorized peace-enforcement mission has been mandated to 'protect' the civilian

---

[767] The Inter-Agency Standing Committee (IASC) was established in 1992 in response to UN General Assembly Resolution 46/182 on the strengthening of humanitarian assistance. It is an inter-agency forum for coordination, policy development and decision-making involving the key UN and non-UN humanitarian partners.

[768] ICRC, *Professional Standards for Protection Work carried out by Humanitarian and Human Rights Actors in Armed Conflict and Other Situations of Violence*, 2nd edition, ICRC, Geneva, 2013, p. 12. See also Inter-Agency Standing Committee, *IASC Operational Guidelines on the Protection of Persons in Situations of Natural Disasters*, The Brookings – Bern Project on Internal Displacement, Bern, January 2011, p. 5. For further details on the concept of impartiality, see paras 794–797.

[769] ICRC Protection Policy, reproduced in *International Review of the Red Cross*, Vol. 90, No. 871, September 2008, pp. 751–775.

[770] The ICRC works on the basis of confidentiality. It should be noted that this confidentiality does not relate only to the ICRC's protection activities, such as in the context of detention; it is a prerequisite for ICRC humanitarian action as a whole. Confidentiality allows the ICRC to have access to victims of armed conflict and other situations of violence, to engage in a bilateral dialogue with relevant authorities and to protect its beneficiaries as well as its staff in the field. For further information, see ICRC, 'The International Committee of the Red Cross's (ICRC's) confidential approach. Specific means employed by the ICRC to ensure respect for the law by State and non-State authorities', Policy document, December 2012, *International Review of the Red Cross*, Vol. 94, No. 887, Autumn 2012, pp. 1135–1144.

population, different activities and approaches may come into play, including the use of armed force. Despite the use of the same term, 'protection' in this sense is very different from the approach of an impartial humanitarian organization when carrying out protection activities.

c. Relief/assistance

819   In its ordinary meaning, 'relief' means 'the alleviation or removal of pain, anxiety, or distress'.[771] As used in the Geneva Conventions, the term 'relief' mostly applies to activities to address humanitarian needs arising in emergency situations. Within the context of Additional Protocol I, this term needs to be read in conjunction with the broader term 'assistance' used in Article 81(1) thereof, which seeks also to cover longer-term as well as recurrent and even chronic needs.[772] As with protection, neither relief nor assistance are defined in the Geneva Conventions or Additional Protocols. The absence of a generic definition, or of a list of specific activities which would be covered by the term 'assistance', is in line with the fact that needs for humanitarian assistance may not necessarily be the same in every context and may evolve over time.

820   'Assistance activities' refers to all activities, services and the delivery of goods carried out primarily in the fields of health, water, habitat (the creation of a sustainable living environment) and economic security (defined by the ICRC as 'the condition of an individual, household or community that is able to cover its essential needs and unavoidable expenditures in a sustainable manner, according to its cultural standards'), which seek to ensure that persons caught up in an armed conflict can survive and live in dignity.[773] In practice, the type of relief activities will differ depending on who the beneficiaries are and the nature of their needs. Relief activities for persons wounded on the battlefield, for example, will not be the same as those undertaken for persons deprived of their liberty. It is one of the core principles of humanitarian law that, whatever the relief activity for persons not or no longer taking a direct part in hostilities, such activities should never be considered as being of a nature to reinforce the enemy's military capabilities, including, for example, the provision of medical aid to wounded fighters.

821   With regard to both protection and assistance activities, the ICRC uses modes of action, such as persuasion, on a bilateral and confidential basis to

---

[771] *Concise Oxford English Dictionary*, 12th edition, Oxford University Press, 2011, p. 1215.
[772] ICRC Assistance Policy, adopted by the Assembly of the International Committee of the Red Cross on 29 April 2004 and reproduced in *International Review of the Red Cross*, Vol. 86, No. 855, September 2004, pp. 677–693.
[773] ICRC Assistance Policy, adopted by the Assembly of the ICRC on 29 April 2004 and reproduced in *International Review of the Red Cross*, Vol. 86, No. 855, September 2004, pp. 677–693, at 678. For examples of specific activities covered by those terms, as undertaken by the ICRC, see ICRC, *Health Activities: Caring for People Affected by Armed Conflict and Other Situations of Violence*, ICRC, Geneva, 2015, and *Economic Security*, ICRC, Geneva, 2013.

induce the authorities to meet their obligation to comply with the rules applicable to them, including those governing the provision of essential services.[774] Where the ICRC considers that its efforts are not going to bring about a satisfactory, timely response from the authorities, and that the problem is a serious one, it may simultaneously engage in appropriate support to, or substitution for, the direct provision of assistance.[775] When this happens, it should still be kept in mind that it is the Parties to the conflict which bear the primary responsibility for ensuring that humanitarian needs are met.[776] When, despite its efforts and in the case of major and repeated violations of humanitarian law, it fails to convince the authorities to assume their responsibilities in this respect, the ICRC may use other modes of action, including, under certain conditions, a public denunciation.[777]

d. Beneficiaries

822 Common Article 3 does not specify which categories of persons may be the beneficiaries of the proposed humanitarian activities. Interpreted in the context of this provision, it must be understood that humanitarian activities can be undertaken in the first place for the benefit of all persons protected by common Article 3, namely '[p]ersons taking no active part in the hostilities, including members of armed forces who have laid down their arms and those placed *hors de combat* by sickness, wounds, detention, or any other cause'.

---

[774] On confidentiality as the ICRC's main working method also in the field of relief activities, see para. 817 and fn. 770.

[775] ICRC Assistance Policy, adopted by the Assembly of the ICRC on 29 April 2004 and reproduced in *International Review of the Red Cross*, Vol. 86, No. 855, September 2004, pp. 677–693, at 682.

[776] The fact that the ICRC or another impartial humanitarian organization undertakes assistance activities and thereby replaces the authorities or supplements their efforts does not mean that it has a legal obligation to do so. This point is further demonstrated by the use of the words 'may offer' in common Article 3. The ICRC Assistance Policy, adopted by the Assembly of the ICRC on 29 April 2004 and reproduced in *International Review of the Red Cross*, Vol. 86, No. 855, September 2004, pp. 677–693, at 683, clarifies the circumstances in which the ICRC will agree to act as a substitute in providing services directly to the population:

> The decision to substitute for the authorities and to provide a direct service for those affected depends on the urgency and gravity of the needs to be met. This mode of action may be considered when:
> – the needs are great and the responsible authorities are not able to meet them, or where no such authorities exist;
> – the needs are great and the responsible authorities are not willing to meet them;
> – security conditions and/or the risk that indirect assistance might be misused or ill received so require;
> – assistance will help protect the persons affected.

[777] For further information, see ICRC, 'Action by the International Committee of the Red Cross in the event of violations of international humanitarian law or of other fundamental rules protecting persons in situations of violence', *International Review of the Red Cross*, Vol. 87, No. 858, June 2005, pp. 393–400.

823   Armed conflicts affect persons other than those explicitly identified in the list of persons protected by common Article 3. The article does not state, however, that those listed are the only ones for whom the ICRC or other impartial humanitarian organizations can offer their services. Further, for persons to benefit from humanitarian activities, it is not required that they be the victims of a violation of an applicable legal standard. This broad interpretation of who can be the beneficiaries of humanitarian activities is reflected in Article 81(1) of Additional Protocol I, which refers to 'the victims of conflicts', and is confirmed by subsequent practice in non-international armed conflicts: when receiving an offer of services, Parties to the conflict typically do not limit their consent for activities only to persons affected by the armed conflict who qualify as persons covered by common Article 3. Lastly, the foregoing remains without prejudice to the fact that other activities of impartial humanitarian organizations, such as those in the realm of prevention (for example, raising awareness of international humanitarian law) can and are exercised for the benefit of able-bodied combatants.

824   While not explicitly mentioned in common Article 3, the right to offer services can also relate to activities for the benefit of dead persons.[778] Similarly, while not mentioned explicitly as such, it flows from the purpose of common Article 3 that the right to offer services can, depending on the circumstances, also be exercised to protect, or safeguard the functioning of, objects benefiting the wounded and sick, such as medical establishments.

6. Addressees of an offer of services

825   Common Article 3 allows impartial humanitarian organizations to offer their services 'to the Parties to the conflict'. In the context of a non-international armed conflict, this entitles such organizations to offer their services both to a High Contracting Party to the Geneva Conventions, when it is a Party to such a conflict, and to any non-State armed group which is a Party to the conflict. Thus, an offer of services on the basis of common Article 3(2) may not be considered as interference in the armed conflict, and 'shall not affect the legal status of the Parties to the conflict'.[779]

826   While the Parties to the conflict are primarily responsible for addressing humanitarian needs, the purpose of this paragraph is to allow impartial humanitarian organizations to supplement the Parties where the latter do not meet their obligations in this regard.

7. Consent

a. Requirement of consent

827   Common Article 3 states that '[a]n impartial humanitarian body, such as the ICRC, may offer its services to the Parties to the conflict', but does not spell out

---

[778] On the protection afforded dead persons on the basis of common Article 3, see para. 760.
[779] See para. 805 and section L.

by whom, nor how, such an offer is to be responded to. In this respect, common Article 3 differs from Article 18(2) of Additional Protocol II, which explicitly addresses the requirement to obtain the consent 'of the High Contracting Party concerned' with regard to a particular type of humanitarian activities, i.e. relief actions.[780]

828 Despite the silence of common Article 3, it is clear from the logic underpinning international law in general,[781] and humanitarian law in particular, that, in principle, an impartial humanitarian organization will only be able to carry out the proposed humanitarian activities if it has consent to do so.

829 Consent may be manifested through a written reply to the organization which has made the offer but can also be conveyed orally. In the absence of a clearly communicated approval, an impartial humanitarian organization can make sure that the Party to the conflict concerned consents at least implicitly, by acquiescence, to the proposed humanitarian activities duly notified to that Party in advance.

830 In exceptional circumstances, however, seeking and obtaining the consent of the Party concerned may be problematic. This may be the case, for example, when there is uncertainty with regard to the government in control, or when the State authorities have collapsed or ceased to function.

831 In addition, there may be cases where the humanitarian needs are particularly important. Whenever such needs remain unaddressed, the humanitarian imperative would require that humanitarian activities be undertaken by impartial humanitarian organizations, such as the ICRC.

b. Consent may not be arbitrarily withheld

832 The Geneva Conventions provide no guidance on whether there are circumstances in which a Party to a non-international armed conflict may lawfully refuse its consent to an offer of services from an impartial humanitarian organization. In 1949, at least with regard to the consent of the High Contracting Party concerned, the understanding of the requirement to obtain the consent of the Parties to the conflict concerned was set in the context of States' nearly unfettered sovereignty: the High Contracting Party to which an offer of services was made did not see its full discretion curtailed by any rules of international law. Already at the time, however, it was understood that when a Party to the conflict refused an offer of services, it would bear a heavy moral responsibility

---

[780] Similarly, for international armed conflicts to which Additional Protocol I applies, see also Article 70(1) and Article 81(1) of that Protocol. See also 'ICRC Q&A and lexicon on humanitarian access', *International Review of the Red Cross*, Vol. 96, No. 893, March 2014, pp. 359–375 and *International Humanitarian Law and the Challenges of Contemporary Armed Conflicts*, Report prepared for the 32nd International Conference of the Red Cross and Red Crescent, Geneva, 2015, pp. 26–30.

[781] This includes a State's sovereign right to regulate access to its territory.

for any ensuing consequences of a nature or effect to violate its own humanitarian obligations towards the intended beneficiaries.[782]

833   Since 1949, international law in general and humanitarian law in particular have evolved considerably to the extent that a Party to a non-international armed conflict, whether a High Contracting Party or a non-State armed group to which an offer of services is made by an impartial humanitarian body, is not at complete liberty to decide how it responds to such an offer. It has now become accepted that there are circumstances in which a Party to a non-international armed conflict is obliged, as a matter of international law, to grant its consent to an offer of services by an impartial humanitarian organization.

834   In particular, international law as informed by subsequent State practice in the implementation of the Geneva Conventions has now evolved to the point where consent may not be refused on arbitrary grounds.[783] Thus, any impediment(s) to humanitarian activities must be based on valid reasons, and the Party to the conflict whose consent is sought must assess any offer of services in good faith[784] and in line with its international legal obligations in relation to the humanitarian needs of the persons affected by the non-international armed conflict. Thus, where a Party to a non-international armed conflict is

---

[782] Pictet (ed.), *Commentary on the First Geneva Convention*, ICRC, 1952, p. 58: 'The Party to the conflict which [when additional help is necessary] refuses offers of charitable service from outside its frontiers will incur a heavy moral responsibility.'

[783] The same evolution has taken place under customary international humanitarian law; see Henckaerts/Doswald-Beck, commentary on Rule 55, pp. 196–197: '[A] humanitarian organization cannot operate without the consent of the party concerned. However, such consent must not be refused on arbitrary grounds.' This statement is made in the context of a rule dealing with 'humanitarian relief for civilians in need'. Logically, the same rule applies with regard to offers to protect or assist the wounded, sick or shipwrecked, as it does with regard to offers of services made to protect or assist prisoners of war. There is no reason why such offers of services should be regulated differently. Otherwise, this would lead to a manifestly absurd and unreasonable situation: a Party to the conflict would be prohibited from arbitrarily refusing an offer of services for civilians, but could do so when the offer of services was intended to benefit other categories of persons affected by the armed conflict. See also *Official Records of the Diplomatic Conference of Geneva of 1974–1977*, Vol. XII, p. 336, where the representative of the Federal Republic of Germany (endorsed on this point by several other delegates) stated with regard to the words 'subject to the agreement of the Party to the conflict concerned in such relief actions': '[T]hose words did not imply that the Parties concerned had absolute and unlimited freedom to refuse their agreement to relief actions. A Party refusing its agreement must do so for valid reasons, not for arbitrary or capricious ones.' See also Guiding Principles on Internal Displacement (1998), Principle 25(2): 'Consent [to an offer of services from an international humanitarian organization or other appropriate actor] shall not be arbitrarily withheld, particularly when authorities concerned are unable or unwilling to provide the required humanitarian assistance.' See also Henckaerts/Doswald-Beck, commentary on Rule 124(B), p. 445. For two recent examples, see UN Security Council, Res. 2139 concerning Syria, 22 February 2014, preambular para. 10: '*condemning* all cases of denial of humanitarian access, and *recalling* that arbitrary denial of humanitarian access and depriving civilians of objects indispensable to their survival, including wilfully impeding relief supply and access, can constitute a violation of international humanitarian law'; and Res. 2216 concerning Yemen, 14 April 2015, preambular para. 10, which contains identical wording as of 'recalling'.

[784] ICRC, *International Humanitarian Law and the Challenges of Contemporary Armed Conflicts*, Report prepared for the 31st International Conference of the Red Cross and Red Crescent, Geneva, 2011, p. 25.

unwilling or unable to address basic humanitarian needs, international law requires it to accept an offer of services from an impartial humanitarian organization. If such humanitarian needs cannot be met otherwise, the refusal of an offer of services would be arbitrary, and therefore in violation of international law.

835   International law does not provide authoritative clarification on how to interpret the criterion of 'arbitrariness'.[785] This assessment remains context-specific. Nevertheless, there are instances in which a refusal to grant consent will clearly not be considered arbitrary. This will be the case, for example, if the Party to which the offer is made is itself willing and able to address the humanitarian needs and actually does so in an impartial manner. Conversely, refusal may be considered arbitrary if it entails a violation of the Party's obligations under humanitarian law or other fields of international law, such as applicable human rights law. This will be the case, for example, when the Party concerned is unable or unwilling to provide humanitarian assistance to the persons affected by the armed conflict, and even more so if their basic needs enabling them to live in dignity are not met.

836   Further, it must be kept in mind that the use of starvation of the civilian population as a method of warfare is prohibited.[786] Therefore, where a lack of supplies is intended to, or can be expected to, result in the starvation of the civilian population, there is no valid reason to refuse an offer to provide humanitarian relief to the population.[787] No valid reasons to refuse such an offer exist either, for example, when the Party to which the offer of services is made is not able to address the humanitarian needs itself. Similarly, the denial of consent for the purpose, implied or express, of exacerbating civilian suffering would also qualify as arbitrary.

837   A refusal to grant consent may also be considered arbitrary when the refusal is based on adverse distinction, i.e. when it is designed to deprive persons of a certain nationality, race, religious beliefs, class or political opinion of the needed humanitarian relief or protection.

838   Military necessity is no valid ground under humanitarian law to turn down a valid offer of services or to deny in their entirety the humanitarian activities proposed by impartial humanitarian organizations.

839   At all times, the consent of a Party to a non-international armed conflict to the undertaking of humanitarian activities remains without prejudice to that Party's entitlement to impose measures of control. Such measures may include: verifying the nature of the assistance; prescribing technical arrangements for

---

[785] See also 'ICRC Q&A and lexicon on humanitarian access', *International Review of the Red Cross*, Vol. 96, No. 893, March 2014, pp. 359–375, at 369.

[786] See Additional Protocol II, Article 14, and ICRC Study on Customary International Humanitarian Law (2005), Rule 53.

[787] ICRC, *International Humanitarian Law and the Challenges of Contemporary Armed Conflicts*, 2011, p. 25.

the delivery of the assistance; and temporarily restricting humanitarian activities for reasons of imperative military necessity.[788] If verification measures result in the conclusion that the activity is not impartial or not humanitarian in nature, access may be denied. The design and implementation of these controls and restrictions may not, however, be such that, for all practical intents and purposes, they amount to a refusal of consent. In other words, the right of control recognized by humanitarian law should not unduly delay humanitarian operations or make their implementation impossible. In this regard, imperative military necessity may be invoked in exceptional circumstances only in order to regulate – but not prohibit – humanitarian access, and can only temporarily and geographically restrict the freedom of movement of humanitarian personnel.[789] Such reasons of imperative military necessity might include, for example, preventing interference with an ongoing or pending military operation.

c. Obligation to allow and facilitate rapid and unimpeded passage

840   Unlike humanitarian law applicable to international armed conflicts,[790] no treaty-based rules specifically address whether High Contracting Parties, other than those which are party to a non-international armed conflict, have an obligation to allow and facilitate the rapid and unimpeded passage of relief consignments, equipment and personnel. It could be argued, at least tentatively, that this may be considered to be compulsory on the basis of the due diligence component enshrined in common Article 1 ('ensure respect'). In any event, when a humanitarian organization can only reach its beneficiaries by crossing through the territory of a particular State, the humanitarian spirit underpinning the Conventions would suggest a legitimate expectation that that State does not abuse its sovereign rights in a manner that would be harmful to those beneficiaries. If those States were to refuse to allow and facilitate the delivery of relief, it would in effect preclude humanitarian needs from being addressed and thus render the consent given by the Parties to the conflict void.

K. Paragraph 3: Special agreements

1. Introduction

841   Paragraph 3 of common Article 3 invites the Parties to the conflict to conclude agreements to apply, in addition to common Article 3, 'other provisions' of the Geneva Conventions that are not formally applicable in a non-international armed conflict. As such, this paragraph reflects the rather rudimentary character of treaty-based humanitarian law applicable in such conflicts. It is

---

[788] See Additional Protocol I, Article 70(3); see also Henckaerts/Doswald-Beck, commentary on Rule 55, p. 198.

[789] See ICRC Study on Customary International Humanitarian Law (2005), Rule 56.

[790] See Additional Protocol I, Article 70(2)–(3), and the commentary on Article 9, para. 1168.

important to recall in this regard that customary international humanitarian law applies even in the absence of a special agreement between the Parties to a non-international armed conflict.

842   Special agreements 'can provide a plain statement of the law applicable in the context – or of an expanded set of provisions of IHL beyond the law that is already applicable – and secure a clear commitment from the parties to uphold that law'.[791] The benefits of negotiating special agreements 'go beyond the formal terms of the document. That the parties to a conflict have been brought together to negotiate the agreement may itself be of value.'[792]

843   The Hague Convention for the Protection of Cultural Property also encourages the Parties to a non-international armed conflict to 'bring into force, by means of special agreements, all or part of the other provisions of' that Convention.[793] The possibility of concluding special agreements in international armed conflicts is set out in common Article 6 (Article 7 of the Fourth Convention).

2. Historical background

844   One of the original proposals for the application of humanitarian law to non-international armed conflicts during the preparation of the draft conventions for the 1949 Diplomatic Conference was that Parties to such conflicts 'should be invited to declare their readiness to apply the principles of the Convention'.[794] This proposal contains the origin of the concept of using a special agreement to bring all of the provisions of the Conventions into force for the Parties to a non-international armed conflict. This possibility found a prominent place in almost all of the iterations of what was at the time the proposed draft article 2(4) during the Diplomatic Conference[795] and was finally retained as paragraph 3 of common Article 3.

845   A historical example of the use of such agreements in a non-international armed conflict, which was not based on any treaty provision as none existed at the time, occurred during the Spanish Civil War (1936–39), when the Parties signed parallel agreements with the ICRC accepting that it provide humanitarian services during that conflict.[796]

[791] ICRC, *Increasing Respect for International Humanitarian Law in Non-International Armed Conflicts*, p. 16.

[792] *Ibid.* p. 17; see also Bell, p. 20.

[793] Hague Convention for the Protection of Cultural Property (1954), Article 19(2). Paragraph 4 of that article furthermore confirms that concluding such agreements does not affect the legal status of the Parties.

[794] *Report of the Preliminary Conference of National Societies of 1946*, p. 15.

[795] *Final Record of the Diplomatic Conference of Geneva of 1949*, Vol. II-B, pp. 120–127. See also Siordet, pp. 198–200.

[796] 'Comité International: Guerre civile en Espagne', *Revue internationale de la Croix-Rouge*, Vol. 67, No. 409, 1936, pp. 758–759. While all the Parties accepted the provision of humanitarian services by the ICRC, in other respects the agreements differed slightly from one another.

3. Discussion

846   Common Article 3(3) states that 'the Parties to the conflict should further endeavour to bring into force, by means of special agreements, all or part of the other provisions of the present Convention'. Read narrowly, the paragraph may seem to suggest that only an agreement that explicitly brings into force other provisions of one or more of the four Geneva Conventions may be considered to be a special agreement and that agreements that go beyond the provisions in the Geneva Conventions may not be considered to be special agreements. As the purpose of the provision is to encourage Parties to an armed conflict to agree to a more comprehensive set of norms that protect those who are not or no longer taking part in hostilities, however, special agreements providing for the implementation of customary international humanitarian law, or which encompass a broader set of norms than those set down in the Geneva Conventions, in particular those of Additional Protocol I, may be considered special agreements under common Article 3. In addition, agreements affirming that the Parties will not use a certain kind of weapon, or confirming or establishing rules on the conduct of hostilities, may also constitute special agreements.

847   Agreements may be merely declaratory in nature, in that they may recognize customary or treaty law obligations that are already applicable, or they may also make more detailed arrangements to implement new or existing obligations. What counts is that the provisions brought into force between the Parties serve to protect the victims of armed conflict. Indeed, a variety of types of agreements can be considered to be special agreements for the purposes of this article. Moreover, in practice a number of different means of expressing a commitment to respect various humanitarian law norms have been used by non-State armed groups and other actors.[797]

848   The Parties 'should...endeavour' to make such agreements. Thus, more than merely pointing out the possibility for the Parties to conclude such agreements, the provision encourages the Parties to make a serious effort to bring into force obligations to protect victims and to limit the suffering caused by the armed conflict. The pressing nature of this exhortation is confirmed by the French version of the article, which uses the word 's'efforceront'.

849   The most straightforward case of a special agreement under common Article 3 is an agreement signed between a non-State armed group and the State against which it is engaged in hostilities or between two non-State armed groups fighting one another. Examples include the agreements concluded between the Parties to the armed conflicts in the former Yugoslavia in the 1990s to bring many provisions of the Geneva Conventions and some provisions of the Additional Protocols into force.[798] Other such agreements include

---

[797] See paras 855–857 of this commentary.
[798] Memorandum of Understanding on the Application of IHL between Croatia and the Socialist Federal Republic of Yugoslavia (1991); Jakovljevic, pp. 108–110.

the Humanitarian Exchange Accord between the Fuerzas Armadas Revolucionarias de Colombia (FARC) and the Government of Colombia, concluded
in 2001;[799] the Humanitarian Cease Fire Agreement on the Conflict in Darfur, concluded in 2004;[800] the Ceasefire Code of Conduct between the Government of Nepal and CPN (Maoist), concluded in 2006;[801] and the Comprehensive Agreement on Respect for Human Rights and IHL in the Philippines,
concluded in 1998.[802] Such agreements have been concluded in the context of
ongoing armed conflicts and aim to regulate hostilities, allow for the delivery
of humanitarian assistance, or lessen the negative effects of the conflict on the
population, among other things.

850   A peace agreement, ceasefire or other accord may also constitute a special
agreement for the purposes of common Article 3, or a means to implement
common Article 3, if it contains clauses that bring into existence further obligations drawn from the Geneva Conventions and/or their Additional Protocols.
In this respect, it should be recalled that 'peace agreements' concluded with a
view to bringing an end to hostilities may contain provisions drawn from other
humanitarian law treaties, such as the granting of an amnesty for fighters who
have carried out their operations in accordance with the laws and customs of
war, the release of all captured persons, or a commitment to search for the
missing.[803] If they contain provisions drawn from humanitarian law, or if they
implement humanitarian law obligations already incumbent on the Parties,
such agreements, or the relevant provisions as the case may be, may constitute
special agreements under common Article 3. This is particularly important
given that hostilities do not always come to an end with the conclusion of a
peace agreement.

851   Likewise, an agreement may contain obligations drawn from human rights
law and help to implement humanitarian law. For instance, it may aim to make
the obligation to conduct fair trials more precise or may draw on international
human rights law in another way.[804] In some cases, a rule under human rights

---

[799] Government-FARC Humanitarian Exchange Accord, 2 June 2001, available at https://www.c-r
.org/accord.

[800] N'Djamena Humanitarian Ceasefire Agreement on the Conflict in Darfur (2004); see also the
accompanying N'Djamena Protocol on the Establishment of Humanitarian Assistance in Darfur (2004).

[801] The Code of Conduct for Ceasefire agreed between the Government of Nepal and the CPN
(Maoist), Gokarna, 25 May 2006.

[802] Comprehensive Agreement on Respect for Human Rights and IHL in the Philippines (1998).

[803] Additional Protocol II, Article 6(5): 'At the end of hostilities, the authorities in power shall
endeavour to grant the broadest possible amnesty to persons who have participated in the
armed conflict, or those deprived of their liberty for reasons related to the armed conflict,
whether they are interned or detained.' See also ICRC Study on Customary International
Humanitarian Law (2005), Rule 159. See e.g. Cotonou Agreement on Liberia (1993). See, however, Comprehensive Agreement on Human Rights in Guatemala (1994), Article IX(2) ('These
statements by the Parties do not constitute a special agreement, in the terms of article 3 (Common), paragraph 2, second subparagraph of the Geneva Conventions of 1949.').

[804] Marco Sassòli, 'Possible Legal Mechanisms to Improve Compliance by Armed Groups with
International Humanitarian Law and International Human Rights Law', Paper presented at

law and humanitarian law may be identical, such that it is immaterial whether the Parties to the agreement have referred to the rule as stemming from one or the other body of law. Again, any provisions in such an agreement that implement or bring into force humanitarian law may constitute special agreements for the purposes of common Article 3.

852   Special agreements may come in a number of different forms and formats. Parallel declarations or 'triangular agreements' between each Party to the conflict and a third Party such as a State or an international organization may also be special agreements, depending on the circumstances. What counts is the expression of consent of the Parties to respect or implement humanitarian law or specific obligations. This may be done via parallel declarations that were negotiated together and that contain terms showing a willingness to be bound.[805] No matter whether these are considered to be special agreements in the sense of common Article 3, when a Party to a conflict concludes an agreement with a humanitarian organization to allow it to perform humanitarian activities, such agreements may help that Party to implement its obligations under humanitarian law or bring into force other provisions of the Conventions.

853   If an agreement is in written form, it will likely be easier to prove the precise terms of the commitments made by the Parties. This is certainly the case for agreements that implement a broad scope of humanitarian law obligations. In addition, agreements setting out safety zones or hospital zones, or setting out judicial guarantees, for example, should be in writing.[806] However, in some circumstances, on a narrow issue, it may not be essential to have an agreement in writing if it is done in such a way that it can be relied upon. Thus, for example, a clear commitment to allow access for the provision of humanitarian relief, agreed by all Parties and widely broadcast or otherwise effectively communicated, will constitute a special agreement for the purposes of common Article 3. That said, the agreement should be sufficiently detailed so that obligations and expectations are clear.[807]

---

the Armed Groups Conference, Vancouver, 13–15 November 2003, p. 10. Confirming the inclusion of human rights law obligations in agreements, Sivakumaran, 2012, pp. 131–132. See also Comprehensive Agreement on Respect for Human Rights and IHL in the Philippines (1998).

[805] This was the case of one of the commonly cited historical examples of a special agreement in a non-international armed conflict, between the ICRC and each of the Parties to the Spanish Civil War. As a more recent example, parallel unilateral declarations were made by the Government of the Democratic Republic of the Congo and the non-State armed group M23 in December 2013: see UN Security Council, *Report of the Secretary-General on the implementation of the Peace, Security and Cooperation Framework for the Democratic Republic of the Congo and the Region*, 23 December 2013, UN Doc. S/2013/773, paras 3–11.

[806] See e.g. the commentaries on Article 23 of the First Convention, and Article 14 of the Fourth Convention.

[807] In addition to the benefits of detailed agreements in general, it is worth recalling that 'mere awareness of IHL . . . [is] not sufficient to produce a direct impact on the behaviour of the combatants'; ICRC, *The Roots of Behaviour in War*, p. 11.

854 It must be underscored that even if the Parties have agreed to a more lim-ited number of additional provisions, they nevertheless remain bound by all applicable humanitarian law norms. Moreover, such agreements cannot dero-gate from applicable humanitarian law so as to lessen the protection of that law. This conclusion flows from a plain reading of the text of common Arti-cle 3, which states that 'each Party to the conflict shall be bound to apply, as a minimum' the provisions of the article.[808] This approach is also taken in common Article 6 (Article 7 in the Fourth Convention), which specifies that special agreements in international armed conflict may not adversely affect the situation of the persons protected by the Conventions, nor restrict the rights conferred upon them.

855 It should be noted in addition that Parties to non-international armed con-flicts often conclude agreements with other Parties to the conflict, with their allies, and with international organizations. Many, but not all, of these agree-ments may constitute special agreements within the meaning of common Arti-cle 3. The purpose of the provision is to encourage Parties to a non-international armed conflict to agree to a more comprehensive set of norms that protect those who are not or no longer taking part in hostilities, as well as to better imple-ment existing obligations. While agreements providing for the implementation of customary international humanitarian law, or which encompass a broader set of norms than those set down in the Geneva Conventions that are con-cluded between allies, rather than between the Parties to the conflict, are not special agreements in the sense of the provision, they may nevertheless be a welcome and effective means to ensure respect for humanitarian law.

856 Non-State armed groups and governments have also signed declarations or agreements with international organizations with special expertise in order to commit the group or State to improving its compliance with respect to a spe-cific issue. Some of these may be construed as a type of unilateral declaration, while others may be two or more party agreements.[809] For example, a faction of the Sudan Liberation Army signed an 'action plan' with UNICEF in which it 'pledged to end recruitment and release all children under the age of 18'.[810] The UN Office of the Special Representative of the Secretary-General for Children

---

[808] Furthermore, Parties may not derogate from obligations under customary international humanitarian law, nor from the provisions of Additional Protocol II where it is applicable, or other humanitarian law treaties applicable in non-international armed conflict.

[809] ICRC, *Improving Compliance with International Humanitarian Law, ICRC Expert Seminars*, October 2003, p. 21; Roberts/Sivakumaran, p. 142.

[810] UN Security Council, Annual report on the activities of the Security Council Working Group on Children and Armed Conflict, established pursuant to resolution 1612 (2005) (1 July 2007 to 30 June 2008), annexed to UN Doc. S/2008/455, 11 July 2008, para. 11(c). In a similar vein, a tripartite agreement between the Government of the Central African Republic, the Union des forces démocratiques pour le rassemblement (UDFR) and UNICEF was signed in June 2007, 'in which the UDFR agreed to separate and release all children associated with its armed group; and facilitate their reintegration'; see also UN General Assembly, *Report of the Secretary-General on children and armed conflict*, UN Doc. A/63/785-S/2009/158, 26 March 2009. The latter two documents are cited in Bellal/Casey-Maslen, p. 190.

and Armed Conflict has signed such 'action plans' with a number of other non-State armed groups and States to prevent and/or halt the use or recruitment of children in armed conflicts.[811] In a similar vein, non-State armed groups have signed deeds of commitment with a non-governmental organization, Geneva Call, in which they pledged their commitment to respect humanitarian law in specific areas.[812] Thus, an express commitment need not be between the Parties to the conflict in order to clarify obligations of humanitarian law for that Party.

857   Indeed, it is not uncommon for non-State armed groups to undertake to respect humanitarian law through various mechanisms. These include the special agreements provided for in common Article 3, as well as unilateral declarations, codes of conduct, or the signing of a 'deed of commitment' or 'action plan', to name a few.[813] All of these mechanisms provide 'an opportunity for a party to a conflict to make an "express commitment" of their willingness or intention to comply with IHL' and should be encouraged.[814] Especially when these are detailed and accompanied by sincere and concrete efforts to implement the commitments contained therein, they can be effective in strengthening respect for humanitarian law.[815] However, the absence of any such commitment does not reduce the obligations of non-State armed groups to abide by treaty and customary international law.

---

[811] UN General Assembly, Report of the Secretary-General on children and armed conflict, UN Doc. A/66/782-S/2012/261, 26 April 2012; *Report of the UN Secretary-General on children and armed conflict*, UN Doc A/67/845-S/2013/245, 15 May 2013 (reissued 30 July 2013). See also Office of the Special Representative of the Secretary-General for Children and Armed Conflict, Action Plans with Armed Forces and Armed Groups, http://childrenandarmedconflict.un.org/our-work/action-plans/.

[812] Geneva Call has three Deeds of Commitment: Deed of Commitment for Adherence to a Total Ban on Anti-Personnel Mines and for Cooperation in Mine Action; Deed of Commitment for the Protection of Children from the Effects of Armed Conflict; and Deed of Commitment for the Prohibition of Sexual Violence in Situations of Armed Conflict and towards the Elimination of Gender Discrimination, http://www.genevacall.org/how-we-work/deed-of-commitment/.

[813] For a list of such commitments, see Sivakumaran, 2012, pp. 143–151, and more generally pp. 107–152. See also ICRC, 'A collection of codes of conduct issued by armed groups', *International Review of the Red Cross*, Vol. 93, No. 882, June 2011. For examples of unilateral declarations, codes of conduct and special agreements, see http://theirwords.org/, a database maintained by the non-governmental organization Geneva Call. See also Ewumbue-Monono, pp. 905–924; Veuthey, pp. 139–147; Roberts/Sivakumaran, pp. 107–152; and ICRC, *Increasing Respect for International Humanitarian Law in Non-International Armed Conflicts*, Geneva, 2008. These references provide some practical examples of the types of subjects on which special agreements have been made.

[814] ICRC, *Increasing Respect for International Humanitarian Law in Non-International Armed Conflicts*. Draft article 38 of Additional Protocol II, which was deleted during the general shortening of the Protocol at the Diplomatic Conference, also provided for the making of unilateral declarations; see *Official Records of the Diplomatic Conference of Geneva of 1974–1977*, Vol. IX, pp. 245–246 paras 45–50. See also 27th International Conference of the Red Cross and Red Crescent, Res. 1, Adoption of the Declaration and the Plan of Action, Annex 2: Plan of Action for the years 2000–2003, para. 1.1.3: 'Organised armed groups in non-international armed conflict are urged to respect international humanitarian law. They are called upon to declare their intention to respect that law and teach it to their forces.'

[815] ICRC, *Increasing Respect for International Humanitarian Law in Non-International Armed Conflicts*; Sassòli 2010, p. 30; Roberts/Sivakumaran, pp. 126–134.

858   Whether a Party has taken on additional obligations under humanitarian law through a special agreement, unilateral declaration or other means of commitment, including in a code of conduct, it should be able to respect the obligations it has undertaken. This ensures that the agreements are not empty words that, in the end, may lessen respect for humanitarian law.

859   An impartial humanitarian organization such as the ICRC may offer its services to facilitate the conclusion of special agreements or to help to implement them.[816] While there may be no general obligation to conclude a special agreement, in some circumstances it may be a vital means of respecting existing obligations under humanitarian law, such as enabling the wounded and sick to be collected and cared for or to address the fate of the missing. It is also important to note that, where Parties to an agreement wish to assign a specific monitoring or oversight role to a third party, they should ensure that they have the consent of that entity for the role in question.

860   Lastly, it is useful to recall that the capacity to make special agreements is closely linked to the observation in common Article 3(4) that 'the application of the preceding provisions shall not affect the legal status of the Parties to the conflict'. Thus, it cannot be deduced that the recognition of the capacity to conclude special agreements bringing into force additional obligations in the Conventions implies recognition of belligerency or in any way signifies that the non-State Party to the agreement possesses full international legal personality.[817] It is not uncommon for Parties to special agreements to reiterate that the agreement does not affect their legal status.[818] Even if it is considered that special agreements do not prevail over national law in the same way that an international treaty might, national law should not be invoked to hinder the implementation of a special agreement negotiated in good faith by the Parties to the conflict.[819]

---

[816] For example, the ICRC was involved in the conclusion of the 1991–92 agreements in the conflicts in the former Yugoslavia. See also common Article 3(2) on the right of an impartial humanitarian body to offer its services to the Parties to the conflict.

[817] See van Steenberghe, pp. 51–65.

[818] In addition, a provision to this effect is included in Geneva Call's standard Deeds of Commitment.

[819] Article 3 of the 1969 Vienna Convention on the Law of Treaties specifies that the Convention does not apply to (but at the same time acknowledges the existence of) 'international agreements concluded between States and other subjects of international law or between such other subjects of international law'. Whether or not they constitute treaties under international law, special agreements concluded between Parties to non-international armed conflicts arguably create obligations under international law. The ICTY considered that at least one of the special agreements between the Parties to the conflict under its jurisdiction was binding and, in the words of one commentator, 'akin to treaties'; the International Commission of Inquiry on Darfur came to a similar conclusion with respect to agreements between the Sudan Liberation Movement/Army and the Justice and Equality Movement; see Sivakumaran, 2012, p. 109. While an ICTY trial chamber relied on a special agreement as a source of legal obligations to sustain a conviction in one case, on appeal the Tribunal preferred to base the same obligation on customary international humanitarian law. See *Galić* Trial Judgment, 2003, and Appeal Judgment, 2006. More frequently, the Tribunal has relied on such agreements for evidentiary purposes; see Vierucci, 2011, p. 423. In some cases, agreements between non-State armed groups

L. Paragraph 4: Legal status of the Parties to the conflict

1. Introduction

861 This clause, which affirms that '[t]he application of the preceding provisions shall not affect the legal status of the Parties to the conflict', is essential. It addresses the fear that the application of the Convention, even to a very limited extent, in cases of non-international armed conflict may interfere with the *de jure* government's lawful suppression of armed activity. This clause makes absolutely clear that the object of the Convention is purely humanitarian, that it is in no way concerned with the internal affairs of States, and that it merely ensures respect for the essential rules of humanity which all nations consider as valid everywhere, in all circumstances.

2. Historical background

862 The drafting history of the provision is straightforward. It was first suggested at the Conference of Government Experts convened by the ICRC in 1947 and was reintroduced with very little change in all successive drafts.[820] Without it, neither common Article 3, nor any other article in its place, could have been adopted. It should be recalled, however, that the scope of humanitarian law that was to apply in non-international armed conflicts changed dramatically from the beginning of the process to the end. The original proposal for paragraph 4 of draft article 2 discussed at the 1949 Diplomatic Conference stated:

In all cases of armed conflict not of an international character which may occur in the territory of one or more of the High Contracting Parties, each of the adversaries shall be bound to implement the provisions of the present Convention. The Convention shall be applicable in these circumstances, whatever the legal status of the Parties to the conflict and without prejudice thereto.[821]

863 For reasons explained above, instead of agreeing to apply the whole of the Conventions in non-international armed conflicts, the delegates at the Diplomatic Conference settled on common Article 3 as we know it today.[822] The assertions by delegates at the Conference of the implications of applying humanitarian law to non-international armed conflicts, in particular that it would 'appear to give the status of belligerents to insurgents, whose right to

and States have not been considered to be treaties under international law, but nevertheless to be 'capable of creating binding obligations and rights between the parties to the agreement in municipal law'; SCSL, *Kallon and Kamara* Decision on Challenge to Jurisdiction, 2004, para. 49. This decision has been criticized, however: Cassese, pp. 1134–1135. See also Colombia, Constitutional Court, *Constitutional Case No. C-225/95*, Judgment, 1995, para. 17. For a discussion of the status of special agreements, see also Vierucci, 2015, pp. 515–517.

[820] *Report of the Conference of Government Experts of 1947*, p. 9.
[821] See *Draft Conventions adopted by the 1948 Stockholm Conference*, p. 10.
[822] For details, see section B.

wage war could not be recognized' must be seen in this light.[823] It was not that the application of any humanitarian law rules whatsoever posed a problem, but in their view applying the whole body of the law could do.[824]

3. Discussion

864   This provision confirms that the application of common Article 3 – or, perhaps more accurately, a State's acknowledgement that common Article 3 and customary international humanitarian law obligations apply to a conflict involving a non-State armed group – does not constitute any recognition by the *de jure* government that the adverse Party has any status or authority of any kind; it does not limit the government's right to fight a non-State armed group using all lawful means; and it does not affect its right to prosecute, try and sentence its adversaries for their crimes, in accordance with its own laws and commensurate with any other international legal obligations that may apply to such procedures.[825] The same holds true in respect of the conclusion of special agreements. Indeed, the application of common Article 3 to a non-international armed conflict does not confer belligerent status or increased authority on the non-State armed group.

865   Despite the clarity of this provision, States sometimes nevertheless continue to have reservations about a situation being classified as a non-international armed conflict, often due to a concern that such classification somehow confers a certain status or legitimacy on non-State armed groups, be it legal or political.[826] This may be due in part to a lack of willingness to sit down to negotiate on a particular issue with a non-State Party to a conflict that a government has labelled as terrorist, or engage with a non-State Party on wider issues such as a peace settlement. Importantly, it is not necessarily because of a lack of willingness to apply and respect humanitarian law.[827] Indeed, although States may continue to deny the existence of a non-international armed conflict for a variety of reasons, including that by doing so they would legitimize the non-State Party to the armed conflict, the principle that the application of

---

[823] *Final Record of the Diplomatic Conference of Geneva of 1949*, Vol. II-B, p. 10.

[824] States were in particular concerned about the application of prisoner-of-war status; *ibid.* pp. 10–11. The fact that the application of humanitarian law has no impact on the legal status of the Parties must thus be understood in the narrower sense relating to the status of belligerents, and not the wider question of the existence (or not) of the international legal personality of non-State armed groups. On this debate, see Moir, pp. 65–66.

[825] See, however, Article 6(5) of Additional Protocol II, which urges the authorities in power, at the end of hostilities, to 'endeavour to grant the broadest possible amnesty to persons who have participated in the armed conflict, or those deprived of their liberty for reasons related to the armed conflict, whether they are interned or detained'. See also ICRC Study on Customary International Humanitarian Law (2005), Rule 159.

[826] United Kingdom, *Manual of the Law of Armed Conflict*, 2004, para. 15.3.1; Fleck, pp. 589–591, para. 1202.

[827] Sivakumaran, 2012, pp. 209 and 546–549.

humanitarian law does not change the status of the Parties is widely accepted today.[828]

866   This provision confirms that, while humanitarian law provides for equal rights and obligations of the Parties to the conflict in the treatment of people in their power, it does not confer legitimacy on non-State armed groups that are Parties to a conflict.

867   Furthermore, it serves to underline that, as international humanitarian law applies based on the facts, regardless of whether a State qualifies the members of a non-State armed group as 'terrorists' or its actions as 'terrorism', humanitarian law applies if and when the conditions for its applicability are met.

868   The denial that groups that a State has labelled as 'terrorist' may be a Party to a non-international armed conflict within the meaning of humanitarian law carries the risk that the non-State armed group loses an incentive to abide by that body of law. This in turn reduces the ability of humanitarian law to serve its protective purpose. Humanitarian law seeks to protect civilians and all those who are not directly participating in hostilities; it does this in part by obliging Parties to distinguish between civilians and civilian objects and military objectives.

869   Nothing since the introduction of common Article 3 in 1949 has altered the fact that the applicability of humanitarian law to situations of non-international armed conflicts does not affect the legal status or enhance the legitimacy of non-State armed groups. This remains as essential today as it was at that time, as any other interpretation will almost inevitably lead States to deny the applicability of common Article 3 and thereby undermine its humanitarian objective.

M. Criminal aspects and compliance

1. Introduction

870   Common Article 3 lacks compliance mechanisms that were included in the Conventions for international armed conflicts, such as the Protecting Powers, the conciliation procedure and the enquiry procedure. Most importantly, it does not provide for the criminal responsibility of individuals who violate its provisions. However, both treaty and customary international law have evolved significantly over the past decades and filled some of these lacunae.

---

[828] A similar provision has been adopted in the context of the 1980 Convention on Certain Conventional Weapons and in other humanitarian law treaties. See Hague Convention for the Protection of Cultural Property (1954), Article 19(4); Amended Protocol II to the Convention on Certain Conventional Weapons (1996), Article 1(6); Second Protocol to the Hague Convention for the Protection of Cultural Property (1999), Article 22(6); and Amendment to Article 1 of the 1980 Convention on Certain Conventional Weapons (2001), Article 1(6). See also the opinion of the Constitutional Court of Colombia on the conformity of Additional Protocol II: *Constitutional Case No. C-225/95*, Judgment, 1995, para. 15.

2. Individual criminal responsibility in non-international armed conflicts

871 The 1949 Diplomatic Conference discussed only briefly the issue of individual criminal responsibility for violations of common Article 3. A few States wished for common Article 3 to include the possibility for States to consider violations of this article as war crimes.[829] These States were mainly those which supported the application of most of the provisions of the 1949 Conventions to non-international armed conflicts. However, at the time, most States rejected this proposal.[830] The majority view was that, except for Article 3, the provisions of the four Geneva Conventions were not applicable in non-international armed conflicts.[831] Similarly, the discussions on the grave breaches provisions during the 1949 Diplomatic Conference show that their application in non-international armed conflicts was not envisaged.[832]

872 Prosecutions of individuals for serious violations of common Article 3 were left to the discretion of States on the basis of their domestic criminal codes. They seldom occurred until the 1990s.[833] The adoption of the Statutes of the International Criminal Tribunals for the former Yugoslavia in 1993 and Rwanda in 1994 marked a turning point in the recognition of individual criminal responsibility in non-international armed conflicts, including for serious violations of common Article 3. The debates in the UN Security Council leading to the establishment of these Tribunals illustrate the change in State practice, as some members of the Security Council understood Article 3 of the ICTY Statute, on violations of the laws or customs of war, to include:

all obligations under humanitarian law agreements in force in the territory of the former Yugoslavia at the time the acts were committed, including common article 3 of the 1949 Geneva Conventions, and the 1977 Additional Protocols to these Conventions.[834]

---

[829] This was the view expressed by the Italian delegate; see *Final Record of the Diplomatic Conference of Geneva of 1949*, Vol. II-B, p. 49.

[830] See La Haye, 2008, p. 133.

[831] See the view expressed by the Rapporteur of the Special Committee, Mr Bolla, during the discussions on common Article 3: 'The Special Committee voiced a definite opinion that the provisions of the Conventions were, on principle, not applicable to civil war, and that only certain stipulations expressly mentioned would be applicable to such conflicts.' *Final Record of the Diplomatic Conference of Geneva of 1949*, Vol. II-B, pp. 36–37.

[832] See e.g. the Fourth Report drawn up by the Special Committee of the Joint Committee, where it is made clear that the grave breaches regime is only applicable to the gravest violations in international armed conflicts; *ibid.* pp. 114–118.

[833] On the absence of domestic prosecutions for serious violations of common Article 3, see Perna, pp. 139–143.

[834] Statement by the US representative in UN Security Council, *Provisional verbatim record of the three thousand two hundred and seventeenth meeting*, UN Doc. S/PV.3217, 25 May 1993, p. 15. See also the statement by France on p. 11 ('[T]he expression "laws or customs of war" used in Article 3 of the Statute covers specifically, in the opinion of France, all the obligations that flow from the humanitarian law agreements in force on the territory of the former Yugoslavia at the time when the offences were committed'), and by the UK on p. 18.

873   The ICTY Appeals Chamber interpreted Article 3 of the ICTY Statute to be 'a general clause covering all violations of humanitarian law' and specifically to include serious violations of common Article 3 and other customary law rules applicable in non-international armed conflicts.[835] It found that:

> [C]ustomary international law imposes criminal liability for serious violations of common Article 3, as supplemented by other general principles and rules on the protection of victims of internal conflict, and for breaching certain fundamental principles and rules regarding means and methods of combat in civil strife.[836]

874   The ICTR Statute is the first international instrument to criminalize serious violations of common Article 3.[837] In 1998, despite the opposition of a small group of States,[838] a large majority of States supported the inclusion of war crimes in non-international armed conflicts within the subject-matter jurisdiction of the ICC, in particular the inclusion of serious violations of common Article 3.[839] As a result, the ICC Statute contains an important list of

---

[835] ICTY, *Tadić* Decision on the Defence Motion for Interlocutory Appeal on Jurisdiction, 1995, para. 89.

[836] *Ibid.* para. 134. These conclusions were shared by the ICTR Trial Chamber in *Akayesu*, where it took the view that: '[I]t is clear that the authors of such egregious violations must incur individual criminal responsibility for their deeds.... The Chamber, therefore, concludes the violation of these norms entails, as a matter of customary international law, individual responsibility for the perpetrator.' *Akayesu* Trial Judgment, 1998, paras 616–617.

[837] See UN Security Council, *Report of the Secretary-General pursuant to paragraph 5 of Security Council Resolution 955 (1994)*, UN Doc. S/1995/134, 13 February 1995, para. 12, stating that 'the [ICTR] statute ... for the first time criminalizes common article 3 of the four Geneva Conventions'. Interestingly, at the time of the adoption of the ICTR Statute in 1994, the Special Rapporteur of the UN Commission on Human Rights on the situation of human rights in Rwanda reported that: 'Many of the acts alleged, such as murder, political assassination, execution of hostages and other inhuman acts committed against the civilian population or unarmed soldiers by the armed forces of the two parties to the conflict constitute war crimes in direct violation of the four Geneva Conventions of 12 August 1949, which have been ratified by Rwanda, and their common article 3.' See UN Commission on Human Rights, *Report on the situation of human rights in Rwanda*, UN Doc. E/CN.4/1995/7, 28 June 1994, para. 54.

[838] See e.g. the statement made by India to the UN Committee of the Whole on 18 June 1998, averring that 'there could not be a homogeneous structure of treatment of international and non-international armed conflicts so long as sovereign States existed'. UN Committee of the Whole, *Summary record of the 5th meeting*, UN Doc. A/CONF.183/C.1/SR.5, 20 November 1998, p. 13.

[839] See e.g. the statement by Bangladesh on 18 June 1998: '[Bangladesh] strongly supported giving full effect to the common article 3 of the 1949 Geneva Conventions.... [T]he distinction between international and non-international conflicts was becoming increasingly irrelevant, viewed in terms of universal peace and security.' UN Diplomatic Conference of Plenipotentiaries on the Establishment of an International Criminal Court, *Summary record of the 7th plenary meeting*, UN Doc. A/CONF.183/SR.7, 25 January 1999, pp. 4–5. On another occasion, the US representative stated: 'The United States strongly believes that serious violations of the elementary customary norms reflected in common Article 3 should be the centerpiece of the ICC's subject matter jurisdiction with regard to non-international armed conflicts.... The United States urges that there should be a section ... covering other rules regarding the conduct of hostilities in non-international armed conflicts.' Statement by the US delegation to the Preparatory Committee on the Establishment of an International Criminal Court, 23 March 1998, http://www.amicc.org/docs/USDel3_23_98.pdf. For more examples and analysis, see La Haye, 2008, pp. 162–164.

war crimes applicable in non-international armed conflicts, including serious violations of common Article 3.[840]

875   Today, the principle of individual criminal responsibility for war crimes in non-international armed conflicts is part of customary international law. A large number of national laws, including ICC implementing legislation and criminal codes, as well as military manuals, qualify serious violations of common Article 3 as war crimes. Numerous unilateral statements made by States in the Security Council or during the negotiations that led to the adoption of the ICC Statute show that, for most States, practice is coupled with a strong belief that perpetrators of serious violations of common Article 3 should be held criminally responsible.[841]

876   The recognition that serious violations of common Article 3 amount to war crimes has opened new avenues for both international courts and tribunals and domestic courts to prosecute alleged offenders. International courts and tribunals, such as the ICTY, the ICTR, the ICC, the SCSL and the Iraqi Special Tribunal, have been set up to prosecute alleged offenders for serious violations of common Article 3, among other international crimes.

877   Alleged perpetrators can be prosecuted by the courts of the State on whose territory the offences were committed, the State of nationality of the victim, or the State of their own nationality. In non-international armed conflicts, these three possible States will mostly be one and the same, namely the territorial State. The national courts of the territorial State, when functioning, seem to be the best fora for such cases. They have direct access to evidence and witnesses and knowledge of local customs and geography. Their judgments carry both a real and symbolic weight: the victims can see justice being done, and this can have a positive impact on reconciliation, while also acting as a deterrent to future criminal conduct.[842] However, governments do not always pursue this solution; those in power might protect suspected criminals, be the perpetrators of war crimes themselves or vote amnesty laws. Even if willing to prosecute, governments may lack the financial, technical or human resources to carry out fair trials.[843]

878   The grave breaches regime has not been extended to serious violations of common Article 3. Thus, States are not obliged, on the basis of the Geneva

---

[840] See ICC Statute (1998), Article 8(2)(c), covering serious violations of common Article 3, and Article 8(2)(e), listing other serious violations of the laws and customs applicable in armed conflicts not of an international character.

[841] For a detailed study of this topic and the establishment of this principle as a customary rule, see La Haye, 2008, pp. 131–251. See also ICRC Study on Customary International Humanitarian Law (2005), Rules 151 and 156; Moir, pp. 233–235; and Sivakumaran, 2012, pp. 475–478.

[842] There have been some national prosecutions in countries that have suffered from non-international armed conflicts, such as Bosnia and Herzegovina, Croatia, Ethiopia, Kosovo and Rwanda. For an overview of national prosecutions, see La Haye, 2008, pp. 256–270. For the many prosecutions carried out in Bosnia and Herzegovina, see http://www.sudbih.gov.ba/?jezik=e.

[843] See La Haye, 2008, p. 216; Morris, pp. 29–39; and Blewitt, pp. 298–300.

Conventions, to search for alleged perpetrators of these serious violations, regardless of their nationality, and to bring them before their own courts.[844] However, it is accepted in customary law that States have a right to vest universal jurisdiction over war crimes, including serious violations of common Article 3, in their domestic courts.[845]

879   Furthermore, States are under an obligation to investigate war crimes allegedly committed by their nationals or armed forces or on their territory and, if appropriate, prosecute the suspects.[846] This customary obligation is applicable in both international and non-international armed conflicts.

880   As at 2015, there seem to have been only 17 reported cases over the previous 60 years where domestic courts or tribunals have exercised universal jurisdiction over perpetrators of war crimes.[847] Interestingly, the vast majority of these cases arose in the last 20 years and concerned events which took place in non-international armed conflicts. This limited number of national prosecutions based on universal jurisdiction can be explained by a variety of factors. The likelihood of prosecutions on the basis of universal jurisdiction is usually dependent on the presence of the alleged offender in a country which is willing and able to extend its jurisdiction over the offender. Some prosecutions on the basis of universal jurisdiction have faced insurmountable problems of proof. Access to evidence and witnesses, and obtaining the cooperation of the authorities of the States where the crimes have been committed, can be difficult. The distance between the domestic courts of a third State and the place and time of the suspected criminal conduct makes the prosecution's work hazardous, and can lead to acquittal for lack of evidence.[848] Lastly, such prosecutions can be costly for the State carrying them out. Nevertheless, prosecutions by the domestic courts of other States can be a valuable alternative in the absence of prosecution in the States where the crimes were committed, as well as a necessary complement to prosecutions by international courts or tribunals.[849]

---

[844] See the discussion of this issue in the commentary on Article 49, section G.

[845] See ICRC Study on Customary International Humanitarian Law (2005), Rule 157. For a contrary view on the customary nature of this rule, see John B. Bellinger III and William J. Haynes II, 'A US Government Response to the International Committee of the Red Cross Study *Customary International Humanitarian Law*', *International Review of the Red Cross*, Vol. 89, No. 866, June 2007, pp. 443–471; but see Jean-Marie Henckaerts, '*Customary International Humanitarian Law*: a Response to US Comments', *International Review of the Red Cross*, Vol. 89, No. 866, June 2007, pp. 473–488.

[846] See ICRC Study on Customary International Humanitarian Law (2005), Rule 158. Note also the preamble to the 1998 ICC Statute, which recalls 'the duty of every State to exercise its criminal jurisdiction over those responsible for international crimes'.

[847] For an overview of these cases, see ICRC, *Preventing and repressing international crimes*, Vol. II, pp. 123–131, and ICRC, National Implementation of IHL database, available at https://www.icrc.org/ihl-nat.

[848] For some examples of domestic prosecutions, see La Haye, 2008, pp. 243–256.

[849] See *ibid.* pp. 270–273.

3. Serious violations of common Article 3 as war crimes

881 The commission of the prohibited acts listed in paragraph 1(a)–(d) of common Article 3 has been found to engage the individual criminal responsibility of perpetrators in non-international armed conflicts. Murder, mutilation, cruel treatment, torture, hostage-taking, outrages upon personal dignity and denial of a fair trial have been explicitly included as war crimes in non-international armed conflicts in the ICTR, ICC and SCSL Statutes.[850] Furthermore, they have been prosecuted as serious violations of the laws or customs of war under Article 3 of the ICTY Statute. These prohibited acts have also been included as war crimes or serious violations of humanitarian law in a great number of national laws.[851]

882 The ICC Elements of Crimes makes no distinction for these offences based on the nature of the armed conflict.[852] Similarly, the international criminal tribunals have applied the same elements of crimes for these offences, whether committed in international or non-international armed conflicts.[853]

883 The list of war crimes applicable in non-international armed conflicts goes beyond the list of prohibited acts contained in common Article 3(1). This list is complemented by the crimes set out in Article 8(2)(e) of the ICC Statute, and by others recognized in treaty or customary law.[854]

884 As to the prohibition of 'violence to life and person', Article 8(2)(c)(i) of the ICC Statute restates common Article 3, listing '[v]iolence to life and person, in particular murder of all kinds, mutilation, cruel treatment and torture' as war crimes under the Statute in non-international armed conflicts. However, the 2002 ICC Assembly of States Parties did not adopt elements of crimes for violence to life and person, but only for the specific crimes of murder, mutilation, cruel treatment and torture. This indicates that the Assembly did not envisage prosecutions for charges of violence to life and person as such under the ICC Statute.

885 Furthermore, a 2002 ICTY judgment took a cautious approach to the war crime of violence to life and person. In *Vasiljević*, the Trial Chamber, in view

---

[850] See ICTR Statute (1994), Article 4(a)–(g); ICC Statute (1998), Article 8(2)(c); and SCSL Statute (2002), Article 3(a)–(g).

[851] For details on these laws, see ICRC, Customary International Humanitarian Law, practice relating to Rules 89 (murder), 90 (torture, cruel treatment and outrages upon personal dignity), 92 (mutilation), 96 (hostage-taking) and 100 (denial of fair trial), section V, available at https://www.icrc.org/customary-ihl/eng/docs/v2_rul.

[852] The sole distinction between the war crimes applicable in international and non-international armed conflict stems from the nature of the victim in question: war crimes in non-international armed conflict are committed against persons protected under common Article 3, whereas war crimes committed in international armed conflict are committed against persons protected under the Geneva Conventions.

[853] For more details on the criminal-law aspects of most of these crimes, see the commentary on Article 50, section D.

[854] See, in particular, Henckaerts/Doswald-Beck, commentary on Rule 156, pp. 597–603.

of the *nullum crimen sine lege* principle – which, *inter alia*, requires criminal law provisions to be sufficiently 'precise to determine conduct and distinguish the criminal from the permissible'[855] – rejected war crimes charges of 'violence to life and person', while convicting the accused of the specific war crime of murder.[856]

886   For the purposes of international criminal law, it is therefore doubtful whether a sufficiently precise definition of a war crime of 'violence to life and person' has developed.[857] However, this has no bearing on the underlying prohibition of violence to life and person under common Article 3. Humanitarian law prohibitions exist independently of whether a violation of these prohibitions has consequences under international criminal law.

887   For the war crime of mutilation, Article 8(2)(c)(i) of the ICC Statute lists mutilation as a serious violation of common Article 3, while Article 8(2)(e)(xi) lists it as a serious violation of the laws and customs of war in non-international armed conflicts. The ICC Elements of Crimes distinguishes between the two offences. As mutilation is a serious violation of common Article 3, it is not necessary to prove that it caused death or seriously endangered the physical or mental health of the victim, while such proof is required for a violation of the laws and customs of war. The fact that this element does not apply to mutilation as a serious violation of common Article 3 has been confirmed by the SCSL Trial Chamber.[858]

888   The choice made by States to criminalize only the prohibitions listed in paragraph 1(a)–(d) of common Article 3 has no impact on the strength of the other obligations contained in the article, including the overarching obligation to treat humanely persons not or no longer taking an active part in hostilities, without any adverse distinction founded on race, colour, religion or faith, sex, birth or wealth, or any other similar criteria.

4. State responsibility for violations of common Article 3

889 A State Party that commits a violation of common Article 3 may be responsible under the rules of State responsibility, in the same way as for any violation

---

[855] See ICTY, *Vasiljević* Trial Judgment, 2002, para. 193.
[856] See *ibid.* paras 193–204 and 307–308. For a different view, see ICTY, *Blaškić* Trial Judgment, 2000, pp. 267–269, where convictions were entered for the war crime of violence to life and person (later reversed on appeal). In its judgment in *Kordić and Čerkez*, the ICTY Trial Chamber agreed with the description of the war crime of violence to life and person used in *Blaškić*; however, considering the parallel war crime charges of 'wilfully causing great suffering' and 'inhuman treatment' as more specific to acts that did not result in the death of the victim, no convictions for violence to life and person were entered; see *Kordić and Čerkez* Trial Judgment, 2001, paras 260 and 821.
[857] Along the same lines, see e.g. SCSL, *Fofana and Kondewa* Trial Judgment, 2007, para. 145, referring to ICTY, *Vasiljević* Trial Judgment, 2002.
[858] SCSL, *Brima* Trial Judgment, 2007, para. 725; *Sesay* Trial Judgment, 2009, para. 182.

of the Geneva Conventions.[859] In some human rights cases, States have been found to have violated common Article 3.[860] States may also be held responsible for the acts of non-State armed groups, if these acts are attributable to it.[861] This will be the case, for example, if the armed group acts in fact on the instructions of or under the direction of that State.

890   The responsibility of armed groups for violations of common Article 3 can also be envisaged if the armed group becomes the new government of a State or the government of a new State. In these circumstances, the conduct of the armed group will be considered as an act of that State under international law.[862]

891   When a non-State armed group is not successful at becoming the new government or the government of a new State, the State Party to that non-international armed conflict will not bear any responsibility for violations of common Article 3 committed by non-State armed groups.[863]

892   International law is unclear as to the responsibility of a non-State armed group, as an entity in itself, for acts committed by members of the group.[864]

5. Preventive measures and monitoring compliance

a. Preventive measures

893   The Geneva Conventions contain a number of measures that Parties to a non-international armed conflict should put in place to enhance respect for common Article 3 and prevent or stop violations thereof.

894   Common Article 3 does not contain an obligation to disseminate the content of the provision. However, Article 47 of the First Convention sets out the obligation to 'disseminate the text' of the Convention, which includes common Article 3, as widely as possible.[865] Spreading knowledge of the content

---

[859] See Draft Articles on State Responsibility (2001), Articles 1 and 4; Henckaerts/Doswald-Beck, commentary on Rule 149, pp. 530–536; and Dinstein, 2014, pp. 116–126.

[860] See Inter-American Commission on Human Rights, *Case 10.480 (El Salvador)*, Report, 1999, para. 82; *Case 10.548 (Peru)*, Report, 1997, para. 88; and *Case 11.142 (Colombia)*, Report, 1997, para. 202; all three cases cited in Sivakumaran, 2015, p. 429, fn. 62.

[861] See Draft Articles on State Responsibility (2001), Article 8, and Henckaerts/Doswald-Beck, commentary on Rule 149, pp. 534–536.

[862] See Draft Articles on State Responsibility (2001), Article 10. See also Dinstein, 2014, pp. 126–130.

[863] State responsibility might be engaged if a State failed to take available steps to protect, for example, the premises of the diplomatic missions of a neutral State (see Draft Articles on State Responsibility (2001), commentary on Article 10, p. 52, para. 15), but it will not be responsible for violations of common Article 3 committed by a non-State armed group.

[864] For an analysis on this issue, see Zegveld, and Annyssa Bellal, 'Establishing the Direct Responsibility of Non-State Armed Groups for Violations of International Norms: Issues of Attribution', in Noemi Gal-Or, Math Noortmann and Cedric Ryngaert (eds), *Responsibilities of the Non-State Actor in Armed Conflict and the Market Place: Theoretical Considerations and Empirical Findings*, Brill, Leiden, 2015, pp. 304–322.

[865] See also the commentary on Article 47, para. 2769; Sivakumaran, 2012, p. 431; Moir, p. 243; and Draper, p. 27.

of the law applicable in non-international armed conflicts to the armed forces of a State and the public at large is a significant step in ensuring the effective application of the law, as well as compliance with the provisions of common Article 3.[866]

895   As the obligation to disseminate contained in Article 47 also covers common Article 3, States Parties are already under an obligation in peacetime to include the study of common Article 3 in programmes of military and, if possible, civil instruction.[867] The methods of dissemination are left to States Parties.[868] Making the content of common Article 3 familiar to the entire population will help create an environment conducive to respect for humanitarian law, should a non-international armed conflict break out.

896   Practice has shown that, once a non-international armed conflict takes place in a State, the dissemination and teaching of humanitarian law, including common Article 3, can also be carried out by entities other than States Parties, such as the ICRC and non-governmental organizations.[869] The inclusion of legal advisers in the armed forces of States and non-State Parties also enhances respect for humanitarian law in such conflicts. Similarly, as States are under an obligation to investigate war crimes and prosecute suspects,[870] they should include serious violations of common Article 3 within the list of war crimes contained in domestic legislation.

897   Raising awareness of humanitarian law among non-State armed groups, the training of their members in how to respect the law, and the imposition of disciplinary sanctions alongside criminal sanctions can play a crucial role in improving compliance with common Article 3 within such groups.[871]

898   Common Article 1 calls on States to respect and ensure respect for the Geneva Conventions in all circumstances. This wording covers the provisions applicable to both international and non-international armed conflicts.[872] Measures to 'ensure respect' for common Article 3 might include diplomatic pressure exerted by third States on Parties which violate common Article 3, the public denunciation of violations of common Article 3, and the

---

[866] See also Article 19 of Additional Protocol II, which states: 'This Protocol shall be disseminated as widely as possible.'

[867] For more details, see the commentary on Article 47.

[868] Traditionally, dissemination is carried out through orders, courses of instruction, or the issuance of manuals, but it can also take place by other means, such as drawings, pictures or comic books, and radio or television programmes; see Sivakumaran, 2012, pp. 433–434.

[869] One non-governmental organization which is particularly active in this field is Geneva Call; see Sivakumaran, 2012, pp. 434–436. See also UN Security Council, *Report of the Secretary-General on the protection of civilians in armed conflict*, UN Doc. S/2001/331, 30 March 2001, Recommendation 10, p. 11.

[870] See ICRC Study on Customary International Humanitarian Law (2005), Rule 158. Note also the preamble to the 1998 ICC Statute, which recalls 'the duty of every State to exercise its criminal jurisdiction over those responsible for international crimes'.

[871] For more details, see Sassòli, 2010; La Rosa/Wuerzner; and Bellal/Casey-Maslen.

[872] For more details, see the commentary on common Article 1, para. 125.

taking of any other measures designed to ensure compliance with common Article 3.[873]

899   It follows from common Article 3, which is binding on all Parties to a non-international armed conflict, that non-State armed groups are obliged to 'respect' the guarantees contained therein.[874] Furthermore, such armed groups have to 'ensure respect' for common Article 3 by their members and by individuals or groups acting on their behalf.[875] This follows from the requirement for non-State armed groups to be organized and to have a responsible command which must ensure respect for humanitarian law. It is also part of customary international law.[876]

b. Monitoring compliance

900   Common Article 3 lacks machinery which could help to ensure compliance with its provisions by Parties to a non-international armed conflict.[877] The compliance mechanisms forming part of the Geneva Conventions, such as the institution of Protecting Powers[878] and the establishment of an enquiry procedure or a conciliation procedure,[879] are applicable only in international armed conflicts.[880] However, Parties to a non-international armed conflict may make special agreements in accordance with Article 3(3) to use these compliance mechanisms or others in non-international armed conflicts.[881]

---

[873]   For a detailed discussion of measures available to States to ensure respect for the Conventions, see *ibid.* paras 146, 150–151 and 181. See also Moir, pp. 245–250.

[874]   For more details on the binding nature of common Article 3 on all Parties to a non-international armed conflict, see paras 505–508.

[875]   See the commentary on common Article 1, para. 132. For some tools, see e.g. ICRC, *Increasing Respect for International Humanitarian Law in Non-International Armed Conflicts*, ICRC, Geneva, 2008, and Sandesh Sivakumaran, 'Implementing humanitarian norms through non-State armed groups', in Heike Krieger (ed.), *Inducing Compliance with International Humanitarian Law: Lessons from the African Great Lakes Region*, Cambridge University Press, 2015, pp. 125–146.

[876]   See ICRC Study on Customary International Humanitarian Law (2005), Rule 139 and commentary (Henckaerts/Doswald-Beck, pp. 497–498).

[877]   See 31st International Conference of the Red Cross and Red Crescent, Geneva, 2011, Res. 1, Strengthening legal protection for victims of armed conflict.

[878]   See the commentaries on Articles 8 and 10.

[879]   See the commentaries on Articles 11 and 52.

[880]   It may be argued that Article 52 (Enquiry procedure) could be used in the context of violations of common Article 3, as the text of Article 52 speaks of 'an enquiry … concerning any alleged violation of the Convention'.

[881]   For further details on special agreement, see section K. For an example of Parties to a non-international armed conflict having considered an enquiry procedure at the relevant time, see Memorandum of Understanding on the Application of IHL between Croatia and the Socialist Federal Republic of Yugoslavia (1991), Article 12, cited in Sassòli/Bouvier/Quintin, pp. 1713–1717:

   12. Request for an enquiry.
   1. Should the ICRC be asked to institute an enquiry, it may use its good offices to set up a commission of enquiry outside the institution and in accordance with its principles.
   2. The ICRC will take part in the establishment of such a commission only by virtue of a general agreement or an ad hoc agreement with all the parties concerned.

901   The International Humanitarian Fact-Finding Commission (IHFFC), established in 1991 pursuant to Article 90 of Additional Protocol I, is competent to
enquire into alleged grave breaches or other serious violations of the Geneva
Conventions or Additional Protocol I. Its competence is constrained by the
scope of application of Additional Protocol I.[882] However, some authors have
considered that the wording of Article 90(2)(c)(i) of the Protocol could encompass serious violations of common Article 3.[883] The Commission itself indicated 'its willingness to enquire into alleged violations of humanitarian law,
including those arising in non-international armed conflicts, so long as all Parties to the conflict agree'.[884] All Parties to a non-international armed conflict
would need to provide the IHFFC with their consent before an enquiry could
take place. This has not occurred to date.[885]

902   Other organizations have been instrumental in enhancing compliance with
humanitarian law in non-international armed conflicts. In particular, common
Article 3 grants impartial humanitarian bodies, such as the ICRC, the right to
offer their services to the Parties to such a conflict.[886] In pursuing its protection activities, the ICRC seeks to prevent violations of the law and to ensure
that the Parties to a non-international armed conflict cease any violations that
may occur.[887] In carrying out these activities, the ICRC focuses on a bilateral dialogue with each Party to the armed conflict with the aim of persuad-
ing those responsible for violations to change their behaviour and meet their

---

See also some unilateral declarations, such as the 'Deed of Commitment under Geneva Call
for adherence to a total ban on anti-personnel mines and for cooperation in mine action', signed
by more than 30 non-State armed groups, which provides in its Article 3 for monitoring and
verification tools.

[882] See Bothe/Partsch/Solf, p. 543; Françoise J. Hampson, 'Fact-Finding and the International Fact-
Finding Commission', in Hazel Fox and Michael A. Meyer (eds), *Armed Conflict and the
New Law*, Vol. II, *Effecting Compliance*, British Institute of International and Comparative
Law, London, 1993, p. 76; Heike Spieker, 'International (Humanitarian) Fact-Finding Commis-
sion', version of March 2013, in Rüdiger Wolfrum (ed.), *Max Planck Encyclopedia of Public
International Law*, Oxford University Press, http://opil.ouplaw.com/home/EPIL and Pfanner,
p. 299.

[883] See Sivakumaran, 2012, pp. 459–462; Luigi Condorelli, 'La Commission internationale humanitaire d'établissement des faits : un outil obsolète ou un moyen utile de mise en œuvre du droit
international humanitaire ?', *Revue internationale de la Croix-Rouge*, Vol. 83, No. 842, June
2001, pp. 393–406, at 401; and Aly Mokhtar, 'To Be or Not to Be: The International Humanitarian Fact-Finding Commission', *Italian Yearbook of International Law*, Vol. XII, 2002, pp. 69–
94, at 90.

[884] International Humanitarian Fact-Finding Commission (IHFFC), *Report of the International
Fact-Finding Commission 1991–1996*, Bern, 1996, p. 2. See also *Report on the work of the
IHFFC on the Occasion of its 20th Anniversary*, Bern, 2011, pp. 15, 17, 19 and 28.

[885] See Sivakumaran, 2012, p. 461.   [886] For more details, see section J.

[887] This is done in furtherance of the ICRC's mandate as contained in Article 5(2) of the 1986
Statutes of the International Red Cross and Red Crescent Movement, which states that the
ICRC is mandated to work for the 'faithful application of international humanitarian law' and
the 'understanding and dissemination of knowledge of international humanitarian law'. For a
discussion of protection activities, see paras 814–818.

obligations.[888] While engaging with all the Parties, the ICRC also issues public statements and appeals for respect for humanitarian law, provides training and capacity-building, and assists in the integration of humanitarian law into official, legal, educational and operational curricula.[889]

903   The work of other organizations, such as the United Nations, also contributes to greater respect for humanitarian law in non-international armed conflicts.[890] The Security Council has a long practice of calling upon Parties to non-international armed conflicts to respect humanitarian law, of condemning serious violations and of recalling the obligation to prosecute the perpetrators of such violations.[891] The Council sets up fact-finding missions to look into violations of humanitarian and human rights law in non-international armed conflicts, and it established the innovative monitoring and reporting mechanism on children and armed conflict under its resolution 1612 (2005).[892] UN human rights mechanisms also aim to ensure better respect for humanitarian law in non-international armed conflicts, in particular as they consider issues of humanitarian law in their special procedures mechanisms or set up commissions of enquiry in certain contexts.[893]

---

[888] This dialogue is, in principle, of a confidential nature. Except in strictly defined circumstances, it is not the ICRC's practice to publicly condemn authorities responsible for violations of humanitarian law; see 'Action by the ICRC in the event of violations of international humanitarian law or of other fundamental rules protecting persons in situations of violence', *International Review of the Red Cross*, Vol. 87, No. 858, June 2005, pp. 393–400.

[889] For more details on the ICRC's engagement with armed groups, see e.g. ICRC, *Increasing Respect for International Humanitarian Law in Non-International Armed Conflicts*, and Sivakumaran, 2012, pp. 467–472.

[890] See, in general, David S. Weissbrodt, 'The Role of International Organizations in the Implementation of Human Rights and Humanitarian Law in Situations of Armed Conflict', *Vanderbilt Journal of Transnational Law*, Vol. 21, 1988, pp. 313–365.

[891] For an overview of the work of the UN Security Council in this area since 1989, see La Haye, 2008, pp. 166–167. See also Sivakumaran, 2012, pp. 465–466, and Stephen M. Schwebel, 'The Roles of the Security Council and the International Court of Justice in the Application of International Humanitarian Law', *New York University Journal of International Law and Politics*, Vol. 27, No. 4, 1995, pp. 731–759. As an example, the UN Security Council referred the situations of Darfur and Libya to the ICC.

[892] The UN Security Council has set up numerous fact-finding missions in Burundi, Darfur (Sudan), Rwanda, the former Yugoslavia and elsewhere. For information on the monitoring and reporting mechanism on grave violations against children in armed conflict, see https://childrenandarmedconflict.un.org/.

[893] See e.g. the request in Human Rights Council, Res. S-16/1, The current human rights situation in the Syrian Arab Republic in the context of recent events, 29 April 2011, pursuant to which the UN High Commissioner for Human Rights established a fact-finding mission to investigate alleged violations of international human rights and humanitarian law in Syria. See also Sivakumaran, 2012, p. 467; Daniel O'Donnell, 'Trends in the application of international humanitarian law by United Nations human rights mechanisms', *International Review of the Red Cross*, Vol. 38, Special Issue No. 324, September 1998, pp. 481–503; Theo C. van Boven, 'Reliance on norms of humanitarian law by United Nations' organs', in Astrid J.M. Delissen and Gerard J. Tanja (eds), *Humanitarian Law of Armed Conflict: Challenges Ahead: Essays in Honour of Frits Kalshoven*, Martinus Nijhoff Publishers, Dordrecht, 1991, pp. 495–513; and Fanny Martin, 'Le droit international humanitaire devant les organes de contrôle des droits de l'homme', *Droits fondamentaux*, No. 1, July–December 2001, pp. 119–148.

6. The concept of belligerent reprisals in non-international armed conflicts

904 Belligerent reprisals are measures taken in the context of an international armed conflict by one of the Parties to the conflict in response to a violation of humanitarian law by an adverse Party. Such measures aim to put an end to the violation and to induce the adverse Party to comply with the law. These measures would be contrary to international law if they were not taken by the injured State in response to an internationally wrongful act committed by a responsible State.[894] Where not prohibited by international law, the use of belligerent reprisals is subject to stringent conditions in international armed conflicts.[895]

905   Both common Article 3 and Additional Protocol II are silent on the issue of belligerent reprisals in non-international armed conflicts. In the view of the ICRC, there is insufficient evidence that the concept of belligerent reprisals in non-international armed conflicts ever materialized in international law.[896] Historically, the practice describing the purpose of reprisals and conditions for resorting to them refers only to inter-State relations.[897] During the negotiations on Additional Protocol II, a number of States thought that the very concept of reprisals had no place in non-international armed conflicts.[898] Extending the concept of belligerent reprisals to non-international armed conflicts might grant a legal status or legitimacy under international law to non-State armed groups,[899] and would also give such groups the right to take belligerent reprisals against the State, all of which States are reluctant to grant.[900] Many military manuals do not apply this concept to non-international armed conflicts, and define belligerent reprisals as a measure of enforcement by one State against another.[901] Furthermore, there does not seem to be recorded instances of actual resort to reprisals by States in non-international armed conflicts in

---

[894] For more details, see the commentary on Article 46, section A.

[895] See ICRC Study on Customary International Humanitarian Law (2005), Rule 145. For more details, see the commentary on Article 46, paras 2731–2732.

[896] See Henckaerts/Doswald-Beck, commentary on Rule 148, p. 527. This point of view is not shared by Sivakumaran, who cites the Spanish Civil War as an example where belligerents felt entitled to use belligerent reprisals; see Sivakumaran, 2012, p. 449.

[897] See Henckaerts/Doswald-Beck, commentary on Rule 148, p. 527.

[898] See *ibid.* citing e.g. the statements made by Canada, Iran, Iraq, Mexico, Nigeria and the United States. For a full review of the preparatory work for Additional Protocol II on this issue, see Henckaerts/Doswald-Beck, commentary on Rule 148, pp. 528–529, and Bílková, pp. 44–47.

[899] See the statement of Germany during the negotiations which led to the adoption of Additional Protocol II: this term could give 'the Parties to a conflict the status under international law which they had no right to claim'; *Official Records of the Diplomatic Conference of Geneva of 1974–1977*, Vol. VIII, p. 325, para. 11.

[900] Milanovic/Hadzi-Vidanovic, p. 273, and De Hemptinne, p. 588.

[901] See Henckaerts/Doswald-Beck, commentary on Rule 148, p. 528, citing e.g. the military manuals of Australia, Canada, Germany, the United Kingdom and the United States. See also Bílková, pp. 50–51.

the last 60 years.[902] Acts of so-called 'reprisals' allegedly committed in non-international armed conflicts have been condemned, and the importance of protecting civilians and persons *hors de combat* has been stressed.[903] These considerations led the ICRC Study on Customary International Humanitarian Law to conclude that Parties to non-international armed conflicts do not have the right to resort to belligerent reprisals under customary international law.[904]

906   Some authors believe, however, that belligerent reprisals are a tool open to Parties to a non-international armed conflict as a necessary consequence of the fact that such Parties are bound by the primary norms of humanitarian law.[905] Some ICTY Chambers have also looked at the issue whether the concept of reprisal was applicable in non-international armed conflicts.[906]

907   However, whichever view is taken, it is clear that common Article 3 prohibits violence to life and person, the taking of hostages, outrages upon personal dignity, in particular humiliating and degrading treatment, and the denial of fair trial 'at any time and in any place whatsoever'. Any 'reprisal' that would entail these acts would therefore be prohibited.[907] Similarly, common Article 3 provides that all persons not or no longer taking active part in the hostilities must be treated humanely 'in all circumstances'. Any 'reprisal' that would be incompatible with the requirement of humane treatment would therefore be unlawful.[908]

---

[902] See Bílková, p. 49. This author argues, however, that 'the fact that States do not resort to reprisals in non-international armed conflict, or at least do not publicly claim to do so, does not necessarily mean that they are persuaded that they lack the right to do so'.

[903] See Henckaerts/Doswald-Beck, commentary on Rule 148, p. 527 (citing examples in the context of conflicts in Chad, Colombia, the Democratic Republic of the Congo, Mali and Rwanda).

[904] See ICRC Study on Customary International Humanitarian Law (2005), Rule 148. See also De Hemptinne, pp. 587–591, and Shane Darcy, 'The Evolution of the Law of Belligerent Reprisals', *Military Law Review*, Vol. 175, March 2003, pp. 184–251, at 216–220.

[905] For details, see Bílková, pp. 31–65, and Sivakumaran, 2012, pp. 449–457. Bílková considers this right of reprisal not to be unlimited; see, in particular, pp. 40–41. Sivakumaran believes that the 'prohibition on the use of belligerent reprisals through common Article 3 has to be limited to the acts prohibited by that article' (p. 451).

[906] It is interesting to note that the earlier findings by the ICTY in *Martić* Rule 61 Decision, 1996, paras 15–17, and *Kupreškić* Trial Judgment, 2000, paras 527–536 – that, under customary law, reprisals against the civilian population were prohibited in all armed conflicts – were not followed by the *Martić* Trial and Appeals Chambers; see *Martić* Trial Judgment, 2007, paras 464–468, and Appeal Judgment, 2008, paras 263–267. Judges in those cases examined whether the shelling of Zagreb by the defendant could be considered a lawful reprisal. In so doing, it applied the conditions or limitations imposed on reprisals, usually recognized to be applicable in international armed conflicts, in a conflict of a non-international character, apparently rejecting therefore the conclusion reached in the *Kupreškić* Trial Chamber that reprisals against the civilian population are prohibited under customary law in all circumstances.

[907] See Pictet (ed.), *Commentary on the First Geneva Convention*, ICRC, 1952, p. 55, and Henckaerts/Doswald-Beck, commentary on Rule 148, p. 526.

[908] *Ibid.* Similarly, Article 4 of Additional Protocol II allows no room for reprisals against persons not or no longer taking a direct part in hostilities; see Sandoz/Swinarski/Zimmermann (eds), *Commentary on the Additional Protocols*, ICRC, 1987, para. 4530.

Select bibliography

Section B. Historical background

Abi-Saab, Rosemary, *Droit humanitaire et conflits internes : Origines et évolution de la réglementation internationale*, Henry Dunant Institute, Geneva, 1986.

Ador, Gustave and Moynier, Gustave, 'Les destinées de la Convention de Genève pendant la guerre de Serbie', *Bulletin international des sociétés de secours aux militaires blessés*, Vol. 7, No. 28, 1876, pp. 164–176.

Duculesco, Victor, 'Effet de la reconnaissance de l'état de belligérance par les tiers, y compris les Organisations internationales, sur le statut juridique des conflits armés à caractère non international', *Revue générale de droit international public*, Vol. 79, 1975, pp. 125–151.

Lauterpacht, Hersch, *Recognition in International Law*, Cambridge University Press, 1947.

– (ed.), *Oppenheim's International Law*, 7th edition, Longmans, Green and Co., London, 1952.

Milanovic, Marko and Hadzi-Vidanovic, Vidan, 'A taxonomy of armed conflict', in Nigel D. White and Christian Henderson (eds), *Research Handbook on International Conflict and Security Law*: Jus ad Bellum, Jus in Bello *and* Jus post Bellum, Edward Elgar, Cheltenham, 2013, pp. 256–314.

Moir, Lindsay, *The Law of Internal Armed Conflict*, Cambridge University Press, 2002.

Moynier, Gustave, *Étude sur la Convention de Genève pour l'amélioration du sort des militaires blessés dans les armées en campagne (1864 et 1868)*, Librairie de Joël Cherbuliez, Paris, 1870.

Neff, Stephen C., *War and the Law of Nations: A General History*, Cambridge University Press, 2005.

O'Connell, Mary Ellen, 'Historical Development and Legal Basis', in Dieter Fleck (ed.), *The Handbook of International Humanitarian Law*, 3rd edition, Oxford University Press, 2013, pp. 1–42.

Oppenheim, Lassa, *International Law: A Treatise*, Vol. II, *War and Neutrality*, 2nd edition, Longmans, Green and Co., London, 1912.

Padelford, Norman J., 'The International Non-Intervention Agreement and the Spanish Civil War', *American Journal of International Law*, Vol. 31, No. 4, 1937, pp. 578–603.

Ramelli Arteaga, Alejandro, *Derecho Internacional Humanitario y Estado de Beligerancia*, 2nd edition, Externado University of Colombia, Bogotá, 2004.

Sivakumaran, Sandesh, *The Law of Non-International Armed Conflict*, Oxford University Press, 2012.

Section C. Paragraph 1: Scope of application of common Article 3

Abi-Saab, Rosemary, *Droit humanitaire et conflits internes : Origines et évolution de la réglementation internationale*, Henry Dunant Institute, Geneva, 1986.

Akande, Dapo, 'Classification of Armed Conflicts: Relevant Legal Concepts', in Elizabeth Wilmshurst (ed.), *International Law and the Classification of Conflicts*, Oxford University Press, 2012, pp. 32–79.

Anderson, Kenneth, 'Targeted Killing and Drone Warfare: How We Came to Debate Whether There is a "Legal Geography of War"', *American University Washington College of Law Research Paper*, No. 2011–16, 2011, pp. 1–17.

Arimatsu, Louise, 'Territory, Boundaries and the Law of Armed Conflict', *Yearbook of International Humanitarian Law*, Vol. 12, 2009, pp. 157–192.

Bartels, Rogier, 'Transnational Armed Conflict: Does it Exist?', in *Scope of Application of International Humanitarian Law*, Proceedings of the 13th Bruges Colloquium, 18–19 October 2012, College of Europe/ICRC, Collegium No. 43, Autumn 2013, pp. 114–128.

– 'From Jus In Bello to Jus Post Bellum: When Do Non-International Armed Conflicts End?', in Carsten Stahn, Jennifer S. Easterday and Jens Iverson (eds), *Jus Post Bellum: Mapping the Normative Foundations*, Oxford University Press, 2014, pp. 297–314.

Bianchi, Andrea, 'Terrorism and Armed Conflict: Insights from a Law & Literature Perspective', *Leiden Journal of International Law*, Vol. 24, No. 1,

Blank, Laurie R., 'Defining the Battlefield in Contemporary Conflict and Counterterrorism: Understanding the Parameters of the Zone of Combat', *Georgia Journal of International and Comparative Law*, Vol. 39, No. 1, 2010, pp. 1–38.

Bothe, Michael, 'War Crimes', in Antonio Cassese, Paola Gaeta and John R.W.D. Jones (eds), *The Rome Statute of the International Criminal Court: A Commentary*, Vol. IA, Oxford University Press, 2002, pp. 379–426.

Bothe, Michael, Partsch, Karl Josef and Solf, Waldemar A., *New Rules for Victims of Armed Conflicts: Commentary on the Two 1977 Protocols Additional to the Geneva Conventions of 1949*, Martinus Nijhoff Publishers, The Hague, 1982.

Cassese, Antonio, 'The *Nicaragua* and *Tadić* Tests Revisited in Light of the ICJ Judgment on Genocide in Bosnia', *European Journal of International Law*, Vol. 18, No. 4, 2007, pp. 649–668.

Condorelli, Luigi, 'War Crimes and Internal Conflicts in the Statute of the International Criminal Court', in Mauro Politi and Giuseppe Nesi (eds), *The Rome Statute of the International Criminal Court: A Challenge to Impunity*, Ashgate, Aldershot, 2001, pp. 107–117.

Corn, Geoffrey S., 'Hamdan, Lebanon, and the Regulation of Hostilities: The Need to Recognize a Hybrid Category of Armed Conflict', *Vanderbilt Journal of Transnational Law*, Vol. 40, No. 2, 2007, pp. 295–355.

– 'Geography of Armed Conflict: Why it is a Mistake to Fish for the Red Herring', *International Law Studies*, U.S. Naval War College, Vol. 89, 2013, pp. 77–107.

Corn, Geoffrey S. and Jensen, Eric Talbot, 'Transnational Armed Conflict: A "Principled" Approach to the Regulation of Counter-Terror Combat Operations', *Israel Law Review*, Vol. 42, 2009, pp. 1–34.

Cullen, Anthony, *The Concept of Non-International Armed Conflict in International Humanitarian Law*, Cambridge University Press, 2010.

David, Eric, *Principes de droit des conflits armés*, 5th edition, Bruylant, Brussels, 2012.

Droege, Cordula, 'Get off my cloud: cyber warfare, international humanitarian law, and the protection of civilians', *International Review of the Red Cross*, Vol. 94, No. 886, June 2012, pp. 533–578.

Ferraro, Tristan, 'The geographic reach of IHL: The law and current challenges', in *Scope of Application of International Humanitarian Law*, Proceedings of the 13th Bruges Colloquium, 18–19 October 2012, College of Europe/ICRC, *Collegium*, No. 43, Autumn 2013, pp. 105–113. (2013a)

– 'The applicability and application of international humanitarian law to multinational forces', *International Review of the Red Cross*, Vol. 95, No. 891, December 2013, pp. 561–612. (2013b)

Fleck, Dieter, 'The Law of Non-International Armed Conflict', in Dieter Fleck (ed.), *The Handbook of International Humanitarian Law*, 3rd edition, Oxford University Press, 2013, pp. 581–610.

Gasser, Hans-Peter, 'International humanitarian law: An introduction', in Hans Haug (ed.), *Humanity for All: The International Red Cross and Red Crescent Movement*, Henry Dunant Institute, Geneva, 1993, pp. 491–592.

Grignon, Julia, *L'applicabilité temporelle du droit international humanitaire*, Schulthess, Geneva, 2014.

Henckaerts, Jean-Marie and Doswald-Beck, Louise, *Customary International Humanitarian Law, Volume I: Rules*, ICRC/Cambridge University Press, 2005, available at https://www.icrc.org/customary-ihl/eng/docs/v1.

ICRC, *International Humanitarian Law and the Challenges of Contemporary Armed Conflicts*, Report prepared for the 28th International Conference of the Red Cross and Red Crescent, ICRC, Geneva, 2003.

– *International Humanitarian Law and the Challenges of Contemporary Armed Conflicts*, Report prepared for the 30th International Conference of the Red Cross and Red Crescent, ICRC, Geneva, 2007.

– *Interpretive Guidance on the Notion of Direct Participation in Hostilities under International Humanitarian Law*, by Nils Melzer, ICRC, Geneva, 2009.

– *International Humanitarian Law and the Challenges of Contemporary Armed Conflicts*, Report prepared for the 31st International Conference of the Red Cross and Red Crescent, ICRC, Geneva, 2011.

– *The Use of Force in Armed Conflicts: Interplay between the Conduct of Hostilities and Law Enforcement Paradigms*, Expert Meeting, Report prepared and edited by Gloria Gaggioli, ICRC, Geneva, 2013.

– *International Humanitarian Law and the Challenges of Contemporary Armed Conflicts*, Report prepared for the 32nd International Conference of the Red Cross and Red Crescent, ICRC, Geneva, 2015.

Kleffner, Jann K., 'Scope of Application of International Humanitarian Law', in Dieter Fleck (ed.), *The Handbook of International Humanitarian Law*, 3rd edition, Oxford University Press, 2013, pp. 43–78. (2013b)

Koh, Harold Hongju, 'Keynote Address: The Obama Administration and International Law', *Proceedings of the Annual Meeting of the American Society of International Law*, Vol. 104, 2010, pp. 207–221.

Kolb, Robert and Hyde, Richard, *An Introduction to the International Law of Armed Conflicts*, 3rd edition, Hart Publishing, Oxford, 2008.

Kreß, Claus, 'Some Reflections on the International Legal Framework Governing Transnational Armed Conflicts', *Journal of Conflict and Security Law*, Vol. 15, No. 2, 2010, pp. 245–274.

Melzer, Nils, *Targeted Killing in International Law*, Oxford University Press, 2008.

Meron, Theodor, 'The Humanization of Humanitarian Law', *American Journal of International Law*, Vol. 94, No. 2, 2000, pp. 239–278.

Milanovic, Marko, 'State Responsibility for Genocide', *European Journal of International Law*, Vol. 17, No. 3, 2006, pp. 553–604.

– 'State Responsibility for Genocide: A Follow-Up', *European Journal of International Law*, Vol. 18, No. 4, 2007, pp. 669–694. (2007a)

– 'Lessons for human rights and humanitarian law in the war on terror: comparing Hamdan and the Israeli Targeted Killings case', *International Review of the Red Cross*, Vol. 89, No. 866, June 2007, pp. 373–393. (2007b)

- 'End of IHL application: Overview and challenges', in *Scope of Application of International Humanitarian Law*, Proceedings of the 13th Bruges Colloquium, 18–19 October 2012, College of Europe/ICRC, *Collegium*, No. 43, Autumn 2013, pp. 83–94.
- 'The Applicability of the Conventions to "Transnational" and "Mixed" Conflicts', in Andrew Clapham, Paola Gaeta and Marco Sassòli (eds), *The 1949 Geneva Conventions: A Commentary*, Oxford University Press, 2015, pp. 27–50.

Milanovic, Marko and Hadzi-Vidanovic, Vidan, 'A taxonomy of armed conflict', in Nigel D. White and Christian Henderson (eds), *Research Handbook on International Conflict and Security Law: Jus ad Bellum, Jus in Bello and Jus post bellum*, Edward Elgar, Cheltenham, 2013, pp. 256–314.

Moir, Lindsay, 'The Concept of Non-International Armed Conflict', in Andrew Clapham, Paola Gaeta and Marco Sassòli (eds), *The 1949 Geneva Conventions: A Commentary*, Oxford University Press, 2015, pp. 391–414.

Pejic, Jelena, 'Status of armed conflicts', in Elizabeth Wilmshurst and Susan Breau (eds), *Perspectives on the ICRC Study on Customary International Humanitarian Law*, Cambridge University Press, 2007, pp. 77–100.

- 'The protective scope of Common Article 3: more than meets the eye', *International Review of the Red Cross*, Vol. 93, No. 881, March 2011, pp. 189–225.

Radin, Sasha, 'Global Armed Conflict? The Threshold of Extraterritorial Non-International Armed Conflicts', *International Law Studies*, U.S. Naval War College, Vol. 89, 2013, pp. 696–743.

Sassòli, Marco, 'Transnational Armed Groups and International Humanitarian Law', *HPCR Occasional Paper Series*, Winter 2006, pp. 1–43.

Sassòli, Marco, Bouvier, Antoine A. and Quintin, Anne, *How Does Law Protect in War?*, Vol. I, 3rd edition, ICRC, Geneva, 2011.

Schindler, Dietrich, 'The Different Types of Armed Conflicts According to the Geneva Conventions and Protocols', *Collected Courses of the Hague Academy of International Law*, Vol. 163, 1979, pp. 117–164.

Schmitt, Michael N., 'Charting the Legal Geography of Non-International Armed Conflict', *International Law Studies*, U.S. Naval War College, Vol. 90, 2014, pp. 1–19.

Schöndorf, Roy S., 'Extra-State Armed Conflicts: Is There a Need for a New Legal Regime?', *New York University Journal of International Law and Politics*, Vol. 37, No. 1, 2004, pp. 1–78.

Shraga, Daphna, 'The United Nations as an Actor Bound by International Humanitarian Law', *International Peacekeeping*, Vol. 5, No. 2, 1998, pp. 64–81.

- 'The applicability of international humanitarian law to peace operations, from rejection to acceptance', in Gian Luca Beruto (ed.), *International Humanitarian Law, Human Rights and Peace Operations*, Proceedings of the 31st Round Table on Current Problems of International Humanitarian Law, 4–6 September 2008, International Institute of Humanitarian Law, San Remo, 2008, pp. 82–89.

Shraga, Daphna and Zacklin, Ralph, 'The Applicability of International Humanitarian Law to United Nations Peacekeeping Operations: Conceptual, Legal and Practical Issues', *Report to the Symposium on Humanitarian Action and Peacekeeping Operations*, 22–24 June 1994, ICRC, Geneva, 2004, pp. 39–48.

Sivakumaran, Sandesh, *The Law of Non-International Armed Conflict*, Oxford University Press, 2012.

Stewart, James G., 'Towards a single definition of armed conflict in international humanitarian law: A critique of internationalized armed conflict', *International Review of the Red Cross*, Vol. 85, No. 850, June 2003, pp. 313–350.

Vité, Sylvain, 'Typology of armed conflicts in international humanitarian law: legal concepts and actual situations', *International Review of the Red Cross*, Vol. 91, No. 873, March 2009, pp. 69–94.

von Hebel, Herman and Robinson, Darryl, 'Crimes within the Jurisdiction of the Court', in Roy S. Lee (ed.), *The International Criminal Court: The Making of the Rome Statute – Issues, Negotiations, Results*, Kluwer Law International, The Hague, 1999, pp. 79–126.

Section D. Paragraph 1: Binding force of common Article 3

Bugnion, François, *The International Committee of the Red Cross and the Protection of War Victims*, ICRC/Macmillan, Oxford, 2003. (2003a)

Cassese, Antonio, 'The status of rebels under the 1977 Geneva Protocol on Non-International Armed Conflicts', *International and Comparative Law Quarterly*, Vol. 30, No. 2, 1981, pp. 416–439.

Dinstein, Yoram, *Non-International Armed Conflicts in International Law*, Cambridge University Press, 2014, pp. 173–199.

Elder, David A., 'The Historical Background of Common Article 3 of the Geneva Convention of 1949', *Case Western Reserve Journal of International Law*, Vol. 11, No. 1, 1979, pp. 37–69.

Engdahl, Ola, 'Compliance with International Humanitarian Law in Multinational Peace Operations', *Nordic Journal of International Law*, Vol. 78, No. 4, 2009, pp. 513–526.

Ferraro, Tristan, 'The applicability and application of international humanitarian law to multinational forces', *International Review of the Red Cross*, Vol. 95, No. 891, December 2013, pp. 561–612.

Kleffner, Jann K., 'The applicability of international humanitarian law to organized armed groups', *International Review of the Red Cross*, Vol. 93, No. 882, June 2011, pp. 443–461.

Kolb, Robert, Porretto, Gabriele and Vité, Sylvain, *L'application du droit international humanitaire et des droits de l'homme aux organisations internationales: Forces de paix et administrations civiles transitoires*, Bruylant, Brussels, 2005.

Moir, Lindsay, *The Law of Internal Armed Conflict*, Cambridge University Press, 2002.

Murray, Daragh, 'How International Humanitarian Law Treaties Bind Non-State Armed Groups', *Journal of Conflict and Security Law*, Vol. 20, No. 1, 2015, pp. 101–131.

Naert, Frederik, *International Law Aspects of the EU's Security and Defence Policy, with a Particular Focus on the Law of Armed Conflict and Human Rights*, Intersentia, *Antwerp*, 2010.

Schindler, Dietrich, 'The Different Types of Armed Conflicts According to the Geneva Conventions and Protocols', *Collected Courses of the Hague Academy of International Law*, Vol. 163, 1979, pp. 117–164.

Shraga, Daphna, 'The United Nations as an Actor Bound by International Humanitarian Law', *International Peacekeeping*, Vol. 5, No. 2, 1998, pp. 64–81.

Sivakumaran, Sandesh, *The Law of Non-International Armed Conflict*, Oxford University Press, 2012.
– 'The Addressees of Common Article 3', in Andrew Clapham, Paola Gaeta and Marco Sassòli (eds), *The 1949 Geneva Conventions: A Commentary*, Oxford University Press, 2015, pp. 415–431.
Zegveld, Liesbeth, *The Accountability of Armed Opposition Groups in International Law*, Cambridge University Press, 2002.

Section E. Sub-paragraph (1): Persons protected

Abresch, William, 'A Human Rights Law of Internal Armed Conflict: The European Court of Human Rights in Chechnya', *European Journal of International Law*, Vol. 16, No. 4, 2005, pp. 741–767.
Bond, James E., 'Application of the Law of War to Internal Conflict', *Georgia Journal of International and Comparative Law*, Vol. 3, No. 2, 1973, pp. 345–384.
Bothe, Michael, Partsch, Karl Josef and Solf, Waldemar A., *New Rules for Victims of Armed Conflicts: Commentary on the Two 1977 Protocols Additional to the Geneva Conventions of 1949*, Martinus Nijhoff Publishers, The Hague, 1982.
Cassese, Antonio, 'The Geneva Protocols of 1977 on the Humanitarian law of Armed Conflict and Customary International Law', *UCLA Pacific Basin Law Journal*, Vol. 3, 1984, pp. 55–118.
Dörmann, Knut, *Elements of War Crimes under the Rome Statute of the International Criminal Court: Sources and Commentary*, Cambridge University Press, 2003.
Draper, Gerald I.A.D., 'The Geneva Conventions of 1949', *Collected Courses of the Hague Academy of International Law*, Vol. 114, 1965, pp. 59–165.
Gasser, Hans-Peter, 'Remarks of Hans-Peter Gasser', in The Sixth Annual American Red Cross-Washington College of Law Conference on International Humanitarian Law: A Workshop on Customary International Law and the 1977 Protocols Additional to the 1949 Geneva Conventions, *American University Journal of International Law and Policy*, Vol. 2, No. 2, 1987, pp. 477–481.
Henckaerts, Jean-Marie and Doswald-Beck, Louise, *Customary International Humanitarian Law, Volume I: Rules*, Cambridge University Press, 2005, available at https://www.icrc.org/customary-ihl/eng/docs/v1.
ICRC, *Interpretive Guidance on the Notion of Direct Participation in Hostilities under International Humanitarian Law*, by Nils Melzer, ICRC, Geneva, 2009.
– *International Humanitarian Law and the Challenges of Contemporary Armed Conflicts*, Report prepared for the 31st International Conference of the Red Cross and Red Crescent, ICRC, Geneva, 2011.
Kleffner, Jann K., 'Friend or Foe? On the Protective Reach of the Law of Armed Conflict: a Note on the SCSL Trial Chamber's Judgment in the Case of "Prosecutor v. Sesay, Kallon and Gbao"', in Mariëlle Matthee, Brigit Toebes and Marcel Brus (eds), *Armed Conflict and International Law: In Search of the Human Face, Liber Amicorum in Memory of Avril McDonald*, Asser Press, The Hague, 2013, pp. 285–302. (2013c)
– 'The Beneficiaries of the Rights Stemming from Common Article 3', in Andrew Clapham, Paola Gaeta and Marco Sassòli (eds), *The 1949 Geneva Conventions: A Commentary*, Oxford University Press, 2015, pp. 433–447.
Melzer, Nils, *Targeted Killing in International Law*, Oxford University Press, 2008.

Meron, Theodor, 'Application of Humanitarian Law in Non-international Armed Conflicts: Remarks by Theodor Meron', *Proceedings of the Annual Meeting of the American Society of International Law*, Vol. 85, 1991, pp. 83–85.

Pejic, Jelena, 'The protective scope of Common Article 3: more than meets the eye', *International Review of the Red Cross*, Vol. 93, No. 881, March 2011, pp. 189–225.

Rogers, A.P.V., *Law on the Battlefield*, 3rd edition, Manchester University Press, 2012.

Sassòli, Marco, 'Terrorism and War', *Journal of International Criminal Justice*, Vol. 4, No. 5, 2006, pp. 959–981.

– 'The Role of Human Rights and International Humanitarian Law in New Types of Armed Conflicts', in Orna Ben-Naftali (ed.), *International Humanitarian Law and International Human Rights Law*, Oxford University Press, 2011, pp. 34–94.

Sivakumaran, Sandesh, *The Law of Non-International Armed Conflict*, Oxford University Press, 2012.

Watkin, Kenneth, '21st Century Conflict and International Humanitarian Law: Status Quo or Change?', in Michael N. Schmitt and Jelena Pejic (eds), *International Law and Armed Conflict: Exploring the Faultlines, Essays in Honour of Yoram Dinstein*, Martinus Nijhoff Publishers, Leiden, 2007, pp. 265–296.

Zegveld, Liesbeth, *The Accountability of Armed Opposition Groups in International Law*, Cambridge University Press, 2002.

Section F. Sub-paragraph (1): Fundamental obligations under common Article 3

Bugnion, François, 'Jus ad bellum, jus in bello and non-international armed conflicts', *Yearbook of International Humanitarian Law*, Vol. 6, 2003, pp. 167–198. (2003b)

Condorelli, Luigi and Boisson de Chazournes, Laurence, 'Quelques remarques à propos de l'obligation des Etats de "respecter et faire respecter" le droit international humanitaire "en toutes circonstances"', in Christophe Swinarski (ed.), *Etudes et essais sur le droit international humanitaire et sur les principes de la Croix-rouge en l'honneur de Jean Pictet*, ICRC/Martinus Nijhoff Publishers, The Hague, 1984, pp. 17–35.

Elder, David A., 'The Historical Background of Common Article 3 of the Geneva Convention of 1949', *Case Western Reserve Journal of International Law*, Vol. 11, No. 1, 1979, pp. 37–69.

Kalshoven, Frits and Zegveld, Liesbeth, *Constraints on the Waging of War: An Introduction to International Humanitarian Law*, 4th edition, ICRC/Cambridge University Press, 2011.

Kleffner, Jann K., 'Protection of the Wounded, Sick, and Shipwrecked', in Dieter Fleck (ed.), *The Handbook of International Humanitarian Law*, 3rd edition, Oxford University Press, 2013, pp. 321–357. (2013a)

Lindsey, Charlotte, *Women facing war: ICRC study on the impact of armed conflict on women*, ICRC, Geneva, 2001.

– 'The Impact of Armed Conflict on Women', in Helen Durham and Tracey Gurd (eds), *Listening to the Silences: Women and War*, Martinus Nijhoff Publishers, Leiden, 2005, pp. 21–35.

Moir, Lindsay, *The Law of Internal Armed Conflict*, Cambridge University Press, 2002.

Nowak, Manfred, *U.N. Covenant on Civil and Political Rights, CCPR Commentary*, 2nd revised edition, N.P. Engel, Kehl am Rhein, 2005.

O'Connell, Mary Ellen, 'Historical Development and Legal Basis', in Dieter Fleck (ed.), *The Handbook of International Humanitarian Law*, 3rd edition, Oxford University Press, 2013, pp. 1–42.

Pejic, Jelena, 'Non-discrimination and armed conflict', *International Review of the Red Cross*, Vol. 83, No. 841, March 2001, pp. 183–194.

Rogers, A.P.V., *Law on the Battlefield*, 3rd edition, Manchester University Press, 2012.

Rona, Gabor and McGuire, Robert J., 'The Principle of Non-Discrimination', in Andrew Clapham, Paola Gaeta and Marco Sassòli (eds), *The 1949 Geneva Conventions: A Commentary*, Oxford University Press, 2015, pp. 191–205.

Sassòli, Marco, Bouvier, Antoine A. and Quintin, Anne, *How Does Law Protect in War?*, Vol. I, 3rd edition, ICRC, Geneva, 2011.

Sivakumaran, Sandesh, *The Law of Non-International Armed Conflict*, Oxford University Press, 2012.

Tams, Christian J., 'The Use of Force against Terrorists', *European Journal of International Law*, Vol. 20, No. 2, 2009, pp. 359–397.

Section G. Sub-paragraph (1): Acts prohibited under common Article 3

Violence to life and person, murder

Ambos, Kai, 'Article 25: Individual criminal responsibility', in Otto Triffterer and Kai Ambos (eds), *The Rome Statute of the International Criminal Court: A Commentary*, 3rd edition, Hart Publishing, Oxford, 2016, pp. 979–1029.

Bellal, Annyssa, Giacca, Gilles and Casey-Maslen, Stuart, 'International law and armed non-state actors in Afghanistan', *International Review of the Red Cross*, Vol. 93, No. 881, March 2011, pp. 47–79.

Bothe, Michael, 'The status of captured fighters in non-international armed conflict', in Christian Tomuschat, Evelyne Lagrange and Stefan Oeter (eds), *The Right to Life*, Martinus Nijhoff Publishers, Leiden, 2010, pp. 195–214.

Cassese, Antonio, 'The Geneva Protocols of 1977 on the Humanitarian law of Armed Conflict and Customary International Law', *UCLA Pacific Basin Law Journal*, Vol. 3, 1984, pp. 55–118.

Dörmann, Knut, *Elements of War Crimes under the Rome Statute of the International Criminal Court: Sources and Commentary*, Cambridge University Press, 2003.

 – 'Wilful killing', in Otto Triffterer and Kai Ambos (eds), *The Rome Statute of the International Criminal Court: A Commentary*, 3rd edition, Hart Publishing, Oxford, 2016, pp. 329–331.

Doswald-Beck, Louise, 'The right to life in armed conflict: does international humanitarian law provide all the answers?', *International Review of the Red Cross*, Vol. 88, No. 864, December 2006, pp. 881–904.

Gasser, Hans-Peter, 'The Sixth Annual American Red Cross-Washington College of Law Conference on International Humanitarian Law: A Workshop on Customary International Law and the 1977 Protocols Additional to the 1949 Geneva Conventions; Remarks of Hans-Peter Gasser', *American University Journal of International Law and Policy*, Vol. 2, No. 2, 1987, pp. 415–538, at 477–481.

Gowlland-Debbas, Vera, 'The right to life and the relationship between human rights and humanitarian law', in Christian Tomuschat, Evelyne Lagrange and Stefan Oeter (eds), *The Right to Life*, Martinus Nijhoff Publishers, Leiden, 2010, pp. 121–150.

Horder, Jeremy (ed.), *Homicide Law in Comparative Perspective*, Hart Publishing, Oxford, 2007.

ICRC, *The Use of Force in Armed Conflicts: Interplay between the Conduct of Hostilities and Law Enforcement Paradigms*, Expert Meeting, Report prepared and edited by Gloria Gaggioli, ICRC, Geneva, 2013.

Knuckey, Sarah, 'Murder in Common Article 3', in Andrew Clapham, Paola Gaeta and Marco Sassòli (eds), *The 1949 Geneva Conventions: A Commentary*, Oxford University Press, 2015, pp. 449–467.

Meron, Theodor, 'Application of Humanitarian Law in Non-international Armed Conflicts: Remarks by Theodor Meron', *Proceedings of the Annual Meeting of the American Society of International Law*, Vol. 85, 1991, pp. 83–85.

Nowak, Manfred, *U.N. Covenant on Civil and Political Rights, CCPR Commentary*, 2nd revised edition, N.P. Engel, Kehl, 2005.

Ovey, Clare and White, Robin C.A., *Jacobs & White: The European Convention on Human Rights*, 4th edition, Oxford University Press, 2006.

Watkin, Kenneth, '21st Century Conflict and International Humanitarian Law: Status Quo or Change?', in Michael N. Schmitt and Jelena Pejic (eds), *International Law and Armed Conflict: Exploring the Faultlines, Essays in Honour of Yoram Dinstein*, Martinus Nijhoff Publishers, Leiden, 2007, pp. 265–296.

Zegveld, Liesbeth, *The Accountability of Armed Opposition Groups in International Law*, Cambridge University Press, 2002.

Zimmermann, Andreas and Geiss, Robin, 'Mutilations', in Otto Triffterer and Kai Ambos (eds), *The Rome Statute of the International Criminal Court: A Commentary*, 3rd edition, Hart Publishing, Oxford, 2016, pp. 528–568.

Mutilation

Dörmann, Knut, *Elements of War Crimes under the Rome Statute of the International Criminal Court: Sources and Commentary*, Cambridge University Press, 2003.

Henckaerts, Jean-Marie and Doswald-Beck, Louise, *Customary International Humanitarian Law, Volume I: Rules*, Cambridge University Press, 2005, available at https://www.icrc.org/customary-ihl/eng/docs/v1.

La Haye, Eve, 'Mutilation and medical or scientific experiments: Article 8(2)(b)(x)', in Roy S. Lee and Hakan Friman (eds), *The International Criminal Court: Elements of Crimes and Rules of Procedure and Evidence*, Transnational Publishers, 2001, pp. 164–167. (2001a)

 – 'Violations of Common Article 3', in Roy S. Lee and Hakan Friman (eds), *The International Criminal Court: Elements of Crimes and Rules of Procedure and Evidence*, Transnational Publishers, 2001, pp. 207–213. (2001b)

Zimmermann, Andreas and Geiss, Robin, 'Mutilations', in Otto Triffterer and Kai Ambos (eds), *The Rome Statute of the International Criminal Court: A Commentary*, 3rd edition, Hart Publishing, Oxford, 2016, pp. 528–568, at 551.

Cruel treatment, torture and outrages upon personal dignity

Bank, Roland, 'Das Verbot von Folter, unmenschlicher oder erniedrigender Behandlung oder Strafe', in Rainer Grote and Thilo Marauhn (eds), *EMRK/GG, Konkordanzkommentar zum europäischen und deutschen Grundrechtsschutz*, Mohr Siebeck, Tübingen, 2006, pp. 479–534.

Burgers, J. Herman and Danelius, Hans, *The United Nations Convention against Torture: A Handbook on the Convention against Torture and Other Cruel, Inhuman or Degrading Treatment or Punishment*, Martinus Nijhoff Publishers, Dordrecht, 1988.

Dewulf, Steven, *The Signature of Evil: (Re)Defining Torture in International Law*, Intersentia, Antwerp, 2011.

Dörmann, Knut, *Elements of War Crimes under the Rome Statute of the International Criminal Court: Sources and Commentary*, Cambridge University Press, 2003.

Doswald-Beck, Louise, *Human Rights in Times of Conflict and Terrorism*, Oxford University Press, 2011, pp. 194–227.

Droege, Cordula, '"In truth the leitmotiv": the prohibition of torture and other forms of ill-treatment in international humanitarian law', *International Review of the Red Cross*, Vol. 89, No. 867, September 2007, pp. 515–541.

Evans, Malcolm, 'Getting to Grips with Torture', in *The Definition of Torture: Proceedings of an Expert Seminar*, Association for the Prevention of Torture, Geneva, 2001, pp. 33–49.

Henckaerts, Jean-Marie and Doswald-Beck, Louise, *Customary International Humanitarian Law, Volume I: Rules*, Cambridge University Press, 2005, available at https://www.icrc.org/customary-ihl/eng/docs/v1.

Nowak, Manfred, 'Challenges to the absolute nature of the prohibition of torture and ill-treatment', *Netherlands Quarterly of Human Rights*, Vol. 23, No. 4, 2005, pp. 674–688.

– 'What Practices Constitute Torture?: US and UN standards', *Human Rights Quarterly*, Vol. 28, No. 4, 2006, pp. 809–841.

Nowak, Manfred and Janik, Ralph R.A., 'Torture, Cruel, Inhuman or Degrading Treatment or Punishment', in Andrew Clapham, Paola Gaeta and Marco Sassòli (eds), *The 1949 Geneva Conventions: A Commentary*, Oxford University Press, 2015, pp. 317–342.

Nowak, Manfred and McArthur, Elizabeth, *The United Nations Convention Against Torture: A Commentary*, Oxford University Press, 2008.

Reyes, Hernán, 'The worst scars are in the mind: psychological torture', *International Review of the Red Cross*, Vol. 89, No. 867, September 2007, pp. 591–617.

Rodley, Nigel S., 'The definition(s) of torture in international law', *Current Legal Problems*, Vol. 55, 2002, pp. 467–493.

– 'The prohibition of torture: absolute means absolute', *Denver Journal of International Law and Policy*, Vol. 34, No. 1, 2006, pp. 145–160.

Rodley, Nigel S. and Pollard, Matt, *The Treatment of Prisoners under International Law*, 3rd edition, Oxford University Press, 2009.

Röling, B.V.A. and Rüter, C.F., *The Tokyo Judgment: The International Military Tribunal for the Far East (I.M.T.F.E.), 29 April 1946–12 November 1948*, 2 volumes, University Press, Amsterdam, 1977.

Sivakumaran, Sandesh, *The Law of Non-International Armed Conflict*, Oxford University Press, 2012.

Taking of hostages

Dörmann, Knut, *Elements of War Crimes under the Rome Statute of the International Criminal Court: Sources and Commentary*, Cambridge University Press, 2003.

Elliott, H. Wayne, 'Hostages or Prisoners of War: War Crimes at Dinner', *Military Law Review*, Vol. 149, 1995, pp. 241–274.

Gasser, Hans-Peter and Dörmann, Knut, 'Protection of the Civilian Population', in Dieter Fleck (ed.), *The Handbook of International Humanitarian Law*, 3rd edition, Oxford University Press, 2013, pp. 231–320, at paras 508 and 535.

Gucciardo, Dorotea, 'Hostages', in Jonathan F. Vance (ed.), *Encyclopedia of Prisoners of War and Internment*, 2nd edition, Grey House Publishing, Millerton, New York, 2006, pp. 183–186.

Hammer, Ellen and Salvin, Marina, 'The Taking of Hostages in Theory and Practice', *American Journal of International Law*, Vol. 38, No. 1, 1944, pp. 20–33.

Henckaerts, Jean-Marie and Doswald-Beck, Louise, *Customary International Humanitarian Law, Volume I: Rules*, Cambridge University Press, 2005, available at https://www.icrc.org/customary-ihl/eng/docs/v1.

Herrmann, Irène and Palmieri, Daniel, 'A haunting figure: The hostage through the ages', *International Review of the Red Cross*, Vol. 87, No. 857, March 2005, pp. 135–145.

Kuhn, Arthur K., 'Editorial Comment: The Execution of Hostages', *American Journal of International Law*, Vol. 36, 1942, pp. 271–274.

Lambert, Joseph J., *Terrorism and Hostages in International Law: A Commentary on the Hostages Convention 1979*, Grotius Publications, Cambridge, 1990.

Pilloud, Claude, 'La question des otages et les Conventions de Genève', *Revue internationale de la Croix Rouge*, Vol. 32, No. 378, June 1950, pp. 430–447.

Rosenstock, Robert, 'International Convention Against the Taking of Hostages: Another International Community Step Against Terrorism', *Denver Journal of International Law and Policy*, Vol. 9, No. 2, 1980, pp. 169–195.

Salinas Burgos, Hernán, 'The taking of hostages and international humanitarian law', *International Review of the Red Cross*, Vol. 29, No. 270, June 1989, pp. 196–216.

Sivakumaran, Sandesh, 'War Crimes before the Special Court for Sierra Leone: Child Soldiers, Hostages, Peacekeepers and Collective Punishments', *Journal of International Criminal Justice*, Vol. 8, No. 4, 2010, pp. 1009–1034. (2010a)
– *The Law of Non-International Armed Conflict*, Oxford University Press, 2012.

Tuck, David, 'Taking of Hostages', in Andrew Clapham, Paola Gaeta and Marco Sassòli (eds), *The 1949 Geneva Conventions: A Commentary*, Oxford University Press, 2015, pp. 297–316.

Wright, Lord, 'The Killing of Hostages as a War Crime', *British Yearbook of International Law*, Vol. 25, 1948, pp. 296–310.

Requirement of a regularly constituted court affording all the indispensable judicial guarantees

Barber, Rebecca, 'Facilitating humanitarian assistance in international humanitarian and human rights law', *International Review of the Red Cross*, Vol. 91, No. 874, June 2009, pp. 371–397.

Bond, James E., 'Application of the Law of War to Internal Conflict', *Georgia Journal of International and Comparative Law*, Vol. 3, No. 2, 1973, pp. 345–384.

Bothe, Michael, Partsch, Karl Josef and Solf, Waldemar A., *New Rules for Victims of Armed Conflicts: Commentary on the Two 1977 Protocols Additional to the Geneva Conventions of 1949*, Martinus Nijhoff Publishers, The Hague, 1982.

Doswald-Beck, Louise, *Human Rights in Times of Conflict and Terrorism*, Oxford University Press, 2011, pp. 331–344.

– 'Judicial Guarantees', in Andrew Clapham, Paola Gaeta and Marco Sassòli (eds), *The 1949 Geneva Conventions: A Commentary*, Oxford University Press, 2015, pp. 469–494.

Henckaerts, Jean-Marie and Doswald-Beck, Louise, *Customary International Humanitarian Law, Volume I: Rules*, Cambridge University Press, 2005, available at https://www.icrc.org/customary-ihl/eng/docs/v1.

Sassòli, Marco, 'Taking Armed Groups Seriously: Ways to Improve Their Compliance with International Humanitarian Law', *Journal of International Humanitarian Legal Studies*, Vol. 1, No. 1, 2010, pp. 5–51.

Sivakumaran, Sandesh, 'Courts of Armed Opposition Groups: Fair Trials or Summary Justice?', *Journal of International Criminal Justice*, Vol. 7, No. 3, 2009, pp. 489–513.

– *The Law of Non-International Armed Conflict*, Oxford University Press, 2012.

Somer, Jonathan, 'Jungle justice: passing sentence on the equality of belligerents in non-international armed conflict', *International Review of the Red Cross*, Vol. 89, No. 867, September 2007, pp. 655–690.

Willms, Jan, 'Justice through Armed Groups' Governance – An Oxymoron?', *SFB-Governance Working Paper Series*, No. 40, October 2012.

Sexual violence

Bastick, Megan, Grimm, Karin and Kunz, Rahel, *Sexual Violence in Armed Conflict: Global Overview and Implications for the Security Sector*, Geneva Centre for the Democratic Control of Armed Forces, 2007.

Brammertz, Serge and Jarvis, Michelle (eds), *Prosecuting Conflict-Related Sexual Violence at the ICTY*, Oxford University Press, 2016.

Durham, Helen, 'International Humanitarian Law and the Protection of Women', in Helen Durham and Tracey Gurd (eds), *Listening to the Silences: Women and War*, Martinus Nijhoff Publishers, Leiden, 2005, pp. 95–107.

Gardam, Judith G. and Jarvis, Michelle J., *Women, Armed Conflict and International Law*, Kluwer Law International, The Hague, 2001.

Haeri, Medina and Puechguirbal, Nadine, 'From helplessness to agency: examining the plurality of women's experiences in armed conflict', *International Review of the Red Cross*, Vol. 92, No. 877, March 2010, pp. 103–122.

Henckaerts, Jean-Marie and Doswald-Beck, Louise, *Customary International Humanitarian Law, Volume I: Rules*, Cambridge University Press, 2005, available at https://www.icrc.org/customary-ihl/eng/docs/v1.

Inter-Agency Standing Committee, *Guidelines for Integrating Gender-based Violence Interventions in Humanitarian Action: Reducing risk, promoting resilience and aiding recovery*, 2015.

Lindsey, Charlotte, *Women facing war: ICRC Study on the impact of armed conflict on women*, ICRC, Geneva, 2001.

Sivakumaran, Sandesh, 'Lost in translation: UN responses to sexual violence against men and boys in situations of armed conflict', *International Review of the Red Cross*, Vol. 92, No. 877, March 2010, pp. 259–277. (2010b)

Solangon, Sarah and Patel, Preeti, 'Sexual violence against men in countries affected by armed conflict', *Journal of Conflict, Security and Development*, Vol. 12, No. 4, 2012, pp. 417–442.

Viseur Sellers, Patricia, 'The Context of Sexual Violence: Sexual Violence as Violations of International Humanitarian Law', in Gabrielle Kirk McDonald and Olivia Swaak-Goldman (eds), *Substantive and Procedural Aspects of International Criminal Law*, Kluwer Law International, The Hague, 2000, pp. 263–332.

Viseur Sellers, Patricia and Rosenthal, Indira, 'Rape and Other Sexual Violence', in Andrew Clapham, Paola Gaeta and Marco Sassòli (eds), *The 1949 Geneva Conventions: A Commentary*, Oxford University Press, 2015, pp. 343–368.

World Health Organization, *World report on violence and health*, Report edited by Etienne G. Krug *et al.*, WHO, Geneva, 2002.
 – *Guidelines for medico-legal care for victims of sexual violence*, WHO, Geneva, 2003.

Non-refoulement

Bellinger III, John B. and Padmanabhan, Vijay M., 'Detention Operations in Contemporary Conflicts: Four Challenges for the Geneva Conventions and Other Existing Law', *American Journal of International Law*, Vol. 105, No. 2, 2011, pp. 201–243.

Byers, Michael, 'Legal Opinion on the December 18, 2005 "Arrangement for the Transfer of Detainees between the Canadian Forces and the Ministry of Defence of the Islamic Republic of Afghanistan"', Liu Institute for Global Issues, 7 April 2006.

Droege, Cordula, 'Transfers of detainees: legal framework, non-refoulement and contemporary challenges', *International Review of the Red Cross*, Vol. 90, No. 871, September 2008, pp. 669–701.

Gillard, Emanuela-Chiara, 'There's no place like home: States' obligations in relation to transfers of persons', *International Review of the Red Cross*, Vol. 90, No. 871, September 2008, pp. 703–750.

Gisel, Laurent, 'The principle of non-refoulement in relation to transfers', in *Detention in Armed Conflicts*, Proceedings of the 15th Bruges Colloquium, 16–17 October 2014, College of Europe/ICRC, *Collegium*, No. 45, Autumn 2015, pp. 113–130.

Hathaway, James C., 'Leveraging Asylum', *Texas International Law Journal*, Vol. 45, No. 3, 2010, pp. 503–536.

Horowitz, Jonathan, 'Transferring Wartime Detainees and a State's Responsibility to Prevent Torture', *American University National Security Law Brief*, Vol. 2, No. 2, 2012, pp. 43–66.

Lauterpacht, Elihu and Bethlehem, Daniel, 'The scope and content of the principle of non-refoulement: Opinion', in Erika Feller, Volker Türk and Frances Nicholson (eds), *Refugee Protection in International Law: UNHCR's Global Consultations on International Protection*, Cambridge University Press, 2003, pp. 87–177.

Meron, Theodor, 'The Humanization of Humanitarian Law', *American Journal of International Law*, Vol. 94, No. 2, 2000, pp. 239–278.

Sanderson, Mike, 'The Syrian Crisis and the Principle of Non-Refoulement', *International Law Studies*, U.S. Naval War College, Vol. 89, 2013, pp. 776–801.

Sassòli, Marco and Tougas, Marie-Louise, 'International Law Issues Raised by the Transfer of Detainees by Canadian Forces in Afghanistan', *McGill Law Journal*, Vol. 56, No. 4, 2011, pp. 959–1010.

Skoglund, Lena, 'Diplomatic Assurances Against Torture – An Effective Strategy? A Review of Jurisprudence and Examination of the Arguments', *Nordic Journal of International Law*, Vol. 77, No. 4, 2008, pp. 319–364.

Section H. Detention outside criminal process

Debuf, Els, *Captured in War: Lawful Internment in Armed Conflict*, Hart Publishing, Oxford, 2013.

Deeks, Ashley S., 'Administrative Detention in Armed Conflict', *Case Western Reserve Journal of International Law*, Vol. 40, No. 3, 2009, pp. 403–436.

Dingwall, Joanna, 'Unlawful confinement as a war crime: the jurisprudence of the Yugoslav Tribunal and the common core of international humanitarian law applicable to contemporary armed conflicts', *Journal of Conflict and Security Law*, Vol. 9, No. 2, 2004, pp. 133–179.

Dörmann, Knut, 'Detention in Non-International Armed Conflicts', in Kenneth Watkin and Andrew J. Norris (eds.), *Non-International Armed Conflict in the Twenty-first Century*, International Law Studies, U.S. Naval War College, Vol. 88, 2012, pp. 347–366.

Hampson, Françoise J., 'Is Human Rights Law of Any Relevance to Military Operations in Afghanistan?', in Michael N. Schmitt (ed.), *The War in Afghanistan: A Legal Analysis*, International Law Studies, U.S. Naval War College, Vol. 85, 2009, pp. 485–524.

Heffes, Ezequiel, 'Detentions by Armed Opposition Groups in Non-International Armed Conflicts: Towards a New Characterization of International Humanitarian Law', *Journal of Conflict and Security Law*, Vol. 20, No. 2, 2015, pp. 229–250.

ICRC, 'Procedural principles and safeguards for internment/administrative detention in armed conflict and other situations of violence', in *International Humanitarian Law and the challenges of contemporary armed conflicts*, Report prepared for the 30th International Conference of the Red Cross and Red Crescent, Geneva, 2007, Annex 1, reproduced in *International Review of the Red Cross*, Vol. 87, No. 858, June 2005, pp. 375–391.

 – *Internment in Armed Conflict: Basic Rules and Challenges*, Opinion Paper, November 2014.

Pejic, Jelena, 'Procedural principles and safeguards for internment/administrative detention in armed conflict and other situations of violence', *International Review of the Red Cross*, Vol. 87, No. 858, June 2005, pp. 375–391.

 – 'Conflict Classification and the Law Applicable to Detention and the Use of Force', in Elizabeth Wilmshurst (ed.), *International Law and the Classification of Conflicts*, Oxford University Press, 2012, pp. 80–116.

Rona, Gabor, 'Is There a Way Out of the Non-International Armed Conflict Detention Dilemma?', *International Law Studies*, U.S. Naval War College, Vol. 91, 2015, pp. 32–59.

Rowe, Peter, 'Is There a Right to Detain Civilians by Foreign Armed Forces during a Non-International Armed Conflict?', *International and Comparative Law Quarterly*, Vol. 61, No. 3, 2012, pp. 697–711.

Section I. Sub-paragraph (2): Collection of and care of the wounded and sick

See also the select bibliography of the commentary on Article 12 of the First Convention.

Bothe, Michael, Partsch, Karl Josef and Solf, Waldemar A., *New Rules for Victims of Armed Conflicts, Commentary on the Two 1977 Protocols Additional to the Geneva Conventions of 1949*, Martinus Nijhoff Publishers, The Hague, 1982.

Breau, Susan C., 'Commentary on selected Rules from the ICRC Study: Protected persons and objects', in Elizabeth Wilmshurst and Susan C. Breau (eds), *Perspectives on the ICRC Study on Customary International Humanitarian Law*, Cambridge University Press, 2007, pp. 169–203.

Dörmann, Knut, *Elements of War Crimes under the Rome Statute of the International Criminal Court: Sources and Commentary*, Cambridge University Press, 2003.

Dunant, Henry, *A Memory of Solferino*, ICRC, Geneva, reprint 1986.

Henckaerts, Jean-Marie and Doswald-Beck, Louise, *Customary International Humanitarian Law, Volume I: Rules*, Cambridge University Press, 2005, available at https://www.icrc.org/customary-ihl/eng/docs/v1.

ICRC, *Management of Dead Bodies after Disasters: A Field Manual for First Responders*, ICRC, Geneva, 2009.
  – *War Surgery: Working with Limited Resources in Armed Conflict and Other Situations of Violence*, Vol. 1 by Christos Giannou and Marco Baldan and Vol. 2 by Christos Giannou, Marco Baldan and Åsa Molde, ICRC, Geneva, 2009 and 2013 respectively.
  – *First Aid in Armed Conflicts and Other Situations of Violence*, ICRC, Geneva, 2010.
  – *Health Care in Danger: Violent Incidents Affecting the Delivery of Health Care*, January 2012 to December 2013, ICRC, Geneva, 2014.
  – *Promoting Military Operational Practice that Ensures Safe Access to and Delivery of Health Care*, ICRC, Geneva, 2014.

Kleffner, Jann K., 'Protection of the Wounded, Sick, and Shipwrecked', in Dieter Fleck (ed.), *The Handbook of International Humanitarian Law*, 3rd edition, Oxford University Press, 2013, pp. 321–357. (2013a)

Lindsey, Charlotte, *Women facing war: ICRC Study on the impact of armed conflict on women*, ICRC, Geneva, 2001.

Müller, Amrei, *The Relationship between Economic, Social and Cultural Rights and International Humanitarian Law: An Analysis of Health-Related Issues in Non-International Armed Conflicts*, Martinus Nijhoff Publishers, Leiden, 2013.

Sivakumaran, Sandesh, *The Law of Non-International Armed Conflict*, Oxford University Press, 2012.

Section J. Paragraph 2: Offer of services by an impartial humanitarian body such as the ICRC

Barrat, Claudie, *Status of NGOs in International Humanitarian Law*, Brill Nijhoff, Leiden, 2014.

Blondel, Jean-Luc, 'L'assistance aux personnes protégées', *Revue internationale de la Croix-Rouge*, Vol. 69, No. 767, October 1987, pp. 471–489.

– 'The meaning of the word "humanitarian" in relation to the Fundamental Principles of the Red Cross and Red Crescent', *International Review of the Red Cross*, Vol. 29, No. 273, December 1989, pp. 507–515.

– 'Genèse et évolution des Principes fondamentaux de la Croix-Rouge et du Croissant-Rouge', *Revue internationale de la Croix-Rouge*, Vol. 73, No. 790, August 1991, pp. 369–377.

Bouchet-Saulnier, Françoise, 'Consent to humanitarian access: An obligation triggered by territorial control, not States' rights', *International Review of the Red Cross*, Vol. 96, No. 893, March 2014, pp. 207–217.

Bugnion, François, *The International Committee of the Red Cross and the Protection of War Victims*, ICRC/Macmillan, Oxford, 2003, Book II, Part Two. (2003a)

de Geouffre de La Pradelle, Paul, 'Une conquête méthodique : le droit d'initiative humanitaire dans les rapports internationaux', in Christophe Swinarski (ed.), *Études et essais sur le droit international humanitaire et sur les principes de la Croix-Rouge en l'honneur de Jean Pictet*, ICRC/Martinus Nijhoff Publishers, The Hague, 1984, pp. 945–950.

Fast, Larissa, 'Unpacking the principle of humanity: Tensions and implications', *International Review of the Red Cross*, Vol. 97, Nos 897/898, Spring/Summer 2015, pp. 111–131.

Forsythe, David P., 'International Humanitarian Assistance: The Role of the Red Cross', *Buffalo Journal of International Law*, Vol. 3, No. 2, 1996–1997, pp. 235–260.

Gentile, Pierre, 'Humanitarian organizations involved in protection activities: a story of soul-searching and professionalization', *International Review of the Red Cross*, Vol. 93, No. 884, December 2011, pp. 1165–1191.

Gillard, Emanuela-Chiara, 'The law regulating cross-border relief operations', *International Review of the Red Cross*, Vol. 95, No. 890, June 2013, pp. 351–382.

Harroff-Tavel, Marion, 'Neutrality and Impartiality – The importance of these principles for the International Red Cross and Red Crescent Movement and the difficulties involved in applying them', *International Review of the Red Cross*, Vol. 29, No. 273, December 1989, pp. 536–552.

Henckaerts, Jean-Marie and Doswald-Beck, Louise, *Customary International Humanitarian Law, Volume I: Rules*, Cambridge University Press, 2005, available at https://www.icrc.org/customary-ihl/eng/docs/v1.

ICRC, 'ICRC Q&A and lexicon on humanitarian access', *International Review of the Red Cross*, Vol. 96, No. 893, March 2014, pp. 359–375.

– *The Fundamental Principles of the International Red Cross and Red Crescent Movement*, ICRC, Geneva, August 2015.

ICRC and International Federation of Red Cross and Red Crescent Societies, *The Fundamental Principles of the International Red Cross and Red Crescent Movement: Ethics and Tools for Humanitarian Action*, ICRC, November 2015.

Junod, Sylvie S., 'Le mandat du CICR durant un conflit armé. Le mandat et les activités du Comité international de la Croix-Rouge', *The Military Law and Law of War Review*, Vol. 43, 2004, pp. 103–110.

Kalshoven, Frits, 'Impartiality and Neutrality in Humanitarian Law and Practice', *International Review of the Red Cross*, Vol. 29, No. 273, December 1989, pp. 516–535.

Kolb, Robert, 'De l'assistance humanitaire : la résolution sur l'assistance humanitaire adoptée par l'Institut de droit international à sa session de Bruges en

2003', *Revue international de la Croix-Rouge*, Vol. 86, No. 856, December 2004, pp. 853–878.

Kuijt, Emilie Ellen, *Humanitarian Assistance and State Sovereignty in International Law: Towards a Comprehensive Framework*, Intersentia, Cambridge, 2015.

Labbé, Jérémie and Daudin, Pascal, 'Applying the humanitarian principles: Reflecting on the experience of the International Committee of the Red Cross', *International Review of the Red Cross*, Vol. 97, Nos 897/898, Spring/Summer 2015, pp. 183–210.

Lattanzi, Flavia, 'Humanitarian Assistance', in Andrew Clapham, Paola Gaeta and Marco Sassòli (eds), *The 1949 Geneva Conventions: A Commentary*, Oxford University Press, 2015, pp. 231–255.

Nishat, Nishat, 'The Right of Initiative of the ICRC and Other Impartial Humanitarian Bodies', in Andrew Clapham, Paola Gaeta and Marco Sassòli (eds), *The 1949 Geneva Conventions: A Commentary*, Oxford University Press, 2015, pp. 495–508.

Oxford Guidance on the Law Relating to Humanitarian Relief Operations in Situations of Armed Conflict, by Dapo Akande and Emanuela-Chiara Gillard, commissioned and published by the UN Office for the Coordination of Humanitarian Affairs, 2016.

Plattner, Denise, 'Assistance to the civilian population: the development and present state of international humanitarian law', *International Review of the Red Cross*, Vol. 32, No. 288, June 1992, pp. 249–263.

Ryngaert, Cédric, 'Humanitarian Assistance and the Conundrum of Consent: A Legal Perspective', *Amsterdam Law Forum*, Vol. 5, No. 2, 2013, pp. 5–19.

Sandoz, Yves, 'Le droit d'initiative du Comité international de la Croix-rouge', *German Yearbook of International Law*, Vol. 22, 1979, pp. 352–373.

Schwendimann, Felix, 'The legal framework of humanitarian access in armed conflict', *International Review of the Red Cross*, Vol. 93, No. 884, December 2011, pp. 993–1008.

Spieker, Heike, 'Humanitarian Assistance, Access in Armed Conflict and Occupation', version of March 2013, in Rüdiger Wolfrum (ed.), *Max Planck Encyclopedia of Public International Law*, Oxford University Press, http://www.mpepil.com.

Stoffels, Ruth Abril, 'Legal regulation of humanitarian assistance in armed conflict: Achievements and gaps', *International Review of the Red Cross*, Vol. 86, No. 855, September 2004, pp. 515–546.

Swinarski, Christophe, 'La notion d'un organisme neutre et le droit international', in Christophe Swinarski (ed.), *Études et essais sur le droit international humanitaire et sur les principes de la Croix-Rouge en l'honneur de Jean Pictet*, ICRC/Martinus Nijhoff Publishers, The Hague, 1984, pp. 819–835.

Swiss Confederation, Federal Department of Foreign Affairs, *Humanitarian Access in Situations of Armed Conflict: Practitioners' Manual*, 2014.

Toebes, Brigit, 'Health and Humanitarian Assistance: Towards an Integrated Norm under International Law', *Tilburg Law Review*, Vol. 18, No. 2, 2013, pp. 133–151.

Vukas, Budislav, 'Humanitarian Assistance in Cases of Emergency', version of March 2013, in Rüdiger Wolfrum (ed.), *Max Planck Encyclopedia of Public International Law*, Oxford University Press, http://www.mpepil.com.

Section K. Paragraph 3: Special agreements

Aïvo, Gérard, 'Le rôle des accords spéciaux dans la rationalisation des conflits armés non internationaux', *Revue québécoise de droit international*, Vol. 27, No. 1, 2014, pp. 1–30.

Bell, Christine, 'Peace Agreements: Their Nature and Legal Status', *American Journal of International Law*, Vol. 100, No. 2, 2006, pp. 373–412.
– *On the Law of Peace: Peace Agreements and the Lex Pacificatoria*, Oxford University Press, 2008.

Cassese, Antonio, 'The Special Court and International Law: The Decision Concerning the Lomé Agreement Amnesty', *Journal of International Criminal Justice*, Vol. 2, No. 4, 2004, pp. 1130–1140.

Corten, Olivier and Klein, Pierre, 'Are Agreements between States and Non-State Entities Rooted in the International Legal Order?', in Enzo Cannizzaro (ed.), *The Law of Treaties: Beyond the Vienna Convention*, Oxford University Press, 2011, pp. 3–24.

Ewumbue-Monono, Churchill, 'Respect for international humanitarian law by armed non-state actors in Africa', *International Review of the Red Cross*, Vol. 88, No. 864, December 2006, pp. 905–924.

ICRC, *The Roots of Behaviour in War: Understanding and Preventing IHL Violations*, by Daniel Muñoz-Rojas and Jean-Jacques Frésard, ICRC, Geneva, October 2005.
– *Increasing Respect for International Humanitarian Law in Non-International Armed Conflicts*, ICRC, Geneva, February 2008.
– 'A collection of codes of conduct issued by armed groups', *International Review of the Red Cross*, Vol. 93, No. 882, June 2011, pp. 483–501.

Jakovljevic, Bosko, 'Armed conflict in Yugoslavia: Agreements in the field of international humanitarian law and practice', *Journal of International Law of Peace and Armed Conflict*, Vol. 5, No. 3, 1992, pp. 108–111. (1992a)
– 'The Agreement of May 22, 1992, on the Implementation of International Humanitarian Law in the Armed Conflict in Bosnia-Herzegovina', *Jugoslovenska Revija za Medunarodno Pravo*, Nos 2–3, 1992, pp. 212–221. (1992b)

Ramelli Arteaga, Alejandro, *Derecho Internacional Humanitario y Estado de Beligerancia*, 2nd edition, Externado University of Colombia, Bogotá, 2004, pp. 45–53.

Roberts, Anthea and Sivakumaran, Sandesh, 'Lawmaking by Nonstate Actors: Engaging Armed Groups in the Creation of International Humanitarian Law', *The Yale Journal of International Law*, Vol. 37, No. 1, 2012, pp. 107–152.

Sassòli, Marco, 'Taking Armed Groups Seriously: Ways to Improve their Compliance with International Humanitarian Law', *International Humanitarian Legal Studies*, Vol. 1, No. 1, 2010, pp. 5–51.

Sassòli, Marco, Bouvier, Antoine A. and Quintin, Anne, *How Does Law Protect in War?*, Vol. I, 3rd edition, ICRC, Geneva, 2011, pp. 1713–1717.

Sassòli, Marco and Tougas, Marie-Louise, 'International Law Issues Raised by the Transfer of Detainees by Canadian Forces in Afghanistan', *McGill Law Journal*, Vol. 56, No. 4, 2011, pp. 959–1010.

Siordet, Frédéric, 'Les Conventions de Genève et la guerre civile (suite)', *Revue internationale de la Croix-Rouge et Bulletin international des Sociétés de la Croix-Rouge*, Vol. 32, No. 375, March 1950, pp. 187–212.

Sivakumaran, Sandesh, 'Lessons for the law of armed conflict from commitments of armed groups: identification of legitimate targets and prisoners of war', *International Review of the Red Cross*, Vol. 93, No. 882, June 2011, pp. 463–482.
– *The Law of Non-International Armed Conflict*, Oxford University Press, 2012.
van Steenberghe, Raphaël, 'Théorie des sujets', in Raphaël van Steenberghe (ed.), *Droit international humanitaire : un régime spécial de droit international ?*, Bruylant, Brussels, 2013, pp. 15–71.
Veuthey, Michel, 'Learning from History: Accession to the Conventions, Special Agreements, and Unilateral Declarations', in *Relevance of International Humanitarian Law to Non-State Actors*, Proceedings of the Bruges Colloquium, 25–26 October 2002, College of Europe/ICRC, *Collegium*, No. 27, Spring 2003, pp. 139–151.
Vierucci, Luisa, 'Special Agreements between Conflicting Parties in the Case-law of the ICTY', in Bert Swart, Alexander Zahar and Göran Sluiter (eds), *The Legacy of the International Criminal Tribunal for the Former Yugoslavia*, Oxford University Press, 2011, pp. 401–433.
– 'Applicability of the Conventions by Means of Ad Hoc Agreements', in Andrew Clapham, Paola Gaeta and Marco Sassòli (eds), *The 1949 Geneva Conventions: A Commentary*, Oxford University Press, 2015, pp. 509–522.

Section L. Paragraph 4: Legal status of the Parties to the conflict

Fleck, Dieter, 'The Law of Non-International Armed Conflict', in Dieter Fleck (ed.), *The Handbook of International Humanitarian Law*, 3rd edition, Oxford University Press, 2013, pp. 581–610.
Moir, Lindsay, *The Law of Internal Armed Conflict*, Cambridge University Press, 2002.
Sivakumaran, Sandesh, *The Law of Non-International Armed Conflict*, Oxford University Press, 2012.

Section M. Criminal aspects and compliance

Bellal, Annyssa and Casey-Maslen, Stuart, 'Enhancing Compliance with International Law by Armed Non-State Actors', *Goettingen Journal of International Law*, Vol. 3, No. 1, 2011, pp. 175–197.
Bílková, Veronika, 'Belligerent reprisals in non-international armed conflicts', *International and Comparative Law Quarterly*, Vol. 63, No. 1, 2014, pp. 31–65.
Blewitt, Graham T., 'The Necessity for Enforcement of International Humanitarian Law', *Proceedings of the Annual Meeting (American Society of International Law)*, Vol. 89, 1995, pp. 298–300.
Bothe, Michael, Partsch, Karl Josef and Solf, Waldemar A., *New Rules for Victims of Armed Conflicts: Commentary on the Two 1977 Protocols Additional to the Geneva Conventions of 1949*, Martinus Nijhoff Publishers, The Hague, 1982.
De Hemptinne, Jérôme, 'Prohibition of Reprisals', in Andrew Clapham, Paola Gaeta and Marco Sassòli (eds), *The 1949 Geneva Conventions: A Commentary*, Oxford University Press, 2015, pp. 575–596.
Dinstein, Yoram, *Non-International Armed Conflicts in International Law*, Cambridge University Press, 2014, pp. 173–199.

Draper, Gerald I.A.D., 'The implementation and enforcement of the Geneva Conventions of 1949 and of the Two Additional Protocols of 1978' (sic), *Collected Courses of the Hague Academy of International Law*, Vol. 164, 1979, pp. 1–54.

Henckaerts, Jean-Marie and Doswald-Beck, Louise, *Customary International Humanitarian Law, Volume I: Rules*, Cambridge University Press, 2005, available at https://www.icrc.org/customary-ihl/eng/docs/v1.

ICRC, *Increasing Respect for International Humanitarian Law in Non-International Armed Conflicts*, ICRC, Geneva, February 2008.

– Advisory Service on International Humanitarian Law, *Preventing and repressing international crimes: Towards an 'integrated' approach based on domestic practice*, Report of the Third Universal Meeting of National Committees for the Implementation of International Humanitarian Law, prepared by Anne-Marie La Rosa, Vols I–II, ICRC, Geneva, February 2014.

La Haye, Eve, *War Crimes in Internal Armed Conflicts*, Cambridge University Press, 2008.

La Rosa, Anne-Marie and Wuerzner, Carolin, 'Armed groups, sanctions and the implementation of international humanitarian law', *International Review of the Red Cross*, Vol. 90, No. 870, June 2008, pp. 327–341.

Meron, Theodor, 'International Criminalization of Internal Atrocities', *American Journal of International Law*, Vol. 89, No. 3, 1995, pp. 554–577.

Milanovic, Marko and Hadzi-Vidanovic, Vidan, 'A taxonomy of armed conflict', in Nigel D. White and Christian Henderson (eds), *Research Handbook on International Conflict and Security Law: Jus ad Bellum, Jus in Bello and Just post bellum*, Edward Elgar, Cheltenham, 2013, pp. 256–314.

Moir, Lindsay, *The Law of Internal Armed Conflict*, Cambridge University Press, 2002.

Morris, Madeline H., 'International Guidelines Against Impunity: Facilitating Accountability', *Law and Contemporary Problems*, Vol. 59, No. 4, 1996, pp. 29–39.

Perna, Laura, *The Formation of the Treaty Law of Non-International Armed Conflicts*, Martinus Nijhoff Publishers, Leiden, 2006.

Pfanner, Toni, 'Various mechanisms and approaches for implementing international humanitarian law and protecting and assisting war victims', *International Review of the Red Cross*, Vol. 91, No. 874, June 2009, pp. 279–328.

Plattner, Denise, 'The penal repression of violations of international humanitarian law applicable in non-international armed conflicts', *International Review of the Red Cross*, Vol. 30, No. 278, October 1990, pp. 409–420.

Sassòli, Marco, 'Taking Armed Groups Seriously: Ways to Improve Their Compliance with International Humanitarian Law', *Journal of International Humanitarian Legal Studies*, Vol. 1, No. 1, 2010, pp. 5–51.

Sassòli, Marco, Bouvier, Antoine A. and Quintin, Anne, *How Does Law Protect in War?*, Vol. I, 3rd edition, ICRC, Geneva, 2011.

Sivakumaran, Sandesh, *The Law of Non-International Armed Conflict*, Oxford University Press, 2012.

– 'The Addressees of Common Article 3', in Andrew Clapham, Paola Gaeta and Marco Sassòli (eds), *The 1949 Geneva Conventions: A Commentary*, Oxford University Press, 2015, pp. 415–431.

ARTICLE 4

APPLICATION BY NEUTRAL POWERS

❖ Text of the provision

Neutral Powers shall apply by analogy the provisions of the present Convention to the wounded and sick, and to members of the medical personnel and to chaplains of the armed forces of the Parties to the conflict, received or interned in their territory, as well as to dead persons found.

❖ Reservations or declarations

None

Contents

A. Introduction

908 The outbreak of an international armed conflict triggers the applicability of specific rules of international law. Without prejudice to other rules of international law, international law applicable to international armed conflicts, as traditionally understood, is composed of both international humanitarian law

326

and the law of neutrality. These are separate yet complementary legal frameworks, in that the law of neutrality, at least in part, has the same object and purpose as international humanitarian law of mitigating and containing the adverse effects of an international armed conflict.[1]

909   The law of neutrality regulates relations between States which are Parties to an international armed conflict and States which are not Parties to the conflict (neutral Powers).[2] Thus, the law of neutrality is composed of rules applicable to both categories of States. While the entire body of the law of neutrality is applicable to every international armed conflict, in practice the full panoply of rights conferred by this body of international law will not always be invoked or enforced by the neutral Powers or the Parties to the armed conflict. This is because many of these rights apply only to specific types of events, which do not necessarily arise in every international armed conflict. Nonetheless, some of the obligations contained in the law of neutrality, such as respect for the inviolability of neutral territory, will apply in every such conflict.

910   The Geneva Conventions contain several rules in which the terms 'neutral Powers', 'neutral countries' or 'neutral States' are used interchangeably.[3] By referring to these terms in 1949, the Conventions acknowledged, for the purposes of international humanitarian law, the continued validity of the law of neutrality following the adoption in 1945 of the UN Charter and its system of collective security.[4] The same conclusion can also be drawn from the provisions of the Geneva Conventions which regulate the system of 'Protecting Powers', since these provisions presuppose the existence of neutral Powers.[5] Nevertheless, the drafters of the 1949 Geneva Conventions

---

[1] See ILC, *Draft articles on the effects of armed conflicts on treaties, with commentaries*, 2011, page 21, where the Draft Articles speak of 'treaties on the law of armed conflict, *including* treaties on international humanitarian law' (emphasis added). See also Christopher Greenwood, 'Historical Development and Legal Basis', in Dieter Fleck (ed.), *The Handbook of International Humanitarian Law*, 2nd edition, Oxford University Press, 2008, pp. 1–43, at 11: 'International humanitarian law thus includes most of what used to be known as the laws of war, although strictly speaking some parts of those laws, such as the law of neutrality, are not included since their primary purpose is not humanitarian.'

[2] For the definition of 'neutral Powers', see paras 916–919. For the definition of 'international armed conflict', as well as for a discussion of when a State becomes a 'Party to an international armed conflict', see the commentary on common Article 2, section D.2. The criteria for determining whether a neutral State has become a Party to an international armed conflict are found exclusively in international humanitarian law, not in the law of neutrality.

[3] See First Convention, Article 4 ('neutral Powers'), Article 8(1) ('neutral Powers'), Article 10 ('neutral State' in 10(2) and 'neutral Power' in 10(4)), Article 11(2) ('neutral territory' and 'neutral Power'), Article 27 ('neutral country' in 27(1), 'neutral Government' in 27(2) and 'neutral country' in 27(4)), Article 37 ('neutral Power' in 37(1) and 'neutral territory' in 37(3)) and Article 43 ('neutral countries').

[4] See the prominent treatment accorded to the 'principle of neutrality' in ICJ, *Legality of the Threat or Use of Nuclear Weapons*, Advisory Opinion, 1996, paras 88–89. See also Edward R. Cummings, 'The Evolution of the Notion of Neutrality in Modern Armed Conflicts', *Military Law and Law of War Review*, Vol. 17, 1978, pp. 37–69, at 46–47.

[5] See common Article 8 (Article 9 in the Fourth Convention). See also Bindschedler, p. 33. When a neutral State performs the role of a Protecting Power in the sense of Article 8, this cannot be considered a violation of the obligations applicable to it on the basis of the law of neutrality, see United States, *Law of War Manual*, 2015, para. 15.3.2.4.

deliberately refrained from addressing questions regarding the substantive rules of the law of neutrality.[6]

911   Article 4 is an example of a rule of the Geneva Conventions which applies to neutral Powers. It regulates situations in which persons protected by the First Convention are in the territory of a neutral Power. With regard to these persons, the neutral Power is bound to apply, in its own territory, the provisions of the First Convention by analogy. This obligation reflects the Convention's purpose: to ensure that persons protected by the Convention receive that protection wherever they may be.

912   The Second Convention contains a provision (Article 5) which – apart from the logical addition of the 'shipwrecked' – is identical to the present article. Additional Protocol I contains a similar rule, but with a much wider scope of beneficiaries.[7] The absence of similar provisions in common Article 3 and in Additional Protocol II is explained by the fact that the law of neutrality does not apply in non-international armed conflicts.

B. Historical background

913   The 1907 Hague Convention (V) is the only treaty dealing specifically with the law of neutrality applicable to land warfare. Article 15 states that '[t]he [1906] Geneva Convention applies to sick and wounded interned in neutral territory'.[8] Thus, the law of neutrality applicable to land warfare referred to the applicability of the Geneva Convention. The Geneva Conventions of 1864, 1906 and 1929 did not contain any such rule.

914   In the draft of the First Convention submitted to the 1948 Stockholm Conference, the ICRC proposed, as a novelty, the insertion of the following rule: 'Neutral Powers shall apply the stipulations of the present Convention by analogy to the wounded and sick, as also to members of the medical personnel and to chaplains, who are members of belligerent armies and who may be interned in their territories.'[9] The incorporation of this rule in the First Convention was considered necessary to ensure that the most recent (1949) version of the Convention would be the instrument of reference for neutral Powers in such circumstances. Furthermore, the proposed wording ensured that the rule would apply not only to the wounded and sick, as was already the case under the 1907 formulation, but also to the armed forces' medical personnel and chaplains. A slightly reworded proposal was accepted by the Stockholm Conference.[10]

---

[6] For detailed references on this point, see paras 934–935.   [7] Additional Protocol I, Article 19.
[8] Similar statements can be found in Article 56 of the 1874 Brussels Declaration, in Article 82 of the 1880 Oxford Manual and in Article 60 of the 1899 Hague Regulations.
[9] *Draft Conventions submitted to the 1948 Stockholm Conference*, draft article 3, pp. 6–7.
[10] *Draft Conventions adopted by the 1948 Stockholm Conference*, draft article 3, p. 10: 'Neutral Powers shall apply by analogy the provisions of the present Convention to the wounded and sick, and to members of the medical personnel and to chaplains of belligerent armed forces interned in their territory.'

915   At the 1949 Diplomatic Conference, the rule was extended to include protected persons 'received'[11] and 'dead persons found'[12] in neutral territory.

C. Discussion

1. Neutral Powers

916   Article 4 binds neutral Powers.[13] This term is used in several provisions of the 1907 Hague Convention (V) and of the 1949 Geneva Conventions.[14] The notion of 'neutral Power' is not defined anywhere in these treaties. As a matter of customary international law, 'neutral Power' refers to a State which is not a Party to an international armed conflict.[15] Thus, Article 4 can be considered to bind all States which are not Parties to an international armed conflict in the sense of common Article 2.[16]

917   The binding nature of Article 4 with regard to all these States does not depend on how they view or characterize their status as not being Parties to a particular conflict, i.e. whether they consider or have declared themselves to be 'neutral' in the sense of being bound by the rights and obligations of the law of neutrality. Nor is it affected if a State chooses to adopt a stance of so-called

---

[11] *Final Record of the Diplomatic Conference of Geneva of 1949*, Vol. II-A, p. 46. For a substantive analysis of this modification, see para. 923.

[12] *Final Record of the Diplomatic Conference of Geneva of 1949*, Vol. II-B, pp. 157 and 165.

[13] See also Article 5 of the Second Convention, which applies equally to 'neutral Powers'. The Geneva Conventions also use the phrase 'neutral or non-belligerent Powers' on two occasions; see Third Convention, Articles 4(B)(2) and 122. This terminological difference has no substantive implications; see Sandoz, pp. 92–93. Furthermore, Article 19 of Additional Protocol I applies to '[n]eutral and other States not Parties to the conflict'. The use of this different terminology in Additional Protocol I does not affect the meaning of the term 'neutral Powers' in the Conventions; see Sandoz/Swinarski/Zimmermann (eds), *Commentary on the Additional Protocols*, ICRC, 1987, p. 61. See also Kussbach, pp. 232–235, and Heintschel von Heinegg, p. 554. See also Sandoz, p. 93, who concludes: 'We can confirm that when an [international armed conflict] breaks out, states are either belligerent or neutral.'

[14] For an overview of the provisions of the First Convention in which this term, along with its substantively identical counterparts, is used, see fn. 3.

[15] This definition corresponds to the ones reflected in recent restatements of international law drafted by independent groups of experts. See San Remo Manual on International Law Applicable to Armed Conflicts at Sea (1994), Rule 13(d); Manual on International Law Applicable to Air and Missile Warfare (2009), Rule 1(aa); and Helsinki Principles on the Law of Maritime Neutrality, adopted by the International Law Association at its 68th Conference, Taipei, 30 May 1998, Article 1.1. Similarly, see Australia, *Manual of the Law of Armed Conflict*, 2006, para. 11.3; Canada, *LOAC Manual*, 2001, paras 1302–1303; and United States, *Naval Handbook*, 2007, para. 7.1. Article 19 of Additional Protocol I similarly speaks of '[n]eutral and other States not Parties to the conflict' without affecting the meaning of the term 'neutral Power' in the Geneva Conventions; see fn. 13. See also Bothe, 2011, p. 1: 'Neutrality means the particular status, defined by international law, of a State not a party to an armed conflict.' The Russian Federation's *Regulations on the Application of IHL*, 2001, refers to 'neutral States' without defining the term.

[16] For an international armed conflict in the sense of common Article 2(1) to exist, there is no requirement for there to have been a declaration of war; see the commentary on that article, section D.1.

'non-belligerency', regardless of whether doing so is lawful as a matter of international law.[17]

918   These considerations are immaterial when it comes to determining the scope of application of Article 4, a provision dealing solely with obligations of a humanitarian nature. Thus, the scope of application of Article 4 includes, but is not limited to, States considering themselves permanently neutral, States proclaiming themselves non-belligerent, and States serving as Protecting Powers within the framework of Article 8. The same holds true if the UN Security Council has taken binding preventive or enforcement measures, such as sanctions or the authorization of the use of force, against a particular State under Chapter VII of the UN Charter. The exercise of these measures may lead to, or occur in the context of, a situation which qualifies as an international armed conflict. Irrespective of whether the law of neutrality needs to be complied with in these circumstances, Article 4 binds all States which are not Parties to that international armed conflict.

919   Two further considerations are equally immaterial for the applicability of Article 4: first, whether diplomatic relations exist between the neutral Power and the Party to the armed conflict; and second, whether the persons covered by Article 4 are entitled to be treated as prisoners of war.[18] The opposite view would run counter to the purpose of Article 4, a provision inspired exclusively by humanitarian considerations, which is to ensure that persons protected by the First Convention receive the protection of the Convention wherever they may be.

2. Conditions for the applicability of Article 4

920   Article 4 requires a neutral Power to apply, by analogy, the relevant provisions of the First Convention when (a) persons protected under the First Convention are (b) received, interned or found in its territory.

a. Persons covered

921   Four categories of persons protected under the First Convention are potential beneficiaries of the obligation laid down in Article 4:

(i) Wounded and sick. The term 'wounded and sick' refers to the persons covered by Article 12(1): members of the armed forces and of groups assimilated

---

[17] As indicated above, the criteria for determining whether a neutral State has become a Party to an international armed conflict are found exclusively in international humanitarian law, not in the law of neutrality. With regard to so-called 'non-belligerency', see, with further references, Heintschel von Heinegg, p. 544: 'there is no basis for concepts such as "benevolent neutrality" or "non-belligerency"'; see also Sandoz, p. 93. For a different view, see Natalino Ronzitti, 'Italy's Non-Belligerency during the Iraqi War', in Maurizio Ragazzi (ed.), *International Responsibility Today: Essays in Memory of Oscar Schachter*, Martinus Nijhoff, Leiden, 2005, pp. 197–207.

[18] On the latter, see Article 4(B)(2) of the Third Convention.

thereto who are covered by Article 13 and who are wounded or sick.[19] From the moment these persons cease to qualify as 'wounded' or 'sick', they are no longer protected by the First Convention, and their status in neutral territory will be regulated on the basis of the law of neutrality, along with other applicable norms of international and domestic law.[20]

The Third Convention provides for the possibility that seriously wounded and seriously sick prisoners of war be accommodated in a neutral country.[21] While Article 4 of the First Convention may also be applicable in such circumstances, the neutral Power must discharge its obligations under the Geneva Conventions by applying the more detailed rules of the Third Convention.[22]

(ii) Members of the medical personnel of the armed forces of the Parties to the conflict. This category includes persons covered by Articles 24 and 25, i.e. permanent military medical and religious personnel and auxiliary medical personnel. In view of the object and purpose of Article 4, based on the provision's drafting history, and since they are entitled to protection under the First Convention, persons covered by Articles 26 or 27 – who are not members of the armed forces of the Parties to the conflict but civilians – are also included within the notion of 'medical personnel' covered by Article 4.[23]

(iii) Chaplains of the armed forces of the Parties to the conflict. This category refers to the religious personnel covered by Article 24. In view of the object and purpose of Article 4, based on the provision's drafting history, and since they are entitled to protection under the First Convention, persons covered by Article 26 or 27 – who are not members of the armed forces of the Parties to the conflict but civilians – are also included within the notion of 'chaplains of the armed forces of the Parties to the conflict' covered by Article 4.

[19] For the definition of 'wounded and sick' in the First Convention, see the commentary on Article 12, section D.2.

[20] On the question of whether the neutral Power must intern them, see paras 934–935.

[21] See Third Convention, Articles 109–117.

[22] The need for the neutral Power to comply with the Third Convention if seriously wounded and seriously sick prisoners of war are accommodated in its territory flows from Article 12(2) of that Convention. While both the First and Third Conventions may – at least temporarily – be applicable simultaneously to persons who are wounded and sick upon falling into enemy hands (see the commentary on Article 14, section C.1), the latter's rules are much more detailed. This question does not arise for persons who become wounded or sick after having acquired prisoner-of-war status: in that case, they benefit only from the protection of the Third Convention.

[23] Article 26 regulates the status of personnel of National Red Cross or Red Crescent Societies and of other voluntary aid societies recognized and authorized to assist the medical services of their State's armed forces. Article 27 regulates the personnel of a recognized society of a neutral country lending the assistance of its medical personnel and units to a Party to the conflict. Support for the interpretation that persons covered by Article 26 or 27 benefit from Article 4 when they are in the territory of a neutral Power flows from the discussion on Article 4 during the 1949 Diplomatic Conference; see *Final Record of the Diplomatic Conference of Geneva of 1949*, Vol. II-A, pp. 188 and 190.

(iv) Dead persons. This category, in line with the scope of application of the First Convention, and in particular its Articles 16 and 17, is limited to deceased persons belonging to one of the categories listed in Article 13.

922   If persons do not fall into one of the above categories, including when they are wounded or sick, the neutral Power has no obligations towards them on the basis of Article 4. Accordingly, except with regard to persons specifically covered by Article 13 of the First Convention, a neutral Power has no obligations on the basis of this provision towards civilians of a Party to an international armed conflict present in its territory, including when they are wounded or sick. A neutral Power has no obligations either, on the basis of Article 4, towards missing persons who may be in its territory.[24] However, the neutral Power may have obligations towards those persons on the basis of other provisions of international humanitarian law, such as Articles 24(2) and 132(2) of the Fourth Convention and Article 19 of Additional Protocol I. Further, the neutral Power may also have obligations vis-à-vis such persons on the basis of other branches of international law, such as human rights law and refugee law.[25]

b. Received, interned or found in the territory of a neutral Power

923   The obligation contained in Article 4 is activated from the moment persons covered by this provision are 'received or interned' or, in the case of dead persons, 'found' in the territory of a neutral Power. In its report to the 1949 Diplomatic Conference, the committee in charge of drafting Article 4 explained that '[t]he words "received" or "interned" shall apply, as regards the first, to the medical personnel and chaplains who are not necessarily to be interned, and as regards the second, to wounded and sick persons'.[26] In other words, the two concepts refer to the different substantive rules with which the neutral Power needs to comply in respect of persons protected by Article 4.[27]

924   For Article 4 to apply, the mere presence of persons covered by this provision in the territory of a neutral Power arguably suffices.[28] It is immaterial which factors explain this presence, and whether such presence is lawful or

---

[24] Missing persons in the territory of a neutral Power are included, however, within the category of 'persons protected by this Part who may be received or interned within their territory, and to any dead of the Parties to that conflict whom they may find' referred to in Article 19 of Additional Protocol I. Article 32 of Additional Protocol I also refers to 'the activities of the High Contracting Parties', including neutral Powers, in the context of the 'general principle' underpinning the section dealing with 'missing and dead persons'. For a discussion of the missing on the territory of a neutral Power, see Sandoz, pp. 105–106.

[25] Similarly, see *ibid.* p. 102.

[26] *Final Record of the Diplomatic Conference of Geneva of 1949*, Vol. II-A, p. 190. See also p. 46.

[27] For a discussion of these substantive rules, see section C.3.c.

[28] See, in this context, United States, *Law of War Manual*, 2015, para. 3.7.1: neutral Powers 'must apply by analogy the rules relating to the treatment of the wounded and sick and of POWs [prisoners of war] when interning such persons under their duties of neutrality'.

unlawful as a matter of international or national law. Among other conceivable scenarios, their presence may be the result of a previous arrangement involving the consent of the neutral Power, for example with regard to the passage of wounded or sick persons through its territory[29] or through its airspace in a medical aircraft.[30] Their presence may also be due to an unexpected situation, such as distress, or to the persons seeking shelter in the territory of the neutral Power.[31] In practical terms, of course, the obligation to apply by analogy the provisions of the First Convention can only be considered to have been activated once the neutral Power's authorities have been made aware of such presence.

925   Article 4 does not preclude the simultaneous applicability of more detailed rules regulating the status and treatment of persons covered by this provision in neutral territory. This would be the case, for example, for seriously wounded and seriously sick prisoners of war accommodated in a neutral country.[32]

3. Substantive obligation: 'shall apply by analogy the provisions of the present Convention'

a. General considerations

926   During the 1949 Diplomatic Conference, one delegation suggested that affirming the substantive requirement which is at the heart of Article 4 may be redundant (i) in view of common Article 1, which requires all 'High Contracting Parties', including neutral Powers, to 'respect and to ensure respect for the [four Geneva Conventions] in all circumstances'; and (ii) in cases where the Parties to the armed conflict already have diplomatic representatives in the territory of the neutral Power, since these representatives 'could look after the welfare of their nationals'.[33] Despite these arguments, it was considered beneficial to state explicitly that, each time the conditions of applicability of Article 4 are fulfilled, a neutral Power must comply with the provisions of the First Convention.

927   Contrary to Article 4(B)(2) of the Third Convention, Article 4 of the First Convention does not explicitly state that the obligation for neutral Powers to apply the relevant provisions of the First Convention by analogy is 'without prejudice to any more favourable treatment which these Powers may choose to give'. Nevertheless, a neutral Power may decide to give more favourable treatment at its own initiative.

---

[29] See Hague Convention (V) (1907), Article 14.   [30] See First Convention, Article 37.
[31] Similarly, see Sandoz, p. 95.
[32] See Third Convention, Articles 109–117. For the status of the persons in such scenarios, see also Third Convention, Article 4(B)(2).
[33] *Final Record of the Diplomatic Conference of Geneva of 1949*, Vol. II-A, p. 119.

928   When persons covered by Article 4 are in its territory, the neutral Power is to 'apply by analogy the provisions of the present Convention'. In other words, it needs to recognize that these persons are protected by the First Convention, and accord them the respect and protection associated with that status. Since, by definition, neutral Powers are not Parties to the international armed conflict, the application expected of them is 'by analogy', as if they were Parties to the conflict (*mutatis mutandis*).[34]

929   The application of the provisions of the First Convention by analogy means that the neutral Power will need to undertake certain activities with regard to the persons referred to in Article 4. Doing so cannot be considered as interference in the conflict, as a contribution to the belligerent State or as turning the neutral Power into a Party to the conflict.[35] Therefore, compliance with Article 4 cannot be considered as a violation of a neutral Power's obligations under the law of neutrality, for example with regard to the classic requirement to treat both Parties to an international armed conflict impartially. The inclusion of Article 4 in the First Convention, in other words, serves 'to protect [neutral Powers] from criticism by belligerent Powers regarding favourable treatment accorded by a neutral Power to the wounded and sick of an enemy belligerent'.[36]

930   The obligation on a neutral Power to apply the relevant provisions of the First Convention is without prejudice to the fact that the persons in question may, in the territory of that Power, benefit from the applicability of other legal frameworks, such as human rights law, refugee law, diplomatic protection and domestic law. Moreover, it in no way qualifies or suspends the obligation on the neutral Power to bring before its courts persons alleged to have committed, or to have ordered to be committed, grave breaches of the Conventions.[37]

931   The First Convention does not contain a list of specific articles which have to be implemented by analogy by neutral Powers.[38] In each instance, based on the

---

[34]   See e.g. United States, *Law of War Manual*, 2015, para. 3.7: 'In some cases, a rule developed specifically for one situation may be a useful and appropriate standard to apply in a different situation. This is sometimes called an application of a rule by analogy', referring to Article 4 as an example of a 'treaty requirement to apply rules by analogy'. See also Jean Salmon, *Dictionnaire de Droit International Public*, Bruylant, Brussels, 2001, p. 63: 'on transpose l'application d'une règle d'une relation juridique qu'elle vise expressément à une relation juridique qu'elle ne vise pas expressément' ('application by analogy: applying a rule that expressly governs one legal relationship to another not expressly governed by it').

[35]   See also Hague Convention (XIII) (1907), Article 26.

[36]   *Final Record of the Diplomatic Conference of Geneva of 1949*, Vol. II-A, p. 47. See also *Minutes of the Diplomatic Conference of Geneva of 1949*, Committee I, Vol. I, meeting held on 26 April 1949, p. 19.

[37]   See Article 49(2).

[38]   During the 1949 Diplomatic Conference, a proposal was made to have a 'complete list' of the provisions of the First Convention that the neutral Power would need to comply with. This proposal was rejected, for 'no list could provide for all possible cases'; see *Final Record of the Diplomatic Conference of Geneva of 1949*, Vol. II-A, pp. 103 and 119. As for the absence of a list of provisions which do not need to be implemented, Article 4 of the First Convention follows, in this respect, the same approach as Article 5 of the Second Convention. Both provisions

specific circumstances, application will depend on the object of the relevant rules.

932 Article 4 does not address the rights and obligations of the neutral Power with regard to objects protected under the First Convention, such as mobile medical units or military medical transports. In light of the object of the First Convention, however, whenever objects entitled to protection under that Convention are present in neutral territory, the neutral Power will need to apply the relevant rules by analogy.[39] With regard to medical aircraft, Article 37 applies.

933 Article 4 is silent as to which State, in the end, bears the costs, for example of hospital accommodation or internment, incurred by the implementation of this provision. Resort can be had to the logic underpinning provisions such as Article 37(3) of the First Convention, which stipulates that the relevant costs 'shall be borne by the Power on which they depend'.[40] In most circumstances, this will be the State of their nationality. However, where someone fights on behalf of a State other than the State of his or her nationality, the costs of accommodation or internment must be borne by the State on whose behalf the person was fighting.

b. Application by analogy with regard to the wounded and sick

934 With regard to the wounded and sick, the key point is that the neutral Power has to apply the provisions of the First Convention regulating their status and treatment. This means that the neutral Power must 'respect and protect' them in the sense of Article 12. For example, when wounded and sick persons are in its territory, the neutral Power must record 'any particulars which may assist in [their] identification' as required under Article 16. Furthermore, if the possibility of the persons' presence on its territory is known, the neutral Power must also, and this in accordance with Article 15, 'take all possible measures to search for and collect' them. Article 4 does not address the question of whether the neutral Power has to ensure that the wounded and sick of a Party to the conflict in its territory take no further part in operations of war. Contrary to

---

differ on this point from Article 4(B)(2) of the Third Convention, which gives a list of specific articles which, in certain circumstances, do not need to be applied to persons covered by that provision. By comparison, Article 19 of Additional Protocol I refers to the 'relevant provisions' of the Protocol which a neutral Power must apply.

[39] Article 35(1) (transports of wounded and sick or of medical equipment) and Articles 36–37 (medical aircraft).

[40] The same principle is reflected in Article 17(2) of the Second Convention with regard to 'wounded and sick or shipwrecked persons who are landed in neutral ports'. See also Hague Convention (V) (1907), Article 12: 'In the absence of a special convention to the contrary, the neutral Power shall supply the interned with the food, clothing, and relief required by humanity. At the conclusion of peace the expenses caused by the internment shall be made good.' See also Hague Convention (X) (1907), Article 15(2). Other provisions of the Geneva Conventions informed by this logic are Article 116 of the Third Convention and Article 36 of the Fourth Convention. See also Sandoz, p. 94, who nevertheless offers some mitigating considerations.

Article 37(3) of the First Convention, the fact that there are circumstances in which international law may require a neutral Power to detain the wounded and sick is not mentioned in this provision.[41] The circumstances in which this is required are exclusively regulated by the law of neutrality, not by international humanitarian law. While the Geneva Conventions were drafted on the assumption that there are circumstances in which a neutral Power is required to do this, the drafters chose not to explicitly address this issue within the context of the Conventions.[42] Indeed, during the 1949 Diplomatic Conference, it was emphasized that 'each Contracting Party would have complete liberty of interpretation', as far as how each Contracting Party viewed the rules of the law of neutrality when called upon to apply them in any given context in the future.[43]

935   In Article 11 of the 1907 Hague Convention (V), the requirements of international law on this matter with regard to able-bodied combatants were stated as follows: 'A neutral Power which receives on its territory troops belonging to the belligerent armies shall intern them, as far as possible, at a distance from the theatre of war'.[44] Article 14 of the same Convention requires that the neutral Power guard the wounded and sick of a Party to the conflict which it has authorized to pass over its territory, as well as those 'who may be committed to its care', so as 'to ensure their not taking part again in the military operations'. It is outside the scope of this commentary to examine the current status of these rules of the Hague Convention (V).[45] It can only be observed that, since 1907, States themselves have not publicly re-examined whether these rules still reflect the law.

936   Persons who have been received by a neutral Power in its territory and whom the neutral Power is required to intern on the basis of international law must be treated as prisoners of war, in line with Article 4(B)(2) of the Third Convention.[46] This reflects the application of Article 14 of the First Convention by analogy. Of course, the requirement to treat them as prisoners of war

---

[41] This is different from some other provisions of the Geneva Conventions which, while not addressing the substantive rules either, do acknowledge that there are circumstances in which a neutral Power may be required to ensure that wounded and sick of the Parties to the conflict are precluded from taking part in 'operations of war'. See e.g. Article 37(3) of the First Convention, as well as Articles 15 and 17(1) of the Second Convention.

[42] On the fact that the drafters of the Geneva Conventions chose not to address the substantive rules of the law of neutrality, see *Final Record of the Diplomatic Conference of Geneva of 1949*, Vol. II-A, pp. 103 and 220–221, and Vol. II-B, p. 240.

[43] *Ibid.* Vol. II-A, pp. 105–107.

[44] See also Hague Convention (X) (1907), Article 15, and Hague Rules of Air Warfare (1923), Article 43.

[45] For a historical analysis, see Mears. See also K.V.R. Townsend, 'Aerial Warfare and International Law', *Virginia Law Review*, Vol. 28, 1941–1942, pp. 516–527, at 518–520.

[46] Connected to this article, Article 122 of the Third Convention requires that neutral Powers 'who may have received within their territory persons belonging to one of the categories referred to in Article 4 [of the Third Convention]' 'institute an official Information Bureau for prisoners of war who are in [their] power'.

remains without prejudice to the possibility that the neutral Power may decide to grant them more favourable treatment.

c. Application by analogy with regard to medical and religious personnel

937 Persons covered by Article 24 (permanent medical and religious personnel who are members of the armed forces) or by Article 26 (staff of National Red Cross or Red Crescent Societies and of other voluntary aid societies assisting the medical services of their own State's armed forces) who are in the territory of a neutral Power must be allowed to return to the Party to the conflict to which they belong (Article 30). These persons must be treated by the neutral Power, pending their return, at least in the same way as prisoners of war.[47] However, applying the text of the Convention at face value, the conclusion may be reached that they may be retained by the neutral Power on the basis of Article 28, if required by 'the state of health, the spiritual needs and the number of' the wounded and sick of the Parties to the conflict.[48] It has been observed that, in practice, the retention-regime is 'not really adapted to a neutral state'. On the basis of this observation, the argument has been made that, unless the Party to the conflict on which they depend has given its consent to the effect that they can be retained, persons covered by Articles 24 and 26 must be freed by the neutral Power.[49]

938 Persons covered by Article 25 (auxiliary medical personnel) who are in the territory of a neutral Power may be detained by that Power so that they cannot again take part in military operations. Based on the combined application of Article 29 of the First Convention and Article 4(B)(2) of the Third Convention, they must be treated as prisoners of war.[50]

939 Persons covered by Article 27 (medical personnel of a recognized society of a neutral country which assist the medical services of a Party to the conflict) who are in the territory of another neutral Power may not be detained or retained by that Power. In accordance with Article 32, they must be allowed to return to their country.

d. Application by analogy with regard to the dead

940 When persons belonging to one of the categories in Article 13 are found dead in the territory of a neutral Power, Articles 16 and 17 apply by analogy. Thus, for example, when dead persons of one of the Parties of the conflict fall into its hands, the neutral Power must record 'any particulars which may assist in [their] identification' as required by Article 16. On the basis of the application by analogy of Article 15(1), the neutral Power must also 'search for the dead'.[51]

---

[47] *Final Record of the Diplomatic Conference of Geneva of 1949*, Vol. II-A, p. 188.
[48] See United States, *Law of War Manual*, 2015, para. 15.16.6.
[49] Sandoz, pp. 97–98.   [50] *Ibid.* p. 189.
[51] For a discussion of the obligations of neutral Powers with regard to missing persons, see fn. 24.

Select bibliography

Bindschedler, Rudolf L., 'Die Neutralität im modernen Völkerrecht', *Zeitschrift für ausländisches öffentliches Recht und Völkerrecht*, Vol. 17, 1956, pp. 1–37.

Bothe, Michael, 'Neutrality: Concept and General Rules', version of April 2011, in Rüdiger Wolfrum (ed.), *Max Planck Encyclopedia of Public International Law*, Oxford University Press, http://www.mpepil.com.

– 'The Law of Neutrality', in Dieter Fleck (ed.), *The Handbook of International Humanitarian Law*, 3rd edition, Oxford University Press, 2013, pp. 549–580.

Castrén, Erik, *The Present Law of War and Neutrality*, Suomalaisen Tiedeakatemian Toimituksia, Helsinki, 1954, pp. 421–492.

Chadwick, Elizabeth, 'Neutrality Revised?', *Nottingham Law Journal*, Vol. 22, 2013, pp. 41–52.

de Preux, Jean, 'Conventions et Etats neutres', *Revue internationale de la Croix-Rouge*, Vol. 71, No. 776, April 1989, pp. 132–143.

Gioia, Andrea, 'Neutrality and Non-Belligerency', in Harry H.G. Post (ed.), *International Economic Law and Armed Conflict*, Martinus Nijhoff Publishers, Dordrecht, 1994, pp. 51–110.

Heintschel von Heinegg, Wolff, '"Benevolent" Third States in International Armed Conflicts: The Myth of the Irrelevance of the Law of Neutrality', in Michael N. Schmitt and Jelena Pejic (eds), *International Law and Armed Conflict: Exploring the Faultlines, Essays in Honour of Yoram Dinstein*, Martinus Nijhoff Publishers, Leiden, 2007, pp. 543–568.

Hostettler, Peter, 'Neutrals, Disarming and Internment of Belligerents', version of June 2006, in Rüdiger Wolfrum (ed.), *Max Planck Encyclopedia of Public International Law*, Oxford University Press, http://www.mpepil.com.

Hostettler, Peter and Danai, Olivia, 'Neutrality in Land Warfare', version of September 2013, in Rüdiger Wolfrum (ed.), *Max Planck Encyclopedia of Public International Law*, Oxford University Press, http://www.mpepil.com.

Kussbach, Erich, 'Le Protocole additionnel I et les Etats neutres', *Revue internationale de la Croix-Rouge*, Vol. 62, No. 725, October 1980, pp. 231–251.

Mears, Dwight S., 'Neutral States and the Application of International Law to United States Airmen during World War II. To Intern or Not to Intern?', *Journal of the History of International Law*, Vol. 15, No. 1, 2013, pp. 77–101.

Monnier, Jean, 'Développement du droit international humanitaire et droit de la neutralité', in *Quatre Etudes du droit international humanitaire*, Henry Dunant Institute, Geneva, 1985.

Neff, Stephen C., *The Rights and Duties of Neutrals: A General History*, Manchester University Press, 2000, pp. 191–217.

Norton, Patrick M., 'Between the Ideology and the Reality: The Shadow of the Law of Neutrality', *Harvard International Law Journal*, Vol. 17, No. 2, 1976, pp. 249–311, especially at 254–257.

Ochsner, Richard, *Der Transit von Personen und Gütern durch ein neutrales Land im Falle des Landkrieges*, Polygraphischer Verlag A.G., Zurich, 1948, pp. 72–80.

Sandoz, Yves, 'Rights, Powers and Obligations of Neutral Powers under the Conventions', in Andrew Clapham, Paola Gaeta and Marco Sassòli (eds), *The 1949 Geneva Conventions: A Commentary*, Oxford University Press, 2015, pp. 86–108.

Schindler, Dietrich, 'Aspects contemporains de la neutralité', in *Recueil des cours de l'Académie de droit international de La Haye*, Vol. 121, 1967, pp. 220–321.
 – 'Transformations in the Law of Neutrality since 1945', in Astrid J.M. Delissen and Gerard J. Tanja (eds), *Humanitarian Law of Armed Conflict: Challenges Ahead, Essays in Honour of Frits Kalshoven*, Martinus Nijhoff Publishers, Dordrecht, 1991, pp. 367–386.
Seger, Paul, 'The Law of Neutrality', in Andrew Clapham and Paola Gaeta (eds), *The Oxford Handbook of International Law in Armed Conflict*, Oxford University Press, 2014, pp. 248–270.

DURATION OF APPLICATION

❖ Text of the provision

For the protected persons who have fallen into the hands of the enemy, the present Convention shall apply until their final repatriation.

❖ Reservations or declarations

None

Contents

A. Introduction

941 There are a number of articles in the Geneva Conventions and Additional Protocols that set out these instruments' temporal scope of application.[1] Those provisions stipulate from when the Conventions and Protocols become applicable and until when they apply, in whole or in part. Indeed, although some provisions of the Conventions and Protocols may cease to be applicable at the end of a conflict, many continue to apply even after that time.[2] In this vein, Article 5 affirms that wounded and sick combatants and medical and religious personnel who have fallen into enemy hands remain protected by the Convention until their final repatriation.

942 Serious disputes during the Second World War as to from when and until when the 1929 Geneva Conventions were applicable made it necessary to add a provision to this effect in the Third and Fourth Conventions of 1949. Certain belligerents, denying the sovereignty, or even any legal existence, of the defeated enemy had claimed the right to deal with prisoners of war as they saw

---

[1] In addition to this article, see, in particular, common Article 2; Third Convention, Article 5; Fourth Convention, Article 6; and Additional Protocol I, Articles 1 and 3. For non-international armed conflicts, see common Article 3, and Additional Protocol II, Articles 1(1) and 2(2).

[2] For a discussion of the temporal scope of application of the First Convention, see the commentary on common Article 2, section D.2.c.

fit and to deprive them of their treaty safeguards.[3] The provisions that were subsequently adopted are phrased in broad terms and go beyond that particular situation. Alongside the articles on the non-renunciation of rights and special agreements,[4] Article 5 precludes a Party to a conflict from invoking any excuse for denying the protection of the Conventions to protected persons for as long as they are in enemy hands.

B. Discussion

943   Article 5 was included in the First Convention in order to ensure the uniformity of the Conventions and so that each Convention would be complete in itself. This article is thus similar to Article 5 of the Third Convention and Article 6 of the Fourth Convention; however, it differs from the other two in that it does not specify the moment when the First Convention begins to apply to the protected persons. The reason for this is that the persons protected by the First Convention already enjoy its protection while they are with their own armed forces. In other words, combatants are protected as soon as they are wounded or sick, and medical personnel are protected as soon as they comply with the conditions set down in the Convention.[5] Thus, unlike the duration of protection, the beginning of protection does not depend on their being in enemy hands.[6]

944   Wounded and sick combatants who have fallen into enemy hands are prisoners of war.[7] They will thus be covered by both the First and Third Conventions. The wounded and sick who do not recover from their initial wounds or sickness even by the end of the conflict and who are still in enemy hands remain protected by the First Convention until the moment specified in Article 5 – their final repatriation.

945   When wounded and sick prisoners of war have recovered, the First Convention no longer applies to them, but they remain protected by the Third Convention until their final release and repatriation.[8] If they are wounded or fall sick again while prisoners of war, they are protected only by the Third Convention, which in any case requires a standard of health care and hygiene that is at least equivalent to that set down in the First Convention. In either case, wounded and sick persons in enemy hands must be given the treatment their condition requires.[9] It follows, therefore, that the point at which a person in enemy hands

---

[3]   See François Bugnion, *The International Committee of the Red Cross and the Protection of War Victims*, ICRC/Macmillan, Oxford, 2003, pp. 686–687; Catherine Rey-Schyrr, *De Yalta à Dien Bien Phu: Histoire du Comité international de la Croix-Rouge 1945–1955*, ICRC/Georg, Geneva, 2007, pp. 138 and 164–167.

[4]   See common Articles 7 and 6, respectively (Articles 8 and 7 in the Fourth Convention).

[5]   See Articles 12 and 24, respectively.

[6]   For when the Convention begins to apply, see Article 2 and its commentary, sections C and D.

[7]   See Article 14.

[8]   See Article 5. See also *Final Record of the Diplomatic Conference of Geneva of 1949*, Vol. II-A, p. 143.

[9]   See, in particular, First Convention, Article 12, and Third Convention, Articles 29–31.

is deemed to have been restored to health is of no real significance. Article 5 is thus most relevant for retained medical or religious personnel as it ensures that they are protected by the First Convention until their final repatriation.

946   The word 'final' pre-empts or excludes any subterfuge involving releasing wounded prisoners of war or retained medical or religious personnel but returning them to captivity under some other name. In this way, it corresponds to Article 5 of the Third Convention.[10] Article 5 of the First and Third Conventions ensures that persons remain protected as long as they are in enemy hands, even if active hostilities have ceased and, in some cases, even long after the end of the conflict.

947   The First Convention requires Parties to return medical and religious personnel who are not indispensable for the care of prisoners of war 'as soon as a road is open for their return and military requirements permit'.[11] This may be well before the end of active hostilities. The significance of Article 5 is that even if a Party fails to fulfil its obligation to repatriate such personnel within the prescribed time, it may not change their status or deny them the protection and treatment due to them.

948   Moreover, the Third Convention requires Parties to release and repatriate prisoners of war 'without delay after the cessation of active hostilities'.[12] For retained medical and religious personnel, this entails that the conditions for their retention and return apply even after the end of hostilities.[13] In other words, a Party which continues to detain prisoners of war (for whatever reason) may only retain the number of medical and religious personnel indispensable to the care of those prisoners.[14] This was an issue during and after the conflict between India and Pakistan in 1971, when prisoners of war continued to be detained and medical personnel retained.[15] While neither Party disputed that the retained medical personnel remained protected by the First Convention, it was questioned whether all of the retained medical personnel were actually indispensable to the care of the prisoners of war. Failing to return superfluous medical and religious personnel could be construed as tantamount to an attempt to change their status.

949   In short, Article 5 affirms the key tenet of international humanitarian law: that the Convention applies based on the facts on the ground. The protection conferred by the Geneva Conventions stands for as long as the protected

---

[10] See the commentary on Article 5 of the Third Convention for a more detailed discussion of the duration of application of that Convention.

[11] See the commentary on Article 30, section C, regarding return and repatriation of medical and religious personnel.

[12] Third Convention, Article 118.

[13] See First Convention, Articles 28, 30 and 31, and Third Convention, Article 33.

[14] This number is to be determined in accordance with the specific conditions and requirements set down in Article 28.

[15] François Bugnion, *The International Committee of the Red Cross and the Protection of War Victims*, ICRC/Macmillan, Oxford, 2003, p. 478; ICRC, *Annual Report 1972*, ICRC, Geneva, 1973, p. 51.

persons remain in circumstances requiring that protection and does not hinge on formalities regarding the beginning or end of a conflict.

Select bibliography

Grignon, Julia, *L'applicabilité temporelle du droit international humanitaire*, Schulthess, Geneva, 2014.

SPECIAL AGREEMENTS

❖ Text of the provision*

(1) In addition to the agreements expressly provided for in Articles 10, 15, 23, 28, 31, 36, 37 and 52, the High Contracting Parties may conclude other special agreements for all matters concerning which they may deem it suitable to make separate provision. No special agreement shall adversely affect the situation of the wounded and sick, of members of the medical personnel or of chaplains, as defined by the present Convention, nor restrict the rights which it confers upon them.

(2) Wounded and sick, as well as medical personnel and chaplains, shall continue to have the benefit of such agreements as long as the Convention is applicable to them, except where express provisions to the contrary are contained in the aforesaid or in subsequent agreements, or where more favourable measures have been taken with regard to them by one or other of the Parties to the conflict.

❖ Reservations or declarations

None

Contents

* Paragraph numbers have been added for ease of reference.

A. Introduction

950 Agreements may be concluded between belligerents during armed conflicts. While ceasefires and peace agreements may be the best known among these, they are not the only ones. Parties to armed conflicts may reach agreements on various subjects, both in the course of hostilities and, especially in relation to protected persons who have been detained, after the end of a conflict. Thus, this article, common to all four of the 1949 Geneva Conventions,[1] recognizes that, despite the detailed nature of the Conventions and their Additional Protocols, the Parties to a conflict, as well as other High Contracting Parties, may wish to develop more specific rules to govern particular situations. Special agreements can be a means of adapting certain provisions of the Conventions and Protocols to specific situations, in the light of prevailing circumstances and modern technology, a feature that was foreseen and provided for in the Conventions themselves.[2]

951 Article 6 confirms that the High Contracting Parties may conclude such agreements, sets an important limit with respect to the substance of those agreements, and clarifies their duration.

952 With regard to non-international armed conflicts, it is important to recall that common Article 3 also encourages the Parties to such conflicts to conclude special agreements to bring into force all or part of the provisions of the Conventions.

953 Article 6 is the keystone of the system of protection afforded by the Conventions and Protocols because it safeguards, as a minimum, the protections enshrined therein and prohibits any derogation from them. When special agreements are negotiated and concluded, no matter their form, it is imperative that the Parties act in good faith in all regards.

B. Historical background

954 The conclusion of special agreements between belligerent Parties has long been a feature of armed conflicts. In fact, prior to the codification of international humanitarian law, such agreements played a significant role in governing relations between the Parties.[3] Perhaps not surprisingly, therefore, each

---

[1] Article 6 of the First, Second and Third Conventions and Article 7 of the Fourth Convention.

[2] See e.g. Article 44 of the Second Convention and Article 60(2) of the Third Convention.

[3] See, in particular, Véronique Harouel-Bureloup, *Traité de droit humanitaire*, Presses Universitaires de France, 2005, pp. 85 and 92–98, in relation to accords on the treatment of medical facilities and wounded and sick members of the armed forces. Regarding historical examples of agreements on the exchange, release and treatment of prisoners of war, see Stephen C. Neff, 'Prisoners of War in International Law: The Nineteenth Century', in Sibylle Scheipers (ed.), *Prisoners in War*, Oxford University Press, 2010, pp. 57–73. Older agreements include, for example, the Convention between Great Britain and France respecting Prisoners of War, London, 10 May 1854 (PRO FO 93/33/55A). In relation to armed conflicts at sea, an excellent example is the treaty for the exchange of all prisoners taken at sea, concluded between France and England on

of the Conventions that preceded the Geneva Conventions of 1949 provided for – or at the very least, anticipated – the conclusion of special agreements to fill out the regimes set down therein. For example, the 1864 Geneva Convention anticipated the conclusion of agreements in arranging for the mutual return of wounded combatants,[4] while the 1906 Geneva Convention stipulated that '[t]he belligerents remain free, however, to mutually agree upon such clauses ... in relation to the wounded or sick as they may deem proper', and went on to specify areas in which they 'shall especially have authority to agree'.[5] The 1929 Geneva Convention on the Wounded and Sick also contained specific articles providing for the conclusion of such agreements.[6]

955   During the First World War, the Parties negotiated and concluded many agreements in relation to prisoners of war over the course of the conflict, there being relatively few treaty rules in this regard at the time.[7] In fact, the provisions of the 1929 Geneva Convention on Prisoners of War were largely based on those agreements. At the same time, the High Contracting Parties to the 1929 Convention reserved 'the right to conclude special conventions on all questions relating to prisoners of war concerning which they may consider it desirable to make special provisions'.[8] Unfortunately, however, during the Second World War some States concluded agreements that modified the protections of the 1929 Convention in important respects,[9] such that prisoners of war lost some of their essential rights. The ICRC therefore proposed in 1947 that the Conventions expressly state that special agreements concluded between belligerents should in no circumstances reduce the standard of treatment of prisoners of

---

12 March 1780. That treaty set forth a number of protections, including for vessels carrying persons being repatriated and for medical and religious personnel tending to the naval personnel of either Party. See Pictet (ed.), *Commentary on the Second Geneva Convention*, ICRC, 1960, p. 3, citing Georges Cauwès, *L'extension des principes de la Convention de Genève aux guerres maritimes*, L. Larose, Paris, 1899, p. 16, and Ernst Julius Gurlt, *Zur Geschichte der internationalen und freiwilligen Krankenpflege*, F.C.W. Vogel, Leipzig, 1873, pp. 29 and 31. Agreements are also concluded between belligerent Parties and neutral States. See also Riccardo Monaco, 'Les conventions entre belligérants', *Recueil des cours de l'Académie de droit international de La Haye*, Vol. 75, 1949, pp. 274–362.

[4] Geneva Convention (1864), Article 6.
[5] Geneva Convention (1906), Article 2.
[6] In particular, Article 2(2) provided: 'Belligerents shall, however, be free to prescribe, for the benefit of wounded or sick prisoners such arrangements as they may think fit beyond the limits of existing obligations.' See also Geneva Convention on the Wounded and Sick (1929), Articles 3, 12 and 13.
[7] There was no treaty relating exclusively to prisoners of war at the time. The pertinent rules in the 1907 Hague Convention IV were Articles 4–20. For the agreements, see, for example, Agreement between the British and Turkish Governments respecting Prisoners of War and Civilians, Bern, 28 December 1917 (PRO FO 93/110/79). Pictet (ed.), *Commentary on the Third Geneva Convention*, ICRC, 1960, p. 79, provides a short list of such agreements. See also Alan R. Kramer, 'Prisoners in the First World War', in Sibylle Scheipers (ed.), *Prisoners in War*, Oxford University Press, 2010, pp. 75–90, especially at 76–77; Allan Rosas, *The Legal Status of Prisoners of War: A Study in International Humanitarian Law Applicable in Armed Conflicts*, Åbo Akademi, Helsinki, 1976, reprinted 2005, pp. 51–69.
[8] Geneva Convention on Prisoners of War (1929), Article 83(1).
[9] See Catherine Rey-Schyrr, *De Yalta à Dien Bien Phu: Histoire du Comité international de la Croix-Rouge 1945–1955*, ICRC/Georg, Geneva, 2007, pp. 165–167; Bugnion, pp. 436–437.

war or of any other protected persons.[10] Although some concerns were raised by one delegation,[11] this view was approved by the Diplomatic Conference in 1949.[12]

956   In the post-1949 era, special agreements have been concluded in relation to the repatriation of wounded and sick prisoners of war.[13] A number of others have been concluded in relation to the general repatriation and exchange of prisoners of war and detained civilians and the exchange or return of dead bodies.[14] In other contexts, attempts have been made to conclude special agreements to evacuate wounded and sick members of the armed forces and civilians from encircled areas.

C. Discussion

For a discussion of the substance of special agreements related to specific articles of the Conventions, see the commentaries on those articles.

1. The irrelevance for Article 6 of the form and timing of an agreement

957   Any agreement between the High Contracting Parties affecting or relating to the rights of protected persons under the Geneva Conventions and Additional Protocol I is governed by Article 6. It makes no difference whether an agreement is bilateral or multilateral, nor does it have to relate solely to a particular Convention or to a particular right for it to qualify as a special agreement. For example, a ceasefire or armistice agreement will constitute a 'special agreement' within the meaning of Article 6 if it contains clauses relating to the rights of protected persons set down in any of the Conventions or Additional Protocol I.[15]

958   A wide variety of agreements may be considered to be 'special agreements' for the purposes of Article 6. The diversity of those listed in the article itself testifies to this fact.[16] The First Convention expressly provides for the conclusion of agreements in the following domains:

---

[10] Wilhelm, pp. 561–590, especially at 573–576.

[11] For a discussion of a proposed amendment seeking to circumscribe the limitation, see section C.6.

[12] See *Report on the Conference of Government Experts of 1947*, p. 259; see also *Final Record of the Diplomatic Conference of Geneva of 1949*, Vol. II-B, p. 109.

[13] For example, the repatriation of wounded Egyptian prisoners of war from Israel in 1956, in Françoise Perret and François Bugnion, *De Budapest à Saigon: Histoire du Comité international de la Croix-Rouge*, ICRC/Georg, Geneva, 2009, p. 93.

[14] See Bugnion, Appendix I, Table of Special Agreements, pp. 1029–1043.

[15] This is also the interpretation of the United Kingdom: see *Manual of the Law of Armed Conflict*, 2004, para. 10.24. That said, such agreements may lead to changes which end the applicability of certain rules of international humanitarian law, although it is the actual change in factual circumstances and not the mere existence of an agreement that has this effect.

[16] Each version of Article 6 (Article 7 of the Fourth Convention) lists a number of the articles referring to special agreements specific to the Convention concerned, further underlining the broad scope of topics on which such agreements may be concluded.

a. appointment of an impartial organization as a substitute for a Protecting Power (Article 10(1));
b. removal, exchange and transport of the wounded left on the battlefield (Article 15(2));
c. evacuation of the wounded and sick from a besieged area, and passage of medical personnel and equipment on their way to that area (Article 15(3));
d. establishment and recognition of hospital zones and localities (Article 23(2) and (3));
e. relief of retained medical personnel (Article 28(3));
f. determination of the percentage of medical and religious personnel to be retained (Article 31(2));
g. protection of medical aircraft (Article 36(1) and (3));
h. protection of medical aircraft flying over the territory of neutral Powers (Article 37(1));
i. establishment of an enquiry procedure concerning any alleged violation of the Convention (Article 52).

959   The above list serves merely as an indication of the kinds of agreements possible under the Convention, for there are other articles that refer to agreements between the belligerents, be they to encourage such arrangements, to prohibit them, or to ensure that they have no impact on the rights of protected persons.[17] For example, the following situations may also involve the conclusion of agreements:

a. establishment of a conciliation procedure for the application or interpretation of the Convention (Article 11(2));
b. return of the personnel of National Red Cross or Red Crescent Societies of neutral countries (Article 32(2)).

In addition, there are cases where, although the Convention does not include any express provision to that effect, the conclusion of special agreements may be necessary or helpful. For example, special agreements could be useful in arranging procedures for handling the dead and their burial.[18]

960   Additional Protocol I also recognizes the possibility of concluding special agreements,[19] and a number of articles in the Protocol provide for the conclusion of agreements on specific topics. As Protocol I supplements the Geneva Conventions of 1949,[20] such agreements are also covered by common Article 6 (Article 7 of the Fourth Convention). This understanding also flows from the

---

[17] See also Article 10(5) (prohibition on any derogation from the provisions relating to substitutes for Protecting Powers if one of the Powers is restricted in its freedom to negotiate).
[18] See Article 17.   [19] Additional Protocol I, Article 4.
[20] Article 96(1) of Additional Protocol I states: 'When the Parties to the Conventions are also Parties to this Protocol, the Conventions shall apply as supplemented by this Protocol.'

object and purpose of the Conventions and the Protocol, which is to set a minimum standard of protection in times of armed conflict. It is therefore understood that no special agreement concluded in respect of matters addressed in the Protocol can adversely affect the situation of protected persons as regulated by the Conventions or, when applicable, Additional Protocol I. Special agreements are provided for in Protocol I in relation to the following:

a. conditions governing the employment of trained, qualified personnel facilitating the application of the Conventions and the Protocol outside national territory (Article 6(4));
b. the protection of medical aircraft (Articles 25, 26, 27, 28, 29 and 31);[21]
c. arrangements for teams to search for, identify and recover the dead from battlefield areas (Article 33(4));
d. facilitating access to gravesites, protecting them, and facilitating the return of the remains of the deceased (Article 34(2));
e. providing additional protection for objects containing dangerous forces (Article 56(6));
f. the establishment of non-defended localities (Article 59(5) and (6));
g. the establishment, marking, use and protection of demilitarized zones (Article 60);
h. the use of distinctive signals by civil defence organizations for identification purposes (Article 66(5));
i. relief actions for populations in territory other than occupied territory (Article 70(1));
j. supervision by the Protecting Power of the evacuation of children (Article 78);
k. the International Fact-Finding Commission (Article 90).

961   Lastly, Additional Protocol III stipulates that the 'medical services and religious personnel participating in operations under the auspices of the United Nations may, with the agreement of participating States, use one of the distinctive emblems' (i.e. the red cross, the red crescent, the red lion and sun, or the red crystal),[22] thereby allowing for the conclusion of agreements in this respect.[23]

962   These examples illustrate that the term 'agreement' encompasses a wide range of possibilities. It can refer to purely local or provisional agreements (e.g. on the evacuation of the wounded), to what would amount to regulations (e.g. on medical personnel), or indeed to more formal agreements (e.g. on a substitute for a Protecting Power or on an enquiry procedure). Thus, the notion of special

---

[21] See also Additional Protocol I, Annex I, Article 6(3).
[22] Additional Protocol III (2005), Article 5.
[23] No other special agreements on the emblem are foreseen in the Geneva Conventions or their Additional Protocols.

agreements must be interpreted in a very broad sense, with no limitation on form or timing.[24]

963   Furthermore, Article 6 applies to agreements regardless of whether they are written, unwritten, tacit,[25] bilateral, multilateral, limited or unlimited in their duration, or even arrived at through the use of signals.[26] While such agreements will only be governed by the 1969 Vienna Convention on the Law of Treaties if they are in written form,[27] general international law recognizes that agreements that are not set down in writing or otherwise recorded may also be treaties.[28] In this vein, it must be pointed out that, even if unilateral declarations by States might not amount to 'agreements' in the formal sense, in view of the capacity of such statements to create binding legal obligations on the States formulating them, they must respect the requirements of Article 6.[29] Special agreements may also be made through mutual and concordant declarations of intent, issued orally and without any other formality, but they may need to be particularly clear and precise in order to be viable.[30] As a matter of policy, it is desirable to set down special agreements in writing wherever possible.[31]

---

[24] Other instruments relating to protection in armed conflicts also refer to specific areas in respect of which agreements may be concluded. For example, Article 24 of the 1954 Hague Convention for the Protection of Cultural Property is a general provision similar to Article 6. The 1994 San Remo Manual on International Law Applicable to Armed Conflicts at Sea refers to a number of areas in which the Parties to a conflict are encouraged to conclude agreements (see, in particular, Rules 11, 47(c), 53, 91 and 177). Rule 99 of the 2009 Manual on International Law Applicable to Air and Missile Warfare also affirms the possibility of concluding agreements to protect persons or objects not covered by the Manual. When such agreements relate in substance to protections set down in the Geneva Conventions, they will also be governed by Article 6.

[25] For example, in the conflict between Argentina and the United Kingdom in 1982, the Parties resorted to tacit agreements to create pauses in the hostilities in order to collect the wounded. See Sylvie S. Junod, *Protection of the Victims of Armed Conflict, Falkland-Malvinas Islands (1982)*, ICRC, Geneva, 1984, p. 26. See also United States, *Law of War Deskbook*, 2010, p. 56, note 16.

[26] Specifically on tacit agreements and signals, see Verdross/Simma, pp. 440–443, paras 683–689. See also the commentaries by Philippe Gauthier, '1969 Vienna Convention. Article 2: Use of terms', in Corten/Klein, pp. 38–40, paras 14–18, and by Yves Le Bouthillier and Jean-François Bonin, '1969 Vienna Convention. Article 3: International agreements not within the scope of the present Convention', in Corten/Klein, pp. 66–76.

[27] Vienna Convention on the Law of Treaties (1969), Article 2. Other questions of general treaty law may also be relevant.

[28] *Ibid*. Article 3. See Yves Le Bouthillier and Jean-François Bonin, '1969 Vienna Convention. Article 3: International agreements not within the scope of the present Convention', in Corten/Klein, pp. 69–70, para. 9, and Hollis, pp. 23–24.

[29] See International Law Commission, 'Guiding Principles applicable to unilateral declarations of States capable of creating legal obligations, with commentaries thereto', *Yearbook of the International Law Commission*, 2006, Vol. II, Part II. See also ICJ, *Nuclear Tests case (Australia v. France)*, Judgment, 1974, p. 253, and *Nuclear Tests case (New Zealand v. France)*, Judgment, 1974, p. 457.

[30] The ICJ has stated that a joint communiqué by States may constitute an international agreement. See *Aegean Sea Continental Shelf case*, Judgment, 1978, para. 96. As a German ambassador wrote in regard to declarations of intent expressed in joint communiqués, 'Everything depends on content and circumstances.' Hartmut Hillgenberg, 'A Fresh Look at Soft Law', *European Journal of International Law*, Vol. 10, 1999, pp. 499–515, at 507, note 42.

[31] When it comes to prisoners of war, there is, in addition, an obligation to post any special agreements – in a language the prisoners understand – alongside the text of the Third Geneva Convention in prisoner-of-war camps. See Article 41 of the Third Convention.

964 Special agreements create binding legal obligations on States.[32] Agreements must be 'scrupulously adhered to'.[33] This is the case whether they are concluded between government representatives with full treaty-making powers or by belligerent commanders on the battlefield in respect of a particular issue or locality.[34] Some military manuals nonetheless point out that it is fairly uncommon nowadays for commanders on the battlefield to enter into direct negotiations with one another, and that communication between belligerents tends to occur at an 'intergovernmental level'.[35]

965 In terms of timing, it is important to note that an agreement need not be concluded *during* an armed conflict in order to be a special agreement. It is not when the agreement is concluded that matters, but whether its terms in substance affect a right afforded by one of the Conventions or the Protocol. Some agreements will be concluded during the conflict – for example with respect to access to besieged or encircled areas or pauses in hostilities to collect the wounded and sick – whereas others may be arrived at after the end of hostilities. Agreements relating to prisoners of war, for example, have even been concluded long after the end of a conflict but while the Third Convention was still applicable.[36] In addition, some special agreements could be concluded between the High Contracting Parties even when there is no armed conflict.[37] All of these agreements, no matter when they are concluded, are subject to the rules laid down in Article 6.

966 Ideally, in order to ensure that different perspectives are identified and addressed in the agreements, negotiations should include persons of different genders and backgrounds.[38]

---

[32] See Julius Stone, *Legal Controls of International Conflict*, Maitland Publications, Sydney, 1954, p. 636; Fitzmaurice, p. 309; and Verdross/Simma, p. 443, para. 687, with further references. But see Baxter, p. 366, for a more ambiguous view. At the very least, even Baxter admits that 'there may be an obligation upon the part of States not to take measures that would prejudice the carrying into effect of these undertakings'.

[33] United Kingdom, *Manual of the Law of Armed Conflict*, 2004, para. 10.13; United States, *Field Manual*, 1956, para. 453: 'It is absolutely essential in all nonhostile relations that the most scrupulous good faith shall be observed by both parties, and that no advantage not intended to be given by the adversary shall be taken.'

[34] On the possibility for military commanders to negotiate and conclude binding agreements, see Peter Kovacs, 'Article 7. Full powers', in Corten/Klein, p. 143, para. 67, and Verdross/Simma, p. 443, para. 687, with further references.

[35] Canada, *LOAC Manual*, 2001, para. 1401.2; United Kingdom, *Manual of the Law of Armed Conflict*, 2004, para. 10.3.1.

[36] See e.g. ICRC, Press Release, 'Iran: 20th anniversary of prisoner-of-war repatriation', 16 August 2010. See also Harroff-Tavel, pp. 465–496, especially at 475–78.

[37] See e.g. in relation to zones (Article 23 of the First Convention, Article 14 of the Fourth Convention and Article 60 of Additional Protocol I).

[38] See UN Security Council, Res. 1325, 31 October 2000, para. 1. There is a growing acknowledgement that women, men, girls and boys are affected by armed conflict in different ways, and that, accordingly, the representation of both women and men at all decision-making levels in national, regional and international institutions and mechanisms for conflict prevention, management and resolution benefits the process. The application of international humanitarian law should also reflect this understanding.

967   With regard to agreements between an Occupying Power and local authorities in the territory it occupies, Article 47 of the Fourth Convention will govern the interpretation of such agreements together with Article 6.[39]

968   Lastly, Article 6 refers to all special agreements concluded between the High Contracting Parties and not just to those between Parties to a conflict. This was a conscious choice of the drafters in order to allow, for example, for agreements between Parties to a conflict and neutral States in regard to the transfer of prisoners of war to be subject to the requirements of the article.[40]

2. Special agreements and non-State entities

969   Article 6 applies to agreements between High Contracting Parties, meaning States.[41] At times, however, special agreements will be concluded between States party to a conflict and signed also by non-State entities, such as the ICRC or another organization.[42] The participation of an organization such as the ICRC in the conclusion of an agreement in itself does not affect the application of Article 6 to that agreement between the High Contracting Parties. Indeed, there is no reason why Article 6 would not apply formally to agreements concluded between a High Contracting Party and an international organization such as the United Nations. Whatever the case, in substance such agreements must respect the principle that they may not in any way diminish the protection afforded by the Conventions.

970   There have also been cases where 'two belligerents reach separate agreements with the ICRC in order to resolve some specific humanitarian issue, while refusing any direct contact with each other'.[43] It goes without saying that the ICRC would not agree to participate in such an agreement if it considered that the proposed agreement would derogate impermissibly from international humanitarian law. In cases where the Parties to the conflict conclude parallel, complementary agreements on their conduct in fields regulated by the First Convention with an organization such as the United Nations or the ICRC, these agreements would be treated as special agreements for the purposes of Article 6. In other words, Parties to a conflict cannot circumvent the

---

[39] John Quigley, 'The Israel-PLO Agreements Versus the Geneva Civilians Convention', *Palestine Yearbook of International Law*, Vol. 7, 1992–1994, p. 45. (This will mostly arise in relation to Article 7 of the Fourth Convention and not Article 6 of the First, Second or Third Conventions.)

[40] *Final Record of the Diplomatic Conference of Geneva of 1949*, Vol. II-B, p. 109.

[41] In circumstances where Article 96(3) of Additional Protocol I applies, Article 6 may also apply to agreements concluded between '[t]he authority representing a people engaged [in an armed conflict] against a High Contracting Party' and other High Contracting Parties. For special agreements between States and organized armed groups in the context of non-international armed conflicts, see the commentary on common Article 3, section K.

[42] See ICRC, Press Release, 'Iran/Iraq: significant step forward in search for missing persons from 1980–1988 war', 16 October 2008, regarding the conclusion of a memorandum of understanding between Iran, Iraq and the ICRC.

[43] Bugnion, pp. 392–394.

requirements of Article 6 by concluding parallel agreements via the intermediary of an organization, even if that organization appears as the counterpart to the agreement. Pure legal formalism cannot circumvent the purpose of this provision and the Geneva Conventions in general.

971   Agreements between Parties to a non-international armed conflict are governed by common Article 3.[44]

3. Special agreements and third parties

972 Under the general rules of international treaty law, international agreements do 'not create either obligations or rights for a third State without its consent'.[45] Obligations may only arise under certain circumstances and if the third State 'expressly accepts that obligation in writing',[46] but it is possible to create rights for third States without their express consent.[47] When it comes to international organizations, the treaty regime is similar, but, unlike for States, the assent of an organization to a right accorded to it is not presumed.[48] The assent of the organization is 'governed by the rules of the organization'.[49]

973   From the perspective of the ICRC, this can be relevant. It is not unusual for High Contracting Parties to conclude special agreements that set out a role for the ICRC in supervising or assisting in the implementation of the accord. Where the ICRC has not been involved in the negotiation of such an agreement and/or has not had an opportunity to consent to or refuse such a role, it is not bound by the terms of that agreement. This occurred, for example, in the context of the 1948 agreement with respect to a truce in Palestine.[50] As the ICRC had misgivings about the role provided for it in that agreement, it instead took on a role that was more in line with its method of working in conformity with the principles of neutrality, impartiality and independence.[51] On other occasions, the ICRC has accepted roles set down for it in agreements to which it was not a party.[52] In principle, the ICRC is likely to accept a role

---

[44] For further details, see the commentary on common Article 3, section K.

[45] Vienna Convention on the Law of Treaties (1969), Article 34.

[46] *Ibid.* Article 35.   [47] *Ibid.* Article 36.

[48] Vienna Convention on the Law of Treaties between States and International Organizations (1986), Articles 34–36.

[49] *Ibid.* Article 36(2).

[50] Paragraph 8 of that agreement stated: 'Relief to populations of both sides in municipal areas ... shall be administered by an International Red Cross Committee [sic] in such a manner as to ensure that reserves of stocks of essential supplies shall not be substantially greater or less at the end of the truce than they were at its beginning.' UN Doc S/829, 8 June 1948, p. 3.

[51] The ICRC 'decided to confine its assistance to transporting supplies for hospitals' as it was concerned that the other role provided for it could lead it to provide food for combatants; see Bugnion, p. 391. See also 'The International Committee of the Red Cross in Palestine', *Revue internationale de la Croix-Rouge et Bulletin des Sociétés de la Croix-Rouge*, Supplement No. 8, August 1948, pp. 128–137, especially at 132–133.

[52] For example, when formally requested to fulfil the role set out for it in the New Delhi Agreement of 28 August 1973 between Pakistan and Bangladesh, the ICRC agreed; see Bugnion, p. 392.

conferred on it through a special agreement that respects international humanitarian law, including Article 6, that conforms to its working methods based on
the principles of neutrality, impartiality and independence, and to which it has
consented.

4. Special agreements and amendments

974   An additional issue arising from general treaty law is the distinction between
an amendment to a treaty and an agreement that modifies the treaty between
the Parties to the agreement. Additional Protocol I contains an amending formula but has no general article on special agreements,[53] whereas the Geneva
Conventions contain no amending formula but have a general article on
special agreements (the present Article 6, Article 7 of the Fourth Convention). The distinction between amendment and modification of a treaty has
significant consequences: under treaty law, amendments become automatically applicable to new Parties to a treaty, whereas special agreements that
modify the treaty between existing Parties remain applicable only between
them.[54]

975   There should be no cause for confusing a special agreement with an amendment. As outlined in Article 97 of Protocol I, the process for adopting an amendment is more formal and rigorous than for special agreements and it does not
apply to the Geneva Conventions. In most cases, special agreements simply
add to the existing set of applicable rules, help to implement them and bind
only the Parties to them. As such, it would be rare that a special agreement
would amount even to a modification of the Geneva Conventions. This interpretation holds true also in respect of special agreements specifically provided
for in the Conventions and the Protocols: for example, the agreements provided
for in Article 56 of Protocol I would constitute special agreements in the sense
of Article 6 and not amendments.

5. Special agreements and the threat or use of force

976   Special agreements are usually concluded in the context of armed conflict,
where, almost inevitably, force is used. Article 52 of the 1969 Vienna Convention on the Law of Treaties stipulates that a treaty is void 'if its conclusion has been procured by the threat or use of force in violation of the principles of international law embodied in the Charter of the United Nations'.[55]
How does this rule relate to special agreements? Since the determination of the

---

[53] Nevertheless Additional Protocol I recognizes the possibility of concluding special agreements;
see Article 4. The procedure for amendment is contained in Article 97 of the Protocol.
[54] See Vienna Convention on the Law of Treaties (1969), Articles 40 and 41.
[55] In addition, according to Article 44(5) of the 1969 Vienna Convention on the Law of Treaties,
'no separation of the provisions of the treaty is permitted' in such cases.

applicability of the rule in Article 52 depends on an appraisal of the *jus ad bellum*, the ICRC will not engage in such analysis, but will consider an agreement on its own terms, including its conformity with Article 6.

977   Other bodies may engage in such analysis, however. It may therefore be helpful to note that, according to one view, '[a] treaty is only procured by coercion if the use or threat of force is directly intended to bring about the treaty or if the treaty is aimed at maintaining a situation which was created by an illegal use of force'.[56] Another view is that 'a treaty is only invalid if the victim of the coercion did not have any other choice but to conclude the treaty', thus very narrowly construing the rule.[57] In the context of Article 6, it can be anticipated that ambiguity in the validity of an agreement in the light of this rule will most likely arise in relation to ceasefire agreements.[58] The mere fact that an agreement was concluded in the context of an unlawful use of force or to mitigate the consequences of such a use of force does not make it void. This flows from the total separation between the *jus ad bellum* and the *jus in bello*, as agreements on humanitarian issues are independent of the use of force.

6. Limitations regarding special agreements

978 The second sentence of Article 6(1) effectively confirms the 'non-derogability' of the rights enshrined in the Geneva Conventions.[59] It states that '[n]o special agreement shall adversely affect the situation of [protected persons]... nor restrict the rights which it confers upon them'. By virtue of this clause, States willingly accepted to curb their freedom to conclude agreements that would diminish the protections afforded by the Conventions to persons affected by armed conflicts. This intent was clearly expressed during the negotiation of the Conventions, in particular in the reactions of States to the proposal by one State to reduce the scope of the 'safeguard' or limitation clause so as to prohibit only agreements that would undermine 'fundamental' provisions of the Conventions. That proposal was firmly rejected by other States on the basis of two principal objections: first, that 'it would be difficult to distinguish between rights of protected persons which were fundamental and those which were not'; and second, that '[s]uch a distinction might open the way to all kinds of abuse, and the purpose of the Conventions was to secure minimum guarantees for the persons which they were intended to protect'.[60] In addition, one delegate

---

[56] Michael Bothe, 'Consequences of the Prohibition of the Use of Force', *Zeitschrift für ausländisches öffentliches Recht und Völkerrecht*, Vol. 27, 1967, pp. 507–519, at 513.

[57] Olivier Corten, '1969 Vienna Convention. Article 52: Coercion of a State by the threat or use of force', in Corten/Klein, pp. 1201–1220, especially at 1219, para. 39.

[58] *Ibid.* pp. 1217–1220.

[59] On the fact that the Conventions confer rights on individuals, see the commentary on Article 7, section C.2.

[60] See *Final Record of the Diplomatic Conference of Geneva of 1949*, Vol. II-B, p. 109.

insisted that 'in no case may it be permitted to derogate from the rules established by the Conventions'.[61] This 'non-derogability' of international humanitarian law is nowadays widely accepted[62] and may be seen as an indication of the *jus cogens* character of its rules.

979   What of special agreements that do not conform to the requirements of Article 6? As Meron states, 'treaties or agreements by which states themselves purport to restrict the rights of protected persons under the Conventions will have no effect'.[63] In addition, under general international law, any treaty contrary to existing *jus cogens* norms is void according to the 1969 Vienna Convention on the Law of Treaties.[64] The same can be said for unilateral declarations of States.[65] For special agreements that purport to derogate from any norms of humanitarian law which amount to *jus cogens*, those rules provide an extra layer of protection.

980   The tenor of that debate also underscores the broad scope of the 'safeguard clause'; it encompasses all of the rights and mechanisms contained in the Conventions and Protocol I, when applicable. Indeed, 'the rights which it confers upon them' refers to the whole body of safeguards which the Conventions afford to protected persons – in this case, the wounded and sick, medical personnel and chaplains. These safeguards reside likewise in all the arrangements

---

[61] Our translation of 'en aucun cas il ne doit pouvoir être dérogé aux règles fixées par les Conventions' (France). Similarly, the delegate from Monaco stated: '[N]ous sommes en présence...de conventions qui seront des conventions humanitaires, des conventions qui ne vivent que si...nous assurons aux maximum le fonctionnement de la clause de sauvegarde.' ('[W]e are in the presence...of humanitarian conventions which will only be brought to life, if...we ensure the fullest application of the safeguard clause.' *Minutes of the Diplomatic Conference of Geneva of 19*, Mixed Committee, meeting held on 29 April 1949, pp. 11 and 17. This concern was depicted thus in the Pictet commentaries:

> When the Governments which met in Geneva in 1949 expressly prohibited any derogatory agreement, they did so because they were aware of a great danger – namely, that the product of their labours, which had been patiently drafted in the best possible conditions (viz. in peacetime) might be at the mercy of modifications dictated by chance or under the pressure of wartime conditions. They were courageous enough to recognize this possible eventuality, and to set up safeguards against it. In that sense Article 6 is a landmark in the process of the renunciation by States of their sovereign rights in favour of the individual and of a superior juridical order.

Pictet (ed.), *Commentary on the First Geneva Convention*, ICRC, 1952, pp. 74–75.

[62] See e.g. ICTY, *Tadić* Decision on the Defence Motion for Interlocutory Appeal on Jurisdiction, 1995, para. 73. See also Meron, pp. 251–253. Where the Conventions allow a derogation, it is explicitly provided for. See Article 5 of the Fourth Convention.

[63] Meron, p. 252.

[64] Article 53 states, in part: 'A treaty is void if, at the time of its conclusion, it conflicts with a peremptory norm of general international law.' Article 53 is described as an 'emerging rule of customary international law' (Mark E. Villiger, *Commentary on the 1969 Vienna Convention on the Law of Treaties*, Martinus Nijhoff Publishers, Leiden, 2009, pp. 676–677) and as having 'gradually acquired the status of a customary rule' (Eric Suy, '1969 Vienna Convention, Article 53: Treaties conflicting with a peremptory norm of general international law ('jus cogens'), in Corten/Klein, pp. 1224–1233, at 1226, para. 5). See also Meron, p. 252.

[65] International Law Commission, 'Guiding Principles applicable to unilateral declarations of States capable of creating legal obligations, with commentaries thereto', *Yearbook of the International Law Commission*, 2006, Vol. II, Part II, Principle 8.

which are stipulated in the interest of these persons, such as the distinctive emblem, protection of members of the population who aid victims of armed conflicts, supervision by the Protecting Powers, or penalties in cases of violations. In short, it may be said that the principle applies to all the rules of the Conventions – except perhaps the purely formal provisions contained in the last section – since the application of any one of these rules represents, directly or indirectly, a benefit for protected persons and a guarantee to which they are entitled. In addition, some provisions of the Conventions have specific rules on the permitted or prohibited content of special agreements. Of course, nothing prevents the Parties from undertaking further and wider obligations in favour of protected persons, but the obligations under the Geneva Conventions must be considered as representing a minimum.

981   Here, as with common Article 7 (Article 8 of the Fourth Convention), the question may sometimes arise as to whether a proposed special agreement would put protected persons in a better or worse situation than that prescribed in the Conventions. It may not always be possible to determine immediately whether or not a special agreement 'adversely affects the situation of protected persons'. What happens when the situation is improved in some respects and adversely affected in others? In this respect, the corollary that special agreements may not 'restrict the rights' the Conventions confer on protected persons was designed to buttress this general safeguard. In the majority of cases, deterioration in the situation of the persons protected will be an immediate or delayed consequence of derogation. In practice, in its representations to the Parties, the ICRC will invoke special agreements that conform to humanitarian law and that enhance protection.

982   An additional complicating factor when assessing whether special agreements conform to the requirements of the Conventions may sometimes arise in relation to the classification of a conflict as international or non-international. In the context of non-international armed conflicts, common Article 3(3) encourages Parties to conclude agreements bringing into force all or parts of the Geneva Conventions. Thus, the special agreements concluded in such circumstances may not comprise all of the protections laid down in the Conventions. In situations where the classification of a conflict as international or non-international may be highly controversial, and in the absence of an international body able to make a binding decision in this respect, it remains possible to conclude an agreement bringing into force large parts of the Conventions, but not all of them, despite the existence of common Article 6.[66]

983   A special circumstance may exist, however. If, as a result of rare, specific circumstances, the application of a provision under the Convention entailed serious disadvantages for protected persons, would the 'safeguard clause' debar the

---

[66] For a contrary view, see ICTY, *Tadić* Decision on the Defence Motion for Interlocutory Appeal on Jurisdiction, 1995, para. 73.

Powers concerned from endeavouring to remedy the situation by an agreement departing from that provision? This is a question which the States concerned cannot settle on their own account. In such a situation, it would be for the neutral, impartial and independent humanitarian organizations responsible for looking after the protected persons to give their opinion, which itself should be based on the rule that is inherent in the safeguard clause that the situation of protected persons must not be adversely affected. In that case, they could tolerate certain measures of derogation which the States concerned might take, either separately or by mutual agreement, with a view to remedying the situation.

984   Certainly, if two belligerents were to agree to subject their nationals to treatment contrary to the Convention, it might be difficult for the protected persons concerned to oppose the conclusion and consequences of such an agreement. But it would then be the duty of the organizations responsible for scrutinizing the application of the Conventions to remind the belligerents of their obligations. Other factors too will doubtless enter into consideration, such as pressure by third States not involved in the conflict, pressure of public opinion, or the fear of prosecution. The correct application of the Conventions is not a matter for the belligerents alone; it concerns the whole community of States.[67]

7. Duration of special agreements

985   Article 6(2) confirms that, except where otherwise provided in the agreement itself or in subsequent agreements, or where 'more favourable measures have been taken with regard to [the protected persons]', special agreements remain applicable for as long as the Geneva Conventions and Additional Protocol I apply.[68] This paragraph had been introduced in the 1929 Geneva Convention on Prisoners of War at the request of Germany, since the Armistice Agreement of 1918 (Article 10) had abrogated the agreements concluded between the belligerents in the First World War with regard to prisoners of war.[69] It prevents a victorious Party from rescinding via an armistice agreement any better treatment it may have accorded to protected persons during the conflict. This may in particular be important for prisoners of war who have not yet been repatriated.

986   Each of the Geneva Conventions and Additional Protocol I specifies the duration of its application to the persons it protects; Article 6 affirms that the same

---

[67] See also the commentary on common Article 1, section A.

[68] In this light, it is helpful to recall that the content or text of special agreements must be posted in prisoner-of-war camps and in places where civilians are interned (Article 41 of the Third Convention and Article 99 of the Fourth Convention). For prisoners of war, the content of the agreements must be posted in their own language, and for civilian internees in a language they understand. See also Article 5 of the First and Third Conventions and Article 6 of the Fourth Convention.

[69] *Proceedings of the Geneva Diplomatic Conference of 1929*, p. 511.

standard applies in regard to special agreements, unless they have been superseded by agreements providing better protection. Thus, this paragraph serves to
underline that the protections in the Conventions are the minimum standard
required.

Select bibliography

Baxter, Richard R., 'Armistices and other forms of suspension of hostilities', *Collected Courses of the Hague Academy of International Law*, Vol. 149, 1976,
pp. 353–400.

Bugnion, François, *The International Committee of the Red Cross and the Protection of War Victims*, ICRC/Macmillan, Oxford, 2003 (especially Part I,
Chapter V).

Corten, Olivier and Klein, Pierre (eds), *The Vienna Conventions on the Law of
Treaties: A Commentary*, Oxford University Press, 2011.

Fitzmaurice, Sir Gerald, 'The juridical clauses of the peace treaties', *Collected
Courses of the Hague Academy of International Law*, Vol. 73, 1948, pp. 255–
367.

Harroff-Tavel, Marion, 'Do wars ever end? The work of the International Committee of the Red Cross when the guns fall silent', *International Review of the
Red Cross*, Vol. 85, No. 851, September 2003, pp. 465–496.

Hollis, Duncan, 'Defining Treaties', in Duncan B. Hollis (ed.), *The Oxford Guide
to Treaties*, Oxford University Press, 2012, pp. 11–45.

Meron, Theodor, 'The Humanization of Humanitarian Law', *American Journal of
International Law*, Vol. 94, No. 2, 2000, pp. 239–278.

Verdross, Alfred and Simma, Bruno, *Universelles Völkerrecht, Theorie und Praxis*,
Duncker & Humblot, Berlin, unchanged reprint of the 3rd edition, 2010, p. 443.

Wilhelm, René-Jean, 'Le caractère des droits accordés à l'individu dans les Conventions de Genève', *Revue internationale de la Croix-Rouge et Bulletin
international des Sociétés de la Croix-Rouge*, Vol. 32, No. 380, August 1950,
pp. 561–590.

NON-RENUNCIATION OF RIGHTS

❖ Text of the provision

Wounded and sick, as well as members of the medical personnel and chaplains, may in no circumstances renounce in part or in entirety the rights secured to them by the present Convention, and by the special agreements referred to in the foregoing Article, if such there be.

❖ Reservations or declarations

None

Contents

A. Introduction

987 Common Article 7 (Article 8 in the Fourth Convention) is a cornerstone of the regime established by the Geneva Conventions. Its purpose is to ensure that protected persons enjoy the protection of the Conventions until the last moment when international humanitarian law applies to them or to their situation. It states that the rights of protected persons are inalienable. Together with common Article 1 and the articles setting out the duration of application of each Convention,[1] as well as common Article 6 (Article 7 in the Fourth Convention) prohibiting special agreements that would derogate from the Conventions, this article was designed to ensure that the protection of the Conventions would be inviolable.

---

[1] In particular, Article 5 common to the First and Third Conventions and Article 6 of the Fourth Convention.

988   Article 7 acts as a safeguard so that a State may not excuse a failure to respect its obligations under the Conventions on the grounds that it was acting based on the will of the protected person(s) concerned. Of course, if the Conventions provide individual protected persons with a choice in regard to their treatment, States that give effect to such choices do not thereby violate the Conventions. Common Article 7 embodies the presumption that in most cases the statuses, rights and mechanisms established by the Conventions, properly applied, afford the best protection for protected persons in situations of armed conflict. For the First Convention, this applies, in particular, to the wounded and sick, as well as to medical and religious personnel.

989   In acknowledging that individuals have rights, but not the right to renounce those rights, this provision displays a degree of tension. It is best understood as a mechanism to ensure the inviolability of rights even in the extreme circumstances of armed conflict, when the exercise of 'free choice' can be severely compromised.

B. Historical background

990 Common Article 7 was a new addition to the Geneva Conventions in 1949. It was adopted largely in response to the practice of some States during the Second World War of putting pressure on prisoners of war to abandon their prisoner-of-war status and become civilians, who at the time did not benefit from the protection of their own Geneva Convention.[2] Those who did so found themselves rapidly in a much worse situation than they had imagined, having no protection against arbitrary treatment and falling outside the reach of ICRC activities.[3] At the 1948 International Conference of the Red Cross in Stockholm, the ICRC proposed a draft article common to the four Conventions stipulating that protected persons 'may in no circumstances be induced by constraint, or by any other means of coercion, to abandon partially or wholly the rights conferred on them by the present Convention'.[4] At the Diplomatic Conference in 1949, the ICRC recommended wording aimed at prohibiting coercion or constraint but allowing for a certain degree of free choice. In adopting common Article 7 with its present, more categorical, wording, the delegates in Stockholm and subsequently at the Diplomatic Conference sought to avoid a twofold danger: first, the physical or psychological harm caused by any pressure put on a protected person to opt for a change in status or protection; and

---

[2] See the explanation by Claude Pilloud in the discussion of the draft article by the Joint Committee, *Final Record of the Diplomatic Conference of 1949*, Vol. II-B, p. 17.

[3] See François Bugnion, *The International Committee of the Red Cross and the Protection of War Victims*, ICRC/Macmillan, Oxford, 2003, pp. 437–438.

[4] *Draft Conventions submitted to the 1948 Stockholm Conference*, draft article 5 of the First Convention and draft article 6 of the Second, Third and Fourth Conventions, pp. 7, 36, 55 and 156.

second, the harm caused by the actual loss of protection. The inherent difficulty in proving coercion was also a factor in making the prohibition absolute.
No similar article was proposed or included in Additional Protocol I; however,
as Protocol I 'supplements' the Geneva Conventions of 1949, logically common
Article 7 also applies to the rights of protected persons set down therein.

C. Discussion

991   Common Article 7 has often been invoked in relation to whether prisoners
of war may consent to treatment or to a change in status that diverges from
that prescribed under the Third Convention. As an article common to all four
Conventions, it also has important implications for the treatment of civilians
and other categories of protected persons.

1. Prohibition of a partial or total renunciation

992   Already at the time of the negotiation of the Conventions, the drafting committee acknowledged that an absolute rule could entail harsh consequences for
some individuals in some circumstances, but it nevertheless decided to accept
that risk.[5] In fact, this article has been labelled by some as 'paternalistic' and
as introducing an 'excessive rigidity' into the Conventions.[6] It is important to
bear in mind, however, that the article flows from the paramount concern that
in situations of armed conflict persons who are in vulnerable situations (and
especially if detained) are unlikely to be in a position to truly consent freely to
a loss of protection. Experience has shown that this concern is no less relevant
today than it was many years ago.

993   This is not to say that the application of the Geneva Conventions allows
protected persons no free choice whatsoever. In a number of places in respect
to prisoners of war and protected civilians, the Conventions establish that on
certain specific points the treatment accorded will depend on the choice of
the persons concerned. For prisoners of war, this is the case, for instance, with
regard to release on parole, assembly in camps, organization of leisure, participation in dangerous labour, performance of religious duties and attendance
at the services of their faith, and repatriation when wounded or sick.[7] In the
Fourth Convention, several articles provide for the exercise of a certain amount
of choice on the part of protected persons. For example, the Parties to the conflict are invited to authorize protected persons to leave the territory if they so

---

[5] See the summary of the discussion on the draft article 5/6/6/6 by the Joint Committee, *Final
Record of the Diplomatic Conference of 1949*, Vol. II-B, pp. 17–18; see also Pictet (ed.), *Commentary on the Fourth Geneva Convention*, ICRC, 1958, p. 75.
[6] Esgain/Solf, p. 544.
[7] See Articles 21(2), 22, 38, 52, 34 and 109(3), respectively, of the Third Convention.

desire.[8] Civilian internees are similarly afforded a degree of choice in certain situations: they 'shall enjoy complete latitude in the exercise of their religious duties'; they must have access to intellectual, educational and recreational pursuits but may not be compelled to partake in them; and a Detaining Power may not employ them as workers unless they want to work.[9] In general, however, the standards of treatment in the Conventions are designed to depend as little as possible for their application on the wishes of protected persons. In particular, the choices exercised by individuals may not lead to the displacing of the Conventions entirely.

994 The thrust of common Article 7 is that the acts or statements of protected persons may not be interpreted as a renunciation of their protected status, nor construed as a reason to rescind that status. For example, if at some point during captivity – other than at the time of general repatriation – a prisoner of war expresses a wish not to be repatriated, that real or purported severance of ties or allegiance does not affect a person's status as a prisoner of war.[10] Moreover, persons who express a desire to desert at some point during captivity remain prisoners of war until their release and repatriation.[11] In short, common Article 7 entails that no effect may be given by the Detaining Power to any real or purported renunciation of rights.[12]

995 Some interpret Article 7 of the Third Convention to mean that a Detaining Power may not accept the voluntary enlistment of any of the prisoners of war it detains into its armed forces (or forces affiliated to it).[13] Where the

---

[8] Fourth Convention, Article 35.

[9] See Articles 93, 94 and 95, respectively, of the Fourth Convention. Article 32(2) of the First Convention also allows personnel of neutral National Societies to choose to continue their work even after they have fallen into the hands of the adverse Party, even though the normal rule is that they be allowed to return to their home countries if possible. Article 32 does not specify whether it is the individual, the National Society, or the States involved that have the decision-making power. See also Christophe Lanord, *Le statut juridique des Sociétés nationales de la Croix-Rouge et du Croissant-Rouge*, Editions de la Chapelle, Geneva, 1999, p. 69.

[10] See Marco Sassòli, 'The status, treatment and repatriation of deserters under international humanitarian law', *Yearbook of the International National Institute of Humanitarian Law*, 1985, pp. 9–36, at 21–24. See also L.B. Schapiro, 'Repatriation of Deserters', *British Yearbook of International Law*, Vol. 29, 1952, pp. 310–324; Esgain/Solf, pp. 537–596, at 554–563; Australia, *Manual of the Law of Armed Conflict*, 2006, para. 10.32; and Canada, *LOAC Manual*, 2001, para. 1011. See Article 4 of the Third Convention and its commentary for a discussion of prisoner-of-war status.

[11] See also L.B. Schapiro, 'Repatriation of Deserters', *British Yearbook of International Law*, Vol. 29, 1952, pp. 310–324; Esgain/Solf, p. 554; and Australia, *Manual of the Law of Armed Conflict*, 2006, paras 10.11 and 10.32.

[12] Sandra Krähenmann, 'Protection of Prisoners in Armed Conflict', in Dieter Fleck (ed.), *The Handbook of International Humanitarian Law*, 3rd edition, Oxford University Press, 2013, pp. 359–411, at 375: 'Article 7 GC [Geneva Convention] III prevents the detaining power from relying on consent by the prisoner. Prisoners cannot, even partially, renounce their rights under GC III.' See also e.g. United Kingdom, *Manual of the Law of Armed Conflict*, 2004, para. 8.1: 'Prisoners of war may in no circumstances renounce their rights under the law of armed conflict. They remain members of the armed forces of the state on which they depend and cannot agree to change their status' (footnote omitted).

[13] Eric David and Howard Levie both argue that Article 7 renders unlawful any recruitment of prisoners of war, even as volunteers, into the armed forces of the Detaining Power. See David,

ICRC has nevertheless encountered such situations, it has, as a minimum, sought to independently verify the wishes of the prisoners of war concerned through interviews without witnesses. This kind of procedure undertaken by a neutral, impartial and independent humanitarian organization such as the ICRC helps to check that the enlistment was not forced. Even with a protective mechanism such as this in place, however, considering the vulnerable and often desperate situation of persons in enemy hands during an armed conflict, it is highly doubtful whether they can make decisions based on 'free will' in such circumstances.[14] Even where the free will of an individual in choosing to renounce protection could be ascertained by an independent body or mechanism, the overall protection regime may be weakened by a few individuals 'opting out'.[15]

996   Some have argued that common Article 7 prohibits the renunciation of rights but does not limit the 'acquisition of more rights'.[16] This argument is sustained by the fact that States may conclude special agreements as long as they do not diminish the protections of the Conventions. While this interpretation may be correct, often the problem lies in knowing whether the additional rights in question will actually benefit the protected persons. It may be a matter of having to wait and see. Although this may seem unsatisfactory on some levels, it may only be with the passage of time that one is able to determine whether a grant of what appear to be more rights does not in the long run result in a diminution of protection.[17] Each such situation has to be carefully observed and weighed.

997   The concern is that in wartime, protected persons who fall into the hands of the enemy are most often not in a position to fully know, evaluate or anticipate the implications of a renunciation of their rights – and in particular of their status – under the Conventions. Some consider that the way common Article 7 operates is to impede States from giving effect to decisions by individuals that would amount to a renunciation of their rights.[18] Thus, States may not rely on the 'voluntariness' of the decision or choice of protected persons to defend violations of their Convention rights. In addition, one may not renounce

---

para. 2.408; Howard S. Levie, *Prisoners of War in International Armed Conflict*, International Law Studies, U.S. Naval War College, Vol. 59, 1978, p. 362.

[14] This concern, specifically related to this context, is reflected in Australia, *Manual of the Law of Armed Conflict*, 2006, para. 10.18.

[15] This is not a purely humanitarian concern: from a military perspective, there may be strong pressure on members of the armed forces to show solidarity with their fellow prisoners and to refuse special treatment. This can also be the case for renunciation of rights which do not affect the status of protected persons, such as prisoners of war consenting to their images being broadcast or published in the media, in violation of Article 13 of the Third Convention.

[16] Rup Hingorani, *Prisoners of War*, 2nd edition, Oceana Press, Dobbs Ferry, 1982, pp. 183–184.

[17] An example might be a Detaining Power granting prisoner-of-war treatment to persons not entitled to it, which could lead to a lengthy detention not subject to review procedures or, conversely, to better material conditions of detention.

[18] Hersch Lauterpacht, *Oppenheim's International Law*, 7th edition, Longmans, Green and Co., London, 1952, p. 396, note 1.

rights under one of the Geneva Conventions, such as the right to prisoner-of-war status, in favour of a different legal regime.[19]

998   When it comes to civilians, Article 8 of the Fourth Convention operates in conjunction with other articles of the Convention to ensure that protected persons are not, for example, compelled to participate in military operations.[20] While the Fourth Convention does permit an Occupying Power to compel protected civilians to do some kinds of work, 'Article 8 is meant to preclude forced participation [in military operations] in the guise of voluntary participation'.[21] Practices such as giving individuals the chance to choose between remaining in administrative detention or being released on the condition that they accept transfer or deportation (even temporary) from the territory in which they normally live are other examples of a situation in which protected persons are being asked to renounce their rights under the Fourth Convention.[22] Lastly, it should be pointed out that in respect to both prisoners of war and civilians, a change in nationality – for example, adopting or being given the nationality of the Detaining Power or Occupying Power during the conflict – may not deprive a protected person of the protection of the Conventions.

999   There is nonetheless one exception to an 'absolutist' application of the rule, which is in relation to the right of prisoners of war to be repatriated at the end of hostilities (Article 118 of the Third Convention). Indeed, Articles 7 and 118 of the Third Convention, if interpreted and applied according to the letter, could mean that a prisoner of war may not refuse to be repatriated.[23] However, prisoners of war must be permitted to make an individual decision as to whether or not they wish to be repatriated, an exception which has existed for as long as the Third Convention has been in force and which is intrinsically linked with the principle of *non-refoulement*.[24] The same applies in respect to

---

[19] This implies that individuals whose status as prisoners of war has been properly recognized by a Detaining Power remain prisoners of war even in view of any proceeding they may undertake to challenge their status or deprivation of liberty.

[20] See Otto, pp. 776–781. See also Fourth Convention, Article 51.

[21] Otto, p. 779. In a similar vein, Otto argues that Article 8 of the Fourth Convention makes clear that the voluntary presence of protected civilians as 'human shields' does not affect the prohibition on their use in Article 28 (pp. 780–81).

[22] See, in particular, their rights under Article 49 of the Fourth Convention; ICRC, *General problems in implementing the Fourth Geneva Convention*, 27 October 1998, Meeting of Experts, Geneva, 27–29 October 1998 (Report), section 5(b)(ii): 'Other detainees have been released but only on condition that they leave the territory, which violates Article 8 regarding non-waiver of rights.' See also ICRC Press Release, Jerusalem: Palestinian detainee transferred to Gaza, 1 April 2012, and BBC, 'Palestinian hunger striker Hana Shalabi exiled to Gaza', 2 April 2012.

[23] See Charmatz/Wit, pp. 394–396, setting out the position of those who advocated that interpretation at the time of the Korean War.

[24] See Pictet (ed.), *Commentary on the Third Geneva Convention*, ICRC, 1960, pp. 542–549. In fact, the need for this exception arose in relation to the Korean War even before many States had ratified the 1949 Geneva Conventions: see Jaro Mayda, 'The Korean Repatriation Problem and International Law', *American Journal of International Law*, Vol. 47, No. 3, July 1953, pp. 414–438, and L.B. Schapiro, 'Repatriation of Deserters', *British Yearbook of International Law*, Vol. 29, 1952, pp. 322–324. For more recent practice, see John Quigley, 'Iran and Iraq and the Obligations to Release and Repatriate Prisoners of War after the Close of Hostilities',

civilians being repatriated following detention or internment,[25] but for them, the prohibition of *refoulement* is explicitly set down in Article 45 of the Fourth Convention. The crucial element in allowing for this exception lies in the fact that, at the end of hostilities, prisoners of war must be able – with no restrictions – to choose between returning to their normal life, in accordance with what the Convention guarantees to them, and another option such as resettlement. The same rule applies in regard to the return of the wounded and sick and medical and religious personnel.[26]

2. Rights secured by the Convention

1000 The initiators of the earliest Geneva Conventions wished to safeguard the dignity of the human person, in the profound conviction that imprescriptible and inviolable rights are attached to it even when hostilities are at their height.[27] Initially, however, the treatment which belligerents were required to accord to persons referred to in the Conventions was not presented, nor indeed clearly conceived, as constituting a body of 'rights'. In 1929, the word 'right' appeared in several provisions of the Geneva Convention on Prisoners of War,[28] but it was with the adoption of the 1949 Conventions that the existence of rights conferred on protected persons was confirmed.[29] The notion that the rights

---

American University International Law Review, Vol. 5, No. 1, 1989, pp. 73–86, especially at 83. Note, however, that a prisoner of war will not have to make out a successful asylum claim in order to refuse repatriation. On the principle of *non-refoulement*, see Emanuela-Chiara Gillard, 'There's no place like home: States' obligations in relation to transfers of persons', *International Review of the Red Cross*, Vol. 90, No. 871, September 2008, pp. 703–750; Cordula Droege, 'Transfers of detainees: legal framework, *non-refoulement* and contemporary challenges', *International Review of the Red Cross*, Vol. 90, No. 871, September 2008, pp. 669–701; Elihu Lauterpacht and Daniel Bethlehem, 'The scope and content of the principle of *non-refoulement*: Opinion', in Erika Feller, Volker Türk and Frances Nicholson (eds), *Refugee Protection in International Law: UNHCR's Global Consultations on International Protection*, Cambridge University Press, 2003, pp. 87–177; and David, section 2.409.

25 See Fourth Convention, Article 134. See also e.g. ICRC Press Release, Azerbaijan: civilian internee transferred under ICRC auspices, 19 August 2008; ICRC Press Release, Israel-Lebanon: transfer operation completed, 16 July 2008; and ICRC, *Annual Report 2005*, ICRC, Geneva, 2006, p. 313.

26 See the commentaries on Articles 15 and 30 of the First Convention and Article 109(3) of the Third Convention.

27 See Max Huber, *The Red Cross: Principles and Problems*, ICRC, Geneva, 1941, pp. 105–133; Jean S. Pictet, 'La Croix-Rouge et les Conventions de Genève', *Recueil des cours de l'Académie de droit international de La Haye*, Vol. 76, 1950, pp. 5–119, at 27–34.

28 For example, Article 42 of the 1929 Geneva Convention on Prisoners of War stipulates: 'Prisoners of war shall have the right to bring to the notice of the military authorities, in whose hands they are, their petitions concerning the conditions of captivity to which they are subjected. They shall also have the right to communicate with the representatives of the Protecting Powers.' Article 62 of the same Convention states: 'The prisoner of war [who is subject to judicial proceedings] shall have the right to be assisted by a qualified advocate of his own choice, and, if necessary, to have recourse to the offices of a competent interpreter. He shall be informed of his right by the Detaining Power in good time before the hearing.' Article 64 sets out a 'right of appeal' against a sentence for prisoners of war.

29 Indeed, the National Red Cross Societies had unanimously recommended in 1946 to confer upon the rights recognized by the Conventions 'a personal and intangible character' that would enable the beneficiaries 'to claim them irrespective of the attitude adopted by their home country'.

attached directly to individuals was clearly present at the time of the drafting of the Conventions: for example, during the discussion of common Article 6 on special agreements, one delegation proposed replacing the phrase 'the rights which it confers upon them' with 'the rights stipulated on their behalf'. This proposal, which would have implied that individuals benefited only indirectly from obligations owed to States, was rejected by the Diplomatic Conference.[30]

1001   The Geneva Conventions thus confer rights on individuals.[31] Whether these are international legal rights in the sense of rights protected by international treaties and enforced or supervised by courts or treaty bodies does not influence the character of the interests protected.[32] Without prejudice to other mechanisms of implementing and enforcing international humanitarian law, the rights protected by the Conventions carry their own enforcement mechanisms, which are adapted to the context of armed conflict. In particular, the ability of prisoners of war to petition the Detaining Power and of prisoners of war and protected civilians directly to contact supervisory powers provides them with a more immediate means to ensure the protection of their rights than would the ability to petition an international court.[33] Common Article 7 allows protected persons to claim the protection of the Conventions, not as a favour, but as a right, and enables them to use the mechanisms in the Conventions or any other available procedure to demand respect for the Conventions. The term

---

Report of the Preliminary Conference of National Societies of 1946, p. 71. See also the remarks of the delegate from France in *Final Record of the Diplomatic Conference of Geneva of 1949*, Vol. II-B, p. 10; and Pictet (ed.), *Commentary on the First Geneva Convention*, ICRC, 1952, especially pp. 82–84.

[30]   *Final Record of the Diplomatic Conference of Geneva of 1949*, Vol. II-B, p. 76. On the other hand, various delegates pointed out that even in its present wording, common Article 7 is addressed first and foremost to States Parties.

[31]   See also Christopher Greenwood, 'Human Rights and Humanitarian Law – Conflict or Convergence?', *Case Western Reserve Journal of International Law*, Vol. 43, 2010, pp. 491–512, at 499; George Aldrich, 'Individuals as Subjects of International Humanitarian Law', in Jerzy Makarczyk (ed.), *Theory of International Law at the Threshold of the 21st Century: Essays in Honour of Krzysztof Skubiszewski*, Kluwer, The Hague, 1996, pp. 851–858, especially at 856; and René Cassin, 'L'homme, sujet de droit international et la protection des droits de l'homme dans la société universelle', in *La technique et les principes du Droit public. Etudes en l'honneur de Georges Scelle*, L.G.D.J., Paris, 1950. Contra see Kate Parlett, *The Individual in the International Legal System: Continuity and Change in International Law*, Cambridge University Press, 2011, p. 187.

[32]   Lauterpacht has described rights which individuals cannot necessarily enforce in courts as 'imperfect legal rights'; see Hersch Lauterpacht, *International Law and Human Rights*, Stevens & Sons, London, 1950, p. 34. In monist States, treaties may be 'self-executing' and may not necessarily require implementing legislation; see Anthony Aust, *Modern Treaty Law and Practice*, 3rd edition, Cambridge University Press, 2013, pp. 163–167, and David Sloss, 'Domestic Application of Treaties', in Duncan B. Hollis (ed.), *The Oxford Guide to Treaties*, Oxford University Press, 2012, pp. 367–395, at 373–376.

[33]   See e.g. Article 78 of the Third Convention and Article 30 of the Fourth Convention, which allow protected persons to petition directly for assistance. As Schindler observed, 'Persons protected by humanitarian law usually are helpless and defenceless and not in a position to resort to any legal process. The rights of victims of armed conflicts are, therefore, better secured by an impartial body that acts on its own initiative than by a system in which the persons whose rights are violated have to institute judicial proceedings.' (Dietrich Schindler, 'Human Rights and Humanitarian Law: Interrelationship of the Laws', *American University Law Review*, Vol. 31, No. 4, summer 1982, pp. 935–943, at 941.)

'rights' refers to the entire system of protection under the Conventions and not only 'fundamental rights'. In the discussion regarding special agreements, it was determined that the rights conferred by the Conventions refer to the whole system and not just to a set of 'fundamental rights'. This logic applies here as well.[34] Hence the importance of the dissemination of the Conventions,[35] with special reference to the individual character of the rights which the Convention confers.

1002   As for what is meant by 'the rights secured by the present Convention', one authority, writing on the protection of civilians in the context of occupation, asserts that '[t]his principle [of non-renunciation of rights] applies to the entirety of international humanitarian law'.[36] Thus, according to that view, whether a right is protected through treaty law or customary international law, or in international or non-international armed conflict, is immaterial to whether it may be renounced. That interpretation may seem contrary to the strict wording of the article but it could nevertheless be sustained by a teleological approach.

Select bibliography

Charmatz, Jan P. and Wit, Harold M., 'Repatriation of Prisoners of War and the 1949 Geneva Convention', *Yale Law Journal*, Vol. 62, No. 3, February 1953, pp. 391–415.

d'Argent, Pierre, 'Non-Renunciation of the Rights Provided by the Conventions', in Andrew Clapham, Paola Gaeta and Marco Sassòli (eds), *The 1949 Geneva Conventions: A Commentary*, Oxford University Press, 2015, pp. 145–153.

David, Eric, *Principes de droit des conflits armés*, 5th edition, Bruylant, Brussels, 2012.

Esgain Albert J. and Solf, Waldemar A., 'The 1949 Geneva Convention Relative to the Treatment of Prisoners of War: Its Principles, Innovations, and Deficiencies', *North Carolina Law Review*, Vol. 41, No. 3, 1963, pp. 537–596.

Otto, Roland, 'Neighbours as human shields? The Israel Defense Forces' "Early Warning Procedure" and international humanitarian law', *International Review of the Red Cross*, Vol. 86, No. 856, December 2004, pp. 771–787.

Wilhelm, René-Jean, 'Le caractère des droits accordés à l'individu dans les Conventions de Genève', *Revue internationale de la Croix-Rouge et Bulletin international des Sociétés de la Croix-Rouge*, Vol. 32, No. 380, August 1950, pp. 561–590.

---

[34] See *Final Record of the Diplomatic Conference of Geneva of 1949*, Vol. II-B, pp. 73 and 74.

[35] See First Convention, Article 47; Second Convention, Article 48; Third Convention, Article 127; Fourth Convention, Article 144; and, if applicable, Additional Protocol I, Article 83, and Additional Protocol II, Article 19.

[36] Hans-Peter Gasser and Knut Dörmann, 'Protection of the Civilian Population', in Dieter Fleck (ed.), *The Handbook of International Humanitarian Law*, 3rd edition, Oxford University Press, 2013, pp. 231–320, at para. 539.

PROTECTING POWERS

❖ Text of the provision*

(1) The present Convention shall be applied with the cooperation and under the scrutiny of the Protecting Powers whose duty it is to safeguard the interests of the Parties to the conflict. For this purpose, the Protecting Powers may appoint, apart from their diplomatic or consular staff, delegates from amongst their own nationals or the nationals of other neutral Powers. The said delegates shall be subject to the approval of the Power with which they are to carry out their duties.

(2) The Parties to the conflict shall facilitate, to the greatest extent possible, the task of the representatives or delegates of the Protecting Powers.

(3) The representatives or delegates of the Protecting Powers shall not in any case exceed their mission under the present Convention. They shall, in particular, take account of the imperative necessities of security of the State wherein they carry out their duties. Their activities shall only be restricted, as an exceptional and temporary measure, when this is rendered necessary by imperative military necessities.

❖ Reservations or declarations

None

Contents

* Paragraph numbers have been added for ease of reference.

A. Introduction

1003 Article 8 regulates the appointment, role and functioning of the Protecting Powers. This provision is common to the four Conventions.[1]

1004   The Diplomatic Conference of 1949 made the Protecting Powers the lynch-pin of the system for monitoring compliance with the Geneva Conventions in international armed conflict. Indeed, concluding a treaty implies a minimum of mutual trust; implementing it requires a minimum of mutual scrutiny. After all, what State would agree to fulfil in good faith the commitments it has undertaken if it is not convinced that its enemies will do the same?

1005   In peacetime, it is up to diplomatic and consular missions to keep their government informed of how the receiving State is observing its commitments vis-à-vis the sending State. In the event of a failure to fulfil those obligations, the sending State may use diplomatic channels to assert its rights.

1006   Common Article 8 (Article 9 in the Fourth Convention) is based on the assumption, largely supported by State practice at the time of the 1949

[1] Article 8 of the First, Second and Third Conventions and Article 9 of the Fourth Convention.

Diplomatic Conference, in particular during the two world wars, that war implies the breaking off of both diplomatic and consular relations. Nowadays, this assumption is not always valid as there have been instances where Parties to an international armed conflict have maintained such relations. However, even then, most members of the diplomatic and consular missions of the Parties to the conflict had been withdrawn and the freedom of movement of those remaining severely restricted, so that they were no longer in a position to observe and report on the way the State of residence was respecting its obligations towards the sending State, nor to provide effective protection to the latter's nationals. Can it be expected that a treaty will be respected in such circumstances?

1007   This difficulty was not foreseen by the drafters of the 1864 Geneva Convention, which was the starting point for international humanitarian law as we know it today. They had planned to rely on the vigilance of the commanders-in-chief to oversee the implementation of the new treaty, whose Article 8 provided that:

> The implementing of the present Convention shall be arranged by the Commanders-in-Chief of the belligerent armies following the instructions of their respective Governments and in accordance with the general principles set forth in this Convention.[2]

1008   Accordingly, the new Convention did not establish any mechanism for supervising the implementation of its provisions. It was thought that all States would be keen to ensure their own compliance with the treaty and that none would risk, by violating its provisions, being banished from what were referred to at the time as the 'civilized nations'.

1009   But those expectations were soon confounded. During the 1870–71 Franco-Prussian War – the first conflict during which the new Convention was in force – the Parties to the conflict accused each other of violating its provisions. This was a situation that would be repeated in subsequent conflicts.

1010   Humanitarian law, which had not initially made provision for any mechanism to supervise its implementation, turned instead to an institution enshrined in diplomatic law.

1011   It was accepted that a State that was not represented in a given country could ask another Power that was represented in that country to safeguard its interests and those of its citizens. The same was true if diplomatic relations were broken off, particularly in wartime, in which case this role extended to monitoring the fate of soldiers and civilians who had fallen into enemy hands – whether sick or wounded soldiers and members of the medical services protected by the Geneva Convention, prisoners of war or civilians held by the adverse Party.

---

[2] Nowadays, see Article 45 of the First Convention and Article 46 of the Second Convention.

1012   This system became further consolidated in the second half of the 19th century, but it was during the two world wars that the work of the Protecting Powers saw the biggest growth in scope.

1013   By stipulating that the new Conventions would be implemented 'with the cooperation and under the scrutiny of the Protecting Powers whose duty it is to safeguard the interests of the Parties to the conflict', the Diplomatic Conference of 1949 made it compulsory to rely on Protecting Powers to monitor their implementation. With a view to making sure that those protected by the new Conventions were not left without protection, the Conference also provided for a substitution mechanism in case no Protecting Power was appointed.[3]

1014   Practice since 1949 has not developed in the direction envisioned by the drafters of the Geneva Conventions: the appointment of Protecting Powers in case of an international armed conflict has been the exception rather than the rule. Seemingly, practice since 1949 has evolved to the point of considering the appointment of Protecting Powers as optional in nature. This does not preclude, however, that Protecting Powers may still be appointed in future international armed conflicts on the basis of Article 8.

1015   Since humanitarian law borrowed the Protecting Power system from diplomatic law, this provision is only applicable in international armed conflicts. Neither common Article 3 nor Additional Protocol II make any mention of a role for Protecting Powers in non-international armed conflicts. Nothing precludes Parties to such a conflict, however, from concluding a special agreement to put into place a system akin to that of Protecting Powers.[4]

B. Historical background

1. Practice until the Second World War

1016   Throughout history, States have entrusted their diplomatic and consular staff with the task of safeguarding their interests and those of their citizens in the receiving State. This is a mission fully recognized by treaty and customary law.[5]

1017   However, this activity is not always limited to protecting the nationals of the sending State. It may be that a State (known as the 'Power of Origin') entrusts another State (known as the 'Protecting Power') with safeguarding its interests and those of its nationals in a country where it is not itself represented (the 'receiving State').

---

[3] See common Article 10 (Article 11 of the Fourth Convention).
[4] On the topic of special agreements in a non-international armed conflict, see the commentary on common Article 3, section K.
[5] According to Article 3 of the 1961 Vienna Convention on Diplomatic Relations:

1. The functions of a diplomatic mission consist, inter alia, in:
     . . .
       (b) Protecting in the receiving State the interests of the sending State and of its nationals, within the limits permitted by international law.

1018   This function came about in the 16th century, at a time when permanent diplomacy was becoming more widespread. Only the great Powers had the financial means to maintain embassies. To make sure that their nationals were given protection, smaller States agreed to entrust this task to other States.[6] There are still today many cases in which States ask another State to represent them and protect their interests in countries where they are not represented.[7]

1019   Similarly, if diplomatic relations were broken off, it was accepted that a State could request a third State to safeguard its interests and protect its nationals in the country where it was no longer represented.[8] This included safeguarding the interests of foreign nationals in wartime and, in particular, protecting persons held by the enemy. This practice gained broad acceptance in the second half of the 19th century[9] and became increasingly widespread during the First World War.[10] Following negotiations in late 1914 and into 1915, representatives of the Protecting Powers were granted permission to visit prisoner-of-war camps. Their representations – and those of the ICRC, undertaken at the same time – helped break the cycle of retaliations and counter-retaliations in which the Parties had become trapped and brought about major improvements for the prisoners.[11]

1020   The Diplomatic Conference of 1929 paid tribute to the work of the Protecting Powers during the First World War by setting out a legal basis for their actions in future. Article 86 of the 1929 Geneva Convention on Prisoners of War provided in its first paragraph that:

The High Contracting Parties recognize that a guarantee of the regular application of the present Convention will be found in the *possibility* of collaboration between the protecting Powers charged with the protection of the interests of the belligerents; in this connexion, the protecting Powers may, apart from their diplomatic personnel, appoint delegates from among their own nationals or the nationals of other neutral Powers. The appointment of these delegates shall be subject to

---

[6] See Pictet (ed.), *Commentary on the First Geneva Convention*, ICRC, 1952, p. 87; Franklin, pp. 8–9; and Siordet, pp. 4–5.

[7] For example, Italy represents San Marino in many countries, while Switzerland represents Liechtenstein in countries where the Principality is not represented (Salmon, p. 118).

[8] Thus, Switzerland represented the interests of the United States in Cuba from 1961 to 2015 and in Iran since 1980, those of Iran in Egypt (since 1979), those of Russia in Georgia (since 2008) and those of Georgia in Russia (since 2009). For further details, see https://www.eda.admin .ch/eda/en/fdfa/foreign-policy/human-rights/peace/protective-power-mandates.html and 'La diplomatie suisse en action pour protéger des intérêts étrangers', *Politorbis*, No. 56, 2014.

[9] Franklin, pp. 30–88; Wyler, pp. 23–39.   [10] Franklin, pp. 88–104 and 243–256.

[11] US diplomats posted to Berlin and London played a key role in these negotiations because of the privileged position of the United States, which simultaneously represented UK interests in Germany and German interests in the British Empire. See *Papers relating to the Foreign Relations of the United States*, 1914, Supplement, The World War, United States Government Printing Office, Washington, 1928, pp. 731–756, and *Papers relating to the Foreign Relations of the United States*, 1915, Supplement, The World War, United States Government Printing Office, Washington, 1928, pp. 997–1023.

the approval of the belligerent with whom they are to carry out their mission.[12] [Emphasis added.]

1021   This provision did not place any obligations on the High Contracting Parties; it was nevertheless to prove extremely useful during the Second World War, when most of the belligerents called upon the services of a Protecting Power. Switzerland protected the interests of 35 States, including most of the major Powers: the British Empire (in relation to 11 States or territories), France (17), United States (12), Germany (15), Japan (15) and Italy (14). Sweden protected the interests of 28 States, including the USSR. And the United States, prior to joining the war, represented a dozen States.[13]

1022   However, major difficulties became apparent. There were no treaty-based provisions authorizing the Protecting Powers to act on behalf of enemy civilians. No provision was made for Protecting Powers to take action in occupied territory; thus Japan, for example, declared all the territories it occupied to be zones of military operation and refused the Protecting Powers access to them.[14] Lastly, the work of the Protecting Powers was not accepted when it was to be performed on behalf of governments without official recognition (such as the Allied Governments in exile that were not recognized by Germany).[15]

2. Preparatory work for the 1949 Conventions

1023   The above mentioned difficulties prompted the ICRC, when it initiated preparations for the adoption of new Geneva Conventions in the aftermath of the Second World War, to set itself the following objectives: to extend to all four Conventions the supervision exercised by the Protecting Powers; to make such supervision compulsory; and to make arrangements for providing a substitute in the absence of a Protecting Power.[16]

1024   The war had brought to light in a dramatic way two very different situations: when the Geneva Convention on Prisoners of War had been implemented with the backing of a Protecting Power, its provisions (or at least the key ones) had largely been respected; whereas, when the supervision of a Protecting Power had been lacking, serious abuses had taken place. The three objectives the ICRC set itself found widespread support when it came to the negotiations that resulted in the adoption of the new Geneva Conventions.

1025   The question of supervising the implementation of the Geneva Conventions was brought first before the Preliminary Conference of National Societies, which took place in Geneva in 1946. However, the Conference focused on the

---

[12] For the legislative history of Article 86 of the 1929 Geneva Convention on Prisoners of War, see Bugnion, 2003, p. 855, fn. 6.

[13] Franklin, pp. 261–277; Janner, pp. 68–70.   [14] Janner, pp. 17 and 27.   [15] *Ibid.* pp. 21–22.

[16] Pictet (ed.), *Commentary on the First Geneva Convention*, ICRC, 1952, p. 92. See also de La Pradelle, 1951, pp. 221–225 and 234–243.

ICRC's role and requested that ICRC delegates enjoy the same rights and remit as the representatives of the Protecting Powers.[17] Otherwise, the Conference merely underlined the importance of supervising the implementation of the new Conventions and of punishing violations of their provisions.[18]

1026   The issue was then addressed by the 1947 Conference of Government Experts. The main focus was on revising Article 86 of the 1929 Geneva Convention on Prisoners of War. The crux of the discussion was the possibility of a procedure for appointing a substitute in the absence of a Protecting Power, and the ICRC's role in supervising the implementation of the Geneva Conventions.[19] The Conference also found that the words 'as a general rule' in Article 86(2) of the Convention on Prisoners of War, which had been seized upon to restrict the activities of delegates of Protecting Powers, particularly in the Far East, should be deleted. The Conference also raised and then rejected the possibility of delegates of Protecting Powers being permanently based in prisoner-of-war camps, and instead placed the emphasis on short-term visits. For the Conference, therefore, it was these visits and the possibility of holding interviews without witnesses with the prisoners that was foreseen as the cornerstone of the implementation of the new Conventions. This function was to be entrusted to the Protecting Powers.[20]

1027   In relation to the protection of civilians, the Conference envisaged the Protecting Powers' involvement in a wide range of specific areas, including dealing with voluntary applications for internment, processing appeals against internment decisions, and supervising transfers and evacuations. However, despite the atrocities committed during the Second World War, particularly against populations in occupied territories, it does not seem that the Conference envisaged giving Protecting Powers a general mandate to work towards the implementation of, and compliance with, any new convention for the protection of civilians in wartime – something that had been so sorely lacking during the Second World War.[21]

1028   In the draft conventions submitted to the 17th International Conference of the Red Cross, held in Stockholm in 1948, the ICRC inserted the following draft common article:

The present Convention shall be applied with the co-operation and under the control of the Protecting Powers, whose duty it is to safeguard the interests of the Parties to the conflict. To this end, the Protecting Powers may appoint, besides their diplomatic staff, delegates among their own nationals, or among nationals of

---

[17] *Report of the Preliminary Conference of National Societies of 1946*, pp. 73–74.
[18] *Ibid.* p. 68.
[19] For the appointment of substitutes, see common Article 10 (Article 11 in the Fourth Convention).
[20] *Report of the Conference of Government Experts of 1947*, pp. 262–268.
[21] For a complete overview of the discussions on these aspects, see *ibid.* pp. 284–347, in particular at 298–300 and 304–305.

other neutral Powers. These delegates shall be subject to the approval of the Power in whose territory they are to carry out their duties.

The Parties to the conflict shall facilitate to the greatest extent possible the task of the representatives or delegates of the Protecting Powers.[22]

1029   When this draft was studied by the Legal Commission of the Stockholm Conference, the Canadian Government's representative spoke out against the fact that the French word 'contrôle' had been translated by 'control' in English. He pointed out that the term 'control' in English was much stronger than its French equivalent and, if it were to be kept, it would give the impression that the Protecting Power was entitled to direct the actions of one of the Parties to the conflict. Following this discussion, the Stockholm Conference replaced the word 'control' in English by 'supervision', while keeping the word 'contrôle' in French at the ICRC's request. Subject to this change, the Conference agreed to the ICRC's proposals without hesitation.[23]

1030   During the 1949 Diplomatic Conference, the task of studying draft article 6/7/7/7 was entrusted to the Conference's Joint Committee, which was responsible for considering all the draft articles common to the four Conventions. The discussions mainly focused on two points.

1031   First, the delegations from English-speaking countries objected to the aforementioned translation of the term 'contrôle' in the first sentence of draft article 6/7/7/7 by 'supervision'. In their view, this accorded the Protecting Power the right to give the Detaining Power or the Occupying Power instructions with which the latter would be obliged to comply. This, they believed, far exceeded the role of the Protecting Power as it had developed in practice during the two world wars. After hesitating between several translations, the Conference finally settled on the term 'scrutiny'.[24] This discussion is interesting because it offers an insight into the meaning that the Diplomatic Conference intended to give to the terms 'contrôle' and 'scrutiny' in the first sentence of Article 8.

1032   Second, the Soviet delegation tabled an amendment stipulating that the delegates of the Protecting Power may not infringe the sovereignty of the receiving State. The amendment was put to the vote and rejected because many delegations feared that the reference to national sovereignty would be invoked to arbitrarily limit the activities of the Protecting Powers and nullify the scrutiny that the Diplomatic Conference wished to establish.[25]

1033   However, the Committee which examined the draft article deemed it advisable to offer the receiving State some safeguards for dealing with the

---

[22] *Draft Conventions submitted to the 1948 Diplomatic Conference*, draft common article 6/7/7/7, pp. 8, 36, 56 and 156.

[23] *Minutes of the Legal Commission at the 1948 Stockholm Conference*, pp. 70–73; *Draft Conventions adopted by the 1948 Diplomatic Conference*, pp. 11, 33, 54 and 115–116.

[24] *Final Record of the Diplomatic Conference of Geneva of 1949*, Vol. II-B, pp. 18–20, 57–59, 89 and 110–111.

[25] *Ibid.* pp. 28–29, 38, 57–59, 74, 89, 110–111 and 130.

Protecting Power. It therefore agreed to add what has become, with editorial changes only, paragraph 3 of Article 8.[26] One sentence in this paragraph, however, only appears in the First and Second Conventions, but has been deliberately removed from the text of the Third and Fourth Conventions.[27]

C. Sources of international law governing Protecting Powers

1034 The status and duties of Protecting Powers are governed essentially by customary law and by two groups of treaties: (i) treaties of international humanitarian law, in particular the 1949 Geneva Conventions and the 1977 Additional Protocol I;[28] and (ii) treaties of diplomatic and consular law, in particular the 1961 Vienna Convention on Diplomatic Relations and the 1963 Vienna Convention on Consular Relations, as well as the 1969 Convention on Special Missions.[29]

1035 On this basis, a distinction is usually made between the 'Geneva mandate', which sets out the duties of the Protecting Powers under humanitarian law, and the 'Vienna mandate', which sets out the activities arising more specifically from diplomatic and consular law and practice.[30] Both have in common that, on the basis of Article 45 of the Vienna Convention on Diplomatic Relations,

---

[26] *Ibid.* p. 111.   [27] For details, see paras 1111–1113.

[28] Common Article 8 (Article 9 in the Fourth Convention) and Article 5 of Additional Protocol I. Article 2(c) of Protocol I defines 'Protecting Power' as 'a neutral or other State not a Party to the conflict which has been designated by a Party to the conflict and accepted by the adverse Party and has agreed to carry out the functions assigned to a Protecting Power under the Conventions and this Protocol'. The mechanisms established by Articles 21–22 of the 1954 Hague Convention for the Protection of Cultural Property are largely inspired by those of the Geneva Conventions.

[29] See Vienna Convention on Diplomatic Relations (1961), Articles 45(b)–(c) and 46. Article 45(b)–(c) reads:

If diplomatic relations are broken off between two States, or if a mission is permanently or temporarily recalled:

. . .

(b) the sending State may entrust the custody of the premises of the mission, together with its property and archives, to a third State acceptable to the receiving State;
(c) the sending State may entrust the protection of its interests and those of its nationals to a third State acceptable to the receiving State.
Article 46 reads:
A sending State may with the prior consent of the receiving State, and at the request of a third State not represented in the receiving State, undertake the temporary protection of the interests of the third State and of its nationals.
Article 27 of the 1963 Vienna Convention on Consular Relations establishes similar rules to be applied if consular relations are broken off. Article 1(a) of the 1969 Convention on Special Missions defines a 'special mission' as 'a temporary mission, representing the State, which is sent by one State to another State with the consent of the latter for the purpose of dealing with it on specific questions or of performing in relation to it a specific task.'

[30] This distinction is also reflected in the last sentence of Article 4(B)(2) of the Third Convention: '[T]he Parties to a conflict on whom these persons depend shall be allowed to perform towards them the functions of a Protecting Power as provided in the present Convention, without prejudice to the functions which these Parties normally exercise in conformity with diplomatic and consular usage and treaties.'

the tasks of the Protecting Power may be performed by that Power's diplomatic officials. Therefore, they will be subject to diplomatic law.

1036   Yet the distinction between the 'Geneva mandate' and the 'Vienna mandate' matters in several instances. First, when diplomatic relations are broken off between two States without there being an international armed conflict in the sense of the Geneva Conventions between them,[31] only the Vienna mandate may be applicable. Furthermore, some of the tasks of the Protecting Power on the basis of the Vienna mandate are not found in the Geneva Conventions, for instance the protection of the premises and archives of the mission, as provided for in Article 45(b) of the Vienna Convention on Diplomatic Relations.[32]

1037   Another scenario in which the distinction matters is when an international armed conflict breaks out, but the States involved maintain diplomatic relations. In that case, there may be no need to appoint a Protecting Power in the sense of the Vienna Convention on Diplomatic Relations. However, because of the armed conflict, it would still be useful to appoint a Protecting Power in the sense of the Geneva Conventions.[33] Indeed, even where diplomatic or consular staff remain, they are still likely to have their freedom of movement restricted.[34] More generally, in practice it will be very difficult to implement all the provisions of diplomatic law, which are mostly designed for peacetime situations.[35]

---

[31] For examples, see Lord Gore-Booth (ed.), *Satow's Guide to Diplomatic Practice*, 5th edition, Longman, London, 1979, p. 188, and Salmon, pp. 499–502.

[32] For the text of that provision, see fn. 29.

[33] Additional Protocol I, Article 5(6), which makes it clear that '[t]he maintenance of diplomatic relations between Parties to the conflict or the entrusting of the protection of a Party's interests and those of its nationals to a third State in accordance with the rules of international law relating to diplomatic relations is no obstacle to the designation of Protecting Powers for the purpose of applying the Conventions and this Protocol'. On this point, see Kolb, p. 551.

[34] During the 1962 international armed conflict between India and the People's Republic of China, for example, the ICRC pointed out that – despite diplomatic relations being maintained between the two countries – neither the Indian prisoners of war in China nor the Chinese civilian internees in India had been visited by representatives of their countries of origin; see *International Review of the Red Cross*, Vol. 3, No. 24, March 1963, p. 149, and ICRC, *Annual Report 1962*, ICRC, Geneva, 1963, p. 27.

[35] See Eritrea-Ethiopia Claims Commission, *Diplomatic Claim, Eritrea's Claim*, Partial Award, 2005, paras 4–6:

> 4.... [A]t the outset, the Commission wishes to stress the Parties' commendable decisions not to sever diplomatic links despite the armed conflict. One need only recall Oppenheim to appreciate the truly exceptional character of this situation.
>
> ...
>
> 6.... [T]his unusual situation has created unusual challenges for the application of diplomatic law. Certain of the core functions of a diplomatic mission – for example, 'promoting friendly relations between the sending State and the receiving State' as set out in Article 3, paragraph (c), of the Vienna Convention on Diplomatic Relations – become obviously incongruous in wartime. Certain of the premises of effective diplomatic representation – for example, free travel, for access, intelligence gathering, ability to influence public opinion – cannot be presumed to continue without strain during hostilities.

See also Smolinska/Boutros/Lozanorios/Lunca, pp. 93–94.

1038   Until at least the Second World War, the outbreak of war between two States
was generally considered to automatically imply the breaking off of diplomatic relations between those States.[36] Nowadays, however, 'the situation is
less clear when an armed conflict takes place without a formal declaration
of war.... [C]ontrary to a declared war, an armed conflict does not necessarily
induce by itself the breaking off of diplomatic relations. This has the advantage
of leaving the countries concerned with the possibility of keeping in diplomatic
contact over the issues at stake.'[37] In practice since 1949, while it has happened
that States maintained diplomatic relations despite their being adversaries in
an international armed conflict, such relations have been broken off at the outset of, or during, a number of other such conflicts.[38] Lastly, there have also
been instances where an international armed conflict has broken out between
States which did not have diplomatic relations at the time of the outbreak.[39] In
all these instances, the continued usefulness of appointing Protecting Powers
goes without saying.

1039   The question of whether an international armed conflict automatically leads
to the breaking off of diplomatic relations needs to be kept separate from the
question of whether the outbreak of such a conflict has any impact on the continued applicability between them of the Vienna Convention on Diplomatic
Relations: whether or not diplomatic relations have been broken off between
the Parties to the conflict, that Convention remains applicable.[40]

1040   When an international armed conflict breaks out between two States *and*
diplomatic relations are broken off between those same States, the distinction
loses its legal bearing in practice if Protecting Powers are appointed in the sense
of the Geneva Conventions. The way State practice developed over time, particularly during the two world wars, meant that the mandate of the Protecting
Powers formed a cohesive whole: where Protecting Powers are appointed in the
sense of the Geneva Conventions, the officials of the Protecting Power will be

---

[36] See Oppenheim, p. 301, para. 98; see also Sfez, p. 388, and Papini/Cortese, pp. 137–138.

[37] See Ludwik Dembinski, *The Modern Law of Diplomacy: External Missions of States and International Organizations*, Martinus Nijhoff Publishers, Dordrecht, 1988, p. 96. On the concept
of declared war, see the commentary on common Article 2, section D.1.

[38] On the breaking off of diplomatic relations, see Sfez, p. 361, and Smolinska/Boutros/Lozanorios/
Lunca, p. 108.

[39] Salmon, p. 498, listing international armed conflicts in which the States involved broke off their
diplomatic relations, and international armed conflicts in which the States involved maintained
them. See also Smolinska/Boutros/Lozanorios/Lunca, p. 92, and Papini/Cortese, p. 138. See also
fn. 35 regarding the conflict between Eritrea and Ethiopia.

[40] See e.g. Vienna Convention on Diplomatic Relations (1961), Articles 44 and 45(a), and Vienna
Convention on Consular Relations (1963), Articles 26 and 27(a). See also ILC, *Draft articles
on the effects of armed conflicts on treaties, with commentaries*, 2011, pp. 11, 20 and 38–40,
which lists 'treaties relating to diplomatic or consular relations' among the 'treaties the subject
matter of which involves an implication that they continue in operation, in whole or in part,
during armed conflict', and Fifty-seventh session, 'The effect of armed conflict on treaties: an
examination of practice and doctrine', Memorandum by the Secretariat, UN Doc. A/CN.4/550,
1 February 2005, p. 25.

largely occupied with the duties common to both the Geneva mandate and the Vienna mandate.

1041   The drafting of Article 8 clearly shows that the 1949 text intended to preserve the unity of the Protecting Power's mandate since it stipulated that the new Conventions would be implemented 'with the cooperation and under the scrutiny of the Protecting Powers whose duty it is to safeguard the interests of the Parties to the conflict'. The fact that that mandate is now enshrined in two different legal instruments does not alter the fact that these mandates were meant to be cohesive.

1042   Indeed, Article 45(c) of the Vienna Convention on Diplomatic Relations stipulates that, if diplomatic relations are broken off, '[t]he sending State may entrust the protection of its interests *and those of its nationals* to a third State acceptable to the receiving State' (emphasis added). In wartime, those nationals whose interests need protecting include wounded and sick members of the armed forces, prisoners of war and civilians in the hands of the adverse Party – in other words, those protected by the Geneva Conventions. Where Protecting Powers are appointed, the two mandates therefore overlap to a large extent. Of course, international humanitarian law will contain the more detailed rules with regard to the tasks the Protecting Power can perform for the protection of the victims of the international armed conflict.

D. Appointment of Protecting Powers

1043   The first sentence of Article 8(1) stipulates that '[t]he present Convention shall be applied with the cooperation and under the scrutiny of the Protecting Powers whose duty it is to safeguard the interests of the Parties to the conflict'.

1044   The use of the word 'shall' indicates that the appointment of the Protecting Powers is not an optional form of assistance available to the Parties to an international armed conflict, but an obligation.[41] In 1949, as was also the case for Article 5 of Additional Protocol I when adopted in 1977, it is clear that this was the intention of the drafters.

1045   Over the decades since 1949, however, States have come to a different understanding of this provision. As discussed below (see section H), the appointment of Protecting Powers since 1949 has been the exception rather than the rule in international armed conflicts. Absent any protest, therefore, it would seem that the failure to appoint a Protecting Power is not, at least in the eyes of most States, seen as a violation of their treaty obligations.[42] At the same time, there

---

[41] The French text is equally clear. It reads: 'La présente Convention sera appliquée avec le concours et sous le contrôle des Puissances protectrices.'

[42] See also Kolb, p. 559: 'state practice has turned the original duty to nominate a Protecting Power into a *mere option*'; see also p. 552.

is no indication that the High Contracting Parties consider that Article 8 has fallen into desuetude.[43]

1046   Article 10, dealing with the appointment of substitutes for Protecting Powers, was not conceived by the drafters of the Geneva Conventions as an alternative to Article 8. Indeed, Article 10 was essentially meant to cover situations in which no Protecting Power could be appointed, for example because of the disappearance of the Power of Origin or because the latter could no longer fulfil its duties.[44] The existence of Article 10, therefore, may not be used as an argument to corroborate the view that the system of Protecting Powers is defunct.

1047   The Conventions do not set out a procedure for the appointment of Protecting Powers. That said, humanitarian law did not create the Protecting Powers system; it simply called upon an institution that was already well established in diplomatic and consular practice. It is therefore customary law, arising from this practice, that provides this procedure. This also explains why only a State can be appointed as a Protecting Power under Article 8.

1048   The appointment of a Protecting Power presupposes the conclusion of two agreements: one between the Power of Origin and the Protecting Power; and the other between the Protecting Power and the receiving State. No agreement between the opposing High Contracting Parties is necessary.

1. Agreement between the Power of Origin and the Protecting Power

1049   No State can name itself Protecting Power on its own initiative. At the same time, nothing prevents a State from approaching a Party to a conflict to propose itself as a Protecting Power. The Protecting Power must receive from the State that calls upon its services a mandate that sets out the scope of the protection it may exercise. It acts by delegation, meaning that it can only, as a general rule, act within the rights to which the State it represents is entitled. Lastly, it is expected that the State represented will not entrust to the Protecting Power tasks that would clearly be detrimental to the latter's interests.[45]

1050   The Protecting Power may not exceed the terms of the mandate entrusted to it. It has also traditionally been expected to regularly submit reports to the Power of Origin on its activities and the situation of that State's nationals in the receiving State.[46] When and how such reports are to be submitted

---

[43] See *ibid.* pp. 558–559:

> Overall, there is an impressive array of reasons that explain why the institution of Protecting Powers has fallen into disuse. Legally, this clearly does not connote any idea of obsolescence or desuetude. The legal institution of Protecting Power has not, to any extent, been abrogated. Hence, a state could perfectly well appoint a Protecting Power today and seek the agreement of the opposing Party.

[44] See the commentary on Article 10, para. 1211.   [45] Franklin, pp. 119–124; Janner, pp. 11–15.

[46] Janner, pp. 12–13. For military personnel, the 'Power of Origin' is the State in whose armed forces a person served before being rendered *hors de combat* by wounds, illness or capture; for

will depend on the agreement between the Power of Origin and the Protecting Power.

1051   A neutral State is not legally obliged to accept the mandate of Protecting Power when asked.[47] Nevertheless, diplomatic tradition and international comity dictate that, provided the receiving State agrees, neutral States will accede to such requests.

1052   However, shortly after the end of the Second World War, Switzerland unilaterally renounced its safeguarding of German interests in view of the disappearance of the Reich Government. Similarly, Switzerland refused to safeguard certain Japanese interests because it no longer enjoyed free communication with the Japanese Government, which was controlled by the Allied Powers at the time. These two examples show that, at least in Swiss practice, a Protecting Power's purpose depends on having a mandate from a government.[48]

1053   Nothing in the Geneva Conventions or diplomatic law or practice obliges two States at war to appoint the same State as Protecting Power. Thus, in September 1939, the United Kingdom and France appointed the United States to safeguard their interests in Germany, while Germany called upon Switzerland to protect its interests in the United Kingdom, and on Spain to protect its interests in France.[49] Experience has shown, however, that if adversaries appoint the same State as Protecting Power, it is easier for that State to be effective than if it is appointed by just one of the Parties to the conflict. This is because it has an overview of the entire situation and can easily communicate with each adversary.[50]

2. Agreement between the Protecting Power and the receiving State

1054   A State approached about being a Protecting Power cannot accept the mandate without the approval of the receiving State;[51] generally speaking, it will even

---

civilians, the term refers to the State of which they are nationals, or, in the case of refugees or stateless persons, the State which granted them asylum.

[47] It might, however, be argued that the High Contracting Parties undertook, under common Article 1, 'to respect and to ensure respect for' the Conventions 'in all circumstances', and that this also imposes an obligation on neutral States to accept and discharge the mandate of Protecting Power if asked to do so. Nevertheless, a neutral State can always question why it was asked to take on this role rather than another State. For a discussion of which States qualify as 'neutral Powers', see the commentary on Article 4, section C.1.

[48] Janner, pp. 12 and 29–30.

[49] See Swiss Federal Council, Minutes of the session of 1 September 1939, *Documents diplomatiques suisses*, Vol. 13, 1991, pp. 331–332; *Journal de Genève*, 3 September 1939, p. 8, and 9 September 1939, p. 4; ICRC, *Report of the International Committee of the Red Cross on its Activities during the Second World War (September 1, 1939–June 30, 1947), Volume I: General Activities*, ICRC, Geneva, May 1948, pp. 358–359; and Franklin, p. 267. After the United States entered the war, Switzerland took over most of the protection mandates carried out up to then by US diplomatic staff; Franklin, pp. 266–268.

[50] Note from J. de Saussure, Deputy Head of the Foreign Interests Division, Political Department, to D. Secretan, Head of the International Unions Section, Political Department, 22 January 1946, *Documents diplomatiques suisses*, Vol. 16, 1997, pp. 166–169, at 167; Janner, pp. 24–25 and 52.

[51] Swiss Federal Council, Minutes of the session of 1 September 1939, *Documents diplomatiques suisses*, Vol. 13, 1991, pp. 331–332; Note from M. Pilet-Golaz, Head of the Political Department,

try to reach a formal agreement with that State guaranteeing that it will be able to satisfactorily perform the duties entrusted to it.[52]

1055   The receiving State may refuse the services of the Protecting Power appointed by the adverse Party; it may not, however, act in such a way that the interests and nationals of another State are left without protection.[53] In international armed conflict, such an attitude would clearly run counter to Article 8 and to a number of specific provisions of the Geneva Conventions, in particular Article 126 of the Third Convention and Article 143 of the Fourth Convention.

1056   The appointment of the delegates of the Protecting Power must be approved by the Party to the conflict with which they will carry out their mission. The final sentence of Article 8(1) states that '[t]he said delegates shall be subject to the approval of the Power with which they are to carry out their duties'.

1057   This rule is in line with diplomatic law and practice, from where the Protecting Power system is derived. It enables the receiving State to reject a delegate's appointment if it has good reason to do so, for instance if the individual put forward had made statements casting doubt on his or her neutrality or impartiality.

1058   But this provision does not allow the receiving State to refuse all delegates appointed by the Protecting Power, because such an attitude would prevent the Protecting Power from fulfilling its mandate. Under Article 8(1), the States party to the Geneva Conventions undertake to implement the Conventions 'with the cooperation and under the scrutiny of the Protecting Powers whose duty it is to safeguard the interests of the Parties to the conflict'. Systematically refusing all the delegates appointed by the Protecting Power is tantamount to preventing it from carrying out its mission.

1059   With a view to fostering compliance with the Geneva Conventions, and aware that to do so it was essential to make available enough individuals capable of shouldering the task entrusted to the Protecting Powers of impartially scrutinizing the implementation of the Conventions, the 20th International Conference of the Red Cross in 1965 invited the States party to the Conventions to envisage the possibility of setting up groups of competent persons to supervise the implementation of the Conventions, and invited the ICRC to contribute to their training.[54] Subsequently, Article 6(1) of Additional Protocol

---

to D.V. Kelly, UK minister in Bern, 28 July 1941, *Documents diplomatiques suisses*, Vol. 14, 1997, pp. 263–264.

[52] Franklin, pp. 124–134; Janner, pp. 16–18.

[53] Janner, p. 16; Heintze, para. 11: 'The permanent rejection of protection violates the minimum standards requirements concerning the treatment of aliens in international humanitarian law.' For examples, see Cahier, p. 138; Salmon, p. 122; and Smolinska/Boutros/Lozanorios/Lunca, p. 106.

[54] 20th International Conference of the Red Cross, Vienna, 1965, Resolution XXII, Personnel for the Control of the Application of the Geneva Conventions; Austrian Red Cross, *Twentieth International Conference of the Red Cross, Vienna, October 2–9, 1965, Report*, Vienna, 1965, pp. 78–79 and 106.

I required the High Contracting Parties to endeavour to train qualified personnel, in particular to carry out 'the activities of the Protecting Powers'.

3. Terms of reference

1060   Lastly, the appointment of a Protecting Power presupposes some common ground between the Parties to the conflict, at least when it comes to agreeing on the duties of the Protecting Power(s). Under humanitarian law, it is naturally the Geneva Conventions that are the basis for that mandate.[55] Additional duties beyond those outlined in Article 8 or in the Vienna Convention on Diplomatic Relations may be agreed upon in a special agreement between the Parties concerned. However, no bilateral agreement between the Parties is required for Protecting Powers to be appointed and take up their duties, nor is any direct communication between the Parties to the conflict necessary.

E. Paragraph 1: Duties of the Protecting Powers under the Geneva Conventions

1. In general

1061   Generally speaking, the mission of the Protecting Powers revolves around two tasks that emerge from the first sentence of Article 8(1): to cooperate in the implementation of the Geneva Conventions; and to scrutinize that implementation.

1062   While the duties of the Protecting Powers can be considered to be a form of 'diplomatic protection', they go beyond the specific definition of this notion as it appears in the ILC's 2006 Draft Articles on Diplomatic Protection. The Draft Articles define this notion 'for the purposes of the present draft articles' thus:

[D]iplomatic protection consists of the invocation by a State, through diplomatic action or other means of peaceful settlement, of the responsibility of another State for an injury caused by an internationally wrongful act of that State to a natural or legal person that is a national of the former State with a view to the implementation of such responsibility.[56]

1063   In the above sense, 'diplomatic protection' is an action whereby a State attempts, after the facts, to have the responsibility of another State established for a violation, by that State, of a rule of international law applicable to it. The activities of a Protecting Power, on the other hand, are mostly preventive in nature: through scrutiny, the aim is to pre-empt violations. Lastly, a key requirement of 'diplomatic protection' in the sense of the Draft Articles is that '[a] State may not present an international claim in respect of an injury to

---

[55] See Dominicé, p. 431: '[W]hile its power to act as a Protecting Power is indubitably founded upon the particular mandate entrusted to it by a specific State, its responsibilities under the Geneva Conventions are assigned to it by all of the Contracting Parties.'

[56] Draft Articles on Diplomatic Protection (2006), Article 1.

a national ... before the injured person has ... exhausted all local remedies'.[57] This requirement does not apply to the activities of a Protecting Power, i.e. a Protecting Power may act, for example for the protection of a prisoner of war, without the prisoner of war having to have exhausted all local remedies.

a. Cooperation

1064 The idea of 'cooperation' implies that the Protecting Power should work with the Power of Origin of the protected persons and with the receiving State in order to implement the Geneva Conventions.

1065 The Protecting Power is supposed to provide a channel for communication between the Power of Origin and the receiving State. The Geneva Conventions contain several provisions stipulating that information about prisoners of war and about civilians protected by the Fourth Convention should be transmitted via the Protecting Power.[58] In other cases, however, the Geneva Conventions state that it is obligatory to transmit certain information without specifying the means of transmittal.[59] These omissions might be read to suggest that the Protecting Powers would only transmit information when it was expressly indicated that they should do so. But this interpretation would ignore the fact that the Diplomatic Conference of 1949 decided that the new Geneva Conventions would be implemented 'with the cooperation and under the scrutiny of the Protecting Powers whose duty it is to safeguard the interests of the Parties to the conflict'. This general obligation was enough, in the minds of the drafters of the Geneva Conventions in 1949, to make the Protecting Power the primary – but by no means the exclusive – channel for information exchange between the Parties to the conflict, without there being a need to remind the Parties each time that such an exchange could take place through the Protecting Powers. In addition, long before 1949 it had become regular practice for the Protecting Power to be a channel for communication between the Power which appointed it and the receiving State, for matters within both the Vienna mandate and the Geneva mandate. Thus, in October 1918 the Government in Berlin asked Switzerland – the Protecting Power for German interests in the United States – to pass on its request for an armistice to President Wilson. Switzerland thus became the intermediary for the negotiations that resulted

---

[57] *Ibid.* Article 14(1).

[58] Thus, Article 122(3) of the Third Convention states that all information regarding the identity, detention, transfer, release or death of a prisoner of war must be immediately forwarded by the most rapid means to his or her country of origin 'through the intermediary of the Protecting Powers and likewise of the Central Agency provided for in Article 123'. Article 137 of the Fourth Convention includes a similar provision regarding civilians protected by the Convention.

[59] Thus, Articles 22 and 24 of the Second Convention make the protection of military hospital ships and hospital ships utilized by National Red Cross or Red Crescent Societies or other officially recognized relief societies subject to the 'condition that their names and descriptions have been notified to the Parties to the conflict ten days before those ships are employed', but do not specify by what channel that notification should be communicated to the adverse Party. The Protecting Powers, where they have been appointed, may be asked to undertake this task (Janner, p. 61).

in the armistice agreement of 11 November 1918.[60] Furthermore, the Protecting Power can be entrusted with passing on remittances or relief consignments from the Power of Origin to its nationals who are prisoners of war or civilian internees.[61]

1066   The Protecting Power mandate therefore encompasses the role of intermediary between the Parties to the conflict. The Protecting Power facilitates communication between the Parties and can also be called upon to lend its good offices in the event of disputes over the interpretation or implementation of treaty provisions[62] or as part of reaching agreements that fill any gaps in humanitarian law or facilitate its implementation.[63]

1067   While there is no evidence of the Protecting Powers organizing meetings between adverse Parties during the Second World War, they lent their good offices in order to reach agreements on improving the lot of the wounded, prisoners of war and civilians. Those agreements resulted in many repatriation operations for the seriously injured, medical personnel and civilians. The most significant operation in terms of numbers was the repatriation, while the hostilities were ongoing, of some 28,000 Italian civilians from Eritrea and Ethiopia following the defeat of Italian forces in Eastern Africa.[64]

1068   In so far as the Protecting Power mandate encompasses the role of good offices, it also includes a right of initiative inherent to that role.[65] Offers made by the Protecting Power exercising this right can therefore under no circumstances be regarded as an unfriendly act.[66] But there are definite limits to this right of initiative, as Article 8 makes clear: 'The representatives or delegates of the Protecting Powers shall not in any case exceed their mission under the present Convention.'

b. Scrutiny

1069 The interpretation of the word 'scrutiny' is more complicated. However, the discussions that took place at the 1949 Diplomatic Conference concerning

---

[60] Pierre Renouvin, *La crise européenne et la Première Guerre mondiale*, 5th edition, Presses universitaires de France, Paris, 1969, p. 613. When it learned of the request of the German Government, the Swiss Federal Council observed that, since it represented German interests in the United States, it had a duty to follow through on that request straight away. Swiss Federal Council, Minutes of the session of 4 October 1918, *Documents diplomatiques suisses*, Vol. 6, 1981, pp. 799–800. The reaction of the Federal Council shows that, as far it was concerned, the Protecting Power mandate encompassed this role of neutral intermediary.

[61] Janner, pp. 41–42 and 54.   [62] See common Article 11 (Article 12 of the Fourth Convention).

[63] See e.g. Agreement between France and Germany concerning Prisoners of War (1918) and Second Agreement between France and Germany concerning Prisoners of War and Civilians (1918). These agreements were signed in Bern under the auspices of Switzerland. Switzerland had been responsible for protecting German interests in France since the United States entered the war. See Renée-Marguerite Frick-Cramer, 'Le Comité international de la Croix-Rouge et les Conventions internationales pour les prisonniers de guerre et les civils', *Revue internationale de la Croix-Rouge*, Vol. 25, No. 293, 1943, pp. 386–402, at 388–389.

[64] Janner, pp. 45–46.

[65] See e.g. Article 11 of the First Convention on the lending of good offices by Protecting Powers to settle disagreements between the Parties to a conflict.

[66] First Convention, Article 3(3).

the translation of the French word 'contrôle' clarified what was meant. The English-speaking delegations observed that the term 'supervision' – used to translate 'contrôle' in the draft conventions approved by the Stockholm Conference – would give the Protecting Power the right to issue instructions to the receiving State. By creating a hierarchical relationship, such a remit would exceed the limits of the Protecting Power mandate as it had developed in practice. Following those discussions, the term 'scrutiny' was chosen as the equivalent of the French 'contrôle'.[67]

1070   The idea behind scrutiny was explained during the 1949 Diplomatic Conference as follows:

> The fundamental concept was that the Protecting Power could not give orders or directives to the Detaining Power. It was entitled to verify whether the Convention was applied and, if necessary, to suggest measures on behalf of protected persons.[68]

1071   Scrutiny implies that the Protecting Powers are entitled to know the condition of protected persons and report this information to their Power of Origin. This means that they have access to the people protected by the Geneva Conventions to assess whether those people are indeed treated in accordance with the relevant provisions of the Conventions. To this end, the Protecting Power's delegates or representatives must have access to all places of detention holding prisoners of war or civilians protected by the Third or Fourth Convention, respectively, who are nationals of the country whose interests the Protecting Power safeguards. And it must be granted permission to meet in private with those detainees. Furthermore, the Detaining Power has a duty to provide the Protecting Power with the information required to identify the prisoners of war and civilian internees, and to notify it of changes to their status, such as transfers, releases, repatriations, escapes, hospitalizations or deaths. The Protecting Power must also be kept informed of any legal action taken against a prisoner of war, protected by the Third Convention, or again a civilian protected by the Fourth Convention, and its representatives have the right to attend those proceedings. In addition, the Protecting Power's representatives are entitled to hear any complaints passed on to them by the representatives of the prisoners of war or by internee committees. The Third and Fourth Conventions refer to these tasks in great detail (see sections E.4 and E.5).

1072   Should the provisions of the Geneva Conventions be violated, the Protecting Power may be requested to communicate the protests of the Power of Origin of the protected persons. The Protecting Power may also make representations on its own initiative, particularly if the violation affects the rights

---

[67] *Final Record of the Diplomatic Conference of Geneva of 1949*, Vol. II-B, pp. 57–58 and 110–111. For a definition of the French word 'contrôle', see also Jean Salmon, *Dictionnaire de Droit International Public*, Bruylant, Brussels, 2001, pp. 261–262. For the full discussion, see paras 1028–1031.

[68] *Final Record of the Diplomatic Conference of Geneva of 1949*, Vol. II-B, p. 110.

conferred upon it by the Geneva Conventions or its ability to carry out its duties thereunder.[69]

1073   The words 'cooperation' and 'scrutiny', both of which appear in Article 8(1), therefore indicate the cooperative nature of the relationship between the receiving State and the Protecting Power: the receiving State agrees to take into account the observations of the Protecting Power, but the latter does not control the activity observed.

1074   In addition to the general scope indicated by the terms 'cooperation' and 'scrutiny', the Geneva Conventions entrusted specific tasks to, and therefore recognized the remit of, the Protecting Powers. Those tasks and remit are governed by many different provisions of the Geneva Conventions. The following paragraphs summarize the key elements of these provisions.

2. Tasks common to the four Geneva Conventions

1075   The main task of the Protecting Powers is to cooperate in implementing the Geneva Conventions and to scrutinize their application. To this end, they have an extensive remit, in particular the right for their representatives to visit all places of internment, detention and work where the adverse Party is holding wounded, sick or shipwrecked members of the armed forces, medical personnel, prisoners of war, and civilians protected by the Fourth Convention (Third Convention, Article 126; Fourth Convention, Article 143).

1076   In the event of a disagreement about the interpretation or application of the Geneva Conventions, the Protecting Powers lend their good offices with a view to settling the disagreement (common Article 11 (Article 12 in the Fourth Convention)).

1077   During hostilities, the Protecting Powers transmit the official translations of the Geneva Conventions, as well as the laws and regulations adopted to ensure their application (First Convention, Article 48; Second Convention, Article 49; Third Convention, Article 128; Fourth Convention, Article 145).

3. Tasks related to wounded, sick and shipwrecked members of the armed forces and medical personnel

1078   The Protecting Power may be involved in activities such as: (i) forwarding particulars to help in the identification of wounded, sick and shipwrecked members of the armed forces and information about the dead (First Convention, Articles 16 and 17; Second Convention, Articles 19 and 20); and (ii) notifying the adverse Party of the names of the relief societies authorized to assist the armed forces' medical service (First Convention, Article 26), and of the employment of hospital ships (Second Convention, Articles 22, 24 and 25). The

---

[69] Thus, during the Second World War, the Swiss Delegation in Tokyo made more than 400 written representations about Allied prisoners of war and passed on 240 protests from the US Department of State (Janner, p. 51).

Protecting Power is invited to lend its good offices in order to facilitate the setting up and recognition of hospital zones and localities (First Convention, Article 23).

4. Tasks related to prisoners of war

1079 To scrutinize the implementation of the Third Convention, the Protecting Power's representatives may go to all places where prisoners of war may be, particularly to places of internment, imprisonment and work; they are also allowed to interview the prisoners, and in particular the prisoners' representatives, without witnesses (Article 126). The Protecting Power's representatives should receive records of the labour detachments dependent on the camps visited (Article 56). Furthermore, the Protecting Power's representatives may receive requests and complaints addressed to them by prisoners of war, as well as periodic reports from the prisoners' representatives (Article 78). All material facilities should be granted to prisoners' representatives for communication with the Protecting Power's representatives (Articles 79 and 81). Where the Detaining Power refuses to approve or dismisses a representative elected by his or her fellow prisoners of war, it must inform the Protecting Power of the reasons for such action (Article 79(4); Article 81(6)). Lastly, the Protecting Power should be notified of all the particulars required for the identification of prisoners of war, as well as information regarding transfers, releases, repatriations, escapes, admissions to hospital, and deaths (Article 122); it must also be informed if an escaped prisoner is recaptured (Article 94).

1080 If prisoners of war are transferred from one Detaining Power to another, the Protecting Power must, if the Power to which they have been transferred fails to meet its obligations in any important respect, notify the Power which transferred the prisoners of war. This notification triggers that Power's obligation to take effective measures to correct the situation or request the return of the prisoners of war. Such requests must be complied with (Article 12).

1081 In terms of the financial resources of prisoners of war, the Protecting Power is involved in determining the maximum amount of money that prisoners may have in their possession (Article 58(2)), is informed of any limitations on that amount (Article 60(4)), and may inspect the prisoners' accounts (Article 65(2)).

1082 The Protecting Power must be consulted on the restrictions imposed on the correspondence of the prisoners of war (Article 71(1)) or on their relief shipments (Article 72(3)); it supervises the distribution of that relief (Article 73(3)), and may organize special shipments when the conveyance of relief is disrupted (Article 75). If necessary, the Protecting Power ensures the distribution of collective relief by any means that it deems useful (Annex III, Article 9).

1083 The Protecting Power's representatives may inspect the record of disciplinary punishments ordered against prisoners of war (Article 96(5)), and may talk freely to prisoners undergoing such punishment (Article 98(1)).

1084   The Protecting Powers' rights are particularly extensive in the area of criminal penalties applicable to prisoners of war. The Protecting Power must be
informed as soon as possible of the offences which are punishable by the
death sentence (Article 100(1)). It must be notified of any legal proceedings
taken against prisoners of war (Article 104(1)), of judgments and sentences
pronounced upon a prisoner of war (Article 107), especially in the case of
the death penalty (Article 101), and of any appeals made by sentenced prisoners (Article 107(1)). If the death sentence is handed down, the sentence
may not be carried out before a period of at least six months from the
date when the Protecting Power receives the notification of this sentence
(Article 101). If the accused does not appoint a legal counsel, it is up to the
Protecting Power to do so (Article 105(2)). The representatives of the Protecting Power are entitled to attend the trial of the case, unless, exceptionally, this is held 'in camera' in the interest of State security (Article 105(5)).
The representatives of the Protecting Power may visit sentenced prisoners
(Article 108(3)).

1085   The Protecting Power should receive a report following the official enquiry
into every death or serious injury of a prisoner of war caused or suspected to
have been caused by a sentry, another prisoner of war, or any other person
(Article 121(2)).

1086   The Protecting Power also has a role to play with regard to the appointment
of the neutral members of the Mixed Medical Commissions provided for in
Article 112.[70]

1087   Lastly, the Protecting Powers are intermediaries for passing on information
regarding the geographical location of prisoner-of-war camps (Article 23(3)), the
rate of working pay (Article 62(1)), payment notifications (Article 63(3)), lists of
prisoners' credit balances (Article 66(1)), measures taken regarding correspondence (Article 71), legal documents (Article 77(1)) and wills (Article 120(1)). The
Protecting Power should receive all the information required to identify prisoners of war and any information about a change in their status, namely transfers, releases, repatriations, escapes, admissions to hospital and deaths (Article 122(3) and (4)).

5. Tasks related to civilians

a. In general

1088   In order to scrutinize the implementation of the provisions of the Fourth Convention, representatives of the Protecting Power may go to all places where
protected persons are, particularly to places of internment, detention and work.

---

[70] Third Convention, Annex II: Regulations concerning Mixed Medical Commissions, Articles 2
and 5.

They should have access to all premises occupied by protected persons and be able to interview them without witnesses (Article 143). The Protecting Power may receive any request or complaint addressed to it by protected persons (Article 30(1); Article 40(4); Article 52(1); and Article 101(2)). The Protecting Power must be informed of any measure taken concerning any protected persons who are kept in custody for more than two weeks, subjected to assigned residence or interned. It should also be informed of any changes in the status of protected persons, especially transfers, releases, escapes, births and deaths (Articles 136–137).

1089   As regards protecting the civilian population from the effects of war, the Protecting Power is invited to lend its good offices in order to facilitate the setting up and recognition of hospital and safety zones and localities (Article 14(3)). The Protecting Power may be entrusted with transmitting information about the establishment of neutralized zones (Article 15(1)). It may also be called upon to appoint the members of the special commissions responsible for checking whether the hospital and safety zones meet the conditions and obligations set out in Annex I of the Fourth Convention (Draft Agreement relating to Hospital and Safety Zones and Localities, Article 10).

1090   The Protecting Power may be called upon to supervise the distribution of shipments of medical supplies and objects for religious worship intended only for civilians, as well as consignments of foodstuffs, clothing and tonics intended for women and children (Article 23(3)).

1091   In order to protect from the effects of the hostilities children under 15 orphaned or separated from their families as a result of the war, the Parties to the conflict must facilitate the reception of such children in a neutral country for the duration of the conflict. This can only be done with the consent of the Protecting Power, if any (Article 24).

b. Foreign nationals in the territory of the Parties to the conflict

1092 As a general rule, the Protecting Power should be informed of the reasons for refusing a protected person's request to leave the territory of a Party to the conflict, and be given the names of those denied permission to leave (Article 35(3)). The Protecting Power should be given the names of any civilians who have been interned or subjected to assigned residence, and be notified of any legal and administrative decisions about their cases (Article 43(2)). The Protecting Power passes on voluntary applications for internment (Article 42(2)).

1093   The Protecting Power may pay allowances to protected persons (Article 39(3)).

1094   If protected persons are transferred from one Detaining Power to another, the Protecting Power carries out the same tasks as in the case of transfers of prisoners of war (Article 45(3)).

c. Civilians in occupied territory

1095 The Protecting Power must be immediately informed of any transfers or evacuations of protected persons (Article 49(4)).

1096   The Protecting Power may, at any time, verify the state of the food and medical supplies in occupied territories (Article 55(3)). When the population of an occupied territory is inadequately supplied, the Occupying Power should agree to and, wherever possible, facilitate relief schemes (Article 59(1)). The Protecting Power may be called upon to certify that the relief shipments will be used for humanitarian purposes (Article 59(4)) or, exceptionally, to give its consent to divert relief consignments from their original purpose (Article 60). The Protecting Power supervises the distribution of the relief consignments or delegates this task to an impartial humanitarian body such as the ICRC (Article 61(1)).

1097   In terms of judicial guarantees, the Protecting Power must be informed of any legal proceedings taken against protected persons when the charges could result in the death penalty or imprisonment of two years or more (Article 71(2) and (3)). The Protecting Power should be notified of any judgment involving such a sentence; other judgments must be detailed in the court's records and be open to inspection by the representatives of the Protecting Power (Article 74(2)). Apart from the exceptional circumstances set out in Article 75, no death sentence may be carried out for at least six months from the date when the Protecting Power is notified of the judgment; the Protecting Power must be notified of any reduction in that time-frame (Article 75(2) and (3)). If the accused does not appoint a legal counsel, the Protecting Power may do so (Article 72(2)). The representatives of the Protecting Power are entitled to attend the trial unless, exceptionally, this is held 'in camera' in the interests of the security of the Occupying Power (Article 74(1)). The representatives of the Protecting Power may visit accused and sentenced prisoners (Article 76(6)).

d. Civilian internees

1098 Here the tasks of the Protecting Power are comparable to those it carries out for prisoners of war.

1099   In addition to the visits to places of internment provided for in Article 143, the representatives of the Protecting Power are entitled to receive any complaints or requests from internees (Article 101(2)). They are in contact with the internee committees (Articles 102(1) and 104(3)) and are informed of the reasons for any refusals or dismissals of members of those committees (Article 102(2)). They receive a list of the labour detachments dependent upon the places of internment they visit (Article 96).

1100   The Protecting Power may pay allowances to internees and check their individual accounts (Article 98(2) and (3)).

1101   The Protecting Power must be duly notified of any restrictions placed on relief shipments for internees (Article 108(2)).

1102   The Protecting Power's representatives are entitled to supervise the distribution of relief supplies to internees (Article 109(3); Annex II, Article 8). In certain circumstances, the Protecting Power may organize special means of transport to deliver relief shipments to internees (Article 111(1)).

1103   The Protecting Power's representatives may inspect the record of disciplinary punishments ordered against internees (Article 123(5)), and may talk freely to internees undergoing such punishment (Article 125(4)).

1104   In terms of judicial guarantees for civilian internees in the national territory of the Detaining Power, the Protecting Power enjoys the same rights as it does in relation to civilians in occupied territory (Article 126).

1105   The Protecting Power should receive a report following the official enquiry into every death or serious injury of an internee caused or suspected to have been caused by a sentry, another internee, or any other person (Article 131).

1106   Lastly, the Protecting Powers are intermediaries for passing on information regarding the geographical location of places of internment (Article 83(2)), measures concerning the internees' contact with the outside world (Article 105), legal documents addressed to or dispatched by internees (Article 113(1)), death certificates (Article 129(3)) and information about the identity of internees (Article 137(1)).

F. Paragraph 2: Facilitation of the task of the representatives or delegates of the Protecting Powers

1107 Article 8(2) obliges the Parties to the conflict to facilitate 'to the greatest extent possible' the task of the representatives or delegates of the Protecting Powers. This is the logical consequence of the obligation set out in the first paragraph.

1108   This obligation includes facilitating visa applications and travel arrangements (except in exceptional circumstances) and, in particular, access to protected persons as set out under Article 126 of the Third Convention and Article 143 of the Fourth Convention.

1109   It may also be useful for a Protecting Power to be granted access to persons near the front line, such as wounded enemy personnel, prisoners of war or civilians who have not yet been evacuated from that area.

G. Paragraph 3: Limitations on the role of representatives or delegates of the Protecting Powers

1110 Article 8(3) is intended to safeguard the rights of the State wherein the Protecting Power's representatives or delegates carry out their duties. Through this paragraph, the 1949 Diplomatic Conference wished to strike a balance between the requirements of humanity and those of national sovereignty.[71]

---

[71] Pictet (ed.), *Commentary on the First Geneva Convention*, ICRC, 1952, p. 99.

Nevertheless, the Conventions impose this obligation on the Protecting Power's representatives or delegates, making them responsible for assessing the imperative security needs of the receiving State and acting accordingly. The reasons for this are clear. If it was up to the receiving State alone to assess its own imperative security needs, that could give rise to abuses and would give that State an easy way to elude the scrutiny of the Protecting Power.

1111   In the First and Second Conventions, paragraph 3 also contains the following sentence: 'Their activities shall only be restricted as an exceptional and temporary measure when this is rendered necessary by imperative military necessities.' Thus, a Party to a conflict may not invoke the 'imperative military necessities' it claims to be facing in order to restrict the activities of the Protecting Power in relation to prisoners of war or civilians protected by the Fourth Convention and thereby prevent the Protecting Power from carrying out its duties as enshrined in the Third and Fourth Conventions.

1112   This provision, which appears only in the First and Second Conventions, protects the receiving State and enables it to restrict the activities of the Protecting Power's representatives or delegates.[72] However, such restrictions may only be an exceptional and temporary measure used in the event of 'imperative military necessities'. The idea of 'military necessity' or 'military requirement' is a key component of the law of armed conflict[73] and appears in many provisions of the Geneva Conventions.[74] Here, however, only 'imperative military necessities' may be invoked in order to restrict the activities of the Protecting Power's representatives or delegates on an exceptional and temporary basis. Although the Geneva Conventions do not give a definition of the term 'imperative', the meaning refers to an absolute constraint that leaves the Party in question with no choice. In addition, those restrictions only apply to the Protecting Power's tasks – in any case limited – involved in helping wounded, sick and shipwrecked military personnel under the First and Second Conventions.

1113   The difference between the First and Second Conventions, on the one hand, and the Third and Fourth, on the other, is deliberate. In draft common article 6/7/7/7, adopted by the Joint Committee of the 1949 Diplomatic Conference, the wording '[t]heir activities shall only be restricted as an exceptional and temporary measure when this is rendered necessary by imperative military necessities' appeared in the four draft Conventions.[75] But when the draft came to

---

[72] For an example of a situation in which it has been stated that this ground can be invoked, see United States, *Law of War Manual*, 2015, para. 4.25.3.

[73] The 1868 St Petersburg Declaration aimed to reach a common agreement on 'the technical limits at which the necessities of war ought to yield to the requirements of humanity'. Similarly, the 1907 Hague Convention (IV) stated that the drafting of the Convention had been inspired 'by the desire to diminish the evils of war, as far as military requirements permit'.

[74] See e.g. First Convention, Articles 12(4), 30(1), 32(2), 33(2) and 50; Second Convention, Articles 28 and 51; Third Convention, Article 126(2); and Fourth Convention, Articles 16(2), 18(4), 49(2) and (5), 53, 143(3) and 147.

[75] *Final Record of the Diplomatic Conference of Geneva of 1949*, Vol. III, pp. 29–30.

be studied in the plenary meeting of the Diplomatic Conference, the delegate from New Zealand pointed out that it was reasonable that imperative military necessity would cause restrictions to be imposed on the activities of the Protecting Powers in the case of the First and Second Conventions, which were mainly to be implemented on the battlefield or in sea warfare, but that such restrictions could not be invoked in the case of the Third and Fourth Conventions, which were mainly to be implemented in the rear zone, in the territory of the Parties to the conflict or in occupied territory, i.e. after the prisoners of war and the civilian internees had been evacuated from the combat zone. In that case, the restrictions might weaken the new Conventions. His statement gave rise to a discussion, at the end of which the Diplomatic Conference voted to remove this proviso from the Third and Fourth Conventions.[76]

H. Developments since 1949

1114 While the Geneva Conventions foresee that the Parties to an international armed conflict entrust a Protecting Power with safeguarding the interests of their nationals in the hands of the adverse Party, the Conventions leave it up to each Party to decide on the course of action to achieve that. In the minds of the drafters of the 1949 Geneva Conventions it was taken for granted that the Parties to the conflict would be keen to take initiatives to ensure the protection of their nationals in the hands of the adverse Party and that the procedure envisaged would be universally followed. This assumption was based on the fact that during the two world wars practically all belligerents had entrusted the protection of their interests and of their nationals to Protecting Powers and on the fact that the State is the natural protector of its nationals. This feature of international armed conflicts was to change dramatically in the era after the end of the Second World War.

1115 Since the 1949 Conventions were adopted, Protecting Powers are only known to have been appointed in five conflicts:[77]

– the Suez conflict (1956) between Egypt on one side and France and the United Kingdom on the other;[78]
– the conflict (July 1961) between France and Tunisia over Bizerte;[79]

---

[76] *Ibid.* Vol. II-B, pp. 344–346.
[77] Even in these five cases, the Protecting Powers were not always able to carry out all the tasks set out in the Geneva Conventions, nor to act on behalf of all the belligerents; see Sandoz/Swinarski/Zimmermann (eds), *Commentary on the Additional Protocols*, ICRC, 1987, p. 77.
[78] Switzerland represented the interests of France and the United Kingdom in Egypt, while India represented Egyptian interests in France and the United Kingdom (*Keesing's Contemporary Archives*, 1956, p. 15181; Knellwolf, pp. 291–294). No Protecting Power represented Egyptian interests in Israel, nor vice versa.
[79] Sweden protected Tunisian interests in France, while Switzerland protected French interests in Tunisia (*Keesing's Contemporary Archives*, 1961, p. 18343 A).

- the Goa crisis (1961) between India and Portugal;[80]
- the conflict (December 1971) between India and Pakistan;[81]
- the Falkland/ Malvinas Islands' conflict (1982)[82] between Argentina and the United Kingdom.[83]

1116   However, no Protecting Power was appointed during the other conflicts since 1949, depriving millions of war victims of the assistance of a third State and of such form of scrutiny of their circumstances, without which the protection afforded by the Geneva Conventions is all too often illusory. Ultimately, such shortcomings can undermine the whole treaty-based protection system. The efficacy of the rules is at risk when the mechanisms designed to ensure that the rules are implemented are regularly brought to a standstill.

1117   It is therefore necessary to ask why no Protecting Power was appointed in all other international armed conflicts since 1949. In the lead-up to and during the 1977 Diplomatic Conference, many experts and government representatives questioned whether the procedure for appointing Protecting Powers was fit for purpose or overly cumbersome. They highlighted the supposedly optional nature of appointing Protecting Powers, the difficulty of agreeing on a neutral State acceptable to both Parties,[84] the maintaining of diplomatic relations between adversaries, and the financial burden that the activities of the

[80] The United Arab Republic protected Indian interests in Portugal, while Brazil had protected Portuguese interests in India since diplomatic relations had broken off in 1955 (*Keesing's Contemporary Archives*, 1961, p. 18635 B).

[81] Both States appointed Switzerland as Protecting Power (*Keesing's Contemporary Archives*, 1972, p. 25054 A; Knellwolf, pp. 294–298). However, Switzerland was only requested to lend its good offices between Pakistan and Bangladesh. Following the suspension of active hostilities, India claimed that Switzerland had been appointed as Protecting Power as defined under diplomatic law only. It used that argument to restrict the activities that the Protecting Power wished to carry out for the 90,000 Pakistani prisoners of war and civilian internees being held in India. Invoking Article 8, Switzerland contested this position and asserted that it was entitled to carry out all the tasks entrusted to Protecting Powers by the Geneva Conventions in the interest of those prisoners of war and civilian internees (Abi-Saab, 1979, pp. 323–324; Knellwolf, pp. 294–298).

[82] The boundaries, names and designations used in this commentary do not imply official endorsement, nor express an opinion on the part of the ICRC, and are without prejudice to claims of sovereignty over the territories mentioned. Whenever a disputed territory is given different names by the parties concerned, the ICRC uses those names together, in French alphabetical order.

[83] Switzerland represented UK interests in Argentina, while Brazil represented Argentine interests in the United Kingdom. In both cases they were charged with representing foreign interests; neither had been formally appointed as Protecting Powers within the meaning of the Geneva Conventions. Nevertheless, the two States worked towards the implementation of the Conventions by performing some of the tasks assigned to Protecting Powers, in particular by forwarding the notification of the commissioning of hospital ships (Sylvie S. Junod, *Protection of the Victims of Armed Conflict, Falkland-Malvinas Islands (1982): International Humanitarian Law and Humanitarian Action*, ICRC, Geneva, 1984, pp. 20–21; Knellwolf, pp. 305–306).

[84] This argument assumes that both adversaries must agree on the same State to be appointed as Protecting Power to safeguard their interests and those of their nationals. This is not the case.

Protecting Power could place on the State calling upon its services.[85] Article 5 of Additional Protocol I was meant to address some of the shortcomings which had been identified with regard to the implementation of Article 8.

1118   In truth, however, the obstacles do not appear to result from the inadequacy of the procedures nor from the financial burden, but are more likely to be related to political considerations. Among the difficulties encountered were the fear that appointing a Protecting Power would be interpreted as implicitly bestowing recognition on an adversary whose legal existence was disputed; the questioning of the applicability of the Geneva Conventions in the case in point; and a dispute over the existence of an armed conflict or over a Party's involvement in the conflict. Furthermore, the possibility, provided for in common Article 10 (Article 11 in the Fourth Convention), to appoint substitutes for a Protecting Power may also reflect the fact that the drafters anticipated that there might be situations in which the system would not work as intended.[86]

1119   Lastly, most armed conflicts since 1949 have been non-international armed conflicts, for which the Protecting Power mechanism was not as such intended.[87]

Select bibliography

Abi-Saab, Georges, 'Le renforcement du système d'application des règles du droit humanitaire', *Revue de droit pénal militaire et de droit de la guerre*, Vol. XII, No. 2, 1973, pp. 223–235.
- 'Les mécanismes de mise en œuvre du droit humanitaire', *Revue générale de droit international public*, Vol. 82, No. 1, 1978, pp. 103–129.
- 'The Implementation of Humanitarian Law', in Antonio Cassese (ed.), *The New Humanitarian Law of Armed Conflict*, Vol. I, Editoriale scientifica, Naples, 1979, pp. 310–346.
Bertschy, Ruth, *Die Schutzmacht im Völkerrecht: ihre rechtliche und praktische Bedeutung*, Paulusdruckerei, Fribourg, 1952.
Bouffanais, Pierre, *Les consuls en temps de guerre et de troubles*, Les Éditions Domat Montchrestien, Loviton & Cie, Paris, 1933.
Bugnion, François, 'Le droit humanitaire applicable aux conflits armés internationaux, Le problème du contrôle', *Annales d'études internationales*, Vol. 8, 1977, pp. 29–61.
- *The International Committee of the Red Cross and the Protection of War Victims*, ICRC/Macmillan, Oxford, 2003, pp. 848–859.
Cahier, Philippe, *Le droit diplomatique contemporain*, 2nd edition, Librairie Droz, Geneva, 1964.
Calmy-Rey, Micheline, 'La protection dans la politique extérieure suisse d'aujourd'hui', *Relations internationales*, No. 144, 2010, pp. 93–103.

---

[85] *Official Records of the Diplomatic Conference of Geneva of 1974–1977*, Vol. VIII, pp. 80, 88, 142–143 and 148–150; Abi-Saab, 1979, pp. 323–325.

[86] For a further analysis as to why the appointment of Protecting Powers has been the exception rather than the rule in international armed conflicts since 1949, see also Kolb, pp. 557–558.

[87] For details, see para. 1015.

Cortese, Gaetano, *La potenza protettrice nel diritto internazionale: elementi per uno studio sistematico dell'azione della potenza protettrice nel caso di una rottura delle relazioni diplomatiche*, Edizioni Bizzarri, Rome, 1972.
- 'La potenza protettrice in case di rottura delle relazioni diplomatiche', *Revue de droit international, de sciences diplomatiques et politiques*, Vol. 54, 1976, pp. 96–106.

Coulibaly, Hamidou, 'Le rôle des Puissances protectrices au regard du droit diplomatique, du droit de Genève et du droit de La Haye, in Frits Kalshoven and Yves Sandoz (eds), *Mise en œuvre du droit international humanitaire*, Martinus Nijhoff Publishers, Dordrecht, 1989, pp. 69–78.

de La Pradelle, Paul, *La Conférence diplomatique et les nouvelles Conventions de Genève du 12 août 1949*, Les Éditions internationales, Paris, 1951, pp. 221–243.
- 'Le contrôle de l'application des conventions humanitaires en cas de conflit armé', *Annuaire français de droit international*, Vol. II, 1956, pp. 343–352.
- 'Une institution en question du droit international humanitaire: la puissance protectrice', *Studies in Honour of Maulio Udina*, Vol. I, A. Giufré, Milan, 1975, pp. 409–419.

de Preux, Jean, 'Puissance protectrice', *Revue international de la Croix-Rouge*, Vol. 67, No. 752, April 1985, pp. 86–95.

Döhring, Karl, 'Schutzmacht', in Karl Strupp and Hans-Jürgen Schlochauer (eds), *Wörterbuch des Völkerrechts*, Vol. III, De Gruyter, Berlin, 1962, pp. 218–222.

Domb, Fania, 'Supervision of the Observance of International Humanitarian Law', *Israel Yearbook on Human Rights*, Vol. 8, 1978, pp. 178–221.

Dominicé, Christian, 'The implementation of humanitarian law', in Karel Vasak (ed.), *The International Dimensions of Human Rights*, Vol. II, UNESCO, Paris, 1982, pp. 427–447.

Dominicé, Christian and Patrnogic, Jovica, 'Les Protocoles additionnels aux Conventions de Genève et le système des puissances protectrices', *Annales de droit international médical*, Vol. 28, 1979, pp. 24–50, at 24–29.

Draper, Gerald I.A.D., 'The implementation of international law in armed conflicts', *International Affairs* (London), Vol. 48, 1972, pp. 46–59.
- 'The implementation and enforcement of the Geneva Conventions of 1949 and of the Two Additional Protocols of 1978' (sic), *Collected Courses of the Hague Academy of International Law*, Vol. 164, 1979, No. III, pp. 1–54.

Escher, Alfred, *Der Schutz der Staatsangehörigen im Ausland durch fremde Gesandtschaften und Konsulate* (Zürcher Beiträge zur Rechtswissenschaft, neue Folge, Heft 16), Graphische Werkstätten H.R. Sauerländer & Co, Aarau, 1929.

Forsythe, David P., 'Who Guards the Guardians, Third Parties and the Law of Armed Conflicts', *American Journal of International Law*, Vol. 70, No. 1, 1976, pp. 41–61.

Franklin, William Mc Henry, *Protection of Foreign Interests: A Study in Diplomatic and Consular Practice*, United States Government Printing Office, Washington, 1946.

Gasser, Hans-Peter, 'Scrutiny', *Australian Year Book of International Law*, Vol. 9, 1985, pp. 345–358.
- 'Ensuring respect for the Geneva Conventions and Protocols: The Role of Third States and the United Nations', in Hazel Fox and Michael A. Meyer (eds), *Armed Conflict and the New Law, Vol. II: Effecting Compliance*, The British Institute of International and Comparative Law, London, 1993, pp. 15–49.

Guggenheim, Paul, *Traité de droit international public*, Vol. II, Georg & Cie, Geneva, 1953, pp. 332–337.

Hackworth, Green H., *Digest of International Law*, 8 volumes, United States Government Printing Office, Washington, 1940–1944, Vol. IV, pp. 485–506, and Vol. VI, pp. 282–286.

Heintze, Hans-Joachim, 'Protecting Power', version of July 2009, *Max Planck Encyclopedia of Public International Law*, http://www.mpepil.com.

Janner, Antonino, *La Puissance protectrice en droit international d'après les expériences faites par la Suisse pendant la seconde guerre mondiale*, Verlagv on Helbingund Lichtenhahn, Basel, 1948 (reprint 1972).

Knellwolf, Jean-Pierre, *Die Schutzmacht im Völkerrecht unter besonderer Berücksichtigung der schweizerischen Verhältnisse*, Ackermanndruck, Bern, 1985.

Kolb, Robert, 'Protecting Powers', in Andrew Clapham, Paola Gaeta and Marco Sassòli (eds), *The 1949 Geneva Conventions: A Commentary*, Oxford University Press, 2015, pp. 549–560.

Laitenberger, Birgit, "Die Schutzmacht", *German Yearbook of International Law*, Vol. 21, 1978, pp. 180–206.

Lauterpacht, Hersch, (ed.), *Oppenheim's International Law*, 7th edition, Longmans, Green and Co., London, 1952, pp. 374–376.

Levie, Howard S., 'Prisoners of War and the Protecting Power', *American Journal of International Law*, Vol. 55, No. 2, 1961, pp. 374–397.

– *Prisoners of War in International Armed Conflict*, International Law Studies, U.S. Naval War College, Vol. 59, 1977, pp. 255–293.

Lowe, A.V., Warbrick, Colin and Lowe, Vaughan, 'Diplomatic Law: Protecting Powers', *International and Comparative Law Quarterly*, Vol. 39, No. 2, 1990, pp. 471–474.

Nordmann, François, 'La représentation des intérêts étrangers au Département fédéral des Affaires étrangères : témoignage d'un diplomate', *Relations internationales*, No. 144, 2010, pp. 87–92.

Papini, Roberto and Cortese, Gaetano, *La rupture des relations diplomatiques et ses conséquences*, Pedone, Paris, 1972.

Patrnogic, Jovica, 'Internationalisation du contrôle des Conventions humanitaires en cas de conflit armé', *Annales de droit international médical*, No. 21, April 1971, pp. 33–51.

– 'Implementation of the Geneva Conventions of 1949 and Additional Protocols of 1977', *European Seminar on Humanitarian Law* (JagelloneanUniversity, Krakow, 1979), Polish Red Cross/ICRC, Warsaw/Geneva, 1979, pp. 87–100.

Peirce, Captain George A.B., 'Humanitarian Protection for the Victims of War: The System of Protecting Powers and the Role of the ICRC', *Military Law Review*, Vol. 90, 1980, pp. 89–162.

Pictet, Jean S., 'Les Conventions de Genève de 1949: Aperçu des règles d'application', *The Military Law and the Law of War Review*, Vol. XII, No. 2, 1973, pp. 59–99.

– *Humanitarian Law and the Protection of War Victims*, A.W. Sijthoff, Leiden, 1975, pp. 61–67.

Rasmussen, Gustav, *Code des prisonniers de guerre : Commentaire de la Convention du 27 juillet 1929 relative au traitement des prisonniers de guerre*, Levin & Munksgaard, Copenhagen, 1931, pp. 56–62.

Rousseau, Charles, 'Les consuls en temps de guerre', *Revue générale de droit international public*, Vol. 40, No. 4, 1933, pp. 506–519.

– *Le droit des conflits armés*, Pedone, Paris, 1983, pp. 34–39 and 94–95.

Salmon, Jean, *Manuel de droit diplomatique*, Bruylant, Brussels, 1994, pp. 118–124.

Sandoz, Yves, 'Implementing international humanitarian law', *International Dimensions of Humanitarian Law*, Henry Dunant Institute, Geneva, 1988, pp. 259–282.

Sassòli, Marco, 'Mise en œuvre du droit international humanitaire et du droit international des droits de l'homme: Une comparaison', *Annuaire suisse de droit international*, Vol. XLIII, 1987, pp. 24–61.

Sereni, Angelo Piero, 'La représentation en droit international', *Recueil des cours de l'Académie de droit international de La Haye*, Vol. 73, 1948, pp. 69–166.

Sfez, Lucien, 'La rupture des relations diplomatiques', *Revue générale de droit international public*, Vol. 70, 1966, pp. 359–430.

Siordet, Frédéric, *The Geneva Conventions of 1949: The Question of Scrutiny*, ICRC, Geneva, 1953.

Smolinska, Anna Maria, Boutros, Maria, Lozanorios, Frédérique and Lunca, Mariana (eds), *Droit international des relations diplomatiques et consulaires*, Bruylant, Brussels, 2015.

Takemoto, Masayuki, 'The Scrutiny System under International Humanitarian Law – An Analysis of Recent Attempts to Reinforce the Role of Protecting Powers in Armed Conflicts', *Japanese Annual of International Law*, Vol. 19, 1975, pp. 1–23.

Vourkoutiotis, Vasilis, 'What the Angels Saw: Red Cross and Protecting Power Visits to Anglo-American POWs, 1939–45', *Journal of Contemporary History*, Vol. 40, 2005, pp. 689–706.

Wyler, Éric, 'La protection des intérêts étrangers : origines et signification de l'institution', *Relations internationales*, No. 143, 2010, pp. 23–39.

Wylie, Neville, 'Protecting Powers in a Changing World', *Politorbis*, No. 40, 2006, pp. 6–14.

– 'Une évaluation du parcours de la Suisse en tant que puissance protectrice à "double mandat" pour le Royaume-Uni et l'Allemagne durant la Seconde Guerre mondiale', *Relations internationales*, No. 144, 2010, pp. 3–19.

ACTIVITIES OF THE ICRC AND OTHER IMPARTIAL HUMANITARIAN ORGANIZATIONS

❖ Text of the provision

The provisions of the present Convention constitute no obstacle to the humanitarian activities which the International Committee of the Red Cross or any other impartial humanitarian organization may, subject to the consent of the Parties to the conflict concerned, undertake for the protection of wounded and sick, medical personnel and chaplains, and for their relief.

❖ Reservations or declarations

None

Contents

A. Introduction

1120   Article 9 grants impartial humanitarian organizations the right to offer, to the Parties to an international armed conflict, to undertake humanitarian activities. The International Committee of the Red Cross (ICRC) is explicitly mentioned as an example of an entity entitled to rely on this provision. Humanitarian activities can take the form of relief or protection.

1121   Access to the potential beneficiaries of humanitarian activities is subject to the consent of the Parties to the conflict concerned. Since 1949, however, international law in general, and international humanitarian law in particular, has evolved to the extent that a Party to an armed conflict is not completely at liberty to decide how it responds to an offer of services made by an impartial humanitarian organization to undertake humanitarian activities. Rather, at all times, the Party must assess the offer in good faith and in line with its international legal obligations with regard to humanitarian needs. Thus, where a Party is unable or unwilling to address the humanitarian needs of such persons, international law requires it to respond positively to an offer by an impartial humanitarian organization to do so in its place. If the humanitarian needs cannot be met otherwise, the refusal of such an offer would be considered arbitrary, and therefore inconsistent with international law. The foregoing is without prejudice to the right of the consenting Party, for reasons of imperative military necessity, to impose measures of control on the humanitarian activities.

1122   The treaty-based right of impartial humanitarian organizations to offer, to the Parties to an armed conflict, to undertake humanitarian activities is often referred to as the right to offer services. In respect of international armed conflict, it has been enshrined in all four Geneva Conventions as common Article 9 (Article 10 in the Fourth Convention). However, the category of persons for whom the said activities may be undertaken differs in each Convention: in the First Convention, it is 'wounded and sick, medical personnel and chaplains'; in the Second Convention, it is 'wounded, sick and shipwrecked persons, medical personnel and chaplains'; in the Third Convention, it is 'prisoners of war'; and lastly, in the Fourth Convention, it is 'civilian persons'. The difference in wording merely reflects the distinct categories of persons protected by each Convention. That is the case, at least, for the first three Conventions. In the Fourth Convention, however, the category of persons benefiting from the provision in Article 10 ('civilian persons') is wider in scope than the category of persons who qualify as 'protected persons' on the basis of Article 4. The categories referred to in all four Conventions are not restrictive, however, in that international law has evolved to the point where the right to offer services can be exercised for all persons affected by an armed conflict.

1123   In addition to its Article 10, which relates to international armed conflict in general, the Fourth Convention deals with this topic more specifically, and more forcefully, in the context of an occupation.[1] Additional Protocol I further expands upon the right to offer services in international armed conflict.[2] In parallel, rules governing the right to offer services also exist for non-international armed conflict, as set forth both in common Article 3 of the Geneva Conventions and in Additional Protocol II.[3] This broad legal foundation is unsurprising, and merely reflects the axiom that, irrespective of its legal characterization, every armed conflict generates needs for humanitarian assistance and protection. States have thus recognized that, as a matter of international law, the ICRC and other impartial humanitarian organizations may have a role to play in addressing those humanitarian needs, regardless of how the armed conflict is categorized. As Article 9 applies only to international armed conflict, this commentary does not address humanitarian activities undertaken in the context of a non-international armed conflict.

1124   The ability and willingness of impartial humanitarian organizations to carry out humanitarian activities do not detract from the fact that, as a matter of international law, the primary responsibility for meeting the humanitarian needs of persons affected by an international armed conflict lies with the Parties to the conflict. The activities of impartial humanitarian organizations should only complement, where necessary, the State's efforts to address those needs itself. This is also why impartial humanitarian organizations have no obligation under international law to offer their services, as is clear from the wording 'may ... undertake' in Article 9. They can do so at their discretion. For their part, National Red Cross and Red Crescent Societies nevertheless have a duty to consider seriously any request by their own public authorities to carry out humanitarian activities falling within their mandate, provided these activities can be implemented in accordance with the Fundamental Principles of the International Red Cross and Red Crescent Movement (hereinafter 'the Movement').[4] This duty stems from the National Societies' special status and unique auxiliary role to their own public authorities in the humanitarian field – a status articulated in the Movement's Statutes.[5] The Fundamental Principles are listed in the preamble to the Statutes, adopted by the International

---

[1] See, in particular, Articles 59 and 63 of the Fourth Convention (expanded upon by Article 69 of Additional Protocol I).

[2] See Additional Protocol I, Article 81. The Protocol also expands upon the rules applicable to humanitarian relief operations in international armed conflict; see Articles 70–71.

[3] See common Article 3(2) of the Geneva Conventions and Article 18(1) of Additional Protocol II.

[4] 30th International Conference of the Red Cross and Red Crescent, Geneva, 2007, Res. 2, Specific nature of the International Red Cross and Red Crescent Movement in action and partnerships and the role of National Societies as auxiliaries to the public authorities in the humanitarian field, para. 4(a).

[5] Statutes of the International Red Cross and Red Crescent Movement (1986), Article 4(3).

Conference of the Red Cross and Red Crescent, which brings together the States party to the 1949 Geneva Conventions, as well as the components of the Movement, and can therefore be considered authoritative.[6]

1125   The rules pertaining to the right of impartial humanitarian organizations to offer their services are distinct from the rules obliging the Parties to an international armed conflict, along with other High Contracting Parties to the Geneva Conventions, to allow and facilitate the rapid and unimpeded passage of relief consignments. Whereas the former permit the Parties to the conflict, in certain circumstances, to lawfully refuse an offer of services, the latter stipulate the obligation of these Parties, once they have given their consent to the delivery of humanitarian assistance, to allow and facilitate the passage of such assistance. In other words, having accepted an offer of services, the Party concerned must allow it to be implemented, even if the humanitarian activities are intended for the population under enemy control, but without prejudice to that Party's right to impose measures of control.[7]

1126   The right to offer services, which is also sometimes referred to as the 'right of humanitarian initiative', is not to be confused with the so-called 'right of humanitarian intervention' nor with the 'responsibility to protect' (R2P), two distinct concepts which have engendered much debate, for example as to whether international law permits measures such as the threat or the use of force against another State when motivated by humanitarian considerations.[8] Similarly, the analysis of Article 9 remains without prejudice to the UN Security Council's entitlement to act, on the basis of the 1945 UN Charter and in line with the effect of its decisions under international law, as it deems fit with regard to humanitarian activities. These issues are regulated by international law in general and the law on the use of force (*jus ad bellum*) in particular. Thus, they have to be viewed separately from the issue of humanitarian activities carried out within the framework of Article 9.

---

[6] The Fundamental Principles were first proclaimed by the 20th International Conference of the Red Cross in Vienna in 1965. They were then integrated into the preamble to the Statutes of the International Red Cross and Red Crescent Movement, adopted by the 25th International Conference of the Red Cross in 1986 and amended in 1995 and 2006. See also the mention of the 'principles laid down by the International Red Cross Conferences' in Article 44(2) of the First Convention. Similarly, Article 81(2) of Additional Protocol I speaks of 'the fundamental principles of the Red Cross as formulated by the International Conferences of the Red Cross'.

[7] See Article 23 of the Fourth Convention and Articles 70–71 of Additional Protocol I (in particular with regard to the obligation of the Parties to the conflict and each High Contracting Party to 'allow and facilitate rapid and unimpeded passage of all relief consignments, equipment and personnel'; see Article 70(2)–(3) of Additional Protocol I). See also ICRC Study on Customary International Humanitarian Law (2005), Rules 55 and 56 (applicable in both international and non-international armed conflict). For a further discussion, see para. 1179.

[8] Vaughan Lowe and Antonios Tzanakopoulos, 'Humanitarian Intervention', version of May 2011, in Rüdiger Wolfrum (ed.), *Max Planck Encyclopedia of Public International Law*, Oxford University Press, para. 2, http://opil.ouplaw.com/home/EPIL.

B. Historical background

1127 As early as the 1870–71 Franco-Prussian War, the ICRC initiated activities to restore links between soldiers who had fallen into enemy hands and their families.

1128 The first treaty-based recognition of the work of 'relief societies for prisoners of war' that had the 'object of serving as the channel for charitable effort' can be found in both the 1899 and the 1907 Hague Regulations.[9] This was the first time a treaty reflected the role of specific humanitarian activities in times of armed conflict.

1129 Work of this nature increased significantly when, during the First World War, the ICRC set up and ran the International Prisoners-of-War Agency.[10] The Agency's activities involved not only restoring family links, but also the transmission of correspondence, parcels and money to prisoners of war, as well as the repatriation or internment in a neutral country of seriously sick or wounded military personnel. The Agency also developed activities for civilian internees.[11]

1130 In the light of this experience, the 1929 Geneva Convention on Prisoners of War contained the first explicit mention of the ICRC's right to offer services in relation to the protection of prisoners of war.[12] Article 88 of the 1929 Convention can be considered the direct precursor of Article 9 of the Third Convention. It stated that '[t]he foregoing provisions [dealing with the execution of the Convention] do not constitute any obstacle to the humanitarian work which the International Red Cross Committee [sic] may perform for the protection of prisoners of war with the consent of the belligerents concerned'.[13]

1131 When comparing Article 88 of the 1929 Convention and common Article 9 of the 1949 Conventions, three differences can be identified:

(i) The 1929 text confers the right to offer services only on the ICRC, whereas the 1949 text confers this right both on the ICRC and on 'any other

---

[9] Article 15 of the 1899 Hague Regulations and (substantively identical) Article 15 of the 1907 Hague Regulations.

[10] For a historical overview, see Gradimir Đjurović, *The Central Tracing Agency of the International Committee of the Red Cross: Activities of the ICRC for the Alleviation of the Mental Suffering of War Victims*, Henry Dunant Institute, Geneva, 1986; and André Durand, *History of the International Committee of the Red Cross, Volume II: From Sarajevo to Hiroshima*, Henry Dunant Institute, Geneva, 1984, pp. 34–48. During the Second World War, the ICRC operated the 'Central Agency for Prisoners of War'. In 1960, the name was changed to the 'Central Tracing Agency', which exists to this day. For details, see the commentary on Article 123 of the Third Convention.

[11] See Gradimir Đjurović, *The Central Tracing Agency of the International Committee of the Red Cross: Activities of the ICRC for the Alleviation of the Mental Suffering of War Victims*, Henry Dunant Institute, Geneva, 1986, pp. 50–62.

[12] See Geneva Convention on Prisoners of War (1929), Articles 79 and 88. With some changes, Article 79 became Article 123 of the Third Convention.

[13] During the 1929 Diplomatic Conference, Article 88 was adopted without any substantive discussion. See *Proceedings of the Geneva Diplomatic Conference of 1929*, p. 520.

impartial humanitarian organization'. This addition was the result of a proposal submitted during the 1949 Diplomatic Conference and adopted with
little substantive discussion.[14] The drafters of the Geneva Conventions
deliberately chose the language 'any other impartial humanitarian organization' and did not indicate a need for this organization to have been previously 'internationally recognized'[15] nor to be of an international character.
Hence, the organization wishing to qualify on the basis of common Article 9 does not have to be active on the territory of more than one State.[16]

(ii) The 1929 text speaks only of 'protection' as a humanitarian activity,
whereas the 1949 text added 'relief'.[17] While all impartial humanitarian
organizations are entitled to offer their services in the fields of humanitarian relief and protection, it must be stressed that the High Contracting Parties have, through various provisions of the Geneva Conventions in which
the ICRC has explicitly been mentioned, conferred a unique mandate on
the ICRC for certain activities falling within the realm of humanitarian
protection. This is the case, for example, for visits to prisoners of war (see
Article 126(4) of the Third Convention). For a discussion of the differences
yet close link between the humanitarian activities of 'relief' and of 'protection', see section C.2.a.

(iii) The 1929 text conferred the right to offer services only in connection
with the protection of 'prisoners of war' (Third Convention), whereas this
right has now, in the 1949 text, been inserted in all four Geneva Conventions, making it possible to offer also to undertake humanitarian activities for the 'wounded and sick, medical personnel and chaplains' (First
Convention), for 'wounded, sick and shipwrecked persons, medical personnel and chaplains' (Second Convention), and for 'civilian persons' (Fourth
Convention).[18]

C. Discussion

1. 'The provisions of the present Convention constitute no obstacle'

1132 The significance of the opening words of Article 9 resides in the affirmation that
nothing in the Geneva Conventions may be interpreted as restricting the right
of impartial humanitarian organizations to offer their services to all Parties to

---

[14] *Final Record of the Diplomatic Conference of Geneva of 1949*, Vol. II-B, pp. 21, 60 and 111.
[15] *Ibid.* p. 60.   [16] *Ibid.* p. 111.
[17] The word 'relief' was added by the 1947 Conference of Government Experts in connection with
the Prisoner of War Convention; see *Report of the Conference of Government Experts of 1947*,
p. 268.
[18] *Final Record of the Diplomatic Conference of Geneva of 1949*, Vol. II-B, p. 21. As of 1930,
Article 5(2) of the Statutes of the ICRC contained the predecessor of Article 5(3) of the current
Statutes of the International Red Cross and Red Crescent Movement. In the 1934 Tokyo Draft
Convention on the Protection of Civilians, three rules dealing with humanitarian activities for
civilians had been proposed; see draft articles 8, 19 and 25 of that convention.

the conflict. Indeed, both the Geneva Conventions and their Additional Protocols contain a number of provisions which explicitly foresee a role for the ICRC, National Red Cross and Red Crescent Societies and other relief societies.[19] The specific feature of the right to offer services, as enshrined in Article 9, is that an offer of services need not be restricted to the activities referred to in such provisions; rather, the High Contracting Parties have explicitly recognized that impartial humanitarian organizations are legally entitled to offer to perform *any* humanitarian activity which they deem pertinent to meet the humanitarian needs engendered by the armed conflict. Similarly, for the ICRC or any other impartial humanitarian organization to make an offer of services on the basis of common Article 9, it does not need to be acting as a substitute for the Protecting Powers in the sense of common Article 10(3). The right to offer services confers an autonomous mandate on the ICRC or any other impartial humanitarian organization to offer to assist and protect persons affected by an armed conflict. This mandate is separate from the ICRC's potential role as a substitute for the Protecting Powers.[20]

1133   Article 9 confers on the ICRC or any other impartial humanitarian organization the right to offer its services even in the absence of any prior approach or request made by the Party to the conflict concerned. When an offer of services is made, it may be regarded neither as an unfriendly act, nor as an unlawful interference in a State's domestic affairs in general or in the conflict in particular. Nor may it be regarded as recognition of or support to a Party to the conflict.[21] Therefore, an offer of services and its implementation may not be prohibited or criminalized by virtue of legislative or other regulatory acts. Conversely, nothing precludes a Party to an armed conflict from inviting the ICRC or another impartial humanitarian organization at any time to undertake certain humanitarian activities. However, as a matter of international law, these organizations are not obliged to accept such a request; it is at their discretion to decide whether or not to respond positively to it.[22] For the treaty-based right

---

[19] Examples of such provisions are: common Article 10(3) (Article 11(3) of the Fourth Convention); Article 125(1) of the Third Convention; Article 142 of the Fourth Convention; Article 5(3) and (4) of Additional Protocol I; and Article 18 of Additional Protocol II. With regard to the ICRC, Article 81(1) of Additional Protocol I introduces the following distinction: for tasks explicitly assigned to the ICRC by the Geneva Conventions and Additional Protocol I, it uses the term 'humanitarian functions'; for all other activities which the ICRC may offer to perform, the provision uses the term 'any other humanitarian activities'.

[20] On the relationship between the right to offer services and the role of the ICRC as a substitute for the Protecting Powers, see the commentary on Article 10, section J.

[21] See Additional Protocol I, Article 70(1), second sentence: 'Offers of such relief shall not be regarded as interference in the armed conflict or as unfriendly acts.' See also ICJ, *Military and Paramilitary Activities in and against Nicaragua case*, Merits, Judgment, 1986, para. 242: 'There can be no doubt that the provision of strictly humanitarian aid to persons or forces in another country, whatever their political affiliations or objectives, cannot be regarded as unlawful intervention, or as in any other way contrary to international law.'

[22] As to the special status of National Red Cross and Red Crescent Societies in this regard, see para. 1124.

to offer services to be effective, however, a High Contracting Party which is a Party to an international armed conflict must make sure that those in charge of making the decision in this regard are available to receive it.

1134   For the purposes of Article 9, there is no need for the organization offering its services and for the entity receiving the offer to agree on the legal classification of the situation, i.e. whether it qualifies as an armed conflict and, if so, if it is international or non-international in character. Similarly, an offer to undertake humanitarian activities has no bearing on the international legal status of the entity to which the offer is made.[23] Thus, the fact that the offer is made to the government of a State which some States do not recognize as the legitimate government has no impact on that government's claim for recognition.[24] Nor may it be interpreted as endorsement of the reasons for which the entity is engaged in an armed conflict.

2. Humanitarian activities undertaken for protected persons

a. Humanitarian activities

1135   The scope of application of Article 9 is limited to humanitarian activities to be undertaken in international armed conflict. The text of the First Convention indicates that 'humanitarian activities' can be for the 'protection' and for the 'relief' of the wounded and sick, medical personnel and chaplains, although no definition of these concepts is given in the Geneva Conventions.[25]

1136   While 'protection' and 'assistance' (a term which can be used interchangeably with the term 'relief') are separate notions, they frequently interconnect and overlap in practice: assisting persons affected by an armed conflict also protects them, and vice versa.[26] When persons affected by an armed conflict receive assistance, they are protected in the sense that impartial humanitarian organizations are present in their midst and may thus help to deter violations of the legal framework protecting the wounded and sick, medical personnel and chaplains. Conversely, better compliance with the First Convention by the Parties to a conflict could mean, for example, that the medical service has

---

[23] This point is made explicitly in the second sentence of common Article 3(4), which also applies in connection with the exercise of the right to offer services in non-international armed conflict; see the commentary on common Article 3, para. 825.

[24] See also the first sentence of Article 4 of Additional Protocol I, which at least indirectly makes the same point: 'The application of the Conventions and of this Protocol, as well as the conclusion of the agreements provided for therein, shall not affect the legal status of the Parties to the conflict.'

[25] The concept of 'humanitarian activities' is similarly used without being defined in Article 81 of Additional Protocol I.

[26] Since 1949, both the term 'protection' and the term 'relief' – along with the various activities that are included within these respective notions – have come to mean different things to different actors. For an interpretation of the term 'protection' in the context of the right to offer services, see section C.2.b; for an interpretation of the term 'relief' in the context of the right to offer services, see section C.2.c.

access to adequate medical supplies with which to tend to the wounded and sick.

1137   Indeed, the aim of both types of humanitarian activities is to safeguard the lives and dignity of persons affected by an armed conflict. It will depend on individual circumstances whether one or other type of humanitarian activity suffices to achieve that objective, or whether both types of activities are needed simultaneously. An indication of what qualifies as 'humanitarian' can be found in the definition of the Fundamental Principle of 'humanity'. This principle, which has also been endorsed by the International Court of Justice,[27] is the first of the Movement's seven Fundamental Principles. From the definition of humanity, it can be inferred that humanitarian activities are all activities which 'prevent and alleviate human suffering wherever it may be found', and the purpose of which is to 'protect life and health and to ensure respect for the human being'.[28]

1138   Various documents emanating from the humanitarian community contain similar definitions of 'humanitarian'.[29] The definitions of some of the other Fundamental Principles, such as impartiality (see paras 1160–1162), have been similarly adopted. Thus, concepts which originated in international humanitarian law have been mainstreamed as operational concepts for the wider humanitarian community, including for activities undertaken in peacetime.

1139   In the context of an armed conflict, 'humanitarian activities' are those that seek to preserve the lives, security, dignity, and mental and physical well-being of persons affected by the conflict, or to restore that well-being if it has been infringed upon. These activities must be concerned with human beings as such. Thus, as also informed by the requirement of 'impartiality' (see paras 1160–1162), humanitarian activities and the way in which they are conducted must not be affected by any political or military consideration, or by any consideration related to the person's past behaviour, including behaviour which is

---

[27] ICJ, *Military and Paramilitary Activities in and against Nicaragua case*, Merits, Judgment, 1986, para. 242.

[28] A further discussion of the principle of 'humanity' and related terms can be found in Jean S. Pictet, 'Commentary on the Fundamental Principles of the Red Cross (I)', *International Review of the Red Cross*, Vol. 19, No. 210, June 1979, pp. 130–149. The use of the term 'life' in this definition is without prejudice to the fact that humanitarian activities may also be undertaken for the benefit of dead persons, for example the handling of human remains, which must also be done with respect for the person's dignity (see paras 1145 and 1150). See also Larissa Fast, 'Unpacking the principle of humanity: Tensions and implications', *International Review of the Red Cross*, Vol. 97, Nos 897/898, Spring/Summer 2015, pp. 111–131.

[29] Another definition of the term 'humanitarian' can be found in the Sphere Project's Humanitarian Charter and Minimum Standards in Humanitarian Response, which refers to the 'humanitarian imperative' in terms of 'that action should be taken to prevent or alleviate human suffering arising out of disaster or conflict' (The Humanitarian Charter, para. 1). On the 'humanitarian imperative', see also the Code of Conduct for the International Red Cross and Red Crescent Movement and Non-Governmental Organisations (NGOs) in Disaster Relief, Geneva, 1994, p. 3: 'The humanitarian imperative comes first'.

potentially punishable on the basis of criminal or disciplinary norms. Humanitarian activities seek to preserve human life, security, dignity and physical
and mental well-being with no other motive than to accomplish this objective.
Lastly, those offering to undertake humanitarian activities focus solely on the
needs of the persons affected by an armed conflict, irrespective of the rights
which these persons may additionally have on the basis of applicable human
rights law.

1140   Besides the above conceptual guidance, the High Contracting Parties have
not drawn up a list of activities which may qualify in their eyes as humanitarian activities. This is in line with the fact that it is impossible to anticipate
the humanitarian needs that might arise in a particular armed conflict; as the
nature of armed conflicts may change, so may the humanitarian needs they
engender. It is impossible to generically define, especially when an armed conflict lasts for several years, or even decades, which activities are, in a particular
context, of a nature to safeguard the lives, security, dignity, and mental and
physical well-being of the affected persons.

1141   Article 9 confers the right to offer to conduct humanitarian activities only on
the 'International Committee of the Red Cross or any other impartial humanitarian organization' (for an analysis of these terms, see section C.3). However,
it should be noted that relief activities may also be carried out by other actors,
such as State organs, that do not qualify as impartial humanitarian organizations. While such activities may alleviate human suffering, they are not covered
by common Article 9.[30]

b. Protection

1142 Article 9 entitles the ICRC or any other impartial humanitarian organization
to offer to undertake humanitarian activities for the 'protection' of certain
categories of persons affected by an international armed conflict. In its ordinary meaning, to 'protect' means to 'keep safe from harm or injury'.[31] For its
part, humanitarian law has as one of its core objectives to 'protect' people
in situations of armed conflict against abuses of power by the Parties to the
conflict.

1143   Article 9 provides no guidance on exactly which activities impartial humanitarian organizations may undertake to ensure that the authorities and other
relevant actors protect people by complying with the applicable legal framework. Even among impartial humanitarian organizations themselves there are

---

[30] When a High Contracting Party offers to undertake humanitarian activities itself in connection
with an international armed conflict opposing two other High Contracting Parties, for example
through a specialized ministry, these activities are not covered by Article 9. This point also
flows from the use of the disjunctive in Article 59(2) of the Fourth Convention: 'by States *or* by
impartial humanitarian organizations' (emphasis added).

[31] *Concise Oxford English Dictionary*, 12th edition, Oxford University Press, 2011, p. 1153.

differing views on what constitute protection activities. For the ICRC and the Inter-Agency Standing Committee,[32] the concept of 'protection' encompasses all activities aimed at ensuring full respect for the rights of the individual in accordance with the letter and spirit of the relevant bodies of law, including international humanitarian law, international human rights law and refugee law.[33]

1144 Accordingly, in the context of humanitarian law, 'protection activities' refer to all activities that seek to ensure that the authorities and other relevant actors fulfil their obligations to uphold the rights of individuals affected by the armed conflict (beyond their mere survival).[34] Protection activities include those which seek to prevent violations of humanitarian law from being committed in the first place, for example by making representations to the authorities or by making the law better known, and those which seek to ensure that the authorities cease or put a stop to any violations of the norms applicable to them.

1145 When pursuing its protection activities in the context of an armed conflict, the ICRC aims to ensure that the relevant rules of humanitarian law or other fundamental rules protecting persons in situations of violence are observed and implemented by the authorities. Such activities may include visits to persons deprived of their liberty.[35] The ICRC may also offer its good offices to the Parties to the conflict, including to facilitate the settlement of disagreements as to the application or interpretation of the provisions of the First Convention or the implementation of any arrangement concluded by the Parties.[36] Within the context of the First Convention, offers of services may also pertain to activities such as the removal of the wounded, sick and dead from the battlefield.[37] More generally, the ICRC may propose to undertake any activity which it deems relevant for the monitoring of the implementation of the applicable rules of humanitarian law or of other fundamental rules protecting persons in situations of violence.[38]

1146 For its part, both in its protection and its assistance activities, the ICRC uses various approaches, such as persuasion, on a bilateral and confidential basis to

[32] The Inter-Agency Standing Committee (IASC) was established in 1992 in response to UN General Assembly Resolution 46/182 on the strengthening of humanitarian assistance. It is an inter-agency forum for coordination, policy development and decision-making bringing together all the key UN and non-UN humanitarian actors.

[33] See ICRC, *Professional Standards for Protection Work Carried Out by Humanitarian and Human Rights Actors in Armed Conflict and Other Situations of Violence*, 2nd edition, ICRC, Geneva, 2013, p. 12, and Inter-Agency Standing Committee, *IASC Operational Guidelines on the Protection of Persons in Situations of Natural Disasters*, The Brookings – Bern Project on Internal Displacement, Bern, January 2011, p. 5.

[34] ICRC Protection Policy, April 2008, p. 3.

[35] See Third Convention, Article 126(4), and Fourth Convention, Article 143(5).

[36] See the commentary on Article 6, para. 973 and the commentary on Article 11, section E.6.

[37] See the commentary on Article 15, paras 1490 and 1518.

[38] See also Statutes of the International Red Cross and Red Crescent Movement (1986), Article 5(2)(c)–(d) and (g).

induce the authorities to comply with the rules applicable to them, including those regarding the provision of essential services.[39] Where the ICRC considers that its efforts are not going to bring about a satisfactory, timely response from the authorities, and that the problem is a serious one, it may simultaneously engage in appropriate support to and/or substitution for the direct provision of such services.[40] When this happens, it should still be kept in mind that it is the Parties to the conflict which bear the primary responsibility for ensuring that the humanitarian needs are met.[41] When, despite its efforts and in the case of major and repeated violations of humanitarian law, it fails to convince the authorities to assume their responsibilities in this respect, the ICRC may resort to other methods, including, under certain conditions, public denunciation.[42]

1147   Beyond the Geneva Conventions, the term 'protection' has come to mean different things to different actors, and not all such activities fall within the scope of Article 9. In practice, this complicates the conceptual analysis. For example, when a military actor such as a UN-authorized peace-enforcement mission has been mandated to 'protect' the civilian population, different activities and approaches may come into play, including the use of armed force. Despite the use of the same term, the approach of an impartial humanitarian organization to 'protection' activities will be very different.

---

[39] The ICRC works on the basis of confidentiality as its main working method. Its confidential approach, however, does not relate only to protection activities, such as in the context of detention. It is a prerequisite for its humanitarian activities as a whole. Confidentiality allows the ICRC to have greater access to victims of armed conflict and other situations of violence, to engage in a bilateral dialogue with the relevant authorities so as to be able to fulfil its humanitarian mission, and to improve the security of its beneficiaries and staff in the field. For further information, see ICRC, 'The International Committee of the Red Cross's (ICRC's) confidential approach. Specific means employed by the ICRC to ensure respect for the law by State and non-State authorities', reproduced in *International Review of the Red Cross*, Vol. 94, No. 887, September 2012, pp. 1135–1144. For further information, see ICRC, 'Action by the International Committee of the Red Cross in the event of violations of international humanitarian law or of other fundamental rules protecting persons in situations of violence', *International Review of the Red Cross*, Vol. 87, No. 858, June 2005, pp. 393–400.

[40] ICRC Assistance Policy, adopted by the Assembly of the ICRC on 29 April 2004 and reproduced in *International Review of the Red Cross*, Vol. 86, No. 855, September 2004, pp. 677–693, at 682.

[41] The fact that the ICRC or another impartial humanitarian organization undertakes assistance activities and thereby replaces the authorities or supplements their efforts does not mean that it has a legal obligation to do so. This point is further demonstrated by the use of the words 'may … undertake' in Article 9. See also para. 1133 of this commentary. The ICRC Assistance Policy, adopted by the Assembly of the ICRC on 29 April 2004 and reproduced in *International Review of the Red Cross*, Vol. 86, No. 855, September 2004, pp. 677–693, at 683, clarifies the circumstances in which the ICRC will agree to act as a substitute and provide services directly to the population.

[42] For further information, see ICRC, 'Action by the International Committee of the Red Cross in the event of violations of international humanitarian law or of other fundamental rules protecting persons in situations of violence', *International Review of the Red Cross*, Vol. 87, No. 858, June 2005, pp. 393–400.

c. Relief/assistance

1148 Article 9 entitles the ICRC or any other impartial humanitarian organization to offer to undertake relief activities for persons affected by an international armed conflict. In its ordinary meaning, 'relief' means 'the alleviation or removal of pain, anxiety, or distress'.[43] As used in the Geneva Conventions, the term 'relief' mostly applies to activities to address humanitarian needs arising in emergency situations. It should be read in conjunction with the broader term 'assistance' used in Article 81(1) of Additional Protocol I, which seeks also to cover longer-term as well as recurrent and even chronic needs.[44] Neither relief nor assistance are defined in the aforementioned treaties. The absence of a generic definition, or of a list of specific activities which would be covered by the term 'assistance', is in line with the fact that needs for humanitarian assistance may not necessarily be the same in every context and may evolve over time.

1149 'Assistance activities' refers to all activities, services and the delivery of goods, carried out primarily in the fields of health, water, habitat (the creation of a sustainable living environment) and economic security (defined by the ICRC as 'the condition of an individual, household or community that is able to cover its essential needs and unavoidable expenditures in a sustainable manner, according to its cultural standards').[45] All of these activities seek to ensure that persons caught up in an armed conflict are able to survive and live in dignity. In practice, the type of relief activities will differ depending on who the beneficiaries are and the nature of their needs. Relief activities for persons wounded on the battlefield, for example, will not be the same as those undertaken for the benefit of prisoners of war in a camp. It is one of the core principles of humanitarian law that, whatever the relief activity, it should never be considered as being of a nature to reinforce the enemy's military capabilities, including, for example, the provision of medical aid to wounded combatants.

d. Beneficiaries

1150 In Article 9 of the First Convention, the persons for whom humanitarian activities may be undertaken are the 'wounded and sick, medical personnel and chaplains'. The term 'wounded and sick' refers to the persons covered by Articles 12

---

[43] *Concise Oxford English Dictionary*, 12th edition, Oxford University Press, 2011, p. 1215.

[44] ICRC Assistance Policy, adopted by the Assembly of the ICRC on 29 April 2004 and reproduced in *International Review of the Red Cross*, Vol. 86, No. 855, September 2004, pp. 677–693, at 677.

[45] ICRC Assistance Policy, adopted by the Assembly of the ICRC on 29 April 2004 and reproduced in *International Review of the Red Cross*, Vol. 86, No. 855, September 2004, pp. 677–693, at 678. For examples of specific activities covered by those terms, as undertaken by the ICRC, see ICRC, *Health Activities: Caring for People Affected by Armed Conflict and Other Situations of Violence*, ICRC, Geneva, 2015, and *Economic Security*, ICRC, Geneva, 2013.

and 13. The term 'medical personnel' refers to the persons covered by Articles 24, 25, 26 and 27. The term 'chaplains' refers to 'chaplains attached to the armed forces' covered by Article 24 and, where applicable, to religious personnel working on the basis of Article 26 or 27.[46] While not explicitly mentioned in Article 9, the right to offer services can also relate to activities for the benefit of dead persons, since a range of obligations are mentioned in their regard in Articles 15, 16 and 17. Similarly, while not mentioned explicitly as such, it flows from the logic of the First Convention that the right to offer services can, depending on the circumstances, also be exercised to protect, or safeguard the functioning of, objects protected under the First Convention (such as military medical establishments and medical aircraft). These objects are protected because of their benefit to the persons protected under the First Convention.[47]

1151   Armed conflict affects persons other than those explicitly identified as falling into, and meeting the conditions of, the categories of beneficiaries enumerated in the four different versions of common Article 9 (Article 10 of the Fourth Convention). Nowhere is it stated that these categories of persons are the only ones for whom the ICRC or any other impartial humanitarian organization may offer its services.[48] Furthermore, the right to offer services can be exercised for the benefit of persons regardless of whether they qualify as 'protected persons' in the sense of one of the four Geneva Conventions. This is demonstrated by Article 10 of the Fourth Convention, which uses the term 'civilian persons' rather than the narrower term 'protected persons' as defined in Article 4 of the Fourth Convention.

1152   Further, for persons to benefit from humanitarian activities, they do not have to be the victims of a violation of an applicable legal standard. This broad interpretation of who may be the beneficiaries of humanitarian activities is reflected in Article 81(1) of Additional Protocol I, which refers to 'the victims of conflicts', and is confirmed by subsequent State practice: when consenting to an offer of services, Parties to a conflict typically do not limit their consent for the humanitarian activities to those persons who qualify as 'protected persons' in the sense of the Geneva Conventions. Lastly, the foregoing remains without prejudice to the fact that other activities of impartial humanitarian

---

[46] For the purposes of Additional Protocol I, see the definitions of 'wounded' and 'sick' in Article 8(a), of 'medical personnel' in Article 8(c) and of 'religious personnel' in Article 8(d).

[47] For further details on this link, see for example the commentaries on Article 19 (fixed establishments and mobile medical units), para. 1772, and on Article 35 (transports of wounded and sick or of medical equipment), para. 2363.

[48] Note that common Article 3(2) remains silent on this particular question, stating only that '[a]n impartial humanitarian body, such as the International Committee of the Red Cross, may offer its services to the Parties to the conflict'. See also Article 81 of Additional Protocol I, which refers to the 'victims of conflicts' as the beneficiaries of humanitarian activities, as well as Article 5(2)(d) of the 1986 Statutes of the International Red Cross and Red Crescent Movement. For an illustration, see Guiding Principles on Internal Displacement (1998), Principle 25(2): 'International humanitarian organizations and other appropriate actors have the right to offer their services in support of the internally displaced.'

organizations, such as those in the realm of prevention (for example: raising awareness of international humanitarian law) can and are exercised for the benefit of able-bodied combatants.

3. The ICRC or any other impartial humanitarian organization

a. The International Committee of the Red Cross

1153 The ICRC is the only organization mentioned by name in both Article 9 and common Article 3(2) regarding the right to offer services. In these contexts, the ICRC is referred to as an example of an organization which qualifies as an impartial humanitarian organization. For the drafters of the Conventions, the ICRC epitomizes the essential characteristics of an impartial humanitarian organization. That said, having conferred on the ICRC, as an example of an impartial humanitarian organization, the right to offer its services, States have signalled that this explicit mention is contingent upon the ICRC operating at all times in that capacity. This requirement extends, by inference, to any other organization seeking to fall within the scope of Article 9.

1154   In the 1949 Geneva Conventions and their 1977 Additional Protocols as they apply to international armed conflict, there are a considerable number of provisions in which the High Contracting Parties have explicitly granted the ICRC the right to offer to perform specific humanitarian activities.[49] In parallel, the Statutes of the International Red Cross and Red Crescent Movement also provide a legal basis for the ICRC to offer its services in such conflicts.[50] Article 5(3) of the Statutes states that '[t]he International Committee [of the Red Cross] may take any humanitarian initiative which comes within its role as a specifically neutral and independent institution and intermediary, and may consider any question requiring examination by such an institution'.[51]

b. Other impartial humanitarian organizations

1155 The ICRC has no monopoly on the right to offer services. Article 9 confers the same right on 'any other impartial humanitarian organization'. This concept has not been defined, nor further clarified, in the Geneva Conventions.[52]

1156   When these words were inserted in the text during the 1949 Diplomatic Conference, the type of organizations the High Contracting Parties had in mind was limited mostly to National Red Cross and Red Crescent Societies.[53] Since

---

[49] For the difference between the right to offer services and the provisions in which the role of the ICRC has been explicitly mentioned in connection with a specific activity, see para. 1132.

[50] With regard to the background and status of these Statutes, see para. 1124.

[51] Statutes of the International Red Cross and Red Crescent Movement (1986), Article 5(3). Other relevant provisions of these Statutes can be found in Article 5(2).

[52] See, however, the references to the 1949 Diplomatic Conference in para. 1131.

[53] For further information, see para. 1131.

1949, the number and diversity of organizations which consider themselves to be impartial humanitarian organizations in the sense of Article 9, and which are recognized as such by Parties to an armed conflict, have grown significantly to include both certain non-governmental organizations and certain intergovernmental organizations.

1157   For an organization to qualify as a 'humanitarian organization', there is no requirement that the scope of its activities be limited to humanitarian activities.[54] Thus, an organization that focused solely on development activities prior to the outbreak of the armed conflict may subsequently become, for the purposes of Article 9, a humanitarian organization, without prejudice to the possibility of the organization concurrently pursuing activities of a different nature elsewhere. Article 9 does, however, require that the entity wishing to offer its services be an 'organization'. Thus, a loose association of individuals, while their activities may alleviate human suffering, would not qualify on the basis of this provision.[55] Nor would a private person wishing to engage in charitable activities. At all times, an organization wishing to qualify as a 'humanitarian organization in the sense of this provision ought to be capable of complying with professional standards for humanitarian activities.[56] Otherwise, in practice there is a risk that the authorities to whom the offer of services is made may doubt the impartial and humanitarian nature of the organization.

1158   Humanitarian organizations require financial means to sustain their staff and operations and to purchase the necessary goods and services. Therefore, the fact that money is involved can by no means be considered as depriving a qualifying organization or its activities of their 'humanitarian' character. Further, provided the organization continues to act as an impartial humanitarian organization nothing precludes it from having a relationship with an economic actor such as a private or a State-owned corporation. Examples of such relationships include: when economic actors with the capacities to deliver humanitarian services, such as a commercial aviation company used for the transport of relief goods, sell their services to impartial humanitarian organizations at a profit; or when economic actors offer their services for free to impartial humanitarian organizations, for example as part of corporate social responsibility programmes.

---

[54] For an analysis of which activities qualify as 'humanitarian activities', see section C.2.
[55] Common Article 3(2) uses the wording 'impartial humanitarian body', which can be considered substantively identical to the term 'impartial humanitarian organization'; see the commentary on that article, para. 788.
[56] See e.g. ICRC, *Professional Standards for Protection Work Carried Out by Humanitarian and Human Rights Actors in Armed Conflict and Other Situations of Violence*, 2nd edition, ICRC, Geneva, 2013. These standards, adopted through an ICRC-led consultation process, reflect shared thinking and common agreement among humanitarian and human rights agencies (UN agencies, components of the Movement, and non-governmental organizations). The ICRC is of the view that the standard of protection that an agency provides should not fall below those set out in this document.

1159   While there are a wide variety of instances in which economic actors can be involved in humanitarian activities, even when they provide free services within the framework of a particular humanitarian activity, for example as part of a corporate social responsibility programme, their otherwise profit-making profile would preclude them from qualifying in their own right as a humanitarian organization. An example of such involvement would be the delivery of humanitarian services directly by an economic actor, either based on a contractual relationship with an impartial humanitarian organization or on its own initiative. Thus, by not qualifying as an impartial humanitarian organization, an economic actor may not invoke the right to offer services in the sense of Article 9.

1160   The Geneva Conventions require a humanitarian organization wishing to offer its services on the basis of Article 9 to be 'impartial'. Impartiality refers to the attitude to be adopted vis-à-vis the persons affected by the armed conflict when planning and implementing the proposed humanitarian activities. As one of the Fundamental Principles applicable to all components of the Movement, 'impartiality' is the requirement not to make any 'discrimination as to nationality, race, religious beliefs, class or political opinions' or, for that matter, any other similar criteria.[57] Further, the Fundamental Principle of impartiality, which has also been endorsed by the International Court of Justice,[58] requires the components of the Movement to 'endeavou[r] to relieve the suffering of individuals, being guided solely by their needs, and to give priority to the most urgent cases of distress'. As a matter of good practice, this definition is applied also by many actors outside the Movement.

1161   For an organization to qualify as an 'impartial humanitarian organization', it does not suffice for it to claim unilaterally that it qualifies as such: it will need to make sure that it operates at all times in an impartial and humanitarian manner. In practice, it matters that the Party to the armed conflict to which the offer of services is made perceives the organization to be both impartial and humanitarian, and that the Party also trusts that it will behave accordingly.

1162   The principle of impartiality applies at both the planning and the implementation stages of any humanitarian activity: only the needs of the persons affected by the conflict may inspire the proposals, priorities and decisions of humanitarian organizations when determining which activities to undertake

---

[57] While the words 'any other similar criteria' do not appear in Article 9, they do in other provisions of the Geneva Conventions. See e.g. Article 12(2) of the First Convention.

[58] ICJ, *Military and Paramilitary Activities in and against Nicaragua case*, Merits, Judgment, 1986, para. 242. See also the Sphere Project's Humanitarian Charter, para. 6, which states:

  [Humanitarian] assistance must be provided according to the principle of impartiality, which requires that it be provided solely on the basis of need and in proportion to need. This reflects the wider principle of non-discrimination; that no one should be discriminated against on any grounds of status, including age, gender, race, colour, ethnicity, sexual orientation, language, religion, disability, health status, political or other opinion, national or social origin.

and where and how to implement them (for example, who receives medical assistance first).

1163   In order for an impartial humanitarian organization to qualify as such in the sense of Article 9, there is no requirement as to where it has its headquarters, which may be outside the territory of the States that are party to the conflict in question.[59]

1164   The concept of impartiality is distinct from that of neutrality. Article 9 does not require organizations wishing to qualify on the basis of this provision to be 'neutral'. In the context of humanitarian activities, 'neutrality' refers to the attitude to be adopted towards the Parties to the armed conflict. Neutrality is also one of the Movement's Fundamental Principles, described as follows: 'In order to continue to enjoy the confidence of all, the Movement may not take sides in hostilities or engage at any time in controversies of a political, racial, religious or ideological nature.' Although not a requirement of this provision, in practice there are contexts in which a proven attitude of neutrality will facilitate an organization's acceptance by the Parties to the conflict concerned. By the same token, an impartial humanitarian organization which is, or is perceived to be, in favour of one of the Parties to the conflict may not be so accepted.

4. 'subject to the consent of the Parties to the conflict concerned'

a. Requirement of consent

1165   Since the adoption of the 1949 Geneva Conventions, the treaty-based requirement to seek and obtain the consent of the Parties to the conflict concerned has become the most debated aspect of the legal framework applicable to humanitarian activities in armed conflict.[60] On the one hand, the High Contracting Parties have conferred on the ICRC and on other impartial humanitarian organizations the right to offer unilaterally to undertake humanitarian activities. On the other hand, a plain reading of Article 9 indicates that this right does not necessarily constitute a right of access, i.e. a guarantee of being able to carry out the proposed humanitarian activities. Access is conditional on the 'consent of the Parties to the conflict concerned'.

1166   For the purpose of this provision, the words 'the Parties to the conflict concerned' need to be construed narrowly; consent only needs to be sought and obtained from the High Contracting Party which (i) qualifies as a 'Party' to the international armed conflict in question, and (ii) is 'concerned' because the

---

[59] See also para. 1131 regarding the discussion which took place on this topic during the 1949 Diplomatic Conference.

[60] This requirement also appears in other treaty-based provisions dealing with the right to offer services; see the commentary on common Article 3, section J.6.a. See also Article 70(1) of Additional Protocol I and Article 18(2) of Additional Protocol II.

proposed humanitarian activities will take place on its territory or in an area under its control, as is the case for an Occupying Power.[61] Thus, the opposing Party to the international armed conflict does not need to be asked for its consent on the basis of Article 9. This is the case even when, for example, the proposed relief convoys need to pass through the opposing Party's territory. In that instance – while a different set of rules regulate its position with regard to its obligation to allow and facilitate 'passage' (see para. 1168) – that Party is not, for the purpose of Article 9, 'concerned' because the proposed humanitarian activities are not going to take place on its territory.[62] However, its consent will need to be sought on the basis of general international law.[63]

1167   Similarly, as a matter of law applicable to international armed conflict, consent on the basis of Article 9 for humanitarian activities to be undertaken on the territory or in an area under the control of a Party to the conflict will not need to be sought and obtained from a neutral Power when the proposed humanitarian activities leave from, or transit through, its territory: it is not 'concerned' in the sense of Article 9. Again in this case, however, the neutral Power's consent will need to be sought on the basis of general international law.[64]

1168   It is at this juncture that the distinction – already referred to in the introduction (see para. 1125) – between seeking and obtaining the consent of a Party to the conflict for access to undertake humanitarian activities, on the one hand, and a Party's obligation to allow and facilitate the passage of humanitarian activities, on the other hand, comes into play. On the basis of and under the conditions set down in Article 23 of the Fourth Convention and Article 70(2) of Additional Protocol I, all High Contracting Parties, whether or not they qualify as Parties to the conflict, have an obligation to allow and facilitate the rapid and unimpeded passage of relief consignments, equipment and personnel destined for the civilian population, even that of an opposing Party, i.e. they must allow the acceptance of an offer of services to be implemented.[65] If those States were to refuse to allow and facilitate relief schemes, it would in effect preclude the humanitarian needs of the persons affected by the armed conflict from

---

[61] Humanitarian activities in the context of an occupation are more tightly regulated than those in the context of an international armed conflict not amounting to an occupation. See Fourth Convention, Articles 55 and 59.

[62] Similarly, see Article 70(1) of Additional Protocol I, which has further clarified this by requiring only the 'agreement of the Parties concerned in such relief actions' when referring to relief action in an area under the control of a Party to the conflict.

[63] See, however, *Oxford Guidance on the Law Relating to Humanitarian Relief Operations in Situations of Armed Conflict*, pp. 36–38.

[64] For an interpretation of the term 'neutral Powers', see the commentary on Article 4, section C.1.

[65] See Fourth Convention, Article 23, and Additional Protocol I, Article 70(3). See also ICRC Study on Customary International Humanitarian Law (2005), Rules 55 and 56 (applicable in both international and non-international armed conflict).

being addressed and thus render the consent given by the Parties to the conflict void.

1169   Article 9 does not indicate how consent is to be manifested. This may be through a written reply to the organization which has made the offer of services but can also be conveyed orally. In the absence of a clearly communicated approval, the impartial humanitarian organization can make sure that the Party to the conflict concerned consents at least implicitly, by acquiescence, to the proposed humanitarian activities of which that Party has been duly notified in advance.

b. Consent may not be arbitrarily withheld

1170 The Geneva Conventions provide no guidance as to whether there are circumstances in which a Party to the conflict may lawfully refuse its consent to an offer to undertake humanitarian activities which, in the context of the First Convention, will be those carried out for the benefit of the wounded and sick and medical and religious personnel covered by the First Convention.

1171   The legal assessment of the situation differs depending on whether the offer of services is made to an Occupying Power (not dealt with here)[66] or to a Party to an international armed conflict other than an Occupying Power (the situation dealt with here).

1172   In 1949, the understanding of the requirement to seek and obtain the consent of the Parties to the conflict concerned was set in the context of States' nearly unfettered sovereignty: a Party to the armed conflict receiving an offer of services did not see its full discretion curtailed by any rules of international law. Already at the time, however, it was understood that when a Party to the conflict refused an offer of services, it would bear international legal responsibility for any ensuing consequences of a nature or effect to violate its own humanitarian obligations towards the intended beneficiaries.[67]

1173   Since 1949, international law in general, and humanitarian law in particular, has evolved to the extent that a Party to an international armed conflict to which an offer of services is made by an impartial humanitarian body is not at complete liberty to decide how to respond to such an offer. It has now become accepted that there are circumstances in which a Party is obliged, as a matter of international law, to grant its consent to an offer of humanitarian

---

[66] For a situation of occupation, Article 59(1) of the Fourth Convention provides for more stringent criteria. See also Article 69 of Additional Protocol I.

[67] Pictet (ed.), *Commentary on the First Geneva Convention*, ICRC, 1952, pp. 110–111:

> All these humanitarian activities are subject to one final condition – the consent of the Parties to the conflict concerned. This condition is obviously a harsh one. But one might almost say that it follows automatically. A belligerent Power can obviously not be obliged to tolerate in its territory activities of any kind by any foreign organization. That would be out of the question. The Powers do not have to give a reason for their refusals. The decision is entirely theirs. But being bound to apply the Convention, they alone must bear the responsibility if they refuse help in carrying out their engagements.

activities by an impartial humanitarian organization. In other words, there are circumstances in which a refusal of such an offer will entail that Party's international legal responsibility.

1174 In particular, humanitarian law, as informed by subsequent State practice, has evolved to the point where one can conclude that consent may not be refused on arbitrary grounds.[68] Thus, any impediment(s) to humanitarian activities must be based on valid reasons, and the Party to the conflict whose consent is sought must assess any offer of services in good faith[69] and in line with its international legal obligations in relation to humanitarian needs. Thus, where a Party to an international armed conflict is unwilling or unable to address those persons' humanitarian needs, it must accept an offer of services from an impartial humanitarian organization. If humanitarian needs cannot be met otherwise, the refusal of an offer of services would be arbitrary, and therefore in violation of international law.

1175 International law does not provide authoritative clarification on how to interpret the criterion of 'arbitrariness'.[70] This assessment remains context-specific. Nevertheless, there are instances in which a refusal to grant consent will clearly not be considered arbitrary. This will be the case, for example, if the State to which the offer is made is itself able and willing to address the humanitarian needs and, importantly, actually does so in an impartial manner.

[68] The same evolution has taken place under customary international humanitarian law; see Henckaerts/Doswald-Beck, commentary on Rule 55 (dealing with humanitarian relief for civilians in need), pp. 196–197: '[A] humanitarian organization cannot operate without the consent of the party concerned. However, such consent must not be refused on arbitrary grounds.' This statement in the customary law study is made in the context of a rule dealing with 'humanitarian relief for civilians in need'. Logically, the same rule applies with regard to offers to protect or assist the wounded, sick or shipwrecked, as it does with regard to offers of services made to protect or assist prisoners of war. There is no reason why such offers of services should be regulated differently. Otherwise, this would lead to a manifestly absurd and unreasonable situation: a Party to the conflict would be prohibited from arbitrarily refusing an offer of services for civilians, but could do so when the offer of services was intended to benefit other categories of persons affected by the armed conflict. See also *Official Records of the Diplomatic Conference of Geneva of 1974–1977*, Vol. XII, p. 336, where the representative of the Federal Republic of Germany (endorsed on this point by several other delegates) stated with regard to the words 'subject to the agreement of the Party to the conflict concerned in such relief actions': 'those words did not imply that the Parties concerned had absolute and unlimited freedom to refuse their agreement to relief actions. A Party refusing its agreement must do so for valid reasons, not for arbitrary or capricious ones.' See also Guiding Principles on Internal Displacement (1998), Principle 25(2): 'Consent [to an offer of services from an international humanitarian organization or other appropriate actor] shall not be arbitrarily withheld, particularly when authorities concerned are unable or unwilling to provide the required humanitarian assistance.' For two recent examples, see: UN Security Council, Res. 2139 of 22 February 2014 concerning Syria, preambular para. 10: '*condemning* all cases of denial of humanitarian access, and *recalling* that arbitrary denial of humanitarian access and depriving civilians of objects indispensable to their survival, including wilfully impeding relief supply and access, can constitute a violation of international humanitarian law'; and Res. 2216 of 14 April 2015 concerning Yemen, preambular para. 10, which contains identical wording as of 'recalling'.

[69] ICRC, *International Humanitarian Law and the Challenges of Contemporary Armed Conflicts*, report prepared for the 31st International Conference of the Red Cross and Red Crescent, Geneva, 2011, p. 25.

[70] See also ICRC, *Q&A and lexicon on humanitarian access*, June 2014, p. 11.

Conversely, refusal may be considered arbitrary, and therefore unlawful, if it entails a violation of the Party's legal obligations under humanitarian law or other fields of international law, including applicable human rights law. This will be the case, for example, when the Party concerned is unable or unwilling to provide humanitarian assistance to the persons affected by the armed conflict, and even more so if their basic needs enabling them to live in dignity are not met.

1176   Further, it must be kept in mind that the use of starvation of the civilian population as a method of warfare is prohibited.[71] Therefore, where a lack of supplies is intended to, or can be expected to, result in the starvation of the civilian population, there is no valid reason to refuse an impartial humanitarian organization's offer to undertake humanitarian activities.[72] Under the 1998 ICC Statute, '[i]ntentionally using starvation of civilians as a method of warfare by depriving them of objects indispensable to their survival, including wilfully impeding relief supplies as provided for under the Geneva Conventions' is a war crime in international armed conflict.[73]

1177   Similarly, the denial of consent for the purpose, implied or express, of exacerbating civilian suffering would also qualify as arbitrary. A refusal to grant consent may also be considered arbitrary when it is based on adverse distinction, i.e. when it is designed to deprive persons of a certain nationality, race, religious beliefs, class or political opinion of needed humanitarian relief or protection.

1178   Military necessity is no valid ground under humanitarian law to turn down a valid offer of services or to deny in their entirety the humanitarian activities proposed by an impartial humanitarian organization.

1179   At all times, the consent of a Party to the undertaking of humanitarian activities remains without prejudice to that Party's entitlement to impose measures of control. Such measures may include: verifying the nature of the assistance; prescribing technical arrangements for the delivery of the assistance; and temporarily restricting humanitarian activities for reasons of imperative military necessity.[74] If verification results in the conclusion that the activity is neither impartial nor humanitarian in nature, access may be denied. The design and implementation of these controls and restrictions may not, however, be such that, for all practical intents and purposes, they amount to a refusal of consent. In other words, the right of control recognized by humanitarian law should not unduly delay relief operations or make their implementation impossible.

[71] See Additional Protocol I, Article 54(1), and ICRC Study on Customary International Humanitarian Law (2005), Rule 53.
[72] ICRC, *International Humanitarian Law and the challenges of contemporary armed conflicts*, report prepared for the 31st International Conference of the Red Cross and Red Crescent, Geneva, 2011, p. 25.
[73] See ICC Statute (1998), Article 8(2)(b)(xxv).
[74] See Additional Protocol I, Article 70(3); see also Henckaerts/Doswald-Beck, commentary on Rule 55, p. 198.

In this regard, imperative military necessity may be invoked in exceptional circumstances only in order to regulate – but not prohibit – the access of impartial humanitarian organizations, and can only temporarily and geographically restrict the freedom of movement of humanitarian personnel.[75] Such reasons of imperative military necessity might include, for example, preventing interference with an ongoing or imminent military operation.

1180   Humanitarian law does not indicate what happens when a State party to an international armed conflict refuses its consent in circumstances which violate its international legal obligations. Lastly, the lawfulness of an impartial humanitarian organization undertaking humanitarian activities in defiance of an arbitrary refusal of its offer of services would need to be assessed on the basis of other applicable rules of international and domestic law.[76]

Select bibliography

Barrat, Claudie, *Status of NGOs in International Humanitarian Law*, Brill Nijhoff, Leiden, 2014.

Blondel, Jean-Luc, 'L'assistance aux personnes protégées', *Revue international de la Croix-Rouge*, Vol. 69, No. 767, October 1987, pp. 471–489.

– 'The meaning of the word "humanitarian" in relation to the Fundamental Principles of the Red Cross and Red Crescent', *International Review of the Red Cross*, Vol. 29, No. 273, December 1989, pp. 507–515.

– 'Genèse et évolution des principes fondamentaux de la Croix-Rouge et du Croissant Rouge', *Revue international de la Croix-Rouge*, Vol. 73, No. 790, August 1991, pp. 369–377.

Bouchet-Saulnier, Françoise, 'Consent to humanitarian access: An obligation triggered by territorial control, not States' rights', *International Review of the Red Cross*, Vol. 96, No. 893, March 2014, pp. 207–217.

de Geouffre de La Pradelle, Paul, 'Une conquête méthodique : le droit d'initiative humanitaire dans les rapports internationaux', in Christophe Swinarski (ed.), *Études et essais sur le droit international humanitaire et sur les principes de la Croix-Rouge en l'honneur de Jean Pictet*, Martinus Nijhoff Publishers, The Hague, 1984, pp. 945–950.

Fast, Larissa, 'Unpacking the principle of humanity: Tensions and implications', *International Review of the Red Cross*, Vol. 97, Nos 897/898, Spring/Summer 2015, pp. 111–131.

Forsythe, David P., 'International Humanitarian Assistance: The Role of the Red Cross', *Buffalo Journal of International Law*, Vol. 3, No. 2, 1996–1997, pp. 235–260.

Gentile, Pierre, 'Humanitarian organizations involved in protection activities: a story of soul-searching and professionalization', *International Review of the Red Cross*, Vol. 93, No. 884, December 2011, pp. 1165–1191.

---

[75] See ICRC Study on Customary International Humanitarian Law (2005), Rule 56.

[76] As to international law, see in particular Article 71(4) of Additional Protocol I. As to national legislation, domestic regulations with regard to entry into national territory would need to be considered.

Gillard, Emanuela-Chiara, 'The law regulating cross-border relief operations', *International Review of the Red Cross*, Vol. 95, No. 890, June 2013, pp. 351–382.

Harroff-Tavel, Marion, 'Neutrality and Impartiality – The importance of these principles for the International Red Cross and Red Crescent Movement and the difficulties involved in applying them', *International Review of the Red Cross*, Vol. 29, No. 273, December 1989, pp. 536–552.

Heintze, Hans-Joachim and Lülf, Charlotte, 'Non-State Actors Under International Humanitarian Law', in Math Noortmann, August Reinisch and Cedric Ryngaert (eds), *Non-State Actors in International Law*, Hart Publishing, Oxford, 2015, pp. 97–111.

Institute of International Law, 'Humanitarian Assistance', Resolution of the Bruges Session, 2 September 2003, available at http://www.idi-iil.org/idiE/resolutionsE/2003_bru_03_en.PDF.

ICRC, 'ICRC Q&A and lexicon on humanitarian access', *International Review of the Red Cross*, Vol. 96, No. 893, March 2014, pp. 359–375.

– *The Fundamental Principles of the International Red Cross and Red Crescent Movement*, ICRC, Geneva, 2015.

Junod, Sylvie S., 'Le mandat du CICR durant un conflit armé. Le mandat et les activités du Comité international de la Croix-Rouge', *The Military Law and Law of War Review*, Vol. 43, 2004, pp. 103–110.

Kalshoven, Frits, 'Impartiality and Neutrality in Humanitarian Law and Practice', *International Review of the Red Cross*, Vol. 29, No. 273, December 1989, pp. 516–535.

Kolb, Robert, 'De l'assistance humanitaire : la résolution sur l'assistance humanitaire adoptée par l'Institut de droit international à sa session de Bruges en 2003', *Revue international de la Croix-Rouge*, Vol. 86, No. 856, December 2004, pp. 853–878.

Kuijt, Emilie Ellen, *Humanitarian Assistance and State Sovereignty in International Law: Towards a Comprehensive Framework*, Intersentia, Cambridge, 2015.

Labbé, Jérémie and Daudin, Pascal, 'Applying the humanitarian principles: Reflecting on the experience of the International Committee of the Red Cross', *International Review of the Red Cross*, Vol. 97, No. 897/898, Spring/Summer 2015, pp. 183–210.

Lattanzi, Flavia, 'Humanitarian Assistance', in Andrew Clapham, Paola Gaeta and Marco Sassòli (eds), *The 1949 Geneva Conventions: A Commentary*, Oxford University Press, 2015, pp. 231–255.

Oxford Guidance on the Law Relating to Humanitarian Relief Operations in Situations of Armed Conflict, by Dapo Akande and Emanuela-Chiara Gillard, commissioned & published by the UN Office for the Coordination of Humanitarian Affairs, 2016.

Plattner, Denise, 'Assistance to the civilian population: the development and present state of international humanitarian law', *International Review of the Red Cross*, Vol. 32, No. 288, June 1992, pp. 249–263.

Ryngaert, Cédric, 'Humanitarian Assistance and the Conundrum of Consent: A Legal Perspective', *Amsterdam Law Forum*, Vol. 5, No. 2, 2013, pp. 5–19.

Sandoz, Yves, 'Le droit d'initiative du Comité international de la Croix-Rouge', *German Yearbook of International Law*, Vol. 22, 1979, pp. 352–373.

Schwendimann, Felix, 'The legal framework of humanitarian access in armed conflict', *International Review of the Red Cross*, Vol. 93, No. 884, December 2011, pp. 993–1008.

Spieker, Heike, 'Humanitarian Assistance, Access in Armed Conflict and Occupation', version of March 2013, in Rüdiger Wolfrum (ed.), *Max Planck Encyclopedia of Public International Law*, Oxford University Press, http://www.mpepil .com.

Stoffels, Ruth Abril, 'Legal regulation of humanitarian assistance in armed conflict: Achievements and gaps', *International Review of the Red Cross*, Vol. 86, No. 855, September 2004, pp. 515–546.

Swinarski, Christophe, 'La notion d'un organisme neutre et le droit international', in Christophe Swinarski (ed.), *Études et essais sur le droit international humanitaire et sur les principes de la Croix-Rouge en l'honneur de Jean Pictet*, ICRC/Martinus Nijhoff Publishers, The Hague, 1984, pp. 819–835.

Swiss Confederation, Federal Department of Foreign Affairs, *Humanitarian Access in Situations of Armed Conflict: Practitioners' Manual*, 2014.

Toebes, Brigit, 'Health and Humanitarian Assistance: Towards an Integrated Norm under International Law', *Tilburg Law Review*, Vol. 18, No. 2, 2013, pp. 133–151.

Vukas, Budislav, 'Humanitarian Assistance in Cases of Emergency', version of March 2013, in Rüdiger Wolfrum (ed.), *Max Planck Encyclopedia of Public International Law*, Oxford University Press, http://opil.ouplaw.com/home/ EPIL.

SUBSTITUTES FOR PROTECTING POWERS

❖ Text of the provision*

(1) The High Contracting Parties may at any time agree to entrust to an organization which offers all guarantees of impartiality and efficacy the duties incumbent on the Protecting Powers by virtue of the present Convention.

(2) When wounded and sick, or medical personnel and chaplains do not benefit or cease to benefit, no matter for what reason, by the activities of a Protecting Power or of an organization provided for in the first paragraph above, the Detaining Power shall request a neutral State, or such an organization, to undertake the functions performed under the present Convention by a Protecting Power designated by the Parties to a conflict.

(3) If protection cannot be arranged accordingly, the Detaining Power shall request or shall accept, subject to the provisions of this Article, the offer of the services of a humanitarian organization, such as the International Committee of the Red Cross, to assume the humanitarian functions performed by Protecting Powers under the present Convention.

(4) Any neutral Power, or any organization invited by the Power concerned or offering itself for these purposes, shall be required to act with a sense of responsibility towards the Party to the conflict on which persons protected by the present Convention depend, and shall be required to furnish sufficient assurances that it is in a position to undertake the appropriate functions and to discharge them impartially.

(5) No derogation from the preceding provisions shall be made by special agreements between Powers one of which is restricted, even temporarily, in its freedom to negotiate with the other Power or its allies by reason of military events, more particularly where the whole, or a substantial part, of the territory of the said Power is occupied.

(6) Whenever in the present Convention mention is made of a Protecting Power, such mention applies to substitute organizations in the sense of the present Article.

---

* Paragraph numbers have been added for ease of reference.

❖ Reservations or declarations

(a) High Contracting Parties for which a reservation is in force at the time of publication: Albania; Democratic People's Republic of Korea; Guinea-Bissau; People's Republic of China; Portugal; The former Yugoslav Republic of Macedonia; Russian Federation; and Viet Nam. For the text and an analysis of these reservations, see section E.

(b) High Contracting Parties which previously had a reservation in force: Belarus (withdrawn 7 August 2001); Bulgaria (withdrawn 9 May 1994); Czechoslovakia (withdrawn 27 September 2001 by the Czech Republic and 5 June 2000 by Slovakia); German Democratic Republic (until unification with the Federal Republic of Germany); Hungary (withdrawn 31 May 2000); Poland (withdrawn 22 September 2004); Romania (withdrawn 24 June 2002); Ukraine (withdrawn 30 June 2006); and Yugoslavia (declaration of succession to the former Socialist Federal Republic of Yugoslavia deposited by the Federal Republic of Yugoslavia 'without any reservation' on 16 October 2001).**

Contents

** Country names at the time the reservation was made.

A. Introduction

1181   Article 10 regulates the conditions under which a substitute for a Protecting Power may be appointed, which organizations may qualify as such, and how and for what purpose they should function. This provision is common to the four Conventions.[1]

1182   The Diplomatic Conference of 1949 made the Protecting Powers the lynchpin of the system for monitoring compliance with the Geneva Conventions[2] and set out a procedure for appointing a substitute in the absence of a Protecting Power.

1183   The Second World War had provided stark proof of the importance of the task – entrusted to the Protecting Powers – of scrutinizing the implementation of humanitarian rules. However, it had also shown that, even in situations where the 1929 Geneva Convention on Prisoners of War was applicable, captives could be denied the help of a Protecting Power.

1184   The 1949 Diplomatic Conference therefore envisaged a procedure in the event that protected persons were not, or no longer, able to benefit from that regime. In order to understand the logic underpinning the Geneva Conventions in this regard, it is important to emphasize that the drafters of the Geneva Conventions were familiar with the scenario in which, when a Protecting Power can no longer fulfil its mandate, for example when it is itself drawn into the conflict, that Power would seek to appoint a new Protecting Power. The Power of Origin asks another neutral State to act as Protecting Power; that State, if it consents, asks for the approval of the State (known as the host or receiving State) where it is to carry out the Protecting Power mandate. Once that approval is given, the new Protecting Power takes up office. It then has all the rights and duties of a Protecting Power and cannot be called a substitute. These were the circumstances in which Switzerland took over from the United States as a Protecting Power in 1917 and 1941.[3]

1185   The debates leading to the adoption of common Article 10 (Article 11 in the Fourth Convention) addressed the completely different situation arising when, for whatever reason, the usual procedure cannot be followed, for example because the Power of Origin ceases to exist or because the international status

---

[1] See Second Convention, Article 10; Third Convention, Article 10; and Fourth Convention, Article 11.

[2] For more information about the appointment and mandate of Protecting Powers, see common Article 8 (Article 9 in the Fourth Convention).

[3] See William McHenry Franklin, *Protection of Foreign Interests, A Study in Diplomatic and Consular Practice*, United States Government Printing Office, Washington, 1946, pp. 254–256 and 266–268, and Janner, p. 24.

of one of the Parties to the conflict is disputed or because there are no neutral States left. These were, in the minds of the drafters of the Geneva Conventions, the circumstances for which a substitution procedure was introduced.

1186   Establishing procedures for substituting for Protecting Powers was high on the agenda of the Diplomatic Conference of 1974–1977. This resulted in paragraphs 4 and 7 of Article 5 of Additional Protocol I, which complement common Article 10 of the 1949 Conventions.[4]

1187   Although it is not specified in Article 10, it is clear that the substitution possibilities it sets out, like the Protecting Power mechanism it is intended to replace, are foreseen only to apply in international armed conflict. Neither common Article 3 nor Additional Protocol II make any mention of a role for a substitute for Protecting Powers in non-international armed conflict. However, nothing precludes the Parties to such a conflict from concluding a special agreement to put in place a similar system, akin to that of the substitutes of Protecting Powers.[5]

B. Historical background

1. Historical precedents

1188 Two particularly significant precedents should be mentioned: the mission to protect Russian prisoners of war in Germany after the First World War; and the ICRC's activities during the Second World War to protect members of the Free French Forces in captivity in Germany and German prisoners held by the Free French Forces.[6]

a. Practice after the First World War

1189 Shortly after the signing of the Armistice agreement of 11 November 1918, which put an end to the First World War, the victorious powers imposed an Inter-Allied Commission on Germany to control the situation of Russian prisoners of war. As it was suspected that most of these prisoners supported the Bolsheviks and were likely, if repatriated, to swell the ranks of the Red Army, the Inter-Allied Commission forbade repatriations to Soviet Russia. The Commission was dissolved in February 1920, shortly after the signing of the Treaty of Versailles; Germany regained its freedom of action but was left with an extremely volatile situation on its hands. Disheartened by captivity and seeing no prospect of it ending, disgusted by broken promises and convinced that the Allies would prevent their return home, the Russian prisoners were on

---

[4] Article 2(d) of Additional Protocol I defines 'substitute' as 'an organization acting in place of a Protecting Power in accordance with Article 5'.

[5] On special agreements in non-international armed conflict, see the commentary on common Article 3, section K.

[6] For historical references to these two cases, see Bugnion, 2003, p. 903, fn. 3.

the brink of revolt. Meanwhile tens of thousands of German, Austrian and Hungarian prisoners of war were trapped in Russia, the Soviet Government refusing to repatriate them until Germany allowed the Russian prisoners to return. The German Government therefore sought to appoint a neutral body to assist in supervising the prisoner-of-war camps and negotiating exchanges of German and Russian prisoners of war, a body that could guarantee that Russian prisoners would all be repatriated in accordance with their own free will, and with whose help any disputes between Russian prisoners of war and the camp authorities could be settled. In short, it envisaged an intermediary role between the Detaining Power, the Power of Origin and the States of transit, to be combined with a mandate to inspect prisoner-of-war camps and mediate between the captives and the detaining authority.

1190   These tasks obviously fell within the remit of a Protecting Power, but no State at that time had diplomatic relations with the Soviet regime. The German Government therefore requested the services of the ICRC, which sent to Germany a delegation that soon numbered about 20 delegates and interpreters. This extensive deployment made it possible to carry out regular inspections of the main prisoner-of-war camps. Repatriation began in May 1920 and went on until July 1921, after which the ICRC mission was phased out.[7]

1191   Although the term 'substitute for a Protecting Power' does not appear in the documents of the time, there can be little doubt that, circumstances having prevented the appointment of such a Power, the ICRC acted as the *de facto* Protecting Power of Russian prisoners of war in Germany.

b. Practice during the Second World War

1192 In the Second World War, too, many prisoners of war were deprived of the help of a Protecting Power even where the 1929 Geneva Convention on Prisoners of War was applicable.[8] Those needing legal assistance were the worst affected, for under Articles 60–67 of the 1929 Convention it was the responsibility of the Protecting Power to see to it that prisoners of war prosecuted by the Detaining Power enjoyed the legal safeguards to which they were entitled. The 1929 Convention did not recognize the ICRC as competent to act in such matters, but whenever prisoners of war received no help from a Protecting Power the ICRC did its utmost to make up for this deficiency.

---

[7] See *ibid.* pp. 869–870.

[8] For example, in December 1941 the Reich opposed Switzerland taking over several protection mandates previously exercised by the United States on the pretext that Germany no longer recognized as a belligerent State any country whose government had left the national territory (the case of Belgium, the Netherlands and Norway, among others); see Rousseau, p. 87, and Janner, p. 23. Further, following the capitulation of Germany and Japan, Switzerland decided to renounce protecting German interests because the Reich Government had disappeared and to give up protecting Japanese interests because Japan had been forced to sever all diplomatic relations. See Janner, pp. 12 and 29–30.

1193   The question of whether the ICRC should exercise the functions normally assigned to Protecting Powers arose most acutely in respect of relations
between Germany and the Free French Forces. In the eyes of the Reich Government, neither the French Committee of National Liberation in Algiers, nor the
Provisional Government of the French Republic that succeeded it once Paris
was liberated, had any legal existence, and only the Vichy regime was qualified
to represent French interests.[9] Subsequently, the agreement of 16 November
1940 between the Third Reich and the Vichy authorities established an illusory
national monitoring system for the welfare of French prisoners in Germany –
the Scapini mission – in the place of a Protecting Power. This proved utterly
ineffective.[10]

1194   It was not long before this position recoiled upon those who had formulated
it. When the Axis forces in North Africa surrendered in May 1943, the Free
French Forces took thousands of prisoners who did not benefit from the activity of a Protecting Power.[11] The authorities in Algiers suggested that Spain –
which until the armistice of June 1940 had been charged with representing
German and Italian interests in France – should act as Protecting Power for
these prisoners, provided that Germany and Italy agreed to the appointment
of a Protecting Power to look after French prisoners. The German Government rejected the proposal and the Italian Government failed to reply. However, in November 1943 the German Government asked the ICRC to provide
legal assistance to German prisoners of war held by the French forces in North
Africa. On humanitarian grounds, 'and in view of the fact that these PW [pris-
oners of war] had no Protecting Power', the ICRC gave its consent, while stressing 'that it could not assume any official mandate and remained sole judge of
its own actions'. Having made arrangements with the authorities in Algiers to
enable it to carry out this mission, the ICRC requested Berlin to make similar arrangements for offering equivalent legal assistance to French prisoners on
trial in German courts. Negotiations continued until April 1945, but no agreement was reached enabling the ICRC to give legal protection to the prisoners
of war on both sides.[12]

1195   The ICRC nevertheless performed many of the tasks usually assigned to Protecting Powers. In November 1944, for example, the Provisional Government
of the French Republic asked the ICRC to notify the Reich Government and
the authorities of the 'Italian Social Republic' of the commissioning of the hospital ship *Canada*. With the backing of the French authorities, the ICRC was
able to give substantial legal assistance to German prisoners of war being tried
in French courts. In February 1944 the Spanish Consul in Algiers informed
the ICRC delegation there that he would in future hand over to it all original

---

[9] Bugnion, 2003, p. 871.   [10] *Ibid.* p. 868.   [11] *Ibid.* p. 871.
[12] *Report of the International Committee of the Red Cross on its Activities during the Second
World War (September 1, 1939–June 30, 1947), Volume I: General Activities*, ICRC, Geneva,
May 1948, pp. 352–353, 357 and 359.

documents received from the French authorities, since the German Government had notified the Spanish Government that it had 'commissioned the
ICRC to take the place of the Protecting Power'.[13]

1196   The German capitulation greatly increased the ICRC's work as a substitute
for a Protecting Power, particularly as large numbers of German prisoners of
war were put on trial by Allied courts for war crimes or other offences and
Switzerland had ceased to act as Protecting Power, since there was no longer
a German Government. The ICRC therefore set up a legal assistance service,
which continued to work for several years after the end of hostilities.[14]

1197   So, without any formal agreement, the ICRC in fact exercised many of the
humanitarian functions of Protecting Powers in relations between the Free
French authorities and the Third Reich.

1198   It was therefore not surprising that, when it came to the process of revising
the humanitarian conventions after the end of the Second World War, provision
was made for the ICRC, or other impartial humanitarian organization, to act as
a substitute in case no Protecting Power had been appointed, in order to assume
the humanitarian functions performed by Protecting Powers under the Geneva
Conventions.

2. Preparatory work for the 1949 Geneva Conventions

1199   Almost 70 per cent of the prisoners of war captured during the Second World
War were denied the assistance of a Protecting Power for some or all of their
time in captivity.[15] Small wonder, therefore, that part of the work leading up
to the revision of the humanitarian conventions involved striving to establish
substitution procedures should the appointment of a Protecting Power meet
insurmountable obstacles. The Conference of Government Experts which met
in Geneva in April 1947 took a first step in that direction by stipulating that, in
the absence of a Protecting Power, the ICRC (or 'some other impartial humanitarian organization') could agree to transmit the notifications and information
between the belligerents as provided for in the prisoners of war convention.[16]

1200   Encouraged by this, the ICRC inserted a common article in the four draft
conventions submitted to the 17th International Conference of the Red Cross
held in Stockholm in August 1948, in which it set out a real substitution
procedure.[17] The idea was to replace a Protecting Power that could not, or no
longer, operate either by a body offering every guarantee of impartiality and
efficacy and approved by the Parties to the conflict or by a neutral State or

---

[13] Bugnion, 2003, pp. 871–872.

[14] *Ibid.* p. 872. See also Catherine Rey-Schyrr, *De Yalta à Dien Bien Phu: Histoire du Comité
international de la Croix-Rouge 1945–1955*, ICRC/Georg, Geneva, 2007, pp. 160–163.

[15] *Final Record of the Diplomatic Conference of Geneva of 1949*, Vol. II-B, p. 21 (ICRC statement).

[16] *Report of the Conference of Government Experts of 1947*, pp. 262–267 and 270–271.

[17] For further historical information, see also de La Pradelle, 1951, pp. 225–234.

a humanitarian organization such as the ICRC, appointed unilaterally by the Detaining Power if the Parties were unable to reach an agreement.

1201 Draft article 8 stated that:

The Contracting Parties may, at all times, agree to entrust to a body which offers all guarantees of impartiality and efficacy the duties incumbent on the Protecting Powers by virtue of the present Convention.

Moreover, if [protected persons] do not benefit, or cease to benefit by the activities of a Protecting Power or of the said body, the Party to the conflict in whose hands they may be, shall be under the obligation to make up for this lack of protection by inviting either a neutral State or an impartial humanitarian agency, such as the International Committee of the Red Cross, to assume in their behalf the duties devolving by virtue of the present Convention on the Protecting Powers.

Whenever the Protecting Power is named in the present Convention, such reference also designates the bodies replacing it under the terms of the present Article.[18]

1202 This draft was adopted with no substantive changes by the Stockholm Conference[19] and was then submitted to the 1949 Diplomatic Conference.[20]

1203 Like all the draft common articles, draft article 8 was submitted to the Joint Committee of the 1949 Diplomatic Conference, which entrusted the task of studying it to the Special Committee. The Special Committee devoted seven meetings to it.[21] The draft then came back before the Joint Committee before being adopted in the Conference's Plenary Assembly.[22]

1204 The discussions at the Diplomatic Conference were long and rather muddled. Although no-one was disputing the need for a substitution procedure in the absence of a Protecting Power, the delegates had divergent views about the bodies that could be called upon as substitutes, about how they should be appointed and about the scope of their mandate. Moreover, the very expression 'substitute for Protecting Powers' was used to refer to organizations that differed radically in nature and in terms of the scope of the tasks that they were to perform. Thus, while some delegations basically envisaged entrusting to the ICRC the humanitarian tasks usually assigned to Protecting Powers,[23]

---

[18] See *Draft Conventions submitted to the 1948 Stockholm Conference*, pp. 8–9, 36–37, 57 and 157. The designation of the protected persons is adapted to each Convention.

[19] *Minutes of the Legal Commission at the 1948 Diplomatic Conference*, pp. 73–79.

[20] *Draft Conventions adopted by the 1948 Stockholm Conference*, draft article 8/9/9/9, pp. 11–12, 34, 55 and 116.

[21] The 13th, 14th, 15th, 16th, 17th, 18th and 19th meetings of the Special Committee.

[22] *Final Record of the Diplomatic Conference of Geneva of 1949*, Vol. I, pp. 48, 62, 75, 114, 206, 226–227, 245–246, 299, 343–357 and 361; Vol. II-A, pp. 208–209, 222–223, 578 and 849; Vol. II-B, pp. 21–23, 60–69, 74–75, 80, 89, 110–112, 27, 92–93, 96–97, 118–119, 106, 29–30, 34, 130–131, 38–39, 158, 166, 172, 190, 346–352, 487–489 and 521–524; Vol. III, pp. 30–34, 102–103 and 182.

[23] 'M. de Alba was of the opinion that the functions of humanitarian organizations and particularly the ICRC should be extended in order to enable them to take the place of Protecting Powers as far as possible', *Final Record of the Diplomatic Conference of Geneva of 1949*, Vol. II-B, p. 22 (Mexico).

others ruled out the possibility of entrusting such a mandate to the ICRC.[24] The French delegation, for its part, suggested setting up an ad hoc international body to shoulder all the tasks of the Protecting Power, including those arising essentially from diplomatic law. France suggested that this 'High International Committee for the Protection of Humanity' would have 30 members recruited from among political, religious and scientific figures, senior judges and Nobel Peace Prize winners. The members would be elected by an assembly made up of representatives of all the States party to the Geneva Conventions. In situations where no Protecting Power had been appointed, this body would take over all the tasks normally entrusted to Protecting Powers under the Geneva Conventions.[25]

1205   In an attempt to clarify the issue, the delegation of the United Kingdom to the Stockholm Conference suggested splitting paragraph 2 of draft article 8 into three separate paragraphs.[26] This new draft was the basis for the deliberations of the Diplomatic Conference.[27] For its part, concerned that a Detaining Power would appoint as a substitute for the Protecting Power a State or international organization biased in its favour, the Soviet delegation was firmly opposed to the unilateral designation of a substitute by the Detaining Power as set forth in both the Stockholm draft and the UK amendment.[28] In the end, the Conference adopted common Article 10 (Article 11 in the Fourth Convention) by 30 votes to 8.[29] At the signing ceremony for the new Geneva Conventions, the Soviet Union and its allies at the time made a reservation to the article.[30]

1206   Article 10 bears the marks of the uncertainty and imprecision that characterized the discussions that gave rise to it.

C. The structure of Article 10

1207 Article 10 sets out the framework for the appointment and the work of the substitute for the Protecting Powers.

1208   The article provides for three substitution scenarios:

(a) the Protecting Powers are replaced by an organization offering every guarantee of impartiality and efficacy, appointed by agreement between the High Contracting Parties (paragraph 1);

---

[24] 'The role of the ICRC is totally different from that of a Protecting Power', *Final Record of the Diplomatic Conference of Geneva of 1949*, Vol. II-B, p. 22 (France); 'the Australian Government considers that the ICRC cannot serve as a substitute for the Protecting Power', *ibid.* pp. 22–23 (Australia).

[25] The French proposal is published in *ibid.* Vol. III, pp. 30–31; for the minutes of the deliberations, see *ibid.* Vol. II-B, pp. 22, 60–63, 110–112, 27, 92–93, 96–97, 118–119, 106, 34, 130–131 and 487–489; for Resolution 2 of the Diplomatic Conference, see *ibid.* Vol. I, p. 361.

[26] The UK amendment is published in *ibid.* Vol. III, pp. 31–32.

[27] *Ibid.* Vol. II-B, pp. 60–69.   [28] *Ibid.* pp. 22, 29–30, 130, 347–348, 350–351 and 352.

[29] *Ibid.* p. 352.

[30] *Ibid.* Vol. I, p. 355, and Vol. II-B, pp. 537–538. For a discussion of this reservation, see section E.

(b) if no such agreement can be reached, the Protecting Powers are replaced by a neutral State or by an organization offering every guarantee of impartiality and efficacy, appointed unilaterally by the Detaining Power (paragraph 2);

(c) if protection cannot be arranged accordingly, the Protecting Powers are replaced by a humanitarian organization such as the ICRC, appointed by the Detaining Power, or the Detaining Power accepts an offer of services from such an organization (paragraph 3).

1209   It is clear from the letter and the structure of Article 10 that these possibilities have to be explored in the order given above: when the first is exhausted by default, the second automatically applies, and when the second is exhausted the third applies.[31]

1210   While Article 10 does not detail the conditions of application of the substitution mechanisms, the deliberations of the Diplomatic Conference made those conditions quite clear. When introducing draft article 8, the ICRC expert explicitly stated that its purpose was 'to make up for the too frequent absence of a Protecting Power',[32] and most of the delegates who took the floor during the opening debate at the fifth meeting of the Joint Committee stressed this point.[33]

1211   The situations in which the substitution procedure was foreseen by the drafters to be applicable were: a large-scale conflict in which there were no longer any neutral Powers able to carry out the role of Protecting Power effectively; the disappearance of the detainees' Power of Origin, or at least of the government representing that Power (the case of Germany following its capitulation on 8 May 1945); or the ability of one of the belligerents to force the adverse Party to put an end to the work of the Protecting Power (the case of Vichy France).[34]

1212   Article 5 of Additional Protocol I has introduced further clarity with regard to the procedure for appointing Protecting Powers or their substitute.

D. Paragraph 1: Appointment of substitutes by agreement between the High Contracting Parties

1213 Article 10(1) outlines the framework for appointing, at any time, a general substitute for Protecting Powers. It does not impose any obligation on the High Contracting Parties, in the absence of a Protecting Power, to entrust an organization with performing the duties incumbent on such a Power, but it does give them the possibility to do so (see the use of 'may').

[31] The same interpretation is given in the Joint Committee's report to the Plenary Assembly of the Diplomatic Conference of 1949, *ibid.* Vol. II-B, p. 130.
[32] *Ibid.* p. 21 (ICRC statement).
[33] *Ibid.* pp. 21–23 (Australia, France, United Kingdom and USSR).
[34] *Ibid.* pp. 21–23 (Canada, France).

1214   This paragraph provides for a substitution based on the agreement of the High Contracting Parties.[35] The intention here was primarily – but not exclusively – to incorporate France's proposal that a 'High International Committee for the Protection of Humanity' be set up.

1215   In fact, however, this proposal was greeted with scepticism because of the difficulty of setting up a body fulfilling all the requirements and capable of working effectively, while made up of members from different States. The Soviet delegation also underlined the artificial nature of this High International Committee, whose members would have to be acknowledged and accepted by all States and 'would . . . be in some way outside and superior to the existing world'. When – in response to the question of where such a learned body could meet if there were no neutral States left – the French representative stated that '[i]t could meet on a piece of internationalized territory, or on several such territories in different parts of the world', it became clear that the proposal relied on mere word-play and that it was out of touch with reality.[36]

1216   At the 1949 Diplomatic Conference, the International Refugee Organization, a predecessor of UNHCR, asked to be expressly mentioned in Article 10 as an organization that could be called upon in the absence of a Protecting Power, in particular when it came to protecting refugees and stateless persons.[37] While refusing to specifically mention the International Refugee Organization, the 1949 Diplomatic Conference acknowledged that the organization perfectly matched the definition of an organization offering every guarantee of impartiality and efficacy.[38]

1217   The Conference eventually concluded that it was not mandated to create a new international organization and merely adopted a resolution that recommended looking into the possibility of setting up an international body tasked with carrying out the duties of Protecting Powers in their absence. Resolution 2 of the 1949 Diplomatic Conference, entitled 'Creation of an international body in the absence of a Protecting Power', stated:

Whereas circumstances may arise in the event of the outbreak of a future international conflict in which there will be no Protecting Power with whose cooperation and under whose scrutiny the Conventions for the Protection of Victims of War can be applied; and

[35] Although the wording of paragraph 1 leaves room for interpretation, the use of the article in the opening phrase, '*The* High Contracting Parties' (emphasis added), seems to indicate that the 1949 Diplomatic Conference foresaw a meeting or consultation of all the Contracting Parties to set up a new organization or to entrust to an existing organization the duties incumbent on the Protecting Powers under the Conventions. If the Conference had envisaged that a limited number of High Contracting Parties were entitled to set up such a body or to entrust the duties incumbent on the Protecting Powers to an existing organization, it would not have used the initial article.

[36] *Final Record of the Diplomatic Conference of Geneva of 1949*, Vol. II-B, pp. 92–93 (Denmark, USSR, France).

[37] *Ibid.* Vol. II-B, p. 80; Vol. III, pp. 32–33.   [38] *Ibid.* Vol. II-B, p. 80.

whereas [common Article 10 (Article 11 in the Fourth Convention) provides] that the High Contracting Parties may at any time agree to entrust to a body which offers all guarantees of impartiality and efficacy the duties incumbent on the Protecting Powers by virtue of the aforesaid Conventions,

the Conference recommends that consideration be given as soon as possible to the advisability of setting up an international body, the functions of which shall be, in the absence of a Protecting Power, to fulfil the duties performed by Protecting Powers in regard to the application of the Conventions for the Protection of War Victims.[39]

1218   Drawing upon this last paragraph, it was logically up to France to undertake consultations to bring its idea to fruition. However, after a few half-hearted attempts, France abandoned the project.[40] Thus, the first possibility of substitution set forth in Article 10 refers to a body that – at least so far and in terms of what the drafters of the Geneva Conventions had in mind – has not seen the light of day.

1219   Although Article 10(1) undoubtedly refers chiefly to the international body that was to be set up to replace Protecting Powers, in accordance with Resolution 2, the wording of the paragraph is not restricted solely to that body, since it refers to 'an organization which offers all guarantees of impartiality and efficacy'.[41] Given that the text of paragraph 1 does not refer to an idea which never materialized, nothing precludes the High Contracting Parties from using this paragraph in the future to create a new body which, as the wording 'organization' indicates, cannot be a neutral State. This also flows from the phrase 'at any time' used in this paragraph.

E. Paragraph 2: Unilateral appointment of a substitute by the Detaining Power

1220 Article 10(2) is the result of the fusion of the provision from the Stockholm draft and a proposal made by the United Kingdom. If in a given international armed conflict no Protecting Power is appointed or in case the appointed Protecting Power ceases its activities and cannot be replaced by another one, this

---

[39] *Ibid.* Vol. I, p. 361.
[40] For a description of the French Government's attempts to canvass support for its proposal after the 1949 Conference and an explanation of why they failed, see de La Pradelle, 1956.
[41] Although the International Red Cross and Red Crescent Movement referred to the principle of impartiality right from its foundation in 1863, this principle was only authoritatively defined in the Declaration of the Fundamental Principles of the Red Cross adopted by the 20th International Conference of the Red Cross which met in Vienna in 1965: 'Impartiality: [The International Red Cross and Red Crescent Movement] makes no distinction as to nationality, race, religious beliefs, class or political opinions. It endeavours to relieve the suffering of individuals, being guided solely by their needs, and to give priority to the most urgent cases of distress.' For further analysis of the notion of 'impartiality', see the commentary on Article 9, para. 1160. The word 'efficacy' belongs to common language and has to be interpreted according to its usual meaning.

paragraph requires the Detaining Power to ask either a neutral State or 'an organization which offers all guarantees of impartiality and efficacy'[42] to undertake
the tasks entrusted to Protecting Powers under the Geneva Conventions.

1221   It may seem surprising that the Conventions maintained the solution of
a unilateral appointment of the substitute for the Protecting Power by the
Detaining Power alone, given that the French delegation had warned the Conference about the risk of the Detaining Power appointing 'some puppet body'.[43]
But this decision is explained by the hypothetical scenarios that the substitution procedures were intended to cover, in particular the disappearance of the
Power of Origin of the protected persons or the disappearance of any government able to speak freely on behalf of that Power.

1222   To overcome the risk of abuse inherent in a unilateral appointment, the UK
delegation had envisaged entrusting the ICRC with the task of designating
the neutral State to which the Detaining Power would have recourse, but the
ICRC delegate stated that it was not up to the ICRC to do so.[44] That being
the case, and in the light of the situations that the substitution procedure
was intended to cover, the only remaining solution was to entrust this task to
the Detaining Power. The Diplomatic Conference considered that Article 10(4)
would be a safeguard against the risk of potential abuse arising from unilateral
designation.

1223   However, these precautions were not enough to reassure the USSR and its
allies, as well as the People's Republic of China and a number of other States,
which feared that the Detaining Power would designate a State or an organization biased in its favour, and that the protection afforded to victims would be
illusory.[45] Thus, when signing the Geneva Conventions, the USSR made the
following reservation:

The Union of Soviet Socialist Republics will not recognize the validity of requests
by the Detaining Power to a neutral State or to a humanitarian organization, to
undertake the functions performed by a Protecting Power, unless the consent of
the Government of the country of which the protected persons are nationals has
been obtained.[46]

---

[42] Article 10(2), itself speaking only of 'such an organization', insofar refers back to the qualities
described in paragraph 1.
[43] *Final Record of the Diplomatic Conference of Geneva of 1949*, Vol. II-B, p. 22 (France).
[44] *Ibid.* pp. 65–66.
[45] For further historical background, see Wylie, p. 11:

> While most states were willing to embrace third party assistance, Moscow's reluctance to
> countenance the presence of neutral protecting powers in the Soviet Union, especially if they
> were to enjoy far-reaching powers to act on behalf of POWs [prisoners of war], proved a major
> stumbling block when the status of protecting powers came up for discussion at the 1949
> diplomatic conference. It also became clear that Moscow was unwilling to allow states to
> nominate agencies to protect the prisoners in their custody, without obtaining the prior con-
> sent of the prisoner's own government.

[46] *Final Record of the Diplomatic Conference of Geneva of 1949*, Vol. I, p. 355. See also see Claude
Pilloud, 'Reservations to the Geneva Conventions of 1949', *International Review of the Red*

1224   The essential element of this reservation, which was formulated in identical wording by the other reserving States, is that the implementation of paragraph 3 remains subject to the consent of the Power of Origin of the protected persons. The logic underpinning this reservation was that, since it is up to the Power of Origin of the protected persons to appoint a Protecting Power, then this Power should also be involved in the appointment of its substitute.

1225   This reservation – the logic of which also applies to the third paragraph of the article – was confirmed when the Conventions were ratified. In the early 1990s, most successor States to the former USSR chose to accede to the Geneva Conventions without making any reservation to Article 10. Similarly, several other States revoked the reservation at the end of the Cold War.[47] However, at the time of writing the reservation remains in force for eight States.[48]

1226   According to the 1969 Vienna Convention on the Law of Treaties, '[a] reservation established with regard to another party … (a) modifies for the reserving State in its relations with that other party the provisions of the treaty to which the reservation relates to the extent of the reservation; and (b) modifies those provisions to the same extent for that other party in its relations with the reserving State'.[49] Therefore, with regard to all those States for which the reservation used to be, or still is, in force, the paragraph was largely ineffectual for any international armed conflict to which they might become party.

1227   But even the States which did not express a reservation with regard to Article 10 did not resort to actually using it: as with paragraph 1, there is also an absence of practice when it comes to the substitution procedure set out in paragraph 2. It is therefore the solution provided for in paragraph 3, namely replacing the Protecting Power by a humanitarian organization such as the ICRC, which should be considered in more detail.

Cross, Vol. 16, No. 180, March 1976, pp. 117–120, and Vol. 16, No. 181, April 1976, pp. 163–187, especially at 117–120.

[47]   Information taken from the ICRC's Treaties and Documents database, available on the ICRC website https://www.icrc.org/.

[48]   For details, see above 'Reservations or declarations' to Article 10.

[49]   Vienna Convention on the Law of Treaties (1969), Article 21(1)(a)–(b). See also International Law Commission, *Report of the Sixty-Third Session*, A/66/10/Add. 1, 2011, p. 454, para. 4.2.4 sub 3:

> To the extent that an established reservation modifies the legal effect of certain provisions of a treaty, the author of that reservation has rights and obligations under those provisions, as modified by the reservation, in its relations with the other parties with regard to which the reservation is established. Those other parties shall have rights and obligations under these provisions, as modified by the reservation, in their relations with the author of the reservation.

For further analysis of this 'principle of reciprocal application of reservations', see pp. 459–464.

F. Paragraph 3: Replacement of the Protecting Power by a humanitarian organization such as the ICRC

1. Discussion of the law

1228   Article 10(3) applies to situations in which none of the substitution possibilities provided for in paragraphs 1 and 2 could be implemented. If there is no Protecting Power, and if the other substitution possibilities have been exhausted, paragraph 3 foresees that the Detaining Power must turn to an impartial humanitarian organization, such as the ICRC, to assume the humanitarian tasks normally undertaken by Protecting Powers or that it must accept an offer of services from such an organization to assume those tasks. As indicated above, the reservations formulated by some States with regard to this article also apply to paragraph 3.[50]

1229   The mention of the ICRC here, as an example of a humanitarian organization, is an express recognition by the Conventions of the ICRC's qualification to assume the humanitarian tasks normally assigned to Protecting Powers. However, nothing prevents an impartial humanitarian organization other than the ICRC from making an offer of services in the sense of paragraph 3.[51] Given that the first three paragraphs of Article 10 do not contain any conditions or restrictions, the clause 'subject to the provisions of this Article' clearly refers to the conditions set out in paragraphs 4 and 5.

1230   Where paragraph 3 applies, the Detaining Power is bound to accept an offer of services from the ICRC to undertake the humanitarian tasks of a Protecting Power. That obligation emerges from the wording of the article itself ('shall accept'). This was indeed the understanding of the government representatives at the Diplomatic Conference.[52] This understanding was also confirmed by the report of the Special Committee of the Joint Committee as well as by the Joint Committee's report to the Plenary Assembly of the Diplomatic Conference:

> It was only if such protection could not be thus ensured, that the Detaining Power would have to apply to a humanitarian body such as the ICRC ... If the Detaining Power did not, on its own initiative, apply to a humanitarian body in the circumstances envisaged, any body of this kind might offer it its services, and it might not refuse them. This latter obligation laid upon the Detaining Power was offset by the condition that the body offering its services should be able to afford sufficient guarantees of its ability to perform the duties in question and to fulfil them with impartiality.[53]

1231   It was, moreover, a necessary consequence of the Diplomatic Conference's desire to ensure that protected persons were not deprived of the protection provided by the functions of a Protecting Power or, failing that, an organization

---

[50] For details, see para. 1225.
[51] For further details on the notion of impartial humanitarian organizations, see the commentary on Article 9, section C.3.b.
[52] *Final Record of the Diplomatic Conference of Geneva of 1949*, Vol. II-B, p. 29 (USSR).
[53] *Ibid.* pp. 111 and 130 (both reports have identical wording on this point).

standing in for such a Power, with the ICRC being included.[54] The ICRC is therefore positioned, alongside other humanitarian organizations, as a kind of 'goalkeeper' of humanitarian protection. If all the other substitution possibilities prove ineffectual, the Detaining Power is obliged to call upon the ICRC, or another humanitarian organization, or to accept an offer of services from such an organization to carry out the humanitarian tasks normally undertaken by the Protecting Powers.

1232   The ICRC, however, has always believed that it would be unable to offer its services unless it was certain of the agreement of the Parties to the conflict.[55] This position, which is a return to the basically consensual nature of the institution of Protecting Powers, makes the ICRC's appointment subject to the consent of the belligerents, whereas paragraph 3 was intended precisely to avoid such a state of affairs. This is in the nature of things and stems from common sense – after all, it is hard to imagine how a humanitarian organization such as the ICRC could exercise the mandate of the substitute for a Protecting Power without the agreement of the belligerents. This understanding was subsequently confirmed in Article 5(4) of Additional Protocol I.

2. Scope of the mandate of a substitute: 'humanitarian functions'

1233 As regards the scope of the tasks that could be entrusted to the ICRC or to any other humanitarian organization appointed as a substitute for Protecting Powers under the terms of this article, paragraph 3 clearly states that it is restricted to 'the humanitarian functions' performed by Protecting Powers. While the substitution scenarios set out in paragraphs 1 and 2 envisage assuming 'the duties' or 'the functions' performed under the Geneva Conventions by a Protecting Power, paragraph 3 refers to 'humanitarian functions'.

1234   No indication, definition, or list of treaty provisions is given in the Conventions, or can be found in the preparatory work, that clarifies which of the various functions entrusted to the Protecting Powers under the Geneva Conventions are 'humanitarian' and which are not.

1235   At the 1949 Diplomatic Conference, the ICRC representative repeatedly stressed that the ICRC could not be a 'genuine substitute' and could only carry out some of the tasks incumbent upon a Protecting Power.[56] The Conference acknowledged that the ICRC could not be expected to assume all the tasks of the Protecting Powers, but only those of a humanitarian nature.[57]

1236   As to what exactly the ICRC understands by the notion of 'humanitarian functions', its position on this point has changed profoundly over time. In a

---

[54] See also Dominicé, p. 428.
[55] For references on this point, see Bugnion, 2003, pp. 905–906, fn. 44.
[56] *Final Record of the Diplomatic Conference of Geneva of 1949*, Vol. II-B, pp. 61 and 63 (ICRC statement).
[57] *Ibid.* p. 130.

memorandum in 1951 the ICRC set out which tasks it was prepared to perform while acting as a substitute for a Protecting Power, and the conditions under which it would do so.[58] It ruled out most of the work of scrutinizing the implementation of the Geneva Conventions, in the belief that such an activity was incompatible with the purpose, the nature and the limits of the ICRC's work as a 'quasi-substitute'.[59] It accordingly refused to supervise the implementation of the provisions governing: the attitude to be observed by belligerents in areas of military operations; the measures belligerents should adopt regarding their own nationals and property (e.g. issuing identity documents to the armed forces or use of the emblem); and many of the provisions relating to occupied territory.[60]

1237   The ICRC also pointed out other activities that could give rise to difficulty.[61] Admittedly, after all these reservations, there was little left of the duties of a substitute for Protecting Powers for the ICRC to perform.

1238   As ICRC practice since 1951 in large measure nullified the relevance of the reservations formulated in the aforementioned memorandum, the ICRC reviewed its position and stated categorically at the 1971 Conference of Government Experts that it was prepared to undertake all the tasks incumbent on Protecting Powers under the Geneva Conventions:

> [T]he representative of the ICRC explained that the Committee had recently given careful attention to this question and that it had arrived at the conclusion that all the tasks falling to a Protecting Power under the Conventions could be considered humanitarian functions. In other words, the ICRC was ready to take upon itself all the functions envisaged for Protecting Powers in the Conventions.[62]

This position was confirmed several times both before and during the 1977–1974 Diplomatic Conference.[63] This understanding is further confirmed by Article 10(6).

3. Subsequent practice

1239 Although most armed conflicts since 1949 have been non-international, there have also been a substantial number of international armed conflicts. And yet,

---

[58] 'Memorandum sur l'activité du Comité international de la Croix-Rouge en l'absence d'une Puissance protectrice', Document D 141, 1 May 1951.

[59] *Ibid.* p. 18. The ICRC used the term 'quasi-substitute' to designate the mandate that might be entrusted to it under Article 10(3) and to emphasize the difference between that limited mandate, covering only some of the tasks incumbent on Protecting Powers, and the mandate of a genuine substitute, which would be required to perform all the tasks incumbent on Protecting Powers under the Geneva Conventions. But the term 'quasi-substitute' is not used in the Conventions, and merely confuses the issue.

[60] *Ibid.* pp. 18–20.   [61] *Ibid.* pp. 20–24.

[62] *Report of the Conference of Government Experts of 1971*, p. 109, para. 553.

[63] See *ibid.*; *Report of the Conference of Government Experts of 1972* p. 180, para. 4.71, and pp. 207–208, para. 5.46; ICRC, *Draft Additional Protocols to the Geneva Conventions of August 12, 1949: Commentary*, October 1973, p. 13; and *Official Records of the Diplomatic Conference of Geneva of 1974–1977*, Vol. 8, p. 146. See also Bugnion, 2003, pp. 884–885.

Protecting Powers were only appointed in five of those conflicts.[64] Thus, there has been no shortage of opportunities to implement the substitution procedures envisaged by the Geneva Conventions.

1240 Yet, in none of those conflicts was an organization formally appointed as a substitute for Protecting Powers. The possibility of appointing the ICRC in this capacity has been raised in a few cases only, including the Suez crisis (1956), the Irian Jaya affair (1961–62), the Vietnam War, the Arab-Israeli conflict, and the conflict between India and Pakistan.[65]

1241 However, since no Protecting Powers have been appointed in most conflicts since 1949, the ICRC has progressively extended the scope of its activities and assumed more and more of the duties normally assigned to them. As discussed below, this has been done on the basis of its right of humanitarian initiative (see para. 1258).

G. Paragraph 4: Assurances required from neutral Powers or humanitarian organizations acting as substitutes

1242 Article 10(4) is intended to prevent any abuses that could arise from the unilateral appointment of a substitute for the Protecting Power by the Detaining Power (as foreseen in paragraphs 2 and 3). This provision has its origins in the draft put forward by the United Kingdom during the 1949 Diplomatic Conference.[66] It imposes a twofold obligation on the neutral State or the organization mandated by the Detaining Power.

1243 First, the substitute unilaterally designated by the Detaining Power must be mindful of its responsibility to the Power of Origin of the captives. Second, the substitute must provide sufficient assurances that it is able to assume the tasks being entrusted to it and to discharge them impartially.

1244 It is, however, by no means certain that these safeguards will prevent the risk – mentioned by the French representative during the opening debate – of the Detaining Power appointing 'some puppet body'. Ultimately, it is the State or organization in question that is subject to the twofold obligation set out in paragraph 4, and not the Detaining Power appointing it.

1245 However, if the neutral State or the organization appointed wishes to carry out its mission in good faith, paragraph 4 is extremely useful because it can be invoked to defend the substitute's independence against any attempts by the Detaining Power to interfere with its work.

1246 As to the question of who is to decide whether the conditions of paragraph 4 are fulfilled, one delegation during the 1949 Diplomatic Conference stated that 'this decision should be taken by the Powers concerned, i.e. the Detaining

---

[64] For details of these five conflicts, see the commentary on Article 8, para. 1115.
[65] For further analysis, see Bugnion, 2003, pp. 889–894.
[66] *Final Record of the Diplomatic Conference of Geneva of 1949*, Vol. III, pp. 31–32.

Power and the Power to which the person to be protected belonged, if such existed'.[67]

H. Paragraph 5: The prohibition of derogations

1247 Article 10(5) provides another safeguard against abuse with regard to the unilateral appointment of a substitute. It provides that no derogation may be made by special agreements from the requirements of Article 10 to qualify as a substitute.

1248   This paragraph originates in a proposal put forward by France during the 1949 Diplomatic Conference. It is intended to prevent the recurrence of a situation that arose during the Second World War.[68] Through an agreement signed on 16 November 1940, the Reich Government forced Vichy France to put an end to the protection of French prisoners of war by the Protecting Power appointed at the outbreak of the war – the United States – and to accept instead a pseudo national monitoring mechanism in the form of a French committee headed by Ambassador Scapini.[69] Given the dependence of the Vichy regime on the Reich Government, this committee was powerless to prevent violations of the 1929 Geneva Convention on Prisoners of War, in particular the changing of prisoners of war into civilian workers so that they could be put to work in the Reich's war industries.

1249   This historical background explains why the wording refers to a special agreement 'between Powers one of which is restricted, even temporarily, in its freedom to negotiate with the other Power or its allies by reason of military events, more particularly where the whole, or a substantial part, of the territory of the said Power is occupied'. The restriction in the freedom to negotiate may be particularly evident in the case of occupation. However, on the basis of the principle of non-derogation by way of the special agreements enshrined in common Article 6 (Article 7 in the Fourth Convention), the prohibition would apply regardless of whether such a specific situation would arise.

I. Paragraph 6: Equivalence of rights and responsibilities of Protecting Powers and their substitutes

1250 Article 10(6) deals with both the rights and the duties of the substitute for the Protecting Power. This provision has its origins in the Stockholm draft. There should be no problems of interpretation regarding the prerogatives and tasks of a substitute designated on the basis of Article 10(1) and (2), since they are exactly the same as those of the Protecting Power itself. The wording of

---

[67] *Ibid.* Vol. II-B, p. 69.   [68] *Ibid.* Vol. III, p. 31.
[69] Protocol of 16 November 1940 between Germany and Vichy France, Berlin, 16 November 1940, quoted by Georges Scapini, *Mission sans gloire*, Morgan, Paris, 1960, pp. 36–37.

paragraph 6 therefore means that the rights and responsibilities of the Protecting Power and its substitute appointed in accordance with paragraphs 1 and 2 of the article are identical.[70]

1251   The issue becomes more complex in relation to the prerogatives and tasks of the ICRC or another organization appointed on the basis of paragraph 3. When such an organization is designated as substitute accordingly, it is tasked with assuming 'the humanitarian functions' performed by Protecting Powers. For a substantive discussion, including on the evolution of the ICRC's position in this regard, which has rendered this distinction irrelevant, see section J.

J. Developments since 1949

1252 Since 1949, Article 10 has evolved in much the same way as Article 8. Going by the use of the word 'shall' in paragraphs 2 and 3, it could be concluded that the appointment of a substitute for Protecting Powers is not an option for the Parties to a conflict but an obligation. In other words, whenever an international armed conflict breaks out, and no Protecting Power or substitute in the sense of paragraph 1 has been appointed, the Parties to the conflict are obliged to appoint a substitute of the Protecting Powers on the basis of either paragraph 2 or paragraph 3. It is clear that, in 1949, this was indeed the intention of the drafters.

1253   However, since 1949 it appears that the interpretation of Article 10 as being compulsory is no longer in line with States' current understanding of this provision, nor with the ICRC's operational practice. Substitutes for the Protecting Powers have not been formally appointed when they should have been in accordance with the letter of the Conventions. Thus, given the absence of any protest, it seems that in the view of most States the failure to appoint a Protecting Power in each international armed conflict is not a violation of the High Contracting Parties' treaty obligations: as with Article 8, the application of Article 10 appears to have been interpreted as being optional. The absence of practice has not been matched, however, by any indication that the High Contracting Parties would consider that Article 10 has fallen into desuetude.[71]

1254   It is possible to identify three – very different – reasons for this development. First, the article is overly complicated and sets out multiple substitution options. Yet, the starting point was a very simple idea drawn from past practice: if no Protecting Power was appointed, allow a humanitarian organization such as the ICRC to carry out some of the tasks normally entrusted to Protecting Powers. Unfortunately, a misconception overshadowed all the deliberations on

---

[70] For a summary of the tasks entrusted to Protecting Powers under the 1949 Geneva Conventions, see the commentary on Article 8, section E.
[71] See also Kolb, pp. 558–559.

this matter: that the greater the number of organizations empowered to assume this role, the more the Parties to a conflict would be prepared to accept the work of a substitute. As a result, other proposals came to be tagged on to the original idea. This was particularly the case for France's proposal to set up a High International Committee for the Protection of Humanity, which actually aimed to replace the Protecting Powers with an international body responsible for overseeing the implementation of the Geneva Conventions. Multiplying the possibilities of substitution meant more uncertainties, sidetracks and interpretation difficulties. Weighed down by all this baggage, the proposed body never materialized.

1255   Second, the same political difficulties that all too often prevented the appointment of a Protecting Power also hindered the appointment of a substitute body.[72] Ultimately, this is what led to the failure of the substitution procedures set out in Article 10: when it would have been possible to appoint a substitute it was not necessary, because then there was no obstacle to appointing Protecting Powers; and when it was necessary, it was not possible, because the obstacles to the appointment of Protecting Powers also stood in the way of the appointment of a substitute.

1256   Third, it is undeniable that, on the basis of its right of humanitarian initiative as enshrined in the Geneva Conventions, the ICRC has expanded the scope of its activities tremendously since 1949. This development has occurred to such an extent that the ICRC already performs many – and in some situations most – of the tasks normally entrusted to Protecting Powers. When there is no Protecting Power, therefore, States have little motivation to seek a substitute organization.

1257   Both constructs are distinct: the possibility for the ICRC or other humanitarian organization to act as a substitute for the Protecting Power remains separate from the right of an impartial humanitarian organization such as the ICRC to offer its services on the basis of what is frequently referred to as the right of humanitarian initiative.[73] Thus, the ICRC retains its right of humanitarian initiative independently of whether and when, in a given international armed conflict, Protecting Powers or their substitutes have formally been appointed.

1258   In general, the ICRC prefers to act on the basis of the right of humanitarian initiative conferred on it by the Geneva Conventions and their Additional Protocols. Thus, instead of acting as a substitute of the Protecting Power, i.e. representing the interests of a particular Party to an international armed

---

[72] For an analysis of these difficulties, see the commentary on Article 8, paras 1117–1118.

[73] As to the legal basis of the ICRC's right of humanitarian initiative, see in particular common Article 3(2), common Article 9 (Article 10 in the Fourth Convention), and Article 81 of Additional Protocol I. See also Article 5(3) of the 1986 Statutes of the International Red Cross and Red Crescent Movement.

conflict on the basis of Article 10, the ICRC prefers to work on the basis of its mandate to protect and assist all persons affected by an armed conflict.[74]

Select bibliography

Abi-Saab, Georges, 'Le renforcement du système d'application des règles du droit humanitaire', *Revue de droit pénal militaire et de droit de la guerre*, Vol. XII, No. 2, 1973, pp. 223–235.

– 'Les mécanismes de mise en œuvre du droit humanitaire', *Revue générale de droit international public*, Vol. 82, No. 1, 1978, pp. 103–129.

– 'The Implementation of Humanitarian Law', in Antonio Cassese (ed.), *The New Humanitarian Law of Armed Conflict*, Vol. I, Editoriale scientifica, Naples, 1979, pp. 310–346.

Bugnion, François, 'Le droit humanitaire applicable aux conflits armés internationaux, Le problème du contrôle', *Annales d'études internationales*, Vol. 8, 1977, pp. 29–61.

– *The International Committee of the Red Cross and the Protection of War Victims*, ICRC/Macmillan, Oxford, 2003, pp. 845–910.

de La Pradelle, Paul, *La Conférence diplomatique et les nouvelles Conventions de Genève du 12 août 1949*, Les Éditions internationales, Paris, 1951, pp. 221–243.

– 'Le contrôle de l'application des conventions humanitaires en cas de conflit armé', *Annuaire français de droit international*, Vol. II, 1956, pp. 343–352.

Domb, Fania, 'Supervision of the Observance of International Humanitarian Law', *Israel Yearbook on Human Rights*, Vol. 8, 1978, pp. 178–221.

Dominicé, Christian, 'The implementation of humanitarian law', in Karel Vasak (ed.), *The International Dimensions of Human Rights*, Vol. II, UNESCO, Paris, 1982, pp. 427–447.

Draper, Gerald I.A.D., 'The implementation of international law in armed conflicts', *International Affairs* (London), Vol. 48, 1972, pp. 46–59.

– 'The implementation and enforcement of the Geneva Conventions of 1949 and of the Two Additional Protocols of 1978' (sic), *Collected Courses of the Hague Academy of International Law*, Vol. 164, 1979, No. III, pp. 1–54.

Forsythe, David P., 'Who Guards the Guardians, Third Parties and the Law of Armed Conflicts', *American Journal of International Law*, Vol. 70, No. 1, 1976, pp. 41–61.

Gasser, Hans-Peter, 'Scrutiny', *Australian Year Book of International Law*, Vol. 9, 1985, pp. 345–358.

Guggenheim, Paul, *Traité de droit international public*, Vol. II, Georg & Cie, Geneva, 1953, pp. 332–337.

---

[74] See also Marco Sassòli, Antoine A. Bouvier and Anne Quintin, *How Does Law Protect in War?*, Vol. I, 3rd edition, ICRC, Geneva, 2011, p. 366: 'The ICRC, for its part, has no interest in acting as a substitute Protecting Power, as it can fulfil most of the latter's functions in its own right, without giving the impression that it represents only one State and not all the victims.'; and Kolb, pp. 557–558: 'In all [cases in which no Protecting Power has been appointed] the ICRC has acted as a sort of *de facto* substitute for a Protecting Power. However, it has performed the functions in its own name, and according to its own mandate, rather than stressing that it acted as the representative of a particular state.'

Janner, Antonino, *La Puissance protectrice en droit international d'après les expériences faites par la Suisse pendant la seconde guerre mondiale*, Verlag von Helbing und Lichtenhahn, Basel, 1948 (reprint 1972).

Kolb, Robert, 'Protecting Powers', in Andrew Clapham, Paola Gaeta and Marco Sassòli (eds), *The 1949 Geneva Conventions: A Commentary*, Oxford University Press, 2015, pp. 549–560.

Levie, Howard S., 'Prisoners of War and the Protecting Power', *American Journal of International Law*, Vol. 55, No. 2, 1961, pp. 374–397.

– *Prisoners of War in International Armed Conflict*, International Law Studies, U.S. Naval War College, Vol. 59, 1977, pp. 255–293.

Patrnogic, Jovica, 'Internationalisation du contrôle des Conventions humanitaires en cas de conflit armé', *Annales de droit international médical*, No. 21, April 1971, pp. 33–51.

– 'Implementation of the Geneva Conventions of 1949 and Additional Protocols of 1977', *European Seminar on Humanitarian Law* (Jagellonean University, Krakow, 1979), Polish Red Cross/ICRC, Warsaw/Geneva, 1979, pp. 87–100.

Peirce, Captain George A.B., 'Humanitarian Protection for the Victims of War: The System of Protecting Powers and the Role of the ICRC', *Military Law Review*, Vol. 90, 1980, pp. 89–162.

Pictet, Jean S., 'Les Conventions de Genève de 1949: Aperçu des règles d'application', *The Military Law and the Law of War Review*, Vol. XII, No. 2, 1973, pp. 59–99.

– *Humanitarian Law and the Protection of War Victims*, A.W. Sijthoff, Leiden, 1975, pp. 61–67.

Sandoz, Yves, 'Implementing international humanitarian law', *International Dimensions of Humanitarian Law*, Henry Dunant Institute, Geneva, 1988, pp. 259–282.

Sassòli, Marco, 'Mise en œuvre du droit international humanitaire et du droit international des droits de l'homme : Une comparaison', *Annuaire suisse de droit international*, Vol. XLIII, 1987, pp. 24–61.

Siordet, Frédéric, *The Geneva Conventions of 1949: The Question of Scrutiny*, ICRC, Geneva, 1953.

Takemoto, Masayuki, 'The scrutiny system under international humanitarian law: An analysis of recent attempts to reinforce the role of protecting powers in armed conflicts', *Japanese Annual of International Law*, Vol. 19, 1975, pp. 1–23.

Vourkoutiotis, Vasilis, 'What the Angels Saw: Red Cross and Protecting Power Visits to Anglo-American POWs, 1939–45', *Journal of Contemporary History*, Vol. 40, No. 4, 2005, pp. 689–706.

Wylie, Neville, 'Protecting powers in a changing world', *Politorbis*, No. 40, 2006, pp. 6–14.

CONCILIATION PROCEDURE

❖ Text of the provision*

(1) In cases where they deem it advisable in the interest of protected persons, particularly in cases of disagreement between the Parties to the conflict as to the application or interpretation of the provisions of the present Convention, the Protecting Powers shall lend their good offices with a view to settling the disagreement.

(2) For this purpose, each of the Protecting Powers may, either at the invitation of one Party or on its own initiative, propose to the Parties to the conflict a meeting of their representatives, in particular of the authorities responsible for the wounded and sick, members of medical personnel and chaplains, possibly on neutral territory suitably chosen. The Parties to the conflict shall be bound to give effect to the proposals made to them for this purpose. The Protecting Powers may, if necessary, propose for approval by the Parties to the conflict, a person belonging to a neutral Power or delegated by the International Committee of the Red Cross, who shall be invited to take part in such a meeting.

❖ Reservations or declarations

None[1]

Contents

---

* Paragraph numbers have been added for ease of reference.
[1] At signature, Hungary entered the following reservation: 'The Government of the Hungarian People's Republic cannot approve the provisions of Article 11 of the Wounded and Sick, Maritime Warfare and Prisoners of War Conventions and of Article 12 of the Civilians Convention, according to which the competence of the Protecting Power extends to the interpretation of the Convention.' (see United Nations *Treaty Series*, Vol. 75, 1950, p. 436). The reservation was confirmed at the time of ratification (see United Nations *Treaty Series*, Vol. 198, 1954, pp. 384, 386, 388 and 390) but withdrawn in 2000 (see United Nations *Treaty Series*, Vol. 2117, 2003, pp. 301, 303, 305 and 307).

449

A. Introduction

1259 Article 11 lays down the legal basis for the establishment of a 'conciliation procedure' in the interest of protected persons. The notion of 'conciliation' appears
in the marginal title of the provision, which bears no official status,[2] but is
not used in the text itself. This characterization of the procedure, however, has
been widely used since the adoption of the Convention and has not raised major
controversy.[3] The same provision appears, in almost identical terms, in all four
of the 1949 Geneva Conventions.[4]

1260   In international law, conciliation was originally conceived as a method of
peaceful settlement of disputes between States and has been recognized as such
in numerous international treaties and other documents. In this context, conciliation usually involves powers of investigation and active participation in
finding a solution to the dispute that is acceptable to all Parties to the procedure. The outcome of the procedure is not binding, the Parties remaining free
to accept or not the terms of the settlement.[5]

---

[2] The marginal titles were drafted by the depositary following the adoption of the Convention.
[3] During the drafting process of Article 11, one delegation argued, however, that the characteriza-
    tion of the procedure as a 'conciliation' was not appropriate; see *Final Record of the Diplomatic
    Conference of Geneva of 1949*, Vol. II-B, p. 23; see also Vol. II-A, p. 34.
[4] See Second Convention, Article 11; Third Convention, Article 11; and Fourth Convention, Arti-
    cle 12. A very similar procedure also exists in Article 22 of the 1954 Hague Convention for the
    Protection of Cultural Property, as well as in Article 35 of its Second Protocol of 1999.
[5] The Institut de Droit International defines conciliation as 'a method for the settlement of inter-
    national disputes of any nature according to which a Commission set up by the Parties, either
    on a permanent basis or on an ad hoc basis to deal with a dispute, proceeds to the impartial
    examination of the dispute and attempts to define the terms of a settlement susceptible of being
    accepted by them, or of affording the Parties, with a view to its settlement, such aid as they may
    have requested' (Institut de Droit International, International Conciliation, Session of Salzburg,

1261   In the Geneva Conventions, however, the notion of conciliation entails a different procedure. First, it does not necessarily suppose a disagreement between the Parties involved, but may be used, more generally, each time that it is 'advisable in the interest of protected persons'. Second, the procedural steps foreseen in Article 11 are not exactly the same as those traditionally foreseen in the context of the peaceful settlement of international disputes. The purpose of Article 11 is to determine the conditions for establishing a dialogue between Parties to an international armed conflict. Paragraph 1 invites Protecting Powers to facilitate such a dialogue through their 'good offices'. Paragraph 2 describes one possible way to proceed, namely the organization of a meeting of the representatives of the Parties to the conflict. Article 11 does not, however, suppose the creation of a panel of experts tasked with examining the dispute and proposing the terms of a settlement, as would be the case under the traditional conciliation procedure. In other words, the mechanisms established under Article 11 may involve less formal diplomatic means, as indicated by the notion of 'good offices' in paragraph 1. Thus, despite its marginal title, Article 11 provides for a mechanism that is not identical to the 'conciliation procedure' as defined in the framework of international dispute settlement.

1262   Article 11 is part of the compliance mechanisms elaborated in the four Geneva Conventions of 1949, and subsequently in Additional Protocol I of 1977.[6] In the First Convention it appears under the heading 'General Provisions'. It must be read in relation to Articles 8 and 10 of the Convention,[7] as well as to Article 5 of Protocol I where applicable. While these three provisions define in general terms the role of the Protecting Powers and their substitutes,[8] Article 11 provides some specific detail, focusing on the 'good offices' function.

1263   Article 11 is also related to Article 6, which encourages the High Contracting Parties to conclude 'special agreements for all matters concerning which they may deem it suitable to make separate provision'. The procedure in Article 11 is a tool that may be used to facilitate the conclusion of such agreements between the Parties to the conflict on any question of application or interpretation of the Convention.

1961, Article 1 (official translation of the authoritative French text). For a presentation of the conciliation procedure as a method of peaceful settlement of international disputes, see Malanczuk, pp. 279–281, and Cot.

[6]   This system foresees a certain number of mechanisms, such as the Protecting Powers and their substitutes (common Article 8 and 10 (Article 9 and 11 in the Fourth Convention) and Additional Protocol I, Article 5), the ICRC or any other impartial humanitarian organization (common Article 9 (Article 10 in the Fourth Convention)), the enquiry procedure (First Convention, Article 52; Second Convention, Article 53; Third Convention, Article 132; and Fourth Convention, Article 149) and the International Humanitarian Fact-Finding Commission (Additional Protocol I, Article 90).

[7]   Respectively, Second Convention, Articles 8 and 10; Third Convention, Articles 8 and 10; and Fourth Convention, Articles 9 and 11.

[8]   See Article 8(1): 'The present Convention shall be applied with the cooperation and under the scrutiny of the Protecting Powers whose duty it is to safeguard the interests of the Parties to the conflict.'

1264   Neither common Article 3 nor Additional Protocol II make any mention of conciliation methods to address humanitarian issues in non-international armed conflicts. This does not mean, however, that mechanisms similar to those described in Article 11 may not be used in such situations. Common Article 3(3) encourages the Parties to the conflict to 'endeavour to bring into force, by means of special agreements, all or part of the other provisions of the present Convention'. This may include the establishment of a conciliation procedure. In addition, the law governing non-international armed conflicts leaves room for conciliation efforts by actors other than the Protecting Powers or their substitutes. Common Article 3(2) provides that the ICRC, or any other impartial humanitarian body, 'may offer its services to the Parties to the conflict'. This may include lending good offices and facilitating the organization of a meeting of the representatives of the Parties to the conflict, following the model of Article 11.

1265   In practice, the 'conciliation procedure', as established under Article 11, has never been used. The main reason for this is that the system of Protecting Powers has almost never been activated since 1949. At the same time, conciliation efforts to improve the situation of victims of armed conflicts were made possible under other mechanisms.

B. Historical background[9]

1266 Participants of the Diplomatic Conference of 1949 examined the conciliation procedure within the framework of a more general discussion on the settlement of disputes arising between Parties to international armed conflicts.[10] As summarized by the Rapporteur of the Joint Committee charged with the study of the articles common to all four Conventions, this debate sought to address two main questions:

> [I]n the event of a violation of a Convention, how is the injured State to obtain justice? In cases of differences of opinion as to the interpretation of the text, how can the law be declared, and how can a dispute with regard to the interpretation of one of our Conventions be settled by arbitration while the two parties are at war with one another?[11]

1267   The delegations to the Diplomatic Conference studied three proposals foreseeing distinct procedures, namely 'good offices and consultation', 'enquiry and

---

[9] For a detailed account of the drafting process of Article 11, see Paul de La Pradelle, *La Conférence diplomatique et les nouvelles Conventions de Genève du 12 août 1949*, Les Éditions internationales, Paris, 1951, pp. 265–286.

[10] See Sixth Report drawn up by the Special Committee of the Joint Committee, *Final Record of the Diplomatic Conference of Geneva of 1949*, Vol. II-B, pp. 119–120, at 119, and Report drawn up by the Joint Committee and presented to the Plenary Assembly, *ibid.* pp. 128–133, at 131.

[11] See Report drawn up by the Joint Committee and presented to the Plenary Assembly, *ibid.* p. 131.

conciliation' and 'judicial settlement'.[12] The debate resulted in the adoption of Article 11, which creates a 'conciliation procedure' including 'good offices', and Article 52, which institutes the 'enquiry procedure'.[13] The draft provision on judicial settlement was not retained in the Convention; it was adopted instead as a resolution of the Diplomatic Conference.[14]

1268   The 'conciliation procedure' in the context of the 1949 Geneva Conventions is largely inspired by Article 87 of the 1929 Geneva Convention on Prisoners of War. This provision required the Protecting Powers to lend their good offices to the belligerents in settling disputes that might occur between them regarding the application of the Convention. For this purpose, Article 87 foresaw the possibility of holding a 'conference' of representatives of the belligerents. In its new version of 1949, the procedure was modified, taking elements from Article 83 of the 1929 Convention, which encouraged the belligerents to authorize 'meetings of representatives of the respective authorities charged with the administration of prisoners of war' with a view to ensuring the application of the Convention and to facilitating the conclusion of 'special conventions'. Unlike Article 87, Article 83 did not introduce a procedure for the settlement of disputes but aimed to foster dialogue between the belligerents, whenever necessary, to promote implementation of and respect for the Convention. Article 11 of the 1949 Convention is thus based on a merger of two originally separate and distinct procedures.

1269   Article 83 of the 1929 Convention was also a source for the drafting of Article 6 of the 1949 Convention on 'special agreements'. Article 83 explicitly provides that meetings of representatives of the Parties to the conflict may be authorized with a view to facilitating the conclusion of such agreements (or 'special conventions' in the wording of the 1929 Convention). The historical context thus highlights the connection between Article 11 and Article 6 of the 1949 Convention.

1270   There was little discussion on draft article 11 during the 1949 Diplomatic Conference. The provision was adopted by the participants almost without alteration. The main issue of contention during the debates related to the role that the new provision would confer on the Protecting Powers.[15]

---

[12] See Sixth Report drawn up by the Special Committee of the Joint Committee, *ibid.* pp. 119–120.

[13] For further details, see the commentary on Article 52.

[14] Resolution 1 reads: 'The Conference recommends that, in the case of a dispute relating to the interpretation or application of the present Conventions which cannot be settled by other means, the High Contracting Parties concerned endeavour to agree between themselves to refer such dispute to the International Court of Justice'; see *Final Record of the Diplomatic Conference of Geneva of 1949*, Vol. I, p. 361. Unlike the provisions inserted in the Convention, the resolution has no legally binding effect. However, it constitutes a pressing recommendation addressed to the States Parties. For a discussion leading to this resolution, see *ibid.* Vol. II-B, pp. 365–371. See also Paul de La Pradelle, *La Conférence diplomatique et les nouvelles Conventions de Genève du 12 août 1949*, Les Éditions internationales, Paris, 1951, pp. 277–284.

[15] See section D.1.

C. Overview

1271   Article 11 proposes two ways of facilitating dialogue between the Parties to an international armed conflict in the interest of protected persons. Paragraph 1 focuses on informal diplomacy by allowing the Protecting Powers to lend their 'good offices'. Paragraph 2 proposes a more formal approach through the organization of a meeting of the representatives of the Parties to the conflict. The Protecting Powers are entitled to propose such a meeting, either at the invitation of one Party or on their own initiative. They may also suggest that third parties, such as a neutral Power or the ICRC, be invited to participate. The Protecting Powers are thus given a central role in ensuring the effective use of the conciliation procedure.

1272   Article 11 is a particular illustration of the role of Protecting Powers established by Article 8.[16] Article 8(1) provides in general terms that the Convention 'shall be applied with the cooperation and under the scrutiny of the Protecting Powers whose duty it is to safeguard the interests of the Parties to the conflict'.[17] The conciliation procedure is one of several tools available to these Powers in fulfilling this task.

1273   In initiating the procedure, each of the Protecting Powers concerned may act individually. The use of the plural for 'Protecting Powers' in Article 11(1) does not mean that they must act in concert. While the Geneva Conventions attribute responsibilities to the 'Protecting Powers' in a number of other provisions, this does not necessarily suppose common action.[18] While, for instance, Article 8(1) provides that the Convention 'shall be applied with the cooperation and under the scrutiny of the Protecting Powers', in the plural, practice has shown that States usually exercise such supervisory functions individually.[19] In addition, Article 11(2) explicitly provides that 'each of the Protecting Powers' may propose a meeting of the Parties to the conflict, thus confirming that this procedure may be initiated unilaterally. Of course, it may be preferable to secure the support of all the Protecting Powers concerned in order to ensure the successful outcome of the conciliation.[20]

---

[16] The compatibility of the two articles was challenged during the drafting process, the delegate of the USSR arguing that these provisions were contradictory. As stressed by the Rapporteur of the Joint Committee, it was considered, however, that the wording of draft article 8 was general enough to include conciliation functions by the Protecting Powers. See *Final Record of the Diplomatic Conference of Geneva of 1949*, Vol. II-B, p. 354 (Colonel Du Pasquier (Switzerland), Rapporteur of the Joint Committee).

[17] See the commentary on Article 8, section E as well as Additional Protocol I, Article 5(2). See further Bugnion, pp. 845–910; Coulibaly, pp. 69–78; and, in general, Heintze.

[18] See Pictet (ed.), *Commentary on the First Geneva Convention*, ICRC, 1952, pp. 86–103. Similarly, visits to prisoners of war or civilian internees by 'representatives or delegates of the Protecting Powers', as foreseen in Article 126 of the Third Convention and Article 143 of the Fourth Convention, respectively, do not suppose the participation of all the Protecting Powers designated in relation to the conflict concerned.

[19] See the commentary on Article 8.

[20] See Pictet (ed.), *Commentary on the First Geneva Convention*, ICRC, 1952, p. 127.

D. Paragraph 1: Good offices of the Protecting Powers

1. *Initiating a conciliation procedure*

1274 Article 11(1) leaves the Protecting Powers a wide margin of discretion in determining when to initiate a conciliation procedure. It allows them to initiate the procedure whenever 'they deem it advisable in the interest of protected persons'.

1275 This means, first, that the Protecting Powers may decide, according to their own assessment of the situation, whether the interest of protected persons is indeed at stake. The answer to this question should be positive at least each time that the conciliation procedure is considered as a means to ensure better respect for the provisions of the Convention. The Conventions constitute binding obligations determining the minimum level of protection and assistance that Parties to the Convention undertook to ensure for protected persons. However, the use of the conciliation procedure need not necessarily be limited to instances of non-observance of the Convention. The word 'interest' suggests that this procedure may be used to resolve any issue affecting protected persons. It may even be used to address humanitarian issues that are not necessarily covered by the Convention. This interpretation is in line with Article 6(1), which confirms that the High Contracting Parties may conclude special agreements 'for all matters' that in their view require further regulation.

1276 Second, even when action is needed in the interest of protected persons, the Protecting Powers must also determine whether the conciliation procedure is indeed the most appropriate mechanism to address the problem. This may not be the case in practice. Depending on the circumstances, it may be that the ICRC or another impartial humanitarian organization is in a better position to meet the needs of protected persons.[21]

1277 The mechanism of Article 11 aims to safeguard the interest of 'protected persons'. This wording is first a reference to Article 13, which determines which individuals, once wounded or sick, are covered by the provisions of the Convention: they include members of the armed forces and other categories of persons who, while not being members of the armed forces, have the right to prisoner-of-war status upon capture.[22] In addition, the object and purpose of Article 11 suggests that the conciliation procedure may be used in the interest of groups other than those explicitly mentioned in Article 13. This procedure is a tool to ensure better implementation of and respect for the Convention as such, and should not be limited to provisions applying to the groups categorized as

---

[21] See Article 9. Another option under Additional Protocol I is the International Humanitarian Fact-Finding Commission, which is empowered to make enquiries into alleged serious violations of the Geneva Conventions of 1949 or their Additional Protocol I of 1977 and to 'facilitate, through its good offices' an attitude of respect for these instruments; see Additional Protocol I, Article 90.

[22] For further details, see the commentary on Article 13.

'protected persons' under the non-official, marginal title of Article 13. This means that the procedure does not apply only to the 'wounded and sick' but extends to all other individuals enjoying protection under the Convention, including medical and religious personnel.[23] Article 11(2) confirms in this regard that conciliation meetings may involve the participation of authorities responsible not only for the 'wounded and sick' but also for 'members of medical personnel and chaplains'. For the same reason, the conciliation procedure should also apply to issues related to the treatment of the dead.[24]

1278   A tension seemingly arises when comparing Articles 11 and 8, which provide, respectively, that the Protecting Powers must act 'in the interest of protected persons', on the one hand, and 'safeguard the interests of the Parties to the conflict', on the other hand. These provisions are not contradictory, however. The fact that a Protecting Power may represent one of the Parties to the conflict does not mean that it may act against the interest of any person protected under the Convention. Article 8 makes clear that the overarching objective of the system of Protecting Powers is to ensure the proper application of the Convention.[25] This objective would obviously not be achieved if activities undertaken on the basis of Article 8 would be detrimental to protected persons or would lead to disregard for the provisions of the Conventions. The general tendency of the 1949 Conventions is indeed to entrust Protecting Powers with rights and duties considerably more extensive than those which would devolve upon them as mere agents of the Power whose interest they safeguard, as well as according them a certain power of initiative. They thus become, as it were, the agents or trustees of all the High Contracting Parties and act in such cases solely according to their own consciences.

2. Types of situation benefiting from a conciliation procedure

1279   Various types of situation may benefit from conciliation efforts. Article 11 is flexible enough to adapt in practice to different needs and circumstances. While the 1929 Geneva Convention on Prisoners of War restricted the good offices of the Protecting Powers to 'dispute[s] between the belligerents',[26] Article 11 extends such possibility to all cases where the Protecting Powers 'deem it advisable in the interest of protected persons'. The occurrence of a dispute is therefore no longer a condition for resorting to this procedure. While paragraph 1 refers to the possibility of 'a disagreement between the Parties to

---

[23] See, especially, Articles 24–27. In this sense, see Pictet (ed.), *Commentary on the First Geneva Convention*, ICRC, 1952, p. 371.

[24] See Article 17.

[25] The first sentence of Article 8(1) reads: 'The present Convention shall be applied with the cooperation and under the scrutiny of the Protecting Powers whose duty it is to safeguard the interests of the Parties to the conflict'.

[26] Geneva Convention on Prisoners of War (1929), Article 87(1).

the conflict', it does so as a specific illustration of a broader category of situations in which the procedure may apply. It clearly states that the conciliation procedure may be used 'in particular', but not exclusively, in case of such disagreement. The reason for this change is that Article 11, as explained before, merges two distinct procedures, which were originally inserted in different sections of the 1929 Convention, namely Article 83 (Application of the Convention) and Article 87 (Settlement of disputes). Therefore, while the conciliation procedure in the 1949 Convention may seek to reconcile divergent views between opposing Parties regarding the application or interpretation of the Convention, this need not necessarily be the case.

1280   The mechanism provided for in Article 11 may be used, for instance, to bring humanitarian issues to the attention of certain authorities, to facilitate dialogue between these authorities, and to propose ways to improve the situation of protected persons. The Convention itself foresees a number of situations in which the intervention of a third party or, more particularly, a Protecting Power may help to foster discussion and the conclusion of arrangements between Parties to armed conflicts, even in the absence of a disagreement. Article 23(3), for instance, invites the Protecting Powers (and the ICRC) to 'lend their good offices' to facilitate the institution and recognition of hospital zones and localities. The conciliation procedure may also be used to help the Parties to the conflict conclude, for example, arrangements for the search and evacuation of the wounded and sick from the battlefield or besieged areas, for the search and collection of the dead, or for relieving or returning retained medical or religious personnel.[27]

1281   Another innovation introduced in 1949 is the possibility, not provided for in Article 87 of the 1929 Convention, to use the conciliation procedure in case of disagreement on the 'interpretation' and not just the 'application' of the provisions of the Convention. In some situations, the interest of protected persons may indeed require that Parties to the conflict seek a common understanding of some of the provisions. This innovation was challenged during the drafting process of Article 11. One delegation argued that the conciliation procedure would 'make the Protecting Powers responsible for functions which are not within their competence, namely the participation in the interpretation of the stipulations of the Convention, and in the solution of differences which may arise between the Parties to the conflict'.[28] It therefore recommended that the procedure be limited to issues related to the 'application' of the Convention and not refer to the 'interpretation' of the Convention or to the settlement

---

[27] See Articles 15(2)–(3), 28(3) and 31(2). Other provisions foreseeing agreements between the Parties to the conflict to extend or implement protections under the First Convention include Articles 6, 36(2), 37(3) and 52.

[28] See *Final Record of the Diplomatic Conference of Geneva of 1949*, Vol. II-B, p. 353 (USSR). See also the reservation entered by Hungary upon signature of the 1949 Geneva Conventions (fn. 1).

of disagreements.[29] The Diplomatic Conference did not endorse these views, however. It was argued during the debate that the new wording would not create additional responsibilities for the Protecting Powers, as 'there is no clear line of demarcation between the application and the interpretation of legal or treaty texts'.[30] It was also stressed that, under the new conciliation procedure, the Protecting Powers would act as intermediaries only, and thus would not provide authoritative interpretation of the Convention or impose any solution in case of disagreement between the Parties.[31] Reference to the 'interpretation' of the Convention was thus maintained in the final version of the text.

3. Lending good offices

1282   Article 11(1) suggests that the Protecting Powers are bound to ('shall') lend their good offices when it appears that conciliation between Parties to an international armed conflict is needed to improve the situation of protected persons in a given case. However, this obligation must be put into perspective as its practical application depends, as explained previously, on an independent assessment of the situation by the Protecting Powers. It is only when a Protecting Power believes that conciliation efforts are advisable in the interest of protected persons in a particular situation that it becomes bound to undertake the procedure. The obligation also amounts to explicit recognition of the right of the Protecting Power to initiate the procedure. Thus, exercising this right does not constitute an inappropriate or unfriendly act towards any of the Parties to the conflict. If a Protecting Power decides to offer its good offices, it does so on the basis of a competence that each State has accepted when becoming a Party to the Convention.[32]

1283   The activities that the Protecting Powers are entitled to undertake under Article 11(1) are characterized as 'good offices'. In international law, good offices are usually defined as a diplomatic tool of peaceful dispute settlement.[33] This notion 'designates the action by a third party who merely encourages the disputing subjects to resume negotiations or helps them to get together. The third party is not supposed to participate in the negotiations.'[34] This traditional

---

[29] See *Final Record of the Diplomatic Conference of Geneva of 1949*, Vol. II-B, p. 353 (USSR).

[30] See *ibid.* p. 353 (Colonel Du Pasquier (Switzerland), Rapporteur of the Joint Committee).

[31] See *ibid.* p. 354. Along the same line, see also the views expressed by Claude Pilloud, Director of the ICRC, in 'Les réserves aux Conventions de Genève de 1949', *Revue internationale de la Croix-Rouge*, Vol. 39, No. 464, 1957, pp. 409–437, at 418, and 'Reservations to the Geneva Conventions of 1949', *International Review of the Red Cross*, Vol. 16, No. 180, March 1976, pp. 107–124, at 121.

[32] See United Kingdom, *Manual of the Law of Armed Conflict*, 2004, para. 16.7: 'Good offices and mediation by neutral states for the purpose of settling differences are friendly acts.' This rule was also explicitly recognized in the context of the peaceful settlement of international disputes; see Hague Convention (I) (1907), Article 3, para. 3.

[33] See Hague Convention (I) (1907), Articles 2–8.

[34] Lapidoth, para. 1. See also Malanczuk, p. 276: 'A third party (as a "go-between") is said to offer its good offices when it tries to persuade disputing states to enter into negotiations; it passes

approach, in which the third party is seen only as an intermediary between opposing States, served as a model for the drafting of Article 11 in 1949.[35]

1284   However, practice arising from procedures other than Article 11 indicates that good offices are often used more flexibly, especially when related to humanitarian issues.[36] In a number of instances, good offices have not been limited to activities purely facilitating contacts between opposing Parties, but have involved a more active role by the individual or organism activating the procedure.[37] This role may include diplomatic dialogue to persuade relevant authorities to respect their obligations, or any form of assistance in finding a suitable framework for resolving the issue at stake.[38] As expressed by an observer of UN diplomatic activities, good offices include all kinds of 'informal contacts and friendly suggestions made as far as circumstances allow'.[39]

1285   Taking into account this evolution, as well as the humanitarian purpose of Article 11, reference to 'good offices' in paragraph 1 should not be understood restrictively. Activities undertaken by the Protecting Powers on the basis of this provision require a flexible approach allowing for the use of any diplomatic initiatives that may serve the interest of protected persons. The Protecting Powers have the possibility not only of acting as intermediaries between opposing Parties, but also of submitting concrete proposals to them, whenever necessary, with a view to facilitating agreed solutions. This proactive role is confirmed and illustrated in Article 11(2), which authorizes each Protecting Power to propose 'on its own initiative' the organization of a meeting of the representatives of the Parties to the conflict. Moreover, the marginal title of Article 11, although not formally binding, further supports this view. Characterizing the procedure as 'conciliation' suggests that the Protecting Powers are expected to play a role that goes beyond the functions traditionally understood as 'good offices'.

1286   Whatever the precise activities undertaken in this framework or the possible outcome of the procedure, the key characteristic of 'good offices' is that the Protecting Powers may only propose, and not impose, any solution to the Parties.[40] This was also noted during the 1949 Diplomatic Conference.[41]

4. Purpose of the conciliation procedure

1287 While Article 11 provides that the good offices must be lent 'with a view to settling the disagreement', the procedure is not limited to this purpose. As

---

messages and suggestions back and forth and when the negotiations start, its functions are at an end.'

[35] See *Final Record of the Diplomatic Conference of Geneva of 1949*, Vol. II-B, p. 354 (Colonel Du Pasquier (Switzerland), Rapporteur of the Joint Committee).

[36] See Ramcharan, in particular pp. 35–51.   [37] See Lapidoth.

[38] This practice was particularly in relation to the role of the UN Secretary-General; see Pěchota, pp. 13–18. See also Ramcharan, pp. 35–36, and Franck/Nolte, pp. 143–182.

[39] Pěchota, p. 2.   [40] See also Hague Convention (I) (1907), Article 6.

[41] See *Final Record of the Diplomatic Conference of Geneva of 1949*, Vol. II-B, p. 23 (Monaco).

explained earlier, the application of this provision does not necessarily require a 'disagreement' between the Parties to the conflict. Arrangements may be needed, for example, to clarify conditions for the practical implementation of the Convention, which does not necessarily mean that the States concerned have opposing views in this respect. Thus, the Protecting Powers may lend their good offices not only with a view to settling disagreements between the Parties, but, more generally, each time 'they deem it advisable in the interest of protected persons'.

E. Paragraph 2: Meeting of the representatives of the Parties to the conflict

1. Purpose of the meeting

1288   Article 11(2) describes a more formal way of operationalizing the 'conciliation procedure'. It suggests practical conditions for the organization of a meeting of the representatives of the Parties to the conflict. Such a meeting shares the same objective as the good offices foreseen in paragraph 1, namely to safeguard the interest of protected persons. While the wording '[f]or this purpose' at the beginning of paragraph 2 may be interpreted as referring to the last part of paragraph 1, i.e. that the good offices must be lent 'with a view to settling the disagreement', the conciliation procedure, as already explained, does not necessarily require divergent views between the Parties to an international armed conflict. These meetings may thus aim to address any issue in the interest of protected persons that must be discussed by the Parties, even in the absence of a disagreement.

2. Initiating the meeting

1289   Article 11(2) foresees two ways of initiating the procedure. According to the first, each of the Protecting Powers may propose a meeting 'at the invitation of one Party'. While the text is not perfectly clear on this point, the historical background of the provision would indicate that this wording refers to a Party 'to the conflict' rather than to a Party 'to the Convention'. Article 83(3) of the 1929 Convention was less ambiguous in this regard, as it provided that those entitled to initiate the procedure were the 'belligerents'. Nothing in the preparatory work for the 1949 Convention suggests that the participants of the Diplomatic Conference intended to modify the rule when they decided to replace the word 'belligerents' by the word 'Party'. In addition, the Convention, when referring to its States Parties, always uses the full expression 'High Contracting Party', and not the word 'Party' by itself. There is no reason why Article 11(2) would be an exception in this regard. The text makes it clear that the initiative may come from 'one' Party only. While for political or practical reasons it may be preferable to involve all Parties concerned in the proposal, this is not a legal requirement.

1290 The second option for a Protecting Power is to propose a meeting 'on its own initiative'. The prior request of a Party to the conflict is thus not a prerequisite. Moreover, Article 11(2) specifies that 'each' of the Protecting Powers is entitled to exercise this competence. This means that the proposal may be made unilaterally, without the accord of other Protecting Powers.

1291 While Article 11(2) focuses on the organization of a meeting of the Parties to the conflict, it also makes clear that this mechanism is not the only option. It provides that the Protecting Powers 'may' propose such a meeting, which implies that other methods are also possible, if more appropriate in the prevailing circumstances. The Protecting Powers thus enjoy a margin of discretion in deciding not only whether the conciliation procedure should be used, but also which specific measure should be proposed in the interest of protected persons.[42]

1292 Article 11(2) does not indicate any specific time for initiating the procedure. Unlike Article 83(3) of the 1929 Geneva Convention on Prisoners of War, which stated that the meetings were to be organized 'at the commencement of hostilities', the 1949 Convention is silent on this point. The Protecting Powers are thus free to activate the procedure at any time. As already stated, the interest of protected persons may require concerted measures, not only at the beginning of the conflict, for instance for the creation of hospital zones and localities,[43] but also at any time thereafter, including possibly once the conflict has ended.[44]

3. Parties' representatives in the meeting

1293 While the meeting foreseen in Article 11(2) must involve the participation of 'representatives' of the Parties to the conflict, the provision does not specify who those persons should be. The wording used in this paragraph, however, is broad enough to cover all kinds of 'representatives' from different spheres of the State, as long as they are entitled to express the views of their government in their respective fields of responsibility. It is also conceivable that they include members of non-State organisms, such as medical or religious associations, with particular expertise in the issues at hand and duly authorized by their government to participate in the meeting. In order to ensure that different perspectives are taken into account, the composition of the

---

[42] This was stressed during the drafting of Article 11. The Rapporteur of the Joint Committee argued that the good offices of a Protecting Power could lead not only to the meeting foreseen in paragraph 2, but also to alternative procedures, such as 'the nomination of a person who could act as an arbitrator'; see *Final Record of the Diplomatic Conference of Geneva of 1949*, Vol. II-B, p. 354.

[43] See Article 23.

[44] For instance, to facilitate transportation of the dead to their home country, as foreseen in Article 17(3).

meeting should be of mixed gender and, ideally, include representatives of diverse backgrounds.[45]

1294   The level of participation will depend on the nature of the issue and the possible outcome of the meeting. If the issue relates to specific situations and may be solved through ad hoc arrangements, for instance the evacuation of wounded and sick combatants from the battlefield, the most appropriate persons to participate may be local military commanders.[46] If the interest of protected persons requires the conclusion of more general and formal agreements, it may be necessary to ensure the participation of representatives empowered to negotiate and adopt such agreements.[47]

1295   Article 11(2) suggests that the 'representatives' may include 'in particular...authorities responsible for the wounded and sick, members of medical personnel and chaplains'. The words 'in particular' mean that the list is not exhaustive but rather illustrative. The naming of these authorities is the only part of this article which is not identical in the four Conventions. The reason for this is that the protected persons to whom it relates are different in each Convention, so the scope of the article is adapted accordingly.[48] Should the need arise, persons in charge of the search for and management of the dead could also be included.

4. Venue of the meeting

1296   With respect to the venue, Article 11(2) suggests that the meeting take place 'possibly on neutral territory suitably chosen'.[49] This option is not mandatory and the Parties concerned may decide otherwise. The territory of a neutral country may be appropriate when the procedure involves lengthy discussions on general questions of interpretation or application of the Convention. The evocation of this possibility is largely the result of experience gained during the First World War, when special agreements on the treatment of prisoners of war and other issues of a humanitarian nature were negotiated and adopted thanks to the diplomatic efforts and on the territory of neutral States.[50] However, when specific humanitarian problems require ad hoc solutions, less formal meetings in the area where hostilities are taking place may be more appropriate.

---

[45] See UN Security Council, Res. 1325, 31 October 2000, in particular, paras 1 and 8.

[46] For further details, see the commentary on Article 15.

[47] A number of such agreements were concluded during the First World War to clarify certain questions related to the treatment of prisoners of war and other problems of a humanitarian nature; see Frick-Cramer, pp. 388–389.

[48] On this point, the other Geneva Conventions read: 'authorities responsible for the wounded, sick and shipwrecked, medical personnel and chaplains' (Second Convention, Article 11); 'authorities responsible for prisoners of war' (Third Convention, Article 11); and 'authorities responsible for protected persons' (Fourth Convention, Article 12).

[49] Neutral territory refers to the territory of a neutral State. For a discussion of the concept of neutral State, see the commentary on Article 4, section C.1.

[50] These included Denmark, the Netherlands, Sweden and Switzerland; see Frick-Cramer, p. 389.

5. Obligation to 'give effect' to the proposal of a meeting

1297   Article 11(2) provides that the Parties to the conflict 'shall be bound to give effect to the proposals made to them' by a Protecting Power for the purpose of organizing a meeting of representatives. This means that the Parties are not allowed to ignore the proposal; they have a legal obligation (they 'shall be bound') to respond. This also supposes that they must at least accept to participate in the meeting. Failing that, the invitation would be without 'effect'. The procedure of Article 11(2) may thus be activated automatically, as the initiative and organization of the meeting as such does not suppose the consent of the Parties to the conflict.

1298   However, the obligation to 'give effect' to the proposal of a meeting does not mean that the Parties are bound to accept the outcome of the discussions. The very nature of conciliation supposes that any decision that might result from the procedure must be agreed by the Parties. The Protecting Power may formulate recommendations but can in no way impose binding conclusions.

1299   The drafting history of Article 87 of the 1929 Geneva Convention on Prisoners of War also supports this view. As explained in section B, this provision was the main source of inspiration for the drafting of common Article 11 of the 1949 Geneva Conventions (Article 12 of the Fourth Convention). During the 1929 Diplomatic Conference, the representative of the ICRC, referring to the possibility of holding conferences of representatives of the Parties to the conflict on the initiative of the Protecting Powers, stated that '[l]es belligérants ne sont tenus que de se rendre à ces réunions; la Convention ne peut leur imposer quoi que ce soit en ce qui concerne ce qui serait décidé dans ces réunions' ('The belligerents are bound only to attend these meetings; the Convention cannot impose on them any decision whatsoever reached during these meetings.').[51]

6. Participation of a neutral Power or the ICRC

1300   The last sentence of Article 11(2) mentions the possible participation of a neutral Power or the ICRC in the meeting. As indicated by the wording of the provision, the Protecting Powers are not bound to invite these other actors, but will do it only if they deem it 'necessary'. In addition, such participation is subject to the approval of the Parties to the conflict. The Protecting Powers are allowed to 'propose', but not impose, the participation of third parties in the meeting. The wording of the provision ('shall be invited to take part') also indicates that the neutral State concerned or the ICRC is not obliged to respond positively to the invitation.[52]

---

[51] *Proceedings of the Geneva Diplomatic Conference of 1929*, p. 520 (unofficial translation).

[52] The ICRC retains at all times its discretion, based on its own criteria of engagement, to decide whether it will undertake an activity in a given situation; see the commentary on Article 9, para. 1133.

1301   Article 11(2) does not specify the purpose of the invitation addressed to the neutral Power or the ICRC. There are indeed a variety of reasons why the presence of these actors may be beneficial. The Convention itself mentions some of these reasons, when it explicitly requires the involvement of a neutral country in safeguarding the interest of protected persons. It will obviously be 'necessary', for instance, to ensure the participation of a neutral country in the meeting if the discussion is aimed at organizing the reception or internment of protected persons on its territory.[53] This will also be the case if the neutral country is expected to play a decisive role in the nomination of the 'Special Commissions' in charge of supervising hospital zones and localities.[54] However, nothing precludes a neutral State from participating in the meeting for other reasons not related to specific provisions of the Convention, as long as this is deemed necessary in the interest of protected persons.

1302   Reasons for inviting the ICRC to the meeting are related to its diverse activities for the victims of armed conflict, as determined by its mandate and mission.[55] Parties to the conciliation procedure may wish to solicit the ICRC's operational expertise or to entrust it with a role in the implementation of the agreement adopted as a result of the procedure. If, for instance, the purpose of the meeting is to conclude a local arrangement to allow the removal, exchange and transport of the wounded, sick or dead left on the battlefield,[56] the Parties may decide to invite the ICRC to carry out this task.

1303   The ICRC may also be invited to the meeting to share its legal expertise on questions related to the application or interpretation of the Convention, as foreseen in Article 11(1). It is one of the main roles of the ICRC, recognized by the Statutes of the International Red Cross and Red Crescent Movement, to work for the faithful application, understanding and dissemination of international humanitarian law.[57]

1304   The question arises whether third parties other than those explicitly mentioned in Article 11(2) may be invited to participate in the meeting. Given that such participation would be subject anyway to the agreement of the Parties to the procedure, this question should be answered affirmatively. Nothing in Article 11(2) suggests that the reference to a neutral Power or the ICRC was meant to be exhaustive. On the contrary, the object and purpose of this

---

[53] See Article 4 and its commentary, in particular section C.2.b.
[54] See Draft agreement relating to hospital zones and localities, Annex I to the First Convention, Article 10.
[55] The mandate and mission of the ICRC are based mainly on the 1949 Geneva Conventions and their Additional Protocols of 1977, the Statutes of the ICRC, the 1986 Statutes of the International Red Cross and Red Crescent Movement, and the resolutions of the International Conferences of the Red Cross and Red Crescent.
[56] See Article 15(2).
[57] See Statutes of the International Red Cross and Red Crescent Movement (1986), Article 5(2)(c) and (g).

provision suggests that the Protecting Powers are entitled to propose any other participant, as long as such proposal may serve the interest of protected persons. Article 11(2) provides guidance for the organization of the meeting, but does not prohibit other avenues, on condition that the Parties to the procedure have given their agreement. Examples of possible participants other than those mentioned in Article 11(2) are representatives of the United Nations, other intergovernmental organizations, third States, non-governmental organizations or independent experts.

F. Developments since 1949

1305 The mechanism established under Article 11 has to date never been used.[58] During the First World War, a number of meetings of representatives of Parties to the conflict were organized on neutral territory and resulted in the conclusion of special agreements on various humanitarian issues, such as the repatriation of seriously sick or wounded prisoners of war.[59] However, this experience has not been repeated since.

1306 The non-use of the conciliation procedure is a direct consequence of the lack of effectiveness of the system of Protecting Powers. Protecting Powers have been appointed on only five occasions since the adoption of the Geneva Conventions in 1949[60] and they have never had the opportunity to apply their formal competence based on Article 11. However, States may also lend their good offices outside the specific framework of Article 11, i.e. even if they are not formally designated as Protecting Powers.

1307 Furthermore, Article 11 does not preclude other actors, nominated as substitutes for the Protecting Powers, from resorting to the conciliation procedure whenever authorized by the Convention.[61] However, this alternative has never been applied in practice.[62]

1308 This problem is also related to the particular context in which the conciliation procedure is supposed to be implemented. It is indeed extremely difficult to convince States, once they are opposed in an armed conflict, to take an active part in a conciliation procedure and reach agreement on humanitarian issues.[63] The fact that they were not able to settle their original dispute through peaceful means would suggest that room for diplomatic dialogue during the conflict is limited.

---

[58] The similar conciliation procedure provided for in the 1954 Hague Convention for the Protection of Cultural Property and its 1999 Second Protocol has also remained dormant to this day; see O'Keefe, p. 126.

[59] For further details, see Pictet (ed.), *Commentary on the First Geneva Convention*, ICRC, 1952, pp. 128–129, and Frick-Cramer, pp. 388–389.

[60] See the commentary on Article 8, para. 1115; see also Bugnion, p. 864.

[61] See Article 10(1).   [62] See the commentary on Article 10, section F.3.

[63] See Sassòli/Bouvier/Quintin, Vol. I, pp. 386–387.

1309   The lack of effectiveness of the procedure set down in Article 11 does not mean, however, that good offices are not a relevant means of safeguarding the interest of protected persons. On the contrary, a number of actors other than the Protecting Powers are entitled to and do resort to such means for humanitarian purposes. Their activities extend both to international and non-international armed conflicts.

1310   It is one of the ICRC's functions to act as a neutral intermediary to provide support to persons in need of protection and assistance. To this end, the ICRC may offer its good offices to the Parties to the conflict to facilitate the settlement of disagreements or the conclusion and implementation of arrangements benefiting protected persons. In practice, the ICRC accepts to play this role only if it is in the interest of the victims of the conflict and with the consent of all the Parties concerned.[64]

1311   The ICRC has lent its good offices for a variety of purposes, such as ensuring respect for international humanitarian law beyond the rules formally binding the Parties to the conflict,[65] creating hospital and safety zones and localities,[66] concluding truces to allow the evacuation of victims of armed conflicts from combat zones,[67] facilitating the passage of relief supplies to besieged areas,[68] and facilitating the release and repatriation of prisoners of war.[69]

---

[64] This role is principally based on the 1949 Geneva Conventions and the 1986 Statutes of the International Red Cross and Red Crescent Movement (see, in particular, Articles 3(2) and 9 of the First Convention and Article 5(2)(d) and (3) of the Statutes). For a more detailed analysis of the legal basis and practice of the ICRC's offers of services, see Bugnion, pp. 403–465. The role of the ICRC, however, is not exclusive. The Convention clearly states that any other impartial humanitarian organization may undertake humanitarian activities, subject to the agreement of the Parties to the conflict concerned; see Articles 3(2) and 9.

[65] When civil war broke out in Yemen in 1962, for instance, the ICRC obtained commitments from both Parties to the conflict to respect the main provisions of the 1949 Geneva Conventions; see Bugnion, p. 414. See also Memorandum of Understanding on the Application of IHL between Croatia and the Socialist Federal Republic of Yugoslavia (1991), following discussions held under the auspices of the ICRC, reproduced in Sassòli/Bouvier/Quintin, pp. 1713–1717, and Agreement on the Application of IHL between the Parties to the Conflict in Bosnia and Herzegovina (1992), following discussions held at the invitation of the ICRC, reproduced in Sassòli/Bouvier/Quintin, pp. 1717–1721.

[66] See Bugnion, pp. 480–483 and 748–763.

[67] See *ibid.* pp. 484–493 and 744–748. Practice shows that Parties to armed conflict often request the ICRC to evacuate wounded, sick or dead persons, in which case the ICRC obtains assurances from both sides that it will have sufficient security to carry out this task.

[68] See *ibid.* pp. 515–516.

[69] See *ibid.* pp. 692–696. In relation to these activities, Bugnion explains, at 694:

This is therefore an essentially diplomatic task in which good offices are combined with the role of conciliator, a role which the ICRC has played in many conflicts since the First World War. Although it was mostly performed off stage and records of it, if any, are hard to trace, in some cases it was acknowledged more officially and the belligerents themselves invited the ICRC to help them to find a solution.

For an example of the ICRC's use of good offices in the context of a non-international armed conflict, see Mégevand, pp. 94–108.

1312   The United Nations, other intergovernmental and non-governmental organizations and individual States may also play a key role in bringing Parties to armed conflicts together to discuss humanitarian issues. Diplomatic dialogue is a tool that the High Contracting Parties to the Geneva Conventions of 1949 may wish to call upon, either individually or collectively, to fulfil their obligation to 'ensure respect' for the Conventions as required by common Article 1.[70]

Select bibliography

Boutruche, Théo, 'Good offices, Conciliation and Enquiry', in Andrew Clapham, Paola Gaeta and Marco Sassòli (eds), *The 1949 Geneva Conventions: A Commentary*, Oxford University Press, 2015, pp. 561–574.

Bugnion, François, *The International Committee of the Red Cross and the Protection of War Victims*, ICRC/Macmillan, Oxford, 2003, pp. 480–493, 515–516, 692–696, 744–763 and 845–910.

Cot, Jean-Pierre, 'Conciliation', version of April 2006, *Max Planck Encyclopedia of Public International Law*, Oxford University Press, http://opil.ouplaw.com/home/EPIL.

Coulibaly, Hamidou, 'Le rôle des Puissances protectrices au regard du droit diplomatique, du droit de Genève et du droit de La Haye', in Frits Kalshoven and Yves Sandoz (eds), *Implementation of International Humanitarian Law/Mise en œuvre du droit international humanitaire*, Martinus Nijhoff Publishers, Dordrecht, 1989, pp. 69–78.

Franck, Thomas M. and Nolte, Georg, 'The Good Offices Function of the UN Secretary-General', in Adam Roberts and Benedict Kingsbury (eds), *United Nations, Divided World: The UN's Roles in International Relations*, 2nd edition, Oxford University Press, 1993, pp. 143–182.

Frick-Cramer, Renée-Marguerite, 'Le Comité international de la Croix-Rouge et les Conventions internationales pour les prisonniers de guerre et les civils', *Revue internationale de la Croix-Rouge*, Vol. 25, No. 293, 1943, pp. 386–402.

Heintze, Hans-Joachim, 'Protecting Power', version of July 2009, *Max Planck Encyclopedia of Public International Law*, Oxford University Press, http://www.mpepil.com.

Lapidoth, Ruth, 'Good Offices', version of December 2006, *Max Planck Encyclopedia of Public International Law*, Oxford University Press, http://opil.ouplaw.com/home/EPIL.

Malanczuk, Peter, *Akehurst's Modern Introduction to International Law*, 7th edition, Routledge, London, 1997, pp. 276–279.

Mégevand, Béatrice, 'Between Insurrection and Government – ICRC action in Mexico', *International Review of the Red Cross*, Vol. 35, No. 304, January-February 1995, pp. 94–108.

O'Keefe, Roger, *The Protection of Cultural Property in Armed Conflict*, Cambridge University Press, 2006, p. 126.

---

[70] See also the commentary on common Article 1, section E.3.d.

Pěchota, Vratislav, *The Quiet Approach: A Study of the Good Offices Exercised by the United Nations Secretary-General in the Cause of Peace*, United Nations Institute for Training and Research, New York, 1972, pp. 13–18.

Ramcharan, Bertrand G., *Humanitarian Good Offices in International Law: The Good Offices of the United Nations Secretary-General in the Field of Human Rights*, Martinus Nijhoff Publishers, The Hague, 1983.

Sassòli, Marco, Bouvier, Antoine A. and Quintin, Anne, *How Does Law Protect in War?*, 3rd edition, ICRC, Geneva, 2011, Vol. I, pp. 386–387, and Vol. III, pp. 1713–1721.

CHAPTER II

WOUNDED AND SICK

1313 This chapter is one of the most important in the Convention. The Convention may even be said to rest upon it, since it embodies the essential idea championed by the founders of the International Red Cross and Red Crescent Movement, an idea that has dominated all of the Geneva Conventions since 1864 – namely, that the person of the soldier who is wounded or sick, and who is therefore *hors de combat*, is from that moment inviolable. The wounded and sick, whether friend or foe, must be tended with the same care.

1314 Article 12 is the foundation on which today's legal protection of the wounded and sick is built. It lays down a system of complementary positive and negative obligations pertaining to the wounded and sick and establishes the fundamental provisions on how they are to be treated and cared for. It also imposes certain obligations with respect to the dead.

1315 Article 15 complements Article 12 by imposing an obligation 'to search for and collect' the wounded and sick in order to remove them from the immediate danger zone and to enable them to receive the necessary medical treatment and care. This is further complemented by Article 18, which contains the kernel of Henry Dunant's idea for civilians to take action to assist and care for wounded and sick members of the armed forces, whether in response to an appeal by the military commander or spontaneously. A Party to the conflict must consider these options when taking 'all possible measures' to search for and collect the wounded and sick and in ensuring that they receive the medical care their condition requires.

1316 The purpose of Article 13 is to specify which persons, on their being wounded or falling sick, the First Convention protects. The list includes members of the armed forces and other categories of persons who, while not being members of the armed forces, either have combatant status or are otherwise entitled to prisoner-of-war status.

1317 Article 14 defines the status of a wounded or sick member of the armed forces who falls into enemy hands. In that situation, a member of the armed forces is both a wounded or sick person needing treatment and an individual who is entitled to become – and thus becomes – a prisoner of war.

1318 Article 16 regulates three cardinal issues: the recording and forwarding of information concerning wounded, sick and dead persons who have fallen into the hands of the adverse Party; the preparation and forwarding of death certificates; and the collection and forwarding of the deceased's personal items. The importance of this provision cannot be underestimated, as without identification and reporting requirements and procedures it is difficult, if not impossible, to account for persons who are missing or to provide information to their families.

1319   Article 17 deals exclusively with the treatment of the dead; it sets out a number of rules regarding burial or cremation, examination of the body prior to burial or cremation, and the maintenance and marking of graves. This provision is essential to guarantee respect for the dignity of the dead and to ensure that they do not go missing.

1320   Some of these provisions were already included in the 1864, 1906 and 1929 Conventions, but they were greatly clarified in 1949 and further complemented by Part II, Section I, of Additional Protocol I.

PROTECTION AND CARE OF THE WOUNDED AND SICK

❖ Text of the provision*

(1) Members of the armed forces and other persons mentioned in the following Article, who are wounded or sick, shall be respected and protected in all circumstances.

(2) They shall be treated humanely and cared for by the Party to the conflict in whose power they may be, without any adverse distinction founded on sex, race, nationality, religion, political opinions, or any other similar criteria. Any attempts upon their lives, or violence to their persons, shall be strictly prohibited; in particular, they shall not be murdered or exterminated, subjected to torture or to biological experiments; they shall not wilfully be left without medical assistance and care, nor shall conditions exposing them to contagion or infection be created.

(3) Only urgent medical reasons will authorize priority in the order of treatment to be administered.

(4) Women shall be treated with all consideration due to their sex.

(5) The Party to the conflict which is compelled to abandon wounded or sick to the enemy shall, as far as military considerations permit, leave with them a part of its medical personnel and material to assist in their care.

❖ Reservations or declarations

None

Contents

* Paragraph numbers have been added for ease of reference.

A. Introduction

1321 '[M]itigating, as far as possible, the sufferings inseparable from war'[1] is a fundamental imperative of international humanitarian law. The protection of the wounded and sick, therefore, has been at the heart of humanitarian law since its modern inception. Wounded and sick military personnel, along with the medical personnel assigned to their care, were the first category of 'protected persons' to benefit from special legal protection by virtue of the 1864 Geneva Convention. Since then, the legal regime pertaining to the wounded and sick has undergone various revisions, namely in 1906,[2] 1929,[3] 1949,[4] and again in 1977,[5] all with the aim of adapting it to the changing nature of armed conflict and of making the protection of the wounded and sick more complete.

1322 Owing to the overall structure of the Geneva Conventions and their Additional Protocols, the legal regime pertaining to the wounded and sick is

---

[1] *Final Record of the Diplomatic Conference of Geneva of 1949*, Vol. II-A, p. 9.
[2] Geneva Convention (1906).   [3] Geneva Convention on the Wounded and Sick (1929).
[4] First Geneva Convention.   [5] Additional Protocol I.

dispersed across various instruments that regulate different aspects of their protection. Article 12 of the First Convention, however, is the foundation on which today's legal protection of the wounded and sick is built. It lays down a system of complementary positive and negative obligations with regard to the wounded and sick and establishes the fundamental provisions on how they are to be treated and cared for.

1323   Article 12 of the First Convention applies in international armed conflict to the wounded and sick who are members of the armed forces or otherwise entitled to prisoner-of-war status.[6] Article 12 of the Second Convention extends protection to wounded, sick and shipwrecked members of the armed forces and other persons at sea entitled to prisoner-of-war status. Article 16(1) of the Fourth Convention provides for the protection and respect of wounded and sick civilians. Article 10 of Additional Protocol I contains a similar provision.

1324   The treatment of the wounded and sick in non-international armed conflict is dealt with in common Article 3 of the Geneva Conventions and Article 7 of Additional Protocol II.

1325   Today, however, the legal regime applicable to the wounded and sick in any given conflict is more comprehensive. The obligations to treat the wounded and sick humanely and to provide them with medical care are mandatory by virtue not only of the Geneva Conventions and their Additional Protocols, but also of customary international humanitarian law.[7] These fundamental obligations apply in both international and non-international armed conflict and regardless of whether the wounded or sick person is military or civilian.[8]

1326   Violations of these obligations can amount to grave breaches of the Geneva Conventions when committed in the context of an international armed conflict.[9] They are punished as war crimes in both international and non-international armed conflict.[10] Reprisals against the wounded and sick are prohibited under Article 46 of the First Convention and customary international law.[11]

B. Historical background

1327 Historical descriptions of past battles show that the practice of caring for wounded and sick combatants from both sides of a conflict occurred in

---

[6] See Article 13.

[7] ICRC Study on Customary International Humanitarian Law (2005), Rules 109–111.

[8] *Ibid.*

[9] Such grave breaches include wilful killing, torture or inhuman treatment, including biological experiments, or wilfully causing great suffering or serious injury to body or health. See First Convention, Article 50, and Second Convention, Article 51.

[10] See ICC Statute (1998), e.g. under Article 8(2)(a)(i)–(iii), (b)(vi) and (x), and (c)(i)–(ii) and (e)(xi).

[11] ICRC Study on Customary International Humanitarian Law (2005), Rule 146: 'Belligerent reprisals against persons protected by the Geneva Conventions [including the wounded and sick] are prohibited.'

various instances across space and time.[12] However, although some kings or commanders may have ordered such charitable actions, for a long time they were not systematic and did not arise from an international legal obligation. The Crimean War (1853–1856) revealed dramatic shortcomings in the treatment of the battlefield wounded and sick.[13] Soon after, a Swiss businessman, Henry Dunant, shocked by the appalling conditions of the wounded on the battlefield of Solferino (1859), where 40,000 fallen Austrian, French and Italian soldiers lay unattended, resolved to remedy these deficiencies.[14] In his book, *A Memory of Solferino*, Dunant proposed the conclusion of an international convention to protect wounded and sick soldiers and suggested the setting up of relief societies that would operate on the basis of this convention 'for the purpose of having care given to the wounded in wartime by zealous, devoted and thoroughly qualified volunteers'.[15] Dunant's initiative led to the establishment in 1863 of the 'International Committee for Relief to the Wounded',[16] initially also referred to as the 'Geneva Committee' or the 'Committee of Five', which in 1876 was renamed the International Committee of the Red Cross (ICRC).[17] At the impetus of the Committee, the Swiss Government convened a Diplomatic Conference in Geneva, which led to the adoption in 1864 of the Geneva Convention for the Amelioration of the Condition of the Wounded in Armies in the Field.

1328   The 1864 Geneva Convention, consisting merely of ten articles, marked a turning point in the laws and customs of war. Previously, limited protections for wounded soldiers and army surgeons had sporadically been included in bilateral agreements between warring Parties.[18] At the national level the so-called Lieber Code, adopted by the United States of America on 24 April 1863, had provided that '[e]very *captured* wounded enemy shall be medically treated, according to the ability of the medical staff' (emphasis added).[19] However, the 1864 Geneva Convention was the first multilateral convention proclaiming – as a matter of law – that '[w]ounded or sick combatants, to whatever nation they may belong, shall be collected and cared for'.[20] In 1868 another set of 15 articles, entitled the 'Additional Articles relating to the Condition of the Wounded in War', aiming to extend the rules of the 1864 Geneva Convention to naval forces

---

[12]   See John F. Hutchinson, *Champions of Charity: War and the Rise of the Red Cross*, Westview Press, Boulder, Colorado, 1996, pp. 24–27; Henri Coursier, 'L'évolution du droit international humanitaire', *Recueil des cours de l'Académie de droit international de La Haye*, Vol. 99, 1960, pp. 357–466, at 364–369; P.M. Bogaïewsky, 'Les secours aux militaires malades et blessés avant le XIXe siècle', *Revue générale de droit international public*, Vol. 10, 1903, pp. 202–221. See also Bugnion, pp. 11–13.

[13]   John F. Hutchinson, *Champions of Charity: War and the Rise of the Red Cross*, Westview Press, Boulder, Colorado, 1996, p. 26. See also Novak, para. 2, and Geiss, 2009, para. 5.

[14]   Bugnion, p. 7.   [15]   Dunant, p. 115.   [16]   Bugnion, pp. 8–9, note 11.

[17]   Jean S. Pictet, 'The foundation of the Red Cross: Some important documents', *International Review of the Red Cross*, Vol. 3, No. 23, February 1963, pp. 60–75, at 60–61.

[18]   Lauterpacht, p. 353.   [19]   Lieber Code (1863), Article 79.

[20]   Geneva Convention (1864), Article 6 (57 States Parties).

(the shipwrecked) and to make some of the provisions of the earlier convention more specific, were adopted but never entered into force.[21] Similarly, neither the Brussels Declaration of 1874 nor the Oxford Manual of 1880, both of which contained sections on the wounded and sick, were adopted as binding texts.[22] Nonetheless, these instruments marked important steps towards an enhanced codification of these rules at the multilateral level.

1329 The 1864 Geneva Convention (10 articles, 57 States Parties) was revised and superseded by the 1906 Geneva Convention for the Amelioration of the Condition of the Wounded and Sick in Armies in the Field (33 articles, 52 States Parties).[23] The 1906 Convention was in turn superseded by the 1929 Geneva Convention for the Amelioration of the Condition of the Wounded and Sick in Armies in the Field (39 articles, 60 States Parties).

1330 After the Second World War, the 1929 Geneva Convention was superseded by the 1949 Geneva Convention for the Amelioration of the Condition of the Wounded and Sick in Armed Forces in the Field (First Convention). The legal protections pertaining to the wounded and sick were comprehensively extended to the maritime context by the 1949 Geneva Convention for the Amelioration of the Condition of Wounded, Sick and Shipwrecked Members of Armed Forces at Sea (Second Convention). And for the first time, legal protections pertaining to wounded and sick civilians were codified in the 1949 Geneva Convention relative to the Protection of Civilian Persons in Time of War (Fourth Convention).[24] In addition, the special protection of female prisoners of war first provided for in the 1929 Geneva Convention on Prisoners of War was transposed to the wounded, sick and shipwrecked.[25]

1331 Owing to the universal ratification of the 1949 Geneva Conventions, the 1864, 1906 and 1929 Geneva Conventions, as well as the 1899 Hague Convention III and 1907 Hague Convention X, are no longer in operation today.[26]

1332 Article 12 of the First Convention was uncontroversial at the time of its drafting. It builds on earlier provisions contained in the 1864, 1906 and 1929 Geneva Conventions on the Wounded and Sick, while providing further specification and broadening its protective ambit. Thus, the scope *ratione personae* of Article 12 is broader than that of its predecessors. Notably, the 1864 Geneva Convention, according to its Article 6, applied only to wounded or sick combatants.

---

[21] See Additional Articles relating to the Condition of the Wounded in War (1868), Introduction. Only the United States ratified this treaty, although in the Franco-German War of 1870–71 and in the Spanish-American War of 1898 the belligerents agreed bilaterally to observe its provisions.

[22] See Brussels Declaration (1874), Articles 35 and 56, and Oxford Manual (1880), Articles 10–18. By and large these instruments referred to and repeated the provisions of the 1864 Geneva Convention.

[23] For more on the history, see Davis, and Sperry, pp. 33–35.

[24] Fourth Convention, Articles 16–17. See, generally, Pictet, 1951, pp. 462–475.

[25] See First Convention, Article 12(4), and Second Convention, Article 12(4). See also Articles 16 and 17 of the Fourth Convention in relation to expectant mothers and maternity cases.

[26] See the commentaries on Article 59 of the First Convention and Article 58 of the Second Convention.

The 1906 Geneva Convention, according to its Article 1, applied to wounded or sick '[o]fficers, soldiers, and other persons officially attached to armies'. Similarly, the 1929 Geneva Convention on the Wounded and Sick applied, also according to its Article 1, to wounded or sick '[o]fficers and soldiers and other persons officially attached to the armed forces'.

1333   Owing to the revised structure of the 1949 Geneva Conventions, which begin with a number of common and general provisions, the provision on the protection of the wounded and sick was moved to Article 12. Notwithstanding this editorial change, Article 12 remains a central provision governing the protection of the wounded and sick and indeed a core provision of the First Convention.[27]

C. Addressees of the obligations

1334 Paragraphs 2 and 5 of Article 12 refer explicitly to the 'Party to the conflict' as the bearer of the obligations to care for the wounded and sick and to treat them humanely. While the other paragraphs do not specify to whom the obligations contained therein are addressed, it is clear that Article 12 as a whole concerns the High Contracting Parties when they are party to an international armed conflict.

1335   In addition, Article 4 of the First Convention requires neutral Powers to apply by analogy the provisions of the Convention to, *inter alia*, the wounded and sick received or interned in their territory.[28]

D. Scope of application

1336 In terms of personal scope of application, Article 12 applies when two distinct criteria are cumulatively fulfilled.

1337   The first criterion is status-based (see section 1 below). It requires a person either to be a member of the armed forces or to belong to one of the other categories of persons listed in Article 13 of the First Convention.[29] It does not matter to which Party to a conflict the person belongs. Article 12 applies to a State's own wounded and sick personnel as well as to the wounded and sick of an adverse Party or co-belligerent.

1338   According to the second criterion, the person has to qualify as wounded or sick in the legal sense (see section 2 below).

---

[27] See Pictet (ed.), *Commentary on the First Geneva Convention*, ICRC, 1952, pp. 133–134.

[28] For an analysis as to what qualifies as a neutral State, see the commentary on Article 4, section C.1.

[29] See the commentary on Article 13, section C.2. Notably, in view of its restriction to certain categories of persons, Article 12 of the First Convention is more limited than Article 10 of Additional Protocol I and the corresponding rules of customary international humanitarian law, which apply to both military and civilian persons; see ICRC Study on Customary International Humanitarian Law (2005), Rules 109–111.

1339   For the application of Article 12(1), it does not matter whether the person in question has been captured or is otherwise in the power of a Party to the conflict. Conversely, the obligations contained in Article 12(2) only extend to the wounded and sick who are in the power of a Party to the conflict.

1. Categories of persons covered

1340 Article 12 applies to persons who are either members of the armed forces or who belong to the other categories of persons mentioned in Article 13 of the First Convention. In addition, Article 4(2) of the Second Convention makes clear that once naval forces are put ashore they immediately become subject to the provisions of the First Convention. Similarly, members of air forces found on land are also covered.[30] Article 12(4) contains an additional obligation with a specific personal scope of application: the wording of this provision indicates that female members of the armed forces or of the categories of persons mentioned in Article 13 are entitled to specific protections.

2. The wounded and sick

1341 In order to benefit from the protections provided for in Article 12, a person has to qualify as wounded or sick. For legal purposes there is no difference between the concepts of 'wounded' and 'sick'. Throughout the First Convention the two terms are used together. The same legal consequences attach to both conditions. The consistent reference in Article 12 to both concepts reinforces the notion that a wide variety of medical conditions can trigger the protected status granted by this provision. Qualifying as wounded or sick in the context of international humanitarian law requires the fulfilment of two cumulative criteria: a person must require medical care and must refrain from any act of hostility. In other words the legal status of being wounded or sick is based on a person's medical condition *and* conduct. The humanitarian law definition of 'wounded and sick' is therefore both narrower and wider than the ordinary meaning of these words. The definition is wider for the medical conditions covered than the colloquial sense of these terms might suggest, while it is narrower because the abstention from any act of hostility is a legal requirement for protection as a wounded or sick person.

1342   The First Convention in general and Article 12 in particular do not specify when a person may be considered to be wounded or sick. Starting from the ordinary meaning of these words, a person would normally be considered wounded or sick if he or she suffers from either a wound or a sickness. The wording is sufficiently open to accommodate a wide range of medical conditions. The decisive criterion for determining when a person is wounded or sick in the sense of

---

[30] See the commentary on Article 13, section C.2.

Article 12 – in addition to refraining from any act of hostility – is that of being in need of medical care. It is this particular need, and the specific vulnerability that comes with it, that the legal regime protecting the wounded and sick aims to address. Indeed, such a reading is also in line with the wording of Article 8(a) of Additional Protocol I. Therefore, as far as the relevant medical condition is concerned, the terms 'wounded' and 'sick' are to be interpreted broadly.

1343   In fact, the understanding of what constitutes 'wounded' or 'sick' under humanitarian law may be wider than the medical or ordinary meanings of these terms.[31] For the purpose of Article 12 it is irrelevant whether a certain physical or mental condition qualifies as a wound or sickness in the ordinary sense of these terms. For example, trauma is a medical condition that is typically found on the battlefield, but as Article 8(a) of Additional Protocol I indicates, any other 'physical ... disorder or disability' suffices as long as there is a need for medical care.[32] Similarly, mental or psychological conditions, including post-traumatic stress disorder, qualify, provided that they require medical care.

1344   It has been suggested that Article 12 only pertains to those persons whose medical condition is of such severity that they are physically incapable of continuing to fight.[33] Such an interpretation is too limiting. A definition which refers only to physically incapacitating medical conditions would equate being wounded or sick with being *hors de combat*, which does not provide an all-encompassing definition of 'wounded or sick' for the purposes of Article 12.[34] While a narrow reading may arguably enhance legal certainty on the battlefield, it would not address all of the cases Article 12 is designed to cover. In particular, it would exclude all those who are wounded or sick, whether severely or not, but who are not (yet) incapacitated by their medical condition. Furthermore, it would *de facto* reduce the obligation to care for the wounded and sick to an obligation of first aid. After all, if being wounded or sick required an incapacitating medical condition, the legal status of being 'wounded or sick' and the obligations that hinge on it would cease as soon as the medical condition is no longer incapacitating – including when a person is in the power of his or her own armed forces. At such a point, and given that being wounded or sick is typically a transitory status, a person may, however, still require medical care. Thus, globally for Article 12, any medical condition requiring care, no matter the severity, suffices to trigger the application of the article. In a combat situation, however, the fact that a combatant is wounded or sick must be visible or

---

[31] See Kleffner, p. 324; Kalshoven/Zegveld, p. 125; and Sandoz/Swinarski/Zimmermann (eds), *Commentary on the Additional Protocols*, ICRC, 1987, para. 301.

[32] The fact that a person is 'wounded or sick' under the First Convention is thus without prejudice to the fact that he or she may simultaneously qualify as a person with a disability under the 2006 Convention on the Rights of Persons with Disabilities, where that Convention applies.

[33] See Spaight, p. 421, and Sivakumaran, p. 274.

[34] For a definition of '*hors de combat*', see Additional Protocol I, Article 41(2).

have some outward manifestation such that an opposing combatant is able to be aware of it.

1345 In addition to being in need of medical care, in order to qualify as wounded or sick in the sense of Article 12, a person must also refrain from any act of hostility. Thus, contrary to the ordinary meanings of the terms 'wounded' and 'sick', persons who continue to engage in hostilities do not qualify as wounded or sick under humanitarian law, no matter how severe their medical condition may be. Unlike the definition of 'wounded and sick' contained in Article 8(a) of Additional Protocol I,[35] this criterion does not appear in the wording of Article 12 of the First Convention. However, given that Article 12 only applies to categories of persons, who, as a general rule, may lawfully be targeted, this limitation must form part of the definition of 'wounded and sick' for the purposes of the article. Otherwise every combatant who is in need of medical care would automatically be entitled to be respected and protected and could thus no longer lawfully be attacked. Such far-reaching protection for combatants would be unrealistic and impossible to uphold in the context of an armed conflict. On the basis of this reasoning, while the definition contained in the first sentence of Article 8(a) of Additional Protocol I is not directly applicable to Article 12 of the First Convention (as the definitions contained in Article 8 of the Protocol were drafted '[f]or the purposes of this Protocol'), the rationale spelled out explicitly in Article 8(a) is implicitly contained in Article 12 of the First Convention.

1346 Thus, for example, a combatant who is with his or her own forces and is recovering from a battle wound, still requires medical care and has not yet begun to engage in hostilities, but who, for example, performs weapons maintenance, can no longer be said to abstain from hostile acts and therefore does not qualify as wounded or sick in the legal sense of the term. If, however, a combatant is being treated in a first-aid clinic or hospital, for example for pneumonia or wounds requiring medical care or supervision, and is not or no longer engaging in acts of hostility, he or she may not be attacked. In practice, in such circumstances, attacking forces may primarily – but not exclusively – be able to distinguish wounded or sick combatants from their able-bodied comrades by the fact that they are being treated in a medical facility. Such persons are entitled to receive the medical care required by their condition. When they recover and resume normal military duties within the armed forces, they are no longer wounded or sick for the purposes of Article 12.

1347 The determination of whether a person is (or is still) wounded or sick may raise considerable difficulties in practice. Of course, the circumstances under which such decisions have to be made may vary significantly. In particular, this

---

[35] The relevant part of Article 8(a) of Additional Protocol I reads: '"wounded" and "sick" mean persons ... who, because of trauma, disease or other physical or mental disorder or disability, are in need of medical assistance or care and who refrain from any act of hostility'.

is because one may encounter wounded or sick persons throughout a theatre of military operations, from the front lines to rear areas. Interpretation of the meaning of 'wounded and sick' is a matter of common sense and good faith. A combatant must take into account all the information reasonably available at the time before making a determination of whether a person is wounded or sick in the sense of Article 12.[36] Those who have to apply these terms in practice, i.e. those who have the task of determining a person's status on the battlefield, may not proceed with an attack if they recognize or would have reason to believe that a person is wounded or sick. From a practical perspective, the *hors de combat* standard may provide helpful guidance in a combat situation.

1348   During hostilities, when a combatant is wounded in battle, whether lightly or severely, there may be a moment when an attacker must cease the attack on that person and begin to respect and protect him or her. Under combat conditions, in the very moment that a person is injured, it may be extremely difficult to determine with any degree of certainty whether that person is wounded in the legal sense, and in particular whether he or she is refraining from any hostile act. This may be especially the case when the person is only lightly wounded. However, even on the basis of a relatively light wound, a combatant may stop all acts of hostility. It is clear in such situations that persons who, for example, are rendered unconscious by wounds, or who are otherwise incapacitated, may not be attacked since they abstain from any acts of hostility.[37] On the other hand, persons who continue to fight, even if they are severely wounded, will not qualify as wounded or sick in the legal sense. There is no obligation to abstain from attacking persons who require medical care but who are preparing to engage in hostilities, or who are actually doing so, regardless of the severity of their wounds or sickness.

1349   In the context of ongoing hostilities, a combatant's status may change within seconds from being a lawful target to being a protected person by reason of wounds. Therefore, the attacking force must be alert to a possible cessation of acts of hostility by an injured combatant and be prepared to suspend or cease an attack at any moment. The visible abandonment of all hostile acts by a wounded combatant must put an end to all hostile acts against that person.

1350   In sum, being wounded or sick is typically, albeit not necessarily always,[38] a transitory status. For legal purposes, the protected status begins as soon as the cumulative requirements of being wounded or sick are fulfilled, i.e. as soon as a condition exists that requires medical care and provided the person concerned refrains from any act of hostility. In a combat situation, however, medical

---

[36] See Sandoz/Swinarski/Zimmermann (eds), *Commentary on the Additional Protocols*, ICRC, 1987, paras 2195–2197.

[37] ICRC Study on Customary International Humanitarian Law (2005), Rule 47. See also Additional Protocol I, Article 41(2)(c).

[38] Certain medical conditions may be chronic or lifelong, such as wounds leading to disability.

conditions must be detected or detectable based on the information reasonably available in the circumstances. If this is the case, protected status is automatically activated; surrender or any other additional activity is not required. Protected status as wounded or sick ends as soon as the protected person engages in hostile acts, dies or recovers, i.e. when the necessity to provide medical care no longer exists.[39]

1351   Wounded or sick combatants who die or are taken prisoner fall under the regimes protecting the dead and prisoners of war, respectively.[40] Once an enemy combatant is captured, the status of being wounded or sick and the status of being a prisoner of war are not mutually exclusive. As specified in Article 14 of the First Convention, they may exist simultaneously.[41] The Third Convention contains a more specific set of obligations than Article 12 of the First Convention with respect to certain aspects of the medical treatment of prisoners of war.[42] Wounded prisoners of war who recover but remain in captivity will no longer be covered by the First Convention but will continue to benefit from the protections accorded to prisoners of war under the Third Convention. Similarly, a combatant may simultaneously qualify as wounded or sick in the sense of Article 12 of the First Convention and as *hors de combat* in accordance with Article 41 of Additional Protocol I. According to Article 7 of the First Convention, the status of being wounded or sick and the rights that that status endows cannot be renounced. For the wounded and sick, this excludes renunciations by word but not by deed, because if a wounded or sick person starts fighting again the protected status would be lost.

E. Paragraph 1: The obligation to respect and protect

1352   Article 12(1) provides that the wounded and sick 'shall be respected and protected in all circumstances'. The article thus contains two distinct obligations: an obligation to respect, i.e. not to attack or otherwise harm the wounded and sick;[43] and an obligation to protect, i.e. to take (pro)active measures for the protection of the wounded and sick against various dangers arising in the context of an armed conflict.[44]

---

[39] See also Kleffner, p. 324. If, however, the person has fallen into the hands of the enemy, he or she will be a prisoner of war; see Article 14.

[40] See e.g. Article 17 of the First Convention regarding the dead and, more generally, the Third Convention regarding prisoners of war.

[41] See the commentary on Article 14, section C.1.

[42] See Third Convention, Articles 29–31.

[43] Bothe, p. 55: 'L'expression "respectés et protégés" implique ... ce qui a été expliqué à diverses reprises dans les débats ... [que] les personnes et objets protégés ne doivent pas être sciemment attaqués.' ('The expression "respected and protected" implies ... as was explained several times during the debates ... [that] protected persons and objects may not be knowingly attacked.')

[44] See Breau, p. 169, and Bugnion, p. 471.

1. The obligation to respect

1353   The obligation 'to respect' imposes a duty of abstention. It is an obligation of result. As such it is violated whenever the persons protected under Article 12 are not 'respected' by the bearer of the obligation.[45]

1354   First of all, the obligation to respect imposes an obligation not to directly or indiscriminately attack the protected person.[46] Thus, the wounded and sick may never be considered lawful targets under the law regulating the conduct of hostilities.

1355   A question that arises is whether the obligation to respect the wounded and sick entails that they must be taken into consideration for the purposes of the proportionality assessment.[47] This is controversial and of particular relevance in the context of Article 12, which refers exclusively to wounded and sick members of the armed forces and other persons mentioned in Article 13. Article 51(5)(b) of Additional Protocol I, which is part of a specific chapter on 'Civilians and Civilian Protection', mentions civilians but not the wounded and sick specifically.[48] The omission of the wounded and sick from this provision might have been for editorial reasons, given the subject matter of the chapter, rather than the intentional exclusion of certain categories of protected persons from the proportionality assessment.

1356   The preparatory work for Article 12 is silent on the matter.[49] This is not surprising given that in 1949 the relevant rules regarding the conduct of hostilities had not been spelled out in as much detail as they are today. However, one might have expected such a discussion in 1977, when simultaneously both the obligation to respect and protect the wounded and sick (Article 10 of Additional Protocol I) and specific rules pertaining to the conduct of hostilities (Articles 51, 57 and 58 of Additional Protocol I) were at issue. Nevertheless, the preparatory work for Article 10 of the Protocol is likewise silent on the matter.[50]

1357   However, in view of the specific protections accorded to the wounded and sick, namely the obligation to respect (and to protect) them in all

---

[45]   Draft Articles on State Responsibility (2001), Chapter II. See also James R. Crawford, *The International Law Commission's Articles on State Responsibility: Introduction, Text and Commentaries*, Cambridge University Press, 2002, pp. 91–123.

[46]   See Pictet (ed.), *Commentary on the First Geneva Convention*, ICRC, 1952, pp. 134–135, and Bothe/Partsch/Solf, p. 537.

[47]   On the concept of proportionality in armed conflict, see Additional Protocol I, Article 51(5)(b), and ICRC Study on Customary International Humanitarian Law (2005), Rule 14. See also Sandoz/Swinarski/Zimmermann (eds), *Commentary on the Additional Protocols*, ICRC, 1987, paras 1976–1981, and William J. Fenrick 'The Rule of Proportionality and Protocol I in Conventional Warfare', *Military Law Review*, Vol. 98, 1982, pp. 91–127.

[48]   Nor are the wounded and sick explicitly mentioned in relation to the obligation to take precautions in attack and against the effects of attacks; see Additional Protocol I, Articles 57 and 58. See also ICRC Study on Customary International Humanitarian Law (2005), Rules 15 and 22.

[49]   See Henderson, p. 196. See also the commentaries on Article 19, para. 1797, and Article 24, para. 1987, respectively. See further Laurent Gisel, 'Can the incidental killing of military doctors never be excessive?', *International Review of the Red Cross*, Vol. 95, No. 889, March 2013, pp. 215–230.

[50]   See *Official Records of the Diplomatic Conference of Geneva of 1974–1977*, Vol. XI, pp. 64–79.

circumstances, *a fortiori* they should also benefit from the protection accorded to civilians. In other words, if civilians are to be included in the proportionality assessment all the more so should the wounded and sick. Indeed, if the wounded and sick were not to be considered for purposes of the proportionality principle, their presence in the vicinity of legitimate military objectives would be legally irrelevant. However, this would contradict the explicit obligation to respect them in all circumstances and the basic rationale of according special protection to them. It would be unreasonable to consider that direct or indiscriminate attacks against the wounded and sick would be strictly prohibited and would amount to a grave breach, while incidental harm and even excessive incidental casualties would not be prohibited. Accordingly, the presence of wounded and sick members of the armed forces in the vicinity of a military objective is to be taken into consideration when carrying out a proportionality assessment prior to an attack. In addition, and on the basis of the same rationale, an attacker must take precautions in accordance with Article 57 of Additional Protocol I in relation not only to civilians but also to wounded and sick members of the armed forces, to protect them from direct attack and collateral damage.[51]

1358   The obligation to respect is not confined solely to the prohibition of direct or indiscriminate attacks. It applies also to other forms of harmful conduct outside the conduct of hostilities. The purpose of Article 12 is to protect the wounded and sick in the light of their specific vulnerability, such that the obligation to respect merits a broad interpretation as a general prohibition on intentionally harming the wounded and sick.[52] Such an interpretation is supported by a comparison between paragraphs 1 and 2 of Article 12. Paragraph 2 contains details of the general obligation to respect by prescribing that the wounded and sick be treated humanely and by providing examples of strictly prohibited behaviour. As the wording 'in particular' in the second sentence makes clear, the list is not exhaustive. Thus, while the enumeration of examples in Article 12(2) indicates conduct that violates the obligation to respect, the obligation to respect itself is broader and prohibits any form of intentional ill-treatment of the wounded and sick, including less severe violations. In addition, certain particularly serious forms of ill-treatment are sanctioned as grave breaches.[53]

---

[51] Given that the obligation to take feasible precautions is a positive obligation, unlike the proportionality principle, which requires Parties to an armed conflict not to cause excessive damage to civilians and civilian objects, it makes sense to include it under the general obligation to protect the wounded and sick. See, however, United States, *Law of War Manual*, 2015, pp. 418–419, para. 7.3.3.1.

[52] In this regard, an awareness of how the situation of the wounded and sick may differ according to their gender, age or background may help to better identify specific vulnerabilities. For further details, see section H. See also e.g. Lindsey-Curtet/Holst-Roness/Anderson; Coomaraswamy; and Lindsey, 2001.

[53] See First Convention, Article 50, and ICC Statute (1998), Article 8(2)(a).

1359   Where armed forces encounter abuse by an opponent of the status of 'wounded' or 'sick', the uncertainty it can engender may complicate the determination of such status in future engagements and thus undermine respect for the genuinely wounded or sick. The war crime of perfidy is therefore an important corollary to the protection of the wounded and sick.[54] For example, Article 37(1)(b) of Additional Protocol I lists as an example of perfidy 'the feigning of an incapacitation by wounds or sickness' with the intent to kill, injure or capture an adversary. While perfidy is only prohibited if it is used to kill, injure or capture an adversary, credible and effective protection of the wounded and sick requires that no one feign being wounded or sick to gain protection.

2. The obligation to protect

1360   According to Article 12(1), the wounded and sick 'shall be . . . protected in all circumstances'. The obligation to protect is complementary to the obligation to respect. It requires Parties to the conflict to take active steps to protect the wounded and sick from harm. The obligation to protect is an obligation of conduct. The Parties to the conflict are therefore obliged not only to refrain from attacking or otherwise harming the wounded and sick through their own organs (to respect), but also to exercise due diligence in preventing the wounded and sick from being harmed in other ways (to protect).

1361   Article 12(1) does not specify against which kinds of harm or danger the wounded and sick must be protected. The obligation to protect could be taken to imply protection of the wounded and sick against harm posed by others, namely a Party's own soldiers and enemy soldiers or civilians (of whichever nationality). In addition, the obligation to protect could be interpreted as requiring protective measures against other dangers arising in the context of an armed conflict, for example from ongoing hostilities, from natural hazards or from explosive remnants of war. Moreover, the obligation to protect could be interpreted as a requirement to protect them from the dangers arising from their medical condition, i.e. to provide medical treatment.

1362   From 1864 through 1906 and 1929 to 1949, the regime governing the wounded and sick has been consecutively revised with the declared purpose of maximizing the protection of this category of persons.[55] Against this background, the obligation to protect the wounded and sick should be interpreted broadly to include all the forms of harm or danger described above. This is further supported by the object and purpose of the First Convention and of Article 12 in particular, and the absence of any indication to the contrary,

---

[54] See Additional Protocol I, Article 37; ICC Statute (1998), Article 8(2)(b)(xi); and ICRC Study on Customary International Humanitarian Law (2005), Rule 65.

[55] *Final Record of the Diplomatic Conference of Geneva of 1949*, Vol. II-A, pp. 184–185; See also *Official Records of the Diplomatic Conference of Geneva of 1974–1977*, Vol. III, pp. 57–59, and Vol. XI, pp. 64–65.

either in the wording, the preparatory work or subsequent State practice. The wounded and sick may be susceptible to harm because they are too weak to defend themselves against ill-treatment by others, because they are impaired in their mobility and therefore less able to evade certain dangers arising on the battlefield, or because their medical condition, if left untreated, will worsen. It is also important to take into account the specific vulnerabilities of the wounded and sick.[56]

1363   Thus, paragraph 1 sets out a general obligation to protect the wounded and sick against harm, irrespective of its source. Other provisions pertaining to the wounded and sick specify particular aspects of this general obligation. For example, the obligation to collect them (Article 15) aims to protect them against the dangers arising from the battlefield (and to enable their medical treatment) and the obligation to protect them against pillage and ill-treatment (Article 15) aims to protect them from specific forms of harm by others.

1364   The fact that these different aspects of the general obligation are spelled out more specifically in subsequent provisions does not render the more general stipulations in paragraph 1 redundant or in any way restrict these obligations. On the contrary, they serve as catch-all clauses that are sufficiently broad to close any protective gaps and to take account of the vagaries and uncertainties inherent in armed conflict.

1365   The obligation to protect requires positive steps to protect the wounded and sick against any harm or dangers. The exact kind of conduct owed by Parties in a given situation depends on a variety of parameters, ranging from the imminence, the type and the extent of the harm, a State's capacity and available resources, its relationship with the transgressor, and its capacity to exert influence or to intervene, which in turn depends on factors such as geographical proximity, as well as military and humanitarian considerations.[57] Thus, the more grave and imminent the danger, the more will generally be required of States. Evidently, once the wounded and sick are in the power of a Party to the conflict, the Party will have better options to protect them against the worsening of their medical condition and other dangers.

1366   Lastly, with regard to the temporal scope of the provision, the obligation to protect could be understood either narrowly, as an obligation only to stop ongoing harm, or more broadly, as an obligation to proactively prevent or mitigate the harm or dangers posed to the wounded and sick. According to Article 14(3) of the 2001 Draft Articles on State Responsibility, '[t]he breach of an international obligation requiring a State to prevent a given event occurs

---

[56] See fn. 52.
[57] Kessler, p. 506. One example of measures necessary to protect the wounded and sick include taking precautions such as marking hospitals and medical units and transports, as well as the requirement to situate those facilities away from military objectives. See e.g. Articles 19, 36 and 42. Similar obligations apply with respect to prisoner-of-war camps; see Third Convention, Article 23.

when the event occurs and extends over the entire period during which the event continues'. The obligation to protect in Article 12 arises 'at the instant that the State learns of, or should normally have learned of, the existence of a serious risk' that any of the harms described above may occur.[58]

3. In all circumstances

1367   The obligations laid out in Article 12(1) apply 'in all circumstances', a phrase used in other provisions.[59] As is the case with common Article 1, for example,[60] a variety of legal meanings can be accorded to this formula as it is used in Article 12.[61] First of all, it is often argued that the formula underlines the non-reciprocal nature of the Geneva Conventions,[62] meaning that even if the enemy fails to respect its humanitarian law obligations, one's own obligations vis-à-vis the wounded and sick remain intact. Second, it is argued that the formula aims to prevent the invocation of the notion of military necessity or any other pretext – including *jus ad bellum* considerations – to justify non-compliance with the rules protecting the wounded and sick.[63] Indeed, since the end of the Second World War it has become universally accepted that military necessity may not be invoked to override rules of humanitarian law unless specifically provided for.[64] Moreover, the formula could also be interpreted as having geographical and temporal connotations requiring respect and protection of the wounded and sick in all places where the First Convention applies, i.e. in the actual combat zone as well as in places far from the combat zone (the rear), and at all times for the duration of an international armed conflict.

1368   In the light of the ordinary meaning of the wording 'in all circumstances' and in view of the purpose of Article 12, the phrase should be interpreted broadly

---

[58] See ICJ, *Application of the Genocide Convention case*, Merits, Judgment, 2007, para. 431.

[59] Historically, see e.g. Article 9 of the 1906 Geneva Convention and Articles 1, 9 and 25(1) of the 1929 Geneva Convention on the Wounded and Sick. See also e.g. Article 24 of the First Convention, Article 12 of the Second Convention, Article 14 of the Third Convention, Article 27 of the Fourth Convention, Articles 1(1), 10(2), 51(1) and 75(1) of Additional Protocol I and Articles 4(1), 7(2) and 13 of Additional Protocol II, as well as common Article 3(1).

[60] Nevertheless, Article 12(1) relates to a rather different context: whereas Article 12 concerns respect for and protection of a specific category of persons, the obligation to respect and ensure respect in common Article 1 concerns compliance with all legal provisions laid down in the Geneva Conventions.

[61] See the commentary on common Article 1, section F. See also Geiss, 2015, pp. 132–133, and Focarelli, pp. 125–171.

[62] This argument is commonly made with respect to the use of the formula in common Article 1. See e.g. Sandoz/Swinarski/Zimmermann (eds), *Commentary on the Additional Protocols*, ICRC, 1987, paras 47–51; ICTY, *Kupreškić* Trial Judgment, 2000, para. 517; and Condorelli/Boisson de Chazournes, p. 19. This finding is confirmed by Resolution 3 of the 30th International Conference of the Red Cross and Red Crescent, Geneva, 2007, which emphasizes that the obligation to respect in common Article 1 'is not based on reciprocity' (preambular para. 12). See also Vienna Convention on the Law of Treaties (1969), Article 60(5).

[63] See also Kleffner, pp. 326–327.

[64] See United States, Military Tribunal at Nuremberg, *Hostages case*, Judgment, 1948, p. 647. It may only be considered where humanitarian law provisions make explicit provision for the exception of military necessity; see Geiss, 2010, p. 558.

to encompass all the aforementioned meanings. The wounded and sick are to be respected just as much when they are with their own armed forces or in no man's land as when they have fallen into the hands of the enemy. The obligation applies to all combatants in any armed force, whoever they may be, and also to non-combatants. It applies also to civilians, in regard to whom Article 18 specifically states that 'the civilian population shall respect these wounded and sick, and in particular abstain from offering them violence'. A clear statement to that effect was essential in view of the special character that modern warfare is liable to assume (dispersion of combatants, isolation of units, mobility of fronts, etc.) and that may lead to closer and more frequent contacts between military and civilians. It was necessary, therefore, that the principle of the inviolability of wounded and sick combatants be brought home, not only to the fighting forces, but also to the general public. For all these reasons, the phrase should be understood literally.

F. Paragraph 2: Treatment and care of the wounded and sick

1. Humane treatment and medical care without adverse distinction

1369   According to the first sentence of Article 12(2), the wounded and sick 'shall be treated humanely and cared for by the Party to the conflict in whose power they may be'. The word 'shall' leaves no doubt as to the obligatory character of this paragraph.

1370   Paragraph 2 applies to situations where the wounded and sick are in the power of a Party to the conflict. For the purposes of this provision, the notion of being in the power of a Party to the conflict includes being in the power of one's own Party. Hence, the obligations in Article 12(2) apply to a State in relation to the wounded and sick of its own armed forces (and those persons listed in Article 13) as well as to the wounded and sick of the adverse Party. Indeed, in relation to wounded and sick enemy personnel who simultaneously qualify as prisoners of war, Article 14 uses the phrase 'who fall into enemy hands'. From this it may be inferred that at least for the purposes of the First Convention, the notion of being in the power of a Party to the conflict in Article 12 has a different meaning to falling into enemy hands as used in Article 14 and includes being in the power of one's own State. In a nutshell, if a State is factually in a position to treat a wounded or sick person inhumanely, that person must be considered to be in the power of that Party.

1371   A comparison between Article 12(2) and Article 15(1) indicates that while the latter primarily envisages the provision of medical first aid in the immediate aftermath of hostilities,[65] the former pertains primarily to the provision of more comprehensive and longer-term medical care under more secure conditions.

---

[65] See the commentary on Article 15, paras 1481–1482.

a. Humane treatment

1372 According to Article 12(2), the wounded and sick 'shall be treated humanely'. The obligation of humane treatment of protected persons is a cornerstone of international humanitarian law. It is to be found in various humanitarian treaties, past and present,[66] as well as in customary international law.[67]

1373 The obligation imposes a minimum standard, namely a duty to respect the inherent human dignity of the wounded and sick,[68] their inviolable quality as human beings.[69] The obligation thus pervades all aspects of treatment of the wounded and sick; it is relevant in a myriad of circumstances and it would be impossible and even unduly restrictive to attempt a comprehensive definition of humane treatment. It is for this reason that the Geneva Conventions and their Additional Protocols – like human rights treaties – have wisely abstained from providing such a definition.[70] That said, it should be recalled that in order to treat people humanely, it is important to understand and take into account the ways in which gender, economic, cultural and political factors shape social structures and affect men and women differently.[71] The requirement of humane treatment imposes an obligation of result. Thus, any treatment that falls below the standard of humane treatment violates the obligation.

1374 Because of its broad protective dimension and so as to make its application to a specific situation more manageable in judicial practice, the obligation of humane treatment is sometimes depicted merely as a prohibition of 'inhuman treatment'.[72] Hence, the obligation to treat the wounded and sick humanely logically includes all prohibitions on treatment that is inhuman or degrading.

1375 The use of the wording 'in particular' in paragraph 2 indicates that this list is not exhaustive. Other forms of ill-treatment not explicitly listed in Article 12, but mentioned in Article 50, such as wilfully causing great suffering, are also

---

[66] See Hague Regulations (1899), Article 4; Hague Regulations (1907), Article 4; Geneva Convention on the Wounded and Sick (1929), Article 1; and Geneva Convention on Prisoners of War (1929), Article 2. See also Article 13 of the Third Convention, Article 27 of the Fourth Convention and Articles 10 and 75 of Additional Protocol I, which uphold the principle of humane treatment of persons not or no longer directly participating in the hostilities. In the context of non-international armed conflict, see, in particular, common Article 3 and Article 4(1) of Additional Protocol II.

[67] ICRC Study on Customary International Humanitarian Law (2005), Rule 87.

[68] See Henckaerts/Doswald-Beck, commentary on Rule 87, fn. 42 and the references contained therein.

[69] See e.g. Colombia, Constitutional Court, *Constitutional Case No. C-291/07*, 2007, section III-D, Heading 5: 'The general guarantee of humane treatment provides the overall guiding principle behind the Geneva Conventions, in the sense that the object itself is the humanitarian task of protecting the individual as a person, safeguarding the rights derived from it.' See also United States, *Naval Handbook*, 2007, pp. 11–1–11–2.

[70] A comparison with paragraph 3, in which the word 'treatment', in the light of the reference to 'medical reasons', is evidently used in a medical sense, supports the view that in the first sentence of paragraph 2 the word 'treatment' is used in a more general sense. A clearer distinction was included in Article 1 of the 1929 Geneva Convention on the Wounded and Sick, which stated that '[the wounded and sick] shall be treated with humanity, and cared for medically, without distinction of nationality, by the belligerent in whose power they may be'.

[71] See fn. 52.   [72] ICTY, *Delalić* Trial Judgment, 1998, paras 520–543.

prohibited. Reference can also be made to common Article 3, which also gives expression to particular aspects of what humane treatment requires and what kind of actions or behaviour would clearly fall below that standard.

1376   More importantly, however, other forms of treatment that cannot be readily subsumed under any of the existing explicit prohibitions may also violate the obligation of humane treatment. For example, the Eritrea-Ethiopia Claims Commission – albeit with regard to the humane treatment of prisoners of war – held that the evacuation of prisoners of war from the battlefield after their footwear had been seized, forcing them to walk barefoot through harsh terrain, which 'unnecessarily compounded their misery', was in violation of Article 20 of the Third Convention requiring evacuations to be 'effected humanely'.[73]

1377   Given that it is based on the fundamental concept of human dignity, the standard of humane treatment is the same for all categories of protected persons and applies equally in international and non-international armed conflict. Thus, practice regarding other humanitarian law provisions may serve as useful guidance on what humane treatment requires under Article 12(2) and on what kind of treatment would fall below that threshold.

1378   For example, some obligations in the Third Convention can be understood as specifications of the obligation to treat persons humanely for the wounded and sick covered by Article 12 who are in enemy hands. Thus, such persons must be provided, *inter alia*, with: appropriate accommodation that offers sufficient health and hygiene standards;[74] sufficient food and water;[75] clothing appropriate to the climate;[76] suitable medical care;[77] protection from the rigours of the climate;[78] protection from the effects of armed conflict;[79] freedom in the exercise of religious duties;[80] and protection from insults and public curiosity.[81]

---

[73] See Eritrea-Ethiopia Claims Commission, *Prisoners of War, Eritrea's Claim*, Partial Award, 2003, para. 68.

[74] Third Convention, Articles 22(1) and 29; Fourth Convention, Article 85. See also United States, *Naval Handbook*, 2007, para. 11.2: 'Humane Treatment . . . All detainees shall: . . . b. Receive sufficient food, drinking water, shelter, and clothing'.

[75] Third Convention, Article 26; Fourth Convention, Article 89. See also the examples of humane treatment given, albeit in the context of international armed conflict, in Burundi, *Regulation on International Humanitarian Law*, 2007, p. 15: 'Les ennemis capturés sont faits P.G. [prisonniers de guerre] Il est interdit de les tuer ou de les torturer. Il faut les traiter humainement (les nourrir, les habiller, . . .)' ('Captured enemy combatants become POWs [prisoners of war]. It is prohibited to kill or torture them. They must be treated humanely (fed, clothed, . . .)). See also United States, *Naval Handbook*, 2007, para. 11.2.

[76] Third Convention, Article 27; Fourth Convention, Article 90. See also e.g. Burundi, *Regulation on International Humanitarian Law*, 2007, p. 15. See also United States, *Naval Handbook*, 2007, para. 11.2.

[77] Third Convention, Articles 15, 30 and 31; Fourth Convention, Articles 91 and 92. See also e.g. United States, *Naval Handbook*, 2007, para. 11.2: 'Humane Treatment . . . All detainees shall: a. Receive appropriate medical attention and treatment'.

[78] Third Convention, Article 22(2); see also Article 27(1).

[79] Third Convention, Article 23(1)–(2).

[80] Third Convention, Article 34; Fourth Convention, Articles 86 and 93. See also e.g. United States, *Naval Handbook*, 2007, para. 11.2: 'Humane Treatment . . . All detainees shall: . . . c. Be allowed the free exercise of religion, consistent with the requirements for safety and security'.

[81] Third Convention, Article 13(2); Fourth Convention, Article 27(1). According to Canada, *Code of Conduct*, 2007, p. 2–9, para. 5, this is to be applied to all persons detained by Canadian forces

Protected persons must be treated with all due regard to their sex[82] and must not be used as human shields.[83] As the commentary on common Article 3 explains, persons protected under that article who are deprived of their liberty also benefit from these protections, among others, by virtue of the right to be treated humanely.

1379   In the context of Article 12(2), such a broad understanding of the notion of humane treatment *prima facie* partially overlaps with the obligation to care for the wounded and sick. This is no defect, however. Rather, this interplay between the two obligations creates a comprehensive system of protection that heeds the realities of armed conflict. The obligation to treat the wounded and sick humanely imposes an obligation of result and as such constitutes an irreducible minimum. Humane treatment is to be expected in any circumstances. At the same time, the obligation to care for the wounded and sick, especially in terms of medical care, is an obligation of means, subject to the best that can be done in the prevailing security situation and with available capacities. While the expected standard of medical and other care may vary depending on the circumstances (in particular, it may be significantly higher than the minimum standard imposed by the requirement of humane treatment), it must never under any circumstances fall below the threshold of humane treatment.

b. The obligation to care for the wounded and sick

1380   The obligation to care for the wounded and sick requires the Parties to an international armed conflict to provide medical care, i.e. to take active steps to

---

personnel carrying out military operations other than Canadian domestic operations as an element of the rule to 'treat all detained persons humanely in accordance with the standard set by the Third Geneva Convention'.

[82]   Third Convention, Article 14(2); Fourth Convention, Article 27(2). See also e.g. Djibouti, *Manual on International Humanitarian Law*, 2004, p. 23: 'Les femmes ont droit également, en application du DIH [droit international humanitaire], à certaines formes de protection spécifiques à leur sexe, qui sont les suivantes: – Traitement humain des femmes combattantes, notamment des prisonnières de guerre' ('Women also have the right, in accordance with IHL [international humanitarian law], to certain kinds of protection specific to their sex. These are the following: – Humane treatment of female combatants, notably female prisoners of war'). According to Canada's *Code of Conduct*, 2007, p. 2–9, para. 5, the following applies as an element of the rule to 'treat all detained persons humanely in accordance with the standard set by the Third Geneva Convention' to the treatment of all persons detained by Canadian forces personnel carrying out military operations other than Canadian domestic operations: 'Detained persons shall be treated with all due regard to their gender. Searches will be conducted by persons of the same sex unless, in exceptional circumstances, they have to be conducted by a member of the opposite sex. Searches conducted by members of the opposite sex will be carried out in a respectful manner.' See also Additional Protocol I, Article 76(1).

[83]   Third Convention, Article 23(1); Fourth Convention, Article 28. See also ICC Statute (1998), Article 8(2)(b)(xxiii); ICRC Study on Customary International Humanitarian Law (2005), Rule 97; and United Kingdom, *Manual of the Law of Armed Conflict*, 2004, Chapter 15: Internal Armed Conflict, p. 392, para. 15.14.2: 'Recent armed conflicts have been blighted by the use of "human shields" to protect military installations from attack.... These practices violate the basic law of armed conflict principles of targeting, discrimination and *humane treatment* of those *hors de combat*' (emphasis added).

ameliorate the condition of the wounded and sick. It is an obligation which must be carried out with due diligence.[84]

i. Content of the obligation to care for the wounded and sick

1381 The exact content of this obligation depends on what kind of medical care can reasonably be expected under the specific circumstances of each case. For example, a severely wounded soldier will require greater medical care than a soldier with minor injuries. Even in the case of fatal wounds, some treatment to ease pain and distress is required.[85]

1382 In addition, the medical personnel of a Party which has significant resources at its disposal can be expected and will therefore be required to do more than the medical personnel of a Party which has limited means.[86] If medical personnel are available, higher standards of medical care can similarly be expected than if no such personnel are available. Even regular soldiers, however, can be expected to deliver first aid and basic care. Similarly, when medical care has to be administered on the battlefield, due diligence does not require the same standard of medical treatment as that required once the wounded and sick have been transferred to the relative security of a medical facility at sufficient distance from the fighting.

1383 With respect to the kind and quality of medical care that is due, the basic rule is that the wounded and sick must receive the 'medical care and attention required by their condition'. Albeit not explicitly mentioned in Article 12, this is provided for in Article 10(2) of Additional Protocol I and is generally accepted.[87] The obligation to provide the care required by the person's condition is nuanced in Article 10(2) of Protocol I by the qualification that care must be provided 'to the fullest extent practicable', which was added in recognition of the fact that not all States have the same resources and that it might not be possible for a State to provide all the wounded and sick with the medical care

---

[84] Sassòli, p. 412. Regarding the due diligence standard, see Dupuy, p. 384; Riccardo Pisillo-Mazzeschi, 'The Due Diligence Rule and the Nature of the International Responsibility of States', *German Yearbook of International Law*, Vol. 35, 1992, pp. 9–51, at 41; Jan Arno Hessbruegge, 'The Historical Development of the Doctrines of Attribution and Due Diligence in International Law', *New York University Journal of International Law & Politics*, Vol. 36, Nos 2 & 3, 2004, pp. 265–306; Rüdiger Wolfrum, 'Obligation of Result Versus Obligation of Conduct: Some Thoughts About the Implementation of International Obligations', in Mahnoush H. Arsanjani *et al.* (ed.), *Looking to the Future: Essays on International Law in Honor of W. Michael Reisman*, Martinus Nijhoff Publishers, Leiden, 2011, pp. 363–384; and Timo Koivurova, 'Due Diligence', version of February 2010, in Rüdiger Wolfrum (ed.), *Max Planck Encyclopedia of Public International Law*, Oxford University Press, http://opil.ouplaw.com/home/EPIL. See also James R. Crawford, 'Second report on State responsibility', UN Doc. A/CN.4/498, 17 March 1999, pp. 23–40, and ICJ, *Application of the Genocide Convention case*, Merits, Judgment, 2007, para. 430.

[85] United States, *Law of Armed Conflict Deskbook*, 2012 p. 49.

[86] See e.g. Lindsey, 2001, p. 112: 'Especially in armed conflicts, the necessary resources for providing safe blood donations may be limited.'

[87] See also ICRC Study on Customary International Humanitarian Law (2005), Rule 110.

required by their condition.[88] Nevertheless, the requirement to provide care 'to the fullest extent practicable' means that it is not sufficient for a Party to do only the minimum necessary for a person's survival; rather, it must do everything it reasonably can to care for that person. Caring for the wounded and sick also entails providing rehabilitation for persons with disabilities. While for the wounded and sick of enemy armed forces this obligation flows from Article 30 of the Third Convention, it is important to recall that it applies also to the wounded and sick of a State's own armed forces. In addition, it follows from the principle of non-discrimination that the standard of care of the wounded and sick must be the same for one's own and the enemy's personnel.[89]

1384   Although the highest standards of medical care would be desirable, the First Convention requires only what can reasonably be expected in the given circumstances, taking into consideration the available resources in terms of personnel and equipment as well as the security conditions. The kind of medical care that can reasonably be expected in a given situation, therefore, will depend on the availability of medical personnel and whether medical care is administered by qualified doctors, paramedics, or soldiers or other persons without any medical qualification. If sufficient medical equipment and personnel are available, a high standard of medical care is expected. Under less optimal conditions, the expected standard would be lower. Thus, the Eritrea-Ethiopia Claims Commission held that 'the requirement to provide . . . medical care during the initial period after capture must be assessed in light of the harsh conditions on the battlefield and the limited extent of medical training and equipment available to front line troops'.[90]

1385   Specific medical standards may change over time and there may be differences from country to country.[91] Nevertheless, some general guidance regarding the applicable standards of medical ethics and professional medical conduct may be derived from universally applicable, general stipulations and instruments adopted by the World Medical Association.[92] There are many studies on

---

[88] *Official Records of the Diplomatic Conference of Geneva of 1974–1977*, Vol. XI, pp. 76–77.
[89] See section F.1.c.
[90] Eritrea-Ethiopia Claims Commission, *Prisoners of War, Ethiopia's Claim*, Partial Award, 2003, para. 70. Ethiopia had alleged that Eritrea had 'failed to provide necessary medical attention to Ethiopian POWs [prisoners of war] after capture and during evacuation, as required under customary international law reflected in Geneva Conventions I (Article 12) and III (Articles 20 and 15)'. Ethiopia argued that '[m]any Ethiopian declarants testified that their wounds were not cleaned and bandaged at or shortly after capture, leading to infection and other complications'. Eritrea responded that 'its troops provided rudimentary first aid as soon as possible, including in transit camps'; *ibid.* para. 69. While the Commission came to the general conclusion that there was no violation, logistical and resource constraints may not excuse a failure to provide even basic care.
[91] See *ibid.* para. 106.
[92] Instruments concerning medical ethics in times of armed conflict, especially: the World Medical Association's Regulations in Times of Armed Conflict (adopted by the 10th World Medical Assembly, Havana, Cuba, October 1956, as amended or revised in 1957, 1983, 2004, 2006 and 2012); Rules Governing the Care of Sick and Wounded, Particularly in Time of Conflict (adopted by the 10th World Medical Assembly, Havana, Cuba, October 1956, edited and amended in 1957 and 1983); Standards of Professional Conduct regarding the Hippocratic Oath and its modern

the type of equipment and techniques that medics should use and on the procedures they should follow. In all cases, the provision of care must always be in accordance with the rules of medical ethics.[93]

1386   Article 10(2) of Additional Protocol I further stipulates that care must be provided 'with the least possible delay'. The parameters set out in that article can be understood as specifications of the due diligence character of the obligation to care for the wounded and sick; as such, they are inherent in the obligation set out in Article 12 of the First Convention.

1387   The obligation to care for the wounded and sick also includes other – similarly essential – forms of non-medical care, such as the provision of food, shelter, clothing and hygiene items.[94] This is because exclusively medical treatment of a wound or sickness is not sufficient to ameliorate the condition of the wounded and sick. Indeed, it would be meaningless to provide medical care if adequate food, shelter, clothing and hygiene items were not provided simultaneously.[95]

1388   This is especially true when severely wounded soldiers are being treated in hospital for a longer period of time. The reason why it was not specifically spelled out in Article 12 may be because Article 14 stipulates that the wounded and sick 'who fall into enemy hands shall be prisoners of war' and as such they benefit, *inter alia*, from Articles 25, 26, 27 and 29 of the Third Convention regarding the provision of adequate quarters, food, clothing and hygiene. However, no such specifications exist with respect to a Party's obligations to its own wounded and sick personnel.

ii. The obligation to have medical services

1389 Given that the quality of medical care hinges on a functioning medical service, including the availability of qualified medical personnel and equipment, it is of particular relevance to consider whether the obligation to provide medical care for the wounded and sick also requires Parties to an armed conflict to put medical services in place and to equip and staff their medical units in

---

version, the Declaration of Geneva, and its supplementary International Code of Medical Ethics (adopted by the 3rd WMA General Assembly, London, England, October 1949, as amended in 1968, 1983 and 2006). See also ICRC, *Health Care in Danger: The Responsibilities of Health-Care Personnel Working in Armed Conflicts and Other Emergencies*, ICRC, Geneva, 2012, pp. 55–62.

[93] Bothe/Partsch/Solf, p. 108, para. 2.3 (end). See also the explicit references to medical ethics in Article 16(1) and (2) of Additional Protocol I.

[94] At the time of drafting of Additional Protocol I, the Holy See proposed an amendment to make it clear that all the needs of the wounded and sick should be attended to and not just medical needs. This proposal – which was only made during the oral deliberations and not submitted formally – was not ultimately adopted. As far as can be seen, this was solely because of editorial considerations and not because it was considered that the wounded and sick should not be entitled to the provision of food, shelter, clothing and hygiene items. The Holy See's proposal was supported by the United States and Belgium; Iraq argued that the use of the term 'medical care' rather than 'medical treatment' encompassed the broader meaning. *Official Records of the Diplomatic Conference of Geneva of 1974–1977*, Vol. XI, pp. 69, 73, 77 and 78.

[95] For further details on women's specific hygiene and nutritional needs, see para. 1434.

accordance with the anticipated number of wounded or sick people. In this regard, the Secretary-General of the 1906 Diplomatic Conference already pointed out that the onus was on all Parties to a conflict to make provision in advance for medical personnel and equipment sufficient to ensure that all wounded and sick persons could be cared for.[96] There is evidence that many States do make such preparations in advance.[97]

1390   Indeed, the obligation to provide the wounded and sick with medical care can only be effectively fulfilled if an adequate medical service exists. Therefore, because the availability of medical personnel and equipment is a prerequisite for medical care, States party to the Convention have to take the preparatory and organizational steps that can reasonably be expected of them.

1391   No precise rule exists that would require the deployment of X number of medical personnel if X number of wounded people are to be expected. However, in the extreme case that a Party to an armed conflict neglects to provide any medical personnel or medical equipment and facilities whatsoever, that failure would violate the obligation to care for the wounded and sick. This was confirmed by the Eritrea-Ethiopia Claims Commission, which held that:

> Eritrea and Ethiopia cannot, at least at present, be required to have the same standards for medical treatment as developed countries. However, scarcity of finances and infrastructure cannot excuse a failure to grant *the minimum standard of medical care* required by international humanitarian law. The cost of such care is not, in any event, substantial in comparison with the other costs imposed by the armed conflict.[98] [Emphasis added.]

The Claims Commission thus confirmed that a basic minimum of medical care can reasonably be expected whatever the circumstances, even when a State lacks significant resources. What may reasonably be expected may vary according to each State's resources and level of development in other fields; expectations may also change over time. States have to create a medical service that allows them to fulfil their obligations under humanitarian law.[99]

c. The prohibition of any adverse distinction

1392   According to Article 12(2), the wounded and sick must be cared for 'without any adverse distinction founded on sex, race, nationality, religion, political

---

[96] Röthlisberger, pp. 18–20.

[97] See Israel, Supreme Court sitting as High Court of Justice, *Physicians for Human Rights* v. *Prime Minister of Israel and others*, Judgment, 2009, para. 9; 'The respondents provided details of the measures adopted before and during the military operations in order to maintain and improve the coordination of the evacuation of the wounded.' See also United Kingdom, *Joint Medical Doctrine*, 2011, Chapter 5, Operations, and para. 1A5.

[98] Eritrea-Ethiopia Claims Commission, *Prisoners of War, Eritrea's Claim*, Partial Award, 2003, paras 138 and 115–119; *Prisoners of War, Ethiopia's Claim*, Partial Award, 2003, paras 104–107.

[99] See also International Covenant on Economic, Social and Cultural Rights (1966), Article 12(2)(c) and (d), and UN Economic and Social Council, *General Comment No. 14, The Right to the Highest Attainable Standard of Health*, UN Doc. E/C.12/2000/4, 11 August 2000.

opinions, or any other similar criteria'. Historically, the idea behind the non-discrimination clause was to ensure that the wounded and sick of the adverse Party received the same treatment and care as members of a Party's own armed forces. Accordingly, previous provisions in the 1906 and 1929 Geneva Conventions referred exclusively to the prohibited criterion of 'nationality'.[100] Over time and in line with developments in the area of human rights law,[101] the list of prohibited criteria for discrimination was extended.

1393   Whereas the prohibition of discrimination on grounds of sex, race, nationality, religion and political opinion is self-explanatory,[102] the reference to 'any other similar criteria' requires further explanation. It indicates that the list in paragraph 2 is not exhaustive. The drafters wisely anticipated a dynamic evolution of the catalogue of prohibited criteria and chose a sufficiently open formulation which could accommodate additional grounds.[103] The determination of which criteria qualify as prohibited at a given time is central to determining the scope of the prohibition of adverse distinction. Article 9 of Additional Protocol I requires the application of the provisions which are intended to ameliorate the condition of the wounded and sick 'without any adverse distinction founded on race, colour, sex, language, religion or belief, political or other opinion, national or social origin, wealth, birth or other status, or on any other similar criteria'.[104] The open wording of Article 12(2) and situating paragraph 2 in the context of contemporary listings of prohibited criteria allows for the consideration of the additional criteria spelled out in Additional Protocol I.

1394   The non-discrimination clause in Article 12 does not prohibit each and every distinction, but only 'adverse distinctions' based on prohibited criteria.[105] In

---

[100] See Geneva Convention (1906), Article 1; see also Geneva Convention on the Wounded and Sick (1929), Article 1.

[101] See in particular Universal Declaration of Human Rights (1948), Article 2.

[102] On Article 2, para. 1, of the 1966 International Covenant on Civil and Political Rights, see UN Human Rights Committee, *General Comment No. 18, Non-discrimination*, 10 November 1989. On Article 14 of the 1950 European Convention on Human Rights and its Protocol 12 of 2000, see Heiko Sauer, 'Art. 14: Diskriminierungsverbot', in Ulrich Karpenstein and Franz C. Mayer (eds), *EMRK. Konvention zum Schutz der Menschenrechte und Grundfreiheiten. Kommentar*, Beck, Munich, 2012, pp. 340–358.

[103] See *Final Record of the Diplomatic Conference of Geneva of 1949*, Vol. II-A, pp. 190–191.

[104] Article 75(1) of Additional Protocol I requires protection be provided 'without any adverse distinction based upon race, colour, sex, language, religion or belief, political or other opinion, national or social origin, wealth, birth or other status, or on any other similar criteria'. See also ICRC Study on Customary International Humanitarian Law (2005), Rule 88. The human rights law principle of non-discrimination refers to similar criteria, see e.g. UN Charter (1945), Article 1(3); Convention on the Elimination of Racial Discrimination (1965), Article 2; International Covenant on Civil and Political Rights (1966), Article 2(1); International Covenant on Economic, Social and Cultural Rights (1966), Articles 2(2) and 3; Convention on the Elimination of Discrimination against Women (1979), Article 2; Convention on the Rights of the Child (1989), Article 2(1); European Convention on Human Rights (1950), Article 14; American Convention on Human Rights (1969), Article 1(1); and African Charter on Human and Peoples' Rights (1981), Article 2.

[105] Moreover, paragraph 2 prohibits adverse distinction only with regard to a specific group of persons, namely the wounded and sick. It is therefore more limited in scope than the general rule laid down in customary international humanitarian law, according to which '[a]dverse

particular, as far as the obligation to provide (medical) care for the wounded and sick is concerned, it is clear that different medical conditions require different forms of medical treatment and that certain distinctions are unavoidable. This rationale is also reflected in Article 12(3) which provides that urgent medical reasons are a ground for priority in treatment. Moreover, such an interpretation is in line with Article 10(2) of Additional Protocol I, which requires that '[t]here shall be no distinction among [the wounded and sick] founded on any grounds other than medical ones', as well as with the contemporary rule of customary international law.[106]

1395   Non-adverse distinctions necessary to give the wounded and sick equal treatment and care are not prohibited, but are instead important to fulfil the obligation without discrimination. This might include taking steps to ensure that all persons who are wounded or sick are able to seek and receive equal care when their social, economic, cultural or political situation or status might otherwise deter them from doing so.[107]

1396   One difficult question that arises is whether the prohibition of 'adverse distinction' prohibits preferential treatment for one's own personnel in situations where enemy personnel receive an acceptable standard of medical care. Reportedly, during the armed conflicts in Iraq and Afghanistan, wounded US soldiers were stabilized and shipped to Germany or the United States as quickly as possible for further treatment, but 'Iraqi prisoners and civilians, on the other hand, receive[d] all their care in Iraq'.[108] In view of the wording of the first sentence of paragraph 2, this arguably amounts to a distinction on the basis of nationality and as such it might seem to qualify as a prohibited 'adverse distinction'. However, it could also be argued that as long as Iraqi soldiers in the power of the United States received the same standard of medical care as US soldiers who were being cared for in Iraq, there is no *adverse* distinction in the sense of paragraph 2. The gist of the prohibition of adverse distinction is not to prevent one's own soldiers from receiving the best possible medical care, but to ensure that enemy soldiers receive the kind of care required by their medical condition and that the standard of care that enemy soldiers receive is not lowered

---

distinction in the application of international humanitarian law ... is prohibited' (ICRC Study on Customary International Humanitarian Law (2005), Rule 88).

[106] *Ibid.* Rule 110.

[107] In order to fulfil the obligations under Article 12, it is important to identify and assess, drawing on the experience of people with different perspectives, how social and cultural barriers associated with the fear of stigma, social consequences or discrimination might hinder equal treatment or care. For example, in a given context men and women might deal differently with psychological problems, stigmatized diseases or sexual or gender-based violence. Typical non-adverse distinctions could include, if possible: only female health workers tending to the needs of wounded and sick women, where culturally appropriate; the availability of separate male/female consulting rooms; and awareness of the need to handle gender-specific health problems or experiences of violence with sensitivity and discretion.

[108] Gawande, p. 2473.

in order to make personnel and other resources available for the treatment of one's own forces.

2. Specifically prohibited forms of conduct

1397 Article 12(2) '*strictly*' prohibits 'any attempts upon [the] lives [of the wounded and sick], or violence to their persons' (emphasis added).[109] Use of the word 'strictly' emphasizes the absolute nature of these prohibitions, which admit of no exception. The word 'any' indicates that these general prohibitions are to be interpreted broadly to cover any form of violence, whether lethal or non-lethal, physical or psychological, against the wounded and sick.

1398   The second sentence of paragraph 2 lists specific examples of these general prohibitions, namely murder, extermination, torture, biological experiments, wilfully leaving the wounded and sick without medical assistance and care, and the creation of conditions exposing them to contagion or infection. These forms of prohibited conduct are specific expressions of the obligation to treat the wounded and sick humanely.

1399   The list of prohibited forms of conduct is not exhaustive. As the wording 'in particular' indicates, other forms of conduct may be prohibited as well. This holds true especially with regard to prohibited forms of conduct that are not explicitly mentioned in Article 12(2) but that are listed as grave breaches in Article 50 of the Convention.[110] In particular, this applies with regard to the grave breaches of 'inhuman treatment' and 'wilfully causing great suffering, or serious injury to body or health'.[111]

1400   The same holds true for sexual violence and 'outrages upon personal dignity, in particular humiliating and degrading treatment'.[112] These forms of prohibited conduct can be subsumed under the prohibition of 'violence to their persons' or the general prohibition of inhuman treatment in the first sentence of paragraph 2.

a. Murder

1401 While murder is prohibited in the Geneva Conventions and Additional Protocols,[113] it is not defined therein. It has been stated that '[m]urder is a crime

---

[109] The equally authentic French version of Article 12 reads: 'Est strictement interdite toute atteinte à leur vie et à leur personne.'

[110] See also ICC Statute (1998), Article 8(2)(a).   [111] See Article 50.

[112] See ICC Statute (1998), Article 8(2)(b)(xxi) and (xxii). See also Roberta Arnold and Stefan Wehrenberg, 'Outrages upon personal dignity', in Triffterer/Ambos, pp. 469–476, and Michael Cottier and Sabine Mzee, 'Rape and other forms of sexual violence', in Triffterer/Ambos, pp. 476–503.

[113] As well as under Article 12 of the First Convention, murder is prohibited under Article 12 of the Second Convention and Article 32 of the Fourth Convention. The Third Convention contains no specific prohibition of murder, but its Article 13 generally prohibits '[a]ny

that is clearly understood and well defined in the national law of every State. This prohibited act does not require any further explanation.'[114] However, conceptions of the notion of murder may vary in domestic legislation, influenced by national criminal law traditions.[115]

1402   According to the ICTY, 'there can be no line drawn between "wilful killing" and "murder" which affects their content',[116] the only difference being that in non-international armed conflict 'the offence need not have been directed against a "protected person" but against a person "taking no active part in the hostilities"'.[117] This approach, consistently asserted in case law, was affirmed in 2002 by the ICC Assembly of States Parties, which for the war crimes of 'wilful killing' in international armed conflict and 'murder' in non-international armed conflict adopted substantively identical elements of crimes, with the exception of the victims of the crimes.[118] International case law on 'wilful killing' can therefore be consulted for the meaning of 'murder' and vice versa.[119]

1403   Based on the above, the following elements of the prohibition of 'murder' in Article 12 can be identified:

– It is prohibited to kill, or cause the death of, a wounded or sick member of the armed forces or other wounded or sick person mentioned in Article 13 of the First Convention.[120]

unlawful act or omission by the Detaining Power causing death or seriously endangering the health of a prisoner of war in its custody' and requires that 'prisoners of war must at all times be protected, particularly against acts of violence'; for details, see the respective commentaries on these provisions. Murder is also prohibited under Article 75(2)(a) of Additional Protocol I, under common Article 3, and under Article 4(2)(a) of Additional Protocol II, as well as under customary international humanitarian law (ICRC Study on Customary International Humanitarian Law (2005), Rule 89).

[114] See ILC Draft Code of Crimes against the Peace and Security of Mankind (1996), p. 48, para. 7, commenting on 'murder' as a crime against humanity.

[115] For an overview of some systems, see e.g. Jeremy Horder (ed.), *Homicide Law in Comparative Perspective*, Hart Publishing, Oxford, 2007.

[116] See ICTY, *Mucić* Trial Judgment, 1998, para. 422.

[117] See ICTY, *Kordić and Čerkez* Trial Judgment, 2001, para. 233.

[118] Under the 2002 Elements of Crimes, the elements adopted for the war crime of wilful killing in Article 8(2)(a)(i) of the 1998 ICC Statute read in part:
1. The perpetrator killed one or more persons. [footnote: The term 'killed' is interchangeable with the term 'caused death'. This footnote applies to all elements which use either of these concepts.]
2. Such person or persons were protected under one or more of the Geneva Conventions of 1949.
    The elements adopted for the war crime of murder in Article 8(2)(c)(i) of the 1998 ICC Statute read in part:
1. The perpetrator killed one or more persons.
2. Such person or persons were either *hors de combat*, or were civilians, medical personnel, or religious personnel [footnote omitted] taking no active part in the hostilities.

[119] For further details, see the commentary on Article 50, section D.1.

[120] For details, see *ibid.*

- Murder is prohibited whether committed by act or omission.[121] The conscious failure, for example, to provide, when possible to do so, sufficient food or medical care to the wounded and sick in the sense of the First Convention who are under one's responsibility, leading to their death, can therefore also fall under the prohibition of murder under Article 12.[122]
- Prohibited as 'murder' – as opposed to other forms of attempts upon their lives – is the intentional killing or causing of death of such persons, as well as the reckless killing or causing of their deaths. An act or omission does not need to be premeditated to be covered by the prohibition of 'murder' in Article 12. On the other end of the spectrum, deaths that are purely accidental or the unforeseeable consequences of a person's negligent act or omission do not fall under the prohibition of 'murder'.[123] In this respect, however, it needs to be kept in mind that in many situations the wounded and sick in the sense of the First Convention are under the complete control of a Party to a conflict and are therefore dependent on that Party for their survival. A certain degree of care and diligence can therefore be expected for an act or omission leading to death not to be regarded as reckless.[124]

1404   Murder is prohibited whatever the motivation may be. Thus, so-called 'mercy killings', i.e. killings to put wounded or sick combatants 'out of their misery' are in contravention of Article 12 and amount to the grave breach of wilful killing. Moreover, it has been suggested that the practice of so-called 'dead-check', which involves the 'shooting of wounded or apparently dead [enemies] to insure that they are dead', is not uncommon on the battlefield.[125] Whatever the validity of these claims, the practice is prohibited.[126] Once persons are wounded or sick as defined by humanitarian law, attempts on their

---

[121] This is independent of the question of whether the violation of the prohibition will lead to international criminal responsibility. For details, see *ibid.*

[122] See the commentary on the grave breach of 'wilful killing' in Article 50, section D.1. The ECCC found an accused guilty of the grave breach of wilful killing as detainees died 'as the result of omissions known to be likely to lead to death and as a consequence of the conditions of detention imposed upon them'; *Kaing* Trial Judgment, 2010, para. 437. See further Article 12's specific prohibition of wilfully leaving the wounded and sick without medical assistance or care, which, if it leads to death, can overlap with murder by omission.

[123] For details, see the commentary on Article 50, section D.1.

[124] See Dörmann, p. 43, referencing, *inter alia*, United Kingdom, British Military Court at Brunswick, *Gerike case*, Trial, 1946, pp. 76–81, in which the accused had been charged with and several of them found guilty of committing a war crime 'in that they at Velpke, Germany, between the months of May and December, 1944, in violation of the laws and usages of war, were concerned in the killing by wilful neglect of a number of children, Polish Nationals'. While not dealing with the wounded and sick in the sense of the First Convention, the situation is comparable.

[125] Solis, pp. 327–330, and Simpson, p. 751.

[126] See also the equally authentic French version of Article 12: 'Est strictement interdite toute atteinte à leur vie et à leur personne et, entre autres, *le fait de les achever ou de les exterminer...*' (emphasis added). As one of its meanings, 'achever' implies 'donner le dernier coup qui tue' ('delivering the final blow that kills') (*Le Petit Larousse*, 2008, p. 11).

lives are prohibited by Article 12 and are considered as wilful killing if they fulfil the elements of that crime.

b. Extermination

1405   Extermination is not defined in the Geneva Conventions.[127] The ordinary meaning of the term 'exterminate' indicates that it refers to complete destruction or eradication.[128]

1406   The prohibition of extermination in Article 12 would therefore seem to cover instances where killings are directed against whole groups of wounded and sick persons protected under the First Convention, while the prohibition of murder can cover the killing of a single wounded or sick person.

1407   Such an understanding of extermination can be confirmed by a comparison with the use of the term in other international instruments. Extermination is a crime against humanity according to the Statutes of the ICTY, the ICTR, the ICC, the Extraordinary Chambers in the Courts of Cambodia (ECCC) and the SCSL.[129] International case law regarding extermination frequently refers to the killing of a large number of persons.[130] The ICC Elements of Crimes also defines the crime against humanity of extermination, as the killing of one or more persons, 'including by inflicting conditions of life calculated to bring about the destruction of part of a population'.[131] The ICC Elements of Crimes indicates that 'the infliction of such conditions could include the deprivation of access to food and medicine'.[132] The ICC Elements of Crimes further confirms the understanding of extermination as conduct directed against

---

[127] As well as in Article 12 of the First Convention, extermination is prohibited in Article 12 of the Second Convention and Article 32 of the Fourth Convention. The Third Convention contains no specific prohibition of extermination, but its Article 13 generally prohibits '[a]ny unlawful act or omission by the Detaining Power causing death or seriously endangering the health of a prisoner of war in its custody' and requires that 'prisoners of war must at all times be protected, particularly against acts of violence'; for details, see the commentaries on these provisions.

[128] *Concise Oxford English Dictionary*, 12th edition, Oxford University Press, 2011, p. 504.

[129] See ICTY Statute (1993), Article 5(b); ICTR Statute (1994), Article 3(b); ICC Statute (1998), Article 7(1)(b); Cambodia, *Law on the Establishment of the ECCC*, 2001, as amended, Article 5; and SCSL Statute (2002), Article 2(b). See also, in this respect, extermination as a crime against humanity under Article 6(c) of the 1945 Nuremberg Charter.

[130] See e.g. ICTY, *Vasiljević* Trial Judgment, 2002, para. 229; *Krstić* Trial Judgment, 2001, para. 498; *Stakić* Appeal Judgment, 2006, para. 252; ICTR, *Bisengimana* Trial Judgment, 2006, para. 72; *Gacumbitsi* Trial Judgment, 2004, para. 309; *Rutaganda* Trial Judgment, 1999, para. 82; *Nahimana* Trial Judgment, 2003, para. 1061; *Ntagerura* Trial Judgment, 2004, para. 701; *Ntakirutimana* Appeal Judgment, 2004, para. 521; *Rutaganira* Trial Judgment, 2005, paras 49–50; *Bagilishema* Trial Judgment, 2001, para. 87; *Kamuhanda* Trial Judgment, 2004, para. 692; and *Kayishema and Ruzindana* Trial Judgment, 1999, para. 145. For a commentary, see Christopher K. Hall and Carsten Stahn, 'Extermination', in Triffterer/Ambos, pp. 250–258.

[131] See ICC Elements of Crimes (2002), Article 7(1)(b), and ICC Statute (1998), Article 7(2)(b). The use of the language 'inflicting on the group conditions calculated to bring about the destruction of part of a population' can also be found in Article 2(c) of the 1948 Genocide Convention. Genocide, contrary to extermination, however, is committed with the intent to destroy, in whole or in part, a national, ethnical, racial or religious group as such.

[132] ICC Elements of Crimes (2002), Article 7(1)(b), para. 1, note 9.

more than one person by requiring that the conduct of the perpetrator constituted, or took place as part of, a mass killing of members of a civilian population.[133]

1408   Extermination is not as such listed as a grave breach in Article 50 of the First Convention. Article 50 refers to 'wilful killing'. Like murder, extermination of wounded and sick persons protected under the First Convention would therefore fall under the grave breach of wilful killing and would need to be repressed as such by the States party to the First Convention.

c. Torture

1409   Although the prohibition of torture is clearly established in humanitarian law,[134] it is not defined in the Geneva Conventions or the Additional Protocols. The first definition in international treaty law is set forth in the 1984 Convention against Torture.[135] On this basis, the ICTY defined torture for the purposes of humanitarian law as the intentional infliction, by act or omission, of severe pain or suffering, whether physical or mental, with the aim of obtaining information or a confession, punishing, intimidating or coercing the victim or a third person, or of discriminating, on any ground, against the victim or a third person. This list is not, however, exhaustive.[136]

1410   The difference between 'torture' and 'inhuman treatment', both of which are listed as grave breaches in Article 50, is that for torture there is a higher threshold of pain or suffering, which must be 'severe' rather than 'serious', and the infliction of such pain or suffering must be the result of a specific purpose or motivation. Humanitarian law does not require an official involvement in the act of torture.

1411   Mental pain and suffering on its own can be severe enough to amount to torture.[137] The Third Convention and Additional Protocol I state explicitly that both physical and mental torture are prohibited.[138] Psychological methods of

---

[133] See ICC Elements of Crimes (2002), Article 7(1)(b).

[134] In addition to Article 12, torture is set down as a grave breach in Article 50/51/130/147, respectively, of the four Geneva Conventions. It is also prohibited in common Article 3, Article 75(2)(a) of Additional Protocol I and Article 4(2)(a) of Additional Protocol II, as well as under customary international humanitarian law (ICRC Study on Customary International Humanitarian Law (2005), Rule 90).

[135] Convention against Torture (1984), Article 1(1).

[136] Initially, the ICTY, in *Kunarac*, listed the purposes in a closed list; Trial Judgment, 2001, para. 497. At the time, the Trial Chamber was satisfied that these purposes had become part of customary international law and it did not need to look into other possible purposes for the particular case on trial; *ibid.* para. 485. Since then, the ICTY has recognized that the list of purposes is not exclusive; see e.g. *Brđanin* Trial Judgment, 2004, para. 487; *Limaj* Trial Judgment, 2005, para. 235; and *Mrkšić* Trial Judgment, 2007, para. 513.

[137] ICTY, *Kvočka* Trial Judgment, 2001, para. 149. See also *Limaj* Trial Judgment, 2005, para. 236; *Haradinaj* Retrial Judgment, 2012, para. 417; and *Mrkšić* Trial Judgment, 2007, para. 514.

[138] Third Convention, Article 17; Additional Protocol I, Article 75(2)(a)(ii).

torture as well as the psychological effects of torture can cause suffering as severe as physical torture and its physical effects.[139]

1412   Based on both treaty and customary international law, the war crime of torture covers the same acts regardless of whether the armed conflict is international or non-international.[140] The ICC Elements of Crimes also makes no distinction for this offence based on the nature of the armed conflict.[141]

d. Biological experiments

1413 Carrying out biological experiments on protected persons such as the wounded and sick violates the obligation to treat those persons humanely. The 1949 Diplomatic Conference explicitly sought to prohibit biological experiments 'with a view to preventing a recurrence of the cruel experiments which had been made in concentration camps during the last war'.[142]

1414   Neither the Geneva Conventions nor the Additional Protocols define the concept of 'biological experiment'. However, in its ordinary meaning, the term 'biological experiment' refers to conduct the primary purpose of which is to study the effects, at that time unknown, of a product or a situation (e.g. extreme cold or altitude) on the human body. Like medical or scientific experiments prohibited by the Third Convention,[143] biological experiments are prohibited unless they are justified by the medical, dental or hospital treatment of the protected person and carried out in such person's or persons' interest.[144] Unless the experiment is done to improve the state of mental or physical health of protected persons and is in their interest, it is unlawful and constitutes a grave breach under Article 50 of the Convention.

1415   Accordingly, Article 12 prohibits any medical procedure which is not indicated by the state of health of the wounded or sick person and which is not consistent with generally accepted medical standards that would be applied under similar medical circumstances to persons who are nationals of the Party conducting the procedure and who are in no way deprived of liberty.[145]

---

[139] Inter-American Court of Human Rights, *Maritza Urrutia* v. *Guatemala*, Judgment, 2003, para. 93. On this subject, see Hernán Reyes, 'The worst scars are in the mind: psychological torture', *International Review of the Red Cross*, Vol. 89, No. 867, September 2007, pp. 591–617.

[140] ICTY, *Brđanin* Trial Judgment, 2004, para. 482. See also ICTY, *Krnojelac* Trial Judgment, 2002, para. 178; *Furundžija* Trial Judgment, 1998, para. 139; *Kunarac* Trial Judgment, 2001, para. 497; *Kvočka* Trial Judgment, 2001, para. 158; *Stanišić and Župljanin* Trial Judgment, 2013, para. 54; and ECCC, *Kaing* Trial Judgment, 2010, para. 439. For more details on torture as a grave breach in international armed conflict, see the commentary on Article 50, section D.2.

[141] Dörmann, p. 401. Confirmed by ICTY, *Brđanin* Trial Judgment, 2004, para. 482, and *Stanišić and Župljanin* Trial Judgment, 2013, para. 54. For further information, see also the discussion of torture in the commentary on common Article 3, section G.2.e.

[142] *Final Record of the Diplomatic Conference of Geneva of 1949*, Vol. II-A, p. 248.

[143] For the prohibition of scientific or medical experiments, see Article 13 of the Third Convention.

[144] See *Final Record of the Diplomatic Conference of Geneva of 1949*, Vol. II-A, p. 191.

[145] This wording is borrowed from Article 11(1) of Additional Protocol I and fn. 46 of the 2002 ICC Elements of Crimes regarding the war crime of medical or scientific experiments under

1416   This prohibition is absolute, as wounded or sick or detained persons cannot validly give consent to a particular biological experiment.[146] The prohibition of biological experiments should not, however, be understood as outlawing therapeutic or clinical research.[147] Nor does it prevent doctors in charge of wounded and sick persons from trying new therapeutic methods which are justified on medical grounds and are dictated solely by a desire to improve a patient's condition. Patients are entitled to freely consent to drug trials aimed at improving their health, provided they are offered in the same manner and under the same conditions as to regular citizens.[148]

1417   In terms of the humanitarian law prohibition, a biological experiment is outlawed even if it does not cause death or seriously endanger the health of the victim.[149]

1418   For more details on biological experiments as a grave breach in international armed conflict, see the commentary on Article 50, section D.4.

e. Wilfully leaving the wounded and sick without medical assistance and care

1419 Wilfully leaving the wounded and sick without medical assistance and care is likewise strictly prohibited under Article 12(2). Although not listed as such in the Geneva Conventions as a grave breach such conduct may amount to inhuman treatment, wilfully causing great suffering or serious injury to body or health or, depending on the circumstances, wilful killing.[150]

---

the 1998 ICC Statute. For a full explanation, see the commentary on Article 50 of the First Convention, section D.4.

[146] See Henckaerts/Doswald-Beck, commentary on Rule 92, p. 322, making reference to many international instruments, official statements and case law which refer to this prohibition without making any specific mention of a possible exception if the detained person consented to the procedure. For further information, see the commentary on Article 50, section D.4.

[147] See *Final Record of the Diplomatic Conference of Geneva of 1949*, Vol. II-A, p. 191:

Biological experiments. The Committee discussed at great length whether these words required definition, and more particularly whether their scope ought not to be restricted by adding, for example: "not necessary for their medical treatment". In reality, however, the word biological, in its generally accepted sense, does not apply to therapeutic treatment, whether medical or surgical.

[148] For more details, see the commentary on Article 50, section D.4.

[149] The grave breach of biological experiments requires that the conduct seriously endangered the health or integrity of the protected person. See *ibid.* In this respect, the scope of criminal responsibility for conducting biological experiments is more restricted than the scope of the prohibition on carrying out experiments in humanitarian law.

[150] The ECCC found an accused guilty of the grave breach of wilful killing as detainees died 'as the result of omissions known to be likely to lead to death and as a consequence of the conditions of detention imposed upon them'; *Kaing* Trial Judgment, 2010, para. 437. The ICTY and the ICTR have both accepted commission by omission for the purposes of Article 7(1); see ICTY, *Tadić* Appeal Judgment, 1999, para. 188; *Kordić and Čerkez* Trial Judgment, 2001, paras 375–376; and ICTR, *Musema* Trial Judgment, 2000, para. 123.

f. Creation of conditions exposing the wounded and sick to contagion or infection

1420 Paragraph 2 states that Parties shall not create conditions exposing the wounded and sick to contagion or infection. For the delegates at the Diplomatic Conference, the word 'contagion applies to diseases communicated from one human being to another, while the word infection . . . applies more particularly to an infection caused artificially, for example by injections'.[151] The prohibition should serve as a reminder that any wilful exposure of the wounded and sick to such intolerable conditions is clearly prohibited and could amount to a grave breach. In any case, the obligation to care for the wounded and sick requires Parties to an armed conflict to do much more than simply not expose the wounded and sick to contagion or infection. They must act with due diligence and endeavour to create the best possible conditions of hygiene under the circumstances.

G. Paragraph 3: Permitted prioritization regarding medical treatment

1421 According to paragraph 3, '[o]nly urgent medical reasons will authorize priority in the order of treatment to be administered'. The word 'only' indicates that criteria other than 'urgent medical reasons' are not permitted. The most obvious example would be prioritizing care based on the nationality of the patient in a manner that deprives enemy personnel of adequate care. Article 12(2) prohibits any adverse distinction with regard to the care of the wounded and sick in all its various facets. It follows, therefore, that decisions of triage must never be based on any of the criteria listed in that paragraph. Paragraph 3 sets out a clear rule specifically in regard to distinction in the 'priority in the order of treatment'.

1422   Which kinds of 'urgent medical reasons' may be invoked in this regard is not specified in humanitarian law. It is generally accepted that the rules of medical ethics and the accepted standards of the medical profession govern this decision.[152] Thus, it can be justified to give priority in a temporal sense to patients with severe injuries over those with minor injuries. Moreover, if the supply of analgesics is low, it would also seem justifiable to provide pain relief to a severely injured soldier in place of a soldier with minor injuries.

1423   Paragraph 3 allows individual as well as collective distinctions based on medical grounds.[153] Medical grounds that may be invoked to justify prioritization

---

[151] *Final Record of the Diplomatic Conference of Geneva of 1949*, Vol. II-A, p. 191. Nowadays it is recognized that disease can be communicated also between animals and humans.

[152] Bothe/Partsch/Solf, p. 108, para. 2.3. See also World Medical Association, International Committee of Military Medicine, International Council of Nurses and International Pharmaceutical Federation, *Ethical Principles of Health Care in Times of Armed Conflict and Other Emergencies*, 2015, Principle 7, https://www.icrc.org/en/document/common-ethical-principles-health-care-conflict-and-other-emergencies.

[153] See also ICRC Study on Customary International Humanitarian Law (2005), Rule 110.

may also be derived from the principles of medical triage. Medical triage is of particular relevance in times of armed conflict where there may be significant numbers of wounded and sick people, while medical personnel and equipment may be limited. Under such circumstances, it would be justifiable to devote more resources in terms of time, personnel and equipment to severely wounded soldiers than to soldiers who have light wounds. Indeed, in such situations triage will be a necessary precondition for ensuring the most efficient provision of medical care for the greatest number of people.[154] According to the ICRC:

The ultimate objective of triage is to achieve optimal use of the available personnel and resources so as to benefit the greatest number of casualties who have the best chance of survival. As a consequence:

– choices are made to achieve the greatest good not for any particular individual but for the greatest number of people;
– because of limited time and resources, some casualties do not even begin to receive treatment, or their treatment is interrupted, or their evacuation is never considered.

Triage might be difficult to perform. The decisions involved are the most difficult in all health care.[155]

1424   The aim of caring for the greatest possible number of wounded and sick people is in line with the purpose of Article 12 and is also consistent with medical ethics. Against this background, the permitted criterion of 'urgent medical reasons' must be interpreted to comprise both individual and collective medical reasons and therefore also permits the practice of medical triage, provided that it is conducted exclusively on medical grounds.

1425   Paragraph 3 makes it clear that factors other than urgent medical reasons cannot justify prioritization in the order of treatment. It follows that military necessity may never be invoked to justify such distinctions. While it is permissible to accord quick medical treatment to lightly injured soldiers in so-called 'battle dressing stations' in order to enable them to return to the battlefield as rapidly as possible, prioritizing those soldiers who merely require a light patching up at the expense of severely injured soldiers who will not be able to return immediately to the battlefield is not permitted.

---

[154] Generally on triage, see Kenneth V. Iserson and John C. Moskop, 'Triage in Medicine, Part I: Concept, History, and Types', *Annals of Emergency Medicine*, Vol. 49, No. 3, March 2007, pp. 275–281; Jonathan P. Wyatt *et al.* (eds), *Oxford Handbook of Emergency Medicine*, 4th edition, Oxford University Press, 2012, p. 7; and Vivienne Nathanson, 'Medical ethics in peacetime and wartime: the case for a better understanding', *International Review of the Red Cross*, Vol. 95, No. 889, March 2013, pp. 189–213, especially at 199–200.

[155] ICRC, *First Aid in Armed Conflicts and Other Situations of Violence*, ICRC, Geneva, 2010, p. 116.

H. Paragraph 4: Treatment of women

1426 The principle that women are to be accorded specific respect in armed conflict when they find themselves in the power of a Party to the conflict first found expression in Article 3 of the 1929 Geneva Convention on Prisoners of War.[156] That provision was largely informed by the fact that a significant number of women were involved in the First World War. Since then, the participation of women in armed conflict has grown, in terms both of the numbers of women serving in armed forces and the variety of roles they play on and off the battlefield.[157] Although war is often considered a masculine domain, women are increasingly involved in close combat functions on the front line.[158]

1427   Since 1949 there have been a number of social and international legal developments in relation to equality of the sexes.[159] Today there is also a deeper understanding that women, men, girls and boys may have specific needs and capacities linked to the different ways armed conflict may affect them.[160] Singling out women in no way implies that they have less resilience, agency or capacity within the armed forces or as civilians, but rather acknowledges that women have a distinct set of needs and may face particular physical and psychological risks.[161]

---

[156] Geneva Convention on Prisoners of War (1929), Article 3: 'Prisoners of war are entitled to respect for their persons and honour. Women shall be treated with all consideration due to their sex. Prisoners retain their full civil capacity.'

[157] According to official defence force websites, the percentage of women engaged full time in large State armed forces, such as Australia (approximately 14%), United Kingdom (approximately 9%) and United States of America (14.6%), is increasing steadily, with less gender-based restrictions on certain combat functions. For example, in Australia, all employment categories are being opened up to women between 2011 and 2016 to ensure that career choices will only be restricted by an individual's ability to meet all the demands of the role, not on the basis of their gender. Field studies carried out by the ICRC indicate that in some conflicts, female fighters can comprise up to 30% of certain non-State armed groups.

[158] Women are allowed in combat roles in several countries – Canada, Denmark, Finland, France, Germany, Israel, the Netherlands, New Zealand, Norway, Poland, Romania, Spain, Sweden and, most recently, Australia.

[159] In 1966 the UN General Assembly adopted the International Covenant on Civil and Political Rights (ICCPR), enshrining the principles of equality between men and women (Article 3) and non-discrimination (Articles 2 and 26). This was followed in 1979 by the adoption of the Convention on the Elimination of Discrimination against Women (CEDAW). More recently, the international community has recognized the link between inequality and discrimination in peacetime and violence against women in armed conflict. UN Secretary-General, *Report of the Secretary-General on women, peace and security*, UN Doc S/2002/1154, 16 October 2002, para. 5.

[160] A number of UN Security Council resolutions focus on the effects of armed conflict on women: see UN Security Council resolutions 1325 (2000), 1820 (2008), 1888 (2009), 1889 (2009), 1960 (2010), 2106 (2013) and 2122 (2013). For more information, see Tengroth/Lindvall; Lindsey, 2005; Coomaraswamy; and Gardam. See also Lindsey, 2001.

[161] In comparison, the original commentary on Article 12(4) was a product of the social and historical context of the time, and the reference to women as 'weaker than oneself and whose honour and modesty call for respect' would no longer be considered appropriate (Pictet (ed.), *Commentary on the First Geneva Convention*, ICRC, 1952, p. 140). For a more detailed debate and feminist critiques of humanitarian law, see Gardam/Jarvis, Haeri/Puechguirbal, and Durham.

1428   The Geneva Conventions and their Additional Protocols are based on the principle that respect for, protection and care of the wounded and sick must be applied without adverse distinction. Article 12 not only contains essential provisions relating to that respect, protection and care, but also lays down how they should be applied. In Article 12(2) adverse distinction based on sex is explicitly prohibited. Within the requirement of equality of protection, Article 12 also allows for favourable distinction based on the specific needs that may arise from the sex of the wounded or sick combatant. Article 12(4) acknowledges that women have specific needs and face particular risks for which a 'blanket' protection may not be adequate. Such needs and risks may be physical or physiological, but they may also stem from social, economic, cultural and political structures in a society. With women increasingly playing a diverse range of roles in times of armed conflict, Article 12(4) is more relevant than ever.

1429   Article 12(4) requires Parties to the conflict to treat female wounded or sick members of the armed forces with 'all consideration due to their sex'. Likewise, Article 12(3) allows for favourable distinction to be based on urgent medical reasons, another needs-based criterion. In the light of the purpose of Article 12, namely to address the specific vulnerability of the wounded and sick and to establish a comprehensive regime for their protection, the distinct set of needs of and particular physical and psychological risks facing women, including those arising from social structures, have to be taken into account in order to comply with the obligation in paragraph 4.

1430   Article 12(4), read together with Article 12(2), sets a requirement for equal respect, protection and care based on all the needs of women. The obligation to identify responses to the specific needs of women – which may not fall below the basic humanitarian standards already articulated in the Conventions – is reinforced by other articles requiring that female members of the armed forces be treated 'with all the regard due to their sex' and 'in all cases benefit by treatment as favourable as that granted to men'.[162]

1431   In Article 12(4) the word 'treat' encompasses not only the provision of immediate and necessary medical attention and material, but also, within the context of the whole article, respect for and the protection of female wounded or sick combatants.[163]

1432   As explained above, in order to qualify as wounded or sick, a person has to fulfil two cumulative criteria: to require medical care and to refrain from any act of hostility. As a result, the category of 'wounded and sick' also includes maternity cases and expectant mothers as they are in need of medical assistance or care. This is explicitly recognized in the definition of 'wounded and sick' in

---

[162] See Third Convention, Article 14(2).
[163] For a discussion of the terms 'respect' and 'protect', see section E.

Additional Protocol I.[164] In the context of Article 12(4), therefore, the specific needs of women while pregnant or after childbirth, such as for additional food or specific hygiene requirements, have to be addressed.

1433   As noted earlier, the protected status accorded to a wounded or sick person ends as soon as that person engages in hostile acts, dies or recovers, i.e. when the condition requiring medical assistance or care no longer exists. In the context of the particular female conditions of pregnancy and childbirth, this means that the obligation to protect women extends beyond the end of the convalescence after the delivery. As long as the mother and child are in need of medical assistance or care, the obligation persists.[165]

1434   In order to treat female wounded or sick combatants 'with all consideration due to their sex', Parties to an armed conflict must ensure that their protection and care takes into account their specific needs with regard to hygiene, ante- and post-natal care and gynaecological and reproductive health, including physiological factors that may heighten the risk of anaemia and mineral deficiencies. If members of the fighting force are pregnant or have recently given birth at the time of injury or illness, they will require specific medical attention. Furthermore, the impact of particular weapons or methods used by belligerents may have distinct implications for female members of the military owing to body mass and other physiological differences.[166] In a practical sense, Article 12(4) requires military medical services to be multidisciplinary in their approach and to have a range of expertise and skills to hand to deal with both male and female patients.[167]

1435   In order to implement the aforementioned obligation, including planning and analysis of the types of health care provided, the Parties to an armed conflict need to consider how the roles and patterns formed by the social, economic, cultural or political context and resulting in different statuses, needs and capacities among women and men of different ages and backgrounds could hamper the safe access to care of any one group. This may include a reluctance to seek or receive medical care, possibly owing to discrimination or a stigma of being

---

[164] See Additional Protocol I, Article 8(a).

[165] The definition of 'wounded and sick' in Article 8(a) of Additional Protocol I also includes 'newborn babies and other persons who may be in need of immediate medical assistance or care'.

[166] See Sweden, Ministry of Foreign Affairs, *International Humanitarian Law and Gender*, Report Summary, International Expert Meeting: 'Gender Perspectives on International Humanitarian Law', 4–5 October 2007, Stockholm, Sweden; and Tengroth/Lindvall, chapter 14.

[167] Conflicts exacerbate existing gender inequalities, often placing women at heightened risk. Women are increasingly deliberately targeted for and subject to distinct forms of violence and abuse in armed conflict, including sexual violence, torture and mutilation, from which they suffer a wide array of physical and psychological effects. (See the reaffirmation of this point in e.g. Committee on the Elimination of Discrimination against Women General Recommendation No. 30, pp. 9–10.) It has been suggested that '[e]fforts to end sexual violence in conflicts must include scrutiny of how gender roles are shaped and upheld in peacetime. Societies that view men as superior create an environment that is conducive to sexual violence in armed conflict.' (Joint Nordic statement at UN Security Council Open Debate on Women, Peace and Security, 24 June, 2013.

wounded or sick. Knowledge of how social structures influence the situation should be taken into account in order to ensure that health care is fully accessible to both women and men and minimizes the risks of any group being subject to discrimination, lack of respect, harm or danger before, during or after the care.[168]

1436   The obligation to ensure the equal treatment of female and male combatants, while paying attention to the specific needs of women, is a continuous theme in the Geneva Conventions and is also applicable under Article 14 of the First Convention when wounded or sick female members of the armed forces fall into enemy hands. Moreover, it appears throughout the Third Convention in relation to the treatment of prisoners of war.[169]

1437   Ensuring that women receive the respect and protection, as well as humane treatment and the care required by their specific needs, is an essential feature of the Geneva Conventions. In armed conflicts today, the relevance and importance of Article 12(4) has never been greater. With women increasingly taking on a range of combat roles, Parties to an armed conflict are required to take into account the concept of favourable distinction in their regard. Treating female members of the armed forces with all consideration due to their sex involves ensuring that Parties have both the capacity and the wider understanding to meet the range of specific needs of women when wounded or sick.

I. Paragraph 5: Compelled to abandon the wounded and sick to the enemy

1438   Paragraph 5 refers to situations in which a Party to an international armed conflict is compelled to abandon the wounded and sick to the enemy and requires, with the caveat 'as far as military considerations permit', that the Party 'leave with them a part of its medical personnel and material to assist in their care'. As far as can be seen, the provision has never been applied or invoked in modern practice. The very premise of this provision, namely that the wounded and sick may be abandoned, is at odds with the obligations laid out in paragraphs 1 and 2. Use of the word 'compelled' indicates that, if at all, the wounded and sick may only be abandoned in the most extreme circumstances. Paragraph 5

---

[168] Assessments should be made as to whether wounded or sick members of the armed forces might be exposed to specific risks of discrimination, violence of any kind, or humiliating or other degrading treatment during armed conflict, taking into account the possibility that inherent gendered discrimination or risks in the society may increase during the armed conflict. For example, if the society itself silently accepts discrimination, violence or rape against women, or if the culture dictates that women and men may only be treated by personnel of the same sex, consideration must be given to what precautions need to be taken when planning and providing health care to ensure that female members of the armed forces are fully protected and respected and receive the same standard of care as their male counterparts. For guidance equally applicable to preventive efforts under the present article, see e.g. Lindsey-Curtet/Tercier Holst-Roness/Anderson, chapter 1.1, Personal safety, and chapter 1.2, Sexual violence; and Tengroth/Lindvall, Recommendations, and chapter 6, Checklist – a gender perspective in the application of IHL.
[169] See Third Convention, Articles 3(1), 14(2), 16, 25(4), 29, 49(1), 88(2), 88(3), 97(4) and 108(2).

should therefore not be understood as a legal basis for abandoning the wounded and sick but as a safeguard provision of last resort, applicable to scenarios where there is no other option but to leave the wounded and sick behind.

1439   Although the wording of paragraph 5 makes no distinction between the wounded and sick of one's own armed forces and those of the enemy's armed forces, the primary focus of the provision is the necessity ('compelled to') of abandoning one's own wounded and sick personnel under extreme circumstances. This interpretation derives from the historical context of paragraph 5, namely Article 1(2) of the 1906 Convention, which provided that '[a] belligerent, however, when compelled to leave *his* wounded in the hands of his adversary, shall leave with them, so far as military conditions permit, a portion of the personnel and "matériel" of his sanitary service to assist in caring for them' (emphasis added). In this context, paragraph 5 stipulates an obligation ('shall') to continue to assist in their treatment, 'as far as military considerations permit'. Thus, even though the other Party to the conflict into whose power the abandoned wounded and sick personnel will soon fall is obliged to care for them by virtue of paragraph 2, paragraph 5 requires the abandoning Party to contribute to the medical care of its wounded and sick personnel by the other Party.

1440   The commentary on the 1929 Geneva Convention on the Wounded and Sick stated:

> This obligation, natural and necessary as it is, may be a heavy charge if, for example, a retreating belligerent is compelled to abandon several groups of wounded in turn, leaving medical personnel and equipment with them each time. He runs the risk in such a case of having no medical personnel or equipment left for those of his troops who are the last to fall. That cannot be helped. It is his duty to provide for present needs without keeping back the means of relieving future casualties. If as a result he has no more medical personnel or equipment for subsequent casualties, he will have to do all he can to ensure that they receive relief, even appealing, in such a case, to the charity of the inhabitants, as he is entitled to do under Article 5 [of the 1929 Geneva Convention].[170]

1441   Such a rigid interpretation, however, goes too far. It is not supported by the wording of paragraph 5. The caveat 'as far as military considerations permit' leaves military commanders with a margin of discretion as to how many medical personnel and how much material is to be left behind. In this respect, Article 28(1) of the First Convention is also relevant. According to this provision, medical personnel designated in Articles 24 and 26 'who fall into the hands of the adverse Party, shall be retained only in so far as the state of health, the spiritual needs and the number of prisoners of war require'. Moreover, according to Article 28(3), '[d]uring hostilities the Parties to the conflict shall make

---

[170] Des Gouttes, *Commentaire de la Convention de Genève de 1929 sur les blessés et malades*, ICRC, 1930, pp. 15–16.

arrangements for relieving where possible retained personnel'.[171] Thus, military commanders are not under an absolute obligation to leave medical personnel and material behind. Rather, the obligation depends on the circumstances of each case, taking into consideration humanitarian as well as military interests, including the anticipated treatment to be provided by the opposing Party once the abandoned personnel are in its power. Thus, an arbitrary decision not to leave behind any medical personnel would be in violation of paragraph 5. Conversely, a decision that is based on considerations that any reasonable military commander would accept under the given circumstances, including the expectation of a large number of wounded military personnel in an upcoming battle, may justify the decision not to leave any medical personnel or material behind.

1442   Given that, as far as can be seen, paragraph 5 has never been applied or invoked in modern practice, it could be argued that the provision has fallen into disuse or even desuetude, that any abandonment of the wounded and sick – even in extreme circumstances – would violate the obligation to treat them humanely, and that this obligation does not admit of any exception, not even by virtue of a specific humanitarian law provision such as paragraph 5. However, since paragraph 5 was designed from the outset as a provision of last resort, the absence of any State practice is not surprising and, without more evidence, cannot be taken as an indication that the provision is no longer valid.[172]

Select bibliography

Bellal, Annyssa, 'Who Is Wounded and Sick?', in Andrew Clapham, Paola Gaeta and Marco Sassòli (eds), *The 1949 Geneva Conventions: A Commentary*, Oxford University Press, 2015, pp. 757–765.

Benoit, James P., 'Mistreatment of the Wounded, Sick and Shipwrecked by the ICRC Study on Customary International Humanitarian Law', *Yearbook of International Humanitarian Law*, Vol. 11, 2008, pp. 175–219.

Bothe, Michael, 'Le statut de la profession médicale en temps de conflit armé', *Annales de droit international médical*, Vol. 28, 1979, pp. 52–59.

Bothe, Michael and Janssen, Karin, 'Issues in the protection of the wounded and sick', *International Review of the Red Cross*, Vol. 26, No. 253, August 1986, pp. 189–199.

Bothe, Michael, Partsch, Karl Josef and Solf, Waldemar A., *New Rules for Victims of Armed Conflicts: Commentary on the Two 1977 Protocols Additional to the Geneva Conventions of 1949*, Martinus Nijhoff Publishers, The Hague, 1982.

Breau, Susan C., 'Commentary on selected Rules from the ICRC Study: Protected persons and objects', in Elizabeth Wilmshurst and Susan C. Breau (eds),

---

[171] See the commentary on Article 28, section E. With regard to the retention regime, see also Articles 30 and 31 of the First Convention and Article 33 of the Third Convention.

[172] See United Kingdom, *Manual of the Law of Armed Conflict*, 2004, para. 7.7, and United States, *Law of Armed Conflict Deskbook*, 2012, p. 49.

Perspectives on the ICRC Study on Customary International Humanitarian Law, Cambridge University Press, 2007, pp. 169–203.

Bugnion, Francois, *The International Committee of the Red Cross and the Protection of War Victims*, ICRC/Macmillan, Oxford, 2003.

Committee on the Elimination of Discrimination against Women, *General recommendation No. 30 on women in conflict prevention, conflict and post-conflict situations*, CEDAW/C/GC/30, 18 October 2013.

Condorelli, Luigi and Boisson de Chazournes, Laurence, 'Quelques remarques à propos de l'obligation des États de "respecter et faire respecter" le droit international humanitaire "en toutes circonstances"', in Christophe Swinarski (ed.), *Etudes et essais sur le droit international humanitaire et sur les principes de la Croix-Rouge en l'honneur de Jean Pictet*, ICRC/Martinus Nijhoff Publishers, The Hague, 1984, pp. 17–35.

Coomaraswamy, Radhika, 'Sexual Violence during Wartime', in Helen Durham and Tracey Gurd (eds), *Listening to the Silences: Women and War*, Martinus Nijhoff Publishers, Leiden, 2005, pp. 53–66.

Davis, George B., 'The Geneva Convention of 1906', *American Journal of International Law*, Vol. 1, No. 2, 1907, pp. 409–417.

Detter, Ingrid, *The Law of War*, 2nd edition, Cambridge University Press, 2000.

Dörmann, Knut, *Elements of War Crimes under the Rome Statute of the International Criminal Court: Sources and Commentary*, Cambridge University Press, 2003.

Dunant, Henry, *A Memory of Solferino*, ICRC, Geneva, reprint 1986.

Dupuy, Pierre-Marie, 'Reviewing the Difficulties of Codification: On Ago's Classification of Obligations of Means and Obligations of Result in Relation to State Responsibility', *European Journal of International Law*, Vol. 10, No. 2, 1999, pp. 371–385.

Durham, Helen, 'International Humanitarian Law and the Protection of Women', in Helen Durham and Tracey Gurd (eds), *Listening to the Silences: Women and War*, Martinus Nijhoff Publishers, Leiden, 2005, pp. 95–107.

Focarelli, Carlo, 'Common Article 1 of the 1949 Geneva Conventions: A Soap Bubble?', *European Journal of International Law*, Vol. 21, No. 1, 2010, pp. 125–171.

Gardam, Judith, 'Women and Armed Conflict: The Response of International Humanitarian Law', in Helen Durham and Tracey Gurd (eds), *Listening to the Silences: Women and War*, Martinus Nijhoff Publishers, Leiden, 2005, pp. 109–123.

Gardam, Judith G. and Jarvis, Michelle J., *Women, Armed Conflict and International Law*, Kluwer Law International, The Hague, 2001.

Gawande, Atul, 'Casualties of War – Military Care for the Wounded from Iraq and Afghanistan', *The New England Journal of Medicine*, Vol. 351, 2004, pp. 2471–2475.

Giacca, Gilles, 'The Obligations to Respect, Protect, Collect, and Care for the Wounded, Sick, and Shipwrecked', in Andrew Clapham, Paola Gaeta and Marco Sassòli (eds), *The 1949 Geneva Conventions: A Commentary*, Oxford University Press, 2015, pp. 781–806.

Geiss, Robin, 'Land Warfare', version of September 2009, in Rüdiger Wolfrum (ed.), *Max Planck Encyclopedia of Public International Law*, Oxford University Press, http://opil.ouplaw.com/home/EPIL.

– 'Military Necessity: A Fundamental "Principle" Fallen into Oblivion', in Hélène Ruiz Fabri, Rüdiger Wolfrum and Jana Gogolin (eds), *Select Proceedings* of the European Society of International Law, Vol. 2, 2008, Hart Publishing, Oxford, 2010, pp. 554–568.

– 'The Obligation to Respect and to Ensure Respect for the Conventions', in Andrew Clapham, Paola Gaeta and Marco Sassòli (eds), *The 1949 Geneva Conventions: A Commentary*, Oxford University Press, 2015, pp. 111–134.

Haeri, Medina and Puechguirbal, Nadine, 'From helplessness to agency: examining the plurality of women's experiences in armed conflict', *International Review of the Red Cross*, Vol. 92, No. 877, March 2010, pp. 103–122.

Henckaerts, Jean-Marie and Doswald-Beck, Louise, *Customary International Humanitarian Law, Volume I: Rules*, ICRC/Cambridge University Press, 2005, available at https://www.icrc.org/customary-ihl/eng/docs/v1.

Henderson, Ian, *The Contemporary Law of Targeting: Military Objectives, Proportionality and Precautions in Attack under Additional Protocol I*, Martinus Nijhoff Publishers, Leiden, 2009.

Jakovljevic, Bosko, 'The protection of the wounded and sick and the development of International Medical Law', *International Review of the Red Cross*, Vol. 5, No. 48, March 1965, pp. 115–122.

Kalshoven, Frits and Zegveld, Liesbeth, *Constraints on the Waging of War: An Introduction to International Humanitarian Law*, 4th edition, ICRC/Cambridge University Press, 2011.

Kessler, Birgit, 'The duty to "ensure respect" under common Article 1 of the Geneva Conventions: its implications on international and non-international armed conflicts', *German Yearbook of International Law*, Vol. 44, 2001, pp. 498–516.

Kleffner, Jann K., 'Protection of the Wounded, Sick, and Shipwrecked', in Dieter Fleck (ed.), *The Handbook of International Humanitarian Law*, 3rd edition, Oxford University Press, 2013, pp. 321–357.

Kolb, Robert and Hyde, Richard, *An Introduction to the International Law of Armed Conflicts*, 3rd edition, Hart Publishing, Oxford, 2008.

Krieger, Heike, 'Protected Persons', version of March 2011, in Rüdiger Wolfrum (ed.), *Max Planck Encyclopedia of Public International Law*, Oxford University Press, http://opil.ouplaw.com/home/EPIL.

Krill, Françoise, 'The Protection of Women in International Humanitarian Law', *International Review of the Red Cross*, Vol. 25, No. 249, December 1985, pp. 337–363.

Lauterpacht, Hersch (ed.), *Oppenheim's International Law*, 7th edition, Longmans, London, 1952.

Lindsey, Charlotte, *Women facing war: ICRC study on the impact of armed conflict on women*, ICRC, Geneva, 2001.

– 'The Impact of Armed Conflict on Women', in Helen Durham and Tracey Gurd (eds), *Listening to the Silences: Women and War*, Martinus Nijhoff Publishers, Leiden, 2005, pp. 21–35.

Lindsey-Curtet, Charlotte, Tercier Holst-Roness, Florence and Anderson, Letitia, *Addressing the Needs of Women Affected by Armed Conflict: An ICRC Guidance Document*, ICRC, Geneva, 2004.

Mehring, Sigrid, 'Medical War Crimes', in Armin von Bogdandy and Rüdiger Wolfrum (eds), *Max Planck Yearbook of United Nations Law*, Vol. 15, 2011, pp. 229–279.

ICRC, *Interpretive Guidance on the Notion of Direct Participation in Hostilities under International Humanitarian Law*, by Nils Melzer, ICRC, Geneva, 2009.

Novak, Gregor, 'Wounded, Sick, and Shipwrecked', version of December 2013, in Rüdiger Wolfrum (ed.), *Max Planck Encyclopedia of Public International Law*, Oxford University Press, http://opil.ouplaw.com/home/EPIL.

Pictet, Jean S., 'The New Geneva Conventions for the Protection of War Victims', *American Journal of International Law*, Vol. 45, No. 3, 1951, pp. 462–475.

Röthlisberger, Ernst, *Die neue Genfer Konvention von 6. Juli 1906*, A. Francke, Bern, 1908.

Sassòli, Marco, 'State responsibility for violations of international humanitarian law', *International Review of the Red Cross*, Vol. 84, No. 846, June 2002, pp. 401–434.

Schmitt, Michael N., 'Deconstructing Direct Participation in Hostilities: The Constitutive Elements', *New York University Journal of International Law and Politics*, Vol. 42, No. 3, 2010, pp. 697–739.

Scobbie, Iain, 'Smoke, Mirrors and Killer Whales: The International Court's Opinion on the Israeli Barrier Wall', *German Law Journal*, Vol. 5, No. 9, 2004, pp. 1107–1131.

Simpson, Stephen W., 'Shoot First, Ask Questions Later: Double-Tapping Under the Laws of War', *West Virginia Law Review*, Vol. 108, No. 3, 2006, pp. 751–775.

Sivakumaran, Sandesh, *The Law of Non-International Armed Conflict*, Oxford University Press, 2012.

Solf, Waldemar A., 'Development of the protection of the wounded, sick and shipwrecked under the Protocols Additional to the 1949 Geneva Conventions', in Christophe Swinarski (ed.), *Studies and Essays on International Humanitarian Law and Red Cross Principles in Honour of Jean Pictet*, ICRC/Martinus Nijhoff Publishers, The Hague, 1984, pp. 237–248.

Solis, Gary D., *The Law of Armed Conflict: International Humanitarian Law in War*, Cambridge University Press, 2010.

Spaight, James Molony, *War Rights on Land*, Macmillan, London, 1911.

Sperry, Charles S., 'The Revision of the Geneva Convention, 1906', *Proceedings of the American Political Science Association*, Vol. 3, 1907, pp. 33–57.

Tengroth, Cecilia and Lindvall, Kristina, *IHL and gender – Swedish experiences*, Swedish Red Cross and Swedish Ministry for Foreign Affairs, Stockholm, 2015.

Triffterer, Otto and Ambos, Kai (eds), *The Rome Statute of the International Criminal Court: A Commentary*, 3rd edition, Hart Publishing, Oxford, 2016.

PROTECTED PERSONS

❖ Text of the provision

The present Convention shall apply to the wounded and sick belonging to the following categories:

(1) Members of the armed forces of a Party to the conflict, as well as members of militias or volunteer corps forming part of such armed forces.

(2) Members of other militias and members of other volunteer corps, including those of organized resistance movements, belonging to a Party to the conflict and operating in or outside their own territory, even if this territory is occupied, provided that such militias or volunteer corps, including such organized resistance movements, fulfil the following conditions:

(a) that of being commanded by a person responsible for his subordinates;

(b) that of having a fixed distinctive sign recognizable at a distance;

(c) that of carrying arms openly;

(d) that of conducting their operations in accordance with the laws and customs of war.

(3) Members of regular armed forces who profess allegiance to a Government or an authority not recognized by the Detaining Power.

(4) Persons who accompany the armed forces without actually being members thereof, such as civil members of military aircraft crews, war correspondents, supply contractors, members of labour units or of services responsible for the welfare of the armed forces, provided that they have received authorization from the armed forces which they accompany.

(5) Members of crews, including masters, pilots and apprentices of the merchant marine and the crews of civil aircraft of the Parties to the conflict, who do not benefit by more favourable treatment under any other provisions in international law.

(6) Inhabitants of a non-occupied territory who, on the approach of the enemy, spontaneously take up arms to resist the invading forces, without having had time to form themselves into regular armed units, provided they carry arms openly and respect the laws and customs of war.

❖ Reservations or declarations

Guinea-Bissau,[1] rejected by the Federal Republic of Germany,[2] the United States of America[3] and the United Kingdom of Great Britain and Northern Ireland.[4]

Contents

A. Introduction

1443   The purpose of Article 13 is to specify which persons, on their being wounded or falling sick, the First Convention protects.[5] The list includes members of

---

[1] United Nations *Treaty Series*, Vol. 920, 1974, pp. 280–282, at 281:

> The Council of State of the Republic of Guinea-Bissau does not recognize the 'conditions' provided for in subparagraph (2) of this article concerning members of other militias and members of other volunteer corps, including those of organized resistance movements, because these conditions are not suited to the people's wars waged today.

[2] *Ibid.* Vol. 970, 1975, pp. 366–367:

> The reservations formulated in this connexion by the Republic of Guinea-Bissau concerning...*Article 13(2)* of the first Geneva convention for the Amelioration of the Condition of the Wounded and Sick in Armed Forces in the Field...exceed, in the opinion of the Government of the Federal Republic of Germany, the purpose and intent of these Conventions and are therefore unacceptable to it. This declaration shall not otherwise affect the validity of the said Geneva Conventions under international law as between the Federal Republic of Germany and the Republic of Guinea-Bissau.

[3] *Ibid.* pp. 367–368:

> The Department of State refers to the note of March 5, 1974 from the Embassy of Switzerland enclosing the notification of the Swiss Federal Political Department concerning the accession of the Republic of Guinea-Bissau to the Geneva Conventions of August 12, 1949 for the protection of war victims, subject to certain reservations.
>
> The reservations are similar to reservations expressed by others previously with respect to the same or different conventions and concerning which the Government of the United States has previously declared its views. The attitude of the Government of the United States with respect to all the reservations by the Republic of Guinea-Bissau parallels its attitude toward such other reservations. The Government of the United States, while rejecting the reservations, accepts treaty relations with the Republic of Guinea-Bissau.

[4] *Ibid.* Vol. 995, 1976, p. 394.

[5] The Convention protects other persons as well – in particular medical and religious personnel – but their protection is not conditioned on their being wounded or falling sick; see especially Articles 24–27.

the armed forces and other categories of persons who, while not being members of the armed forces, either have combatant status or are otherwise entitled to prisoner-of-war status. The enumeration of protected persons in Article 13 is thus deliberately almost the same as that adopted for prisoners of war in Article 4 of the Third Convention. Reliance in Article 13 on the definition of prisoners of war provided in Article 4 of the Third Convention ensures consistency in the Conventions.[6]

1444   However, there are some differences between Article 13 of the First Convention and Article 4 of the Third Convention. For instance, Article 13 does not take into account Article 4B of the Third Convention, which deals with belligerents who have been re-interned in occupied territory or in a neutral or non-belligerent territory. This is because the First Convention relates primarily to treatment of the wounded and sick who are in the immediate vicinity of hostilities, whereas the categories of persons listed in Article 4B of the Third Convention are not relevant to that context.[7] In addition, there is no requirement in Article 13 that a person be in enemy hands in order to be covered by the First Convention. Nevertheless, as soon as wounded or sick persons covered by the First Convention fall into the hands of the enemy, they are also protected as prisoners of war as affirmed by Article 14. In such cases, the First and Third Conventions apply simultaneously.[8]

1445   Other than the limited number of civilians who fall under paragraphs 4 and 5 of Article 13, the First Convention does not apply to civilians who are wounded or sick. Civilians who are wounded or sick are entitled to protection under the Fourth Convention and other rules of international humanitarian law.[9]

B. Historical background

1446 The first Geneva Convention (1864) was concerned with the protection of the wounded and sick in armies in the field. That Convention set up a system for

---

[6] For example, obligations relating to the recording and forwarding of information on wounded and sick persons and prescriptions regarding the dead are similar in the First and Third Conventions. Compare, for example, Article 17 of the First Convention and Article 120 of the Third Convention.

[7] Article 4B concerns persons already in enemy hands or under the control of a neutral or non-belligerent Power. As such persons are not likely to be found wounded or sick on battlefields or near hostilities, these categories were not included in Article 13 of the First Convention.

[8] See the commentary on Article 14, section C.1.

[9] See Articles 16 and 17 of the Fourth Convention. For those States party to Additional Protocol I, Article 8(a) makes no distinction between wounded and sick military personnel and civilians for the purposes of the Protocol. According to the ICRC study on customary international humanitarian law, no distinction should be made between wounded or sick combatants, military personnel and civilians in respect of the obligations owed to them under that body of law; see ICRC Study on Customary International Humanitarian Law (2005), Rules 109–111. In the context of non-international armed conflicts, common Article 3 specifies that the wounded and sick must be collected, cared for and treated humanely. Article 7 of Additional Protocol II also does not distinguish between wounded and sick military personnel and civilians.

the protection of '[w]ounded or sick combatants, to whatever nation they may belong'.[10] When the Convention was revised in 1906, it protected wounded or sick '[o]fficers, soldiers, and other persons officially attached to armies', thus extending protection to all members of the armed forces, including non-combatants such as medical personnel and any others who were officially part of the armed forces without being combatants.[11] When the Convention was revised again in 1929, the scope of application remained unchanged.[12]

1447   In 1929 there was no attempt to harmonize the categories of persons to whom the Geneva Convention on the Wounded and Sick would apply with those to whom the new Geneva Convention on Prisoners of War was to apply, even though both Conventions were being negotiated at the same time.[13] This was intentional, as there was concern that some States which were already party to the 1906 Convention would not wish to become party to the revised convention if it adopted a definition of a prisoner of war which they did not espouse.[14] In 1949, however, the delegates preferred to harmonize the Conventions to the greatest extent possible.[15]

1448   At the same time, the protection of civilians who were wounded or sick because of or during armed conflicts became a pressing concern. During the preparatory work for the Conventions prior to the 1949 Diplomatic Conference, the possibility of extending the protection of the whole of the First Convention to civilians was debated.[16] Instead of taking that approach, the Fourth

---

[10] Geneva Convention (1864), Article 6.

[11] Geneva Convention (1906), Article 1. See Des Gouttes, *Commentaire de la Convention de Genève de 1929 sur les blessés et malades*, ICRC, 1930, p. 15. The term 'non-combatants' here is used in the narrow sense, as it was meant in Article 3 of the 1907 Hague Regulations. To give an example, at that time cooks who were members of the armed forces were not considered combatants.

[12] Geneva Convention on the Wounded and Sick (1929), Article 1. In 1929, the English translation was slightly revised, to '[o]fficers *and* soldiers and other persons...' but otherwise remained identical to that of 1906. The French version of all three Conventions used the word 'militaires'.

[13] *Proceedings of the Geneva Diplomatic Conference of 1929*, pp. 88–90. In the end, the 1929 Geneva Convention on Prisoners of War relied on the definition in the 1907 Hague Convention (IV), but could also apply to certain categories of civilians; see Geneva Convention on Prisoners of War (1929), Articles 1 and 81.

[14] There was discussion during the 1929 Diplomatic Conference as to whether the definition, for the purposes of the Geneva Convention on the Wounded and Sick, would be identical to that being negotiated for prisoners of war. See *Proceedings of the Geneva Diplomatic Conference of 1929*, pp. 88–89 (delegate of the United Kingdom: 'Je crois que le même texte se trouvera dans le Code des prisonniers de guerre' ('I believe that the same text will be found in the code for prisoners of war.'). However, the President of the Diplomatic Conference counselled against harmonizing the two treaties on this point; see p. 89. At the time, the definition of prisoners of war was that found in Articles 1–3 of the 1907 Hague Regulations.

[15] They also sought to harmonize the definition with that in Article 1 of the 1907 Hague Regulations; see *Final Record of the Diplomatic Conference of Geneva of 1949*, Vol. II-A, pp. 237, 239–242, 386–387, 413–414 and 420–423.

[16] This idea was considered during the 1937 Commission of Experts (National Societies), but it was not adopted by the 17th International Conference of the Red Cross; see *Report of the Preliminary Conference of National Societies of 1946*, pp. 16–18.

Convention was developed as a separate treaty and the scope of protection of the First Convention was essentially maintained.

1449   The development of the categories which were ultimately adopted in Article 13 of the First and Second Conventions and in Article 4A of the Third Convention occurred entirely within the context of the revision of the Geneva Convention on Prisoners of War.

For a more detailed discussion of the historical development of the categories as they pertain to prisoners of war, see the commentary on Article 4 of the Third Convention.

C. Discussion

1. Scope of application: 'wounded and sick belonging to the following categories'

1450   The introductory paragraph of Article 13 provides that the First Convention applies to 'the wounded and sick belonging to the following categories'. The meaning of the term 'wounded and sick' in this context is set out in the commentary on Article 12.[17]

1451   In addition to the requirement that a person be wounded or sick, Article 13 is distinct from Article 4 of the Third Convention in a subtle but important way: as noted above, it does not require a wounded or sick person to have fallen into enemy hands in order to be protected. This means that the First Convention also applies to wounded and sick members of a Party's own armed forces, in addition to those of the armed forces of the adverse Party.[18] This is the way in which the obligations now enshrined in the First Convention have been understood since their adoption in 1864.[19] Furthermore, it underscores that Parties to a conflict have obligations towards wounded and sick persons, such as the obligation in Article 15 of the First Convention to search for and collect the wounded and sick, even when such persons are not in their hands.

---

[17] See the commentary on Article 12, section D.2.

[18] This is also affirmed in Article 10 of Additional Protocol I, and the 1987 commentary reiterates this point; see Sandoz/Swinarski/Zimmermann (eds), *Commentary on the Additional Protocols*, ICRC, 1987, para. 445:

> The inclusion of the expression 'to whichever Party they belong' ensures that 'it is clearly stated that every Party to the conflict must respect and protect its own wounded, sick and shipwrecked – which may seem self-evident, though it is perhaps a useful reminder...' In spite of this, the First Convention retains the wording 'Detaining Power' in paragraph 3 of Article 13, even though that formulation is technically inaccurate for the situation of the wounded and sick.

[19] See Des Gouttes, *Commentaire de la Convention de Genève de 1929 sur les blessés et malades*, ICRC, 1930, pp. 13–14.

2. *The different categories in Article 13*

1452 Article 13 includes members of the armed forces of Parties to the conflict and also a number of other categories of persons. The first paragraph refers to '[m]embers of the armed forces of a Party to the conflict, as well as members of militias or volunteer corps forming part of such armed forces'. The term 'armed forces' was specifically chosen to encompass all military personnel, no matter to which service they belong, be it land, sea or air forces.[20] It should be noted that the incorporation of individuals into State armed forces, including militia and volunteer corps that are part of such armed forces, is not regulated under international law and depends on the internal laws of States.[21]

1453 Paragraph 2 sets out the criteria that 'other militias' must meet in order to have prisoner-of-war status.[22] The four conditions listed in that paragraph for militias and volunteer forces which belong to a Party to a conflict but are not part of its regular armed forces have been recognized since at least 1899, when they were enumerated in the Hague Regulations.[23] The innovation in 1949 was to extend those conditions to cover organized resistance groups fighting against Occupying Powers, including when the Occupying Power had established full control over the whole territory.

1454 Paragraph 3 protects regular armed forces fighting for a government not recognized by the opposing forces.[24] This provision applies to situations where a State exists but where the government in power may not be recognized as the legitimate government of the territory by other States that are Parties to the conflict. This was the case during the international armed conflict between the Taliban and the US-led coalition in Afghanistan in 2001–2002.[25] While the Taliban controlled 90 per cent of the territory of the country, it was recognized as the legitimate government of Afghanistan by only a few States.[26]

1455 The wording in Article 13(3) warrants additional clarification. Article 13(3) refers to the 'Detaining Power' instead of 'opposing forces', which suggests that,

---

[20] In the English translation of the 1929 Geneva Convention on the Wounded and Sick, the expression 'armed forces' was already in use, whereas in the French version of that Convention, the term 'armies' was used.

[21] See Knut Ipsen, 'Combatants and Non-Combatants', in Dieter Fleck (ed.), *The Handbook of International Humanitarian Law*, 3rd edition, Oxford University Press, 2013, pp. 79–113, at 86.

[22] See also the commentary on Article 4 of the Third Convention.

[23] Hague Regulations, 1899, Article 1. The same conditions were also listed in Article 9 of the 1874 Brussels Declaration.

[24] Its inclusion in 1949 was inspired by a need to protect the members of armed forces such as those fighting under General Charles de Gaulle during the Second World War.

[25] Issues relating to the prisoner-of-war status of the participants in that conflict are discussed in the commentary on Article 4 of the Third Convention.

[26] See Stephane Ojeda, 'US Detention of Taliban Fighters: Some Legal Considerations', in Michael N. Schmitt (ed.), *The War in Afghanistan: A Legal Analysis*, International Law Studies, U.S. Naval War College, Vol. 85, 2009, pp. 357–369, at 358–359.

to fall under it, the wounded and sick must be detained. This is technically incorrect; the use of the term might be due to an oversight when the drafters transposed the article from the Third Convention to the First.[27] In any case, the term should be interpreted in the light of the aim of the provision, which is to ensure that assistance is provided without exception. Thus, wounded and sick persons covered by the First Convention, including those mentioned in this paragraph, benefit from the protection owed to them by enemy forces even when they are not (yet) in their hands or detained.

1456   Paragraph 4, which affirms that persons 'who accompany the armed forces without actually being members thereof' are protected, extends the protection of the First Convention to some civilians in specific roles.[28] This category may include journalists 'embedded' with armed forces, as well as private contractors who supply services to armed forces and who are authorized to do so by a Party to the conflict.[29]

1457   There is a minor distinction in the wording of Article 13(4) of the First Convention compared with the equivalent text in Article 4A(4) of the Third Convention. Article 4A(4) adds that the armed forces which have authorized persons to accompany them 'shall provide them ... with an identity card similar to the annexed model'. The omission of this phrase in Article 13 is logical, as it may not be feasible, in practice, to check for an identity card before or even while respecting and collecting the wounded and sick, whereas such checks can be made once a person is in the power of the enemy. In any case, the preparatory work on Article 4 indicates that possession of an identity card should not be taken as a necessary element for prisoner-of-war status.[30] Even so, since such cards are sufficient to identify persons as accompanying the armed forces,

---

[27] A delegate to the 1949 Diplomatic Conference pointed out that 'the words "Detaining Power" would have to be replaced by "adverse Party"', but this seems to have been forgotten in the end; see *Final Record of the Diplomatic Conference of Geneva of 1949*, Vol. II-A, p. 50.

[28] Those civilians were accorded prisoner-of-war status in the 1899/1907 Hague Conventions (II/IV) and the 1929 Geneva Convention on Prisoners of War, but it was only with the 1949 Convention that the protections for the wounded and sick were extended to them. Article 13 of the 1899 and the 1907 Hague Regulations reads: 'Individuals who follow an army without directly belonging to it, such as newspaper correspondents and reporters, sutlers, contractors, who fall into the enemy's hands, and whom the latter think fit to detain, have a right to be treated as prisoners of war, provided they can produce a certificate from the military authorities of the army they were accompanying.' Article 81 of the 1929 Geneva Convention on Prisoners of War maintained prisoner-of-war status for this group. For further analysis, see the commentary on Article 4 of the Third Convention.

[29] Not all private contractors fall within this category, however. For example, it is unlikely that private military and security contractors hired by non-governmental organizations, by private companies, or even by government agencies other than defence departments (depending on internal laws) would meet the requirements to be considered to be civilians accompanying the armed forces. See Lindsey Cameron and Vincent Chetail, *Privatizing War: Private Military and Security Companies under Public International Law*, Cambridge University Press, 2013, pp. 419–421.

[30] See *Final Record of the Diplomatic Conference of Geneva of 1949*, Vol. II-A, pp. 416–418. The preparatory work is silent as to why the card is not mentioned in Article 13.

States are required to issue them to protect those persons. Nevertheless, the fact that no card is mentioned in Article 13(4) makes no practical difference in terms of who may fall under this article.

1458   Paragraph 5 stipulates that the civilian crews of merchant ships and civilian aircraft of a Party to the conflict who are wounded or sick also enjoy the protection of the Convention if they 'do not benefit from more favourable treatment under any other provisions in international law'. This clause is relevant primarily for the application of Article 14 of the First Convention to this category of persons. The 'more favourable treatment' clause refers to the 1907 Hague Convention (XI), which provides that certain merchant seamen must not be made prisoners of war.[31] They must, however, be respected, collected and cared for in accordance with the First Convention. The crews of *neutral* merchant vessels and civilian aircraft are not protected by the First Convention, but they may be protected by the Fourth Convention.[32] Lastly, Article 13(6) protects the wounded and sick who were participating in a 'levée en masse' (mass rising). This last category was already considered to be essentially archaic in 1949, but was included in the Conventions as a long-standing category of persons whose belligerent status is recognized provided that they fulfil certain conditions.[33]

1459   The debates during the 1949 Diplomatic Conference regarding the development of the list of protected persons in Article 4 of the Third Convention (Article 13 of the First Convention) were primarily concerned with the question of who should be entitled to prisoner-of-war status, in view of the benefits of such status. This is still the case today: controversy related to the interpretation of the concepts embodied in both Article 4 of the Third Convention and Article 13 of the First Convention is often linked to the question of prisoner-of-war status, i.e. a question relevant for the application of the Third Convention. In contrast, controversy has not arisen in relation to the status and protection of wounded or sick persons under the First Convention.[34]

For a more comprehensive discussion of the different categories of persons, especially in relation to prisoner-of-war status, see the commentary on Article 4 of the Third Convention.

---

[31] See Hague Convention (XI) (1907), Articles 5–8. For a discussion, see *Final Record of the Diplomatic Conference of Geneva of 1949*, Vol. II-A, pp. 418–419. See also Hague Convention (XI) (1907), Articles 3 and 4, which stipulate that certain vessels are exempt from capture. On vessels exempt from capture, see also San Remo Manual on International Law Applicable to Armed Conflicts at Sea (1994), Rule 136.

[32] If they are not protected persons under the Fourth Convention, they are entitled to protection under Article 75 of Additional Protocol I.

[33] See *Final Record of the Diplomatic Conference of Geneva of 1949*, Vol. II-B, p. 239.

[34] This was confirmed in part in 1970 by the report of the UN Secretary-General, 'Respect for Human Rights in Armed Conflicts', UN Doc. A/8052 (1970), 18 September 1970, para. 99: '[T]here seems to be no pressing need for revision of the Geneva Conventions on the protection of wounded, sick and ship-wrecked combatants.'

*3. Protection of the wounded and sick who are not covered by
   the First Convention*

1460   Article 13 defines which persons, if they are wounded or sick, benefit from the
protection of the First Convention. It must be emphasized, however, that all
wounded or sick persons, including civilians, are entitled to respect, humane
treatment, and the care which their condition requires. Anyone in need of
medical attention is entitled to receive it. When a wounded or sick person falls
into enemy hands, the priority must be to provide medical care with the least
possible delay.[35] The determination as to whether that person meets the conditions for being a prisoner of war can be made later, at an appropriate time
and place. Moreover, some obligations in the First Convention – such as the
obligation to search for and collect the wounded and sick – must be carried out
before it is possible to determine whether these persons meet the criteria in
Article 13.[36]

1461   At the Diplomatic Conference in 1949, it was emphasized that 'it is of course
clearly understood that those not included in this enumeration [of Article 13]
still remain protected, either by other Conventions, or simply by the general
principles of International Law'.[37] Thus, Article 13 cannot in any way entitle
a Party to a conflict to fail to respect a wounded person, or to deny the requisite treatment, even where the person does not belong to one of the categories
specified in it.

1462   The significance of this approach has only increased over time. With the
many changes in the way in which armed conflicts have been conducted over
the past 150 years, civilians have become even more likely than members of
the armed forces to suffer injury during hostilities.[38] In addition, many conflicts
nowadays are of a mixed character, with non-international armed conflicts – in
which there is no prisoner-of-war status as a matter of law – occurring alongside international armed conflicts. When it comes to respecting and protecting
the wounded and sick, providing them with medical care and treating them

---

[35] For details, see Fourth Convention, Article 16, and Additional Protocol I, Articles 8(a)–(b) and
    10. See also ICRC Study on Customary International Humanitarian Law (2005), Rules 109–111.
[36] See Article 15.
[37] See *Final Record of the Diplomatic Conference of Geneva of 1949*, Vol. II-A, p. 191 (regarding
    Article 10A). There was a proposal by the Drafting Committee to add a paragraph to Article 13
    'specifying that the provisions of Article [13] should not deprive the wounded and sick, whatever
    their category, of the protection to which they were entitled according to the general principles
    of the law of nations'. That proposal, which was brought forward before Article 4 of the Third
    Convention was finalized, was rejected by vote, but the rejection was due to problems with
    translation regarding the proposed text and principle; see *Final Record of the Diplomatic Con-
    ference of Geneva of 1949*, Vol. II-A, p. 158. See also *Minutes of the Diplomatic Conference of
    Geneva of 1949*, Commission I, Vol. III, meeting held on 30 July 1949, pp. 35–46.
[38] This was already the case in the 1930s and 1940s when the revision of the Geneva Convention
    on the Wounded and Sick was being discussed; see *Report of the Preliminary Conference of
    National Societies of 1946*, pp. 16–18.

humanely, the inclusion of Article 13 in the First Convention does not mean that these obligations are excluded with respect to persons not covered by the article.[39]

[39] See e.g. United Kingdom, *Manual of the Law of Armed Conflict*, 2004:

> 7.3. The wounded and sick are to be protected and respected. They may not be attacked. They must be treated humanely. They must be provided with medical care. They may not wilfully be left without medical assistance nor exposed to contagious diseases or infection. Priority of treatment is dictated by medical reasons only....
> 7.3.2. Paragraph 7.3 applies to all wounded and sick, whether United Kingdom, allied or enemy, military or civilian.

STATUS OF THE WOUNDED AND SICK WHO HAVE FALLEN INTO ENEMY HANDS

❖ Text of the provision

Subject to the provisions of Article 12, the wounded and sick of a belligerent who fall into enemy hands shall be prisoners of war, and the provisions of international law concerning prisoners of war shall apply to them.

❖ Reservations or declarations

None

Contents

A. Introduction

1463 Article 14 defines the status of a wounded or sick member of the armed forces who falls into enemy hands.[1] In that situation, a member of the armed forces is both a wounded or sick person needing treatment and an individual who is entitled to become – and thus becomes – a prisoner of war. The First and Third Conventions will therefore apply simultaneously.

B. Historical background

1464 Both the 1906 and 1929 Geneva Conventions on the Wounded and Sick contained a provision affirming that a wounded or sick member of the armed forces

---

[1] For the purposes of the commentary on this article, the phrase 'member of the armed forces' includes those persons who are not members of the armed forces of a Party to a conflict but who nevertheless come within the scope of Article 13 of the First Convention.

who falls into enemy hands is a prisoner of war and that 'the general provisions of international law concerning prisoners of war shall be applicable to them'.[2] Article 14 was thus included in the 1949 First Convention without controversy.

1465   As a point of historical interest, in the deliberations on this issue during the negotiation of the 1929 Convention, one delegation proposed that while wounded or sick prisoners of war were hospitalized they should have a special, privileged status distinct from that of prisoners of war.[3] The proposal was rejected for a number of reasons, not least because of the endless conundrums and inequalities that such a status might create. Moreover, it was agreed that if the existing rules on the treatment of the wounded and sick and prisoners of war were observed conscientiously, no special status should be necessary to ensure that the wounded and sick received all the care required by and appropriate to their condition.[4]

C. Discussion

1. Simultaneous application of the Conventions

1466   As wounded and sick combatants who have fallen into enemy hands are prisoners of war, they are covered by both the First and Third Conventions. Those who do not recover from their initial wounds or sickness by the end of the conflict and are still in enemy hands remain protected by the First Convention until the moment specified in Article 5 – their final repatriation.

1467   When wounded or sick prisoners of war have recovered, the First Convention no longer applies to them, but they remain protected by the Third Convention until the moment specified in Article 5 of that Convention – their final release and repatriation.[5] If they are wounded or fall sick again while prisoners of war, they are protected only by the Third Convention, which in any case requires a standard of medical care and hygiene that is at least equivalent to that set down in the First Convention.[6] In either case, wounded and sick persons in enemy hands must be provided with the treatment their condition requires.[7]

---

[2] Geneva Convention on the Wounded and Sick (1929), Article 2. The wording of Article 2 of the 1906 Geneva Convention is almost identical, stipulating that 'the general rules of international law concerning prisoners become applicable to them'. The 1864 Geneva Convention did not address the subject.

[3] *Proceedings of the Geneva Diplomatic Conference of 1929*, pp. 102–103 and 108–115.

[4] *Ibid.* pp. 142–144 and 600–601. See also Des Gouttes, *Commentaire de la Convention de Genève de 1929 sur les blessés et malades*, ICRC, 1930, pp. 19–21.

[5] Third Convention, Article 5. See also *Final Record of the Diplomatic Conference of Geneva of 1949*, Vol. II-A, p. 143.

[6] Many provisions in the Third Convention relate to the medical care of prisoners of war: see, for example, Article 15, as well as Articles 19–20, 29–32, 46–47, 49, 54, 55, 98, 109–110, 112–114 and all other provisions relating to a healthy environment, sufficient food, etc. for prisoners of war.

[7] See, in particular, Article 12 of the First Convention and Articles 29–31 of the Third Convention.

1468   The First Convention relates primarily to the wounded and sick in armed forces *in the field*, whereas the Third Convention regulates the treatment of prisoners of war, and includes a whole series of detailed provisions relating to the various aspects of their captivity. The level of detail in each Convention is tailored to the circumstances and context in which it is anticipated to apply. Thus, during hostilities or in their immediate aftermath, the obligations set out in the First Convention would predominate. The further removed the hostilities are in time and space, the more the detailed provisions of the Third Convention gain precedence.

2. 'Subject to the provisions of Article 12'

1469   The clause '[s]ubject to the provisions of Article 12' makes clear that the paramount concern in regard to wounded or sick members of the armed forces who fall into enemy hands is that they are respected and protected, treated humanely and cared for, as required by Article 12. Thus, for example, in urgent cases a Power detaining wounded or sick persons must prioritize medical care over measures to restrict their liberty.

3. Falling into enemy hands

1470   Article 14 stipulates that the 'wounded or sick of a belligerent who *fall into enemy hands*' are prisoners of war. The phrase 'fall into enemy hands' is sufficiently broad to cover capture or surrender and the taking of wounded persons into the enemy's medical units to care for them. It also encompasses the mere act by the opposing forces of providing treatment on the battlefield: when wounded combatants are being tended to by the adverse Party, that Party is in a position to exert a degree of control over them, amounting to a situation that entails prisoner-of-war status.

1471   The 1929 Geneva Convention on the Wounded and Sick uses the phrase 'fall into the hands of the enemy', while the 1929 Geneva Convention on Prisoners of War uses the word 'capture'.[8] During the Second World War, some Detaining Powers denied prisoner-of-war status to combatants who had surrendered, arguing that surrender was not the same as 'capture'.[9] To avoid the recurrence of such situations, Article 4 of the Third Convention adopted the wording 'fallen

---

[8] Geneva Convention on the Wounded and Sick (1929), Article 2; Geneva Convention on Prisoners of War (1929), Articles 1 and 2, respectively.

[9] See Pictet (ed.), *Commentary on the Third Geneva Convention*, ICRC, 1960, p. 50. See also Bugnion, p. 194: '[I]n 1945 the Allies refused prisoner-of-war status for German and Japanese soldiers who fell into their hands after the capitulation of their respective countries, claiming that their situation was not covered by the 1929 Convention. Instead, they were classed as "Surrendered Enemy Personnel".'

into the power of the enemy', such that the First and Third Conventions are now, in essence, identical on this point.[10]

1472   As noted in the commentary on Article 13, the interpretation of the criteria for determining whether a person is entitled to prisoner-of-war status has been the subject of some controversy. These debates are most relevant to – and can best be understood in the context of – provisions relating to prisoners of war and are therefore discussed in the commentary on Article 4 of the Third Convention.

1473   Lastly, although in setting down who is a prisoner of war Article 14 uses the looser formulation 'the wounded and sick of a belligerent' rather than the more technical terms used in Article 13, the definition of prisoners of war in the First Convention is not meant to diverge from that in the Third Convention. This understanding is confirmed by the placement of Article 14 in sequence after Article 13, combined with the desire of the drafters to ensure coherence across the Conventions.

4. Protection afforded to prisoners of war under international law

1474   Article 14 states not only that the wounded and sick who fall into enemy hands 'shall be prisoners of war', but that all 'the provisions of international law concerning prisoners of war shall apply to them'. This phrase was chosen over a reference only to the Third Convention to make clear that all international law related to the protection of prisoners of war would remain applicable, in particular in the event that some States became Parties to the First Convention but not the Third or that the text of the Third Convention was revised but not that of the First Convention.[11] That fear did not materialize, however, as States have ratified the four Geneva Conventions together, such that the detailed provisions of the Third Convention will apply.[12] In any case, the Third Convention is also generally considered to reflect customary international law.[13]

1475   Unlike its predecessors in the 1906 and 1929 Conventions, Article 14 does not specifically provide for the conclusion of special agreements on matters such as the return of the wounded or their transfer to a neutral State. However, common Article 6 of the 1949 Conventions (Article 7 in the Fourth Convention) provides for the possibility of concluding such agreements with respect to

---

[10] *Final Record of the Diplomatic Conference of Geneva of 1949*, Vol. II-A, p. 237. The French text of Article 14 of the First Convention and Article 4 of the Third Convention is even closer: 'tombés au pouvoir de l'adversaire' (Article 14) and 'tombées au pouvoir de l'ennemi' (Article 4).

[11] *Draft Conventions submitted to the 1948 Stockholm Conference*, commentary on draft article 11, pp. 10–11.

[12] Where applicable, Additional Protocol I may also be relevant to determine who is entitled to prisoner-of-war status. See also ICRC Study on Customary International Humanitarian Law (2005), Rule 106.

[13] See Eritrea-Ethiopia Claims Commission, *Prisoners of War, Eritrea's Claim*, Partial Award, 1 July 2003, para. 41, and *Prisoners of War, Ethiopia's Claim 4*, Partial Award, 1 July 2003, para. 32.

protected persons as long as they do not derogate from the protections afforded by the Conventions.[14]

Select bibliography

Bugnion, François, *The International Committee of the Red Cross and the Protection of War Victims*, ICRC/Macmillan, Oxford, 2003, pp. 192–194.

---

[14] For the predecessors of Article 14, see Geneva Convention (1906), Article 2, second paragraph, and Geneva Convention on the Wounded and Sick (1929), Article 2, second paragraph. As regards the 1949 Conventions, Article 15 of the First Convention affirms that agreements can be made to exchange the wounded on the battlefield, and Articles 109–111 of the Third Convention regulate the return of sick or wounded prisoners of war and provide for the conclusion of agreements in that regard.

SEARCH FOR CASUALTIES. EVACUATION

❖ Text of the provision*

(1) At all times, and particularly after an engagement, Parties to the conflict shall, without delay, take all possible measures to search for and collect the wounded and sick, to protect them against pillage and ill-treatment, to ensure their adequate care, and to search for the dead and prevent their being despoiled.

(2) Whenever circumstances permit, an armistice or a suspension of fire shall be arranged, or local arrangements made, to permit the removal, exchange and transport of the wounded left on the battlefield.

(3) Likewise, local arrangements may be concluded between Parties to the conflict for the removal or exchange of wounded and sick from a besieged or encircled area, and for the passage of medical and religious personnel and equipment on their way to that area.

❖ Reservations or declarations

None

Contents

* Paragraph numbers have been added for ease of reference.

A. Introduction

1476 Article 15 complements Article 12 and sets out certain core obligations on Parties to an international armed conflict vis-à-vis the wounded and sick. Obligations similar to those in Article 15 are contained in the Second Convention, the Fourth Convention, the Additional Protocols and customary international humanitarian law.[1] In particular, Article 15 fleshes out the general obligation laid down in Article 12 to protect the wounded and sick in all circumstances. Thus, Article 15(1) imposes an obligation 'to search for and collect' the wounded and sick, in order to remove them from the immediate danger zone and to enable them to receive the necessary medical treatment. Paragraph 1 also imposes certain obligations with regard to the dead. Paragraph 2 provides for arrangements to be made, for example a suspension of fire, to facilitate the execution of the obligations in paragraph 1. Lastly, paragraph 3 envisages such arrangements in particular situations, namely with respect to besieged and encircled areas.

1477   Article 15 is closely related to the original regime of legal protection for the wounded and sick on land as it was laid out in the 1864, 1906 and 1929 Geneva Conventions. Thus, like Article 12, Article 15 applies only during international armed conflict and only to the wounded and sick (and dead) who are members of the armed forces or otherwise entitled to prisoner-of-war status.

1478   Today, however, the obligation to search for and collect the wounded and sick, including civilians, is part of customary international humanitarian law, applicable in both international and non-international armed conflict.[2] The same holds true for the obligations to provide the wounded and sick with medical care and attention[3] and to protect them against pillage and ill-treatment.[4] Moreover, customary international humanitarian law today imposes obligations on the Parties to an armed conflict to search for and collect the dead,[5] to prevent them from being despoiled,[6] and to dispose of them in a respectful manner.[7]

---

[1] Second Convention, Article 18; Fourth Convention, Articles 16–17; Additional Protocol I, Article 10; Additional Protocol II, Article 8; ICRC Study on Customary International Humanitarian Law (2005), Rules 109–113.

[2] ICRC Study on Customary International Humanitarian Law (2005), Rule 109. For a different view, see Benoit. For those States party to it, Additional Protocol I also extends this obligation to all wounded and sick civilians. See also United States, *Law of War Manual*, 2015, pp. 477–478.

[3] ICRC Study on Customary International Humanitarian Law (2005), Rule 110.

[4] *Ibid.* Rule 111.   [5] *Ibid.* Rule 112.   [6] *Ibid.* Rule 113.   [7] *Ibid.* Rule 115.

B. Historical background

1479 The obligation to collect the wounded and sick has been part of international humanitarian law since its inception as treaty law in 1864.[8] This is only logical, given that Henry Dunant's proposal for an international convention to ameliorate the condition of wounded and sick soldiers was inspired by the appalling conditions he witnessed on the battlefield of Solferino, where some 40,000 fallen Austrian, French and Italian soldiers lay unattended.[9] The provision was expanded upon in the 1906, 1929 and 1949 Geneva Conventions.[10] The basic humanitarian rationale has, however, remained constant: that the wounded and sick must not be left to suffer without medical care.

C. Scope of application

1480 Article 15 applies 'at all times' to the 'Parties to the conflict' during an international armed conflict. More specifically, it applies in relation to the wounded and sick as defined by Articles 12 and 13 and to the dead falling within the scope of the First Convention.

1481   The 1952 commentary asserted that 'Article 15 applies exclusively to operations which take place at the front'.[11] Articles 12 and 15 are often perceived as regulating two distinct situations. According to this view, Article 12 would apply to the 'rear' and to situations where the wounded and sick are in the power of a Party to the conflict, while Article 15 would be confined to the front line of combat and to the area 'between the lines'.[12] However, while in practice these are the typical fields of application, neither of the provisions is legally confined in such a way. Article 12(2) is the exception, as the text explicitly requires the wounded and sick to be in the power of a Party to the conflict.[13] The wording in Article 15(1) – '[a]t all times, and particularly after an engagement' – rather suggests a broad interpretation and does not imply any geographical limitation. It would be inconsistent with the purpose of Article 15, which is to ensure that the wounded and sick receive the medical care their condition requires, if they had to be collected only in the actual zone of combat, which in any case defies a clear-cut definition or geographical delimitation. Especially in

---

[8] Geneva Convention (1864), Article 6(1).   [9] Dunant, p. 126.

[10] Geneva Convention (1906), Article 3; Geneva Convention on the Wounded and Sick (1929), Article 3. Moreover, in 1899, the principles of the 1864 Geneva Convention were adapted for the first time to maritime warfare and to wounded, sick and shipwrecked members of the armed forces and sailors at sea by virtue of the Hague Convention (III), which was superseded in 1907 by the Hague Convention (X) (see Article 25 of the 1907 Hague Convention (X)).

[11] Pictet (ed.), *Commentary on the First Geneva Convention*, ICRC, 1952, p. 150.

[12] *Ibid.* pp. 150–151. The 1929 Geneva Convention on the Wounded and Sick had already attempted, for the sake of clarity, to draw a distinction between these different stages by dealing first with operations taking place at the front and then with those in the rear, where it is possible to have recourse to installations of a more permanent character.

[13] See the commentary on Article 12, para. 1370.

the context of contemporary armed conflicts, where there is often no front line in the traditional sense and where hostilities frequently shift from one location to another, such a qualification would be unduly restrictive.[14] Thus, even though the wording 'particularly after an engagement' in paragraph 1, 'battlefield' in paragraph 2 and 'besieged or encircled area' in paragraph 3 indicates that the combat zone is the primary field of application of Article 15, this reflects a pragmatic emphasis and not a legal limitation. Therefore, the territorial scope of application of Article 15 follows that of the First Convention as a whole in respect of persons who are wounded or sick as a result of the conflict, or whose access to medical treatment or care is affected by the conflict.

1482   That said, the standard of medical care that is owed in a given situation may vary depending on where the wounded and sick are found. Thus, it is clear that the kind of medical care that can be expected under secure conditions, for example when the wounded and sick are in a hospital, cannot be expected in close proximity to the combat zone, where the obligation to provide care typically concerns the administration of first aid. Under combat conditions more than that would appear to be unrealistic. Thus, Article 15(1) will require different kinds and levels of care in the immediate danger zone compared to those in the more secure conditions of a hospital further away from this zone, where other resources in terms of medically qualified personnel and equipment are available.

D. Paragraph 1: Search, collection and care

1. The obligation to search for and collect the wounded and sick

1483 Under paragraph 1, Parties to an armed conflict are obliged to search for and collect the wounded and sick. The two obligations are complementary: in order to collect the wounded and sick, logically one must first search for them. The purpose of this provision is to remove the wounded and sick from the immediate danger zone and to enable them to receive adequate medical treatment as rapidly as possible and under better and more secure conditions.

1484   It is therefore logical to understand the seemingly distinct obligations of 'to search for' and 'to collect' as a single obligation to carry out search and rescue activities. Likewise, it is evident that merely collecting the wounded and sick without a corresponding obligation to evacuate them to a more secure place would be meaningless, particularly in the light of the well-established medical understanding that treatment within the first hour of injury often increases the likelihood of survival exponentially.[15] Therefore, regardless of the specific

---

[14] See Bart, pp. 33–43, especially at 43.
[15] Atul Gawande, 'Casualties of War – Military Care for the Wounded from Iraq and Afghanistan', *The New England Journal of Medicine*, Vol. 351, 2004, pp. 2471–2475.

language used, the obligation in each case entails search, collection and evacuation. Accordingly, the rule as formulated in the ICRC's study on customary international humanitarian law has not added a new dimension to this obligation; rather, by including a mention of 'to evacuate', it merely specifies an important aspect of this obligation that has been part and parcel of previous references to the obligation to search and collect.[16]

1485   The obligation to search and collect, i.e. to carry out search and rescue activities, is an obligation of conduct. This character of the obligation is made clear by the wording 'take all possible measures'. As such, it is to be exercised with due diligence.[17] Precisely what due diligence requires in a given situation depends on the elements set down in the primary norm and on the circumstances.[18] The relevant point of reference is what would be expected of a reasonable commander under the given circumstances.[19] In addition to the timing of search and rescue activities, this applies to the kind of measures to be taken, such as the number of suitably qualified personnel and the type of equipment to be deployed.

1486   The following general parameters of the obligation to search and collect can be discerned. First, searching for and collecting the wounded and sick is a continuous obligation. As indicated by the wording 'at all times', it applies for the duration of the entire armed conflict. This does not mean, however, that Parties must search actively for the wounded and sick at all times, as that would be unrealistic. Yet whenever there is an indication that there may be wounded or sick people in an area, and circumstances permit, a reasonable commander should commence search and rescue activities. With regard to the precise point in time at which a duty to take all possible measures arises, the International Court of Justice held in the *Application of the Genocide Convention* case that 'a State's ... duty to act, *arise[s] at the instant* that the State learns of, or should normally have learned of, the existence of a *serious risk ...*' (emphasis added).[20] In this regard, Article 15(1) imposes an obligation to take steps 'particularly after an engagement' because of the likelihood that wounded, sick or dead persons may be present at that time. The term 'engagement' describes

---

[16] In addition, Article 16(1) of the First Convention requires Parties to the conflict to 'record as soon as possible ... any particulars which may assist in [the] identification [of the wounded and sick]', which implies that any belongings of the wounded or sick should also be collected.

[17] See Koivurova, paras 1–3; Dupuy, pp. 378 and 384; Pisillo-Mazzeschi, pp. 41–46; and Hessbruegge, p. 270.

[18] See ICJ, *Application of the Genocide Convention case*, Merits, Judgment, 2007, para. 430, and Pisillo-Mazzeschi, p. 44.

[19] Pisillo-Mazzeschi, pp. 44–45.

[20] ICJ, *Application of the Genocide Convention case*, Merits, Judgment, 2007, para. 431. However, as far as State responsibility for the breach of the obligation to prevent is concerned, the ICJ was more cautious and, in accordance with Article 14(3) of the 2001 Draft Articles on State Responsibility, ruled that 'a State can be held responsible for breaching the obligation to prevent genocide only if genocide was actually committed. It is at the time when commission of the prohibited act ... begins that the breach of an obligation of prevention occurs.' For a critique, see Dupuy, pp. 381–384.

any kind of combat activity that may result in persons being wounded, sick or killed. Hence, it can be inferred that unless there are clear indications that combat activity has *not* given rise to any wounded, sick or dead, search and rescue activities are normally required after every engagement.

1487 Second, the measures that must be taken in each case have also to be determined on the basis of what may reasonably be expected. A variety of factors may need to be considered, which may include security considerations and the availability of (medical) personnel and of medical and other rescue equipment, in addition to such factors as the terrain and weather conditions. There are times when security considerations may, at least temporarily, make the obligation to search for the fallen impracticable. There will be cases which exceed the limits of what the medical personnel can be expected to do, however great their courage and devotion. It is for this reason that the obligation in the article is not absolute and that it provides that 'Parties to the conflict shall, without delay, take all possible measures...'. The obligation to act without delay is strict, but the action to be taken is limited to what is feasible, in particular in the light of security considerations. The military command must judge reasonably and in good faith, based on the circumstances and the available information, what is possible and to what extent it can commit its medical personnel. In all cases, the operation must be conducted in full compliance with the principle of non-discrimination.

1488 Third, given that the obligation to search for and collect applies 'at all times', it applies even during an engagement. However, it may at times be difficult to strike a balance between the acceptable level of risk to one's own life (or the lives of medical personnel) and performing search, collection and evacuation activities as rapidly as possible. That said, if during an engagement on the ground it becomes apparent that there are wounded soldiers in the area and if a Party to the conflict can locate and evacuate them without any major risk to its personnel, it would be required to do so. Especially during ongoing hostilities, when there is an increased likelihood that people will be wounded, the quick delivery of first aid is essential and often life-saving. The urgency of the task needs to be taken into consideration when deciding on whether to conduct search and rescue activities. Article 15 therefore emphasizes that search and rescue activities have to be commenced 'without delay', i.e. as soon as possible. The relevant reference point, therefore, is not only 'after every engagement' but rather every time there is reason to believe that there are wounded and sick people in the area and as soon as circumstances permit.[21] This reading is confirmed by Article 15(1) itself, which by using the word 'particularly' clarifies that the obligation is not in any way confined to post-engagement situations.

1489 Fourth, logically, a greater number of wounded and sick people may require greater search and rescue resources than a smaller number. A similar logic

---

[21] ICJ, *Application of the Genocide Convention case*, Merits, Judgment, 2007, para. 431.

applies for search and rescue activities carried out in difficult terrain. If significant resources in terms of personnel and equipment are available, their deployment would be required in so far as it would be reasonable to use them. This is especially relevant when the known or suspected casualties are the result of an attack by air or other long-range/stand-off assets. In such cases, a commander may know or expect that the attack will result in casualties, but it may not be feasible for the attacking force to engage in search and rescue activities.

1490   Fifth, the Parties to an international armed conflict are the ones responsible for searching for and collecting the wounded and sick. However, Article 15 does not specify who has to carry out these activities. The typical scenario that paragraph 1 envisages involves soldiers or military medical personnel carrying out search and rescue activities, although the Convention also provides for the possibility of civilians helping to collect and care for the wounded and sick.[22] In situations in which multinational or coalition forces are engaged as Parties to a conflict, it may also mean that a Party that has not participated in a particular engagement nevertheless needs to assist in search, collection and evacuation activities if it is present in the area of an engagement. Armed forces remain responsible for search activities; however, those lacking the means to evacuate the wounded and sick should rely on external help. Practice shows that the ICRC in particular has frequently engaged in the evacuation of the wounded and sick in a variety of conflict settings.[23] Therefore, a Party to the conflict, knowing that wounded and sick people are in the vicinity, may be required, at a minimum, to inform other actors, especially neutral humanitarian organizations, of their presence and, if possible, to provide more detailed information (geographical coordinates) on their exact whereabouts. In addition, an offer of services from impartial humanitarian organizations to collect or evacuate the wounded and sick and the dead must not be refused on arbitrary grounds.[24] In practice, such organizations will seek the consent of the Parties to the conflict. This interpretation of paragraph 1 is based on the text, which explicitly requires Parties 'to take *all possible* measures to search for and collect the wounded and sick' (emphasis added) and also follows from the purpose of paragraph 1.

1491   Lastly, there may be limits as to what can be expected in terms of search, collection and evacuation in certain circumstances, for example if one side in an armed conflict engages exclusively in long-distance (aerial) operations,

---

[22] See Article 18. See also Giacca, para. 29.
[23] See e.g. Henckaerts/Doswald-Beck, commentary on Rule 109, p. 398. For example: during the Palestinian conflict (between June and August 1948) (*Revue internationale de la Croix-Rouge et Bulletin international des Sociétés de la Croix-Rouge*, Vol. 30, No. 354, June 1948, pp. 401–407 and further references); during the conflict between the armed forces of France and Tunisia in Bizerte (July 1961) (*Revue internationale de la Croix-Rouge*, Vol. 43, No. 515, November 1961, p. 530; *Keesing's Contemporary Archives*, 1961, pp. 18341–18343); and during the war between Egypt and Israel (November 1973 and January 1974) (*Revue internationale de la Croix-Rouge*, Vol. 55, No. 660, December 1973, p. 728).
[24] See also the commentary on Article 9, section C.4.b.

without any forces on the ground. Still, at a minimum, after an engagement and as far as military considerations permit, the geographical location of the (aerial) attacks should be disclosed to third actors, namely impartial humanitarian organizations or other States that are in the vicinity and that can begin evacuation activities, normally with the agreement of the Party under whose jurisdiction the wounded are found. It would also appear essential for the Party that conducted the attacks to guarantee in advance that it will not attack while such activities are ongoing.

2. The obligation to protect the wounded and sick against pillage and ill-treatment

1492 Parties to the conflict are obliged to ('shall') protect the wounded and sick against pillage and ill-treatment. The 1906 and 1929 Geneva Conventions contained the same obligation.[25] The obligation to protect in Article 15(1) is closely related to the obligation to respect and protect in Article 12(1), but Article 15(1) identifies concretely some of the dangers against which the wounded and sick are to be protected.

1493 Owing to their medical condition, the wounded and sick are particularly vulnerable to various kinds of ill-treatment. The obligation to protect them directly addresses this vulnerability and logically, therefore, ill-treatment should be interpreted broadly. In this light, the Parties to the conflict must take all possible measures to protect the wounded and sick against any form of ill-treatment, in particular the types of conduct listed in Article 12(2) and Article 50.

1494 'Pillage' can be defined as the appropriation or obtaining of public or private property by an individual without the owner's consent, in violation of international humanitarian law.[26] The appropriation or obtaining of the property is not necessarily done by force or violence but is carried out without the owner's implied or express consent.[27]

---

[25] Geneva Convention (1906), Article 3; Geneva Convention on the Wounded and Sick (1929), Article 3.

[26] The ICTY discussed the definition of plunder or pillage in the following judgments: *Delalić* Trial Judgment, 1998, paras 587–591; *Simić* Trial Judgment, 2003, para. 99; *Kordić and Čerkez* Appeal Judgment, 2004, paras 79–84; *Naletilić and Martinović* Trial Judgment, 2003, paras 612–615; and *Hadžihasanović* Trial Judgment, 2006, paras 49–51. The SCSL discussed the war crime of pillage in the following cases, among others: *Brima* Trial Judgment, 2007, para. 754; *Fofana and Kondewa* Trial Judgment, 2007, para. 160; and *Taylor* Trial Judgment, 2012, para. 452. The ICC discussed the war crime of pillage in *Bemba* Trial Judgment, 2016, paras 113–125 and 639–648.

[27] ICTY, *Delalić* Trial Judgment, 1998, para. 591. See also France, Permanent Military Tribunal at Metz, *Bommer case*, Judgment, 1947. During the negotiation of the elements of the war crime of pillage under the 1998 ICC Statute, States rejected the element of 'force', concentrating instead on the 'absence of consent'. See the commentary on Article 33 of the Fourth Convention.

1495   The prohibition of pillage covers both organized pillage, such as authorized or ordered forms of pillage, and individual acts.[28] Pillage can be carried out either by combatants or by civilians.

1496   It is important to distinguish between the unlawful appropriation of property that amounts to pillage, on the one hand, and the appropriation of property that is considered lawful under international humanitarian law, on the other hand. First, there is a recognized right in international armed conflict to capture as war booty any movable property belonging to the enemy State.[29] Booty of war covers all types of enemy movable public property that can be used for military operations, such as arms and munitions. If individuals were to take these types of public goods from a wounded or sick person on the battlefield, it might not amount to pillage if it is handed over to the State. If such goods are taken for private use, however, that would constitute pillage and would contravene the prohibition in Article 15. Second, in the conduct of hostilities, there are situations of lawful appropriation of property that are derived from Article 23(g) of the 1907 Hague Regulations. That article allows for the seizure of enemy property when such seizure is imperatively demanded by the necessities of war. Other than these listed exceptions,[30] appropriation of property during armed conflict without the consent of the owner constitutes pillage.[31]

1497   Article 15 refers specifically to the pillage of the wounded and sick, i.e. the unlawful appropriation of their property. The taking of property belonging to wounded or sick persons without their consent, unless it falls within one of the listed exceptions of legal appropriation of private and public property under the law of armed conflict, is prohibited by Article 15.

1498   Paragraph 1 does not specify against whom the wounded and sick must be protected. However, in the light of the purpose of this provision, and given that the wording of paragraph 1 does not contain any restrictions, they must be protected against ill-treatment or pillage no matter by whom committed. Thus, Parties to an armed conflict are obliged to protect the wounded and sick against ill-treatment and pillage by their own and enemy forces, as well as by civilians.

1499   The obligation to protect the wounded and sick is an obligation of conduct, to be carried out with due diligence. As far as protection against a State's own forces is concerned, proactive steps must be taken to prevent any form of

---

[28] See e.g. ICTY, *Delalić* Trial Judgment, 1998, para. 590, and ICC, *Bemba* Trial Judgment, 2016, para. 117.

[29] See ICRC Study on Customary International Humanitarian Law (2005), Rule 49: 'The parties to the conflict may seize military equipment belonging to an adverse party as war booty.'

[30] An additional exception in international armed conflict is that the prohibition of pillage does not affect the right of an Occupying Power to use the resources of the occupied territory for the maintenance and needs of the army of occupation within the limits of the law of occupation. See Articles 52, 53 and 55 of the 1907 Hague Regulations, as well as Articles 55 and 57 of the Fourth Convention. See also the commentary on Article 33 of the Fourth Convention.

[31] This presupposes, of course, that a link can be established between the act of pillage and the armed conflict. This nexus is what distinguishes pillage from theft in domestic law.

ill-treatment or pillage, including by ensuring that armed forces receive proper instruction and by punishing abuses. On the battlefield, Article 15 requires a Party to an armed conflict to guard the wounded and sick in order to prevent their ill-treatment or pillage. In case medical personnel need to resort to the use of their weapons in order to defend the wounded and sick in their charge against such acts, they do not thereby forfeit their protected status.[32]

3. *The obligation to ensure adequate care of the wounded and sick*

1500 By virtue of paragraph 1, Parties to an armed conflict are under an obligation to 'take all possible measures . . . to ensure . . . adequate care' of the wounded and sick.

1501 In view of the wording 'particularly after an engagement', it appears that the typical – albeit not the only – situation that Article 15(1) envisages is the delivery of first aid on the battlefield. As noted, first aid is essential and often life-saving.[33]

1502 The obligation to *ensure* adequate care entails taking steps in advance to put in place the medical supplies and personnel necessary for the care of the wounded and sick under the anticipated conditions of hostilities. That is, it implies a double obligation, not only to provide care, but also to ensure that care can be provided. Given that medical care may have to be administered in the battle space after or possibly even during an engagement, it is clear that the Convention does not impose the same standard of treatment as would be required once the wounded and sick have been transferred to a hospital or to a more secure medical facility.

1503 The wounded and sick must receive the medical care and attention that their condition requires.[34] Even though medical care in accordance with the highest medical standards would be the most desirable, Article 15 requires that care be 'adequate'. The exhortation to take all possible measures demands that Parties to a conflict do everything that can reasonably be expected of them in the circumstances to provide appropriate care. The kind of medical treatment that can reasonably be expected in a given situation depends on the availability of qualified personnel and on whether medical care is administered by doctors or paramedics or by ordinary soldiers or other persons without any medical training. The absence of qualified medical personnel may not, however, justify a failure to provide care, which must be provided with whatever resources are available.

---

[32] First Convention, Article 22(1). See also the commentary on Article 24, paras 2005–2006.
[33] See Atul Gawande, 'Casualties of War – Military Care for the Wounded from Iraq and Afghanistan', *The New England Journal of Medicine*, Vol. 351, 2004, pp. 2471–2475.
[34] See the commentary on Article 12, para. 1383.

1504   The relevant standards and procedures may change over time and there may be differences from country to country.[35] Nevertheless, some general guidance regarding the applicable standards of medical ethics and professional medical conduct may be derived from universally applicable, general stipulations and documents adopted by the World Medical Association (WMA).[36] There are many studies on the type of equipment and techniques that medical personnel should use and on the procedures they should follow. Again, it must be underscored that the provision of care must always be in accordance with the applicable standards of medical ethics.[37]

1505   The Eritrea-Ethiopia Claims Commission held that 'the requirement to provide...medical care during the initial period after capture must be assessed in light of the harsh conditions on the battlefield and the limited extent of medical training and equipment available to front line troops'.[38] Caring for the wounded and sick may give rise to an array of questions. Thus, it may also be necessary to distinguish between decisions that need to be taken by a military commander, in which case the relevant point of reference will be a reasonable military commander, and decisions that need to be taken by a doctor, which are to be measured against the standard of a reasonable medical practitioner.[39]

---

[35] Eritrea-Ethiopia Claims Commission, *Prisoners of War, Ethiopia's Claim*, Partial Award, 2003, para. 106.

[36] Instruments concerning medical ethics in times of armed conflict, especially: the World Medical Association's Regulations in Times of Armed Conflict (adopted by the 10th World Medical Assembly, Havana, Cuba, October 1956, as amended or revised in 1957, 1983, 2004, 2006 and 2012); Rules Governing the Care of Sick and Wounded, Particularly in Time of Conflict (adopted by the 10th World Medical Assembly, Havana, Cuba, October 1956, edited and amended in 1957 and 1983); Standards of Professional Conduct regarding the Hippocratic Oath and its modern version, the Declaration of Geneva, and its supplementary International Code of Medical Ethics (adopted by the 3rd WMA General Assembly, London, England, October 1949, as amended in 1968, 1983 and 2006). See also ICRC, *Health Care in Danger: The Responsibilities of Health-Care Personnel Working in Armed Conflicts and Other Emergencies*, ICRC, Geneva, 2012, pp. 55–62.

[37] See also Additional Protocol I, Article 16(1)–(2); ICRC Study on Customary International Humanitarian Law (2005), Rule 26; and Bothe/Partsch/Solf, p. 108, para. 2.3 (end).

[38] Eritrea-Ethiopia Claims Commission, *Prisoners of War, Ethiopia's Claim*, Partial Award, 2003, paras 69–70. Ethiopia had alleged that Eritrea had 'failed to provide necessary medical attention to Ethiopian POWs [prisoners of war] after capture and during evacuation, as required under customary international law reflected in Geneva Conventions I (Article 12) and III (Articles 20 and 15)'. Ethiopia further argued that '[m]any Ethiopian declarants testified that their wounds were not cleaned and bandaged at or shortly after capture, leading to infection and other complications'. Eritrea responded that 'its troops provided rudimentary first aid as soon as possible, including in transit camps'. While the Commission came to the general conclusion that there was no violation, logistical and resource constraints may not excuse a failure to provide even basic care.

[39] Israel, Supreme Court sitting as High Court of Justice, *Physicians for Human Rights* v. *Prime Minister of Israel and others*, Judgment, 2009, para. 23:

The respondents said that on 5 January 2009 a special health operations room was established, under the command of an officer with the rank of major, who is responsible for...coordinating the evacuation of the wounded and the dead from the area where fighting is taking place. Professional matters that arise in the operations room are decided by a doctor, who is an officer with the rank of lieutenant-colonel.

1506   As noted above, the obligation to *'ensure'* the 'adequate care' of the wounded and sick implies having the necessary personnel and equipment in place before the outbreak of an armed conflict, i.e. it requires the establishment of a medical service. Furthermore, the considerations relating to the obligation to have medical services discussed in the commentary on Article 12 of the First Convention also apply, *mutatis mutandis*, to Article 15.[40]

1507   The obligation to care for the wounded and sick also includes the provision of other – similarly essential – forms of non-medical care, such as food, shelter, clothing and hygiene. This is because the exclusively medical treatment of a wound or sickness is not sufficient to ameliorate the condition of the wounded and sick. Indeed, it would be meaningless to provide medical care if food, shelter, clothing and hygiene were denied. Hence, the provision merely of medical care would not qualify as 'adequate care' because the wounded and sick are unlikely to recover if their other basic needs are not met. Accordingly, by virtue of the obligation to ensure adequate care, Parties are under a due diligence obligation to provide the wounded and sick also with food, shelter, clothing and hygiene items.

4. The obligation to search for the dead and to prevent their being despoiled

1508   Paragraph 1 stipulates two distinct obligations regarding the dead, namely to search for them and to prevent their being despoiled. These obligations are important in ensuring respect for the dignity of the dead, which is crucial, not least because disrespect for the dead might set off a cycle of barbarity.[41] In addition, the search for and collection of the dead helps to prevent people from going 'missing'. The obligation to search for the dead in international armed conflict was first codified in the 1929 Geneva Convention on the Wounded and Sick.[42] The obligation to protect the dead 'from robbery and ill treatment' had already been included in the 1906 Geneva Convention.[43]

1509   The two obligations laid out in paragraph 1 in relation to the dead are similar to the obligations to search for the wounded and sick and to protect them against pillage and ill-treatment.[44] In both cases, they are obligations of conduct. This may include permitting and facilitating the search for the dead by other actors, notably impartial humanitarian organizations. In practice, the ICRC has frequently been engaged in the collection of the dead.[45] A Party may not arbitrarily withhold consent for such organizations to carry out collection

---

[40] See the commentary on Article 12, paras 1389–1391.   [41] See also Article 17.

[42] Geneva Convention on the Wounded and Sick (1929), Article 3.

[43] Geneva Convention (1906), Article 3. This obligation was maintained in 1929 (Article 3).

[44] This is the case notwithstanding the slight difference in wording: Article 15(1) uses 'prevent' instead of 'protect' in relation to the dead.

[45] Henckaerts/Doswald-Beck, commentary on Rule 112, p. 407. For example, ICRC delegates recovered the war dead in Bosnia and Herzegovina (UN Secretary-General, Report pursuant to Security Council resolution 752 (1992), UN Doc. S/24000, 26 May 1992, para. 9).

and evacuation activities.[46] Moreover, in situations in which Parties' resources in terms of personnel and equipment are scarce and where there are dead and wounded soldiers in the area, the wounded and sick must be given priority.

1510   Although Article 15 states an obligation to search for the dead, that obligation logically also comprises their collection.[47] The obligation to search for and collect the dead is complemented by the obligations set forth in Article 17 to identify them, ensure their honourable burial, and mark their graves. These measures aim to avoid people going missing.[48]

1511   The obligations in Article 15(1) apply regardless of the Party to which the dead belong and whether or not they have taken a direct part in the hostilities. The obligations set out in Article 15(1) do not apply as such to dead civilians; nevertheless, other treaty provisions and customary international law contain corresponding obligations in respect of dead civilians.[49]

1512   Parties must prevent the dead from being despoiled. Despoilment is a form of pillage and, as such, prohibited.[50] In the *Pohl* case in 1947, for example, the US Military Tribunal at Nuremberg stated that robbing the dead 'is and always has been a crime'.[51] Moreover, it should be noted that, under Additional Protocol I, the protection of the dead goes further than their protection against despoilment: Parties to an armed conflict are obliged more broadly to 'respect' the dead.[52] Although not specifically provided for in Article 15, the mutilation of dead bodies is prohibited under customary international law and is covered by the war crime of 'committing outrages upon personal dignity' under the 1998 ICC Statute.[53]

E. Paragraph 2: Arrangements to permit the removal, exchange and transport of the wounded and sick

1513 Paragraph 2 aims to enable and facilitate the evacuation of the wounded so that they can receive adequate treatment.[54] To this end, paragraph 2 lists different

---

[46] See the commentary on Article 9, section C.4.b.
[47] Similarly, albeit in relation to non-international armed conflict, see Sivakumaran, pp. 280–281. See also ICRC Study on Customary International Humanitarian Law (2005), Rule 112.
[48] See also the commentary on Article 17, para. 1663.
[49] See Fourth Convention, Article 16; Additional Protocol I, Articles 33(4) and 34(1); Additional Protocol II, Article 8; and ICRC Study on Customary International Humanitarian Law (2005), Rules 112–113.
[50] Hague Regulations (1907), Article 28; see also ICRC Study on Customary International Humanitarian Law (2005), Rule 52.
[51] United States, Military Tribunal at Nuremberg, *Pohl case*, Judgment, 1947, p. 996.
[52] See Additional Protocol I, Article 34, and Petrig, pp. 350–351.
[53] ICRC Study on Customary International Humanitarian Law (2005), Rule 113; ICC Elements of Crimes (2002), Definition of the war crime of outrages upon personal dignity (ICC Statute (1998), fn. 49 relating to Article 8(2)(b)(xxi)). For a commentary on this war crime, see Dörmann, p. 314, and Roberta Arnold and Stefan Wehrenberg, 'Outrages upon personal dignity', in Triffterer/Ambos, pp. 469–476.
[54] See also Articles 19 and 20 of the Third Convention, which specify conditions for the evacuation of wounded and sick prisoners of war.

mechanisms, namely the conclusion of an armistice, a suspension of fire, or local arrangements, which can create the (security) conditions needed to carry out search and rescue activities. It is thus complementary to the obligations laid out in paragraph 1.

1514 The provision stipulates that 'a suspension of fire *shall be arranged'* to permit the removal of the wounded from the battlefield (emphasis added). The seemingly imperative character of this obligation is qualified by the phrase 'whenever circumstances permit', leaving the Parties with a significant margin of discretion. It is nevertheless an urgent and important recommendation from the humanitarian point of view for the welfare and even the survival of the wounded. Commanders are therefore urged to keep this possibility always in mind, to have recourse to it whenever they are able, and to bring it to the attention of their troops at all levels in the chain of command.

1515 Unlike paragraph 1, paragraph 2 only refers to the wounded, without explicitly mentioning the sick or the dead. Logically, the sick can also be included in such agreements. The preparatory work contains no evidence of any intentional omission.[55] In the light of the scope of the First Convention as a whole and of paragraphs 1 and 3 specifically, which consistently refer to the 'wounded and sick', and given that there is not always a clear distinction between persons who are wounded and persons who are sick, paragraph 2 should be understood to apply also to the sick. This view is supported by the reference in the corresponding provision in the Second Convention, Article 18(2), to both the wounded and the sick. Moreover, paragraph 2 complements the obligations set down in paragraph 1, which mentions the wounded, the sick and the dead. In practice, the same search and rescue activities for the wounded and sick might also be used to search for and collect the dead, although different procedures may need to be followed.[56] According to Additional Protocol I, Parties must endeavour to agree on arrangements for teams to search for and recover the dead from the battlefield areas.[57]

1516 In terms of the agreements that are to be concluded, paragraph 2 explicitly mentions an armistice, a suspension of fire or local arrangements.[58] For the purposes of paragraph 2, the exact (legal) differentiation between these various forms of agreements is irrelevant.[59] In any case, an authoritative legal definition of either an armistice or a suspension of fire does not exist. In practice, a

---

[55] *Final Record of the Diplomatic Conference of Geneva of 1949*, Vol. II-B, pp. 155–156.
[56] For example, ambulances should usually not be used to collect the dead, as the collection of dead bodies should not take priority over the collection of the wounded. See also ICRC, *Management of Dead Bodies after Disasters: A Field Manual for First Responders*, ICRC, Geneva, 2009, pp. 7–8.
[57] Additional Protocol I, Article 33(4).
[58] See Ary, pp. 192–195 and 233–242, and Dinstein, 2000, pp. 146–151.
[59] For example, Canada's military manual stipulates: 'In the case of a land engagement, agreements between commanders, whether by armistice or by cease-fire, may be made for the exchange, removal and transport of the wounded left on the field' (Canada, *LOAC Manual*, 2001, para. 904.3).

number of terms, such as armistice, ceasefire, suspension of fire or hostilities and cessation of hostilities, are used interchangeably.[60] Today, an armistice is commonly understood as a more formal agreement concluded between two or more States waging war against each other and denoting the end of war without, however, restoring peace in the full sense of that term.[61] A suspension or cessation of hostilities or a ceasefire, on the other hand, is more informal and may be a preliminary step towards a more formal agreement.[62] The term 'suspension of fire' may be understood as a synonym for the terms 'suspension of hostilities' or ceasefire.[63] As such, it is understood as an agreed cessation, local or general, of the fighting within a period of armed conflict.[64] It does not necessarily terminate the armed conflict existing between the belligerents, either *de jure* or *de facto*.[65]

1517   The aforementioned agreements are specifically covered by Article 6 of the First Convention. Such special agreements create binding legal obligations for States. This is the case whether they are concluded between commanders with full treaty-making powers or by commanders on the battlefield in regard to a particular issue or locality.[66]

1518   The explicit reference to 'local arrangements' indicates that paragraph 2 covers all agreements between the Parties to an armed conflict that will bring about the necessary conditions for the removal, exchange and transport of the wounded and sick, regardless of their precise legal qualification or designation. Indeed, by including 'local arrangements' in paragraph 2, the Diplomatic Conference of 1949 specifically intended to respond to practical needs and to allow even the commanders of small units to make arrangements that would enable search and rescue activities to be carried out.[67] Thus, paragraph 2 covers international treaties negotiated by plenipotentiaries and concluded in a formalized procedure between States, as well as impromptu, informal oral agreements reached by local commanders. In fact, the latter kind of informal agreements with a limited scope of application *ratione loci* are typical for the situation envisaged in paragraph 2, namely agreements that aim to respond to humanitarian needs as they arise in a particular location.[68] In practice, neutral

---

[60] See Dinstein, 2000, p. 140.

[61] See Dinstein, 2009, para. 1, and Bell, para. 5. Until the two world wars, an armistice meant an agreement designed to bring about a mere suspension of hostilities between belligerent Parties, which remained locked in a state of war, and the expression was synonymous with truce. Its meaning has since evolved from suspension of hostilities to termination of war. See also Levie, pp. 884–888.

[62] See Bell, para. 6, and Dinstein, 2009, paras 25–27.   [63] See Azarov/Blum, paras 1, 2 and 8.

[64] See *ibid.* para. 1.   [65] See Levie, p. 884.

[66] See the commentary on Article 6, paras 963–964.

[67] In relation to Article 15 of the First Convention, see Pictet (ed.), *Commentary on the First Geneva Convention*, ICRC, 1952, p. 154. In relation to Article 12 of the Fourth Convention, see Pictet, *Commentary on the Fourth Geneva Convention*, ICRC, 1958, p. 139.

[68] See Germany, *Military Manual*, 1992, p. 238. Dinstein notes that: 'The area of application of a limited armistice shall be defined as precisely as possible. If, for instance, wounded persons are to be recovered it must be clear if and up to what line bombardments further to the rear

intermediaries such as the ICRC,[69] National Red Cross and Red Crescent Societies[70] and Médecins Sans Frontières[71] have played an important role in initiating or facilitating such agreements between the Parties to a conflict.

1519   Paragraph 2 is not limited to agreements between the Parties to a conflict nor does it require that the Parties themselves carry out the removal and transport of the wounded and sick and the dead. Of course, it is evidently inherent in any armistice or suspension of fire that it is concluded between the belligerent Parties. However, the term 'local arrangements' is broad enough to also cover agreements with third parties. Thus, if Parties to an armed conflict, rather than concluding an agreement with each other, enter into an agreement with an impartial humanitarian organization (thus creating a triangular relationship) in order to facilitate the removal, exchange and transport of the wounded and sick and the dead, this would appear to suffice. The purpose of paragraph 2 is to enable and facilitate the evacuation of the wounded and sick so that they can be adequately treated (and the dead identified and thereby prevented from going 'missing', as well as honourably interred). It therefore covers any kind of arrangement that will help to achieve these goals. Indeed, in practice, Parties to an armed conflict may often be more inclined to contact an impartial human-itarian organization for help in evacuating the wounded and sick and the dead than to enter into direct contact with one another to make local arrangements for a ceasefire.[72] It is important for the terms of such agreements to be clearly communicated to all who are in a position to comply with or violate them if they are to fulfil their purpose.

1520   Lastly, unlike the corresponding provision in the 1929 Geneva Conven-tion on the Wounded and Sick,[73] paragraph 2 also envisages the 'exchange' of the wounded left on the battlefield. This had also been provided for in the 1864 Geneva Convention,[74] but was omitted in 1929 because the immediate

---

remain permissible. Sometimes it will also be necessary to coordinate the utilization of the airspace and the passage of ships.' (Yoram Dinstein, *War, Aggression and Self-Defence*, 5th edi-tion, Cambridge University Press, 2011, p. 52.) This is also evidenced by the fact that the histor-ical predecessor of paragraph 2, namely Article 3(2) of the Geneva Convention on the Wounded and Sick (1929), spoke of the conclusion of a 'local armistice'; see Pictet (ed.), *Commentary on the First Geneva Convention*, ICRC, 1952, p. 154.

[69] For an example from a non-international armed conflict, see Stephanie Nebehay, 'Syria, rebels agree truce for Homs evacuation: ICRC', *Reuters*, 20 June 2012.

[70] For example, the Norwegian Red Cross has done so; see ICRC, *Annual Report 2011*, ICRC, Geneva, 2012, p. 369.

[71] Médecins Sans Frontières, *Activity Report 2011*, pp. 14–15.

[72] Médecins Sans Frontières has also carried out large-scale medical evacuations, e.g. in Libya in March 2011; see *ibid.* pp. 72–73.

[73] Article 3 of the 1929 Geneva Convention on the Wounded and Sick provided for the conclu-sion of a local armistice or a suspension of fire merely 'to permit the removal of the wounded remaining between the lines'.

[74] Article 6 of the 1864 Geneva Convention provided that: 'Commanders-in-Chief may hand over immediately to the enemy outposts enemy combatants wounded during an engagement, when circumstances allow and subject to the agreement of both parties.'

exchange of the wounded on the battlefield was perceived as utopian.[75] Paragraph 2 clarifies that exchanging the wounded and sick, albeit rare in practice,[76] is a feasible option and does not conflict with a Party's obligations under paragraph 1. Nothing would seem to bar a broad interpretation of the term 'exchange', which thus also comprises the unilateral cession of the wounded (and sick) by one Party to another Party. Exchange of the (untreated) wounded (and sick) on the spot is different from the situation envisaged by Article 109 of the Third Convention, where 'seriously wounded and seriously sick prisoners of war', after Parties have cared for them and provided they are fit to travel, have to be sent back to their home countries. In paragraph 2, 'exchange' of the wounded is mentioned as one possibility for removing the wounded from the battlefield and ensuring that they will be cared for under more secure conditions.

F. Paragraph 3: Arrangements for the removal or exchange of the wounded and sick from besieged or encircled areas

1521   Paragraph 3 focuses on the conclusion of local arrangements for the exchange of the wounded and sick or their removal from besieged or encircled areas and the passage of medical and religious personnel and equipment into those areas.[77] The terms of such arrangements should, like more formal agreements, also be clearly communicated to anyone in a position to either comply with or violate them. Like paragraph 2, paragraph 3 aims to enable and facilitate care of the wounded and sick, either by removing them from an area where such care is no longer possible or by creating conditions in the area which will again allow the provision of both medical and spiritual care. In the light of the purpose of this paragraph, it should also be applied in relation to the dead.

1522   Paragraph 3 strongly encourages the Parties to conclude local arrangements to allow the removal of the wounded or sick and the passage of medical and religious personnel and their equipment to such areas, 'whenever circumstances permit'. It follows from paragraph 3 that the strategic aim of burdening the besieged Party with the wounded and sick is not a legitimate consideration. If it were, the obligation to facilitate the exchange of the wounded and sick or their removal from besieged or encircled areas would be meaningless.

1523   Paragraph 3 explicitly mentions the 'sick', making it clear that they may also be the subject of an arrangement to evacuate them from a besieged or encircled area. Paragraph 3 mentions only 'local arrangements' and explicitly refers to the Parties to the conflict. The term 'local arrangements' is broad enough to cover

---

[75] Des Gouttes, *Commentaire de la Convention de Genève de 1929 sur les blessés et malades*, ICRC, 1930, p. 24.

[76] During the Falklands/Malvinas conflict, the hospital ships in the Red Cross Box apparently did exchange war casualties; see http://blog.usni.org/2011/06/29/the-red-cross-box.

[77] See also Fourth Convention, Article 17.

armistices and ceasefires. Given its purpose, it also allows for the conclusion of other agreements and arrangements – possibly with third actors, such as impartial humanitarian organizations – to enhance the care of the wounded and sick and facilitate the removal of the dead.

1524   The concept of a 'besieged or encircled area' has not been defined under international humanitarian law.[78] Although not prohibited as such, it follows from various provisions of international humanitarian law, including those pertaining to the conduct of hostilities – for example, the prohibition against attacking or rendering useless objects indispensable to the survival of the civilian population or against starving the civilian population[79] – that many aspects of traditional siege warfare are no longer permissible today. Furthermore, the provisions of international law applicable to humanitarian activities also need to be considered.[80] Starvation of the civilian population as a method of warfare by depriving it of objects indispensable to its survival, including wilfully impeding relief supplies as provided for under the Geneva Conventions, would amount to a war crime.[81] In the light of the purpose of Article 15 as a whole, it is of little relevance whether an area is 'besieged' or 'encircled'. Rather, what matters is whether the wounded and sick have been cut off from adequate medical or spiritual care owing to ongoing hostilities. Conversely, if the wounded and sick are trapped by the hostilities in a location where medical treatment is still adequate, there may be no humanitarian need to evacuate them.

1525   Paragraph 3 envisages arrangements that will allow for the exchange of the wounded and sick or their removal from the area in question or permit 'the passage of medical and religious personnel and equipment on their way to that area'. The nationality of such personnel is not specified.[82] With regard to the removal of people, it is important to note that paragraph 3 applies only to those

---

[78] Although Article 27 of the 1907 Hague Regulations refers to 'sieges', the term is not defined. A siege is a concept confined to land warfare. The equivalent in a naval or aerial context would be a blockade. For a restatement of the rules applicable to a naval blockade, see San Remo Manual on International Law Applicable to Armed Conflicts at Sea (1994), Rules 93–104; for a restatement of the rules applicable to an aerial blockade, see Manual on International Law Applicable to Air and Missile Warfare (2009), Rules 147–159. In the latter, Rule 147 defines an 'aerial blockade' as 'a belligerent operation to prevent aircraft (including [Unmanned Aerial Vehicles/Unmanned Combat Aerial Vehicles] from entering or exiting specified airfields or coastal areas belonging to, occupied by, or under the control of the enemy'. The term 'encircled area' only appears in the Geneva Conventions; see Article 18(2) of the Second Convention and Article 17 of the Fourth Convention.

[79] Additional Protocol I, Article 54(1)–(2); ICRC Study on Customary International Humanitarian Law (2005), Rules 54 and 53.

[80] See Article 9.

[81] ICC Statute (1998), Article 8(2)(b)(xxv). On starvation, see Michael Cottier and Emilia Richard, 'Starvation of civilians as a method of warfare', in Triffterer/Ambos, pp. 508–519. See also Dinstein, 2010, pp. 220–223.

[82] With regard to religious personnel, the Pictet commentary held: 'As for religious personnel, the most elementary sentiments of humanity and respect for the individual demand that they should always be allowed free access when their presence is required, in order that they may bring the consolations of religion to all, whether wounded or fit.' (Pictet (ed.), *Commentary on the First Geneva Convention*, ICRC, 1952, p. 157.)

who qualify as wounded or sick under Article 12.[83] A similar provision regarding civilians is contained in Article 17 of the Fourth Convention. In any case, neither Article 15(3) nor Article 17 may be used as a legal pretext to implement a policy of ethnic cleansing and to justify the removal of parts of the population from specific areas.[84]

1526   Whenever a situation exists in which the wounded and sick cannot be retrieved, arrangements must be made to enable them to receive the care their condition requires, either by sending medical personnel or by allowing the wounded and sick to be removed to an area where they can receive treatment. In cases where such situations persist, a one-time agreement would not suffice.

Select bibliography

Ary, Vaughn A., 'Concluding Hostilities: Humanitarian Provisions in Cease-Fire Agreements', *Military Law Review*, Vol. 148, 1995, pp. 186–273.

Azarov, Valentina and Blum, Ido, 'Suspension of Hostilities', version of March 2011, in Rüdiger Wolfrum (ed.), *Max Planck Encyclopedia of Public International Law*, Oxford University Press, http://www.mpepil.com.

Bart, Gregory Raymond, 'Special Operations Commando Raids and Enemy *Hors de Combat*', *The Army Lawyer*, July 2007, pp. 33–44.

Bell, Christine, 'Ceasefire', version of December 2009, in Rüdiger Wolfrum (ed.), *Max Planck Encyclopedia of Public International Law*, Oxford University Press, http://www.mpepil.com.

Benoit, James P., 'Mistreatment of the Wounded, Sick and Shipwrecked by the ICRC Study on Customary International Humanitarian Law', *Yearbook of International Humanitarian Law*, Vol. 11, 2008, pp. 175–219.

Bothe, Michael, Partsch, Karl Josef and Solf, Waldemar A., *New Rules for Victims of Armed Conflicts: Commentary on the Two 1977 Protocols Additional to the Geneva Conventions of 1949*, Martinus Nijhoff Publishers, The Hague, 1982, pp. 107–108.

de Mulinen, Frédéric, *Handbook on the Law of War for Armed Forces*, ICRC, Geneva, 1987.

Dinstein, Yoram, 'The Initiation, Suspension, and Termination of War', in Michael N. Schmitt (ed.), *International Law Across the Spectrum of Conflict: Essays in Honour of Professor L.C. Green on the Occasion of his Eightieth Birthday*, International Law Studies, U.S. Naval War College, Vol. 75, 2000, pp. 131–160.

– 'Armistice', version of April 2009, in Rüdiger Wolfrum (ed.), *Max Planck Encyclopedia of Public International Law*, Oxford University Press, http://www.mpepil.com.

– *The Conduct of Hostilities under the Law of International Armed Conflict*, 2nd edition, Cambridge University Press, 2010.

Dörmann, Knut, *Elements of War Crimes under the Rome Statute of the International Criminal Court: Sources and Commentary*, Cambridge University Press, 2003.

Dunant, Henry, *A Memory of Solferino*, ICRC, Geneva, reprint 1986.

---

[83] See the commentary on Article 12, section D.2.   [84] Geiss, paras 3–8.

Dupuy, Pierre-Marie, 'Reviewing the Difficulties of Codification: On Ago's Classification of Obligations of Means and Obligations of Result in Relation to State Responsibility', *European Journal of International Law*, Vol. 10, No. 2, 1999, pp. 371–385.

Geiss, Robin, 'Ethnic Cleansing', version of April 2013, in Rüdiger Wolfrum (ed.), *Max Planck Encyclopedia of Public International Law*, Oxford University Press, http://opil.ouplaw.com/home/EPIL.

Giacca, Gilles, 'The Obligations to Respect, Protect, Collect, and Care for the Wounded, Sick, and Shipwrecked', in Andrew Clapham, Paola Gaeta and Marco Sassòli (eds), *The 1949 Geneva Conventions: A Commentary*, Oxford University Press, 2015, pp. 781–806.

Henckaerts, Jean-Marie and Doswald-Beck, Louise, *Customary International Humanitarian Law, Volume I: Rules*, ICRC/Cambridge University Press, 2005, available at https://www.icrc.org/customary-ihl/eng/docs/v1.

Hessbruegge, Jan Arno, 'The Historical Development of the Doctrines of Attribution and Due Diligence in International Law', *New York University Journal of International Law & Politics*, Vol. 36, Nos 2 & 3, 2004, pp. 265–306.

Koivurova, Timo, 'Due Diligence', version of February 2010, in Rüdiger Wolfrum (ed.), *Max Planck Encyclopedia of Public International Law*, Oxford University Press, http://opil.ouplaw.com/home/EPIL.

Levie, Howard S., 'The Nature and Scope of the Armistice Agreement', *American Journal of International Law*, Vol. 50, 1956, pp. 880–906.

Petrig, Anna, 'The war dead and their gravesites', *International Review of the Red Cross*, Vol. 91, No. 874, June 2009, pp. 341–369.

Pisillo-Mazzeschi, Riccardo, 'The Due Diligence Rule and the Nature of the International Responsibility of States', *German Yearbook of International Law*, Vol. 35, 1992, pp. 9–51.

Röthlisberger, Ernst, *Die neue Genfer Konvention von 6. Juli 1906*, A. Francke, Bern, 1908.

Sivakumaran, Sandesh, *The Law of Non-International Armed Conflict*, Oxford University Press, 2012.

Triffterer, Otto and Ambos, Kai (eds), *The Rome Statute of the International Criminal Court: A Commentary*, 3rd edition, Hart Publishing, Oxford, 2016.

RECORDING AND FORWARDING OF INFORMATION

❖ Text of the provision*

(1) Parties to the conflict shall record as soon as possible, in respect of each wounded, sick or dead person of the adverse Party falling into their hands, any particulars which may assist in his identification.

(2) These records should if possible include:

    (a) designation of the Power on which he depends;

    (b) army, regimental, personal or serial number;

    (c) surname;

    (d) first name or names;

    (e) date of birth;

    (f) any other particulars shown on his identity card or disc;

    (g) date and place of capture or death;

    (h) particulars concerning wounds or illness, or cause of death.

(3) As soon as possible the above mentioned information shall be forwarded to the Information Bureau described in Article 122 of the Geneva Convention relative to the Treatment of Prisoners of War of August 12, 1949, which shall transmit this information to the Power on which these persons depend through the intermediary of the Protecting Power and of the Central Prisoners of War Agency.

(4) Parties to the conflict shall prepare and forward to each other through the same bureau, certificates of death or duly authenticated lists of the dead. They shall likewise collect and forward through the same bureau one half of a double identity disc, last wills or other documents of importance to the next of kin, money and in general all articles of an intrinsic or sentimental value, which are found on the dead. These articles, together with unidentified articles, shall be sent in sealed packets, accompanied by statements giving all particulars necessary for the identification of the deceased owners, as well as by a complete list of the contents of the parcel.

❖ Reservations or declarations

None

---

* Paragraph numbers have been added for ease of reference.

Contents

A. Introduction

1527   Article 16 regulates three issues: the recording and forwarding of information concerning wounded, sick and dead persons who have fallen into the hands of the adverse Party; the preparation and forwarding of death certificates; and the collection and forwarding of the deceased's personal items.

1528   The information to be recorded relates to identification. It serves several purposes, principal amongst which are to protect the persons concerned, to provide information to the Power on which they depend, and to provide information to their families. Recording this information and subsequently forwarding it to the State on which the persons depend and to their families, serves to account for their whereabouts, and thus to prevent them from going missing or forcibly disappearing.[1] For details on how this issue is dealt with in non-international armed conflict, see the commentary on common Article 3, section I.

1529   In the case of dead persons, the collection and forwarding of their personal items are also important for their loved ones. These items may be the very last belongings of the deceased that the family will receive and be all the more precious for having been on the person at the time of his or her death.

1530   Article 16 is related to the other provisions of international humanitarian law on the wounded and sick and on the dead, as well as to those on the missing and the right of families to know the fate of their loved ones.[2] In particular, there is a close relationship between the present provision and several provisions of the Third Convention.

1531   Wounded and sick members of the armed forces and certain other persons who have fallen into the hands of the adverse Party are prisoners of war and, as such, also benefit from the protections afforded by the Third Convention.[3] Given that most of the provisions of Article 16 are also to be found in Articles 17, 120 and 122 of the Third Convention, it might have been thought that there was no need for the First Convention to contain an article of this sort. However, despite the overlap, the present article remains important for two reasons in particular.

1532   First, the wounded and sick often find themselves outside the usual locations established for prisoners of war, such as in a field hospital rather than in a prisoner-of-war camp. Likewise, they do not always go through the same processes as other prisoners of war; for example they may be diverted to a military hospital immediately upon capture instead of first being processed at a transit

---

[1] See also Convention on Enforced Disappearance (2006), Article 17(3), which provides that each State Party to the Convention 'shall assure the compilation and maintenance of one or more up-to-date official registers and/or records of persons deprived of liberty, which shall be made promptly available, upon request, to any judicial or other competent authority or institution authorized for that purpose by the law of the State Party concerned or any relevant international legal instrument to which the State concerned is a party'.

[2] See e.g. First Convention, Article 17, and Additional Protocol I, Article 32.

[3] Third Convention, Article 4. On the division between the First and Third Conventions, see Article 14 of the First Convention.

or prisoner-of-war camp. Thus, the persons who come into contact with the wounded and sick will likely be more familiar with the provisions of the First Convention than of the Third Convention. Accordingly, it was thought necessary to include in the First Convention provisions similar to those of the Third Convention. This is also in conformity with the general approach of making each Convention, as far as possible, complete in itself.

1533   Second, in addition to the wounded and sick, the present article covers the dead, including persons who died prior to falling into the hands of the adverse Party. At no stage would such persons have been prisoners of war.

1534   Those two points notwithstanding, the close relationship between the present article and various provisions of the Third Convention means that regard must also be had to that Convention and its commentary.

B. Historical background

1535   The need to identify wounded, sick or dead members of the armed forces and certain other persons has long been recognized, as has the need to transmit death certificates and certain possessions of the deceased to the Party on whom the deceased depended.

1536   The 1880 Oxford Manual provided that '[t]he dead should never be buried until all articles on them which may serve to fix their identity, such as pocket-books, numbers, etc., shall have been collected'. It added that '[t]he articles thus collected from the dead of the enemy are transmitted to its army or government'.[4]

1537   Article 4 of the 1906 Geneva Convention covered similar matters. It also required the belligerents to forward to the authorities a list of the names of the wounded and sick in their charge, thus extending the requirement of identification to the wounded and sick. However, it provided little in the way of detail.

1538   The 1929 Geneva Convention on the Wounded and Sick expanded upon the provisions of the 1906 Convention. Article 4 required the communication of the names of the wounded, the sick and the dead to the adverse Party, together with anything that might assist in their identification; the transmittal of death certificates; and the collection and transmittal of certain personal items of the deceased, including one half of the identity disc. Transmittal of personal items was considered of particular importance given that they might be all the family of the deceased had to remember their loved one by.[5]

1539   The 1929 Convention contains the core of the protections that are to be found in Article 16 of the present Convention, to which further details were added.

---

[4] Oxford Manual (1880), Article 20.
[5] Des Gouttes, *Commentaire de la Convention de Genève de 1929 sur les blessés et malades*, ICRC, 1930, p. 31.

The 1929 Convention was limited in a number of respects, omitting to mention what information might assist in the identification of the deceased or the manner in which it was to be transmitted to the adverse Party,[6] and lacking guidance on which of the deceased's belongings to transmit. Article 16 expands upon these aspects and takes into account practice from the Second World War, as well as its shortcomings.[7]

C. Paragraph 1: Recording of information[8]

1. Nature of the obligation

1540   The Parties to the conflict are under an obligation to record, as soon as possible, any particulars that may assist in the identification of wounded, sick or dead persons of the adverse Party who have fallen into their hands. The obligation is an absolute one as is evident from the wording 'shall record'.[9] Accordingly, certain particulars must be recorded and there is no excuse for the failure to do so. The precise particulars to be recorded are set out in the second paragraph and the ability to record some of them will vary according to the situation.

1541   Two aspects of the recording and forwarding of information are of particular importance, namely speed and accuracy.[10] Speedy recording of information is of the essence, as it reduces the risk of persons going missing, especially if they are moved from place to place. Delay in forwarding the recorded information exacerbates the suffering of the families and friends of persons who are unaccounted for. Accuracy is also critical. Only when the details are recorded with care and precision can an individual's identity be ascertained correctly and accurate information passed on to the family.

1542   Accordingly, the Parties must take the necessary preparatory steps in good time, and even before the commencement of hostilities, in order to ensure that the competent authorities are in a position to perform their duties. These steps include, for example, deciding on the form the records are to take, instructing

---

[6] However, the 1929 Geneva Convention on Prisoners of War contained provisions on the creation of national information bureaux (Article 77) and a Central Agency (Article 79), and those bodies were implicitly entrusted with matters concerning the wounded and dead collected on the battlefield; see *ibid.*

[7] On which, see ICRC, *Report of the International Committee of the Red Cross on its Activities during the Second World War (September 1, 1939–June 30, 1947), Volume I: General Activities* and *Volume II: The Central Agency for Prisoners of War*, ICRC, Geneva, 1948.

[8] The equally authoritative French text is set out in a slightly different format. The first and second paragraphs of the English text are combined to form the first paragraph of the French text. Accordingly, the third paragraph of the English text corresponds to the second paragraph of the French text, and the fourth paragraph of the English text corresponds to the third paragraph of the French text.

[9] The recording of this information in respect of the dead and the detained is also an obligation under customary international law; see ICRC Study on Customary International Humanitarian Law (2005), Rules 116 and 123.

[10] Durand, p. 416.

and training the relevant personnel in the recording of information, and establishing speedy identification and processing procedures.

2. Personal scope of application

1543   The obligation is vested in the 'Parties to the conflict' and not in particular individuals. Nonetheless, by necessity, it can only be fulfilled by individuals. It is only they who will be able to question wounded or sick persons about their identity or to read their identity cards or discs. Thus, the obligation concerns all levels of the Parties to the conflict and all forces,[11] the determining factor being whether wounded, sick or dead persons have fallen into their hands. Accordingly, the persons who carry out the obligation of the Party in the first paragraph, i.e. the recording of information, might not be the same ones who undertake the tasks required by the third paragraph, namely the forwarding of the information to the information bureau. Who actually fulfils these tasks will depend on each Party's procedure for forwarding information to the information bureau. Nonetheless, States must organize and structure the competent authorities and institutions in such a way as to be able to comply fully with the obligations set forth in Article 16. This means that, for example, if the individuals are not the same at each stage of the process, the Party has to ensure, including through training and regulations, that the information is properly transmitted along the chain.

1544   Article 16 does not place any duty on States not Parties to the conflict to record information. However, pursuant to Article 4 of the First Convention, '[n]eutral Powers shall apply by analogy the provisions of the present Convention to the wounded and sick . . . received or interned in their territory, as well as to dead persons found'. Accordingly, Article 16 read together with Article 4 of the First Convention makes clear that neutral States that receive or find wounded, sick or dead persons in their territory are under the same obligation to record the necessary information.

1545   The particulars are to be recorded in respect of 'each wounded, sick or dead person of the adverse Party falling into [the] hands' of a Party to the conflict. The particulars must be recorded individually, regardless of the number of persons concerned. This follows from the requirement to record the information in respect of 'each' wounded, sick or dead person. Individual recording is of particular importance given that a group of people might be split up when moved. Furthermore, it is essential for establishing individual identities.

1546   This is one of the few provisions of the First Convention that covers the wounded and sick and the dead together;[12] other provisions relate either to the

---

[11] See also Katz, p. 409.

[12] See also First Convention, Articles 4 and 15. For the meaning of the term 'wounded and sick', see the commentary on Article 12, section D.2.

wounded and sick or to the dead.[13] They are treated together in the present article given the need to identify all three categories of persons. Further obligations
that concern the deceased exclusively are set out in the fourth paragraph.

1547   The obligation is limited to 'each wounded, sick or dead person *of the adverse
Party*' (emphasis added). Thus, unlike the provisions on the search for wounded,
sick or dead persons and on the burial of the dead,[14] the obligation in the
present article does not extend to wounded, sick or dead members of the Party's
own forces. The limitation can be explained by the obligation that follows
the recording of information, namely that it be forwarded to the adverse Party
through the procedure set out in the third paragraph. Obligations under international humanitarian law on providing information in respect of the Party's
own forces stem from different rules.[15]

1548   The identities of the wounded, sick or dead will not always be easy to determine, and it may also be unclear whether they belong to the adverse Party.
Given that one of the purposes of this provision is to assist in the identification of such persons, it follows that, where there is doubt as to which Party a
person belongs, particulars that could assist in his or her identification should
still be recorded.

1549   The obligation is further limited to the wounded, sick or dead persons of the
adverse Party 'falling into [the] hands' of a Party to the conflict. For the meaning
of that phrase, see the commentary on Article 14, section C.3.

3. Recording of particulars

1550 The Parties to the conflict are required to 'record' certain particulars. The word
'record' means 'to make a record of',[16] and it is that action and the content of
the record that are of particular importance. This record will enable the Party
to keep a constant check on wounded, sick or dead enemy personnel who have
fallen into its hands, and will furnish the particulars that are to be forwarded
to the adverse Party. The precise form that the record takes is of lesser significance and can be either electronic or paper. Nonetheless, there are certain matters that follow from the requirement. First, there must actually be a record: it
is not sufficient for the individuals into whose hands the persons have fallen to
simply memorize the particulars. Memorizing will inevitably result in inaccu-
racies or loss of information. Second, the record must be as accurate as possible.
Although 100 per cent accuracy may not be achievable, given the situation, the
persons recording the information must do so with due diligence. Third, the

---

[13] On the wounded and sick, see in particular Chapter II of the First Convention; on the dead, see
Article 17 of the First Convention.
[14] First Convention, Articles 15 and 17.
[15] See e.g. Additional Protocol I, Article 32. See also ICRC Study on Customary International
Humanitarian Law (2005), Rule 117.
[16] *Concise Oxford English Dictionary*, 12th edition, Oxford University Press, 2011, p. 1202.

record must be able to withstand the conditions of an armed conflict and the vagaries of the climate. Fourth, the Party must have a standard approach to the recording of information. This will assist in the timely transmission of information along the chain.[17] And lastly, once the record is made, it must be stored securely and sent as soon as possible to the information bureau, pursuant to the third paragraph of the present article.

1551   The processing of data for the purposes envisaged in this article is consistent with legal bases for processing generally found in data protection legislation. These include compliance with a legal obligation, in this case Article 16 itself; the vital interests of the data subjects, in this case to ensure that they do not go missing; and important grounds of public interest, in the present case the performance of a humanitarian activity foreseen by the Geneva Conventions, their Additional Protocols and the Statutes of the International Red Cross and Red Crescent Movement, and of the mandates of the information bureau and of the Central Tracing Agency derived therefrom.[18] It is the responsibility of States party to the Geneva Conventions to ensure that if they adopt data protection legislation, such legislation does not bar compliance with Article 16.

1552   The first paragraph of Article 16 sets out the information to be recorded, while the second paragraph sets out in detail the particulars to be recorded.

1553   Article 16(1) provides that 'any particulars which may assist in' the identification of the wounded, sick or dead must be recorded. The primary purpose of the provision therefore is the identification of the wounded, sick or dead person in the hands of the adverse Party. Accordingly, 'any' particulars which 'may assist' in identification must be recorded, no matter how trivial they may seem. This point is expanded on in the second paragraph but, in general terms, the Party should err on the side of inclusion. The summary recording of information does not meet the requirements of this provision.

4. Timing

1554 The Parties to the conflict are required to record the particulars 'as soon as possible'. The need for speedy fulfilment of the obligation is evident from its rationale.[19] Parties to the conflict have obligations in respect of persons who are missing.[20] Families and friends have an interest in knowing whether their loved ones are alive or dead. Timely recording of information also serves to protect individuals, by accounting for their whereabouts. Moreover, speed in

---

[17] On which, see para. 1588.
[18] See e.g. Council of Europe, Convention for the Protection of Individuals with regard to Automatic Processing of Personal Data, Convention No. 108, Strasbourg, 28 January 1981, Article 5(a).
[19] See para. 1541.
[20] See Fourth Convention, Article 26; Additional Protocol I, Article 33; and ICRC Study on Customary International Humanitarian Law (2005), Rule 117.

establishing the necessary records will assist the Party in its task of distributing the wounded to their various places of accommodation while keeping a
careful check on their movements. This is of particular importance given that
Parties sometimes find it difficult to account for wounded and sick enemy personnel who are in their hands but outside the usual prisoner-of-war handling
processes.[21]

1555   Further precision in regard to the time allowed to fulfil this obligation could
not be included in the provision as this will vary according to circumstances.
In particular, the timing will depend on the number of persons who have fallen
into the hands of the adverse Party, the number of persons who receive them
and the period of time involved.[22] Nonetheless, some guidance can be provided.
To the extent possible, the information must be recorded at the moment the
wounded, sick or dead person first falls into the hands of the adverse Party
and prior to any transfer, be it internal or external. This last requirement is of
particular importance given that there is a greater chance of a person becoming unaccounted for if there is a transfer to or from, for example, temporary
holding facilities, hospitals or prisoner-of-war camps, and this chance increases
substantially if the person is transferred to a facility outside the control of the
adverse Party.[23]

1556   Both humanitarian and military considerations may make it impossible to
record the information immediately upon the person falling into the hands of
the adverse Party. For example, the wounded and sick may require urgent medical treatment or rapid evacuation from the battlefield in conditions that do
not allow for the immediate recording of information.[24] Although this creates
a gap between the moment when the person falls into enemy hands and the
moment when the information is recorded, it does not vitiate the obligation,
albeit deferred, to record the information. Some States operate a multi-stage
system: a truncated documentation, involving the recording of basic details at
the point of capture, and a more detailed documentation as soon as reasonably
practical thereafter, usually at subsequent stages of the processing of captured
personnel.[25]

5. *Capture cards*

1557 As noted earlier, members of the armed forces and certain other persons who
are wounded or sick and who have fallen into the hands of the adverse Party are
prisoners of war and benefit also from the Third Convention. The attention of

---

[21] Ary, p. 25.   [22] See also *ibid.* p. 21.
[23] See also the safeguards in Article 12 of the Third Convention.
[24] See also the obligation to respect and protect the wounded and sick (Article 12) and the obligation to search for and evacuate them (Article 15). See also Article 19 of the Third Convention,
and Ary, pp. 25–26.
[25] See e.g. United Kingdom, *Joint Doctrine Captured Persons*, 2015.

the authorities responsible for applying the First Convention should therefore be drawn to Article 70 of the Third Convention, pursuant to which prisoners of war must be enabled to write directly to their families and to the Central Prisoners of War Agency, now known as the Central Tracing Agency.[26]

D. Paragraph 2: Content of the record

1558 Article 16(2) provides a list of the particulars that are required for the identification of the wounded, sick or dead who have fallen into the hands of the adverse Party. It was felt that everything possible should be done to ensure that persons falling into enemy hands were duly identified; and it was desired that the process of identification should, if possible, be the same for all categories of persons protected under the four Conventions. Hence, similar detailed provisions are included in all four Conventions.[27]

1. Nature of the content

1559 The list of particulars set out in Article 16(2) is illustrative and not exhaustive, as follows from the use of the phrase 'should if possible include'. The guiding principle in this area is that as much information as possible that may assist in the identification of the wounded, sick or dead person is to be recorded. Accordingly, items or particulars that are not mentioned in the article, such as photographs, fingerprints, body measurements, names and addresses of next of kin,[28] and distinguishing features or markings such as scars or tattoos,[29] may be included in the record. Recording these items will be of particular importance where certain details listed in the paragraph are unobtainable. They are also important given that errors sometimes occur in the recording or transmittal of information.[30] These errors may be due to linguistic differences such as different alphabets, the similarity of certain names, whether phonetic (e.g. Hussein, Hussain and Hossein) or graphic (e.g. Ferrand and Ferraud), or common names (e.g. John Smith).[31] The items listed in the article are the ones that will be

---

[26] For details concerning timing, content of writing, and transmission of cards, see Article 70 of the Third Convention and its commentary. On the name change, see para. 1591.

[27] Second Convention, Article 19; Third Convention, Article 122; Fourth Convention, Article 138.

[28] The names and addresses of next of kin were included, for example, in some of the death certificates that were forwarded by Ethiopia during the armed conflict between Eritrea and Ethiopia. Although the wording used is 'next of kin', it refers to the general notion of the family of the deceased and is not limited to the stricter meaning of 'closest immediate relative'.

[29] See, with respect to the dead, ICRC, *Operational Best Practices Regarding the Management of Human Remains and Information on the Dead by Non-Specialists*, ICRC, Geneva, 2004, pp. 41–42.

[30] For example, during the conflict in Cyprus in 1974, some of the lists transmitted 'were only of partial use because the misspelling of names made identification of the prisoners impossible'; Djurović, p. 232.

[31] This was a particular problem during the Second World War. See ICRC, *Report of the International Committee of the Red Cross on its Activities during the Second World War (September 1,*

most useful in identifying individuals, in contacting the Power on which they depend and in accounting for their whereabouts.

1560   Article 16(2) provides that the listed items 'should if possible' be included in the record. The use of this wording indicates that it may not be possible to record all of the listed items in respect of each and every wounded, sick or dead person. It will not be possible, for example, to include the particulars shown on the identity card or disc if no such card or disc is present. Likewise, it may not be possible to record persons' names and date of birth if they are unconscious and not carrying any form of identification.[32] Thus, if it is possible to do so, the information must be recorded, and the notion of 'possibility' is to be interpreted strictly. The sheer number of wounded, sick or dead people or lack of manpower does not release the Party from its obligation. It may take the Party longer than would ordinarily be the case, but in that case the standard of 'as soon as possible' will be interpreted accordingly. Likewise, the absence of one particular does not excuse the Party from recording all the other information that is available.

2. Types of particulars

1561   The listed particulars are of different sorts. Most of them relate to the identification of the individual: name, date of birth, other particulars shown on the identity card or disc, and army or other number. Other particulars relate to the identification ('designation') of the Power on which the person depends, so that it may be duly notified. This item of information is of particular importance in a conflict that involves several Parties so that the correct Party and, in turn, the person's family can be informed and the obligations contained in the third and fourth paragraphs be fulfilled. Other particulars relate to the circumstances in which the person fell into enemy hands. This is the case for the date and place of capture or death and details of wounds, illness or cause of death. These last particulars are related to the obligations contained in related provisions, in particular Article 17 of the First Convention.

3. The listed particulars

a. Designation of the Power on which the person depends

1562   'Designation of the Power on which [the person] depends' means naming the Party to the conflict to which the individual was attached. This will usually be

---

1939–June 30, 1947), *Volume II: The Central Agency for Prisoners of War*, ICRC, Geneva, 1948, pp. 105–106.

[32]   See Henckaerts/Doswald-Beck, commentary on Rule 123, p. 440 ('As to the extent of the information to be recorded, the duty of the State cannot exceed the level of information available from detainees or from documents they may carry.')

the same as the person's State of nationality. However, in certain situations, a person may be fighting on behalf of a State of which he or she is not a national.

b–e. Number, names and date of birth

1563　The particulars of 'army, regimental, personal or serial number', 'surname', 'first name or names' and 'date of birth' are everyday concepts and need no further explanation. All names must be written in full. Shortened forms may cause unnecessary delay in identification and have the potential to mislead.

f. Particulars on the identity card or disc

1564　Although the paragraph refers to an 'identity card or disc', an identity disc is preferable, given that an identity card is more easily lost, damaged or destroyed amid the turmoil of conflict.

i. Identity card

1565　Article 17(3) of the Third Convention requires that States furnish 'persons under [their] jurisdiction who are liable to become prisoners of war, with an identity card'. The persons to whom Article 17 is referring are those listed in Article 4A and B of the Third Convention. The categories of persons listed in Article 4A of the Third Convention are the same as those listed in Article 13 of the First Convention, which sets out the categories of persons to which the Convention applies. Accordingly, every wounded or sick person who benefits from the present Convention should be carrying an identity card, unless it has been lost or destroyed during the conflict.

1566　While there is considerable overlap with the particulars listed in Article 16(2), identity cards have to contain several additional pieces of information not specified in the present provision. These are the person's rank, signature, fingerprints (optional) and other unspecified information, and, in the case of persons who accompany but who are not members of the armed forces, also the name of the military authority issuing the card, place of birth, date of issue, photograph, blood type, religion, imprint of official seal, and marks of identification.[33] These items equate to the 'any other particulars' to which item (f) of the present article refers. Each of these details can be recorded, in the case of the signature and fingerprints through scans, digitization or photographs, and these will then afford a valuable means of identification in the absence of general particulars, for example in cases where the card is partially destroyed. These further particulars help ensure that the correct individual is identified and can be cross-checked against the records held by the Power on which the person depends.

---

[33]　Third Convention, Article 4A(4) and Annex IV.

1567   In practice, States do not always issue identity cards, and this has led to great difficulties in identifying individuals, particularly when they are deceased. Indeed, in some cases, persons have remained unidentified for want of this type of information. Consequently, it is important for Parties to issue identity cards and for members of the armed forces always to carry one.

1568   Should the person be carrying another form of identification, for example a driver's licence or a national identity card, any further particulars provided by those documents should also be recorded.

ii. Identity disc

1569 The practice of providing each member of the armed forces with an identity disc became widespread during the First World War, and the need for standardization of the disc became apparent shortly after.[34] A model identity disc, which could be divided in two, each part bearing the same information, one of which was to remain on the body of the deceased and the other detached from the body and sent to the State on which the individual depended,[35] was approved by the 13th International Conference of the Red Cross,[36] and reference to the identity disc was included in Article 4 of the 1929 Geneva Convention on the Wounded and Sick. Identity discs have since become widely used by State armed forces. In 1981, the 24th International Conference of the Red Cross urged all Parties to armed conflict, without distinction between international and non-international armed conflict, 'to take all necessary steps to provide the members of their armed forces with identity discs and to ensure that the discs are worn during service'.[37]

1570   To be effective for identification purposes, these double discs must be made with the greatest care. The inscriptions must be indelible. The substance of the disc must be as resistant as possible to the destructive effects of chemical and physical agents, especially fire and heat,[38] and be unaffected by the climate and bodily contact. This will usually be a durable metal. Although there is a model identity disc, different armed forces follow their own preferences. The precise

---

[34] On the use of the disc prior to the First World War, see Capdevila/Voldman, 2006, pp. 22–26.

[35] See Commission internationale pour la standardisation du matériel sanitaire, 2nd Session, 24–31 October 1927, Resolution III, reproduced in *Revue internationale de la Croix-Rouge et Bulletin international des Sociétés de la Croix Rouge*, Vol. 9, No. 107, November 1927, pp. 770–771, and 3rd Session, 16–23 July 1928, Resolution VIII, reproduced in *Revue internationale de la Croix-Rouge et Bulletin international des Sociétés de la Croix Rouge*, Vol. 10, No. 115, July 1928, p. 583.

[36] 13th International Conference of the Red Cross, The Hague, 1928, Resolution X, reproduced in *Revue internationale de la Croix-Rouge et Bulletin international des Sociétés de la Croix Rouge*, Vol. 10, No. 119, November 1928, p. 1019.

[37] 24th International Conference of the Red Cross, Manila, 1981, Resolution I, reproduced in *International Review of the Red Cross*, Vol. 21, No. 225, December 1981, p. 318.

[38] This passage, originally from Pictet (ed.), *Commentary on the First Geneva Convention*, ICRC, 1952, p. 171, was reiterated in Resolution I of the 24th International Conference of the Red Cross, Manila, 1981, reproduced in *International Review of the Red Cross*, Vol. 21, No. 225, December 1981, p. 318.

form of the disc may thus vary between States, for example in its shape (oval, rectangular, etc.), the particular metal used, and the manner in which the two halves of the disc are attached (by chain, directly to each other, etc.). This object is sometimes referred to as 'a disc' (i.e. a single item but with two halves) or 'discs' (i.e. a reference to two parts of a whole). Whether in the singular or the plural, it is basically the same thing.

1571   The disc should be worn on the person, usually around the neck, and not be attached to an item of clothing, for example the lace of a boot, or to another belonging such as a rucksack. It is all too easy to become separated from one's belongings, especially during hostilities, vastly reducing the utility of the disc if it is not worn on the person.[39] Likewise, it is imperative for individuals to wear their own discs and not those of others.

1572   The precise information inscribed on the identity disc varies between States. The 24th International Conference of the Red Cross recommended that the discs 'give all the indications required for a precise identification of members of the armed forces such as full name, date and place of birth, religion, serial number and blood group'.[40] Some States include other particulars, for example the person's social security/insurance number or the branch of the armed forces in which he or she serves. It goes without saying that the details inscribed on the disc must be genuine and not contain false information designed, for example, to mislead the adverse Party. It should also be inscribed in a manner that can easily be understood by others, for example not in code.

1573   The identity disc should be issued as soon as the individual enters the armed forces. This is one of the measures States Parties can take in peacetime. Delay in issuing the identity disc until the outbreak of hostilities may result in the identity disc being issued too late or not at all owing to the speedy deployment of forces or preoccupation with military matters.[41]

1574   It may be argued that, for practical reasons, there is an obligation on States to issue identity discs to members of their armed forces. This follows from the obligation on Parties to conflicts in Article 17(3) of the Third Convention 'to furnish the persons under [their] jurisdiction who are liable to become prisoners of war, with an identity card', coupled with the preference for identity discs over identity cards expressed in Resolution I of the 24th International Conference.[42] However, Article 16 does not as such spell out an obligation to

---

[39] In certain older conflicts, 'paybooks' were issued to soldiers and served as identity documents, but these were carried in soldiers' packs and were not taken into battle with them. '[E]quipment was stamped with a personal number whose holder could in theory be identified from the quartermaster's records. But the morning after a big battle many of the dead on the battlefield were left naked, having been stripped by looters during the night.' Accordingly, it was recognized that some form of identification needed to be carried on the person. See Bugnion, p. 499.

[40] 24th International Conference of the Red Cross, Manila, 1981, Resolution I, reproduced in *International Review of the Red Cross*, Vol. 21, No. 225, December 1981, p. 318.

[41] See Bugnion, p. 502.

[42] Furthermore, Article 40(2) of the First Convention provides that medical personnel 'in addition to wearing the identity disc mentioned in Article 16, shall also carry a special identity card'.

issue identity discs or to wear them.[43] Regardless, the importance of such discs and the desirability of their adoption by all armed forces and of all individuals becoming familiar with them cannot be overstated. The absence of identity discs in certain conflicts has led to numerous problems with the identification of dead bodies and the tracing of missing persons.[44]

g–h. Details concerning capture, wounds, illness or death

1575   It is largely within the ability of the Party into whose hands the individual has fallen to determine the information required under the items '(g) date and place of capture or death' and '(h) particulars concerning wounds or illness, or cause of death'. Accordingly, such information must be recorded to the extent possible, regardless of the person's condition and the presence of any identity disc or card. The required information is related to Article 17 of the present Convention (prescriptions regarding the dead) and thus to associated obligations on the Party.

1576   In so far as item (g) is concerned, it will not always be possible to give the exact date on which death occurred, for example when the individual was already deceased when picked up on the battlefield. But the date is nevertheless of great importance for reasons mainly connected with civil and family law, for example in relation to the deceased's family receiving due benefits or for testate matters. The date must therefore be determined with all the precision which present-day medical science affords, to the extent such science is available and practical, and mention should be made of any medical examination, together with the results, in the details that are forwarded.[45]

1577   The date and place of capture must also be recorded. This holds true for situations in which a person falls into enemy hands in a manner other than capture (e.g. surrender). It should be recalled that the first paragraph sets out the scope of the provision and refers to wounded, sick or dead individuals falling into the hands of the adverse Party generally. In referring only to capture, the second paragraph does not serve to limit the scope of the provision. Rather, it lists the particulars that are to be recorded 'if possible'. In the absence of an identity card or disc, a record of the time and place that the persons fell into the Party's hands, for example through GPS coordinates, may assist in their identification. Families of missing persons sometimes contact the Central Tracing Agency with information that their loved ones were picked up by the adverse Party at a particular time and place. This information can then

---

[43] See also H. Wayne Elliott, 'Identification', in Roy Gutman, David Rieff and Anthony Dworkin (eds), *Crimes of War: What the Public Should Know*, 2nd edition, W.W. Norton & Company, New York, 2007, pp. 232–234.

[44] This was the case, for example, in the 1991 Gulf War, as the Iraqi armed forces did not use identity discs.

[45] On the examination of the body, see also the commentary on Article 17, section C.2.

be cross-checked against the equivalent information provided by the Party in question.

1578   The information required under item (h) is medical in nature and should be supplied by a doctor. Provision should in consequence be made for the constant presence of a doctor with the competent administrative authorities. If no doctor is present, the information should be provided by another suitably qualified person. The Parties to the conflict must endeavour to supply these particulars, only in so far as they have a bearing on the identification of the individual.[46] According to contemporary standards of medical ethics, doctors must treat all medical information with absolute confidentiality,[47] unless the patient has capacity and consents to the disclosure/sharing of the information, 'it is required by law' (in this case Article 16 itself) or 'it is justified in the public interest'.[48] It is a delicate matter, which must be handled with the utmost care in the light of the person's high degree of vulnerability.

4. Means of obtaining the particulars

1579   Collecting information on wounded, sick or dead persons can be difficult. However, the Party into whose hands an individual has fallen can obtain the information required by Article 16(2) in different ways.

1580   Items (a) to (f) in the list can be obtained most readily from the identity card or disc, where present, while items (g) and (h) are supplied by the Power into whose hands the individual has fallen. It should be recalled that the identity card or disc cannot be confiscated at any time, even to obtain the relevant information. This is stated explicitly in Article 17(2) of the Third Convention, a rule which applies with equal force in the present context given that to confiscate the card or disc would be to obviate its very rationale.

1581   The information can also be obtained by questioning the person concerned. Pursuant to Article 17(1) of the Third Convention, prisoners of war are required to provide their 'surname, first names and rank, date of birth, and army, regimental, personal or serial number, or failing this, equivalent information'. In this scenario, Article 17(4) prohibits torture or coercion to secure information from prisoners of war and provides that '[p]risoners of war who refuse to answer may not be threatened, insulted, or exposed to any unpleasant or

---

[46]   See also, in respect of the deceased, Article 17 of the First Convention.

[47]   World Medical Association, International Code of Medical Ethics, adopted by the 3rd General Assembly of the World Medical Association, October 1949, as amended; ICRC, *Health Care in Danger: The Responsibilities of Health-Care Personnel Working in Armed Conflicts and Other Emergencies*, ICRC, Geneva, 2012, p. 77

[48]   British Medical Association, *Ethical decision-making for doctors in the armed forces: a tool kit*, London, 2012, p. 25; ICRC, *Health Care in Danger: The Responsibilities of Health-Care Personnel Working in Armed Conflicts and Other Emergencies*, ICRC, Geneva, 2012, pp. 76–78. See also Additional Protocol I, Article 16(3).

disadvantageous treatment of any kind'. In the present context, this means, in particular, that medical treatment cannot be made contingent on the answering of questions. Likewise, the failure to answer questions cannot lead to disadvantageous treatment of any sort, including inferior medical treatment. Furthermore, the questioning must not in any way hinder or interfere with the required medical care. Accordingly, acts such as delaying necessary medical treatment in order to make the person feel more vulnerable or stretching out the journey to the medical facility in order to have more time for questioning are prohibited.

1582   Although the provisions of Article 17 of the Third Convention are not contained in the present article, they nonetheless apply to persons covered by it.[49] The wounded and sick who have fallen into the hands of the adverse Party are prisoners of war and the First and Third Conventions apply simultaneously to them. It is therefore essential that the authorities and all persons who are called upon to apply the First Convention are fully conversant with the provisions of Article 17 of the Third Convention and that they strictly observe them. Furthermore, pursuant to Article 12 of the First Convention, the wounded and sick must be treated humanely and cared for.

1583   If the information cannot be obtained by the above means, for example if the person is unconscious or refuses to provide the information, or when an identity card or disc is not present, it does not follow that a record cannot be made. As indicated above, some of the information required is largely within the control of the Party into whose hands the wounded, sick or dead have fallen.[50] Accordingly, this information can usually be provided and there will not normally be a reasonable excuse for failing to record it.

1584   Other information can be obtained by different means. According to the Third Convention, 'all possible means' must be used to identify '[p]risoners of war who, owing to their physical or mental condition, are unable to state their identity', but these means must not amount to, or involve, torture, coercion, threats, insults or exposure to unpleasant or disadvantageous treatment of any kind.[51] Thus, an individual may be fingerprinted or photographed.[52] A DNA sample may not be taken without the person's consent, unless there is a legal justification, such as in the case of a criminal investigation, or to identify remains.[53]

---

[49] On the division between the First and Third Conventions, see Article 14 of the First Convention.
[50] See also Sassòli, p. 11.
[51] Third Convention, Article 17(4)–(5).
[52] See e.g. United Kingdom, *Manual of the Law of Armed Conflict*, 2004, para. 8.33.2, which lists these as examples of measures that may be taken.
[53] In such cases, the DNA sample must be taken solely for the purpose of identifying the individual, collected by qualified persons, destroyed after the purpose is served, analysed in laboratories working according to accredited standards, and protected from unauthorized access and use. See ICRC, *Missing People, DNA Analysis and Identification of Human Remains*, 2nd edition, ICRC, Geneva, 2009, p. 42.

E. Paragraph 3: Forwarding and transmittal of information

1585　Article 16(3) describes what has to be done with the information that has been collected. It fills an important gap in the previous Geneva Conventions, none of which specified how or to whom the information was to be transmitted.[54] The provision is now quite clear. The information is to be forwarded as soon as possible, by the persons or authorities who collected it, to the information bureau which the Party to the conflict is required to establish. The information bureau will transmit it to the Protecting Power, should one exist, and to the Central Tracing Agency, while the Protecting Power and the Central Tracing Agency will each pass it on to the Power on which the wounded, sick or dead persons depend. This process, aside from the appointment of Protecting Powers, has generally been followed in all major international armed conflicts since the adoption of the Convention.

1. Forwarding to the information bureau

1586　The information collected pursuant to the first and second paragraphs of Article 16 is to be forwarded to the information bureau described in Article 122 of the Third Convention. Pursuant to that article, the Parties to the conflict are required to establish an information bureau upon the outbreak of the conflict and in cases of occupation. The purpose of the information bureau is to centralize all information relating to prisoners of war, such as information on their movements, releases, illnesses or deaths. This is necessary both for administrative reasons and to enable particulars to be forwarded to the Power on which the prisoners of war depend and, in turn, to their families. It also follows from the principle that prisoners of war are in the hands of the adverse Party rather than of the individuals who captured them.[55] Given the overlap between the First and Third Conventions,[56] the mandate of the information bureau extends to certain aspects of the First Convention. Indeed, it was only logical to centralize all the information concerning prisoners of war, advising one and the same office of everything happening to them, be they wounded, sick or in good health, regardless of whether they came under the First, Second or Third Convention.

1587　For the information bureau to carry out its tasks, the Party to the conflict must have a procedure in place for the forwarding of information. This will require 'clear lines of communication'[57] between the individuals into whose hands the persons have fallen, hospitals or other facilities for the treatment

---

[54] See Geneva Convention on the Wounded and Sick (1929), Article 4; *Report of the Preliminary Conference of National Societies of 1946*, p. 22; and *Report of the Conference of Government Experts of 1947*, p. 17.
[55] Third Convention, Article 12.　　[56] See the commentary on Article 14, section C.1.
[57] Ary, pp. 21–22.

of the wounded and sick, prisoner-of-war camps and the information bureau. This is the only way to ensure that those who actually record the information forward it to the information bureau.

1588   The information is to be forwarded 'as soon as possible' for the reasons set out above.[58] The likely existence of a chain of transmission makes its timeliness all the more important. The phrase 'as soon as possible' implies that the forwarding of the information must take place by the most rapid means available, for example electronically.

2. Transmittal to the Protecting Power and the Central Tracing Agency

1589   Once the information bureau receives the information, it is required to transmit it to the Protecting Power and the Central Tracing Agency. This dual line of reporting has proved useful given the relatively few conflicts in which Protecting Powers have been appointed.[59] In conflicts in which Protecting Powers exist, the information will reach the adverse Party through two distinct channels.

1590   The transmission to the Protecting Power will usually be effected by communicating the information to the diplomatic staff which the Protecting Power maintains in the country concerned for the purpose of exercising its protective functions. It is then incumbent on the diplomatic staff to arrange for the information to be transmitted as quickly as possible to its own authorities, who will pass it on to the Party on whose behalf it is acting as Protecting Power.

1591   The Central Prisoners of War Agency, renamed the Central Tracing Agency in 1960, is a standing division of the ICRC based in Geneva. As its original name suggests, one of its primary functions is to centralize information on prisoners of war and to transmit that information to the country of origin of the prisoners of war or to the Power on which they depend.[60] In so far as the present provision is concerned, one of the Agency's functions is to receive particulars relating to the wounded, sick and dead, and to forward them to the Power on which they depend.[61] In practice, the particulars have taken a variety of forms, including individual identity cards, lists, death certificates, letters and telegrams.

---

[58] See section C.4. Katz, p. 409, frames it as 'with the utmost speed'. Article 122 of the Third Convention requires that the equivalent obligation in respect of prisoners of war be fulfilled '[w]ithin the shortest possible period'. Each of these phrases means essentially the same thing.

[59] See the commentary on Article 8, section H.   [60] Third Convention, Article 123.

[61] Although Article 123 might appear broader, in that it provides also for the transmission of information to 'the country of origin of the prisoners of war', in practice there is little difference between it and the provision under discussion. Ordinarily, the person's country of origin will be the same as the Power on which the person depends. In cases where the two States are not the same, the Central Agency will not transmit the information to the country of origin unless the person consents, given that to do so may be to inform the State concerned that one of its nationals was a member of the armed forces of a foreign State. See Sassòli, p. 12, fn. 26.

1592   The information bureau must transmit the information 'as soon as possible'.[62] The equivalent provision in Article 122(3) of the Third Convention requires that it be done 'immediately'. In practice, at this stage of the transmission process, there will be little difference between 'as soon as possible' and 'immediately'. Immediacy is subject to putting the information in an appropriate form, cross-checking it against other information received, and making a copy for the records of the Party to which the information bureau belongs.

1593   The information must be forwarded using 'the most rapid means' available. This standard is set out in the equivalent provision in Article 122(3) of the Third Convention and applies equally to the present provision. The precise means of transmission will depend on the relevant State's level of technical progress. In practice, this has included the postal service, telegram, electronic communication and hand delivery. However, some of these means (e.g. telegram) are now mostly redundant and the requirement to use the most rapid means available suggests that, in most cases, this will be, and in practice often has been, electronic means such as email. On occasion, the information is handed over to delegates of the ICRC or of another impartial humanitarian organization on the ground.

3. Obligatory nature of forwarding and transmittal of information

1594   Both stages in the transmittal process, i.e. from those who record the information to the information bureau and from the information bureau to the Protecting Power (if any) and the Central Tracing Agency, are obligatory. This is evident from the word 'shall', which is used twice in the paragraph and in relation to both stages. Accordingly, the individuals who record the information cannot use their discretion in deciding whether to forward the information to the information bureau. Likewise, the information bureau cannot use its discretion in deciding whether to transmit the information to the Protecting Power and the Central Tracing Agency. This is the case regardless of the circumstances, for example if equivalent information has been provided by the adverse Party.[63] The provision, like all of international humanitarian law, does not operate on the basis of reciprocity.[64]

4. Transmittal to the Power on which the persons depend

1595   The Protecting Power and the Central Tracing Agency act as intermediaries between the Parties in regard to the transmittal of information. Accordingly,

---

[62] Katz, p. 409, frames it as 'without delay'.
[63] However, in practice in certain conflicts, Parties have occasionally conditioned the sending of information on the adverse Party doing the same.
[64] See Vienna Convention on the Law of Treaties (1969), Article 60(5). See also ICTY, *Kupreškić* Trial Judgment, 2000, paras 510–520.

they do not keep the information for themselves; rather, they are required to forward that information to the Power on which the persons depend. The Agency does, however, record and keep a copy of the information for its files,[65] for example in case the information is lost en route to the Power. This also allows the Agency to respond to queries from concerned families.[66]

1596   An exception to this rule, in so far as the Agency is concerned, is where the Power on which the persons depend systematically uses the information to harm the persons concerned or their families,[67] such as to make accusations of desertion or to intimidate or persecute families. Transmittal may also be suspended where the information is repeatedly (mis)used for propaganda purposes, such as to accuse the adverse Party of torturing or murdering the persons in its hands. This is also consistent with the notion that personal data may not be used for purposes other than those for which they were collected or for compatible further processing.[68] Accordingly, if the Power on which the persons depend uses that information to harm them or their families, it is only proper that transmittal be suspended. Such suspension is a matter for the Agency and not for the Power into whose hands the persons have fallen; it remains incumbent on the latter to transmit the information to the Agency. Nor does it mean that the families of persons who have fallen into the hands of the adverse Party will be deprived of news of their loved ones. The Agency may communicate the information directly to the families concerned if it considers that it can so act without prejudice to anyone.

1597   The situation is more difficult in so far as the Protecting Power is concerned. Unlike the Central Tracing Agency, which is a purely humanitarian body concerned exclusively with the fate of victims of armed conflict, the Protecting Power, through a sort of agreement between itself and the Power that it is protecting, undertakes the forwarding of the most varied kinds of documents without necessarily considering whether it is expedient to forward them or not. However, if the interests of the persons in the hands of the adverse Party or their families are being harmed, the Protecting Power would be well advised to adopt, at least temporarily, a position similar to that of the Agency.

1598   The transmittal of information must be carried out 'as soon as possible'. The paragraph commences with these words and they can be read as applying to both the Protecting Power and the Central Tracing Agency. This is confirmed

---

[65] Bugnion, p. 501. See also Djurović, p. 231, on the Indo-Pakistan conflict of the early 1970s.
[66] Bugnion, p. 501.
[67] An exception to this effect in respect of civilian internees is set out explicitly in Articles 137(2) and 140(2) of the Fourth Convention.
[68] See e.g. Guidelines for the Regulation of Computerized Personal Data Files, adopted by UN General Assembly, Res. 45/95, 14 December 1990, Annex, Principle 3(b); OECD Guidelines on the Protection of Privacy and Transborder Flows of Personal Data, C(80)58/FINAL, 23 September 1980, Annex, as amended by C(2013)79, 11 July 2013, para. 9; and Council of Europe, Convention for the Protection of Individuals with regard to Automatic Processing of Personal Data, Convention No. 108, Strasbourg, 28 January 1981, Article 5(b).

by Article 123 of the Third Convention, which provides that the Agency must 'transmit [the information] as rapidly as possible'. The information is transmitted in the same manner as noted above, for example by email or hand, depending on the context.[69]

5. *Communication to the family*

1599 Although nowhere stated in the paragraph, the Power on which the persons depend must inform the families of the wounded, sick or dead who are in the hands of the adverse Party of the fate of their loved ones.[70] Indeed, the system is established in the interest of the State on which the individuals depend and their families. Article 122(4) of the Third Convention provides that the equivalent information required by that article 'shall make it possible quickly to advise the next of kin concerned'. Although it may have been unclear at the time of the adoption of the Convention whether the provision constituted a recommendation that the belligerents advise the next of kin of prisoners of war, given that these are matters which are solely within the purview of the Power on which prisoners of war depend, international humanitarian law has since developed. Additional Protocol I provides that application of its provisions on the missing and the dead 'shall be prompted mainly by the right of families to know the fate of their relatives',[71] a point which holds true also for the provisions of the Conventions relating to the wounded, sick and dead.

1600 Other instruments also provide for a right of families to know the fate of missing relatives.[72] Under customary international law, each Party to the conflict must provide family members of missing persons with any information it has on their fate.[73] Indeed, one State has expressed the view that the need to establish an individual's identity is 'to enable his capture to be reported to the authorities in his own country and to his family';[74] another stipulates that one of the tasks of the national information bureau is to 'transmit ... the information received to the families concerned'.[75] Deliberately withholding information about missing persons contravenes the right of families to know the fate of their loved ones. This does not mean that every single piece of information has to be communicated to the family, as a Party might have a legitimate

---

[69] See section E.2, and para. 1593 in particular.
[70] The capture card mentioned in Article 70 of the Third Convention should help to provide this information. Precisely which family member is to be informed depends on the person's situation. In practice, this tends to be the spouse, the parents or, failing those, another family member.
[71] Additional Protocol I, Article 32.
[72] See e.g. UN Secretary-General's Bulletin (1999), Section 9.8; Guiding Principles on Internal Displacement (1998), Principles 16(1) and 17(4); and Henckaerts/Doswald-Beck, commentary on Rule 117, pp. 423–426.
[73] ICRC Study on Customary International Humanitarian Law (2005), Rule 117.
[74] United Kingdom, *Manual of the Law of Armed Conflict*, 2004, para. 8.33.1.
[75] Belgium, *Specific Procedure on the Prisoners of War Information Bureau*, 2007, section 7(d).

interest in withholding certain types of information. Nonetheless, the general fate of individuals, such as their death or capture, must be communicated to the family.

F. Paragraph 4: Forwarding of death certificates and personal items

1601 Article 16(4) deals with the forwarding of documents and items that relate exclusively to the dead.

1602   The present provision embodies the practice of a number of belligerents and of the Central Prisoners of War Agency during the Second World War, and introduces the precision which was lacking in the 1929 Geneva Convention on the Wounded and Sick.

1. Certificates of death or lists of deceased

1603 Pursuant to the first sentence of Article 16(4), the Parties to the conflict 'shall prepare and forward to each other . . . certificates of death or duly authenticated lists of the dead' (hereinafter shortened to 'death certificates or lists').

a. The obligation

1604 The Parties to the conflict are required to prepare and forward death certificates or lists, as is evident from use of the word 'shall'.[76] The obligation is one of result and there is no excuse for failure to meet this requirement. This does not mean that the Party is under an obligation to identify every single deceased person so that it can prepare death certificates. The obligation of identification is one of conduct, to be carried out with due diligence, as it may not be possible to identify the deceased, for example if no identity disc or card was on the person and he or she did not regain consciousness whilst in the hands of the Party.[77] In respect of persons who have not been identified, as much information as possible is to be provided on the death certificates or lists.

1605   Given that the obligation to prepare the death certificates or lists is so that they can be forwarded, the Party whose task it is must not use them for such other purposes as propaganda or intimidation.

b. Timing

1606 Although not stated explicitly in the paragraph, the death certificates or lists are to be prepared and forwarded as soon as possible. This is because it is in the

---

[76] The obligation applies also to neutral States in the situation referenced in and pursuant to Article 4 of the First Convention.

[77] See also the commentary on Article 17, para. 1664.

interests of the family to receive the death certificate as soon as possible following notification of the death so that testate and other civil law matters can start to be addressed. Likewise, Article 120(2) of the Third Convention requires that death certificates of prisoners of war or certified lists of dead prisoners of war be forwarded 'as rapidly as possible'. In many cases, it may be possible to prepare and transfer the record of death and the death certificate at the same time. Indeed, with respect to persons who died immediately upon falling into the hands of the adverse Party and before the record required by the second paragraph can be made, the Party may decide to record the required information in the form of a death certificate.

c. Procedure

1607 The death certificates or lists are to be forwarded 'through the same bureau', that is to say the information bureau referred to in the third paragraph. In practice, death certificates or lists are not always transmitted through the information bureau. They are sometimes handed over in person to ICRC delegates on the ground, who forward them to the Central Tracing Agency in Geneva, or they are sometimes handed over to the ICRC in Geneva by the permanent mission of the State in question.

d. Documents and items for forwarding

i. Death certificates

1608 Article 4, paragraph 2, of the 1929 Geneva Convention on the Wounded and Sick referred to 'certificates of death', without specifying their content or how they were to be made out. During the Second World War, the procedure for the preparation and transmission of death certificates varied, but some States made use of a detailed standard form proposed by the ICRC.[78] Despite the existence of this form, the First Convention does not specify the content of the death certificate or the form it should take, so reference should be made to the Third Convention in this regard. Article 120(2) of the Third Convention sets out the requirements for death certificates in respect of prisoners of war. While there are differences in a Party's duty of care to a person who dies on the battlefield and one who dies whilst a prisoner of war,[79] the provisions of Article 120 apply largely to both categories, at least in so far as circumstances allow.

---

[78] See ICRC, *Report of the International Committee of the Red Cross on its Activities during the Second World War (September 1, 1939–June 30, 1947), Volume I: General Activities*, ICRC, Geneva, 1948, pp. 301–302. See also *ibid. Volume II: The Central Agency for Prisoners of War*, p. 33.

[79] For example, Article 121 of the Third Convention requires that an official enquiry be conducted in the case of prisoners of war killed or seriously injured in certain circumstances.

1609   This means that the death certificates of persons who die on the battlefield should follow the model annexed to the Third Convention (Annex IVD) and contain three kinds of information.

1610   The first set of particulars relates to the identity of the deceased and includes: surname and first name; rank; army, regimental, personal or serial number, or equivalent information; and date of birth. The second set relates to the death itself and includes the date and place of death and the cause of death. The third and final set relates to the burial site and includes the date and place of burial and all particulars necessary to identify the grave. If the body has been cremated, the fact is to be stated, together with the reasons for such exceptional treatment, as provided in Article 17(2) of the First Convention.[80] All these particulars, with the exception of the last set, are the same as those required by Article 16(1) and (2).

1611   The model death certificate includes, in addition to the above particulars, two headings of the greatest interest to the families of the deceased, namely a reference to the possible existence of personal effects, which is further discussed below, and a few details about the last moments of the deceased. It will no doubt only be rarely that particulars can be given under the latter heading in the case of dead picked up on the battlefield. But the responsible authorities should nevertheless endeavour to give as many details as possible, in view of their sentimental and human value.

ii. Authenticated lists of the dead

1612   As an alternative to the preparation and forwarding of death certificates, the paragraph provides for the preparation and forwarding of duly authenticated lists of the dead. This was done, for example, during the conflicts in the Middle East in the late 1960s and early 1970s.[81] The lists must be authenticated, i.e. certified, which requires both that an individual of sufficient authority authenticates the lists[82] and that a process of authentication be undertaken, for example checking the information contained in the lists against other records in the Party's possession. Authentication will usually take place through a signature together with a stamp or seal.[83]

1613   Although presented as an alternative, death certificates are by far preferable to certified lists, as individual death certificates are generally required by the national legislation of the Power on which the individual depends, for example to legally confirm death and to issue benefits to the family of the deceased or for testate matters. The reason for the provision of an alternative was the view that death certificates could not be made obligatory owing to the additional

---

[80] For further details, see Article 120 of the Third Convention.   [81] Djurović, p. 226.
[82] Article 120(2) of the Third Convention requires that the lists be certified 'by a responsible officer'.
[83] Article 122(8) of the Third Convention provides that '[a]ll written communications made by the Bureau shall be authenticated by a signature or a seal'.

work they involved.[84] If authenticated lists of the dead are used, they must, as far as possible, be consistent with the model death certificate and contain the same kinds of information.

2. Identity disc, wills and personal items

a. The obligation

1614   Pursuant to the second sentence of Article 16(4), the Parties to the conflict are required to collect, i.e. to 'bring or gather together',[85] and forward the items mentioned in the paragraph. The obligation is evident from the use of the word 'shall'. The items in question are: 'one half of a double identity disc, last wills or other documents of importance to the next of kin, money and in general all articles of an intrinsic or sentimental value, which are found on the dead'.[86]

b. Timing

1615   Although not set out explicitly in the paragraph, the listed items are to be collected and forwarded as soon as possible. This obligation is based on the needs of the family. For example, the wills will be required for the possessions of the deceased to be distributed in accordance with their wishes. In many cases, it may be possible to forward the items to the information bureau at the same time as the information specified in the second paragraph, or at the same time as the death certificates or lists of the dead specified in the fourth paragraph. This may not be possible in all cases, for example if the information can be transmitted electronically but there are no physical means by which to send the items. It should also be recalled that the individuals into whose hands the deceased have fallen are not permitted to keep the items for any reason, including, for example, as souvenirs.[87]

c. Procedure

1616   The items are to be forwarded 'through the same bureau', that is to say through the information bureau, which in turn has to transmit them to the Central Tracing Agency or the Protecting Power. As the items are unique tangible objects, they can only be transmitted through one of these two channels. The choice between the two is for the relevant information bureau to make but, in

---

[84] For the debate on this topic in the context of the Third Convention, see *Report of the Conference of Government Experts of 1947*, p. 247.

[85] *Concise Oxford English Dictionary*, 12th edition, Oxford University Press, 2011, p. 281.

[86] See also ICRC Study on Customary International Humanitarian Law (2005), Rule 114 (Parties to the conflict must return the personal effects of the deceased to their next of kin.).

[87] This would amount to looting/pillage and is prohibited under Articles 28 and 47 of the 1907 Hague Regulations and Article 15 of the First Convention, as well as under customary international law (see ICRC Study on Customary International Humanitarian Law (2005), Rule 52).

practice, it is the Agency which is usually chosen, either because there are no Protecting Powers or, in conflicts in which Protecting Powers are used, because the Agency has prepared especially for this task. The Central Tracing Agency and Protecting Power will, in turn, transmit the items to the family of the deceased.

d. Items for forwarding

1617   The paragraph provides an exhaustive list of items to be forwarded, although two of the items – documents of importance to the next of kin and articles of an intrinsic or sentimental value – are general in nature. In practice, States have interpreted the list broadly, requiring that 'personal effects' be collected and forwarded, and this is reflected in the customary international law standard.[88]

1618   What is common to each of the listed items is that they are 'found on the dead'. The phrase includes items that are physically on the body, for example one half of the double identity disc, a ring or a wristwatch. It also includes items that are on, or in, the clothes that are worn by the deceased, for example in a pocket or affixed to a lapel. It further covers items that are being carried by the deceased, for example in a rucksack, as those too are 'found on the dead'. Lastly, the phrase extends to objects that are in the immediate vicinity of the dead.[89] It would be unfortunate if a strict reading of the provision led to the conclusion, for example, that an item otherwise falling within the scope of the paragraph but lying just beyond the reach of the deceased's outstretched hand was not collected and forwarded as it was not found 'on the dead'. While the Party is not under an obligation to search the surroundings for valuables belonging to the deceased, the phrase must be interpreted with the purpose of the provision in mind,[90] namely to return items of value and/or importance to the families of the deceased. Accordingly, where it is clear that an item not found on the deceased nonetheless belongs to him or her and is of value or importance to

---

[88] ICRC Study on Customary International Humanitarian Law (2005), Rule 114. See Benin, *Law of Armed Conflict Manual*, 1995, Fascicule III, p. 13; Cameroon, *Instructor's Manual*, 2006, pp. 122 and 164; Chad, *Instructor's Manual*, 2006, p. 94; Croatia, *LOAC Compendium*, 1991, p. 21; France, *LOAC Teaching Note*, 2000, p. 3; Hungary, *Military Manual*, 1992, p. 38; Israel, *Manual on the Rules of Warfare*, 2006, p. 39; Kenya, *LOAC Manual*, 1997, p. 12; Madagascar, *Military Manual*, 1994, para. 23; Netherlands, *Military Manual*, 2005, para. 610; Peru, *IHL and Human Rights Manual*, 2010, para. 69(c); Senegal, *IHL Manual*, 1999, p. 18; Spain, *LOAC Manual*, 2007, paras 5.2.d.(6) and 6.2.b.(3); Togo, *Military Manual*, 1996, Fascicule II, p. 12; and United Kingdom, *Manual of the Law of Armed Conflict*, 2004, para. 7.34. This is consistent with Article 4 of the 1929 Geneva Convention on the Wounded and Sick, which referred to 'articles of a personal nature'.

[89] The ICRC had suggested that the words 'or in the immediate vicinity' be included in the provision 'as the articles in question need not be actually found on the dead'; see *Draft Conventions adopted by the 1948 Stockholm Conference*, p. 11. Article 4 of the 1906 Geneva Convention referred to items 'which are found upon the field of battle, or have been left by the sick or wounded who have died in sanitary formations or other establishments'.

[90] Vienna Convention on the Law of Treaties (1969), Article 31(1).

the family, it must be forwarded.[91] Indeed, in practice, and reflected in the customary international law standard, States have omitted the condition that the personal effects be 'found on the dead', instead referring to a more general obligation to collect and forward the items.[92]

i. One half of the double identity disc

1619 One half of the double identity disc is to remain around the neck of the deceased, while the other half is to be detached and sent to the State on which he or she depended.[93] Article 17(1) provides for the possibility of soldiers being issued only with single discs. In such cases, the whole disc must remain with the body, as it is essential for the body to be identifiable at any time. But the use of a single disc will deprive the Power on which the individual depended of an additional, and often very valuable, means of identification. Accordingly, the disc should be composed of two separable parts.

ii. Last wills

1620 In collecting the documents that are on the person of the deceased, the preservation and forwarding of those which have legal value, particularly wills, are important. Only in this way can the possessions of the deceased be disposed of in the manner intended. Although the practice of conflicts suggests that the Geneva Conventions' provisions on wills rarely need to be resorted to, such is the importance of the issue that the topic is mentioned in all four Conventions.[94]

1621 The reference to a 'will' is to 'a legal document containing instructions for the disposition of one's money and property after one's death',[95] howsoever characterized. The document that passes for a will may not look like one, for example it might be scrawled on a scrap of paper, it might not use the language of the law (testator, beneficiary, and so on), and witnesses might not have attested to it. This does not prevent it from having to be forwarded. It is not for the Party to judge the validity of the will, only to forward to the information bureau that which resembles a will.[96]

1622 Should there be multiple wills of differing dates, all such wills must be forwarded. The reference to 'last will' is simply to the will, 'last will' or 'last will and testament' being alternative names for the document. The reference does

---

[91] See also the last paragraph of Article 122 of the Third Convention, which requires that 'personal valuables' of prisoners of war be collected and forwarded and that their 'other personal effects' be transmitted.

[92] ICRC Study on Customary International Humanitarian Law (2005), Rule 114 and related practice.

[93] On the identity disc, see paras 1569–1574.

[94] Second Convention, Article 19; Third Convention, Articles 77 and 120; Fourth Convention, Article 129.

[95] *Concise Oxford English Dictionary*, 12th edition, Oxford University Press, 2011, p. 1651.

[96] Indeed, even if the document does not legally constitute a will, it might amount to an article of sentimental value.

not mean that the individuals of the Party into whose hands the deceased have fallen are to select and forward only the most recently dated will. As already noted, the choice between wills, their validity and so forth are not matters for the Party concerned; all that is required of the Party in this regard is that the will(s) are forwarded to the information bureau. Decisions on the validity of the will and other matters fall within the domestic legal framework of the State in which the will is to be given effect.

iii. Other documents of importance

1623 The documents to be forwarded are not limited to wills; they include 'other documents of importance to the next of kin'. This is a broad category that is defined by three salient features. First, the item must be of a documentary nature, i.e. it must be 'a piece of written, printed, or electronic matter that provides information or evidence'.[97] Second, the item must be important to the next of kin.[98] This category thus includes such documents as instructions for the disposal of the body and arrangements for the care of children. It also excludes certain documents, such as those of intelligence or military value. As the importance of a document is relative and, aside from certain documents such as a will or those of military value, may not be immediately apparent, the individuals of the Party into whose hands the deceased have fallen should err on the side of forwarding the document. Indeed, the provision should be read as requiring the forwarding of documents that are not obviously unimportant to the next of kin. Where a bundle of papers, or files on a USB drive, contain documents of military value as well as documents of importance to the next of kin, the documents should be separated if, and to the extent, possible.

iv. Money

1624 '[M]oney . . . which [is] found on the dead' must also be forwarded. As this category is not narrowed down further, aside from it being found on the dead, all money is to be forwarded regardless of the amount and currency. Likewise, it is not limited to cash, that is to say banknotes and coins, but extends to cheques, money orders and any other monetary items.

v. Articles of intrinsic or sentimental value

1625 The final category listed is 'in general all articles of an intrinsic or sentimental value'. This comprises, in fact, two categories – objects of an intrinsic value and objects of sentimental value. The two categories are to be interpreted broadly, as is evident by the words 'in general' and 'all'. The defining feature of both

---

[97] *Concise Oxford English Dictionary*, 12th edition, Oxford University Press, 2011, p. 421.
[98] Some States interpret 'importance' broadly, as equivalent to 'useful'. See, regarding the parallel provision in the Third Convention, Canada, *LOAC Manual*, 2001, para. 1036.

categories is the value of the object, although one category is judged by its monetary worth and the other by its sentimental worth. Selection in the latter case will sometimes be more difficult; it must be borne in mind that articles which have little or no apparent value may, for sentimental reasons, be highly prized by near relatives. Likewise, what is considered to be of sentimental value will also vary by individual and also possibly by culture. Accordingly, and given also that what might be considered valuable for monetary reasons by one person might be considered near worthless by another, the individuals of the Party into whose hands the deceased have fallen should err on the side of forwarding the objects and leave it to the families of the deceased to judge whether or not they wish to retain the objects.[99] Indeed, the very fact that the object was on the person of the deceased at the moment he or she passed away might make it of sentimental value to the family. In general terms, though, articles of sentimental value include personal letters,[100] personal photographs, a wallet, a wristwatch, items of jewellery such as a ring or a chain, and religious artefacts. Also in general terms, items that would not fall within this category include weapons,[101] other military materiel, and photographs of military use, for example those taken on a scouting expedition.

vi. Unidentified articles

1626 One further category of items to be forwarded is listed, albeit in the final sentence of the paragraph and not in the sentence that contains the other items to be forwarded. This category is termed 'unidentified articles' and by default does not include any of the categories discussed above. It must be recalled that, under customary international law, all 'personal effects' and not only those items listed in the paragraph under discussion are to be collected and forwarded. Through the inclusion of the category 'unidentified articles', the conventional and customary law standards are not far apart.

3. Transmittal of the items

1627 The final sentence of Article 16(4) provides details concerning the transmittal of the items listed in the paragraph. The Parties to the conflict are to send the objects in sealed packets, accompanied by a statement on the identity of the deceased owner, as well as by a complete list of the contents.

---

[99] The difficulties of leaving the adverse Party to determine the intrinsic or sentimental value of items was noted by one delegation during the Conference of Government Experts in June 1947 and which accordingly proposed the words be deleted; see *Draft Conventions submitted to the 1948 Stockholm Conference*, Document No. 4a, p. 12. The phrase was nonetheless retained.

[100] This was expressly included in Article 4 of the 1906 Geneva Convention.

[101] This will be the case even if the particular weapon can be said to be of sentimental value to the deceased.

1628   The items in question are those set out in the first two sentences, together with 'unidentified articles'. They are to be 'sent' through the information bureau. As the items in question are physical objects rather than pieces of information, it will be necessary for them to be physically transported, first to the information bureau and then to the Central Tracing Agency or Protecting Power. This will usually be done through the postal system, and the Third Convention provides that the information bureau 'shall enjoy free postage for mail'.[102] However, provided that the items are 'sent', it is not required that this be done via the postal system; other means, such as personally conveying the items to the information bureau and to the Protecting Power or Agency, are just as acceptable. Regardless of the precise means used, the method and manner of sending must be reliable. Reliability operates at different levels, including that the items are actually received in the ordinary course of things, that they are received in good order, and that their receipt is not unduly delayed. All feasible precautions must be taken to ensure that parcels of such value are not lost or opened 'en route'. In time of armed conflict, postal communications are uncertain and often roundabout, and the risk of damage or deterioration is correspondingly increased.

1629   The items are to be sent 'in sealed packets'. This reduces the chance of interference with or damage to the items. It further reduces the chances of them being mixed up with the belongings of other persons transmitted at the same time.

1630   The sealed packets must be 'accompanied by' certain pieces of information. Thus, the required information must be packaged alongside the items and should not follow later. The information must also be attached to the items or clearly indicate the item to which it belongs; otherwise, the very purpose behind the sending of the information is negated. The information in question is 'statements giving all particulars necessary for the identification of the deceased owners' and 'a complete list of the contents of the parcel'. The former is required in order to match the deceased owners with their property, while the latter is required to ensure that all the items that are sent reach their final destination. In the event that the property was found on a person who could not be identified, the information concerning the deceased owner will relate to the particulars that the Party was able to record.

1631   The Central Tracing Agency or Protecting Power that receives the items sends them unopened to the family of the deceased. Precisely which family member receives the items depends on the individual's circumstances. In practice, this tends to be the spouse, the parents or, failing these, another family member. In so far as the Central Agency is concerned, if the ICRC has already

---

[102] Third Convention, Article 124. This provision is given effect *inter alia* through the Universal Postal Convention, Article 7.2.1–7.2.3, the Letter Post Regulations, Rules 111–112, and the Postal Payment Services Regulations, Article 1005. See Universal Postal Union, *Postal Payment Services Manual*, Berne, 2013, para. 10.4–10.6.

had contact with the family of the deceased, the items are sent to the ICRC delegation or the National Red Cross or Red Crescent Society of the State in question, rather than through the Power on which the deceased depended, for transmittal to the family. If there has been no such contact, the ICRC discusses the matter with the Power on which the deceased depended or sends the items to it, for onward transmittal to the family.

Select bibliography

Ary, Vaughn A., 'Accounting for Prisoners of War: A Legal Review of the United States Armed Forces Identification and Reporting Procedures', *Army Lawyer*, No. 261, August 1994, pp. 16–26.

Bugnion, François, *The International Committee of the Red Cross and the Protection of War Victims*, ICRC/Macmillan, Oxford, 2003, pp. 498–507.

Capdevila, Luc and Voldman, Danièle, 'Du numéro matricule au code génétique: la manipulation du corps des tués de la guerre en quête d'identité' ('From regimental number to genetic code: The handling of bodies of war victims in the search for identity'), *International Review of the Red Cross*, Vol. 84, No. 848, December 2002, pp. 751–765.

– (eds), *War Dead: Western Societies and the Casualties of War*, Edinburgh University Press, 2006.

Đjurović, Gradimir, *The Central Tracing Agency of the International Committee of the Red Cross*, Henry Dunant Institute, Geneva, 1986.

Durand, André, *History of the International Committee of the Red Cross, Volume II: from Sarajevo to Hiroshima*, Henry Dunant Institute, Geneva, 1984, pp. 34–48 and 413–441.

Geiss, Robin, 'Name, rank, date of birth, serial number and the right to remain silent', *International Review of the Red Cross*, Vol. 87, No. 860, December 2005, pp. 721–735.

Henckaerts, Jean-Marie and Doswald-Beck, Louise (eds), *Customary International Humanitarian Law, Volume I: Rules*, ICRC/Cambridge University Press, 2005, available at https://www.icrc.org/customary-ihl/eng/docs/v1.

Katz, Monique, 'The Central Tracing Agency of the ICRC', *International Review of the Red Cross*, Vol. 17, No. 199, October 1977, pp. 407–412.

Petrig, Anna, 'Search for Missing Persons', in Andrew Clapham, Paola Gaeta and Marco Sassòli (eds), *The 1949 Geneva Conventions: A Commentary*, Oxford University Press, 2015, pp. 257–276.

Sassòli, Marco, 'The National Information Bureau in Aid of the Victims of Armed Conflicts', *International Review of the Red Cross*, Vol. 27, No. 256, February 1987, pp. 6–24.

PRESCRIPTIONS REGARDING THE DEAD. GRAVES REGISTRATION SERVICE

❖ Text of the provision*

(1) Parties to the conflict shall ensure that burial or cremation of the dead, carried out individually as far as circumstances permit, is preceded by a careful examination, if possible by a medical examination, of the bodies, with a view to confirming death, establishing identity and enabling a report to be made. One half of the double identity disc, or the identity disc itself if it is a single disc, should remain on the body.

(2) Bodies shall not be cremated except for imperative reasons of hygiene or for motives based on the religion of the deceased. In case of cremation, the circumstances and reasons for cremation shall be stated in detail in the death certificate or on the authenticated list of the dead.

(3) They shall further ensure that the dead are honourably interred, if possible according to the rites of the religion to which they belonged, that their graves are respected, grouped if possible according to the nationality of the deceased, properly maintained and marked so that they may always be found. For this purpose, they shall organize at the commencement of hostilities an Official Graves Registration Service, to allow subsequent exhumations and to ensure the identification of bodies, whatever the site of the graves, and the possible transportation to the home country. These provisions shall likewise apply to the ashes, which shall be kept by the Graves Registration Service until proper disposal thereof in accordance with the wishes of the home country.

(4) As soon as circumstances permit, and at latest at the end of hostilities, these Services shall exchange, through the Information Bureau mentioned in the second paragraph of Article 16, lists showing the exact location and markings of the graves together with particulars of the dead interred therein.

❖ Reservations or declarations
None

---

* Paragraph numbers have been added for ease of reference.

Contents

A. Introduction

1632 Article 17 deals exclusively with the treatment of the dead. It is closely related to the last paragraph of Article 16, for after laying down rules in regard to the belongings of the deceased, and to the information found on their persons, it was still necessary to say what was to become of the bodies. Article 17 therefore sets out a number of rules relating to the burial or cremation of the deceased, examination of the body prior to burial or cremation, and the maintenance and marking of graves.

1633   The first paragraph contains two principal obligations. First, the Parties to the conflict are required to ensure that the dead are buried or cremated. The burial or cremation must take place individually as far as circumstances permit. Second, a careful examination of the body must be undertaken prior to burial or cremation. Although this paragraph refers to 'burial or cremation', the second paragraph indicates a preference for burial, allowing for cremation only in two limited situations. The third paragraph sets out a number of related obligations. The Parties must ensure that the dead are honourably interred, if possible according to the rites of the religion to which the deceased belonged. They must ensure respect for the graves, group them if possible according to nationality, and maintain and mark them. The Parties are also required to set up an official graves registration service at the outset of hostilities, enabling them to exchange 'lists showing the exact location and markings of the graves together with particulars of the dead interred therein'.

1634   The underlying purpose of the provisions relating to the dead – in this and other provisions of international humanitarian law[1] – is to preserve the dignity of the dead. Thus, their bodies are to be treated honourably and with respect,[2] their identities ascertained and their graves marked and respected.

1635   The provisions regarding the dead, for example those on establishing identity and marking graves, are related to those concerning missing persons and the right of families to know the fate of their loved ones.[3]

1636   For information on the treatment of the dead in non-international armed conflicts, see the commentary on common Article 3, section I.

B. Historical background

1637 Throughout history, the treatment of the dead in times of armed conflict has been a subject of concern, pronounced on by a variety of cultures and religions. International humanitarian law also has a long history of regulating the treatment of the dead, dating back at least to the 1880 Oxford Manual.[4]

1638   The 1906 Geneva Convention also contained provisions relating to the treatment of the dead. It provided that 'the belligerent who remains in possession of the field of battle...will see that a careful examination is made of the bodies of the dead prior to their interment or incineration'.[5] It also provided that '[a]s soon as possible each belligerent shall forward to the authorities of their country or army the marks or military papers of identification found upon the bodies of the dead'.[6] The Convention was interpreted at the time by one State as requiring the taking of 'the necessary measures for the...examination and identification of the dead'.[7]

---

[1] Second Convention, Articles 18 and 20; Third Convention, Article 120; Fourth Convention, Articles 129 and 130; Additional Protocol I, Article 34.

[2] See also First Convention, Article 15 (protection of the dead against despoliation).

[3] See Additional Protocol I, Articles 32–33; see also ICRC Study on Customary International Humanitarian Law (2005), Rule 117.

[4] Oxford Manual (1880), Articles 17 and 20.   [5] Geneva Convention (1906), Article 3.

[6] Ibid. Article 4.

[7] 'Geneva (Red Cross) Conference of 1906', in Papers relating to the Foreign Relations of the United States with the Annual Message of the President transmitted to Congress December 3, 1906, Government Printing Office, Washington, 1909, Part Two, p. 1557.

1639   Although explicitly requiring a 'careful examination...of the bodies of the dead prior to their interment or incineration', it was unclear whether or not the Convention also imposed an obligation on the belligerent itself to bury or cremate the dead. Such an obligation was not specified in the text of the Convention, and at least one State took the view that the Convention contained no such obligation.[8] However, the obligation to bury or cremate the dead, in so far as possible, was considered a norm of customary international law in academic writings even by 1906.[9]

1640   The provisions of the 1906 Convention were expanded upon in the 1929 Geneva Convention on the Wounded and Sick.[10] The 1929 Convention contains the core of the protections that are to be found in Article 17 of the present Convention.

C. Paragraph 1: Examination of the body and establishing identity

1641   Article 17(1) contains two principal obligations. First, the Parties to the conflict are required to ensure the burial or cremation of the dead. As far as circumstances permit, such burial or cremation must be carried out individually. Second, the Parties must undertake a careful examination of the body prior to burial or cremation, to confirm death, establish the person's identity and enable a report to be made.

1642   In addition, Article 4 of the First Convention requires neutral Powers to apply by analogy the provisions of the Convention to, *inter alia*, the dead found in their territory.[11]

1. Burial or cremation

a. The obligation

1643   The Parties to the conflict must ensure that the dead are buried or cremated. The second and third paragraphs of Article 17 set out in detail how the burial or cremation should be performed, including ensuring 'that the dead are honourably interred'. The 1929 Convention also required that the dead be

---

[8]   United Kingdom, War Office, *Manual of Military Law*, London, 1914, p. 267.

[9]   See Lassa Oppenheim, *International Law: A Treatise*, Vol. II, *War and Neutrality*, Longmans, Green and Co., London, 1906, p. 128, and James Molony Spaight, *War Rights on Land*, Macmillan, London, 1911, p. 431 (implicitly). See also United Kingdom, War Office, *Manual of Military Law*, London, 1914, p. 267 (implicitly – 'the principle that even the enemy's dead should be given burial is generally admitted').

[10] Geneva Convention on the Wounded and Sick (1929), Article 4. In addition to the obligations repeated from the 1906 Geneva Convention, the 1929 Convention required, *inter alia*, that the dead be honourably interred, that their graves be respected and marked, and that a graves registration service be created.

[11] See the commentary on Article 4, para. 940.

'honourably interred'.[12] Honourable interment is of particular importance given that, all too often, bodies are left on the battlefield.[13] State practice confirms the obligation to ensure the actual burial or cremation of the dead.[14]

1644   The obligation to ensure that the dead are buried or cremated can be satisfied in different ways. The Party in question may itself honourably inter the deceased. Alternatively, it may return the bodies of the deceased to their families for burial or cremation. The ICRC can act as a neutral intermediary in this regard.[15] The choice of means follows from the wording of the provision, which states that the Parties 'shall ensure' the burial or cremation of the deceased rather than that the Parties 'shall bury or cremate' the deceased.

1645   The preferred option is the return of the remains of the deceased to their families so that they may bury or cremate them in accordance with their religious beliefs and practices. Another reason why this option is preferable is that it enables the families to mourn their loved ones.[16] Indeed, return of the dead to their families can be considered a basic humanitarian goal, recognized in both conventional and customary humanitarian law.[17]

1646   'Burial' is defined as 'the burying of a dead body' and 'to bury' as 'to place (a dead body) in the earth or a tomb'.[18] Burial usually involves placing the body of the deceased in a coffin or body bag, or wrapping it in a shroud, and then depositing it in the earth. 'Cremate' means to 'dispose of a dead person's body

---

[12] Geneva Convention on the Wounded and Sick (1929), Article 4.

[13] See e.g. Sophie Martin, 'The Missing', *International Review of the Red Cross*, Vol. 84, No. 848, December 2002, pp. 723–726, at 723 and 725.

[14] See e.g. Australia, *Manual of the Law of Armed Conflict*, 2006, paras 9.103–9.104 ('The minimum respect for the remains of the dead is a decent burial or cremation'); Canada, *LOAC Manual*, 2001, para. 925.5 ('Parties to the conflict shall ensure that the dead are honourably interred, if possible according to the rites of the religion to which they belong'); Croatia, *Commanders' Manual*, 1992, para. 76 ('As a rule, the dead shall be identified and buried, cremated or buried at sea individually'); Italy, *LOAC Elementary Rules Manual*, 1991, para. 76 ('As a general rule, the dead shall be... buried, cremated or buried at sea individually'); Russian Federation, *Regulations on the Application of IHL*, 2001, para. 164 ('Search for, collection, identification and burial of the dead members of the enemy armed forces as well as of other victims of armed conflicts shall be organized immediately, as soon as the situation permits, and carried out to... bury them with due dignity and respect as required by ethical principles'); Spain, *LOAC Manual*, 1996, Vol. I, para. 5.2.d.(6) ('The dead shall be buried, cremated or buried at sea as soon as the tactical situation and other circumstances permit'); Ukraine, *Manual on the Application of IHL Rules*, 2004, paras 1.4.12 ('As soon as the circumstances allow, all parties to an armed conflict shall... organize the search for the dead to... ensure their proper burial'); and United States, *Operational Law Handbook*, 1993, p. Q-185 ('The Parties must ensure proper burial.').

[15] For instance, following the conflict between Armenia and Azerbaijan in the early 1990s, the ICRC acted as a neutral intermediary in the return of the remains of the deceased. See ICRC, *Annual Report 2010*, ICRC, Geneva, 2011, p. 315.

[16] ICRC, *Accompanying the Families of Missing Persons: A Practical Handbook*, ICRC, Geneva, 2013, pp. 36, 57–58 and 134.

[17] See Additional Protocol I, Article 34(2), and ICRC Study on Customary International Humanitarian Law (2005), Rule 114.

[18] *Concise Oxford English Dictionary*, 12th edition, Oxford University Press, 2011, pp. 187 and 189.

by burning it to ashes';[19] this includes both cremation in a formal crematorium and cremation on a hand-built pyre.

1647   Although the first paragraph refers to 'burial or cremation', it is clear from the second paragraph that the two options are not equal and that the Parties to the conflict are not able to choose freely between them. Burial is the preferred option, while cremation is allowed only in exceptional circumstances.[20]

b. Individual burial or cremation

1648   Burial or cremation of the dead is to be carried out individually 'as far as circumstances permit'. This is an aspect of the requirement that the dead be honourably interred. A common grave conflicts with the sentiment of respect for the dead, yet, all too often, the dead are 'thrown pell-mell in a common grave'.[21] Although that observation was made in 1930, it remains true today. Practical reasons also favour burial in an individual grave or individual cremation. Burial in an individual grave makes possible the eventual return of the remains of the deceased to the family or home country, it facilitates any later exhumation and identification, and it avoids the disturbance of the final resting place of the other deceased. The requirement of burial in an individual grave does not preclude the interment of several bodies at the same time or in a common funeral but ensures that each body is committed separately. Individual cremation is of particular importance, as it would prove impossible otherwise to return the ashes of each deceased to their respective families.

1649   Reflecting the realities of armed conflict, the obligation of burial in an individual grave or of individual cremation is not an absolute one. Rather, it is to be fulfilled 'as far as circumstances permit'. There is thus a presumption that burial or cremation will be carried out individually, and it will be up to the Party departing from the obligation to demonstrate that circumstances did not so permit. Burial in a collective grave or collective cremation should be an exceptional measure. Use of the word 'circumstances' makes clear that the reasons for burial in a collective grave or collective cremation are not limited to military ones. Such circumstances may include the sheer number of deceased, lack of manpower and military necessity.[22] Public health grounds do not generally justify burial in a collective grave.[23] Despite the sometimes ingrained fear

---

[19] *Ibid.* p. 336.   [20] See section D.

[21] Des Gouttes, *Commentaire de la Convention de Genève de 1929 sur les blessés et malades*, ICRC, Geneva, 1930, p. 32.

[22] Wisner/Adams, p. 199 (referring to number of deaths, climatic or other constraints).

[23] Tidball-Binz, p. 426, notes:

> Research has shown that the dead, including decomposing bodies, do not spread diseases after catastrophes unless they are in direct contact with drinking water. Instead, the surviving population is the most likely source of epidemics. The unfounded belief that the dead spread diseases is swiftly disseminated by the weary public after catastrophes and is often promoted by the media and on occasions even by misled sanitary authorities. The political pressure brought about by this belief too often causes authorities to call for hasty mass burials and

that dead bodies will cause epidemics, the risk to health from dead bodies is negligible.[24]

1650   The obligation to bury or cremate the dead individually is to be construed strictly. If circumstances do 'permit' burial in an individual grave or individual cremation, that is required as a matter of legal obligation. Circumstances that merely make burial in an individual grave or individual cremation more difficult do not excuse the Parties from their obligations under the article. This will be a question of fact. Burial in a collective grave is also rendered unnecessary if facilities for temporary conservation of the bodies, such as ice, electricity or embalming fluids, are available.[25] Burial in an individual grave or individual cremation is necessarily a more onerous and time-consuming task than burial in a collective grave or collective cremation. This does not, by itself, excuse the Parties from their obligation as the obligation would then be vitiated; it only excuses the Parties if this transforms the circumstances into ones that do not permit individual burial or cremation. It is only in such cases that burial in a collective grave is permitted as it is preferable to the deceased being left on the battlefield.

1651   If the circumstances do not permit burial in an individual grave, certain requirements of burial in a common grave should be respected as an absolute minimum. The choice is not between individual burial and dumping bodies in a mass grave. The dead should be buried in a trench, in one layer only and not on top of one another; bodies should be interred at certain intervals, parallel with one another, and ideally in separate body bags or shrouds.[26] They should be 'laid out in a recognizable sequence, preferably side by side', with a marker indicating the start of the sequence. Two lists indicating the sequence should be drawn up, one being left beneath the marker, the other with the record of the grave.[27] The Party might not be able to provide a separate grave for each deceased, nor might it be able to perform individual funeral ceremonies. However, it must do

cremations of unidentified bodies and for the use of ineffective 'sanitary' measures, such as the use of masks and spraying the dead with so-called 'disinfectants', which may truly pollute water sources.
    The mismanagement of dead bodies resulting from such hasty procedures may cause serious and long-lasting mental distress to bereaved families and communities exposed to the undignified handling of their dead and left unable to mourn their loved ones.

[24] See Morgan/Tidball-Binz/van Alphen, pp. 5–6 ('The risk to the public is negligible because they do not touch dead bodies'); WHO Regional Office for South-East Asia, *Disposal of Dead Bodies in Emergency Conditions*, WHO/SEARO Technical Notes for Emergencies, Technical Note 8, p. 1 ('health-related risks are likely to be negligible'); Harvey/Baghri/Reed, p. 135 ('in the vast majority of situations, the health hazard associated with dead bodies is negligible'); and Tidball-Binz, p. 426. See also Wisner/Adams, p. 198:

    Dead or decayed human bodies do not generally create a serious health hazard, unless they are polluting sources of drinking-water with faecal matter, or are infected with plague or typhus, in which case they may be infested with the fleas or lice that spread these diseases.

[25] See Wisner/Adams, p. 199.

[26] See Tidball-Binz, p. 436, and ICRC, *Operational Best Practices Regarding the Management of Human Remains*, Annex E.

[27] ICRC, *Operational Best Practices Regarding the Management of Human Remains*, Annex H.

its utmost to ensure that subsequent exhumation and identification of every individual will be possible and that each deceased is treated with respect. Such precautions will also assist in establishing that circumstances genuinely did not permit individual burial and that the Party was not intending, rather, to hide evidence of a violation of the law or to ignore its obligations.

1652   Given that cremation is only permitted in exceptional cases,[28] and that collective burial of the dead is also exceptional, collective cremation would be justified under the law only in the rarest of circumstances. As collective cremation makes subsequent identification and the return of the ashes to the family or home country impossible, it is to be hoped that a Party to a conflict will never resort to it.

c. Personal scope of application

1653   The obligation to bury or cremate the dead is vested in the 'Parties to the conflict'. Accordingly, the Parties cannot assume that the dead will be honourably interred by other persons or entities, such as the National Red Cross or Red Crescent Society, but will have to 'ensure' that those persons or entities take on this responsibility.

1654   The phrase 'shall ensure' is employed here for the first time in the Convention. It is not new, however, having been used to introduce the same provision in the Conventions of 1929 and 1906. The verb 'to ensure' means 'to make certain that (something) will occur or be so'.[29] The compulsory nature of the obligation is reinforced by the preceding word, 'shall'. This does not mean that the Parties have to bury or cremate the dead personally; the obligation can be delegated to other persons or entities. However, if they do, the Parties are required to make certain that the obligation is fulfilled. Alternatively – and this is the preferred option – the Parties may return the bodies of the deceased to their families for burial or cremation. Accordingly, there is no justification for thinking that the task is optional. On the contrary, in calling upon the Parties to the conflict to ensure that it is carried out, the Convention is once more drawing attention to the importance of the task and to the necessity of accomplishing it.

1655   In contrast with Article 16, which refers to the dead 'of the adverse Party falling into [the] hands' of a Party to the conflict, reference in the present provision is made simply to 'the dead'. The different scope of application of the two provisions can be explained by the fact that Article 16 relates to records of the dead which are then forwarded to the other side through intermediaries.[30] There is thus no reason to include the dead of the side of the Party in question within the scope of that article, given that such records would not be forwarded

---

[28] See section D.
[29] *Concise Oxford English Dictionary*, 12th edition, Oxford University Press, 2011, p. 475.
[30] See the commentary on Article 16, section E.

to the adverse Party. Article 17, for its part, contains obligations of a different sort, namely respect for the dead, such respect being equally applicable to all the dead regardless to which Party they belong. Their differing subject matters thus explain why Article 16 refers to the dead 'of the adverse Party', whereas Article 17 refers to the dead without further qualification.[31] Likewise, Article 15, on the search for the dead, applies to the dead generally and not only to the dead of the adverse Party.[32] While it may be commonly assumed that Parties will always treat their own forces humanely, the history of international humanitarian law has proved otherwise. After all, it was concern for the wounded, sick and dead of both Parties to the Battle of Solferino that moved Henry Dunant to call for the creation of relief societies and not just one Party's treatment of those of the adverse Party.[33]

1656   The present provision is closely related to the equivalent provision in Article 120 of the Third Convention, with both provisions governing the treatment of dead combatants. Their application differs in that the present provision is essentially concerned with the dead picked up on the battlefield, whereas Article 120 of the Third Convention is essentially concerned with prisoners of war who have died in captivity. However, the substantive rules contained in the present article and in Article 120 of the Third Convention are largely the same.

2. Examination of the body prior to burial or cremation

a. The obligation

1657   The Parties to the conflict are under an obligation to ensure that bodies undergo a 'careful examination' prior to their burial or cremation.[34] The examination serves to confirm death, establish identity and enable a report to be made.

1658   The Parties to the conflict 'shall ensure' a careful examination is carried out. The phrase 'shall ensure', as used here, has the same meaning as that discussed above.[35] Accordingly, while the Parties do not have to undertake the examination themselves, referring it, for example, to a competent medical examiner outside the armed forces, they must make sure that the examination is carried out. The obligation exists regardless of whether the burial is in an individual or a common grave. The task in question is not optional. On the contrary, in calling upon the Parties to the conflict to ensure that it is carried out, the

---

[31] See also Thomas Erskine Holland, *The Laws of War on Land*, Clarendon Press, Oxford, 1908, p. 29, distinguishing between the obligations in Articles 3 and 4 of the 1906 Geneva Convention, the latter being considered to relate to the dead of the enemy alone. Article 3 of the 1906 Convention is equivalent to Article 17 of the present Convention, in relevant part, and Article 4 of the 1906 Convention to Article 16 of the present Convention.

[32] See the commentary on Article 15, para. 1511. See also Petrig, pp. 349–350.

[33] Henry Dunant, *A Memory of Solferino*, ICRC, Geneva, reprint 1986.

[34] On the meaning of 'careful', see paras 1670–1671.   [35] See para. 1654.

Convention is once more drawing attention to the importance of the task and to the necessity of accomplishing it.

b. Purpose of the examination

1659   The requirement of an examination of the body serves a particular purpose. This is evident from the language of the provision, which states that the examination is to be undertaken 'with a view to' reaching certain conclusions. The purpose is threefold: 'confirming death, establishing identity and enabling a report to be made'. Each component is important, although the last follows on from the first two.

1660   Death must be confirmed in order to avoid the terrible tragedy of burial or cremation of a person who appears to be dead but is in fact alive. The term 'dead' is thought to be self-explanatory.[36] Medically, death is understood as the permanent cessation of all vital functions of the body, including the heartbeat, brain activity, including the brain stem, and breathing.[37]

1661   The identity of the deceased is to be established with as much certainty as possible. All feasible measures must be taken in this respect.[38] They include a thorough examination of all documents and other objects found on the deceased's person. Besides examining such items, recourse must be had to other methods which will make it possible to establish the person's identity. In the past, measurements and description of the body and its physical features and examination of the teeth were the methods of choice. Since then, methods of identification have evolved considerably, and a wider range of possibilities is available today to assist Parties in complying with this obligation. These include taking photographs and/or video of the body and the face, taking prints of all the fingers, and collecting a hair sample (including the roots) for later DNA analysis.[39] However, a description of the person's physical features remains important,[40] while the more recent means of identification should be regarded as complementary. A holistic approach to identification is required,

---

[36] Petrig, p. 344.

[37] Elizabeth A. Martin (ed.), *Concise Medical Dictionary*, Oxford University Press, 8th edition, 2010.

[38] 'The Missing: Action to resolve the problem of people unaccounted for as a result of armed conflict or internal violence and to assist their families', International Conference of Governmental and Non-Governmental Experts, Geneva, 19–21 February 2003, Observations and Recommendations, Point 11.1, reproduced in *International Review of the Red Cross*, Vol. 85, No. 849, March 2003, pp. 185–193, at 185.

[39] ICRC, *Operational Best Practices Regarding the Management of Human Remains*, Annex D. See also ICRC, *Missing People, DNA Analysis and Identification of Human Remains*, 2nd edition, ICRC, Geneva, 2009.

[40] These include: sex, approximate age, height, build, skin colour, hair colour and style, facial hair, eye colour, ethnic appearance, clothing and insignia, jewellery, tattoos, birthmarks, scars, visible dental abnormalities, unusually distributed hair, nicotine staining on fingers, condition of fingernails, and obvious deformities or malformations. See ICRC, *Operational Best Practices Regarding the Management of Human Remains*, Annex I. For further practical guidance, see Tidball-Binz, pp. 430–433.

as visual recognition on its own, including through photographs, can be unreliable. Although not all Parties may have access to all forms or means of identification, the absence of a qualified forensic service or poor technical capabilities cannot excuse a Party's failure to comply with the underlying principles on which the provisions are built. Organizations such as the ICRC can also assist Parties with the development and dissemination of protocols, capacity building and the acquisition of the necessary equipment.

1662   Identification must be carried out in a manner that respects the Party's other obligations under international humanitarian law. Thus, for example, if photographs or video footage are taken of the deceased, these must not be made public or used for propaganda purposes.[41] Sensitivity is required if the images are shown to the family of the deceased.

1663   The person's identity is to be established in order to account for the missing and provide information to the families, in the light of one of the central principles of this area of the law, namely 'the right of families to know the fate of their relatives'.[42]

1664   The obligation is one of conduct, to be carried out with due diligence, rather than one of result.[43] Accordingly, failing to identify the deceased after taking all feasible measures to do so, does not constitute a violation of the article.

1665   The obligation to take all feasible measures to identify the deceased extends beyond the conclusion of the conflict. This is evident from the obligations in respect of the missing.[44]

1666   Also for reasons of identification, one half of the double identity disc, or the identity disc itself if it is a single disc, should remain on the body at all times.[45] A tag bearing a unique identifying reference number on a waterproof label should be attached to the body.[46] Both of these measures will assist with any later establishment or confirmation of identity of the deceased, for example

---

[41] See Article 13 of the Third Convention and its commentary.

[42] See Additional Protocol I, Article 32. See also Henckaerts/Doswald-Beck, commentary on Rule 117, pp. 423–426, and Elliott, p. 11, noting that 'part of the motivation for identifying the dead is to let their next of kin know their fate'. The uncertainty surrounding the fate of missing relatives causes real anguish for families. See also ICRC, *Accompanying the Families of Missing Persons: A Practical Handbook*, ICRC, Geneva, 2013, pp. 35 and 40–56.

[43] See Sassòli/Tougas, p. 731, and Petrig, p. 352. This is the case despite the seeming suggestion in the military manuals of certain States that the obligation is one of result. Examples of results-based obligations may be found in the military manuals of Argentina, Belgium, Benin, Burundi, the Central African Republic, Italy, Kenya, Madagascar, Senegal, Spain, and Togo. Military manuals indicating a conduct-based obligation include Cameroon, Canada, Cote d'Ivoire, Croatia, France, Germany, Hungary, Mexico, the Netherlands, New Zealand, Nigeria, Peru, the Philippines, Poland, the Russian Federation, Switzerland, Ukraine, the United Kingdom and the United States. See ICRC, Customary International Humanitarian Law, Practice relating to Rule 116, section A(III), available at https://www.icrc.org/customary-ihl/eng/docs/v2_rul.

[44] Additional Protocol I, Article 33 ('As soon as circumstances permit, and at the latest from the end of active hostilities.'). See also Henckaerts/Doswald-Beck, commentary on Rule 117, pp. 426–427.

[45] On the identity disc, see the commentary on Article 16, paras 1569–1574.

[46] This number must be clearly marked at ground level and mapped for future reference. See Morgan/Tidball-Binz/van Alphen, p. 22.

in the case of exhumation. The effect of this provision is that no members of the armed forces, living or dead, may be deprived of their identity disc. The fact that military authorities may thus be certain of always being able to identify their own personnel again, unless in very exceptional circumstances, should encourage those of them who have not already done so to make universal use of the identity disc, preferably a double one.

1667   A report must be made to provide a record of the confirmation of death and of the identity of the deceased or, as the case may be, of the inability to determine such identity. The report should include the means by which the individual was identified, such as through the identity papers found on the body and the information contained in them.[47] The report should also give the location of death or where the body was found, as precisely as possible, including in the form of GPS coordinates where available. This will help to prevent misidentification of the person in question as well as, at the domestic level, allow for more detail to be issued in a death certificate. Later, the place of burial – in the form of GPS coordinates or other salient markings – and the particulars of the grave will be added, so that the grave can always be found. These initial measures will enable the death to be conveyed with the least possible delay to the national information bureau, which will in turn inform the adverse Party. They will further facilitate the subsequent work of the graves registration service, one of the principal tasks of which is to group the graves and draw up lists of them.[48] The report will also enable any follow-up, such as exhumation and the possible return of the body to the family or to the home country. It might also have consequences at the domestic level, such as enabling a death certificate to be issued and, in turn, the family to receive benefits to which they are entitled.

1668   Although the article explicitly mentions only the three aforementioned purposes, examination of the body also serves other purposes. For example, it should, if possible, establish the date and time of death of the individual as accurately as possible and the cause of death, which are mentioned in Article 16. A statement of the date and time of death – or, where the date or time is only presumed, the reasons for this presumption – should be included in the report.

1669   The purposes set out in the article have implications for the nature of the examination.

c. Nature of the examination

1670 A 'careful examination' is required. Accordingly, a perfunctory examination will not suffice, nor will an examination that is designed merely to 'tick the box' that the Party in question complied with its obligations under the present

---

[47] See also Article 16 and its commentary.   [48] See section F.

article. The examination must be a genuine and thorough one that aims to serve the purposes set out in the article and discussed above.[49]

1671   The phrase a 'careful examination' has a second meaning. The body of the deceased is also to be treated with care and respect at all times – before, during and after the examination. The examination cannot result in mutilation or despoliation for example.[50] Medical or scientific experiments on the body are prohibited.[51] The examination must not be used as an opportunity to display the body to the public at large as this would be inconsistent with the requirement that the dead be 'honourably interred'.[52]

1672   The examination of the body of the deceased should be a medical one. Article 17 refers to 'a careful examination, if possible...a medical examination'. The term 'if possible' does not mean that Parties are free to choose whether or not to undertake a medical examination. Rather, it allows for situations in which a medical examination is not feasible. This may arise, for example, where there are no, or not enough, medical examiners available and burial has to take place rapidly. In many situations, a medical examination will be possible. If a military medical examiner is not available, a civilian examiner may be. If neither is available, burial may be able to be delayed until an examiner can be reached. Refrigeration, for example, allows for the temporary storage of bodies. A medical examination is important also because in most States, a death certificate can only be issued following such an examination, and a death certificate might be needed, for example for the family to receive benefits to which they are entitled.

1673   Where a medical examination is not possible, the Party to the conflict must endeavour to carry out an examination akin to a medical examination. This may be undertaken, for example, by a person who has medical training but who is not a qualified medical examiner. Certain members of the armed forces may have received instruction in how to treat bodies prior to the arrival of the forensic services,[53] and they may have to be called upon if the forensic services cannot be reached. Even if a medical examination cannot be undertaken, the Party must still seek to establish the identity of the deceased, for example by measuring and describing the body, taking photographs or video, collecting DNA samples and so on, and a report must still be made. At the very least, the Party must take all possible measures to 'maximize the chances of systematic

---

[49] See section C.2.b.

[50] On despoliation, see also the commentary on Article 15, section D.4. See also Additional Protocol I, Article 34(1) and ICRC Study on Customary International Humanitarian Law (2005), Rule 113.

[51] Pursuant to Article 50 of the First Convention, 'biological experiments' constitute grave breaches of the Convention.

[52] See Article 17(3); see also ICRC Study on Customary International Humanitarian Law (2005), Rule 115.

[53] See e.g. Colombia, *Operational Law Manual*, 2009, pp. 121–125.

evaluation of the event and identification at a later date'.[54] The report should also specify that a medical examination could not be carried out and the reasons for this. This may also allow a medical examination to be performed at a later date if appropriate.

1674   It is imperative that the examination be carried out in a timely manner. It follows from the threefold purpose of an examination that it be carried out as soon as possible following the incident leading to the death. The notion of a 'timely' examination is inherently variable and will depend on the facts at hand. Military considerations or practical difficulties may affect the timing of the examination. For example, ensuing hostilities may delay the search for the dead.[55] The terrain, the available transport, or the distance from qualified examiners may also affect the timeliness of the examination. Nonetheless, these considerations do not detract from the need for a timely examination, and unnecessary delay is to be avoided. The number of dead may also affect the timeliness of the examination. However, it does not remove in its entirety the obligation to carry out the examination.

D. Paragraph 2: Cremation of bodies

1675 Although the first paragraph refers to 'burial or cremation', it is evident from the language of Article 17(2) – '[b]odies shall not be cremated except for...' – that burial is the norm. The fact that the reasons for cremation have to be provided 'in detail', whereas no such reasons have to be provided in the case of burial, confirms this conclusion.

1676   The main reason why burial is favoured over cremation today is that the latter is irreversible. Should the family of the deceased wish to cremate their loved one, it remains possible for them to do so, even if the deceased was previously buried. It is also easier for a Party to hide violations of the law by cremation than by burial. As happened in the Second World War, the traces of crimes under international law were effaced by cremation,[56] a situation that was fresh in the minds of those attending the Diplomatic Conference.[57] Confirmation of the identity of the deceased is also rendered impossible in the case of cremation and, therefore, unidentified individuals must in no circumstances be cremated.

1677   Article 17 allows for cremation only in two limited situations, namely 'imperative reasons of hygiene' and 'for motives based on the religion of the deceased'.

1678   Historically, certain beliefs regarding hygiene may have led to the choice of cremation over burial. However, science has since proven these beliefs to

---

[54] ICRC, *Operational Best Practices Regarding the Management of Human Remains*, para. 3.2.
[55] On the search for the dead, see the commentary on Article 15, section D.4.
[56] See e.g. United Kingdom, Military Court at Hamburg, *Stalag Luft III case*, Trial, 1947.
[57] ICRC, *Report of the Commission on the Religious and Intellectual Needs of Prisoners of War and Civilian Internees of 1947*, pp. 4–5. See also Elliott, p. 11.

be unfounded. The wording of the article suggests that a high threshold must be met, for it is not simply any reason of hygiene but 'imperative' reasons of hygiene. The qualifier 'imperative' in this context indicates that the Party must be left with no other choice than to cremate. The imperative reasons of hygiene are not limited to the threat to the health of the Party alone but also to the health of, for example, civilians in the vicinity. In the past, hygiene considerations were prompted mainly by the fear of outbreaks of disease. Today, it is recognized that such concerns do not necessitate cremation rather than burial,[58] as the risk to public health from dead bodies is negligible.[59] Accordingly, based upon medical insights gained since 1949, the first situation justifying cremation rarely applies.

1679   The second exceptional situation, relating to the religion of the deceased,[60] is linked to the third paragraph, concerning the honourable interment of the dead in accordance with the rites of their religion.[61] Certain knowledge that the deceased belonged to a religion that favours cremation would militate for cremation of the body.[62] Ultimately, however, the decision of whether or not to cremate should be based on the individual's wishes, if expressed, or beliefs and not on the preferences of the Party on whose behalf the deceased was fighting. Today, many States are multicultural, so the religion of the majority may not be that of the deceased. As is clear from Article 17(2), the exception for religion relates to the religion 'of the deceased' and not to the primary religion of the State concerned or of its armed forces. It would be difficult to determine the religion of a particular individual based on physical appearance so other factors must be considered in reaching a conclusion. If the deceased's religion cannot be ascertained or the person is found to be an agnostic or an atheist, burial must be the preferred choice. Likewise, in case of doubt, the Party must err on the side of burial. All this follows from the preference expressed in the article for burial over cremation. Thus, only in limited situations will the exception for cremation based on religion apply. Even then, for the reasons mentioned above,[63] it would be preferable for the body of the deceased to be returned to the family for cremation.

---

58   Tidball-Binz, p. 435; Harvey/Baghri/Reed, p. 135 ('Health considerations alone provide no justification for cremation.').

59   ICRC, *Management of Dead Bodies after Disasters*, pp. 5–6. See also Wisner/Adams, p. 198 ('Dead or decayed human bodies do not generally create a serious health hazard, unless they are polluting sources of drinking-water with faecal matter, or are infected with plague or typhus, in which case they may be infested with the fleas or lice that spread these diseases'); WHO Regional Office for South-East Asia, *Disposal of Dead Bodies in Emergency Conditions*, p. 1 ('health-related risks are likely to be negligible'); Harvey/Baghri/Reed, p. 135 ('the health hazard associated with dead bodies is negligible'); and Claude de Ville de Goyet, 'Epidemics caused by dead bodies: a disaster myth that does not want to die', *Pan-American Journal of Public Health*, Vol. 15, No. 5, May 2004, pp. 297–299.

60   The phrase '*motives* based on the religion of the deceased' (emphasis added) simply means *reasons* based on the religion of the deceased.

61   See section E.1.

62   For a list of religions and their preferences for burial or cremation, see Froidevaux, pp. 800–801.

63   See para. 1645.

1680   A third exceptional situation exists, although the article does not mention it explicitly, namely the wish to be cremated expressed by the individual, not necessarily motivated by religious reasons.[64] The reason why there is no mention of this additional exception in this article, unlike in the Third Convention, is likely to be because it was felt that the present provision was essentially concerned with the dead picked up on the battlefield. Nonetheless, the situation can arise even in respect of the First Convention, for example when a person expresses the desire to be cremated shortly before passing away on the battlefield or on the way to medical treatment. In such cases, the Party to the conflict may choose to respect the wish of the deceased. It is imperative that the person's wish be explicit. Certain safeguards should also be in place to ensure that the wish is freely expressed. This may take the form of an independent witness or the desire expressed in writing by the deceased, although these will not always be to hand. Again, in such a situation, it would be preferable for the body of the deceased to be returned to the family to perform the cremation.

1681   If the deceased is cremated, Article 17 requires that the circumstances surrounding the cremation and the reasons for cremation be given. This requirement demonstrates the exceptional nature of cremation. The circumstances and reasons are to be provided 'in detail'. Accordingly, it will not suffice to specify solely that the reason for cremation was the 'religion of the deceased'. Rather, the various factors that led to the finding of the religion of the deceased need to be spelled out. This also applies in the case of the wish of the individual; indeed, a greater level of detail would be expected to be provided in such a case. Sufficient detail should be given to satisfy the Party's obligations under the article and to provide information to the adverse Party and the family of the deceased. The level of detail will vary according to the situation. The circumstances and reasons are to be provided 'in the death certificate or on the authenticated list of the dead'. If the wish was manifested in writing, this should be appended to the death certificate or enclosed with the authenticated list of the dead.

E. Paragraph 3: Honourable interment

1682 Article 17(3) contains a number of related obligations for the Parties. First, they must ensure that the dead are honourably interred, if possible according to the rites of the religion to which they belonged. Second, they have certain obligations in respect of the graves, namely to ensure they are respected, grouped if possible according to the nationality of the deceased, and maintained and marked. To fulfil the second set of obligations, the Parties must organize, 'at the commencement of hostilities', an official graves registration service, which has specific functions.

---

[64] See Article 120(5) of the Third Convention, in which the exception can be found alongside the two mentioned in the present article.

1. Honourable interment

1683   The Parties to the conflict shall ensure that the dead are honourably interred. This obligation constitutes the minimum respect for the remains of the deceased,[65] and is of long standing.[66] The language 'shall ensure' has been discussed above and applies equally here.[67]

1684   The obligation to inter the dead honourably is an absolute one. It has both positive and negative aspects. Parties must respect the body of the deceased, the burial site and the interment ceremony. This includes, for example, choosing an appropriate site for burial if the body of the deceased is not returned to the family.[68] It also prohibits the deliberate contamination of the site and offensive acts on the site, such as littering or urination. It prohibits burial of the deceased with, for example, items that may be considered offensive to the deceased such as the insignia of the adverse Party. It involves respecting and not disrupting the interment ceremony, for example observing a minute's silence if that is a feature of the ceremony. The Party must also ensure that other persons respect the interment process.

1685   Criminal prosecutions have been brought for preventing the honourable burial of the dead.[69]

1686   The interment is to take place, if possible, according to the rites of the religion to which the deceased belonged. The inclusion of the phrase 'if possible' confirms that this obligation is not an absolute one; the situation may preclude the interment of the dead in this manner. However, as indicated above where the phrase is discussed in greater detail,[70] the language 'if possible' also makes clear that the Parties are not given a free choice in the matter. Where interment according to the rites of the religion of the deceased is 'possible', Parties must act accordingly. Nonetheless, in certain situations, it will not be possible. It may not be possible to ascertain the religion to which the deceased belonged. If it can be ascertained, the Party may not be able to locate an appropriate

---

[65] See e.g. Australia, *Manual of the Law of Armed Conflict*, 2006, paras 9.103–9.104.

[66] Elliott, p. 10, describes it as being present 'from antiquity and recognized as part of the law of nature'.

[67] See para. 1654.

[68] The 'Checklist on the emergency or temporary burial of human remains' also provides:

> There should be soil in which to bury the remains; The soil should be well drained and due consideration should be given to avoiding contamination of the water table (this might include sprinkling lime in the grave); The site should be easily reached by vehicles; The site should not be in a strategically or tactically significant area; The site should be located at a reasonable distance from sources of water for human consumption, in order to prevent those sources from being contaminated.

> ICRC, *Operational Best Practices Regarding the Management of Human Remains*, Annex H. Although disregard for these factors cannot be considered a dishonourable burial, they should be respected as far as possible.

[69] United States, Military Commission at the Mariana Islands, *Yochio and others case*, Trial, 1946.

[70] See para. 1672.

religious figure or a necessary component of the rite.[71] In such a case, the Party may well be able to comply with certain aspects of the rites of the religion but not others, for example the saying of a prayer, or burial facing a particular direction. A religious figure may preside over the burial, even if not of the religion of the deceased; if no religious figure is available, another individual may preside over the burial.[72] Accordingly, the phrase 'if possible' is to be read as meaning 'as far as possible', demonstrating that it is not a choice between all of the rites of the religion to which the deceased belonged and none of them.

2. Graves

1687 The Parties have particular obligations in respect of the graves of the deceased. A grave is understood to be 'a hole dug in the ground to receive a coffin or corpse',[73] and thus relates to that part of the earth that houses the deceased – or part of the remains of the deceased if, for example, the body does not consist of a single whole. It is not limited to formal burial grounds, such as a cemetery. Collective graves fit this description as much as individual ones do. As is evident from the definition, the earth in question must house the remains of the deceased. Thus, an empty tomb does not constitute a grave, whereas a monument containing the bones of a deceased does. If a monument and a grave together form a single whole, the entire object must be treated as a grave.[74] Likewise, a temporary grave from which the deceased has been removed does not constitute a grave as from the time of removal.[75] This does not mean that that site should not be afforded certain special treatment, for example a prohibition on building on the site; however, that is a matter for domestic law.

a. Respect for graves

1688 The Parties to the conflict are to ensure that the graves are 'respected'. This can be derived from the obligation to respect the dead. The principle of unqualified respect for fallen enemies holds good even after death.

1689 The obligation to ensure respect for the graves has both negative and positive components. The Parties themselves must not disrespect the graves, a point that applies also to all entities and individuals whose conduct can be

---

[71] Examples given during the drafting of the equivalent article in the Third Convention were the use of a rare substance and the sacrifice of an animal. ICRC, 'Rapport sur les travaux de la Commission constituée pour étudier les dispositions conventionnelles relatives aux besoins religieux et intellectuels des prisonniers de guerre et des civils internés', *Revue internationale de la Croix-Rouge et Bulletin international des Sociétés de la Croix-Rouge*, Vol. 29, No. 341, May 1947, pp. 399–421, at 402.

[72] ICRC, *Operational Best Practices Regarding the Management of Human Remains*, Annex H.

[73] *Concise Oxford English Dictionary*, 12th edition, Oxford University Press, 2011, p. 622.

[74] See also Petrig, p. 345. Each case will have to be judged on its facts.

[75] But see *ibid.* considering it 'sufficient that the gravesite contained some mortal remains at some point in time'.

attributed to the Parties. This prohibits such actions as vandalizing or removing headstones, razing or dismantling gravesites, and disinterring bodies, unless exhumation is authorized by international humanitarian law.[76] Importantly, the article does not limit this obligation to the Parties' own conduct; rather, they are obliged to 'ensure' that the graves of the dead are respected.[77] Consequently, the Parties must take measures to prevent other persons or entities from disrespecting the graves. This obligation includes such actions as adopting legislation protecting graves and taking measures to ensure the security of graves, for example by constructing a security perimeter, particularly during and immediately after a conflict, when tensions may remain high.

1690   One aspect of respecting the graves is specifically mentioned in the article, namely maintenance.[78]

b. Grouping of graves

1691   The Parties are to ensure that the graves are 'grouped if possible according to the nationality of the deceased'. The obligation has two aspects: the obligation to group the graves and, if possible, to group them according to the nationality of the deceased. Of the two aspects, it is the grouping of the graves that is the more important. This is demonstrated by the inclusion of the words 'if possible' in relation to the manner in which the graves are to be grouped. The provision was aimed at avoiding the hasty roadside burials which were so frequent a feature of the wars that were fought immediately prior to the Diplomatic Conference of 1949. Grouping of graves is thus related to respect for the dead and an honourable interment, transforming a stretch of land into a cemetery rather than a series of ad hoc individual graves. It also facilitates later exhumation.

1692   The second aspect refers to the manner in which the graves are to be grouped: if possible according to the nationality of the deceased. Grouping on the basis of nationality is the one which military authorities will most naturally select. Grouping in this manner will make it possible for countries to pay collective tribute to their dead at a later date. It also assists with later exhumations and the return of remains to the home country.[79] The phrase 'if possible' makes clear that the obligation is not an absolute one but will depend on the situation at hand. Military considerations or the sheer number of bodies may make grouping according to nationality impossible. Likewise, the Parties may be unable to identify the nationality of the deceased, for example in a conflict with numerous Parties and where the bodies could not be identified.

1693   Grouping according to nationality is particularly important in the case of burial in a collective grave. As burial in a collective grave is allowed only where

---

[76] On the last point, see Additional Protocol I, Article 34(4).
[77] For a discussion of the term 'shall ensure', see para. 1654.   [78] See section E.2.c.
[79] See Additional Protocol I, Article 34.

circumstances do not permit individual burial,[80] time will likely be a key factor. Nonetheless, there may be situations in which time does not allow for individual burial but does allow for grouping according to the nationality of the deceased.

c. Maintenance and marking of graves

1694 The Parties shall ensure that the graves are 'properly maintained and marked so that they may always be found'. The Parties are thus under two distinct but interrelated obligations: the obligation properly to maintain graves and the obligation to mark graves. The two are also linked to the broader obligation to respect the graves. If graves are not properly maintained, for example by being allowed to become overgrown with vegetation, the presence of the grave may be obscured, making respect for the grave more difficult. Proper maintenance also means that headstones must be repaired or replaced if necessary. Likewise, if a grave is not marked, it would be difficult to ensure respect for it as it might not be identifiable as a grave.

1695 In addition, the article provides that the graves be marked so that they 'may always be found'. Thus, name plates on graves must be maintained and must not be removed. Physical marking of the grave is important given that memories fade with the passage of time and what was once known to be a grave may later be forgotten.[81] That graves may always be found is also important for future exhumations,[82] which may take place years or decades after the burial. Proper marking of a grave is also necessary so that the family may visit it.[83]

1696 The brief reference in the article to the matter of marking gives no exact indication of what the marking should be. The essential point is that it should always be possible to find the grave. A mere number or group of symbols on the marker, corresponding to the particulars in the record, is hardly enough for the purpose, for the record may be destroyed. The reference number in the record can, and should, appear on the gravestone; but it is essential that the surname (family name) and first names and, if possible, the date of birth and date of death should also figure in the inscription. This is all the more essential in the case of common graves. The information should be inscribed in such a way as to be indelible and non-perishable in order to withstand the vagaries of the weather.

1697 All the above provisions, adapted accordingly, apply equally to ashes, as stated in the last sentence of the paragraph, which is discussed below.[84]

1698 Reference in the paragraph to the maintenance and marking of graves so that they 'may always be found' indicates that the obligation persists after the cessation of hostilities. The paragraph does not specify for how long the

---

[80] See section C.1.b.
[81] See also ICRC Study on Customary International Humanitarian Law (2005), Rule 116, which links the marking of the location of the grave with the identification of the dead.
[82] On which, see Additional Protocol I, Article 34.   [83] See *ibid.*   [84] See section E.3.c.

obligation continues. As the requirement of marking and maintaining gravesites involves financial expenditure, particularly where there are a great many deceased on the territory, the State on whose territory the graves are located cannot be expected to bear the cost ad infinitum for the maintenance of the graves of foreign nationals. Article 34 of Additional Protocol I sets out a procedure for this and, in the practice relating to the maintenance of graves, little differentiation is made between graves in respect of which the Protocol applies and graves in respect of which it does not. Agreements have been concluded on the subject in respect of conflicts that ended before the entry into force of the Protocol.[85] Furthermore, graves commissions tend to maintain graves from a variety of conflicts.[86]

3. Graves registration service

a. Creation of an official graves registration service

1699 In order to facilitate the fulfilment of the obligations described above, the Parties must establish an official graves registration service. Such a service may be vested in the armed forces; it may be another part of government; or it may take the form of a non-governmental entity.[87] If the last, it needs to be 'official' in the sense of being created by the Party to the conflict or having sufficient connections with the Party to be able to carry out its functions, and the State would remain responsible for it. The graves registration service need not be called a 'graves registration service' in order to be one. However, it must carry out the functions set out in the article, and the Party as well as other Parties should be aware that, although named differently, it is the equivalent of the graves registration service envisaged in the article.

1700 In practice, the majority of States have permanent military graves services which are responsible in peacetime for the maintenance of the graves of members of armed forces who have fallen in battle. After all, the obligation was first

---

[85] See e.g. Agreement concerning the Treatment of War Graves of Members of the UK Armed Forces in the German Democratic Republic, Berlin, 27 April 1987, relating to war graves resulting from the First and Second World Wars; Agreement between the Government of the USSR and the Government of Japan regarding persons who were detained in prisoner-of-war camps, Tokyo, 18 April 1991; and Agreement between the Russian Federation and the Government of the Republic of Turkey on Russian burial sites on the territory of the Republic of Turkey and Turkish burial sites on the territory of the Russian Federation, Istanbul, 3 December 2012. See also Agreement between the Russian Federation and the Government of the Republic of Hungary to perpetuate the memory of the fallen soldiers and civilian victims of war and the status of graves, Moscow, 6 March 1995, which refers to and applies the provisions of the Geneva Conventions and Additional Protocols to military personnel killed during the First and Second World Wars and the inter-war period.

[86] See the commentary on Article 34 of Additional Protocol I.

[87] Bothe, p. 316, gives as examples the tasks being carried out by ministerial departments in France and Italy, an agency of the executive branch of the Federal Government in the United States, and a private body in Germany charged with this task by the State.

contained in the 1929 Geneva Convention on the Wounded and Sick.[88] These services are very well equipped, and are in a position on the outbreak of hostilities either to take over themselves the maintenance and listing of enemy graves or to form a special section for the purpose. Although States are free to decide how to implement this obligation, in view of the specialized nature of the duties involved, the military authorities should entrust the work to individuals or organizations familiar with it rather than set up new bodies which may not have the desired experience or competence.

1701   According to Article 17(3), the graves registration service is to be established 'at the commencement of hostilities'. In certain circumstances, the Parties ought to establish the graves registration service even prior to the commencement of hostilities, such as following a declaration of war.[89] Persons may be killed at any time, resulting in obligations for the Parties in respect of those deceased also at any time. In light of the functions of the service, it is too late to establish it part way through the conflict or, worse, at the conclusion of the conflict. For this reason, there is a practical need to make preparations for a graves registration service in peacetime.

1702   The article does not stipulate an end date for the operations of the graves registration service. Given its functions, it is evident that the service does not – indeed cannot – cease to exist at the conclusion of the conflict. Exhumation and possible repatriation of bodies may take place more frequently after a conflict than during it. For this reason, graves registration services created during the First World War, such as the Commonwealth War Graves Commission (previously the Imperial War Graves Commission) exist to this day. This does not mean, however, that services are intended to carry out their functions ad infinitum. The temporal considerations discussed above apply here.[90]

1703   The article provides for specific functions of the graves registration service, namely to allow exhumations, ensure identification of bodies and facilitate possible transportation of the body to the home country. The functions of the service are also linked to the obligations of the Parties in respect of the graves, discussed above.[91]

b. Functions of the graves registration service

1704 The graves registration service has two sets of functions. The first set relates to the obligations of the Parties discussed above, namely to ensure respect for the graves, their grouping, and their proper maintenance and marking so that they may always be found. Hence, the article provides that it is '[f]or this purpose' that an official graves registration service must be created. During the conflict, the service will prove important for all three of this set of functions;

---

[88] Geneva Convention on the Wounded and Sick (1929), Article 4.
[89] On the concept of declared war, see the commentary on common Article 2, section D.1.
[90] See para. 1698.   [91] See section E.2.

after the conflict is over, as time passes, the last of these functions will take precedence. The service thus has to mark clearly any graves which have not yet been marked or which have been marked inadequately. It also has to maintain a list showing the exact location and markings of the graves, which will be exchanged with the equivalent list maintained by the graves registration service of the adverse Party.[92]

1705   During the 1949 Diplomatic Conference, a proposal was made to add further details to the duties of the graves registration service. In particular, it was proposed that the service would be tasked with 'record[ing] particulars of all cremations and burials including the location of graves'.[93] The proposal was not adopted as it was thought that the duties of the service were 'already clearly implied by the very name of the Service'.[94] Either way, it is evident that recording particulars of cremations and burials, including the location of graves constitutes an important function of the service.

1706   The second set of functions is noted in the context of the creation of the graves registration service. These functions are also threefold, namely to allow subsequent exhumations, to ensure the identification of the bodies and to assist in the possible transportation to the home country. Exhumations of the buried may take place at a later date, for example to confirm the identity of the individual or to repatriate the remains. It will be important to have a centralized body that can assist with such exhumation. The service is also to ensure the identification of the body. As identification should have taken place at the time of the examination of the body,[95] the service will be responsible primarily for keeping track of any change in the burial site or the transfer of the body.

1707   Both the function of subsequent exhumation and the function of identifying the bodies arise 'whatever the site of the graves'. Although an ambiguous reference, the phrase is merely an updating of the 1929 Convention, which contained the associated phrase 'whatever may be the subsequent site of the grave'.[96] This, together with the phrase 'dead interred in their cemeteries and elsewhere' in the subsequent paragraph of the 1929 Convention, reveals that the phrase is intended to cover bodies that are buried in graves other than in cemeteries, that is to say all graves.

1708   Lastly, the service is to assist in the possible transportation of the body to the home country. This allusion to the possible return of bodies was introduced for the first time at the Diplomatic Conference. Certain delegations at the Conference proposed making the provision imperative; others wished to omit it altogether.[97] It is the custom in some countries to bring the dead home at the

---

92 See section F.
93 *Final Record of the Diplomatic Conference of Geneva of 1949*, Vol. II-A, p. 155 (United Kingdom).
94 *Ibid.* (Netherlands).   95 See section C.2.b.
96 Geneva Convention on the Wounded and Sick (1929), Article 4.
97 See *Final Record of the Diplomatic Conference of Geneva of 1949*, Vol. II-A, pp. 154–155.

close of hostilities, while others prefer to have them buried in the actual theatre where they have fallen. To satisfy both customs, the clause was left optional and the wording 'possible return' used. Article 34 of Additional Protocol I contains further provisions on the return of the remains of the deceased.[98]

1709   Agreements have been concluded to allow graves registration services to carry out these functions.[99]

c. Treatment to be afforded to ashes

1710 In light of the possibility in certain circumstances of cremation rather than burial of the dead, Article 17 also provides for the treatment to be afforded to the ashes of the cremated. As stated in the final sentence of the paragraph, the foregoing provisions apply also in respect of the ashes. The ashes are to be kept by the graves registration service until their proper disposal in accordance with the wishes of the home country.

1711   Until such time as this can be ascertained, the ashes are to be treated with the same respect as the buried given the equivalence, in this regard, between burial and cremation. This means, for example, that the ashes must be collected, preferably in urns. They are to be stored in an appropriate place with suitable surroundings and not be discarded or forgotten about. Given that the article provides for the keeping of the ashes until their proper disposal, the service must not scatter the ashes. The ashes must also be protected against sacrilege of any kind and from the climate. They must be clearly marked to denote their contents as ashes and with all the particulars for which provision is made in the case of graves.

1712   Although the article refers to the proper disposal of the ashes in accordance with 'the wishes of the home country', wherever possible the home country should take into account the wishes of the family of the deceased. Indeed, the equivalent provision of the Fourth Convention provides that the ashes 'shall be transferred as soon as possible to the next of kin on their request',[100] and such a position ought to be adopted also in this context.

---

[98] See the commentary on Article 34 of Additional Protocol I.
[99] See e.g. Panmunjom Armistice Agreement (1953), Article II(13):

> The Commanders of the opposing sides shall: . . . f. In those cases where places of burial are a matter of record and graves are actually found to exist, permit graves registration personnel of the other side to enter, within a definite time limit after this armistice agreement becomes effective, the territory of Korea under their military control, for the purpose of proceeding to such graves to recover and evacuate the bodies of the deceased military personnel of that side, including deceased prisoners of war.

> For further analysis, see the commentary on Article 34 of Additional Protocol I.

[100] Fourth Convention, Article 130. Although the term used is 'next of kin', it refers to the general notion of the family of the deceased and is not limited to the stricter meaning of closest immediate relative. See also Article 34(2)(c) of Additional Protocol I and its commentary.

F. Paragraph 4: Exchange of lists showing the location and marking of graves

1713 The graves registration services of the Parties to the conflict are to exchange 'lists showing the exact location and markings of the graves together with particulars of the dead interred therein'. The 1929 Convention provided only for the exchange of 'the list of graves and of dead interred'.[101] This was not sufficiently explicit and lists giving only these particulars would undoubtedly have been incomplete, and would not always have made it possible to locate the exact site of a particular grave or to identify the body contained in it. Accordingly, the present article provides that the lists must show the 'exact' location and markings of the graves. This may be assisted by the provision of maps, GPS coordinates and the like. The particulars of the dead are those mentioned in Article 16 of the First Convention.

1714   Article 17 sought to provide more information on the graves and the dead interred in them to the adverse Party than the 1929 Convention. It did not seek to limit the information to be provided. Accordingly, any other pertinent information, such as the report drawn up following the examination of the body of the deceased,[102] should also be provided. Indeed, during the latter part of the Second World War, '[a] regular exchange of photographs of graves was established'.[103]

1715   The exchange of lists is to take place through the information bureaux mentioned in Article 16(2) of the First Convention, i.e. each Party's information bureau for prisoners of war.[104] Although the word 'exchange' is used, suggesting that there should be a simultaneous handing over of information, there is no reason why the communication of these particulars should take the form of an exchange in the strict sense of the word. There would not appear to be any necessity for them to be communicated simultaneously by the Parties. Indeed, the handing over of information other than in a simultaneous manner is to be encouraged given that international humanitarian law does not operate on the basis of *de jure* reciprocity and the failure of one side to live up to its obligations does not excuse the other side from complying therewith. Likewise, reference to the information bureau in the article does not mean that, should one side not establish one, the relevant information cannot be exchanged. For example, it has also been done through the intermediary of the ICRC.

1716   The exchange is to take place '[a]s soon as circumstances permit, and at latest at the end of hostilities'. Reference in the article to 'as soon as circumstances permit' confirms that the obligation is a pressing one, owing to the right of

---

[101] Geneva Convention on the Wounded and Sick (1929), Article 4.
[102] This report is discussed in para. 1667.
[103] ICRC, *Report of the International Committee of the Red Cross on its Activities during the Second World War (September 1, 1939–June 30, 1947), Volume I: General Activities*, ICRC, Geneva, May 1948, p. 303.
[104] For more details, see Article 122 of the Third Convention.

the families to know the fate of their relatives,[105] the desire of the Parties to know the whereabouts of their personnel, and the obligations of the Parties in relation to the missing.[106] At the same time, the clause recognizes that the exigencies of the conflict might make the immediate exchange of lists impossible. For example, the sheer number of deceased may require the graves registration service to focus its attention on the grouping and marking of graves. Such exigencies no longer exist once hostilities are over, and the article provides for this with its statement that the lists must be exchanged 'at latest at the end of hostilities'. The term 'the end of hostilities' is ambiguous but refers to the cessation of hostilities rather than the conclusion of hostilities. The equivalent provision in the 1929 Convention states explicitly '[a]fter the cessation of hostilities',[107] and the wording of the 1949 Convention was intended only to reflect the fact that exchanges could take place during hostilities, as was the case during the Second World War,[108] and was not limited to the aftermath of the hostilities. Furthermore, the exigencies of the situation following the cessation of hostilities would likely make the exchange of lists possible.

1717   The exchange of lists is not a one-off obligation; rather, it is an ongoing obligation. In practice, lists are provided by the Parties, or requested by the ICRC, as soon as it is known that a person has died.

Select bibliography

Bothe, Michael, 'War Graves', in Rudolf Bernhardt (ed.), *Encyclopedia of Public International Law*, Vol. 4, North-Holland Publishing Company, Amsterdam, 2000, pp. 1373–1374.

Capdevila, Luc and Voldman, Danièle (eds), *War Dead: Western Societies and the Casualties of War*, Edinburgh University Press, 2006.

Elliott, H. Wayne, 'The Third Priority: The Battlefield Dead', *Army Lawyer*, July 1996, pp. 3–20.

Froidevaux, Sylvain, 'L'humanitaire, le religieux et la mort', *International Review of the Red Cross*, Vol. 84, No. 848, December 2002, pp. 785–801.

Gavshon, Daniela, 'The Dead', in Andrew Clapham, Paola Gaeta and Marco Sassòli (eds), *The 1949 Geneva Conventions: A Commentary*, Oxford University Press, 2015, pp. 277–296.

Harvey, Peter, Baghri, Sohrab and Reed, Bob, *Emergency Sanitation: Assessment and Programme Design*, Water, Engineering and Development Centre, Loughborough University, 2002.

---

[105] See Additional Protocol I, Article 32; see also Henckaerts/Doswald-Beck, commentary on Rule 117, pp. 423–426.

[106] See Additional Protocol I, Article 33; see also ICRC Study on Customary International Humanitarian Law (2005), Rule 117.

[107] Geneva Convention on the Wounded and Sick (1929), Article 4.

[108] See *Report of the Preliminary Conference of National Societies of 1946*, p. 24, and *Report of the Conference of Government Experts of 1947*, p. 20.

Henckaerts, Jean-Marie and Doswald-Beck, Louise, *Customary International Humanitarian Law, Volume I: Rules*, ICRC/Cambridge University Press, 2005, available at https://www.icrc.org/customary-ihl/eng/docs/v1.

ICRC, *Operational Best Practices Regarding the Management of Human Remains and Information on the Dead by Non-Specialists*, ICRC, Geneva, 2004.

Morgan, Oliver, Tidball-Binz, Morris and van Alphen, Dana (eds), *Management of Dead Bodies after Disasters: A Field Manual for First Responders*, Pan American Health Organization/World Health Organization/ICRC/International Federation of Red Cross and Red Crescent Societies, Geneva, 2009.

Petrig, Anna, 'The war dead and their gravesites', *International Review of the Red Cross*, Vol. 91, No. 874, June 2009, pp. 341–369.

Sassòli, Marco and Tougas, Marie-Louise, 'The ICRC and the missing', *International Review of the Red Cross*, Vol. 84, No. 848, December 2002, pp. 727–750.

Tidball-Binz, Morris, 'Managing the dead in catastrophes: guiding principles and practical recommendations for first responders', *International Review of the Red Cross*, Vol. 89, No. 866, June 2007, pp. 421–442.

Wisner, Benjamin and Adams, John (eds), *Environmental health in emergencies and disasters: A practical guide*, World Health Organization, Geneva, 2002.

ROLE OF THE POPULATION

❖ Text of the provision*

(1) The military authorities may appeal to the charity of the inhabitants voluntarily to collect and care for, under their direction, the wounded and sick, granting persons who have responded to this appeal the necessary protection and facilities. Should the adverse Party take or retake control of the area, he shall likewise grant these persons the same protection and the same facilities.

(2) The military authorities shall permit the inhabitants and relief societies, even in invaded or occupied areas, spontaneously to collect and care for wounded or sick of whatever nationality. The civilian population shall respect these wounded and sick, and in particular abstain from offering them violence.

(3) No one may ever be molested or convicted for having nursed the wounded or sick.

(4) The provisions of the present Article do not relieve the occupying Power of its obligation to give both physical and moral care to the wounded and sick.

❖ Reservations or declarations

None

Contents

* Paragraph numbers have been added for ease of reference.

A. Introduction

1718   Article 18 contains the kernel of Henry Dunant's idea for civilians to take action to assist and care for wounded and sick members of the armed forces, whether in response to an appeal by the military commander or spontaneously. Since the adoption of the first Geneva Convention in 1864, the provision of medical care by military medical personnel in armed conflict has become more sophisticated and regimented in many places, to the extent that such individual civilian assistance may seem less likely to be needed. At the same time, the capacity of local organizations to respond effectively to needs in emergencies is gaining recognition.[1] Under Article 18, the possibility thus remains for a military commander to appeal to civilians or relief societies to help care for wounded or sick military personnel.

1719   The right of local civilians and relief societies present in the territory to tend to wounded or sick combatants on their own initiative was reaffirmed in 1949 and extended in 1977, in Article 17 of Additional Protocol I, to the right to provide care to wounded or sick civilians. A Party to the conflict must consider these options when taking 'all possible measures' to search for and collect the wounded and sick and in ensuring that they receive the medical care their condition requires.[2] The two options enshrined in Article 18 – to request assistance from civilians and to permit civilians or civilian organizations to provide assistance spontaneously – are reiterated in some military manuals and armed forces training materials, often without specifying whether the persons to be cared for are military or civilian.[3]

---

[1] The effectiveness of local organizations in addressing needs generated by disasters and situations of armed conflict has been acknowledged in a number of reports. See e.g. Tsunami Evaluation Coalition, *Joint evaluation of the international response to the Indian Ocean tsunami: Synthesis Report*, July 2006, pp. 91–92 and 110–111; United Kingdom (Lord Ashdown), *Humanitarian Emergency Response Review*, July 2011, pp. 33–34.

[2] First Convention, Articles 12 and 15.

[3] See e.g. Argentina, *Law of War Manual*, 1969, para. 3.006; Cameroon, *Instructor's Manual*, 1992, p. 96, and *Instructor's Manual*, 2006, p. 81, para. 401; Canada, *LOAC Manual*, 2001, para. 906.1; Germany, *Military Manual*, 1992, para. 632; Kenya, *LOAC Manual*, 1997, Précis No. 3, p. 11;

1720   Civilians are under a direct obligation not to harm the wounded and sick. By the same token, carers may not be harmed or harassed for coming to the assistance of the wounded and sick. In contemporary situations, the principle enshrined in Article 18 serves as a reminder to military authorities or Parties to the conflict that civilians will often rush to help wounded survivors of an attack and have a right to do so; the presence of these rescuers must be taken into account in subsequent attacks.

B. Historical background

1721   The principle that no wounded or sick combatant should be left on the battlefield for lack of personnel to care for them was a central element of the very first Geneva Convention of 1864. Article 5 of that Convention permitted and encouraged the local population to come to the aid of wounded and sick combatants.[4] With some modifications, this notion has been maintained in all subsequent versions of the Geneva Conventions on the Wounded and Sick,[5] including in the present article, and is reaffirmed in Article 17 of Additional Protocol I.

1722   However, early controversy about the utility of such aid providers, in terms of both efficacy and risks, almost led to the deletion of the article and, some argue, to the demise of the fledgling red cross initiative.[6] Article 5 of the 1864 Convention provided for certain protections and immunities for spontaneous rescuers that were reportedly abused during the Franco-Prussian War. Some people were said to have set up fake ambulances and hospitals in order to benefit from the protection of the emblem and escape their obligations to billet troops or pay war taxes, while others, wearing the emblem on their arms,

---

New Zealand, *Military Manual*, 1992, para. 1003(4); Russian Federation, *Military Manual*, 1990, para. 15; Switzerland, *Basic Military Manual*, 1987, Article 75; Turkey, LOAC Manual, 2001, p. 70; and United Kingdom, Military Manual, 1958, para. 345, and Manual of the Law of Armed Conflict, 2004, para. 7.38.1. In its Law of War Deskbook, 2012, p. 47, the United States warns against treating wounded or sick civilians differently from wounded or sick combatants in practice, even though it might not recognize this as a legal obligation, it not being currently party to Additional Protocol I. The manual also reiterates the voluntary participation of the local population in relief efforts.

[4]   Geneva Convention (1864), Article 5:

Inhabitants of the country who bring help to the wounded shall be respected and shall remain free. Generals of the belligerent Powers shall make it their duty to notify the inhabitants of the appeal made to their humanity, and of the neutrality which humane conduct will confer. The presence of any wounded combatant receiving shelter and care in a house shall ensure its protection. An inhabitant who has given shelter to the wounded shall be exempted from billeting and from a portion of such war contributions as may be levied.

[5]   Geneva Convention (1906), Article 5; Geneva Convention on the Wounded and Sick (1929), Article 5.

[6]   Hutchinson, pp. 126–133. See also Charles Sperry, 'The Revision of the Geneva Convention, 1906', *Proceedings of the American Political Science Association*, Vol. 3, 1907, p. 37. The preparatory documents for the 1906 Diplomatic Conference to revise the 1864 Convention recommended that Article 5 be deleted, and a motion to this effect was made during the conference. *Proceedings of the Geneva Diplomatic Conference of 1906*, pp. 17 and 161.

pillaged the wounded on the battlefield under the pretext of searching for them.[7] Meanwhile, the apparently successful organization of aid for the wounded and sick under the military authority on the Prussian side suggested that militarily organized action led to better results – and better care – than an appeal to kind-hearted but ill-trained and poorly equipped civilian charity.[8]

1723   The delegates to the Diplomatic Conference in 1906 thought that deleting the article entirely, as had been proposed in the light of the abuses encountered, would not send the right message.[9] Thus, the concerns raised were addressed in the 1906 and 1929 Conventions by making civilian assistance subject to military supervision and control and by limiting the immunities or incentives granted to persons responding to an appeal for assistance.[10] Moreover, new rules governing the use of the emblem were set out in detail and a prohibition on misuse or abuse of the emblem was added.[11] At the same time, medical assistance provided within the armed forces to the wounded and sick became increasingly professionalized, reducing reliance on civilian assistance more generally.

1724   The experience of the Second World War reinforced the utility of the principle enshrined in Article 5 of the 1929 Geneva Convention on the Wounded and Sick. It even illustrated that in some respects it did not go far enough, as demonstrated by the plight of the crews of aircraft that were shot down and of wounded parachutists who fell into enemy territory. Two key elements were felt to be missing: first, that enemy or occupying authorities must also recognize the 'neutrality' of civilians assisting the wounded and sick; and second, that civilians and relief societies should be allowed to provide care 'spontaneously' to the wounded and sick.[12] Article 18 of the 1949 First Convention addresses these shortcomings.

C. Paragraph 1: Appeal to the charity of the inhabitants

1725 Parties to a conflict have an obligation to take 'all possible measures' to search for and collect wounded and sick members of armed forces and to care for

---

[7] Hutchinson, pp. 109–117.

[8] *Ibid.* pp. 117–138. Other commentators argued that changes in the way battles were fought made it unlikely that civilians would be in a position to undertake such roles. See Auguste-Raynald Werner, *La Croix-Rouge et les conventions de Genève : Analyse et synthèse juridiques*, Geneva, Georg & Cie, 1943, pp. 194–195.

[9] See also *Proceedings of the Geneva Diplomatic Conference of 1906*, pp. 182–184 and 198–200.

[10] Geneva Convention (1906), Article 5; Geneva Convention on the Wounded and Sick (1929), Article 5. See also *Proceedings of the Geneva Diplomatic Conference of 1906*, pp. 182–184 and 198–200.

[11] See Geneva Convention (1906), Articles 18–23, and Geneva Convention on the Wounded and Sick (1929), Articles 19–24.

[12] These elements are evident from statements made during the expert meetings held to prepare the new conventions for the Diplomatic Conference, although no detail was provided. *Report of the Preliminary Conference of National Societies of 1946*, pp. 24–25, and *Report of the Conference of Government Experts of 1947*, pp. 20–23.

them.[13] Making use of the voluntary resources of local inhabitants or capable organizations present in the territory, or granting such organizations access to areas where wounded and sick people are located, can be a valuable means of meeting this obligation.

1. Voluntary response to an appeal

1726 Article 18(1) provides military authorities who find themselves without sufficient resources to collect and care for wounded and sick members of the armed forces with the option to appeal for assistance from the local civilian population.[14] Local civilians may, in turn, choose to respond to such an appeal. The military authorities are not bound to appeal to the inhabitants, and, under international law, the inhabitants are not bound to respond to their appeal.[15] There may nevertheless be a strong moral imperative for military authorities to use this option if they themselves are unable to provide care for the wounded and sick. Civilians, however, cannot be compelled to agree to such a request: the word 'voluntarily' was inserted in Article 18 specifically 'with a view to preventing any abuse', particularly on the part of an Occupying Power.[16]

1727 The possibility of requesting voluntary assistance was maintained in Article 17 of Additional Protocol I and, in line with the general thrust of the Protocol, extended to the collection and care of wounded and sick civilians. That extension remedied a gap in the protection of civilians, as the Fourth Convention has no equivalent of Article 18 of the First Convention. Article 17 of Protocol I also expands the activities for which local civilian assistance may

---

[13] First Convention, Articles 15 and 12. See also Additional Protocol I, Article 10.

[14] In Article 17 of Additional Protocol I, when indicating who may make such an appeal, the term 'Parties to the conflict' was chosen in order to encompass civilian as well as military authorities. See Sandoz/Swinarski/Zimmermann (eds), *Commentary on the Additional Protocols*, ICRC, 1987, para. 720.

[15] Despite finding that medical care for wounded prisoners of war just after capture was inadequate on both sides in the 1998–2000 Ethiopia-Eritrea conflict (although not to the extent of being a violation of the Convention), the Claims Commission does not appear to have enquired into whether commanding officers had sought to alleviate shortages by requesting assistance from the local population. Eritrea-Ethiopia Claims Commission, *Prisoners of War, Ethiopia's Claim*, Partial Award, 2003, paras 69–70; *Prisoners of War, Eritrea's Claim*, Partial Award, 2003, paras 64–65.

[16] *Final Record of the Diplomatic Conference of Geneva of 1949*, Vol. II-A, p. 143. At *ibid.* p. 192, the Drafting Committee explained: 'The Committee wished to make special provision for the case of occupied countries and to prevent, under the guise of an appeal to charitable zeal, the Occupying Authority from bringing pressure to bear on the population in order to induce them, even against their own will, to give prolonged treatment to the wounded, and thus relieve the Occupying Power of one of its principal responsibilities.' Belligerents and Occupying Powers may compel protected persons to undertake certain forms of work, for which they must be compensated (Fourth Convention, Articles 40 and 51). They may not compel such persons to take part in military operations. The fact that civilians cannot be compelled to respond to an appeal to assist the wounded and sick does not mean that collecting and caring for the wounded and sick entails taking part in military operations; rather, compelled labour must be compensated, whereas Article 18 allows for an appeal to 'charity', implying that it is not necessary to provide compensation for such acts.

be requested to include searching for the dead and reporting their location.[17] Importantly, the drafters of the Protocol sought to maintain the voluntary nature of the provision.[18]

2. Addressees of an appeal for assistance

1728   The first paragraph refers to 'the inhabitants', meaning the local population of an occupied territory or a territory in which an armed conflict is occurring, regardless of their nationality. Indeed, it refers only to 'the inhabitants' without mentioning the organizations or relief societies referred to in the second paragraph. Logically, however, an appeal to local civilians encompasses also civilians who have organized themselves into an aid society. For States party to Additional Protocol I, any doubt in this regard was removed in the corresponding paragraph of Article 17, which expressly refers also to aid societies.[19]

1729   A further clarification is apposite in regard to the inhabitants to which such an appeal may be made. In particular, it should be recalled that this cohort of persons can include medical professionals who have not been assigned to specific medical tasks by a Party to the conflict. An appeal for their assistance would not render such persons permanent medical personnel in the sense of the Convention, nor temporary medical personnel for the purposes of Additional Protocol I.[20]

3. To collect and care for the wounded and sick

1730   Nowadays, individuals are more likely to collect wounded or sick persons and bring them to a medical facility than to care for them in their own homes. That said, if they do take the wounded or sick into their homes, or if a relief organization provides care in its own facilities, that care may go beyond urgent first aid. The word 'care' thus also covers all reasonable measures necessary to improve the condition of wounded or sick persons, including the provision of food, shelter, clothing, blankets and hygiene items.[21] At the Diplomatic Conference, the wording 'collect and care for' was preferred over 'give first aid to' to avoid restricting the care that could be provided, as long as it was provided voluntarily.[22]

---

[17]   Additional Protocol I, Article 17(2).

[18]   *Official Records of the Diplomatic Conference of Geneva of 1974–1977*, Vol. XI, pp. 242–243.

[19]   In addition, there is nothing in the preparatory work for the First Convention to indicate that the drafters sought to exclude the possibility for military authorities to request assistance from local aid agencies or relief organizations. For the debates concerning Article 18, see *Final Record of the Diplomatic Conference of Geneva of 1949*, Vol. II-A, pp. 49 and 51–52, and Vol. III, p. 35, amendments 30 and 31 to the Wounded and Sick Convention.

[20]   First Convention, Article 24; Additional Protocol I, Article 8(k). See also the discussion of 'control', section C.5.

[21]   See also Article 12 and its commentary, para. 1387.

[22]   *Final Record of the Diplomatic Conference of Geneva of 1949*, Vol. II-A, pp. 51 and 143.

1731   Collecting wounded or sick persons may need to be preceded by searching for them. Following an attack or a military engagement, the existence and location of injured or dead persons may not be immediately apparent. In order to be able to collect and care for them, rescuers will have to search for them. The purpose of Article 18, which is to ensure that wounded or sick persons receive timely and life-saving treatment, necessarily also encompasses the search for such persons.[23]

1732   As noted above, Article 17 of Additional Protocol I adds a third task that the civilian population may be called upon to undertake, provided, as always, it is undertaken voluntarily: to search for the dead and report their location to the authorities. It is important to emphasize that civilians may not be requested to *collect* the dead.[24]

4. Necessary protection and facilities

1733 When a Party appeals to local inhabitants or relief societies to assist in collecting and caring for the wounded and sick, it must grant the protection and facilities without which the task of the population or the relief societies would be too difficult or dangerous. The assessment of such necessity is left in the first instance to the competent authorities of the Party to the conflict that made the appeal, but that Party must take into account, as far as possible, the wishes and views of the persons or relief organizations prepared to respond to the appeal. Such protection and facilities will essentially depend on the circumstances, and therefore all of the possibilities cannot be listed exhaustively.[25] 'Facilities' may include guarantees of as much freedom of movement as possible to carry out the tasks in question, facilities to transmit correspondence by any means, and facilities to transmit relief supplies and funds. It does not mean, however, that freedom of movement cannot be limited where military operations genuinely impede such access. 'Facilities' may include the provision of vehicles or other means of transport, as well as guarantees of safe conduct. Organizations receiving medical or other humanitarian supplies from outside the territory should also be exempted from customs and transport duties.[26]

1734   'Protection' refers in part to the conditions of security necessary to collect and care for the wounded and sick. What measures are necessary and

---

[23] See also Article 15 and its commentary, paras 1483–1484.

[24] The collection of the dead was considered too onerous a task for local inhabitants to undertake: see *Official Records of the Diplomatic Conference of Geneva of 1974–1977*, Vol. XI, p. 486. The UK delegation 'felt that it was not right that civilian populations and relief societies should be expected to collect the dead, with the possible exception of those at sea'.

[25] Article 5 of the 1906 Geneva Convention used the term 'immunities' instead of 'facilities'. There was some debate over the meaning of the word 'immunities' and whether it included a dispensation from a requirement to billet troops. See Des Gouttes, *Commentaire de la Convention de Genève de 1929 sur les blessés et malades*, ICRC, 1930, pp. 37–38.

[26] See e.g. Third Convention, Article 74(1); Fourth Convention, Article 61(3); and Additional Protocol I, Article 70(2).

appropriate for ensuring the safety of humanitarian aid workers is a complex issue that the Convention does not address.[27] One aspect of protection involves ensuring that one's own forces know not to – and do not – attack persons or organizations carrying out medical or humanitarian tasks. Protection can also mean, among other things, making local arrangements or agreeing cease-fires with the enemy to allow for medical or humanitarian activities to take place.[28] It also entails preventing, or taking steps to prevent, attacks by others. Furthermore, the requirement to grant protection reinforces the provision in Article 18(3) that '[n]o one may ever be molested or convicted for having nursed the wounded or sick'.[29]

1735   It is important to note that the protection which can be granted in this context does not include the right to use the red cross, red crescent or red crystal emblem. This restriction is justified because the risk of abuse is so great.[30] The use of the emblem must be restricted to situations explicitly provided for in the Conventions and Protocols, under the control of the competent military or civilian authorities. Persons or organizations responding to an appeal for assistance by a military authority thus cannot display the emblem on houses or buildings in which the wounded are cared for unless a Party to the conflict designates those buildings as medical facilities under the First or Fourth Conventions.[31]

1736   As for individuals wearing the emblem themselves, there is no mechanism in the First Convention for increasing the number of military medical personnel through the assignment of temporary medical personnel; however, States party to Additional Protocol I do have that option.[32] Thus, under Protocol I, the Parties to the conflict may increase the strength of their temporary medical personnel or the number of their temporary medical units, and such persons would be

---

[27] See Kate Mackintosh, 'Beyond the Red Cross: the protection of independent humanitarian organizations and their staff in international humanitarian law', *International Review of the Red Cross*, Vol. 89, No. 865, March 2007, pp. 113–130; Abby Stoddard, Adele Harmer and Katherine Haver, *Aid Worker Security Report 2011, Spotlight on security for national aid workers: Issues and perspectives*, Humanitarian Outcomes, 2011. Note, however, that Article 71(2) of Additional Protocol I states that '[relief personnel] shall be respected and protected'.

[28] See First Convention, Article 15. In addition, it should be recalled that '[i]ntentionally directing attacks against personnel, installations, material, units or vehicles involved in a humanitarian assistance...mission..., as long as they are entitled to the protection given to civilians or civilian objects under the law of armed conflict' is a war crime under Article 8(2)(b)(iii) of the 1998 ICC Statute.

[29] See section E.

[30] See section B for early examples of abuses of the emblem in relation to this article. However, some relief societies, in particular National Red Cross and Red Crescent Societies, are entitled to use or wear the emblem on a separate legal basis. For details, see Article 44 and its commentary, section D. See also the specific regime of Article 26 of the First Convention.

[31] First Convention, Article 21; Fourth Convention, Article 18. Or, if Additional Protocol I applies, Article 18 of the Protocol.

[32] Additional Protocol I, Article 8. The First Convention does, however, allow for increasing the number of medical personnel in a given situation via auxiliary medical personnel (Article 25) or use of the medical services of National Red Cross or Red Crescent Societies (Articles 26 and 27).

entitled to use the emblem. However, such measures imply strict supervision. Even for those States that are party to the Protocol, persons who respond to an appeal by the military authorities may not be equated to temporary medical personnel unless they are explicitly given an assignment as temporary medical personnel.[33] It is important to recall that not everyone carrying out medical activities in an area of armed conflict qualifies as 'medical personnel' in the sense of the Conventions and the Protocol.

1737   Lastly, Article 18(1) stipulates that if the adverse Party takes control of an area, it must grant the same protection and facilities to the inhabitants who have responded to an appeal for assistance. This obligation was added in 1949 as it was perceived as a significant gap in the 1929 Convention that had led to negative repercussions for persons who had responded to such an appeal.

5. Under the direction of the military authorities

1738   Volunteers who respond to an appeal for help with the wounded and sick must do so 'under the direction' of the military authorities (the equally authentic French text says 'sous son contrôle'). This requirement was inserted in response to the abuses that occurred during the Franco-Prussian War and has endured in subsequent iterations of the Conventions.[34]

1739   The provision makes it clear that even if local inhabitants or relief organizations come to the aid of the wounded, it is the military authorities who remain responsible for their condition and medical treatment. In particular, when it comes to the enemy wounded, the State authorities must inform the Power of Origin of their identity and capture and arrange for their protection under the Third Convention relative to the treatment of prisoners of war.[35] Wounded enemy personnel in the care of local inhabitants or relief organizations acting in response to a request by and under the direction or control of the military authorities must be considered to have fallen into the hands of the enemy and to be prisoners of war.[36]

1740   The military authorities may prescribe the nature and extent of the measures of control they consider necessary. In practice, once the particulars with regard

---

[33] Additional Protocol I, Article 8(k). It should be noted, however, that the rules on the use of the emblem do not prohibit other humanitarian organizations from using their own signs, flags, or clothing with their own logos identifying them, as long as those items will not lead to confusion with the red cross, red crescent or red crystal emblems. See especially Article 53 of the First Convention and its commentary, section D.

[34] The stipulation that the military authorities were responsible for supervising the collection and care of the wounded and sick by the local inhabitants was added in Article 5 of the 1906 Convention.

[35] Pictet (ed.), *Commentary on the First Geneva Convention*, ICRC, 1952, pp. 187–188. On the need to record and forward information, see Article 16 and its commentary. Article 14 of the First Convention stipulates that the wounded or sick who fall into enemy hands are prisoners of war; Article 12 of the Third Convention affirms that prisoners of war 'are in the hands of the enemy, but not of the individuals or military units who have captured them'.

[36] See the commentary on Article 4 of the Third Convention.

to identity have been collected and transmitted, this control may consist in ensuring that the wounded receive proper care and are treated humanely and with the respect to which they are entitled.

1741   For States party to Additional Protocol I, it may not always be easy to draw the line between stringent measures of control in relation to a general appeal for assistance from the local population and an assignment of one's own citizens to act as temporary medical personnel. Temporary medical personnel should be clearly and explicitly assigned as such. In this light, and with respect to any use of the emblem by persons responding to an appeal, the Party to the conflict which is responsible for preventing the misuse of the protective emblem must retain the power to decide who is entitled to the protection reserved for medical personnel.

D. Paragraph 2: Spontaneous collection and care of the wounded or sick by civilians and relief societies

1742 Article 18(2) makes it mandatory for authorities to permit spontaneous relief action. Local inhabitants and relief societies have a right to come to the aid of wounded and sick combatants, including enemy combatants.[37] This possibility was maintained and affirmed in Article 17 of Additional Protocol I, including in relation to wounded and sick civilians. Parties to a conflict have an obligation to take 'all possible measures' to search for and collect wounded and sick members of armed forces and to care for them.[38]

1743   The second sentence of paragraph 2 contains an important admonition: civilians and relief societies coming to the aid of the wounded and sick must 'abstain from offering them violence'. This obligation is addressed to civilians and applies directly to them. At the same time, it denotes an important responsibility for States, in that authorities remain obliged to protect wounded and sick members of the armed forces from third parties, including civilians purporting to act as their rescuers but who mistreat or harm them instead. States have an obligation to make sure that the wounded and sick are treated humanely, whether they are in the hands of State agents or private citizens.[39]

1. Inhabitants and relief societies

1744 The First Convention specifies that, in addition to the inhabitants, the authorities must permit relief societies to care for the wounded and sick. This addition was made in 1949 because the right of relief societies to so act was at times contested during the Second World War.[40] However, it does not define what

---

[37] *Final Record of the Diplomatic Conference of Geneva of 1949*, Vol. II-A, p. 51.
[38] First Convention, Articles 15 and 12. See also Additional Protocol I, Article 10.
[39] See First Convention, Article 12.
[40] Pictet (ed.), *Commentary on the First Geneva Convention*, ICRC, 1952, p. 191.

constitutes a relief society for the purposes of this article and there was no discussion on the matter at the Diplomatic Conference in 1949.[41] There are some indications that the term should be construed to mean local organizations such as National Red Cross or Red Crescent Societies, but not be limited to them. In particular, Article 17 of Additional Protocol I, which extends the principle to wounded and sick civilians without altering the meaning of Article 18 of the First Convention, states, '*such as* national Red Cross (Red Crescent, Red Lion and Sun) Societies', suggesting that those organizations are included but do not have an exclusive right of action in this regard. When Article 17 was adopted at the Diplomatic Conference in 1977, the Holy See stated that it had joined the consensus 'in the conviction that the reference to the national Red Cross (Red Crescent, Red Lion and Sun) Societies does not imply any limitation on the initiative and the action of *other* aid societies' (emphasis added).[42]

1745   The parallel right of individuals is accorded to 'the inhabitants', meaning persons already relatively close to the hostilities or to places where the wounded and sick require assistance. Logically, the right is not limited to relief organizations in the immediate vicinity of the wounded or sick, but to those present in the territory where the conflict is occurring. It does not extend to foreign or international organizations, which are covered by other provisions.[43] Article 18 affirms, moreover, that the military authorities shall permit relief societies to carry out activities for the wounded and sick in occupied or invaded territories.[44]

1746   When relief organizations spontaneously provide assistance to the wounded and sick, they should adhere to humanitarian principles, in particular impartiality.[45] Especially for organizations providing medical relief, impartiality coincides with medical ethics and the principle that those whose needs are greatest must be treated first, no matter to which side they belong.[46]

1747   When individual civilians spontaneously assist the wounded and sick, they are under no obligation to be strictly impartial in their sentiments, but they must be so in their actions. In addition, they must be 'humanitarian'. Thus, like any other persons providing medical care, they should not view a wounded combatant as an enemy but simply as a human being in need of care. This is further emphasized in paragraph 2 by the admonition that civilians must not harm the wounded and sick.

---

[41] The possibility for relief societies to act spontaneously in this manner was suggested during the 1947 Conference of Government Experts. Pictet (ed.), *Commentary on the First Geneva Convention*, ICRC, 1952, p. 191.

[42] *Official Records of the Diplomatic Conference of Geneva of 1974–1977*, Vol. VI, p. 78.

[43] In particular, common Article 9 (Article 10 in the Fourth Convention) and Article 81 of Additional Protocol I. For non-international armed conflict, see common Article 3(2) and Additional Protocol II, Article 18(2).

[44] For a definition of occupation, see the commentary on common Article 2, section E.

[45] For more details on humanitarian principles, including the principle of impartiality, see the commentary on Article 9.

[46] See Article 12 and its commentary, section G.

1748   Again, it must be stressed that individuals and members of aid societies may not use the emblem on their facilities or their persons unless they have been specifically authorized to do so by the competent authorities.[47]

2. Spontaneous action by inhabitants and relief societies

1749   Article 18 stipulates that individuals and relief societies may act 'spontaneously' to collect and care for the wounded and sick. Read in the light of the first paragraph, which allows such actions to be undertaken in response to an appeal, 'spontaneously' in the second paragraph may logically be interpreted to mean that individuals and relief societies may also take such actions on their own initiative. This interpretation is further supported by discussions during the Diplomatic Conference in 1977 in relation to Article 17 of Additional Protocol I, when the word 'spontaneously' was discussed in detail. Delegates in 1977 were concerned that the word 'spontaneously' could be interpreted narrowly so as to exclude *organized* relief efforts.[48] However, there is no indication in the record that Article 18 of the First Convention had been interpreted in that manner.[49] Their concerns were not therefore a reaction to how Article 18 had been applied in practice. Nevertheless, to ensure that organized relief action, in particular by aid societies, could not be excluded from the purview of Article 17 of Additional Protocol I, delegates to the 1977 Diplomatic Conference preferred the formulation 'on their own initiative' to 'spontaneously'. They wanted to make sure that any relief society that was organized would not be prevented from providing aid on the grounds that it was not 'spontaneous', while preserving the freedom of individual persons to offer assistance of their own accord.[50] Therefore, 'spontaneously' in Article 18 of the First Convention should be interpreted as having the same meaning as 'on their own initiative' in Article 17 of Protocol I.

1750   The word 'spontaneously' serves another important purpose, which is to remind Parties to conflicts that local civilian inhabitants can – and often do – rush to the site of an attack or explosion to collect and care for wounded persons. However, follow-up attacks, described as 'explosions intended to cause as many injuries and deaths as possible, including amongst those assisting the victims of a previous explosion', have become a worrying phenomenon in recent times.[51] Such attacks, which have been known to target first responders directly, arguably deter civilians from going to the aid of the wounded and

---

[47] Article 18 of the Fourth Convention provides that the competent authorities (who may be military or civilian) may recognize and authorize civilian hospitals to use the emblem. See also Article 18 of Additional Protocol I.

[48] *Official Records of the Diplomatic Conference of Geneva of 1974–1977*, Vol. XI, pp. 237–244.

[49] *Ibid.*   [50] *Ibid.*

[51] ICRC, *Health Care in Danger: Violent Incidents Affecting Health Care, January to December 2012*, ICRC, Geneva, 2013, p. 9; *Health Care in Danger: Violent Incidents Affecting the Delivery of Health Care, January 2012 to December 2013*, ICRC, Geneva, 2014, p. 13.

sick, and this may be contrary to the spirit of the Convention in general and Article 18 in particular. The express recognition of the right – and by implication the likelihood – of spontaneous civilian response in areas affected by hostilities must also be considered by attacking commanders, especially when assessing the legality of a follow-up attack against non-wounded combatants or a military objective. That response will influence the assessment of the necessary precautionary measures to be taken and of the expected incidental harm to civilians.[52] When considering or engaging in follow-up attacks, attackers must take into account the presence of all first responders, from trained medical personnel to local civilians who happen to be present, and take all necessary precautions to avoid or minimize incidental harm to them. An attacker should wait until first responders 'have collected and evacuated the wounded and sick from the scene of a prior attack'.[53]

3. To collect and care for the wounded and sick

1751 To what has already been stated regarding the collection and care of the wounded and sick, it should be added that the drafters of Article 17(1) of Additional Protocol I supported a notion of spontaneous 'care' that is broader than strict medical assistance. In their view, such care may also include immediate humanitarian relief, including clothing or food.[54] This understanding is consistent with the humanitarian purpose of Article 18.

4. Relationship with the military authorities

1752 Unlike the first paragraph, the second paragraph of Article 18 does not mention that spontaneous relief efforts are subject to the direction of the military authorities. This is not an oversight; it is, rather, the reflection of a choice explicitly made by the Diplomatic Conference in 1949. The drafting history reveals an important and principled stance.

1753 The conferences of experts that had prepared the draft conventions for the Diplomatic Conference had thought it desirable to reconcile charitable with military requirements, and had agreed after long discussion to propose a provision whereby the inhabitants could not withhold the wounded and sick they had collected from possible control by the military authorities.[55] That

---

52 Additional Protocol I, Article 57(2)(a)(iii).   53 Breitegger, pp. 109–110.

54 See also para. 1730. See also *Official Records of the Diplomatic Conference of Geneva of 1974–1977*, Vol. XI, pp. 159–163. This interpretation was advanced by the delegate of the Holy See and supported by the Swiss delegate; it encountered no opposition.

55 *Report of the Preliminary Conference of National Societies of 1946*, pp. 24–25; *Report of the Conference of Government Experts of 1947*, pp. 20–23. This suggestion was already controversial during the 1947 Conference of Government Experts. The relevant part of the proposed article adopted at the 1948 Stockholm Conference stipulated: 'The military authorities shall permit the inhabitants and relief societies, even in invaded or occupied areas, to offer in collecting and

condition appeared in the draft that was discussed at the Diplomatic Conference in 1949; however, the Diplomatic Conference insisted that the condition be deleted. Delegates at the conference refused to make the permission granted to the inhabitants to give spontaneous help dependent on the acceptance of military supervision, or on any kind of compulsory disclosure of information related to the wounded or sick.[56] At the time, the drafters were influenced by concerns, based on the experience of the Second World War, that informing the authorities could lead to negative repercussions for the wounded and for their rescuers. Such control is not prohibited, however, but the drafters felt that 'it would be extremely undesirable that this should be mentioned in a humanitarian Convention'.[57] It may also be more difficult in practice for the authorities to exercise control over spontaneous relief efforts than when they have appealed for help.

1754   It is important to recall that Article 18 of the First Convention can apply to medical professionals. Some concern has been expressed that an obligation to denounce wounded or sick members of the adverse Party in such a person's care could clash with the principle of medical secrecy.[58] The absence of a specific rule in the Convention thus led to some debate over the relationship between medical ethics – and in particular the rules governing medical secrecy – and a hypothetical obligation in national law (or created by occupying authorities) to report a wounded or sick person to the authorities.[59] Indeed, requiring medical personnel to report persons who are treated for specific types of wounds (e.g. bullet or stab wounds) is common in national legislation, in case a criminal investigation is warranted.

1755   The issue of medical secrecy was revisited in Additional Protocol I. Article 16(3) of the Protocol states:

No person engaged in medical activities shall be compelled to give to anyone belonging either to an adverse Party, or to his own Party except as required by the law of the latter Party, any information concerning the wounded and sick who are, or who would have been, under his care, if such information would, in his opinion, prove harmful to the patients concerned or to their families. Regulations for the compulsory notification of communicable diseases shall, however, be respected.[60]

---

giving first aid to wounded or sick members of the armed forces, of whatever nationality, on condition that the latter shall not be withheld from the possible control of national or occupying authorities.' *Draft Conventions adopted by the 1948 Stockholm Conference*, pp. 14–15.

[56] *Final Record of the Diplomatic Conference of Geneva of 1949*, Vol. II-A pp. 51–52. The record states that the UK representative observed that 'under the second paragraph [of the draft text] the civilian population would be obliged to hand over the wounded in their care to the enemy occupying their territory – and that, by virtue of a humanitarian Convention!' The record adds: 'He pressed for the omission of any such obligation.'

[57] *Ibid.* pp. 51–52 and 143; Remarks of the Rapporteur of the First Commission of the Diplomatic Conference, *ibid*, p. 192. See also Additional Protocol I, Article 16(3).

[58] International Law Association, *International Medical Law, Conference Report (Buenos Aires)*, 1968, Vol. 53, pp. 539–588, especially at 542–549 and 558–573.

[59] *Ibid.*

[60] See the commentary on Article 16 of Additional Protocol I for a discussion of the content of this provision.

5. *Respect for the wounded and sick by the civilian population*

1756 The admonition that 'the civilian population shall respect wounded and sick, and in particular abstain from offering them violence' is the sole provision in the First Convention addressed specifically to the civilian population. Of course, there are many obligations in the Conventions and Protocols governing the *protection* of civilians, but this article is unique in setting an explicit standard of care that civilians themselves must meet when dealing with wounded and sick persons.[61] This sentence reiterates the basic principle set out in Article 12 of the First Convention and clarifies that civilian persons are also bound to respect and protect the wounded and sick. Its equivalent became the first line of Article 17 of Additional Protocol I.

1757 The existence of this obligation, coupled with the right of local inhabitants to collect and care for wounded and sick persons, highlights the importance of raising awareness of international humanitarian law, including among the general public, in order to promote respect for this rule and the Geneva Conventions more generally.[62] In this light, it should be recalled that wilful killing, torture, inhuman treatment and wilfully causing great suffering or serious injury to body or health of the wounded and sick are grave breaches of the Convention, including when they are committed by civilians.[63] In any case, doing violence to an incapacitated individual, even an individual associated with the armed forces of an enemy State, is so inherently inhumane that the prohibition in Article 18 should be self-evident, even if it bears repeating.

E. Paragraph 3: No punishment for caring for the wounded or sick

1758 Paragraph 3 states that 'no one may ever be molested or convicted for having nursed the wounded or sick'. This provision was included in Article 18 in the light of the practice of some States during the Second World War of executing doctors and others for caring for wounded enemy personnel, particularly resistance fighters in occupied territories.[64] Caring for the wounded or sick must not be regarded as an offence under any circumstances.[65] The right not to be

---

[61] Nevertheless, it should be recalled that, since the trials following the Second World War, the fact that civilians can also be perpetrators of war crimes more generally has been accepted. See, in particular, France, Permanent Military Tribunal at Metz, *Bommer case*, Judgment, 1947, pp. 65–66. On potential perpetrators, see Knut Dörmann, *Elements of War Crimes under the Rome Statute*, Cambridge University Press, 2003, pp. 34–37. See also the commentary on Article 50, section C.3.

[62] See the commentary on Article 47.   [63] See Article 50 and its commentary.

[64] See François Bugnion, *The International Committee of the Red Cross and the Protection of War Victims*, ICRC/Macmillan, Oxford, 2003, pp. 478–479.

[65] States may have legislation prohibiting the performance of specific medical acts by persons who are not registered medical doctors or health practitioners, which, however, makes an exception for the provision of emergency medical care under certain conditions. Some States also have 'Good Samaritan' laws that may be relevant in these circumstances. For example, such laws may require people to go to the aid of a person in distress, or they may provide that rescuers who voluntarily and in good faith give first aid to a person in need are not liable for shortcomings in the care provided, unless there is gross negligence.

harmed, harassed or convicted for exercising the right set down in the previous paragraph is crucial to protect those caring for the wounded and sick. It is in line with the overall object and purpose of the Convention: in order to protect the wounded and sick, those who collect and care for them, including civilian volunteers and relief societies, must also be respected and protected. Indeed, the aim of the provision is to prevent any repression or retaliation for such activities, via judicial or other mechanisms.

1759   The term 'molested' is broad. Although today it tends to connote sexual abuse, the word as used in the Convention means more generally to 'pester or harass in a hostile way'.[66] It thus prohibits any form of harassment and prevents any criminal or administrative proceedings being brought against a person solely for having cared for the wounded or sick. The provision also prohibits extrajudicial forms of repression. It prevents any administrative measure (in particular a disciplinary measure) from being taken, or any form of annoyance, threat or harassment. Clearly, as it prohibits harassment on that level, it also prohibits any form of ill-treatment or violence to life as proscribed by international law. In the same context, Article 17(1) of Additional Protocol I uses the terms 'harmed, prosecuted...or punished'. Those terms were added for the sake of completeness, but such acts are encapsulated in the term 'molested'. If the specific terms of Article 17 of Protocol I are taken as additional concrete examples of behaviour that constitutes 'molesting' carers, 'prosecute' refers in particular to the examining magistrate and the public prosecutor, who should not bring such a case before the court, while 'harm' may refer to the investigation stage, which should not be embarked upon only for such a reason. 'Molesting' can also include detaining such persons at checkpoints unnecessarily or arresting them solely on the grounds that they collect and/or care for the wounded and sick. Actions such as confiscating medical records, in violation of humanitarian-law protections against disclosure of medical information to authorities, and disrupting the functioning of medical facilities are also prohibited forms of molestation. While armed entry into medical facilities in order to detain or question persons present there is not prohibited *per se*, the manner in which such entries are conducted must ensure that the wounded and sick continue to receive proper medical care. In short, it encompasses all acts that aim to deter or impede the provision of care to the wounded and sick for fear of attracting negative repercussions.[67]

1760   Lastly, a court should acquit anyone brought before it on a charge of having nursed the wounded or sick when the accused has acted in accordance with international humanitarian law and in compliance with medical ethics.

---

[66] *Concise Oxford English Dictionary*, 12th edition, Oxford University Press, 2011, p. 921.
[67] Threats against health-care personnel often have a negative effect on the delivery of care; see ICRC, *Health Care in Danger: A Sixteen-Country Study*, ICRC, Geneva, 2011, p. 10.

1761 Moreover, although it is stated in Article 18 in relation to the civilian population, the prohibition applies broadly to any person who cares for the wounded and sick. For States party to Additional Protocol I, this is clarified by Article 16(1) of the Protocol, which provides that '[u]nder no circumstances shall any person be punished for carrying out medical activities compatible with medical ethics, regardless of the person benefiting therefrom'.

F. Paragraph 4: Continued responsibilities of the Occupying Power

1762 The final paragraph of Article 18 affirms that an Occupying Power is not released from its obligations to care for the wounded and sick if it relies on local inhabitants and relief societies. It continues to bear full responsibility for the fate of the wounded and sick. It is for the Occupying Power to see that their treatment is in all respects in conformity with the Convention, and to furnish the means necessary to achieve this. Indeed, the same is true when it comes to employing retained medical and religious personnel for the benefit of prisoners of war.[68]

Select bibliography

Breitegger, Alexander, 'The legal framework applicable to insecurity and violence affecting the delivery of health care in armed conflicts and other emergencies', *International Review of the Red Cross*, Vol. 95, No. 889, March 2013, pp. 83–127.

Hutchinson, John F., *Champions of Charity: War and the Rise of the Red Cross*, Westview Press, Boulder, Colorado, 1996.

---

[68] See Article 28(4).

CHAPTER III

MEDICAL UNITS AND ESTABLISHMENTS

1763   The rationale for the protection of medical units and establishments used by the armed forces' medical service is the same as for medical personnel, material and transports: they are protected on account of the functions they perform, i.e. providing medical care to wounded and sick soldiers, which is a central aim of the First Convention.

1764   Article 19 deals with medical establishments and units used by the armed forces' medical service. The first paragraph outlines the protection granted to these establishments and units and prescribes the treatment to be accorded to their personnel if they fall into enemy hands. The second paragraph sets out a specific obligation to take precautionary measures to protect these establishments and units from the effects of attacks against military objectives.

1765   Article 21 lays down the conditions under which military medical establishments and units covered by Article 19 lose their protection, i.e. if they are 'used to commit, outside their humanitarian duties, acts harmful to the enemy'. It also regulates the stringent criteria that must be met before such loss of protection occurs: a warning must be given, providing, in all appropriate cases, a reasonable time limit. Protection ceases only 'after such warning has remained unheeded'.

1766   Article 22 supplements Article 21 by listing five 'conditions', i.e. specific factual scenarios, which must not be regarded as acts harmful to the enemy, in spite of certain appearances which may lead to the opposite conclusion or at least create some doubt. Consequently, conduct falling within the list of acts specified in Article 22 does not lead to a loss of protection of the military medical establishment or unit in question.

1767   Article 20 prohibits any attacks launched from land against hospital ships at sea. Article 20 goes hand in hand with Article 23 of the Second Convention: the former prohibits attacks from land against hospital ships entitled to the protection of the Second Convention, while the latter prohibits attacks from the sea against land-based establishments entitled to the protection of the First Convention.

1768   Lastly, Article 23 provides for the establishment of hospital zones and localities outside areas where fighting is taking place, in order to enhance the protection of the wounded and sick from the effects of war. Together with the safety zones and neutralized zones regulated in Articles 14 and 15 of the Fourth Convention, Article 23 forms part of a wider system of protected zones laid down in the Geneva Conventions and further developed in Additional Protocol I.

1769   This chapter is further complemented by a number of provisions contained in Part II, Section I, of Additional Protocol I.

ARTICLE 19

PROTECTION OF MEDICAL UNITS AND ESTABLISHMENTS

❖ Text of the provision*

(1) Fixed establishments and mobile medical units of the Medical Service may in no circumstances be attacked, but shall at all times be respected and protected by the Parties to the conflict. Should they fall into the hands of the adverse Party, their personnel shall be free to pursue their duties, as long as the capturing Power has not itself ensured the necessary care of the wounded and sick found in such establishments and units.

(2) The responsible authorities shall ensure that the said medical establishments and units are, as far as possible, situated in such a manner that attacks against military objectives cannot imperil their safety.

❖ Reservations or declarations

None

Contents

* Paragraph numbers have been added for ease of reference.

A. Introduction

1770 Article 19 deals with medical establishments and units of the armed forces' medical services. The first paragraph outlines the extent of the protection granted to these facilities in international armed conflict and prescribes the treatment to be accorded to medical personnel associated with them if such establishments or units fall into enemy hands. The second paragraph sets out a specific obligation to take precautionary measures to protect these establishments and units from the effects of attacks against military objectives.

1771   For details on how such facilities are protected in non-international armed conflicts, see the commentary on common Article 3, section I.

1772   The fundamental rationale for the protection of military medical establishments and units is the same as for medical personnel, material and transports of the armed forces' medical services: they are protected on account of the functions they perform, i.e. providing medical care to the military wounded and sick, which is the central aim of the First Convention.[1] Wounded and sick civilians, as well as civilian hospitals, their personnel and specific types of transports for wounded and sick civilians, are protected on the basis of the Fourth Convention, as well as of Additional Protocol I.[2]

B. Historical background

1773 The obligation to respect and protect military medical establishments and units is among the oldest rules of international humanitarian law. It was first set out in the Geneva Convention of 1864 in relation to military hospitals. However, at the time the hospitals' protection was conditioned upon the presence of the wounded and sick within them.[3] With the adoption of the Geneva Convention of 1906, such presence was no longer a requirement for protection. Moreover, that Convention for the first time introduced the distinction between 'mobile sanitary formations' and 'fixed establishments' of the 'sanitary service', which is relevant in that, when these establishments or units fall into enemy hands, they are treated differently depending on whether they belong to one category or the other.[4] The Geneva Convention of 1929 contains provisions virtually identical to those of the 1906 Geneva Convention.[5]

---

[1] See Article 12.
[2] See Fourth Convention, Articles 16 and 18–22, and Additional Protocol I, Articles 8(e) and 12–13.
[3] Geneva Convention (1864), Article 1.
[4] Geneva Convention (1906), Article 6. For their respective treatment when they fall into enemy hands, see Articles 14 and 15.
[5] Geneva Convention on the Wounded and Sick (1929), Article 6. The question of how these establishments and units should be dealt with when they fall into enemy hands is covered in Articles 14 and 15 of that Convention.

C. Paragraph 1: Respect for and protection of medical units

1. First sentence: Basic rule

a. Fixed establishments and mobile medical units

1774 While the two categories of 'fixed establishments' and 'mobile medical units' generally enjoy the same protection under this article, the distinction between them is relevant since they will be treated differently if they fall into enemy hands, in accordance with Chapter V, Articles 33 and 34, of the First Convention.

1775 The Convention does not define the notions of 'fixed establishments' and 'mobile medical units'. However, in accordance with their ordinary meaning, 'fixed' can be understood as attached or positioned securely,[6] and 'establishments' as something 'set up on a firm or permanent basis'.[7] Because buildings such as hospitals are immovable, they would undoubtedly fall within this category.

1776 In contrast, the term 'mobile' means 'able to move or be moved freely or easily'.[8] For instance, field hospitals accommodated in tents or containers, as well as other open-air installations which can be set up and taken down in accordance with medical needs, would qualify as mobile medical units.

1777 The text of Article 19 provides no guidance on what medical purposes fixed establishments and mobile medical units are to fulfil. However, the activities in which military medical personnel engage, as spelled out in Article 24 of the First Convention, form the context for the interpretation of Article 19, i.e. the search for, or the collection, transport or treatment of the wounded or sick, or the prevention of disease. The relevance of the medical purposes set out in Article 24 has also been confirmed by their subsequent inclusion in the definition of 'medical units' in Additional Protocol I, which also encompasses military medical establishments and units covered by the present article.[9]

1778 Clearly, the medical purpose of *treatment* of the wounded and sick will be fulfilled in fixed establishments, such as hospital buildings, as well as in mobile medical units. The degree of treatment is not important and could, for instance, range from first aid and triage, which may be performed at a first-aid post, to psychological care, such as relieving combat-induced stress, or it could also include general surgery performed in field hospitals. It could also encompass more specialized surgery, such as cardiac or neurosurgery, and rehabilitative care, including physiotherapy, which may be performed in fixed establishments such as general military hospitals, sometimes far from the battlefield.

---

[6] *Concise Oxford English Dictionary*, 12th edition, Oxford University Press, 2011, p. 538.
[7] *Ibid.* p. 488.　[8] *Ibid.* p. 918.
[9] See Additional Protocol I, Article 8(e), and Henckaerts/Doswald-Beck, commentary on Rule 28, p. 95.

1779   Also, a medical or pharmaceutical depot or a laboratory attached to a field hospital would fall within the category of 'mobile medical units', since such units may either be free-standing or constitute an integral part of the field hospital which serves to treat the wounded and sick. In addition, mobile medical units or fixed establishments dedicated to dental care are recognized as fulfilling the medical purpose of treatment.[10]

1780   *Collection* of the wounded and sick is also a relevant medical purpose, e.g. for first-aid stations. Such stations may be either fixed or mobile. The latter may be inflatable and transported to the battlefield in or attached to a vehicle. At times, first-aid stations perform the dual functions of collection and treatment. But even if the wounded and sick are merely collected and not actually cared for by the first-aid station, this would not hinder their qualification for protection under Article 19.

1781   *Prevention of disease* is another recognized function of medical personnel. It is relevant for fixed establishments and mobile medical units providing, for example, vaccinations, carrying out awareness-raising or training with regard to communicable diseases (such as Ebola, cholera, dysentery or sexually transmitted diseases), or performing activities for the prevention of psychological trauma, including for the benefit of able-bodied combatants.[11]

1782   The *search* for and *transport* of the wounded and sick would primarily be relevant for military medical personnel and/or military medical transports. However, mobile medical units may, for instance, also include vehicles, and by that nature may also serve to transport wounded and sick or medical personnel alongside the functions of collection, treatment, or prevention of disease.[12] This raises the question as to the difference between the 'mobile medical units' examined here and 'transports' protected under Article 35. Indeed, medical transports will usually also contain at least rudimentary equipment for providing first aid to the wounded and sick being conveyed. While these two categories generally enjoy the same protection on the battlefield, the difference becomes relevant when they fall into enemy hands. Whereas the 'mobile medical units' of the armed forces' medical services remain reserved for the wounded and sick within them and may not be converted to other purposes, including military ones, by the Party into whose hands they fall,[13] military 'medical transports' may be converted to other uses, as long as the wounded and sick within them are taken care of elsewhere.[14] A way of differentiating between the two categories is to determine which medical purpose is more dominant:

---

[10] *Minutes of the Diplomatic Conference of Geneva of 1949*, p. 30.
[11] For more details, see the commentary on Article 24, para. 1958.
[12] See *Final Record of the Diplomatic Conference of Geneva of 1949*, Vol. II-A, p. 104, and *Minutes of the Diplomatic Conference of Geneva of 1949*, pp. 6 and 9.
[13] See Article 33(1). This is to be distinguished from the case where the Party to a conflict that uses these 'mobile medical units' transforms them itself at the outset into units dedicated to non-medical, including military, purposes.
[14] See Article 35(2).

the transport function in principle prevails in the case of 'transports', while the possibility of administering care prevails in the case of 'mobile medical units'.

b. *Part of the medical service*

1783 Fixed establishments and mobile medical units are entitled to protection under this provision only if they are 'of the Medical Service'. However, this does not mean that they have to be owned by the medical service. Rather, for their conduct to be attributable to the armed forces, they must form an integral part of those forces, be empowered to exercise medical functions on their behalf or be under their control. In this regard, the term 'Medical Service' denotes the section of the armed forces, or of other militias or volunteer corps, dealing with their medical needs. In addition, the fixed establishments and mobile medical units of a National Red Cross or Red Crescent Society, or of another voluntary aid society, which is assisting the medical service on the basis of Article 26 or 27 of the First Convention, short of thereby themselves becoming military organs, are also covered.[15]

1784 Also, it is for each Power to decide on the composition of its medical service. There are no requirements as to the form of this decision nor when it has to be taken; it can range from a law, a regulation or a decree to a simple declaration in the midst of hostilities that a given object will henceforth form part of the medical service. This gives the authorities the flexibility to designate fixed establishments and mobile medical units before an armed conflict occurs, as well as to decide, as the need arises, to transform objects serving a non-medical purpose into a medical establishment or unit during an armed conflict: for example, to use a military barracks, a tent where ammunition has been stored in the past, or a school or religious building henceforth as a makeshift medical establishment or unit.[16]

1785 Such flexibility means that there are no requirements as to the level of sophistication or organization of the medical capacity that a medical establishment or unit needs to have in order to qualify for protection under Article 19. Any establishment or unit serving at least one of the medical purposes detailed above is covered.[17]

1786 The only substantive restriction on the authorities' discretion as to which fixed establishments and mobile medical units form part of the medical service

---

[15] Similarly, see the commentary on Article 26, para. 2080.
[16] See e.g. Israel, *Manual on the Rules of Warfare*, 2006, p. 27: in the case of a large military base converted into a clearing station for the wounded, 'it must not be attacked, as it is a medical facility (on the assumption that no military activities are conducted therein, being disguised as treatment for the wounded)'.
[17] In this regard, Article 18(1) of the Fourth Convention on the protection of civilian hospitals, as well as the definition of 'medical units' in Article 8(e) of Additional Protocol I, require that they be 'organized' for the medical purposes enumerated in those paragraphs. On the interpretation given to the term 'organized' in those contexts, see the commentaries on those articles.

is that the establishments or units must be *exclusively assigned* to one or more of the aforementioned medical purposes.

1787   While Article 19 does not expressly state that the criterion of 'assignment' must be met because, as *military* medical establishments or units, they are assigned *ex officio* by the competent authorities, this interpretation results again from the relevant context of Article 24 of the First Convention.[18] It must also be emphasized that this restriction on the authorities' discretion as to what forms part of the military medical service is necessary, as establishments or units of that service may be assigned to a purpose which is considered military medicine, but which does not fall under one or more of the specified medical purposes, such as health examinations in the selection of combatants for a mission. Importantly, this restriction is also necessary to prevent misuse of the distinctive emblems by limiting the establishments and units entitled to use them.[19]

1788   Further, by analogy with Article 24, once military medical establishments and units have been so assigned, their assignment must also be 'exclusive', i.e. they may not serve any purpose other than one or more of the permitted medical purposes.[20] This does not mean that the establishments or units must actually be used for such purposes at all times: a given establishment or unit may qualify for protection under Article 19 even if it has not yet received any wounded or sick people or no longer has any wounded or sick people within it, or if no doctors or other medical personnel are present at a certain time, as long as its assignment does not extend to any other, non-medical purposes.

1789   Article 19 is silent about whether military medical establishments and units must be assigned exclusively to medical purposes on a permanent basis, or whether they can be so assigned on a temporary basis while still being protected under this provision. In the context of Article 19, it must be emphasized that, both for personnel (by virtue of the specific category of auxiliary personnel covered under Article 25) and for transports (including all vehicles employed, temporarily or permanently), the possibility of temporary assignment to medical purposes is recognized under the First Convention.[21] Moreover, the purpose of this provision is to ensure the care of the military wounded and sick. The recognition of temporarily assigned establishments or units increases the likelihood that the wounded and sick receive the necessary treatment where permanent establishments or units are not available. For instance, this leaves enough flexibility to spontaneously convert a building to medical purposes,

---

[18] See the commentary on Article 24, section D.1.
[19] The display of the distinctive emblems on military medical establishments and units is governed by Article 42.
[20] Besides exclusive assignment, the other requirements of recognition, authorization and placement under military laws and regulations must be fulfilled for establishments and units of National Red Cross or Red Crescent Societies or other voluntary aid societies auxiliary to the armed forces' medical services, by analogy with Article 26 of the First Convention.
[21] See the commentaries on Article 35, para. 2380, and Article 36, para. 2445.

and to so assign it only for a limited period of time. After this period, if there is no indication that the assignment has been renewed, the facility returns to its initial, non-medical purpose.

1790   While the preparatory work suggests that military medical establishments and units intended only *temporarily* to serve medical purposes are excluded from protection under Article 19,[22] this reflects the dominant view at the time, i.e. that an exclusive assignment implies that it has to be permanent. However, this paradigm has shifted with subsequent State practice. In the context of the preparatory work for Additional Protocol I, State representatives, including those of States which have, since the Diplomatic Conference of Geneva of 1974–1977, not become party to Additional Protocol I, agreed at an early stage that the definition of 'medical units' contained in Article 8(e) of the Protocol, a definition that includes military medical establishments or units falling under Article 19, would extend to *temporary* establishments and units.[23]

1791   Neither the term 'permanent' nor its opposite, 'temporary', is defined in the Geneva Conventions. Article 8(k) of Additional Protocol I generally defines 'permanent medical units' as 'those assigned exclusively to medical purposes for an indeterminate period'. The standard of assignment for an indeterminate period is met where, at the outset, the idea is to make the assignment of units to medical purposes definitive (i.e. without imposing any time limit). 'Temporary medical units' are defined in Article 8(k) as 'those devoted exclusively to medical purposes for limited periods during the whole of such periods'.

2. Obligation to respect and protect

1792   The obligation to respect and protect fixed establishments and mobile medical units dates from the 1864 Geneva Convention, where it was enshrined in relation to military hospitals. This obligation is also set out in the specific provisions relating to the wounded and sick and to medical personnel and transports. In this regard, 'to respect' entails obligations of a negative nature, i.e. to refrain from engaging in certain conduct, while 'to protect' implies obligations of a positive nature, i.e. to take certain active measures.

a. Prohibition of attack

1793   The wording 'may in no circumstances be attacked', which precedes the obligation to respect and protect, was added in 1947, following the Conference of Government Experts, to reflect the increasing scale of aerial bombardment,[24]

---

[22] See *Final Record of the Diplomatic Conference of Geneva of 1949*, Vol. II-A, p. 193.

[23] See *Report of the Conference of Government Experts of 1972*, Vol. I, p. 32 (India and the United States, among others, participated in the conference as States which have not become party to Additional Protocol I). For the negotiations, see *Official Records of the Diplomatic Conference of Geneva of 1974–1977*, Vol. XI, in particular pp. 22–23 and 221.

[24] See *Report of the Conference of Government Experts of 1947*, p. 24.

then a recent development. While from a contemporary perspective this is no longer a new development, the specific mention of a prohibition of attack is important within the framework of the codification, in Additional Protocol I, of the rule of distinction between civilian objects and military objectives in the conduct of hostilities.

1794   Furthermore, for an object to qualify as a 'military objective' in accordance with Additional Protocol I (Article 52(2)) and its customary law equivalent, it is not sufficient that it belongs to, or is used by, armed forces. In order to so qualify, it must also be shown that it makes an 'effective contribution to military action' and that its 'total or partial destruction, capture or neutralization, in the circumstances ruling at the time, offers a definite military advantage'. In principle, military medical units do not fulfil any of these criteria. Therefore, for the purpose of the law regulating the conduct of hostilities, military medical objects are civilian objects.

1795   Therefore, the prohibition on attacking[25] fixed establishments and mobile medical units of the *military* medical services confirms that these are civilian objects.

1796   The proposition that military medical objects are not military objectives is furthermore supported by Additional Protocol I, which requires attackers to take all feasible precautions to verify, *inter alia*, that objectives to be attacked are not subject to special protection but are military objectives.[26] Undoubtedly, military medical establishments and units qualify as objects entitled to special protection for the purposes of the conduct of hostilities.[27]

1797   The prohibition on attacking military medical establishments and units means, first, that attacks must not be directed against them. Moreover, indiscriminate attacks affecting such establishments and units, as well as attacks that may be expected to cause excessive incidental damage to them in relation to the concrete and direct military advantage anticipated, may be deemed prohibited.[28] This view is supported by the stringent character of the obligations to respect and protect which form the immediate context in which the prohibition on attacking military medical establishments and units is embedded. It results, moreover, from the aforementioned determination that these establishments and units in principle constitute civilian objects.[29] Besides, the

---

[25] The notion of attack is defined in Article 49 of Additional Protocol I as 'acts of violence against the adversary, whether in offence or defence'.

[26] Additional Protocol I, Article 57(2)(a)(i).

[27] See the commentary on Article 21, para. 1841. There is a higher threshold for the loss of protection of medical establishments and units than for civilian objects in general. The conditions that must be fulfilled before an attack on medical establishments and units can take place include an advance warning and a time limit for the warning to be observed, compared with the general precautionary obligation under Article 57(2)(c) of Additional Protocol I for an attacker to issue an advance warning, but only 'unless circumstances do not permit'.

[28] On the prohibition on indiscriminate and disproportionate attacks affecting military medical establishments and units, see Articles 12(4) and 48–58 of Additional Protocol I.

[29] Gisel, pp. 215–230.

view that these establishments or units are also protected from attacks that may be expected to cause excessive incidental damage to them in relation to the concrete and direct military advantage anticipated is supported by certain States,[30] as well as by a number of leading commentators.[31] However, according to other views, the expected incidental harm to these establishments or units is not to be included as relevant harm under the principles of proportionality and precautions for the purposes of the conduct of hostilities, since medical units positioned near military objectives are deemed to have accepted the risk of death or injury due to their proximity to military operations.[32]

b. Respect and protection

1798   Both obligations – to respect and to protect – apply to a Party to the conflict's own medical establishments and units as well as to those of the enemy.[33]

1799   As regards the obligation to respect, the explicit mention of the prohibition of attack before the obligation is stated implies that it encompasses broader commitments than simply to refrain from attack in the context of the conduct of hostilities. To respect medical units also means not interfering with their work in order to allow them to continue to treat the wounded and sick in their care.

1800   This precludes the intentional destruction of medical establishments and units,[34] as well as practices such as plunder of their medical equipment. Moreover, using such establishments or units for military purposes is subject to stringent restrictions, in particular the principle – in line with the requirement to ensure continued medical care for the wounded and sick found therein – as enshrined in Article 33(2) of the First Convention.[35] In this vein, absent any arrangements for the continued care of the wounded and sick in a medical establishment or unit, the seizure of an entire medical facility by an opposing

---

[30] See e.g. Australia, *Manual of the Law of Armed Conflict*, 2006, para. 5.9; Canada, *LOAC Manual*, 2001, para. 204.5; Hungary, *Military Manual*, 1992, p. 45; New Zealand, *Military Manual*, 1992, para. 207; Philippines, *Air Power Manual*, 2000, paras 1–6.4 and 1–6.5; and United Kingdom, *Manual of the Law of Armed Conflict*, 2004, para. 5.32.5.

[31] See Michael Bothe, Karl Josef Partsch, and Waldemar A. Solf, *New Rules for Victims of Armed Conflicts: Commentary on the Two 1977 Protocols Additional to the Geneva Conventions of 1949*, Martinus Nijhoff Publishers, The Hague, 1982, pp. 118–119, and Yoram Dinstein, *The Conduct of Hostilities under the Law of International Armed Conflict*, 2nd edition, Cambridge University Press, 2010, p. 172. See also Manual on International Law Applicable to Air and Missile Warfare (2009), Rule 1(1).

[32] See United Sates, *Law of War Manual*, 2015, p. 445, para. 7.10.1.1, and Ian Henderson, *The Contemporary Law of Targeting: Military Objectives, Proportionality and Precautions in Attack under Additional Protocol I*, Martinus Nijhoff Publishers, Leiden, 2009, pp. 195–196.

[33] With respect to wounded and sick personnel, see the commentary on Article 12, paras 1337, 1368 and 1370. See also United Kingdom, *Manual of the Law of Armed Conflict*, 2004, para. 7.3.2. Furthermore, see Mikos-Skuza, p. 213.

[34] Subject to the specific provisions of Article 33(3) of the First Convention, which does not categorically exclude the intentional destruction of buildings composing fixed medical establishments. See the commentary on that provision, section B.3.

[35] See the commentary on Article 33, section B.2.

Party with a view to using it for military purposes, such as for the storage of weapons, the setting up of a military command and control centre or the launch of military operations, or for interrogations or detention,[36] raises issues under the obligation to respect. This is because such seizure may impede the functioning of the facility and the continued provision of medical care for the wounded and sick. In addition, it will lead to the loss of the facility's specific protection and moreover, upon fulfilling the relevant criteria under humanitarian law, to its also becoming a military objective, thus endangering any wounded or sick people and medical personnel within it.[37]

1801   That said, temporary entry by armed forces or law enforcement officials that falls short of taking control of the medical establishment or unit may be conducted for legitimate purposes based on military necessity. Such purposes include interrogating or detaining wounded or sick military personnel, verifying that a medical unit is not used for military purposes, or searching for suspects alleged to have committed a crime in relation to an armed conflict.[38]

1802   However, the obligation to respect requires that such activities be avoided before completion of the necessary treatment of the wounded and sick or, at the very least, that their continued treatment be ensured. Similarly, a good-faith interpretation of the obligation to respect medical establishments and units, i.e. not to unduly impede the treatment of the wounded and sick, leads to the conclusion that the possibility of inspecting a medical unit must not be abused.[39] Assessing whether an inspection constitutes an abuse will inevitably depend on the circumstances, but one that would result in the wounded and sick no longer being able to receive the necessary medical treatment would not be in keeping with the said obligation.[40]

1803   Therefore, entry into a military medical establishment or unit for any of the aforementioned purposes – given that such operations may disrupt its functioning and therefore its ability to provide the wounded and sick with medical care they need – must strike a reasonable balance between military necessity and the potential humanitarian impact. Specific procedures could assist in

---

[36] On the scenario of armed takeovers of hospitals and other health-care facilities and incidents collected by the ICRC in this regard, see ICRC, *Health Care in Danger: Violent Incidents Affecting the Delivery of Health Care, January 2012 to December 2014*, ICRC, Geneva, 2014, p. 13.

[37] On the loss of protection of military medical establishments and units, see Article 21.

[38] See the practice of some States recognizing the possibility of inspecting medical units to ascertain their contents and actual use: e.g. Nigeria, *IHL Manual*, 1994, p. 45, para. (f); Senegal, *IHL Manual*, 1999, p. 17; Togo, *Military Manual*, 1996, Fascicule II, p. 8; and United States, *Field Manual*, 1956, para. 221.

[39] At the same time, such an interpretation may also be based on the obligation to respect the wounded and sick under Article 12.

[40] In this regard, the practice of Senegal requires that such an inspection be ordered explicitly by the authority responsible for the maintenance of law and order; see Senegal, *IHL Manual*, 1999, p. 17.

achieving this balance so that non-medical personnel do not remain for longer than necessary within the establishment or unit.[41]

1804   Lastly, the obligation to respect means that an intentional disruption of these units' ability to communicate for medical purposes with other components of the armed forces is also prohibited.

1805   The obligation to protect means taking feasible measures, depending on the circumstances, to facilitate the functioning of military medical establishments and units and to prevent their being harmed.[42] While the wording of this obligation does not *per se* suggest an obligation of conduct, its practical implementation, which would depend on a Party's capacity to implement such measures and on the prevailing security situation, makes such nuancing necessary.

1806   It is not specified which Party to the conflict has the obligation to protect military medical establishments and units from harm – the adverse Party or the Party to which the establishments or units are attached. Given that the discharge of this obligation is dependent on what is feasible in the circumstances, the obligation may apply to one or the other. The determination of which Party that would be hinges on a variety of factors, such as who controls the territory where the facility is located, the Party's influence over the potential perpetrators of harm, geographical proximity and humanitarian and military considerations.

1807   As regards the content of the obligation to protect, the taking of feasible measures to support the functioning of medical establishments and units means that a Party must actively help to ensure the delivery of medical supplies or equipment or ensure more generally that the medical units are not deprived of other vital resources such as electricity or water.[43]

1808   The obligation to prevent medical establishments and units from being harmed entails taking all feasible measures to ensure that such establishments and units are respected. Thus, preventive measures may be called for to ensure that their mission is not jeopardized by third parties, for example private persons such as looters or rioters who are not attributable to a Party to the conflict. Moreover, where the functioning of a medical establishment or unit

---

[41] See, in this regard, also the recommendations of military experts elaborated as part of the Health Care in Danger initiative for minimizing the negative humanitarian effects of search operations in health-care facilities by State armed forces; ICRC, *Promoting Military Operational Practice that Ensures Safe Access to and Delivery of Health Care*, ICRC, Geneva, 2014, pp. 25–27 and 36–38.

[42] See e.g. Peru, *IHL Manual*, 2004, para. 88(b).

[43] See Sandoz/Swinarski/Zimmermann (eds), *Commentary on the Additional Protocols*, ICRC, 1987, para. 518. For recommendations that could be usefully taken into account (while not necessarily legally binding), see those elaborated by experts as part of consultations conducted in the context of the Health Care in Danger initiative to ensure the supply chain of health-care facilities with essential goods and equipment; ICRC, *Ensuring the Preparedness and Security of Health-Care Facilities in Armed Conflict and Other Emergencies*, ICRC, Geneva, 2015, pp. 49–54.

is already impeded by looters or rioters, the fulfilment of this obligation may require coming to the aid of the affected facility.

c. The terms 'in no circumstances' and 'at all times'

1809 The fact that medical establishments and units may *in no circumstances* be attacked, and that the obligations to respect and protect must be observed *at all times*,[44] reaffirms the non-reciprocal character of these rules.[45] This also means that such establishments and units enjoy protection even when they contain no wounded or sick people or any medical personnel at a given time. Furthermore, the stringent character of the prohibition of attack and of the obligations to respect and protect these establishments and units, which is apparent from the terms 'in no circumstances' and 'at all times', also explains why reprisals against them are prohibited under Article 46 of the First Convention.

1810   However, the terms 'in no circumstances' and 'at all times' are without prejudice to the possibility that medical establishments and units may lose their specific protection if they are used to commit acts harmful to the enemy, outside their humanitarian duties.[46] These terms are also without prejudice to the specific rules that apply to medical establishments and units under Articles 33 and 34 of the First Convention.

d. Criminal aspects of a violation

1811 Since military medical establishments and units constitute property protected under the First Convention, violations of the prohibition of attack and of the obligation to respect under Article 19 may give rise to the grave breach of 'extensive destruction and appropriation, not justified by military necessity and carried out unlawfully and wantonly', pursuant to Article 50 of the Convention.[47] Furthermore, under the ICC Statute it is a war crime to '[i]ntentionally direc[t] attacks against...hospitals and places where the wounded and sick are collected, provided they are not military objectives'.[48] Attacks directed against protected medical establishments and units displaying the distinctive emblem may also amount under the Statute to the war crime of '[i]ntentionally directing attacks against buildings,...medical units...using

---

[44] In the light of this stringent formulation, the usefulness of Article 23 of the Second Convention, pursuant to which medical establishments on land must be protected from bombardment or attack from the sea, was challenged during the drafting debates on that provision. See the commentary on Article 23 of the Second Convention.

[45] This is a specific expression of this principle, which can be found in the obligation to 'respect and ensure respect for the present Convention in all circumstances' in common Article 1. On the interpretation of this notion, see the commentary on that article, para. 188.

[46] For further details on these notions, see Articles 21 and 22.

[47] Such actions are also included as a grave breach in the list of war crimes in Article 8(2)(a)(iv) of the 1998 ICC Statute. See also Mikos-Skuza, pp. 225–227.

[48] This is a war crime in both international and non-international armed conflict; see ICC Statute (1998), Article 8(2)(b)(ix) and (e)(iv).

the distinctive emblems of the Geneva Conventions in conformity with international law'.[49]

3. Second sentence: Medical units falling into enemy hands

1812   The second sentence of Article 19(1), which was added in 1949, deals with the scenario in which military medical establishments or units fall into enemy hands. The very existence of the sentence implies that this possibility is not *per se* precluded by humanitarian law and that there may be circumstances in which an enemy Power legitimately takes over such an establishment or unit, including through capture.[50] The sentence does not specify how military medical establishments or units must fall into enemy hands in order for this provision to apply. Therefore, all possible scenarios are covered, including where the enemy forcibly takes possession of a medical establishment or unit or where its personnel voluntarily surrender.

1813   This sentence provides guidance on how a Party to the conflict is to implement its obligations vis-à-vis wounded or sick enemy combatants found in medical establishments and units, given that the Power into whose hands they have fallen may not immediately be in a position to ensure their continued care. Thus, it reflects the principle that, while implicitly recalling the obligations of the Detaining Power with respect to the wounded and sick in its hands, until such time as the Detaining Power is capable of assuming these obligations, medical establishments and units of the adversary falling into its hands must be able to continue to operate.[51]

1814   The wording 'their personnel shall be free to pursue their duties' is actually centred on medical personnel rather than on the medical establishments or units in which they work. In this way, this provision is related to the 'retention' regime of medical personnel covered by Articles 24 and 26, which makes the possibility of depriving such personnel of their liberty dependent on whether this is necessary for the continued medical or spiritual care of prisoners of war.[52]

---

[49] This, too, is a war crime in both international and non-international armed conflict; see ICC Statute (1998), Article 8(2)(b)(xxiv) and (e)(ii). Paragraph 1 of the 2002 ICC Elements of Crimes adds, in this connection, that attacks directed against buildings, medical units or other objects using another *method of identification indicating protection under the Geneva Conventions* are also covered by this war crime. This formulation takes into account the additional means of identification created for medical units, including those covered by Article 19 of the First Convention and by Annex I to Additional Protocol I, in particular light signals, radio signals and electronic identification. See Additional Protocol I, Annex I, Articles 6–9.

[50] Mikos-Skuza, p. 221.

[51] See *Final Record of the Diplomatic Conference of 1949*, Vol. II-A, p. 193.

[52] See First Convention, Articles 28 and 30–31, and Third Convention, Article 33. This is without prejudice to the fact that the primary responsibility for the medical care of prisoners of war remains with the Detaining Power, and not with the retained medical personnel. See First Convention, Article 28(4).

1815   The principle of continued care of wounded and sick members of the armed forces in enemy hands also informs the regulation of medical establishments and units in which they are found and their material.[53] Even where the Party into whose hands they have fallen uses such objects for non-medical purposes or requisitions property of aid societies in case of urgent necessity,[54] it may do so only *after* ensuring the care of the wounded and sick within them.

D. Paragraph 2: Positioning of medical units

1816   Article 19(2) was newly included in 1949 and is one of the few provisions of the Conventions dealing explicitly with the conduct of hostilities. It precedes the inclusion of the more elaborate rules on the conduct of hostilities in Additional Protocol I. The obligation contained in this paragraph is intended essentially to benefit a belligerent's own medical establishments and units, and ultimately its own wounded and sick personnel (or those establishments and units of the enemy that are under its control), unlike many rules in the First Convention, which address exclusively the relationship between a Party to a conflict and wounded and sick enemy personnel.

1817   The character of the obligation to 'ensure that medical establishments and units are, as far as possible, situated in such a manner that attacks against military objectives cannot imperil their safety' is a specific precaution against the effects of attacks on military objectives.[55] The obligation is a responsibility both for the commanders of medical units and for the commanders of combatant units.[56]

1818   The obligation under discussion here relates to the location of medical establishments and units in relation to military objectives. Inasmuch as the term 'military objective' was not defined in 1949, and in view of the intricate links between this obligation and the aforementioned obligations under Additional Protocol I, this term must now be understood in accordance with the definition contained in Additional Protocol I or its customary international law equivalent.[57]

1819   While the obligation would best be discharged if such establishments and units were situated far away from any military objective, such a strict interpretation does not follow from the explicit wording of this provision, nor may

---

[53] This principle is also reflected in Articles 28, 30, 33 and 34 of the First Convention.

[54] See the commentaries on Articles 33 and 34 for an explanation of the different regimes applying to mobile medical units, fixed medical establishments and the real and personal property of aid societies.

[55] See also Article 12(4) of Additional Protocol I, which states: 'Whenever possible, the Parties to the conflict shall ensure that medical units are so sited that attacks against military objectives do not imperil their safety.'

[56] See United States, *Law of War Manual*, 2015, para. 7.10.2.2.

[57] See Additional Protocol I, Article 52(2), and ICRC Study on Customary International Humanitarian Law (2005), Rule 8.

this always be feasible in practice. First, it is not as explicit as the comparable provision of Article 18(5) of the Fourth Convention, which stipulates that 'such hospitals be situated as far as possible from such objectives'.[58] The preparatory work indicates that this was a deliberate choice, since it was pointed out that it was unrealistic to adopt too strict a standard requiring the remoteness of military medical establishments and units from military objectives. It was argued, during the 1949 Diplomatic Conference, that it was common practice to place military hospitals near military objectives, and that such proximity was even necessary to ensure rapid access to them by the wounded and sick.[59] This argument remains valid, as further underscored by the contemporary practice of some States of locating their military medical establishments inside military bases.[60] In this case also, the conditions set down in Article 19(2) apply. Thus, Parties locating medical establishments inside military bases must ensure they are as far away as possible from high value targets, such as an ammunition depot. In such a scenario, the need for the medical establishment to display the distinctive emblem is particularly compelling. Similarly, Parties may wish to establish a system of layered security, for example placing heavy armaments at the outside perimeter of the base. The important point is that, once the immediate perimeter of the medical facility is reached, the rules pertaining to the siting of medical establishments apply, regardless of its location within a military base.

1820　　Second, the obligation is subject to the caveat 'as far as possible'. Parties to the conflict should always situate medical establishments and units away from military objectives to the best of their ability. As in the case of the equivalent obligations under Additional Protocol I,[61] this means that this obligation should be taken into account in peacetime for military medical establishments in a State's own territory. However, the caveat indicates that this obligation is not absolute and that there might be circumstances in which it might not be feasible, for example, to avoid the construction of a hospital next to a barracks, or vice versa.[62] Even more importantly, in the light of contemporary warfare, with frequently shifting front lines during hostilities, it may not always be feasible to keep a distance from military objectives, in particular in the case of mobile medical units, which often operate near the battlefield. Therefore, the mere fact that a medical establishment has been built, or a mobile medical unit happens to be near, a military objective cannot in and of itself be interpreted

---

[58] Note, however, that the wording of Article 18(5) of the Fourth Convention is purely hortatory, i.e. it is merely 'recommended' to do so.

[59] The UK delegation even proposed deleting this provision entirely. Furthermore, because of the range of modern explosives, it was considered physically impossible to ensure that attacks could not endanger medical units. See *Minutes of the Diplomatic Conference of Geneva of 1949*, pp. 26–27.

[60] United States, *Law of War Manual*, 2015, para. 7.10.2.1.

[61] See Additional Protocol I, Article 12(4).

[62] See United States, *Law of War Manual*, 2015, para. 7.10.2.1. See also Mikos-Skuza, p. 213.

as a violation of the specific precautionary obligation discussed here, nor as an 'act harmful to the enemy' outside its humanitarian duties[63] leading to the loss of protection of the establishment or unit.

1821   The proximity of military medical establishments or units to military objectives may thus be a result of the impracticability, whether dictated by humanitarian considerations or by battlefield conditions, of doing otherwise. Such proximity must be distinguished from the question of whether the positioning results from an intention to shield a military objective from attack. Article 19(2) does not contain an explicit prohibition to that effect, but doing so would run counter to the purpose of this provision. An explicit prohibition exists in Article 12(4) of Additional Protocol I, which states: 'Under no circumstances shall medical units be used in an attempt to shield military objectives from attack.' In addition, such conduct would amount to an 'act harmful to the enemy' entailing a loss of protection, in accordance with Article 21 of the First Convention.[64] This does not automatically mean that in this situation a medical establishment or unit becomes a military objective. It must also meet the requirements of a 'military objective' under Article 52(2) of Additional Protocol I or its customary international law equivalent.

Select bibliography

Bart, Gregory Raymond, 'The Ambiguous Protection of Schools Under the Law of War – Time for Parity with Hospitals and Religious Buildings', *Georgetown Journal of International Law*, Vol. 40, No. 2, Winter 2009, pp. 321–358.

Gisel, Laurent, 'Can the incidental killing of military doctors never be excessive?', *International Review of the Red Cross*, Vol. 95, No. 889, March 2013, pp. 215–230.

Henckaerts, Jean-Marie and Doswald-Beck, Louise, *Customary International Humanitarian Law, Volume I: Rules*, ICRC/Cambridge University Press, 2005, available at https://www.icrc.org/customary-ihl/eng/docs/v1, Rule 28, pp. 91–97.

Kleffner, Jann K., 'Protection of the Wounded, Sick, and Shipwrecked', in Dieter Fleck (ed.), *The Handbook of International Humanitarian Law*, 3rd edition, Oxford University Press, 2013, pp. 321–357.

Mikos-Skuza, Elżbieta, 'Hospitals', in Andrew Clapham, Paola Gaeta and Marco Sassòli (eds), *The 1949 Geneva Conventions: A Commentary*, Oxford University Press, 2015, pp. 207–229.

Principe, Philip R., 'Secret Codes, Military Hospitals, and the Law of Armed Conflict: Could Military Medical Facilities' Use of Encrypted Communications Subject Them to Attack Under International Law?', *University of Arkansas at Little Rock Law Review*, Vol. 24, 2002, pp. 727–750.

---

[63] On the conditions governing the loss of protection of military medical establishments and units, see Article 21.

[64] For further details, see the commentary on Article 21, section C.1.

Smith, Michael Sean, *The Protection of Medical Units Under the Geneva Conventions in the Contemporary Operating Environment*, thesis submitted in partial fulfilment of the requirements for the degree of Master of Military Art and Science, US Army Command and General Staff College, Fort Leavenworth, 2008, http://www.dtic.mil/dtic/tr/fulltext/u2/a501873.pdf.

Vollmar, Lewis C., Jr., 'Development of the laws of war as they pertain to medical units and their personnel', *Military Medicine*, Vol. 157, 1992, pp. 231–236.

PROTECTION OF HOSPITAL SHIPS

❖ Text of the provision

Hospital ships entitled to the protection of the Geneva Convention for the Amelioration of the Condition of Wounded, Sick and Shipwrecked Members of Armed Forces at Sea of August 12, 1949, shall not be attacked from the land.

❖ Reservations or declarations

None

Contents

A. Introduction

1822 This provision of the First Convention deals with a very specific scenario: attacks launched from land against hospital ships at sea. The provision prohibits such attacks. If launched from any platform at sea, be it beneath the surface, e.g. a submarine, or above, including from an aircraft, the attack would be prohibited on the basis of Articles 22, 24 or 25 of the Second Convention. Thus, an attack on a hospital ship is prohibited, regardless of its geographic point of departure.

1823 Article 20 goes hand in hand with Article 23 of the Second Convention: the former prohibits attacks from land against hospital ships entitled to the protection of the Second Convention, while the latter prohibits attacks from the sea against land-based establishments entitled to the protection of the First Convention.

B. Historical background

1824 Article 20 has no precursor in previous treaties. It originates from an amendment introduced by the United Kingdom during the 1949 Diplomatic

Conference.[1] In the initial version, the amendment combined the substantive elements of what eventually became Article 20 of the First Convention and Article 23 of the Second Convention. In the UK proposal the amendment was to be included in the Second Convention.[2]

1825   When the amendment was discussed, some delegations questioned whether it had any added value. Did it not state the obvious in that the three categories of hospital ships recognized under the Second Convention 'may in no circumstances be attacked . . . but shall *at all times* be respected and protected' (emphasis added)?[3] It was felt that the more generally phrased rule aptly captured the protection of hospital ships, and that there was no need to go into particular scenarios. Indeed, an attack from land is only one among several possible scenarios in which hospital ships might find themselves attacked. One of these is attack from an aircraft, which is equally prohibited, irrespective of whether the aircraft is flying above land (in which case the First Convention applies) or above sea (in which case the Second Convention applies).[4]

1826   When a proposal by one delegation to delete the UK amendment was put to a vote, it failed to attract sufficient support.[5] Other than a sense that the provision undoubtedly reflected the humanitarian considerations which the Convention sought to turn into binding law, the main reason the article was retained seems to have been an excess of caution. The delegates at the 1949 Diplomatic Conference who opted in favour of including the amendment were concerned that commanders of 'armed forces in the field' would not be familiar with the substantive rules of the Second Convention and that commanders of 'armed forces at sea' would not be familiar with the substantive rules of the First Convention.[6]

1827   In line with this concern, it was decided to split the substance of the amendment into two parts, becoming Article 20 of the First Convention and Article 23 of the Second Convention, respectively. Thus, the message could be delivered where it was felt to be most needed.

C. Discussion

1. The prohibition on attacking hospital ships

1828 Under Article 20, it is prohibited to 'attack' 'from the land' '[h]ospital ships entitled to the protection of' the Second Convention. Each of these three terms is analysed below.

---

[1] The historical record of the Second World War reveals numerous instances of attacks against hospital ships, albeit launched mostly from aircraft or submarines; see Philippe Eberlin, *Crimes de Guerre en Mer 1939–1945*, MDV – Maîtres du Vent, 2007, pp. 115–124.

[2] *Final Record of the Diplomatic Conference of Geneva of 1949*, Vol. II-A, p. 146.

[3] Second Convention, Article 22(1), to which both Articles 24 and 25 refer on this point.

[4] *Minutes of the Diplomatic Conference of Geneva of 1949*, Commission I, Vol. I, 12th session held on 9 May 1949, p. 48.

[5] *Final Record of the Diplomatic Conference of Geneva of 1949*, Vol. II-A, p. 147.   [6] *Ibid.*

1829   The words 'from the land' need to be understood in their ordinary meaning, i.e. in geographic terms, starting as of the coast. In line with this approach, islands, including rocks, equally qualify as 'land' for the purposes of interpreting this provision.[7]

1830   Article 20 applies to any persons on land or in the air while flying over land, and this irrespective of the branch of the armed forces they belong to. This understanding also flows from the logic underpinning Article 4 of the Second Convention.[8]

1831   The prohibition only covers attacks against '[h]ospital ships entitled to the protection of' the Second Convention. The three categories of vessels concerned are dealt with in Articles 22, 24 and 25 of the Second Convention, respectively.[9] By adopting the wording 'entitled to the protection of', the rule remains without prejudice to circumstances in which hospital ships might lose their protection.[10]

1832   Under the Geneva Conventions, no definition exists of the verb '[to] attack'.[11] Under Additional Protocol I, the noun 'attack' is defined as 'acts of violence against the adversary, whether in offence or in defence'.[12]

2. The place of Article 20 in contemporary international humanitarian law

1833   The stated rationale for including Article 20 in the First Convention stemmed from the desire to ensure that armed forces on land – familiar with the First Convention – were aware of the protection due to hospital ships under the Second Convention. The prohibition on attacking hospital ships is also contained in the much more generally phrased, and wider, obligation to 'respect and protect' them, which flows from Articles 22–24 and 25 of the Second Convention.

1834   The insertion of Article 20 in the First Convention was done at a time when – at least in terms of treaty law – the law applicable to the conduct of hostilities had not yet undergone the development and refinement it would eventually undergo in Articles 48–58 of Additional Protocol I. In the framework of Additional Protocol I, it is clear that hospital ships 'entitled to the protection of' the Second Convention cannot be considered military objectives.[13] Furthermore, a

---

[7] Article 121(1) of the 1982 United Nations Convention on the Law of the Sea defines an 'island' as 'a naturally formed area of land, surrounded by water, which is above water at high tide'. While Article 121(3) of the same Convention stipulates that '[r]ocks which cannot sustain human habitation or economic life of their own shall have no exclusive economic zone or continental shelf', this has no implications for the provision commented upon here. Thus, 'rocks' at sea qualify as being 'land' for the purposes of Article 20 of the First Convention.

[8] For details, see the commentary on Article 4 of the Second Convention.

[9] Article 22(1)–(2) of Additional Protocol I further expands the categories of vessels entitled to the protection of the Second Convention.

[10] For details on loss of protection, see the commentary on Article 34 of the Second Convention.

[11] It should be noted that Article 23 of the Second Convention (which mirrors Article 20 of the First Convention for all armed forces at sea) speaks of 'bombardment or attack'. For a discussion, see the commentary on Article 23 of the Second Convention.

[12] Additional Protocol I, Article 49(1).

[13] Technically speaking, Articles 48–67 of Additional Protocol I do not apply – as a matter of treaty law – to the scenario in Article 20 of the First Convention, i.e. an attack by armed forces on

violation of Article 20 of the First Convention may amount to the war crime of intentionally directing attacks against medical transports using the distinctive emblems of the Geneva Conventions in conformity with international law.[14]

1835   Since Article 20 states an obvious point, it has attracted no debate or controversy. The provision remains valid but stands in the shadow of more generally phrased rules (such as Article 22(1) of the Second Convention), of which it is simply an illustration of a particular point.

1836   Hospital ships are but one of the categories of vessels which may not be attacked from the land. Any type of vessel which does not qualify as a 'military objective' must not be the object of such an attack.[15] The 1994 San Remo Manual on International Law Applicable to Armed Conflicts at Sea lists no less than nine other classes of enemy vessels which are exempt from attack and whose protection can only be lost if they qualify as a military objective and provided additional conditions are met.[16]

---

land against a hospital ship at sea. See Article 49(3) of Additional Protocol I, which states: 'The provisions of this section apply to any land, air or sea warfare which may affect the civilian population, individual civilians or civilian objects *on land*. They further apply to all attacks from the sea or from the air against objectives *on land* but do not otherwise affect the rules of international law applicable in armed conflict at sea or in the air.' (Emphasis added.) Despite this technicality, it is nowadays uncontroversial to conclude that the rule embedded in Article 20 of the First Convention is in line with contemporary customary international humanitarian law applicable to the conduct of hostilities, regardless of the interaction between land, sea and air components of modern warfare.

[14] See ICC Statute (1998), Article 8(2)(b)(xxiv).

[15] Under the Second Convention, it is similarly prohibited to attack lifeboats of hospital ships (Article 26) and small craft employed by the State or by the officially recognized lifeboat institutions for coastal rescue operations (Article 27).

[16] Rule 47 of the 1994 San Remo Manual on International Law Applicable to Armed Conflicts at Sea states:

The following classes of enemy vessels are exempt from attack:
- (a) hospital ships;
- (b) small craft used for coastal rescue operations and other medical transports;
- (c) vessels granted safe conduct by agreement between the belligerent parties including:
  - (i) cartel vessels, e.g., vessels designated for and engaged in the transport of prisoners of war;
  - (ii) vessels engaged in humanitarian missions, including vessels carrying supplies indispensable to the survival of the civilian population, and vessels engaged in relief actions and rescue operations;
- (d) vessels engaged in transporting cultural property under special protection;
- (e) passenger vessels when engaged only in carrying civilian passengers;
- (f) vessels charged with religious, non-military, scientific or philanthropic missions, vessels collecting scientific data of likely military applications are not protected;
- (g) small coastal fishing vessels and small boats engaged in local coastal trade, but they are subject to the regulations of a belligerent naval commander operating in the area and to inspection;
- (h) vessels designed or adapted exclusively for responding to pollution incidents in the marine environment;
- (i) vessels which have surrendered;
- (j) life rafts and life boats.

DISCONTINUANCE OF PROTECTION OF MEDICAL UNITS AND ESTABLISHMENTS

❖ Text of the provision

The protection to which fixed establishments and mobile medical units of the Medical Service are entitled shall not cease unless they are used to commit, outside their humanitarian duties, acts harmful to the enemy. Protection may, however, cease only after a due warning has been given, naming, in all appropriate cases, a reasonable time limit and after such warning has remained unheeded.

❖ Reservations or declarations

None

Contents

A. Introduction

1837   Article 21 lays down the conditions under which military medical establishments and units covered by Article 19 of the First Convention[1] lose their protection, i.e. if they are 'used to commit, outside their humanitarian duties, acts harmful to the enemy'. It also regulates the stringent criteria that must be met before such a loss of protection becomes effective: a warning which provides, in all appropriate cases, a reasonable time limit has to be given. Protection ceases only 'after such a warning has remained unheeded'. These specific conditions are reiterated in several provisions of the Geneva Conventions and their

---

[1] Article 19 also covers medical establishments and units of National Societies and other voluntary aid societies auxiliary to or assisting the military medical services, to the extent that they fulfil the conditions of Articles 26 or 27 of the First Convention. See the commentary on Article 19, para. 1783.

Additional Protocols.[2] The requirement of a warning, coupled with an appropriate time limit, sets a higher threshold for the loss of protection of these specifically protected objects than that governing civilian objects under general protection.[3]

B. Historical background

1838 As early as 1906, the Geneva Convention provided that the protection of 'sanitary formations' and establishments ceases if they are used to commit 'acts injurious to the enemy'.[4] The 1929 Geneva Convention introduced a minor change to this wording by using the term 'acts harmful to the enemy' for the first time in international treaty law.[5] The same formulation also appears in the provision under discussion here, with the addition of 'outside their humanitarian duties'.

C. Discussion

1. *Acts harmful to the enemy, outside their humanitarian duties*

1839 Article 21 specifies that the protection of military medical establishments and units may not cease '*unless* they are used to commit, outside their humanitarian duties, acts harmful to the enemy' (emphasis added). The wording makes it clear that this is the sole criterion by which military medical establishments or units may lose protection. From a humanitarian perspective, both the word 'unless' and the addition of 'outside their humanitarian duties' constitute important safeguards in view of the adverse consequences for the wounded and sick that such a loss of protection would entail.

1840   The formulations 'acts harmful to the enemy' and 'outside their humanitarian duties' are not defined in the Convention. The preparatory work shows that there was a controversy over whether to adopt the concept of 'acts harmful to the enemy' or that of 'acts incompatible with their humanitarian duties'.

---

[2] See Second Convention, Article 34; Fourth Convention, Article 19; Additional Protocol I, Articles 13 and 65; and Additional Protocol II, Article 11(2). Article 13(1) of Additional Protocol I and Article 11(2) of Additional Protocol II speak of 'humanitarian function' instead of 'humanitarian duties', while Article 11(2) of Additional Protocol II speaks of 'hostile acts' instead of 'acts harmful to the enemy'. These terminological differences have no substantive implications. On the applicability of these criteria with regard to medical personnel, see the commentary on Article 24, section F. That these conditions also apply to medical transports is evident from the fact that their protection is expressly the same as that of mobile medical units. See Article 35 of the First Convention and Article 21 of Additional Protocol I. Therefore, the rules regarding their loss of protection are also the same.

[3] On the general protection of civilian objects, see the commentary on Article 52 of Additional Protocol I.

[4] Geneva Convention (1906), Article 7.

[5] Geneva Convention on the Wounded and Sick (1929), Article 7.

Therefore, these two notions were initially perceived to be alternatives.[6] While the ICRC expressed its preference for 'acts harmful to the enemy' over 'acts incompatible with their humanitarian duties', it prepared an alternative proposal in case the wording 'acts harmful to the enemy' did not meet with States' approval at the 1949 Diplomatic Conference. This proposal read in part as follows: 'acts the purpose or effect of which is to harm the adverse Party, by facilitating or impeding military operations'.[7] In the end, the Drafting Committee at the 1949 Diplomatic Conference decided, as a compromise, to combine the two formulations 'acts harmful to the enemy' and 'acts incompatible with their humanitarian function', rather than deciding in favour of one or the other or providing a definition of acts leading to a loss of protection, as in the above ICRC proposal.[8] Therefore, both the wording and the preparatory work make it clear that acts must fulfil the two cumulative criteria of being harmful to the enemy and being committed outside their humanitarian duties for a military medical establishment or unit to lose its protection.

1841   Notwithstanding the lack of an agreed definition of 'acts harmful to the enemy', the rationale for a loss of protection is clear. Military medical establishments and units enjoy protection because of their function of providing care for the wounded and sick. When they are used, outside their function, to interfere, *directly or indirectly*, in military operations and thereby cause harm to the enemy, the rationale for their specific protection is removed. Furthermore, an act harmful to the enemy, which may render a military medical establishment or unit liable to attack, may seriously endanger the wounded and sick entrusted to its care.[9] Lastly, such an act may also engender distrust of the work of military medical establishments or units in other cases, and thus may lessen the protective value of the Convention in general.

1842   Any use by a Party to the conflict of military medical establishments or units for military purposes may be considered an 'act harmful to the enemy'.[10]

---

[6] Originally, the draft text of the Convention submitted to the 1949 Diplomatic Conference, which had resulted from the 1948 International Conference of the Red Cross in Stockholm, had replaced the notion of 'acts harmful to the enemy', proposed in a draft text prepared for that conference, with 'acts incompatible with their humanitarian duties'; see *Draft Conventions adopted by the 1948 Stockholm Conference*, draft article 16, p. 15. However, at the 1949 Diplomatic Conference, the United Kingdom proposed an amendment, namely to revert to the wording 'acts harmful to the enemy'; see *Final Record of the Diplomatic Conference of Geneva of 1949*, Vol. II-A, p. 58.

[7] For the text of this proposal, see *ICRC Remarks and Proposals on the 1948 Stockholm Draft*, p. 12. This definition is furthermore referred to in Belgium, *Law of Armed Conflict Training Manual*, 2009, Course V, p. 16, and United States, *Army Health System*, 2013, para. 3–26.

[8] See *Final Record of the Diplomatic Conference of Geneva of 1949*, Vol. II-A, p. 132.

[9] Even in such a case, however, the enemy must take all feasible precautions to avoid or minimize incidental loss of life of, or injury to, wounded and sick within the military medical establishment or unit that has lost its protection. See para. 1854.

[10] The practice of a number of States supports this broad understanding. See e.g. Cameroon, *Disciplinary Regulations*, 2007, Article 31 ('It is evidently necessary that structures and buildings are not being used for military purposes'); Ecuador, *Naval Manual*, 1989, para. 8.5.1.4 ('If medical facilities are used for military purposes inconsistent with their humanitarian mission, and if appropriate warnings that continuation of such use will result in loss of protected status are unheeded, the facilities become subject to attack'); and United States, *Naval Handbook*, 2007,

Examples of such use include firing at the enemy for reasons other than individual self-defence, installing a firing position in a medical post,[11] the use of a hospital as a shelter for able-bodied combatants,[12] as an arms or ammunition dump,[13] or as a military observation post,[14] or the placing of a medical unit in proximity to a military objective with the intention of shielding it from the enemy's military operations.[15] Furthermore, scenarios that are recognized as being 'acts harmful to the enemy' in the context of hospital ships under the Second Convention (transmitting information of military value) and of civilian hospitals under the Fourth Convention (use of a civilian hospital as a centre for liaison with fighting troops) may also constitute 'acts harmful to the enemy' in the context of military medical establishments and units under the First Convention. Engaging in such acts may not only lead to a loss of protection, but may also qualify, where the establishments and units were displaying the distinctive emblems, as improper use of the emblems or as the war crime of perfidy, if done in order to kill or injure an enemy combatant.[16]

1843   In contrast to the provisions of the Second Convention relating to hospital ships, the First Convention does not contain any prescriptions for how military medical establishments or units must communicate with other departments of the armed forces. This issue arises in connection with the use of 'encrypted communications', i.e. communication in a form that is unintelligible to the enemy, which is expressly prohibited for hospital ships under the Second Convention.[17] Where such encrypted communications are used, the enemy might not have the means to verify whether the encrypted data contain

---

para. 8.9.1.4 ('If medical facilities are used for military purposes inconsistent with their humanitarian mission, and if appropriate warnings that continuation of such use will result in loss of protected status are unheeded, the facilities become subject to attack.').

[11] See Switzerland, *Basic Military Manual*, 1987, Article 83. The issue of arming military medical establishments or units is dealt with in greater detail in the commentary on Article 22, section C.

[12] See e.g. Netherlands, *Military Handbook*, 2003, p. 7–44; Switzerland, *Basic Military Manual*, 1987, Article 83; and United States, *Law of War Manual*, 2015, para. 7.10.3.1.

[13] See e.g. South Africa, *LOAC Manual*, 1996, Appendix A, Chapter 4, para. 59; Switzerland, *Basic Military Manual*, 1987, Article 83; and United States, *Law of War Manual*, 2015, para. 7.10.3.1.

[14] See e.g. Switzerland, *Basic Military Manual*, 1987, Article 83, and United States, *Air Force Pamphlet*, 1976, para. 3–2(d).

[15] See e.g. Belgium, *Law of Armed Conflict Training Manual*, 2009, Course V, p. 16, and Peru, *IHL Manual*, 2004, Chapter V, para. 88(b)(2).

[16] Article 38 of Additional Protocol I prohibits any improper use of the emblems. In addition, the perfidious use, in violation of Article 37 of Additional Protocol I, of one of the distinctive emblems or protective signs recognized by the Conventions or by that Protocol amounts to a grave breach, in accordance with Article 85(3)(f) of Additional Protocol I. See also ICRC Study on Customary International Humanitarian Law (2005), Rules 59 and 65. In addition, under the 1998 ICC Statute, making improper use of the distinctive emblems of the Geneva Conventions, resulting in death or serious injury, is also a war crime in international armed conflict (Article 8(2)(b)(vii)), and treacherously killing or wounding individuals belonging to the hostile nation/army/adversary is a war crime in both international and non-international armed conflict (Article 8(2)(b)(xi) and (e)(ix), respectively).

[17] Article 34(2) of the Second Convention states: 'In particular, hospital ships may not possess or use a secret code for their wireless or other means of communication.' See the commentary on that article for how this prohibition is interpreted today.

only medical information, or whether it is used for transmitting information of military value. Thus, there is the potential for abuse. On the other hand, encryption may protect the confidentiality of medical data and may thereby serve a humanitarian purpose. For this reason, the use of encrypted information *per se* would not necessarily lead to the conclusion that an 'act harmful to the enemy' has been committed. Without being legally obliged to do so, a Party to an armed conflict may decide that (at least part of) the communications of a military medical establishment be transmitted via an unencrypted channel, to allow the adverse Party to verify that the establishment is not being used to commit acts harmful to the enemy.

1844   The wording 'outside their humanitarian duties', as an additional requirement for concluding that 'acts harmful to the enemy' have been committed, serves to prevent an overly broad understanding of such acts. Even if a particular type of conduct may appear to constitute an 'act harmful to the enemy', it will still not result in a loss of protection where it remains within the humanitarian duties of the military establishment or unit. One scenario might occur where a mobile medical unit accidentally breaks down while it is being moved in accordance with its humanitarian function and thereby obstructs a crossroads of military importance. More generally, as mobile medical units will need to be able to move near the front line, this additional caveat would preclude their mere presence on or close to the battlefield from being interpreted as an 'act harmful to the enemy'. In interpreting the present provision, one must bear in mind that it is based on humanitarian considerations. Therefore, in case of doubt as to whether a particular type of conduct amounts to an 'act harmful to the enemy', it should not be considered as such.

1845   Hence, the conditions entailing a loss of protection under the First Convention must be interpreted strictly. The examples of 'acts harmful to the enemy' must be read together with the non-exhaustive list of conditions in Article 22 of the Convention that are not to be considered such acts. Thus, Article 22 provides further guidance to prevent too broad an understanding of the term 'acts harmful to the enemy'.

2. Warning and time limit

1846 The requirement that protection may cease 'only after a due warning has been given, naming, in all appropriate cases, a reasonable time limit and after such warning has remained unheeded' was introduced by the 1949 Geneva Conventions.[18] These conditions highlight the specific protection to which medical establishments and units are entitled, as compared with the general

---

[18] The same requirements are stated in Article 34 of the Second Convention for hospital ships, Article 19 of the Fourth Convention for civilian hospitals, Article 13(1) of Additional Protocol I for civilian medical units, and Article 11(2) of Additional Protocol II for medical units and transports.

protection enjoyed by civilian objects under Additional Protocol I and customary international law.[19]

1847   In the first place, loss of protection does not necessarily mean that the establishment will be attacked, in that it also includes the possibility that its functioning may be interfered with. This follows from the basic obligation to respect and protect military medical establishments and units, which also requires Parties to the conflict to do more than merely refrain from attacking them.[20] The question of whether such an establishment or unit may be the object of an attack in turn depends on it fulfilling the criteria for qualifying as a 'military objective'. In practice, however, it is hard to conceive of circumstances in which the commission of an 'act harmful to the enemy' would not transform the facility in question into a military objective.

1848   Second, the stipulation that protection may cease 'only after a due warning has been given' establishes that such a warning must be issued even where an 'act harmful to the enemy, outside their humanitarian function' has occurred. The wording indicates a strict interpretation of the 'due warning' requirement which is not subject to the caveat 'in all appropriate cases', as this comes after the further requirement of naming a reasonable time limit.[21] However, certain States are explicit in recognizing that there may be situations where a warning is not 'due' owing to overriding military necessity or the exercise of the right of combatants' self-defence, such as may occur when combatants approaching a military medical establishment or unit come under fire from persons inside it.[22]

---

[19] See Additional Protocol I, Articles 48–58, and ICRC Study on Customary International Humanitarian Law (2005), Rules 1–24.

[20] On the meaning of the obligation to respect and protect military medical establishments and units, see the commentary on Article 19, section C.2.

[21] In contrast, Article 57(2)(c) of Additional Protocol I provides, with respect to the general precautionary obligations regarding civilians, that 'effective advance warning shall be given of attacks which may affect the civilian population, unless circumstances do not permit', thereby generally subjecting the warning requirement to the caveat 'unless circumstances do not permit'. This would, in particular, allow combatants to dispense with a warning where surprise is of the essence in an attack.

[22] See e.g. Australia, *Manual of the Law of Armed Conflict*, 2006, para. 9.69 ('Military medical personnel, facilities and equipment are also entitled to general protection under the Geneva Conventions. However, they may lose this protection if they engage in acts harmful to the enemy. Before the protection of medical personnel and facilities is lost, a warning will normally be provided and reasonable time allowed to permit cessation of improper activities. In extreme cases, overriding military necessity may preclude such a warning.'). See also the decision of the Israeli Supreme Court sitting as the High Court of Justice in *Physicians for Human Rights* v. *Commander of the IDF Forces in the West Bank*, Judgment, 2002, which states that:

> The instructions which are to be given to soldiers should deal with, among other things, the reasonable and fair warnings which should be given to medical teams. These guidelines should be subject to the circumstances, and should be carried out by the IDF in a way that balances the threat of Palestinian fighters camouflaged as medical teams against the legal and moral obligation to uphold humanitarian rules regarding the treatment of the sick and wounded. Such a balance should take into consideration, among other things, the imminence and severity of any threat.

1849   The purpose of issuing a warning is to allow those committing an 'act harmful to the enemy' to terminate such act, or – if they persist – to ultimately allow for safe evacuation of the wounded and sick who are not responsible for such conduct and who should not become the victims of it. Against that background, a decision to dispense with the warning requirement must be taken with extreme caution, giving due consideration to the risk that this entails for wounded and sick people. Such a decision can only be allowed on an exceptional basis, in the extreme circumstances of an immediate threat to the lives of advancing combatants, where it is clear that a warning would not be complied with.

1850   Article 21 does not specify what is meant by a 'due warning', including what form it must take. The absence of a further definition of this concept has the advantage of allowing a determination to be made about how to implement this requirement in the light of concrete circumstances and the technologies available. The warning may take various forms. In many cases, it could simply consist of an order, transmitted on the spot, to cease the harmful act within a specified period. In other instances, it could also consist of an email addressed to the military authorities in charge of the establishment or unit, a radio message or a press release.[23] Whatever the method selected, it must reach those committing an 'act harmful to the enemy' in order to achieve the purpose of the warning, i.e. to allow for termination of the act or, failing that, the safe evacuation of the wounded and sick.

1851   In contrast to the warning requirement, the formulation 'reasonable time limit' is subject to the caveat 'in all appropriate cases'. In the original draft submitted to the 1949 Diplomatic Conference, this condition was not included. However, it was inserted, following one delegation's proposal to delete the requirement of naming a time limit, because of the concern that it would not always be feasible to grant such a time limit.[24] The example repeatedly given was the same scenario described above, i.e. a number of troops approaching a hospital being met by heavy fire from every window. In such a case, after the issuance of a warning, fire could be returned without delay. In other words, it is uncontroversial to dispense with the requirement of setting a time limit in cases where an imminent and severe threat emanates from a military medical establishment or unit that is used for committing an act harmful to the enemy, outside its humanitarian duties.

Further, see United States, *Law of Armed Conflict Deskbook*, 2012, p. 146, which states: 'When receiving fire from a hospital, there is no duty to warn before returning fire in self-defense'. It goes on to cite US battlefield practice in Grenada and Operation Iraqi Freedom in this regard. See also United States, *Law of War Manual*, 2015, para. 7.10.3.2.

[23] See e.g. Tallinn Manual on the International Law Applicable to Cyber Warfare (2013), Rule 73, para. 5, p. 210.

[24] See *Final Record of the Diplomatic Conference of Geneva of 1949*, Vol. II-A, pp. 58 and 193.

1852   In cases where it is appropriate to issue a time limit, Article 21, rather than laying down a precise deadline, states that that limit must be 'reasonable'. While thus allowing for sufficient flexibility to accommodate specific circumstances, the time limit must be long enough to achieve the purpose of a warning. The time limit should also allow those in charge of the military medical establishment or unit enough time to reply to the accusations that have been made.

1853   In accordance with Article 21, the loss of specific protection of military medical establishments or units will only become effective when the warning that protection will cease 'has remained unheeded', i.e. where the act harmful to the enemy is not terminated. Obviously, where the warning has been heeded, the military medical establishment or unit remains protected and the enemy may not take any adverse measure against it that it would otherwise be entitled to take had the loss of protection become effective. Thus, any adverse measure, including an attack directed against the establishment or unit, is unlawful when those committing the act harmful to the enemy ceased doing so after the warning.

1854   Where such a warning has remained unheeded, the enemy is no longer obliged to refrain from interfering with the work of a medical establishment or unit, or to take positive measures to assist it in its work. Even then humanitarian considerations relating to the welfare of the wounded and sick being cared for in the facility may not be disregarded. This is evident from the fundamental obligation – one not based on reciprocity – to respect and protect the wounded and sick *in all circumstances*. Wounded and sick persons must be spared and, as far as possible, active measures for their safety taken, including in the conduct of hostilities.[25] The same conclusion can be drawn from the general rules on the conduct of hostilities that apply to attacks on any military objective, including attacks on a military medical establishment or unit that has forfeited its protection, notably the rule on proportionality and the obligation to take all feasible precautions to avoid or at least minimize incidental loss of life of, and injury to, the wounded and sick.[26]

1855   A loss of specific protection means that a military medical establishment or unit will also become liable to attack, once it fulfils the criteria for being qualified as a military objective, which will, as stated earlier, often likely be

---

[25] See, for further details, the commentary on Article 12, section E. See also Peru, *IHL Manual*, 2004, Chapter V, para. 88(b)(2), which states explicitly that, in the context of an attack as a result of a loss of protection of a medical unit, '[i]n any event, an attempt must be made to protect the wounded and sick'.

[26] See Laurent Gisel, 'Can the incidental killing of military doctors never be excessive?', *International Review of the Red Cross*, Vol. 95, No. 889, March 2013, pp. 215–230. See also Alexandra Boivin, 'The Legal Regime Applicable to Targeting Military Objectives in the Context of Contemporary Warfare', *Research Paper Series*, No. 2, University Centre for International Humanitarian Law, Geneva, 2006, p. 56, and Kleffner, p. 344.

the case.[27] The above-mentioned restraints for the benefit of the wounded and sick will nonetheless apply.

1856   The stipulation in Article 21 that protection will 'cease', without any further qualification, appears to suggest that once protection is lost, it cannot be regained for the duration of hostilities. However, this conclusion might be unjustified, given the purpose of a loss of specific protection, especially where a single 'act harmful to the enemy' does not produce any further harmful consequences for the enemy that would render an attack necessary. Moreover, for protection to be regained after the harmful consequences of an 'act harmful to the enemy' have ceased might be deemed desirable from the point of view of the wounded and sick, who once again could benefit from an unhindered provision of medical care. Neither the preparatory work nor subsequent State practice in the interpretation of this provision allows definite conclusions to be drawn on this question.[28]

1857   One argument in favour of a temporary rather than a permanent loss of specific protection is that the status of an object during hostilities may change from a civilian object to a military objective, depending on the circumstances prevailing at a given time. Therefore, an object, including a military medical establishment or unit, which at the outset is not a military objective, may become one for such time as the criteria of a 'military objective' are fulfilled. Subsequently, when these conditions no longer exist, it will cease being a 'military objective' and will again enjoy protection from attack.[29]

1858   On the other hand, the enemy may normally assume that military medical establishments or units do not abuse their function, and on that basis must accord specific protection to them. In this regard, as has been noted, any 'act harmful to the enemy' engenders distrust and, consequently, may lessen the protective value of the Convention in general. In the context of discouraging

---

[27] See para. 1847. Furthermore, the relevance of the general definition of 'military objective' for attacks on civilian hospitals that have lost their specific protection is apparent from Article 8(2)(b)(ix) and (e)(iv) of the 1998 ICC Statute, which characterizes as a war crime 'intentionally directing attacks against . . . hospitals and places where the sick and wounded are collected, *provided they are not military objectives*' (emphasis added). This in turn is based on Article 27 of the Hague Convention (IV), which states: 'In . . . bombardments all necessary steps must be taken to spare, as far as possible, . . . hospitals, and places where the sick and wounded are collected, provided they are not being used at the time for military purposes.' See also Tallinn Manual on the International Law Applicable to Cyber Warfare (2013), p. 209.

[28] But see the following statement of one delegation, in the context of a debate on whether it would be appropriate for a time limit to accompany a warning when there is a loss of specific protection: ' . . . such acts destroy *ipso facto* all entitlement to protection'; *Minutes of the Diplomatic Conference of Geneva of 1949*, p. 43. It is also noted here that, in the case of civil defence buildings which also lose protection when 'acts harmful to the enemy' are committed, the agreed interpretation at the Diplomatic Conference leading to the adoption of the Additional Protocols was that such loss of protection would be final. See Michael Bothe, Karl Josef Partsch and Waldemar A. Solf, *New Rules for Victims of Armed Conflicts: Commentary on the Two 1977 Protocols Additional to the Geneva Conventions of 1949*, Martinus Nijhoff Publishers, The Hague, 1982, Vol. 2, p. 412.

[29] See the commentary on Article 19 of the Fourth Convention, and especially the ICTY jurisprudence quoted in it. See also Haeck, p. 847.

the further commission of 'acts harmful to the enemy', a definitive loss of protection may be justified. Especially where such acts are not confined to isolated or sporadic incidents, but have been committed repeatedly, the enemy's trust may not be easily regained.

1859   Were one to accept the possibility of protection being regained in such cases, something more might be required to justify renewed protection than simply switching back to medical activities. For example, the military medical establishment or unit could reorganize or remove the persons who committed 'acts harmful to the enemy', thereby making the intention clear to the enemy that, in the future, the establishment or unit will again be exclusively dedicated to medical purposes.[30]

Select bibliography

Haeck, Tom, 'Loss of Protection', in Andrew Clapham, Paola Gaeta and Marco Sassòli (eds), *The 1949 Geneva Conventions: A Commentary*, Oxford University Press, 2015, pp. 839–854.

Henckaerts, Jean-Marie and Doswald-Beck, Louise, *Customary International Humanitarian Law, Volume I: Rules*, Cambridge University Press, 2005, Rule 28, pp. 91–97, available at https://www.icrc.org/customary-ihl/eng/docs/v1.

Kleffner, Jann K., 'Protection of the Wounded, Sick, and Shipwrecked', in Dieter Fleck (ed.), *The Handbook of International Humanitarian Law*, 3rd edition, Oxford University Press, 2013, pp. 321–357.

Principe, Philip R., 'Secret Codes, Military Hospitals, and the Law of Armed Conflict: Could Military Medical Facilities' Use of Encrypted Communications Subject Them to Attack Under International Law?', *University of Arkansas at Little Rock Law Review*, Vol. 24, 2002, pp. 727–750.

Smith, Michael Sean, *The Protection of Medical Units Under the Geneva Conventions in the Contemporary Operating Environment*, thesis submitted in partial fulfillment of the requirements for the degree of Master of Military Art and Science, US Army Command and General Staff College, Fort Leavenworth, 2008, http://www.dtic.mil/dtic/tr/fulltext/u2/a501873.pdf.

---

[30] For a similar case involving civil defence personnel, see Michael Bothe, Karl Josef Partsch and Waldemar A. Solf, *New Rules for Victims of Armed Conflicts: Commentary on the Two 1977 Protocols Additional to the Geneva Conventions of 1949*, Vol. 2, Martinus Nijhoff Publishers, The Hague, 1982, p. 413.

CONDITIONS NOT DEPRIVING MEDICAL UNITS AND ESTABLISHMENTS OF PROTECTION

❖ Text of the provision

The following conditions shall not be considered as depriving a medical unit or establishment of the protection guaranteed by Article 19:

(1) That the personnel of the unit or establishment are armed, and that they use the arms in their own defence, or in that of the wounded and sick in their charge.
(2) That in the absence of armed orderlies, the unit or establishment is protected by a picket or by sentries or by an escort.
(3) That small arms and ammunition taken from the wounded and sick and not yet handed to the proper service, are found in the unit or establishment.
(4) That personnel and material of the veterinary service are found in the unit or establishment, without forming an integral part thereof.
(5) That the humanitarian activities of medical units and establishments or of their personnel extend to the care of civilian wounded or sick.

❖ Reservations or declarations

None

Contents

A. Introduction

1860 Article 22 expressly sets out five 'conditions', i.e. specific factual scenarios, which must not be regarded as acts harmful to the enemy, in spite of certain appearances which may lead to the opposite conclusion or at least create some doubt. Consequently, conduct falling within the list of acts specified in Article 22 does not lead to a loss of protection of the military medical establishment or unit in question. In this sense, this article supplements Article 21 of the First Convention, which contains the principle that only acts harmful to the enemy, committed outside their humanitarian duties, may lead military medical establishments or units to lose their protection. The list of factual scenarios described in Article 22 merely gives an illustration of situations that may not be considered as acts harmful to the enemy; as such, it is not an exhaustive list.[1] Similar illustrative lists are to be found in the Second and Fourth Conventions, as well as in Additional Protocol I.[2]

B. Historical background

1861 Virtually all of the factual scenarios included in Article 22 of the First Convention had already appeared in previous international treaties. Provisions equivalent to Article 22(1)–(3) may be found in both the 1906 Geneva Convention[3] and the 1929 Geneva Convention on the Wounded and Sick, while the 1929 Convention also contains a provision corresponding to Article 22(4).[4] Therefore, the only addition in 1949 was Article 22(5) of the First Convention. Its inclusion was necessary, since in practice civilians may receive care in military medical establishments and units in the same way as wounded or sick combatants, and since, for the first time, an international treaty, the Fourth Convention, was exclusively devoted to civilians.

---

[1] See also, in this respect, Switzerland, *Military Manual*, 1984, Article 83, which paraphrases the scenarios contained in Article 22 and refers to them as '*examples* of cases that do not give rise to a loss of protection' (emphasis added). This is also evident from Sierra Leone's military manual, which considers the following scenario, spelt out neither in Article 22 nor in any other provision of international humanitarian treaty law, as not leading to a loss of protection of a medical unit: 'The delivery to [a] medical unit of wounded and sick personnel is in non-medical transport[s], such as ordinary, unmarked military vehicle[s] or helicopters'; see Sierra Leone, *Instructor Manual*, 2007, p. 59.

[2] The lists of acts not leading to a loss of protection for hospital ships under Article 35 of the Second Convention and for civilian hospitals under Article 19 of the Fourth Convention overlap with Article 22(1), (3) and (5) and with Article 22(3) and (5), respectively. Furthermore, the list of acts not constituting acts harmful to the enemy for civilian medical units under Article 13(2) of Additional Protocol I corresponds to the scenarios addressed by Article 22(1), (2) and (3).

[3] Geneva Convention (1906), Article 8.

[4] Geneva Convention on the Wounded and Sick (1929), Article 8.

C. Paragraph 1: Carrying or use of arms in self-defence or defence of the wounded and sick

1862 Article 22(1) governs the issue of the arming of medical, auxiliary medical, and religious personnel associated with a military medical establishment or unit and what this entails for the protection of the establishment or unit.[5] This paragraph makes it clear that such personnel may be armed and that they may, in case of need, use these arms in their own defence or in that of the wounded and sick in their charge.

1863   While this paragraph expressly refers only to the 'wounded and sick in their charge', the fact that religious personnel generally enjoy the same protection as medical personnel under Article 24 of the First Convention supports the conclusion that religious personnel may also be armed. Furthermore, the principle of defending oneself or those in one's spiritual charge would so dictate. In any event, the decision on whether medical or religious personnel are entitled to be armed lies with national authorities, and, with regard to religious personnel, certain countries have chosen not to equip them with weapons.[6]

1864   Article 22(1) does not specify what type of arms personnel associated with a medical establishment or unit may carry. However, in the context of hospital ship personnel under the Second Convention, it was made clear that such personnel will need only individual portable weapons, such as pistols or rifles.[7] The understanding of the type of permitted weapons reached in the context of the Second Convention also applies to personnel associated with medical establishments or units for the purposes of Article 22(1). This was subsequently clarified during the negotiations, in connection with civilian medical units under Additional Protocol I, and in State practice.[8] Additional Protocol I

---

[5] While the subjects of this factual scenario are personnel, the relevant Articles 24 and 25 of the First Convention are not explicit as to which acts would not result in a loss of protection, including whether the respective personnel may be armed. But see, on the analogous applicability of Article 22(1) to personnel, the commentaries on Article 24, section F, and Article 25, paras 2040–2042.

[6] See Stefan Lunze, 'Serving God and Caesar: Religious personnel and their protection in armed conflict', *International Review of the Red Cross*, Vol. 86, No. 853, March 2004, pp. 69–90, at 76, and Nilendra Kumar, 'Protection of Religious Personnel', in Dieter Fleck (ed.), *The Handbook of International Humanitarian Law*, 3rd edition, Oxford University Press, 2013, pp. 413–424, at 420.

[7] Pictet (ed.), *Commentary on the Second Geneva Convention*, ICRC, 1960, commentary on Article 35, p. 194. See also the commentary on Article 35 of the Second Convention.

[8] See e.g. Belgium, *Law of Armed Conflict Training Manual*, 2009, Course V, p. 13 ('Le personnel sanitaire doit pouvoir assurer sa propre sécurité et protection ainsi que celles des blessés et des malades dont il a la charge, et ce, contre des actes de pillage, de brigandage ou simplement pour maintenir l'ordre et la discipline parmi les blessés (Ex: garde de PG blessés). Il s'agit, donc, d'une mission de police et non de combat. A cet effet, il peut être en possession d'armes légères individuelles (Ex: pistolets et fusils)') ('Medical personnel must be able to ensure their own safety and protection, and those of the wounded and sick in their charge, against looting and robbery, or simply to maintain order and discipline among the wounded (e.g. while guarding wounded prisoners of war). To this end, they may be in possession of individual light weapons

extends the right to carry 'light individual weapons' for self-defence or defence of the wounded and sick in their charge to personnel of civilian medical units.[9] When personnel associated with military medical establishments or units were allowed to be armed in 1949, the views expressed regarding the lawful use that such personnel could make of these arms implied that they must be light individual weapons. Thus, carrying weapons which are portable by one individual yet which go beyond the purpose of self-defence, such as a man-portable missile or an anti-tank missile, would lead to a loss of specific protection. Furthermore, as the tasks to be carried out by military medical personnel covered by Article 22(1) are the same as for civilian medical personnel, any weapons heavier than those stipulated for civilian medical personnel under Additional Protocol I could not be allocated to military personnel under Article 22(1) of the First Convention, i.e. weapons that cannot easily be transported by an individual and which have to be operated by several persons, without incurring the loss of specific protection of the military medical unit in which such personnel operate.

1865   Moreover, personnel associated with medical establishments and units must make use of these 'light individual weapons' only for the purposes expressly permitted. Any use going beyond these permitted purposes, even with 'light individual weapons', would constitute an act harmful to the enemy, and, upon fulfilling the further conditions of Article 21, would result in a loss of protection of the medical establishment or unit in question.

1866   The term 'defence' must be understood restrictively in the sense of individual defence against unlawful violence directed either at medical personnel

---

(e.g. pistols and rifles)'); Peru, *IHL Manual*, 2004, paras 83(c) and (d) and 88(b)(2) ('Medical personnel may only carry light individual weapons and are only permitted to use them to defend themselves and the wounded in their charge. The circumstances of armed conflict often lead to a state of internal disruption which, in addition to the conflict itself, results in acts of violence, such as looting, rape and pillage. The weapons carried by medical personnel are limited to light, individual firearms, which can only be used for the purposes mentioned above . . . The following are not considered harmful to the adverse Party: medical personnel equipped with light individual weapons for their own defence or for that of the wounded and sick in their charge (defence against an offence committed against them, but not against an attack by the enemy)'; United Kingdom, *Manual of the Law of Armed Conflict*, 2004, paras 7.15 and 7.15.1 ('Medical personnel may be equipped with "light individual weapons for their own defence or for that of the wounded and sick in their charge". Light individual weapons are those that can be handled and fired by one person and primarily intended for personnel targets. It follows that medical personnel may be armed with sub-machine guns, self-loading rifles, and handguns'); and United States, *Army Health System*, 2013, para. 3–31 ('Medical personnel are not authorized crew-served or offensive weapons. They may carry small arms, such as rifles, pistols, squad automatic weapons, or authorized substitutes in the defense of medical facilities, equipment, and personnel/patients without surrendering the protections afforded by the Geneva Conventions.'). For details on the type of weapons permissible under Additional Protocol I, see the commentary on Article 13 of Additional Protocol I.

[9] Additional Protocol I, Article 13(2)(a).

themselves or at the wounded and sick only.[10] The unlawful violence contemplated here may manifest itself, for example, in attacks by rioters or pillagers, or in unlawful attacks by enemy soldiers against the medical establishment or unit as such or against the wounded and sick, or other medical personnel, contained therein.[11]

1867   In delimiting the permissible scope of 'defence', it must always be borne in mind that the use of light individual weapons by medical personnel must not result in the commission of an act harmful to the enemy. The scope of defence would not cover cases of enemy military advances aimed at taking control over the area where the medical establishments or units are located, nor would the use of force to prevent the capture of their unit by the enemy be permitted.[12] In a similar vein, medical personnel also may not resist by force of arms inspections by the enemy that have the purpose of verifying whether the medical establishment or unit is truly engaged in medical tasks.[13] Such weapon use would go beyond the permitted defensive purposes and would result in the commission of an act harmful to the enemy.[14]

1868   Similar considerations apply to mounting weaponry, for instance on mobile military medical units. On this basis, heavy weapons, such as 'crew-served'

---

[10] This implies that no defence against violence directed at other persons, including combatants, would be covered. For further details, see the commentary on Article 24.

[11] See Belgium, *Law of Armed Conflict Training Manual*, 2009, Course V, p. 13; Peru, *IHL Manual*, 2004, paras 83(c) and (d) and 88(b)(2); and United States, *Army Health System*, 2013, para. 3–31 ('In recognition of the necessity of self-defense, however, medical personnel may be armed for their own defense or for the protection of the wounded and sick under their charge. To retain this privileged status, they must refrain from all aggressive action and may only employ their weapons if attacked in violation of the Conventions.'). See also Hyder Gulam, 'Medical personnel and the law of armed conflict', *Australian Defence Forces Health Journal*, Vol. 6, 2005, pp. 31–32.

[12] See e.g. Belgium, *Law of Armed Conflict Training Manual*, 2009, Course V, p. 16 ('le personnel ne peut toutefois pas s'opposer par les armes à la capture pacifique de son unité par l'adversaire') ('the personnel may not, however, resist by force of arms the peaceful capture of their unit by the enemy'); Netherlands, *Military Handbook*, 2003, p. 7–45; Peru, *IHL Manual*, 2004, para. 83(d) ('If they try to resist a military advance using weapons, they lose their "neutrality" in the conflict and, therefore, their right to protection, unless the enemy deliberately tries to kill the wounded and sick or the medical personnel themselves'); South Africa, *LOAC Manual*, 1996, para. 59 ('A medical unit must not be defended against the enemy in the event of penetration by the enemy into the territory where it is located. Such defence would constitute a hostile act, causing the unit to forfeit its right to protection'); and United States, *Army Health System*, 2013, para. 3–31 ('They may not employ arms against enemy forces acting in conformity with the Law of Land Warfare and may not use force to prevent the capture of their unit by the enemy.').

[13] As has been observed in the context of Article 19 of the First Convention, such inspections are, in principle, compatible with the obligation to respect that establishment or unit. See the commentary on that article, paras 1800–1803.

[14] International humanitarian law recognizes the possibility of withdrawing in the face of an advancing enemy. See e.g. Belgium, *Law of Armed Conflict Training Manual*, 2009, Course V, p. 16 ('le personnel ne peut toutefois pas s'opposer par les armes à la capture pacifique de son unité par l'adversaire. Il peut, néanmoins, tenter d'échapper à celle-ci par un repli') ('the personnel may not, however, resist by force of arms the peaceful capture of their unit by the enemy. Nevertheless, they may try to escape such capture by withdrawing'); and United States, *Army Health System*, 2013, para. 3–31 ('it is, on the other hand, perfectly legitimate for a medical unit to withdraw in the face of the enemy'). This possibility may, however, be precluded by national military laws and regulations.

machine guns (requiring a team of at least two people to operate them), could not be mounted on a mobile military medical unit without that unit losing its specific protection. Moreover, the strictly defensive purposes for which personnel could use 'light individual weapons' would dictate additional constraints on mounting weapons on military medical units. Ultimately, in the light of these strictly defensive purposes but also to avoid the perception that a military medical unit is armed in a manner beyond that necessary for defensive purposes, a narrow interpretation of what constitutes a 'light' versus a 'heavy' weapon is called for: the larger the weapon system, the greater the risk that its presence on the military medical unit could lead an adversary to conclude that the unit might be used to commit 'acts harmful to the enemy', and thus no longer be entitled to protection. The way in which the weapons are displayed, in other words, must not lead the enemy to believe that the medical unit is equipped with offensive weaponry.[15] In sum, medical units protected by Article 19 should not be armed to the extent that they could be interpreted as being capable of inflicting harm on the adversary, because this would amount to an act the purpose or effect of which is to facilitate or impede military operations of a Party to the conflict.

1869   Contrary to the Second Convention,[16] Article 22(1) does not mention, as one of the permitted purposes for bearing or using weapons, the 'maintenance of order' in the unit. However, it has also been recognized in the context of this provision that it is necessary for medical personnel to be in a position to ensure the maintenance of order and discipline in the units under their charge, for instance among the convalescent wounded and sick.[17]

D. Paragraph 2: Protection of a unit or establishment by a picket, sentries or an escort

1870 This paragraph complements Article 22(1) in that it relates to armed protection of the military medical establishment or unit, and specifically to the defence of the wounded and sick contained therein. Article 22(2) addresses the question

---

[15] See the commentary on Rule 74(c)(i) of the 2009 Manual on International Law Applicable to Air and Missile Warfare. Transposed to the situation of military medical units, see also San Remo Manual on International Law Applicable to Armed Conflicts at Sea (1994), para. 170.2 ('[A]s there is no prohibition on [such units] defending themselves, it would be unreasonable not to allow them to do so as long as it is in a way that cannot be interpreted as being potentially aggressive'), and Canada, *Code of Conduct*, 2007, p. 2–16, para. 6 ('As a general rule medical transports should not have any weapons "mounted" on them to avoid being mistaken for fighting vehicles.')

[16] Second Convention, Article 35(1).

[17] In this regard, see Netherlands, *Military Manual*, 2005, para. 1058: 'The following do not constitute grounds for the ending of protection [of medical units]: – if the personnel of the medical unit are equipped with personal small arms for their own defence or for that of the wounded and sick in their charge, *and for the preservation of order and calm within the unit*' (emphasis added). See also Belgium, *Law of Armed Conflict Training Manual*, 2009, Course V, pp. 13 and 16.

of such protection by medical and non-medical personnel, and does so from the angle of a particular scenario, namely that 'in the absence of armed orderlies, the unit or establishment is protected by a picket or by sentries or by an escort'.

1871   None of the above terms is defined in the Convention. In accordance with its ordinary meaning, while acknowledging differences may exist at the national level, 'orderly' may be understood as an attendant in a hospital who assists in the medical care of patients as well as with cleaning and other non-medical tasks,[18] 'picket' as 'a soldier or small body of troops sent out to watch for the enemy',[19] 'sentry' as 'a soldier stationed to keep guard or to control access to a place',[20] and an 'escort' as 'a person, vehicle, or group accompanying another to provide protection or as a mark of rank'.[21] Therefore, Article 22(2) is broader than Article 22(1), in that the protection of a medical establishment or unit by non-medical members of the armed forces is also envisaged.

1872   The formulation 'in the absence of armed orderlies' may give the impression that the simultaneous presence of armed orderlies and a military guard is prohibited. However, the intention was that the guard of a medical unit would, as a rule, be provided by its own personnel, but that armed soldiers would be brought in to help in exceptional cases, when this was necessary, e.g. where the orderlies were too few in number.[22] Whether there is such a need for protection of a medical establishment or unit by external military guards may depend on such factors as the importance of the establishment or unit for the delivery of medical care to the wounded and sick, the severity of the threat, and the number of wounded and sick people to be cared for.[23]

1873   Article 22(2) does not specify whether there are restrictions as to the number of non-medical members of the armed forces who could be employed to protect a medical establishment or unit without that establishment or unit losing protection. While this leaves the authorities in charge with some discretion in the light of particular circumstances, the aforesaid intention behind this paragraph, i.e. that non-medical members of the armed forces would be assigned guard duties only in exceptional cases, where this is necessary, would call for a certain restraint in this regard. Such restraint is also required given that the presence of a large number of combatants in or around a medical establishment or unit will likely lead the enemy to perceive this presence as an act

---

[18] *Concise Oxford English Dictionary*, 12th edition, Oxford University Press, 2011, p. 1007. It should be noted that 'orderlies' are recognized, for the purposes of Article 24 of the First Convention, as capable of falling within the category of medical personnel proper, i.e. those 'exclusively engaged in the search for, or the collection, transport or treatment of the wounded and sick, or in the prevention of disease'. Depending on the circumstances, they may also fall within the category of auxiliary medical personnel of the armed forces under Article 25 of the First Convention. See the commentaries on Article 24, para. 1955, and Article 25, para. 2029.

[19] *Concise Oxford English Dictionary*, 12th edition, Oxford University Press, 2011, p. 1083.

[20] *Ibid.* p. 1312.   [21] *Ibid.* p. 487.

[22] Pictet (ed.), *Commentary on the First Geneva Convention*, ICRC, 1952, commentary on Article 22, pp. 203–204.

[23] See e.g. Belgium, *Law of Armed Conflict Training Manual*, 2009, Course V, p. 13.

harmful to the enemy, thus putting the establishment or unit at greater risk of attack.[24]

1874　Therefore, the underlying assumption of Article 22(2) is that, as a rule, the medical personnel of the medical establishment or unit would be sufficient to ensure its defence against attacks by rioters or pillagers and unlawful attacks by enemy soldiers, as well as the defence of the wounded and sick therein, or to ensure the maintenance of order.[25] Yet where armed orderlies are not sufficient to ensure the protection of the establishment or unit, non-medical members of the armed forces may also be called upon to reinforce their protective presence. It is clear that, regardless of whether protection is ensured by armed orderlies or by non-medical members of the armed forces, only the same type of weapons, notably 'light individual weapons', may be carried and, where necessary, used for defensive purposes only. Therefore, in the same way as armed orderlies, those non-medical members of the armed forces who have been assigned to protect the unit must not attempt to prevent or resist capture by the enemy by force.[26] Moreover, escort vehicles dedicated exclusively to protecting a mobile medical unit must not have heavy weapons, such as crew-served automatic machine guns, mounted on them, in the same way as such weapons cannot be mounted on medical establishments or units themselves. Where combatants are assigned to provide protection for a medical establishment or unit as well as for military objectives surrounding it, this constitutes an act harmful to the enemy and must be avoided in order to prevent the whole establishment or unit from losing protection.[27] In such circumstances, there would also be a

---

[24] Subsequent to the adoption of the First Convention, during the preparatory work on Article 13(2)(b) of Additional Protocol I, the paragraph equivalent to Article 22(2) of the First Convention, Cuba submitted a proposed amendment specifying that a civilian medical unit under the Protocol could only be guarded by 'a reasonable number of' sentries. See *Official Records of the Diplomatic Conference of Geneva of 1974–1977*, Vol. XI, pp. 127–128 and 230. See also United Kingdom, *Manual of the Law of Armed Conflict*, 2004, para. 7.18 ('medical personnel must be careful that the protected status of their unit is not put at risk by the presence of a disproportionate number of . . . combatants').

[25] The scenarios arising under the 'maintenance of order' purpose mentioned earlier in the context of Article 22(1) are of particular relevance in this context, since the 'maintenance of order' is even one of the tasks included in the definition of 'orderly'.

[26] United Kingdom, *Manual of the Law of Armed Conflict*, 2004, para. 7.16 ('However, the guard also may only act in a purely defensive manner and may not oppose the occupation or control of the unit by the enemy'); United States, *Army Health System*, 2013, para. 3–32 ('But, as in the case of medical personnel, the Soldiers may only act in a purely defensive manner and may not oppose the occupation or control of the unit by an enemy who is respecting the unit's privileged status.'). If captured, these non-medical members of the armed forces are prisoners of war. For an elaboration of the individual status of medical personnel and non-medical members of armed forces assigned to guard duties, see the commentary on Article 24, para. 2007.

[27] See Belgium, *Law of Armed Conflict Training Manual*, 2009, Course V, p. 13 ('Le personnel sanitaire ne peut pas être utilisé à la garde d'autres installations que des installations sanitaires. Cela constituerait une participation aux hostilités qui lui ferait perdre sa protection et constituerait, aux yeux de l'ennemi, un précédent mettant en cause la confiance réciproque') ('Medical personnel may not be used to guard facilities other than medical facilities. This would constitute participation in hostilities, which would cause them to lose their protection and would, in the enemy's eyes, set a precedent undermining mutual confidence.'). See also Peter De Waard

real danger of the medical establishment or unit incurring collateral damage as a result of attacks on the combatants in their vicinity.

1875   Apart from these traditional ways of physically protecting medical establishments or units, when it comes to protecting computers which process medical data forming an integral part of the functioning or the administration of a medical establishment or unit, there are, for instance, non-physical means of protecting these data. This could include software applications, such as the installation of intrusion detection or prevention software designed to prevent and react to harmful interferences with data by the enemy. The reactions to harmful interferences may consist in resetting the connection or reprogramming the software to block traffic from a suspected malicious source. Such blocking of access may be regarded as serving the function of an electronic guard of the protected computer system. The installation and operation of such software applications would be compatible with the strictly defensive purposes for which physical guards could be employed in the context of Article 22(2), even if the effects of these methods could be perceived as impeding the adversary's military operations.[28]

E. Paragraph 3: The presence of small arms and ammunition

1876   This paragraph is a reminder of the fact that the First Convention is essentially concerned with the protection of wounded and sick members of armed forces. Therefore, when such wounded and sick persons arrive in a military medical establishment or unit, they may still be in possession of small arms or ammunition, which will be taken from them and handed to the proper service, i.e. authorities outside the medical establishment or unit. However, this may take some time, and it may happen that the establishment or unit falls into the hands of the enemy or is searched by the enemy before those in charge of the establishment or unit have had an opportunity to hand over the weapons collected. In that scenario, this paragraph makes it clear that the temporary presence of small arms and ammunition found inside a military medical establishment or unit may not be considered an act harmful to the enemy.

1877   Article 22(3) does not define the term 'small arms or ammunition'. However, the equally authentic French text uses the term 'armes portatives' (portable weapons). Therefore, the decisive criterion for these weapons is that of being capable of being carried by people, i.e. portability. The category of portable arms is to be understood more broadly here than in Article 22(1) and (2). As emphasized above in relation to Article 22(1), the understanding of the type of arms that medical personnel may carry is that these are *individual* portable weapons.

and John Tarrant, 'Protection of Military Medical Personnel in Armed Conflicts', *University of Western Australia Law Review*, Vol. 35, No. 1, 2010, pp. 157–183, at 176.

[28] See Tallinn Manual on the International Law Applicable to Cyber Warfare (2013), p. 209.

Moreover, this has been explicitly confirmed in the case of civilian medical units under Additional Protocol I. That treaty contains the exact same grounds as Article 22(3) for not entailing a loss of protection, and, in that context, the arms concerned are small arms, in other words, arms which can be carried by people. On the other hand, there is no indication that they must be individual arms. Thus, some weapons which are slightly heavier than those which are authorized for medical personnel could be involved, such as, for example, small machine guns, provided that they are portable, even if this should require two or three soldiers. This difference between Article 22(1) and (3) in the type of weapons covered can also be found in State practice.[29] Therefore, certain weapons that may temporarily be found inside the medical establishment or unit without entailing an act harmful to the enemy would constitute such an act were they to be used by personnel associated with such an establishment or unit. On the other hand, the presence of any weapons other than portable weapons inside a medical establishment or unit could not be justified even on a temporary basis.

1878   While the temporary presence of portable arms that are heavier than light individual weapons may be allowed, the personnel of a medical establishment or unit are well advised to hand over those weapons and ammunition to authorities outside the unit as soon as possible to dispel any doubt about their intention not to commit an act harmful to the enemy. Arrangements should thus be made by the authorities in charge to avoid an excessive accumulation of portable arms inside the establishment or unit, in particular where a large number of wounded and sick people will likely be cared for therein.[30]

F. Paragraph 4: The presence of personnel and material of the veterinary service

1879 This particular condition not entailing a loss of protection of a military medical establishment or unit goes back to the 1929 Geneva Convention.[31] At the

---

[29] See e.g. Germany, *Military Manual*, 1992, para. 619 ('To this effect, the following acts shall not be considered as hostile acts: – that medical personnel use arms for their own protection, and that of the wounded and sick; ... – that *war material* taken from the wounded and sick is retained') (emphasis added); the Netherlands, *Military Manual*, 2005, para. 622 ('The following do not constitute grounds for the ending of protection: – if the personnel of the medical unit are equipped with *personal small arms* ... ; – if *small arms and ammunition*, taken from the wounded and sick and not yet handed in, are found in the units') (emphasis added); and Sierra Leone, *Instructor Manual*, 2007, p. 59 ('However, their [medical units'] protection will not be lost if: a. They are armed only with *light individual weapons*. ... c. *Small arms and equipment* taken from patients are stored temporarily in the medical unit pending their return to combat unit') (emphasis added). While historically, notably in the context of the 1929 Geneva Convention, the understanding was effectively that of *individual portable arms*, that can be regarded as outdated in the light of these subsequent developments. On this historical understanding, see Des Gouttes, *Commentaire de la Convention de Genève de 1929 sur les blessés et malades*, ICRC, 1930, pp. 45–46.

[30] See e.g. United Kingdom, *Manual of the Law of Armed Conflict*, 2004, para. 7.17.

[31] Geneva Convention on the Wounded and Sick (1929), Article 8(4).

time, it was deemed necessary to specify that, while members of the veterinary service may be found inside medical formations or establishments without forming an integral part thereof, those formations or establishments would not lose protection. This took into account the evolution of tasks that veterinarians performed within State armed forces, from a traditional role of purely combat-related activities to activities that also fall under protected medical services.[32]

1880   The activities of veterinarians have evolved from caring for horses used by cavalries, to training or caring for dogs used for combatant purposes, such as demining, searching or guarding, to inspecting food supplies to prevent contamination with animal disease agents, or taking vector-control measures such as delousing or disinfection.[33] While food inspections or the performance of delousing or disinfection may fall within the medical purpose of 'prevention of disease' (such as diseases transmitted by animals (e.g. rabies), cholera or dysentery, in line with comprehensive public health measures) under Article 24 of the First Convention, the other activities mentioned above would not serve any medical purposes. Both combat purposes, such as training and caring for watchdogs or demining dogs, and the medical tasks associated with 'prevention of disease' remain relevant in today's armed forces.

1881   Where veterinarians are assigned to duties not covered by Article 24, they would be considered combatants.[34] On the other hand, where they are exclusively assigned to medical purposes, they may be considered 'medical personnel' in accordance with Article 24.[35] The assumption underlying Article 22(4) is, however, that they would not qualify as medical personnel within the meaning of Article 24, but that they might be closely associated with medical establishments or units without being part of them. In that sense, Article 22(4) makes it clear that the mere presence of such personnel inside a medical establishment or unit could not be regarded as an act harmful to the enemy.

---

[32] Another proposal to place the veterinary service on the exact same footing as the medical service was rejected at the 1929 Diplomatic Conference. See Des Gouttes, *Commentaire de la Convention de Genève de 1929 sur les blessés et malades*, ICRC, 1930, p. 46.

[33] On the evolution of the tasks of veterinarians, see Eric Darré and Emmanuel Dumas, 'Vétérinaires et droit international humanitaire: réflexions sur une controverse', *Revue de Droit Militaire et de Droit de la Guerre*, Vols 3–4, No. 43, 2004, pp. 111–136, at 116–121. For a contemporary understanding of the activities encompassed by veterinary health, see Food and Agriculture Organization, *Veterinary Public Health and Control of Zoonoses in Developing Countries*, Rome, 2003.

[34] See e.g. United States, *Veterinary Service Manual*, 2004, para. 1–4. See also Yoram Dinstein, *The Conduct of Hostilities under the Law of International Armed Conflict*, 2nd edition, Cambridge University Press, 2010, p. 165.

[35] For a discussion of the current legal status of members of the armed forces' veterinary service, see the commentary on Article 24, para. 1959.

G. Paragraph 5: Care for wounded and sick civilians

1882 While the First Convention is concerned with wounded and sick members of the armed forces, and the protection of wounded and sick civilians is regulated in the Fourth Convention, Article 22(5) makes it clear that, where the humanitarian activities of military medical establishments or units extend to wounded and sick civilians, this would not constitute an act harmful to the enemy. This paragraph has its counterpart in Article 19(2) of the Fourth Convention, which does not regard as an act harmful to the enemy leading to a loss of protection of civilian hospitals the fact that 'sick or wounded members of the armed forces are nursed in these hospitals'.

1883   One may wonder if inclusion of this paragraph was even necessary, since the activities described would undoubtedly be humanitarian, and could not in any event be interpreted as acts harmful to the enemy outside the humanitarian duties of medical establishments and units. Still, at the time of the adoption of the Conventions, the reason for this additional paragraph was that, in view of the changes seen in warfare – the effects of which often struck civilians as much as members of armed forces – it had to be explicitly made possible for wounded and sick soldiers and civilians to be treated in the same medical establishments or units. This humanitarian principle, i.e. that all wounded and sick people, including civilians, who do not fall within the scope of the protection afforded by the First Convention, may be cared for in a military medical establishment or unit, is now uncontested. Furthermore, for States party to Additional Protocol I, Article 22(5) of the First Convention and Article 19(2) of the Fourth Convention have been overtaken by the fact that the definition of the 'wounded and sick' under Additional Protocol I expressly applies to both military and civilian wounded and sick, all of whom enjoy the same protection.[36]

Select bibliography

See the select bibliography of the commentary on Article 19 of the First Convention.

---

[36] Additional Protocol I, Article 8(a). See also Article 13(2)(d) of the Protocol, which provides that, for the purposes of this treaty, the presence of combatants in the unit for medical reasons must not be considered an act harmful to the enemy on the part of civilian medical units.

HOSPITAL ZONES AND LOCALITIES

❖ Text of the provision*

(1) In time of peace, the High Contracting Parties and, after the outbreak of hostilities, the Parties thereto, may establish in their own territory and, if the need arises, in occupied areas, hospital zones and localities so organized as to protect the wounded and sick from the effects of war, as well as the personnel entrusted with the organization and administration of these zones and localities and with the care of the persons therein assembled.

(2) Upon the outbreak and during the course of hostilities, the Parties concerned may conclude agreements on mutual recognition of the hospital zones and localities they have created. They may for this purpose implement the provisions of the Draft Agreement annexed to the present Convention, with such amendments as they may consider necessary.

(3) The Protecting Powers and the International Committee of the Red Cross are invited to lend their good offices in order to facilitate the institution and recognition of these hospital zones and localities.

❖ Reservations or declarations

None

Contents

* Paragraph numbers have been added for ease of reference.

A. Introduction

1884 Article 23 provides for the establishment of hospital zones and localities outside areas where fighting is taking place, in order to enhance the protection of the wounded and sick from the effects of war. Together with safety zones and neutralized zones regulated in Articles 14 and 15 of the Fourth Convention, respectively, Article 23 forms part of a wider system of protected zones laid down in the 1949 Geneva Conventions. This system was further developed in Additional Protocol I, which affords special protection to non-defended localities and demilitarized zones.[1]

1885 International humanitarian treaty law makes provision for hospital zones and localities only in the context of international armed conflict. Parties to a non-international armed conflict wishing to make the protection of the wounded and sick more effective in practice can, however, make Article 23 applicable by means of a special agreement, as provided for in common Article 3(3).[2] Furthermore, the prohibition on directing attacks against zones established to shelter the wounded and sick from the effects of hostilities is part of customary international law, applicable in both international and non-international armed conflicts.[3]

1886 Since its adoption in 1949, Article 23 has not been extensively applied. Practice has shown, however, that Parties to armed conflicts have made use of the general concept of protected zones provided for in the Conventions both in international and non-international conflicts.[4] In December 1991, for example,

---

[1] See Additional Protocol I, Articles 59 and 60.
[2] See Kleffner, pp. 347–348; see also the commentary on common Article 3, section K.
[3] ICRC Study on Customary International Humanitarian Law (2005), Rule 35.
[4] Frequently cited examples of protected zones include: Dhaka (1971), Nicosia (1974), Saigon (1975), Phnom Penh (1975), Managua (1979), N'Djamena (1980), Port Stanley/Puerto Argentino

an agreement declaring the hospital of Osijek and its surroundings 'a protected zone according to the principles of Article 23 of the First Geneva Convention of 1949 and of Articles 14 and 15 of the Fourth Geneva Convention' was concluded under the auspices of the ICRC.[5] Although there were some violations, the agreement was generally respected.[6]

1887   Another example of a protected zone was the so-called 'Red Cross Box', an area agreed upon by Argentina and the United Kingdom during the 1982 Falklands/Malvinas conflict. Even though protected zones are not mentioned in the Second Convention governing the protection of the wounded, sick and shipwrecked at sea, the Parties made use of the concept to designate an area with a diameter of approximately 20 nautical miles located on the high seas north of the islands to allow hospital ships to hold position and to exchange the wounded.[7]

1888   The system of protected zones under international humanitarian law must be distinguished from the zones established on the basis of UN Security Council resolutions in the 1990s, referred to variously as 'security zones', 'safe corridors' or 'safe areas'.[8] These zones were created in response to armed conflicts in which the civilian population had become a systematic target and in which 'ethnic cleansing' and genocide were committed.[9] While protected zones under international humanitarian law depend for their establishment and effectiveness on their recognition by the Parties to the conflict, these zones were created without the Parties' consent, and in some cases, when other cooperative

---

(1982), Tripoli (Lebanon) (1983), Jaffna (1990) and Chiapas (1994). Regardless of their denomination, these examples predominantly had the characteristics of a neutralized zone rather than of a hospital or safety zone or locality, having been established, on a temporary basis, close to where the fighting was taking place, for the protection of the civilian population. For the most part, these zones did not arise from the initiative of the Parties to the conflict but of a third party, notably the ICRC. For an overview, see e.g. Bouvier, pp. 258–259; Bugnion, pp. 484 and 755–761; Lavoyer, p. 266; Sandoz, pp. 908–911 and 913–916; and Torrelli, pp. 799–801.

[5] Agreement between Croatia and the Socialist Federal Republic of Yugoslavia on a Protected Zone around the Hospital of Osijek (1991), para. 1. A few days earlier, a monastery and a hospital in Dubrovnik had already been declared protected zones; they, too, were generally respected; see Lavoyer, pp. 267–268.

[6] For further details and a discussion of less successful attempts at establishing protected zones or localities, e.g. at the Vukovar hospital, see Lavoyer, pp. 266–270, and Sandoz, pp. 920–921. See also ICRC, Communication to the press No. 92/1, 'Conflict in Yugoslavia: Review of ICRC activities', 2 January 1992.

[7] See Junod, p. 26 (a 'neutral zone at sea'); Sandoz, pp. 915–916 ('In purpose and use, the Red Cross Box was therefore rather like a hospital zone as provided for in Article 23 of the First Convention for war on land'); and United Kingdom, Manual of the Law of Armed Conflict, 2004, p. 372, fn. 130. See also San Remo Manual on International Law Applicable to Armed Conflicts at Sea (1994), Rule 160: 'The parties to the conflict may agree, for humanitarian purposes, to create a zone in a defined area of the sea in which only activities consistent with those humanitarian purposes are permitted.'

[8] See, in particular, UN Security Council Res. 687 (1991) (Iraq-Kuwait); Res. 819 (1993) (Srebrenica); Res. 824 (1993) (Sarajevo, Tuzla, Žepa, Goražde, Bihać, Srebrenica); and Res. 925 and 929 (1994) (Rwanda). See also McDonald/Brollowski, paras 10–12.

[9] For further details, see Bouvier, p. 260; Landgren; Lavoyer, pp. 270–275; Sandoz, pp. 919–925; Simon; and Torrelli, pp. 787–847.

solutions were not forthcoming, were imposed on the Parties on the basis of Chapter VII of the UN Charter.[10]

B. Historical background

1889   The provision on hospital zones and localities, like the system of protected zones in general, was a new addition to the body of humanitarian treaty law in 1949. However, as early as 1870, six years after the adoption of the very first Geneva Convention, Henry Dunant had suggested the 'neutralization' of certain areas for the benefit of wounded soldiers during the Franco-Prussian War. This proposal, which came to nothing owing to rapid military developments, foreshadowed what is today Article 23.[11]

1890   In view of the codification of international humanitarian law around that time focusing on the protection of certain categories of persons based on their personal inviolability, the idea of establishing designated areas to enhance the protection of specific groups receded into the background.[12]

1891   After the First World War the notion of geographically defined protected zones for groups of vulnerable persons – notably wounded and sick soldiers, but also civilians – was revived by various initiatives.[13] These were prompted by new technologies that extended the range of weapons beyond the immediate front, increasingly putting at risk persons protected from the effects of hostilities under international humanitarian law. Following a recommendation by the 16th International Conference of the Red Cross in 1938, a commission of military and legal experts drew up a 'Draft Convention for the Creation of Hospital Localities and Zones in Wartime', known as the 1938 Draft.[14] This draft convention, which addressed the issue of protected zones for wounded and sick military personnel, was intended to serve as a basis for the work of the Diplomatic Conference proposed for the beginning of 1940. That Conference, however, was postponed owing to the outbreak of the Second World War.[15]

---

[10] For further details, see Lavoyer, pp. 275–276, and Sandoz, pp. 925–927. For a reflection on the differences between the various zones, as well as on past experiences and the conclusions to be drawn, see *Report of the Secretary-General to the Security Council on the protection of civilians in armed conflict*, UN Doc. S/1999/957, 8 September 1999, p. 21.

[11] For further details, see Rittberg, pp. 19–20, and ICRC, *Hospital Localities and Safety Zones*, pp. 1–2.

[12] On the protection of military victims of war and of the personnel involved in their care, see the 1899 Hague Convention (III), as well as the 1906 Geneva Convention. Basic provisions with protective effect for civilians during hostilities were adopted in the form of Articles 25–27 of the 1899/1907 Hague Regulations. For further details, see Rittberg, pp. 23–25; ICRC, *Hospital Localities and Safety Zones*, p. 4; and Simon, pp. 49–51.

[13] For further details, see Pictet (ed.), *Commentary on the First Geneva Convention*, ICRC, 1952, pp. 208–209. See also Bugnion, pp. 480–481 and 748–749; ICRC, *Hospital Localities and Safety Zones*, pp. 4–12; Rittberg, pp. 26–69 and 71–82; Sandoz, pp. 901–903; and Simon, p. 52.

[14] See ICRC, 'Rapport du Comité international de la Croix-Rouge sur le projet de convention pour la création de localités et zones sanitaires en temps de guerre'.

[15] For further details, see Rittberg, pp. 59–69, and ICRC, *Hospital Localities and Safety Zones*, pp. 11–12.

1892   During the Second World War, the ICRC suggested on several occasions that the Parties to the conflict conclude agreements on protected zones based on the 1938 Draft.[16] The Draft would have been applied by analogy to zones for the protection of certain categories of the civilian population. But although a number of States sent favourable replies to the ICRC, none of them acted upon the suggestion.[17]

1893   In 1945, the ICRC took the 1938 Draft as the basis for its preparatory work for the revision and development of the Geneva Conventions, extending the draft to cover also certain categories of civilians. However, the 1947 Conference of Government Experts showed that States were not inclined to adopt clauses of a mandatory nature in this regard. The most the experts would agree to was that the Geneva Conventions should provide for the optional creation of protected zones. Furthermore, their recognition by the enemy was to be made dependent upon the conclusion of special agreements.[18] The ICRC accordingly drafted two articles for insertion in, respectively, the draft revised 1929 Geneva Convention on the Wounded and Sick and the draft new Convention relative to the Protection of Civilian Persons in Time of War. To encourage the creation of protected zones or localities, it proposed that a draft agreement, which States could use as a model for establishing and recognizing such zones or localities, be annexed to the two Conventions.[19]

1894   In addition, experiences of temporary protected zones, for example in Madrid in 1936, in Shanghai in 1937 and in Jerusalem in 1948, led to the realization of their usefulness in providing shelter for all wounded and sick and for the local civilian population endangered by military operations in the vicinity.[20] The ICRC accordingly prepared an additional draft article for insertion in the draft civilians convention, providing for the setting up of neutralized zones.[21]

1895   The three draft articles, together with the draft agreement, were approved with no fundamental changes by the International Conference of the Red Cross in Stockholm in 1948 and a year later by the Diplomatic Conference as Article 23 of the First Convention ('Hospital zones and localities') and as Article 14 ('Hospital and safety zones and localities') and Article 15 ('Neutralized zones') of the Fourth Convention. The Diplomatic Conference divided the draft agreement, which had previously been common to the First and Fourth

---

[16] See the memorandum sent by the ICRC to all the governments of States party to the conflict on 15 March 1944, discussed in ICRC, *Hospital Localities and Safety Zones*, pp. 17–20.

[17] See Rittberg, pp. 69–71 and 87–93; ICRC, *Hospital Localities and Safety Zones*, pp. 16–20; and ICRC, *Report concerning Hospital and Safety Localities and Zones*, pp. 3–7.

[18] For further details, see *Report of the Conference of Government Experts of 1947*, pp. 26–29, 74 and 300, and ICRC, *Hospital Localities and Safety Zones*, pp. 36–40.

[19] See *Draft Conventions submitted to the 1948 Stockholm Conference*, pp. 15 and 158–159; see also ICRC, *Hospital Localities and Safety Zones*, pp. 40–41.

[20] For details on the Madrid, Shanghai and Jerusalem zones, see e.g. Bugnion, pp. 749–751, and ICRC, *Hospital Localities and Safety Zones*, pp. 13–16 and 23–36.

[21] For further details, see the commentary on Article 15 of the Fourth Convention. See also ICRC, *Hospital Localities and Safety Zones*, pp. 23–36 and 41–42.

Conventions, into two distinct documents: one annexed to the First Convention, and the other annexed to the Fourth Convention.[22]

C. Paragraph 1: Establishment of hospital zones and localities

1. Circumstances of the establishment of hospital zones and localities

a. In peacetime and after the outbreak of hostilities

1896   Article 23 mentions the possibility of hospital zones and localities being established already 'in time of peace' by all 'High Contracting Parties'. This underlines the importance of preparatory measures taken in peacetime by the States party to the Convention. The many aspects of setting up and managing a hospital zone or locality risk being neglected during the early days of an armed conflict. These aspects should therefore be looked at in detail before hostilities break out, so that the zones can be activated immediately if an armed conflict erupts.

1897   States may be reluctant to set up hospital zones or localities in peacetime because they do not want to see themselves or appear to others as preparing for armed conflict. However, they should consider such preparations as an expression of their general readiness to limit the effects of armed conflict, should it arise. Furthermore, given that hospital zones and localities are intended to be established at some distance from the combat areas, a practical difficulty – apart from potentially the limited availability of suitable areas – may be predicting where exactly the fighting might be taking place. States may therefore make provision for a number of zones or localities, only some of which might be activated during an armed conflict.[23]

1898   Article 23 also envisages the establishment of hospital zones or localities by the Parties to the conflict 'after the outbreak of hostilities'. The explicit reference to this possibility makes clear that efforts to increase the protection of the wounded and sick in practice should also be made while an armed conflict is ongoing.

b. Optional nature of hospital zones and localities

1899   Article 23 creates no obligation to set up hospital zones or localities. The article's use of the word 'may' indicates the optional nature of the provision. However, by including it in the First Convention, the drafters wished to draw

---

[22] For further details, see *ibid.* pp. 42 and 57.

[23] Practice over the past decades has nevertheless shown a clear reticence of States to establish protected zones, especially already in peacetime. See e.g. national responses to question 3.8 of the questionnaire on 'The implementation of international humanitarian law at the national level with special reference to developments of modern warfare', *Military Law and Law of War Review*, Vol. 28, 1989, pp. 51–308.

attention to the humanitarian value of such zones and to recommend they be set up in practice.

1900   The establishment of a hospital zone or locality by a High Contracting Party or a Party to a conflict is initially a unilateral measure that is only binding on the adverse Party once that Party has recognized the zone or locality.[24] This does not mean, however, that in the absence of recognition such zones or localities, or the persons and objects assembled therein, are without protection: the general rules of international humanitarian law apply in any case.[25]

c. Placement of hospital zones and localities

1901   According to Article 23, hospital zones or localities may be established in a State's own territory or in occupied areas. There is also the possibility that an Occupying Power finds a pre-existing hospital zone or locality in the territory it occupies. In this respect, the Draft Agreement annexed to the First Convention provides:

> In the case of occupation of a territory, the hospital zones therein shall continue to be respected and utilized as such.
> Their purpose may, however, be modified by the Occupying Power, on condition that all measures are taken to ensure the safety of the persons accommodated.[26]

1902   Having been approved by States at the 1949 Diplomatic Conference, the Draft Agreement gives useful guidance on various aspects of the creation of hospital zones or localities, even though its provisions are not binding.

2. Purpose and nature of hospital zones and localities

a. Purpose

1903   The purpose of the hospital zones and localities provided for in Article 23 is to 'protect' certain categories of persons 'from the effects of war'.

1904   This broad wording is intentional. While not apparent from the text of Article 23, hospital zones and localities were envisaged as being placed some distance from the areas where fighting is taking place.[27] They were intended in

---

[24] For details, see section D.

[25] See First Convention, Articles 12, 19, 21–22 and 24–26, Fourth Convention, Articles 16 and 18–20, and Additional Protocol I, Articles 48, 51, 52 and 57, and the pertinent rules of customary international humanitarian law. For further details, see section C.2. With regard to the comparable context of neutralized and demilitarized zones, see also United States, *Air Force Commander's Handbook*, 1980, para. 3–6.

[26] First Convention, Annex I: Draft agreement relating to hospital zones and localities, Article 12.

[27] See ICRC, 'Rapport du Comité international de la Croix-Rouge sur le projet de convention pour la création de localités et zones sanitaires en temps de guerre', p. 173. In contrast, 'Neutralized zones', according to Article 15 of the Fourth Convention, are expressly meant to be established 'in the regions where fighting is taking place'.

particular to shelter persons from dangers that may arise from aerial bombardments, long-range artillery fire or missiles launched against military objectives far behind the front, even though dangers arising from fighting close at hand are, of course, also included.[28]

1905   Hospital zones and localities can also help address other effects of armed conflict, such as a shortage of medical supplies or a breakdown of health services. Assembling the wounded and sick in a specially prepared and equipped area facilitates their care and treatment.[29]

1906   It follows from the purpose of hospital zones or localities that they must be respected and protected and that attacks against them are prohibited.[30] This understanding is reflected in Article 11 of the Draft Agreement: 'In no circumstances may hospital zones be the object of attack. They shall be protected and respected at all times by the Parties to the conflict.'[31]

1907   The prohibition on directing attacks against protected zones also forms part of customary international humanitarian law in respect of both international and non-international armed conflicts.[32]

1908   Violations of hospital zones and localities can have consequences under international criminal law. Attacks on them can fall within the war crime of '[i]ntentionally directing attacks against . . . places where the sick and wounded are collected'.[33] The war crime of '[a]ttacking or bombarding, by whatever means, towns, villages, dwellings or buildings which are undefended and which

---

[28] See ICRC, *Hospital Localities and Safety Zones*, p. 46.

[29] The experts involved in the development of the 1938 Draft underlined the usefulness of hospital zones and localities placed at some distance from the fighting, pointing out that the medical treatment of wounded and sick soldiers would be facilitated by the setting up of such zones and localities because of the greater degree of security provided and because the recovery of those concerned would likely be enhanced by the feeling of additional protection. See ICRC, 'Rapport du Comité international de la Croix-Rouge sur le projet de convention pour la création de localités et zones sanitaires en temps de guerre, p. 166.

[30] See Kleffner, p. 350.

[31] On the meaning of the obligation to respect and protect, see, in particular, the commentaries on Articles 12 and 24. See also Pictet (ed.), *Commentary on the First Geneva Convention*, ICRC, 1952, pp. 427–428, commenting on Article 11 of the Draft agreement relating to hospital zones and localities:

> As a natural consequence of their being declared neutral, hospital zones must never be attacked. There is also a positive obligation; they are to be protected and respected by the belligerents at all times.
>
> The authors have deliberately used the phrase *protected and respected*, which the Geneva Convention applies consistently to the persons, buildings and objects which it safeguards. The 1938 Draft referred expressly to the Convention, saying: 'they shall be respected and protected in accordance with Article 6 of the Geneva Convention of 1929'.
>
> The traditional sense attaching to these two words creates positive obligations of wider implication than a mere prohibition of attack. Protection must be extended, in particular, to the arrangements for supplying the zones and possibly also to the communications leading to them. In case of occupation, the enemy will, moreover, be responsible for the welfare of persons residing in the zone. This responsibility also falls on the Power establishing the zone.

[32] ICRC Study on Customary International Humanitarian Law (2005), Rule 35.

[33] See ICC Statute (1998), Article 8(2)(b)(ix) and (e)(iv). For a commentary, see Dörmann, pp. 215–228 and 458–463.

are not military objectives' can also be applicable.[34] In addition, attacks against a hospital zone or locality, or the persons or objects sheltered therein, could constitute other war crimes, such as attacks on the civilian population, on civilian objects or on buildings using the distinctive emblems of the Geneva Conventions.[35]

1909   Additional Protocol I explicitly states that 'making non-defended localities and demilitarized zones the object of attack' is a grave breach, 'when committed wilfully, in violation of the relevant provisions of this Protocol, and causing death or serious injury to body or health'.[36]

1910   It should be noted that persons sheltered in hospital zones or localities are not dependent for their protection on the establishment of such zones or localities. All the military or civilian wounded and sick and the persons engaged in their care, as well as civilians not taking a direct part in hostilities, are protected under international humanitarian law and must not be made the object of attack.[37] Hospital zones and localities are merely a concrete means of providing such protection and of making it more effective in practice. The same applies to objects assembled in a protected zone or locality for the benefit of the persons sheltered therein, such as medical units or civilian objects. Thus, the existence of hospital zones or localities must not be construed as entailing a reduction in the protection due to these persons or objects when they are not assembled in a protected zone or locality.[38]

1911   Accordingly, in the event of a protected zone or locality losing its protected character, persons or objects assembled therein continue to benefit from protection under international humanitarian law,[39] unless they fulfil the criteria of a military objective.[40]

---

[34]   See ICC Statute (1998), Article 8(2)(b)(v); see also ICTY Statute (1993), Article 3(c).

[35]   See ICC Statute (1998), Article 8(2)(b)(i) and (e)(i), (b)(ii), and (b)(xxiv) and (e)(ii).

[36]   Additional Protocol I, Article 85(3)(d). See also Additional Protocol I, Articles 59 and 60, which are generally understood as complementing Article 15 of the Fourth Convention. Article 59, in particular, is regarded as a development of Article 25 of the 1907 Hague Regulations; see e.g. Sandoz, pp. 911–912.

[37]   For details on the persons intended for shelter in a hospital zone or locality, see section C.3.

[38]   See Articles 12, 19, 21–22 and 24–26 of the First Convention and, as applicable, Articles 48, 51–52 and 57 of Additional Protocol I, as well as the pertinent rules of customary international humanitarian law. See also ICRC, 'Rapport du Comité international de la Croix-Rouge sur le projet de convention pour la création de localités et zones sanitaires en temps de guerre', pp. 167 and 171.

[39]   Articles 59(7) and 60(7) of Additional Protocol I explicitly provide with respect to non-defended localities and demilitarized zones that if such a locality or zone loses its protected status it 'shall continue to enjoy the protection provided by the other provisions of this Protocol and the other rules of international law applicable in armed conflict'. For further details on these considerations, see ICRC, *Hospital Localities and Safety Zones*, pp. 47–48, as well as Gasser/Dörmann, pp. 248–249; Kleffner, p. 350; Lavoyer, p. 276; Rittberg, pp. 124–125; and Sandoz, p. 926. See also Pictet (ed.), *Commentary on the First Geneva Convention*, ICRC, 1952, pp. 425–426, commenting on Article 9(2) of the Draft Agreement annexed to the First Convention. The same considerations apply to the zones imposed by the UN Security Council discussed in section A. See Lavoyer, pp. 275–276, and Sandoz, pp. 925–927.

[40]   For the definition of military objectives, see Additional Protocol I, Article 52(2); see also ICRC Study on Customary International Humanitarian Law (2005), Rule 8.

b. Nature

1912 The nature of hospital zones and localities is determined by their purpose. They are to be 'so organized as to' fulfil their protective function.

1913 The protective function is to be taken into consideration, for example, when deciding on the size of a proposed hospital zone or locality. In this context, 'locality' should be taken to mean a specific place of limited area, generally containing buildings. The term 'zone' is used to describe a relatively large area of land and may include one or more localities.

1914 It is a characteristic of protected zones and localities under international humanitarian law that they require recognition as such by the adverse Party.[41] For the adverse Party to be willing to recognize it, the zone or locality will usually need to be 'demilitarized', both at the time of the initial recognition and thereafter.[42] The zone or locality must contain no military objectives. This characteristic corresponds to the status of the persons intended for shelter within a protected zone, who are themselves not lawful targets. The Draft Agreement annexed to the First Convention provides guidance on how such demilitarization can be achieved with respect to both persons and objects.[43]

1915 An important implication of the demilitarized character of hospital zones and localities is that they must not be defended militarily.[44] The adverse Party is not prohibited from taking over the zone or locality but remains bound to respect all its obligations towards the protected zone or locality and the persons and objects sheltered therein.[45]

3. Beneficiaries of hospital zones and localities

1916 The categories of persons who may find shelter in hospital zones or localities are the following:

a. The wounded and sick

1917 Article 23 does not specify who are the wounded and sick who may be sheltered in a hospital zone or locality. However, the article's position in the First Convention indicates that they are the wounded and sick of the armed forces or belonging to one of the other categories of persons listed in Article 13.

---

[41] For details, see section D.

[42] In this context 'demilitarized' should not be understood in the technical legal sense of Article 60 of Additional Protocol I, but in its common meaning, as a place from which all military forces have been removed; see *Concise Oxford English Dictionary*, 12th edition, Oxford University Press, 2011, p. 380. The conditions for non-defended localities and demilitarized zones listed in Articles 59(2) and 60(3) of Additional Protocol I, respectively, are nevertheless informative.

[43] See First Convention, Annex I: Draft agreement relating to hospital zones and localities, Articles 2–5.

[44] See *ibid.* Article 5(b). See also Gasser/Dörmann, pp. 248–249, in the context of protected zones under Article 14 of the Fourth Convention. Compare also Article 21 of the First Convention.

[45] This is underlined in Article 12 of the Draft agreement relating to hospital zones and localities.

1918   This reading is confirmed by Article 14 of the Fourth Convention, which also envisages the establishment of protective areas for 'wounded [and] sick...persons'. Article 14, like Article 23, does not specify who these persons are. However, its placement in Part II of the Fourth Convention, addressing the 'General protection of populations against certain consequences of war', indicates that it refers to wounded and sick civilians.[46]

1919   However, the system of protected zones laid down in the Geneva Conventions allows for flexibility. Nothing in the Conventions speaks against a hospital zone or locality providing shelter for both wounded and sick military personnel and civilians. On the contrary, the First Convention provides in Article 22(5) that a medical unit or establishment shall not be deprived of protection if its humanitarian activities extend to the care of wounded and sick civilians. This approach would apply to a hospital zone or locality established by virtue of Article 23.[47] Furthermore, the understanding of the terms 'wounded' and 'sick' in Additional Protocol I as covering both military and civilian persons may have made the distinction between Article 23 of the First Convention and Article 14 of the Fourth Convention 'somewhat obsolete even in theoretical terms'.[48]

1920   Admission to a hospital zone or locality must be accorded 'without any adverse distinction founded on sex, race, nationality, religion, political opinions, or any other similar criteria'. This follows from the prohibition of adverse distinction as expressed in Article 12(2) of the First Convention.[49]

b. The personnel entrusted with the care of the wounded and sick

1921   Medical personnel protected under the First Convention are entitled to be present in hospital zones and localities.[50] This applies also to personnel exclusively engaged in the administration of medical units and establishments,[51] as well as to religious personnel attached to the armed forces.[52]

---

[46] For further details, see the commentary on Article 14 of the Fourth Convention.

[47] In this context, see also Article 19(2) of the Fourth Convention.

[48] Sandoz, p. 913.

[49] Insofar as a hospital zone or locality shelters both military and civilian wounded and sick, see also Article 13 of the Fourth Convention, prohibiting 'any adverse distinction based, in particular, on race, nationality, religion or political opinion'.

[50] See Articles 24–27. In view of the possibility to combine Article 23 of the First Convention and Article 14 of the Fourth Convention, the presence of medical personnel protected under the Fourth Convention can also be envisaged; see Article 20 of the Fourth Convention. Furthermore, medical personnel protected under Additional Protocol I can also be regarded as lawfully present in a hospital zone or locality; see Additional Protocol I, Articles 8(c) and 15.

[51] See Article 24. In view of the possibility to combine Article 23 of the First Convention and Article 14 of the Fourth Convention, see also Article 20 of the Fourth Convention, with respect to '[p]ersons regularly and solely engaged in the operation and administration of civilian hospitals' and '[o]ther personnel who are engaged in the operation and administration of civilian hospitals...while they are employed on such duties'. Medical personnel protected under Additional Protocol I may also be regarded as lawfully present in a hospital zone or locality; see Articles 8(c) and 15 of Additional Protocol I.

[52] See Article 24. Religious personnel protected under Additional Protocol I may also be regarded as lawfully present in a hospital zone or locality; see Additional Protocol I, Articles 8(d) and 15.

c. The personnel entrusted with the organization and administration of the zones

1922 Depending on the size, complexity and duration of hospital zones and localities, it may be necessary to employ special personnel for their organization and administration, in addition to personnel entrusted with the care of the wounded and sick. It has been noted that:

> the expression 'personnel entrusted with the organization and administration of the zones' must be taken in a fairly broad sense, to include, for example, the police, the services responsible for preventing the entry into the zone of persons who have no right to reside there, and the fire and passive defence services, as well as members of the Commissions of control provided for in Article 8 of the Draft Agreement.[53]

1923 The inclusion of such personnel ensuring security within a zone or locality, or preventing access of persons not entitled to be present there, must not lead to a – real or perceived – undermining of the demilitarized and non-defended character of the zone or locality. Like any other person present in a hospital zone or locality, such personnel must not engage in acts that might compromise the zone's or locality's protected status.[54] Furthermore, in order to avoid any misperception in practice, clear agreement between the Parties to the conflict on the presence of such personnel in the hospital zone or locality is essential.[55]

d. The local civilian population

1924 Although Article 23 itself makes no mention of this category of persons, they must necessarily be taken into consideration, especially when a hospital zone is of a considerable size.

1925 In this sense, Article 1 of the Draft Agreement expressly provides that:

> Hospital zones shall be strictly reserved for the persons named in Article 23 of the Geneva Convention for the Amelioration of the Condition of the Wounded and Sick in Armed Forces in the Field of August 12, 1949, and for the personnel entrusted with the organization and administration of these zones and localities and with the care of the persons therein assembled.

---

[53] Pictet (ed.), *Commentary on the First Geneva Convention*, ICRC, 1952, p. 416, commenting on Article 1 of the Draft agreement relating to hospital zones and localities. Recognition of the lawful presence of, among others, 'police forces retained for the sole purpose of maintaining law and order' in non-defended localities and demilitarized zones is also contained in Articles 59(3) and 60(4) of Additional Protocol I.

[54] Gasser/Dörmann, pp. 248–249, explain, in the comparable context of hospital and safety zones and localities pursuant to Article 14 of the Fourth Convention: '[M]easures shall be taken to provide protection for all, in the sense of ensuring personal security against acts of violence. However, defence of the zone or locality as a whole, with the aim of preventing enemy forces from taking it over, is prohibited'. In this context, compare also Article 22(1) and (2) of the First Convention.

[55] In this sense, Article 60(3) of Additional Protocol I explicitly provides, in the context of demilitarized zones: 'The Parties to the conflict shall agree ... upon persons to be admitted to the demilitarized zone other than those mentioned in paragraph 4.' Paragraph 4 mentions 'persons specially protected under the Conventions and this Protocol, and ... police forces retained for the sole purpose of maintaining law and order'.

Nevertheless, persons whose permanent residence is within such zones shall have the right to stay there.

1926   Like any other person present in a hospital zone or locality, members of the local civilian population must not engage in acts that might lead to the loss of the zone's or locality's protected status. In order to avoid any misperception in practice, clear agreement between the Parties to the conflict on the presence of such persons in the zone or locality is essential.

4. Marking of hospital zones and localities

1927   Article 23 does not address the question of marking. However, in so far as the personnel entrusted with the care of the wounded and sick, as well as the objects used for such care, are entitled to display the distinctive emblem, nothing speaks against the visible demonstration of the zone's or locality's protected status by marking it with the distinctive emblem.[56]

D. Paragraph 2: Recognition of hospital zones and localities

1. Recognition

1928   Hospital zones and localities established in accordance with Article 23(1) will not enjoy protection as a protected area until such time as they have been recognized by the adverse Party.[57]

1929   For such recognition to be obtained, their demilitarized and non-defended character is therefore usually decisive.[58]

1930   Recognition will typically entail the conclusion of an agreement between the Parties to the conflict. While such an agreement can be more or less formal and detailed, in the interest of the effectiveness of the protected zone, it should address, at a minimum, the most relevant points relating to the definition of the zone, the persons to be sheltered therein, and its organization and marking.

1931   Depending on the circumstances, such as the urgency of recognition, the agreement may not necessarily be discussed at government level but by the military authorities on the ground. In that case, the military authorities are regarded as competent to negotiate and to enter into agreements binding on

---

[56] See Article 6 of the Draft agreement relating to hospital zones and localities. According to Additional Protocol III, marking by means of the red crystal is also possible.

[57] This is without prejudice to the protection due under other rules of international humanitarian law, see section C, para. 1910.

[58] In this context, 'non-defended' and 'demilitarized' are not to be understood in the technical legal sense of Articles 59 and 60 of Additional Protocol I, but in their common meaning as places which offer no resistance against attacks and from which all military forces have been removed; see *Concise Oxford English Dictionary*, 12th edition, Oxford University Press, 2011, pp. 375 and 380.

the respective Parties to the conflict.[59] Ideally, in order to ensure that different perspectives are identified and addressed in the agreements, negotiations should include persons of different genders and backgrounds.[60]

2. Draft agreement relating to hospital zones and localities

1932   With the object of promoting the establishment of hospital zones and localities and to facilitate negotiations, the Diplomatic Conference decided to annex to the First Convention the 'Draft agreement relating to hospital zones and localities', which States could use as a model with whatever amendments they considered necessary.

1933   The above analysis of the various elements necessary for setting up an effective hospital zone or locality has shown that the Draft Agreement is a useful guidance tool.[61]

E. Paragraph 3: Good offices to facilitate the setting up of hospital zones and localities

1934   The establishment and recognition of hospital zones and localities by the Parties to an armed conflict usually call for the availability of a neutral intermediary. In accordance with the general thrust of the Geneva Conventions, it was natural to specifically mention the Protecting Powers and the ICRC in this connection and to invite them to lend their good offices in this matter. This

---

[59] On the capacity of military commanders to negotiate and conclude binding agreements, see Kovacs, p. 143, para. 67, commenting on Article 7(1)(b) of the 1969 Vienna Convention on the Law of Treaties, and Alfred Verdross and Bruno Simma, *Universelles Völkerrecht: Theorie und Praxis*, 3rd edition, Duncker & Humblot, Berlin, 1984, p. 443, para. 687, with further references. Canada's military manual provides: 'Any agreement made by belligerent commanders must be adhered to, and any breach of its conditions would involve international responsibility if ordered by a government, and personal liability, (which might amount to a war crime) if committed by an individual on his or her own authority'; *LOAC Manual*, 2001, para. 1403.1. Note, however, that some military manuals also indicate that, owing, for example, to modern telecommunications, commanders on the ground today only rarely directly enter into negotiations; see Canada, *LOAC Manual*, 2001, para. 1401.2, and United Kingdom, *Manual of the Law of Armed Conflict*, 2004, para. 10.3.1. For further details on the conclusion of agreements between Parties to a conflict, see the commentary on common Article 6 (Article 7 in the Fourth Convention).

[60] See UN Security Council, Res. 1325, 31 October 2000, para. 1. There is a growing acknowledgement that women, men, girls and boys are affected by armed conflict in different ways, and that, accordingly, the representation of both women and men at all decision-making levels in national, regional and international institutions and mechanisms for conflict prevention, management and resolution benefits the process. The application of international humanitarian law should also reflect this understanding.

[61] A commentary on the Draft agreement relating to hospital zones and localities can be found in Pictet (ed.), *Commentary on the First Geneva Convention*, ICRC, 1952, pp. 415–429. Agreements on protected zones over the past decades have reflected elements of the Draft agreement relating to hospital zones and localities, even if the Agreement was not used as such; it should be noted that many of the examples of protected zones in practice predominantly had the characteristics of a neutralized zone in the sense of Article 15 of the Fourth Convention, for which no Draft Agreement was attached to the Convention.

also means that, when they think it advisable, they may themselves take the initiative and put forward proposals to governments. Practice in recent decades has shown that it has indeed often been on the initiative of the ICRC that the concept of protected zones has been put into practice.[62]

Select bibliography

Bouvier, Antoine, 'Zones protégées, zones de sécurité et protection de la population civile', in Katia Boustany and Daniel Dormoy (eds), *Perspectives humanitaires entre conflits, droit(s) et action*, Bruylant, Brussels, 2002, pp. 251–269.

Bugnion, François, *The International Committee of the Red Cross and the Protection of War Victims*, ICRC/Macmillan, Oxford, 2003, pp. 480–484 and 748–762.

Dörmann, Knut, *Elements of War Crimes under the Rome Statute of the International Criminal Court: Sources and Commentary*, Cambridge University Press, 2003, pp. 215–228 and 458–463.

Gasser, Hans-Peter and Dörmann, Knut, 'Protection of the Civilian Population', in Dieter Fleck (ed.), *The Handbook of International Humanitarian Law*, 3rd edition, Oxford University Press, 2013, pp. 231–320, at 247–251.

ICRC, 'Rapport du Comité international de la Croix-Rouge sur le projet de convention pour la création de localités et zones sanitaires en temps de guerre, adopté par la commission d'experts réunie à Genève les 21 et 22 octobre 1938', reproduced in *Revue internationale de la Croix-Rouge et Bulletin international des Sociétés de la Croix-Rouge*, Vol. 21, No. 243, March 1939, pp. 161–201.

– *Report concerning Hospital and Safety Localities and Zones*, ICRC, Geneva, 1946.

– *Hospital Localities and Safety Zones*, ICRC, Geneva, 1952.

International Society for Military Law and the Law of War, Questionnaire on the Implementation of international humanitarian law at the national level with special reference to developments of modern warfare, *Military Law and Law of War Review*, Vol. 28, 1989, pp. 51–308.

Junod, Sylvie S., *Protection of the Victims of Armed Conflict, Falkland-Malvinas Islands (1982): International Humanitarian Law and Humanitarian Action*, ICRC, Geneva, 1984.

Kleffner, Jann K. 'Hospital and Safety Zones and Localities; Neutralized Zones', in Dieter Fleck (ed.), *The Handbook of International Humanitarian Law*, 3rd edition, Oxford University Press, 2013, pp. 347–351.

Landgren, Karin, 'Safety Zones and International Protection: A Dark Grey Area', *International Journal of Refugee Law*, Vol. 7, No. 3, 1995, pp. 436–458.

Lavoyer, Jean-Philippe, 'International humanitarian law, protected zones and the use of force', in Wolfgang Biermann and Martin Vadset (eds), *UN Peacekeeping in Trouble: Lessons Learned from the Former Yugoslavia*, Ashgate, Aldershot, 1998, pp. 262–279.

---

[62] For an overview, see e.g. Bugnion, pp. 755–759. When a protected zone or locality is set up exclusively under the ICRC's responsibility, its work can be based on its general right of humanitarian initiative laid down in common Article 9 (Article 10 in the Fourth Convention). In the context of a non-international armed conflict, the basis of an initiative taken by the ICRC can be found in common Article 3(2).

McDonald, Avril and Brollowski, Hanna, 'Security zones', version of April 2011, in Rüdiger Wolfrum (ed.), *Max Planck Encyclopedia of Public International Law*, Oxford University Press, http://opil.ouplaw.com/home/EPIL.

Rittberg, Jochen Graf von, *Schutzzonen für die Zivilbevölkerung*, Dissertation, Mainz, 1967.

Ronzitti, Natalino, 'Protected Areas', in Andrew Clapham, Paola Gaeta and Marco Sassòli (eds), *The 1949 Geneva Conventions: A Commentary*, Oxford University Press, 2015, pp. 369–387.

Sandoz, Yves, 'The establishment of safety zones for persons displaced within their country of origin', in Najeeb Al-Nauimi and Richard Meese (eds), *International Legal Issues Arising under the United Nations Decade of International Law*, Martinus Nijhoff Publishers, The Hague, 1995, pp. 899–927.

Sassòli, Marco, Bouvier, Antoine A. and Quintin, Anne, *How Does Law Protect in War?*, Vol. III, 3rd edition, ICRC, Geneva, 2011, pp. 1713–1717.

Simon, Annette, *UN-Schutzzonen – Ein Schutzinstrument für verfolgte Personen?*, Springer, Berlin, 2005.

Torrelli, Maurice, 'Les zones de securité', *Revue générale de droit international public*, Vol. 99, No. 4, 1995, pp. 787–848.

CHAPTER IV

PERSONNEL

1935 The medical and religious personnel referred to in this chapter are those forming part of the armed forces in the field. The chapter also covers certain civilians
working under the auspices of the armed forces in the field. It does not include
civilian staff not working under the auspices of the armed forces in the field
or medical personnel and chaplains of forces at sea, such personnel being dealt
with in the Second and Fourth Geneva Conventions, as well as in Additional
Protocol I.

1936   The personnel protected under this chapter comprise the following six categories:

1. Medical personnel of the armed forces exclusively engaged in the search for,
   or the collection, transport or treatment, of the wounded or sick, or in the
   prevention of disease (Article 24).
2. Personnel of the armed forces exclusively engaged in the administration of
   medical units and establishments (Article 24).
3. Religious personnel of the armed forces (Article 24).
4. The staff of National Red Cross Societies and other recognized relief societies, who are employed for the benefit of their own State's armed forces on
   the same duties as the personnel mentioned under 1, 2 and 3, and are subject
   to military laws and regulations (Article 26).
5. Personnel of relief societies of a neutral country who lend their assistance
   to a Party to the conflict and are duly authorized to do so (Article 27).
6. Members of the armed forces specially trained for employment, should
   the need arise, as hospital orderlies, nurses or auxiliary stretcher-bearers
   (Article 25).

1937   The personnel in the last of these categories are known as 'auxiliary personnel', as opposed to 'permanent personnel'– a term which is sometimes used to
describe the personnel in the first five categories.

1938   These personnel are protected because of the functions they perform: attending to the wounded and sick, or meeting the spiritual needs of members of
the armed forces. They must be respected and protected in all circumstances.
Articles 24, 25, 26 and 27 delineate which persons are covered by the protection they confer, what that protection entails and under what conditions they

may benefit from that protection. Protection may also be lost, namely when these persons commit, outside their humanitarian duties, acts harmful to the enemy.

1939   Article 30 contains the basic rule which must be complied with when military medical or religious personnel (covered by Article 24) or staff of National Red Cross or Red Crescent Societies, or of other voluntary aid societies, assisting the medical services of their own State's armed forces (covered by Article 26), fall into enemy hands: they must be returned to the Party to the conflict to which they belong. The purpose of this provision is to ensure that medical and religious personnel can continue at all times to provide their services to those who need them.

1940   Article 31 sets out the criteria for determining which medical or religious personnel should be returned on the basis of Article 30 and provides for the possibility for the Parties to the conflict to conclude special agreements covering the practical aspects of their retention.

1941   Article 28 is the centrepiece of the regime for the retention of persons covered by Articles 24 and 26, in that it sets forth the conditions under which retention is permissible. It also clarifies the status of retained personnel, their role, and the treatment and facilities to which they are entitled, so as to ensure that prisoners of war receive the necessary medical and spiritual care. Retention is contemplated as an exception to Article 30, requiring the return of such personnel to the Party to the conflict to which they belong. The retention regime rests on the principle that medical and religious personnel may not be retained unless the state of health, the spiritual needs and the number of prisoners of war so require.

1942   Article 29 applies to all '[m]embers of the personnel designated in Article 25 who have fallen into the hands of the enemy', whether or not they are carrying out their medical duties 'at the time when they come into contact with the enemy or fall into his hands'. When this occurs, they are prisoners of war covered by the Third Convention, but they 'shall be employed on their medical duties in so far as the need arises'. The aim is to avoid the possibility that medical expertise which may be needed for the care of prisoners of war will remain unused.

1943   Finally, Article 32 deals with the scenario in which the medical personnel of a recognized society of a neutral country, covered by Article 27, fall into the hands of the adversary of the Party to the conflict they are assisting. They may not be detained but must, in principle, be permitted to return to their country.

1944   The rules of this chapter are complemented by a number of provisions contained in Part II, Section I, of Additional Protocol I.

1945   For ease of reference, the table below gives an overview of the interlinkages between all provisions of the First Convention dealing with medical and religious personnel.

1946

Category of personnel	Articles of the First Convention			
	Definition and status	Status when falling into enemy hands	Material	Identification
Permanent military medical and religious personnel	24	28, 30–31	33	40
Auxiliary medical personnel	25	29	33	41
Personnel of voluntary aid societies	26	28, 30–31	34	40
Personnel of recognized societies of neutral countries	27	32	34	40

PROTECTION OF PERMANENT PERSONNEL

❖ Text of the provision

Medical personnel exclusively engaged in the search for, or the collection, transport or treatment of the wounded or sick, or in the prevention of disease, staff exclusively engaged in the administration of medical units and establishments, as well as chaplains attached to the armed forces, shall be respected and protected in all circumstances.

❖ Reservations or declarations

None

Contents

A. Introduction

1947 Article 24 deals with the official medical and religious personnel of the armed forces, i.e. those members of the armed forces who have been assigned exclusively and permanently to certain duties of a medical or religious nature. It delineates which persons are covered by the protection it confers, what that protection entails and under what conditions they may benefit from that protection.

1948 Persons covered by Article 24 are protected because of the functions they perform: attending to the wounded and sick or meeting the spiritual needs of members of the armed forces. Thus, from the perspective of alleviating human suffering in armed conflict, Article 24 is of paramount importance: when military medical personnel are unable to assist the wounded and sick – because they are attacked or otherwise prevented from carrying out their work – the adverse consequences may be wide-ranging.[1] In the spiritual realm, the same holds true for the religious personnel of the armed forces.

1949 The symbiotic and functional nature of the relationship between medical and religious personnel and the persons they attend to informs the protection due when such personnel fall into enemy hands: they do not become prisoners of war – and may not be 'detained' as such – but fall under a specific 'retention' regime, whereby they can be 'retained only in so far as the state of health, the spiritual needs and the number of prisoners of war require'.[2]

1950 One of the distinctive features of Article 24 is that the High Contracting Parties have agreed to confer specific protection on certain members of the enemy's armed forces, even when they are not in their hands. As can be deduced from the terms of Article 24, medical and religious personnel are entitled to be 'respected and protected in all circumstances'; this protection also applies, and indeed is acutely needed, during active hostilities.

1951 Persons covered by Article 24 are one of the categories of persons protected under the First Convention.[3] With regard to their identification, see Article 40.

B. Historical background

1952 The obligation to 'respect and protect' the medical and religious personnel of the enemy's armed forces is a longstanding rule of international humanitarian law. The essence of this rule already appeared in the first Geneva Convention of 1864.[4] Largely similar provisions can be found in the Geneva Conventions of

---

[1] This reality is one of the factors which prompted the International Red Cross and Red Crescent Movement to initiate its 'Health Care in Danger' campaign in 2011; for details of this campaign and associated publications, see http://www.icrc.org/eng/what-we-do/safeguarding-health-care/index.jsp. See also World Health Organization, Resolution 55.13, 'Protection of Medical Missions during Armed Conflict', adopted by the 55th World Health Assembly, 18 May 2002, and Resolution 46.39, 'Health and Medical Services in Times of Armed Conflict', adopted by the 46th World Health Assembly, 14 May 1993.
[2] Article 28(1). For full details, see Articles 28, 30 and 31 of the First Convention and Articles 4(C) and 33 of the Third Convention.
[3] For the relevant provisions in Additional Protocol I, see Articles 8(c)(i) and 43(2).
[4] Geneva Convention (1864), Article 2.

1906[5] and 1929.[6] It eventually crystallized as Article 24 of the First Convention of 1949. The substance of Article 24 also belongs to customary international law.[7]

C. The three categories of persons covered

1. Medical personnel engaged in the search, collection, transport or treatment of the wounded or sick, or in the prevention of disease

1953   The Convention defines the first category of persons covered by Article 24 by reference to the types of activities performed: the 'search for', 'collection', 'transport' or 'treatment' of the 'wounded or sick' or the 'prevention of disease'. Therefore, the first criterion for determining if members of the armed forces fall under this category is whether they perform one or more of the activities listed.

1954   Provided all the conditions of Article 24 are fulfilled, a person can be covered by this provision without belonging, in terms of internal administrative structure, to the medical service of the armed forces.[8] Conversely, being a member of the armed forces' medical service, or being involved in activities which professionals involved in 'military medicine' consider covered by that discipline, does not automatically mean a person is engaged in one or more of the activities protected by Article 24. For example, members of the armed forces' medical service who deal both permanently and exclusively with training activities seeking to enhance the combat-related performance of able-bodied combatants are not protected under Article 24. Similarly, psychologists involved in, for example, the design of detainee interrogation techniques or in the selection of combatants who are psychologically apt to undertake certain missions are not covered by Article 24. However, 'prevention of disease' is included in the list of protected activities, and this activity may very well be undertaken for the benefit of all members of the armed forces (see para. 1958).

1955   Persons who perform the activities of search for, collection or transport of the wounded or sick may include, for example, hospital orderlies, nurses, auxiliary stretcher-bearers, ambulance drivers and pilots of medical aircraft. It should be noted that 'hospital orderlies, nurses or auxiliary stretcher-bearers' also come within the scope of application of Article 25, in which provision they constitute the only persons covered. However, their activities can equally be covered by Article 24, provided they meet all the prescribed conditions. Once they do, the

---

[5] Geneva Convention (1906), Article 9.
[6] Geneva Convention on the Wounded and Sick (1929), Article 9(1).
[7] See ICRC Study on Customary International Humanitarian Law (2005), Rules 25 and 27.
[8] The term 'medical service' is used in both Article 19 and Article 21 of the First Convention. A High Contracting Party is at liberty to use a different term. It is, in any event, for each Power to decide the composition of its medical service and to say who shall be employed in it.

regime of Article 24 applies. This has significant implications in terms of their status if they fall into enemy hands.[9]

1956   The phrase 'treatment of the wounded or sick' encompasses the entire spectrum of medical activities performed by medical doctors, both general practitioners and specialists, as well as by surgeons, dentists, pharmacists, nurses, and staff operating medical equipment or devices. 'Treatment' can be both physical and psychological. It covers diagnostic activities, first-aid treatment[10] and rehabilitation, including physiotherapy. With regard to rehabilitation – which may last for a long time and take place far from the battlefield – it is immaterial that it could result in the person regaining the ability to return to combat duty; the medical personnel involved are nonetheless protected under Article 24. This holds true more generally for all activities protected on the basis of this provision, even if they might lead to persons regaining their ability to fight.

1957   The activities of search for, collection, transport and treatment are to be undertaken for the benefit of the wounded and sick. Within the context of the First Convention, the concept of 'wounded and sick' has to be understood in its technical sense, i.e. as referring to the wounded and sick belonging to the categories identified in Articles 12 and 13 of the Convention. However, the fact that the medical personnel extend their activities to wounded and sick civilians does not deprive them of their entitlement to be respected and protected.[11]

1958   In 1949, 'prevention of disease' was added to the list of protected activities. The result is that Article 24 is not limited to curative medicine. By its nature, the prevention of disease can be undertaken for the benefit of all members of the armed forces, i.e. not only for the wounded and sick but also for able-bodied combatants. 'Prevention of disease' includes hygienic and prophylactic measures (for example delousing or the disinfection of the water supply; some of these activities may be undertaken by veterinarians, see para. 1959), administration of vaccines, disinfection of barracks, and training in the prevention of sexually transmitted diseases. The activities of psychologists involved in the prevention of trauma, such as combat-related stress and mental disorders, can also fall within the term 'prevention of disease', as well as of the term 'treatment' once the trauma is present.

1959   The activities of veterinarians – even when they are members of the armed forces' medical service – will, in principle, fall outside those listed in Article 24, particularly when they exclusively involve animal health care.[12] Indeed, a veterinarian who, as a member of the armed forces, takes care of

---

[9] Personnel covered by Article 24 would fall under the 'retention' regime provided for in Articles 28, 30 and 31, while personnel covered by Article 25 would fall under the regime provided for in Article 29.

[10] Both 'diagnosis' and 'first-aid treatment' are listed in the definition of 'medical purposes' in Article 8(e) of Additional Protocol I.

[11] See also Article 22(5).

[12] The status of veterinarians who are members of the armed forces is dealt with in greater detail in the commentary on Article 22, section F.

animals that are deployed to assist combat activities would, for example, be deemed a combatant. Historically, this has been the dominant paradigm. However, when a veterinarian engages exclusively in the protected activity of 'prevention of disease' vis-à-vis human beings, for example when inspecting the hygiene of food supplies for able-bodied combatants, as more and more veterinarians who are members of the armed forces do, this person qualifies to be 'respected and protected' in the sense of Article 24.

2. Staff engaged in the administration of medical units and establishments

1960 Protection is not only accorded to those in direct contact with the wounded and sick. It is also accorded to members of the armed forces whose work is necessary for the functioning of the medical units and establishments in which the wounded and sick are treated. These members of the armed forces may, but need not, be part of the armed forces' medical service. Provided they are serving exclusively in support of medical units, for example the procurement of medical supplies or other administrative functions, or, for example, as cooks or cleaners, they fulfil the conditions for protection under Article 24.

1961   As can be deduced from the words 'of medical units and establishments', the protection accorded to administrative staff on the basis of Article 24 does not extend to those providing administrative support to religious personnel (dealt with below). Based on humanitarian considerations, it can only be hoped that, as long as they are exclusively engaged in such tasks, they will nevertheless be treated as being protected.

1962   The notion of 'medical units and establishments' has to be understood in the technical sense of Article 19 of the First Convention. Staff engaged in similar activities for civilian hospitals may be covered by Article 20 of the Fourth Convention.

1963   Of note in this context is Article 8(c) of Additional Protocol I, which has adopted in this respect a wider scope than Article 24 of the First Convention. This provision includes, within the definition of 'medical personnel' in the sense of the Protocol, those assigned exclusively not only to 'the administration of medical units' but also to 'the operation or administration of medical transports'. This could be the case, for example, for a member of the armed forces exclusively assigned to the maintenance of medical aircraft.[13]

3. Religious personnel attached to the armed forces

1964 By virtue of Article 24, 'chaplains attached to the armed forces' are entitled to the same protection as the two categories of medical personnel described above. As with those two categories, Article 24 only deals with members of the armed forces who are permanently and exclusively assigned to meeting the spiritual

---

[13] For details on the legal status of medical aircraft under the First Convention, see Article 36.

needs of the armed forces as a whole.[14] Members of the armed forces who have prior qualifications in this field without having been exclusively assigned to perform religious duties are not covered by Article 24. They are combatants, and if they fall into enemy hands, will be prisoners of war.[15]

1965   Article 24 only applies to persons who are members of the armed forces and who serve in religious functions. By contrast, Article 8(d) of Additional Protocol I defines 'religious personnel' more broadly to include civilian religious personnel.[16] See, moreover, the additional possibility created by Article 8(d) and (k) of the Protocol of having religious personnel assigned on a temporary basis.

1966   The scope of beneficiaries for whom 'chaplains attached to the armed forces' may exercise their services is different to that of the two categories of medical personnel referred to above. While military medical personnel may only work for the benefit of the wounded or sick (except when they are engaged in the 'prevention of disease'), religious personnel may extend their activities to the armed forces as a whole, be they wounded, sick or able-bodied.[17]

1967   The term 'chaplains' as used in this provision is dated. The notion is not confined to religious personnel of the Christian faith, who are but one example of religious personnel.[18] Therefore, as a practical matter, the reference to 'chaplains attached to the armed forces' should be understood as referring to all religious personnel attached to the armed forces.

1968   The Geneva Conventions do not provide any criteria for who qualifies as 'religious' personnel. It is left to the discretion of each High Contracting Party to designate such personnel as it sees fit. The reference to 'religious' does not presuppose the traditional understanding of the term. Some High Contracting Parties have appointed humanist, non-confessional counsellors,[19] who are equally protected by Article 24.[20]

---

[14] See, however, the additional possibility, created under Article 8(d) and (k) of Additional Protocol I, of having religious personnel assigned on a temporary basis.

[15] Article 36 of the Third Convention deals specifically with the situation of such 'ministers of religion'.

[16] On respect for and protection of civilian religious personnel, see Article 15(5) of Additional Protocol I.

[17] This logic is extended into the 'retention' regime to which religious personnel covered by Article 24 are entitled under Article 28 (and related provisions). If retained, religious personnel can look after the religious needs of all prisoners of war, i.e. not only the wounded and sick. See Articles 33 and 35 of the Third Convention.

[18] Article 8(d) of Additional Protocol I makes this point clear in its definition of 'religious personnel' with the words 'such as chaplains'. For further analysis, see Claudie Barrat, *Status of NGOs in International Humanitarian Law*, Brill Nijhoff, Leiden, 2014, pp. 123–125.

[19] See e.g. Netherlands, *Military Manual*, 2005, para. 616:

Religious personnel are not considered medical personnel, but enjoy the same protection. They may be military or civilian. They include almoners, field pastors and rabbis whose sole duty is to act as ministers. They are attached to the armed forces of one party to the conflict, to medical corps or to civil defence institutions. Although less well known outside the Netherlands, humanist counsellors and life coaches also belong to the category of religious personnel.

[20] See also ICC Elements of Crimes (2002), p. 31, which, in a footnote to the war crime of murder, states that '[t]he term "religious personnel" includes those non-confessional non-combatant

D. Conditions for coverage by Article 24

1969 While Article 24 does not explicitly state it, only members of the armed forces of a Party to a conflict fall within its scope of application.[21] While they are members of the armed forces, persons covered by Article 24 are not combatants.[22]

1970   When it comes to a State's regular armed forces, Article 24 has a broad scope of application. Provided its requirements are met, it can cover medical and/or religious personnel of all branches of a State's armed forces (army, navy, air force or other), regardless of the terminology actually used and where they are deployed. Thus, medical personnel on board a medical aircraft will be covered by Article 24.

1971   For the purposes of Article 24, the term 'armed forces' does not need to be understood as being confined to the regular armed forces of a Party to the conflict. All groups referred to in Article 13(1)–(3) of the First Convention are entitled to assign some of their members to the functions described in Article 24.[23] While not explicit in Article 24, this interpretation is justified for two reasons. First, members of these groups are among the persons who can qualify as 'wounded and sick' in the sense of Article 13. Thus, the functional nature of the protection accorded to medical and religious personnel entails that – for humanitarian reasons – these groups be able to resort to the services of those personnel. Second, when they fall into enemy hands, members of the groups covered by Article 13(1)–(3) are entitled to prisoner-of-war status. Therefore, the medical and religious personnel of all groups referred to in Article 13(1)–(3) of the First Convention deserve protection equal to that of similar personnel of the regular armed forces of a Party to the conflict.

1. Assignment to medical or religious duties

1972 Article 24 requires that the persons covered by this provision be 'engaged in' a given range of activities. The equally authentic French text requires them to

---

military personnel carrying out a similar function'. The same understanding exists in the context of international human rights law; see International Covenant on Civil and Political Rights (1966), Article 18. See also UN Human Rights Committee, *General Comment No. 22, Article 18 (Freedom of Thought, Conscience or Religion)*, UN Doc. CCPR/C/21/Rev.1/Add.4 (1993), 30 July 1993, para. 2:

> Article 18 protects theistic, non-theistic and atheistic beliefs, as well as the right not to profess any religion or belief. The terms 'belief' and 'religion' are to be broadly construed. Article 18 is not limited in its application to traditional religions or to religions and beliefs with institutional characteristics or practices analogous to those of traditional religions.

[21] The term 'armed forces of a Party to a conflict' has been defined, for States Parties, in Article 43(1) of Additional Protocol I.

[22] See Article 3 of the 1907 Hague Regulations and Article 43(2) of Additional Protocol I. See also ICRC Study on Customary International Humanitarian Law (2005), Rule 3.

[23] In the 'levée en masse' scenario referred to in Article 13(6), it seems unlikely that the persons involved would have had time to assign medical personnel. However, should they do so, these persons will equally qualify for protection on the basis of Article 24.

be 'affecté à' ('assigned to') such activities. The difference is not just semantic: one can be 'engaged in' a given activity without having been 'assigned to' it. Over time, it has come to be widely understood that the requirement is one of 'assignment': mere 'engagement' in certain activities does not suffice as such. Article 8(c) of Additional Protocol I reflects this understanding: for all categories of 'medical personnel' there is a requirement to be exclusively 'assigned, by a Party to the conflict' to medical or religious duties.

1973   The requirement of 'assignment' means that members of the armed forces can only fall within the scope of application of this provision if they have been assigned – by the authority on whom they depend – to one or more of the medical activities (exhaustively referred to in Article 24) and/or to the functions of religious personnel attached to the armed forces. Article 24 defers the practical details of this assignment (who takes the decision, in what form, etc.) to the domestic level. In all cases, the essential requirement is that the person assigned is subject to the control of that authority. This is important in view of the other aspects of the law applicable to them, such as the 'retention' regime and the rules regarding the wearing of the distinctive emblem.[24]

1974   Members of the armed forces cannot assign themselves to the medical or religious service.[25] Training or special qualifications, for example as a surgeon or priest, do not do away with the need to be assigned to those functions by the relevant authorities. Members of the armed forces who have specific qualifications in the medical or religious field but who have not been assigned to the functions described in Article 24 remain combatants and are not covered by this provision.[26] Similarly, combatants who have not been 'assigned' in the sense of Article 24 but who, on their own initiative, care for fellow combatants who are wounded or sick are not entitled to the protection of Article 24. While this holds true as a matter of law, it is hoped that the enemy – prompted by humanitarian considerations – will nevertheless refrain from attacking combatants while engaged in such activities.

1975   The Geneva Conventions do not specify the level of medical training or other qualifications which members of the armed forces must have in order to be eligible to be 'assigned' as medical personnel. The same is true for religious personnel. Yet, in line with the obligation to implement all treaty obligations in good faith, the assignment must be genuine, i.e. the person needs to have the required degree and/or qualifications.

1976   The requirement that a person be 'assigned' by the competent domestic authorities does not imply that those covered by Article 24 necessarily become

---

[24] With regard to the 'retention' regime, see Articles 28, 30 and 31. With regard to the identification of persons covered by Article 24, see Article 40.

[25] See United States, *Law of War Manual*, 2015, para. 4.9.2.2.

[26] If such persons fall into enemy hands, they will become prisoners of war, who are covered by the applicable detention regime rather than the 'retention' regime to which persons covered by Article 24 are entitled. For their situation, Articles 32 and 36 of the Third Convention provide a specific arrangement.

part of the military chain of command or carry military rank, nor that they would be subject to the military justice system. The Geneva Conventions leave that choice to each High Contracting Party. Thus, a High Contracting Party can decide how to organize its armed forces' medical and religious services. The same applies to whether or not these persons wear the uniform of the armed forces and, if so, whether the uniform is identical to that worn by combatants.[27]

2. The exclusive nature of the assignment

1977   The assignment to the activities referred to in Article 24 needs to be 'exclusive'. While a narrow reading of the provision would seem to suggest that the requirement of 'exclusivity' only applies to medical personnel, logic dictates that this requirement applies to all three categories of personnel covered by Article 24.

1978   The importance of this requirement is significant. It entails that, once assigned, a person can only undertake one or more of the prescribed activities. A person may be assigned, for example, to both the treatment of the wounded and sick and the prevention of disease. Conversely, the assignment cannot cover activities that are not mentioned in Article 24. An activity not listed in Article 24 may even, depending on the circumstances, amount to an 'act harmful to the enemy outside their humanitarian duties' which could entail a loss of protection (see section F).

1979   Once a member of the armed forces has been assigned on an exclusive basis to one or more of the activities explicitly referred to in Article 24, the entitlement to be 'respected and protected' exists regardless of whether or not the person is actually carrying out those activities at any given time. The protection conferred by Article 24 (and by the related 'retention' regime) is status-based, i.e. based on the permanent and exclusive nature of the assignment. This feature distinguishes Article 24 from Article 25 on auxiliary medical personnel; the latter is conduct-based, i.e. it only grants protection when medical activities are actually being carried out.

1980   In the logic of Article 24, as it was understood in 1949, the exclusivity of the assignment implies that it has to be not only of an exclusive but also of a permanent nature. As regards the interpretation of the term 'permanent', no definition exists in the Geneva Conventions. For the purposes of Additional Protocol I, Article 8(k) thereof refers to 'an indeterminate period' in order to delineate the concept of 'permanent'. While Article 24 does not mention the

---

[27] For identification of the persons covered by Article 24, see Article 41, which does not mention that they wear a military uniform. See also Article 21(3) of the 1929 Geneva Convention on the Wounded and Sick, which indicates that medical and religious personnel 'who have no military uniform shall be provided with a certificate of identity'.

concept of 'permanent', it has traditionally been read into this provision by contrasting this Article with the logic of Article 25.[28]

1981   Article 24 is silent as to the way in which persons covered by this provision need to exercise the activities referred to. In this respect, Article 12 is of paramount importance, including its paragraph 3, whereby 'only urgent medical reasons will authorize priority in the order of treatment to be administered'. This may require treating the wounded and sick of the adverse Party first. Of further importance are the rules of international humanitarian law dealing with medical ethics.[29]

E. The obligation to respect and protect in all circumstances

1982   The obligation to 'respect and protect' is a term of art that appears frequently in the Geneva Conventions and their Additional Protocols. It was first introduced in treaty law in the 1906 Geneva Convention, replacing earlier terms such as 'immunity', 'inviolability' and 'neutrality'. While those terms may still be used to describe the status of persons covered by Article 24, they are no longer used in contemporary treaties.

1983   The requirement to respect and protect 'in all circumstances' implies that the obligation is not subject to a yardstick of feasibility. It can only be deviated from if the behaviour of the person in question amounts to an 'act harmful to the enemy outside [his or her] humanitarian duties' (see below). Thus, operational reasons or military necessity do not, as such, create any ground to deviate from the obligation to respect and protect.

1984   The requirement to respect and protect triggers obligations of a dual nature. First, to 'respect' implies a series of obligations of a negative nature, i.e. to refrain from engaging in certain types of behaviour, such as attacks, vis-à-vis the protected persons. Second, to 'protect' implies a series of obligations of a positive nature, i.e. to take certain steps to the benefit of those persons, such as reacting against third parties seeking to interfere with their ability to carry out their work.

1985   The multi-faceted nature of what it means to 'respect and protect' cannot be reduced to a checklist of measures to take or actions from which to abstain. Furthermore, it is frequently impossible to clearly separate the obligation to 'respect' from the obligation to 'protect'. The same behaviour may reflect an expression of both obligations. The following paragraphs, therefore, merely

---

[28] See also Article 9(2) of the 1929 Geneva Convention on the Wounded and Sick which, for its part, explicitly uses the term 'permanent medical personnel'.

[29] See Additional Protocol I, Article 16. See also Sigrid Mehring, *First Do No Harm: Medical Ethics in International Humanitarian Law*, Brill, Boston, 2014, pp. 22–26, for a discussion of what the author calls the 'dual-loyalty' conflict facing military physicians: '[A]re military physicians soldiers first and physicians second, or *vice versa*?', and p. 429: 'physicians should be physicians first and as such dedicated to those needing medical care, and soldiers second'. See also Toebes, p. 173.

serve to highlight, by way of example, some of the dimensions inherent in the practical implementation of the requirement to 'respect and protect in all circumstances'. Depending on the circumstances, additional steps may be required in order to come to a meaningful implementation of this obligation. Conversely, some of the steps outlined in what follows may be irrelevant in certain situations.

1986   The obligation to 'respect' and the obligation to 'protect' both apply in two different types of relationships. First, they apply in the relationship between a Party to the conflict and the medical and religious personnel of the enemy's armed forces. Second, they apply in the relationship between a High Contracting Party and the medical and religious personnel of its own armed forces. The latter dimension may be particularly relevant when it comes to the duty to 'protect'.

1987   At a minimum, 'respect' requires compliance with the duties of abstention, such as not to attack medical and religious personnel (be it directly, indiscriminately or in violation of the principle of proportionality),[30] kill them if they fall into one's hands, or ill-treat, harm in any way, injure, kidnap, threaten, intimidate, physically assault, or subject them to arbitrary arrest.[31] Respect for the legal framework protecting the medical ethics under which they operate is also required. In this regard, Article 16 of Additional Protocol I contains the rule that i.e. medical personnel may not be forced to act contrary to the applicable ethics. Thus, for example, medical personnel are not to be harassed or threatened with punishment in order to obtain information about the wounded and sick they may have treated.[32]

1988   Furthermore, medical and religious personnel may not be made to renounce the rights secured to them by the applicable law.[33]

1989   For all of the foregoing acts, the mere threat of such action is equally unlawful, even if the threat is not carried out. Thus, for example, it is prohibited to threaten to attack medical personnel in order to discourage them from carrying out their work.[34] The obligation to 'respect' applies both to the State and to its organs, each of which may bear responsibility under applicable international law, be it State responsibility or individual criminal or disciplinary responsibility. Lastly, the fact that persons covered by Article 24 may be retained only

---

[30] See Gisel. For a different view, see United States, *Law of War Manual*, 2015, paras 4.10.1, 7.8.2.1 and 7.8.2.1.

[31] Arbitrary arrest would cover, for example, arrests carried out unlawfully or for purposes of intimidation. That said, the arrest of medical personnel who have committed a violation of applicable law remains lawful. However, depending on the circumstances (e.g. when carried out on a wide scale or under false pretences), the latter may still amount to a violation of the obligation to 'respect' medical personnel.

[32] Breitegger, pp. 118–121.   [33] See Article 7.

[34] In this context, Article 18(3) is relevant: 'No one may ever be molested or convicted for having nursed the wounded or sick.' See also Article 16 of Additional Protocol I on the 'General protection of medical duties'.

under certain conditions (see Articles 28 and 30) can be seen as flowing directly from the requirement to 'respect' them 'in all circumstances'.

1990   It should be kept in mind that medical and religious personnel are required to wear the distinctive emblem.[35] Under the ICC Statute it is a war crime in both international and non-international armed conflict to 'intentionally direc[t] attacks against … personnel using the distinctive emblem of the Geneva Conventions in conformity with international law'.[36] Similarly, the obligation to respect will be violated if the personnel are made the object of belligerent reprisals.[37] In this context, it bears recalling that persons covered by Article 24 are persons protected under the First Convention. Therefore, the acts listed in Article 50 of the First Convention, if committed against them, may qualify as grave breaches of the Convention.

1991   The obligation to 'protect' medical and religious personnel entails, at a minimum, an obligation to take steps to ensure that they can carry out their work and to refrain from unduly interfering with their work, such as by arresting them simply for performing their assigned duties.[38] As with the obligation to 'respect', the obligation to 'protect' applies both to the State and to its organs, each of which may bear responsibility under applicable international law, i.e. be it State responsibility or individual criminal or disciplinary responsibility. The overarching objective of the obligation to protect is to ensure that medical personnel can reach those in need – that is, in the case of medical personnel, the wounded and sick.

1992   Depending on the circumstances, the obligation to 'protect' may equally entail an obligation to 'ensure respect' by third parties. This may be relevant where looters or marauders seek to interfere with the ability of medical or religious personnel to carry out their work. In such cases, practical steps must be taken to put a stop to the interference. In short, one needs to come to the defence, assistance or rescue of medical and religious personnel.

1993   Without prejudice to the absolute nature of both the obligation to 'respect' and the obligation to 'protect', it must be acknowledged that the practical implementation of the obligation to allow them to fulfil their medical duties may, in some circumstances, have to be temporarily delayed for reasons of military necessity.[39] In this regard, the obligation to 'respect' is different from the

---

[35] The display of the emblem, in and of itself, does not confer protection; it is merely an outward sign indicating the protected status of the person displaying it. For details, see the commentary on Article 40, section B.4.

[36] See ICC Statute (1998), Article 8(2)(b)(xxiv) and (e)(ii).   [37] See also Article 46.

[38] More broadly, within the context of Additional Protocol I, this entails an obligation to comply with its Article 16 (General protection of medical duties). This obligation applies vis-à-vis both one's own medical personnel and enemy medical personnel, for example when retained.

[39] See e.g. Benin, *Law of Armed Conflict Manual*, 1995, Fascicule III, p. 5 ('Specially protected persons may not take a direct part in hostilities and must not be attacked. They shall be allowed to carry out their tasks as long as the tactical situation permits.'); Croatia, *Commanders' Manual*, 1992, paras 7 and 12 ('Specifically protected persons may not participate directly in hostilities and may not be attacked. They shall be allowed to perform their tasks, when the tactical

obligation to 'protect' because it suffers no exception whatsoever, not even in case of urgent military necessity.

1994   The phrase 'in all circumstances' serves not only to underscore the stringent nature of the substantive obligation contained in Article 24, but also to highlight that it applies at all times and in all places, both on the battlefield and behind the lines, and whether the medical or religious personnel are retained only temporarily by the enemy or for a lengthy period. Lastly, the phrase emphasizes the argument that the obligation exists for a Party to the armed conflict regardless of whether or not the enemy complies with it. The term 'in all circumstances' is without prejudice, however, to the possibility that the entitlement to be 'respected and protected' can be lost in certain specific and limited circumstances.

F. Loss of protection: Acts harmful to the enemy outside humanitarian duties

1995   Article 24 is silent on the question of whether or not the entitlement to be 'respected and protected in all circumstances' can be lost in certain circumstances. Despite this silence, the logic of the protective regime for medical and religious personnel entails that, under certain circumstances, protection can be lost. The reasons for this position are that on the basis of Article 24, the High Contracting Parties confer protection on certain members of the enemy armed forces. Such a privileged position comes with corresponding duties that preclude abuse of that protection. The repeated use of the word 'exclusively' in Article 24 underscores this point.

1996   The entitlement to be 'respected and protected' can be lost only if the persons in question commit an 'act harmful to the enemy' and if the commission of that act takes place 'outside their humanitarian duties'. It bears emphasis that an 'act harmful to the enemy outside their humanitarian duties' is the sole legal criterion whereby the said entitlement can be lost. No other reasons, such as military necessity, may be invoked to justify the loss of protection.

1997   The criterion of 'acts harmful to the enemy outside their humanitarian duties' is also used in Article 21 of the First Convention, in connection with the loss of protection of fixed establishments and mobile medical units of the medical service.[40] Article 22 of the Convention provides, also in connection with those establishments and units, a non-exhaustive list of 'conditions' which may not be considered as leading to a loss of protection. While both provisions

situation permits.'); and Nigeria, *IHL Manual*, 1994, p. 45, para. (f) ('Specifically protected persons...recognised as such must be respected. Specifically protected persons are to be allowed to fulfil their activity unless the tactical situation does not permit.')

[40] Article 13(1) of Additional Protocol I speaks of 'humanitarian function' instead of 'humanitarian duties'; Article 11(2) of Additional Protocol II speaks of 'hostile acts' instead of 'acts harmful to the enemy'. These small terminological differences have no substantive implications.

have been written from the perspective of the loss of protection of medical establishments and units, the same criteria should be applied *mutatis mutandis* to persons providing medical or religious services. Thus, for example, the fact that they carry 'small arms and ammunition taken from the wounded and sick and [which are] not yet handed to the proper service' and the fact that their 'humanitarian activities...extend to the care of civilian wounded and sick' cannot be considered as acts harmful to the enemy.[41]

1998   In practice, it is of critical importance to know what exactly amounts to an 'act harmful to the enemy outside their humanitarian duties'. At the level of treaty law, outside the list of 'conditions' in Article 22, no definition exists and little work has been undertaken to clarify the notion. The absence of a treaty-based definition may lead to some uncertainty. Therefore, in view of the humanitarian values at stake, in case of doubt as to whether a particular type of behaviour qualifies as an act harmful to the enemy, it ought not to be considered as such.

1999   During the negotiation of the Geneva Conventions, the ICRC proposed the following definition of the term 'acts harmful to the enemy': 'acts the purpose or the effect of which is to harm the adverse Party, by facilitating or impeding military operations'.[42] While this proposal was not incorporated into the text of the Conventions, it remains useful to gain a better understanding of the notion. The following examples were provided by the ICRC in the initial commentary, albeit in relation to objects: 'the use of a hospital as a shelter for able-bodied combatants or fugitives, as an arms or ammunition dump, or as a military observation post; another instance would be the deliberate siting of a medical unit in a position where it would impede an enemy attack'.[43]

2000   As is clear from the words 'purpose or effect' in the ICRC proposal, the criterion of 'acts harmful to the enemy' is to be understood broadly: every form of behaviour – outside the humanitarian duties of medical or religious personnel – which harms the enemy may be considered as an act harmful to the enemy. Depending on the particular circumstances of the case, this criterion may be fulfilled in such cases where a person covered by Article 24 takes up arms against the enemy (other than in self-defence),[44] assists in the operation of a weapon system or in the planning of a military operation, or transmits intelligence of military value.[45] Another scenario which may amount to an act

---

[41] See Article 22(3) and (5), respectively.

[42] *Final Record of the Diplomatic Conference of Geneva of 1949*, Vol. II-A, p. 59. See also *Draft revision of the 1929 Geneva Convention submitted by the ICRC to National Societies in 1937*, p. 3.

[43] Pictet (ed.), *Commentary on the First Geneva Convention*, ICRC, 1952, pp. 200–201.

[44] For a discussion of the contours of the notion of 'self-defence', see the commentary on Article 22(1).

[45] For example, for the US armed forces, see *Religious Affairs in Joint Operations*, 2013, p. I-2, stating: '[C]haplains must not engage directly or indirectly in combatant duties; will not conduct activities that compromise their noncombatant status; must not function as intelligence

harmful to the enemy is when medical personnel help able-bodied combatants of their State to hide for a while in a hospital. Depending on the circumstances, and provided the constitutive requirements have been met, engaging in any of the foregoing may also qualify as prohibited perfidy and/or, separately, as an improper use of the distinctive emblem.[46]

2001   The phrase 'outside their humanitarian duties' makes clear that certain acts may fulfil the criterion of 'acts harmful to the enemy' without entailing a loss of protection.[47] As explained earlier, persons covered by Article 24 are entitled to carry out certain activities, such as disease prevention and provision of religious services, to the benefit of able-bodied combatants. Such activities fall within the humanitarian duties of medical and religious personnel, even if their effect may be harmful to the enemy. Hence, these activities do not lead to a loss of protection. Even if a particular act may be considered as an 'act harmful to the enemy', it will still not lead to a loss of protection if it was committed as part, or as a result of, the exercise of the said 'humanitarian duties'. This nuance is important in that the work of medical and religious personnel may at times temporarily inconvenience military operations, for example when they perform their duties close to military operations or when the collection of the wounded and sick impedes the enemy's advances. Provided they remain within the boundaries of the prescribed 'humanitarian duties', the acts in question do not lead to a loss of protection.

2002   The criterion of 'acts harmful to the enemy outside their humanitarian duties' bears some similarity to the criterion of 'taking a direct part in the hostilities'. However, the two notions are separate, have their own scope of applicability and engender different consequences. The criterion of 'taking a direct part in the hostilities' only applies to civilians and not to persons covered by Article 24. Thus, these notions are not to be conflated.[48]

2003   In terms of acts covered, the scope of application of the notion of 'acts harmful to the enemy' is broader than that of 'direct participation in hostilities'.[49]

---

collectors or propose combat target selection; and will not advise on including or excluding specific structures on the no-strike list or target list.'

[46] As to the types of perfidious conduct which qualify as prohibited perfidy, see the first sentence of Article 37(1) of Additional Protocol I. For proper and improper use of the distinctive emblem, see Articles 40 and 44 of the First Convention and Article 38(1) of Additional Protocol I, respectively.

[47] For further details, see the commentary on Article 21, para. 1844.

[48] ICRC, *Interpretive Guidance on the Notion of Direct Participation in Hostilities under International Humanitarian Law*, by Nils Melzer, ICRC, Geneva, 2009, p. 20: 'Where IHL provides persons other than civilians with immunity from direct attack, the loss and restoration of protection is governed by criteria similar to, but not necessarily identical with, direct participation in hostilities.'

[49] See United States, *Law of War Manual*, 2015, para. 7.8.3; See also Michael Bothe, Karl Josef Partsch and Waldemar A. Solf, *New Rules for Victims of Armed Conflicts: Commentary on the Two 1977 Protocols Additional to the Geneva Conventions of 1949*, Martinus Nijhoff Publishers, The Hague, 1982, p. 411; Robert W. Gehring, 'Loss of Civilian Protections under the Fourth Geneva Convention and Protocol I', *Military Law Review*, Vol. 90, 1980, pp. 49–87; Nils Melzer, *Targeted Killing in International Law*, Oxford University Press, 2008, p. 329.

Thus, every single act, if committed by civilians, which qualifies as 'taking a direct part in hostilities', will qualify as an 'act harmful to the enemy outside their humanitarian duties' if it is committed by a person entitled to respect and protection under Article 24. The opposite is not the case, however, as not every 'act harmful to the enemy' would constitute a 'direct participation in hostilities' if committed by a civilian.

2004   While the notion of 'acts harmful to the enemy' is broad, it is not open-ended. Frequently, medical personnel of the armed forces may be near combatants and travel in the same vehicles as them. The mere fact that medical personnel of the armed forces travel in the same vehicle as combatants, or that they may even be incorporated into a unit of combatants, must not be considered an 'act harmful to the enemy outside their humanitarian duties'.[50] This very proximity may serve to facilitate access to the wounded and sick. However, the prohibition on using the presence of medical or religious personnel in an attempt to shield military objectives from attack needs to be respected.[51] Similarly, the mere fact that such personnel wear the uniform of the enemy armed forces cannot be considered, as such, to be an 'act harmful to the enemy outside their humanitarian duties'.[52]

2005   In line with the conditions listed in Article 22(1), all medical and religious personnel of the armed forces can be equipped with light individual weapons without losing their protection.[53] It is the sole remit of the national authorities to decide whether or not such personnel are entitled to be armed.[54] If it is decided at the domestic level to authorize (or compel)[55] medical and religious

---

[50] Similarly, see Henckaerts/Doswald-Beck, commentary on Rule 25, p. 85:

   [T]he equipment of medical personnel with small arms to defend themselves or their patients and the use of such arms for this purpose do not lead to loss of protection. Furthermore, in analogous application of the similar rule applying to medical units, it is not to be considered a hostile act if medical personnel are escorted by military personnel or such personnel are present or if the medical personnel are in possession of small arms and ammunition taken from their patients and not yet handed over to the proper service.

[51] See Additional Protocol I, Article 12(4). See also ICC Statute (1998), Article 8(2)(b)(xxiii) and Customary International Humanitarian Law (2005), Rule 97.

[52] For a further discussion of this issue, see the commentary on Article 39(2) of Additional Protocol I.

[53] For a further discussion of this issue, including the types of permissible weapons, see the commentary on Article 22, section C. See also Breitegger, p. 112:

   [T]he mere use by medical personnel ... of personal protective equipment such as helmets, bulletproof vests, or gas masks, or the use of armoured vehicles, would not go beyond the permissible limits of individual defence, as such items serve the exclusively defensive purpose of absorbing the impact of explosive devices or reducing exposure to chemicals or hazardous material.

[54] For an overview of the type of considerations which may inform this decision, see ICRC, *Ambulance and Pre-Hospital Services in Risk Situations*, ICRC, Geneva, 2013, pp. 35–38, under the heading 'The question of personal protective equipment (PPE) should be analysed by country and/or context and proper training provided'.

[55] At the domestic level, a decision may be taken whereby medical or religious personnel are not just entitled, but compelled, to carry weapons within the limits of what is permissible under international humanitarian law. It may also happen that the personnel in question would prefer not to follow this order (for example, for religious reasons). However, as long as the order

personnel to carry permitted types of weapons, the mere fact of their being so armed cannot be considered an 'act harmful to the enemy outside their humanitarian duties'. The weapons in question, however, can only be used for two specific purposes: for the persons' 'own defence' or for the defence of the 'wounded and sick in their charge'. Thus, even when the use of the weapons is defensive in nature, they may not be used for the defence of other persons, let alone for the defence of military objectives.[56] If this were allowed to occur, the line dividing medical and religious personnel from combatants would become all too easily blurred. Further, such personnel may not take up arms on their own initiative, for example for offensive purposes, or in a defensive military operation in which the 'defensive' element would go beyond the bounds of the two permitted purposes.[57] When they take up arms for offensive or for non-recognized defensive purposes, that action may be considered as an 'act harmful to the enemy outside their humanitarian duties', but in any case it will depend on the circumstances.

2006   The entitlement to use arms for the two permitted purposes – self-defence and defence of the wounded and sick – may result in these persons becoming actively engaged in the fighting, not only against marauders but also in situations that may resemble combat. Medical and religious personnel therefore need to be aware at all times of the potential danger inherent in using their weapons in self-defence and defence of the wounded and sick in their charge. Doing so too quickly – even when for permitted purposes – may engender widespread distrust of their position as persons protected under the First Convention.

2007   In practice, questions have arisen as to whether the assignment of medical and religious personnel to sentry or picket duty constitutes, in and of itself, an 'act harmful to the enemy outside their humanitarian duties'. As this is a borderline case, it is recommended that commanders avoid assignment of medical and religious personnel to such duties in order not to compromise the protection of such personnel.[58] Whether persons assigned as sentries or pickets

---

remains within the limits of international humanitarian law, they would have no legal basis under international law for not complying with it.

[56] United Kingdom, *Allied Joint Doctrine for Medical Support, with UK National Elements*, 2015, p. 1–98: 'Medical personnel must not be used to support the collective protection of non-medical facilities and assets. Commanders at all levels have a responsibility to ensure that the protected status of medical personnel is maintained.'

[57] See also United Kingdom, *Manual of the Law of Armed Conflict*, 2004, para. 7.16: 'The [medical] unit may be "guarded by a picket or by sentries or by an escort" [footnote *inter alia* referring to Article 22(2) of the First Convention]. However, the guard also may only act in a purely defensive manner and may not oppose the occupation or control of the unit by the enemy.'

[58] See United States, *Navy Regulations*, 1990, para. 1063:

While assigned to a combat area during a period of armed conflict, members of Medical, Dental, Chaplain, Medical Service, Nurse or Hospital Corps and Dental Technicians shall be detailed or permitted only such duties as are related to medical, dental or religious service and the administration of medical, dental or religious units and establishments. This restriction is necessary to protect the non-combatant status of these personnel under the Geneva Conventions of August 12, 1949.

can be considered to be engaged in an 'act harmful to the enemy outside their humanitarian duties' depends on the circumstances. Of particular relevance is the nature of the facility which the person has been assigned to guard. If it is a military objective, such assignment (especially as picket, because it enables intelligence about advancing troops to be passed on, for example) could be considered an 'act harmful to the enemy outside their humanitarian duties'. If it is a medical unit, however, the assignment ought not to be considered as an 'act harmful to the enemy outside their humanitarian duties'. In this context, reference can be made to Article 22(2), which prohibits considering as an 'act harmful to the enemy' the fact that 'in the absence of armed orderlies, the unit or establishment is protected by a picket or by sentries or by an escort'. Thus, serving as sentry or picket for a medical unit does not lead, in and of itself, to a loss of protection.

2008   The consequences of medical or religious personnel committing an 'act harmful to the enemy outside their humanitarian duties' need to be measured in a nuanced way. On the battlefield, the commission of such an act will in any event lead to the loss of the entitlement to be 'protected'. This means, for example, that the enemy can no longer be expected to facilitate that person's work. That said, when it comes to the loss of the entitlement to be 'respected', the commission of an 'act harmful to the enemy' does not, in and of itself, mean that the person automatically becomes a lawful target. In practice, however, it is hard to conceive of circumstances in which it would not do so, i.e. generally, engaging in an act harmful to the enemy will lead to the loss of the entitlement to be protected. However, when this happens, the requirements of Article 21 apply above and beyond the general provisions of the law on the conduct of hostilities: 'Protection may, however, cease only after a due warning has been given, naming, in all appropriate cases, a reasonable time limit and after such warning has remained unheeded.'[59] Thus, in accordance with the conditions discussed in the commentary on Article 21, the person needs to be given an opportunity to cease the behaviour in question. At all times, medical and religious personnel of the armed forces need to be aware of the dangers inherent in committing acts harmful to the enemy. These may quickly taint other protected personnel, resulting in a weakening of the overall protection regime.

2009   If just one act harmful to the enemy has been committed, the loss of protection is arguably only temporary, i.e. the protection provided for in Article 24 is regained once that act has ceased to produce its effects.[60] In other words, the

---

Gary D. Solis, *The Law of Armed Conflict: International Humanitarian Law in War*, Cambridge University Press, 2010, p. 193, reports a US directive which includes the following sentence: 'Corpsmen may not man defensive positions of checkpoint/control points.'

[59] See the commentary on Article 21, section C.2.

[60] For an overview of the same question with regard to military medical units and establishments, the considerations of which apply *mutatis mutandis* here too, see the commentary on Article 21, paras 1856–1859.

commission of a single act harmful to the enemy would not lead to a permanent loss of protection for that person for the remainder of the armed conflict.

2010   Independent of the battlefield status of medical or religious personnel who commit one or more acts harmful to the enemy, the question arises as to what happens to such persons when they fall into enemy hands. In particular, do they forfeit their entitlement to return on the basis of Article 30 or, if retained on the basis of Article 28, their entitlement to work only on medical or spiritual duties? If they have been instructed by their commander to conduct the act(s) in question, the assignment to medical duties has been withdrawn. Thus, they become combatants and are no longer entitled to display the distinctive emblem. Upon falling into enemy hands, they would become prisoners of war entitled to combatant immunity for the lawful acts committed after the initial instruction. However, if they were to commit one or more acts harmful to the enemy on their own initiative, there is no agreed rule settling the question.[61] In the case of a single act harmful to the enemy, one might argue that the status remains unchanged, and the provisions of Articles 28 and 30 would remain applicable. However, this logic may be harder to defend when that person has committed several acts harmful to the enemy. In practice, a competent tribunal in the sense of Article 5 of the Third Convention would be the appropriate, and arguably required, authority to decide upon the person's status, taking into account all the circumstances of the case.

Select bibliography

Baccino-Astrada, Alma, *Manual on the Rights and Duties of Medical Personnel in Armed Conflicts*, ICRC, Geneva, 1982.

Breitegger, Alexander, 'The legal framework applicable to insecurity and violence affecting the delivery of health care in armed conflicts and other emergencies, *International Review of the Red Cross*, Vol. 95, No. 889, March 2013, pp. 83–127.

Casey-Maslen, Stuart, 'The Status, Rights, and Obligations of Medical and Religious Personnel', in Andrew Clapham, Paola Gaeta and Marco Sassòli (eds), *The*

---

[61] See, however, United States, *Law of War Manual*, 2015, para. 4.9.2.3: military medical personnel committing acts harmful to the enemy 'would not be entitled to military medical status'. Similarly, at para. 4.10.1: 'Military medical and religious personnel who take actions outside their role as military medical and religious personnel forfeit the corresponding protections of their special status and may be treated as combatants or auxiliary medical personnel, as appropriate.' Under this interpretation, the status of this person when falling into enemy hands will be that of a prisoner of war; see para. 9.3.2, including under the list of persons entitled to prisoner-of-war status that of 'military medical and religious personnel not entitled to retained personnel status (e.g., those not exclusively engaged in medical duties at the time of their capture)'. See also United States, *Medical Evacuation in a Theater of Operations*, 2000, para. A-6, suggesting, in case of a violation of the Convention by military medical personnel, that there is a risk of 'captured medical personnel becoming prisoners of war rather than retained persons. They may not be permitted to treat fellow prisoners.' For alternative options explored in the literature, see Haeck, pp. 848–849, and Sassòli, pp. 55–57.

1949 Geneva Conventions: A Commentary, Oxford University Press, 2015, pp. 807–824.

Commission médico-juridiquede Monaco, 'Le statut de la profession médicale en temps de conflit armé', Compte-rendu de sa VIIIe session, *Annales de droit international médical*, No. 28, July 1979, pp. 52–88.

Darré, Eric and Dumas, Emmanuel, 'Vétérinaires et droit international humanitaire: réflexions sur une controverse', *Revue de Droit Militaire et de Droit de la Guerre*, Vols 3–4, No. 43, 2004, pp. 111–136.

Darré, Eric, Alsina, Teniente Coronel Javier and Bonventre, Eugene, 'L'armement du personnel sanitaire: une contrainte nécessaire', *Revue internationale des services de santé des forces armées*, Vol. 78, 2005, pp. 193–202.

Desch, Thomas, 'Militärseelsorgepersonal – Tragen von Waffen', in Peter Steiner and Karl-Reinhart Trauner (eds), *Humanitäres Völkerrecht und seine Wurzeln*, Evangelischen Militärsuperintendentur No. 3, Vienna, 2005, pp. 25–27.

De Waard, Peter and Tarrant, John, 'Protection of Military Medical Personnel in Armed Conflicts', *University of Western Australia Law Review*, Vol. 35, 2010, pp. 157–183.

Gisel, Laurent, 'Can the incidental killing of military doctors never be excessive?', *International Review of the Red Cross*, Vol. 95, No. 889, March 2013, pp. 215–230.

Green, Leslie C., 'War Law and the Medical Profession', *Canadian Yearbook of International Law*, Vol. 17, 1979, pp. 159–205.

Haeck, Tom, 'Loss of Protection', in Andrew Clapham, Paola Gaeta and Marco Sassòli (eds), *The 1949 Geneva Conventions: A Commentary*, Oxford University Press, 2015, pp. 839–854.

Hampson, Françoise J., 'Conscience in Conflict: The Doctor's Dilemma', *The Canadian Yearbook of International Law*, 1989, pp. 203–225.

Henckaerts, Jean-Marie and Doswald-Beck, Louise, *Customary International Humanitarian Law, Volume I: Rules*, ICRC/Cambridge University Press, 2005, available at https://www.icrc.org/customary-ihl/eng/docs/v1.

Hiebel, Jean-Luc, 'Droit de l'aumônerie, droit de l'assistance spirituelle', *Annuaire français des droits de l'homme*, Vol. I, 1974, pp. 531–543.

– *Assistance spirituelle et conflits armés*, Henry Dunant Institute, Geneva, 1980.

– 'Human rights relating to spiritual assistance as embodied in the Geneva Conventions of 1949', *International Review of the Red Cross*, Vol. 20, No. 214, February 1980, pp. 3–28.

ICRC, *Rights and Duties of Nurses, Military and Civilian Personnel under the Geneva Conventions of August 12, 1949 (Extracts of the Geneva Conventions with Comments)*, ICRC, Geneva, 1970.

– *Health Care in Danger: The Responsibilities of Health-Care Personnel Working in Armed Conflicts and Other Emergencies*, ICRC, Geneva, 2012.

Ishan Jan, Mohammad Naqib and Ansari, Abdul Haseeb, 'The care of wounded and sick and the protection of medical personnel in time of armed conflict', *ISIL Yearbook of International Humanitarian and Refugee Law*, Vol. XI, 2011, pp. 47–73.

Jeanty, Bernard, *La protection du personnel sanitaire dans les conflits armés internationaux*, Thèse de Licence, Université de Neuchâtel, 1990.

Kalshoven, Frits, 'Noncombatant Persons: A Comment to Chapter 11 of the Commander's Handbook on the Law of Naval Operations', in Horace B. Robertson

Jr. (ed.), *The Law of Naval Operations*, International Law Studies, U.S. Naval War College, Vol. 64, 1999, pp. 300–330.

Koerber, H.E., 'Probleme der Bestimmungen über die Militärgeistlichen in den Genfer Abkommen vom 12. August 1949', *The Military Law and the Law of War Review*, Vol. 5, 1966, pp. 417–428.

Kounda, Abderrahim, *Le personnel et la logistique sanitaires au regard du droit international humanitaire*, Mémoire pour l'Obtention du Diplôme des Etudes Supérieures en Sciences Politiques, Doctorat de 3ᵉ Cycle, Université Hassan II, Casablanca, 1999.

Lavergne, Hervé, *La protection et le respect du médecin au cours des hostilités*, Pierre Moulin, Lyon, 1954.

Lunze, Stefan, *The Protection of Religious Personnel in Armed Conflict*, Peter Lang Europäischer Verlag der Wissenschaften, 2004.

– 'Serving God and Caesar: Religious personnel and their protection in armed conflict', *International Review of the Red Cross*, Vol. 86, No. 853, March 2004, pp. 69–90.

Nahlik, E., 'Le statut du personnel sanitaire dans les conflits armés', Contribution du 'Séminaire de Varsovie sur les milieux médicaux, Novembre 1980', unpublished, available at the ICRC library.

Nicolas, Claude, *L'assistance spirituelle dans le droit de la guerre – Contribution à l'étude comparée des statuts juridiques et canoniques des aumôneries et de leur personnel*, Thèse de doctorat en Droit publique, Université de Paris XI, 1991.

O'Brien, Roderick, *A Manual of International Humanitarian Law for Religious Personnel*, Australian Red Cross Society, Adelaide, 1993.

Odier, Lucie, 'Medical Personnel Assigned to the Care of the Wounded and Sick in the Armed Forces (Training, Duties, Status and Terms of Enrolment)', *International Review of the Red Cross*, Supplement, Vol. VI, No. 10, October 1953, pp. 175–183.

Odom, Jonathan G., 'Beyond Arm Bands and Arms Banned: Chaplains, Armed Conflict, and the Law', *Naval Law Review*, Vol. 49, 2002, pp. 1–70.

Parks, Hays W., 'Memorandum of Law: Status of Certain Medical Corps and Medical Service Corps Officers Under the Geneva Conventions', *The Army Lawyer*, April 1989, pp. 5–6.

Pictet, Jean, S., 'La profession médicale et le droit international humanitaire', *Revue internationale de la Croix-Rouge*, Vol. 67, No. 754, August 1985, pp. 195–213.

Sassòli, Marco, '"Acts harmful to the enemy" versus "direct participation in hostilities" or when does medical and religious personnel lose protection against attack?', in *Vulnerabilities in Armed Conflicts: Selected Issues*, Proceedings of the 14th Bruges Colloquium, 17–18 October 2013, Collegium No. 44, Autumn 2014, pp. 50–57.

Schlögel, Anton, 'Schutz der Seelsorge im humanitären Völkerrecht', in Yvo Hangartner and Stefan Trechsel (eds), *Völkerrecht im Dienste des Menschen: Festschrift für Hans Haug*, Verlag Paul Haupt, 1986, pp. 259–278.

Schoenholzer, Jean-Pierre, 'Le médecin dans les Conventions de Genève de 1949', *Revue internationale de la Croix-Rouge et Bulletin international des Sociétés de la Croix-Rouge*, Vol. 35, Nos 410/411, February/March 1953, pp. 94–126 and 169–194.

– 'Le soldat sanitaire n'est pas un combattant', *Revue internationale de la Croix-Rouge et Bulletin international des Sociétés de la Croix-Rouge*, Vol. 37, No. 436, April 1955, pp. 241–244.
– *Nurses and the Geneva Conventions of 1949*, ICRC, Geneva, 1957.
Servais, Olivier, *The Military Medical Officer and the Geneva Conventions*, International Committee of Military Medicine and Pharmacy, Liège, 1988.
Stadlmeier, Sigmar, 'Die Stellung des Militärseelsorgers im Humanitären Völkerrecht', in Hans Walther Kaluza *et al.* (eds), *Pax et Iustitia, Festschrift für Alfred Kostelecky zum 70. Geburtstag*, Duncker & Humblot, Berlin, 1990, pp. 521–534.
Toebes, Brigit, 'Doctors in Arms: Exploring the Legal and Ethical Position of Military Medical Personnel in Armed Conflict', in Mariëlle Matthee, Brigit Toebes and Marcel Brus (eds), *Armed Conflict and International Law: In Search of the Human Face, Liber Amicorum in Memory of Avril McDonald*, Asser Press, 2013, pp. 169–194.
Torrelli, Maurice, 'La protection du médecin dans les conflits armés', in Christophe Swinarski (ed.), *Etudes et essais sur le droit international humanitaire et sur les principes de la Croix-Rouge en l'honneur de Jean Pictet*, ICRC/Martinus Nijhoff Publishers, The Hague, 1984, pp. 581–601.
Vollmar, Lewis C., Jr., 'Development of the laws of war as they pertain to medical units and their personnel', *Military Medicine*, Vol. 157, 1992, pp. 231–236.
– 'Military Medicine in War: The Geneva Conventions Today', in Thomas E. Beam and Linette R. Sparacino (eds), *Military Medical Ethics*, Vol. 2, Office of The Surgeon General, United States Army, Washington D.C., 2003, pp. 739–771.
Voncken, Jules, 'Le médecin, un combattant?', *Revue internationale de la Croix-Rouge et Bulletin international des Sociétés de la Croix-Rouge*, Vol. 37, No. 436, April 1955, pp. 245–249.
Watson, Liselotte B., 'Status of Medical and Religious Personnel in International Law', *Judge Advocate General Journal*, Vol. 20, 1965, pp. 41–59.
Wilson, Robert R., 'Status of chaplains with armed forces', *American Journal of International Law*, Vol. 37, 1943, pp. 490–494.

PROTECTION OF AUXILIARY PERSONNEL

❖ Text of the provision

Members of the armed forces specially trained for employment, should the need arise, as hospital orderlies, nurses or auxiliary stretcher-bearers, in the search for or the collection, transport or treatment of the wounded and sick shall likewise be respected and protected if they are carrying out these duties at the time when they come into contact with the enemy or fall into his hands.

❖ Reservations or declarations

None

Contents

A. Introduction

2011 Article 25 regulates a distinct category of persons who, as members of the armed forces, are entitled to be 'respected and protected' under certain conditions. While the term does not appear as such in the First Convention, these persons are traditionally referred to as 'auxiliary medical personnel' or simply 'auxiliary personnel'. Unlike the permanent medical personnel covered by Article 24, auxiliary medical personnel are only employed on medical duties for part of the time. For the remainder of their time they will be assigned to duties as combatants, in which case they are to be treated as such. Auxiliary medical personnel are distinct from permanent medical personnel; therefore, their status when they fall into enemy hands and their means of identification

714

are regulated in provisions separate from those regulating the same issues for permanent personnel.[1]

2012   The possibility created by Article 25 is appealing for a number of reasons. From the perspective of the armed forces, the use of auxiliary personnel enables the pool of permanent medical personnel to be supplemented in a flexible and possibly cost-efficient manner. Moreover, since auxiliary medical personnel are likely to be in even closer proximity to combatants than permanent medical personnel, they may be more effective in carrying out, for example, the obligations contained in Article 15(1).

2013   From the perspective of the wounded and sick in the field, the presence of auxiliary personnel (drawn from among their units) enhances their chances of receiving swift access to medical care, i.e. immediate attention on the battlefield, followed by rapid transport to a health-care facility. Indeed, depending on the type of injury sustained, such care will be much more effective, even life-saving, if it can be administered within what is often referred to as the critical 'ten platinum minutes' or, in certain cases, as the 'golden hour'. Auxiliary medical personnel may be uniquely placed to administer first aid within the first ten minutes, and may subsequently be able to transport the casualty to a medical unit within the next hour.

2014   The situation of auxiliary personnel is dynamic in nature, in that the applicable regime can change: they are protected as medical personnel if they are carrying out the duties referred to in Article 25 at the time they come into contact with the enemy, but revert to combatant status whenever they are not carrying out these duties. When they fall into enemy hands, they revert in any event to their initial status as combatants and as such are entitled to prisoner-of-war status (see Article 29) and not to the retention regime governing personnel designated in Articles 24 and 26 (see Article 28). Thus, protection on the basis of Article 25 is conduct-based, as opposed to the protection of Articles 24 and 26, which is status-based.[2]

2015   Both in the past and nowadays, it seems that very few armed forces actually make use of the possibility created by Article 25.[3] Certainly, in a good number of them, some or even a significant share of combatants (sometimes referred to as 'combat lifesavers') are trained to perform medical tasks on the battlefield.[4] However, they do not claim these combatants to be covered by Article 25, and do not give them the specific means of identification provided for in Article 41.

---

[1] *Final Record of the Diplomatic Conference of Geneva of 1949*, Vol. II-A, pp. 120–122 and 194. For when persons covered by Article 24 fall into enemy hands, see Articles 28, 30 and 31 of the First Convention (as well as Article 33 of the Third Convention). For means of identification for persons covered by Article 24, see Article 40 of the First Convention.

[2] See the commentary on Article 24, para. 1979 and the commentary on Article 26, para. 2074.

[3] See also Pictet (ed.), *Commentary on the First Geneva Convention*, ICRC, 1952, p. 221: this category 'has not up to the present been very numerous in practice'.

[4] Geoffrey S. Corn *et al.*, *The Law of Armed Conflict: An Operational Approach*, Wolters Kluwer Law & Business, New York, 2012, pp. 255–256.

As a result, 'combat lifesavers' are not entitled to the protection conferred by Article 25: they remain combatants even when they perform medical tasks.

2016   Of further relevance, Article 8(k) of Additional Protocol I has created the category of 'temporary medical personnel', defined as persons 'devoted exclusively to medical purposes for limited periods during the whole of such periods'. While members of the armed forces covered by Article 25 qualify as 'temporary medical personnel' in the sense of Article 8(k), the latter category is broader. Members of the armed forces who qualify as 'temporary medical personnel' are protected on the basis of Additional Protocol I even when they do not fulfil the conditions of Article 25. As a result, States have an alternative way of ensuring that auxiliary medical personnel are protected without having to meet the strictures of Article 25. At the same time, nothing prevents States, in the future, from resorting to Article 25.[5]

B. Historical background

2017   During the 1906 Diplomatic Conference, it was considered 'unreasonable' to grant protection to auxiliary medical personnel, and this in view of their being combatants when their medical skills were not required.[6] What was eventually to become Article 9(2) of the 1929 Geneva Convention on the Wounded and Sick (the direct precursor of Article 25) arose from a proposal submitted by the US delegation during the 1929 Diplomatic Conference.[7] The proposal initially met with criticism: given the hybrid nature of auxiliary medical personnel, some delegations feared that the concept would create difficulties and controversies in practice.[8] In the end, however, the proposal was accepted since it was felt to provide protection to a category of persons that already existed in the practice of certain States, e.g. members of the armed forces who are musicians and who have also been trained to perform certain medical tasks.[9] Thus, unlike permanent medical personnel, who had to be 'exclusively' engaged in one or more of a series of enumerated activities of a medical nature, auxiliary medical personnel did not have to be so exclusively engaged.

2018   The status of auxiliary medical personnel, as regulated in the 1929 Geneva Convention, was markedly different from their status under the 1949 Geneva Convention. Under the 1929 regime, auxiliary medical personnel were entitled to the same treatment as permanent medical personnel if they fell into enemy

---

[5] See United States, *Law of War Manual*, 2015, para. 4.13.1; see also United States, *Army Health System*, 2013, pp. 3.5–3.6.
[6] See *Proceedings of the Diplomatic Conference of 1906*, Report of the Drafting Committee, p. 253.
[7] See *Proceedings of the Geneva Diplomatic Conference of 1929*, pp. 127 and 129.
[8] See *ibid.* pp. 129–130 (comments by the Swiss and Dutch delegations).
[9] See *ibid.* p. 130 (US delegation), p. 168 (French delegation) and p. 169 (Swiss delegation). For the discussion leading to the adoption of Article 9(2) of the 1929 Geneva Convention on the Wounded and Sick, see *ibid.* pp. 183–189.

hands,[10] but they did not explicitly enjoy any form of specific protection on the battlefield.[11] The First Convention of 1949 has inverted this logic. As a result, the current regime provides for an entitlement to be 'respected and protected' when auxiliary medical personnel perform certain medical duties on the battlefield, but does not provide for coverage by the retention regime if they fall into enemy hands.

2019   Both during the 1946 Preliminary Conference of National Societies[12] and during the 1947 Conference of Government Experts,[13] proposals were made to delete this separate category of auxiliary medical personnel. The 1947 Conference of Government Experts advanced three arguments to support the deletion of Article 9(2) of the 1929 Convention: (i) the difficulty of providing them with identification certificates; (ii) the fact that many combatants were trained to provide medical care; and (iii) 'most importantly', that when prisoners are taken in large numbers, it is impossible to know who among the combatants was engaged in medical activities.[14] In the drafts both submitted to and adopted by the 1948 International Conference of the Red Cross in Stockholm, Article 9(2) of the 1929 Convention remained deleted.[15]

2020   During the 1949 Diplomatic Conference, it remained an issue of controversy whether the First Convention should retain this separate category. The main concern – raised by those who wished to abolish this category – was that it was prone to abuse. For example, a combatant might falsely claim to have been active in a medical capacity at the moment of capture. Another concern was that, when a large number of enemy combatants were captured at once, it would be difficult to know who was actually engaged in medical activities at that time. These concerns were, of course, fuelled by the fact that the 1929 Convention foresaw an entitlement to privileged treatment – identical to the one for permanent medical personnel – when they fell into enemy hands.

---

[10] See Geneva Convention on the Wounded and Sick (1929), Article 12(1).

[11] However, as noted in Pictet (ed.), *Commentary on the First Geneva Convention*, ICRC, 1952, p. 222: 'This did not mean that the enemy had the right to fire deliberately upon auxiliary personnel collecting the wounded. If he has by chance recognized them for what they are, he is bound to respect their status.'

[12] See *Minutes of the Preliminary Conference of National Societies of 1946*, Vol. I, pp. 59–66. See also *ibid.* Vol. V, pp. 21–22. In the end, however, the 1946 Conference maintained this category of auxiliary medical personnel, while wishing to ensure that such personnel would be able to prove their identity through an identity card. See also *Report of the Preliminary Conference of National Societies of 1946*, p. 28.

[13] The 1947 Conference of Government Experts proposed the deletion of this category of medical personnel; see *Minutes of the Conference of Government Experts of 1947*, Vol. II, p. 5. For the discussion, see *Minutes of the Preliminary Conference of National Societies of 1946*, Vol. I, pp. 149–151 and 187–189.

[14] *Report of the Conference of Government Experts of 1947*, p. 33.

[15] *Draft Conventions submitted to the 1948 Stockholm Conference*, pp. 15–16, retaining only Article 9(1) of the 1929 Convention. Further, see *Draft Conventions adopted by the 1948 Stockholm Conference*, p. 17, retaining just the precursor of what eventually became Article 24 of the First Convention. See also *ICRC Remarks and Proposals on the 1948 Stockholm Draft*, p. 13, proposing an amendment in connection with what eventually became Article 24, but with no mention of reviving what eventually became Article 25.

2021   In the end, the category of auxiliary medical personnel was maintained in the First Convention based on the consideration that the activities mentioned in Article 25 could meet a definite humanitarian need: their proximity to the wounded and sick, who might have been fellow combatants up until minutes before, would enable auxiliary medical personnel to carry out certain, well-defined medical tasks, such as the swift removal of the wounded from the battlefield.[16]

2022   The concern that combatants might be tempted to claim the status of auxiliary medical personnel once they fall into enemy hands is fully addressed in the new regime: the treatment to which they are entitled in enemy hands is the one applicable to combatants, and not the one for permanent medical personnel (see Article 29). This is in line with the purpose of the protection of medical personnel under the Geneva Conventions, namely to allow adequate medical care of the wounded and sick.

C. Discussion

1. Persons covered

2023   Persons covered by Article 25 are combatants who are temporarily, and functionally, protected as medical personnel.

2024   The category of 'auxiliary medical personnel' can only consist of certain members of the armed forces. It does not apply to staff of National Red Cross or Red Crescent Societies or of other voluntary aid societies.[17] In this respect, the term 'auxiliary medical personnel' is not to be confused with the role of National Red Cross and Red Crescent Societies as auxiliaries to the public authorities in the humanitarian field.[18]

2025   Article 25, together with the related provisions of Articles 29 and 41, most naturally applies to land-based units of the armed forces. But its scope of application is not confined to these: auxiliary medical personnel may also be on board medical aircraft, and their status will be regulated by Article 29 if they fall into enemy hands.[19]

---

[16] *Final Record of the Diplomatic Conference of Geneva of 1949*, Vol. II-A, p. 68. See also *Minutes of the Diplomatic Conference of Geneva of 1949*, Vol. I, 10th meeting, pp. 27–29. Two amendments were made with a view to resurrecting Article 9(2) of the 1929 Convention: see the amendment by the United Kingdom, *Final Record of the Diplomatic Conference of Geneva of 1949*, Vol. III, p. 35, Annex 32, and the amendment by Switzerland, *ibid.* Vol. III, p. 37, Annex 33. The principle of these amendments was accepted by the Drafting Committee; see *ibid.* Vol. II-A, pp. 77–78. For the text proposed by the Drafting Committee, see *ibid.* pp. 120–122 and, for the final changes to the text, see *ibid.* Vol. II-B, pp. 213–214.

[17] Note, however, the possibility created for States party to Additional Protocol I by the addition of 'temporary medical personnel' in Article 8(k) of the Protocol. These may, but need not, be members of the armed forces.

[18] See the commentary on Article 26, para. 2087.

[19] See Article 36(5), which refers to the eventuality of a medical aircraft having to make an 'involuntary landing in enemy or enemy-occupied territory'. In that case '[t]he medical personnel

2026 The fact that they are and remain combatants when not carrying out their duties, as well as the fact that they do not become members of the medical service of the armed forces, can be derived not only from Article 29, but also *a contrario* from Article 43(2) of Additional Protocol I: 'Members of the armed forces of a Party to a conflict (other than medical personnel and chaplains covered by Article 33 of the Third Convention) are combatants, that is to say, they have the right to participate directly in hostilities.' Since persons covered by Article 25 of the First Convention are not covered by Article 33 of the Third Convention, their status remains one of combatants, whose entitlement to participate directly in hostilities becomes temporarily suspended: once they commit an 'act harmful to the enemy', they lose their protection.[20]

2027 The medical functions in which auxiliary medical personnel are allowed to participate are restricted to just three: hospital orderly, nurse or auxiliary stretcher-bearer.[21] This list is exhaustive. Thus, it is much narrower than the list of activities provided for under Article 24. Surgeons, for example, or staff engaged in the administration of medical units and establishments would not fall within the scope of application of Article 25. Therefore, under the First Convention, such persons cannot perform their activities on a temporary basis.[22]

2028 Conversely, the fact that a member of the armed forces serves in one of the functions set out in Article 25 does not necessarily mean that he or she will be covered by that provision. If the respective conditions of Article 24 of the First Convention are fulfilled, coverage under that provision is equally possible: all three categories covered by Article 25 also come within the scope of application of Article 24. The choice of whether a person will be governed by

---

shall be treated according to Article 24, and the Articles following'. This implies that personnel covered by Article 25 may be on board medical aircraft. See also the commentary on Article 25, para. 2025. When medical personnel on board a medical aircraft fall into enemy hands at sea, Article 39(5) of the Second Convention stipulates that they be treated according to Articles 36 and 37 of that Convention. This works for persons covered by Article 36, i.e. the religious, medical and hospital personnel of hospital ships and their crews. It does not work, however, for persons covered by Article 37, since that provision provides for the retention regime. If persons covered by Article 25, who were on board a medical aircraft, fall into enemy hands at sea, their status and treatment would be best regulated by Article 29 of the First Convention, applicable by analogy. See also Article 30(4) of Additional Protocol I dealing with the conditions under which a medical aircraft may be seized. If that happens, '[i]ts occupants shall be treated in conformity with the relevant provisions of the Conventions and of this Protocol'.

20 Regarding loss of protection for the commission of acts harmful to the enemy, see the commentary on Article 24, section F.

21 Although the French text of the First Convention mentions only 'infirmiers ou brancardiers auxiliaires', the category of 'hospital orderlies' is understood to be included; see *Final Record of the Diplomatic Conference of Geneva of 1949*, Vol. II-A, p. 122. See also the commentary on Article 55, section B.2.

22 Additional Protocol I has changed this, in that it explicitly allows for military medical personnel to be temporary; see Article 8(c)(i) and (k) of the Protocol. See also Article 20(3) of the Fourth Convention, which provides persons working in a civilian hospital with a status that resembles that provided by Article 25 of the First Convention: persons, other than persons regularly and solely engaged in the operation and administration of civilian hospitals, 'who are engaged in the operation and administration of civilian hospitals shall be entitled to respect and protection and to wear the armlet . . . while they are employed on such duties'.

Article 24 or by Article 25 is to be made by the national authorities, who must designate the person on this basis, and will be reflected in the means of identification provided (see Articles 40 and 41).[23] When they fall into enemy hands, permanent medical personnel covered by Article 24 would be governed by the 'retention' regime provided for in Articles 28, 30 and 31 of the First Convention (along with Article 33 of the Third Convention), while auxiliary medical personnel covered by Article 25 would be governed by the regime provided for in Article 29.

2029   As to the meaning of the three functions referred to in Article 25, it is immaterial whether the terms 'hospital orderly', 'nurse' or 'auxiliary stretcher-bearer' are actually used under domestic law (such as in internal administrative regulations). The term 'orderly', in this context, is defined as 'an attendant in a hospital responsible for cleaning and other non-medical tasks'.[24] The term 'stretcher-bearer' refers to a person who carries 'sick, injured, or dead people lying down' on a stretcher.[25] In practice, what matters in this respect is the activity performed (i.e. the conveyance of such persons) rather than whether it involves the carrying of a stretcher. Thus, for example, a person aboard a medical aircraft who operates the rescue harness can qualify as auxiliary personnel (provided all other conditions of Article 25 are met).

2030   In terms of the activities that can be performed by 'hospital orderlies, nurses or auxiliary stretcher-bearers', the four listed in Article 25 ('the search for or the collection, transport or treatment of the wounded and sick') also appear in Article 24, and need to be interpreted identically.[26] As was the case with Article 24, the deliberately disjunctive nature of the list (by the use of 'or') allows for the same person to be engaged in more than one of the said activities.[27]

2031   At the same time, however, there are three differences between Articles 24 and 25 in terms of the activities that can be performed by persons covered by either provision. First, 'prevention of disease' is mentioned only in Article 24.[28] Second, staff engaged in the administration of medical units and establishments cannot function on the basis of Article 25. And lastly, military religious personnel (referred to as 'chaplains attached to the armed forces' in Article 24) cannot function on the basis of Article 25 either. Additional Protocol I takes

---

[23] See United States, *Law of War Manual*, 2015, para. 4.13.2.

[24] *Concise Oxford English Dictionary*, 12th edition, Oxford University Press, 2011, p. 1007. For further details on the term 'orderly', see the commentary on Article 22, para. 1871.

[25] *Concise Oxford English Dictionary*, 12th edition, Oxford University Press, 2011, pp. 118 and 1428.

[26] See the commentary on Article 24, section C.1. The term 'search' did not appear in Article 9(2) of the 1929 Convention. It was added by the 1946 Preliminary Conference of National Societies; see *Report of the Preliminary Conference of National Societies of 1946*, p. 28.

[27] *Final Record of the Diplomatic Conference of Geneva of 1949*, Vol. II-B, pp. 213–214.

[28] This was deliberate; see *Minutes of the Diplomatic Conference of Geneva of 1949*, Tome I, 26th meeting, p. 58.

a different approach in this regard by allowing both medical and religious personnel to carry out their duties on a temporary basis.[29]

2032   As mentioned earlier, the term 'auxiliary medical personnel' does not appear as such in the First Convention but has traditionally been used to refer to persons covered by Article 25. This term may convey the wrong impression. While the word 'auxiliary' is suggestive of a support or subsidiary role, the activities performed by 'auxiliary medical personnel' may be anything but: in some cases they can be life-saving. In the context of Article 25, the word 'auxiliary' refers to the place of the person vis-à-vis the (permanent) medical service, not to the nature (nor the effect) of the activities performed.

2033   An essential precondition for auxiliary medical personnel to be covered by Article 25 is that they be 'specially trained for employment, should the need arise, as hospital orderlies, nurses or auxiliary stretcher-bearers'.[30] It is left to the national authorities to decide on the content and length of the training. It does not have to be conducted by the armed forces themselves, i.e. qualifications obtained outside the armed forces may suffice. Nor does the training need to have taken place prior to the outbreak of the armed conflict: one reason for the usefulness of Article 25 is the possibility of training combatants for particular medical functions in response to needs as they arise during the armed conflict, for example to make up for a shortage of medical personnel.

2034   However, the training must result in a certain level of skill and specialization. It needs to render the person qualified to perform the tasks required of 'hospital orderlies, nurses or auxiliary stretcher-bearers'. Thus, basic first-aid training, which most combatants receive as part of their regular training, will not necessarily suffice.[31]

2035   Furthermore, the mere fact of being 'specially trained for employment, should the need arise, as hospital orderlies, nurses or auxiliary stretcher-bearers' does not necessarily nor automatically mean that persons will be covered by Article 25: they must be so designated on the basis of Article 25.[32] No member of the armed forces will be covered by Article 25 merely based on a willingness to act in an 'auxiliary medical' capacity. In practice, certain armed forces train some combatants as 'combat lifesavers' without claiming that these persons would be covered by Article 25. Therefore, these armed forces do not give these persons the means of identification provided for in Article 41.

2036   Further, should a commander decide to assign a combatant who has not received the requisite training to look after a fallen comrade, that person would not be covered by Article 25. Likewise, a combatant not designated as 'auxiliary

---

[29] See Additional Protocol I, Article 8(k).
[30] See also Article 41(2), requiring that the '[m]ilitary identity documents to be carried' by persons covered by Article 25 'shall specify what special training they have received'.
[31] *Final Record of the Diplomatic Conference of Geneva of 1949*, Vol. II-A, p. 194.
[32] See United States, *Law of War Manual*, 2015, para. 4.13.2.

medical personnel' on the basis of Article 25 who spontaneously assists a fallen comrade is acting at his or her own risk. While it is hoped that the enemy, out of goodwill and prompted by humanitarian considerations, would refrain from attacking such a person, he or she is not entitled to any specific protection.

2037   The beneficiaries of the medical activities performed by auxiliary personnel are the 'wounded and sick'. Within the context of the First Convention, the concept of 'wounded and sick' has to be understood in its technical sense, i.e. as referring to the wounded and sick belonging to the categories identified in Articles 12 and 13. However, the fact that auxiliary medical personnel extend their activities to civilian wounded and sick does not deprive them of their entitlement to be respected and protected.[33]

2. Scope of protection

2038   Auxiliary personnel must be respected and protected if they are carrying out their medical duties 'at the time when they come into contact with the enemy or fall into his hands'. Hence, they are not entitled to the protection of Article 25 if this occurs when they are not carrying out their medical duties.[34]

2039   The meaning of the notion of 'fall into [enemy] hands' is dealt with in the commentary on Article 14, section C.3. As to the notion of 'come into contact with the enemy', no physical or otherwise direct contact is required. From the moment the enemy identifies a person as being entitled to the protection of Article 25, they 'come into contact'.

2040   The notions of respect and protection are to be understood in the same way as in Article 24 (as indicated by the term 'likewise'). This applicability *mutatis mutandis* means that persons covered by Article 25 are – for as long as they are carrying out their medical duties – one of the categories of persons protected under the First Convention. As a result, reprisals against them are prohibited.[35] When acts referred to in Article 50 are committed against persons covered by Article 25, they would be considered grave breaches. Further, attacks intentionally directed against auxiliary medical personnel may qualify as a war crime under the 1998 ICC Statute.[36] In addition, the conditions and

---

[33] See also Article 22(5).

[34] This scenario does not preclude that, once they have fallen into enemy hands, auxiliary medical personnel become prisoners of war who, in view of their medical skills 'shall be employed on their medical duties in so far as the need arises'; see Article 29, which speaks of 'members of the personnel designated in Article 25 who have fallen into the hands of the enemy', without requiring them to have been 'carrying out [their] duties at the time when they come into contact with the enemy or fall into his hands'. For details, see the commentary on Article 29, para. 2210.

[35] See Article 46.

[36] Article 8(2)(b)(xxiv) of the 1998 ICC Statute includes in the list of 'war crimes': '[i]ntentionally directing attacks against buildings, material, medical units and transport, and personnel using the distinctive emblems of the Geneva Conventions in conformity with international law'. The 2002 ICC Elements of Crimes, para. 1, states in connection with this war crime: 'The perpetrator attacked one or more persons, buildings, medical units or transports or other objects using,

restrictions under which permanent medical personnel may carry arms, and use them, apply *mutatis mutandis* to auxiliary personnel.[37] Lastly, where that provision applies (either as a matter of treaty law or of customary law), persons covered by Article 25 are entitled to the 'general protection of medical duties' provided for in Article 16 of Additional Protocol I, this provision being applicable to any 'person engaged in medical activities'.

2041 Conversely, the entitlement to be 'respected and protected' entails the similar applicability of the conditions under which that entitlement may be lost.[38] In this regard, the hybrid nature of auxiliary medical personnel is somewhat sensitive. In particular, the fact that they may switch from the role of, for example, a nurse temporarily protected under Article 25 to that of combatant may engender distrust.[39] The particular feature of Article 25 is that it obliges a Party to the conflict to 'respect and protect' members of the enemy's armed forces who may have been in active combat just before they start carrying out their duties as auxiliary medical personnel and who may resume combat activity the next day, or even some hours later. In order to maintain the integrity of, and trust in, the system, it is advisable that combatants designated as auxiliary medical personnel do not switch status repeatedly, for example within the same day.

2042 Given the sensitive nature of the role of auxiliary medical personnel, a State deploying persons on the basis of Article 25 must make them aware of the need to refrain scrupulously, while fulfilling that role, from any act which may be perceived as 'harmful to the enemy'.[40] The prohibition of perfidy is particularly pertinent in this context, especially since auxiliary personnel may, albeit under certain restrictions, be armed.[41]

2043 The system has a built-in corrective in this regard: protection on the basis of Article 25 is limited *ratione temporis* to those points in time when 'they are carrying out' their medical duties. In this respect, Article 25 differs markedly from Article 24, where the entitlement to be 'respected and protected' exists 'in all circumstances'.

---

in conformity with international law, a distinctive emblem or other method of identification indicating protection under the Geneva Conventions.' While the method of identification provided for under Article 41 of the First Convention does not belong to 'the distinctive emblem[s] of the Geneva Conventions', it can be understood to qualify as one of the 'other method[s] of identification indicating protection under the Geneva Conventions'.

[37] For further details, see the commentary on Article 24, para. 2005.
[38] See *ibid.* section F.
[39] There is a notable difference in this regard between 'auxiliary medical personnel' (covered by Article 25 of the First Convention) and 'members of the armed forces and military units assigned to civil defence organizations' (covered by Article 67(1) of Additional Protocol I). One of the requirements applicable to the latter (and not to the former) is that 'such personnel do not perform any other military duties during the conflict'.
[40] Peter de Waard and John Tarrant, 'Protection of Military Medical Personnel in Armed Conflicts', *University of Western Australia Law Review*, Vol. 35, 2010, pp. 157–183, at 181.
[41] See Additional Protocol I, Article 37(1). On the entitlement of auxiliary personnel to be armed, see para. 2040.

2044   Absent from Article 25 is the 'exclusivity' requirement which appears in Article 24.[42] However, logic dictates that, for as long as auxiliary personnel are carrying out their duties of a medical nature, they must comply with this requirement *mutatis mutandis*. Persons covered by Article 25 can be considered as one of the categories of persons included in the notion of 'temporary medical personnel' in the sense of Article 8(k) of Additional Protocol I. Thus, they can only expect to be 'respected and protected' on the battlefield if they are 'devoted exclusively to medical purposes for limited periods during the whole of such periods'. In real-life battlefield situations, it is hoped that the requirement to respect and protect auxiliary medical personnel only when 'they are carrying out these duties at the time when they come into contact with the enemy or fall into his hands' will be interpreted in good faith, on the one hand, and that auxiliary personnel will act in compliance with the constraints flowing from this provision, on the other hand.

Select bibliography

See the select bibliography of the commentary on Article 24 of the First Convention.

[42] See the commentary on Article 24, section D.2.

ARTICLE 26

PERSONNEL OF AID SOCIETIES

❖ Text of the provision*

(1) The staff of National Red Cross Societies and that of other Voluntary Aid Societies, duly recognized and authorized by their Governments, who may be employed on the same duties as the personnel named in Article 24, are placed on the same footing as the personnel named in the said Article, provided that the staff of such societies are subject to military laws and regulations.

(2) Each High Contracting Party shall notify to the other, either in time of peace or at the commencement of or during hostilities, but in any case before actually employing them, the names of the societies which it has authorized, under its responsibility, to render assistance to the regular medical service of its armed forces.

❖ Reservations or declarations

None

Contents

---

* Paragraph numbers have been added for ease of reference.

725

A. Introduction

2045 Article 26 regulates a specific type of humanitarian activity. This activity occurs when the staff of a National Red Cross or Red Crescent Society, or of another voluntary aid society, are entrusted with assisting the medical services of their own country's armed forces in the context of an international armed conflict.[1] This provision is of key significance for National Red Cross and Red Crescent Societies (hereinafter referred to as 'National Societies') since it has anchored in international humanitarian law their distinct status and roles in support of the public authorities' humanitarian tasks.

2046   Under the conditions set forth in Article 26, the staff of these Societies are placed on the same footing as military medical and religious personnel covered by Article 24 of the First Convention.[2] As a result, such persons, although not members of the armed forces, are brought under the protective regime afforded by the First Convention to military medical and religious personnel.[3]

2047   Since the adoption of the Geneva Conventions in 1949, there have been relatively few occasions on which Article 26 played a role in practice.

B. Historical background

2048 The genesis of Article 26 can be traced back to the origins of the International Red Cross and Red Crescent Movement (hereinafter referred to as 'the

---

[1] The situation regulated by Article 26 must be distinguished from the one regulated by Article 27, in which a recognized society of a neutral country provides its medical personnel and units to a Party to the conflict. When the Second Convention applies, Article 24 of that Convention provides for a similar regime as far as hospital ships utilized by, *inter alia*, National Societies are concerned. Article 26 does not preclude voluntary aid societies from carrying out the role foreseen by this provision in a non-international armed conflict. However, a National Society carrying out such a role in such a context would need to be particularly attentive to the implications this might carry for the National Society's image and reputation as an independent, neutral and impartial humanitarian actor and for the perception of the International Red Cross and Red Crescent Movement as a whole. These are concerns which were noted in the context of the ICRC's Safer Access Project, see *Safer access: A Guide for all National Societies. Practical Resource Pack*, ICRC, October 2013.

[2] The material of voluntary aid societies acting on the basis of Article 26 (such as a mobile medical unit) will equally be entitled to respect and protection under the First Convention; see below, para. 2085.

[3] The results of their being placed on the same footing as persons covered by Article 24 are discussed below, see section E.

Movement').[4] The idea arose of establishing what would come to be called National Red Cross or Red Crescent Societies, i.e. privately founded voluntary aid organizations entrusted with supplementing and assisting, as auxiliaries, the medical services of the armed forces in caring for wounded soldiers.[5] The idea was favourably received by a number of influential people in Geneva. Thanks to their efforts, the Geneva International Conference took place in 1863. Article 1 of the resolution adopted at this Conference states: 'Each country shall have a Committee whose duty it shall be, in time of war and if the need arises, to assist the Army Medical Services by every means in its power.'[6]

2049 The next year, a diplomatic conference convened by the Swiss Federal Council adopted the first Geneva Convention (1864). However, this Convention contains no language similar to Article 1 of the 1863 resolution. This was deliberate: in 1864, States and their military authorities were not yet ready to confer an official function, by means of a treaty, on these new societies.[7] While these societies were ready to take on and to cover the costs of tasks that would benefit the armed forces, their reliability still had to be tested. Some States were not yet certain that private volunteers would constitute a useful supplement to the official medical services of the armed forces.[8] In the years and decades following 1864, these newly established National Societies proved, through their practice, to be useful assets to the military authorities.[9]

2050 As a result, the distrust which a number of military authorities harboured in 1864 vis-à-vis private voluntary aid societies gave way to a somewhat more open attitude when States convened in 1906 to revise the 1864 Geneva Convention. On that occasion, the decision was made to recognize their role in

[4] See Dunant, especially pp. 85–86. For detailed historical accounts of the first decades of the International Red Cross and Red Cross Movement, see Boissier, Hutchinson, and Reid/Gilbo. See also the three articles grouped together under 'Turning points in the history of the ICRC and the Movement', *International Review of the Red Cross*, Vol. 94, No. 888, December 2012, pp. 1273–1347.

[5] Initially, the idea was that the National Societies would be not only privately founded, but also privately funded. While privately founded in terms of their origin, National Societies are generally recognized at the domestic level through a legislative or similar act. In terms of funding, many National Societies nowadays receive some measure of public funding for their activities.

[6] Reproduced in ICRC/International Federation of Red Cross and Red Crescent Societies, *Handbook of the International Red Cross and Red Crescent Movement*, 2008, p. 515.

[7] See *Proceedings of the Geneva Diplomatic Conference of 1906*, pp. 113 and 254. Paradoxically, while States in 1864 were not yet ready to confer an official status on these newly formed national societies, the first sentence of Article 5 of the Geneva Convention of 1864 states that '[i]nhabitants of the country who bring help to the wounded shall be respected and shall remain free'. On this point, see Werner, p. 210. See also the commentary on Article 18, section B.

[8] See Boissier, pp. 75 and 116; Hutchinson, p. 48; Lueder, p. 297; and Noailly, p. 182.

[9] It is interesting to note that, in the naval context, the step of officially recognizing the role of private aid societies was taken much more quickly: see Additional Articles relating to the Condition of the Wounded in War (1868), Article 13. For a discussion, see the commentary on Article 24 of the Second Convention. Although it is the result of a private initiative, see also Oxford Manual (1880), Article 13.

Article 10, which, importantly, is nearly identical to the current formulation of Article 26.[10] During the 1906 Diplomatic Conference, several conditions nevertheless proved critical for the provision to become acceptable: first, the requirement that the staff of National Societies and of other voluntary aid societies be 'subject to military laws and regulations' and, second, the restriction of the provision's application to those societies which had been 'duly recognized and authorized by their own governments'. In consideration of these conditions, the military authorities were assured that they would remain firmly in control as to which private persons would see their status and treatment placed on the same footing as the members of the armed forces' official medical services.[11]

2051   During both the Italo-Turkish War (1911)[12] and the First World War (1914–18), the National Societies of several States involved in those conflicts played an important role as auxiliaries to their armed forces' medical services. This period saw the greatest use of private aid societies (including National Societies) serving as auxiliaries to the armed forces' medical services, while operating subject to military laws and regulations – a condition considered critical.[13] With regard to the requirement that the National Society personnel be subject to military laws and regulations, it was already understood, in the formative years of the Movement, that this condition should not entail total subservience to the military authorities.[14] During the First World War, however, a closeness was observed between some National Societies and the military hierarchy of the armed forces' medical services, leading some historians to criticize certain aspects of the role played by National Societies in that conflict.[15]

2052   At around the same time, the scope of activities undertaken by the National Societies broadened considerably beyond the narrow ambit of Article 10 of

---

[10] See *Proceedings of the Geneva Diplomatic Conference of 1906*, especially, on p. 16, the Swiss Federal Council's questionnaire, the third question of which reads: '*Y a-t-il lieu de mentionner le personnel des Sociétés de secours volontaires et de déterminer les conditions auxquelles ce personnel sera neutralisé?*' (Is it necessary to mention the staff of the voluntary aid societies and to determine the conditions on which these staff shall be accorded neutral status?) For a substantive discussion, see *ibid.* p. 113. See also Best, p. 151. Semantics aside, there are two substantive differences between Article 10 of the 1906 Convention and Article 26 of the 1949 Convention, which are discussed below (see paras 2053–2054 and fn. 53). A decision was taken not to include the status of private aid societies in a separate chapter of the 1906 Geneva Convention, but to deal with it in the chapter on 'personnel', i.e. alongside the status of the official personnel of the armed forces' medical services; see *Proceedings of the Geneva Diplomatic Conference of 1906*, p. 246.

[11] *Ibid.* p. 254. See also Hutchinson, p. 350; Lanord, 1999, pp. 43–44; Lueder, pp. 296–298; and Werner, p. 32. As early as the resolution of the Geneva International Conference of 1863, one finds the following idea: 'On the request or with the consent of the military authorities, Committees may send voluntary medical personnel to the battlefield where they shall be placed under military command.' See 'Resolutions and Recommendations of the Geneva International Conference of 1863', Article 6, reproduced in ICRC/International Federation of Red Cross and Red Crescent Societies, *Handbook of the International Red Cross and Red Crescent Movement*, 2008, p. 516.

[12] See Durand, pp. 16–17.   [13] Noailly, pp. 49–50.   [14] See Reid, p. 10.

[15] See e.g. Best, pp. 141–142, and Hutchinson, pp. 275–276.

the 1906 Geneva Convention. Activities were developed, first, for the benefit of soldiers in captivity, and second, for the benefit of civilians. The National Societies also carried out charitable activities in peacetime. This broadening of activities coincided with the development of the medical services of a number of States' armed forces, which became better equipped and resourced, rendering the initial role of voluntary aid societies in supplementing such services less prominent, while allowing them to pursue other forms of cooperation with their State's armed forces.[16]

2053   During the negotiation of the Geneva Convention on the Wounded and Sick in 1929, it was proposed that Article 10 of the 1906 Geneva Convention should be maintained, with only one substantive change.[17] Under the 1929 Geneva Convention, only the activities of recognized aid societies acting as auxiliaries (subject to military laws and regulations) to the armed forces' medical services are addressed and specifically protected.[18] During the Second World War, further examples can be found of National Societies serving as auxiliaries to the armed forces' medical services.[19]

2054   During the preparations for the 1949 Diplomatic Conference, only one substantive change was introduced to the 1929 Geneva Convention: whereas the 1906 and 1929 Geneva Conventions spoke generically of 'volunteer aid societies' and of 'Voluntary Aid Societies', respectively, pursuant to a deliberate

---

[16] An example of such cooperation is the organization by the National Societies of training courses for members of the armed forces in fields such as first aid and international humanitarian law. Some National Societies cooperate with the armed forces' medical services, but do so without being subject to military laws and regulations. Other National Societies' relationship to the armed forces is regulated through a broad-ranging memorandum of understanding, pursuant to which they undertake activities such as the dispatch of Red Cross messages, the furnishing of support to soldiers' families at home, and the provision of technical advice on matters of international humanitarian law to the medical services of the armed forces, as requested, in connection with the development of relevant doctrine. Lastly, cooperation can also consist, for example, in the Societies' playing a supporting role in the repatriation and subsequent hospital treatment of wounded and sick soldiers. Article 26 does not apply to any of these forms of cooperation.

[17] Geneva Convention on the Wounded and Sick (1929), Article 10. The substantive change between the 1906 and 1929 versions of the text can be found in the first paragraph: while the 1906 text spoke of those 'who are employed in the sanitary formations and establishments of armies', the 1929 text refers to those 'who may be employed on the same duties as' the personnel of the armed forces' official medical services. The latter formulation is much broader, in that the work in question need not be confined to work physically situated 'in the sanitary formations and establishments of armies'. Thus, while the removal and transportation of wounded and sick soldiers was not covered under the 1906 text, it was covered under the 1929 text. See *Proceedings of the Geneva Diplomatic Conference of 1929*, p. 191, and George B. Davis, 'The Geneva Convention of 1906', *American Journal of International Law*, Vol. 1, No. 2, 1907, pp. 409–417, at 414.

[18] For an overview of the national legislation of that period, see Des Gouttes, 1934.

[19] In April 1940, the Canadian authorities requested the US Government to notify the German Government that, 'pursuant to Article 10 [of the 1929 Convention], . . . the Canadian Government have recognized the Canadian Red Cross Society as a Voluntary Aid Society and that the Society is authorized to render assistance to the regular medical service of the Canadian armed forces'. Examples of other National Societies which served during the Second World War on the basis of Article 10 of the 1929 Geneva Convention are the American Red Cross Society, the Australian Red Cross Society, the British Red Cross Society and the Japanese Red Cross Society.

choice not to mention any such society by name,[20] Article 26 of the First Convention of 1949 speaks of the 'staff of National Red Cross Societies and that of other Voluntary Aid Societies'.[21]

2055   At no point during the preparations for the First Convention was it proposed to expand the scope of the activities of voluntary aid societies referred to in Article 26. As a result, notwithstanding some minor modifications, Article 26 of the First Geneva Convention of 1949 still reflects, by and large, the text as it was drafted for the 1906 Geneva Convention. The latter, in turn, reflects the practice of the last few decades of the nineteenth century and the beginning of the twentieth century.

C. Societies covered

1. 'National Red Cross Societies' and 'other Voluntary Aid Societies'

2056   As is clear from the wording of Article 26(1), National Societies (which are particular examples of voluntary aid societies) have no monopoly on performing the services envisaged by Article 26. This was deliberate: the States negotiating the Geneva Conventions in 1949 wished to preserve their prerogative to choose to work with (or without) their National Society, or with one or more voluntary aid societies other than their National Society.

---

[20] *Proceedings of the Geneva Diplomatic Conference of 1906*, pp. 106 and 124, and *Proceedings of the Geneva Diplomatic Conference of 1929*, pp. 133–135, 191–192 and 606. During the latter conference, an amendment aimed at explicitly mentioning the staff of National Red Cross (Red Crescent, Red Lion and Sun) Societies or of similar societies was rejected by a large majority. See also Des Gouttes, *Commentaire de la Convention de Genève de 1929 sur les blessés et malades*, ICRC, 1930, pp. 65–66, and Lanord, 1999, pp. 34–35.

[21] The proposal for an explicit mention of the role of National Societies was made at the 1946 Preliminary Conference of National Societies. In fact, the Conference wished to restrict the scope of applicability of the provision exclusively to 'National Red Cross (Red Crescent, Red Lion and Sun) Societies'. Should other organizations wish to offer their services, the Conference was of the view that they could do so only with the consent of the above-mentioned Societies. The 1947 Conference of Government Experts not only rejected the latter idea, but actually wished to maintain the approach of the 1929 Geneva Convention, i.e. to speak generically of 'voluntary aid societies'. See *Report of the Preliminary Conference of National Societies of 1946*, pp. 29–30; *Minutes of the Preliminary Conference of National Societies of 1946*, Vol. I, pp. 69–82; *Report of the Conference of Government Experts of 1947*, pp. 34–35; and *Minutes of the Conference of Government Experts of 1947*, Committee I, Vol. II, Tome 1, pp. 152–164. The 1949 Diplomatic Conference accepted this idea, and did so in order to 'pay a special tribute to the Red Cross Societies, thus recognizing the great services they had rendered on all the battlefields of the world', while maintaining the option that 'other national relief organizations' might also qualify; see *Final Record of the Diplomatic Conference of Geneva of 1949*, Vol. II-A, p. 194. There were some initial objections to the proposal to explicitly mention the National Red Cross Societies; see *ibid.* p. 78, as well as *Minutes of the Diplomatic Conference of Geneva of 1949*, Commission I, pp. 21–28. Under the 1949 Geneva Convention, nothing in practice precludes a government wishing to do so from adopting the idea put forward at the 1946 Preliminary Conference, i.e. requesting that other voluntary aid societies work under the supervision of, or through, the National Society. It should be noted that Article 27 of the First Convention speaks generically of 'a recognized Society of a neutral country'. For a discussion of this point, see the commentary on Article 27, paras 2119–2121.

2057   While Article 26 speaks only of 'National Red Cross Societies', this cannot
have been meant to exclude other National Societies, such as National Red
Crescent Societies from the scope of this provision: in the light of its purpose –
allowing each High Contracting Party to supplement its armed forces' medical services with additional staff – each High Contracting Party's National
Society may qualify for the purposes of Article 26. The importance of the fact
that National Societies are explicitly mentioned in Article 26 should not be
underestimated. Through this mention, their distinct position and status under
international humanitarian law is explicitly recognized by the High Contracting Parties. In 1949, this recognition constituted the crystallization of a development which had begun in 1863.[22] In 1949, it was National Societies which
were essentially considered by States as being the ones to act on the basis of
Article 26.

2058   As to the 'other Voluntary Aid Societies' mentioned, although no names
are given, the national associations forming part of the Order of the Knights
of Malta and the national associations forming part of the Order of St. John
of Jerusalem have historically been the most prominent and active in this
regard.[23] While both of these were explicitly referred to during the Diplomatic
Conference of 1949, they are by no means the only voluntary aid societies
which have acted as auxiliaries to their armed forces' medical services.[24]

2059   These historical examples need not necessarily constrain how the term
'voluntary aid society' is construed today, where it may also apply to non-
governmental organizations.[25] Indeed, in the absence of a list of, or criteria

---

[22] As basic units of the International Red Cross and Red Crescent Movement, whose role is explicitly mentioned in several other provisions of the Geneva Conventions and their Additional Protocols, the National Societies' task remains to 'organize, in liaison with the public authorities,
emergency relief operations and other services to assist the victims of armed conflicts as provided in the Geneva Conventions'; see Statutes of the International Red Cross and Red Crescent
Movement (1986), Article 3(2).

[23] See *Final Record of the Diplomatic Conference of Geneva of 1949*, Vol. II-A, p. 78. See also *Proceedings of the Geneva Diplomatic Conference of 1929*, pp. 371–379, and Des Gouttes, *Commentaire de la Convention de Genève de 1929 sur les blessés et malades*, ICRC, 1930, pp. 65–66.
Further see Claudie Barrat, *Status of NGOs in International Humanitarian Law*, Brill Nijhoff,
Leiden, 2014, p. 95. More generally, see Béat de Fischer, 'L'Ordre souverain de Malte', *Recueil
des cours de l'Académie de droit international de La Haye*, Vol. 163, 1979, pp. 1–47.

[24] See ICRC, *Rapport général du CICR sur son activité d'août 1934 à mars 1938*, submitted to
the 16th International Conference of the Red Cross, London, 1938. In this report, on pp. 20–21,
the ICRC lists, for a number of countries, the voluntary aid societies which, in 1938, could offer
their assistance to the armed forces' official medical services. For most countries, this is only the
National Red Cross or Red Crescent Society. For France, the United Kingdom, the Netherlands
and Romania, a number of other societies are listed. For France, for example, these include the
Union des Femmes de France and the Association des Dames françaises.

[25] See *Concise Oxford English Dictionary*, 12th edition, Oxford University Press, 2011, p. 1370,
which defines a 'society' as 'an organization . . . formed for a particular purpose or activity'. Article 24 of the Second Convention foresees the possibility that a 'private person' may offer a
hospital ship to the armed forces of his or her own country. By restricting its scope of application to 'societies', a strict reading of Article 26 of the First Convention leads to the conclusion
that private persons offering, for example, their private staff to assist the armed forces' medical services cannot be covered by this provision. For further analysis of the term 'voluntary aid

for, such organizations in the Geneva Conventions, it remains for each State to decide which societies, if any, it wants to recognize and authorize for this type of work.

2060   The word 'voluntary' refers to the fact that persons working on the basis of Article 26 are doing so based on a personal decision freely reached, and not because they have been compelled to do so by any legal obligation, stemming, for example, from national legislation. The word 'voluntary' does not, however, preclude such persons from receiving compensation for the work they perform. It is immaterial whether the voluntary aid societies have been created by a private or a public initiative, and equally immaterial whether or not they receive all or part of their funding from the State. Lastly, the words 'voluntary aid' do not necessarily restrict the scope of Article 26 to societies which are guided exclusively by not-for-profit motives.

2. The societies have to be 'recognized' and 'authorized' (Article 26(1))

2061   There are two cumulative requirements which must be met before the qualifying staff of a society may be placed on the same footing as, and benefit from the same protection, as the personnel of the armed forces' medical service: namely recognition and authorization by their governments. The requirement of notification, provided for in Article 26(2), is not constitutive of the protection under Article 26 (see below, para. 2072).

2062   First, the society needs to have been 'duly recognized' by its own government. The First Convention provides no guidance as to what form this recognition should take, nor as to which formula or words must be used for the decision to qualify as recognition within the meaning of Article 26.[26] In essence, recognition implies the need for the State to decide that a particular society may or will be called upon to serve as an auxiliary to the armed forces' medical services. The form which this decision should take is left entirely to the national authorities, in accordance with national law and procedures. Domestic law also regulates whether such recognition must be made public. Accordingly, the use of the term 'government' means that recognition must be granted by the public authority responsible for such decisions. This need not necessarily be the executive branch of government, but may also be the legislative authorities. In practice, a National Society's role as auxiliary to the armed forces' medical services is usually foreseen in the national recognition act which establishes the National Society in the domestic legal order.[27]

---

society', see Claudie Barrat, *Status of NGOs in International Humanitarian Law*, Brill Nijhoff, Leiden, 2014, pp. 87–89.
[26] Noailly, pp. 154–156.
[27] One of the 10 conditions for recognition of a National Society by the ICRC is that it must '[b]e duly recognized by the legal government of its country on the basis of the Geneva Conventions and of the national legislation as a voluntary aid society, auxiliary to the public authorities in

2063   It is important in this context to draw a clear distinction between the act of recognition of a National Society by its own public authorities and the process of recognition of a National Society as a component of the Movement by the ICRC in accordance with Article 4 of the Statutes of the Movement.[28] For the purposes of Article 26, only the recognition by a National Society's own government matters. In other words, a National Society which has not been recognized by the ICRC, but which meets the conditions set out in Article 26 could still be recognized and serve as an auxiliary to the armed forces' medical services.

2064   While there can be only one National Society in any given State,[29] nothing precludes a State from recognizing and authorizing, for the purposes of Article 26, one or more other voluntary aid societies, in addition to its National Society.[30] The national authorities retain full discretion in this regard.[31] Their decision to recognize a National Society for the purposes of Article 26 does not depend on the separate question of whether that society has been recognized by the ICRC as a component of the Movement.

2065   Second, the society needs to have been 'duly authorized' by its own government to serve as an auxiliary to the armed forces' medical services. This means that the government gives its official permission for the society to perform the public function of providing medical care to wounded and sick members of the armed forces.[32]

2066   Based on a strict reading of Article 26, recognition and authorization are two distinct steps. In practice, the same act may constitute both the decision to recognize and to authorize for the purposes of Article 26. While the decision to authorize a society to serve as an auxiliary to the armed forces' medical services means that the society has also been recognized for that purpose, the

---

the humanitarian field' (Statutes of the International Red Cross and Red Crescent Movement (1986), Article 4(3)).

[28] See *ibid.* Article 5(2)(b).

[29] The principle of unity is one of the seven Fundamental Principles of the Red Cross and Red Crescent Movement. See also Article 4(2) of the 1986 Statutes of the International Red Cross and Red Crescent Movement: in order to be recognized as a National Society of a State, one of the conditions which needs to be met is to '[b]e the only National Red Cross or Red Crescent Society of the said State and be directed by a central body which shall alone be competent to represent it in its dealings with other components of the Movement'.

[30] Similarly, a State may decide to limit recognition to a single society, e.g. the National Red Cross or Red Crescent Society. This is the case, for example, in the United States; see *Regulations for the American National Red Cross*, in Code of Federal Regulations, 1 July 2013, Title 32: National Defense, Chapter VI: Department of the Navy, Subchapter A: United States Navy Regulations and Official Records, Part 700.816: United States Navy Regulations and Official Records: 'The American National Red Cross is the only volunteer society authorized by the Government to render medical and dental aid to the armed forces of the United States. Other organizations desiring to render medical and dental aid may do so only through the Red Cross.'

[31] The interpretation that a State may recognize and authorize more than one society is further corroborated by the reference in Article 26(2) to 'the names of the societies' in the plural.

[32] See *Concise Oxford English Dictionary*, 12th edition, Oxford University Press, 2011, p. 88: to 'authorize' means to 'give official permission for or approval to'.

reverse is not necessarily true.[33] In order to avoid any ambiguity, it may be preferable for a government wishing to call upon the services of a society on the basis of Article 26 to state explicitly in its decision that it both recognizes and authorizes a given society to act as an auxiliary to its armed forces' medical services.[34]

3. The name of the society has to be notified (Article 26(2))

2067   Article 26(2) requires the High Contracting Parties to notify each other, either in time of peace or at the commencement of or during hostilities, but in any case before employing them, of the names of the societies which have been recognized and authorized on the basis of Article 26 to assist the armed forces' medical services. The requirement of notification applies both to National Societies and to other voluntary aid societies.[35]

2068   Such notification is to be given by the State, and not by the National Society or voluntary aid society in question.[36] As the term 'notification' indicates, the communication is intended purely to inform the other States of the name(s) of the society. Once notification has been received, they have to grant qualifying staff the respect and protection due to them under Article 26, provided that all the conditions of this provision have been met.

2069   While the term 'notification' suggests that information should be given in writing,[37] the Convention does not prescribe how notification must be provided, nor what form it should take. In order to avoid any ambiguity, it is recommended that notification be given in writing, for example through a diplomatic note. At all times, notification may be provided directly, or through an intermediary such as the Protecting Power or the ICRC.[38] While not strictly required on the basis of Article 26, if notification has been given long before

---

[33] Lanord, 1999, p. 30.

[34] For a discussion of State practice, see Lanord, 1999, pp. 31–32. For examples of legislation prior to the Second World War, see Des Gouttes, 1934.

[35] Previous writers took a different approach when it came to the National Red Cross and Red Crescent Societies, arguing that notification would not be necessary in regard to them. See Des Gouttes, p. 67; Pictet (ed.), *Commentary on the First Geneva Convention*, ICRC, 1952, p. 229; and Werner, p. 122. Several decades later, the realities have changed. Since it has become rather exceptional for National Red Cross and Red Crescent Societies to act on the basis of Article 26, the notification requirement also applies with regard to them.

[36] Since notification is to be provided by one State to another, on the assumption that the National Society will follow its armed forces abroad, it does not directly involve, nor is it addressed to, the 'host' National Society, i.e. the National Society of the State on whose territory the activities will take place. On this issue, see para. 2093.

[37] See *Concise Oxford English Dictionary*, 12th edition, Oxford University Press, 2011, p. 978: to 'notify' means to 'inform (someone) of something in a formal or official manner'.

[38] François Bugnion, *The International Committee of the Red Cross and the Protection of War Victims*, ICRC/Macmillan, Oxford, 2003, pp. 477 and 878. See also ICRC, *Rapport présenté par le Comité international sur les mesures à prendre pour communiquer officiellement aux belligérants l'envoi des missions sanitaires de la Croix-Rouge sur les champs de bataille*, submitted to the 9th International Conference of the Red Cross, Washington, 1912, p. 3.

the outbreak of the armed conflict in which the society will act, it might be advisable to renew it 'at the commencement' of hostilities. Whether done in time of peace[39] or at the commencement of or during hostilities, it would be advisable to provide the names of the society or societies not only to the enemy, but also to all other High Contracting Parties, inasmuch as neutral Powers have to apply the First Convention by analogy.[40]

2070   In terms of timing, notification must take place, at the latest, 'before actually employing' the staff of the society. In practical terms, this implies that it must be given at a point in time which will reasonably allow the other Parties to the conflict to inform their echelons, including the lower ones, of the treatment to be accorded to the staff of the National Society or other voluntary aid society in question. In the final analysis, when exactly this needs to occur will depend on the technical, including the communication, capabilities of the State receiving the communication. Beyond that teleological interpretation, however, the formula 'before actually employing them' is not particularly precise.[41] Article 26 does not clarify how many days in advance such notification needs to be provided.[42] The term 'employing' has to be understood in its ordinary meaning, i.e. as 'making use of'.[43] Thus, notification need not yet occur if the steps taken are merely preparatory, for example when the staff receive their training and instructions and are not yet about to be deployed. Conversely, it must be given prior to their actually being operational in the roles envisaged by Article 26.

2071   The term 'employ[ment]' does not imply, nor does it require, that the staff are employed by the State, as the term would be understood within the context of domestic labour law. They may, but need not, be employed or financially remunerated by the voluntary aid society. Whatever the case may be, it is immaterial for the purpose of determining whether they are 'actually employ[ed]' within the meaning of Article 26.[44] Similarly, for the purposes of Article 26, the term 'staff' must be understood to encompass all persons working on the basis of this provision, including the volunteers placed at the disposal of the armed forces' medical services.

2072   The First Convention provides no guidance as to a situation in which notification has not been given. On the one hand, no textual support exists for

---

[39] No practice has been found in which a High Contracting Party provided such notification in time of peace. See also Lanord, 1999, p. 39.

[40] Article 4.   [41] Lanord, 1999, p. 38.

[42] For a different approach, see Article 22 of the Second Convention, which provides, as one of the conditions to be met before military hospital ships are entitled to be respected and protected, that 'their names and descriptions [shall] have been notified to the Parties to the conflict ten days before those ships are employed'.

[43] *Concise Oxford English Dictionary*, 12th edition, Oxford University Press, 2011, p. 468.

[44] The term 'staff' does not require the persons concerned to have a contract that would give them the status which the term 'staff' may confer under domestic legislation. While a person who is considered 'staff' under the domestic legal framework will also be considered staff on the basis of Article 26, other arrangements (such as consultancy, volunteer work, secondment, etc.) are equally possible.

concluding that the staff of the voluntary aid society in such a case would not qualify as persons protected under the First Convention. A lack of notification, in other words, does not deprive the staff of the protection to which they are entitled if all the conditions of Article 26(1) have been fulfilled. Notification under Article 26(2) is, therefore, not constitutive of protection.[45] From a practical standpoint, however, it may be more difficult in that case for the staff of the voluntary aid society concerned to prove their status as persons covered by Article 26.[46]

D. Persons covered

1. Staff employed on the duties named in Article 24

2073   The assessment as to which (paid and volunteer) staff are protected by Article 26 has to be made on an individual basis. Only those staff 'who may be employed on the same duties as the personnel named in Article 24' of the First Convention will be entitled to the protection conferred by Article 26.[47] Not covered by Article 26, therefore, are the societies' staff members who, even while working for the benefit of the members of the armed forces, are not engaged in any of the activities referred to in Article 24.[48] While not protected on the basis of Article 26, they may be protected under other applicable provisions of international humanitarian law.[49]

2074   As is the case with the conditions for protection under Article 24, persons can only be covered by Article 26 if they are exclusively engaged in, and

---

[45] This is corroborated by comparing Article 26 of the First Convention with Article 22 of the Second Convention, where the entitlement of military hospital ships to be respected and protected is made subject to the 'condition' that 'their names and descriptions have been notified to the Parties to the conflict ten days before those ships are employed'.

[46] See Lanord, 1999, p. 40. Proving their status need not be insurmountable, however, especially if they display the means of identification referred to in Article 40(2), which requires the special identity card to mention, among other things, 'in what capacity [the bearer] is entitled to the protection of the present Convention'. In any event, a failure to provide notification of the names of the voluntary aid societies before actually employing them (e.g. at the commencement of an armed conflict) can always be rectified.

[47] In practice, it is conceivable that some staff members of a particular society will qualify as persons protected by Article 26, while other staff members of the same society will not.

[48] *Proceedings of the Geneva Diplomatic Conference of 1929*, pp. 136 and 606. One example would be a staff member of a National Society engaged in dispatching Red Cross messages, i.e. communications which, via the National Society, are sent by or to family members in the home country, for example in order to swiftly inform a member of the armed forces, or his family, of an emergency or another important event. Another example would be a staff member of a National Society involved in providing training to the armed forces' medical services.

[49] Where the relevant conditions are met, they could, for example, qualify as civilian medical personnel (Article 20 of the Fourth Convention and Article 15 of Additional Protocol I), or as protected persons within the meaning of Article 4 of the Fourth Convention. The possibility envisaged by Article 4(A)(4) of the Third Convention also needs to be kept in mind, i.e. 'persons who may accompany the armed forces without actually being members thereof, such as . . . services responsible for the welfare of the armed forces'. Such persons are, subject to certain conditions, covered by the status of prisoner of war when they fall into enemy hands (and they do not come under the retention regime to which persons covered by Article 26 are entitled).

permanently assigned to, one or more of the activities referred to in Article 24.[50] However, as indicated by the term 'may', protection on the basis of Article 26 is status-based, not conduct-based, i.e. a person covered under Article 26 does not need to be actually carrying out the activities referred to in that article in order to remain entitled to the protection it confers.[51] In this respect, Articles 24 and 26 both differ from Article 25.[52]

2075   There is no restriction as to where persons covered by Article 26 can perform the activities referred to in Article 24.[53] Thus, for example, persons involved in welfare visits to the military wounded and sick can be covered under Article 26. As indicated in the commentary on Article 24, whereas the activities of 'prevention of disease', and those of chaplains, can be exercised for the benefit of all members of the armed forces, i.e. not only those who are wounded or sick, other activities, such as the 'search for, or the collection, transport or treatment' of soldiers, need to be exercised for the benefit of the 'wounded and sick'.[54] In line with the general approach of the Geneva Conventions on this point, if a person covered by Article 26 also performs the activities referred to in Article 24 for the benefit of wounded and sick civilians, doing so does not lead to a loss of the protection conferred by Article 26.[55]

2. Staff shall be subject to 'military laws and regulations'

2076   The requirement that the 'staff of such societies [be] subject to military laws and regulations' explains why States were willing to accept, as from the 1906 Geneva Convention, the role of National Societies or of private voluntary aid societies as auxiliaries to the medical services of their State's armed forces.[56]

2077   It must be emphasized that subordination to 'military laws and regulations' applies to the staff, and not to the voluntary aid society as such.

---

[50] For details about the requirements of exclusivity and permanency, which apply here in a similar way as to persons covered by Article 24, see the commentary on Article 24, section D.2.

[51] This situation is similar to that of persons covered under Article 24; see *ibid.* para. 1979.

[52] See also the commentary on Article 25, para. 2014.

[53] This clarification is important in that Article 10(1) of the 1906 Geneva Convention protected only those 'who are employed in the sanitary formations and establishments'. As a result of this restriction, under the regime established by the 1906 Geneva Convention, staff of voluntary aid societies were not protected by that provision in a battlefield role, for example when searching for, collecting or transporting wounded and sick soldiers on the battlefield. This restriction has to be seen against the historical background (see above, section B), which was one of initial distrust. The stricture was deleted in the 1929 Geneva Convention. For a discussion, see Lanord, 1999, p. 42.

[54] See the commentary on Article 24, paras 1957–1958. In the First Convention, the 'wounded and sick' can only be those belonging to the categories referred to in Article 13. On the basis of Article 8(a) of Additional Protocol I, the 'wounded and sick' can be 'military or civilian'.

[55] See the commentary on Article 24, paras 1957 and 1997. See also Article 22(5).

[56] For a detailed discussion, see section B.

2078   In order to be 'subject to military laws and regulations', it is not sufficient for the staff of an aid society to agree at the operational level to abide by security regulations, such as temporary restrictions on movement, issued by the military authorities. Instead, at minimum, for the purposes of Article 26, the staff functioning under the auspices of the armed forces' medical services need to obey the lawful orders given by the authorities to whom they are subject.[57]

2079   The requirement of being 'subject to military laws and regulations' may, but does not need to, imply that the staff in question are subject to the armed forces' military justice system as it applies to the members of the army medical service.[58] The same goes for the option to submit them to the military discipline system as it applies, for example, to civilian employees of the armed forces. Depending on the system that exists at the national level, this may go as far as their being subject to the armed forces' courts-martial jurisdiction,[59] or to any other disciplinary mechanism specifically applicable to members of the armed forces at the national level.[60]

2080   The fact that the staff of voluntary aid societies are subject to military laws and regulations and placed on the same footing as members of the armed forces' medical services does not mean, however, that they actually acquire the status of members of the armed forces.[61] At all times, they remain civilians, with the unique feature that they are entitled to the respect and protection enjoyed by the members of the armed forces' medical services. Further, all other aspects of their treatment – such as whether they are paid, who decides on a request for leave, and whether they enjoy the same benefits as members of the armed forces – are left to the national authorities, in consultation with the voluntary aid society. The requirement that they be subject to military laws and

[57]   Many authors, when discussing Article 26, use the term 'incorporation'. See Des Gouttes, *Commentaire de la Convention de Genève de 1929 sur les blessés et malades*, ICRC, 1930, p. 61; Haug/Gasser, p. 171; and Werner, p. 123.

[58]   See e.g. United States, *Law of War Manual*, 2015, para. 4.11.1: 'American National Red Cross personnel who support the U.S. armed forces in military operations [on the basis of Article 26] are subject to the Uniform Code of Military Justice.' However, the mere fact that the staff of a voluntary aid society work in a military hospital does not suffice to make them subject to military laws and regulations; see *Proceedings of the Geneva Diplomatic Conference of 1929*, p. 132.

[59]   See Rain Liivoja, 'Service Jurisdiction under International Law', *Melbourne Journal of International Law*, Vol. 11, 2010, pp. 309–337, especially at 334.

[60]   See ICRC, *Report on the Interpretation, Revision and Extension of the Geneva Convention of July 27, 1929*, Report prepared for the 16th International Conference of the Red Cross, London, 1938, pp. 15–16, referring to the revision of Article 10 of the 1929 Geneva Convention:

> The International Committee had proposed to substitute, at the end of the paragraph, for the words 'subject to military law and regulations' the wording 'subject to military law and discipline'. The Commission of Experts upheld the present wording, since on the one hand there are far more military regulations than laws, and on the other hand, the notion of 'regulations' is very different from that of military discipline, to which, moreover, Voluntary Aid Societies may not be entirely subject.

> On this point, see also *Draft revision of the 1929 Geneva Convention submitted by the ICRC to National Societies in 1937*, p. 6.

[61]   See United Kingdom, *Military Manual*, 1958, p. 112.

regulations does not necessarily mean, for example, that they must wear a military uniform.[62]

3. Staff work under the responsibility of the State

2081 Article 26(2) mentions, in the context of the requirement to provide notification of the names of the societies recognized and authorized to assist the armed forces' medical services, that these societies are 'under [the] responsibility' of the High Contracting Party which employs or intends to employ them.[63]

2082 While reported State practice does not seem to have clarified what this means, the ordinary meaning of the text warrants the following interpretation: for the purposes of international law dealing with State responsibility, the behaviour of the staff covered by Article 26 can trigger the international responsibility of the High Contracting Party for whom they serve as auxiliaries to the armed forces' medical services. The staff of this society have, after all, been recognized and authorized by their governments to perform the public function of providing medical care to wounded and sick members of the armed forces.[64] As a result, the society acts under the international legal responsibility of that State.[65]

E. Identical protection and treatment as for persons covered by Article 24

2083 Persons covered by Article 26 'are placed on the same footing as the personnel named' in Article 24.[66] This means that their status is assimilated to, and therefore identical to, that of the members of the armed forces' medical services.[67]

2084 The results of their being placed on the same footing as persons covered by Article 24 are threefold. First, they are protected persons within the meaning

---

[62] The question of whether or not persons covered by Article 26 are required to wear the armed forces uniform is left to the national military authorities, in consultation with the voluntary aid society; see Des Gouttes, *Commentaire de la Convention de Genève de 1929 sur les blessés et malades*, ICRC, 1930, p. 61. They may also wear the uniform of their own society, where such uniform exists. In any event, whether or not they wear the distinctive emblem is a matter which is regulated by Article 40 of the First Convention.

[63] These words already appeared in Article 10(2) of the 1906 Convention and in Article 10(2) of the 1929 Geneva Convention.

[64] See Article 26(1).

[65] In view of this potential for State responsibility, the State which will be assisted by the services of a voluntary aid society may wish to ensure that the staff of this society are aware (e.g. through training) of their legal rights and obligations, in particular as regards international humanitarian law. For the same reason, the State may wish to vet the staff of the voluntary aid society, for example by having relevant military or civilian services conduct a background check of each proposed staff member's criminal and/or professional (e.g. medical) record. Whether and how such checks are to be conducted is a matter which remains outside the scope of international humanitarian law; it is left entirely in the hands of the domestic authorities, in consultation with the voluntary aid society.

[66] Under Additional Protocol I, they qualify as 'medical personnel'; see Article 8(c)(ii) of that Protocol.

[67] Where relevant, religious personnel are placed on the same footing as the chaplains attached to the armed forces, as provided by Article 24.

of the First Convention,[68] i.e. persons entitled to be respected and protected in all circumstances.[69] Second, when they fall into the hands of the adverse Party, they shall not be deemed prisoners of war, but shall be returned to the Party to the conflict to whom they belong, unless lawful grounds exist for their retention.[70] Lastly, they shall be entitled to wear the distinctive emblem as a protective device.[71]

2085   Article 26 does not explicitly discuss the status of the facilities and equipment which may be used by the staff of the voluntary aid societies in furtherance of their role.[72] In any event, the silence of Article 26 with regard to the provision, by a voluntary aid society, of 'units' or other forms of equipment does not preclude these from being provided. Indeed, a National Society may offer medical personnel without medical units, or vice versa. Lastly, when it comes to the law applicable to the conduct of hostilities, Articles 19, 21 and 22 of the First Convention arguably apply by analogy, on the basis of logic: since the staff of societies covered by Article 26 are protected and treated in the same way as military medical personnel, these societies' facilities and equipment are also to be treated on the same footing as the fixed establishments and mobile medical units of the medical services.[73] Otherwise, protection would be severely weakened.[74]

---

[68] Since persons covered by Article 26 qualify as protected persons within the meaning of the First Convention, reprisals against them are prohibited (Article 46). Similarly, the acts described in Article 50 qualify as grave breaches if committed against persons covered by Article 26. Since these persons are required to wear the distinctive emblem, it needs to be kept in mind that, under the 1998 ICC Statute, in both international and non-international armed conflicts, it is a war crime to '[i]ntentionally direc[t] attacks against … personnel using the distinctive emblems of the Geneva Conventions in conformity with international law'; see ICC Statute (1998), Articles 8(2)(b)(xxiv) and (e)(ii).

[69] This entitlement to be 'respected and protected in all circumstances' exists irrespective of whether they are active, at a particular point in time, in the role to which they have been assigned. This results from the very wording of Article 26 ('who may be employed'; see para. 2074). Such entitlement can be lost if they commit an act harmful to the enemy. Hence, the protection is status-based, while the loss of protection is conduct-based (for details, see the commentary on Article 24, para. 1979). The fact of being placed on the same footing as personnel of the armed forces' medical services also extends to the possibility of being armed with individual light weapons for the purposes of individual self-defence, or for the defence of the wounded and sick in one's charge. For details, see the commentaries on Article 22(1), section C, and Article 24, paras 2005–2006.

[70] This means that they 'shall be retained only in so far as the state of health, the spiritual needs and the number of prisoners of war require'. For details, see Articles 28, 30 and 31 of the First Convention and on Article 33 of the Third Convention.

[71] Both the personnel and the units are entitled to display the distinctive emblem as a protective device; see Articles 40, 42 and the last sentence of Article 44(1) of the First Convention. See also Emblem Regulations (1991), Articles 9–10 and 14.

[72] In this respect, Article 27(1) of the First Convention is different in that it explicitly refers to the possibility, for a recognized Society of a neutral country, to 'lend the assistance of its medical personnel and units'.

[73] The guarantee of identical protection and treatment holds true only as far as the law applicable to the conduct of hostilities is concerned, as demonstrated by the differences in treatment provided for in Article 33 (applicable to the material of mobile medical units of the armed forces) and in Article 34 (applicable to the real and personal property of aid societies). These articles regulate the status of such property when it falls into enemy hands.

[74] Lanord, 1999, pp. 50–51.

F. Developments since 1949

1. National Red Cross and Red Crescent Societies

2086 Already in 1952, in reply to a survey circulated by the ICRC to National Societies, only six out of 31 National Societies answering the survey indicated that they still expected, or were still expected, to act on the basis of Article 26.[75] At the time of writing, it seems that only four National Societies have active programmes to serve their armed forces' medical services on the basis of Article 26, or have engaged in a dialogue with their national armed forces and the latter's medical services to this end.[76] Clearly, the improvement in the capabilities of many armed forces' medical services can be considered as the main factor explaining this trend.[77]

2087 The scant practice with regard to Article 26 is without prejudice to this provision's continued validity as a matter of treaty law: this provision has not fallen into desuetude.[78] The Model Law on the Recognition of National Societies, for example, attests to the continued validity of Article 26, and that it continues to be one of the National Societies' defining features.[79] The absence of widespread and effective practice, in short, does not limit the possibility for societies to act in the future on the basis of Article 26. Furthermore, acting on the basis of Article 26 needs to be kept separate from another distinct role and function of National Societies, i.e. their role as auxiliaries to the public authorities in the humanitarian field, a role overall much broader and the nature of which has evolved over time.[80]

---

[75] See ICRC, *Report of the International Committee of the Red Cross on the Training, Duties, Status and Terms of Enrolment of the Medical Personnel Assigned to the Care of the Wounded and Sick in the Armed Forces*, 1952, p. 5.

[76] These are the American Red Cross, the Italian Red Cross, Magen David Adom in Israel, and the Swiss Red Cross. For the American Red Cross, for example, the legal basis in domestic law is the *Code for American Red Cross Cooperation and Assistance*, 2011; see also United States, *Law of War Manual*, 2015, para. 4.11.1. For the Swiss Red Cross, the legal basis in domestic law is the *Ordinance on Employees of the Red Cross*, 2006.

[77] While this is not in itself a reason why there is very limited practice with regard to Article 26, it should be kept in mind that the personnel covered by Article 26, when they fall into enemy hands, can be retained on the basis of Article 28 of the First Convention. Certain National Societies may be uncomfortable with the idea that their staff, who are and remain civilians, can be so retained.

[78] For a discussion of the requirements which must be met before a given treaty provision can be considered to have fallen into desuetude, see Introduction, section C.8.

[79] See the Model Law on the Recognition of the (Name of the Red Cross or Red Crescent Society), referred to in the Plan of Action, Final goal 3.3, para. (14)(b), adopted by the 27th International Conference of the Red Cross and Red Crescent, Geneva, 1999, Annex 2 of Res. 1, Article 1(2): 'The Society is a voluntary aid society, auxiliary to the public authorities in the humanitarian field, recognised and authorised on the basis of the Geneva Conventions (and their Additional Protocols) to render assistance to the medical services of the armed forces in times of armed conflict.'

[80] See the last sentence of Article 3(1) of the 1986 Statutes of the Red Cross and Red Crescent Movement. For a number of years, the topic of National Red Cross and Red Crescent Societies as auxiliaries to the public authorities in the humanitarian field has figured prominently on the agenda of both the International Conference of the Red Cross and Red Crescent and of the Council of Delegates. See 30th International Conference of the Red Cross and Red Crescent, Geneva, 2007, Res. 3; 31st International Conference of the Red Cross and Red Crescent, Geneva,

2088   One important factor to include in the assessment of the role of Article 26 since 1949 pertains to the articulation between a National Society's role as auxiliary to the armed forces' medical services, and the commitment of a National Society to abide at all times with the seven Fundamental Principles of the Movement: humanity, impartiality, neutrality, independence, voluntary service, unity and universality.[81] Their normative weight needs to be properly understood: the Principles are rules of behaviour which are internal to the Movement and which must be complied with by the Movement's components in all their actions, including when acting on the basis of Article 26.[82] They have been developed and tested over time as tools critical to ensuring the acceptability of the Movement's humanitarian activities. While the High Contracting Parties to the Geneva Conventions are not themselves components of the Movement, they are nevertheless required, under the Statutes of the Movement, to 'at all times respect the adherence by all the components of the Movement to the Fundamental Principles'.[83] In addition, under the Statutes States have committed themselves to making sure that the National Society has 'an autonomous status which allows it to operate in conformity with the Fundamental Principles of the Movement'.[84]

2089   When a National Society places any of its staff at the disposal of the medical services of its State's armed forces on the basis of Article 26, it may be considered that no challenges would automatically arise in terms of compliance by the National Society with the Fundamental Principles of humanity,[85]

2011, Res. 4; Council of Delegates, Geneva, 2003, Res. 6; Council of Delegates, Seoul, 2005, Res. 9; and Council of Delegates, Geneva, 2007, Res. 3. For further background information, see 'The specific nature of the Red Cross and Red Crescent Movement in action and partnerships and the role of National Societies as auxiliaries to the public authorities in the humanitarian field', Background document prepared for the 30th International Conference of the Red Cross and Red Crescent by the International Federation of Red Cross and Red Crescent Societies in consultation with the ICRC, Geneva, October 2007.

[81]   For a historical overview, see Jean-Luc Blondel, 'Genèse et évolution des Principes fondamentaux de la Croix-Rouge et du Croissant-Rouge', *Revue internationale de la Croix-Rouge*, Vol. 73, No. 790, August 1991, pp. 369–377. Among the most prominent works in this connection is Jean S. Pictet, *Red Cross Principles*, ICRC, Geneva, 1956, in which the author lists seven 'Fundamental Principles' and 10 'Organic Principles'. For the current version of the Fundamental Principles, see the preamble to the 1986 Statutes of the International Red Cross and Red Crescent Movement.

[82]   See 30th International Conference of the Red Cross and Red Crescent, Geneva, 2007, Res. 2, para. 6. See also Statutes of the International Red Cross and Red Crescent Movement (1986), Preamble and Article 3(1).

[83]   Statutes of the International Red Cross and Red Crescent Movement (1986), Article 2(4). For Parties to Additional Protocol I, see Article 81(2) and (3) of that Protocol. See also International Federation of Red Cross and Red Crescent Societies, *National Red Cross and Red Crescent Societies as auxiliaries to the public authorities in the humanitarian field*, 2003, p. 25, and ICRC, *National Red Cross and Red Crescent Societies as auxiliaries to the public authorities in the humanitarian field: Study on situations of armed conflict*, 2005, p. 26. See also UN General Assembly, Res. 55(I), National Red Cross and Red Crescent Societies, 19 November 1946, para. (b).

[84]   Statutes of the International Red Cross and Red Crescent Movement (1986), Article 4(4).

[85]   ICRC, *National Red Cross and Red Crescent Societies as auxiliaries to the public authorities in the humanitarian field: Study on situations of armed conflict*, 2005, p. 25.

impartiality,[86] neutrality,[87] voluntary service, independence, unity and universality.[88]

2090   However, acting on the basis of Article 26 requires that the staff be 'subject to military laws and regulations'. Both conceptually and practically, this may be seen to raise challenges in terms of compliance with the Fundamental Principle of independence. This principle states that '[t]he National Societies, while auxiliaries in the humanitarian services of their governments and subject to the laws of their respective countries, must always maintain their autonomy so that they may be able at all times to act in accordance with the principles of the Movement'. In reality, however, the principle of independence is not automatically violated by the mere fact that the staff of a National Society work on the basis of Article 26. Indeed, the requirement of being 'subject to military laws and regulations' applies only to the staff acting on the basis of Article 26, and not to the society as such.

2091   Having said this, in practice, since these staff members remain the representatives of the National Society for which they work, the perception may be different in the eyes of Parties on the ground. Everything will depend on the practical arrangements made at the national level as to whether the National Society maintains its autonomy – as foreseen by the Fundamental Principle of independence – and whether the staff working on the basis of Article 26 remain able at all times to act in accordance with the Fundamental Principles of the Movement, in particular those of impartiality, neutrality and independence. Should the arrangements not allow for this, the National Society must carefully consider the issue and may have to refrain altogether from serving as an auxiliary to the armed forces' medical services within the framework of Article 26. The way that one component of the Movement is perceived may have repercussions for how other components are perceived.

2092   In order for the military (medical) authorities to see to it that the National Societies are able to comply at all times with the Fundamental Principles, it is important that these authorities have a thorough understanding of these principles.[89] This should notably preclude situations in which they would instruct the National Society and its medical staff to undertake the activities

---

[86] The fact that a National Society serves as an auxiliary to the medical services of its own State's armed forces does not necessarily entail a violation of the principle of impartiality, provided that enemy wounded and sick are also being treated in accordance with that principle.

[87] If a National Red Cross or Red Crescent Society operates on the basis of Article 26, this does not, as such, violate the principle of neutrality. In order to comply with the principle, the National Society will need to refrain from expressing any views about its State's arguments concerning the reasons for the armed conflict. See International Federation of Red Cross and Red Crescent Societies, *National Red Cross and Red Crescent Societies as auxiliaries to the public authorities in the humanitarian field*, p. 25.

[88] Council of Delegates, Seoul, 16–18 November 2005, Summary of the study on situations of armed conflict, Section 5.

[89] Conversely, the arrangements made at the national level between the military authorities and the National Society may require the Society's staff, prior to their deployment on the basis of Article 26, to attend a number of courses organized by the armed forces (e.g. on discipline).

referred to in Article 24 in a way that may lead, or may be perceived as leading, to an infringement of one or more of the Fundamental Principles.[90]

2093   Lastly, when a National Society acts on the basis of Article 26, neither the 1997 Seville Agreement nor its 2005 Supplementary Measures apply to that activity.[91] The scope of the Seville Agreement is limited to 'those international activities which the components are called upon to carry out in cooperation, on a bilateral or multilateral basis, to the exclusion of the activities which the Statutes of the Movement and the Geneva Conventions entrust to the components individually'.[92] Similarly, the requirement for a National Society operating abroad to obtain the consent of the 'host' National Society (i.e. the Society of the State on whose territory the activities take place) would, in principle, not apply when a National Society acts on the basis of Article 26.[93] However, as a matter of good practice, it is advisable to notify the 'host' National Society prior to any activities on the basis of Article 26.

2. Other voluntary aid societies

2094   Conceptually, the National Societies are the most prominent subdivision of the broader category of voluntary aid societies which may act on the basis of Article 26. Among voluntary aid societies other than the National Societies, the national organizations of the Order of the Knights of Malta and of the Order of St. John of Jerusalem are among the most prominent. In recent decades, despite its numerous humanitarian activities worldwide, the Order of the Knights of Malta has not been active on the basis of Article 26. Historically, the Order of St. John of Jerusalem has maintained close links with the British Red Cross Society: the two lie at the origin of today's St. John and Red Cross Defence Medical Welfare Service. Under the legislation of the United Kingdom, that organization can be and is deployed on the basis of Article 26.

2095   Since voluntary aid societies other than National Societies do not qualify as components of the Movement, they are not bound to comply with the Movement's Fundamental Principles, nor with any other aspect of its policy or regulatory framework. However, since the activities referred to in Article 24 of

---

[90] Such a violation would occur, for example, if the military authorities were to prohibit persons covered by Article 26 from providing medical care to enemy wounded and sick. On this point more generally, see 30th International Conference of the Red Cross and Red Crescent, Geneva, 2007, Res. 2, Specific nature of the International Red Cross and Red Crescent Movement in action and partnerships and the role of National Societies as auxiliaries to the public authorities in the humanitarian field, para. 4(b).

[91] See Seville Agreement (1997) and Supplementary Measures to the Seville Agreement (2005).

[92] Seville Agreement (1997), Article 1.1; see also Articles 1.3 and 1.4 of the Agreement.

[93] See also the Statutes of the International Red Cross and Red Crescent Movement (1986), Article 3(3), first subparagraph, and ICRC, *National Red Cross and Red Crescent Societies as auxiliaries to the public authorities in the humanitarian field: Study on situations of armed conflict*, pp. 16–17. For the primary source of this principle, see 10th International Conference of the Red Cross, Geneva, 1921, Res. XI, Relations between National Societies, para. 1, as well as Huber, pp. 35–36.

the First Convention are of a humanitarian nature,[94] these societies will, as a matter of fact, most likely wish to comply with the principles of humanitarian action as they apply to such activities in time of armed conflict, and as equally reflected in certain rules of international law (for example, in Article 12 of the First Convention).[95]

2096   For several decades, the number of organizations involved in humanitarian activities, for example non-governmental organizations, has greatly increased. Many of them, if (some of) their staff are engaged in the activities referred to in Article 24, would qualify as 'Voluntary Aid Societies' within the meaning of Article 26. It can only be observed that States do not use them as societies in that sense, whether because the armed forces' medical services do not need to be supplemented, or because these organizations themselves feel uncomfortable about acting on the basis of the conditions set out in Article 26.

3. Critical assessment

2097   The origins of Article 26 go back to 1863, when the founders of what was eventually to become the Movement successfully called for the establishment of voluntary aid societies at the national level. These societies were intended to compensate for the inadequacies, as they existed at the time, of the armed forces' official medical services. Between 1863 and the Second World War, National Societies came to be the most prominent among these voluntary aid societies, working as auxiliaries to the armed forces' medical services. Provided that they are subject to military laws and regulations, those of their staff members who are engaged in the activities referred to in Article 24 will have their status and treatment placed on the same footing as the members of these medical services. Thus, persons who are not members of the armed forces become covered by the First Convention.

2098   Since the end of the Second World War, Article 26 has played a limited role. Over time, in some countries at least, the armed forces' medical services have improved their capabilities, thus rendering less compelling the initial vision of the Movement's founders. This development has allowed these voluntary aid societies, including the National Societies, to focus their activities in time of armed conflict on other categories of victims. In parallel, the National Societies have developed numerous peacetime activities, which have led to their having been recognized as auxiliaries to the public authorities in the humanitarian field.

2099   Within the Movement, the development of the Fundamental Principles has raised questions about whether a National Society remains in compliance with

---

[94] For a discussion of the concept of 'humanitarian activities', see the commentary on Article 9, section C.2.a.

[95] For a discussion of these principles, see the commentary on Article 9, paras 1124, 1137–1138 and 1160.

these principles while acting on the basis of Article 26. In particular, the requirement for the staff of the National Societies to be subject to military laws and regulations has a potentially uneasy relationship to the principle of independence. Nevertheless, this disjunction in theory need not lead to paralysis in practice: as long as the military authorities ensure that the National Societies are continuously able to comply scrupulously, and to be perceived as complying scrupulously, with all of the Fundamental Principles, it remains possible for them to work on the basis of Article 26, including in States where this is not, or is no longer, the case. The same holds true for other voluntary aid societies, yet the fact remains that, at least for now, this possibility is rarely used.

2100   Even so, in today's environment, the significance and continued relevance of Article 26 for the National Societies should not be underestimated. It still forms the historical basis of their relationship with their State's authorities, including the military authorities and their medical services. Article 26 lies at the origin of the contemporary, much broader role of the National Societies as auxiliaries to the public authorities in the humanitarian field. This role is no longer exclusively linked to the Geneva Conventions, and exists both in time of peace and in time of armed conflict.[96]

Select bibliography

Backus, Johannes, 'Die Weiterentwicklung der zivil-militärischen Zusammenarbeit zwischen dem Zentralen Sanitätsdienst der Bundeswehr und dem Deutschen Roten Kreuz', *Journal of International Law of Peace and Armed Conflict*, Vol. 25, No. 1, 2012, pp. 7–11.

Best, Geoffrey, *Humanity in Warfare: The Modern History of the International Law of Armed Conflicts*, Weidenfeld and Nicolson, London, 1980.

Bogaievsky, P.M., 'Les secours aux militaires malades et blessés avant le XIXe siècle', *Revue générale de droit international public*, Vol. X, 1903, pp. 202–221.

Bohny, Gustav Adolf, *Über die rechtliche Stellung der Rotkeuzorganisationen*, Helbing & Lichtenhahn, Basel, 1922.

Boissier, Pierre, *History of the International Committee of the Red Cross: From Solferino to Tsushima*, ICRC/Henry Dunant Institute, Geneva, 1985.

Borel, Paul, 'L'organisation internationale de la Croix-Rouge', *Recueil des cours de l'Académie de droit international de La Haye*, Vol. 1, 1923, pp. 569–608.

Camporini, Yoland, *National Societies Auxiliaries of the Public Authorities: Their Activities in Time of Armed Conflict*, Henry Dunant Institute *Working Papers*, Vol. 7, No. 87, Geneva, 1987.

---

[96] For a contemporary understanding of this notion, see 30th International Conference of the Red Cross and Red Crescent, Geneva, 2007, Res. 3. See also Statutes of the International Red Cross and Red Crescent Movement (1986), Article 3(1), which contains the following sentence: 'The National Societies support the public authorities in their humanitarian tasks, according to the needs of the people of their respective countries.'

de Fischer, Béat, 'L'Ordre Souverain de Malte aujourd'hui', *Revue internationale de la Croix-Rouge*, Vol. 57, No. 673, January 1975, pp. 5–8.

Des Gouttes, Paul, *La Croix-Rouge internationale avant, pendant et depuis la guerre mondiale*, La Vie des Peuples, Paris, 1923.

– 'La nouvelle Convention de Genève du 27 juillet 1929 et les Sociétés de la Croix-Rouge', *Revue internationale de la Croix-Rouge*, Vol. 12, No. 138, June 1930, pp. 415–423.

– (ed.) *Recueil de textes relatifs à l'application de la Convention de Genève et à l'action des Sociétés nationales dans les Etats parties à cette Convention*, ICRC, Geneva, 1934.

– 'Les grandes étapes de la Croix-Rouge et de la Convention de Genève', *Revue internationale de la Croix-Rouge*, Vol. 19, No. 218, February 1937, pp. 121–153.

Dunant, Henry, *A Memory of Solferino (Un souvenir de Solferino)*, translation from the French of the 1st edition, published in 1862, American National Red Cross, Washington, D.C., 1939.

Durand, André, *History of the International Committee of the Red Cross, Volume II: From Sarajevo to Hiroshima*, Henry Dunant Institute, Geneva, 1984.

Ferrière, Suzanne, 'L'activité de guerre et l'activité de paix des Sociétés nationales de la Croix-Rouge', *Revue internationale de la Croix-Rouge et Bulletin international des Sociétés de la Croix-Rouge*, Vol. 8, No. 86, February 1926, pp. 65–93.

François, Alexis, *Le Berceau de la Croix-Rouge*, Librairie A. Jullien, Geneva, 1918.

Haug, Hans and Gasser, Hans-Peter, *Humanité pour tous: Le Mouvement International de la Croix-Rouge et du Croissant-Rouge*, Institut Henry Dunant/Éditions Paul Haupt, Bern, 1993.

Huber, Max, *Principles, Tasks and Problems of the Red Cross in International Law*, ICRC, Geneva, 1946.

Hutchinson, John F., *Champions of Charity: War and the Rise of the Red Cross*, Westview Press, Boulder, Colorado, 1996.

ICRC, *Report of the International Committee of the Red Cross on the Training, Duties, Status and Terms of Enrolment of the Medical Personnel Assigned to the Care of the Wounded and Sick in the Armed Forces*, reporting on a questionnaire to both National Societies and medical services of the armed forces, 18th International Conference of the Red Cross, Toronto, 20 July–8 August 1952, item III(c) of the agenda of the Health, Medical Personnel and Social Aid Commission, Doc. 20.

– 'La Croix-Rouge et son rôle d'auxiliaire des services de santé militaires', *note technique* [technical memorandum], *Revue internationale de la Croix-Rouge*, Vol. 65, No. 741, June 1983, pp. 143–145.

– *National Red Cross and Red Crescent Societies as auxiliaries to the public authorities in the humanitarian field: Study on situations of armed conflict*, prepared in consultation with a number of National Societies, Council of Delegates, Seoul, 16–18 November 2005.

ICRC and International Federation of Red Cross and Red Crescent Societies, *Handbook of the International Red Cross and Red Crescent Movement*, 14th edition, Geneva, 2008.

International Federation of Red Cross and Red Crescent Societies, *National Red Cross and Red Crescent Societies as auxiliaries to the public authorities in the humanitarian field*, Geneva, 2003.

Karski, Karol, 'The International Legal Status of the Sovereign Military Hospitaller Order of St. John of Jerusalem of Rhodes and of Malta', *International Community Law Review*, Vol. 14, 2012, pp. 19–32.

Lanord, Christophe, *Le statut juridique des Sociétés nationales de la Croix-Rouge et du Croissant-Rouge*, Éditions de la Chapelle, Geneva, 1999.

– 'The legal status of National Red Cross and Red Crescent Societies', *International Review of the Red Cross*, Vol. 82, No. 840, December 2000, pp. 1053–1077.

Lueder, C., *La Convention de Genève au point de vue historique, critique et dogmatique*, E. Besold, Erlangen, 1876.

Moynier, Gustave, *Étude sur la Convention de Genève pour l'amélioration du sort des militaires blessés dans les armées en campagne (1864 et 1868)*, Librairie de Joël Cherbuliez, Paris, 1870.

– *La révision de la Convention de Genève : étude historique et critique, suivie d'un projet de Convention révisée*, ICRC, Geneva, 1898.

Noailly, Frédérique, *La Croix-Rouge au point de vue national et international : son histoire, son organisation*, Librairie générale de droit et de jurisprudence, Paris, 1935.

Perruchoud, Richard, *International Responsibilities of National Red Cross and Red Crescent Societies*, ICRC/Henry Dunant Institute, Geneva, 1982.

Pictet, Jean S., 'La Croix-Rouge et les Conventions de Genève', *Recueil des cours de l'Académie de droit international de La Haye*, Vol. 76, 1950, pp. 5–119.

Reid, Daphne A. and Gilbo, Patrick F., *Beyond Conflict: The International Federation of Red Cross and Red Crescent Societies, 1919–1994*, International Federation of Red Cross and Red Crescent Societies, Geneva, 1997.

Reid, Ian, 'The Evolution of the Red Cross', *Joint Committee for the Re-appraisal of the Role of the Red Cross*, Background Paper Vol. 2, No. 2, ICRC/Henry Dunant Institute, Geneva, 1975.

Rosas, Allan, 'Notes on the Legal Status of National Red Cross Societies', in Christophe Swinarski (ed.), *Studies and Essays on International Humanitarian Law and Red Cross Principles in Honour of Jean Pictet*, Martinus Nijhoff Publishers, The Hague, 1984, pp. 959–973.

Ruegger, Paul, 'The Juridical Aspects of the Organization of the Red Cross', *Collected Courses of the Hague Academy of International Law*, Vol. 82, 1953, pp. 481–586.

Spieker, Heike, 'Die zivil-militärische Zusammenarbeit zwischen Bundeswehr und Deutschem Roten Kreuz', *Journal of International Law of Peace and Armed Conflict*, Vol. 25, No. 1, 2012, pp. 4–6.

Werner, Auguste-Raynald, *La Croix-Rouge et les Conventions de Genève : Analyse et synthèse juridiques*, Georg & Cie, Geneva, 1943.

SOCIETIES OF NEUTRAL COUNTRIES

❖ Text of the provision*

(1) A recognized Society of a neutral country can only lend the assistance of its medical personnel and units to a Party to the conflict with the previous consent of its own Government and the authorization of the Party to the conflict concerned. That personnel and those units shall be placed under the control of that Party to the conflict.

(2) The neutral Government shall notify this consent to the adversary of the State which accepts such assistance. The Party to the conflict who accepts such assistance is bound to notify the adverse Party thereof before making any use of it.

(3) In no circumstances shall this assistance be considered as interference in the conflict.

(4) The members of the personnel named in the first paragraph shall be duly furnished with the identity cards provided for in Article 40 before leaving the neutral country to which they belong.

❖ Reservations or declarations

None

Contents

---

* Paragraph numbers have been added for ease of reference.

A. Introduction

2101   Article 27 sets out the conditions under which a recognized voluntary aid society of a neutral country may lend the assistance of its medical personnel and units to a Party to an international armed conflict. In order for this to occur in line with Article 27, several requirements need to be fulfilled and complied with. When these requirements have been met, the medical personnel and units of the neutral country's recognized society will qualify as persons and objects protected under the First Convention.

2102   Article 27 must be read in conjunction with Article 26, since the former constitutes a variant of the latter. Article 26 deals with the conditions under which National Red Cross and Red Crescent Societies (hereinafter referred to as 'National Societies') – as well as other voluntary aid societies – can serve as auxiliaries to the medical services of their *own* State's armed forces, when that State is a Party to an international armed conflict. Article 27, in turn, deals with the conditions pursuant to which a recognized society of a neutral country can assist the medical services of *another* State's armed forces when that State is a Party to an international armed conflict.

2103   Hence, the commentary on Article 26 with regard to the impact of the Fundamental Principles of the International Red Cross and Red Crescent Movement (hereinafter referred to as 'the Movement'), applicable to National Societies when they act on the basis of that provision, is also applicable when National Societies act on the basis of Article 27. Therefore, this commentary is not repeated here.[1] In this context, special mention must be made of Article 27(3), which underscores, for National Societies, the idea that acting on the basis of Article 27 does not violate the Fundamental Principle of neutrality.[2]

2104   Several other provisions of the First Convention must be mentioned in order to afford a full understanding of the legal situation enjoyed by medical staff and units serving on the basis of Article 27. When these personnel fall into the hands of the adversary of the Party they are assisting, Article 32 applies. The real and personal property of the societies covered by Article 27 is protected by Article 34. When it comes to identification, Article 40 sets out the legal framework for the personnel covered by Article 27.

2105   Article 9(2) of Additional Protocol I also needs to be considered. This provision makes the relevant provisions of Articles 27 and 32 of the First Convention applicable to permanent medical units and transports,[3] and to those of their personnel who are made available to a Party to the conflict for humanitarian purposes by (a) a neutral or other State which is not a Party to that conflict;

---

[1] See the commentary on Article 26, paras 2088–2089.   [2] For details, see section E below.
[3] Other than hospital ships, in respect of which Article 25 of the Second Convention remains the only relevant provision (this clarification can be found in the text of Article 9(2) of Additional Protocol I).

(b) a recognized and authorized aid society of such a State; or (c) an impartial international humanitarian organization.[4]

2106　Since the end of the Second World War, there do not seem to have been any instances in which the potential for assistance provided by Article 27 has been used.

B. Historical background

2107　The historical background of Article 27 needs to be read in conjunction with the parallel section in the commentary on Article 26. Only those elements which are specific to Article 27 will be mentioned here.

2108　While paragraphs 3 and 4 of Article 27 were new additions to the 1949 version of the First Convention, the origins of paragraphs 1 and 2 can be traced back much earlier.

2109　In the Resolutions and Recommendations of the Geneva International Conference of 1863, one finds in embryonic form the current idea underpinning Article 27.[5] In the 1864 Geneva Convention, however, the role of voluntary aid societies (whether of a neutral country or of the Parties to the conflict themselves) as auxiliaries to the armed forces' medical services was left unaddressed.[6]

2110　As early as the 1870–71 Franco-Prussian War, the aid societies of neutral countries (along with some neutral countries themselves) not only supplied relief to both sides, but also dispatched medical teams. Some of the volunteers of these societies, however well-intentioned they may have been, reportedly did not possess sufficient medical skills. As a result, they did not always succeed in having their role accepted by the military authorities.[7] During the 1877–78 armed conflict between Russia and the Ottoman Empire, at the request of the latter and with the agreement of all sides to the conflict, the Netherlands Red Cross Society administered a mobile hospital for the Ottoman Empire.[8]

---

[4] See also Article 12(2)(c) of Additional Protocol I. Under this provision, 'civilian medical units' which have been 'authorized in conformity with Article 9, paragraph 2, of [Additional Protocol I] or Article 27 of the First Convention' shall be respected and protected at all times and may not be the object of attack. See also Article 64 of Additional Protocol I, which is similar to Article 27, although it pertains to different humanitarian tasks. This provision deals with the personnel and *matériel* (materials and equipment) of civilian civil defence organizations of neutral or other States not Parties to the conflict which perform civil defence tasks (as defined in Article 61 of Additional Protocol I) in the territory of a Party to the conflict, with the consent and under the control of that Party.

[5] Article 5(2) of the Resolutions and Recommendations of the Geneva International Conference of 1863 reads: 'In time of war, the Committees of belligerent nations ... may call for assistance upon the Committees of neutral countries.' This concerns, however, assistance provided by one National Society to another, not assistance provided directly to the Party to the conflict.

[6] For details, see the commentary on Article 26, para. 2049.

[7] See Boissier, pp. 254–256, and Hutchinson, p. 125.

[8] See *Bulletin international des Sociétés de la Croix-Rouge*, Vol. 9, No. 33, January 1878, pp. 71–81. See also Frits Kalshoven, 'Impartialité et neutralité dans le droit et la pratique humanitaires', *Revue internationale de la Croix-Rouge*, Vol. 71, No. 780, December 1989, pp. 541–562, at 548–549.

Another example of what eventually became Article 27 of the First Convention can be found in the 1897 Greek-Ottoman war.[9] These three examples developed in practice, before having been formally regulated in treaty law. This state of affairs was undesirable: neither the conditions for such charitable activities, nor the status of the persons and units involved, were clear.

2111   The 1906 Geneva Convention was the first treaty to formally recognize and regulate the role of voluntary aid societies as auxiliaries to the armed forces' medical services.[10] The role of such societies from neutral countries was defined in Article 10 (the precursor of Article 26 of the First Convention of 1949), and further elaborated in Article 11.[11] The reason for the stringency of these conditions is clear: the medical staff and units of neutral voluntary aid societies would only be admitted to the protection of the Convention if the military authorities accepted them in such a role.[12]

2112   During both the Italo-Turkish War (1911–12)[13] and the Balkan Wars (1912–13),[14] the National Societies of several neutral countries sent medical units to the battlefield.

2113   Apart from minor differences in wording, Article 11 of the 1929 Geneva Convention on the Wounded and Sick is identical to Article 11 of the 1906 Geneva Convention. During the Geneva Diplomatic Conference of 1929, a proposal was made to allow for the protection of assistance when it is offered spontaneously, in an urgent situation, by the aid societies of neighbouring neutral countries.[15] The fact that this proposal was unsuccessful is telling: States wanted to maintain the formality of the arrangement, i.e. the protection of the medical personnel and units of recognized societies of neutral countries was to remain subject to a series of approvals and notifications.[16]

2114   After 1929, there seem to have been only three further instances in which a recognized society of a neutral country offered its support to the medical services of another State's armed forces. In 1935, in the context of the armed

---

[9] Des Gouttes, *Commentaire de la Convention de Genève de 1929 sur les blessés et malades*, ICRC, 1930, p. 68.

[10] For details, see the commentary on Article 26, para. 2050.

[11] Article 11 of the 1906 Geneva Convention reads: 'A recognized society of a neutral state can only lend the services of its sanitary personnel and formations to a belligerent with the prior consent of its own government and the authority of such belligerent. The belligerent who has accepted such assistance is required to notify the enemy before making any use thereof.' Here already one notes the restrictive tone of the terms 'can only lend'. The article goes back to a proposal made by the UK delegation; see *Proceedings of the Geneva Diplomatic Conference of 1906*, p. 57, and *Projet de Convention revisée soumis par les plénipotentiaires anglais* (Draft revised convention submitted by the English plenipotentiaries), with proposed Article 6, pp. 60–61.

[12] Best, pp. 152–153.   [13] Durand, p. 16.

[14] See *Bulletin international des Sociétés de la Croix-Rouge*, Vol. 44, No. 173, January 1913, p. 37.

[15] *Proceedings of the Geneva Diplomatic Conference of 1929*, p. 18, proposed article 11*bis*. This proposal was introduced by the Dutch delegation, and had already been submitted to the 10th International Conference of the Red Cross, Geneva, 30 March–7 April 1921. It was inspired by a particular historical example. For a discussion, see *Proceedings of the Geneva Diplomatic Conference of 1929*, p. 139.

[16] See *ibid.* pp. 192–193 and 607.

conflict between Italy and Ethiopia, the United Kingdom made it known, pursuant to the requirements of Article 11 of the 1929 Geneva Convention, that the 'British Ambulance Service in Ethiopia' could provide medical assistance to the Ethiopian armed forces.[17] In connection with the same armed conflict, the Swedish Red Cross also acted on the basis of Article 11 when sending an ambulance brigade and a field hospital.[18] Under the same provision, during the Second World War, the Swiss Red Cross Society provided medical assistance to the German armed forces,[19] and the American Voluntary Ambulance Corps assisted the British and French armed forces before the United States of America became a Party to the conflict.[20]

2115   In terms of treaty development, the 1946 Preliminary Conference of National Societies proposed to add a further procedural requirement, namely that not only the Party to the conflict accepting the assistance, but also the neutral country, would need to notify the adversary of that Party. This requirement was adopted by the Diplomatic Conference of Geneva of 1949 as the first sentence of Article 27(2).[21] The Preliminary Conference of National Societies also added what was to become Article 27(3).[22] Article 27(4) was added by the 1947 Conference of Government Experts.[23] During the 1949 Diplomatic Conference, only one final substantive modification was introduced.[24]

---

[17] US Department of State, *Treaty Information Bulletin*, No. 74, 30 November 1935, Government Printing Office, Washington, D.C., p. 9. See also *Bulletin international des Sociétés de la Croix-Rouge*, Vol. 66, No. 398, October 1935, p. 794, and Vol. 66, No. 399, November 1935, p. 876.

[18] See Viveca Halldin Norberg, *Swedes in Haile Selassie's Ethiopia, 1924–1952: A study in early development co-operation*, Scandinavian Institute of African Studies, Uppsala, 1977, pp. 154–159.

[19] *Minutes of the Conference of Government Experts of 1947*, Committee I, Vol. II, Tome 1, p. 166. For historical references, see Edgar Bonjour, *Histoire de la neutralité suisse pendant la seconde guerre mondiale*, À la Baconnière, Neuchâtel, 1970, pp. 437–449. See also Karl Philipp Behrendt, *Die Kriegschirurgie von 1939–1945 aus der Sicht der beratenden Chirurgen des deutschen Heeres im Zweiten Weltkrieg*, inaugural dissertation submitted for the degree of Doctor of Medicine, University of Freiburg Faculty of Medicine, 2003, pp. 179–183, and Rudolf Bucher, *Zwischen Verrat und Menschlichkeit. Erlebnisse eines Schweizer Arztes an der deutsch-russisschen Front 1941/42*, 3rd edition, Huber, Frauenfeld, 1967, pp. 256–260. More generally, see Reinhold Busch, *Die Schweiz, Die Nazis und die erste Ärztemission an die Ostfront, Schweizer Ärztemissionen im II. Weltkrieg, Teil 1: Robert Nicole, Bericht über die Schweizerische Ärztemission nach Finnland*, Frank Wünsche, Berlin, 2002.

[20] *Minutes of the Diplomatic Conference of Geneva of 1949*, Committee I, Vol. I, 14th session, 11 May 1949, p. 34.

[21] *Minutes of the Preliminary Conference of National Societies of 1946*, Vol. I, pp. 84–86. The proposal dates from the meetings of the Commission of Experts convened by the ICRC in 1937 to discuss the revision of the 1929 Geneva Convention.

[22] *Ibid.* pp. 85–87. See also *Minutes of the Conference of Government Experts of 1947*, Committee I, Vol. II, Tome 1, pp. 164 and 169. In the *Draft Conventions submitted to the 1948 Stockholm Conference*, this notification requirement appeared as the final sentence of the first paragraph (the second paragraph of this draft contained what had already been there since 1906, i.e. the notification requirement as it applies to the State accepting the assistance of the neutral Power's recognized society).

[23] *Minutes of the Conference of Government Experts of 1947*, Committee I, Vol. II, Tome 1, pp. 152–164.

[24] Upon the proposal of one delegation, and without further discussion, the drafters added what became the final sentence of Article 27(1), namely: 'That personnel and those units shall be placed under the control of that Party to the conflict.' See *Final Record of the Diplomatic*

2116   Since the end of the Second World War, no recognized Society of a neutral country has acted on the basis of Article 27. The reasons why this has been the case as far as Article 26 is concerned are equally valid here.[25] The scant practice with regard to Article 27 is without prejudice to this provision's continued validity as a matter of treaty law: this provision has not fallen into desuetude.[26] The absence of past practice, in short, does not limit the possibility for societies to act in the future on the basis of Article 27. Support to the military medical services lies at the origin of the Movement, and could still be of practical value in the future.

2117   Furthermore, National Societies, as well as other voluntary aid societies, today also carry out a wide range of humanitarian activities in support of public authorities other than those defined under Articles 26 and 27, i.e. the armed forces' medical services. As regards National Societies, such activities are nowadays considered to be part of their role and function as auxiliaries to the public authorities in the humanitarian field.[27] However, if ever carried out in support of the public authorities of a foreign State that is a Party to an international armed conflict, none of these activities would be covered by Article 27.

C. Paragraph 1: Basic concepts and rules

2118 Article 27(1) lists the first series of conditions which must be met if a recognized society of a neutral country wishes to offer the assistance of its medical personnel and units to a Party to the conflict. Article 27 is silent on the question of who may take the initiative in this respect. As a result, all scenarios remain possible.[28]

1. First sentence: Consent and authorization

2119 Only a 'recognized Society of a neutral country' can act on the basis of Article 27. A society wishing to qualify to act on the basis of this provision, while it needs to be based in the neutral country, may not be part of its public authorities.[29]

Conference of Geneva of 1949, Vol. II-A, pp. 78, 122 and 212. Lastly, whereas the draft submitted to the 1949 Diplomatic Conference spoke of 'that belligerent', this was modified to read 'that Party to the conflict'.

[25] See the commentary on Article 26, section F.

[26] For a discussion of the requirements which must be met before a treaty provision can be considered to have fallen into desuetude, see the Introduction, section C.8.

[27] See the commentary on Article 26, para. 2087.

[28] *Minutes of the Preliminary Conference of National Societies of 1946*, Vol. I, pp. 83–84.

[29] It should be noted that the idea that a neutral country could offer the services of its own armed forces' medical services to a Party to the conflict was rejected in the period prior to 1949. Indeed, this possibility was discussed in 1937 when the ICRC convened a Commission of Experts to consider the revision of the 1929 Geneva Convention. See *Report on the Interpretation, Revision and Extension of the Geneva Convention of July 27, 1929*, Report prepared for the 26th International Conference of the Red Cross, London, June 1938, p. 16, where the idea was rejected 'in

2120   The meaning of 'recognized Society' is not defined in Article 27. However, when read together with Article 26 it becomes clear that it equally refers to 'National Red Cross Societies and other Voluntary Aid Societies'.[30] As is the case with societies acting on the basis of Article 26, those wishing to act under Article 27 need to have been 'recognized' by their own government.[31] In the case of Article 27, the government referred to is the neutral government. For the meaning of the term 'neutral country', see the commentary on Article 4.[32]

2121   The society not only needs to be recognized by its own neutral government; it also needs to have received this government's previous consent to go abroad to assist the armed forces of a Party to an international armed conflict.[33] While semantically different, this requirement corresponds to the requirement in Article 26 that the society be authorized to assist the armed forces' medical services.[34] This requirement is critical: Article 27 can be applicable only if the neutral government allows a recognized society of its country to serve on the basis of that provision.[35] This consent can be given either on a case-by-case basis or in advance of any specific instance in which the society would be deployed. In all instances, vis-à-vis the adversary of the Party to which the assistance is offered, the requirement to notify pursuant to the first sentence of Article 27(2) persists.

view of the very great difficulties which would follow such practice'. See also *Draft revision of the 1929 Geneva Convention submitted by the ICRC to National Societies in 1937*, p. 6, and *Minutes of the Conference of Government Experts of 1947*, Committee I, Vol. II, Tome 1, p. 170. This possibility is now envisaged in, and regulated by, Article 9(2)(a) of Additional Protocol I.

30   For a discussion of the terms 'National Red Cross Societies and … other Voluntary Aid Societies', see the commentary on Article 26, section C.1. For further analysis, see Claudie Barrat, *Status of NGOs in International Humanitarian Law*, Brill Nijhoff, Leiden, 2014, pp. 89–91.

31   For a discussion of the terms 'recognized' and 'government', see the commentary on Article 26, para. 2062. As is the case under Article 26, nothing precludes a Party to a conflict from being assisted by several recognized societies (of one or more neutral countries, in addition to domestic societies). Here, too, it must be emphasized that the term 'recognition', as used in Article 27, is not to be confused with the entirely separate issue of a society's recognition by the ICRC as the National Red Cross or Red Crescent Society of that State. See the commentary on Article 26, para. 2063.

32   It should be noted that, whereas Article 4 uses the term 'neutral Powers', Article 27 uses the term 'neutral country'. While semantically different, these terms are functionally identical. For a discussion of what qualifies as a 'neutral country', see the commentary on Article 4, section C.1.

33   Where Additional Protocol I applies, note must be taken of Article 81(2), (3) and (4) of that Protocol. These provisions impose certain (and differing) obligations on the Parties to the conflict and on the High Contracting Parties in terms of facilitating the work of Red Cross and Red Crescent Societies and other humanitarian organizations.

34   For a discussion of the term 'authorized', see the commentary on Article 26, section C.2.

35   See *Proceedings of the Geneva Diplomatic Conference of 1906*, pp. 125 and 225. In practice, it may happen that a neutral government not only wishes to withhold such consent, but wishes to go further in terms of barring a society of its country from assisting the armed forces of another State, e.g. by adopting domestic legislation criminalizing its nationals if they should serve in the medical services of a Party to the conflict. This happened in Norway during the Second World War; see *Minutes of the Diplomatic Conference of Geneva of 1949*, Committee I, Vol. I, 11 May 1949.

2122   Article 27 does not prescribe whether such consent – which remains a bilateral arrangement between the neutral government and the recognized society – needs to be expressed in writing. In any event, vis-à-vis the adversary of the State which accepts the society's assistance, the consent will be established on the basis of the notification required by the first sentence of Article 27(2).

2123   Understandably, the Party to the conflict which wishes to accept the assistance of the neutral country's recognized society also needs to authorize this. Article 27 does not prescribe how the authorization is to be given. In practice, it is better for the Party to the conflict which wishes to accept the medical units and personnel of a neutral recognized society to convey the required authorization in writing to the recognized society. In any event, vis-à-vis the adversary of this Party, the authorization will be established by the notification provided to the adversary pursuant to the second sentence of Article 27(2).

2124   On the basis of Article 27, the recognized society may 'lend the assistance of its medical personnel and units'. There is no obligation to offer both medical personnel and medical units. Indeed, a National Society may offer medical personnel without medical units, or vice versa.

2125   The terms 'medical personnel' and 'medical units' are not specifically defined, nor further regulated, for the purposes of Article 27.[36] In line with the logic of the First Convention concerning medical personnel and units, they need to be permanently and exclusively assigned to the medical activities referred to in Article 24.[37] Of note in this respect is Article 12(2)(c) of Additional Protocol I, pursuant to which civilian medical units shall be respected and protected at all times and shall not be the object of attack, *inter alia*, when they 'are authorized in conformity with ... Article 27 of the First Convention'.

2126   The medical personnel of a neutral State's society remain civilians, and do not become members of the armed forces which they assist.[38]

2127   While the term 'transports' does not appear as such in Article 27, for the purposes of that provision 'transports' can be understood to be a subcategory of the category 'medical units'.[39] As a result, a recognized society may offer the assistance of its medical transports on the basis of Article 27.[40]

---

[36] For the term 'fixed establishments and mobile medical units of the Medical Service', see Article 19 and its commentary, section C.1.a. For the term 'medical personnel', see Article 24 and its commentary, section C.1. For the definition of 'medical personnel' in Additional Protocol I, see Article 8(c), which includes, in its subparagraph (ii), the 'medical personnel of national Red Cross (Red Crescent, Red Lion and Sun) Societies and other national voluntary aid societies duly recognized and authorized by a Party to the conflict'. For the definition of 'medical units' in Additional Protocol I, see Article 8(e).

[37] See the commentary on Article 24, section D. As to the fact that persons covered by Article 27 can only be engaged in the activities referred to in Article 24, see below, para. 2133. See also the definition of 'permanent medical personnel' and 'permanent medical units' in Additional Protocol I, Article 8(k).

[38] The same applies to personnel acting under Article 26. See the commentary on Article 26, para. 2080.

[39] See also the commentary on Article 34, para. 2343.

[40] Article 9(2) of Additional Protocol I explicitly includes permanent medical transports.

2128   Article 27 is restricted to situations in which a recognized society of a neutral country offers its medical personnel, units or transports to a Party to an international armed conflict. All other humanitarian activities which may be carried out by a neutral recognized society in the context of an international armed conflict are outside the scope of Article 27.[41] This is true for other activities to benefit the armed forces of a Party to the armed conflict,[42] and especially for activities to benefit other categories of people in need (for example, aid offered through the host National Society).

2129   The assistance offered to one Party to an international armed conflict does not need to be balanced by a similar offer to that Party's adversaries.[43] However, should the society of the neutral State encounter wounded or sick members of the adversary of the State which it is assisting, it goes without saying that the society – like the medical services themselves – must tend to them as well, without any adverse distinction.[44]

2. Second sentence: Control

2130   Pursuant to the last sentence of Article 27(1), the medical personnel and units must be placed 'under the control of' the Party to the conflict which accepts the assistance. This sentence was proposed as late as the 1949 Diplomatic Conference, where it was accepted without further discussion.[45]

2131   Being 'under the control' of the Party to the conflict which accepts such assistance means, in order for the construct of Article 27 to be workable and practicable, that the medical services of this State's armed forces are entitled to direct the activities of the medical personnel and units concerned. Conversely, the latter are not entitled to act unless directed to do so. Therefore, they operate under the responsibility of that State.[46]

2132   The question arises as to whether being 'under the control of' means that persons covered by Article 27 must be 'subject to military laws and regulations', which is a more stringent and formalistic requirement applicable to persons covered by Article 26.[47] Based on the clear textual differences, the conclusion

---

[41] Thus, a recognized society of a neutral country offering its services (for example, offering to distribute food to civilians in need) on the basis of common Article 9 (Article 10 in the Fourth Convention) is not covered by Article 27.

[42] For relief provided to prisoners of war by 'religious organizations, relief societies, or any other organization assisting prisoners of war', see Article 125 of the Third Convention. In contrast to societies covered by Article 27 of the First Convention, societies wishing to act on the basis of Article 125 of the Third Convention do not need to have been specifically recognized to carry out the activities covered by that provision. For a discussion, see Lanord, 1999, p. 91.

[43] Jean S. Pictet, *Red Cross Principles*, ICRC, Geneva, 1956, p. 75.

[44] See Article 12.

[45] *Minutes of the Diplomatic Conference of Geneva of 1949*, Committee I, Vol. I, 11 May 1949.

[46] For the meaning and legal implications of the words 'under its responsibility', see the commentary on Article 26, section D.3.

[47] For the meaning of the words 'subject to military laws and regulations', see the commentary on Article 26, section D.2.

can be reached that if the drafters had meant this to be the case, they would have used identical terminology. This difference in wording also makes sense from the perspective of the law of neutrality, in that a neutral State cannot be expected to agree to have its nationals made 'subject to military laws and regulations' of a Party to an armed conflict.

2133   Those covered by Article 27 can only be 'employed on the same footing as the personnel' covered by Article 24. This limitation on the activities which can be undertaken can also be deduced from the fact that Article 27 speaks only of the assistance of the recognized society's 'medical personnel and units'.[48]

2134   Once the conditions of Articles 27(1) and (2) have been met, the article is silent about the status of the persons and units covered and the protection which they enjoy as a matter of law. In order to ensure consistency between Articles 26 and 27, the only tenable view is that persons covered by Article 27 – like those covered by Article 26 – (a) are granted protection and treatment identical to that of persons covered by Article 24,[49] and (b) are protected persons within the meaning of the First Convention.[50] As a result, they are to be respected and protected in all circumstances, except when their conduct amounts to an act harmful to the enemy.[51]

D. Paragraph 2: Double notification requirement

2135   Under the 1906 and 1929 Geneva Conventions, only a belligerent which had accepted the assistance of the recognized society of a neutral country had an obligation to make this known to its adverse Party, or adverse Parties,[52] before making use of the society. It was reported to the 1946 Preliminary Conference of National Societies that this requirement had frequently not been complied with in practice.[53]

---

[48] The possibility of providing the assistance of religious personnel is not mentioned in Article 27, though it ought to exist.

[49] For a discussion of what this entails, see the commentary on Article 26, section E.

[50] For a discussion of what it means to be a protected person or object under the First Convention, see the commentary on Article 26, para. 2084. When persons covered by Article 27 fall into enemy hands, Article 32 applies. As for objects covered by Article 27, they are protected under the First Convention, and therefore benefit from the additional protection conferred by Article 34.

[51] For a discussion of what type of conduct amounts to an act harmful to the enemy, see the commentary on Article 24, section F. As with persons covered by Article 24 or by Article 26, those covered by Article 27 are entitled to carry individual light weapons for self-defence or for the defence of the wounded and sick in their charge; see the commentary on Article 24, paras 2005–2006. The fact that they may be armed can also be inferred from Article 32(4).

[52] If the State accepting the assistance is engaged in an international armed conflict against more than one other State (for example a coalition of States), both notifications required by Article 27 need to be addressed to all those States. For a discussion of this point, see *Proceedings of the Geneva Diplomatic Conference of 1929*, p. 138.

[53] See *Minutes of the Preliminary Conference of National Societies of 1946*, Vol. I, p. 84. See also *Minutes of the Conference of Government Experts of 1947*, Committee I, Vol. II-1, pp. 164–165.

2136   The 1949 Diplomatic Conference maintained the requirement for the Party to the conflict which accepts the assistance to notify its adversary of this fact,[54] and added a second notification requirement: the government of the neutral country concerned, after giving its consent for a recognized society to act under Article 27, must notify the adversary of the State which accepts such assistance of its consent.[55] Thus, if the Party to the conflict which accepts such assistance fails to notify its adversary, the latter would still be informed. Doing so is also in the neutral Power's own interest.[56] By providing notification, the neutral Power shows that it fully supports its recognized society's intention to act on the basis of Article 27.[57] It is therefore understandable that the drafters of Article 27 rejected a proposal to make the notification by the neutral Power merely optional,[58] and thus made Article 27(2) deliberately rigid.[59]

2137   Notification is to be given by both States to the adversary of the Party to the conflict which accepts the assistance, and not by the recognized society itself. It may be desirable to notify all other High Contracting Parties, or at least all such Parties which might become concerned by the assistance offered (such as neighbouring countries of the Parties to the conflict).[60]

2138   Article 27 does not prescribe how, or in what form, these notifications need to be provided. While parties are not explicitly required to give notification in writing, it is undoubtedly preferable to do so, for example through a diplomatic note or other means, including modern electronic means of communication, in order to avoid any ambiguity. Notification may be given directly, or through an intermediary such as the Protecting Power or the ICRC.[61]

2139   As to when notification needs to occur, Article 27(2) clarifies this only as regards the Party to the conflict which accepts the assistance: notification

---

54 This requirement comes in addition to the obligation, for the State accepting the assistance of the recognized society of the neutral country, to consent to receive this society's services; see Article 27(1).

55 The 'adversary of the State which accepts such assistance' (the term used in Article 27(2)) is not the enemy of the neutral country. The latter wording appeared in an earlier version of the text, but was modified accordingly by the 1947 Conference of Government Experts; see *Report of the Conference of Government Experts of 1947*, p. 36.

56 *Minutes of the Conference of Government Experts of 1947*, Committee I, Vol. II, Tome 1, p. 165.

57 ICRC, *Report of the Conference of Government Experts of 1947*, p. 36. See also ICRC, *Report on the Interpretation, Revision and Extension of the Geneva Convention of July 27, 1929*, Report prepared for the 26th International Conference of the Red Cross, London, 1938, pp. 16–17.

58 *Minutes of the Conference of Government Experts of 1947*, Committee I, Vol. II, Tome 1, pp. 166–169.

59 On this point, see Hutchinson, pp. 197–198: 'Article 11 [of the 1906 Geneva Convention], with its requirement that neutral assistance receive a double authorization, seemed designed to limit rather than encourage participation in wars by the Red Cross societies of neutral countries.'

60 Doing so may be particularly relevant in the event that persons covered by Article 27 fall into the hands of another neutral country. On the basis of Article 4, the latter will need to apply Article 32.

61 It has been reported that this was done prior to the Second World War; see ICRC, *Report on the Interpretation, Revision, and Extension of the Geneva Convention of July 27, 1929*, submitted by the ICRC to the 26th International Conference of the Red Cross, London, 1938, p. 16.

needs to occur 'before [the said Party] mak[es] any use of' the assistance. The time frame is left unaddressed as far as notification by the neutral country is concerned. In practice, it would seem advisable for the latter also to provide notification before the Party to the conflict which receives the recognized society's assistance makes use thereof.[62]

2140   Article 27 recognizes the right of a State to supplement its medical services with the aid of a recognized society of a neutral country. It requires the adversary to be notified of this but does not foresee any other action or reaction by the adversary in this process.[63]

2141   The First Convention does not specify the consequences if only one of the notifications takes place, or if neither does. If the neutral Power does not comply with the notification requirement before the Party to the conflict which accepts such assistance makes use of it, the medical personnel and units of the neutral country's recognized society are formally not entitled to the status of protected persons or objects within the meaning of the First Convention. In that case, indeed, the adversary of the State which accepts such assistance cannot be certain that the neutral country actually approves of its recognized society's acting on the basis of Article 27.[64] This will be so even if the Party to the conflict which accepts such assistance has, for its part, complied with the notification requirement applicable to it.[65] On the other hand, while the medical personnel and units are, in that case, not persons specifically protected under the First Convention, their status remains that of neutral civilians, and they must protected as such.

2142   If the State which receives the neutral society's assistance fails to notify its own adversary before making use of such aid, the adversary will still be required to treat the neutral society's personnel and units in accordance with Article 27, provided that all the other conditions of Article 27 have been met. This includes the requirement for the neutral government to have notified the adversary of the State which accepts the assistance of its consent, as well as the requirement for the personnel and units to be placed under the control of that State. If all the other conditions of Article 27 are complied with, the adversary of the State which accepts the assistance would indeed be acting in bad faith to invoke the absence of notification as a reason to deny these medical personnel and units the protection to which they are entitled under the First Convention.

---

[62] For a discussion of the time frame, see the commentary on Article 26, para. 2070.

[63] See *Proceedings of the Geneva Diplomatic Conference of 1906*, pp. 115, 125 and 255. See also *Minutes of the Conference of Government Experts of 1947*, Committee I, Vol. II, Tome 1, p. 165.

[64] For a further indication that States wished to make sure that the neutral country formally approved of the assistance, and details on the unsuccessful proposal at the 1929 Diplomatic Conference with regard to spontaneously offered help, see paras 2113–2115.

[65] In this respect, Article 27 is more stringent than Article 26, see the commentary on Article 26, para. 2072.

E. Paragraph 3: Humanitarian nature of the activity

2143 Article 27(3) has its origin in the work of the Commission of Experts convened by the ICRC in 1937 to discuss the revision of the 1929 Geneva Convention. Legally speaking, the fact that a recognized society of a neutral Power assists the medical services of a Party to the conflict cannot be considered a violation of the applicable rules of the law of neutrality. The same holds true for the neutral Power which has given its consent for this.[66]

2144 In practice, however, the perception may be different, as demonstrated by the reactions to some of the few instances in which neutral societies have lent their assistance.[67] Article 27(3) therefore makes it clear that these perceptions are without any legal value.

2145 The provision of medical personnel and units to the medical services of a Party to a conflict is, indeed, an activity which is purely humanitarian in nature.[68] This observation also holds true when the recognized society provides its medical personnel and units to only one of the Parties to the conflict. Nothing in Article 27, nor in international law applicable to international armed conflicts, compels a recognized society of a neutral country, or the neutral country itself, to balance or supplement the aid given by a recognized society to only one side of a conflict through aid given by another (or by the same) society to the other side of the conflict.

2146 Lastly, it needs to be kept in mind that National Societies must comply with the Fundamental Principles of the Movement.[69] Their giving assistance to one Party to an armed conflict – which is prompted by purely humanitarian motives, i.e. the desire to reduce the suffering of the wounded and sick – must not be misunderstood as a violation of the Fundamental Principle of neutrality: by doing so, they do not take sides in the conflict.[70] For National Societies,

---

[66] For a discussion of the law of neutrality, see the commentary on Article 4, section A.

[67] See ICRC, *Report on the Interpretation, Revision and Extension of the Geneva Convention of July 27, 1929*, Report prepared for the 26th International Conference of the Red Cross, London, 1938, p. 17. See also *Minutes of the Preliminary Conference of National Societies of 1946*, Vol. I, pp. 86–87. See also *Minutes of the Conference of Government Experts of 1947*, Committee I, Vol. II, Tome 1, p. 165. Similarly, see Lanord, 1999, pp. 67–68.

[68] As far as the National Societies are concerned, see International Federation of Red Cross and Red Crescent Societies, *National Red Cross and Red Crescent Societies as auxiliaries to the public authorities in the humanitarian field*, 2003, p. 25. For further details, see the commentary on Article 26, para. 2095. See also United States, *Law of War Manual*, 2015, paras 15.5.2.1 and 15.6.2.2.

[69] For a discussion of the Fundamental Principles' normative weight, and their impact on the ability of a National Red Cross or Red Crescent Society to act on the basis of Article 26, see the commentary on Article 26, paras 2088–2089. When a National Society acts on the basis of Article 27, the Movement's agreed coordination rules do not apply; see the commentary on Article 26, para. 2093. In particular, the recommendation as a matter of good practice to notify, if this has not already been done as part of the preceding agreement, the 'host' National Society prior to any activities on the basis of Article 26, applies in even stronger terms in the scenario envisioned by Article 27.

[70] See the commentary on Article 26, para. 2089.

therefore, Article 27(3) underscores the idea that acting on the basis of Article 27 does not violate the principle of neutrality.[71]

2147   Furthermore, as indicated above, the members of a neutral State's National Society assisting the medical services of the armed forces of a Party to the conflict must treat all wounded and sick persons, regardless of the Party to the conflict to which they belong, in line with the Fundamental Principle of impartiality, namely without any adverse distinction, 'guided solely by their needs' and giving 'priority to the most urgent cases'.[72] This should not be problematic, in that the military medical service they are assisting is, for its part, bound by the same standards under the First Convention.[73]

2148   Recognized societies that are not components of the Movement are not bound to comply with the Movement's Fundamental Principles, nor with any of its other internal rules. However, since the activities referred to in Article 25 of the First Convention are of a humanitarian nature,[74] these societies will, as a matter of fact, most likely wish to comply with the principles of humanitarian action as they apply to such activities in time of armed conflict, and as equally reflected in certain rules of international law (for example, in Article 12 of the First Convention).[75]

F. Paragraph 4: Identity cards

2149   Article 40 of the First Convention prescribes the means by which persons covered by Article 27 are to be identified.[76] These are a water-resistant armlet bearing the distinctive emblem (Article 40(1)), an identity disc, and a special identity card bearing the distinctive emblem (Article 40(2) and (3)). In respect of the special identity card, Article 27(4) stipulates that the persons covered by Article 27 need to be furnished with these cards before leaving the neutral country to which they belong. The cards in question are to be issued by the military authority of the Party to the conflict to which these personnel will provide assistance and not by the neutral country, or by the recognized society. This authority will therefore need to find a way to make sure that the persons covered by Article 27 receive the special identity card before they leave the neutral country.

---

[71] The Fundamental Principle of neutrality reads: 'In order to continue to enjoy the confidence of all, the Movement may not take sides in hostilities or engage at any time in controversies of a political, racial, religious or ideological nature.'

[72] See the definition of the Fundamental Principle of impartiality in the preamble to the 1986 Statutes of the International Red Cross and Red Crescent Movement.

[73] See Article 12.

[74] For a discussion of the concept 'activities of a humanitarian nature', see the commentary on Article 9, section C.2.a.

[75] For a discussion of these principles, see the commentary on Article 9, para. 1138.

[76] As to the identification of the medical units covered by Article 27, see Article 43.

2150   This paragraph originates in an incident during the Second World War. When members of the 'American Voluntary Ambulance Corps' were on their way to assist the British and French medical services, they were captured by the German armed forces on the grounds that they did not have proper identification cards proving that they intended to serve on the basis of Article 11 of the 1929 Geneva Convention. In light of this experience, it was felt that persons covered by Article 27 needed to receive their identity cards prior to leaving the neutral country,[77] and not just prior to any active employment.[78] Thus, the US delegation at the 1947 Conference of Government Experts proposed the text of what is now Article 27(4).[79] The advantage of this provision is that, if the persons covered by Article 27 fall into the hands of the adversary of the Party they will be assisting prior to reaching that Party's armed forces, their status will be clearly defined.[80]

Select bibliography

See the select bibliography of the commentary on Article 26 of the First Convention.

---

[77] *Minutes of the Diplomatic Conference of Geneva of 1949*, Committee I, Vol. I, 11 May 1949.

[78] For a discussion of this paragraph, see *ICRC Remarks and Proposals on the 1948 Stockholm Draft*, p. 13, and *Minutes of the Diplomatic Conference of Geneva of 1949*, Committee I, Vol. I, 11 May 1949.

[79] *Minutes of the Conference of Government Experts of 1947*, Committee I, Vol. II, Tome 1, p. 164. At the 1947 Conference of Government Experts, the proposal was adopted without any substantive discussion.

[80] *Final Record of the Diplomatic Conference of Geneva of 1949*, Vol. II-A, p. 194. When persons covered by Article 27 fall into the hands of the adversary of the Party they are assisting, Article 32 applies.

RETAINED PERSONNEL

❖ Text of the provision*

(1) Personnel designated in Articles 24 and 26 who fall into the hands of the adverse Party, shall be retained only in so far as the state of health, the spiritual needs and the number of prisoners of war require.

(2) Personnel thus retained shall not be deemed prisoners of war. Nevertheless they shall at least benefit by all the provisions of the Geneva Convention relative to the Treatment of Prisoners of War of 12 August 1949. Within the framework of the military laws and regulations of the Detaining Power, and under the authority of its competent service, they shall continue to carry out, in accordance with their professional ethics, their medical and spiritual duties on behalf of prisoners of war, preferably those of the armed forces to which they themselves belong. They shall further enjoy the following facilities for carrying out their medical or spiritual duties:

(a) They shall be authorized to visit periodically the prisoners of war in labour units or hospitals outside the camp. The Detaining Power shall put at their disposal the means of transport required.

(b) In each camp the senior medical officer of the highest rank shall be responsible to the military authorities of the camp for the professional activity of the retained medical personnel. For this purpose, from the outbreak of hostilities, the Parties to the conflict shall agree regarding the corresponding seniority of the ranks of their medical personnel, including those of the societies designated in Article 26. In all questions arising out of their duties, this medical officer, and the chaplains, shall have direct access to the military and medical authorities of the camp who shall grant them the facilities they may require for correspondence relating to these questions.

(c) Although retained personnel in a camp shall be subject to its internal discipline, they shall not, however, be required to perform any work outside their medical or religious duties.

---

* Paragraph numbers have been added for ease of reference.

(3) During hostilities the Parties to the conflict shall make arrangements for relieving where possible retained personnel, and shall settle the procedure of such relief.

(4) None of the preceding provisions shall relieve the Detaining Power of the obligations imposed upon it with regard to the medical and spiritual welfare of the prisoners of war.

❖ Reservations or declarations

None

Contents

A. Introduction

2151 Article 28 is the centrepiece of the regime for the retention of military medical and religious personnel (covered by Article 24) and staff of voluntary aid societies employed on the same duties (covered by Article 26) in international armed conflicts. Retention is contemplated as an exception to the rule, set out in Article 30, requiring the return of such personnel to the Party to the conflict to which they belong. The special treatment to which qualifying personnel are entitled under this provision is designed to ensure that prisoners of war receive the necessary medical and spiritual care.

2152 The regulation of retention is informed by a balance between competing considerations. On the one hand, the captivity of such personnel hampers the mission of the medical and religious services of their own armed forces, which is to care for the wounded and sick wherever and whenever needed.[1] It is therefore in the interest of the home State to have medical and religious personnel returned as soon as possible. On the other hand, it is equally in the interest of the home State to have prisoners of war from its armed forces cared for by its own medical and religious personnel. However, for this to be possible, the retained personnel must be able to continue to fulfil their medical and religious tasks and not be employed on other duties. In addition, the retention of medical and religious personnel must not become a substitute for the obligation of a Detaining Power to provide for the medical and spiritual welfare of prisoners of war. If the Detaining Power discharges its responsibilities fully towards prisoners of war, there is likely to be no need to exercise the right of retention.

2153   Article 28 sets forth the conditions under which retention is permissible. It also clarifies the status of retained personnel, their role, and the treatment and facilities to which they are entitled. The provision needs to be viewed in conjunction with Articles 30 and 31 of the First Convention, which regulate the return of medical and religious personnel and allow for the possibility of concluding special agreements with regard to their retention. Further, the parts of Article 28 pertaining to the status, treatment and facilities due to retained medical personnel and chaplains are reaffirmed almost verbatim in Article 33 of the Third Convention.[2]

2154   The retention of medical and religious personnel proved to be a contentious issue during the negotiations of the First Convention. However, in contrast to the Second World War, when belligerent Parties retained large numbers of enemy medical personnel over extended periods of time,[3] such practice today is rare.[4] Accordingly, while the provisions governing retention – with Article 28 at their core – remain applicable and relevant to the issue, the number of international armed conflicts in which they have been called upon to play a role has decreased over time.

2155   It appears that the retention regime provided for in the Geneva Conventions, which rests on the principle that medical and religious personnel may not be retained unless the state of health, the spiritual needs and the number of prisoners of war so require, has not been applied by analogy in non-international

---

[1] Bugnion, p. 472: 'For medical personnel to be able to do their job properly it is not enough to protect them against the hazards of battle; the belligerents must also refrain from obstructing their work. The most common impediment of all, and the most likely to bring the work of medical services to a standstill, is captivity. If doctors, medical orderlies, and nurses are thrown into camps and fortresses pell-mell with prisoners of war, they can do nothing for the wounded lying on the field of battle.'

[2] The main differences between the two articles are analysed below; see sections D.2, D.3 and D.4.b. However, these have no substantive implications. See also Sigrid Mehring, *First Do No Harm: Medical Ethics in International Humanitarian Law*, Brill, Boston, 2014, p. 111, fn. 163.

[3] See Pictet (ed.), *Commentary on the First Geneva Convention*, ICRC, 1952, p. 237.

[4] For examples, see Bugnion, p. 478.

armed conflicts. Accordingly, Parties to a non-international armed conflict are under no legal obligation to set captured medical or religious personnel free.[5]

B. Historical background

2156 The legal regulation of the retention of medical and religious personnel has evolved considerably over time. Article 3 of the 1864 Geneva Convention provided that:

> [Medical and religious personnel] may, even after enemy occupation, continue to discharge their functions in the hospital or ambulance with which they serve, or may withdraw to rejoin the units to which they belong. When in these circumstances they cease from their functions, such persons shall be delivered to the enemy outposts by the occupying forces.

The provision led commentators to conclude that Parties to an armed conflict had no unilateral right to retain such personnel.[6]

2157 The 1906 Geneva Convention addressed the subject of retention for the first time in its Article 12, which is a rudimentary precursor of the current rule inasmuch as it contemplated the retention of medical personnel who were to 'continue in the exercise of their functions, under the direction of the enemy, after they ha[d] fallen into his power' for as long as their assistance was indispensable, after which they were to be 'sent back to their army or country'.[7] The rule in the 1929 Geneva Convention on the Wounded and Sick was based on the contrary assumption, namely the principle of return of medical and religious personnel to the Party to which they belong.[8] Belligerents were allowed to abrogate from this rule by way of special agreements on the retention of medical personnel.[9] In the absence of such an agreement, retained personnel were to be sent back to the belligerent to which they belonged 'as soon as a route for their return shall be open and military considerations permit'.[10] However, pending their return, retained medical personnel were to 'continue to carry out their duties under the direction of the enemy' and 'preferably be engaged in the care of the wounded and sick of the belligerent to which they belong'.[11]

---

[5] In this vein, see also Bugnion, p. 473.

[6] *Ibid.* p. 472: 'The 1864 Conference (Art. 3) settled the issue in the clearest possible way: it ruled that medical personnel were not to be taken prisoner; that even under enemy occupation, they must be freely able to continue their work of tending the wounded and sick; and that when their care was no longer required they were to be handed over to the outposts of their own armed forces.'

[7] See also Article 17(2) of the 1906 Geneva Convention pertaining to convoys of evacuation, which reaffirmed 'the obligation to return the sanitary personnel' when their assistance was no longer indispensable.

[8] See Geneva Convention on the Wounded and Sick (1929), Article 12(1).

[9] See *ibid.* Articles 12(2) and 14(4).   [10] See *ibid.* Article 12(2).

[11] *Ibid.* Article 12(3). For an analysis of the provision, see Des Gouttes, *Commentaire de la Convention de Genève de 1929 sur les blessés et malades*, ICRC, 1930, pp. 72–86.

2158   A number of special agreements of the type envisaged in the 1929 Convention were concluded during the Second World War. However, the Convention did not prescribe the procedure to be followed or the treatment and conditions of work to be accorded to retained medical personnel. Belligerents subjected such personnel to the same conditions of captivity as prisoners of war, in some cases considered them as such, and often made them engage in work of a non-medical nature.[12] The ICRC argued against such an equation in terms of their status and treatment.[13] As regards their status, the ICRC's position had a clear basis in two legal precursors, the 1906 and 1929 Geneva Conventions, both of which stipulated that medical personnel who fell into enemy hands were not to be treated as prisoners of war.[14] As regards their treatment, the ICRC pointed out the need for additional privileges and facilities enabling retained medical personnel to carry out their duties.[15] While this request was fully in line with the underlying rationale of retaining medical personnel, it did not have a basis in law at the time.

2159   The retention of medical and religious personnel proved to be one of the most divisive issues during the drafting of the 1949 Geneva Conventions.[16] While agreement on the permissibility of retaining medical personnel was reached relatively soon, a lively discussion continued for several years on the subject of the status of retained personnel.[17] The view of a group of States that retained medical and religious personnel should be treated as prisoners of war was opposed by other States and the ICRC, which were of the opinion that such personnel should be entitled not only to a special status that would confirm their inviolable character as non-combatants but also to a number of privileges and facilities that would allow them to perform their duties efficiently. The discussions eventually culminated in a compromise, largely based on a draft approved by the International Conference of the Red Cross held in Stockholm in 1948, which provided that retained medical and religious personnel should not be considered prisoners of war, while at least benefiting from all the provisions of the Third Convention, as well as from a number of privileges and facilities necessary to the performance of their medical and spiritual duties.[18]

2160   The controversy surrounding the drafting of Article 28 meant that the provision as adopted lacked detail in certain respects. States decided to leave unanswered some of the specifics of the retention regime, such as the ratios between certain types of medical personnel and the number of prisoners of war, and did

---

[12] Vollmar, p. 746.
[13] *Report of the Preliminary Conference of National Societies of 1946*, p. 32.
[14] See Article 9 of both Conventions.
[15] *Report of the Preliminary Conference of National Societies of 1946*, pp. 32–33.
[16] See also Paul de La Pradelle, *La Conférence diplomatique et les nouvelles Conventions de Genève du 12 août 1949*, Les Éditions internationales, Paris, 1951, pp. 114–133.
[17] For an illustration of these discussions and the arguments on both sides, see e.g. the statements made by States during the 1949 Diplomatic Conference, *Final Record of the Diplomatic Conference of Geneva of 1949*, Vol. II-A, pp. 67–71.
[18] *Draft Conventions adopted by the 1948 Stockholm Conference*, draft article 22.

not include details of the relief of retained medical and religious personnel. Instead, the 1949 Diplomatic Conference adopted Resolution 3 entitled 'Preparation of a Model Agreement on the Percentage and Relief of Retained Personnel', requesting the ICRC 'to prepare a model agreement' on the topics of both Articles 28 and 31 of the First Convention, although it was understood that the Model Agreement would not be legally binding.[19] In the same resolution, the ICRC was further requested 'to submit [the Model Agreement] to the High Contracting Parties for their approval'. Resolution 3 resulted in the publication by the ICRC in 1955 of two Model Agreements, one relating to the retention of medical and religious personnel, the other to the relief of such personnel.[20] The same year, the ICRC circulated paper copies of the Model Agreements, accompanied by a commentary, to the Permanent Missions in Geneva, as well as to National Red Cross and Red Crescent Societies. The sole substantive comments received in response were from the United Kingdom, which objected to a number of deviations in the Model Agreements from the original text of the First Convention.[21]

2161   Academic writings in the early years after the adoption of Article 28 display a certain degree of dissatisfaction with the compromise reached. Some commentators lamented the provision's resulting lack of precision. For instance, Article 28 stipulates that, although not deemed prisoners of war, retained medical personnel 'shall at least benefit by all the provisions' of the Third Convention, without specifying which of those provisions are to be considered beneficial, as opposed to detrimental.[22]

C. Paragraph 1: Scope of application

2162 Article 28 applies only to the personnel designated in Articles 24 and 26, i.e. medical and religious personnel attached to the armed forces, and staff of duly

---

[19] As to the intended non-binding nature of the model agreement, see *Final Record of the Diplomatic Conference of Geneva of 1949*, Vol. II-A, p. 170.

[20] ICRC, *The Retention and Relief of Medical Personnel and Chaplains: Model Agreements*, ICRC Doc. D306/2b, 1955.

[21] The most notable inconsistencies between the First Convention and the Model Agreements pointed out by the United Kingdom were: (a) Article 1(1) of the Model Agreement Relating to the Retention of Medical Personnel and Chaplains provides that retained personnel may only 'carry out their duties on behalf of prisoners of war of the armed forces to which they themselves belong', whereas Article 28 contains no such restriction; (b) Article 1(2) of the same Model Agreement stipulates that the staff of National Red Cross and Red Crescent Societies and of other voluntary aid societies 'may only be retained at their own express wish', whereas Article 28 does not require such consent; (c) Article 8 of the same Model Agreement restricts the possibility of transferring retained medical and religious personnel to situations where 'such personnel accompany prisoners of war who have already been in their care and are being transferred under the circumstances provided for in Article 12 of the Third Convention, and only in so far as such care cannot be provided by medical personnel of the new Detaining Power', a restriction that cannot be deduced from Article 28; and (d) Article 5 of the Model Agreement Relating to the Relief of Medical Personnel and Chaplains unduly subjects them to the military laws and regulations of the Retaining Power, in contravention of Article 28.

[22] See e.g. Schoenholzer, pp. 173–174, and Lauterpacht, p. 380. See also, later, Pictet, 1985, p. 203.

recognized and authorized voluntary aid societies employed on the same duties. The status and treatment of other personnel who fall into enemy hands, in particular the staff of voluntary aid societies of neutral States referred to in Article 27 and the auxiliary medical personnel referred to in Article 25, are regulated in separate provisions.[23]

2163   The retention regime is applicable when the personnel designated in Articles 24 and 26 'fall into the hands of the adverse Party'. Article 14 of the First Convention similarly uses the phrase 'fall into enemy hands' in respect of the wounded and sick.[24] Despite the almost identical wording, there are different underlying assumptions in the two cases: pursuant to Article 15 of the First Convention, the Parties to the conflict have an obligation to search for and collect the wounded and sick; a similar duty or, for that matter, a right to search for medical and religious personnel is absent from Article 28, reflecting the incidental nature of their capture and possible subsequent retention. While nothing would prevent the Parties to an international armed conflict from holding, until their status has been determined, medical and religious personnel encountered during the capture or surrender of enemy troops, it would be incompatible with that incidental nature if these Parties were to search actively for such personnel in order to retain them or, to put it otherwise, to engage in a 'medical hunt'.[25] The 'adverse Party' may not be the only one called upon to implement Article 28: where persons covered by Articles 24 or 26 are on the territory of a neutral Power, the latter must apply Article 28 (and its related provisions in Articles 30 and 31) by analogy.[26]

2164   Retention is contemplated as an exception to the rule of return of captured medical and religious personnel to the Party to the conflict to which they belong. This is clear from the phrasing of the first paragraph: 'Personnel . . . shall be retained *only* in so far as' (emphasis added). It is further confirmed by the regulatory context in which Article 28 operates: Articles 30 and 31 provide in detail for the return of personnel 'whose retention is not indispensable by virtue of the provisions of Article 28'. Unless the conditions laid down in Article 28 are met, medical and religious personnel have to be returned in accordance with Articles 30 and 31. In other words, while it is not unlawful *per se* to retain medical and religious personnel, their retention is conditioned on certain requirements.

2165   First and foremost, medical and religious personnel can only be retained for the benefit of prisoners of war. Accordingly, retention would be impermissible if the Power retaining medical or religious personnel is not also a Detaining Power in the technical sense of the Third Convention, i.e. a State Party to an

---

[23] See Articles 32 and 29, respectively.

[24] For an explanation of this notion, see the commentary on Article 14, section C.3.

[25] Pictet (ed.), *Commentary on the First Geneva Convention*, ICRC, 1952, p. 242.

[26] See Article 4, and, importantly, the commentary on that provision at para. 937. See also United States, *Law of War Manual*, 2015, para. 15.16.6.

international armed conflict into whose hands the persons designated in Article 4 of the Third Convention have fallen. This excludes the possibility not only of any 'anticipatory' retention of medical and religious personnel,[27] but also of their retention for the benefit of civilians (unless the civilians in question have prisoner-of-war status).[28] Second, the state of health, the spiritual needs and the number of prisoners of war must require it. As indicated by the use of the word 'require', along with the word 'indispensable' in Article 30(1), the possibility of retaining medical and religious personnel is contingent on meeting a stringent threshold of necessity.[29]

2166   The state of health, the spiritual needs and the number of prisoners of war are inherently context specific. Therefore, the extent to which retention is lawful cannot be determined in the abstract. For instance, the retention of religious personnel may be called for if the Detaining Power's own religious personnel and the prisoners of war are of different faiths, as it would be inappropriate in such a case for the Detaining Power to make its own religious personnel available.[30] Another scenario would be an increase in the need for medical and religious personnel following the capture of a large number of prisoners of war, many of whom may be wounded. Conversely, during a later phase of an armed conflict, the need for retained medical and religious personnel may decrease. In all instances, the situation may evolve to the point where the initial condition for allowing retention may no longer exist, with the legal consequence that retention is no longer permissible. In that case, the right to retain medical and religious personnel will be superseded by the obligation to return them.[31] In any

---

[27] See also Article 5(1) of the Model Agreement Relating to the Retention of Medical Personnel and Chaplains: 'The number of personnel and chaplains liable to be retained, as determined by the foregoing provisions, shall be considered as a maximum, and shall not be exceeded in order to provide for *possible needs arising from the capture, at a later date, of enemy military personnel, or on any other pretext.*' (Emphasis added.) This is subject to the two limited exceptions stipulated in Article 5(2) of the Model Agreement pertaining to the retention of surplus personnel to replace personnel who have been retained for more than one year; and in Article 6 of the Model Agreement pertaining to the increase of the number of retained chaplains by way of mutual agreement between the belligerent Parties.

[28] See Third Convention, Article 4(A)(4)–(5).

[29] See also the commentary on Article 30, para. 2228.

[30] The context-specific nature of these equations is also reflected in the Model Agreement; see e.g. Article 6, allowing the Parties to the conflict to 'agree mutually, in the course of hostilities, to increase the number of chaplains to be retained, should this be necessary, and in the case of a Detaining Power not having ministers of the religion practised by the prisoners, among its own nationals'. Indeed, the retention of religious personnel would facilitate compliance with the obligation of Parties to an international armed conflict to grant prisoners of war 'complete latitude in the exercise of their religious duties', in accordance with Article 34 of the Third Convention.

[31] See Article 30 on the return of medical and religious personnel and Article 31 on the selection of personnel for return. See also Articles 109–117 of the Third Convention on direct repatriation of seriously wounded and sick persons and their accommodation in neutral countries, which may have an impact on the medical and spiritual needs in a prisoner-of-war camp. See, further, Odom, p. 29: 'Likewise, the stated length of such retention of chaplains is not for a set period of time or for the duration of the armed conflict like POWs [prisoners of war]. Instead, the term of their retention is conditionally based upon the "necessity" or "need" for their religious

event, the Detaining Power has to assess in good faith the factual circumstances surrounding the need for retention.

2167   According to Article 31(2) of the First Convention, the proportion of retained medical and religious personnel to prisoners of war and their distribution in prisoner-of-war camps may be the subject of a special agreement between the Parties to the conflict. In this respect, Article 2 of the Model Agreement Relating to the Retention of Medical Personnel and Chaplains suggests some possible ratios between different types of medical and religious personnel, such as general practitioners, specialists, dentists, nurses and chaplains, on the one hand, and the number of prisoners of war, on the other hand.[32] The suggested ratios are a clear reflection of the state of medical and social affairs at the time. From a contemporary perspective, the Model Agreement is conspicuously silent, for instance, on the specific needs of female prisoners of war,[33] whose medical care may differ in some respects from those of male prisoners. For example, it fails to take account of the need for gynaecologists. Furthermore, the Model Agreement is a reflection of the resources of industrialized States rather than the scarcer resources of less-developed States.

2168   It may be that modern medicine requires different ratios from those proposed in the Model Agreement.[34] Ideally, in order to ensure that different perspectives are identified and addressed in the agreements, negotiations should include persons of different genders and backgrounds.[35] In addition, each Party's available resources must be taken into account. While these factors militate against an abstract determination of universally applicable ratios, certain guiding principles can be drawn from Article 28. First, the ratios must ensure that the care of prisoners of war is both timely and sufficient in quality and quantity

---

services. Therefore, if their retention is "not indispensable," then the Conventions mandate that chaplains be returned to their side of the conflict as soon as practicable.'

[32] See also Article 5 of the Model Agreement, stipulating that the numbers of retained personnel specified in Article 2 of the Model Agreement 'shall be considered as a maximum' and lists the conditions for retaining surplus personnel. See further Article 7 of the Model Agreement on the reduction of these numbers in the light of the retention of auxiliary medical personnel and of prisoners of war who, though not attached to the medical service of their armed forces, are physicians, surgeons, dentists, nurses or medical orderlies and are required by the Detaining Power to exercise their medical functions in accordance with Article 32 of the Third Convention.

[33] These needs are partially reflected in Article 12(4) of the First Convention, as well as in Articles 14(2), 25(4) and 29(2) of the Third Convention. For a very limited exception to the neglect of the special needs of women prisoners of war in the Model Agreement, see Article 4(2) pertaining to the retention of female nurses.

[34] As an illustration, see e.g. United States, *Army Regulation on Enemy Prisoners, Retained Personnel, Civilian Internees and Other Detainees*, 1997, section 3-15(k), providing for a ratio of two physicians, two nurses, one chaplain and seven enlisted medical personnel per 1,000 prisoners of war.

[35] See UN Security Council, Res. 1325, 31 October 2000, para. 1. There is a growing acknowledgement that women, men, girls and boys are affected by armed conflict in different ways, and that, accordingly, the representation of both women and men at all decision-making levels in national, regional and international institutions and mechanisms for conflict prevention, management and resolution benefits the process. The application of international humanitarian law should also reflect this understanding.

to meet their health and spiritual needs. Second, medical care must be provided in accordance with contemporary professional ethics. These ethics are set down in the rules and codes of conduct for health-care professionals, the core elements of which include: respect for the dignity and autonomy of persons deprived of their liberty; avoidance of any action detrimental to the patient; provision of relevant and quality medical care; informed consent; and medical confidentiality.[36] Third, the number of retained personnel must not be excessive, i.e. it must not be more than needed in order to ensure adequate care. In determining that need, retention may not be more than a complement to – as opposed to a substitute for – the Detaining Power's obligation to ensure the medical and spiritual welfare of prisoners of war through its own medical and religious personnel, as confirmed in Article 28(4). Thus, when paragraph 1 stipulates that one of the parameters for determining whether and to what extent retention is permissible is the number of prisoners of war, the Detaining Power's own available medical and religious personnel have to be factored in. Retained medical and religious personnel cannot be relied on as substitutes for them.

2169   If, however, the aforementioned conditions are fulfilled, the right to retain arises. That right can be lawfully exercised in good faith unilaterally by the Detaining Power. The consent of the belligerent Party to which the personnel belongs is not required, nor is the consent of the retained personnel.

D. Paragraph 2: Status and treatment of retained personnel

1. First sentence: Exclusion from prisoner-of-war status

2170   Paragraph 2 begins by specifying that retained personnel shall not be deemed prisoners of war.[37] While thus excluding them from prisoner-of-war status, neither Article 28 nor any of the other related provisions of the Geneva Conventions define in positive terms the status of retained personnel in the way the Third Convention does for prisoners of war[38] or the Fourth Convention does for 'protected persons'.[39] Notwithstanding the absence of such a definition, retained personnel constitute a separate category of persons in enemy hands, subject to distinct regulation.[40]

---

[36] For details, see Additional Protocol I, Article 16.

[37] See also Article 4(C) of the Third Convention: 'This Article [definition of prisoners of war] shall in no way affect the status of medical personnel and chaplains as provided for in Article 33 of the present Convention.'

[38] Third Convention, Article 4.   [39] Fourth Convention, Article 4.

[40] See also Pictet (ed.), *Commentary on the Fourth Geneva Convention*, ICRC, 1958, p. 51: 'Every person in enemy hands must have some status under international law: he is either a prisoner of war and, as such, covered by the Third Convention, a civilian covered by the Fourth Convention, or again, a member of the medical personnel of the armed forces who is covered by the First Convention. *There is no* intermediate status; nobody in enemy hands can be outside the law.'

2171   If a person falls into the hands of the adverse Party and claims the status of medical or religious personnel and, as a consequence, the applicability of the rules on return or retention, as opposed to the regime applicable to prisoners of war, the Detaining Power will have to determine the status of that person if any doubt arises as to the merits of his or her claim. A conceivable example would be if a person claims the status of medical or religious personnel and displays the distinctive emblem on an armlet, but fails to produce an identity disc and/or card, claiming to have lost them, or, if an identity disc and/or card is produced, there are doubts as to their authenticity. An obvious body to make such a determination would be a 'competent tribunal' as foreseen in Article 5(2) of the Third Convention.[41] However, Article 5 does not apply as a matter of law unless the person whose status is unclear has 'committed a belligerent act'. Medical and religious personnel are presumed not to engage in such acts and, indeed, are only allowed to use weapons in their personal defence or for the defence of the wounded and sick in their charge.[42]

2172   It would nevertheless be necessary to determine the status of a person who claimed to fall into the category of retained medical or religious personnel, not least to ensure that a Detaining Power meets its relevant legal obligations, including the return of those whose retention is not indispensable in accordance with Article 30 of the First Convention. Consequently, if the Detaining Power decides not to rely on the competent tribunal foreseen in Article 5(2) of the Third Convention, it would have to adopt an alternative procedure able to make an effective and reliable determination of the person's status.

2173   In the course of this determination, the distinctive emblem on the armlet, the identity disc mentioned in Article 16, and an identity card would be important elements in proving the person's status.[43]

2. Second sentence: Benefit by all the provisions of the Third Convention

2174   Retained personnel, while they do not have prisoner-of-war status, 'shall at least benefit by all the provisions' of the Third Convention. The choice of wording indicates that only those provisions of the Third Convention that are advantageous to retained personnel apply.[44] Article 33 of the Third Convention is even more explicit in this respect, inasmuch as it stipulates that retained personnel 'shall...receive as a minimum the benefits and protection' of the Third Convention. By limiting the applicable rules to those that benefit and

---

[41] See also United States, *Human Intelligence Collector Operations*, 2006, p. vii: 'Persons in the custody of the US Armed Forces who have not been classified as an EPW [enemy prisoner of war] (Article 4, GPW [Third Geneva Convention]), retained personnel (Article 33, GPW), and Civilian Internee (Articles 27, 41, 48, and 78, GC [Fourth Geneva Convention]) shall be treated as EPWs until a legal status is ascertained by competent authority; for example, by Article 5 Tribunal.'

[42] See the commentaries on Article 24, paras 2005–2006, and Article 26, para. 2084.

[43] See Article 40 and its commentary, para. 2581.   [44] Schoenholzer, pp. 173–174.

protect prisoners of war – as opposed to those that may be disadvantageous – Article 33 of the Third Convention confirms that the legally required treatment of retained medical and religious personnel differs from that of prisoners of war. At the same time, there is no substantive difference between the phrase 'shall at least benefit' in the present article and 'shall . . . receive as a minimum the benefits and protection' in Article 33 of the Third Convention. The rules that have an element of 'protection' certainly 'benefit' prisoners of war and therefore retained medical and religious personnel as well.

2175   Entitlement to the benefits and protection of the Third Convention means that retained personnel must at all times be humanely treated and protected, and no reprisals may be taken against them.[45] Retained personnel are entitled in all circumstances to respect for their persons and their honour.[46] Retained female personnel must be treated with all the regard due to their sex and in all cases benefit by treatment as favourable as that granted to men.[47] Captured medical and religious personnel retain the full civil capacity which they enjoyed at the time they fell into the hands of the adverse Party.[48] The Detaining Power must also provide retained personnel free of charge with the necessities of life and the medical attention required by their state of health.[49] Like prisoners of war, retained medical and religious personnel are also entitled to equal treatment: while some differential treatment may be accorded to them on the grounds of their rank, sex, state of health, age or professional qualifications, they may be subject to no (other) adverse distinction.[50]

2176   More concretely, when, for example, retained personnel are questioned in order to ascertain their status, they are bound to give only their 'surname, first names and rank, date of birth, and army, regimental, personal or serial number, or failing this, equivalent information'.[51] Likewise, their personnel effects shall remain in their possession, except arms that they may have carried with them for self-defence or for the defence of the wounded and sick in their charge, horses, military equipment and military documents.[52] In a similar vein, the rules governing the evacuation of prisoners of war also apply to retained personnel.[53]

2177   However, the foregoing are relatively clear-cut examples of beneficial rules, as opposed to rules which neither benefit nor protect. In other cases, determining whether a given (part of a) provision of the Third Convention confers a benefit or a protection to retained personnel can be more complex. Some of the rules on penal and disciplinary sanctions as provided for in Articles 82–108 of the Third Convention may serve as examples. The third sentence of Article 28(2) of the First Convention stipulates that retained personnel shall

---

[45] See Third Convention, Article 13.   [46] See *ibid.* Article 14(1).   [47] See *ibid.* Article 14(2).
[48] See *ibid.* Article 14(3).   [49] See *ibid.* Article 15.   [50] See *ibid.* Article 16.
[51] See *ibid.* Article 17(1).   [52] See *mutatis mutandis* Article 18(1) of the Third Convention.
[53] See *ibid.* Articles 19–20.

continue to carry out, in accordance with their professional ethics, their medical and spiritual duties '[w]ithin the framework of the military laws and regulations of the Detaining Power, and under the authority of its competent service'. Accordingly, retained personnel may be subject to judicial or disciplinary measures in respect of violations of such laws and regulations. While a number of the rules in the Third Convention addressing such sanctions are clearly beneficial,[54] others will not necessarily be. Thus, the determination of whether a provision of the Third Convention constitutes a 'benefit' in the sense of the second sentence of Article 28(2) has to be made on a case-by-case basis by the Detaining Power acting in good faith.

2178   As a general rule, however, all provisions of the Third Convention that enable retained personnel to carry out their medical or spiritual duties for the benefit of prisoners of war and that facilitate those tasks, within the confines of the military laws and regulations of the Detaining Power, are applicable to such personnel.[55] Conversely, provisions of the Third Convention that hamper retained personnel in carrying out their duties are not applicable. Thus, although the liberty of retained personnel may be restricted, they may not be interned in the sense of the Third Convention[56] to the extent that such an internment would interfere with the fulfilment of their medical and spiritual duties. Indeed, as they may be retained only to fulfil these duties, the extent of the restrictions on their liberty will vary according to circumstances and may include less severe restrictions, such as supervision and assigned residence, rather than actual internment in a camp.[57]

2179   Similarly, when the state of health, the spiritual needs and the number of transferred prisoners of war so require, retained medical and religious personnel may be transferred to another Detaining Power along with the prisoners of war, while benefiting from the same safeguards as the prisoners of war.[58] Furthermore, the special provisions relating to retained personnel restrict the work which may be assigned to them to medical and spiritual duties,[59] and thus exclude the provisions in the Third Convention dealing with the assignment of work to prisoners of war and the arrangements connected with it. However, retained personnel will benefit from the provisions on working conditions, rest,

---

[54] Examples are the obligation of the Detaining Power to 'ensure that the competent authorities exercise the greatest leniency and adopt, wherever possible, disciplinary rather than judicial measures' (Article 83 of the Third Convention), and the fair trial guarantees referred to in Articles 84(2) and 86 of the Third Convention.

[55] See also Model Agreement Relating to the Retention of Medical Personnel and Chaplains, Article 11.

[56] On internment of prisoners of war, see Third Convention, Article 21(1).

[57] In this vein, see also Pictet (ed.), *Commentary on the First Geneva Convention*, ICRC, 1952, p. 245. On the notions of 'supervision' and 'assigned residence', see *mutatis mutandis* the commentary on Article 41 of the Fourth Convention.

[58] See Third Convention, Article 12, and Model Agreement Relating to the Retention of Medical Personnel and Chaplains, Article 8.

[59] See section D.3.

pay, etc., in so far as the provisions in question are compatible with the carrying out of their medical or spiritual duties.[60] The aforementioned examples show that a detailed analysis is required in order to identify those rules in the Third Convention that are applicable to retained personnel.

2180   It is equally clear from the wording of paragraph 2 that the Detaining Power is in no way prevented from going beyond the beneficial provisions of the Third Convention, i.e. it may grant retained medical and religious personnel more advantageous treatment. However, practice seems to suggest that Detaining Powers rather treat retained personnel on the same footing as prisoners of war in terms of the benefits and protection they accord.[61]

3. *Third sentence: Continuation of medical or spiritual duties*

2181 The third sentence of Article 28(2) confirms that, although the retention of medical and religious personnel places them in a new environment and under a different authority, their essential work of caring for wounded and sick prisoners of war remains unchanged, and should continue without hindrance. Indeed, the stipulation that retained personnel 'shall continue to carry out ... their medical and spiritual duties on behalf of prisoners of war' constitutes the centrepiece of the retention regime and informs the interpretation of the provision. The expression 'medical and spiritual duties' must be understood in its broadest sense to encompass all work that is intrinsically linked to meeting the medical and spiritual needs of prisoners of war.[62] Thus, for instance, personnel who are engaged in the administration of units and hospitals may be required to continue to carry out the duties assigned to them. In addition, it follows that it is impermissible to retain medical and religious personnel for undertaking other (non-medical and non-spiritual) duties, as explicitly stated in Article 28(2)(c). It also means that the Detaining Power may not interfere with the performance of their duties. Rather, it must facilitate the fulfilment of these duties. Accordingly, the Detaining Power may not deprive retained personnel of, but must provide them with, the required medical equipment. Similarly, while Article 18 of the Third Convention allows prisoners of war only to keep certain 'effects and articles of personal use', retained personnel are entitled to keep all articles and equipment needed for their professional use.

2182   Several provisions of the Model Agreement specify how this underlying principle pertains to specific categories of medical personnel, including

---

[60] For further details, see Article 49–57 of the Third Convention. See also Article 9 of the Model Agreement on working pay.

[61] See e.g. United States, *Army Regulation on Enemy Prisoners, Retained Personnel, Civilian Internees and Other Detainees*, 1997, pp. 14–15.

[62] Vollmar, p. 746: '[T]he term "medical duties" must be interpreted broadly to include such work as administration and upkeep of a hospital or clinic in which the medical personnel are working.'

specialists[63] and female nurses.[64] Conversely, the text says they 'shall continue...their duties'. This has been interpreted as implying that persons initially covered by Article 28 yet who refuse to perform such duties 'would not be entitled to retained personnel status'.[65] Where such a refusal takes place even when all the conditions of Article 28 have been complied with, the persons in question will be entitled to prisoner-of-war status.

2183   Once the personnel are retained, their medical and spiritual duties will be carried out under the laws and military regulations of the Detaining Power and under the authority of its competent services.[66] The Detaining Power, being responsible for the state of health of all prisoners of war in its hands,[67] retains full powers of direction and control. The retained personnel whose help it receives are therefore absorbed, as it were, into the larger organization of the Detaining Power, and are subject in their work to the same rules as the regular staff in matters relating to the exercise of their profession. The medical personnel will naturally be placed under the authority of the medical services of the Detaining Power, while religious personnel will come under the same service as that to which the religious personnel of the Detaining Power are attached.

2184   The Convention nevertheless tempers this rule by specifying that medical and religious personnel are to carry out their duties 'in accordance with their professional ethics'. Article 33 of the Third Convention refers instead to 'their professional etiquette', a phrase that is substantively identical. It has been stated that the 'captor's authority ends where questions of medical ethics begin'.[68] Of importance to note is that 'their' professional ethics refers to the ethics of the medical and religious personnel themselves, which are not necessarily identical to those of the retaining power.[69] A central element of the professional ethics of medical personnel is their complete clinical independence in deciding upon the treatment of persons in their care.[70] Thus, a doctor may not be prevented from treating a sick person, or obliged to adopt a certain treatment, although some restrictions to clinical freedom may emanate from factors such as a limited choice of medications or the need to respect standard protocols on the diagnosis and treatment of particular conditions (such as communicable diseases, including tuberculosis and HIV). With regard to the 'professional ethics' of religious personnel, Article 35 of the Third Convention requires that

---

[63] See Article 3(2) of the Model Agreement.   [64] See Article 4 of the Model Agreement.
[65] See United States, Law of War Manual, 2015, paras 4.9.2.3 and 7.9.4.
[66] See also paragraph 2(c) of this article, stating that retained personnel in a camp shall be subject to its internal discipline.
[67] See Third Convention, Article 15.   [68] Vollmar, p. 746.
[69] Of note also is that the French version of Article 28 uses the term 'conscience professionnelle', which introduces a more subjective element; see Sigrid Mehring, 'The Rights and Duties of Physicians in Armed Conflict', Militair Rechtelijk Tijdschrift, Vol. 103, No. 5, 2010, pp. 205–221, at 217–218.
[70] See e.g. World Medical Association, Declaration of Tokyo – Guidelines for Physicians Concerning Torture and other Cruel, Inhuman or Degrading Treatment or Punishment in Relation to Detention and Imprisonment, 2006. See also Article 16 of Additional Protocol I.

they be allowed to minister to the prisoners of war 'in accordance with their religious conscience'.

2185   The text also provides that the prisoners of war on whose behalf retained personnel are to carry out their duties should preferably be 'those of the armed forces to which they themselves belong'.[71] The recommendatory language indicates that it is permissible to retain medical and religious personnel also for the care of prisoners of war of the armed forces of other Parties to the conflict. However, the provision reflects a clear preference of States for prisoners of war to be cared for by medical and religious personnel of their own armed forces, who, for instance, speak the same language and use familiar treatment methods, on the assumption that under these conditions medical care might be better accepted and yield better results. At the same time, the carrying out of medical and spiritual duties for members of the armed forces to which retained personnel themselves belong must not conflict with the principle of non-discrimination which informs the entire regime of care for the wounded and sick[72] or with professional ethics. It would be impermissible to grant preferential treatment to wounded and sick prisoners of war of the armed forces to which retained personnel themselves belong if they are in less urgent need of medical assistance and care than those belonging to other armed forces.

4. Fourth sentence: Facilities for carrying out medical or spiritual duties

2186   The fourth sentence of Article 28(2) sets out the additional facilities which are to be accorded to retained personnel.[73] The wording that retained personnel 'shall further' enjoy the facilities listed – over and above the benefits and protections conferred by the Third Convention – entails that the application of beneficial provisions of the Third Convention to retained personnel is subsidiary to the application of the provisions of the present article relating to retained personnel specifically, even if these provisions are similar to those in the Third Convention. In other words, if a given facility is regulated specifically in Article 28(2), fourth sentence, but the matter is also addressed in a provision of the Third Convention either in a more generic or in a conflicting fashion, the special provisions relating to retained personnel take precedence. Thus, the restriction of work of retained personnel to their medical or religious duties in Article 28(2)(c) takes precedence over Articles 49 and 50 of the Third Convention, which identify certain types of work for which a Detaining Power may utilize prisoners of war 'with a view particularly to maintaining them in a good state of physical and mental health' (and in that sense constituting a 'benefit').

[71] See also the same logic at play in Article 30(3) of the Third Convention.
[72] See Article 12(2) and (3).
[73] See also the additional facilities granted to retained religious personnel by virtue of Article 35 of the Third Convention.

2187   The purpose of the additional facilities foreseen in the fourth sentence of Article 28(2) is to support retained personnel in carrying out their medical or spiritual duties. These facilities thus further underline the rationale of granting medical and religious personnel special status, namely to enable them to carry out their duties under the best possible conditions, and not of according them privileges as individuals. The ultimate justification for their privileged status is the good of the prisoners of war for whose benefit they work.

a. Periodic visits to labour units or hospitals outside the camp

2188   The first facility accorded to retained personnel, in addition to the self-evident right to visit prisoners of war inside a camp, is the right, under sub-paragraph (a), to make periodic visits to prisoners of war in labour units (for instance to conduct the periodic assessments to verify that the prisoners of war are fit for work)[74] or in hospitals outside the camp, and to have the necessary transport for that purpose. The Detaining Power is free to exercise such supervision over these journeys as it considers necessary, and will decide if the circumstances call for an escort or not. Retained personnel cannot misuse the right so conferred on them: they are only entitled to leave the camp and travel in order to visit prisoners entrusted to their care or in need of their services.

b. Senior medical officer responsible to the military authorities of the camp

2189   Under sub-paragraph (b), 'the senior medical officer of the highest rank shall be responsible to the military authorities of the camp for the professional activity of the retained medical personnel'. That medical officer is automatically selected according to his or her highest rank amongst the retained medical personnel. To facilitate the identification of these ranks, the Parties to the conflict are under an obligation to agree, from the outbreak of hostilities, 'regarding the corresponding seniority of the ranks of their medical personnel, including those of the societies designated in Article 26'. The said ranks are also to be communicated with a view to facilitating the determination of who is the senior medical officer.[75] Any resulting agreement is a special agreement and must comply with the requirements of Article 6 of the First Convention. Accordingly, such an agreement may not adversely affect the situation of the wounded and sick or the medical or religious personnel as defined in the First Convention, nor restrict the rights which the Convention confers upon them.[76]

2190   The senior medical officer will perform, on behalf of the retained medical personnel, all the duties which the prisoners' representative performs for

---

[74] See Third Convention, Article 55.
[75] See United States, *Law of War Manual*, 2015, para. 9.4.2.5.
[76] Article 6(1). As to the temporal scope of the applicability of such special agreements, see Article 6(2).

prisoners of war.[77] Accordingly, the senior medical officer will, in fact, be the medical personnel's representative. However, the role of the senior medical officer differs from that of the prisoners' representative inasmuch as Article 28(2)(b) specifies that the former is 'responsible' to the authorities 'for the professional activity of the retained medical personnel'. The responsible officer will therefore effectively act as head of the retained medical personnel in the camp in all professional matters, in so far as this is compatible with the fact that such personnel are placed, in principle, under the authority of the competent services of the Detaining Power. Article 33(2)(b) of the Third Convention, meanwhile, describes the responsibility of the senior medical officer in each camp more loosely as extending to 'everything connected with the activities of retained medical personnel'. However, if considered in the context of the remainder of Article 33(2)(b), where reference is made to the right of the senior medical officer and religious personnel 'to deal with the competent authorities of the camp *on all questions relating to their duties*' (emphasis added), it would stand to reason to interpret the responsibility as limited to the professional activity of the retained medical personnel and thus as being identical to Article 28(2)(b) of the First Convention.

2191   Article 28 gives the senior medical officer two prerogatives: direct access to the camp authorities in all questions arising out of his or her duties, and the necessary facilities for correspondence relating to such questions. As far as direct access is concerned, the English version of Article 33(2)(b) of the Third Convention stipulates more loosely a 'right to deal with the competent authorities of the camp'. However, the French version uses wording identical to Article 28 and provides for 'accès direct'. The meaning which best reconciles these different texts arguably is to understand the English version of Article 33(2)(b) of the Third Convention as also providing for a right of direct access to the camp authorities.[78]

2192   Regarding the necessary facilities for correspondence, no limit may be placed on the number of letters, cards, emails and other communications which it may be necessary for the responsible medical officer to send and receive. This is contrary to what may be the case in certain circumstances with regard to the number of communications sent and received by prisoners of war.[79] It is important that the responsible medical officer remains in close touch with medical circles in his or her own country and with the Protecting Power, the ICRC, relief organizations, the families of captured personnel and others of relevance.

---

[77] On prisoner of war representatives, see, in particular, Third Convention, Articles 79–81, in addition to Articles 28(2), 41(2), 48(4), second sentence, 57(2), 62(3), 65(1), 78(2), 96(4), third sentence, 98(5), second sentence, 104(3) and (4), 107(1), second sentence, 113(1), sub-para. 2, and (4), 125(4), first sentence, and 126(1), second sentence.

[78] See Vienna Convention on the Law of Treaties (1969), Article 33(4). Generally, see also Article 55.

[79] See Third Convention, Article 71(1).

In general, therefore, the facilities for correspondence should be at least as generous as those accorded to prisoners' representatives.[80]

2193   It should be noted that the appointment of a 'responsible' officer only concerns medical personnel and not religious personnel. However, individual religious personnel are, like the responsible medical officer, to have direct access to the camp authorities, who are under an obligation to provide them with the facilities they may require for correspondence relating to questions arising out of their duties. Furthermore, Article 35 of the Third Convention contains additional rules pertaining to religious personnel who are retained to assist prisoners of war, including correspondence, 'subject to censorship, on matters concerning their religious duties with the ecclesiastical authorities in the country of detention and with international religious organizations'.[81]

c. Performance of work outside medical or religious duties

2194   Sub-paragraph (c) stipulates that retained personnel may not be required to perform any work outside their medical or religious duties. That fundamental rule is absolute. Thus, retained personnel may not be obliged to do work outside their medical or religious duties even if they happen to be unoccupied for a brief period of time. During such a brief period of time they may always, of course, volunteer for work outside their medical or religious duties. That said, it is inadvisable for retained personnel to become prisoner of war representatives in the sense of Articles 79 to 81 of the Third Convention.[82]

2195   However, if no work falling within the scope of their medical or religious duties is available for a longer period of time, their retention is no longer indispensable and they have to be returned to the Party to the conflict to which they belong, in accordance with Article 30 of the First Convention.

2196   It follows from sub-paragraph (c) (in addition to the more generic stipulation that retained personnel 'shall continue to carry out . . . their medical and spiritual duties'),[83] that the provisions on the labour of prisoners of war[84] – even to the extent that they are to be considered 'beneficial' in the sense explained above – have to be adapted accordingly: those provisions that identify the type of work to which prisoners of war may be assigned and the arrangements connected with it[85] are generally not applicable to retained personnel. Furthermore, the beneficial provisions pertaining to working conditions, rest, pay,

---

[80] See *ibid.* Article 81(4).   [81] *Ibid.* Article 35, fourth sentence.
[82] United States, *Law of War Manual*, 2015, para. 9.24.1:

> In practice it is advisable for the POW [prisoner-of-war] representative to be a POW as opposed to a retained person. Medical personnel have their own representative for issues related to their activities. In addition, the duties of the POW representative and the duties of retained personnel could interfere with one another, and special provision is made in the [Third Convention] to ensure that other duties [do] not interfere with the duties of retained personnel or the duties of the POW representative.

[83] See section D.3.   [84] Third Convention, Articles 49–57.
[85] See *ibid.* Articles 49, 50, 52, 56 and 57.

etc.[86] are only applicable to the extent that they are compatible with the carrying out of medical and spiritual duties.[87]

2197   The same sub-paragraph provides that retained personnel are to be subject to the internal discipline of the camp. The provision should be read in conjunction with the clause, examined above,[88] that the personnel are to carry out their duties under the authority of the competent service of the Detaining Power. They will thus come under the authority of the commander of the camp except when actually carrying out their duties, in which case they are subject to the authority of the competent medical or religious service of the Detaining Power.

E. Paragraph 3: Arrangements for relieving retained personnel

2198   Article 28(3) requires Parties to the conflict to make arrangements for relieving retained personnel during hostilities, where possible, and to settle the procedure of such relief. In its ordinary meaning, 'to relieve' means 'to release (a person) from a duty by acting or providing a substitute'.[89] The concept of 'relieving' in the present context is thus equivalent to 'substituting' retained personnel. Generally speaking, the substitution of retained personnel can take various forms: retained personnel can be replaced by personnel belonging to the Detaining Power, by new personnel who have fallen into the hands of that Power,[90] or by personnel selected by a Party to the armed conflict for the specific purpose of relieving retained personnel of the same nationality. The 'arrangements' for relief made between the Parties to the conflict contemplated in paragraph 3 only pertain to the last form of relief. The caveat 'where possible' makes clear that there is no obligation to make such arrangements, but that their making as well as their substance will depend on a variety of factors. When drafting the Model Agreement Relating to the Relief of Medical Personnel and Chaplains, the ICRC identified the following factors: 'the circumstances obtaining at the time, the nature of the conflict, the Powers concerned in the relief, their national characteristics, the geographical distances which separate them, the number of prisoners, the actual organization of the Medical Services of the armies concerned and that of the medical profession, the state of mind of the civilian population, and so on'.[91]

2199   The agreements resulting from an application of Article 28(3) are special agreements in the sense of Article 6 of the First Convention, which must comply with the substantive requirements of the latter provision. The Model

---

[86] See *ibid.* Articles 51 and 53–55.
[87] Pictet (ed.), *Commentary on the First Geneva Convention*, ICRC, 1952, p. 254.
[88] See section D.3.
[89] *Concise Oxford English Dictionary*, 12th edition, Oxford University Press, 2011, p. 1215.
[90] See Article 31(1), which provides that the selection of personnel for return under Article 30 shall be made '*preferably according to the chronological order of their capture* and their state of health' (emphasis added).
[91] For the reference to the Model Agreement, see para. 2160.

Agreement Relating to the Relief of Medical Personnel and Chaplains provides a blueprint for such arrangements and the applicable procedure. However, nothing prevents the Parties from diverging from the Model Agreement. Indeed, as the ICRC explained in its commentary on the Model Agreement, opinions on the subject of relief of medical and religious personnel 'varied considerably and were often actually contradictory'.[92] This divergence of views, which 'had already been noted in the course of the 1949 Diplomatic Conference', was 'symptomatic of the special character, highly technical and often varying according to the regions and nationalities concerned, of the problems raised by the organization of a relief operation'.[93] Against the backdrop of the context-specific circumstances of any armed conflict, the ICRC, when drafting the Model Agreement, kept to a few principles which it considered to be 'apparently valid in all cases' at the time.[94] The principles addressed matters such as the period after which retained personnel must be relieved, the equivalence in competence and duties between relieved and relieving personnel, the choice of the personnel to be relieved, certain prioritizations of personnel to be relieved, the authority of the Detaining Power over relieving personnel, the possibility of an overlapping period after the arrival of the relieving personnel before the departure of the retained personnel, safety issues, the issuing of identity cards to relieving personnel, the responsibility for recruiting and selecting relieving personnel, and the establishment of a body to coordinate relief operations.[95]

F. Paragraph 4: Continuation of the obligations of the Detaining Power

2200   Article 28(4) restates the fundamental consideration underlying the retention regime as a whole, which is that retention may not be used as a way to circumvent the Detaining Power's obligations regarding the medical and spiritual welfare of the prisoners of war.[96] These obligations include the provision free of charge for the maintenance of prisoners of war and for the medical attention required by their state of health.[97] This obligation in turn entails that the Detaining Power makes available its own medical and, to the extent appropriate, religious personnel to prisoners of war. The retention of enemy medical and religious personnel is no substitute for this, nor does retention amount to the actual fulfilment of these obligations.[98] Instead, the lawfulness of retention is conditioned on the Detaining Power not being in a position to provide for the medical and spiritual welfare of prisoners of war through its own medical and

---

[92] See the commentary on the Model Agreement, p. 19.   [93] *Ibid.*
[94] *Ibid.*   [95] See *ibid.*
[96] See, in particular, Third Convention, Articles 15 and 34, but also Articles 20(2), 30–31, 46(3), 55 and 108(3). See also United States, *Law of War Manual*, 2015, para. 7.9.6: 'In other words, the fact that the Detaining Power permits and enables retained personnel to care for POWs [prisoners of war] does not relieve the Detaining Power of its own responsibilities to care for POWs.'
[97] Third Convention, Article 15.   [98] Jeanty, p. 65.

religious personnel. Retention is thus envisaged as a complement to, rather than a substitute for, the Detaining Power's own measures.[99] Such an understanding of the nature of retention is entirely in line with other relevant rules, such as Article 19(1) of the First Convention, which stipulates that, should units of the medical service of the armed forces fall into enemy hands, 'their personnel shall be free to pursue their duties, as long as the capturing Power has not itself ensured the necessary care of the wounded and sick found in such establishments and units'.

Select bibliography

Bugnion, François, *The International Committee of the Red Cross and the Protection of War Victims*, ICRC/Macmillan, Oxford, 2003.

ICRC, 'La rétention et la relève du personnel sanitaire et religieux: Accords-types', *Revue internationale de la Croix-Rouge et Bulletin international des Sociétés de la Croix-Rouge*, Vol. 37, No. 433, January 1955, pp. 7–31.

Jeanty, Bernard, *La protection du personnel sanitaire dans les conflits armés internationaux*, Thèse de Licence, Université de Neuchâtel, 1989.

Lauterpacht, Hersch, 'The Problem of the Revision of the Law of War', *British Yearbook of International Law*, Vol. 29, 1952, pp. 360–382.

Odom, Jonathan G., 'Beyond Arm Bands and Arms Banned: Chaplains, Armed Conflict, and the Law', *Naval Law Review*, Vol. 49, 2002, pp. 1–70.

Pictet, Jean S., 'Les nouvelles Conventions de Genève : La rétention du personnel sanitaire des armées tombé au pouvoir de la partie adverse', *Revue internationale de la Croix-Rouge et Bulletin international des Sociétés de la Croix-Rouge*, Vol. 31, No. 371, November 1949, pp. 869–884, and Vol. 31, No. 372, December 1949, pp. 937–976.

 – 'La profession médicale et le droit international humanitaire', *Revue internationale de la Croix-Rouge*, Vol. 67, No. 754, August 1985, pp. 195–213.

Schoenholzer, Jean-Pierre, 'Le médecin dans les Conventions de Genève de 1949', *Revue internationale de la Croix-Rouge et Bulletin international des Sociétés de la Croix-Rouge*, Vol. 35, Nos 410/411, February/March 1953, pp. 94–126 and 169–194.

Vollmar, Lewis C., 'Military Medicine in War: The Geneva Conventions Today', in Thomas E. Beam and Linette R. Sparacino (eds), *Military Medical Ethics*, Vol. 2, Office of The Surgeon General, United States Army, Washington D.C., 2003, pp. 739–771.

---

[99] See also Article 1(1) of the Model Agreement and its commentary, p. 10.

STATUS OF AUXILIARY PERSONNEL WHO HAVE FALLEN INTO ENEMY HANDS

❖ Text of the provision

Members of the personnel designated in Article 25 who have fallen into the hands of the enemy, shall be prisoners of war but shall be employed on their medical duties in so far as the need arises.

❖ Reservations or declarations

None

Contents

A. Introduction

2201 Article 29 is one of three provisions in the First Convention which regulate the protection of auxiliary medical personnel. The other two provisions are Article 25 (setting out who qualifies as auxiliary medical personnel) and Article 41 (setting out their means of identification).

2202 Article 25 provides that members of the armed forces who qualify as auxiliary medical personnel shall be 'respected and protected' if they are carrying out their medical duties 'at the time when they come into contact with the enemy or fall into his hands'.

2203 Article 29 applies to all '[m]embers of the personnel designated in Article 25 who have fallen into the hands of the enemy', whether or not they are carrying out their medical duties 'at the time when they come into contact with the enemy or fall into his hands'. The rationale is clear: to avoid the possibility that medical expertise which may be needed for the care of prisoners of war will remain unused. When members of the armed forces specially trained for employment in one or more of the functions referred to in Article 25 fall into enemy hands, they are prisoners of war covered by the Third Convention, but they 'shall be employed on their medical duties in so far as the need arises' (this being the sole exception to their having to be treated like other prisoners of war on the basis of the Third Convention).

2204   When auxiliary medical personnel fall into enemy hands, their initial status as combatants prevails. Hence, they can be detained, and continue to be detained, as prisoners of war regardless of the number or the state of health of prisoners of war.[1] They are only entitled to return to the Party to which they belong under the conditions generally applicable to all prisoners of war.[2] This is because they are not permanent medical personnel and could always be required to perform combat duties.[3]

B. Historical background

2205   Under the 1929 Geneva Convention on the Wounded and Sick, when medical personnel fell into enemy hands, they could not be detained as prisoners of war nor be retained to assist in caring for prisoners of war. They had, in principle, to be sent back to the belligerent to which they belonged. This prohibition on detaining or retaining them was applicable to all categories of medical personnel recognized under that Convention,[4] and therefore also to auxiliary medical personnel.[5]

2206   The First Convention of 1949 modified this uniform approach by allowing for the retention of (i) military medical and religious personnel, and (ii) the staff of National Societies and other voluntary aid societies assisting the medical services of their State's armed forces under certain conditions.[6] However, when the conditions for retaining these categories of medical personnel do not or no longer exist, they shall be returned to the Party to the conflict to whom they belong.[7]

---

[1] In order to make it clear to readers of the First Convention that permanent medical personnel and auxiliary medical personnel are different categories, it was decided to deal with the various aspects of their status and treatment in separate provisions throughout the First Convention; see *Final Record of the Diplomatic Conference of Geneva of 1949*, Vol. II–A, p. 194.

[2] See Third Convention, Articles 109 and 118.

[3] For permanent military medical personnel (covered by Article 24), see Articles 28 and 30.

[4] On their status and treatment, see Articles 12–13 of the 1929 Geneva Convention.

[5] Auxiliary medical personnel were defined in Article 9(2) of the 1929 Geneva Convention. As discussed in the commentary on Article 25, para. 2017, Article 9(2) of the 1929 Geneva Convention resulted from a proposal introduced during the Diplomatic Conference by the US delegation. The second sentence of that proposal already contained the notion that, should auxiliary personnel fall into enemy hands, they were to be treated as prisoners of war. For the text of the proposal, see *Proceedings of the Geneva Diplomatic Conference of 1929*, p. 127.

[6] The relevant condition can be found in Article 28(1): 'shall be retained only in so far as the state of health, the spiritual needs and the number of prisoners of war require'.

[7] For details, see the commentary on Article 30, section C.

2207   During the Diplomatic Conference of 1949, it was a matter of controversy whether to maintain auxiliary medical personnel as a separate category of protected persons under the First Convention.[8] In the end it was decided to do so.[9] As a result, an additional rule was needed to regulate their status and treatment when they fell into enemy hands. This rule, now Article 29, was formulated by the Drafting Committee and adopted without any discussion.[10] Since 1949, there seems to have been no practice with regard to Article 29. This is related to the fact that very few armed forces have actually used, or intend to use, auxiliary medical personnel within the meaning of Article 25.[11]

C. Discussion

1. Status

2208   Article 25 applies only to 'Members of the armed forces specially trained for employment, should the need arise, as hospital orderlies, nurses or auxiliary stretcher-bearers, in the search for or the collection, transport or treatment of the wounded and sick'.[12]

2209   These combatants are protected as medical personnel under the First Convention if they are carrying out their medical duties at the time when they come into contact with or fall into enemy hands.[13]

2210   When auxiliary medical personnel fall into enemy hands at the time they are carrying out their medical duties,[14] they lose their status as persons temporarily protected under the First Convention. Instead, they 'shall be prisoners of war', covered by the Third Convention, except that they 'shall be employed on their medical duties in so far as the need arises'. Prisoner-of-war status applies even if they were carrying out medical duties at the time of their falling into enemy hands and wearing the armlet provided for in Article 41, and even if the state of health and the number of prisoners of war do not require their medical care.

---

[8] For details of the misgivings expressed regarding the category of auxiliary medical personnel, both before and during the 1949 Diplomatic Conference, see the commentary on Article 25, paras 2019–2020.

[9] For details, see the commentary on Article 25, paras 2020–2021.

[10] See *Final Record of the Diplomatic Conference of Geneva of 1949*, Vol. II-A, p. 140. See also *Minutes of the Diplomatic Conference of Geneva of 1949*, Committee I, Tome I, pp. 63–64.

[11] See the commentary on Article 25, para. 2015.

[12] For the meaning of the terms 'hospital orderlies, nurses or auxiliary stretcher-bearers', see the commentary on Article 25, para. 2029.

[13] Article 25.

[14] For the meaning of the expression 'fall[ing] into enemy hands', see the commentary on Article 14, section C.3. As mentioned in paragraph 2025 of the commentary on Article 25, auxiliary medical personnel may be on board medical aircraft. If such an aircraft involuntarily lands in enemy or enemy-occupied territory, Article 29 applies to them; see the final sentence of Article 36(5), which explicitly states that they 'shall be treated according to Article 24, and the Articles following'.

2211   Because they have the status of prisoners of war, the time of their release and repatriation is governed by the Third,[15] and not by the First Convention.[16] All other aspects of their status and treatment are also regulated by the Third Convention. In contrast to persons covered by the retention regime (who shall 'at least benefit by all the provisions' of the Third Convention)[17], auxiliary medical personnel who have fallen into enemy hands are to be treated on the basis of the Third Convention, there being no injunction to the Party retaining them to go beyond the provisions of the Third Convention as regards the treatment accorded to them. If persons covered by Article 25 are themselves wounded or sick when they fall into enemy hands, the First Convention also applies to them.[18]

2212   The reason why auxiliary medical personnel are given specific protection only if and for as long as they are carrying out their medical duties goes back to the distrust about this category of personnel.[19] After all, since their primary status is that of combatants, they may be deployed again as combatants when they rejoin their armed forces. Therefore, the drafters of the First Convention feared that, if personnel in this category were entitled to repatriation in the same way as permanent medical personnel, this might lead to abuses.[20] This is the difference with the retention regime: persons covered by the retention regime do not have the status of prisoners of war, but shall at least benefit by the treatment to which prisoners of war are entitled on the basis of the Third Convention.

2213   The First Convention does not address the question of whether the detention of auxiliary medical personnel as prisoners of war should lead to a decrease in the number of personnel retained on the basis of Article 28. According to Article 25, auxiliary medical personnel have been trained as 'hospital orderlies, nurses or auxiliary stretcher-bearers'. While the potential role for auxiliary stretcher-bearers inside a prisoner-of-war camp seems rather limited, both hospital orderlies and nurses may have useful services to provide in that context. Their detention might lead to a situation in which the retention of some of the personnel on the basis of Article 28 is no longer necessary, thus requiring their return to the Party to the conflict to which they belong.

---

[15] The relevant provisions are Articles 109–121 of the Third Convention (Part IV: Termination of captivity).

[16] The regime of persons covered by Article 25 differs in this respect from both (i) the regime of persons covered by the retention regime (see Articles 28, 30 and 31 of the First Convention and Article 33 of the Third Convention), and (ii) persons covered by Article 27 when they fall into the hands of the adversary of the Party they are assisting (see Article 32).

[17] See Article 28(1) of the First Convention and Article 33(1) of the Third Convention.

[18] See the commentary on Article 14, section C.1.

[19] See the commentary on Article 25, para. 2020.

[20] *Final Record of the Diplomatic Conference of Geneva of 1949*, Vol. II-A, p. 194–195: 'Whereas the Convention of 1929 provided for [auxiliary medical personnel's] return on the same conditions as those applicable to permanent personnel, Committee I concluded that there was no justification for granting this special favour, and declared that they should also be treated as prisoners of war.'

2214   The matter may, first of all, be addressed in a special agreement, which the Parties to the conflict are invited to conclude on the basis of Article 31(2), with regard to (i) the 'percentage of personnel to be retained, in proportion to the number of prisoners' and (ii) the 'distribution of said personnel in the camps'. Such an agreement may allow the Parties to the conflict to agree upon a formula regarding the degree to which the presence of auxiliary medical personnel should lead to a decrease in retained personnel.[21]

2215   Absent such agreement, reference may be had to the idea contained in Article 7 of the Model Agreement Relating to the Retention of Medical Personnel and Chaplains, pursuant to which the number of auxiliary medical personnel detained 'shall reduce by the same amount that of the regular personnel engaged on similar duties who are liable to be retained'.[22] When interpreting the words 'on similar duties', it must be kept in mind that Articles 25 and 29 apply only to hospital orderlies, nurses or auxiliary stretcher-bearers and not to other medical professionals such as doctors or surgeons.[23] Therefore, in a context in which the conditions for retaining medical personnel are fulfilled,[24] the presence of auxiliary medical personnel is unlikely to make retained personnel redundant altogether.[25]

2. Employment

2216   One of the conditions to be met before members of the armed forces can acquire protected status under Article 25 is that they must have been 'specially trained for employment, should the need arise, as hospital orderlies, nurses or auxiliary stretcher-bearers'.[26] The type of training received needs to be specified on the military identity documents which are to be carried by persons covered under Article 25.[27] By stating that the prisoners of war who, prior to their falling into enemy hands, qualified as auxiliary medical personnel 'shall be employed on their medical duties in so far as the need arises', Article 29 ensures that

---

[21] See the commentary on Article 31, para. 2279. See also the commentary on Article 45, para. 2722.

[22] In this regard, see also the commentary on Article 7 of the Model Agreement Relating to the Retention of Medical Personnel and Chaplains, pp. 9 and 12. The original text of Article 7 of the Model Agreement speaks, in connection with auxiliary medical personnel, of their being 'retained'. This is to be considered a mistake, since persons covered by Article 25 are detained, not retained. For a discussion of the origin and status of this Model Agreement, see the commentary on Article 28, para. 2160.

[23] See the commentary on Article 25, para. 2027.

[24] These conditions are outlined in Article 28(1). In this regard, it must be recalled that the Retaining Power bears the primary responsibility for looking after the medical needs of the prisoners of war; see Article 28(4).

[25] This will in any event apply to religious personnel, who can be retained on the basis of Article 28, but who can never qualify on the basis of Article 25; see the commentary on Article 25, para. 2031.

[26] For a discussion of this requirement, see the commentary on Article 25, paras 2033–2034.

[27] Article 41(2).

their medical skills can be used, as needed, for the benefit of the prisoners of war.

2217   The First Convention does not state explicitly how persons who have been trained as auxiliary medical personnel should be employed if they fall into enemy hands at a time when they are acting as combatants. While it is clear that they become prisoners of war, the question is whether they must also 'be employed on their medical duties in so far as the need arises'. This appears to be the case, since Article 29 refers generically to 'members of the personnel designated in Article 25', without requiring them to have been acting as auxiliary medical personnel at the time of their falling into enemy hands.

2218   The 'need' referred to in Article 29 is only the medical need of the prisoners of war held by the Detaining Power.[28] Persons covered by Article 29 will preferably work on behalf of the prisoners of war of the armed forces to which they themselves belong.[29] The 'medical duties' referred to are the activities of auxiliary medical personnel as hospital orderlies, nurses or auxiliary stretcher-bearers in the treatment of the wounded and sick and – though less likely inside a prisoner-of-war camp – in the search for, the collection or the transport of the wounded and sick.

2219   As indicated by the unconditional use of the word 'shall', the employment of auxiliary medical personnel for medical duties is not left to the discretion of the Detaining Power.[30] It has to be based on a good-faith assessment of the needs of the prisoners of war. This means that, as soon as and for as long as prisoners of war have medical needs which cannot be addressed by the Detaining Power itself, but which can be addressed by the auxiliary medical personnel, the Detaining Power is obliged to make use of them.

2220   In that case, it seems appropriate to apply the provisions of Article 32 of the Third Convention to auxiliary medical personnel:[31] 'they shall continue to be

---

[28] In speaking generically of 'the need', Article 29 does not clarify whose need is covered. All other similar provisions in the First and Third Conventions, however, indicate that medically qualified personnel in the hands of a Party to the conflict must work 'on behalf of prisoners of war, preferably those of the armed forces to which they themselves belong' (Article 28(2) of the First Convention). Similar language can be found in Articles 30(2) and 32(3) of the First Convention and in Articles 32 and 33(2) of the Third Convention.

[29] See the previous footnote for the provisions in both the First and Third Conventions, as well as in the Model Agreement Relating to the Retention of Medical Personnel and Chaplains, which states, in Article 7(1) (even more categorically than the provisions in the First and Third Conventions, in that the word 'preferably' does not appear here): 'Auxiliary medical personnel,... who fall into the hands of the adverse Party, shall be employed on medical duties on behalf of prisoners belonging to the armed forces to which they themselves belong.' For an interpretation of these nuances to the effect that this cannot lead to a violation of the principle of impartiality of care, as enshrined in Article 13(3) of the First Convention, see the commentaries on Article 28(2), para. 2185, Article 30, para. 2250, and Article 32, paras 2306–2308.

[30] See also Article 32 of the Third Convention regarding '[p]risoners of war who, though not attached to the medical service of their armed forces, are physicians, surgeons, dentists, nurses or medical orderlies'. These persons '*may* be required by the Detaining Power to exercise their medical functions in the interests of prisoners of war dependent on the same Power' (emphasis added).

[31] In this context, see also the commentary on Article 45, para. 2724.

prisoners of war, but shall receive the same treatment as corresponding medical personnel retained by the Detaining Power'.[32] This means that they should enjoy the necessary facilities for carrying out their medical duties, as described in Article 33 of the Third Convention.[33] When they are required to carry out such medical duties, they should be paid in line with the Third Convention for such work.[34]

2221   On the other hand, if their fellow prisoners of war have no medical needs, or no longer have such needs, persons covered by Article 29 may be asked to perform non-medical duties.[35] The rules and conditions set out in the Third Convention's section on 'Labour of prisoners of war' apply in this regard.[36]

Select bibliography

See the select bibliography of the commentary on Article 24 of the First Convention.

---

[32] Since Article 32 of the Third Convention applies to prisoners of war who have medical qualifications without being attached to the medical services of their armed forces, it can be argued that it applies, *a fortiori*, to prisoners of war who have such qualifications while having some links with the medical services of their armed forces, without being a member thereof either.

[33] See also the corresponding provision in Article 28(2).

[34] See, in particular, Article 62(2) of the Third Convention.

[35] This is another difference between persons covered by Article 29 and those covered by the retention regime. The latter 'shall not ... be required to perform any work outside their medical or religious duties'; see Article 28(2)(c).

[36] This section, containing Articles 49–57, can be found in Part III, Section III, of the Third Convention.

ARTICLE 30

RETURN OF MEDICAL AND RELIGIOUS PERSONNEL

❖ Text of the provision*

(1) Personnel whose retention is not indispensable by virtue of the provisions of Article 28 shall be returned to the Party to the conflict to whom they belong, as soon as a road is open for their return and military requirements permit.

(2) Pending their return, they shall not be deemed prisoners of war. Nevertheless they shall at least benefit by all the provisions of the Geneva Convention relative to the Treatment of Prisoners of War of August 12, 1949. They shall continue to fulfil their duties under the orders of the adverse Party and shall preferably be engaged in the care of the wounded and sick of the Party to the conflict to which they themselves belong.

(3) On their departure, they shall take with them the effects, personal belongings, valuables and instruments belonging to them.

❖ Reservations or declarations
None

Contents

* Paragraph numbers have been added for ease of reference.

793

A. Introduction

2222 Article 30 contains the basic rule which needs to be complied with when military medical or religious personnel (covered by Article 24) or staff of National Red Cross or Red Crescent Societies or of other voluntary aid societies assisting the medical services of the armed forces (covered by Article 26) fall into enemy hands: they must be returned to the Party to the conflict to which they belong. For the sake of brevity, both categories are subsumed under the phrase 'medical and religious personnel' in the commentary on this article.

2223   The purpose of this provision is to ensure that medical and religious personnel can continue to provide their services at all times to those who need them.[1] In this light, Article 30 regulates the period between their falling into enemy hands and their return to the Party to the conflict to which they belong. During this period, 'they shall continue to fulfil their duties'.

2224   Article 30 should be read in conjunction with two other provisions of the First Convention: Articles 28 and 31. Article 28, the exception to Article 30, allows the Party into whose hands medical or religious personnel have fallen to retain some or all of them if required by the 'state of health, the spiritual needs and the number of prisoners of war' detained by that Party. The principle of return in Article 30 applies both to personnel who may not be retained as of the moment they fall into enemy hands and to personnel who may initially be retained on the basis of Article 28 but who must be returned once the reasons for retaining them no longer exist.

2225   Article 31 sets out the criteria for determining which medical or religious personnel should be returned on the basis of Article 30 and provides for the possibility for the Parties to the conflict to conclude special agreements covering the practical aspects of their retention.

B. Historical background

2226 Predecessors of the first and third paragraphs of Article 30 can be found in both the 1906 Geneva Convention[2] and the 1929 Geneva Convention on the Wounded and Sick.[3] Yet, during the First and Second World Wars, the requirement to return medical and religious personnel was rarely complied with.[4] In light of this experience, while commenting on a proposal almost identical to the

---

[1] *Final Record of the Diplomatic Conference of Geneva of 1949*, Vol. II-A, p. 69. See also *Minutes of the Conference of Government Experts of 1947*, Committee I, Vol. II, p. 140. Similarly, see United States, *Law of War Manual*, 2015, para. 4.10.2.

[2] See Geneva Convention (1906), Article 12.

[3] See Geneva Convention on the Wounded and Sick (1929), Article 12.

[4] *Report of the Preliminary Conference of National Societies of 1946*, p. 32. Similarly, see *Report of the Conference of Government Experts of 1947*, p. 38, and *Final Record of the Diplomatic Conference of Geneva of 1949*, Vol. II-A, p. 66. See also Pictet, 1949, p. 873 (in relation to the First World War), and pp. 876–877 (in relation to the Second World War), and Vollmar, p. 746.

current first and third paragraphs of Article 30, the 1947 Conference of Government Experts stated: 'It should be stressed that this Article (which is applicable only to medical personnel whose retention in captivity is not indispensable...) is categorical. It therefore offers the belligerents no option to conclude agreements forgoing repatriation of Medical Personnel.'[5]

2227   The essence of the first two sentences of Article 30(2) are to be found in the draft submitted to the 17th International Conference of the Red Cross in Stockholm in 1948.[6] The third sentence – 'They shall continue to fulfil their duties...' – was added by the Drafting Committee during the 1949 Diplomatic Conference, and is in line with similar wording found in Article 28.[7]

C. Paragraph 1: Return to the Party to the conflict to which they belong

1. The principle of return

2228 When medical or religious personnel fall into enemy hands, that Party is obliged to return them to the Party to the conflict to which they belong.[8] Retaining them is only lawful if retention is 'indispensable' in view of the state of health, the spiritual needs and the number of prisoners of war already detained by that Party.[9] Medical and religious personnel may only be retained if a stringent threshold is met: that the medical and spiritual welfare of prisoners of war requires it.[10]

2229   Moreover, where persons covered by Articles 24 or 26 are on the territory of a neutral Power, the latter is also under an obligation to apply Article 30 (and its related provisions in Articles 28 and 31) by analogy.[11]

2230   According to Article 31(2), the 'Parties to the conflict may determine by special agreement the percentage of personnel to be retained, in proportion to the number of prisoners and the distribution of the said personnel in the camps'. The absence of such an agreement, the conclusion of which is optional ('may'), cannot be used as a pretext for failing to return personnel who are not indispensable.[12] In that case, it will be up to the Detaining Power to assess whether it may retain medical and religious personnel in line with the conditions set down in Article 28(1). While this assessment can be made unilaterally,

---

[5] *Report of the Conference of Government Experts of 1947*, p. 38.
[6] See *Draft Conventions submitted to the 1948 Stockholm Conference*, p. 18, draft article 23.
[7] *Final Record of the Diplomatic Conference of Geneva of 1949*, Vol. II-A, p. 127.
[8] Article 30 applies to all categories of persons covered by Articles 24 and 26. The idea of limiting the requirement of return to doctors and nurses only (to the detriment of, for example, 'staff exclusively engaged in the administration of medical units and establishments') was unsuccessful; see *Final Record of the Diplomatic Conference of Geneva of 1949*, Vol. II-A, p. 81.
[9] See Article 28(1) of the First Convention and Article 33(1) of the Third Convention.
[10] See the commentary on Article 28, section C.
[11] See the commentary on Article 4, para. 937. See also United States, *Law of War Manual*, 2015, para. 15.16.6.
[12] *Minutes of the Conference of Government Experts of 1947*, Committee I, Vol. II, Tome 1, p. 186.

and does not require the consent of the persons who are to be retained (nor of the Party to which they belong), it needs to be made in good faith.[13] Thus, if the medical and spiritual needs of the prisoners of war in the hands of the Detaining Power are adequately addressed, the Party to which the medical and religious personnel belong can expect them to be returned to it.[14]

2231   The draft article submitted to the 1948 Stockholm Conference contained the following final paragraph: 'Members of this personnel shall not be repatriated against their will.'[15] Although the sentence was not retained, the principle is still valid. A person who refuses to return acquires the status of prisoner of war and will be covered by the Third Convention. While such persons remain in enemy hands, the work they may undertake as prisoners of war is regulated by the relevant provisions of the Third Convention.[16] The Third Convention also regulates when such prisoners of war are to be released and repatriated.[17]

2232   The obligation to return medical and religious personnel to the Party to which they belong can be triggered from the moment they fall into enemy hands.[18] This will be the case, for example, when there are no wounded or sick prisoners of war requiring treatment, or when the Detaining Power has sufficient medical personnel of its own to address the needs of the prisoners of war. The obligation can also arise at a later time, for example when wounded or sick prisoners of war have recovered and no longer need medical care.

2233   The logic of the regime regulating the status and treatment of medical and religious personnel in enemy hands requires strict compliance with Article 30. As discussed in the commentary on Article 28, the compromise underpinning this logic was only reached after a lengthy discussion.[19] The following elements need to be kept in mind in this regard: prisoners of war may be detained until the cessation of active hostilities;[20] and during their detention, they may be compelled to undertake certain categories of work which will benefit the Detaining Power.[21] These rules do not, however, apply to medical and religious personnel in enemy hands: the mere fact that hostilities are ongoing does not

---

[13] For a discussion of an unsuccessful proposal made in this regard, see the *Proceedings of the Geneva Diplomatic Conference of 1929*, p. 150.

[14] In this regard, the Detaining Power has the primary responsibility of ensuring that the medical and spiritual needs of the prisoners of war are taken care of; see Article 28(4). On the question of whether medical and religious personnel can be retained to address the medical and spiritual needs of prisoners of war of a nationality other than their own, see the commentary on Article 28, para. 2185.

[15] *Draft Conventions submitted to the 1948 Stockholm Conference*, p. 18, draft article 23.

[16] These include Article 32 (prisoners engaged on medical duties) and Article 36 (prisoners who are ministers of religion), but also the general provisions regulating the type of work which all prisoners of war may be required to do. Thus, within the limits of Article 49 and subsequent articles of the Third Convention, such prisoners of war may also be required to do work of a non-medical nature.

[17] See Third Convention, Article 118, along with its related provisions.

[18] For an analysis of the term 'fall into enemy hands', see the commentary on Article 14, section C.3.

[19] See the commentary on Article 28, para. 2159.   [20] See Third Convention, Article 118.

[21] See Third Convention, Articles 49–57.

constitute a ground to detain them until the cessation of active hostilities; it is only lawful to retain them if the prisoners of war have medical or spiritual needs which the Detaining Power is unable to address.[22] Thus, if there are no (or no longer) such needs, the Party into whose hands the medical or religious personnel have fallen must return them to the Party to which they belong.[23] After all, when they return to the latter Party it is with a view to resuming their medical or religious duties, which may not be considered detrimental to the interests of the adverse Party.

2234   The Parties to the conflict may not conclude an agreement allowing for medical or religious personnel to be retained in circumstances which do not meet the conditions set out in Article 28(1). Article 30's drafting history confirms the absolute nature of the obligation.[24]

2235   Article 30 requires that personnel whose retention is not indispensable be returned 'to the Party to the conflict to whom they belong'. This wording, which was already introduced in Article 12(2) of the 1929 Geneva Convention on the Wounded and Sick, differs from the wording in Article 12(2) of the 1906 Geneva Convention, whereby such personnel needed to be sent back 'to their army or country'. The words 'to the Party to the conflict to whom they belong' were chosen to enable medical and religious personnel to be returned to a place where they could continue to provide their services. This precludes, for example, an Occupying Power from claiming that medical or religious personnel who have fallen into its hands have no need to leave the territory it occupies since they are already in their own country.[25] Furthermore, if the medical or religious personnel have the nationality of a State other than the State to whose armed forces they belong, they would still need to be returned to the latter. Lastly, the wording makes clear that medical and religious personnel do not necessarily need to be returned to the military unit to which they were originally attached. The mere fact that that military unit happens to be in a place where no 'road is open for their return' would not constitute a ground to delay their return.[26]

---

[22] On the prohibition of 'anticipatory' retention, as well as on the prohibition of retaining medical and religious personnel to meet the medical and religious needs of civilians, see the commentary on Article 28, para. 2165.

[23] For an example, see ICRC, *Annual Report 1972*, ICRC, Geneva, 1973, p. 51.

[24] *Report of the Conference of Government Experts of 1947*, p. 38. See also *Minutes of the Conference of Government Experts of 1947*, Committee I, Vol. II, Tome 1, p. 185 (in particular, United States). This differs from Article 32(2); see the commentary on Article 32, section D.

[25] Des Gouttes, *Commentaire de la Convention de Genève de 1929 sur les blessés et malades*, ICRC, 1930, p. 81; Pictet (ed.), *Commentary on the First Geneva Convention*, ICRC, 1952, p. 262.

[26] In the text adopted by the 11th International Conference of the Red Cross in Geneva in 1923, and which served as the basis for the discussions during the 1929 Diplomatic Conference, the section on this point read that the persons in question must be returned to the (translation) 'military authority to whom they belong'; see *Proceedings of the Geneva Diplomatic Conference of 1929*, p. 18, draft article 12(2). For the discussion which led to the modification as it appears in Article 30(2), see the *Proceedings of the Geneva Diplomatic Conference of 1929*, p. 154.

2236   In the case of staff of National Red Cross or Red Crescent Societies or of other voluntary aid societies assisting the medical services of the armed forces, the requirement that they be returned 'to the Party to the conflict to whom they belong' means that they be returned to the medical service of their State's armed forces. Unless the Party to which they 'belong' so decides, Article 30 does not provide for a repatriation to their home.[27]

2237   When the return of medical and religious personnel occurs at the same time as the repatriation of seriously wounded and sick prisoners of war on the basis of Article 109 of the Third Convention, the former may be called upon to continue to perform their functions for the benefit of the latter during the repatriation.

2. Temporary delay of return

2238   The Party into whose hands medical or religious personnel have fallen is obliged to return these persons to the Party to which they belong 'as soon as a road is open for their return and military requirements permit'. This means that the Party may temporarily delay their return on one of the two aforementioned grounds.[28] However, it is clear from the wording adopted that this may be well before the end of active hostilities.[29]

2239   The first ground relates to a material impossibility, i.e. no route (whether by land, water or air) is open for the return of the medical or religious personnel. This may be the case when hostilities are still ongoing and no safe alternatives exist. In line with the purpose of Articles 28 and 30 that medical and religious personnel be able to continue to use their expertise in the service of those who need it, the absence of a suitable route does not mean the return of such personnel may be delayed indefinitely. If, for example, no options exist for their safe return by means of transport over land, the Parties to the conflict should endeavour to conclude a special agreement to facilitate their return by other means, such as a cartel aircraft or ship.[30]

2240   The second ground allows the Party to invoke 'military requirements' to delay the return of medical or religious personnel. The First Convention does not provide any clarification of the notion of 'military requirements'. The term 'requirements', however, implies that the military reasons invoked need to be serious, not merely a matter of convenience, and of a nature to leave the Party

---

[27] *Final Record of the Diplomatic Conference of Geneva of 1949*, Vol. II-B, p. 220.

[28] While phrased slightly differently, Article 32(1) uses substantively identical grounds with regard to persons covered by Article 27 who fall into the hands of the enemy of the Party they were assisting.

[29] See also the commentary on Article 5, paras 948–949.

[30] The Manual on International Law Applicable to Air and Missile Warfare (2009), Rule 1(g), defines a 'cartel aircraft' as 'an aircraft granted safe conduct by agreement between the Belligerent Parties for the purpose of performing a specific function, such as the transport of prisoners of war or parlementaires'.

with no other choice.[31] This stringent criterion may be fulfilled, for example, if temporarily delaying their return is the only way to prevent persons passing on to their own Party information of military value acquired while they were in enemy hands. Furthermore, the phrase 'military requirements' needs to be interpreted in the light of the purpose of Article 30. Thus, other than physical impediments arising from ongoing hostilities, it is difficult to conceive of a scenario in which 'military requirements' would justify a long-term delay in returning medical or religious personnel.

2241   Even when one or both grounds exists, the delay may only be temporary. As soon as there is no more reason for a delay, the persons must be allowed to return. No grounds other than the two mentioned explicitly in Article 30 may be invoked as a justification for a delay.

2242   Article 30 does not specify who has to cover the cost of transporting the medical and religious personnel to the Party to which they belong. Failing an agreement on this matter, the rules governing the transport of prisoners of war to a neutral country or the return home of civilian internees could be applied by analogy: the Party into whose hands the personnel have fallen has to pay the costs of their transportation only up to its own borders.[32] From there, the Party to whom the personnel belong must pay for their transportation to their final destination.

D. Paragraph 2: Status and treatment pending return

2243   The purpose of Article 30(2) is to settle the status and treatment of medical and religious personnel for the period between when they fall into enemy hands and when they return to the Party to which they belong. With regard to the regulatory framework which is of relevance to this period, mention must be made of the Model Agreement Relating to the Retention of Medical Personnel and Chaplains, which was drafted by the ICRC at the request of the 1949 Diplomatic Conference.[33] Article 12(1) of the Model Agreement states:

The provisions of the present Agreement shall also apply to medical personnel and chaplains who have fallen into the hands of the adverse Party and, not having been retained, are awaiting their return in accordance with Article 30 of the First Convention. They shall be applicable as long as such personnel remain in the territory of the Party into whose hands they have fallen.

2244   The status and treatment of medical and religious personnel will be relevant in every instance in which such persons fall into enemy hands. Even when their return takes place almost immediately, the organization of the actual departure

---

[31] See United States, *Law of War Manual*, 2015, para. 2.2.2.2.
[32] Third Convention, Article 116; Fourth Convention, Article 135(1).
[33] For the background and current status of this Model Agreement, see the commentary on Article 28, para. 2160.

may take a few days, for example because the practical details of the return need to be discussed with the adverse Party. This discussion can take place directly between the Parties or indirectly, for example through a neutral intermediary such as the ICRC.

2245   The first two sentences of Article 30(2) are identical to the first two sentences of Article 28(1). Thus, the basic principles applicable to retained personnel are also applicable to those who may not (or no longer) be retained and are thus awaiting their return: while in enemy hands, they 'shall not be deemed prisoners of war' but 'shall at least benefit by all the provisions' of the Third Convention.[34]

2246   All elements of the third sentence of Article 30(2) also appear in the third sentence of Article 28(2).[35] The latter contains more detail, however: while Article 30(2) states that medical and religious personnel are to continue to work 'under the orders of the adverse Party', Article 28(2) states that they shall do so '[w]ithin the framework of the military laws and regulations of the Detaining Power, and under the authority of its competent service', it being understood that this is tempered by the requirement that they be able to continue to work 'in accordance with their professional ethics'.

2247   There are a priori no reasons why personnel awaiting their return, especially when their return is imminent, should work '[w]ithin the framework of the military laws and regulations of the Detaining Power'. This may change, however, if their return is delayed: in that case, the Party into whose hands they have fallen may subject them to the same regulatory framework as that applicable to retained personnel. In any event, no matter how short their stay, it is the responsibility of the Detaining Power to ensure that medical and religious personnel are, at all times, in a position to work 'in accordance with their professional ethics'.[36]

2248   Article 30 does not confer what Article 28(2) calls the 'facilities for carrying out their medical or spiritual duties' to which retained personnel are entitled on the basis of the latter provision. This is logical since personnel covered by Article 30 are awaiting their return during what should, in principle, be a short period. However, if the Party into whose hands they have fallen exercises its right to delay their return temporarily, they will find themselves in a situation analogous to that of retained personnel. Hence, to the extent such personnel are asked to perform their medical or spiritual duties during that period, they should equally receive all 'facilities for carrying out' those duties.[37] In line with

---

[34] For the meaning of these terms, see the commentary on Article 28, sections D.1 and D.2.

[35] See also Article 32(3), applicable to persons covered by Article 27 who have fallen into the hands of the enemy of the Party they were assisting.

[36] For the meaning of the words 'in accordance with their professional ethics', see the commentary on Article 28, para. 2184.

[37] Final Record of the Diplomatic Conference of Geneva of 1949, Vol. II-A, p. 128 (Canada). See also Jean-Pierre Schoenholzer, 'Le médecin dans les Conventions de Genève de 1949', Revue internationale de la Croix-Rouge et Bulletin international des Sociétés de la Croix-Rouge, Vol. 35, Nos 410/411, February/March 1953, p. 178.

this general principle, it is clear that, when they are asked to perform their duties, they shall be paid on the same basis as retained personnel.[38]

2249 The reference to 'their duties' in Article 30(2) implies that the work medical and religious personnel may be asked to perform pending their return can only be of a medical or religious nature.[39] Thus, when there is no work of such a nature, they may not be required to work at all. If medical or religious personnel covered by Article 30 genuinely volunteer to work in these circumstances, they must benefit by all the relevant provisions of the Third Convention.[40]

2250 According to the third sentence of Article 30(2), personnel covered by Article 30 are 'preferably' to be engaged in the care of the wounded and sick of the Party to the conflict to which they themselves belong.[41] This sentence is the corollary, in the First Convention, of Article 30(3) of the Third Convention, according to which '[p]risoners of war shall have the attention, preferably, of medical personnel of the Power on which they depend and, if possible, of their nationality'. As indicated by the word 'preferably', this is only a recommendation. At all times, as medical professionals, persons covered by Article 30 must act in accordance with medical ethics, which require them to dispense medical care based on actual needs and not on the nationality of the victims. Should the persons covered by Article 26 work for a National Red Cross or Red Crescent Society, the same requirement also flows from the Fundamental Principle of impartiality.[42] Use of the word 'preferably' also implies that the Party to the conflict into whose hands the medical and religious personnel have fallen is entitled to direct them to take care of the medical needs of the wounded and sick of a Party other than that in whose service they were.

E. Paragraph 3: Objects which may be taken on departure

2251 Article 30(3) addresses a practicality with regard to the return of medical and religious personnel who have fallen into enemy hands. This paragraph only appears in Article 30, i.e. in connection with persons who may not be retained.

---

[38] For the payment to which retained personnel are entitled, see the commentary on Article 28, paras 2179 and 2196, and the relevant provisions of the Third Convention (in particular Articles 54 and 62).

[39] This is also the case for retained personnel (see the commentary on Article 28, section D.3) and for persons covered by Article 27 who have fallen into the hands of the adversary of the State they were assisting (see the commentary on Article 32, para. 2305).

[40] See, in particular, Third Convention, Articles 49–57.

[41] Substantively identical terminology can be found in Articles 28(2) and 30(2) of the First Convention, as well as in Article 33(2) of the Third Convention. During the 1929 Diplomatic Conference, this language was questioned, yet in the end maintained. See *Proceedings of the Geneva Diplomatic Conference of 1929*, p. 149 (New Zealand); see also p. 149 (Egypt), and p. 155 (United States). See also the statement of Paul Des Gouttes, p. 160. Despite these reservations, in the end the majority voted in favour of this wording; see *Proceedings of the Geneva Diplomatic Conference of 1929*, p. 162. No explanation was recorded as to why the majority voted the way it did.

[42] For the role of the Fundamental Principles in general, and the formulation of the Fundamental Principle of impartiality in particular, see the commentary on Article 26, paras 2088–2092.

Logically, however, the provision is also relevant to persons initially retained on the basis of Article 28 when they return to the Party to the conflict to which they belong.

2252   First, when leaving, medical and religious personnel who have fallen into enemy hands are entitled to take 'the effects, personal belongings [and] valuables ... belonging to them'.[43] The words 'belonging to them' mean that these 'effects, personal belongings [and] valuables' must be their private property.[44] Thus, objects they were carrying with them at the time they fell into enemy hands, yet which are the property of the Party to which they belong or of a voluntary aid society, do not qualify on the basis of this provision. These objects cannot be taken with them on their departure.

2253   Second, when leaving, medical and religious personnel are entitled to take with them the 'instruments belonging to them'. The 'instruments' referred to must be understood to include the personnel's medical instruments,[45] as well as instruments needed for the celebration of religious services. Also here, the words 'belonging to them' necessarily imply that this is restricted to their private property, i.e. objects given to them by the Power on which they depend for the exercise of their medical duties cannot be taken with them on their departure.

2254   With regard to the objects of a medical or religious nature which cannot be taken with them on their departure, the logic underpinning Articles 33(2) and 35(2) can arguably be considered applicable *mutatis mutandis*. Thus, while they remain in enemy hands, they must continue to be used for the care of the wounded and sick.

2255   Unlike Article 32(4), Article 30(3) does not include the 'arms and if possible the means of transport belonging to them' in the list of objects that medical and religious personnel may take with them. The absence of such an entitlement applies to any type of arms which they may have had on or with them at the time they fell into enemy hands, including: (i) the weapons which they were carrying for their own self-defence or for the defence of the wounded and sick in their charge;and (ii) the arms taken from the wounded and sick prior to their falling into enemy hands.[46] This is logical: Article 32 applies to persons

---

[43] With regard to the personal property of prisoners of war, see Third Convention, Article 18. There is some redundancy in the list provided in Article 30(3): 'effects' and 'personal belongings' mean the same thing, see *Concise Oxford English Dictionary*, 12th edition, Oxford University Press, 2011, p. 456. Similarly, 'valuables' (defined in the *Concise Oxford English Dictionary*, p. 1598, as 'small valuable items of personal property') are but a subcategory of 'effects'.

[44] See *ibid.* p. 124, which defines 'belong to' both as 'be the property of' and as 'be the rightful possession of; be due to'. One can be the rightful possessor of an object without having a property title over it.

[45] See *Proceedings of the Geneva Diplomatic Conference of 1906*, p. 55, at which the changes (to the 1864 Geneva Convention) suggested by the Swiss Federal Council were clarified in this sense. See, similarly, p. 117.

[46] For some of the conditions which may not be considered as depriving medical and religious personnel of the protection to which they are entitled on the basis of these provisions, see Articles 22(1) and 22(3), and the commentaries on Article 24, section F, and Article 26, para. 2084.

covered by Article 27 (i.e. staff of a recognized society of a neutral country when they assist the medical service of a Party to an international armed conflict) when they fall into the hands of the enemy of the Party they were assisting. These persons can neither be detained nor retained, and remain staff working for a recognized society of a neutral country; they are not the enemy of the Party into whose hands they have fallen. As a result, that Party has no grounds for keeping their arms and means of transport.[47] As for medical and religious personnel covered by Article 30, their arms and means of transport (such as ambulances) are typical examples of booty of war. Thus, the ownership of these objects immediately passes to the enemy into whose hands they have fallen.

Select bibliography

See the select bibliography of the commentary on Article 28 of the First Convention.

[47] For details, see the commentary on Article 32, section F.

SELECTION OF PERSONNEL FOR RETURN

❖ Text of the provision*

(1) The selection of personnel for return under Article 30 shall be made irrespective of any consideration of race, religion or political opinion, but preferably according to the chronological order of their capture and their state of health.

(2) As from the outbreak of hostilities, Parties to the conflict may determine by special agreement the percentage of personnel to be retained, in proportion to the number of prisoners and the distribution of the said personnel in the camps.

❖ Reservations or declarations

None

Contents

A. Introduction

2256 The two paragraphs of Article 31 address separate points which aim to regulate and facilitate the implementation of Articles 28 and 30. The first paragraph specifies the order of return of personnel on the basis of Article 30. The second paragraph allows for the conclusion of special agreements to regulate the retention of personnel on the basis of Article 28.

---

* Paragraph numbers have been added for ease of reference.

2257   The personnel covered by these three provisions are those mentioned in Article 24 (military medical and religious personnel) and in Article 26 (staff of National Red Cross and Red Crescent Societies and of other voluntary aid societies assisting the medical services of their own State's armed forces). For the sake of brevity, both categories are subsumed under the phrase 'medical and religious personnel' in the commentary on this article.

B. Historical background

2258   While to a certain extent both Article 28 and Article 30 have predecessors in the 1906 Geneva Convention and the 1929 Geneva Convention on the Wounded and Sick, Article 31(1) does not.[1] The origin of Article 31(1) can be traced back to the 1946 Preliminary Conference of National Red Cross Societies for the study of the Conventions and of various Problems relative to the Red Cross, during which the following paragraph was adopted: 'The choice of persons thus retained shall not be influenced by any consideration of race, or of political opinions'.[2] The text adopted by the 1947 Conference of Government Experts added 'religion' to the list and specified that the selection of 'repatriates' should be done 'preferably according to the chronological order of their capture'.[3] The draft submitted to the Stockholm Conference went further, stipulating that the selection of personnel to be repatriated should preferably be done according not only to 'the chronological order of their capture' but also to 'their state of health'.[4] Following an amendment submitted during the 1949 Diplomatic Conference, the word 'repatriates' was replaced by the words 'personnel for return under Article [30]', leading to the final version of Article 31(1).[5]

2259   Article 31(2) has no predecessor as such in the 1906 Geneva Convention or in the 1929 Geneva Convention on the Wounded and Sick. However, the fourth paragraph of Article 14 of the 1929 Geneva Convention on Prisoners of War stated that '[i]t shall be permissible for belligerents mutually to authorize each other, by means of special agreements, to retain in the camps doctors and medical orderlies for the purpose of caring for their prisoner compatriots'. The 1947 Conference of Government Experts adopted the following paragraph: 'As from the outbreak of hostilities, belligerents may determine by special arrangement the percentage of personnel to be retained in captivity, in proportion to the number of prisoners of war.'[6] The draft adopted by the 1948 Stockholm Conference added that such a 'special arrangement' could also address 'the

---

[1] For details, see the commentaries on Article 28, paras 2156–2158, and Article 30, para. 2226.
[2] *Report of the Preliminary Conference of National Societies of 1946*, p. 34.
[3] *Report of the Conference of Government Experts of 1947*, p. 38.
[4] *Draft Conventions submitted to the 1948 Stockholm Conference*, p. 18, draft article 24.
[5] *Final Record of the Diplomatic Conference of Geneva of 1949*, Vol. II-B, p. 220.
[6] *Report of the Conference of Government Experts of 1947*, p. 19.

distribution of said personnel in the camps',[7] which became the final wording of Article 31(2).

C. Paragraph 1: Selection of personnel for return

2260   Article 31(1) has a dual purpose. First, it regulates how the selection of personnel to be returned on the basis of Article 30 should preferably be made, by requiring that similarly situated persons are treated differently based upon certain considerations.[8] Second, it makes clear by which criteria this selection cannot be made. In this way, Article 31(1) protects medical and religious personnel who have fallen into enemy hands against potential arbitrariness in the decision-making process. It is important for all involved to have legal certainty on this point.

2261   Article 31(1) is closely linked to Article 30. Thus, where Article 31(1) speaks of 'personnel for return' without clarifying to whom or to where this return is to take place, it is referring to the return of the personnel 'to the Party to the conflict to whom they belong', as spelled out in Article 30(1).[9]

1. Prohibited grounds for selection

2262   When selecting personnel for return under Article 30, the Party into whose hands the personnel have fallen is absolutely prohibited from allowing 'considerations of race, religion or political opinion' to play any role in the decision-making.[10] While no practice seems to exist with regard to the interpretation of these three criteria as far as Article 31 is specifically concerned, their meaning is self-explanatory.[11] The exhaustive list of criteria in Article 31 is less elaborate than that in Article 12 of the First Convention dealing with the prohibition of non-adverse distinction, with the former omitting 'sex', 'nationality' and the catch-all phrase 'any other similar criteria'.[12]

---

[7] *Draft Conventions adopted by the 1948 Stockholm Conference*, p. 19.

[8] See also Gabor Rona and Robert J. McGuire, 'The Principle of Non-Discrimination', in Andrew Clapham, Paola Gaeta and Marco Sassòli (eds), *The 1949 Geneva Conventions: A Commentary*, Oxford University Press, 2015, pp. 191–205, at 197.

[9] Whereas the English version of the 1949 Geneva Conventions uses the wording 'for return', the French version speaks of 'le renvoi à la Partie au conflit'. The absence of the words 'to the Party to the conflict' in the English version of Article 31(1) can only be explained as an oversight by the drafters, in view of the close relationship between Article 30 and Article 31(1). Thus, both equally authentic versions of the Geneva Conventions express the common will of the drafters. On this point, see the commentary on Article 55, para. 3129.

[10] See also Model Agreement Relating to the Relief of Medical Personnel and Chaplains, Article 3.

[11] For a human rights law perspective, see UN Human Rights Committee, *General Comment No. 18: Non-discrimination*, 10 November 1989.

[12] For its part, Article 12 lists fewer criteria than Article 9(1) of Additional Protocol I. See also Gabor Rona and Robert J. McGuire, 'The Principle of Non-Discrimination', in Andrew Clapham, Paola Gaeta and Marco Sassòli (eds), *The 1949 Geneva Conventions: A Commentary*, Oxford University Press, 2015, pp. 191–205, at 197.

2263   Thus, considerations of 'nationality', 'sex', age and 'other similar criteria' may be taken into account when selecting which personnel to return, but only when doing so is objectively justified, i.e. when these criteria do not qualify as an adverse distinction.[13] For example, if there are no longer any wounded or sick prisoners of war of a particular nationality, preference may be given to the medical and religious personnel of that nationality when selecting who is to return.[14] Similarly, the sex of the prisoners of war may be a deciding factor. On the basis of Article 12, as well as of similar provisions in the Third Convention, women who are wounded or sick 'shall be treated with all consideration due to their sex'.[15] This requirement may justify retaining female medical or religious personnel to cater to the specific needs of female prisoners of war or, conversely, in the absence of such needs, returning them earlier than their male counterparts.

2. Preferred grounds for selection

2264 The selection of personnel for return needs to be made 'preferably according to the chronological order of their capture and their state of health'. As is clear from the use of 'preferably', these two criteria are neither obligatory nor exclusive. Thus, in a special agreement concluded on the basis of Article 31(2), the Parties to the conflict may decide to include additional or different criteria. If no such agreement exists, however, 'the chronological order of their capture' and 'their state of health' remain the sole criteria by which to determine the order of return of personnel covered by Article 30.

2265   Article 31(1) does not specify a hierarchy between the two criteria for return. However, when medical or religious personnel are themselves wounded or sick, they may not be able to perform their function of catering to the medical or spiritual needs of the prisoners of war. In that case, their retention on the basis of Article 28(1) may no longer be justified.[16] Thus, also in line with the purpose of Articles 28 and 30, priority for return may be granted to wounded or sick medical or religious personnel over able-bodied personnel who may have been captured earlier.

---

[13] For the concept of 'adverse distinction', see the commentary on Article 12, section F.1.c.

[14] On the question of whether persons covered by Articles 24 or 26 can be retained in order to care for the medical or spiritual needs of prisoners of war of a different Party to the conflict, see the commentary on Article 28, para. 2185.

[15] For references to the specific needs of female prisoners of war in the Third Convention, see Articles 3(1), 14(2), 16, 25(4), 29, 49(1), 88(2), 88(3), 97(4) and 108(2) of that convention.

[16] See Model Agreement Relating to the Retention of Medical Personnel and Chaplains, Article 10. For further information, see the commentary on that article, p. 13. See also the logic at work in Article 4 of the Model Agreement Relating to the Relief of Medical Personnel and Chaplains. For the text, origins and status of the Model Agreements, see the commentary on Article 28, para. 2160.

2266   The requirement that the selection be made on the basis of the 'chronological order of their capture' has been referred to as the 'first-in/first-out approach'.[17]

2267   Article 31(1) speaks of the chronological order of 'their' capture and of 'their' state of health without specifying who exactly 'they' are. In order to interpret these references, two separate elements must be kept in mind. The first element is the scope of application *ratione personae* of Articles 24 and 26. These provisions not only cover doctors (general practitioners and specialists) but may also include other categories of personnel such as nurses, staff exclusively engaged in the administration of medical units and establishments, and military religious personnel.[18]

2268   The second element relates to the logic of the provisions in the First Convention regulating the fate of medical and religious personnel who have fallen into enemy hands (Articles 28 and 30): retaining some or all of such personnel is only lawful if justified by, and for as long as there are, medical or spiritual needs of the prisoners of war.[19] Thus, the sole guiding factor in assessing whether medical and religious personnel can be retained remains those needs and if and how they can be addressed by the specific skills of the persons in question.[20] Inherently, this will be a context-specific assessment. Depending on the facts of the case, for example, there may be no need to retain any administrative staff but a need to retain some nurses. The reference to 'their' is, therefore, to be applied to members of the same professional group: doctors vis-à-vis doctors, nurses vis-à-vis nurses, chaplains vis-à-vis chaplains, and so on. In other words, the criteria of 'chronological order of capture' and of 'state of health' cannot be applied vis-à-vis the entirety of the personnel in enemy hands. Thus, if the medical situation of the wounded and sick evolves in such a way that it is no longer required to retain all surgeons, the selection of which surgeons are to be returned has to be made on the basis of the surgeons' chronological order of capture and state of health. This reasoning means that a Party to the conflict cannot seek to retain a surgeon to work as a nurse.[21] Conversely, the methodology of looking at the professional reference group instead of at the entirety of the medical and religious personnel in enemy hands also precludes that persons qualify for return on the basis of the chronological order of their

---

[17] United States, *Law of Armed Conflict Deskbook*, 2012, p. 54.

[18] For a discussion of these provisions' scope of application *ratione personae*, see the commentaries on Article 24, section C, and Article 26, section D.1.

[19] For details, see the commentaries on Article 28, section C, and Article 30, section C.1.

[20] This is without prejudice to the rule in Article 28(4).

[21] See Model Agreement Relating to the Retention of Medical Personnel and Chaplains, Article 3, paras 1 and 2. During the 1949 Diplomatic Conference, a proposal was made (by the French delegation) to include the following sentence: 'Specialists for whose services there is no special call in the camps shall have priority in repatriation.' The proposed amendment was not accepted, but can also be considered redundant in that it flows in any case from a consistent application of Articles 28(1) and 31(1). For details, see *Final Record of the Diplomatic Conference of Geneva of 1949*, Vol. II-A, p. 171.

capture while their services are still objectively required in view of the medical or spiritual needs of the prisoners of war.

D. Paragraph 2: Special agreements on retention

1. General considerations

2269 Article 31(2) allows the Parties to the conflict, from the outbreak of hostilities, to agree on (i) 'the percentage of personnel to be retained, in proportion to the number of prisoners' and (ii) 'the distribution of the said personnel in the camps'.[22] This may allow for a smoother implementation of aspects of the Convention that may otherwise cause dispute between the Parties to the conflict.

2270 An agreement concluded on the basis of Article 31(2) constitutes a special agreement in the sense of Article 6 and therefore needs to comply with the conditions of Article 6.[23] In any event, the agreement also needs to respect the prohibition under Article 31(1) of discrimination on the basis of 'race, religion or political opinion'.[24]

2271 As indicated by the word 'may', the conclusion of a special agreement on the basis of Article 31(2) is not compulsory. Special agreements may be concluded by means of direct contacts between the Parties to the conflict or indirect contacts through a neutral intermediary such as the ICRC.[25] Since 1949, no special agreements appear to have been concluded on the basis of Article 31(2). In this respect, Resolution 3 of the 1949 Diplomatic Conference had noted, explicitly referring to the opening words of Article 31(2) – '[a]s from the outbreak of hostilities' – that 'agreements may only with difficulty be concluded during hostilities'. With this in mind, the Conference requested that the ICRC prepare

---

[22] An alternative reading of Article 31(2) would be that the special agreement only relates to the 'percentage of personnel to be retained' and that this percentage is to be determined 'in proportion to the number of prisoners' as well as 'in proportion to' the 'distribution of the said personnel in the camps'. This reading would not make sense, however: the percentage of personnel to be retained cannot depend on the distribution of personnel (already) in the camps. The understanding that the special agreement can address 'the percentage of personnel to be retained, in proportion to the number of prisoners' and, separately, that it can address how said personnel are to be distributed in the camps, is corroborated by the *Final Record of the Diplomatic Conference of Geneva of 1949*, Vol. II-A, Report of Committee I, p. 196.

[23] Article 31(2) explicitly uses the term 'special agreement', while Article 6(1) explicitly refers to Article 31.

[24] See Gabor Rona and Robert J. McGuire, 'The Principle of Non-Discrimination', in Andrew Clapham, Paola Gaeta and Marco Sassòli (eds), *The 1949 Geneva Conventions: A Commentary*, Oxford University Press, 2015, pp. 191–205, at 197.

[25] See also Jean-Pierre Schoenholzer, 'Le médecin dans les Conventions de Genève de 1949', *Revue internationale de la Croix-Rouge et Bulletin international des Sociétés de la Croix-Rouge*, Vol. 35, Nos 410/411, February/March 1953, pp. 94–126 and 169–194, at 173: 'A défaut d'accord, la puissance détentrice déterminera le pourcentage sur la base de la raison, de l'équité et de l'expérience.' ('In the absence of an agreement the Detaining Power will determine the percentage on the basis of reason, equity and experience.')

a model agreement on the subject. This became the Model Agreement Relating to the Retention of Medical Personnel and Chaplains.[26]

2272   A Party to the conflict may only exercise the right to retain the enemy's med-ical and religious personnel if the conditions of Article 28(1) are met, i.e. 'in so far as the state of health, the spiritual needs and the number of prisoners of war require'. The fact that Article 31(2) invites the Parties to the conflict to agree upon some of the practicalities involved in this exercise does not undermine the validity of these conditions: any special agreement concluded on the basis of this provision needs to respect the conditions of Article 28(1).[27] Similarly, irrespective of whether or not such a special agreement has been concluded, the duty remains to return those who may not or no longer be retained.[28] Thus, the conclusion of a special agreement does not alter the legal framework applicable on the basis of Articles 28 and 30.

2273   Ideally, in order to ensure that different perspectives are identified and addressed in the agreements, negotiations should include persons of different genders and backgrounds.[29]

2. Aspects which can be regulated by special agreement

2274   The first aspect with regard to which Parties to the conflict may conclude a special agreement is the 'percentage of personnel to be retained, in proportion to the number of prisoners'.[30] Such an agreement has the advantage of providing both sides with legal certainty as to the ratios that are mutually considered permissible.

2275   '[P]risoners' refers only to the prisoners of war already in the hands of the enemy. Thus, as is the case with the unilateral exercise of the right to retain medical and religious personnel, 'anticipatory retention' is prohibited even when provided for in a special agreement.[31] Such an agreement, for example

---

[26] For details on the background and status of this Model Agreement, see the commentary on Article 28, para. 2160.

[27] For a specific example, see the discussion on 'anticipatory retention' in para. 2274 and the com-mentary on Article 28, para. 2165.

[28] See *Minutes of the Conference of Government Experts of 1947*, Committee I, Vol. II, Tome 1, p. 186, remarks by Jean Pictet in reaction to a proposal to delete what is now Article 31(2), with a proposal for an additional sentence.

[29] See UN Security Council, Res. 1325, 31 October 2000, para. 1. There is a growing acknowl-edgement that women, men, girls and boys are affected by armed conflict in different ways, and that, accordingly, the representation of both women and men at all decision-making levels in national, regional and international institutions and mechanisms for conflict prevention, man-agement and resolution benefits the process. The application of international humanitarian law should also reflect this understanding.

[30] This wording mirrors the third of the three criteria in Article 28(1) that can be used to justify the retention of medical and religious personnel: 'the state of health, the spiritual needs and the number of prisoners of war'.

[31] As to the unlawfulness of 'anticipatory retention' if exercised unilaterally by a Party to the con-flict, see para. 2275 and the commentary on Article 28, para. 2165. A special agreement allowing the Parties to the conflict to resort to 'anticipatory retention' would equally be unlawful as it

when concluded at the beginning of an armed conflict with a view to the hypothetical, future capture of prisoners of war, would run counter to the purpose of Articles 28 and 30 of the First Convention, which is to ensure that, at all times, the expertise of medical and religious personnel can continue to serve the needs of the wounded and sick, and would thus be unlawful.

2276   The Model Agreement Relating to the Retention of Medical Personnel and Chaplains suggests different ratios between the number of prisoners of war and the number and type of medical and religious personnel who can be retained to cater for their medical and spiritual needs.[32] For a contemporary analysis of how many, and which type of, medical personnel may be retained in relation to a given number of prisoners of war, see the commentary on Article 28, section C.

2277   As with the methodology for implementing Article 31(1), the approach here should take into account the professional qualifications of the various personnel to be retained (x number of nurses per x number of prisoners of war, x number of religious personnel per x number of prisoners of war, etc.).[33] In line with the discussion under Article 31(1) regarding whether specialists can be retained, the third paragraph of Article 3 of the Model Agreement Relating to the Retention of Medical Personnel and Chaplains invites Parties to the conflict to conclude agreements concerning the 'non-retention or immediate repatriation of physicians who are considered to be highly specialized, and whose presence in their country of origin is considered necessary for public health'.

2278   The second aspect with regard to which Parties to the conflict may conclude a special agreement is the distribution of the personnel in the camps. This possibility underscores the fact that retained personnel continue to be in the service of their Power of Origin.[34] With regard to military religious personnel, Article 35 of the Third Convention states that chaplains in enemy hands, including when they are retained to assist prisoners of war, 'shall be allocated among the various camps and labour detachments containing prisoners of war belonging to the same forces, speaking the same language or practising the same religion'.

2279   Special agreements governing the retention of medical and religious personnel need not be restricted to the two aspects mentioned explicitly in Article 31(2). Provided its conditions are complied with, Article 6 allows for the conclusion of special agreements on 'all matters concerning which [the High

would conflict with the conditions of the second sentence of Article 6, according to which 'no special agreement shall adversely affect the situation of . . . members of the medical personnel or of chaplains, as defined by the present Convention, nor restrict the rights which it confers upon them'.

[32] See Model Agreement Relating to the Retention of Medical Personnel and Chaplains, Article 2. See also United States, *Law of Armed Conflict Deskbook*, 2012, p. 54. For historical reference purposes, see *Final Record of the Diplomatic Conference of Geneva of 1949*, Vol. II-A, p. 170 (France).

[33] See para. 2268. See also *Final Record of the Diplomatic Conference of Geneva of 1949*, Vol. II-A, pp. 126–127 (France).

[34] *Final Record of the Diplomatic Conference of Geneva of 1949*, Vol. II-A, p. 196.

Contracting Parties] may deem it suitable to make separate provision'.[35] Since Articles 28, 30 and 31 of the First Convention leave many practical yet important questions unaddressed, a special agreement may be a suitable instrument to determine the way in which such questions are to be dealt with. This may be the case, for example, for settling the question whether the detention of auxiliary medical personnel as prisoners of war on the basis of Article 29 should lead to a decrease in the number of personnel retained on the basis of Article 28;[36] or in order to establish the procedures for repatriation.[37]

Select bibliography

See the select bibliography of the commentary on Article 28 of the First Convention.

[35] For details, see the commentary on Article 6, paras 958–959.
[36] See the commentary on Article 29, paras 2213–2215 and the commentary on Article 45, para. 2722.
[37] See e.g. United States, *Law of War Manual*, 2015, paras 4.10.2 and 9.1.2.2.

RETURN OF PERSONNEL BELONGING TO NEUTRAL COUNTRIES

❖ Text of the provision*

(1) Persons designated in Article 27 who have fallen into the hands of the adverse Party may not be detained.

(2) Unless otherwise agreed, they shall have permission to return to their country, or if this is not possible, to the territory of the Party to the conflict in whose service they were, as soon as a route for their return is open and military considerations permit.

(3) Pending their release, they shall continue their work under the direction of the adverse Party; they shall preferably be engaged in the care of the wounded and sick of the Party to the conflict in whose service they were.

(4) On their departure, they shall take with them their effects, personal articles and valuables and the instruments, arms and if possible the means of transport belonging to them.

(5) The Parties to the conflict shall secure to this personnel, while in their power, the same food, lodging, allowances and pay as are granted to the corresponding personnel of their armed forces. The food shall in any case be sufficient as regards quantity, quality and variety to keep the said personnel in a normal state of health.

❖ Reservations or declarations

None

Contents

* Paragraph numbers have been added for ease of reference.

A. Introduction

2280 Article 32 deals with the specific scenario in which the medical personnel of
a recognized society of a neutral country (persons covered by Article 27) fall
into the hands of the adversary of the Party to the conflict they are assisting.
Article 27, for its part, clarifies the conditions under which such society may
offer the assistance of its medical personnel and units to a Party to the conflict.
When the conditions of Article 27 are fulfilled, these personnel will qualify as
persons protected under the First Convention, i.e. they are to be respected and
protected in all circumstances.[1]

2281   Since the end of the Second World War, there seem to have been no instances
in which Article 27 was implemented; hence, there also seems to be no practice
from this period with regard to Article 32.[2]

2282   When Additional Protocol I applies, Article 9(2) thereof provides that the relevant provisions of Article 32 are applicable to the personnel of permanent medical units and transports made available to a Party to the conflict for humanitarian purposes: (a) by a neutral or other State which is not a Party to that
conflict; (b) by a recognized and authorized aid society of such a State; or (c) by
an impartial international humanitarian organization.[3]

B. Historical background

2283 The origins of Article 32 can be traced back to Articles 12 and 13 of the 1906
Geneva Convention,[4] and especially to Articles 12 and 13 of the 1929 Geneva
Convention on the Wounded and Sick. Article 12 of the latter Convention
established a prohibition on retaining the three categories of personnel for

---

[1] This protection can be lost if such persons commit an act harmful to the enemy. For a discussion of what type of conduct amounts to an act harmful to the enemy, see the commentary on
Article 24, section F.

[2] For a discussion of the absence of practice with regard to Article 27 since 1949, see the commentary on that article, para. 2116. Article 12 of the 1929 Geneva Convention on the Wounded
and Sick, one of the precursors of Article 32, was among the most controversial, and most frequently violated, provisions during the First World War; see Des Gouttes, *Commentaire de la
Convention de Genève de 1929 sur les blessés et malades*, ICRC, 1930, p. 72.

[3] Except hospital ships, to which Article 25 of the Second Convention applies. See Article 9(2) of
Additional Protocol I.

[4] As to Article 32(1), the prohibition on detaining cannot be found in Article 12 of the 1906 Geneva
Convention. That provision was based on the premise that all categories of medical personnel,
when they had fallen into enemy hands, would continue to exercise their medical functions
except when their assistance was no longer necessary. The 1929 Geneva Convention reversed this
logic (which was, in turn, partially reversed in the 1949 Geneva Conventions for two categories
of medical personnel). For details, see the commentary on Article 28, section B.

which it provided: (i) military medical and religious personnel; (ii) the personnel of voluntary aid societies assisting the medical services of their own State's armed forces; and (iii) the personnel of recognized societies of neutral countries assisting the medical services of a Party to an international armed conflict.

2284   The 1949 Diplomatic Conference reversed this logic when it comes to categories (i) and (ii); in other words, when these persons fall into enemy hands, they may be retained, but only in so far as the state of health, the spiritual needs and the number of prisoners of war require.[5] The rule in Article 12 of the 1929 Geneva Convention was kept, however, as far as category (iii) was concerned, resulting in Article 32(1).[6]

C. Paragraph 1: Prohibition on detaining

2285 Article 32 applies to the persons designated in Article 27. Although Article 32(4) deals with certain objects which these persons have with them when they fall into the hands of the adversary of the Party to the conflict they are assisting, the status of these objects (such as medical units and transports) is covered by Article 34.

2286   Article 32 applies only when persons covered by Article 27 fall 'into the hands of the adverse Party'. The circumstances in which these persons fall into the hands of that Party are immaterial. The words 'adverse Party' need to be understood as referring to the adversary of the Party to the conflict whose medical services these persons are assisting.[7] Private individuals of a neutral country are not in an adversarial relationship vis-à-vis that Party to the conflict.

2287   When these persons fall into the hands of the adversary, Article 32 stipulates that the latter has no right to detain them (be it as prisoners of war, civilian internees, or persons having any other status), for example on account of having assisted the medical services of the armed forces of its adversary. At that moment, that Party to the conflict is obliged to implement Article 32(2). Thus, while they are exempt from capture and detention, they may be held temporarily in line with Article 32(2).[8]

2288   While the provision does not say so explicitly, the Party into whose hands they have fallen may not retain (in the sense of Article 28) medical personnel covered by Article 27. This is the case even if the medical needs of the prisoners of war are compelling.

---

[5] For details, see the commentaries on Articles 28–30 and 31 of the First Convention, as well as the commentary on Article 33 of the Third Convention.

[6] 'It was perfectly obvious, in view of the general principles of International Law, that it was quite impossible to contemplate altering the status of medical personnel of neutral countries.' *Final Record of the Diplomatic Conference of Geneva of 1949*, Vol. II-A, p. 196.

[7] The words 'adversary of the State which accepts such assistance' are used in Article 27(2), and describe the relationship more accurately than the term 'adverse Party' used in Article 32(1).

[8] See e.g. United States, *Law of War Manual*, 2015, para. 7.9.1.1.

2289   The rationale for the prohibition on detaining and retaining persons covered by Article 27 is that these are civilians of a neutral country.[9] This neutral country may be either the country of the recognized society covered by Article 27, or any other neutral country. In all instances, as these persons are protected under the First Convention, the State into whose hands they fall does not have the right to detain or retain them. This reading is, of course, without prejudice to the possibility that the State concerned may have a separate legal basis for detaining a given individual, for example if they are suspected of having committed a grave breach or an ordinary crime.

2290   The only exception to the prohibition set forth in Article 32(1) is the existence of an agreement to the contrary, based on Article 32(2).

2291   It is conceivable that a recognized society working on the basis of Article 27 decides to hire one or more private citizens of the same nationality as the Party to the conflict they are assisting. The First Convention does not deal, under this hypothesis, with the status of such persons when they fall into the hands of the Party to the conflict that is their own State's adversary.[10] Since, from the perspective of the Party into whose hands they have fallen, they are enemy nationals, it would be understandable if that Party sought to deny the applicability of Article 32 (a provision based on the assumption that the persons covered by Article 27 are private citizens of a neutral country). However, in that case, the least that can be expected is that Article 28 (which applies to medical personnel working as auxiliaries to the medical services of their own State's armed forces), as well as Articles 30 and 31, will be applied by analogy.

D. Paragraph 2: Permission to return unless agreement to the contrary

2292   The basic premise of Article 32 is that the persons covered by it have permission to leave the territory of the Party into whose hands they have fallen. Ideally, they are entitled to return to the neutral country of which they are nationals.[11] However, if this is not possible, they are entitled to go to the territory of the Party to the conflict they were assisting within the framework of Article 27.[12] The assessment of whether it is 'possible' to return to the neutral country of which they are nationals may depend not only on practical considerations, but also on the wishes of the persons in question. In all instances, upon

---

[9] Persons covered by Article 27 do not become members of the armed forces of the country they assist. See the commentary on Article 27, para. 2126.

[10] Lanord, 1999, p. 69.

[11] As is clear from the word 'permission', persons covered by Article 27 cannot be compelled to return against their will. In this regard, see the commentary on Article 30, para. 2231.

[12] Article 12(2) of the 1929 Geneva Convention states that 'they shall be sent back to the belligerent to which they belong'. The qualifying provision 'return to their country, or if this is not possible, to the territory of the Party to the conflict in whose service they were' was added by the 1947 Conference of Government Experts; see *Minutes of the Conference of Government Experts of 1947*, Vol. II, p. 7.

return, the persons are entitled to resume their duties within the framework of Article 27.

2293   Article 32(2) assumes that the medical personnel have fallen into the hands of the adversary outside the territory of the State they are assisting. Article 32(2) does not clarify what happens if they are captured when on the territory of the State they are assisting, for example when that territory is invaded by an outside force. In such instances, the basic rule applies, i.e. they may not be detained, and must, unless otherwise agreed, have permission to return to their country.

2294   Except when there is an agreement to the contrary, the Party into whose hands persons covered by Article 27 have fallen may unilaterally and temporarily delay their return, either to their country or to that of the Party they are assisting, on two grounds only: when a route is not yet open for their return, or when military considerations do not permit such a return.[13] Articles 32(3) and 32(5) regulate the period prior to the personnel's return.

2295   Article 32 leaves it to the Party into whose hands the medical personnel have fallen to invoke one or both of the aforementioned grounds. Yet that Party is expected to interpret these grounds in good faith, bearing in mind that it has no right to detain or to retain these persons.

2296   The first ground which may be invoked to delay the return of persons covered by Article 32 relates to a material impossibility, i.e. the fact that no route (whether by land, water or air) is open for their return. This may be the case, for example, when hostilities are still ongoing and no safe alternatives exist.

2297   The second ground is more delicate, in that it allows the Party into whose hands the personnel have fallen to invoke 'military considerations' (but no considerations other than those of a military nature). This may be the case when the persons would be in a position to pass on information of military value they acquired to the Party to the conflict they are assisting. Use of the term 'military considerations' makes it clear that this ground is less stringent than if there would have been a requirement of military necessity.

2298   Both grounds only allow the Party into whose hands the persons have fallen to delay their return, not to refuse to allow them to return altogether. As soon as the basis for delay disappears, for example, when a route becomes available or when the information acquired has lost its military value, e.g. because a planned attack has taken place, the persons must be allowed to return.

2299   No grounds other than the two explicitly mentioned in Article 32 may be invoked as a reason to delay the return of persons covered by Article 27. Even when the prisoners of war detained by the Party to the conflict have considerable medical needs, the return of this category of medical personnel may not be refused. In this respect, Article 32 is markedly different from the retention

---

[13] While phrased slightly differently, Article 30(1) envisages essentially identical grounds with regard to persons covered by Articles 24 and 26 who have fallen into enemy hands.

regime,[14] and justifiably so. As neutral nationals, coming from a neutral State which remains entitled to all the protections conferred on it by the law of neutrality, persons covered by Article 27 can indeed not be treated on the same basis as nationals of a Party to the conflict.

2300   Article 32 does not specify who has to pay the costs of the transport. Failing an agreement on this matter, the rules governing the transport of prisoners of war to a neutral country, and those governing the return of civilian internees, could be applied by analogy: the Party into whose hands the personnel have fallen must pay the costs of their transportation only up to its own borders.[15] From there, the neutral country (or its recognized society) will have to pay the costs of transportation to their final destination.

2301   All of the foregoing is without prejudice to the possibility – explicitly provided for through the formula 'unless otherwise agreed'[16] – that an agreement is reached stating that one or more persons covered by Article 32 will stay with the Party into whose hands they have fallen, for example in order to perform medical activities.

2302   For its part, Article 32 provides no guidance as to who needs to be involved in the agreement:[17] the persons covered by Article 32, the recognized society of a neutral country which lends its assistance to a Party to the conflict, the neutral country, the Party whose medical service they are assisting, and/or the Party into whose hands the persons have fallen.[18] First and foremost, since its consent is required for the recognized society to act under Article 27 in the first place, the neutral State will need to agree to allow the staff of the recognized society to continue to serve while they are no longer in the hands of the Party for which the initial consent was given. Second, the Party into whose hands the personnel have fallen will need to be involved in the agreement. No agreement is required, however, of the Party whose medical services the personnel are assisting, since such persons work not only for the wounded and sick of one Party to the conflict, but for the wounded and sick of all sides in a conflict.

E.   Paragraph 3: Work pending release

2303 The third and fifth paragraphs of Article 32 both govern the period during which the medical personnel are awaiting their return. They are relevant both when the return is imminent and when there is an agreement (on the basis of Article 32(2)) for them to stay longer.

---

[14] See Articles 28, 30 and 31, which apply when medical and religious personnel (covered by Article 24) and personnel of voluntary aid societies (covered by Article 26) fall into enemy hands.
[15] See Article 116 of the Third Convention and Article 135(2) of the Fourth Convention.
[16] This possibility derives from an amendment adopted without discussion during the 1929 Diplomatic Conference; see *Proceedings of the Geneva Diplomatic Conference of 1929*, p. 148.
[17] Since such an agreement involves the High Contracting Parties, it is a special agreement within the meaning of Article 6 and, as such, will need to comply with the conditions of that provision.
[18] See Lanord, 1999, p. 69.

2304   These paragraphs fail to address many questions which may arise in terms of the treatment to be accorded to these persons during that period. This will be a matter of particular concern in cases where their return is delayed. As a practical matter, the persons ought to be entitled to the same facilities as those provided for under the retention regime.[19] If an agreement under Article 32(2) exists, such a clarification could be part of it.

2305   The first sentence of Article 32(3) indicates that 'they shall continue their work under the direction' of the Party to the conflict into whose hands they have fallen. As is the case with retained personnel, the work in question can only be of a medical nature,[20] and the Party to the conflict into whose hands they have fallen must allow the medical personnel to carry out their work 'in accordance with their professional ethics'.[21] Persons covered by Article 32 are not subject to 'the framework of the military laws and regulations of the Detaining Power' as required for retained personnel under Article 28. Having said that, they work 'under the direction' of the Party to the conflict into whose hands they have fallen. This implies that they will have to accept a certain amount of oversight.[22]

2306   Pursuant to the second sentence of Article 32(3), the personnel should work 'preferably' for the care of the wounded and sick of the Party to the conflict in whose service they were.[23] From the perspective of contemporary medical ethics, this recommendation makes sense, in that it prohibits the Party into whose hands they have fallen from instructing the persons covered by Article 27 to look after the medical needs of its own armed forces (or of its own civilian population) to the detriment of the 'wounded and sick of the Party to the conflict in whose service they were'.

2307   If the Party into whose hands the medical personnel have fallen detains prisoners of war of several nationalities, the clarification that 'they shall preferably

---

[19] This means that, while they are not to be deemed prisoners of war, they must at least benefit from all the provisions of the Third Convention and, in addition, be entitled to certain facilities for carrying out their medical or spiritual duties; see Article 28 of the First Convention and Article 33 of the Third Convention.

[20] See Article 28(2)(c): '... they shall not ... be required to perform any work outside their medical or religious duties'. As to whether religious personnel may be covered by Article 27, see the commentary on that provision, section D.3.

[21] This wording appears in Article 28(2) of the First Convention (for a discussion, see the commentary on that article, paras 2168 and 2184). See also Article 33(2) of the Third Convention, which uses the phrase 'in accordance with their professional etiquette'.

[22] See *Proceedings of the Geneva Diplomatic Conference of 1906*, p. 125. Initially, it was proposed to use the term 'control'; this was changed to 'direction'; see *ibid.* p. 255. Retained personnel work under the 'authority' (Article 28 of the First Convention) and 'control' of the 'competent service' of the Party retaining them (Article 33 of the Third Convention). Practically speaking, however, the extent to which they must obey the instructions of the Party into whose hands they have fallen is not regulated.

[23] Substantially identical terminology can be found in Articles 28(2) and 30(2) of the First Convention and in Article 33(2) of the Third Convention. During the 1929 Diplomatic Conference, this language was criticized, yet in the end it was maintained. See *Proceedings of the Geneva Diplomatic Conference of 1929*, pp. 149, 160 and 162.

be engaged' ensures that the prisoners of war receive medical care from professionals who speak their own language and are familiar with their culture,[24] to the extent that this is lawful.

2308   However, as indicated by the word 'preferably', their being 'engaged in the care of the wounded and sick of the Party to the conflict in whose service they were' is merely a recommendation. In particular, and at all times, the principle of impartiality of care, as enshrined in Article 12(3), prevails, i.e. '[o]nly urgent medical reasons will authorize priority in the order of treatment to be administered'. This will be so even if the order in which treatment is administered on the basis of such 'medical reasons' leads to a situation in which the personnel in question are unable to prioritize care for the wounded and sick of the Party to the conflict in whose service they were.

2309   Should these persons work for the National Red Cross or Red Crescent Society of a neutral State, the same rule would also flow from their having to comply with the Fundamental Principle of impartiality.

F. Paragraph 4: Objects which may be taken when departing

2310   Article 32(4) addresses a practical matter with regard to the departure of persons covered by this provision. It applies both to persons who leave soon after they fall into the hands of the adversary of the Party they are assisting, and to those who stay longer pursuant to an agreement under Article 32(2).

2311   First, when leaving, they are entitled to take with them 'their effects, personal articles and valuables'.[25] They had to have those objects with them at the time they fell into the hands of the adversary of the Party to the conflict they were assisting. It is immaterial whether these 'effects, personal articles and valuables' are their private property.

2312   Second, when leaving, such persons are entitled to take with them 'the instruments, arms and if possible the means of transport belonging to them'. Here, too, the words 'belonging to them' need to be construed as meaning that they are their personal property. However, it is likely that these instruments, arms and means of transport are not their private property, but rather that of the recognized society of the neutral country or of the medical services of the armed

---

[24] See also, in this regard, Article 30(3) of the Third Convention.

[25] There is some redundancy in the list in Article 32(4), which speaks both of 'effects' and of 'personal articles'; here, 'effects' means 'personal belongings' (see *Concise Oxford English Dictionary*, 12th edition, Oxford University Press, 2011, p. 456). Similarly, 'valuables' ('small valuable items of personal property', *ibid.* p. 1598) are but a subcategory of personal articles. Except for the mention of 'arms' and 'means of transport' in Article 32, a similar list appears in Article 30(3) of the First Convention for personnel whose retention is necessary by virtue of Article 28: 'On their departure, they shall take with them the effects, personal belongings, valuables and instruments belonging to them.' With regard to the personal property of prisoners of war, see Article 18 of the Third Convention.

forces they were assisting.[26] If that is the case, these objects cannot be taken with them when they depart. However, the logic underpinning Article 33(2) and Article 35(2) can arguably be considered applicable *mutatis mutandis*, i.e. while these objects remain in enemy hands, they must continue to be used for the care of the wounded and sick.

2313   However, if persons covered by Article 32 have taken arms from the wounded and sick prior to their falling into the hands of the Party to the conflict they were assisting, these arms cannot be taken with them on their departure. They belong neither to them nor to the recognized society of the neutral country. Nor do they belong to the medical services of the armed forces they were assisting. These arms are booty of war, and can remain with the Party into whose hands the personnel have fallen.

2314   The 'instruments' referred to must be understood to include their medical instruments.[27] As to the 'arms', this refers to the individual light weapons which persons covered by Article 27 may carry in order to defend themselves, or to defend the wounded and sick in their charge.[28] There is no such absolute right to take with them the 'means of transport', such as ambulances, they had with them when they fell into the hands of the adversary. Whether or not they will be able to take such means of transport with them when they depart will depend on whether or not it is possible to do so.[29] If it is not possible in the circumstances (for example, because the person is returning by aeroplane), this does not necessarily mean that the Party to the conflict into whose hands they have fallen acquires any right of ownership of the said means of transport. The rules set forth in Article 34 continue to apply.

G. Paragraph 5: Treatment to be accorded while in the power of the adversary

2315 The third and fifth paragraphs of Article 32 both govern the period during which the medical personnel are awaiting their return.

2316   Article 32(5) prescribes a number of practicalities in terms of the treatment to which persons covered by Article 32 are entitled as long as they remain in the power of the Party to the conflict into whose hands they have fallen.[30] Like Article 32(3), Article 32(5) applies both to persons who will leave soon after they fall into the hands of the adversary of the Party they are assisting, and to

---

[26] In this context, it should be recalled that the real and personal property of aid societies covered by Article 26 or Article 27 is to be regarded as private property. For details, see Article 34(1).

[27] See *Proceedings of the Geneva Diplomatic Conference of 1906*, pp. 55 and 117.

[28] See the commentary on Article 27, para. 2134. Article 27 does not address the issue of whether persons covered by Article 32 are entitled to continue to carry their arms once they have fallen into the hands of the adversary of the Party they are assisting. If one looks for guidance to the regulations for prisoners of war, this is not the case; see Article 18(1) of the Third Convention.

[29] During the 1949 Diplomatic Conference, a proposal to delete the words 'if possible' was not adopted; see *Final Record of the Diplomatic Conference of Geneva of 1949*, Vol. II-A, p. 82.

[30] Paragraph 5 speaks of 'the Parties to the conflict' in the plural. Of course, the obligation pertains only to the Party to the conflict into whose hands the persons covered by Article 27 have fallen.

those who stay longer pursuant to an agreement reached under Article 32(2), in each instance for as long as they are in the power of that Party.

2317   The first sentence of Article 32(5) requires that Party to 'secure to this personnel . . . the same food, lodging, allowances and pay as are granted to the corresponding personnel of their armed forces'.[31] Persons covered by Article 27, however, are civilians and will not necessarily have ranks corresponding to military ranks. Where an agreement is reached on the basis of Article 32(2), it may clarify this point. If no such agreement exists, the Party into whose hands they have fallen could consider granting them the same level of treatment as it accords to its own military medical personnel of approximately the same seniority.

2318   The second sentence of Article 32(5) deals with the amount and type of food which must be given to the personnel as long as they remain in the hands of the adversary of the Party to the conflict they are assisting. This food must 'in any case be sufficient as regards quantity, quality and variety to keep the said personnel in a normal state of health'.[32] The words 'in any case' emphasize that this is a minimum standard of treatment to which the personnel are entitled in all circumstances.

2319   Lastly, with regard to the question of whether the personnel are entitled to fly their national flag, see Article 43(2).[33]

Select bibliography

See the select bibliography of the commentary on Article 26 of the First Convention.

---

[31] This wording is the same as that used in Article 13(1) of the 1929 Geneva Convention on the Wounded and Sick. Article 13(2) of that Convention requires that 'at the outbreak of hostilities the belligerents will notify one another of the grades of their respective medical personnel'. On the issue of pay, see *Proceedings of the Geneva Diplomatic Conference of 1906*, p. 125.

[32] On this point, see *Final Record of the Diplomatic Conference of Geneva of 1949*, Vol. II-A, p. 196.

[33] See also United States, *Law of War Manual*, 2015, para. 4.12.

BUILDINGS AND MATERIAL

2320 The rules governing the protection of fixed and mobile medical units of the armed forces are contained in Chapter III of the First Convention.[1] They may in no circumstances be attacked, but must at all times be respected and protected by the Parties to the conflict. Article 19 specifically provides that, should such units or establishments fall into the hands of the adverse Party, their personnel must be free to pursue their duties, as long as the capturing Power has not itself ensured the necessary care of the wounded and sick they contain.

2321 Chapter V complements Chapter III and contains the rules detailing the fate of buildings and material of medical units of the armed forces and aid societies after they fall into enemy hands.

2322 Article 33 deals with this question in relation to the material of mobile medical units of the armed forces and to the buildings, material and stores of fixed medical establishments of the armed forces. This article does not regulate medical vehicles of the armed forces, which are covered by Article 35.

2323 Article 34 deals with the same question in relation to the buildings and material of aid societies which are admitted to the privileges of the Convention; in this case, the medical transports used by such societies are also covered.

2324 The personal property of medical and religious personnel of the armed forces, as well as of the medical personnel of neutral countries, who fall into enemy hands is dealt with in Articles 30(3) and 32(4).

[1] See, in particular, Articles 19, 21 and 22.

BUILDINGS AND MATERIAL OF MEDICAL UNITS AND ESTABLISHMENTS

❖ Text of the provision*

(1) The material of mobile medical units of the armed forces which fall into the hands of the enemy, shall be reserved for the care of wounded and sick.

(2) The buildings, material and stores of fixed medical establishments of the armed forces shall remain subject to the laws of war, but may not be diverted from their purpose as long as they are required for the care of wounded and sick. Nevertheless, the commanders of forces in the field may make use of them, in case of urgent military necessity, provided that they make previous arrangements for the welfare of the wounded and sick who are nursed in them.

(3) The material and stores defined in the present Article shall not be intentionally destroyed.

❖ Reservations or declarations

None

Contents

A. Introduction

2325 Article 33 governs the fate of medical property belonging to the armed forces when it falls into the hands of the enemy. This may happen either during the conduct of hostilities or in situations of occupation. The provision covers both

---

* Paragraph numbers have been added for ease of reference.

'fixed' and 'mobile' medical units, although the Convention does not define either of these concepts.[1]

2326 In its ordinary meaning, 'mobile' means 'able to move or be moved freely or easily'.[2] Mobile medical units are therefore establishments which can move from place to place as circumstances require and according to the movements of the troops. Field hospitals and any other establishment, however small, where wounded and sick persons are collected and cared for, constitute mobile medical units.

2327 The word 'fixed' can be understood as 'fastened securely in position'.[3] Fixed medical establishments are, therefore, permanent buildings used as hospitals and stores. Stores, in turn, can be defined as the places where pharmaceutical or any other medical equipment or supplies are kept and therefore fall within the category of buildings and material. This article does not regulate medical transports or vehicles of the armed forces, such as ambulances.[4]

B. Discussion

1. Mobile medical units and their material

2328 Article 33(1) deals with the material of mobile medical units.[5] At first, the provision would seem to be silent as to the fate of the mobile medical units themselves. However, in most instances it would be difficult to differentiate between the physical structure of such a unit and the material it contains, as the value of mobile medical units resides in the material contained therein. Accordingly, mobile medical units and all their material are covered by Article 33.[6]

2329 The mobile medical units of the armed forces and their material which fall into the hands of the enemy must be reserved for the care of the wounded and sick. This represents a limitation to the traditionally recognized right of a belligerent to take and use freely any movable public property of the enemy

---

[1] The Diplomatic Conference refrained from adopting specific definitions for 'mobile' and 'fixed' medical units and establishments; see Pictet (ed.), *Commentary on the First Geneva Convention*, ICRC, 1952, p. 195. For more details on these concepts, see the commentary on Article 19, paras 1775–1776.

[2] *Concise Oxford English Dictionary*, 12th edition, Oxford University Press, 2011, p. 918.

[3] *Ibid.* p. 538.

[4] Medical transports are covered by Article 35 of the First Convention, as long as they are exclusively engaged in the transport of the wounded and sick or of medical equipment. If the vehicle has the characteristics of a mobile medical unit and can deliver medical care, it will fall under Article 33.

[5] The fate of the personnel of these mobile medical units is governed by Article 19 of the First Convention.

[6] Such interpretation is supported by the wording of the corresponding provisions (Article 14) of both the 1929 Geneva Convention on the Wounded and Sick and the 1906 Geneva Convention.

as booty of war.[7] Thus, mobile medical units of the armed forces and their material which have fallen into enemy hands must be reserved for the treatment and care of the wounded and sick. They may not be diverted from their original purpose, even in case of urgent military necessity. Such a limitation is not imposed on fixed medical establishments; therein lies the major difference between the regimes for fixed medical establishments and mobile medical units of the armed forces.

2330   The 1949 Diplomatic Conference rejected a proposal put forward by the 1947 Conference of Government Experts to treat the material of mobile and fixed medical units and establishments in the same way. Had the proposal been accepted, it would have meant that the material of mobile medical units and establishments might have been liable to become booty of war.[8]

2331   The wounded and sick present in the mobile medical units must be cared for alongside any other wounded or sick persons, as their medical condition requires. In line with the accepted principle of impartiality of care, any wounded or sick persons must be cared for by the Party to the conflict in whose power they may be.[9]

2332   Unlike the 1906 and 1929 Geneva Conventions on the Wounded and Sick, Article 33(1) does not contain any obligation to restore mobile medical units and their material to their country of origin during hostilities. Under the regime of the 1929 Convention, mobile medical units which had fallen into enemy hands were to be restored, together with their equipment and stores, their means of transport and the drivers employed, under the conditions laid down for medical personnel, as far as possible at the same time as the medical personnel.[10] The 1949 Diplomatic Conference, having changed the rules governing medical personnel, including by creating the possibility of retaining them, chose not to require restoration of mobile medical units and their

---

[7] For the concept of booty of war, see Yoram Dinstein, 'Booty in Warfare', version of March 2008, in Rüdiger Wolfrum (ed.), *Max Planck Encyclopedia of Public International Law*, Oxford University Press, http://opil.ouplaw.com/home/EPIL William Gerald Downey, 'Captured Enemy Property: Booty of War and Seized Enemy Property', *American Journal of International Law*, Vol. 44, 1950, pp. 488–504; Elyce K.D. Santerre, 'From Confiscation to Contingency Contracting: Property Acquisition On or Near the Battlefield', *Military Law Review*, Vol. 124, Spring 1989, pp. 111–161; H.A. Smith, 'Booty of War', *British Yearbook of International Law*, Vol. 23, 1946, pp. 227–239; and Jean-Marie Henckaerts and Louise Doswald-Beck, *Customary International Humanitarian Law, Volume I: Rules*, ICRC/Cambridge University Press, 2005, commentary on Rule 49, pp. 173–175, available at https://www.icrc.org/customary-ihl/eng/docs/v1_rul.

[8] See *Final Record of the Diplomatic Conference of Geneva of 1949*, Vol. II-A, pp. 83–84. Both in 1906 and in 1929, mobile medical units were also considered not to be booty of war and needed to be reserved for the treatment of wounded and sick. See Article 14 of the 1906 Geneva Convention and Article 14 of the 1929 Geneva Convention on the Wounded and Sick, which provided that these units must be restored, as far as possible at the same time as the medical personnel who operate them are returned.

[9] See Article 12.   [10] See Article 14 of 1929 Geneva Convention on the Wounded and Sick.

material to their country of origin during hostilities. The practical difficulties of doing so also influenced the decision.[11]

2333 The First Convention is also silent on the fate of mobile medical units and their material at the end of hostilities. Unless otherwise provided, for example in a peace treaty, their fate is governed by the laws of war. As movable public property, the State which had originally owned the mobile medical units can neither demand their restoration nor request compensation.[12] The absence of practice found since 1949 on this issue has not allowed any further clarification of this point.

2. Fixed medical establishments

2334 The buildings, material and stores of fixed medical establishments of the armed forces which fall into enemy hands remain subject to the laws of war. This means that the material and stores of fixed medical establishments, being movable public property of the enemy State, can be taken as booty of war.[13] A State which takes booty is regarded as acquiring property without any obligation of restitution or compensation. Buildings, on the other hand, being real property of the enemy State, will not be war booty but can be used and administered by the Party into whose hands they have fallen.[14]

2335 The regime is subject to an important limitation as the buildings, material and stores of fixed medical establishments cannot be diverted from their purpose if they are required for the care of the wounded and sick. In other words, the Party into whose hands they have fallen may not make use of them for its own purposes so long as the interests of the wounded and sick demand otherwise. However, contrary to what is provided for mobile medical units, an exception of military necessity applies to fixed medical establishments. In case of urgent military necessity, the enemy can make use of these facilities for other purposes, provided that they make alternative arrangements for the 'welfare' of the wounded and sick who are being cared for therein.[15] As is clear from the words 'urgent military necessity', the use by the enemy of fixed

---

[11] For more details, see Pictet (ed.) *Commentary on the First Geneva Convention*, ICRC, 1952, pp. 272–273, and *Final Record of the Diplomatic Conference of Geneva of 1949*, Vol. II-A, p. 115.

[12] See e.g. Yoram Dinstein, 'Booty in Warfare', in Rüdiger Wolfrum (ed.), Version of March 2008, *Max Planck Encyclopedia of Public International Law*, Oxford University Press, para. 10, http://opil.ouplaw.com/home/EPIL; Elyce K.D. Santerre, 'From Confiscation to Contingency Contracting: Property Acquisition On or Near the Battlefield', *Military Law Review*, Vol. 124, 1989, pp. 113–120; and H.A. Smith. 'Booty of War', *British Yearbook of International Law*, Vol. 23, 1946, pp. 229–230.

[13] See Hague Regulations (1907), Article 53.   [14] See *ibid.* Article 55.

[15] As to the term 'welfare', the equally authoritative French text of the Convention uses the word 'bien-être'. This refers more precisely to the well-being of the wounded and sick rather than the wider concept of welfare.

medical establishments for purposes other than the care of the wounded and sick should be seen as a measure of last resort.

2336   Article 33(2) tries to strike a balance between the necessity of ensuring the care of the wounded and sick present in fixed medical establishments and the realities of war. Thus, the regime governing the buildings, material and stores of fixed medical establishments of the armed forces, while subject to the laws of war, is limited by an exception based on humanitarian considerations. This exception is in turn tempered by a further concession to military realities, which are once again subordinated to humanitarian requirements.

2337   In recent decades, no practice, in particular concerning the circumstances that could amount to 'urgent military necessity', could be found justifying the use of fixed medical establishments for other than medical purposes.

3. Prohibition of intentional destruction of material and stores

2338   The material and stores of mobile and fixed medical establishments must not be intentionally destroyed. This obligation applies equally to the property of the enemy and to a Party's own property.[16]

2339   This provision was a new addition in 1949, not having featured in the 1906 or 1929 Geneva Conventions. It represents an important step forward in international humanitarian law, as it goes further than a simple obligation to protect the material and stores of medical establishments against destruction by the enemy. It also aims to discourage those holding the said material and stores from destroying them to prevent them falling into enemy hands.[17] Article 33(3) would prevent someone from relying in court on the exception of urgent military necessity contained in Article 23(g) of the 1907 Hague Regulations as a pretext for the destruction of the medical material and stores. For example, in the *Hostages case* in 1948, the defendant Rendulic justified his 'scorched earth' policy on the grounds that it was a precautionary measure against an attack by advancing forces. The Tribunal found that the operational conditions as they appeared to Rendulic at the time were sufficient to warrant his belief that urgent military necessity required the destruction of private and public property in the province of Finnmark in Norway.[18]

2340   Article 33(3) covers the material and stores of both mobile and fixed medical establishments. It does not apply to the buildings of fixed medical

---

[16] See *Final Record of the Diplomatic Conference of Geneva of 1949*, Vol. II-A, p. 83.

[17] *Ibid.* This proposal was put forward by the Swedish delegate, who argued that '[i]t was necessary to cover the case of a commander who, forced to withdraw his troops, might attempt to destroy medical supplies which he could not take with him in order to prevent them falling into the hands of the enemy'.

[18] See United States, Military Tribunal at Nuremberg, *Hostages case*, Judgment, 1948, pp. 68–69.

establishments or of stores which remain subject to the law on the conduct of hostilities.[19]

2341   A violation of Article 33(3) could amount to the grave breach of 'extensive destruction of property, not justified by military necessity and carried out unlawfully and wantonly' under Article 50 of the First Convention. Similarly, the grave breach of 'extensive appropriation of property' under this same article could also extend to cases where the medical material of medical units and establishments is seized without the prescribed conditions spelled out in Article 33(1) and (2) being respected.

[19] See e.g. Articles 19, 21 and 22 of the First Convention, as well as Articles 48–58 of Additional Protocol I.

PROPERTY OF AID SOCIETIES

❖ Text of the provision*

(1) The real and personal property of aid societies which are admitted to the privileges of the Convention shall be regarded as private property.

(2) The right of requisition recognized for belligerents by the laws and customs of war shall not be exercised except in case of urgent necessity, and only after the welfare of the wounded and sick has been ensured.

❖ Reservations or declarations

None

Contents

A. Introduction

2342   Article 34 regulates the regime of real and personal property[1] of National Red Cross and Red Crescent Societies and of other aid societies which are admitted to the privileges of the Conventions (hereinafter referred to generically as 'aid societies'). These aid societies include those duly recognized and authorized to render assistance to the medical service of the armed forces under the conditions of Article 26 of the First Convention, as well as those recognized societies of neutral countries which lend the services of their medical personnel and units to a Party to the conflict under the conditions of Article 27.

2343   Article 34 contains rules detailing the fate of buildings and material of medical units and establishments belonging to these aid societies when they fall into enemy hands. The medical transports used by such societies are also covered by this provision.

---

* Paragraph numbers have been added for ease of reference.
[1] 'Real and personal property' means movable and non-movable property. The equally authentic French version of this provision reads 'biens mobiliers et immobiliers'.

B. Discussion

1. Treatment as private property

2344   Property belonging to the societies engaged in caring for the wounded and sick of the armed forces and used in connection with the assistance lent by these societies to the medical service of the armed forces must be regarded as private property and may never be taken as booty of war or confiscated.[2]

2345   It was felt, already in 1906, that if the buildings and material of aid societies were to be treated as booty of war, this would affect the 'development of these societies and make it far more difficult for them to find the resources they require. Private subscribers would not feel encouraged to make the sacrifices needed for the purchase of material, if it was liable to be captured out of hand.'[3]

2346   When aid societies act in accordance with the role envisioned in Articles 26 and 27 of the First Convention, the property of these societies is protected, whatever its nature and wherever it might be. Protection is extended to both fixed and mobile units and establishments, as well as separate objects and vehicles, pharmaceutical products, etc. The Convention does not require that the material be actually owned by the aid societies. Article 34 covers all material used by them, irrespective of ownership. National Red Cross and Red Crescent Societies should therefore mark with the distinctive emblem the material or the premises they own or use in their capacity as auxiliaries to the medical services of the armed forces.[4]

2347   When aid societies are working in functions other than as auxiliaries to the medical service of the armed forces, their property is not deprived of protection, but their protection flows from provisions such as Articles 57 and 63 of the Fourth Convention and Article 81 of Additional Protocol I.

---

[2] As mentioned in the commentary on Article 33, para. 2329, there is a recognized right of belligerents to take and use freely any movable public property of the enemy as booty of war. For the concept of booty of war, see Yoram Dinstein, 'Booty in Warfare', in Rüdiger Wolfrum (ed.), *Max Planck Encyclopedia of Public International Law*, version of March 2008, Oxford University Press, http://opil.ouplaw.com/home/EPIL; William Gerald Downey,'Captured Enemy Property: Booty of War and Seized Enemy Property', *American Journal of International Law*, Vol. 44, 1950, pp. 488–504; Elyce K.D. Santerre, 'From Confiscation to Contingency Contracting: Property Acquisition On or Near the Battlefield', *Military Law Review*, Vol. 124, Spring, 1989, pp. 111–161; H.A. Smith. 'Booty of War', *British Yearbook of International Law*, Vol. 23, 1946, pp. 227–239; and Jean-Marie Henckaerts and Louise Doswald-Beck, *Customary International Humanitarian Law, Volume I: Rules*, ICRC/Cambridge University Press, 2005, commentary on Rule 49, pp. 173–175, available at https://www.icrc.org/customary-ihl/eng/docs/v1_rul. Private property, on the contrary, cannot be confiscated, i.e. appropriated without any form of compensation; see Hague Regulations (1907), Article 46; see also Articles 52 and 53(2).

[3] Louis Renault, rapporteur to the 1906 Diplomatic Conference, cited in Pictet (ed.), *Commentary on the First Geneva Convention*, ICRC, 1952, p. 278. See Geneva Convention (1906), Article 16. There was not much debate on this issue in 1949. However, both in 1906 and in 1929 some States felt that as aid societies were merged into the medical service of the armed forces, their material should be placed on the same footing as that of the armed forces. See the views of the Japanese and UK delegates cited in John F. Hutchinson, *Champions of Charity: War and the Rise of the Red Cross*, Westview Press, Boulder, Colorado, 1996, pp. 198–199. Their view, however, did not prevail.

[4] See, in particular, Article 42 of the First Convention, as well as the 1991 Emblem Regulations.

2. Limitation of the right of requisition

2348   Like all private property, real and personal property of aid societies can be subject to requisition by the adverse Party. The usc of the word 'requisition' indicates that the scope of this paragraph is limited to situations of occupation. The right of requisition is acquired through occupation of enemy territory.[5] If the material in question is necessary to the occupying armed forces, they may requisition it. The consequences of such requisition are governed by Article 52 of the 1907 Hague Regulations. Fair compensation must be paid, however, and receipts given for all material handed over. In some cases, the requisition will involve a transfer of property, such as for medicines or other movable items. In other cases, an aid society's ambulance could be briefly requisitioned and then returned to the aid society once the urgent medical needs have been met.

2349   During the First World War, this right granted to the enemy armed forces was abused by some belligerents, leaving some aid societies unable to care for the wounded and sick of the armed forces once their material had been requisitioned.[6] It was therefore felt necessary to limit this right.[7] Under Article 34, the right of requisition of the real and personal property of aid societies is subject to a twofold limitation: first, it presupposes an urgent medical and not military need, and second, that proper arrangements are made for the care of the wounded and sick concerned.[8]

2350   Accordingly, the right to requisition the real and personal property of aid societies must only be exercised as an exceptional measure, when it is absolutely necessary to do so in order to assist the wounded and sick.[9] A similar

---

[5] See Rudolf Dolzer, 'Requisitions', in Rudolf Bernhardt (ed.), *Encyclopedia of Public International Law*, Vol. III, 1997, pp. 205–208; Santerre, Elyce K.D. 'From Confiscation to Contingency Contracting: Property Acquisition On or Near the Battlefield', *Military Law Review*, Vol. 124, 1989, pp. 111–161, at 112; and Avril McDonald and Hanna Brollowski, 'Requisitions', version of April 2011, in Rüdiger Wolfrum (ed.), *Max Planck Encyclopedia of Public International Law*, Oxford University Press, http://opil.ouplaw.com/home/EPIL.

[6] See *Proceedings of the Geneva Diplomatic Conference of 1929*, p. 201.

[7] See Des Gouttes, *Commentaire de la Convention de Genève de 1929 sur les blessés et malades*, ICRC, 1930, pp. 104–105, and *Proceedings of the Geneva Diplomatic Conference of 1929*, pp. 200–209.

[8] On the imposition of new limitations and the discussions in 1929, see Des Gouttes, *Commentaire de la Convention de Genève de 1929 sur les blessés et malades*, ICRC, 1930, pp. 104–105. See also the wording of Article 16(3) of the 1929 Geneva Convention on the Wounded and Sick.

[9] This understanding was also shared in 1929. The preparatory work for the 1929 Geneva Convention on the Wounded and Sick make it clear that only urgent medical necessity would allow an infringement of the protection of private property and permit requisition of the real and personal property of aid societies. See *Proceedings of the Geneva Diplomatic Conference of 1929*, p. 203, during which the Secretary General of the Conference stated clearly that 'la réquisition est subordonnée aux nécessités des soins immédiats à donner aux blessés. Si c'est pour le soin urgent des blessés que l'on réquisitionne et retient ce matériel, cela se comprend mais si ce matériel n'est pas indispensable, il faut le rendre' ('requisition is subordinated to the necessity of providing immediate care to the wounded. If the requisition and retention of this material takes place in order to dispense urgent care to the wounded, that is understandable, but if this material is not indispensable, it must be returned'); see also the position of the representative of the Netherlands, p. 202.

understanding applies to civilian hospitals. Article 57 of the Fourth Convention provides that the Occupying Power may requisition civilian hospitals only temporarily and only in cases of urgent necessity for the care of wounded and sick military personnel, and on condition that suitable arrangements are made in due time for the care and treatment of the hospitals' existing patients and for the future hospital needs of the civilian population.

2351 Article 34 speaks of the obligation of the belligerents to ensure the 'welfare' of the wounded and sick. The French text speaks only of 'le sort des blessés et des malades' ('the fate of the wounded and sick'). It is submitted that the belligerents must both meet the medical needs and ensure the basic well-being of the wounded and sick before they can requisition, for example, a mobile medical unit belonging to an aid society under Article 34 of the Convention.

2352 Widespread violations of this provision, involving the requisitioning of medical material belonging to aid societies without fulfilling the prescribed conditions spelled out in Article 34, may trigger the individual criminal responsibility of the perpetrator under the grave breach of extensive appropriation of property laid down in Article 50 of the First Convention.

3. Right of seizure

2353 Article 34 is silent as to the right of seizure by belligerents of real and personal property of aid societies both during occupation and outside situations of occupation. In situations of occupation, private property, such as means of transport of persons or things may be seized by the enemy but must be restored and compensation fixed when peace is made.[10] However, it can be assumed that the limitations imposed by Article 34 on the right of requisition would extend to the right of seizure of property belonging to or used by aid societies.[11] In a situation of occupation, there would be no reason to differentiate between a belligerent's right to seize and its right to requisition the real and personal property of aid societies.

2354 As to the right of seizure which exists in military operations outside of a context of occupation, belligerents may seize enemy property when such seizure is imperatively demanded by the necessities of war.[12] The laws of war did not carve out exceptions applicable to the real and personal property of aid societies. Therefore, it does not appear that the limitations imposed on the right of the enemy to requisition property of aid societies contained in Article 34 extend

---

[10] See Hague Regulations (1907), Article 53(2).

[11] This would also be in line with the treatment accorded to civilian hospitals under Article 57 of the Fourth Convention and to National Red Cross and Red Crescent Societies or other relief societies under Article 63 of the Fourth Convention.

[12] Article 23(g) of the 1907 Hague Regulations provides for an exception to the prohibition on destroying or seizing enemy property, when 'such destruction or seizure is imperatively demanded by the necessities of war'.

to seizure of that property outside of situations of occupation.[13] Article 34 is silent as to the right of seizure by belligerents of property of aid societies, and the absence of recent State practice in this respect does not allow for a different conclusion.

[13] While the terms 'seizure' and 'requisition' appear in Section III of the 1907 Hague Regulations in relation to situations of occupation, the definition of these concepts in other contexts, such as military operations or sea prizes, can vary in the literature. See Knut Dörmann, *Elements of War Crimes under the Rome Statute of the International Criminal Court: Sources and Commentary*, Cambridge University Press, 2003, pp. 256–257.

CHAPTER VI

MEDICAL TRANSPORTS

2355   The protection of medical transports is a logical corollary of, and provides functional support for, the First Convention's primary objective, which is 'the amelioration of the condition of the wounded and sick in armed forces in the field'. In order to ensure the respect and protection due to the wounded and sick under Article 12 of the First Convention, it is necessary to grant protection to the means of transport used to convey them to a treatment facility. Military medical transports are thus protected on account of the functions they perform.

2356   Article 35 sets out the legal regime applicable to medical transports on land used by the armed forces. The first paragraph of Article 35 deals with the status and protection of military medical transports, stating that they are governed by the same rules as mobile medical units. The second paragraph regulates what happens when these transports fall into enemy hands. The third paragraph stipulates that requisitioned civilian personnel and means of transport are subject to 'the general rules of international law'.

2357   Often the fastest, and sometimes the only, means of carrying out the evacuation of the wounded and sick is by aircraft, a term which includes helicopters. Rapid evacuation of the wounded and sick is a genuine life-saving measure in modern conflict. Article 36 confers protection on medical aircraft, which are aircraft exclusively employed for the removal of the wounded and sick and the transport of medical personnel and equipment. They must not be attacked and must be respected by all belligerents. Their protection is subject to relatively stringent criteria, spelt out in Article 36.

2358   Many armed forces rely on aircraft to transport the wounded and sick to permanent medical facilities, often situated far from the battlefield. Getting the wounded and sick to these facilities may necessitate extensive flight through the airspace of one or more neutral States. Article 37 tries to reconcile the need to transport the wounded and sick to permanent medical facilities with the rights of neutral States. It grants medical aircraft the right to fly over neutral States' territory, land on it in case of necessity or use it as a port of call. At the same time, it gives neutral States the right to place conditions or restrictions on the passage or landing of medical aircraft on their territory.

2359   This chapter is complemented by a number of provisions contained in Part II, Section II, of Additional Protocol I.

ARTICLE 35

PROTECTION OF MEDICAL TRANSPORTS

❖ Text of the provision*

(1) Transports of wounded and sick or of medical equipment shall be respected and protected in the same way as mobile medical units.

(2) Should such transports or vehicles fall into the hands of the adverse Party, they shall be subject to the laws of war, on condition that the Party to the conflict who captures them shall in all cases ensure the care of the wounded and sick they contain.

(3) The civilian personnel and all means of transport obtained by requisition shall be subject to the general rules of international law.

❖ Reservations or declarations

None

Contents

* Paragraph numbers have been added for ease of reference.

A. Introduction

2360 Article 35 sets out the legal regime applicable to medical transports on land used by the armed forces (hereinafter 'military medical transports').[1]

2361 Article 35(1) deals with the status and protection of military medical transports, stating that they are governed by the same rules as mobile medical units. The second paragraph regulates what happens when these transports fall into enemy hands. The third paragraph stipulates that requisitioned civilian personnel and means of transport are subject to 'the general rules of international law'.

2362 In the context of the First Convention, the reference under Article 35(1) to the 'wounded and sick' must be understood to mean persons falling into the categories defined in Article 13(1), i.e. the wounded and sick belonging to the armed forces of a Party to the conflict or to groups affiliated with such forces. Thus, while care may be dispensed already on board such transports, the primary purpose of Article 35 is to regulate the status and protection of the transports used for conveying the wounded and sick to a place where they can receive medical treatment.

2363 The protection of medical transports in this context is a logical corollary of, and functional support to, the First Convention's primary objective, which is, as the Convention's title indicates, 'the amelioration of the condition of the wounded and sick in armed forces in the field'. In order to ensure the respect and protection due to the wounded and sick under Article 12 of the First Convention, it is necessary also to accord protection to the means of transport used to convey them to a treatment facility. One of the key principles of humanitarian protection of the wounded and sick is that they and the required medical personnel and equipment be transported as quickly as possible to a place where they can receive care. The use, therefore, of medical transports is an essential component of casualty evacuation and treatment.[2] Military medical transports are thus protected on account of the functions they perform. The protection of the wounded and sick would be seriously diluted if analogous protection were not extended to the assets assigned exclusively, on a permanent or temporary basis, to their transport and/or to the transport of the medical personnel and equipment needed for their care.

---

[1] Paragraphs 1 and 3 of Article 35 also apply to medical transports used by voluntary aid societies acting as auxiliaries to the armed forces medical service on the basis of Article 26 or 27; however, that arrangement has rarely occurred in practice since 1949. For details, see the commentaries on Article 26, section F, and Article 27, para. 2116. Article 35(2) does not apply to such transports; see para. 2412.

[2] For example, the United States, *Medical Evacuation Manual*, 2007, para. 1–15, provides:

Ensure that medical evacuation assets are in close proximity to supported elements to enhance response time, increase Soldier confidence and be a combat multiplier. This is accomplished by complementing organic medical evacuation assets with medical evacuation assets placed in DS [Direct Support], GS [General Support], and area support roles.

2364   Article 35 is part of a series of specific provisions in the 1949 Geneva Conventions and their 1977 Additional Protocols regulating and protecting medical transports in international armed conflict. The Second Convention sets down rules for specific types of medical transports at sea, such as hospital ships, coastal rescue craft and ships chartered for the transport of medical equipment.[3] Article 21 of the Fourth Convention regulates '[c]onvoys of vehicles or hospital trains on land or specially provided vessels on sea, conveying wounded and sick civilians'. Using the term 'medical vehicles' (defined in Article 8(h) of the Protocol as 'any medical transports by land'), Article 21 of Additional Protocol I states that they 'shall be respected and protected in the same way as mobile medical units under the Conventions and [the] Protocol'. Lastly, the requirement to 'respect and protect' medical transports has been found to reflect customary international humanitarian law.[4]

2365   For the protection of medical transports in non-international armed conflict, see the commentary on common Article 3, section H.

B. Historical background

2366   The treaty-based protection of means of transport used for the benefit of wounded or sick combatants goes back to the beginnings of contemporary international humanitarian law: the original Geneva Convention of 1864 stipulated that '[a]mbulances . . . shall be recognized as neutral, and, as such, protected and respected by the belligerents'. However, in this initial formulation, the requirement only applied 'as long as [the ambulances] accommodate [the] wounded and sick'.[5]

2367   The 1906 Geneva Convention contained a detailed provision dealing with what were called at the time 'convoys of evacuation'.[6] Since then, military medical transports have been granted protection irrespective of whether or not they actually have wounded or sick persons on board. As is the case with the current formulation in Article 35, Article 17 of the 1906 Convention also stated that the legal regime applicable to 'mobile sanitary formations' applied to such 'convoys of evacuation'. Furthermore, this provision contained rules substantively similar to paragraphs 2 and 3 of the present article.

2368   The 1929 Geneva Convention on the Wounded and Sick provided detailed regulations for '[v]ehicles equipped for the evacuation of [the] wounded and sick'.[7] While under Article 22 of the Second Convention the term 'equipped' still figures among the definitional requirements for a vessel to qualify as a hospital ship, it has been dropped from Article 35 in relation to military

---

[3] See Second Convention, Article 22 (hospital ships), Article 27 (coastal rescue craft) and Article 38 (ships chartered for the transport of medical equipment).
[4] See ICRC Study on Customary International Humanitarian Law (2005), Rule 29.
[5] Geneva Convention (1864), Article 1.   [6] Geneva Convention (1906), Article 17.
[7] Geneva Convention on the Wounded and Sick (1929), Article 17.

medical transports on land. This leaves the Parties to a conflict with significant flexibility with regard to the vehicles which may, at some point, be assigned exclusively to medical transportation.

C. Paragraph 1: Definitions and status

1. Definitions

a. Transports

2369 While the first paragraph of Article 35 speaks of 'transports', the second refers to 'transports or vehicles'. Neither of these terms is defined in the First Convention. As can be deduced from other provisions in the Geneva Conventions and Additional Protocol I, Article 35 is limited to land-based convoys and vehicles used by the armed forces, be it by their medical service or a combat unit, or by an aid society operating on the basis of Article 26 or 27. Transports covered by this provision may, but need not, be the property of the aforementioned categories; they may also, for example, have been rented or leased.

2370 For the purposes of Additional Protocol I, 'medical vehicles' is defined as 'any medical transports by land'. In turn, 'medical transports' is defined as 'any means of transportation, whether military or civilian, permanent or temporary, assigned exclusively to medical transportation and under the control of a competent authority of a Party to the conflict'.[8] The terms 'permanent' and 'temporary' are similarly defined for the purposes of Protocol I.[9] Today, these definitions are viewed as authoritative when considering which objects may qualify as 'transports or vehicles' in the sense of Article 35.[10] For an analysis of the criterion of 'assigned' in relation to military medical assets, and what is required for them to have been 'exclusively' so assigned, see the commentary on Article 19(1), paras 1786–1791.

2371 Article 35 does not specify which persons may use the transports qualifying for protection. Within the context of the First Convention, these are limited to permanent and auxiliary medical personnel of the armed forces or the personnel of voluntary aid societies falling within the scope of Article 26 or 27. Thus, if combatants were to operate medical transports, it would compromise the protection of those transports.

2372 Article 35 covers all vehicles of any type, as long as they are assigned exclusively to the transportation of the wounded and sick or of medical equipment and are not specifically covered by another provision of the Geneva Conventions (such as medical aircraft, dealt with under Article 36, or the various

---

[8] Additional Protocol I, Article 8(g) ('medical transports') and (h) ('medical vehicles'). See also Article 8(f), which defines the overarching notion of 'medical transportation'.
[9] Additional Protocol I, Article 8(k).
[10] See Henckaerts/Doswald-Beck, commentary on Rule 29, p. 100, 'Definition of medical transports', with references to military manuals.

categories of vessels which are protected on the basis of the Second Convention). Accordingly, transports falling within the scope of this article may include automobiles, trucks, trains, motorcycles, small all-terrain vehicles and inland boats. They need not be motorized and can travel either individually or in convoy.

2373   Technological advances may in the future result in new types of transports falling within the scope of Article 35. For example, it is increasingly likely that States will develop and employ unmanned ground and/or air medical evacuation vehicles that are either remotely controlled or autonomous to collect and transport wounded and sick personnel. As long as they meet the requirement for protection set forth in Article 35 (i.e. being assigned exclusively to medical transportation), there is no reason to exclude such transports from the scope of Article 35. Their protection can only contribute to the humanitarian objectives of the Convention.

2374   Unlike under Article 17 of the 1929 Geneva Convention on the Wounded and Sick, medical transports are covered by Article 35 even when they have not been specifically 'equipped' for that purpose. Indeed, as the operational situation and casualty evacuation needs may require the use of any available transport asset for medical purposes, a restrictive definition of a medical transport would be contrary to the purpose of the article and to the overall humanitarian objectives of the Convention. Only medical transports specifically protected by other treaty provisions are excluded from the scope of Article 35. This means that vehicles and other transports normally performing a combat or combat-support function may be assigned, even on a temporary basis, to medical transportation. Once they are assigned to such transportation, however, they need to be exclusively engaged in such function. Conversely, the moment they cease to have a medical function, they lose their protected status. A change of status will also have implications for a medical transport's entitlement to display the distinctive emblem.[11]

2375   Military medical transports covered by Article 35 are different from 'mobile medical units of the Medical Service' covered by Article 19. While they enjoy the same protection on the battlefield, the distinction matters once they have fallen into enemy hands.[12] For a discussion of the difference between the two categories, see the commentary on Article 19, paragraph 1782. In this context, since military medical transports may contain on-board treatment facilities, the guiding principle is that the differentiation takes place on the basis of the more dominant element: the transport element in principle prevails in the case of 'transports', while the possibility of administering care prevails in the case of 'mobile medical units'. This guiding principle may not solve all cases: if in doubt as to the qualification of an object which has fallen into their hands,

---

[11] For details, see section C.2.c.
[12] Compare the second sentence of Article 19(1) with Article 35(2).

Parties to the conflict should presume that the object in question is a mobile medical unit, unless objective information clearly exists to the contrary.[13]

2376 'Medical transports' is a broad term and is intended to cover all vehicles permanently or temporarily employed for such use,[14] whether operating in isolation or in medical convoys, or integrated into non-medical convoys. This is only logical, as tactical and operational considerations will invariably influence the employment of vehicles to transport the wounded and sick and/or medical equipment.[15] Thus, it is the purpose for which the vehicle is used, and not its location or proximity to other military or medical assets, that entitles it to protected status.

2377 In all instances, two cumulative conditions must be met in order for a medical transport to be entitled to protection under Article 35: first, the assignment to medical transportation must be exclusive;[16] and second, the transport must be under the control of a competent authority, which, in the context of the First Convention, will be the armed forces or an aid society operating on the basis of Article 26 or 27.[17] Displaying the emblem, however, is not a prerequisite for protected status.[18]

2378 Transports permanently designated or equipped as ambulances will not always be readily available, which makes it virtually inevitable that other vehicles will be used temporarily for medical transport. Thus, Article 35 anticipates the use of vehicles that would, prior to and upon completion of a medical transport mission, qualify as military objectives. The use of such vehicles is permissible under this article. As long as these vehicles are exclusively engaged in medical transport, they are, for the duration of their use in this capacity, to be respected and protected.

2379 Any interpretation that would limit the protection to 'permanent' medical transport would be inconsistent with the purpose of the article and of the general humanitarian spirit of the First Convention. Such an interpretation would prevent armed forces from using any available vehicle, on a temporary basis, to transport the wounded and sick, which, in the absence of permanent medical transports, could prolong the suffering of victims of an armed conflict.

---

[13] For an explanation of why the rule governing mobile medical units in enemy hands confers more protection than the rule governing military medical transports in enemy hands, see paras 2412–2413.

[14] Langdon/Rogers/Eadie, p. 181. See also Additional Protocol I, Article 8(k).

[15] See e.g. United States, *Medical Evacuation Manual*, 2007, para. 1–10, which provides: 'The location of medical evacuation assets in support of combat operations is dictated by orders and the tactical situation (mission, enemy, terrain and weather, troops and support available, time available, and civil considerations.'

[16] See also the definitions of 'permanent' and 'temporary' in Article 8(k) of Additional Protocol I.

[17] Today, these requirements, set down in Article 8(g) of Additional Protocol I, are viewed as authoritative for the purpose of interpreting what qualifies as 'transports of wounded and sick [persons] or of medical equipment' in the sense of Article 35; see para. 2370.

[18] For details, see the commentary on Article 39, para. 2578.

2380   Accordingly, Article 35 covers all vehicles assigned exclusively to medical transportation, whether on a permanent or temporary basis. The notion of 'permanent' does not mean that a medical transport vehicle may never be converted to a non-medical use. It does suggest, however, that the primary and intended use of the vehicle will be exclusively for medical purposes for an indefinite period of time. An example of such a vehicle would be an ambulance specifically equipped to transport casualties. In contrast, 'temporary' does indicate use in a medical transport capacity at least for a defined, albeit possibly short, period of time. An example of such use would be a military truck assigned on a one-off basis to transport casualties from an area of engagement to a mobile medical unit. However, the Parties to the conflict must keep in mind that the more occasional the use of such vehicles – with or without special markings – the greater the risk they will be mistaken by enemy forces for lawful objects of attack.[19] Temporary use of a vehicle for medical transport must be distinguished from what is pragmatically characterized as a 'mixed' transport mission, i.e. use of a vehicle simultaneously for both a combat or combat-support function and for transporting casualties. Since, in this case, the vehicle is not 'exclusively' engaged in a medical transport function, it does not qualify for protection. Accordingly, it is the 'exclusive' nature of the medical transport mission, even if for a short duration, that triggers the protection of this article. In the same vein, it remains possible to use combat vehicles to transport the wounded and sick. Absent their being exclusively engaged in medical transport, they do not qualify for protection either.[20]

b. Wounded and sick

2381   In the context of the First Convention, the term 'wounded and sick' should be understood as referring to persons belonging to the categories covered by Article 13, i.e. wounded or sick members of the armed forces of a Party to the conflict and members of groups affiliated with them. However, in line with the logic of Article 22(5) with regard to military medical units and establishments, if the humanitarian activities of medical transports covered by Article 35 happen to extend to the transport of wounded or sick civilians, it would not deprive these transports of their protected status. Such transport should not, however, be their primary purpose. If the transport of civilian battlefield casualties is the primary purpose of the vehicle, the appropriate legal provision, as far as the

---

[19] See Langdon/Rogers/Eadie, p. 182.
[20] United States, *Medical Evacuation Manual*, 2007, Section III, 'Medical evacuation versus casualty evacuation', para. 1–27: 'Medical evacuation is performed by dedicated, standardized evacuation platforms'; para. 1–31: 'Casualty evacuation is a term used to refer to the movement of casualties aboard nonmedical vehicles or aircraft'; and para. 1–33: 'Since [casualty evacuation] operations can reduce combat power and degrade the efficiency of the [army health system], units should only use [casualty evacuation] to move Soldiers with less severe injuries when medical evacuation assets are overwhelmed.'

1949 Geneva Conventions are concerned, is Article 21 of the Fourth Convention dealing specifically with '[c]onvoys of vehicles or hospital trains on land or specially provided vessels on sea, conveying wounded and sick civilians, the infirm and maternity cases'. It is also worth noting that Additional Protocol I renders irrelevant the distinction between the transportation of 'military' or 'civilian' wounded or sick persons.[21]

2382   While not explicitly mentioned in Article 35, it is in line with the object and purpose of the First Convention that military medical transports carrying dead persons also qualify for protection.

c. Medical equipment

2383 The 1929 Geneva Convention mentioned only '[v]ehicles equipped for the evacuation of [the] wounded and sick'. This could have been taken to mean that vehicles that carried only medical material were not protected. However, Article 35 is clear on the matter, as it refers expressly to '[t]ransports of [the] wounded and sick or of medical equipment'.

2384   Although not defined in Article 35, medical equipment includes drugs, bandages, medical instruments, stretchers and other supplies needed for the care of the wounded and sick.[22] The logic of extending humanitarian protection to transports carrying such items is obvious,[23] as they are essential for the care of all wounded and sick persons falling under the protection of international humanitarian law.

2. Status

a. Obligation to respect and protect

2385 Transports qualifying as military medical transports on the basis of Article 35 'shall be respected and protected in the same way as mobile medical units'. By these words, Article 35 declares Article 19(1), first sentence, and 19(2) applicable *mutatis mutandis* to military medical transports.[24] This means that they 'may in no circumstances be attacked, but shall at all times be respected and protected'.

2386   As flows from the phrase 'at all times', this requirement applies also at moments when no wounded or sick persons are in the transports. However,

---

[21] See Additional Protocol I, Articles 8 and 21.

[22] In relation to the display of the distinctive emblem, Article 39 speaks of 'all equipment employed in the Medical Service'. For details, see the commentary on that article, section B.3.

[23] See Langdon/Rogers/Eadie, p. 182. See also Michael Bothe, Karl Josef Partsch and Waldemar A. Solf, *New Rules for the Victims of Armed Conflicts: Commentary on the Two 1977 Protocols Additional to the Geneva Conventions of 1949*, Martinus Nijhoff Publishers, The Hague, 1982, p. 101.

[24] There is only one difference, pertaining to what may be done with mobile medical units and medical transports, respectively, when they fall into enemy hands; see paras 2412–2413.

the requirement to 'respect and protect' military medical transports is without prejudice to the entitlement of the Parties to the armed conflict to exercise control rights, for example through a search. The exercise of such rights, however, may not lead to the care of the wounded and sick being jeopardized.[25]

2387   Of particular relevance when it comes to the interpretation of the 'protect' component of this requirement is that Parties to the conflict may not unduly hold up, obstruct the passage of, or otherwise prevent military medical transports from fulfilling their task.[26] They must also actively ensure and enforce respect by any third parties that may seek to unjustifiably interfere with medical transports.[27]

2388   The obligation to respect transports protected on the basis of Article 35 will be violated if belligerent reprisals are directed against them.[28] In this context, it bears recalling that transports covered by Article 35 are protected objects under the First Convention. Therefore, the acts listed in Article 50, if committed against these transports, may qualify as a grave breach of the Convention.

2389   The fact that transports covered by Article 35 'shall be respected and protected in the same way as mobile medical units' entails that the same rules apply to their loss of protection if they are used, outside their humanitarian function, to commit an act harmful to the enemy. What qualifies in this case as 'harmful to the enemy' is inherently fact-specific. However, it is fairly clear that using such vehicles in a capacity inconsistent with their exclusively medical transport function will in many (though not necessarily all) cases qualify as an act harmful to the enemy. Examples of acts harmful to the enemy include the transport of weapons and ammunition (other than weapons or ammunition taken from the wounded and sick occupants of the vehicle and not yet handed over to the proper service) or the use of the vehicle as a mobile military command post or as a base from which to launch an attack. Depending on the circumstances, and provided the constitutive requirements have been met, engaging in any of the foregoing may also qualify as prohibited perfidy, improper use of the distinctive emblem or use of a medical transport in an attempt to shield a military objective from attack.[29]

2390   In contrast, the fact that the availability of such vehicles mitigates the need to use temporarily as medical transports other vehicles normally providing combat support, thereby giving an opponent a tactical benefit, does not qualify as an act harmful to the enemy. Between the two extremes are many potential variables. For example, a military medical transport may be located in a

---

[25] See Spieker, para. 9.
[26] ICRC, *Ambulance and Pre-Hospital Services in Risk Situations*, p. 17. See also Breitegger, pp. 114–115.
[27] See Spieker, para. 11.   [28] See also Article 46.
[29] On conduct which qualifies as prohibited perfidy, see the first sentence of Article 37(1) of Additional Protocol I. For proper and improper use of the distinctive emblem, respectively, see Article 39 of the First Convention and Article 38(1) of Additional Protocol I. As to the prohibition on shielding a military objective from attack, see Article 12(4) of Additional Protocol I.

position that functionally impedes forces engaged in hostilities and thereby provides a benefit to the force to which the vehicle belongs. Whether this is an 'act harmful to the enemy' would depend on how and why the transport is in that position. In many cases, it might be merely incidental to the performance of the transport's legitimate humanitarian function. Ultimately, the Parties to the conflict must have a reasonable basis before concluding that a military medical transport has forfeited the protection provided by this article. Even acts which, legally speaking, do not qualify as harmful to the enemy yet which constitute misuse of the military medical transport, may lead, in practice, to perception problems when it comes to the belligerents' willingness to respect their legal status, thereby diluting the functional protection afforded to all properly marked medical transports.[30]

2391   Where it is established that a vehicle covered by Article 35 is being used, outside its humanitarian function, for the commission of an act harmful to the enemy, the same constraints as those outlined in section C.2 of the commentary on Article 21 apply (warning, time limit, etc.). In particular, regard must be had for the measures which have to be taken to spare, as far as possible, the wounded and sick who may suffer from such an attack.

2392   There is one exception to the logic of extending, *mutatis mutandis*, the rules governing mobile medical units to military medical transports: when the latter fall into enemy hands, Article 35(2) provides for different, and less protective, regulation than that applicable to mobile medical units in similar circumstances (Article 19(1), second sentence).[31]

b. Arming of military medical transports

2393   The question of whether arms may be mounted on medical transports must be distinguished from the question of whether they may be armoured.[32] The latter is generally permitted because it is a purely deflective means of defence.[33]

2394   Article 35 does not specify whether military medical transports covered by this provision may be armed and, if so, with which types of weapons without losing their protection under the Convention. This question should be seen as distinct from that concerning the possibility of the personnel operating those transports being armed, which is addressed in other provisions of the

---

[30] ICRC, *Ambulance and Pre-Hospital Services in Risk Situations*, p. 16:

> [M]isuse can also take less serious forms and the reasons for it may not always be military: even these form[s] of misuse can have serious consequences in terms of public perceptions, effectiveness and security. For instance, ambulances can be misused as personal vehicles for hospital directors or managers, as taxis, or to carry goods. When that happens, they fall under suspicion and are, at best, subjected to delays and obstructed or, at worst, become objects of attack.

[31] See paras 2412–2413.

[32] *Concise Oxford English Dictionary*, 12th edition, Oxford University Press, 2011, p. 71, defining 'armour' as 'the tough metal layer covering a military vehicle or ship'.

[33] See Breitegger, p. 112.

Convention and Protocol I.[34] The reality is that operational considerations may necessitate measures to protect medical transports from unlawful attack. Accordingly, if, when and how military medical transports may be armed must be assessed on a case-by-case basis.[35]

2395   Within certain limits, medical units and establishments are permitted to be armed and to use their weapons, but only for self-defence or for the defence of the wounded and sick in their charge.[36] As under Article 35 military medical transports are afforded the same protections as mobile medical units, permission to use arms in similar circumstances logically extends to them too. Given that medical transports must travel through areas that are often more volatile than those where mobile medical units are located, they may have an even more compelling need to act in self-defence and/or the defence of their wounded and sick occupants against unlawful attack.

2396   As already noted, Article 35 is silent on this issue. Article 22 does not address the arming of medical *transports*, only the arming of the *personnel* of military medical transports. As a result, resolution of the issue is based on analogy with the authority to use weapons to protect mobile medical units. Because there is no internationally accepted categorization of weapon systems, it is difficult to identify, in concrete terms, any clear categories of permissible versus impermissible armaments that may be used for the legitimate and limited purpose of defending a military medical transport against unlawful attack.

2397   As a general rule, however, only 'light' weapons may be mounted on military medical transports. While the nature of the anticipated threat will certainly influence the type of defensive armament used, mounting heavy weapons, sometimes referred to as 'crew served' (meaning they require a team of at least two people to operate them), is inconsistent with the protected status of such transports.[37] Whether every belt-fed machine gun falls into this category is uncertain, as some light, belt-fed machine guns are individually operated. Ultimately, in the light of these strictly defensive purposes and also to avoid the perception that a medical transport, displaying the distinctive emblem, is armed in a manner beyond that necessary for its self-defence, a narrow interpretation of what constitutes a 'light' versus 'heavy' weapon is called for: the larger the weapon system, the greater the risk that its presence on the vehicle could lead an adversary to conclude that the transport may be engaged in 'acts harmful to the enemy', and thus no longer be entitled to protection. The

---

[34] For a discussion, see the commentaries on Article 24, paras 2005–2006, Article 26, section E, and Article 27, section C.2. See also Additional Protocol I, Article 13(2).

[35] For an overview of the type of considerations which may inform this decision, see ICRC, *Ambulance and Pre-Hospital Services in Risk Situations*, pp. 35–38, under the heading 'The question of personal protective equipment (PPE) should be analysed by country and/or context and proper training provided.'

[36] See the commentary on Article 22(1), section C.1.

[37] See Breitegger, p. 112: '[N]o armaments could be mounted that could potentially be used in an offensive fashion. On the other hand, purely deflective means of defence, such as chaff, infrared flares or jammers, may be permissible.'

nature of the display of the weapons, in other words, must not be such as to lead the enemy to believe that the medical transport is equipped with non-defensive weaponry.[38] In short, it must be ensured that transports protected by Article 35 are not armed to an extent that they can be perceived as being capable of inflicting harm on the adversary because this would amount to an act the purpose or effect of which is to facilitate or impede the military operations of a Party to the conflict. Otherwise, there is a risk of their being mistaken for 'fighting vehicles'.[39]

2398   Where a commander anticipates general compliance with international humanitarian law and respect for the medical mission and the distinctive emblem, limiting armaments to light weapons carried by the crew members of the military medical transport would be appropriate, as the anticipated threat to the transport would be minimal.

2399   There may be situations where military medical transports are at particular risk of unlawful attack. In these cases, there may be a genuine need to employ suppressive fire against the attacking force at a range beyond the capability of light individual weapons. Nevertheless, the paramount concern in such situations should be the preservation of respect for the medical mission, for the wounded and sick, and in particular, if used, for the distinctive emblem. For that reason, it would not be appropriate to mark a heavily armed medical transport with the distinctive emblem. When they wish to mount heavy weapons on a military medical transport, commanders must order the distinctive emblem removed or fully concealed.[40] Nothing precludes such an unmarked and heavily armed vehicle, which will not be entitled to the protection of the Convention, from being subsequently embedded in a tactical convoy that includes other vehicles capable of responding to an attack with effective combat power.

2400   As some military transports may be assigned temporarily to medical transportation, it may not always be feasible to remove mounted weapons. Where it is not considered necessary to protect the transport, the weapon should not be left mounted on the vehicle merely because removal would be

---

[38] See the commentary on Rule 74(c)(i) of the 2009 Manual on International Law Applicable to Air and Missile Warfare, p. 217. See also San Remo Manual on International Law Applicable to Armed Conflicts at Sea (1994), para. 170.1, if transposed to the situation of military medical transports: '[A]s there is no prohibition on [such transports] defending themselves, it would be unreasonable not to allow them to do so as long as it is in a way that cannot be interpreted as being potentially aggressive.'

[39] Canada, *Code of Conduct*, 2007, p. 2–16, para. 6.

[40] See e.g. United Kingdom, *Allied Joint Doctrine for Medical Support, with UK National Elements*, 2015, p. 1–99:

Where a threat exists from non-state actors, commanders are empowered, subject to legal and policy advice, to remove the Red Cross insignia, and to fit a mounted weapon system for the protection of that platform and those within their care. However, such a platform will no longer be recognisable as an ambulance and it, and its occupants, will lose the protection that the distinctive emblem would otherwise confer. Under no circumstances may the Red Cross emblem be displayed on an ambulance platform at the same time as a weapon system is mounted on it.

considered inconvenient. However, where the time needed to remove it would interfere with the legitimate medical transport mission of a vehicle temporarily used for that task, and thereby place the wounded and sick in greater jeopardy by delaying their evacuation and treatment, proceeding with the existing armament may be necessary. If the vehicle is marked with the distinctive emblem, this may raise concerns that it is being misused, and therefore any emblem should be removed or concealed. The nature of a combat vehicle may lead to the conclusion that it should not be marked with the distinctive emblem, even if temporarily used exclusively for medical transport. For example, it would be hard to accept the marking of a tank temporarily being used as a medical transport, the risk being too great that the opposing side would perceive it as an improper use of the distinctive emblem. Beyond such extremes, however, the nature of the arming of medical transports must be dictated by considerations such as mission, threat and available transport.

2401   There is no doubt that the improper use of *any* weapon would cause the transport to forfeit the protection provided by this article. Whatever their nature, weapons may be used only to defend the medical transport and/or the wounded and sick from unlawful attack, as is the case for those assigned to the protection of medical establishments.

2402   Like mobile medical units, military medical transports are subject to capture by the enemy and must submit to lawful enemy control (for example at a checkpoint) without resistance. Article 35(2) regulates the fate of military medical transports if they fall into enemy hands. Even if armed, the crew of the vehicle may not use force to prevent such capture, unless they are subject to unlawful attack, in which case they may use force to defend the wounded and sick in their charge. Resistance in other circumstances would render the vehicle and personnel open to lawful attack by the enemy and potential criminal sanction, for example for improper use of the emblem. The prohibition on using force to resist lawful capture includes firing on an enemy attempting to force the transport to cease movement. Refusing to heed a warning issued by the enemy to cease an act harmful to the enemy outside their humanitarian function (such as transporting troops, carrying military supplies, or failing to stop moving across a designated area) will result in forfeiture of the protection provided by this article and may justify an attack against the vehicle, if the vehicle constitutes a lawful target.[41]

c. Display of the distinctive emblem

2403 Article 35 does not say whether the transports covered by its provisions may or may not display the distinctive emblem. In the First Convention, this issue is

[41] See Langdon/Rogers/Eadie, p. 182.

regulated by Article 39: 'Under the direction of the competent military author-ity, the emblem shall be displayed on the flags, armlets and on all equipment employed in the Medical Service.'[42] Military medical transports fall within the term 'equipment' as used in Article 39.[43] Moreover, as flows from the reference to 'in the same way as mobile medical units' in Article 35(1), Article 42 also applies to military medical transports with regard to the display of the distinc-tive emblem. It must be recalled that the distinctive emblem is only intended to facilitate identification and does not, in and of itself, confer protected status.[44]

2404   In order to ensure military medical transports receive the respect and protec-tion due to them under Article 35, Parties to a conflict should strive always to mark them with the distinctive emblem for the entire duration of their being assigned exclusively to medical transportation. Such marking is the only sure and effective method of informing the enemy of the vehicle's protected status. This approach derives from the very purpose of the emblem: to ensure that protected persons and objects are identifiable and spared from attack during hostilities.

2405   On the other hand, there is no rule against using a vehicle to transport the wounded and sick and/or medical equipment *without* it being marked with the distinctive emblem. The emblem, therefore, may be removable.[45] Indeed, there may be situations where a commander determines, based on the infor-mation reasonably available to him or to her at the time, that the removal or concealment of the distinctive emblem on a vehicle assigned temporarily or permanently to medical transportation is essential for tactical reasons. This may be the case, for example, when the medical transport is part of a military convoy attempting to avoid enemy observation or when enemy forces make a point of attacking transports marked with the emblem. In such circumstances, there may be reason to believe that the medical transport will be better pro-tected if it is not marked with the distinctive emblem. In such exceptional cases, removing or concealing the emblem is permissible.

2406   It must be acknowledged that while military medical transports not marked with the emblem remain protected, it will often be very difficult for the oppos-ing Party to distinguish them from other military vehicles, increasing the risk that the vehicle will be subject to attack. This risk may be particularly acute when the medical vehicle operates in close proximity to military objec-tives. The Party using a medical transport that does not display the distinctive emblem therefore accepts the risk that the vehicle may find itself attacked. Provided the attack complies with all the other requirements flowing from the applicable law on the conduct of hostilities, it will be lawful. The attack will be

---

[42] See also Additional Protocol I, Article 18.
[43] See the commentary on Article 39, section B.3.
[44] See *ibid.* section B.4. See also Breitegger, p. 124.   [45] See Langdon/Rogers/Eadie, p. 184.

unlawful, however, if and as soon as the attacking Party knows, or has reason to know, that the vehicle is exclusively engaged in a medical transport function, an unlikely but not impossible scenario.

2407   Although there were good reasons for introducing the principle of a distinctive emblem that can be removed, the risk of abuse of the emblem has certainly increased as a result. After the wounded have been taken to the rear under the protection of the distinctive emblem, it may be tempting to load the empty vehicles returning to the front with war material. If the emblem then remains on the loaded vehicles, this constitutes an improper use of the emblem (and hence prohibited on the basis of Article 38 of Additional Protocol I), even if the sign has simply been left on through negligence or because there has been no time to remove or conceal it. Parties to a conflict must therefore be constantly vigilant in ensuring that the distinctive emblem is immediately removed or concealed whenever a vehicle used for medical transport is no longer exclusively employed for that purpose.

2408   The same rules and considerations apply to temporary military medical transports: normally, it will be necessary to mark the vehicle visibly with the distinctive emblem so that the enemy is aware of its temporary use as a medical transport and thus of its protected status. It is also essential to remove or conceal such markings as soon as the temporary medical use ceases.

2409   No matter how the enemy is made aware of a military medical transport's temporary use – by it being marked with the distinctive emblem or possibly through recognition of its exclusive medical transport purpose – the fact that the vehicle was previously, and may again in the future, be used in a capacity subjecting it to lawful attack may not be used as a pretext for attacking it or for taking any other unlawful action short of attack. Any such action would violate the protection afforded to medical transports and cannot be justified by military necessity. Article 35 reflects the view of the States party to the Convention that no military advantage can be derived from attacking transports abiding by all applicable law in maintaining and making known their protected status.[46]

2410   It must be kept in mind at all times that, under the ICC Statute, it is a war crime in both international and non-international armed conflict to '[i]ntentionally direc[t] attacks against...medical...transport using the distinctive emblems of the Geneva Conventions in conformity with international law'.[47]

---

[46] See Cassese, p. 388 (the Italian Court recognized that military necessity as a defence was not applicable to Article 191 of Italy's *Wartime Military Criminal Code*, 1941, which provides that whoever fires on ambulances, hospitals or other medical facilities where, 'pursuant to the law or international conventions they must be respected and protected', may be punished with imprisonment").
[47] See ICC Statute (1998), Article 8(2)(b)(xxiv) and (e)(ii).

D. Paragraph 2: Military medical transports in enemy hands

2411 Article 35(2) regulates the fate of military medical transports which have fallen into enemy hands. This paragraph applies irrespective of the circumstances in which these transports fell into enemy hands. Thus, included in its scope of application are the capture of military medical transports or the surrender of their crew.

2412 The paragraph applies only to the medical transports used by the armed forces proper and not to those of voluntary aid societies acting on the basis of Article 26 or 27. Under the special provision set down in Article 34 and in common with all other material belonging to these societies, the latter are to be considered as private property and, accordingly, are exempt from capture. However, to maintain their protected status, they must abide by the applicable law in all instances.

2413 As for medical transports employed by the armed forces medical service, the 1949 Diplomatic Conference recognized their military importance in modern warfare and the value of converting them to military use by the Party into whose hands they have fallen. Such military use may, in addition, have been their primary function prior to being assigned to medical transportation. Accordingly, the provision that military medical transports 'shall be subject to the laws of war' means that they – like the material of fixed medical establishments covered by Article 33 but unlike mobile medical units covered by Article 19(1) – may be treated in the same way as any other equipment subject to the laws of war. Thus, once captured, military medical transports become booty of war, and the property title passes to the Power into whose hands they have fallen. Consequently, they may be disposed of (even destroyed) or converted to use by the capturing Power.[48] Notably, such use need not be limited to medical transport, but may extend to any function whatsoever, including combat. However, if a medical transport is used for another purpose, such as military transport, the distinctive emblem must be immediately removed or concealed.[49]

2414 A military medical transport may not be captured and retained unless the capturing force can ensure that its wounded and sick occupants receive the necessary treatment and care in accordance with the non-discrimination principle. The wording 'ensure the care of' must be interpreted as safeguarding the inalienable rights of the wounded and sick: they must receive adequate care and the treatment required by their state of health; and they must not suffer any adverse consequences of the impounding of the vehicles. The Party to the

---

[48] See Schöberl, pp. 829 and 838.
[49] See e.g. United Kingdom, *Allied Joint Doctrine for Medical Support, with UK National Elements*, 2015, p. 1–99: 'Under no circumstances may the Red Cross emblem be displayed on an ambulance platform at the same time as a weapon system is mounted on it.' See also Langdon/Rogers/Eadie, p. 183.

conflict into whose hands the military medical transport has fallen remains bound by the provisions of Article 12 on respect for and protection of the wounded and sick.

2415   If, for any reason, the capturing force is unable to provide the wounded and sick with the care they require, it must allow the medical transport to pursue its journey and return to its own lines. Moreover, the words 'the wounded and sick they contain' must be interpreted broadly to cover all the wounded and sick whose health depends on the transport, including casualties that will be stranded or abandoned if the medical transport is unable to complete its mission. In other words, the capturing force is prohibited from retaining the medical transport if it is incapable of providing care not only of the wounded and sick on board at the moment of capture. Arguably, in view of the purpose of the First Convention, the same considerations should apply as long as the needs of the wounded and sick awaiting collection by that vehicle have not first been taken care of.

2416   Article 35 deals only with the disposal or use of the vehicles themselves when they fall into enemy hands. Should the transports be carrying wounded and sick people, medical personnel or medical material, other rules of international humanitarian law apply. When it comes to determining the status of medical personnel when they fall into enemy hands, the rights of the capturing Power in this respect (for example the retention of enemy medical personnel on the basis of Article 28) are subject, however, to the same limitation as in respect of the vehicles: they may be exercised only if the captor ensures the care of the wounded and sick occupants of the transport. If the inability to provide the necessary care of the wounded or sick occupants prohibits retention of the transport, it is self-evident that the crew must also be permitted to remain with the vehicle, as it would be incapable of performing its humanitarian mission without the services of its operators. The safeguards laid down in the Convention would then become void of any meaningful effect.

E. Paragraph 3: Requisitioned civilian personnel and means of transport

2417   Article 35(3) states that '[t]he civilian personnel and all means of transport obtained by requisition shall be subject to the general rules of international law'. The same rule, with identical wording, appeared as Article 17(6) of the 1929 Geneva Convention on the Wounded and Sick. The interpretation of this sentence, which does not seem to have led to any reported application in practice or been the object of any analysis in the literature, is not clear.

2418   The assumption which seems to underpin this paragraph is the eventuality that a Party to an international armed conflict lacks sufficient military medical transports and/or qualified personnel to operate them and therefore decides to requisition civilian personnel or civilian means of transport. When this occurs, this article suggests that the fate of civilian personnel and means of transport is governed by the general rules of international law. What those 'general rules of international law' are is not further clarified in the article. While this approach has the advantage of allowing for international law to evolve on the matter, it renders the task of the commentator or operational legal adviser all the more difficult.[50]

2419   A scenario in which the paragraph could play a role is when a State would, on the basis of its domestic law, wish to requisition the property or services of persons under its jurisdiction. Through the reference to 'the general rules of international law', it is clear that any applicable human rights law protecting persons in this case must be complied with.

2420   Clearly, the paragraph may also have a role to play in occupied territory, where the Occupying Power may wish to requisition civilian personnel or civilian means of transport. Based on the law of occupation, an Occupying Power is entitled to requisition civilian means of transport or the services of civilian personnel if required to meet the needs of its armed forces. In that case, the reference in Article 35(3) to the 'general rules of international law' is to Articles 52 and 53(2) of the 1907 Hague Regulations. Article 52 of the Regulations provides in relevant part that '[c]ontributions in kind shall as far as possible be paid for in cash; if not, a receipt shall be given and the payment of the amount due shall be made as soon as possible'. According to Article 53(2) of the Regulations, means of transport must be restored and compensation fixed when peace is made.

2421   Where an Occupying Power wishes to requisition the property of aid societies which are admitted to the privileges of the Convention (i.e. those operating on the basis of Article 26 or 27), it must comply with the conditions set down in Article 34(2).

2422   The question could be asked whether the more stringent conditions of Article 34(2) apply to requisition undertaken on the basis of Article 35(3). There is no clear textual basis for answering this question in the affirmative. However, in the light of the object and purpose of the First Convention, the Occupying Power is advised, also in this instance, to requisition civilian personnel and civilian means of transport only 'in case of urgent necessity, and only after the welfare of the wounded and sick has been ensured'.[51] This would be in line with the conditions set down in Article 57 of the Fourth Convention for an Occupying Power to requisition civilian hospitals.

---

[50] In view of the undefined character of the words 'general rules of international law', the added value of this paragraph was already questioned during the 1929 Diplomatic Conference; see *Proceedings of the Geneva Diplomatic Conference of 1929*, p. 219.

[51] Article 34(2).

Select bibliography

Breitegger, Alexander, 'The legal framework applicable to insecurity and violence affecting the delivery of health care in armed conflicts and other emergencies', *International Review of the Red Cross*, Vol. 95, No. 889, March 2013, pp. 83–127.

Cassese, Antonio, 'Under What Conditions May Belligerents be Acquitted of the Crime of Attacking an Ambulance?', *Journal of International Criminal Justice*, Vol. 6, No. 2, 2008, pp. 385–397.

Henckaerts, Jean-Marie and Doswald-Beck, Louise, *Customary International Humanitarian Law, Volume 1: Rules*, ICRC/Cambridge University Press, 2005, available at https://www.icrc.org/customary-ihl/eng/docs/v1.

ICRC, *Ambulance and Pre-hospital Services in Risk Situations*, ICRC, Geneva, 2013.

Langdon, J.B.R.L, Rogers, A.P.V. and Eadie, C.J., 'The use of transport under the additional protocols 1977', in Hazel Fox and Michael A. Meyer (eds), *Effecting Compliance – Armed Conflict and the New Law*, British Institute of International and Comparative Law, London, 1993, pp. 177–193.

Schöberl, Katja, 'Buildings, Material, and Transports', in Andrew Clapham, Paola Gaeta and Marco Sassòli (eds), The 1949 *Geneva Conventions: A Commentary*, Oxford University Press, 2015, pp. 825–838.

Spieker, Heike, 'Medical Transportation', version of March 2013, in Rüdiger Wolfrum, *Max Planck Encyclopedia of Public International Law*, Oxford University Press, http://opil.ouplaw.com/home/EPIL.

ARTICLE 36

MEDICAL AIRCRAFT

❖ Text of the provision*

(1) Medical aircraft, that is to say, aircraft exclusively employed for the removal of wounded and sick and for the transport of medical personnel and equipment, shall not be attacked, but shall be respected by the belligerents, while flying at heights, times and on routes specifically agreed upon between the belligerents concerned.

(2) They shall bear, clearly marked, the distinctive emblem prescribed in Article 38, together with their national colours, on their lower, upper and lateral surfaces. They shall be provided with any other markings or means of identification that may be agreed upon between the belligerents upon the outbreak or during the course of hostilities.

(3) Unless agreed otherwise, flights over enemy or enemy-occupied territory are prohibited.

(4) Medical aircraft shall obey every summons to land. In the event of a landing thus imposed, the aircraft with its occupants may continue its flight after examination, if any.

(5) In the event of an involuntary landing in enemy or enemy-occupied territory, the wounded and sick, as well as the crew of the aircraft shall be prisoners of war. The medical personnel shall be treated according to Article 24, and the Articles following.

❖ Reservations or declaration

None

Contents

* Paragraph numbers have been added for ease of reference.

A. Introduction

2423   Collection and evacuation of the wounded and sick, as well as the transport of medical personnel and equipment, are a vital part of efforts to mitigate the suffering associated with armed conflict. Often the fastest, and sometimes the only, means of carrying out these humanitarian tasks is by aircraft (a term which includes helicopters). It is axiomatic that rapid casualty evacuation is a genuine life-saving measure in modern conflict. Indeed, the decisive effect of evacuating battlefield casualties to a facility able to stabilize their injuries within the shortest possible time is commonly referred to as the critical 'ten platinum minutes' or as 'the golden hour', depending on the type of injury.[1]

2424   Nowadays, evacuation of the wounded and sick by air is an integral component of military medical capabilities for many armed forces possessing rotary and/or fixed-wing air transports. Accordingly, maximizing the protection of aircraft exclusively engaged in the collection, evacuation and treatment[2] of the wounded and sick or in the transport of medical personnel and equipment supports one of the main objectives of international humanitarian law, i.e. to ensure respect for and protection of the wounded and sick. In the context of the First Convention, the wounded and sick are understood to be those who are members of armed forces and of groups affiliated with them.[3]

2425   Article 36 confers protection on medical aircraft but subjects that protection to relatively stringent criteria. The reason for the stringency is that, at the time of drafting the Geneva Conventions, the precise nature of an enemy aircraft was very difficult to ascertain from a distance. Moreover, ever since the advent of aviation, there has been a concern that medical aircraft may be used as a cover for acquiring information of military value.

2426   In many ways, the extent of capabilities and operations involving the transport of the wounded and sick has outpaced the rules established by the Geneva Conventions to accommodate this humanitarian activity. Since 1949, several initiatives to update Article 36 and other provisions of the Geneva Conventions

---

[1] See ICRC, *War Surgery: Working with Limited Resources in Armed Conflict and Other Situations of Violence*, Vol. 1, ICRC, Geneva, 2009, p. 111. For further information on the difference between the concepts of 'medical evacuation' and 'casualty evacuation', see the commentary on Article 35, fn. 20.

[2] While treatment does not appear in the definition of medical aircraft, as found in Article 36, it is nowadays widely accepted that medical aircraft may contain on-board treatment facilities. For a discussion, see para. 2443.

[3] See Articles 12–13.

related to the protection of medical aircraft have resulted in a closer symmetry between international humanitarian law and operational practice.[4] Nowadays, it is therefore impossible to understand the full mosaic of rules applicable to medical aircraft by focusing exclusively on the relevant provisions in the Geneva Conventions.[5] The latter continue, however, to form the foundation for such regulation.

B. Historical background

2427 If regulated effectively, the use of aircraft exclusively employed for medical purposes and the obligation to respect and protect such aircraft clearly contribute to alleviating the suffering of victims of armed conflict.

2428 Aircraft have been used for medical purposes in time of armed conflict since 1910.[6] As a new phenomenon on the battlefield at the time, the employment of medical aircraft naturally triggered questions as to under which conditions they could, if at all, be protected by international humanitarian law. As early as 1912, concerns were raised in legal literature about the intelligence advantage that could potentially be gained by aircraft while searching for the wounded or transporting them from the battlefield.[7] Accordingly, a clear distinction was made between the use of aircraft to collect and evacuate casualties, which was considered to be a protected activity,[8] and the use of aircraft to search for casualties, which was deemed to be an unprotected activity.[9]

2429 After the First World War, the use of aircraft for medical purposes in time of armed conflict became too frequent for it to be addressed solely in academic publications. Thus, in 1923, the (non-binding) Hague Rules of Air Warfare declared that the 'principles' of the 1906 Geneva Convention and of the 1907 Hague Convention (X) applied to what were called at the time 'flying ambulances'.[10]

2430 The topic was subsequently taken up by the International Conference of the Red Cross. The agenda of the 12th International Conference, held in Geneva in 1925, included a discussion on a draft convention for the adaptation of the principles of the 1906 Geneva Convention to aerial warfare.[11] The proposed

---

[4] Most importantly, see Articles 24–31 of Additional Protocol I. See also Manual on International Law Applicable to Air and Missile Warfare (2009), Section L, 'Specific Protection of Medical Aircraft', Rules 75–87, and San Remo Manual on International Law Applicable to Armed Conflicts at Sea (1994), Part VI, Section III, entitled 'Medical Aircraft', Rules 174–183.

[5] These provisions are: Articles 36–37 of the First Convention; Articles 39–40 of the Second Convention; and Article 22 of the Fourth Convention.

[6] Des Gouttes/Julliot, p. 2.

[7] In that year, Julliot considered the use of aircraft for medical evacuation; see Julliot, 1912, pp. 689–710. See also Julliot, 1918, pp. 14–20.

[8] Julliot, 1912, p. 689.   [9] *Ibid.* p. 702. See also Des Gouttes, p. 932.

[10] Hague Rules of Air Warfare (1923), Article 17.

[11] Des Gouttes/Julliot, p. 1: The idea of discussing the legal regime applicable to medical aircraft was raised by the French Government at the 11th International Conference of the Red Cross

text was approved by the International Conference and sent to the Swiss Federal Council to be placed before the Diplomatic Conference. However, when convening the conference in 1929 for the purpose of revising the Geneva Convention and concluding a new convention on the treatment of prisoners of war, the Swiss Government did not think it advisable to add a new and complex problem to the already extensive programme.[12]

2431   Nonetheless, the issue had become so topical and so important that it was deemed impossible to revise the 1906 Geneva Convention without making provision for the use of medical aircraft. However, efforts to address the issue at the 1929 Conference suffered two impediments. First, there was insufficient time to draw up a complete set of detailed provisions. Second, the lack of sufficient notice that the matter would be on the agenda of the Diplomatic Conference prevented governments from including the necessary experts in their delegations.[13] The issue was therefore only settled by including some basic principles in the form of a new Article 18 in the 1929 Geneva Convention on the Wounded and Sick.[14] In recognition of the insufficiency of this solution, the Conference recommended in its Final Act 'that the countries participating in the Geneva Conventions should meet in conference in the near future with the view to regulate as comprehensively as may be necessary the use of medical aircraft in time of war'.[15]

2432   The provision dealing with medical aircraft was arguably the most significant innovation in the 1929 Convention. However, limiting the use of such aircraft

in Geneva in 1923. For an overview of the numerous activities on the subject from that period, see ICRC, *Rapport général du Comité international de la Croix-Rouge sur son activité de 1923 à 1925*, Geneva, 1925, pp. 18–21. See also 13th International Conference of the Red Cross, The Hague, 1928, Res. VII, 'Aviation sanitaire'.

[12] Des Gouttes, *Commentaire de la Convention de Genève de 1929 sur les blessés et malades*, ICRC, 1930, p. 120.

[13] *Ibid.*

[14] Geneva Convention on the Wounded and Sick (1929), Article 18:

> Aircraft used as means of medical transport shall enjoy the protection of the Convention during the period in which they are reserved exclusively for the evacuation of wounded and sick and the transport of medical personnel and material.
>
> They shall be painted white and shall bear, clearly marked, the distinctive emblem prescribed in Article 19, side by side with their national colours, on their lower and upper surfaces.
>
> In the absence of special and express permission, flying over the firing line, and over the zone situated in front of clearing or dressing stations, and generally over all enemy territory or territory occupied by the enemy, is prohibited.
>
> Medical aircraft shall obey every summons to land.
>
> In the event of a landing thus imposed, or of an involuntary landing in enemy territory and territory occupied by the enemy, the wounded and sick, as well as the medical personnel and material, including the aircraft, shall enjoy the privileges of the present Convention.
>
> The pilot, mechanics and wireless telegraph operators captured shall be sent back, on condition that they shall be employed until the close of hostilities in the medical service only.

The full discussion on what eventually became Article 18 of the 1929 Geneva Convention can be found in *Proceedings of the Geneva Diplomatic Conference of 1929*, pp. 221–242 and 613–615. See also de La Pradelle, p. 392.

[15] *Final Act of the Geneva Diplomatic Conference of 1929*, Recommendation No. 3.

was an important aspect of this regulation and reflected the earlier concerns. Subsequently, the ICRC submitted a draft to the 14th International Conference of the Red Cross, held in Brussels in 1930, for a new convention adapting the principles of the Geneva Convention to aerial warfare.[16] The Conference approved this draft, and instructed the ICRC to transmit it to the Swiss Government to be included in the agenda of the next Diplomatic Conference, set for 1940.[17] However, this conference was postponed owing to the outbreak of the Second World War.

2433   After the Second World War, when the ICRC resumed its work on the revision of the Geneva Conventions, the idea of developing a separate treaty dealing exclusively with medical aircraft was again raised.[18] The special draft convention was submitted to the Preliminary Conference of National Red Cross Societies in 1946, with a request for views on possible extensions or modifications, in the light of the various countries' experiences. However, the ICRC proposed to abandon efforts to develop a separate convention, prompted by the recognition that the protection afforded by the Geneva Convention to the wounded and sick as well as to the buildings and personnel exclusively engaged in or devoted to their collection and care was equally applicable to air and to land transport. The ICRC concluded that the special conditions prevailing at sea during armed conflict – which in 1907 prompted the adaptation of the principles of the Geneva Convention to maritime warfare – did not extend to aerial operations. Medical aircraft were understood merely as a means, like any other, of transporting or aiding the wounded and sick.[19]

2434   The 1947 Conference of Government Experts agreed that: (i) Article 18 of the 1929 Geneva Convention on the Wounded and Sick had met with very limited application during the Second World War; (ii) technical progress in fighter aircraft and anti-aircraft artillery rendered somewhat unrealistic any attempt to develop the use of protected medical aircraft on a wide scale; and (iii) that the issue was further complicated by the increasingly common practice of evacuating the wounded by air under fighter escort. Thus, the delegates concluded that medical aircraft should not be dealt with in a separate treaty. Instead, they took the view that the substance of Article 18 of the 1929 Convention

---

[16] Charles-Louis Julliot and Paul Des Gouttes, *La Convention de Genève de 1929 et l'immunisation des appareils sanitaires aériens : Projet d'une convention additionnelle pour l'adaptation à la guerre aérienne des principes de la Convention de Genève*, ICRC, Geneva, 1929.

[17] 'Résolutions et vœux adoptés par la XIVe Conférence internationale de la Croix-Rouge, Résolution No. XXIII, Aviation sanitaire en temps de guerre', in *Revue internationale de la Croix-Rouge et Bulletin international des Sociétés de la Croix-Rouge*, Vol. 12. No. 42, October 1930, p. 863. For a discussion of some of the issues at the time, see *Draft revision of the 1929 Geneva Convention submitted by the ICRC to National Societies in 1937*, pp. 11–12.

[18] See also Paul de La Pradelle, *La Conférence diplomatique et les nouvelles Conventions de Genève du 12 août 1949*, Les Éditions internationales, Paris, 1951, pp. 194–202.

[19] *Minutes of the Preliminary Conference of National Societies of 1946*, Vol. I, p. 41, see also p. 109; *Report of the Preliminary Conference of National Societies of 1946*, pp. 38–40.

could be retained, provided a provision was added governing flights by medical aircraft over the territory of neutral Powers.[20] This last issue was addressed through the inclusion of Article 37 in the First Convention and Article 40 of the Second Convention.

2435   The same view prevailed at the 1949 Diplomatic Conference, despite a proposal put forward by two delegations to allow greater use to be made of medical aircraft. They insisted that aeronautical progress, far from undermining the efficacy of medical aviation, offered excellent possibilities of bringing rapid aid to the wounded and of providing unprecedented speed of evacuation to vital medical treatment, which might be at a great distance away. The draft articles submitted by the two delegations recommended that medical aircraft be used more extensively and that such use should include authorized flight over enemy territory.[21]

2436   These proposals did not lead, however, to extensive revisions to Article 18 of the 1929 Convention. This lack of progress was highlighted in the 1987 commentary on Additional Protocol I, which noted that '[f]ar from developing these rather embryonic provisions of the 1929 Convention, the Diplomatic Conference of 1949 virtually paralyzed medical aviation when it subordinated all activity of medical aircraft of a Party to the conflict to a prior agreement with the adverse Party'.[22]

2437   Articles 24–31 of Additional Protocol I further clarified the rules applicable to medical aircraft in time of armed conflict. In practice, these rules supplement those of the present Convention, as they are binding on the Parties to the Protocol and are widely considered by States not party to the Protocol to provide important and helpful clarification of the existing rules. These more recent provisions indicate the clear and unambiguous objective of ensuring that Parties to a conflict endeavour to maximize the protection of all medical aircraft, even in situations where such aircraft are not necessarily protected through compliance with the strict treaty provisions related to routes and transit over contested or even enemy territory.

C. Definition of medical aircraft

2438   In line with the scope of application of Chapter VI ('Medical transports') as a whole and within the context of the First Convention in particular, Article 36 only applies to medical aircraft used by the armed forces, by groups mentioned in Article 13 and by voluntary aid societies operating under the conditions set down in Article 26 or 27. Medical aircraft so employed may, but need not, be

---

[20] *Report of the Conference of Government Experts of 1947*, pp. 45–46.
[21] *Final Record of the Diplomatic Conference of Geneva of 1949*, Vol. II-A, pp. 85–86 (proposals by Finland and Monaco).
[22] See Sandoz/Swinarski/Zimmermann (eds), *Commentary on the Additional Protocols*, ICRC, 1987, para. 967.

the property of the aforementioned categories; they may also, for example, have been leased.

2439 In time of armed conflict, other actors – such as the ICRC and other impartial humanitarian organizations – may also operate aircraft for medical transport. This may happen pursuant to an agreement with the Parties and as a substitute to their own air transport, for example where they lack such means of transport themselves. Without prejudice to the fact that these aircraft may also be used to transport wounded and sick combatants, as far as the Geneva Conventions are concerned such aircraft are regulated by Article 22 of the Fourth Convention.

2440 The term 'aircraft' encompasses all airborne transports such as planes, airships and helicopters.[23] In practice, helicopters are particularly important for removing the wounded and sick from the battlefield. The law prescribes neither a minimum nor a maximum size as a constitutive criterion for an aircraft to qualify as a medical aircraft. Any kind of aircraft may qualify as a medical aircraft. Thus, so long as it is exclusively employed in a medical capacity for the duration of its medical mission, a military aircraft may be a medical aircraft.[24] The same is true, for example, of State aircraft, civilian aircraft or civilian airliners.[25] Advances in transportation technology may, in the future, result in new types of aircraft (including unmanned aircraft) falling within the scope of Article 36.[26] Once the transport qualifies as a medical aircraft, it will remain protected so long as it does not commit, or is not used to commit, outside its humanitarian duties, an act harmful to the enemy (for the meaning of this term, see section D.2).

2441 In order to qualify as a medical aircraft, an aircraft needs to be 'exclusively employed' for the 'removal of wounded and sick' and/or for the 'transport of medical personnel and equipment'. This is consistent with other definitions of the term 'medical aircraft', which indicate that any aircraft exclusively engaged in, or assigned exclusively to, a medical mission falls within the definition.[27]

---

[23] See Manual on International Law Applicable to Air and Missile Warfare (2009), Rule 1(d): '"Aircraft" means any vehicle – whether manned or unmanned – that can derive support in the atmosphere from the reactions of the air (other than the reactions of the air against the earth's surface), including vehicles with either fixed or rotary wings.'

[24] See also *ibid.* commentary on Rule 1(u), para. 4.

[25] For definitions of these concepts, see *ibid.* Rule 1(h) (civilian aircraft), 1(i) (civilian airliner), 1(x) (military aircraft) and 1(cc) (State aircraft).

[26] See also the commentary on Article 35, para. 2373. See also International Civil Aviation Organization, *Manual Concerning Safety Measures Relating to Military Activities Potentially Hazardous to Civil Aircraft Operations*, Doc 9554-AN/932, 1990.

[27] See Article 8(j) of Additional Protocol I, which defines 'medical aircraft' as 'any medical transports by air'. For its part, Article 8(g) of the Protocol defines 'medical transports' as 'any means of transportation, whether military or civilian, permanent or temporary, assigned exclusively to medical transportation and under the control of a competent authority of a Party to the conflict'. See also Rule 1(u) of the Manual on International Law Applicable to Air and Missile Warfare (2009), which defines 'medical aircraft' as 'any aircraft permanently or temporarily assigned – by the competent authorities of a Belligerent Party – exclusively to aerial transportation or treatment of wounded, sick, or shipwrecked persons, and/or the transport of medical personnel and medical equipment or supplies'. It should be noted that Article 36 of the First Convention speaks

Today, these definitions are viewed as authoritative when considering which objects may qualify as 'transports or vehicles' in the sense of Article 35.[28] An aircraft need not actually be engaged in one or both of these activities in order to qualify as a medical aircraft. An aircraft may also qualify as a medical aircraft, for example, if it is on its way to remove the wounded and sick from the battlefield but does not yet have any wounded or sick on board.

2442   A first activity for which medical aircraft may be employed is the 'removal of wounded and sick'. Within the context of the First Convention, the term 'wounded and sick' primarily refers to the wounded and sick covered by Articles 12 and 13. However, the fact that the medical aircraft's activities may extend to wounded and sick civilians does not disqualify the aircraft as a medical aircraft.[29] Aircraft used for the search and rescue of able-bodied combatants (often referred to as 'combat SAR') or for the transport of such combatants (even when there are wounded and sick on board) do not qualify as medical aircraft.[30]

2443   While the wounded and sick are being removed from the battlefield and conveyed to a land-based medical facility, it is compatible with the purpose of medical transport that they may already receive medical treatment on board the aircraft.[31] Although the drafters of the Geneva Conventions did not envision that medical aircraft would develop to the point of containing full-scale medical treatment capabilities which would go beyond first-aid treatment, subsequent State practice clearly shows that this has become both technically feasible and normatively acceptable. However, except by prior agreement with the enemy, medical aircraft may not be used to search for the wounded and sick.[32]

2444   A second activity for which medical aircraft may be employed is the 'transport of medical personnel and equipment'. Within the context of the First

---

of 'exclusively employed' and not, as is the case with the definitions in Additional Protocol I and the 2009 Manual on International Law Applicable to Air and Missile Warfare, of 'assigned exclusively'.

[28] See Henckaerts/Doswald-Beck, commentary on Rule 29, p. 100, 'Definition of medical transports', with references to military manuals.

[29] See Article 22(5), the logic of which applies also to medical aircraft. Further, for '[a]ircraft exclusively employed for the removal of wounded and sick civilians, the infirm and maternity cases, or for the transport of medical personnel and equipment', see Article 22 of the Fourth Convention. See also the definition of 'wounded and sick' in Article 8(a) of Additional Protocol I, which applies to 'persons, whether military or civilian'.

[30] See the second sentence of Article 28(2) of Additional Protocol I: '[Medical aircraft] are prohibited from carrying any persons or cargo not included within the definition of Article 8, sub-paragraph (f).' Article 8(f) of the Protocol defines 'medical transportation' as 'the conveyance by land, water or air of the wounded, sick, shipwrecked, medical personnel, religious personnel, medical equipment or medical supplies protected by the Conventions and by this Protocol'. See also Manual on International Law Applicable to Air and Missile Warfare (2009), Rule 86(a).

[31] See the definition of 'medical aircraft' in Rule 1(u) of the 2009 Manual on International Law Applicable to Air and Missile Warfare and paragraph 3 of the commentary on that provision. Similarly, see Schöberl, p. 829.

[32] Article 28(4) of Additional Protocol I. See also Rule 86(b) of the 2009 Manual on International Law Applicable to Air and Missile Warfare, the second sentence of which states that '[i]f medical aircraft nevertheless operate for [the purposes of searching for the wounded, sick and shipwrecked within areas of combat operations] they do so at their own risk'.

Convention, the term 'medical personnel' refers to all categories of personnel covered by Chapter IV of the Convention. Where the rules of Additional Protocol I apply, the term 'medical personnel' can also cover other categories of medical personnel (such as civilian medical personnel), as specified in Article 8(c) of the Protocol. The term 'medical equipment' has to be interpreted broadly as including not only the equipment (including surgical equipment) necessary for medical care, but also medicines and heavier equipment such as a field hospital.

2445   There is no requirement that medical aircraft be organized, specially equipped or permanently detailed for medical purposes.[33] This is clearly justified as the exigencies of war may require that aircraft (including military aircraft) be temporarily called upon to perform medical duties. If and for as long as such aircraft are exclusively employed for such duties, they will qualify as medical aircraft. In summary, it can be said that the First Convention, and Additional Protocol I for that matter, provide a great deal of flexibility as to which type of aircraft can qualify as medical aircraft. The same cannot be said of the conditions under which an aircraft, once it qualifies as a medical aircraft, will actually be entitled to protection.

D. Paragraph 1: Conditions for protection

1. General considerations

2446   In order to be respected and protected, a medical aircraft must be exclusively employed for medical purposes. The term 'exclusively employed' means that, in order for an aircraft to qualify as a medical aircraft, it must be used solely for medical purposes.

2447   The word 'exclusively' also implies that a medical aircraft cannot be used to undertake humanitarian activities which are not medical in nature.[34] In addition, it is understood that a medical aircraft may not commit, or be used to commit, an act harmful to the enemy (such as transporting munitions or conducting aerial intelligence operations), without forfeiting protected status. There is no reference to 'acts harmful to the enemy' in Article 36. As far as the First Convention is concerned, this notion only appears in Article 21 in relation to the loss of protection of medical units and establishments of the medical service of the armed forces. Despite the Convention's silence in this

---

[33] See, similarly, the commentary on Article 35, para. 2374. Contrast this, for example, with the definition of 'hospital ships' in Article 22(1) of the Second Convention, which need to have been 'built or equipped by the Powers specially and solely with a view to assisting the wounded, sick and shipwrecked, to treating them and to transporting them', as well as with the definition of 'civilian hospitals' in Article 18(1) of the Fourth Convention, which need to have been 'organized to give care to the wounded and sick'.

[34] For an analysis of the term 'humanitarian activities', see the commentary on Article 9, section C.2.a. Regarding possible consequences of a medical aircraft undertaking humanitarian activities other than medical, see para. 2459.

respect, it is uncontroversial that a medical aircraft may lose its protection if it commits, or is used to commit, acts harmful to the enemy. This is the sole basis on which protection may be lost.[35]

2448   An aircraft need not be exclusively employed for medical purposes for the entire time it is in the service of a Party to the conflict.[36] Rather, for the duration of even one particular flight, an aircraft may qualify for protection as a medical aircraft under the Convention, so long as it complies with the conditions applicable to medical aircraft, primarily among them exclusive employment for medical purposes.[37] Accordingly, belligerents may use aircraft in multiple roles, for example sending transport aircraft to the front line carrying munitions and soldiers and, after unloading that cargo, transporting the wounded and sick or medical personnel and equipment away from the front. In the former case, the aircraft is not entitled to protection, nor to display the distinctive emblem; in the latter case, the aircraft will be entitled to all due protections and to display the distinctive emblem, so long as other articles of the Convention are complied with.

2449   Aircraft exclusively employed for medical purposes, as well as their crew, may within certain limits be armed. While the Geneva Conventions themselves remain silent on the question of whether medical aircraft (and, separately, their personnel) may be armed, both Additional Protocol I and subsequent State practice have introduced helpful clarifications in this regard. First, according to Article 28(3) of Protocol I, there may be 'small arms and ammunition taken from the wounded, sick and shipwrecked on board and not yet handed to the proper service'.[38] Second, like medical personnel covered by Article 24, it is equally lawful, under that provision, for the personnel of medical aircraft to carry 'light individual weapons as may be necessary to enable the medical personnel on board to defend themselves and the wounded, sick and shipwrecked in their charge'. The medical aircraft itself may be equipped with purely deflective means of defence. Furthermore, light individual weapons (such as removable weapons in the door mount of a helicopter) may also be mounted on the aircraft, but can only be used for self-defence, that is for the defence of the personnel on board and of the wounded and sick in their charge.[39]

---

[35] See Manual on International Law Applicable to Air and Missile Warfare (2009), Rule 83: 'Subject to Rule 74, a medical aircraft loses its specific protection from attack if it is engaged in acts harmful to the enemy.'

[36] This may, of course, be the case. See also Article 8(k) of Additional Protocol I, defining, for the purposes of the Protocol, 'permanent medical transports' as 'those assigned exclusively to medical purposes for an indeterminate period'.

[37] See also Article 8(k) of Additional Protocol I, defining, for the purposes of that Protocol, 'temporary medical transports' as 'those devoted exclusively to medical purposes for limited periods during the whole of such periods'.

[38] On this particular scenario, see the commentary on Article 22, section E.

[39] See Manual on International Law Applicable to Air and Missile Warfare (2009), Rule 82:

> A medical aircraft may be equipped with deflective means of defence (such as chaff or flares) and carry light individual weapons necessary to protect the aircraft, the medical personnel and the wounded, sick or shipwrecked on board. Carrying of the individual weapons of the wounded, sick or shipwrecked during their evacuation does not entail loss of protection.

The considerations developed on this topic under Article 35 in connection with military medical transports apply *mutatis mutandis* to medical aircraft.[40]

2450   Most importantly, the plain text of Article 36 confers protection on medical aircraft only 'while flying at heights, times and on routes specifically agreed upon between the belligerents concerned'.[41] The requirement of prior agreement was born out of practical considerations for both the protection of the aircraft and the prevention of abuse. The delegates that recommended this solution explained that, under the conditions of warfare that prevailed while the Geneva Conventions were being discussed prior to 1949, visual identification of aircraft was often impracticable. Aircraft can be fired upon from well beyond visual range, at distances where colour markings are indistinguishable. Even when subject to visual observation, the nature of aircraft will often make it impracticable to positively identify and distinguish between medical aircraft, on the one hand, and aircraft engaged in belligerent activities, on the other hand. The delegates therefore concluded that only previous agreement could afford certainty of protection to medical aircraft.[42] Prior agreement also provides belligerents with adequate safeguards against abuse.

2451   Agreements on the operation of medical aircraft may be concluded on a case-by-case basis, or a general agreement might be reached between the Parties to the conflict. Such agreements would fall within the definition of a special agreement in the sense of common Article 6.[43] In order to reduce the uncertainty associated with the use of medical aircraft and to maximize their protection, Parties to a conflict should endeavour to establish such agreements, which may be facilitated through the good offices of the ICRC or any other impartial humanitarian organization.

2452   The use of medical aircraft is not, however, contingent on such agreements. Parties to a conflict may employ such aircraft without an agreement referred to in Article 36(1). When doing so, these aircraft operate at their own risk.[44] Of course, any attack must be predicated on an assessment that the aircraft qualifies as a military objective and that all other rules on the conduct of hostilities are complied with.[45] In other words, the mere absence of an agreement does not give a Party a licence to attack or capture such aircraft. The lack of an

---

[40] For details, see the commentary on Article 35, section C.2.b.
[41] The same requirement appears in Article 37(1), third sentence.
[42] *Final Record of the Diplomatic Conference of Geneva of 1949*, Vol. II-A, p. 86.
[43] Article 6 of the First, Second and Third Conventions and Article 7 of the Fourth Convention. Article 6 of the First Convention lists agreements under Article 36 as special agreements.
[44] On the implications thereof, see Schöberl, p. 830: 'Aircraft operating without or in violation of an agreement do so "at their own risk and peril" – which arguably refers to a factual risk rather than a loss of immunity in law.'
[45] See also Manual on International Law Applicable to Air and Missile Warfare (2009), Rule 25: 'Aircraft may be the object of attack only if they constitute military objectives.' For a definition of 'military objective', see Article 52(2) of Additional Protocol I and ICRC Study on Customary International Humanitarian Law (2005), Rule 8.

agreement does not in and of itself transform a medical aircraft into a military objective.

2453   Indeed, concern has been expressed that the protected status of medical aircraft seems predicated on the agreement itself.[46] However, the protection of the aircraft and its occupants is not contingent on an agreement. Rather, the wounded and sick, medical personnel and equipment are to be respected and protected, and being aboard a medical aircraft operating in the absence of an agreement does not divest them of this protection.[47] Agreements facilitate the fundamental respect due to medical aircraft by reducing the likelihood of them being misidentified. The absence of an agreement exposes a medical aircraft to the substantial risk that a Party will be unable to positively distinguish it from an enemy aircraft that may be subject to lawful attack. In view of this risk, all Parties to a conflict should be guided by general humanitarian principles and refrain from resorting to extreme measures (for example, an attack on and destruction of an aircraft that cannot be positively identified as a military objective). Instead, they should make all reasonable efforts in the circumstances to verify the status of the aircraft (for example by forcing it to land for the purpose of inspection).[48]

2454   The distinction between the specific protection resulting from prior agreements and the general protection afforded to the wounded and sick, to those exclusively engaged in their collection and care and to medical transports is addressed extensively in Additional Protocol I.[49] While the Protocol includes a rule making maximum protection for medical aircraft flying over territory controlled by an enemy contingent on a prior agreement, it also makes clear that the absence of such an agreement does not release the Parties to a conflict from their obligations to respect and protect the wounded and sick.[50] To that end, the Protocol requires operators of medical aircraft to make every effort to signal to the enemy the protected status of their craft.[51] Furthermore, the Protocol emphasizes that shooting down medical aircraft flying without a prior agreement is a measure of last resort.[52] The codification of this distinction between the general obligations to respect and protect the wounded and sick and medical personnel and equipment, on the one hand, and the enhanced protection derived from prior agreement, on the other hand, represented a significant departure from the 1949 Convention but ultimately reflected the drafters' response to the concerns prompted by the requirement of prior agreement.

---

[46] Doswald-Beck, pp. 159–160.   [47] *Ibid.* p. 161.

[48] In this regard, they are assisted by Article 36(4), first sentence: 'Medical aircraft shall obey every summons to land.'

[49] See Additional Protocol I, Article 27. On the difference between objects and persons entitled to general protection versus those entitled to specific protection, see also Manual on International Law Applicable to Air and Missile Warfare (2009), Section K, commentary, para. 1.

[50] Additional Protocol I, Article 27(2).   [51] *Ibid.*

[52] See Additional Protocol I, Article 27(2), second sentence. See also Sandoz/Swinarski/ Zimmermann (eds), *Commentary on the Additional Protocols*, ICRC, 1987, para. 1033.

2455   Once an aircraft qualifies as a medical aircraft, the protection due to it is identical to that accorded to land-based medical transports, namely they must be respected and protected at all times. Article 36 refers to an obligation to 'respect' such aircraft in addition to the prohibition on attacking them. This means that the obligation to 'respect' extends beyond the prohibition of attack, although Article 36 does not elaborate on what 'respect' entails in practice. Logically, it should include refraining from measures short of attack that interfere with the medical function of the aircraft (such as 'painting' the aircraft with air defence radar in a hostile way which interferes with its ability to operate, visibly training air defence weapons on the aircraft, or capturing it).[53] In addition, a Party to an armed conflict which deploys aircraft (including unmanned aerial vehicles) in the area in which the enemy's medical aircraft is known to be operating should notify, whenever feasible, the enemy of the presence and flight path of these vehicles so as to safeguard the medical aircraft's integrity at all times. However, it is acknowledged that, in particular with regard to the operation of military aircraft, military tactical and operational considerations, including the lack of a viable means of communication, may render such a notification not feasible.

2456   The obligation to 'protect' entails taking positive measures to assist or support the functioning of the medical aircraft. For further analysis of the term 'protect', see the commentaries on Article 19, paras 1805–1808, and Article 35, para. 2387.

2. Loss of protection

2457   The phrase 'act harmful to the enemy', outside the aircraft's medical function, is intentionally broad. Thus, it includes scenarios such as a medical aircraft bearing the protective emblem while parked next to a military objective with the aim of shielding the latter from attack,[54] transporting combatants or ammunition (even when wounded and sick persons or medical equipment are simultaneously on board), or cloaking an intelligence-gathering aircraft with the protective emblem.[55]

2458   While the lack of a definition creates some uncertainty as to the line between permissible activities and activities harmful to the enemy, it is clear that so long as the aircraft is exclusively engaged in a medical function, it may not be considered to be engaged in an act harmful to the enemy. Proximity to non-medical military aircraft may alter this conclusion, as including medical evacuation vehicles among non-medical military vehicles is common operational

---

[53] For further clarification of what exactly is included in the requirement to 'respect' medical objects, see the commentary on Article 19, section C.2.b and the commentary on Article 35, section C.2.a.

[54] See Additional Protocol I, Article 28(1), second sentence.

[55] See also Additional Protocol I, Article 28(2).

practice. Whether such a situation amounts to an 'act harmful to the enemy' depends on factors such as the distance between a medical unit and a military objective and the amount of time the medical aircraft remained adjacent to a military objective. These factors may also be relevant in the assessment of whether there was an intention of shielding a military objective from attack.

2459   Furthermore, if a medical aircraft is being used to undertake a humanitarian activity other than a medical activity, such as the delivery of food to civilians, this does not constitute an act harmful to the enemy. Doing so is not desirable, however, since any deviation from its exclusively medical character may lead to confusion as to the aircraft's true purpose. In order to avoid any confusion, such alternative use should best be covered by a prior agreement.

2460   Provided the grounds for doing so are reasonable, it can be expected that an opponent will construe any activities inconsistent with an aircraft's medical duties as acts harmful to the enemy. Therefore, when a medical aircraft deviates from its strictly medical duties, and when this results in the aircraft qualifying as a military objective in the circumstances ruling at the time, it may be subject to lawful attack. For example, using a medical aircraft to transport combatants or supplies of value for combat operations or engaging in reconnaissance missions with no relation to the transport of the wounded and sick would be inconsistent with an exclusively medical function.[56] It is therefore essential that the Parties to an armed conflict remain constantly aware of the distinction between medical aircraft losing protection by virtue of being used to commit, outside their humanitarian duties, acts harmful to the enemy, and medical aircraft qualifying as military objectives (which may render them liable to attack), which hinges, *inter alia*, upon their making a direct contribution to military action. The assessment of whether the aircraft has lost protection does not *ipso facto* result in the conclusion that the aircraft constitutes a lawful object of attack. Therefore, each of these assessments must be considered distinct, although the second will often be predicated on the first. In practice, however, it is hard to conceive of circumstances in which the commission of an 'act harmful to the enemy' would not transform the aircraft in question into a lawful object of attack.

E. Paragraph 2: Marking and other means of identification

2461   According to the first sentence of Article 36(2), medical aircraft are required to bear the distinctive emblem of the Convention, along with their national colours (e.g. the flag of the State to which the aircraft belongs), clearly marked on their lower, upper and lateral surfaces so that the distinctive emblem and national colours are visible from above, below and the sides. Wings are not

---

[56] See also Additional Protocol I, Article 28(2).

mentioned in this regard, as certain types of aircraft which can qualify as medical aircraft have no wings, such as helicopters.

462   Under the system of the 1929 Convention, the entire aircraft had to be painted white.[57] That provision was not maintained in the 1949 Convention owing to a combination of the increased difficulty of visual identification and the need to allow for greater ease in transforming any aircraft into a medical aircraft, since fitting it with the distinctive emblem is much more feasible than repainting the aircraft in its entirety. Nonetheless, it should be noted that the red cross, red crescent or red crystal emblems must always appear on a white background.[58] Thus, it is not sufficient to merely paint a red cross, red crescent or red crystal on an aircraft if the aircraft itself is not white;[59] a white background must be painted on as well. This clarification is important as any type of aircraft, including a military aircraft, may become a medical aircraft.

2463   The second sentence of Article 36(2) states that medical aircraft are to be provided with 'any other markings or means of identification that may be agreed upon between the belligerents upon the outbreak or during the course of hostilities'. As is clear from the use of the word 'may', it is for the Parties to the conflict to decide whether they wish to conclude a special agreement on this point. This provision left the way open for future technical improvements in this field. Internationally agreed means of identifying medical aircraft include specialized radio codes, a flashing blue light, and use of secondary surveillance radar.[60]

2464   Because it is not uncommon for Parties to a conflict to use aircraft not bearing a distinctive emblem to transport the wounded and sick (for example when properly marked aircraft are unavailable), it is important to note that the mere absence of such markings neither deprives an aircraft of its qualification as a medical aircraft, nor allows the enemy to attack the aircraft.[61] The entitlement to protection under the Convention is inherent to transports assigned exclusively to carrying the wounded and sick or medical personnel.[62] The distinctive

---

[57] See Geneva Convention on the Wounded and Sick (1929), Article 18(2).

[58] An agreement with regard to 'any other markings or means of identification' constitutes a special agreement in the sense of Article 6 of the First Convention, and therefore needs to comply with the conditions of that provision.

[59] For a discussion of the different distinctive emblems, and their equal status under international humanitarian law, see the commentary on Article 38, section C.

[60] Additional Protocol I, Annex I (both in its initial version and as amended in 1993) deals with the identification of medical aircraft. See also Additional Protocol I, Article 18, and Manual on International Law Applicable to Air and Missile Warfare (2009), Rule 76(b): 'A medical aircraft ought to use additional means of identification where appropriate.' For further information, see Eberlin, pp. 7–13.

[61] See also Manual on International Law Applicable to Air and Missile Warfare (2009), Rule 76(c): 'A temporary medical aircraft which cannot – either for lack of time or because of its characteristics – be marked with the distinctive emblem, ought to use the most effective means of identification available.'

[62] The same applies to aircraft which are on their way to collect wounded and sick persons but do not yet have any on board; see para. 2441.

emblem itself, while the visible symbol of that protection, does not confer protection, it merely aids in identification.[63] An aircraft which is exclusively employed in medical activities but which does not bear the distinctive emblem does not therefore forfeit its protection. The critical factor in such cases will be the enemy's knowledge of the aircraft's function. Prior notification of that function would obviously facilitate such awareness.

2465   As already noted, aircraft may be used for non-medical purposes on the inbound flight and subsequently repurposed as a medical aircraft for the out-bound flight or vice versa. The aircraft will, of course, only be protected during the time that it is exclusively engaged in removing or transporting the wounded and sick or medical personnel and equipment. Accordingly, it is essential that the distinctive emblem be removed or fully concealed during any phase of the mission in which the aircraft is not exclusively engaged in a medical function.

F. Paragraph 3: Flight over enemy or enemy-occupied territory

2466   The Convention prohibits flights of medical aircraft over enemy or enemy-occupied territory.[64] The sole exception to this prohibition exists when an agreement (in the sense of Article 6) has been reached between the Parties to the conflict to allow such a flight. The agreement may take the form of 'local arrangements' between the Parties to the conflict 'for the removal or exchange of [the] wounded and sick from a besieged or encircled area, and for the passage of medical and religious personnel and equipment on their way to that area', as provided for in Article 15(3).

2467   The prohibition on medical aircraft flying over enemy or enemy-occupied territory resulted from concerns that such flights, absent prior agreement, com-promised the legitimate needs of military security, specifically through unwar-ranted observation from such an aircraft. However, the requirement to obtain an agreement prior to being allowed to fly over enemy or enemy-occupied

---

[63] See the commentary on Article 39, para. 2578. See also Manual on International Law Appli-cable to Air and Missile Warfare (2009), Rule 76(d): 'Means of identification are intended only to facilitate identification and do not, of themselves, confer protected status.' Similarly, see Rules 72(c) and (d) of the Manual, the latter stating that '[t]he failure of medical and religious personnel, medical units and medical transports to display the distinctive emblem does not deprive them of their protected status'. In practice, if the enemy is aware that the unmarked aircraft is exclusively engaged in a medical function, attack would be prohibited based on the protected status of the aircraft's occupants. Accordingly, while the absence of marking is not dispositive on the issue of whether attacking an aircraft is lawful, it does result in increased risk of misidentification and of the aircraft being construed as a lawful target and therefore attacked.

[64] For a definition of the term 'occupied territory', see the commentary on common Article 2, section E. Further, the Drafting Committee did not assess whether medical aircraft could fly over an enemy's territorial waters, since 'they had not wished to venture onto such uncertain ground'. See Final Record of the Diplomatic Conference of Geneva of 1949, Vol. II-A, p. 141. Under contemporary international law of the sea, ships of all States enjoy the right of innocent passage through the territorial sea of other States (see Articles 17–26 of the 1982 UN Convention on the Law of the Sea). No parallel right exists for aircraft flying through the airspace above the said territorial sea.

territory should not be seen as contrary to the humanitarian objective of this provision, as it might be perceived. Medical aircraft transport the wounded and sick from the front lines and medical personnel and equipment to forward areas. For these purposes, in a given range of conceivable scenarios, medical aircraft will fly over territory controlled by friendly forces.[65] However, if a medical aircraft must fly over enemy-controlled territory, to or from a besieged area for example, an agreement between the belligerents may provide for its safe passage. Such an agreement must specify the altitude, route and time of the aircraft's flight over enemy territory in order to avoid misidentification and ensure its protection from attack.[66]

2468   Failure for any reason, including by mistake, to comply with the prohibition exposes the aircraft to all the dangers inherent in flying over enemy or enemy-occupied territory. Even then, a Party needs to comply with the rules regulating the conduct of hostilities. For example, assuming that the adverse Party can reasonably be expected to know that the aircraft is protected, the belligerent must attempt to warn the offending plane by radio or order it to land before resorting to the extreme measure of attacking it (which will only be permissible if the aircraft qualifies as a lawful object of attack and if all applicable rules regulating the conduct of hostilities have been complied with). In fact, the first response to an offending medical aircraft should be to issue a summons to land under Article 36(4). In this respect, it must be noted that Additional Protocol I substantially modified this rule by lessening the prohibitive aspect and instead highlighting the risk inherent in flying over enemy territory in the absence of a prior agreement.[67] Furthermore, once the aircraft has landed, the craft, its occupants and medical supplies must be accorded the full protection applicable in all circumstances to the wounded and sick and to those exclusively engaged in their collection and care.[68]

G. Paragraph 4: Summons to land

2469   The summons to land provides the adverse Party with a safeguard against abuse; it is the one real means of ensuring that the aircraft is exclusively employed for medical purposes. However, a summons to land may only be

---

[65] While medical aircraft typically have no need for protective agreements when flying over friendly territory, notification is recommended when 'proposed flight plans of medical aircraft will bring them within the range of an adverse party's surface-to-air weapons systems' (United Kingdom, *Manual of the Law of Armed Conflict*, 2004, para. 12.110.1). A similar recommendation existed in the 1929 Convention and largely focused on the concepts of 'the firing line' or 'contact zone'. See Doswald-Beck, p. 169. These are not requirements for medical aircraft, merely suggestions in order to ensure their greater safety when operating in such areas. When medical aircraft need to fly over the territory of a neutral State, Article 37 of the First Convention applies.

[66] Thus, an agreement reached on the basis of Article 36(3) must contain the same details as an agreement reached on the basis of Article 36(1).

[67] See Additional Protocol I, Article 27(2).   [68] See Article 36(5).

issued for the purpose of inspecting an aircraft to ascertain that it is indeed performing a medical function and is not violating any of the restrictions placed on such aircraft; there can be no other reason or justification for a summons to land.[69]

2470   Medical aircraft must obey all summonses to land. This requirement applies to aircraft flying over enemy or enemy-controlled territory, whether authorized to do so or not. The requirement also applies to medical aircraft flying over territory the physical control of which is not clearly established, which may also be the case if they are flying close to enemy lines.[70]

2471   A separate analysis is required for the scenario where, despite reasonable efforts to warn the aircraft, the Party issuing the warning reasonably concludes that the aircraft has received the warning and failed to act on it within a reasonable time, for example by ignoring the summons or by unambiguously making evasive manoeuvres. If that happens, depending on the circumstances the aircraft might qualify as a military objective in accordance with the law applicable to the conduct of hostilities.[71] As indicated by the word 'explicitly', the mere absence of a response to a summons to land cannot be construed as an act harmful to the enemy as the medical aircraft may genuinely not have received the summons.

2472   This scenario, however, needs to be distinguished from that in which a Party realizes that an enemy aircraft has deviated from the conditions of an overflight agreement and has determined that the aircraft is a medical aircraft. In that case, the belligerent must make all reasonable efforts to issue that aircraft with a summons to land. Further, the Party may have other options available, such as forcing the aircraft to land by accompanying it with fighter jets or using close-range communications to convey the summons to land.

2473   There is no set way of delivering a summons. This is a technical question that is not addressed in the Convention, but important and useful guidance can be found in Article 14 of the Regulations concerning identification annexed to Additional Protocol I.

2474   Good practice in delivering a summons to land would include broadcasting the summons on a pre-approved frequency, the specifics of which – in case a prior agreement has been reached to allow the flight over enemy or enemy-occupied territory – would be determined along with the time, route and altitude requirements for all flights over enemy territory. If the medical aircraft flies in the absence of a prior agreement, the Party issuing the summons to land must take all reasonable measures to ensure that the summons actually reaches the persons in control of the aircraft.

---

[69] Doswald-Beck, p. 175.
[70] Similarly, see Additional Protocol I, Article 30(1), and San Remo Manual on International Law Applicable to Armed Conflicts at Sea (1994), Rule 180.
[71] See Additional Protocol I, Article 27(2).

2475   Article 36(4) states that an aircraft which has landed pursuant to a summons may be examined. The provision does not, however, contain any guidance on how such examination is to take place (especially keeping in mind the constraints linked to the presence on board of the wounded and sick), or which purpose it may serve. These considerations, in addition to their flowing from the object and purpose of Article 36, have now been addressed in Article 30 of Additional Protocol I.[72] After obeying a summons to land, a medical aircraft may be inspected by the adverse Party to ensure that it is exclusively employed for medical purposes. Where the aircraft is found to be in compliance with the Convention, it must to be allowed to resume its flight without delay.[73] Inspection should be conducted promptly to enable aircraft operating within the bounds of the law to resume their medical mission quickly. The purpose of the inspection is not to unduly burden the aircraft; rather, it is to enable the enemy to ensure that the provisions of the Convention are being respected, as all Parties to a conflict using medical aircraft benefit if the belligerents adhere to the law. One of the main objectives of medical aviation is to permit the rapid evacuation of the wounded and sick and the transport of medical personnel and equipment. Neither of these categories of protected persons and objects must be allowed to suffer because the enemy has exercised its right of inspection – all the more so if the suspicion of improper activity has been discounted by the inspection. Additionally, good faith compliance by the crew with the summons justifies the obligation to allow the aircraft to resume its medical mission promptly.

2476   If examination reveals that the medical aircraft has been used to commit an 'act harmful to the enemy' outside its humanitarian duties, the aircraft loses its entitlement to be 'respected and protected'. In that case, based on the relevant rule of Additional Protocol I, the aircraft may be seized, the wounded and sick taken prisoner, and the medical personnel and material treated according to the general rules of the Convention.[74] At all times, however, the Party which proceeds to such measures remains responsible for ensuring that the wounded and sick receive the treatment, including medical treatment, to which they are entitled.[75] Furthermore, on the basis of the last sentence of Article 30(4) of Additional Protocol I, '[a]ny aircraft seized which had been assigned as a permanent medical aircraft may be used thereafter only as a medical aircraft'. As indicated, this may be the case for some of the aircraft covered by Article 36.[76]

---

[72] On the impact of the provisions of Additional Protocol I on the interpretation of the Geneva Conventions with regard to the provisions of medical aircraft, see para. 2437.
[73] See Additional Protocol I, Article 30(3).
[74] See Additional Protocol I, Article 30(4).   [75] See Article 12.
[76] In this regard, there is an important difference, when they fall into enemy hands, as compared to the fate of military medical transports; see the commentary on Article 35, paras 2412–2413. Similarly, see Schöberl, p. 830.

2477   Another scenario, with partially similar results in terms of how it is regulated, is when the examination reveals that the aircraft has been employed in activities which, while of a humanitarian nature, are not strictly medical and therefore do not benefit from the protection due under Article 36. In view of their humanitarian nature, it will be hard to argue that these activities are to be considered as acts harmful to the enemy. However, when it comes to aircraft assigned exclusively as medical aircraft on a temporary basis, they may result in the aircraft being treated as booty of war if it is a State aircraft (including a military aircraft) or captured as prize if it is a civilian aircraft. The Party which resorts to such measures remains responsible, at all times, for ensuring that the wounded and sick receive the treatment, including the medical treatment, to which they are entitled.[77]

H. Paragraph 5: Involuntary landing

2478   An involuntary landing in the sense of Article 36(5) occurs when a medical aircraft is obliged to land in enemy or enemy-controlled territory owing to weather conditions, mechanical problems, or any cause (such as an attack directed against it) other than a summons to land issued on the basis of Article 36(4). When such a landing occurs, the adverse Party may take the wounded and sick and, depending on their status, the crew prisoner. The difference in treatment between involuntary landings and landings made in response to a summons was deemed necessary for military security. Provided the adverse Party ensures the care of its wounded and sick occupants, the aircraft itself becomes war booty, as would a medical vehicle on the ground in similar circumstances.[78] However, if the medical aircraft is used by a voluntary aid society acting on the basis of Article 26 or 27, it will be regarded as private property, and the right of requisition 'shall not be exercised except in case of urgent necessity, and only after the welfare of the wounded and sick has been ensured'.[79]

Select bibliography

Cummings, Edward R., 'The Juridical Status of Medical Aircraft Under the Conventional Laws of War', *Military Law Review*, Vol. 66, 1974, pp. 105–141.

de La Pradelle, Paul, 'La protection de l'aviation sanitaire en temps de conflit', *Revue internationale de la Croix-Rouge*, Vol. 49, No. 585, September 1967, pp. 391–405.

Des Gouttes, Paul, 'Essai d'adaptation à la guerre aérienne des principes de la Convention de Genève du 6 juillet 1906', *Revue internationale de la Croix-Rouge et Bulletin international des Sociétés de la Croix-Rouge*, Vol. 6, No. 72, December 1924, pp. 931–944.

---

[77] See Article 12.   [78] See Article 35(2).   [79] Article 34(2).

Des Gouttes, Paul and Julliot, Charles-Louis, *Vers une convention internationale appliquant à la guerre aérienne les principes de la Convention de Genève*, Recueil de documents sur la neutralisation des aéronefs sanitaires, ICRC, Geneva, 1925.

Doswald-Beck, Louise, 'The Protection of Medical Aircraft in International Law', *Israel Yearbook on Human Rights*, Vol. 27, 1998, pp. 151–192.

Eberlin, Philippe, 'The identification of medical aircraft in periods of armed conflict', *International Review of the Red Cross*, Vol. 22, No. 229, August 1982, pp. 202–215.

Evrard, E., 'Legal Protection of Aero-Medical Evacuation in War-Time', *International Review of the Red Cross*, Vol. 6, No. 64, July 1966, pp. 343–361.

Henckaerts, Jean-Marie and Doswald-Beck, Louise, *Customary International Humanitarian Law, Volume 1: Rules*, ICRC/Cambridge University Press, 2009, available at https://www.icrc.org/customary-ihl/eng/docs/v1.

Julliot, Charles-Louis, 'Avions sanitaires et Convention de la Croix-Rouge', *Revue générale de droit international public*, Vol. XIX, 1912, pp. 689–710.

– *Les aéronefs sanitaires et la guerre de 1914*, Pedone, Paris, 1918.

Schöberl, Katja, 'Buildings, Material, and Transports', in Andrew Clapham, Paola Gaeta and Marco Sassòli (eds), The 1949 *Geneva Conventions: A Commentary*, Oxford University Press, 2015, pp. 825–838.

Spieker, Heike, 'Medical Transportation', version of March 2013, in Rüdiger Wolfrum (ed.), *Max Planck Encyclopedia of Public International Law*, Oxford University Press, http://opil.ouplaw.com/home/EPIL.

FLIGHT OVER NEUTRAL COUNTRIES. LANDING OF THE WOUNDED AND SICK

❖ Text of the provision*

(1) Subject to the provisions of the second paragraph, medical aircraft of Parties to the conflict may fly over the territory of neutral Powers, land on it in case of necessity, or use it as a port of call. They shall give the neutral Powers previous notice of their passage over the said territory and obey all summons to alight, on land or water. They will be immune from attack only when flying on routes, at heights and at times specifically agreed upon between the Parties to the conflict and the neutral Power concerned.

(2) The neutral Powers may, however, place conditions or restrictions on the passage or landing of medical aircraft on their territory. Such possible conditions or restrictions shall be applied equally to all Parties to the conflict.

(3) Unless agreed otherwise between the neutral Power and the Parties to the conflict, the wounded and sick who are disembarked, with the consent of the local authorities, on neutral territory by medical aircraft, shall be detained by the neutral Power, where so required by international law, in such a manner that they cannot again take part in operations of war. The cost of their accommodation and internment shall be borne by the Power on which they depend.

❖ Reservations or declarations

None

Contents

* Paragraph numbers have been added for ease of reference.

A. Introduction

2479 New in 1949, Article 37 represented an advance in international humanitarian law. For several years prior to that, the ICRC, faced with certain specific cases, had felt that a provision regulating the flight of medical aircraft over neutral territory was needed.[1] The article is an accommodation between two vital interests: considerations of humanity and the requirement to facilitate care of the wounded and sick during armed conflict, on the one hand, and the rights of neutral Powers, on the other hand.

2480   During an armed conflict, a belligerent Power with the necessary capabilities may seek to move its wounded and sick personnel expeditiously by air from the front line to a hospital in its own territory or elsewhere. The most direct route to a hospital – one that minimizes flight time and maximizes the chances of the wounded reaching life-saving treatment in time – may pass through the airspace of a neutral Power, i.e. a State which is not a Party to the international armed conflict in question.[2]

2481   In such a scenario, absent another international law provision to the contrary, the neutral Power would have the absolute right to deny the passage of the medical aircraft, notwithstanding the potential human suffering engendered by disallowing the flight through its airspace.[3]

2482   Central to the issue is a long-standing principle of international law, codified in Article 1 of the 1907 Hague Convention (V), that '[t]he territory of neutral Powers is inviolable'. This provision, specific to the law of neutrality, is in line with the general rule of international law that any entry into national airspace or territory is subject to the prior authorization of the State concerned.

2483   It might also happen that a belligerent Power's medical aircraft, without initially having planned to do so, enters neutral airspace owing to inclement

---

[1] As the 1929 Geneva Convention on the Wounded and Sick had not addressed this issue, it fell to law of war experts to consider what rules might apply to a medical aircraft overflying the territory of a neutral Power. Among the varying views were: that medical aircraft evacuating the wounded and sick should be able to enter and leave neutral jurisdictions freely; that medical aircraft should seek permission to enter neutral airspace; and that wounded and sick aboard medical aircraft could be subject to internment. See Edward R. Cummings, 'The Juridical Status of Medical Aircraft Under the Conventional Laws of War', *Military Law Review*, Vol. 66, 1974, pp. 105–141, at 122 (citing James Molony Spaight, *Air Power and War Rights*, 3rd edition, Longmans, London, 1947, p. 359).

[2] For further details on which entities qualify as a 'neutral Power', see the commentary on Article 4, section C.1.

[3] See Chicago Convention on International Civil Aviation (1944), Article 1: 'The contracting States recognize that every State has complete and exclusive sovereignty over the airspace above its territory.'

weather or mechanical failure or because a patient on board is suffering severe complications. In this scenario, also absent international law provisions to the contrary, the neutral Power might be tempted to interpret the absolute inviolability of its territory and the restrictions flowing from the law of neutrality as licence to deny the aircraft's passage through its airspace, or to refuse it permission to land in its territory.

2484   In both of the above scenarios, the humanitarian imperative of expeditiously transporting the wounded and sick to medical facilities is in direct conflict with the neutral Power's sovereignty and its concomitant right to exclude entry to aliens. The need to reconcile these two competing interests had been apparent since the discussions in 1907 on the wording of Article 14 of the Hague Convention (V) and of Article 15 of the Hague Convention (X).[4] Article 37 of the First Convention extends the accommodation between these interests to air transport. The provisions of Article 37 have since been further clarified, and expanded upon, in Article 31 of Additional Protocol I.[5]

2485   Lastly, for a certain number of States, it must be emphasized that air 'casualty evacuation' has evolved since 1949 to play a central role in the collection, evacuation and care of the wounded and sick during armed conflict. Such operations are no longer confined to the initial transfer of the casualty from the tactical engagement area to a forward-deployed medical treatment facility. Many armed forces rely on fixed-wing air capabilities to transport casualties to permanent medical facilities, often situated far from the battlefield. Getting the wounded and sick to these facilities may necessitate extensive flight through the airspace of neutral Powers.[6] The coordination of such transit and the setting of clear rules to avoid uncertainty as to the status of medical aircraft while they transit neutral airspace is therefore essential if the humanitarian objectives of the Convention are to be fulfilled.

B. The law of neutrality and medical aircraft

2486 The law of neutrality plays a vital role in the regulation of international armed conflicts by establishing the rights and obligations of neutral Powers, on the one hand, and the belligerent Parties, on the other hand. International customary and treaty law imposes an obligation on neutral Powers to prevent the use

---

4   See Doswald-Beck, p. 176.
5   See also Manual on International Law Applicable to Air and Missile Warfare (2009), Rules 84 and 85, and San Remo Manual on International Law Applicable to Armed Conflicts at Sea (1994), Rules 181, 182 and 183.
6   Furthermore, in relation to Article 37 specifically, it must be noted that when such transport is an aspect of military operations conducted pursuant to a UN Security Council authorization adopted on the basis of Chapter VII of the UN Charter, the characterization of a 'neutral' Power may be complicated by the obligation of UN Member States to act in support of the Security Council authorization. In this respect, see Manual on International Law Applicable to Air and Missile Warfare (2009), Rule 165.

of their territory and the airspace above by the Parties to the conflict for any military purpose.[7] It is self-evident that the use of neutral airspace by military aircraft of the belligerent Powers would amount to a breach of the neutrality obligation, and is therefore prohibited.[8] Failure to comply with this obligation may result in the belligerent Powers taking measures to prevent opponents from benefiting from access to neutral territory for military purposes.[9] It is nonetheless accepted that use of neutral airspace by Parties to an international armed conflict to transport the wounded and sick is not a violation of the law of neutrality by any of the States involved. This is so because such transport cannot be considered as serving a military role as its sole purpose is to alleviate the suffering associated with armed conflict.

2487   Article 37 aims to reconcile the obligation of the neutral Power to prevent abuse of its territory for military gain with the humanitarian objective of enabling the evacuation of the wounded and sick by the fastest means possible, which is most likely to be by air. Accordingly, the article explicitly applies not only to the Parties to an armed conflict, but also to neutral Powers. On the basis of Article 4 of the First Convention, the latter 'shall apply by analogy the provisions of the [First] Convention to the wounded and sick, and to members of the medical personnel ... of the armed forces of the Parties to the conflict, received or interned in their territory'. Neutral Powers are therefore obliged to respect and protect the wounded and sick and the medical personnel of Parties to the conflict in their otherwise inviolable territory. Other conventions have similarly mentioned the right of a neutral Power to allow the wounded and sick to transit its territory, under certain restrictions designed to protect the said Power's neutrality and to prevent the Parties to the conflict from abusing the neutral territory for logistical purposes.[10]

C. Historical background

2488   The 14th International Conference of the Red Cross, held in Brussels in 1930, requested that the matter of medical aircraft flying over neutral territory be regulated. An informal proposal was subsequently developed whereby medical aircraft should be allowed to cross neutral airspace freely, provided that the neutral Power concerned was able to exercise a right of control similar to that

---

[7] See Hague Convention (V) (1907), Articles 1 to 5, and Hague Convention (XIII) (1907), Articles 1, 2 and 5. See also Manual on International Law Applicable to Air and Missile Warfare (2009), Rules 166 and 167(a).

[8] See Manual on International Law Applicable to Air and Missile Warfare (2009), Rule 170(a), first sentence: 'Any incursion or transit by a belligerent military aircraft (including [an Unmanned Aerial Vehicle/Unmanned Combat Aerial Vehicle] or missile into or through neutral airspace is prohibited.'

[9] See Hague Convention (V) (1907), Article 10, and Hague Convention (XIII) (1907), Article 8. See also Manual on International Law Applicable to Air and Missile Warfare (2009), Rules 168 and 169.

[10] Hague Convention (V) (1907), Article 14.

exercised by a belligerent Power over enemy medical aircraft flying above its territory.[11]

2489   Based on this proposal, the Preliminary Conference of National Societies in 1946 recommended that the First Convention include an article analogous to Article 14 of the 1907 Hague Convention (V).[12] This idea was accepted by the 1947 Conference of Government Experts on the cumulative condition that the neutral Power was previously notified of the passage of a medical aircraft over its territory and that the medical aircraft obeyed any summons to land.[13]

2490   The draft approved by the 1948 Stockholm Conference maintained these ideas, while adding that the neutral Power was entitled to formulate, and apply (if it did so equally for all the Parties to the conflict), conditions or restrictions on the passage of medical aircraft through its airspace.[14] A proposal put forward during the 1949 Diplomatic Conference to relax these conditions was unsuccessful.[15]

D. Paragraph 1: Conditions for a medical aircraft to fly over, or land in, the territory of a neutral Power

2491 Although Article 37 reflects an effort to advance the humanitarian purpose of protecting the wounded and sick, it also reflects the need to preserve the rights of neutral Powers. As a result of these competing considerations, it was not possible to impose an unconditional obligation on a neutral Power to allow the flight, over its territory, of an aircraft qualifying as a medical aircraft.[16] At the same time, it was not considered feasible to allow neutral Powers plenary authority to grant or deny medical aircraft use of their airspace.

2492   The agreed solution was to adopt a general rule permitting medical aircraft of a belligerent Power to fly over the territory of a neutral Power, land in case of necessity, or use it as a port of call.[17] Article 37 gives neutral Powers the assurance that allowing medical aircraft to fly over, or land in, their territory does not violate the law of neutrality, while also giving them the right to place restrictions or conditions on those aircraft.

2493   According to Article 37(1), medical aircraft may 'fly over the territory of neutral Powers', i.e. through their national airspace. Interpreted in the context of

---

[11] *Reports and Documents for the Preliminary Conference of National Societies of 1946*, pp. 42–43. See also *Minutes of the Preliminary Conference of National Societies of 1946*, Vol. I, pp. 113–114.

[12] *Minutes of the Preliminary Conference of National Societies of 1946*, p. 114.

[13] *Report of the Conference of Government Experts of 1947*, p. 47.

[14] *Draft Conventions adopted by the 1948 Stockholm Conference*, p. 44.

[15] *Final Record of the Diplomatic Conference of Geneva of 1949*, Vol. II-A, pp. 86–87.

[16] For an analysis of the conditions which need to be complied with for an aircraft to qualify as a medical aircraft, see the commentary on Article 36, sections C and D.1.

[17] The current text thus establishes a right of medical aircraft to overfly neutral countries, subject to the condition of a prior agreement specifying the route, altitude and time of flight. See *Final Record of the Diplomatic Conference of Geneva of 1949*, Vol. II-A, p. 197.

the relevant provisions of international law, the term 'airspace' refers to the national airspace over land areas, internal waters, and the territorial sea.[18]

2494   Moreover, medical aircraft may use the territory of a neutral Power 'as a port of call', i.e. as a stopover before pursuing their journey, for example to transfer the wounded and sick from one aircraft to another or to refuel.[19] In such cases, the rights and obligations flowing from Article 4 come into play.

2495   Article 37(1) imposes three express, and cumulative, conditions on the use of neutral airspace by belligerent Powers, all of which are derived from Article 36.

2496   First, belligerent Powers whose medical aircraft wish to pass safely through the national airspace or land in the territory of a neutral Power must give the latter notice of this intent. Article 37 does not indicate exactly how, when, by whom or to whom such notice must be given. This seems to allow maximum flexibility in complying with this obligation, while requiring good faith on the part of the belligerent Power in ensuring that the neutral Power's competent authorities have truly received the notice. Once notice has been given, Article 37 contains no explicit requirement for the Power operating the medical aircraft to wait until the neutral Power confirms receipt of the notice. However, barring emergency situations, the need to wait for confirmation is implicit in Article 37(2), which allows the neutral Power to place conditions or restrictions on the passage or landing. In keeping with the general obligation to implement treaties in good faith, the pre-planned versus time-sensitive nature of such intrusions into neutral airspace should guide the level of authority and timing of the notice, providing the neutral Power with every opportunity (and obligation) to respond to the notice. As indicated by the text of Article 37(1), landing in the territory of a neutral State is only authorized 'in case of necessity', i.e. it cannot merely be a matter of convenience or preference. The 'necessity' may relate to factors such as the aircraft's technical needs, as it may also relate to the medical needs of the wounded and sick.

2497   Second, medical aircraft must obey any summons to land issued by the neutral Power.[20] Such a summons could be exercised by the neutral Power for the purpose not only of inspecting the aircraft, but also for the purpose of complying with its obligations flowing from the law of neutrality. As with the first condition, Article 37 does not indicate by whom or when such summons must be issued. However, it stands to reason that, like the belligerent Power, the

---

[18]   For the purpose of interpreting Article 37(1), the notion of 'territory of neutral Powers' excludes the airspace above straits used for international navigation, as well as the airspace above designated archipelagic sea lanes, through which medical aircraft are already entitled to fly as per the conditions set out in Articles 38(1) and 53(1)–(3) of the 1982 UN Convention on the Law of the Sea. See also Manual on International Law Applicable to Air and Missile Warfare (2009), Rule 84.

[19]   See also the definition of 'port of call' in *Concise Oxford English Dictionary*, 12th edition, Oxford University Press, 2011, p. 1118.

[20]   For clarification of the article provided in Additional Protocol I, see Doswald-Beck, p. 177 ('there is...a simple reference to the duty of medical aircraft to obey a summons to land without specifying that that summons must only be for inspection').

neutral Power also has an obligation to use good faith in resorting to this provision. Accordingly, such summons should be issued as promptly as feasible in the prevailing conditions and in a manner that maximizes the opportunity for the aircraft to heed the demand.[21] If a medical aircraft is issued with a summons to land, the officer in charge may be hesitant to comply, for example because of concerns that the condition of the wounded and sick could be adversely affected by the delay or that they could be interned by the neutral Power.

2498   As noted below, overflight of a neutral Power's territory by a medical aircraft will ideally occur pursuant to a prior agreement with all the Parties to the conflict. If authorized by such agreement (in other words, the opposing belligerent Power had previously agreed to allow continuation of the flight based on the assurances of the aircraft commander to the authorities of the neutral Power), the neutral Power may grant a request from the officer in charge to continue the flight. Granting such a request does risk conflicting with the neutral Power's international legal obligation to prevent use of its territory by Parties to a conflict for military purposes, as the neutral Power would have to take the aircraft commander's word as to the nature of the occupants and cargo. To reconcile humanitarian interests with its neutrality obligations, the neutral Power may nonetheless order landing and inspection as a precondition for allowing the flight to resume. Even if overflight takes place pursuant to a prior agreement, compliance with a request to land would be required. Ultimately, therefore, including within an agreement between the belligerent Powers and the neutral Power, a 'continuation of flight' provision based on the assurances of the aircraft commander will not completely eliminate the possibility of a summons to land for inspection, but it substantially reduces the likelihood of it happening. In essence, therefore, the agreement reached for each specific case will be the framework in which to assess the question of whether the neutral Power remains entitled to summon the medical aircraft to land for inspection purposes.

2499   Lastly, as specified in the third sentence of Article 37(1), medical aircraft are protected from attack, both by the neutral Power and the Parties to the conflict, only when flying on routes, at heights and at times specifically agreed upon between the Parties to the conflict and the neutral Power.[22] The wording of this requirement mirrors the wording of Article 36(1).

2500   The relationship between the first and the third sentences of Article 37(1) needs to be carefully analysed. Based on the first sentence, medical aircraft have a right to fly over, or land in, neutral territory. Yet, according to the third sentence, their immunity from attack depends on a prior agreement. Implementation of the requirement to obtain an agreement, as provided for in the third sentence, may not negate the right granted by the first sentence.

---

[21] For further details, see the commentary on Article 36, section G.
[22] See *Final Record of the Diplomatic Conference of Geneva of 1949*, Vol. II-A, p. 214.

2501 The agreement referred to in the third sentence of Article 37(1) will be in the form of a special agreement in the sense of Article 6 of the Convention. The wording 'between the Parties to the conflict and the neutral Power concerned' does not necessarily imply that the agreement must be multilateral, i.e. between the neutral State and all the Parties to the international armed conflict. A bilateral agreement, i.e. between the neutral Power and the Party to the conflict concerned, will suffice.[23]

2502 Lastly, allowing the overflight of a medical aircraft of a Party to an armed conflict without a prior agreement does not amount to a violation of the neutral Power's duties under the law of neutrality. Granting such permission cannot be considered to have given the Party to the conflict a military advantage as it is motivated purely by humanitarian considerations.

2503 It must be noted that the prior agreement requirement is a controversial aspect of Article 37, as it may be read by some to imply that, in the absence of such an agreement, the neutral Power has the right to take all measures deemed necessary to prevent use of its airspace by medical aircraft that fail to comply with this requirement.[24] As indicated above, this could potentially negate the right conferred by the first sentence of Article 37(1). At the same time, while the right conferred by the first sentence stands as such, it is clear that the agreement referred to in the third sentence provides the most comprehensive protection against attack or against any other measure that might interfere with the flight of the aircraft. Therefore, with regard to this last condition, it must be emphasized that, consistent with the provisions of Article 36, an attack against such aircraft, even when flying without a prior agreement or deviating from prearranged conditions, should always be considered a measure of last resort to protect the sovereign interests of the neutral Power.

2504 Furthermore, while the law of neutrality dictates whether or not the neutral Power may act to prevent unauthorized overflight of its territory by a medical aircraft, any attack against such an aircraft by the neutral Power must comply with the applicable rules of international humanitarian law. In particular, the terms 'immune from attack only when flying on routes' agreed upon, as used in the third sentence of Article 37(1), in no way releases the neutral Power from its obligation to respect the rules on the conduct of hostilities, such as those restricting attacks to military objectives and those requiring the taking of all feasible precautions in attack. Accordingly, as an aircraft exclusively engaged in a medical (transport) activity does not qualify as a military objective, deliberately attacking such an aircraft, even once it has violated the sovereignty of

---

[23] Pictet (ed.), *Commentary on the First Geneva Convention*, ICRC, 1952, p. 295.

[24] For the scenario in which a medical aircraft flies over the territory of a neutral Power in the absence of an agreement (or in deviation from the terms of an agreement), see Additional Protocol I, Article 31(2)–(3), as well as Manual on International Law Applicable to Air and Missile Warfare (2009), Rule 85, and San Remo Manual on International Law Applicable to Armed Conflicts at Sea (1994), Rule 182.

the neutral Power, must be considered unlawful if the neutral Power is aware or should have been be aware of the status of the aircraft.

2505   The rule regarding overflight by a medical aircraft of the territory of a neutral Power in the absence of an agreement or in deviation from the terms of an agreement has been clarified in Article 31(2) of Additional Protocol I.[25] This provision requires the medical aircraft in these circumstances to make every effort to give the neutral Power notice of its entry into its airspace, and requires the neutral Power to make all reasonable efforts to avoid having to resort to the final option of attacking it, for example by giving medical aircraft an order to land for inspection purposes.[26]

2506   Accordingly, while a special agreement between the neutral Power and the Parties to the conflict is not completely necessary for a medical aircraft to enter neutral airspace, it helps to avoid doubt by putting the neutral Power on notice of its presence and intentions. Informing the neutral Power of the flight's times, route and altitude will minimize the risk of the neutral Power misidentifying the medical aircraft as either a military aircraft of a belligerent Power or as an unknown agent violating its sovereignty.

2507   Additionally, situations may arise in which a medical aircraft enters and/or lands in neutral territory out of necessity and without having planned to do so. Take, for example, a medical aircraft that had intended to fly around neutral territory, rendering prior agreement with the neutral Power unnecessary. However, owing to a navigational error, the aircraft inadvertently flies into neutral airspace, or is forced by mechanical fault to land in neutral territory. The same may arise because of a sudden, unexpected medical emergency for one of the patients on board. While there is no prior agreement between the belligerent Power and the neutral Power, international law prohibits the neutral Power from attacking the medical aircraft as a first resort. The neutral Power would have an independent obligation to identify the aircraft and issue it with a summons to land in order to inspect it.

E. Paragraph 2: Equal application of conditions or restrictions

2508   Article 37(2) allows the neutral Powers to place 'conditions or restrictions on the passage or landing of medical aircraft on their territory'. This would logically take the form of conditions or restrictions concerning route, altitude, landing, inspection or timing, or a combination of them. In keeping with the

---

[25] For a discussion of the impact of the rules in Additional Protocol I dealing with medical aircraft on the interpretation of the rules in the Geneva Conventions dealing with medical aircraft, see the commentary on Article 36, para. 2437.

[26] See also Manual on International Law Applicable to Air and Missile Warfare (2009), Rule 85(a), second sentence: 'Once the aircraft is recognized as a medical aircraft by the Neutral, it must not be attacked but may be required to land for inspection.'

overall nature of neutrality obligations, all conditions and restrictions related to the use of neutral airspace by medical aircraft of a Party to the conflict must not only be the same for all belligerents but also, according to Article 37(2), applied equally to them all.[27]

2509   Equal application of conditions or restrictions to the medical aircraft of any belligerent Power is an important aspect of neutrality and a component of the broader equality of treatment principle inherent in the law of neutrality. A belligerent Power would be likely to consider any differentiation between it and the other belligerent Powers in the formulation or application of such conditions or restrictions to be disadvantageous treatment by the neutral Power. This in turn could result in the neutral Power's neutrality being called into question by the belligerent Power which considers itself aggrieved.

2510   A neutral Power's entitlement to place conditions or restrictions on the passage over or landing of medical aircraft on its territory necessarily implies a good faith obligation to facilitate such passage by formulating appropriate conditions. Accordingly, it would be inconsistent with the object and purpose of Article 37 for a neutral Power to use this entitlement to impose conditions or restrictions which, de facto, render it (next to) impossible for medical aircraft to exercise the rights conferred on them by the first sentence of Article 37(1).

F. Paragraph 3: Actions upon the landing of medical aircraft on the territory of a neutral Power

2511   Once a medical aircraft has landed on the territory of a neutral Power, its authorities may inspect the aircraft, irrespective of the reasons for the landing. The purpose of the inspection is to verify whether the aircraft is, in fact, a medical aircraft. If this is the case, the aircraft may continue its flight. If not, it may be seized.[28] If, whatever the circumstances, the wounded and sick on board disembark with the consent of the local authorities, paragraph 3 applies; conversely, paragraph 3 does not apply if the wounded and sick remain on board.[29] For details with regard to each of those instances pertaining to an inspection, see Article 30 of Additional Protocol I.

2512   Since the neutral Power has the authority to determine whether it is necessary or not to inspect such an aircraft, it would be somewhat illogical if a medical aircraft would be summoned to land without the need for inspection. If the Party requesting the aircraft to land does not proceed to an inspection, it could be construed that the summons was issued for other, possibly

---

[27] See also Additional Protocol I, Article 31(5).

[28] Yves Sandoz, 'Rights, Powers and Obligations of Neutral Powers under the Conventions', in Andrew Clapham, Paola Gaeta and Marco Sassòli (eds), *The 1949 Geneva Conventions: A Commentary*, Oxford University Press, 2015, pp. 85–108, at pp. 100–101.

[29] *Addenda to the Draft Conventions submitted to the 1948 Stockholm Conference*, p. 4.

unlawful, reasons. Accordingly, inspection is probable following a summons to land, but will also be lawful if exercised, for example, following an involuntary landing. Various situations may lead to the disembarkation of the wounded and sick, with the consent of the local authorities. Whatever the preceding circumstances, Article 37(3) stipulates that they 'shall be detained by the neutral Power, where so required by international law, in such a manner that they cannot again take part in operations of war'.

2513   No precise guidance is given as to who exactly is covered by the term 'local authorities'. In practice, which authority is entitled to consent to the disembarkation of the wounded and sick from a medical aircraft on its territory will depend on the country's internal structure. If the wounded and sick's medical needs require such disembarkation, for example because of the delay engendered by the inspection, it seems difficult to imagine how such consent could lawfully be denied in view of Article 4, which requires the neutral Power to 'respect and protect' the wounded and sick on its territory (application by analogy of Article 12).[30] As noted above, absent a special agreement permitting onward flight, Article 37 establishes what appears to be an obligation for the medical aircraft to comply with a summons to land. In such a situation, consent for disembarkation should be implied by the summons. The alternative would lead to an illogical result: the neutral Power would require the aircraft to land, prohibit onward flight because of the absence of a special agreement, and then require the occupants to remain in the aircraft, thus almost certainly causing their medical needs to remain unaddressed. The obligation on the neutral Power to detain, 'in such a manner that they cannot again take part in operations of war', the wounded and sick belonging to a belligerent Power who are disembarked from a medical aircraft is qualified by the words 'where so required by international law'. These words were inserted to ensure the provision's consistency with Article 11 of the 1907 Hague Convention (V), in which general provision is already made for the internment by neutral Powers of belligerent forces who enter its territory.[31] It is outside the scope of this commentary to examine the current status of the said article.[32] It can only be observed that, since 1907, States themselves have not publicly re-examined whether

---

[30] If dead persons are on board the medical aircraft, Article 4 of the First Convention requires the neutral Power to apply, by analogy, the provisions of the Convention applicable to the dead. The same holds true for the military medical and religious personnel on board. For details, see the commentary on that article, sections C.3.c and C.3.d.

[31] A similar rule can be found in Article 15 of the 1907 Hague Convention (X) and in Article 43 of the 1923 Hague Rules of Air Warfare.

[32] For a historical analysis, see Dwight S. Mears, 'Neutral States and the Application of International Law to United States Airmen during World War II. To Intern or Not to Intern?', *Journal of the History of International Law*, Vol. 15, No. 1, 2013, pp. 77–101. See also K.V.R. Townsend, 'Aerial Warfare and International Law', *Virginia Law Review*, Vol. 28, 1941–1942, pp. 516–527, at 518–520.

these rules still reflect the law.[33] Article 37 remains silent as to what needs to occur to the crew if they are civilians, and it has been observed that international law is not clear on this issue.[34]

2514   The objective to be achieved on the basis of the obligation applicable to the neutral Power is that the wounded and sick 'cannot again take part in operations of war'. No guidance is given on the specific measures which need to be taken by the neutral Power in order to achieve that objective. In the Second Convention, with regard to other factual scenarios pursuant to which wounded and sick persons may end up in the hands of a neutral Power, two different formulations can be found. First, Article 15 of the Second Convention states that 'it shall be ensured' by the neutral Power that the wounded, sick and shipwrecked taken on board a neutral warship or a neutral military aircraft 'can take no further part in operations of war'. In addition, Article 17(1) of the Second Convention requires that the wounded, sick and shipwrecked who are landed in a neutral port with the consent of the local authorities 'shall . . . be so guarded' by the neutral Power so that 'the said persons cannot again take part in operations of war'. Since these are related provisions, however, despite the terminological differences, they must be interpreted to imply the same obligation.[35] Otherwise, this would lead to inconsistencies in the interpretation of these three provisions regarding essentially the same situation involving the neutral Power.

2515   The practical question these formulations raise is whether, in order to achieve the stated objective, it is necessary to deprive the persons in question of their liberty, i.e. whether the more stringent term 'detained' as used in Article 37(3) takes precedence with regard to the interpretation of all three provisions. During the 1949 Diplomatic Conference, it was noted that the word 'internment' was not mentioned. At the same time, the question was raised whether, in practical terms, this boils down to the same thing: 'How else can you prevent people from taking part in the war if you do not intern them?'[36] Internment is non-criminal, non-punitive detention for security reasons in situations of armed conflict.[37] Internment, however, is certainly the most

---

[33] The drafters of the Geneva Conventions deliberately chose not to address the substance of the law of neutrality, while cross-referring to it in a number of rules. For details, see the commentary on Article 4, para. 910 and section C.3.b.

[34] Yves Sandoz, 'Rights, Powers and Obligations of Neutral Powers under the Conventions', in Andrew Clapham, Paola Gaeta and Marco Sassòli (eds), *The 1949 Geneva Conventions: A Commentary*, Oxford University Press, 2015, pp. 85–108, at 101.

[35] Vienna Convention on the Law of Treaties (1969), Article 31(1): 'A treaty shall be interpreted in good faith in accordance with the ordinary meaning to be given to the terms of the treaty in their context and in the light of its object and purpose.'

[36] *Final Record of the Diplomatic Conference of Geneva of 1949*, Vol. II-B, p. 249 (Netherlands).

[37] See ICRC Opinion Paper, 'Internment in armed conflict: basic rules and challenges', November 2014, available at www.icrc.org/en/document/internment-armed-conflict-basic-rules-and-challenges.

invasive and severe measure that can be taken to preclude persons from taking any further part in operations of war. Depending on the circumstances, however, internment may not be necessary. Wherever possible, neutral Powers must explore alternative measures, such as requesting the persons in question to submit to regular appearances at a police station or confining them to a living facility while being under electronic surveillance. For a neutral Power assessing its obligations under Article 37(3), internment should only be considered as a last resort, i.e. if it is the only way of achieving the objective.[38]

2516   Where the option of internment is absolutely necessary, and without prejudice to any more favourable treatment which the neutral Power may choose to give, the persons concerned are to be treated as prisoners of war.[39] If the option to intern is taken, the other paragraphs of both Article 11 and Article 12 of the 1907 Hague Convention (V) apply.

2517   Even where required by international law, the wounded and sick may not be detained by the neutral Power if it has been agreed otherwise ('[u]nless agreed otherwise between the neutral Power and the Parties to the conflict'). As is the case with the agreement referred to in Article 37(1), the agreement referred to in this paragraph is not bilateral (between the neutral Power and the Party to the conflict concerned) but multilateral (between the neutral Power and all the Parties to the conflict). At all times, the neutral Power must remain cognizant of and committed to the obligations set forth in Article 4.

2518   Article 37 is silent as to the fate of any medical personnel, or dead persons, who may be on board the medical aircraft.[40] In all instances in which the wounded and sick are accommodated and interned by the neutral Power, the costs incurred are to be borne by the State on which they depend, i.e. the State that they served before coming under the jurisdiction of the neutral Power.[41] In most circumstances, this will be the State of their nationality. However, where a person fights on behalf of a State other than the State of his or her nationality, the costs of accommodation and internment are borne by the State on whose

---

[38] Conférence internationale de la Paix, La Haye, 18 May–29 July 1899, Sommaire général, Troisième Partie, Deuxième Commission, p. 80:

> Ce que le comité de rédaction désire, c'est que les blessés, les malades et les naufragés soient déclarés incapables de servir. Ce n'est pas une raison de les garder indéfiniment sur le territoire neutre. . . . C'est imposer un devoir trop lourd aux neutres que de les obliger à garder pendant toute la durée de la guerre les naufragés, blessés ou malades. Il faudrait trouver des garanties suffisantes sans exiger ce sacrifice des Puissances neutres.
>
> (The drafting committee wants the wounded, sick and shipwrecked to be declared incapable of service. This is not a reason to hold them indefinitely on the neutral territory. . . . This imposes too heavy a burden on neutral countries by obliging them to guard the shipwrecked, injured or sick for the duration of the war. Sufficient guarantees must be found that this sacrifice will not be required on the part of neutral Powers.)

[39] See Third Convention, Article 4(B)(2).
[40] As to their status and treatment, see the commentary on Article 4, sections C.3.c and C.3.d.
[41] See also United States, *Law of War Manual*, 2015, para. 9.1.2.1

behalf he or she is fighting. In most instances, this will be their State of nationality. However, in cases where an individual fights on behalf of a State other than their State of nationality, the costs of accommodation and internment shall be borne by the State on whose behalf they fight.[42]

Select bibliography

See the select bibliography of the commentary on Article 36 of the First Convention.

[42] Similarly, see Article 15(2) of the 1907 Hague Convention (X) and Article 40(3) of the Second Convention.

CHAPTER VII

THE DISTINCTIVE EMBLEM

2519   Chapter VII contains the provisions relating to the use and protection of the distinctive emblem. It reaffirms the protective functions of the emblem and clarifies the restrictions on its use. The word 'distinctive' is used to describe the emblems in both their protective and indicative forms.

2520   Article 38 confirms that the red cross or red crescent on a white ground is the distinctive emblem to be used by the medical service of a country's armed forces.[1] Article 39 sets out how the emblem is to be used by the medical service of the armed forces.

2521   Article 40 elaborates on those articles by describing the means of identification, armlets and identity cards, and their necessary or ideal characteristics. The measures set out in this article are designed to enable permanent medical and religious personnel of the armed forces to be identified as such on the battlefield or when they fall into enemy hands, so that they may benefit from the respect and protection due to them by virtue of Article 24.

2522   Article 41 stipulates that the red cross or red crescent emblem on a white armlet may also be worn by the auxiliary medical personnel covered in Article 25.

2523   Article 42 details how, and under whose control, the emblem as a protective device should be displayed on military medical units and establishments that enjoy respect and protection under Article 19 of the Convention. It requires Parties to the conflict to ensure, subject to military considerations, that the emblem is clearly visible to the enemy armed forces.

2524   Article 43 governs the marking of medical units of National Red Cross and Red Crescent Societies or other voluntary aid societies of neutral countries that have been authorized to lend assistance to a Party to the conflict in accordance with the provisions of Article 27.

2525   Article 44 reiterates the general rule that the emblem may only be used as a protective device for the marking of medical units and establishments, personnel and material as laid down under the First Convention, as well as, where relevant, under the other Geneva Conventions and their Additional Protocols.

---

[1] The red lion and sun emblem, which is also mentioned in Article 38 of the Convention, has not been used by any State since 1980. An additional emblem – the red crystal – was created by Additional Protocol III of 2005. It is subject to the same rules as the original emblems.

Importantly, the article also sets out the circumstances in which the emblem may be used as an indicative device by National Red Cross and Red Crescent Societies and, furthermore, permits the ICRC and the International Federation of Red Cross and Red Crescent Societies to make use of the emblem at all times.

2526   Lastly, it should be noted that Articles 53 and 54 in Chapter IX deal with the misuse of the distinctive emblems and that the present chapter is complemented by Article 18 of Additional Protocol I and its Annex I.

EMBLEM OF THE CONVENTION

❖ Text of the provision*

(1) As a compliment to Switzerland, the heraldic emblem of the red cross on a white ground, formed by reversing the Federal colours, is retained as the emblem and distinctive sign of the Medical Service of armed forces.

(2) Nevertheless, in the case of countries which already use as emblem, in place of the red cross, the red crescent or the red lion and sun on a white ground, those emblems are also recognized by the terms of the present Convention.

❖ Reservations or declarations

Bangladesh: Declaration made on 20 December 1988;[1] Islamic Republic of Iran: Declaration made on 4 September 1980; communication made on 12 September 2000;[2] and Israel: Reservation made on signature on 8 December 1949 and maintained on ratification.[3]

Contents

---

* Paragraph numbers have been added for ease of reference.

[1] Communication from the Swiss Federal Department of Foreign Affairs of 9 January 1989: 'The Permanent Mission of Bangladesh to the United Nations in Geneva has brought to the knowledge of the Swiss Government, by note dated 20 December 1988, the decision of the Government of the People's Republic of Bangladesh to use henceforth the red crescent instead of the red cross as the emblem and distinctive sign.'

[2] On 4 September 1980 the Government of the Islamic Republic of Iran declared that henceforth it wished to use the red crescent as the distinctive emblem and sign instead of the red lion and sun. In its communication of 23 July 2000, the Government of the Islamic Republic of Iran stated that 'in the case of approval and increase of new distinctive emblems', it will 'maintain its right of using the Red Lion and Sun Emblem once again'.

[3] United Nations *Treaty Series*, Vol. 75, p. 436: 'Subject to the reservation that, while respecting the inviolability of the distinctive signs and emblems of the Convention, Israel will use the Red Shield of David as the emblem and distinctive sign of the medical services of her armed forces.'

A. Introduction

2527   Article 38 confirms the red cross on a white ground as the distinctive emblem to be used by the medical service of a country's armed forces. The desirability of creating a single, uniform sign as a means of improving the protection of sick and wounded soldiers and members of the military medical service was first raised prior to the drafting of the original Geneva Convention of 1864. Such a uniform distinctive sign was established in the 1864 Geneva Convention and was included and further developed in subsequent revisions of the Convention. The content of Article 38 reflects these elaborations.

2528   The second paragraph of Article 38 also recognizes the emblems of the red crescent and of the red lion and sun as alternatives to the red cross emblem, for those countries already using either of these two emblems at the time Article 38 was adopted. For those countries, the red crescent emblem and the red lion and sun emblem enjoyed equal status under the First Convention.[4] The intention was that new States party to the Convention would use the red cross emblem, and that the latter two emblems would remain limited exceptions. However, in practice, States adopted the emblem most suitable for their national circumstances. Today, all of the distinctive emblems enjoy equal status.[5]

2529   The formal recognition of distinctive signs additional to the red cross reflects the historical, ideological and/or practical difficulties for some States Parties in using the red cross emblem, and the efforts by those responsible for negotiating the successive Geneva Conventions to find a suitable solution. In practice, the red cross emblem is the distinctive sign most widely used by the medical services of countries' armed forces, although the red crescent emblem is used by a significant number of States Parties.

2530   All of the distinctive emblems are to be understood as signs of neutrality and protection, devoid of any religious, ideological or other partisan significance.

---

[4] Articles in the other 1949 Geneva Conventions concerning the use of the red cross emblem also give equal status to the red crescent and the red lion and sun emblems.

[5] This is confirmed by Article 2(1) of Additional Protocol III. The word 'distinctive' is used to describe the emblems in both their protective and indicative forms. This is confirmed, for example, in preambular paragraphs 7 and 9 of Additional Protocol III, as well as in Article 3 of Protocol III (on the indicative use of the Third Protocol emblem). Article 18(7) of the 1977 Additional Protocol I refers to 'use of the distinctive emblem in peacetime', as prescribed in Article 44 of the First Convention. It may be noted, however, that Article 8(l) of the 1977 Additional Protocol I uses the words 'distinctive emblem' to refer to the emblem in its protective function for the purposes of that Protocol.

In spite of their intended neutrality, the plurality of distinctive emblems confirmed under Article 38 has given rise to a number of practical difficulties, both for States and for the components of the International Red Cross and Red Crescent Movement (hereinafter 'the Movement'). In some cases, misperceptions about the nature of the emblems have served to undermine their protective value and to diminish their purpose of representing universal values. These difficulties were addressed in 2005 when a new and additional distinctive emblem, the red crystal, was adopted. This positive step must be complemented by continuing efforts to ensure wide understanding of the special meaning and neutral status of all the distinctive emblems.

B. Historical background

1. Establishment of the distinctive emblem

2531 Long before the adoption of the original Geneva Convention of 1864, hospitals and ambulances were sometimes marked on the battlefield by a flag of a single colour, which varied according to the occasion and the country. Those responsible for the 1864 Geneva Convention and the founders of the Red Cross Movement recognized the need for a uniform international emblem as the visible sign of the immunity to which medical personnel (and their equipment) and the wounded should be entitled.[6]

2532 The sign of the red cross on a white ground came into being at the first International Conference, which met in Geneva from 26–29 October 1863 and laid the foundations of the International Red Cross and Red Crescent Movement.[7] The Diplomatic Conference which drew up the original Geneva Convention the following year officially adopted the red cross on a white ground as a single distinctive emblem for all army medical personnel, and for military hospitals and ambulances.[8]

2533 The intention of those responsible for establishing the Movement and the original Geneva Convention was to create a sign devoid of any religious, cultural or other partisan significance.[9] However, it soon became clear that certain countries would be unwilling to accept and to use the newly established

---

[6] Even earlier, in 1857, Lucien Baudens, a military doctor operating in the Crimean War, had highlighted the need for a single distinctive sign for the medical personnel of all countries. Bugnion, 2007, p. 3.

[7] Article 8 of the Resolutions of the 1863 Geneva International Conference provided that the voluntary medical personnel attached to armies 'shall wear in all countries, as a uniform distinctive sign, a white armlet with a red cross'. The Recommendations of the Conference included 'that a uniform distinctive sign be recognized for the Medical Corps of all armies, or at least for all persons of the same army belonging to this Service; and, that a uniform flag also be adopted in all countries for ambulances and hospitals'.

[8] Geneva Convention (1864), Article 7.

[9] The 1864 Geneva Convention and indeed the red cross emblem were intended to represent standards felt to be universal in nature. Understandably, the Convention was a product of its time, reflecting the Euro-Christian tradition (Kosuge, p. 75). Of course, the humanitarian values reflected in the original Geneva Convention are found in traditions worldwide.

distinctive sign of a red cross on a white ground. Indeed, it was not long after the adoption of the red cross emblem that a new sign, a red crescent on a white ground, came into use.[10]

2534   While the need for a single unifying emblem was upheld during the 1906 Diplomatic Conference which undertook the first revision of the 1864 Geneva Convention, the red crescent sign continued to be used in practice by the Ottoman Empire, while Persia (now the Islamic Republic of Iran) continued to use the sign of the red lion and sun.[11]

2535   By the time of the 1929 Diplomatic Conference, and on the proposal of the Turkish, Persian and Egyptian delegates, both the red crescent and the red lion and sun emblems were formally adopted under the revised Convention,[12] the intention being that these two emblems would only be used by the three countries that had proposed their inclusion.[13] However, not long after the adoption of the revised Convention, it became apparent that several additional countries wished to use, or in fact were already using, alternative signs.[14]

2536   The wording of the current article, as agreed in 1949, remained very similar to the text included in the 1929 Convention. As in 1929, the intention was that, while the red cross would remain the primary distinctive emblem, the red crescent emblem and the red lion and sun emblem would represent exceptions of limited application. However, in the years following the adoption of the First Convention in 1949, it became clear that the desire to limit the use of these latter emblems could not be maintained if the overall goal was to encourage universal acceptance of the Conventions; this was particularly so in relation to the expanding use of the red crescent emblem. Much later, in 2005, an additional distinctive emblem – the red crystal – was adopted, in part to limit the proliferation of the distinctive emblems.[15] Today, there is no hierarchy between the distinctive emblems, all enjoying equal status.[16]

2. Nature of the emblem

2537 The plurality of distinctive emblems established under Article 38 has both clear advantages and disadvantages, many of these having been borne out in

---

[10] The first instance of such use was during the Russo-Turkish War of 1877–78, when the Ottoman Empire opted to use a red crescent on a white ground for the medical service of its armed forces (despite its having acceded to the 1864 Convention without reservation). The soldiers of the Ottoman Empire felt offended by the red cross emblem, which reminded them of the sign of the medieval crusaders.

[11] The 1906 Diplomatic Conference authorized States to file reservations to the articles relating to the distinctive emblem, the Ottoman Empire and Persia choosing to do so in relation to the red crescent and the red lion and sun, respectively. Bugnion, 2007, p. 11.

[12] Geneva Convention on the Wounded and Sick (1929), Article 19.   [13] Bugnion, 2007, p. 11.

[14] In 1931, the ICRC became aware of the establishment of a relief society in Palestine that was using the red shield of David as its emblem. In 1935, Afghanistan requested recognition of the Red Archway Society (using the emblem of a red mosque on a white ground). Bugnion, 2007, p. 13.

[15] See Additional Protocol III.   [16] For a further discussion, see section C.2.

practice since 1949. Although the red lion and sun emblem has not been used by any State since 1980,[17] the use of the red crescent emblem has increased over time.[18] On the one hand, one may conclude that the formal recognition of the red crescent emblem has enabled wider acceptance of the Geneva Conventions and consequently, the recognition of a greater number of National Societies within the Movement. On the other hand, the coexistence of, in effect, two distinctive emblems may have resulted in somewhat diminishing their neutral significance and protective value, with potentially dangerous consequences.[19]

2538   Practice suggests that, while the red crescent emblem is not used by any States whose populations are not predominantly Muslim, a number of States whose populations are predominantly Muslim choose to use the red cross emblem.[20] Further, there are some States which use the red cross emblem that are primarily Hindu, Buddhist, Shinto or Taoist,[21] that have predominantly indigenous or other beliefs, or that are officially atheist.[22] While these examples serve to reinforce the intended meaning and status of the red cross emblem as a sign of neutrality, the National Societies in some of these countries have, at times, experienced operational difficulties, which may in part be caused by their use of the red cross emblem.

2539   Article 38 makes it clear that the emblem is the distinctive sign of the medical services of armed forces. Other articles of the Geneva Conventions and their Additional Protocols set out those individuals and bodies who are also authorized to use the emblem, including the respective components of the Movement.[23] However, the medical service of the armed forces is considered to be the primary user of the emblem,[24] with several examples of national legislation confirming this position.[25]

---

[17] In 1980 the Islamic Republic of Iran declared its adoption of the red crescent emblem in place of the red lion and sun, while reserving the right to return to the red lion and sun emblem in the future. See fn. 41.

[18] In 2015, 33 States Parties used the red crescent emblem.

[19] Aside from legal concerns, practical experience has shown that the emblems command far less respect on the battlefield when they are identified with one or another Party to the conflict. This is particularly apparent where each Party to the conflict uses a different distinctive emblem. Bugnion, 2007, p. 30. The existence of a plurality of emblems has the potential to work against the unity of the Movement.

[20] These include Burkina Faso, Indonesia, Lebanon, Mali and Niger.

[21] For example, India (predominantly Hindu) and Japan (predominantly Buddhist and Shinto).

[22] For example, the People's Republic of China.

[23] See e.g. Article 44 of the First Convention. Article 18, read together with Article 8, of Additional Protocol I, authorizes users of the emblem to include civilian medical personnel, units and transports.

[24] For the secondary use of the emblem (referred to as 'indicative' use), see the commentary on Article 44, section D. The emblem is normally used indicatively by the organizations of the Movement.

[25] See e.g. the national laws on emblem use in a number of countries, including: Bosnia and Herzegovina, *Emblem Law*, 2002; Georgia, *Emblem Law*, 1997; Guatemala, *Emblem Law*, 1997, as amended; and Kazakhstan, *Emblem Instruction*, 2002.

2540   It is important to note that, while the distinctive emblems are intended to facilitate the identification of certain categories of protected persons and objects under international humanitarian law, they do not in themselves confer such protection.[26]

3. Form and status of the emblem

2541   Article 38 refers to the 'heraldic emblem of a red cross on a white ground, formed by reversing the Federal colours'. The form of the red cross emblem is not rigidly defined, but in practice normally consists of a red cross with arms of equal length, wholly surrounded by a white ground.[27] Article 18 of the 1906 revision of the 1864 Geneva Convention affirmed that the sign of the red cross is intended as a reversal of the flag of Switzerland, which provides some guidance as to its shape or form. The essence of that statement was retained in subsequent revisions and has also been useful in reasserting the non-religious nature of the emblem. The precise forms of the red crescent emblem and of the red lion and sun emblem are similarly undefined.[28] The Convention does not prescribe a particular shade of red for the emblems. National legislation on the use of the emblems may set out more detailed descriptions as to their respective forms.[29]

2542   The intention in using the words 'heraldic emblem' from 1906 onwards was to reinforce the non-religious nature of the red cross sign. In practice, this has also had the effect of giving the red cross emblem the same standing

---

[26] Article 1(2) of Annex 1 to Additional Protocol I (Regulations concerning identification, as amended on 30 November 1993) in effect supports this fundamental point. See also the commentary on Article 39 of the First Convention, paras 2578–2579.

[27] The reference to 'reversing the Federal colours' is not intended to suggest that the form of the red cross emblem should follow the form of the heraldic emblem of the Swiss Confederation (the latter being prescribed). In fact, a measure of flexibility in form was felt preferable in armed conflict and other situations. The reasons are clear. If the form of the cross had been rigidly defined, attempts might have been made to justify attacks on installations protected by the Convention, on the pretext that the emblems displayed were not of the prescribed dimensions. Similarly, unscrupulous persons could have taken advantage of a rigid definition to use a slightly larger or slightly smaller red cross for commercial purposes.

[28] Articles 4–5 of Annex I to Additional Protocol I provide pictorial models of the red cross, red crescent and red lion and sun emblems, which States Parties may use as a guide. More detailed guidance is contained in Philippe Eberlin, *Protective Signs*, ICRC, Geneva, 1983, and Gérald C. Cauderay, *Manual for the Use of Technical Means of Identification by Hospital Ships, Coastal Rescue Craft, Other Protected Craft and Medical Aircraft*, ICRC, Geneva, 1990. See also Emblem Regulations (1991), Article 5.

[29] In common-law countries such as the United Kingdom and Australia, the form of the red cross emblem is specified as comprising vertical and horizontal arms of the same length on, and completely surrounded by, a white ground. The same legislation also defines the form of the other distinctive emblems. As an example regarding the form of the red crescent emblem, Tajikistan's national law on emblem use explains that 'the Red Crescent emblem depicts a red crescent placed on a white background, with its sharp points turned to the right from the one who faces it, not reaching its margins'. In addition, some National Red Cross Societies have defined the form of cross which they themselves will use. The majority appear to have chosen a cross made up of five equal squares (the shape which is most easily mass-produced).

as official arms,[30] thus encouraging States to enact legislation to protect the emblem.[31] However, this has led to some confusion as to whether the red cross emblem is in fact a heraldic sign. The reference to the 'Federal colours' supports the fact that, while the emblem was intended to be equated with the heraldic emblem of the Swiss Confederation, it was not to be considered a heraldic sign itself.[32]

2543   Article 38 also refers to the emblem as the 'distinctive sign' of the medical service of the armed forces. Although it is not clear when or by whom this terminology was first used, it may have been by Dr Lucien Baudens, following his experiences in Crimea, where he witnessed Russian cannons firing, on at least two occasions, on doctors and nurses who were tending to the Russian wounded.[33] Such unfortunate circumstances suggested the need for a widely recognized sign that was also highly visible on the battlefield. Similar terminology was also used by others at the time of the 1863 International Conference.[34] However, the term 'distinctive sign' did not appear in a treaty text until the 1906 revision of the 1864 Geneva Convention.

2544   Some sources indicate that another reason for choosing the red cross is that it was not already used by any State, a factor also seen as lending credibility to its neutral nature.[35] One may also recall that it was common for different nations to use different flags to identify their respective medical services, the lack of recognition of and respect for these flags arguably leading to a greater number of casualties on the battlefield. Consequently, the creation of a sign 'distinctive' in nature addressed the twin concerns of uniformity and uniqueness. Various studies on visibility have concluded that, in practice, the red cross is the most easily distinguishable of the emblems.[36]

2545   In more recent times, States have continued to establish special means of identification for medical units and transports. In addition, a number of distinctive signals were adopted in Additional Protocol I.[37]

---

[30] The 'official arms', for example of a State, would normally consist of a heraldic design (made up of symbols or signs representing that country) on a shield (sometimes also referred to as armorial bearings, armorial devices or heraldic devices). The use of official arms is normally regulated by national legislation.

[31] This is in addition to the specific provisions of the First and Second Conventions. See Articles 53 and 54 of the First Convention and Article 45 of the Second Convention.

[32] The confusion as to the heraldic status of the red cross emblem is exacerbated by the fact that some national laws refer, for example, to the 'heraldic emblems of the Red Cross and Geneva Cross'.

[33] Baudens, p. 20.

[34] It is not entirely clear and undisputed as to who initially proposed the red cross as the 'distinctive emblem' or sign, although it would appear that Louis Appia may have first suggested it. See the records of the 1863 Geneva International Conference (*Compte Rendu de la Conférence internationale réunie à Genève les 26, 27, 28 et 29 octobre 1863 pour étudier les moyens de pourvoir à l'insuffisance du service sanitaire dans les Armées en Campagne*, 1904), pp. 93–94.

[35] The sign was meant to be international and neutral, a symbol of disinterested aid to the wounded soldier, whether friend or foe.

[36] Cauderay, p. 317. For more details, see the commentary on Article 42, para. 2646.

[37] For further information, see Article 18 and Annex I, Chapter III, of Additional Protocol I.

C. Discussion

2546 Article 38 reaffirms the significance and role of the three distinctive emblems – the red cross, the red crescent and the red lion and sun – in international law. It is different from other provisions of the First Convention, in that it is an article of general application, its implementation being dependent upon subsequent articles of the Convention, as well as those of other Geneva Conventions and their Additional Protocols.[38] The main issues in giving effect to Article 38 are set out below.

1. Adoption of a different emblem after 1949

2547 According to a strict reading of Article 38, States Parties are required to adopt the red cross emblem on ratification. As Article 38(2) makes clear, the only States able to use the red crescent emblem or the red lion and sun emblem were those already doing so at the time the 1949 Geneva Conventions were adopted. Such a framework was felt necessary to encourage the desired eventual return to use of a single distinctive emblem.

2548   In practice, a number of States, when adhering to the First Convention, chose to use the red crescent emblem, and did so without objections (at least those of a public nature) being raised by other States Parties.[39] Nor were there formal objections from the ICRC when officially recognizing their respective National Red Crescent Societies.[40] Consequently, one must conclude that a practice or custom at variance with the rule set out in Article 38 has thus been allowed to take root.

2549   The situation has been somewhat similar in relation to States that formally adopted the red cross emblem on their ratification of the Conventions, but later elected to change to the red crescent emblem (that is, such actions have not been publicly opposed). That said, it appears that private reservations by at least one State Party were expressed on one such occasion, while the ICRC has also in the past communicated its concerns directly to relevant States Parties in such circumstances, in particular highlighting the difficulties such a move would create for the efforts to return to a single universal emblem. It would be the responsibility of States party to the Geneva Conventions, if they wish to

---

38 As examples, see First Convention, Articles 39–44; Second Convention, Articles 41–45; and Additional Protocol I, Articles 18(4), 38 and 85(3)(f).

39 Libya and Morocco are two examples where no formal objections were raised to the use of the red crescent emblem following their respective accessions to the Geneva Conventions.

40 Under the 1986 Statutes of the International Red Cross and Red Crescent Movement, the ICRC has the function of recognizing newly established or reconstituted National Societies as components of the Movement (Article 5(2)(b)). A National Red Cross or Red Crescent Society must use the same emblem as the medical service of its country's armed forces. This long-established practice is based on the National Society's role as an auxiliary to the military medical service of its country, and is supported by the relevant provisions of the First Convention, e.g. Articles 26, 40 and 44.

do so, to object or to express reservations to a new State Party adopting the red crescent emblem.

2550   As noted above, one of the distinctive emblems recognized under Article 38(2) is the emblem of the red lion and sun. It has only ever been used by one State Party, the Islamic Republic of Iran, which in 1980 communicated its intention to no longer use the red lion and sun emblem and henceforth to use the red crescent emblem, while reserving the right to return to the use of the red lion and sun should new distinctive emblems be recognized.[41] Since the date of this reservation, the red lion and sun emblem has not been used.

2551   To conclude, practice since the adoption of Article 38 demonstrates that States Parties have taken a more flexible approach to its application.[42] New States Parties have been free to choose any one of the distinctive emblems set out in Article 38. Moreover, States Parties which used a red cross emblem when the First Convention was adopted in 1949 have later been able to change to the red crescent emblem (in effect, moving from the established or default position to the exception). Further, one State Party has been able to change without difficulty from one of the emblems initially defined as a limited exception to another also defined as such (that is, from the red lion and sun emblem to the red crescent emblem).

2. Equal status of the emblems

2552   Article 38 established a hierarchy among the distinctive emblems. As indicated above, the text provided for the red crescent and the red lion and sun emblems to continue to be used only by those States that had utilized one of these signs prior to 1949. For all other States Parties, the use of the red cross emblem was to be the rule. That said, as Article 38 also makes clear, in terms of their use in practice, the emblems were to be understood as sharing an identical meaning and status.[43]

2553   The preceding section demonstrates the practical departure from the rule regarding the hierarchy of the emblems in the years following 1949. Gradually, the officially recognized distinctive emblems acquired *de facto* equal status. The desire to return to a single emblem remained a continuing concern for the ICRC, due to a sense that this would best serve the emblem's universal humanitarian purpose. However, it is clear that a pragmatic approach to the increasing use of the red crescent emblem was also adopted by the organization, in particular in the light of State practice on the matter.

---

[41] Declarations made on 4 September 1980 and 12 September 2000 by the Islamic Republic of Iran.
[42] This flexible approach can be seen as affirmed also with the adoption of Additional Protocol III in 2005.
[43] This is borne out in subsequent articles of the First Convention and the other Geneva Conventions.

2554   The equal status of the emblems under international humanitarian law was formally recognized in 2005 by the adoption of Additional Protocol III. Article 2(1) of Additional Protocol III states that the distinctive emblems enjoy equal status.[44]

3. Use of the 'double emblem'

2555   Article 38 makes it clear that States Parties may use only one of the three distinctive emblems; it does not envisage the possibility of using, for example, the red cross emblem and the red crescent emblem alongside one another. This restriction caused difficulties for two States in the decades following 1949, both of which wished to use the red cross emblem and the red crescent emblem alongside one another for the medical service of their respective armed forces, as well as for their respective National Societies.[45] Based on the conditions for the recognition of new National Societies as defined in the Statutes of the Movement, the ICRC's consistent practice regarding the latter issue is not to recognize a National Society wishing to use a 'double emblem'.[46]

2556   These difficulties were somewhat abated by the adoption in 2005 of Additional Protocol III. Additional Protocol III allows the medical services and religious personnel of States Parties' armed forces to make temporary use of any one of the distinctive emblems, where this may enhance protection.[47] The National Societies of States Parties which decide to use the red crystal emblem may, for indicative purposes only,[48] choose to incorporate within the red crystal a combination of distinctive emblems. This may comprise, for example, the red cross and red crescent emblems alongside one another.[49]

2557   It should be noted that the International Federation of Red Cross and Red Crescent Societies uses as its logo a red cross and a red crescent side by side set on a white background within a red rectangle.[50]

[44] The commentary on Article 2(1) explains that the evolution in the equality of the emblems (including the red crystal emblem provided for in Additional Protocol III) is explicitly acknowledged by the declaration of their equal legal status, and also notes that the paragraph logically employs the plural, i.e. 'distinctive emblems'. See Quéguiner, p. 187.

[45] In 1993, Kazakhstan passed a parliamentary decree setting out its adhesion to the 1949 Geneva Conventions, with a reservation on use of the 'double heraldic emblem of the red crescent and red cross on a white ground'. Eritrea expressed a similar wish in relation to its military medical service and National Society, although it made no reservations in relation to Article 38 when it acceded to the Conventions in 2000. Bugnion, 2007, p. 19.

[46] Article 4 of the 1986 Statutes of the International Red Cross and Red Crescent Movement, which provides under condition 5 that a National Society must '[u]se a name and distinctive emblem in conformity with the Geneva Conventions and their Additional Protocols'. The ICRC first encountered such a proposal when Cyprus achieved independence in the early 1960s. Bugnion, 1977, p. 62.

[47] See Additional Protocol III, Article 2(4).

[48] For an explanation of the use of the emblem for indicative purposes, see the commentary on Article 44, section D.

[49] See Additional Protocol III, Article 3(1)(a).

[50] In 1981, after Iran dropped its use of the red lion and sun, the League of Red Cross Societies (which became the International Federation of Red Cross and Red Crescent Societies in 1991) began using the double emblem. Annex to Rule 1 para. 1.3 of the International Federation's Rules

4. Red crystal emblem

2558 It has been argued that 'the co-existence of the two emblems has had the effect of accentuating their religious connotation in public opinion'.[51] Not only has this resulted in potentially weakening their protective value (in certain contexts), but also in possibly undermining the distinctive signs' claim to universality (that is, by their being misinterpreted as representing two widespread monotheistic religions, to the exclusion of all other faiths).[52]

2559 At least one State has felt unable to adopt any of the formally recognized distinctive emblems, resulting in practical difficulties not only for the medical service of its armed forces, but also for its National Society.[53] Further, as noted above, other States have made the case for using more than one emblem in juxtaposition, in order to represent fully the religious and cultural affiliations of different sections of their populations. The plurality of distinctive emblems has also been viewed as inconsistent with the Fundamental Principle of unity, one of seven foundational principles observed by the Movement.[54] Additionally, in practical terms, since the adoption of the Geneva Conventions, in a minority of cases States Parties and the organizations of the Movement have experienced operational difficulties when using the red cross emblem (as well as when using the red crescent emblem).

2560 For many years, a solution to the above-mentioned difficulties was actively sought by States and by the Movement. As mentioned above, in 2005, a new distinctive emblem was agreed – the 'Third Protocol emblem', i.e. the red crystal – under the auspices of Additional Protocol III.[55] While emphasizing that the distinctive emblems were never intended to have any religious, ethnic, racial, regional or political significance, the signatories to Additional Protocol III also recognized the difficulties that certain States and National Societies may have with their use.[56]

2561 With the adoption of Additional Protocol III, the equal status of the distinctive emblems is confirmed in international law. In addition, the National Societies of those States Parties which decide to use the red crystal emblem may

---

of Procedure, revised and adopted by the 16th Session of the General Assembly, November 2007, pp. 31–32, available at https://www.ifrc.org/Global/Governance/Statutory/RoP_revised-en.pdf.

[51] Sommaruga, pp. 334–335.   [52] *Ibid.*

[53] The Magen David Adom (Red Shield of David), the National Society of Israel, was until 2006 unable to be formally recognized as a member of the Movement, given that it did not use a name and distinctive emblem in conformity with the Geneva Conventions, as required under Article 4 of the Statutes of the International Red Cross and Red Crescent Movement.

[54] Bugnion, 2007, p. 27. The text of the Fundamental Principle of unity is as follows: 'There can be only one Red Cross or one Red Crescent Society in any one country. It must be open to all. It must carry on its humanitarian work throughout its territory.' The text of the Fundamental Principles is set out in the preamble to the 1986 Statutes of the International Red Cross and Red Crescent Movement, as amended in 1995 and 2006.

[55] Article 2(2) of Additional Protocol III describes the red crystal emblem as being composed of 'a red frame in the shape of a square on edge on a white ground'. The Annex to Additional Protocol III provides a pictorial model of the red crystal emblem. See also Emblem Regulations (1991), Article 5.

[56] As set out in the fifth and ninth preambular paragraphs of Additional Protocol III.

choose to incorporate within its frame (for indicative purposes only) one of the other distinctive emblems (or a combination thereof), or their own distinctive sign.[57]

Select bibliography

Baudens, Lucien, *La guerre de Crimée*, Michel Lévy Frères, Paris, 1858.

Bugnion, François, *The emblem of the Red Cross: A brief history*, ICRC, Geneva, 1977.

– *Red Cross, Red Crescent, Red Crystal*, ICRC, Geneva, 2007.

Cauderay, Gérald C., 'Visibility of the distinctive emblem on medical establishments, units, and transports', *International Review of the Red Cross*, Vol. 30, No. 277, August 1990, pp. 295–321.

Kosuge, N. Margaret, 'The "non-religious" red cross emblem and Japan', *International Review of the Red Cross*, Vol. 85, No. 849, March 2003, pp. 75–93.

Meyer, Michael, 'The proposed new neutral protective emblem: a long-term solution to a long-standing problem', in Richard Burchill, Nigel D. White and Justin Morris (eds), *International Conflict and Security Law: Essays in Memory of Hilaire McCoubrey*, Cambridge University Press, 2005, pp. 84–107.

Pictet, Jean S., 'Le signe de la croix rouge', *Revue internationale de la Croix-Rouge*, Vol. 31, No. 363, March 1949, pp. 167–201 (later published in English as 'The sign of the red cross').

Quéguiner, Jean-François, 'Commentary on the Protocol additional to the Geneva Conventions of 12 August 1949, and relating to the Adoption of an Additional Distinctive Emblem (Protocol III)', *International Review of the Red Cross*, Vol. 89, No. 865, March 2007, pp. 175–207.

Sommaruga, Cornelio, 'Unity and plurality of the emblems', *International Review of the Red Cross*, Vol. 32, No. 289, August 1992, pp. 333–338.

---

[57] In accordance with Article 3(1)(b) of Additional Protocol III, such other sign or emblem must have been in 'effective use' by the State Party and such use must have been the subject of a communication to other High Contracting Parties and the ICRC through the depositary prior to the adoption of Additional Protocol III. Only the Red Shield of David (the Magen David Adom) fulfils these conditions.

USE OF THE EMBLEM

❖ Text of the provision

Under the direction of the competent military authority, the emblem shall be displayed on the flags, armlets and on all equipment employed in the Medical Service.

❖ Reservations or declarations

None

Contents

A. Introduction

2562 Article 39 sets out how the distinctive emblem is to be used by the medical service of the armed forces and on what items and equipment it should be displayed. These include, in particular, flags and armlets, such items being recognized as typical examples of the use of the emblem as a protective device.

2563   The placing of the distinctive emblem on the equipment, transports and personnel of the medical service of the armed forces is under the control of the competent military authority. National legislation regarding the distinctive emblem appears, in many cases, to reflect this principle, assigning the responsibility for controlling the use of the emblem to the Ministry of Defence.

2564   Although the emblem is referred to in the singular form, it is clear that Article 39 is intended to apply to the three distinctive emblems established under Article 38, that is, the red cross, the red crescent, and the red lion and sun.[1]

---

[1] It also applies to the additional distinctive emblem, namely the red crystal emblem, established by Additional Protocol III (see Articles 1(2) and 2(3) thereof).

905

2565   It is important at this juncture to refer to the two distinct uses to which the red cross on a white ground, and the other distinctive emblems, may be put, namely the display of the emblem as a protective or as an indicative device.[2] In the first case, this being the one to which Article 39 relates, the emblem is used as the outward and visible sign of protection (and referred to in this instance as the protective sign). It has this meaning when displayed on buildings, persons and objects entitled to respect under the Geneva Conventions and their Additional Protocols.

2566   While it is generally accepted that the emblem should be displayed on all relevant items, so far as possible, such marking does not in itself confer protected status upon an object or person (nor is an object's or a person's protected status lost if the emblem is not displayed, although in practice it may be more difficult to ensure their safety). It is at the military commander's discretion to determine when the emblem will not be displayed on protected objects, for example through the use of camouflage.

2567   In the second case, the sign is purely indicative, that is, it is used only to designate persons or objects connected with the International Red Cross and Red Crescent Movement. This does not, and is not intended to, imply the protection of the Conventions.[3]

2568   The emblem has its essential significance when used as a protective sign, and is referred to as the 'emblem of the Convention'.[4]

B. Discussion

1. Use of the emblem under the direction of the competent military authority

2569   The initial phrase of Article 39 stipulates that the emblem is displayed '[u]nder the direction of the competent military authority'.[5] This wording replaced the text agreed on in the 1929 Geneva Convention on the Wounded and Sick, which read: 'with the permission of the competent military authority'.[6] The new

---

[2]   For further discussion of the two distinct uses of the emblem, see the commentary on Article 44, sections C and D.

[3]   National Red Cross and Red Crescent Societies may also be authorized to use the emblem as a protective device when carrying out the functions set out under Article 26 of the First Convention and with the consent of the military authority. The 'international Red Cross organizations' (in practice, the International Committee of the Red Cross (ICRC) and the International Federation of Red Cross and Red Crescent Societies) may use the distinctive emblem without reservation (that is, as either a protective or an indicative device). For further discussion, see the commentary on Article 44, section E.

[4]   This term is helpful in signifying the essential connection between the red cross emblem and the 1949 Geneva Conventions as part of international treaty law. This is particularly important given the widespread misconception that the emblem 'belongs' to the International Red Cross and Red Crescent Movement.

[5]   The French text of this article states: 'Sous le contrôle de l'autorité militaire compétente' (emphasis added).

[6]   Geneva Convention on the Wounded and Sick (1929), Article 20.

wording adopted in 1949 lays emphasis on the fact that the military authorities, and, in practice, the military commander, must exercise effective control over the use of the emblem (including determining those situations in which it will or will not be displayed).

2570   National legislation regarding the distinctive emblem appears, in many cases, to reflect Article 39, by placing responsibility for controlling the use of the emblem under the Ministry of Defence.[7] Model national legislation on the use of the emblems,[8] produced by the ICRC and intended to assist States, where needed, in developing relevant domestic laws, also places use of the emblem by the medical service of the armed forces under the control of the Ministry of Defence.[9] While some national legislation also sets out the particular post within the relevant ministry where such authority is to be vested, many do not, presumably and at least in part, to allow for flexibility in designating the responsible position.

2. Display of the emblem on flags and armlets

2571 In principle, a distinctive emblem should be displayed on the buildings, persons and objects protected by the Conventions. In practice, in order for enemy troops at a distance to be able to accord these persons, objects or buildings the respect required by the Conventions, they must be in a position to identify them for what they are.

2572   Persons, establishments, units and transports entitled to display the distinctive emblem under the present Convention include the following:

(a) medical and religious personnel of the armed forces (Article 24);
(b) personnel of the armed forces exclusively engaged in the administration of medical units and establishments (Article 24);

---

[7] See e.g. Austria, *Red Cross Protection Law*, 2008, Article 6(1); Bosnia and Herzegovina, *Emblem Law*, 2002, Article 19; Burkina Faso, *Emblem Law*, 2003, Article 4; Central African Republic, *Emblem Law*, 2009, Article 7; Georgia, *Emblem Law*, 1997, Article 6; Mali, *Emblem Law*, 2009, Article 5; Philippines, *Emblem Act*, 2013, section 4; South Africa, *Emblem Act*, 2007, para. 7(c); Uruguay, *Emblem Decree*, 1992, Article 4; and Yemen, *Emblem Law*, 1999, Article 4. Common-law countries such as Australia and the United Kingdom also place the responsibility for regulation of the distinctive emblem under the Ministry of Defence. Still other countries specifically provide that identity cards and brassards (armlets) will be distributed and regulated by the minister of defence, e.g. Georgia, *Emblem Law*, 1997, Article 8; Kyrgyzstan, *Emblem Law*, 2000, Article 3; and Turkmenistan, *Emblem Law*, 2001, Article 10.

[8] See ICRC, Advisory Service on International Humanitarian Law, *Model Law on the Emblems: National Legislation on the Use and Protection of the Emblem of the Red Cross, Red Crescent and Red Crystal*, 15 July 2008.

[9] See *ibid.* Article 3(1). The model law also indicates that use of the emblem by civilian hospitals and other civilian medical units, where authorized in times of armed conflict, should be under the control of the Ministry of Health (which should, in practice, work together with the Ministry of Defence). Such matters will normally be governed by national administrative arrangements. There may be merit in centralizing authorization for emblem use under the Ministry of Defence.

(c) auxiliary medical personnel, i.e. members of the armed forces specially trained for employment, in case of emergency, as hospital orderlies, nurses or auxiliary stretcher-bearers, while so employed (Article 25);

(d) the staff of National Red Cross and Red Crescent Societies and other recognized relief societies serving as auxiliaries to the medical services of the armed forces (Article 26);[10]

(e) personnel of National Societies or other relief societies of neutral countries, who lend their assistance to a belligerent and are duly authorized to do so (Article 27);

(f) fixed establishments and mobile medical units of the medical service of the armed forces (Article 19);

(g) transports used by the armed forces exclusively assigned to transporting the wounded and sick and/or medical equipment (Article 35);

(h) equipment used in the medical service (Article 39); and

(i) aircraft exclusively employed for the removal of the wounded and sick and for the transport of medical personnel and equipment (Article 36).

2573   The 1864 Geneva Convention referred to the use of a red cross on a white ground on a flag and on an armlet.[11] Subsequent revisions of the Convention have made repeated reference to these specific items belonging to the medical service of the armed forces. Armlets and flags marked by the distinctive emblem are recognized as typical examples of the use of the emblem as a protective device.[12]

2574   Flags displaying the distinctive emblem are generally used to identify military medical units and transports. Similarly, military medical personnel often use an armlet marked with a distinctive emblem as a means of identification. This includes the wearing of the armlet by military medical personnel when carrying out their regular duties away from the combat zone. A number of national laws governing the use of the distinctive emblem specify that armlets shall be issued by the relevant authority to those who are entitled to wear them.[13]

---

[10] Since 1949, practice has confirmed that such National Societies also use the distinctive emblem on armlets in armed conflict (to aid identification), even when not operating in their auxiliary role. See fn. 12 below.

[11] See Geneva Convention (1864), Article 7.

[12] National Red Cross and Red Crescent Societies, which are permitted by their national authorities to use the emblem within certain limits, may not place the emblem as an indicative device, i.e. their logo, on armlets when it is used in peacetime (so as to avoid confusion with the use of such items displaying the emblem in armed conflict). See Emblem Regulations (1991), Article 4 and its commentary. See also Article 44 of the First Convention. The same is recommended for flags: the commentary on Article 4 of the 1991 Emblem Regulations recommends that, in peacetime, National Societies 'refrain from placing the emblem on armlets, roofs or even flags'.

[13] Examples include national laws governing emblem use in Burkina Faso, *Emblem Law*, 2003, Article 5; Kyrgyzstan, *Emblem Law*, 2000, Article 3; Lithuania, *Law on the Red Cross Society and Emblems*, 2000, Article 15; and Tajikistan, *Emblem Law*, 2001, Article 7. See also fn. 7. See also Articles 40 and 41 of the First Convention and their commentaries.

2575   As the means and methods of warfare have modernized, practical difficulties have been identified regarding the ability of the armed forces to distinguish accurately personnel and items displaying one of the distinctive emblems.[14] In order to address this important issue, since 1949 additional means of identification have been developed. A number of these are set out in the Regulations concerning identification annexed to Additional Protocol I. These include distinctive signals, such as the use of lights, radio and electronic identification. In addition, specific guidance has been given to enhance the visibility of the emblem used as a protective device.[15] Moreover, it is stipulated that medical personnel carrying out their duties on the battlefield 'shall, as far as possible, wear headgear and clothing bearing the distinctive emblem'.[16]

3. Display of the emblem on 'all' equipment

2576 Article 39 stipulates that the distinctive emblem shall be displayed on flags and on armlets, as well as 'on all equipment employed in the Medical Service'. In practice, it is obvious that it may not be feasible to place the distinctive emblem on every item of equipment.[17] For example, the shape or size of some items, such as surgical instruments, may prevent such display. However, such articles will normally form an integral part of a larger unit, which will be marked.

2577   In principle, the emblem should be displayed prominently on all equipment where such display will help to distinguish relevant items from non-medical military equipment, and therefore to assist in confirming the protection of such equipment under international humanitarian law. Examples may include vehicles, medical equipment such as scanners, small and large containers, bags, rucksacks, kits and other items used to store and carry medical instruments and personnel.

4. Display and non-display of the emblem

2578 It is generally accepted that the emblem should be displayed on all relevant items, so far as possible. However, it is important to recall that such

---

[14] In 1979, Philippe Eberlin discussed 'technical shortcomings in visual markings', saying that '[t]he rule concerning the armlet which medical personnel have to wear on the left arm is quite inadequate to give them protection from all sides, as has become necessary today. A 10 cm red cross on an armlet cannot be distinguished at a distance of more than 50 metres.' See Eberlin, p. 66.

[15] See e.g. Cauderay, and Dominique Loye, *Commentary on Annex I (as amended 30 November 1993) to Additional Protocol I*, ICRC, Geneva, 2002. For certain types of transports, see ICRC, *Manual for the Use of Technical Means of Identification by Hospital Ships, Coastal Rescue Craft, Other Protected Craft and Medical Aircraft*, 2nd edition, ICRC, Geneva, 1995.

[16] Additional Protocol I, Annex I, Regulations concerning identification (as amended in 1993), Article 5(4).

[17] The reference to 'all' stems from the original provision in the 1906 Geneva Convention. Statements from the preparatory work for the Geneva Diplomatic Conference of 1906 indicate that the meaning of 'all' was intentionally left open.

marking does not in itself confer protected status upon an object or person: rather, it facilitates their identification as a protected object or person.[18] The use of camouflage is therefore permitted, although in practice this may affect the protection of such camouflaged objects from attack.[19]

2579   Since the adoption of the First Convention in 1949, in a minority of conflicts, a small number of States have chosen not to display the distinctive emblem on personnel and/or equipment of the military medical services.[20] Evidence suggests that such actions were carried out in contexts where the special meaning and status of the emblem were not observed.[21] This shows the discretion that may be exercised by the military commander in circumstances where the emblem's neutrality may not be respected. Protected objects do not lose their protection under such circumstances, but their safety from attack cannot be guaranteed if they are unable to be identified as such by the adversary.[22]

Select bibliography

Cauderay, Gérald C., 'Visibility of the distinctive emblem on medical establishments, units, and transports', *International Review of the Red Cross*, Vol. 30, No. 277, August 1990, pp. 295–321.

Eberlin, Philippe, 'Modernization of protective markings and signalling', *International Review of the Red Cross*, Vol. 19, No. 209, April 1979, pp. 59–83.

Henckaerts, Jean-Marie and Doswald-Beck, Louise, *Customary International Humanitarian Law, Volume 1: Rules*, ICRC/Cambridge University Press, 2005, available at https://www.icrc.org/customary-ihl/eng/docs/v1.

---

[18] Some States' criminal codes require medical establishments to be properly marked with the distinctive emblem. However, this will be of importance only for criminal responsibility in the event that such units are attacked. See Henckaerts/Doswald-Beck, commentary on Rule 30, pp. 103–104. Article 1(2) of Annex I to Additional Protocol I in effect supports this fundamental point.

[19] United Kingdom, *Manual of the Law of Armed Conflict*, 2004, para. 7.25.

[20] Examples of such armed conflicts include that in Vietnam and, more recently, in Afghanistan.

[21] Practice also shows that, in some cases, the distinctive emblem is not displayed on certain vehicles and personnel because they are required for a dual purpose (that is, to carry out certain medical functions, but also to carry out ordinary military functions). In such cases, the item or individual no longer enjoys protected status under the Geneva Conventions (the removal of the emblem confirming this fact). See also the commentary on Article 22 of the First Convention.

[22] North Atlantic Treaty Organization (NATO) Standardization Agreements (STANAG) provide that medical units and transports may be camouflaged as a temporary measure at the discretion of the competent combat commander, to be exercised on the basis of a balance of due protection and operational need. Such agreements specify that these orders, which are to be made by a commander of brigade level or equivalent, are to be temporary and local in nature, and countermanded as soon as circumstances permit. See e.g. NATO Standardization Agreement 2931 (1998).

ARTICLE 40

IDENTIFICATION OF MEDICAL AND RELIGIOUS PERSONNEL

❖ Text of the provision*

(1) The personnel designated in Article 24 and in Articles 26 and 27 shall wear, affixed to the left arm, a water-resistant armlet bearing the distinctive emblem, issued and stamped by the military authority.

(2) Such personnel, in addition to wearing the identity disc mentioned in Article 16, shall also carry a special identity card bearing the distinctive emblem. This card shall be water-resistant and of such size that it can be carried in the pocket. It shall be worded in the national language, shall mention at least the surname and first names, the date of birth, the rank and the service number of the bearer, and shall state in what capacity he is entitled to the protection of the present Convention. The card shall bear the photograph of the owner and also either his signature or his fingerprints or both. It shall be embossed with the stamp of the military authority.

(3) The identity card shall be uniform throughout the same armed forces and, as far as possible, of a similar type in the armed forces of the High Contracting Parties. The Parties to the conflict may be guided by the model which is annexed, by way of example, to the present Convention. They shall inform each other, at the outbreak of hostilities, of the model they are using. Identity cards should be made out, if possible, at least in duplicate, one copy being kept by the home country.

(4) In no circumstances may the said personnel be deprived of their insignia or identity cards nor of the right to wear the armlet. In case of loss, they shall be entitled to receive duplicates of the cards and to have the insignia replaced.

❖ Reservations or declarations

None

Contents

---

* Paragraph numbers have been added for ease of reference.

A. Introduction

2580 The measures set out in Article 40 are designed to enable permanent medical and religious personnel of the armed forces to be identified as such on the battlefield or when they fall into enemy hands, so that they may benefit from the respect and protection due to them under the Conventions. As medical and religious personnel may wear military uniforms and often work in proximity to combatants on the battlefield, the aim of the armlet (or armband or brassard) is to enable opposing forces to distinguish them from combatants during hostilities and thus avoid attacking them. This somewhat simple system of identification, established 150 years ago, endures today, but it is acknowledged that nowadays the armlet alone may be insufficient as a means of battlefield identification of medical personnel. Field tests have shown that, while the distinctive emblem is visible on the armlet in close combat situations, it is more visible on tabards or bibs and on helmets.[1]

2581 Articles 38 and 39 specify which persons are entitled to wear the protective emblem for the purposes of the First Convention. Article 40 elaborates on those articles by describing the means of identification (armlets and identity cards) and their necessary or ideal characteristics. The provision is detailed for a reason: strict control over who may wear the emblem is designed to ensure trust in the emblem and anyone wearing it so that it will be respected and its wearer will not be targeted during hostilities. When medical personnel fall into enemy hands, proof of their status serves to distinguish them from prisoners of war, enabling them to benefit from the prescribed protection and treatment, including being returned to their own armed forces or retained in accordance with the retention regime.[2] Although identity cards are important for this purpose, the

---

[1] Cauderay, pp. 305–308. More sophisticated technical means, such as lights and signals, have been used to identify medical units and transports. Regarding the marking of medical aircraft and medical units and establishments, see also the commentaries on Article 35, section C.2.c, Article 36, section E, and Article 42, section F.

[2] First Convention, Articles 28, 30 and 31, and Third Convention, Article 33.

status of medical or religious personnel may also be established in the absence of such cards.

2582   For States party to it, Article 18 of Additional Protocol I extends the right to wear the emblem (and carry an identity card bearing the emblem) to permanent and temporary civilian medical and religious personnel as defined in the Protocol.[3] Article 20 of the Fourth Convention sets out the terms of use of the emblem and identity cards by civilian medical and hospital staff. Lastly, for States party to Additional Protocol II, Article 12 provides for the use of the emblem by medical and religious personnel and medical units in non-international armed conflicts.

B. Historical background

2583   The notion that medical personnel should be identifiable on the battlefield to protect them from attack by enemy forces was one of the first ideas of the founders of the ICRC and was enshrined in the first Geneva Convention of 1864.[4] This concept was repeated and developed in the subsequent conventions on the wounded and sick.[5] The requirement that the armlet be not only issued but also stamped by the military authority was introduced in the 1906 Convention. The obligation for medical and religious personnel to carry an identity card was also introduced in 1906, with further details in its respect being added in 1929. In addition, protection was extended to religious personnel in 1906.[6] The 1949 Convention specifies that the armband should be made of water-resistant material and provides yet more detail on the format and contents of the identity cards. However, in essence, the system has remained unchanged since its conception.

C. Paragraph 1: The armlet

1. Introduction

2584   The main purpose of the armlet or other items of clothing or headgear marked with the emblem is to make it easier for enemy armed forces to identify medical personnel on the battlefield in order to avoid attacking them. The use of the emblem by medical personnel as a protective device is therefore strictly controlled to ensure its full respect. The Parties to a conflict must never be given

---

[3] See Additional Protocol I, Articles 8 and 18(3). Article 18(3) applies in particular in occupied territories or areas where hostilities are taking place. See also Article 42 of the Second Convention, which governs the identification of the medical and religious personnel of armed forces at sea.

[4] Article 7 of the 1864 Geneva Convention reads in part: 'An armlet may also be worn by personnel enjoying neutrality but its issue shall be left to the military authorities. Both flag and armlet shall bear a red cross on a white ground.'

[5] Geneva Convention (1906), Article 20; Geneva Convention on the Wounded and Sick (1929), Article 21.

[6] Geneva Convention (1906), Article 9.

reason to doubt that the emblem is being used other than in accordance with the Conventions and their Additional Protocols.

2585   Importantly, the armlet does not in itself confer protection; it is merely an outward sign of a person's protected status. It is, however, a means of facilitating identification. As a visible sign of protected status, the emblem is thus a vitally important means of protection. If not wearing the emblem, the person runs the risk of being mistakenly targeted. Nevertheless, with or without the armlet, medical and religious personnel may not be attacked as long as they act in accordance with their status, i.e. they do not commit acts harmful to the enemy.[7] From the moment medical or religious personnel have been identified as such, shortcomings in the means of identification cannot be used as a pretext for failing to respect them.

2586   The armlet – along with the identity card – also serves to identify personnel entitled to the treatment prescribed by the retention regime when they fall into enemy hands.[8]

2. Personnel entitled to wear the armlet

2587   All permanent medical and religious personnel belonging to the armed forces (i.e. those designated in Article 24) are entitled to wear the armlet.[9] In addition, the personnel of National Red Cross and Red Crescent Societies or of other voluntary aid societies, who, pursuant to Article 26, are employed as permanent medical or religious personnel attached to the armed forces, are entitled to wear the protective emblem.[10] Although in practice this arrangement no longer arises frequently – and for religious personnel has never been known to arise – some States continue to provide for the possibility, including with respect to the use of armlets and identity cards, in their national legislation.[11] The personnel of the National Society of a neutral State may also lend their assistance to a Party to the conflict, pursuant to Article 27, but this has not been known

---

[7] On the notion of acts harmful to the enemy, see the commentary on Article 24, section F.

[8] On the retention regime, see Articles 28, 30 and 31 of the First Convention and Article 33 of the Third Convention, and their respective commentaries.

[9] Auxiliary (temporary) medical personnel may be authorized to wear an armlet bearing the emblem in miniature when they are exclusively engaged in medical activities. See Article 41 and its commentary, in particular, section C. Article 18 of Additional Protocol I, however, does not stipulate a difference in the size of the emblem.

[10] See the commentary on Article 26, para. 2084; see also Emblem Regulations (1991), Articles 8 and 9.

[11] See e.g. Austria, *Red Cross Protection Law*, 2008, Article 6; Burkina Faso, *Emblem Law*, 2003, Article 8; Cameroon, *Emblem Law*, 1997, Section 8; Georgia, *Emblem Law*, 1997, Article 5; Kyrgyzstan, *Emblem Law*, 2000, Article 5; and Panama, *Emblem Law*, 2001, Article 9. Some States provide for assistance by medical personnel of the National Red Cross or Red Crescent Society to 'a relevant executive authority' of the government, such as the minister of health, which would cover medical care or assistance to civilians and civilian hospitals. See e.g. Azerbaijan, *Emblem Law*, 2001, Article 9.

to have occurred since the end of the Second World War and, with very few exceptions, is not provided for in national legislation.[12]

2588   Religious personnel may also wear the protective emblem. However, they are less likely to be present in areas of active combat, reducing the need for them to wear an armlet to distinguish them from combatants. Nevertheless, it remains a useful form of identification, especially when it comes to their treatment if they fall into enemy hands. Given that a variety of faiths may be represented in the armed forces, and although the emblems are meant to be devoid of any religious significance, States may use their discretion in deciding whether to impose the wearing of the emblem on religious personnel.

2589   Civilian medical and religious personnel who have been assigned certain exclusively medical or religious tasks by a Party to a conflict may also be autho- rized to wear the protective emblem in occupied territories or in areas near where hostilities are taking place. However, the wearing of the armlet by these persons is not governed by the First Convention.[13]

2590   Article 40(1) states that medical personnel 'shall wear' an armlet bearing the emblem. Normally, use of the word 'shall' indicates an obligation. How- ever, in the light of the object and purpose of the provision and of the Conven- tions, a more nuanced interpretation is called for. The aim of the armlet is to ensure that medical personnel are identifiable and not attacked during hostil- ities, enabling them to collect and care for the wounded and sick even in the midst of fighting. Logically, where there is reason to conclude that medical per- sonnel will be better protected if they do *not* wear the emblem, the competent military authorities are free to so decide.[14] This might be the case, for example,

---

[12] Two States whose national laws provide for this possibility are Belarus and Tajikistan; see Belarus, *Law on the Emblem*, 2000, Article 12, and Tajikistan, *Emblem Law*, 2001, Article 10. The ICRC's Model Law on the Emblems states that it is possible for personnel of the National Red Cross or Red Crescent Societies of neutral States to lend their assistance to a Party to the conflict and states that '[i]f such an authorization has been granted, or is to be granted, it might be useful to mention this in the [State's emblem] law' (fn. 16 of the Model Law).

[13] See Fourth Convention, Article 20, and Additional Protocol I, Articles 8 and 18. These persons may also carry a special identity card.

[14] The United Kingdom's *Manual of the Law of Armed Conflict*, 2004, for example, while stipu- lating a general duty for personnel to wear the armlet in para. 7.26, also provides in para. 7.25: 'Whilst medical units, personnel, and transport are normally marked with the protective emblem, it is not mandatory to do so. The parties to a conflict are exhorted to "endeavour to ensure" that they are marked.' This implies that the United Kingdom considers that Additional Protocol I has changed the rule in Article 40, such that it is no longer mandatory for personnel to wear the emblem. See also United States, *Army Uniforms and Insignia*, 2005, sections 28– 29, p. 254, which states that '[m]edical personnel wear the brassard, *subject to the discretion of* a competent military authority' (emphasis added). Australia's *Manual of the Law of Armed Conflict*, 2006, para. 9.74, states: 'In the most extreme circumstances, for example where an enemy was unlawfully targeting medical personnel, a military commander may order military personnel to not wear their brassard. The military commander may order the medical personnel to reinstate the brassard without jeopardising their special protection.' See, further, Gary Solis, *The Law of Armed Conflict: International Humanitarian Law in War*, Cambridge University Press, 2010, p. 139. State practice observed by the ICRC furthermore confirms this interpreta- tion of 'shall wear' in this context. But see United States, US Court of Appeals, *Al Warafi case*, Appeal, 2013. See also the commentary on Article 39, section B.4.

in an area where there is a misperception that the red cross is a religious symbol, which may put medical personnel wearing the emblem at greater risk of
attack, in violation of international humanitarian law. Similarly, if a Party to a
conflict adopts an unlawful policy of intentionally attacking medical personnel
out of a belief that it gives a military advantage, it may be better for medical
personnel not to be so identified.

2591   Some military manuals and national legislation nonetheless stipulate that
medical and religious personnel of the armed forces must wear the armlet.[15]
One commentator also holds this view.[16] The concern is that, if medical personnel are perceived by the opposing side to be removing the armlet in order to
participate in hostilities from time to time, it could lead to a general lessening
of respect for the emblem because the other side may think medical personnel are also carrying out 'acts harmful to the enemy'.[17] Wearing the protective
emblem can thus be seen to have a twofold effect: first, it clearly indicates who
is protected, and second, it ensures that those who wear it act in strict compliance with their status, thereby contributing to their own and others' continued
protection. Accordingly, unless there is good reason to fear that the wearing of
the armlet in a particular situation would diminish the protection owed to medical and religious personnel, the imperative language of the Convention should
be respected.

2592   It should be noted that, under certain circumstances, medical units and medical transports may be camouflaged, as may medical personnel.[18]

3. Characteristics of the armlet

2593   The armlet must bear the distinctive emblem, that is, the red cross or red crescent on a white ground.[19] States party to Additional Protocol III may also use
the red crystal.[20]

---

[15] See e.g. Azerbaijan, *Emblem Law*, 2001, Article 6 ('shall wear'); Canada, *LOAC Manual*, 2001,
para. 915.1 ('are required to wear'); Georgia, *Emblem Law*, 1997, Article 7 ('doivent porter',
certified ICRC translation); and Philippines, *Emblem Act*, 2013, section 4 ('shall wear'). Article 5
of the ICRC's Model Law on the Emblems states: 'Such personnel *shall wear armlets* and carry
identity cards' (emphasis added).

[16] Kleffner, p. 352.

[17] This concern was raised in relation to permitting auxiliary or temporary medical personnel to
wear an armlet while carrying out their duties. The paramount concern is to preserve respect
for the emblem and those wearing it by limiting the possibility that an enemy will consider
that combatant forces are inappropriately using the protective emblem to provide cover from
attack. *Minutes of the Diplomatic Conference of Geneva of 1949*, pp. 20–22.

[18] See e.g. Netherlands, *Military Handbook*, 2003, p. 7–44, and United Kingdom, *Manual of the
Law of Armed Conflict*, 2004, para. 7.25. See also the commentary on Article 39, section B.4
and Article 42, section F.

[19] Article 38 of the First Convention (the red lion and sun also specified in the article is no longer in
use). Additional Protocol III provides for one more distinctive emblem, 'Third Protocol emblem',
known as the red crystal. The red cross and red crescent are the two most commonly used
emblems.

[20] Israel, which is the only State to have adopted the red crystal as its emblem, however, 'directs its
uniformed medical personnel to not wear any identifying protective sign in combat [situations]';
see Solis, p. 139.

2594   While the armed forces of some States use a white band that encircles the upper arm, others use a patch bearing a red cross or red crescent on a white background. The Convention does not require that the entire armlet be white, as long as one of the distinctive emblems is present and clearly identifiable on a white background. It is considered important not to be overly prescriptive about the size and colour of the armlet or the material on which it is affixed,[21] to avoid enemy forces claiming that an armlet does not meet certain specifications and therefore need not be respected.

2595   The armlet should be water-resistant to ensure visibility of the emblem even after exposure to the elements. The use of materials or substances that make the emblem more visible to enemy forces, whether through infra-red or thermal imaging or other technology, is also recommended.[22] Since such methods of identification may depend on the use of a particular technology by the enemy forces, it is important that the Parties inform one another of the method or materials in use or how they may best be visible. At the same time, failure to use special materials in no way affects the obligation of enemy armed forces to respect the emblem (and its wearer) as soon as they identify it.

2596   Article 40 further stipulates that the armlet is to be worn on the left arm, a detail that was meant to ensure that combatants knew exactly where to look for it. However, tests conducted in 1972 revealed that '[a]n armlet worn on the left arm is visible at a distance of 50 m only if clean and smooth and if the wearer is standing with his left side to the observer'.[23] Thus, wearing the emblem elsewhere on the body in addition to the armlet, such as on a bib, tabard or helmet, may increase visibility and enhance protection. The wearing of the emblem only on the right arm or elsewhere besides the left arm may not be used by the enemy as justification for attacking protected personnel on the basis that the means of identification is not in conformity with the Convention. Rather, taking steps to improve the visibility of the emblem, especially when it enhances protection, is desirable.

2597   The armlet must be issued and stamped by the military authority. Normally, this will be the competent military authority discussed in more detail in Article 39. In this light, the armlet remains an important means of identification of medical and religious personnel. Clearly, the use of the emblem must be controlled by an official military authority fully aware of its responsibility.

4. *Use by medical personnel of helmets, tabards or bibs, or flags bearing the emblem*

2598 As mentioned above, tests have shown that the emblem on helmets and on bibs or tabards is visible at a greater distance on the ground than the emblem

---

[21] There is no prescribed method for attaching the emblem to a uniform.
[22] Additional Protocol I, Annex I, Regulations concerning identification (amended 30 November 1993).
[23] de Mulinen, p. 483.

on an armlet.[24] In the midst of fighting, wearing the emblem elsewhere on the body may therefore be a useful means of facilitating identification. While these are not prescribed methods of identification, they are also not prohibited, and recourse to them in no way diminishes the protection due to the wearer. In 1972, one expert observed: 'To be really useful, the emblem should be visible at first glance, as soon as its bearer comes into sight and whatever the distance and the mode of observation.'[25] In fact, the amended 'Regulations concerning identification', adopted as Annex I to Additional Protocol I, recommend that '[m]edical and religious personnel carrying out their duties in the battle area shall, as far as possible, wear headgear and clothing bearing the distinctive emblem'.[26] Nevertheless, the wearing of the emblem on an armlet persists as a method of identification of medical personnel for protective purposes.

2599   Medical personnel and orderlies have in the past also adopted the practice of carrying and waving a white flag bearing the emblem.[27] Again, although it is not a prescribed method of identification, it remains perfectly acceptable and is encouraged so long as those bearing the flag are entitled to display the protective emblem and act in accordance with that status.

D. Paragraphs 2 and 3: The identity card

2600   Article 40(2) sets out the format and content of the identity cards to be carried by medical and religious personnel.[28] The provision is very specific and detailed so as to ensure that States adopt practices that are proven to be effective. This is especially important when medical or religious personnel fall into enemy hands, so that they may benefit from the retention regime. In terms of physical characteristics, the card must bear the emblem and be water-resistant and pocket-sized. A water-resistant card is more durable and preserves its legibility if exposed to the elements. Specifications on the size of the card were added because it was found that if identity cards were too big, their owners were apt to keep them in their packs – which are not normally worn on the battlefield – or elsewhere not on their persons.[29] The card must bear the owner's photograph and signature or fingerprints, preferably both. It must also be embossed with the stamp of the military authority. A model identity card can be found in Annex II to the First Convention.

---

[24] Cauderay, pp. 305–308.   [25] de Mulinen, p. 483.

[26] Additional Protocol I, Annex I, Regulations concerning identification (amended 30 November 1993), Article 5(4).

[27] Pictet (ed.), *Commentary on the First Geneva Convention*, ICRC, 1952, p. 312.

[28] Medical personnel of National Red Cross and Red Crescent Societies attached to the armed forces must also be issued with an identity card. If necessary, the National Society should remind the State authorities of this obligation. See Emblem Regulations (1991), Article 9(2) and its commentary.

[29] Pictet (ed.), *Commentary on the First Geneva Convention*, ICRC, 1952, p. 314.

2601   Article 40(3) stipulates that the identity card must be uniform throughout the same armed forces. Therefore, the identity card of personnel of a National Society or other voluntary aid society of the State covered by Article 26 must bear the same distinctive emblem.

2602   Since the adoption of the 1949 Geneva Conventions, there have been many technological developments in relation to identity documents, with the introduction of biometric passports and cards with computer chips able to store large quantities of information. However, 'low-tech' cards continue to serve a valuable purpose because they can be produced – and, more importantly, deciphered – at any time and in any place, without the need for sophisticated equipment.[30]

2603   The card must be written in the bearer's national language. It was originally proposed that English or French be used in addition to the national language but that requirement was dropped during the negotiations.[31] The military manual of one State suggests that, where appropriate, the identity card should also be in the local language of the region concerned.[32] Although not required by the Convention, such a measure is not prohibited and may indeed make the cards more effective.

2604   The particulars that must be included on the identity card are the bearer's surname and first names, date of birth, rank and service number, as well as the capacity in which he or she is entitled to the protection of the Convention. Where the date of birth is unknown, the estimated age of the bearer at time of issue may be substituted.[33] Other particulars, such as blood type, have been suggested as appropriate for inclusion on the card.[34] Some States indeed do this.[35] Moreover, for medical personnel in particular, it may be wise to indicate the medical function for which they have been trained or their area of specialization, as this information may be pertinent in determining whether they may be retained when they fall into enemy hands.[36]

---

[30] Loye, para. 92.

[31] *Final Record of the Diplomatic Conference of Geneva of 1949*, Vol. II-A, p. 116. The reasons for abandoning this requirement are not given in the preparatory work.

[32] Canada, *LOAC Manual*, 2001, p. 4B-1. Article 2(1)(c) of the Regulations concerning identification (as amended on 30 November 2003) also indicates that the identity cards of permanent civilian medical personnel should be worded 'in the local language of the region concerned'. This can include a local language other than the national language of a State, or a predominant language in the area where the conflict is taking place or forces are deployed.

[33] This possibility is also recommended in Article 2(1)(d) of the Regulations concerning identification (as amended on 30 November 2003).

[34] At the 1949 Diplomatic Conference, the delegate of Portugal recommended including this information on the card; see *Final Record of the Diplomatic Conference of Geneva of 1949*, Vol. II-A, p. 93. Article 2(1)(i) of the Regulations concerning identification (as amended on 30 November 2003) also recommends its inclusion on the identity cards of permanent civilian medical personnel.

[35] The United States is one example; see Department of Defense Form, 1934.

[36] The inclusion of this requirement was also suggested during the Diplomatic Conference, but in the end was not retained; see *Final Record of the Diplomatic Conference of Geneva of 1949*, Vol. II-A, p. 116. See also the commentary on Article 31, section C.

2605   Even if a State does not transmit to the other Party the model of the card being used, the identity card remains valid. The model of the card may also be communicated to a third party, such as a neutral State or an international organization, as the purpose of this requirement is simply to engender trust in the cards found on medical or religious personnel. This would enable authorities to verify a document against the model if ever the authenticity of a card is in doubt. Uniformity of cards across armed forces can further help to foster trust in the documents.

2606   The provision states that medical and religious personnel 'shall' carry a special identity card bearing the distinctive emblem. While possession of such a card may indeed be an important means for such personnel to prove their status if they fall into enemy hands, this requirement must not be interpreted in a way that disadvantages medical or religious personnel. That is, it must not be viewed as a *sine qua non* to prove their status.[37] Indeed, Article 40(4) anticipates that cards and insignia might be lost. The loss (or lack of possession) of a card alone cannot be equated with a loss of protected status. The solution prescribed by the Convention is rather that a duplicate be issued.

2607   Moreover, if the card fails in some way to meet the detailed requirements of Article 40, that alone would not render it invalid. What counts is whether the card and the information on it are sufficiently reliable to support a claim by medical or religious personnel in enemy hands that they are entitled to that status.

2608   The idea that a duplicate card be held in the records of the Power on which the medical personnel depend was discussed at length during the Diplomatic Conference.[38] The basis for the proposal was the concern that a Power be able to demonstrate convincingly that the persons it claims are its medical personnel – and who may therefore be entitled to be returned or retained under the conditions set out in Article 28 – were listed as such before they fell into enemy hands.[39] In that case, a retaining Power would have no reason to doubt the authenticity of a claim to that status by medical or religious personnel.

2609   The competent authorities must take steps during peacetime to prepare identity cards, armlets, and the identity discs required by Article 16, so that they

---

[37] But see United States, US Court of Appeals, *Al Warafi case*, Appeal, 2013, pp. 7–8. The Court held:

> In the end, the question of whether Al Warafi has met his burden of establishing his status as permanent medical personnel entitled to protection under the First Geneva Convention is one of fact, or at least a mixed question of fact and law. Although the district court believed, and we agree, that military personnel without appropriate display of emblems can never so establish, it also found facts – e.g., the prior combat deployment – inconsistent with that role.

See the commentary on Article 28, paras 2171–2173.

[38] *Final Record of the Diplomatic Conference of Geneva of 1949*, Vol. II-A, pp. 116–118.

[39] First Convention, Articles 28, 30 and 31, and Third Convention, Article 33.

can be issued without delay in the event of an armed conflict. Furthermore, when new medical and religious personnel are appointed during times of armed conflict, identity cards, armlets and discs must be swiftly issued to them and a list kept.

E. Paragraph 4: Prohibition of confiscation; replacement of lost cards and insignia

2610 Medical personnel may keep their identity papers and wear the armlet in all circumstances, that is, even when retained by the adverse Party to assist their captured compatriots. In both world wars, medical personnel sometimes had their armlets and cards taken from them, which can be a way for the capturing State to attempt to evade its obligations.[40] Such practices are strictly forbidden by the Convention. In 2012, during the armed conflict between Sudan and South Sudan, captured medical personnel reported that their identity cards had been taken away from them or lost; nevertheless, the absence of the identity documents did not prevent the medical personnel from being returned to their own armed forces.[41]

2611 The special insignia and cards of medical personnel can only be withdrawn by the military authorities of their own armed forces. Should the armlet be lost or destroyed, the owner must be issued with a new one. If the identity card is lost, the person is entitled to a duplicate card. This provision lays an obligation not only on the Power on which the personnel depend, but also on the capturing Power, which must do all it can to facilitate the transmission of new cards and armlets for captured enemy medical personnel. In the past, the ICRC has acted as an intermediary for the conveyance of these items.[42]

Select bibliography

Bouvier, Antoine A., 'The Use of the Emblem', in Andrew Clapham, Paola Gaeta and Marco Sassòli (eds), *The 1949 Geneva Conventions: A Commentary*, Oxford University Press, 2015, pp. 855–886.

Cauderay, Gérald C., 'Visibility of the distinctive emblem on medical establishments, units, and transports', *International Review of the Red Cross*, Vol. 30, No. 277, August 1990, pp. 295–321.

de Mulinen, Frédéric, 'Signalling and Identification of Medical Personnel and Material', *International Review of the Red Cross*, Vol. 12, No. 138, September 1972, pp. 479–494.

---

[40] Pictet (ed.), *Commentary on the First Geneva Convention*, ICRC, 1952, p. 316.

[41] For more information on this example, see 'South Sudan shows Sudanese POWs [prisoners of war], as Khartoum urges to protect medical team', *Sudan Tribune*, 16 April 2012, available at http://www.sudantribune.com/spip.php?article42271.

[42] Pictet (ed.), *Commentary on the First Geneva Convention*, ICRC, 1952, p. 316.

Kleffner, Jann K., 'Protection of the Wounded, Sick, and Shipwrecked', in Dieter Fleck (ed.), *The Handbook of International Humanitarian Law*, 3rd edition, Oxford University Press, 2013, pp. 321–357.

Loye, Dominique, *Commentary on Annex I (as amended 30 November 1993) to Additional Protocol I*, ICRC, Geneva, 2002.

IDENTIFICATION OF AUXILIARY PERSONNEL

❖ Text of the provision*

(1) The personnel designated in Article 25 shall wear, but only while carrying out medical duties, a white armlet bearing in its centre the distinctive sign in miniature; the armlet shall be issued and stamped by the military authority.

(2) Military identity documents to be carried by this type of personnel shall specify what special training they have received, the temporary character of the duties they are engaged upon, and their authority for wearing the armlet.

❖ Reservations or declarations

None

Contents

A. Introduction

2612 Under the First Convention, a distinction is made between permanent medical personnel (Article 24) and auxiliary or temporary medical personnel (Article 25) in relation to both their identification on the battlefield and their treatment if they fall into enemy hands.[1] Article 41 stipulates that the emblem on the white armlet worn by auxiliary medical personnel should be 'in miniature'. The rationale for this requirement was to preserve the significance of the armlet of

---

* Paragraph numbers have been added for ease of reference.

[1] The persons covered by Article 25 are commonly referred to as 'auxiliary personnel'. Since the adoption of Additional Protocol I, the term 'temporary (medical) personnel' is used more frequently to describe this category of medical personnel. For a full definition of temporary medical personnel, see Additional Protocol I, Article 8(k).

permanent medical personnel and to avoid abuses of the emblem in the area of hostilities. This concern has now been overridden by the need to ensure that all medical personnel, be they permanent or temporary, are identifiable as such when they are exclusively employed on their duties close to hostilities. In those circumstances, auxiliary medical personnel enjoy the same immunity from attack as permanent medical personnel and must therefore display their status in the same way.

2613   In enemy hands, however, auxiliary medical personnel are not entitled to the same treatment as permanent medical personnel, that is, they are not covered by the retention regime (see Article 28). Instead, like combatants, they become prisoners of war (see Article 29). However, according to Article 29, auxiliary medical personnel who are detained as prisoners of war must be employed on medical duties when necessary. In this regard, it is important for them to carry identity documents certifying their status as auxiliary or temporary medical personnel.

B. Historical background

2614 The protection accorded to auxiliary or temporary medical personnel under the Geneva Conventions has fluctuated over time. In the 1864 and 1906 Conventions, no protection was accorded to such personnel. In the 1929 Geneva Convention on the Wounded and Sick, auxiliary medical personnel who had fallen into enemy hands were entitled to the same treatment under the retention regime as permanent medical personnel but were not authorized to wear the emblem identifying them as temporary medical personnel during hostilities, even when they were exclusively employed on medical duties.[2] In practice, however, it proved difficult to establish what auxiliary medical personnel were doing at the time they fell into enemy hands. With this in mind, the 1949 Convention essentially reversed the provisions of the 1929 Convention, allowing auxiliary medical personnel to wear the emblem but not to benefit from the retention regime.

2615   The 1929 Diplomatic Conference had not granted auxiliary medical personnel the right to wear the emblem on the battlefield because abuses were feared. Delegates to the Conference refused to entertain the idea of the armlet being put on or taken off according to whether the person was acting in a combatant or a medical capacity. In other words, they did not wish to make the emblem 'removable'.[3] The drafters of the 1949 Convention felt that protection could

---

[2] Geneva Convention on the Wounded and Sick (1929), Article 9(2). Under the retention regime, medical personnel may not be held until the end of active hostilities on the same basis as prisoners of war; unless they are needed to care for the wounded and sick, they must be sent back to their own armed forces. See, Articles 28, 30 and 31 of the First Convention.

[3] Des Gouttes, *Commentaire de la Convention de Genève de 1929 sur les blessés et malades*, ICRC, 1930, pp. 154–155; *Proceedings of the Geneva Diplomatic Conference of 1929*, pp. 168–177 and 184–191.

be accorded to auxiliary personnel while they were actually carrying out their medical duties on the battlefield. However, they, too, felt that there was a risk of abuse if such personnel were authorized to use the same armlet as permanent medical personnel.[4] Following a discussion of possible ways to indicate the difference, including by using initials to represent auxiliary medical functions such as 'stretcher bearer', the Diplomatic Conference settled on the same emblem but in a smaller size.[5]

C. Paragraph 1: The armlet

2616 Article 41 sets out the identification measures to be applied by auxiliary or temporary medical personnel as defined in Article 25 of the First Convention.[6]

2617 Under the system set up in the First Convention, auxiliary or temporary medical personnel may be authorized to wear an armlet bearing the emblem in miniature when they are exclusively engaged in medical activities. However, for States party to Additional Protocol I, Article 18(1) provides that '[e]ach Party to the conflict shall endeavour to ensure that medical and religious personnel and medical units and transports are identifiable' and does not specify a difference in the size of the emblem, whether worn by permanent or auxiliary medical personnel.

2618 There is good reason to consider that the requirement set down in Article 41 for the emblem displayed on the armlets of auxiliary medical personnel to be 'in miniature' is obsolete.[7] The fear that medical personnel might abuse the protection symbolized by the emblem by putting on and taking off the armlet at will, which could lead to a lessening of respect for the emblem, has abated. The primary concern today is to promote the visibility of medical personnel in all circumstances where it will facilitate their protection.

2619 The view that the emblem on the armlet worn by auxiliary medical personnel need not be restricted in size is supported by instruments providing further guidance on the use of the protective emblem. The Regulations concerning identification in Annex I of Additional Protocol I state (in relation to Article 18) that '[t]he distinctive emblem shall, whenever possible, be displayed on a flat surface, on flags or in any other way appropriate to the lay of the land, so that it is visible from as many directions and from as far away as possible,

---

[4] *Minutes of the Diplomatic Conference of Geneva of 1949*, pp. 20–22.

[5] *Final Record of the Diplomatic Conference of Geneva of 1949*, Vol. II-A, pp. 116–118 and 198.

[6] Article 8(c) and (k) of Additional Protocol I provides a further definition of temporary medical personnel, which is broader than Article 25 as it encompasses civilian medical personnel who are not members of the armed forces.

[7] Sandoz/Swinarski/Zimmermann (eds), *Commentary on the Additional Protocols*, ICRC, 1987, para. 759, which emphasizes that 'the indications of the Conventions regarding restrictive use of the emblem (armlets) and particularly those imposing on temporary personnel the obligation to wear an emblem smaller in size, must be considered to be obsolete'. Note also that the ICRC's Model Law on the Emblems does not include a provision relating to the use of an armlet with an emblem in miniature. See also ICRC, *Study on the Use of the Emblems*, pp. 47–51.

and in particular from the air'.[8] It also states that '[m]edical and religious personnel carrying out their duties in the battle area shall, as far as possible, wear headgear and clothing bearing the distinctive emblem'.[9] Studies have shown that even the normal-sized emblem on an armlet is often insufficiently visible on the battlefield, prompting the adoption of the more flexible regulations in the Protocol.[10] Requiring auxiliary medical personnel to use an even smaller emblem would only compound the problem. This interpretation is affirmed in academic writing.[11]

2620   While some States may wish nevertheless to continue to use the emblem in miniature on armlets worn by their auxiliary medical personnel,[12] they are not bound to do so.

2621   In view of this development, it is of the utmost importance that auxiliary or temporary medical personnel are not seen to be switching too frequently between the roles of combatant and medic. Indeed, no time limit has been fixed on the duration of the assignment to exclusively medical duties, but common sense dictates that, to the greatest possible extent, there should be no change in the assignment of medical personnel – or, for that matter, medical objects – during a given military operation. If the temporary assignment is too short and changes too often, it could generate mistrust towards the medical personnel and undermine their protection.[13] Moreover, auxiliary medical personnel must comply scrupulously with the conditions under which they are authorized to wear the emblem: they must be specially trained for medical duties and they must only wear the emblem when they are actually engaged in such activities.

2622   The armlet must be issued and stamped by the competent military authority, just as for permanent medical personnel under Article 40.

D. Paragraph 2: Identity documents

2623   Article 41 sets out the specific details to be included on the military identity documents carried by auxiliary or temporary medical personnel. These identity cards should be the same as those required by Article 17(3) of the Third Convention, but include a special entry indicating that the bearer is authorized to wear the armlet.[14] The documents are thus distinct from those carried by permanent medical personnel, underscoring the different regimes that apply to the personnel once they fall into enemy hands. The identity cards of auxiliary

---

[8] Additional Protocol I, Annex I, Regulations concerning identification (amended 30 November 1993), Article 5, para. 1.

[9] *Ibid.* para. 4.   [10] Cauderay, pp. 305–308.

[11] De Waard/Tarrant, p. 167. See also Kleffner, pp. 352–355, and Bouvier, pp. 864–865, who make no mention of a difference in the size of the protective emblem.

[12] See e.g. Belgium, *Law of Armed Conflict Training Manual*, 2009, Course V, p. 10; Netherlands, *Military Manual*, 2005, p. 80; and United States, *Law of War Manual*, 2015, p. 438.

[13] Sandoz/Swinarski/Zimmermann (eds), *Commentary on the Additional Protocols*, ICRC, 1987, para. 395. See also De Waard/Tarrant, pp. 159 and 180–181.

[14] *Final Record of the Diplomatic Conference of Geneva of 1949*, Vol. II-A, p. 198; see also the commentary on Article 17(3) of the Third Convention.

medical personnel must specify the temporary nature of their activities so as to clarify that they are liable to be held as prisoners of war rather than returned to their own forces or retained as medical personnel. At the same time, the cards must indicate the bearers' authority for wearing the armlet and the special training they have received in this respect. The latter may facilitate their employment on medical duties if detained as prisoners of war (see Article 29).

2624   Possession of an identity card is not a *sine qua non* for proving one's authority to wear the protective emblem in every case, especially since documents can be lost or taken; in the absence of such documents, the status of auxiliary medical personnel can be proven by other means when they fall into enemy hands.[15] That said, as the system is based on trust, auxiliary medical personnel would be well advised to carry an identity card demonstrating their authority for wearing the armlet.

2625   The requirement for auxiliary medical personnel to be issued with identity cards in general is set down in Article 17(3) of the Third Convention, as States must provide such documents to any person liable to become a prisoner of war. Article 40(4) of the First Convention prohibits depriving permanent medical personnel of their identity cards and insignia; while Article 41 is silent on the matter, the last sentence of Article 17(3) of the Third Convention clearly establishes the same prohibition in respect of identity cards of prisoners of war, including those of auxiliary medical and religious personnel.

Select bibliography

Bouvier, Antoine A., 'The Use of the Emblem', in Andrew Clapham, Paola Gaeta and Marco Sassòli (eds), *The 1949 Geneva Conventions: A Commentary*, Oxford University Press, 2015, pp. 855–886.

Cauderay, Gérald C., 'Visibility of the distinctive emblem on medical establishments, units, and transports', *International Review of the Red Cross*, Vol. 30, No. 277, August 1990, pp. 295–321.

De Waard, Peter and Tarrant, John, 'Protection of Military Medical Personnel in Armed Conflicts', *University of Western Australia Law Review*, Vol. 35, No. 1, 2010, pp. 157–183.

ICRC, *Study on the Use of the Emblems: Operational and Commercial and Other Non-Operational Issues*, ICRC, Geneva, 2011, pp. 47–51.

Kleffner, Jann K., 'Protection of the Wounded, Sick, and Shipwrecked', in Dieter Fleck (ed.), *The Handbook of International Humanitarian Law*, 3rd edition, Oxford University Press, 2013, pp. 321–357.

---

[15] For a view that the requirement is more stringent, see De Waard/Tarrant, p. 167, who assert: 'This is a critical requirement. If a combatant wearing a distinctive protective armlet or brassard does so without the appropriate documentation, they could be liable for misuse of the protective emblem.'

MARKING OF MEDICAL UNITS AND ESTABLISHMENTS

❖ Text of the provision*

(1) The distinctive flag of the Convention shall be hoisted only over such medical units and establishments as are entitled to be respected under the Convention, and only with the consent of the military authorities.

(2) In mobile units, as in fixed establishments, it may be accompanied by the national flag of the Party to the conflict to which the unit or establishment belongs.

(3) Nevertheless, medical units which have fallen into the hands of the enemy shall not fly any flag other than that of the Convention.

(4) Parties to the conflict shall take the necessary steps, in so far as military considerations permit, to make the distinctive emblems indicating medical units and establishments clearly visible to the enemy land, air or naval forces, in order to obviate the possibility of any hostile action.

❖ Reservations or declarations

None

Contents

A. Introduction

2626 Article 42 details how, and under whose control, the emblem as a protective device should be displayed on military medical units and establishments that

---

* Paragraph numbers have been added for ease of reference.

enjoy respect and protection by virtue of Article 19 of the First Convention.[1] In this respect, Article 42 builds on the provisions of Articles 39 and 44 of the First Convention dealing, respectively, with the use of the emblem as a protective device by the medical services of the armed forces as a whole and the differences between protective and indicative uses.

2627   Article 42 uses the term 'distinctive flag', which is one of the classic forms in which the emblem may be used as a protective device. It also deals with the question of whether or not the emblem may be accompanied by a national flag.

2628   Lastly, consistent with the purpose of the protective emblem as the visible manifestation of the protection of medical establishments and units provided for in the First Convention, Article 42 requires Parties to the conflict to ensure, subject to military considerations, that the emblem is clearly visible to the enemy armed forces.

B. Historical background

2629   The marking of military medical establishments and units with the 'distinctive flag' was first provided for in the 1864 Geneva Convention.[2] The Convention further stipulated that the distinctive flag 'should in all circumstances be accompanied by the national flag'. The 1906 Geneva Convention laid down the general rule that the national flag must accompany the distinctive flag on both mobile units and fixed establishments of the armed forces' medical services.[3] The 1929 Geneva Convention on the Wounded and Sick maintained this rule for fixed establishments only, making it optional in the case of mobile medical units.[4] In the 1949 Convention, flying the national flag became optional for both fixed establishments and mobile medical units.

2630   The rule that medical units which have fallen into enemy hands are not entitled to fly any national flag alongside the distinctive flag was introduced in the 1906 Convention and subsequently retained.[5]

2631   The obligation of the Parties to a conflict to take the necessary steps to ensure the visibility of the emblem on medical units and establishments, in so far as military considerations permit, first found its way into international humanitarian treaty law by virtue of the 1929 Convention.[6]

C. Paragraph 1: Use of the distinctive flag of the Convention

2632   By using the term 'distinctive flag', Article 42(1) reaffirms this traditional means of displaying the emblem of the red cross, the red crescent or, more

---

[1] The use of the emblem on medical units, establishments and transports is also governed by Articles 18, 21 and 22 of the Fourth Convention and Article 18 of Additional Protocol I.
[2] Geneva Convention (1864), Article 7.   [3] Geneva Convention (1906), Article 21.
[4] Geneva Convention on the Wounded and Sick (1929), Article 22(1).
[5] Geneva Convention (1906), Article 21(2); Geneva Convention on the Wounded and Sick (1929), Article 22(2).
[6] Geneva Convention on the Wounded and Sick (1929), Article 22(3).

recently, the red crystal as a protective device.[7] A number of States have also made reference to it as a protective device in their national legislation and military manuals following the adoption of the First Convention.[8] The word 'flag' must not be taken too literally. This is confirmed in the fourth paragraph of the present article, which spells out the purpose of displaying the emblem as a protective device, namely to make military medical units and establishments clearly visible to enemy armed forces. Moreover, Article 44(2), as an example of the difference between the protective and indicative uses of the emblem, explicitly reserves the placement of the emblem on the roofs of buildings to the protective use of the emblem.[9]

2633   Flags as such are not the only method of displaying the emblem as a protective device on medical units or establishments. Other manifestations, such as painting the emblem on the roof, are also possible, as long as the fundamental purpose of visibility is attained.[10] Consequently, the word 'flag' can simply be interpreted as the 'emblem' of the red cross, the red crescent or the red crystal, while leaving it to the discretion of the military authorities to decide on the means of displaying it.

2634   Article 42(1) contains an express limitation on the use of the emblem as a protective device, in that it 'shall be hoisted only over such medical units and establishments as are entitled to be respected under the Convention'. In line with Article 19 of the First Convention, that entitlement is restricted to the fixed establishments and mobile medical units of the armed forces' medical services, as well as to the medical units and establishments of National Red Cross and Red Crescent Societies or of other voluntary aid societies auxiliary to the medical services.[11]

2635   According to this limitation, medical units and establishments that have lost their protection under the First Convention are not entitled to use the emblem

---

[7] Technically, the distinctive flag also includes the red lion and sun as one of the distinctive emblems recognized under Article 38(2) of the First Convention. This symbol, which has only ever been used by one State Party, is no longer in use. Additional Protocol III, adopted in December 2005, recognizes the red crystal as an additional emblem subject to the same conditions of use as those enshrined in the 1949 Geneva Conventions, including the First Convention, and, where applicable, the 1977 Additional Protocols.

[8] See e.g. Australia, *Manual of the Law of Armed Conflict*, 2006, para. 9.75; Colombia, *Emblem Law*, 2004, Article 2(3); Thailand, *Red Cross Act*, 1956, Section 5; United States, *Army Health System*, 2013, para. 3-23; and Uruguay, *Emblem Decree*, 1992, Article 7.

[9] See also Article 4 of the 1991 Emblem Regulations, which enjoin National Red Cross and Red Crescent Societies, when using the emblem as an indicative device, not to place it on roofs.

[10] See e.g. Colombia, *Decree No. 138*, 2005, Article 4(1); Uruguay, *Emblem Decree*, 1992, Article 8; and Uzbekistan, *Law on the Use and Protection of the Red Crescent and Red Cross Emblems*, 2004, Article 7.

[11] See the commentary on Article 19, sections C.1 and C.2. While Article 19 covers the medical establishments and units of National Societies or other voluntary aid societies both of States that are party to the conflict and of neutral States, only the medical establishments and units of the National Society of a Party to the conflict come within the scope of Article 42. Article 43 deals with the use of the emblem as a protective device by medical establishments and units of National Societies of neutral States; see the commentary on that article.

as a protective device.[12] Whenever and for as long as a medical unit or establishment loses its protection, it becomes necessary to remove the flag. Leaving it on would amount to an improper use of the emblem prohibited by international humanitarian law, or even, if the requisite conditions are fulfilled, to the war crime of perfidy.

2636   Article 42(1) also requires that the distinctive flag be used only 'with the consent of the military authorities'. As is the case in Article 39, this provision does not specify who the competent military authorities are. Under the national legislation and regulations of many States, the minister of defence is designated as the competent military authority in this regard.[13] What is essential is that all armed forces are responsible for authorizing and exercising control over every use of the emblem as a protective device by medical units and establishments covered by this paragraph.[14]

D. Paragraph 2: Use of the national flag

2637   As already mentioned, in 1949 it became optional for both fixed medical establishments and mobile medical units to fly the national flag of the State to whose military medical service they were attached.[15] This marked a change from the 1929 Convention, which had made it optional only for mobile medical units to fly the national flag but compulsory for fixed establishments. The justification for the differential treatment in the 1929 Convention was that requiring mobile military medical units to fly the national flag would essentially provide the adversary with a convenient aiming point and invite attack.[16] This rationale was subsequently put forward by the 1937 Commission of Government Experts[17] as applying to both fixed establishments and mobile medical units

---

[12] On the scope of the loss of protection of medical units and establishments, see Articles 21 and 22 of the First Convention, and their commentaries. See also the commentaries on Article 19, paras 1820–1821, and Article 24, section F.

[13] See the commentary on Article 39, section B.1. See also e.g. Bosnia and Herzegovina, *Emblem Law*, 2002, Article 19; Central African Republic, *Emblem Law*, 2009, Article 7; Georgia, *Emblem Law*, 1997, Article 6; Mali, *Emblem Law*, 2009, Article 5; Philippines, *Emblem Act*, 2013, section 4; Uruguay, *Emblem Decree*, 1992, Article 4; and Yemen, *Emblem Law*, 1999, Article 4.

[14] This responsibility cannot be delegated to entities other than military authorities. See ICRC, *Study on the Use of the Emblems: Operational and Commercial and Other Non-Operational Issues*, ICRC, Geneva, 2011, pp. 60 and 64.

[15] Only the emblem as a protective device, i.e. a red cross, a red crescent, a red lion and sun or a red crystal on a white ground, referred to as the 'distinctive flag', can be the visible manifestation of the protection of medical units and establishments under the First Convention. Other flags, in particular national flags, do not have this significance. See, however, the commentary on Article 38 regarding the particular status of the Swiss national flag, of which the red cross emblem is considered to be the reversal.

[16] Des Gouttes, *Commentaire de la Convention de Genève de 1929 sur les blessés et malades*, ICRC, 1930, p. 165.

[17] This commission was convened by the ICRC and produced a report and a draft for revision of the 1929 Geneva Convention on the Wounded and Sick, which was adopted by the 16th International Conference of the Red Cross, London, 1938. It should have been discussed at a

because the national flag was generally considered as a symbol of belligerency that would provoke attacks. The Commission accordingly proposed that the flying of the national flag be made optional in either case, a recommendation which was endorsed by the 1946 Preliminary Conference of National Societies and the 1947 Conference of Government Experts, and adopted in 1949 without further debate.[18] National military manuals mostly reaffirm this as an option rather than an obligation.[19]

2638   Therefore, it is within the discretion of the Parties to the conflict to decide whether the national flag is flown alongside the protective emblem on medical units and establishments. Although not specified in Article 42(2), those competent to take that decision are the same military authorities as the ones responsible for authorizing and controlling the use of the protective emblem itself.[20] Since the use of the emblem as a protective device by medical establishments and units of National Red Cross and Red Crescent Societies or other voluntary aid societies auxiliary to the armed forces' medical services also falls within the scope of Article 42, the competent military authorities may also extend this option to such medical establishments and units.[21]

2639   Article 42 does not address the use of flags other than national ones alongside the protective emblem, for instance, the UN flag by medical establishments and units of troop contributing countries involved in peace operations under UN command and control. The United Nations as an international organization is not entitled as such to use the emblem. However, contributing States participating in UN operations retain their rights and obligations with respect to the emblem, such that the emblem itself may be used.[22] In such cases, should the emblem be displayed on military medical establishments or units in peace operations, care must be taken to avoid placing the emblem in close proximity to the UN flag (or that of any other international organization) and to avoid the use of a double emblem. The red cross, red crescent or red crystal emblems must in all cases retain their original form.[23]

Diplomatic Conference convened by the Swiss Government in 1940, but the conference was postponed owing to the outbreak of the Second World War. The draft then formed the basis of further preparatory work in the run-up to the 1949 Diplomatic Conference. See *Report of the Preliminary Conference of National Societies of 1946*, p. 15.

[18] See *Report of the Conference of Government Experts of 1947*, p. 52.

[19] See e.g. Belgium, *Law of Armed Conflict Training Manual*, 2009, Course V, p. 16; Canada, *LOAC Manual*, 2001, para. 915.2; Switzerland, *Basic Military Manual*, 1987, Article 95; and United States, *Army Health System*, 2013, para. 3-23.

[20] This may be deduced from the context of this paragraph. Article 43(2) deals with the same issue of flying the national flag alongside the protective emblem for medical units of National Red Cross and Red Crescent Societies or other voluntary aid societies of *neutral* countries, and refers to the 'responsible military authorities' as competent to give certain orders in this regard. See the commentary on Article 43, section C.

[21] ICRC, *Study on the Use of the Emblems: Operational and Commercial and Other Non-Operational Issues*, ICRC, Geneva, 2011, pp. 144–146.

[22] See Article 5 of Additional Protocol III and its commentary.

[23] See ICRC, *Study on the Use of the Emblems: Operational and Commercial and Other Non-Operational Issues*, ICRC, Geneva, 2011, Chapter 27, pp. 161–166.

E. Paragraph 3: Medical units in enemy hands

2640 Article 42(3) excludes the use of the national flag alongside the protective emblem by medical units that have fallen into enemy hands.[24] The provision is a consequence of the rule contained in Article 19(1), whereby such units must be allowed to continue to treat the wounded and sick in their care until such time as the Power into whose hands they have fallen can take on this responsibility itself.[25] During this transitional phase, before the capturing Power has made use of the possibility of disposing of medical objects within the limits provided for in Articles 33 and 34, the question arises as to whether medical units should continue to fly the national flag of the State to which they belong or should switch to that of the Power into whose hands they have fallen.[26]

2641 Indeed, it would have been difficult to provide for the use of one or other national flag besides the distinctive flag of the Convention, as there are objections in either case.[27]

2642 Article 42(3) expressly refers only to 'medical units', in contrast to the other paragraphs of this article which refer to both medical establishments and units. On a strict literal reading, this could be taken to mean that the rule at issue only applies to mobile medical units and not to fixed medical establishments. A more nuanced interpretation was already put forward in relation to the identical wording contained in the 1929 Convention. In that Convention, a distinction between fixed establishments and mobile medical units of the armed forces was considered justified. However, such a distinction was not deemed appropriate for fixed establishments and mobile medical units of National Red Cross and Red Crescent Societies or other voluntary aid societies auxiliary to the medical services.[28]

2643 Since the adoption of the 1949 Convention, the expression 'medical units' has been interpreted as covering both fixed establishments and mobile medical units. This change in interpretation was justified by the fact that, when they

---

[24] Medical establishments and units of National Red Cross and Red Crescent Societies or other voluntary aid societies of *neutral* countries are excluded from the scope of this paragraph as they are governed by the specific rule contained in Article 43(2). On the notion of 'falling into enemy hands', see the commentary on Article 19, section C.3.

[25] See *ibid.*

[26] See the commentaries on Article 33 and Article 34 for further details on the treatment of fixed medical establishments, their material and stores, and of mobile medical units and their material belonging respectively to the armed forces and to National Red Cross and Red Crescent Societies or other voluntary aid societies.

[27] That objection had already been expressed in relation to the same wording used in this regard in the 1929 Convention. See Des Gouttes, *Commentaire de la Convention de Genève de 1929 sur les blessés et malades*, ICRC, 1930, p. 166.

[28] See *ibid.* pp. 166–167. The relevant difference between fixed establishments of the medical services of the armed forces and fixed establishments of National Red Cross and Red Crescent Societies or other voluntary aid societies auxiliary to the medical services was that only the former were subject to the law of war, which corresponds to the legal position in Articles 33 and 34 of the 1949 Convention.

fall into enemy hands, the position of fixed establishments and mobile medical units – regardless of whether they belong to the medical service of the armed forces or to National Red Cross or Red Crescent Societies or other voluntary aid societies auxiliary to the medical services – is so similar that a distinction with regard to their use of the flag would be unwarranted.[29]

F. Paragraph 4: Visibility of the emblem as a protective device

2644   The obligation in Article 42(4) on the Parties to the conflict to 'take the necessary steps' to make the emblem as a protective device clearly visible to enemy armed forces is an obligation of conduct rather than of result. This is clear in the light of the provision's ultimate objective to 'obviate the possibility of any hostile action'. This depends not only on those displaying the emblem as a protective device but also on the enemy armed forces honouring their fundamental obligation to take all feasible precautions to verify that the target of an attack is indeed a military objective.[30]

2645   As regards the interpretation of the obligation to 'take the necessary steps', it is clear that if the emblem is to serve its purpose as the visible manifestation of protection and to 'obviate the possibility of any hostile action', it should be visible from as far away, from as many sides and as early as possible, both from the ground and from the air. Neither the distance from which the emblem should be clearly visible nor its size is specified. Indeed, it would be impossible to do so, as the visibility of the emblem as a protective device is highly contextual and depends on a variety of factors, such as the terrain, weather, time of day, and the types of weaponry and observation technology available to the adversary.[31]

2646   However, in 1936, in the 1970s, in 1989 and between 1993 and 1995, the ICRC, in cooperation with armed forces, conducted visibility tests from the air, from the ground and at sea, taking many of these variables into account. In terms of distance and size, the aerial tests in 1936 showed, for example, that in good weather conditions a red cross on a white ground, 5 metres square, placed on a roof, could hardly be distinguished from altitudes above 2,500 metres. This result was essentially confirmed in aerial tests conducted in 1989, with the flag no longer recognizable at a distance of 3,000 metres; a red cross flag measuring 10 metres across was no longer visible from 5,000 metres.[32] The 1989 aerial tests also found that the red crescent was less easily recognizable than the red

---

[29] On the position of fixed medical establishments and mobile medical units under the 1929 Geneva Convention on the Wounded and Sick, see *ibid.* p. 166.

[30] Additional Protocol I, Article 57(2)(a)(i); see also Customary International Humanitarian Law (2005), Rule 16.

[31] See e.g. Sweden, *IHL Manual*, 1991, p. 156.   [32] Cauderay, p. 300.

cross.[33] In terms of ground visibility, the 1989 tests found that any emblem measuring more than 1 metre across was recognizable from up to a distance of 400 metres.[34]

2647   At night or in bad weather, one way of increasing visibility is by lighting or illuminating the emblem. The emblem is 'lit' when receiving light from a projector or a lamp; the white light projected onto it brings out its shape and colours. The emblem is 'illuminated' when red and white lights are placed on it in order to pick out the red emblem against the white ground. This may be done by placing strings of red electric bulbs along the contour of the emblem and white bulbs round the edge of the white ground.

2648   The added value of the tests conducted in the 1970s and thereafter, compared with the 1936 tests, was that they took into account technological developments in electronic observation techniques, including passive infrared, also known as thermal imaging,[35] and image intensifiers, such as night vision devices.[36] These techniques make it possible to identify targets when visibility is reduced, notably in poor weather or at night. The tests conducted in 1989 showed that when image intensifiers are used, the visibility of the emblem may be improved by using paint containing reflective materials.[37] Thermal imaging cameras, meanwhile, do not distinguish differences in colour but instead detect differences in temperature. Therefore, and following aerial, ground and maritime tests performed between 1993 and 1995, the use of special adhesive tapes with a high thermal reflection coefficient was recommended. Thus, the red cross or red crescent can be made up of these special tapes, providing a temperature contrast between the cross or the crescent and its white background. This contrast can then be detected by the thermal imaging camera.[38] Similar tests were carried out in 2000 and 2001 with what was to be adopted as the red crystal on a white ground.[39]

2649   Many findings of these tests have subsequently been incorporated into the Regulations concerning identification annexed to Additional Protocol

---

[33] *Ibid.* pp. 300–308, 315 and 317.   [34] *Ibid.* p. 303.

[35] By this means, the electromagnetic energy emitted in the infrared band by objects is transformed into electrical signals which are then used to draw a map of the hot points on the landscape, thus forming an image which can be observed, for example, through field glasses or on a screen. See Cauderay, p. 297, note 3, and Loye, p. 198, note 1.

[36] These are electro-optical devices which amplify the light levels of objects lit by low light at night. The main component is a light amplification tube which converts a low-level polychromatic image (white light) into an electronic image, which is then electronically amplified and transformed into a more intense, usually dull green, monochromatic image; Cauderay, p. 297, note 4.

[37] *Ibid.* p. 310. See also Colombia, *Decree No. 138*, 2005, Article 4(6), which explicitly provides for the possibility of using reflective materials to ensure visibility at night.

[38] See Loye, pp. 198–202.

[39] Jean-François Quéguiner, 'Commentary on the Protocol additional to the Geneva Conventions of 12 August 1949, and relating to the Adoption of an Additional Distinctive Emblem (Protocol III)', *International Review of the Red Cross*, Vol. 89, No. 865, March 2007, p. 187, note 35.

I.[40] These regulations not only specify measures intended to ensure greater visibility of the protective emblem, but also provide for additional distinctive signals, such as radio and electronic identification, given that purely visual means of identification may be insufficient in circumstances of modern warfare enabling long-range targeting.[41] Parties may also wish to make the presence of medical facilities known by communicating their GPS coordinates to other Parties.

2650   The obligation contained in Article 42(4) is further qualified by the caveat 'in so far as military considerations permit', which recognizes that there may be circumstances in which the emblem as a protective device may not be displayed at all. Pursuant to Article 39, generally the emblem should be displayed, and this is the predominant doctrine and State practice in armed forces. However, a protective emblem does not in and of itself confer protection; it only serves as the visible manifestation of such protection and facilitates identification by enemy armed forces.[42] Therefore, failure to display the protective emblem neither automatically deprives a medical establishment or unit of protection, nor should it automatically lead to the conclusion that a medical establishment or unit has lost its protection.[43]

2651   A commander is accordingly permitted to decide that the emblem as a protective device on certain medical units should be removed or covered up (camouflaged) where military considerations so require. A commander must remove or unambiguously conceal the emblem if he or she considers it necessary to equip a medical unit with heavy weaponry to deter unlawful attacks.[44] Military doctrine and State practice recognize the validity of such a course of action in situations where armed forces are confronted with an enemy that systematically attacks medical units bearing a protective emblem, in clear violation of international humanitarian law.

2652   Moreover, military doctrine and State practice recognize that a Party may choose not to display the emblem where it is necessary to place medical units within or close to military objectives, such as in the case of mobile medical

---

[40] See Additional Protocol I, Annex I, Regulations concerning identification (as amended in 1993), Articles 4 and 5.

[41] *Ibid.* Articles 6–9. Parties may also wish to authorize the use of electronic markings in relation to computer networks and data, for example. See Tallinn Manual on the International Law Applicable to Cyber Warfare (2013), Rule 72, pp. 206–208.

[42] See the commentary on Article 39, section B.4. See also Additional Protocol I, Annex I, Regulations concerning identification (as amended in 1993), Article 1(2), and Additional Protocol III, Preamble, para. 4. The emblem's fundamental purpose as the visible manifestation of protection is also recognized in the national legislation of numerous countries; see e.g. Bosnia and Herzegovina, *Emblem Law*, 2002, Article 2; Colombia, *Emblem Law*, 2004, Article 2(1); Mali, *Emblem Law*, 2009, Article 3; and Philippines, *Emblem Act*, 2013, section 3(f).

[43] See e.g. Australia, *Manual of the Law of Armed Conflict*, 2006, para. 9.3; United Kingdom, *Manual of the Law of Armed Conflict*, 2004, para. 7.25.1; and United States, *Army Health System*, 2013, para. 3-23. See also Vollmar, p. 748.

[44] For a discussion concerning the loss of specific protection if heavy weaponry is mounted on military medical units, see the commentary on Article 22, para. 1868.

units, in order not to reveal the position and number of troops engaged.[45] In addition, it can be deduced from the purpose of the use of the emblem as a protective device, that where there is reason to conclude that medical units and establishments will be better protected if they are *not* marked with the emblem, the competent military authorities may decide that these medical units and establishments will not be marked.[46]

2653   While medical establishments and units of the medical services remain legally protected, regardless of whether or not they are marked with the emblem, in practice this protection will only be effective to the extent that the enemy can recognize them for what they are. Therefore, it is recognized in military doctrine that medical units should not be camouflaged any longer than is absolutely necessary.[47]

Select bibliography

Bouvier, Antoine A., 'The Use of the Emblem', in Andrew Clapham, Paola Gaeta and Marco Sassòli (eds), *The 1949 Geneva Conventions: A Commentary*, Oxford University Press, 2015, pp. 855–886.

Cauderay, Gérald C., 'Visibility of the distinctive emblem on medical establishments, units, and transports', *International Review of the Red Cross*, Vol. 30, No. 277, August 1990, pp. 295–321.

de Mulinen, Frédéric, 'Signalling and Identification of Medical Personnel and Material', *International Review of the Red Cross*, Vol. 12, No. 138, September 1972, pp. 479–494.

Eberlin, Philippe, 'Modernization of protective markings and signalling', *International Review of the Red Cross*, Vol. 19, No. 209, April 1979, pp. 59–83.

– *Protective Signs*, ICRC, Geneva, 1983.

Henckaerts, Jean-Marie and Doswald-Beck, Louise, *Customary International Humanitarian Law, Volume 1: Rules*, ICRC/Cambridge University Press, 2005, available at https://www.icrc.org/customary-ihl/eng/docs/v1.

---

[45] See e.g. Australia, *Manual of the Law of Armed Conflict*, 2006, para. 9.4 (stating that in order to 'conceal a military deployment, a commander may choose not to display the red cross, red crescent or red crystal on field ambulances or medical facilities which by necessity must be located close to a military objective such as a medical transit post adjacent to a military airfield'); Germany, *Military Manual*, 2013, para. 652; Peru, *IHL Manual*, 2004, para. 30(t), Annex 10, Terms of Reference, points 25 and 98; and Philippines, *LOAC Teaching File*, 2006, pp. 5–7, 9–3 and 16–2. However, this course of action is subject to the obligation under Article 19(2) of the First Convention to ensure that medical establishments and units are, as far as possible, situated in such a manner that attacks against military objectives cannot imperil their safety. See the commentary on Article 19, section D.

[46] See also the commentaries on Article 39, sections B.2 and B.3, and Article 40, section C.2, regarding the use of the emblem on flags, emblems and medical equipment and the identification of medical and religious personnel.

[47] See NATO Standardization Agreement 2931 (1998) (providing that an order to camouflage medical facilities is to be temporary and local in nature only and must be rescinded as soon as the security situation on the ground permits. Furthermore, such an order may only be issued at a certain level of the military chain of command, i.e. brigade level or equivalent. However, this possibility is not foreseen for large, fixed medical establishments.) See also Belgium, *Law of Armed Conflict Training Manual*, 2009, Course V, p. 17; United Kingdom, *Manual of the Law of Armed Conflict*, 2004, para. 7.25.2; and United States, *Army Health System*, 2013, para. 3-23.

Loye, Dominique, 'Making the distinctive emblem visible to thermal imaging cameras', *International Review of the Red Cross*, Vol. 37, No. 317, March–April 1997, pp. 198–202.

Vollmar, Lewis C., 'Military Medicine in War: The Geneva Conventions Today', in Thomas E. Beam and Linette R. Sparacino (eds), *Military Medical Ethics*, Vol. 2, Office of The Surgeon General, United States Army, Washington D.C., 2003, pp. 739–771.

MARKING OF UNITS OF NEUTRAL COUNTRIES

❖ Text of the provision*

(1) The medical units belonging to neutral countries, which may have been authorized to lend their services to a belligerent under the conditions laid down in Article 27, shall fly, along with the flag of the Convention, the national flag of that belligerent, wherever the latter makes use of the faculty conferred on him by Article 42.

(2) Subject to orders to the contrary by the responsible military authorities, they may, on all occasions, fly their national flag, even if they fall into the hands of the adverse Party.

❖ Reservations or declarations

None

Contents

A. Introduction

2654 Article 43 governs the marking of medical units of National Red Cross and Red Crescent Societies or other voluntary aid societies of neutral countries that have been authorized to lend their services to a Party to the conflict according to the conditions laid down in Article 27 of the First Convention.[1] This type of arrangement has not occurred since the end of the Second World War but nevertheless remains an option.[2]

---

* Paragraph numbers have been added for ease of reference.
[1] For a discussion of the requirements for such authorization, see the commentary on Article 27, sections C and D.
[2] See the commentary on Article 27, section B. See also François Bugnion, *The International Committee of the Red Cross and the Protection of War Victims*, ICRC/Macmillan, Oxford, 2003, p. 517.

B. Paragraph 1: The flag of the belligerent and the flag of the Convention

2655 Article 43(1) states that medical units of neutral countries shall fly, along with the flag of the Convention, the national flag of the belligerent to which they lend their services if the belligerent commander has decided that medical units shall do so (which, under Article 42, is not compulsory).[3] This means that the medical unit of a National Society or other voluntary aid society of a neutral country would fly the flag of the belligerent Party to which it lends its services.

2656   Such units may also display the protective emblem, referred to in the present article as the 'flag of the Convention', be it the red cross, the red crescent, or the red crystal.[4] The word 'flag' should be interpreted broadly.[5]

C. Paragraph 2: The flag of the neutral country

2657 The right of the medical units of a neutral country to fly their national flag, in addition to those of the Convention and of the belligerent to which they lend their services, was introduced in 1929.[6] At that time, there were misgivings about the wisdom of allowing the medical unit of a National Society to fly its national flag in such circumstances.[7] In the absence of recent practice, however, it is difficult to assess the likely effects of the display of such flags.

2658   Under the 1949 text, a medical unit of a neutral country may fly its national flag even after it falls into enemy hands. This situation thus differs from that of military medical units, which under Article 42(3) may no longer fly their national flags but only the flag of the Convention after they have fallen into enemy hands.

2659   The option for medical units of a neutral country to continue to fly their national flag, however, is made '[s]ubject to orders to the contrary by the responsible military authorities'. This does not mean that the belligerent can decide generally whether or not medical units of neutral countries may or may not fly their national flags.[8] Rather, ordering them not to fly the national flag is

---

[3] See the commentary on Article 42, para. 2637.

[4] Technically, the reference to 'the flag of the Convention' in Article 43(1) also includes the red lion and sun as one of the distinctive emblems recognized under Article 38(2) of the First Convention. This symbol, which has only ever been used by one State Party, is no longer in use. See also the commentary on Article 2(4) of Additional Protocol III. With regard to measures to enhance the visibility of the protective emblem, see also Additional Protocol I, Annex I, Regulations concerning identification (as amended on 30 November 1993), and its commentary.

[5] See the commentary on Article 42, section C.

[6] Geneva Convention on the Wounded and Sick (1929), Article 23.

[7] See, in particular, the concerns listed by Des Gouttes, *Commentaire de la Convention de Genève de 1929 sur les blessés et malades*, ICRC, 1930, pp. 171–172. Among other things, Des Gouttes was particularly concerned that by flying its national flag in these circumstances, a National Society would give the false impression that the State to which it belonged had entered the war. In 1952, however, Pictet wrote that those objections 'for reasons of principle' were 'not convincing' (*Commentary on the First Geneva Convention*, ICRC, 1952, p. 323).

[8] See the commentary on Article 42, section D.

restricted to particular cases and for a limited period only, when there are tactical reasons for not displaying the national flag, such as the need to conceal medical units in forward areas. This interpretation flows from a logical reading of the article. With any other interpretation, use of the phrases 'subject to orders to the contrary' and 'they may, on all occasions' in the same sentence would appear contradictory and the paragraph would have no real meaning.

RESTRICTIONS IN THE USE OF THE EMBLEM. EXCEPTIONS

❖ Text of the provision*

(1) With the exception of the cases mentioned in the following paragraphs of the present Article, the emblem of the red cross on a white ground and the words 'Red Cross', or 'Geneva Cross' may not be employed, either in time of peace or in time of war, except to indicate or to protect the medical units and establishments, the personnel and material protected by the present Convention and other Conventions dealing with similar matters. The same shall apply to the emblems mentioned in Article 38, second paragraph, in respect of the countries which use them. The National Red Cross Societies and other Societies designated in Article 26 shall have the right to use the distinctive emblem conferring the protection of the Convention only within the framework of the present paragraph.

(2) Furthermore, National Red Cross (Red Crescent, Red Lion and Sun) Societies may, in time of peace, in accordance with their national legislation, make use of the name and emblem of the Red Cross for their other activities which are in conformity with the principles laid down by the International Red Cross Conferences. When those activities are carried out in time of war, the conditions for the use of the emblem shall be such that it cannot be considered as conferring the protection of the Convention; the emblem shall be comparatively small in size and may not be placed on armlets or on the roofs of buildings.

(3) The international Red Cross organizations and their duly authorized personnel shall be permitted to make use, at all times, of the emblem of the Red Cross on a white ground.

(4) As an exceptional measure, in conformity with national legislation and with the express permission of one of the National Red Cross (Red Crescent, Red Lion and Sun) Societies, the emblem of the Convention may be employed in time of peace to identify vehicles used as ambulances and to mark the position of aid stations exclusively assigned to the purpose of giving free treatment to the wounded or sick.

---

* Paragraph numbers have been added for ease of reference.

❖ Reservations or declarations

United States of America: Reservation made upon ratification.[1]

Contents

A. Introduction

2660   Article 44 expresses the general rule that, as a protective device, the distinctive emblems may only be used for the marking of medical units and establishments, personnel and material as laid down under the First Convention (Articles 38–43), as well as under the other Geneva Conventions and their Additional Protocols. Importantly, the article also sets out a number of exceptions to this rule, whereby the emblem may be used by certain additional entities, provided that specific conditions are met.

2661   At the outset, it is important to understand that use of the emblems may take two distinct forms, both of which are identified and elaborated under Article 44. First and foremost is the use of the emblem as a protective device, i.e. as the visible sign of the protection accorded by the Convention to certain persons or objects.[2] Second is the use of the emblem as an indicative sign, which shows that a person or object is connected with the organizations of the International Red Cross and Red Crescent Movement (hereinafter 'the Movement'). Use of the emblem as an indicative sign does not imply the protection of the Convention.

B. Historical background

2662 Although earlier versions of the text of Article 44 date from 1906, it was not until the present article was adopted in 1949 that the essential distinction

---

[1] United Nations *Treaty Series*, Vol. 213, 1955, pp. 378–381. For the text of the reservation and a discussion thereof, see the commentary on Article 53, paras 3086–3087.

[2] This does not mean that the protection of such persons or objects is dependent on use of the emblem; protected persons or objects that do not display the emblem do not lose their protected status under the Convention. See the commentary on Article 39, paras 2566 and 2578.

between the protective use and the indicative use of the emblem was made. For example, Article 23 of the 1906 Geneva Convention simply stipulated that the red cross emblem and the words 'Red Cross' or 'Geneva Cross' could only be used, whether in time of peace or war, 'to protect or designate sanitary formations and establishments, the personnel and "matériel" protected by the convention'.

2663   The text of Article 23 was expanded upon in the new Article 24 of the 1929 Geneva Convention on the Wounded and Sick, both to take account of those countries using the red crescent or red lion and sun emblems (these additional distinctive emblems having been formally adopted under the 1929 Convention) and to allow for use of one or other of the emblems by National Red Cross, Red Crescent and Red Lion and Sun Societies (hereinafter 'National Societies') in connection with their humanitarian activities, in accordance with their national legislation. However, failure to recognize the distinction between the protective and the indicative uses of the emblem led the 1929 Diplomatic Conference to decide that, other than when carrying out their work as auxiliaries to the medical service of the armed forces, National Societies should only be entitled to use the emblem in time of peace. Thus, at the outbreak of a conflict, a National Society was required to prevent the use of the emblem by any of its staff or volunteers or on its buildings or objects not used for the military wounded or attached to the medical service of the armed forces. In practice, this stipulation usually remained a dead letter.

2664   Article 44 of the First Convention of 1949 draws a clear distinction between the protective and the indicative uses of the emblem, and successfully reconciles the two needs which had become apparent. On the one hand, there continued to be the need to use the emblem as a protective device, in particular, by the medical services of armed forces, its original and primary function. On the other hand, National Societies continued to use the emblem for activities outside of their auxiliary role to the military medical services, and the emblem was increasingly associated with both the National Society and these general humanitarian activities. A balance needed to be struck. Article 44 imposes the strictest safeguards on the use of the protective emblem, while allowing National Societies to make appropriate use of the emblem as an indicative sign, including during armed conflict, albeit within certain parameters. Conditions on the indicative use have been further developed in additional texts adopted by International Conferences of the Red Cross and Red Crescent and associated Movement meetings.[3]

---

[3] This process of development resulted in the 'Regulations on the Use of the Emblem of the Red Cross or the Red Crescent by the National Societies', adopted by the 20th International Conference of the Red Cross (Vienna, 1965) and revised by the Council of Delegates of the International Red Cross and Red Crescent Movement (Budapest, 1991). The revised text was effectively endorsed through a written procedure by all States party to the Geneva Conventions.

C. Paragraph 1: The primacy of the emblem as a protective device

2665 Article 44(1) confirms the primacy of the protective use of the emblem to mark medical units and establishments, personnel and material protected by the First Convention and other Conventions dealing with similar matters. The paragraph refers to the red cross emblem and to the other recognized emblems set out under Article 38(2) in respect of the countries that use them.[4] The words 'Red Cross' and 'Geneva Cross' are also covered. In effect, while Articles 38 and 39 stipulate that the emblem of the red cross (or one of the other distinctive emblems, where relevant) is the emblem of the medical service of the armed forces and that it should appear on everything connected with them,[5] Article 44 makes clear that, apart from the prescribed exceptions, it should appear on nothing else. All use of the emblem other than as laid down in the Geneva Conventions and their Additional Protocols is strictly forbidden.

2666 A majority of States protect the distinctive emblems and their associated designations in accordance with Article 44(1) in their national legislation, albeit with considerable variations. Mostly, such legislation restricts use of the red cross, red crescent and red lion and sun emblems (although the last is no longer in use).[6] While some States only protect the specific designation of the emblem used in their territory,[7] many extend protection to both the 'Red Cross' and 'Red Crescent' designations (and in some cases also to the designation 'Red Lion and Sun').[8] Few, however, apparently refer explicitly to the use of the designation 'Geneva Cross'.[9]

2667 Article 44(1) stipulates that the emblem and relevant designations may not be employed either in time of peace or in time of war, except as described in Article 44. While the emblem laws of a number of States include references to both armed conflict and peacetime, few define these terms.[10] In addition, the

---

[4] These other recognized emblems are the red crescent and the red lion and sun. Since the adoption of Additional Protocol III in 2005, they include the third Protocol emblem, or 'red crystal'.

[5] See the commentary on Article 39, para. 2572, for a full list of persons, establishments, units and transports entitled to display the distinctive emblems under the present Convention, as well as practical examples of specific items and equipment on which they may be displayed.

[6] This is also in spite of the fact that Article 44(1) applies to the red crescent and red lion and sun emblems only 'in respect of the countries which use them'. In practice, therefore, many States have taken a more expansive view of this paragraph. See the commentary on Article 53, fn. 58, for examples of States which have enacted legislation protecting the red cross, red crescent and red lion and sun emblems.

[7] See e.g. Brunei Darussalam.

[8] This is in spite of the fact that Article 44(1) does not explicitly refer to the designations 'Red Crescent' and 'Red Lion and Sun' (only to the emblems themselves: see fn. 6). More recently, since the adoption of Additional Protocol III in 2005, legislation in some countries has been extended to include the red crystal emblem and one or both of its designations (i.e. 'Red Crystal' and 'Third Protocol Emblem').

[9] See the commentary on Article 53, fn. 16, for examples of States that explicitly refer to the designation 'Geneva Cross' in their national legislation.

[10] Of the few that define 'armed conflict', Belarus applies the definition given in common Article 2 of the Geneva Conventions, Article 1(4) of Additional Protocol I and Article 1 of Additional Protocol II (thereby covering international and certain non-international armed conflicts); see

paragraph contains a reference to 'other Conventions dealing with similar matters', which was a newly suggested inclusion in 1949.[11] The preparatory work indicates that this text refers to the other 1949 Geneva Conventions.[12] Today, it would also refer to the Additional Protocols to the Geneva Conventions.

2668   Article 44 also allows for use of the emblem as a protective device by National Red Cross and Red Crescent Societies, as well as other Societies so designated under Article 26 of the Convention 'within the framework of the present paragraph'.[13] This means that such Societies may employ the protective sign only for that part of their personnel and material which assists the medical service of the armed forces, is employed exclusively for the same purpose, and is subject to military laws and regulations.[14] Even then, they can use it only with the consent of the military authority.[15]

2669   In recent times, few National Societies have deployed as auxiliaries to the medical service of their country's armed forces. More generally, National Societies may act as an auxiliary to their respective public authorities in the humanitarian field.[16] Such a role may also be exercised in the context of an armed conflict, where a National Society may be called upon to provide, for example, psychosocial, family tracing and/or other support to members of the armed forces, to nationals of their country or to others in need of it. However, such activities are distinct from those envisaged under Article 26 of the First Convention, and do not trigger the application of Article 44(1) (i.e. they do not entail an entitlement to use the emblem as a protective device).[17]

Belarus, *Law on the Emblem*, 2000, Article 2. Cameroon specifies both international and non-international armed conflicts; see Cameroon, *Emblem Law*, 1997, Section 8. No definition of 'peacetime' was found in any of the national laws examined (although the term is used extensively). A number of States, in particular those with Geneva Conventions Acts (and some with a Red Cross or Red Crescent Act), do not refer to 'armed conflict' or 'peacetime' in the relevant articles, but do incorporate the texts of the Four Geneva Conventions by reference or in a schedule.

[11] The preparatory work for the 1949 Conventions indicates that a suggestion to include a similar text at this juncture ('this or other international Conventions' in replacement of 'the Convention') was tabled by the delegation of the United States, and accepted unanimously. *Final Record of the Diplomatic Conference of Geneva of 1949*, Vol. II-A, p. 95.

[12] *Minutes of the Diplomatic Conference of Geneva of 1949*, Commission I, Vol. I, pp. 35–36 (US).

[13] See Article 40, which allows the personnel of such organizations to wear an armlet and carry identity cards, both bearing the emblem. In practice, relatively few organizations other than National Red Cross and Red Crescent Societies undertake such auxiliary activities.

[14] For a discussion of these terms, see the commentary on Article 26.

[15] Article 2 of the 1991 Emblem Regulations confirms that National Societies 'may use the emblem as a protective device only with the consent of and in accordance with the conditions laid down by the [competent State] Authority'.

[16] This is a condition for recognition as a National Society: Article 4(3) of the 1986 Statutes of the International Red Cross and Red Crescent Movement. See also Article 3(1) of the Statutes and Resolution 2 of the 30th International Conference of the Red Cross and Red Crescent (Geneva, 2007) and Resolution 4 of the 31st International Conference of the Red Cross and Red Crescent (Geneva, 2011). See also the commentary on Article 26, fns 27 and 79.

[17] In addition, the medical personnel of such National Societies may potentially be authorized to display the emblem as a protective device where they are 'regularly and solely engaged in the operation and administration of civilian hospitals' (Fourth Convention, Article 20(1)). Moreover, under Additional Protocol I, the competent authority may authorize civilian medical personnel (which can include National Society medical personnel who are not attached to the medical

2670 Although Article 44 concerns international armed conflict, in situations of non-international armed conflict a National Society may exercise its status and role as an auxiliary to the medical service of the armed forces in line with the idea underpinning Article 26. It may also do so more generally as an auxiliary to the public authorities in the humanitarian field. While the role of National Societies as auxiliaries has evolved over time, there is a distinct legal regime governing a National Society's use of the emblem in these different roles. Use of the protective emblem is limited to situations that conform to Article 26. Furthermore, in practice, in non-international armed conflicts the National Society may prefer not to act in its auxiliary role, so as to distinguish itself from the government (which may be a Party to the conflict) and thus maintain the confidence of the whole population.[18] Its auxiliary status may nevertheless enable the Society to take on certain functions during the armed conflict, such as the coordination of incoming international humanitarian assistance.[19] In any case, in such situations a National Society may, at most, use its logo, under certain conditions.[20]

2671 More detailed guidance on the appropriate use of the emblem by National Societies (both as a protective device and as an indicative sign) has been provided by successive sessions of the statutory meetings of the Movement, in particular by the International Conference of the Red Cross and Red Crescent, which brings together the States party to the 1949 Geneva Conventions and the components of the Movement every four years. The 20th International Conference in 1965 adopted a set of regulations on the use of the emblem by National Societies, entitled the 'Regulations on the Use of the Emblem of the Red Cross, of the Red Crescent and of the Red Lion and Sun by the National Societies', which were subsequently revised in 1991 by the Movement's Council of Delegates.[21] These Regulations (hereinafter referred to as

---

service of the armed forces (see Article 8(c)) to use the emblem as a protective device (see Article 18 of the Protocol).

[18] For example, this is the reported approach of the Colombian Red Cross Society in relation to the non-international armed conflict in its territory.

[19] If this happens, the National Society must uphold its obligation to respect the Fundamental Principles, in particular impartiality and neutrality. The ability of a National Society to give practical effect to its auxiliary status in a non-international armed conflict in its territory will depend on the national context, will be driven by a range of factors, and may change over time. For example, in the non-international armed conflict in Syria, the Syrian Arab Red Crescent has been able to take on a formally recognized role in humanitarian coordination tasks, in principle (at least in part) owing to its auxiliary status. At the same time, the Society makes every effort to ensure that its adherence to the Fundamental Principles, in particular neutrality and impartiality, is well understood, both within Syria and externally (these efforts being supported by the wider Movement). That said, it is perhaps obvious that the fulfilment of a National Society's auxiliary role, and the management of perceptions by others of this role, will remain highly challenging in the context of a non-international armed conflict.

[20] See ICRC, *Study on the Use of the Emblems*, pp. 122–125.

[21] The Council of Delegates is the forum where the representatives of the components of the Movement meet to discuss matters which concern the Movement as a whole. It does not include the States party to the 1949 Geneva Conventions; however, following their revision by the Council of Delegates, the 1991 Emblem Regulations were forwarded by the ICRC to all States Parties, none of which submitted any formal objections to the amendments.

'the 1991 Emblem Regulations') contain one chapter on the protective use of the emblem and another on its indicative use, as well as a number of general rules pertaining to both. The ICRC has stressed that the 1991 Emblem Regulations are in accordance with the 1949 Geneva Conventions, and that they represent the widest possible interpretation of the relevant treaty rules.[22] The 1991 Emblem Regulations must also be applied within the framework of the relevant national laws on emblem use.

2672   The indicative use of the emblem, as elaborated under the 1991 Emblem Regulations, is examined in greater detail below. Regarding use of the emblem as a protective device by National Societies, the 1991 Emblem Regulations confirm that such use is permissible only with the consent of, and in accordance with, the conditions laid down by the State authority. It is therefore up to States to take the necessary steps to authorize and control the protective use of the emblem. To avoid National Societies being caught unprepared in the event of an armed conflict, the State authority should determine in peacetime the National Society's role as auxiliary to the military medical service and its right to use the emblem for its medical personnel and equipment.[23] This is in keeping with the framework of Article 44(1), whereby National Societies use the protective emblem when operating in their auxiliary role to the medical service of the armed forces. While evidence suggests that formal authorization may not always be provided by a State, the potential for such use may be agreed in practice.[24] In addition, the 1991 Emblem Regulations stipulate that, when used as a protective device by National Societies, the emblem must always retain its original form[25] and be identifiable from as far away as possible and be as large as necessary under the circumstances.[26]

D. Paragraph 2: Use of the emblem by National Societies as an indicative sign

2673 Article 44(2) is concerned with the indicative use of the emblem and name by National Societies.[27] Use of the emblem by the international organizations of

---

[22] See the preamble to the 1991 Emblem Regulations, which also stipulate that, while they develop Article 44 of the First Convention, certain provisions will take on a broader meaning for the National Societies of countries that are party to Additional Protocol I.

[23] Emblem Regulations (1991), Article 2 and its commentary.

[24] In a survey of 20 National Societies on emblem use carried out in 2013 (hereinafter referred to as 'the National Society emblem survey'), the National Societies of the following States reported that they had received no formal authorization to use the emblem as a protective device: Austria, Canada, Chile, Lithuania, South Sudan, Spain and Thailand.

[25] Emblem Regulations (1991), Article 5.

[26] Emblem Regulations (1991), Article 6. In the National Society emblem survey, no responding National Society reported any circumstances in which they used the emblem as a protective device. However, a number reported using a large-sized emblem on various items, either as part of their marque (logo) or on its own, for indicative purposes (and consequently outside the framework of Article 44 and the 1991 Emblem Regulations). The implications of such use are discussed in paras 2677–2678.

[27] Although Article 44(2) refers explicitly to the 'name and emblem of the Red Cross', given its reference to Red Crescent and Red Lion and Sun Societies, in effect it also permits National Red

the Movement (namely the ICRC and the International Federation of Red Cross and Red Crescent Societies (hereinafter 'International Federation')) is dealt with in Article 44(3) and is subject to specific rules.

2674   The emblem has a purely indicative value when it is used to show that a person or object has a connection with one of the organizations of the Movement, without implying protection under the Geneva Conventions or any intention to invoke them. When used in this way, the sign should be small in proportion to the person or object, and must be accompanied by the name or initials of the relevant organization.[28] The conditions under which it is used should preclude any risk of confusion with the emblem as a protective device.[29] The reason for this is the need for stringent control over the use of the emblem as a protective device; it is vital to avoid that any abuse or misuse of the emblem as a protective device by third parties leads to a loss of trust and therefore diminishes its protective value.

2675   On plain reading, Article 44(2) makes a distinction between the indicative use of the emblem in time of peace and its indicative use in time of war, when the latter circumstance additionally requires that the emblem for indicative purposes be comparatively small in size and may not be placed on armlets or on the roofs of buildings. This is to avoid the perception that the emblem as a protective device, which must be as large as necessary to aid identification, is being displayed. However, the stipulations regarding size and non-use of the indicative emblem on certain objects were extended in the 1991 Emblem Regulations as applying to its use both in time of peace and in time of war.[30] This

Crescent Societies to use the name and emblem of the red crescent. Following the discontinuation in 1980 of use of the red lion and sun emblem by the Islamic Republic of Iran, there are currently no National Red Lion and Sun Societies. It should be noted that references to National Red Cross and Red Crescent Societies also include the Magen David Adom (MDA) (Red Shield of David) in Israel; although the Red Shield of David is not a formally recognized distinctive emblem under the 1949 Geneva Conventions, the MDA is an officially recognized National Society and part of the Movement. See Article 3(2) of Additional Protocol III, which, in effect, sets out how the MDA may continue to use its name and associated emblem, while also making use of the red crystal (Third Protocol) emblem. It is the MDA's use of the red crystal emblem that enabled it to be recognized as a National Society.

[28]   The requirement that the emblem, when used as an indicative sign, be accompanied by the name or initials of the National Society is set out in Article 5 of the 1991 Emblem Regulations.

[29]   Even prior to 1949 the disadvantages of having two separate uses of the emblem (protective and indicative) were identified: as Pictet notes, 'it may well be asked whether at the outset it would not have been better to adopt two distinct emblems; one as the visible sign of the protection conferred by the Convention, the other as the flag of the National Red Cross Societies for their work as a whole'. Pictet goes on to note that, in spite of the difficulties, there are some advantages to such use, both for the Red Cross and Red Crescent organizations (which benefit from the prestige of the emblem) and for the emblem itself, where the organizations are held in high esteem. That said, care must always be taken that the distinction between the two uses of the emblem (i.e. protective and indicative) is clearly made. See Pictet (ed.), *Commentary on the First Geneva Convention*, ICRC, 1952, p. 330.

[30]   Regarding indicative use of the emblem, Article 4 of the 1991 Emblem Regulations stipulates that National Societies 'shall endeavour to follow [the rule relating to emblem size and non-use on certain items] in peacetime so as to avoid from the very beginning of a conflict any confusion with the emblem used as a protective device'. The commentary on Article 4 goes on to explain that, in spite of this stipulation, 'the use of a large-size emblem is not excluded in certain cases, such as events where it is important for first-aid workers to be easily identifiable'. Articles 14,

has helped to further obviate the risk of confusion between the protective use and the indicative use of the emblem in the event of an armed conflict.

2676   The fact that National Societies may not display the protective emblem (other than when acting as auxiliaries to the medical services of the armed forces in accordance with Articles 26 or 27) does not mean that they are not protected from attack under humanitarian law. It should be recalled that it is not the display of the emblem as a protective device itself that confers protection. Even without any emblem being displayed, civilians and civilian objects, including the staff and volunteers and property of National Societies, remain, under humanitarian law, protected against direct attack (provided, of course, they do not take a direct part in hostilities).

2677   It has been observed that, in practice, a number of National Societies carrying out their humanitarian activities in insecure operational contexts, including in situations of armed conflict, display the indicative emblem (in the form of the National Society's logo) in a large size, in particular on the uniforms or bibs of personnel and on vehicles, to aid identification. These activities do not fall within the National Society's role as auxiliary to the medical service of the armed forces (although they may well be carried out as part of its broader role as auxiliary to the public authorities in the humanitarian field). There do not seem to have been any objections to this practice by the States concerned. Displaying a large logo may, in certain circumstances, enhance the visibility of the National Society and contribute to its ability to carry out life-saving humanitarian activities. This practice does not conform strictly to the letter of the Convention and is not fully covered by the 1991 Emblem Regulations, which stipulate that the logo should be comparatively small in size.[31] It would therefore seem necessary for each State to determine, with its National Society, whether such practice is permissible in its national context. Use of a large-size logo should occur on an exceptional basis only, and purely for operational purposes (e.g. to ensure visibility or safe access to populations in need). A large-size logo must not be authorized for fundraising or commercial purposes.

2678   If the use of a large-size indicative emblem is permissible for operational purposes, it is important that the name or initials of the National Society always appear. In other words, the National Society must use its official logo, as required by the 1991 Emblem Regulations, and especially when using a large-size emblem for indicative purposes. Otherwise, in practice, it would be impossible to distinguish between the indicative and the protective uses of the emblem.

16, 17, 18, 19, 21 and 23 (the commentary) of the 1991 Emblem Regulations set out specific situations in which the emblem as an indicative device must be relatively small or of reduced dimensions (e.g. when worn by members and employees of the National Society while on duty (Article 14), and when placed on the buildings and premises of the National Society (Article 19)).
[31] See Emblem Regulations (1991), commentary on Article 16(1).

2679   While neither Article 44 nor the 1991 Emblem Regulations provide an exact definition of the term 'comparatively small', national legislation, agreed national practice and/or the internal regulations of the National Society concerning the use of the emblem may expand on this notion.[32]

2680   Paragraph 2 states that National Societies may use the emblem as an indicative sign 'in accordance with their national legislation'. While a majority of countries have introduced some form of legislation on the use of the emblem, a handful have yet to do so.[33] Nevertheless, in a number of the latter cases the relevant National Society uses one of the distinctive emblems, notwithstanding the absence of national legislation governing its use.[34]

2681   Article 44(2) also states that National Societies may use the name and emblem for their activities (outside of those set out in paragraph 1) 'which are in conformity with the principles laid down by the International Red Cross Conferences'. The International Conference of the Red Cross and Red Crescent (the successor to the International Conference of the Red Cross) has long had an interest in matters of emblem protection (both in terms of its use by those authorized to do so, including States and components of the Movement, and instances of misuse). For example, from 1869 onwards, the International Conference has regularly discussed or adopted resolutions regarding abuses of the emblem, concerning itself with matters such as the adoption of national legislative measures to repress such abuses.[35] As noted earlier, the original version of the 1991 Emblem Regulations was adopted in 1965 by the 20th International Conference.

2682   The principles referred to in Article 44(2) were further developed in the years following the adoption of the 1949 Geneva Conventions, and may generally

---

[32] Article 7 of the 1991 Emblem Regulations requires National Societies to establish such regulations or directives, and sets out their possible content. A number of National Societies have agreed national practice (developed in conjunction with their public authorities) or established internal regulations aiming to clarify such matters, for example by setting out the agreed size of the emblem on a range of National Society objects and materials (such as buildings, uniforms, vehicles and documents). According to the National Society emblem survey, examples of countries whose National Societies have done so include Argentina, Austria, Bosnia and Herzegovina, Canada, Chile, Colombia, Denmark, Germany, Indonesia, Norway, Spain, Sweden, South Sudan and Thailand. While national standards are helpful, there can be a lack of uniformity in size (as well as a lack of consistency more generally on matters of emblem use) from one country to another. This can have ramifications in relation to activities that involve a number of National Societies or, for example, for uses of the emblem that can reach a global audience, such as on the internet. These differences in national use of the indicative sign, and the efforts taken by the Movement to address such difficulties, are further discussed in paras 2683–2684.

[33] It is estimated that, at the time of writing, approximately 20 States do not have any form of national legislation on the use of the emblem.

[34] Examples of countries that do not have national legislation on the use of the emblem but do have a recognized National Society using one of the distinctive emblems include Afghanistan, Kuwait, San Marino and Somalia.

[35] Perruchoud, p. 212, reports that, in its consistent efforts to promote the need for stronger national measures to repress abuses of the emblem, the International Conference of the Red Cross and Red Crescent demonstrated one of its essential roles in adopting resolutions, that is, where possible, to create conditions favourable to the development and adoption by States of binding provisions, whether national or international, on areas of humanitarian concern.

be understood as referring to the Fundamental Principles of the Movement, as adopted by the 20th International Conference of the Red Cross in 1965.[36] The requirement that use of the emblem by National Societies be solely for activities that conform to the Fundamental Principles is confirmed and elaborated in the 1991 Emblem Regulations.[37] In addition, National Societies may not use the emblem when carrying out activities which have only a tenuous connection with their essential humanitarian mission.[38]

2683   Since the adoption of the 1949 Geneva Conventions, National Societies, while maintaining their core mission and functions, have greatly diversified their activities.[39] In addition, today there is an acknowledged need for all organizations, including National Societies, to communicate their identity and 'brand' effectively to relevant audiences, for example in traditional media, as well as, increasingly, in the digital sphere.[40] Moreover, many National Societies are experiencing greater competition for resources, owing to a perceived decrease in suitable funding sources for the ever expanding humanitarian needs.[41] Partly as a result of these circumstances, the Movement has developed more detailed guidance on the interpretation of the relevant rules governing indicative use of the emblem (namely the applicable treaty provisions and the 1991 Emblem Regulations). These resources, including a number

[36] The seven Fundamental Principles of the Movement are: humanity, impartiality, neutrality, independence, voluntary service, unity and universality (adopted by the 20th International Conference of the Red Cross, Vienna, 1965, Resolution 8, and incorporated with some amendments into the Statutes of the Movement, adopted by the 25th International Conference of the Red Cross and Red Crescent, Geneva, 1986, Resolution 31).

[37] Article 3 of the 1991 Emblem Regulations confirms this requirement and also adds an obligation on National Societies to ensure, at all times, that nothing tarnishes the prestige of the emblem or reduce respect for it.

[38] Emblem Regulations (1991), commentary on Article 3. One may ask in what circumstances a National Society might engage in activities that depart from its essential humanitarian mission. As National Societies have developed, they have often had to seek to diversify their funding sources. A growing area of focus for many National Societies is the need to engage with third-party (often commercial) organizations both in terms of programme delivery, but also, importantly, for fundraising purposes. Some joint fundraising activities may well have a less direct connection with the humanitarian mission of the Society. A further development is the growing trend of some National Societies to establish and manage their own commercial (i.e. profit-making) enterprises to support their funding needs. While some such enterprises may concern the delivery of health, ambulance or first-aid services, others may involve, for example, the management of retail shops, hotels and other leisure services. For a more full discussion of this issue, see Doole, pp. 4–9.

[39] For example, many National Societies have expanded their activities into areas such as migration and development.

[40] The distinctive emblems are not, in themselves, a 'brand': they must be viewed in terms of their special meaning and purpose under the Geneva Conventions. However, when used as an indicative sign by a National Society, the emblem inevitably becomes part of the visual identity or 'brand' of the Society. The inherent tension between the protective and the indicative uses of the emblem and the care needed to ensure that the two are kept separate has been discussed earlier (see fn. 29).

[41] In 2013, the Council of Delegates acknowledged that the Movement is operating in 'a rapidly changing and increasingly competitive environment, particularly with respect to positioning and obtaining funds' (Council of Delegates, Sydney, 2013, Res. 6, Preamble, para. 1).

of Movement policies[42] and a study by the ICRC concluded in 2009,[43] do not modify or develop the existing legal framework but help to inform practical implementation of the rules and to address those areas of greatest difficulty.[44]

2684 An increasing emphasis on fundraising and communication activities at the global level have, in part, highlighted a lack of uniformity by National Societies in their use of the emblem as an indicative sign.[45] Mindful of the need for greater coherence on emblem use and better adherence to the existing rules, the 2013 Council of Delegates urged the components of the Movement to recognize the existing international provisions governing use of the emblem (including Article 44 of the First Convention), as well as the 1991 Emblem Regulations.[46] The Council also reaffirmed the paramount importance of ensuring understanding of, and respect for, the emblem's functions when used as a protective device or as an indicative sign.[47] Lastly, the crucial role and interest of States,

---

[42] For example, 'Minimum elements to be included in operational agreements between Movement components and their external operational partners' (Council of Delegates, Geneva, 2003, Res. 10 (Annex)), and 'Substantive provisions of the International Red Cross and Red Crescent Movement policy for corporate sector partnerships' (Council of Delegates, Seoul, 2005, Res. 10 (Annex)).

[43] ICRC, *Study on the Use of the Emblems* (welcomed by the Council of Delegates, Nairobi, 2009, Res. 2, Preamble, para. 6).

[44] The ICRC's *Study on the Use of the Emblems* is particularly comprehensive and includes many useful and practical examples. It covers use (both protective and indicative) of the emblem by National Societies and other components of the Movement and provides guidance on the control and use of the emblem by States and (where relevant) third parties. That said, while States (including governmental and military representatives) were consulted in the drafting of the text, they have not formally endorsed it.

[45] In 2013, the Movement noted with concern the 'lack of consistency in the interpretation and practical application of the 1991 Emblem Regulations by National Societies' (Council of Delegates, Sydney, 2013, Res. 6, Preamble, para. 12). Evidence of such inconsistencies had been gathered partly through an 'International Branding Initiative' launched by the Movement in 2010. Two key purposes of the initiative were to examine use of the emblem by National Societies and to provide further guidance on some aspects of the 1991 Emblem Regulations. A series of workshops held as part of the initiative enabled National Societies, the ICRC and the International Federation to share practical experiences and examples of their use of the emblem. Further evidence was also gathered in the National Society emblem survey. These examples revealed a wide variation in interpretation by National Societies of parts of the 1991 Emblem Regulations, as well as some practice that was, regrettably, outside of the Regulations. Two particular discrepancies were use of the emblem for so-called 'decorative purposes' (covered by Article 5 of the 1991 Emblem Regulations) and use of the emblem on third-party products or items for sale (which is prohibited under Article 23 of the 1991 Emblem Regulations). Regarding the former, Article 5 of the 1991 Emblem Regulations allows for limited use of a 'freer design' of the indicative emblem where the purpose is to promote the National Society and the Movement at public events or on the National Society's own promotional materials. However, such use must not be prohibited by national legislation and, importantly, must not tarnish the prestige of the emblem or reduce respect for it (in accordance with Article 3 of the 1991 Emblem Regulations). If a decorative design is permitted for use within the above parameters, it should, as far as possible, be accompanied by the emblem used as an indicative sign (i.e. a small-sized emblem accompanied by the name or initials of the National Society, normally the National Society's ordinary logo).

[46] Council of Delegates, Sydney, 2013, Res. 6, para. 14. Similarly, in 2007 and 2009 the Council of Delegates emphasized the vital importance of respect for the rules governing use of the emblem (Council of Delegates, Geneva, 2007, Res. 7, Preamble, para. 4; Council of Delegates, Nairobi, 2009, Res. 2, para. 5).

[47] Council of Delegates, Sydney, 2013, Res. 6, Preamble, para. 12.

which bear the overall responsibility and authority for controlling use of the emblem and ensuring better compliance with the existing legal framework, cannot be overestimated.[48]

E. Paragraph 3: Use of the emblem by the international Red Cross organizations

2685 A further exception to the general principle set out in Article 44(1) is the permitted use, at all times, of the distinctive emblem by the 'international Red Cross organizations'.[49] Prior to 1949, there was no international provision formally authorizing these organizations to make use of the emblem, even though, in practice, their right to do so was never contested by governments.[50] This omission in earlier versions of the First Convention was therefore helpfully remedied by the inclusion of the third paragraph of Article 44.

2686 At the time of its adoption in 1949, this paragraph applied to the ICRC and to the League of Red Cross Societies (the latter having been established in 1919).[51] Therefore, the paragraph referred only to use of the red cross emblem. In 1983, the League changed its name to the League of Red Cross and Red Crescent Societies,[52] and in 1991 it became formally known as the International

---

[48] States' continuing interest in ensuring adherence to the rules on emblem use is demonstrated, for example, through successive resolutions of the International Conference of the Red Cross and Red Crescent dealing with emblem matters (e.g. 30th International Conference of the Red Cross and Red Crescent, Geneva, 2007, Res. 2, Preamble, para. 11).

[49] Interestingly, unlike the previous paragraph concerning National Societies, there is no explicit reference in Article 44(3) to use of the name of the emblem by the international Red Cross organizations. However, their ability to use the name may be implied, and it is certainly confirmed, through practice.

[50] For example, during the Second World War the ICRC proposed to governments that, in given cases and with States' formal consent, the emblem should be displayed on certain forms of transport (namely ships, but also rail and road convoys) organized by and under the control of the ICRC (or of a National Society); see Pictet (ed.), *Commentary on the First Geneva Convention*, ICRC, 1952, p. 336. For its part, the League of Red Cross Societies, although a partner in the Joint Relief Commission established with the ICRC in 1940, did not supervise the transfer of supplies or conduct negotiations with relevant authorities, but undertook a number of important support tasks, including purchasing supplies and keeping records, where requested; Reid/Gilbo, p. 127.

[51] It might be said that the red cross (or red crescent) emblem could also be used by a third 'international' entity: the International Red Cross and Red Crescent Movement. However, the Movement is not an 'organization' (or a legal or operational entity) in its own right: rather, it is the term used to describe the collective organizations of the Movement (the ICRC, the International Federation of Red Cross and Red Crescent Societies, and the recognized National Red Cross and Red Crescent Societies). In practice, the emblems displayed alongside one another on a white background (accompanied by the name of the Movement) may be used to signify the Movement (this is recognized by implication in preambular paragraph 10 of Additional Protocol III). That said, the Movement is not an 'international organization' in the sense of Article 44(3).

[52] From 1973 to 1976, a process of revision of the Constitution of the League of Red Cross Societies took place, during which, in spite of some support for a change among National Societies, the official name of the League was eventually retained (in part owing to the specific reference to the League of Red Cross Societies in certain articles of the Additional Protocols (e.g. Article 81(3) of Additional Protocol I). However, it was agreed in 1977 to use the title 'International Federation of Red Cross, Red Crescent and Red Lion and Sun Societies' on documents produced by the League (this being facilitated by an amendment to the League's Rules of Procedure), while

Federation of Red Cross and Red Crescent Societies. The logo of the International Federation incorporates the red cross and red crescent emblems side by side.[53] Given these developments, paragraph 3, while not explicitly providing for such use, should be interpreted as including use of the red crescent emblem by the International Federation.[54]

2687   The authorization in paragraph 3 is granted without reservation.[55] Consequently, the present paragraph refers to both the protective and the indicative uses of the emblem by either organization. In practice, the ICRC may use the emblem as a protective device (and therefore during hostilities).[56]

2688   While both the ICRC and the International Federation are permitted to use the emblem under the present paragraph, they are not obliged to do so. This

also retaining the official name 'League of Red Cross Societies'. When the name of the League was officially changed in 1983 to 'League of Red Cross and Red Crescent Societies' through an amendment to its Constitution, the Rules of Procedure were amended accordingly. See Item 16 (Amendments to the Statutory Texts of the League, Report of the Ad-Hoc Working Group), 8th Session of the General Assembly of the League of Red Cross and Red Crescent Societies, Budapest, 1991.

[53] Rule 1.3 of the Rules of Procedure of the International Federation of Red Cross and Red Crescent Societies confirms the official name of the organization. An annex to Rule 1.3 sets out the appropriate form and use, on letterheads and publications, of the International Federation's logo, this being the red cross and red crescent emblems side by side within a rectangular red frame, normally accompanied by the organization's full name.

[54] For its part, although not explicitly authorized to do so under the present paragraph, in principle the ICRC is not prevented from using the red crescent emblem, should it wish to do so. In its *Study on the Use of the Emblems*, the ICRC stated that there may be exceptional circumstances in which it could decide to use the red crescent emblem, out of operational necessity. A distinction should be made between potential use at a specific site or on a specific object, or for a particular activity, and potentially wide use in a given context (e.g. across a country). In the former instance, authority for such use may rest with the head of the relevant ICRC delegation and be limited in time. In the latter case, such use would require authorization from ICRC Headquarters after consultation with the relevant National Society and the Parties to the armed conflict (ICRC, *Study on the Use of the Emblems*, pp. 153–154).

[55] That said, the ICRC and the International Federation have agreed to abide by the aforementioned Emblem Regulations for indicative and so-called 'decorative' uses of the emblem (Council of Delegates, Birmingham, 1993, Res. 8, para. 4). As explained earlier, the Regulations set out various restrictions on use, including size and form. In addition, national legislation governing use of the emblem may be relevant to its use by the ICRC and the International Federation. For the ICRC, indicative use of the emblem normally takes the form of its 'roundel' (consisting of the red cross emblem enclosed in two concentric circles between which are written the words 'COMITE INTERNATIONAL GENEVE') with its initials (in the appropriate language: e.g. CICR, ICRC, MKKK, etc.) beneath. For the agreed form of indicative use by the International Federation, see fn. 53.

[56] The ICRC's *Study on the Use of the Emblems*, p. 156, provides a number of examples. In addition to the use of the red cross emblem (i.e. a red cross on a white ground), the ICRC has developed a longstanding practice of using its 'roundel' (which includes the red cross emblem – see fn. 55) for protective purposes. The ICRC reports that this practice has been developed for reasons of security and identification, and is accepted by States; see ICRC, *Study on the Use of the Emblems*, p. 157, in particular fn. 232. For its part, the International Federation does not stipulate when its own use of the emblems is protective rather than indicative, and its Rules of Procedure do not refer to protective use. On occasion the International Federation has used a large red cross emblem and red crescent emblem side by side within a red rectangle, without the organization's name, in its field operations, reportedly for visibility purposes. Such use of the large-sized Federation logo (without its name) would not constitute use of the emblems as a protective device within the terms of the Geneva Conventions and their Additional Protocols.

means that either organization may choose not to display the emblem, in circumstances where, for example, such use may not be appropriate[57] or in a context where the protective value of the emblem may have been compromised.[58]

2689   Both the ICRC and the International Federation are entitled to use the red crystal emblem by virtue of Article 4 of Additional Protocol III. However, such use may only occur in exceptional circumstances, in order to facilitate their work.[59]

F. Paragraph 4: Marking of third-party ambulances and aid stations

2690   Article 44(4) provides for a limited possibility for third parties to use the emblem for two specific purposes: to identify vehicles used as ambulances and to mark the position of aid stations, where either of these are used to provide free treatment for the wounded or sick. The paragraph, although subject to strict conditions, represents a departure from the general principle that third-party organizations and individuals are not permitted to use the emblem.[60]

2691   A provision allowing for use of the emblem on aid stations providing free treatment was first introduced under Article 24 of the 1929 Geneva Convention on the Wounded and Sick. This text was retained and extended under the present Article 44 to include vehicles used as ambulances.[61] Acknowledging that the possibility of using the emblem in such ways could be open to abuse, the 1929 Diplomatic Conference laid down stringent safeguards that were preserved in the 1949 text. In particular, the paragraph refers only to use of the

---

[57] For example, where such use may contravene the requirements set out under the 1991 Emblem Regulations.

[58] The ICRC reports that, on the whole, it has not run into difficulties when displaying the emblem. However, in exceptional circumstances in which the ICRC and/or the emblem (or the ICRC's logo) might be perceived as having certain connotations that could endanger its staff, it may decide not to use the red cross emblem (whether as a protective or as an indicative device). Such a decision would be based only on operational necessity, taking into account the consistency of the ICRC approach in the field (ICRC, *Study on the Use of the Emblems*, p. 152).

[59] In practice, to date, neither the ICRC nor the International Federation has used the red crystal emblem. In addition, preambular paragraph 10 of Additional Protocol III notes the determination of the ICRC and the International Federation (as well as of the Movement) to retain their current names and emblems. The ICRC has stated that 'it may be necessary for combatants and civilians during armed conflicts, as well as for the civilian population in general, to become familiar with the red crystal as a new protective device' before the ICRC would take the exceptional decision to display it in the field (ICRC, *Study on the Use of the Emblems*, p. 153).

[60] Article 53(1) of the First Convention sets out the broad prohibition on the use of the emblem by a range of third parties, other than those entitled to do so under the Convention.

[61] Both the 1929 and the updated 1949 texts must be understood in the context of relevant practical developments during these periods. While in 1929 the Diplomatic Conference acknowledged the benefits of allowing use of the emblem (subject to the permission of the National Society) on first-aid stations providing free treatment (for example along roadsides and at public events), by 1949 the increasing introduction of motor ambulances and the perceived need for these to be clearly and uniformly marked compelled the Diplomatic Conference to grant the same permission to such vehicles. This extension reflected the apparent practice in the marking of ambulances that had arisen at that time; see Pictet (ed.), *Commentary on the First Geneva Convention*, ICRC, 1952, p. 337.

emblem in peacetime, precluding the possibility of such ambulances and aid stations being marked in time of armed conflict (and therefore avoiding any potential confusion with the use of the emblem as a protective device in such circumstances).[62] In addition, the treatment provided in such cases must be free and exclusively available to the wounded and sick, and the emblem may not be used on any items or objects other than those specified in the paragraph.[63]

2692   Paragraph 4 stipulates that the emblem may be employed for the aforementioned purposes only where they are in conformity with national legislation. In effect, States can limit the scope of this paragraph or introduce extra safeguards through such measures.[64] In addition, express authorization must be given by the National Red Cross or Red Crescent Society,[65] effectively conferring on such Societies a public function not shared by any other organization.

2693   There is evidence that, in some countries, the emblem is used by third-party organizations to provide treatment to the general population in peacetime.[66] However, it is not clear whether these instances are always in conformity with Article 44(4) (and in some cases they may constitute improper use of the emblem).[67] On occasion, the ICRC is approached by a National

---

[62] This means that, where the emblem has been authorized for use in accordance with Article 44(4), the sign must be removed from all such aid stations and ambulances during situations of armed conflict covered by the Geneva Conventions.

[63] Article 44(4) explicitly states that use of the emblem on such aid stations and ambulances, subject to certain conditions, is an 'exceptional measure'. In addition to aid stations and ambulances, Pictet noted that, in some countries, the emblem also appeared on first-aid kits kept in public buildings, on public transport and in large stores and factories, and considered that such use did not infringe 'either the spirit or the letter of the Convention' (although display of the emblem on first-aid kits sold commercially for private use would do so); Pictet (ed.), *Commentary on the First Geneva Convention*, ICRC, 1952, p. 338. Today, one could consider that use of the emblem on freely available public first-aid kits is not an acceptable practical extension of paragraph 4 (and may in any event be limited by national legislation). This is in part owing to the development of specific and widely used symbols to represent, for example, first aid (often a white cross on a green background, accompanied by the words 'First Aid'). The benefits of restricting use of paragraph 4 and of employing other appropriate signs (such as a suitable first-aid sign) for aid stations and ambulances are addressed in para. 2694.

[64] For example, a State may wish to stipulate further supervisory procedures or to exclude such use entirely. For instance, in the United Kingdom, no third-party organizations are permitted to use the emblem in this way.

[65] A plain reading of the text may give the impression that any National Society can provide authorization, but it is clear that the intention is to confer this responsibility on the National Society of the territory in question.

[66] For example, in the National Society emblem survey, the Swiss Red Cross reported that the red cross emblem is used on free first-aid tents at major events (which appears to conform to Article 44(4)). The survey also revealed that the purpose and application of this paragraph may not be well understood; for example, while several National Societies reported that they had authorized certain third parties to use the emblem in conformity with paragraph 4, further information revealed that many of these cases concerned services delivered by a government department or a public body or by entities controlled by or affiliated with the National Society (in some instances a fee was also charged).

[67] In one case, such improper use is enshrined in an international treaty. The 1968 UN Convention on Road Signs and Signals (as well the 1971 European Agreement supplementing the Convention) includes two road signs that wrongly display the emblem: the first is a road sign for first-aid stations and the second is a road sign for civilian hospitals. These road signs are in use in some countries, including Norway and Sweden. The ICRC considers that these provisions of

Society to provide guidance on whether, for example, a specific third party providing ambulance or other relevant services should be permitted to use the emblem. Although paragraph 4 provides for a limited possibility of doing so, the ICRC prefers that such situations be avoided, in order to prevent potentially widespread use of the emblem.[68]

2694   Today, it would seem that there are sound reasons for paragraph 4 to be limited in application, to the extent possible. The purpose of this text, when first introduced and later extended, appears to have been to reflect the increasing improvement in a number of countries in the provision of public first-aid and medical services (such as the introduction of ambulance services) in the first half of the 20th century. In many States these activities are becoming increasingly sophisticated and professionalized, and can involve a range of public and private actors.[69] Given the growth and diversity of these services, restricting the application of paragraph 4 helps to avoid excessive use of the emblem and thereby to preserve its special meaning and unique status.

2695   In addition, considerable effort has been made in recent years in a number of countries to encourage use of dedicated symbols for first-aid activities and for a variety of medical services. For example, in some countries, first aid is now marked with an official sign recognized for that purpose, often incorporating a white cross on a green background.[70] The 'star of life' is also used in some countries to identify emergency medical services, including ambulances.[71] The increasing acceptance and use of such symbols, some of which have been subject to formal recognition and/or standardization at a national, in some cases regional, and even international, level, is a very positive development in terms of maintaining the special significance and status of the emblem. States should

---

the UN Convention are not in conformity with the rules on the use of the emblem under the Geneva Conventions (including Article 44(4)), and has recommended that they be modified. As a practical measure, National Societies should encourage their authorities to use the alternative formal sign for civilian hospitals endorsed by the UN Convention (this being a white capital 'H' on a blue background), and to use a different road sign for first-aid stations, such as the first-aid symbol (a white cross on a green background). See ICRC, *Study on the Use of the Emblems*, pp. 195–202.

[68] In its *Study on the Use of the Emblems*, p. 191, the ICRC recommends that National Societies be 'extremely cautious' when considering such authorization under Article 44(4).

[69] For example, in several countries a number of organizations are involved in the provision of and training in first aid. These can include, for instance, the National Red Cross or Red Crescent Society or the Order of St John (Australia, Canada and the United Kingdom). Many countries have no public ambulance service and may rely purely on private organizations (whether commercial or voluntary) to fulfil this function; others may have a single public service, or use a combination of public and private providers.

[70] For example, in the European Union (EU), the official sign for first aid is the white cross on a green ground, normally accompanied by the words 'First Aid'. The European Council Directive 92/58/EEC standardized the appearance of safety signs, including those relating to first aid, across the EU.

[71] The star of life is a blue, six-pointed star with a white border and the 'rod of Aesculapius' (the symbol associated with medical and health care) in the centre of the star. Originally developed in the United States, the star of life is used to mark emergency medical personnel and vehicles (including ambulances and their crews) in some countries, including Canada, Switzerland, the United Kingdom and the United States.

use and encourage greater use of such signs, where appropriate. National Societies should also promote their use and use them for their own relevant activities, as far as possible alongside their official logo.[72] In addition, the appropriate display of alternative symbols introduced for certain functions, such as the first-aid sign, both by components of the Movement and by third parties, will prevent excessive or improper use of the emblem and help to preserve its unique meaning and status.

Select bibliography

Doole, Claire, 'Humanity Inc.', *Red Cross Red Crescent Magazine*, Issue 3, 2012, pp. 4–9.

ICRC, *First Aid in Armed Conflicts and Other Situations of Violence*, ICRC, Geneva, 2006.

– *Study on the Use of the Emblems: Operational and Commercial and Other Non-Operational Issues*, ICRC, Geneva, 2011.

Meyer, Michael A., 'Protecting the emblems in peacetime: The experiences of the British Red Cross Society', *International Review of the Red Cross*, Vol. 29, No. 272, October 1989, pp. 459–464.

Perruchoud, Richard, *Les résolutions des Conférences internationales de la Croix-Rouge*, Henry Dunant Institute, Geneva, 1979.

Reid, Daphne A. and Gilbo, Patrick F., *Beyond Conflict: The International Federation of Red Cross and Red Crescent Societies, 1919–1994*, International Federation of Red Cross and Red Crescent Societies, Geneva, 1997.

---

[72] For example, it would be very helpful for a National Society that provides first-aid services to display on all relevant materials and objects the appropriate official sign for first aid. This could appear in addition to the logo of the National Society (which normally includes the red cross or red crescent emblem, as appropriate, and the Society's name). Such use by the National Society would help to prevent a misconception that the emblem is a general sign of first aid, and also encourage greater use of the first-aid sign by other first-aid providers in their country (thereby helping to discourage improper use of the emblem). This practice is, for example, employed by the British Red Cross Society, and strongly encouraged by the UK Ministry of Defence. It is also recommended by the ICRC (*First Aid in Armed Conflicts and Other Situations of Violence*, pp. 27–28).

EXECUTION OF THE CONVENTION

2696 The articles grouped under Chapter VIII reaffirm the duty of High Contracting Parties under Article 1 to respect and to ensure respect for the Convention, in particular by prescribing certain measures to be taken for the Convention's effective implementation.

2697 Article 45 obligates Parties to a conflict, acting through their commanders-in-chief, to ensure the detailed execution of the Convention and to provide for unforeseen cases, in conformity with the Convention's general principles. The same obligation is contained in Article 46 of the Second Convention.

2698 Article 46 underlines that reprisals against the wounded, sick, personnel, buildings or equipment protected by the Convention are prohibited. The other Conventions similarly prohibit reprisals against persons and objects protected under the relevant Convention.[1]

2699 Article 47 contains the obligation of High Contracting Parties to disseminate the Convention, in peacetime and during armed conflict, as widely as possible in their respective countries and, in particular, to include its study in military and, if possible, civilian instruction programmes. This provision is common to the Conventions.[2]

2700 Article 48 obligates High Contracting Parties to communicate to one another official translations of the Conventions and of the laws and regulations adopted to ensure their application. This provision is common to the Conventions.[3]

2701 An identical section is contained in the Second Convention, as are similar sections in the Third and Fourth Conventions and Additional Protocol I.[4]

---

[1] See Second Convention, Article 47; Third Convention, Article 13; and Fourth Convention, Article 33.

[2] See Second Convention, Article 48; Third Convention, Article 127; and Fourth Convention, Article 144.

[3] See Second Convention, Article 49; Third Convention, Article 128; and Fourth Convention, Article 145.

[4] See Second Convention, Chapter VII (Execution of the Convention); Third Convention, Part VI, Section I (Execution of the Convention, General provisions); and Fourth Convention, Part IV, Section I (Execution of the Convention, General provisions). See also Additional Protocol I, Part V, Section I (Execution of the Conventions and of this Protocol, General provisions).

DETAILED EXECUTION. UNFORESEEN CASES

❖ Text of the provision

Each Party to the conflict, acting through its Commanders-in-Chief, shall ensure the detailed execution of the preceding Articles and provide for unforeseen cases, in conformity with the general principles of the present Convention.

❖ Reservations or declarations

None

Contents

A. Introduction

2702 Article 45, like its mirror provision Article 46 in the Second Convention, underlines the crucial importance of ensuring respect for the Geneva Conventions during armed conflict and emphasizes the particular role of the military authorities in this regard. While it is during armed conflict that the majority of the provisions must actually be put into effect, failure to take adequate measures during peacetime to ensure their execution directly jeopardizes their observance.

2703   Given that the application of the Conventions in conflict situations falls to a large extent within the scope of responsibility of the military authorities, it is particularly important for commanders of the armed forces to ensure that, in conformity with this article, military doctrine integrates the detailed execution of the Conventions and provides for unforeseen cases.

2704   The obligation in Article 45 to take all necessary measures of execution usefully complements common Article 1 of the four Conventions: 'The High Contracting Parties undertake to respect and to ensure respect for the present Convention in all circumstances.'[1] The general undertaking in common Article 1 'to respect and to ensure respect' is translated into more concrete obligations by a number of other provisions, among which the present article occupies an important place.[2] It deals with one particular aspect of the duty of implementation, namely the obligation to ensure the detailed execution of the Convention during armed conflict through the military chain of command. It thereby focuses on a crucial period of the implementation process, during which a lack of commitment of the Parties to the conflict and their military authorities to ensuring respect for the rules therein may directly translate into violations of the Convention.

2705   It is therefore essential to ensure that respect for international humanitarian law is firmly integrated into the operational practice of the armed forces. This must already be done in peacetime by incorporating respect for humanitarian law into military doctrine, education, training and equipment, and sanctions.[3]

B. Historical background

2706 The obligation to ensure the detailed execution of the Convention and to provide for unforeseen cases has a number of predecessors in earlier treaties. Article 45 largely reproduces the text of Article 26 of the 1929 Geneva

---

[1] See 30th International Conference of the Red Cross and Red Crescent, Geneva, 2007, Res. 3, para. 21, which 'recalls that the obligation to respect international humanitarian law cannot be fulfilled without domestic implementation of international obligations and therefore *reiterates* the need for States to adopt all the legislative, regulatory and practical measures that are necessary to incorporate international humanitarian law into domestic law and practice'.

[2] See also e.g. Articles 47 on dissemination and 48 on communication of translations. For further details, see the commentary on common Article 1.

[3] See ICRC, *Handbook on International Rules Governing Military Operations*, pp. 27–39.

Convention on the Wounded and Sick.[4] A similar provision is to be found in the 1906 Geneva Convention,[5] and even in the 1864 Geneva Convention.[6]

2707   One important difference exists, however, between the present provision and its predecessors. The earlier provisions primarily stipulated obligations of the commanders-in-chief and, by obligating them to act in accordance with the instructions of their respective governments, only hinted at the ultimate responsibility of the Parties to the conflict.[7] The present provision, on the contrary, improves on the previous texts by clearly designating the Parties to the conflict as the responsible entities, mentioning the commanders-in-chief as the organs entrusted with ensuring the detailed execution of the Convention and providing for unforeseen cases.

C. Discussion

1. Scope of application

a. Detailed execution of the Convention during armed conflict

2708   The obligation to ensure the detailed execution of the Convention and to provide for unforeseen cases is addressed to '[e]ach Party to the conflict' rather than to '[t]he High Contracting Parties' more generally, as is the case, for example, in Articles 47 (dissemination) and 48 (translations, implementing laws and regulations). Hence, it applies only to the Convention's execution during armed conflict and thus only to one part of the broader spectrum of necessary measures of implementation. This does not mean, however, that there is no obligation on the High Contracting Parties to take the necessary preparatory measures prior to the outbreak of an armed conflict. That obligation flows from the undertaking to respect and to ensure respect for the Conventions expressed in common Article 1 and a number of specific provisions.[8] Therefore, even though this

---

[4] Geneva Convention on the Wounded and Sick (1929), Article 26: 'The Commanders-in-Chief of belligerent armies shall arrange the details for carrying out the preceding articles as well as for cases not provided for in accordance with the instructions of their respective Governments and in conformity with the general principles of the present Convention.'

[5] Geneva Convention (1906), Article 25: 'It shall be the duty of the commanders in chief of the belligerent armies to provide for the details of execution of the foregoing articles, as well as for unforeseen cases, in accordance with the instructions of their respective governments, and conformably to the general principles of this convention.'

[6] Geneva Convention (1864), Article 8: 'The implementing of the present Convention shall be arranged by the Commanders-in-Chief of the belligerent armies following the instructions of their respective Governments and in accordance with the general principles set forth in this Convention.'

[7] See also Des Gouttes, *Commentaire de la Convention de Genève de 1929 sur les blessés et malades*, ICRC, 1930, pp. 191–192, identifying as one of the obligations of the commanders-in-chief: 'recevoir les instructions de leurs gouvernements, car ce sont ces derniers qui portent en définitive la responsabilité' ('to receive instructions from their governments, for it is the latter which ultimately bear the responsibility').

[8] For more details on 'the provisions which shall be implemented in peacetime', see the commentary on common Article 2, section C.

article places particular emphasis on the obligation of ensuring compliance during conflict situations, it is without prejudice to the preparatory measures which are central to faithful adherence to humanitarian law during actual armed conflict.

2709   Each Party to the conflict must ensure the detailed execution of 'the preceding Articles'. Based on the ordinary meaning of these words, this formulation covers all the provisions of the Convention, including common Article 3. Given that Article 3 contains obligations for both State and non-State Parties to a conflict, Article 45 should be construed as covering non-State Parties as well.

b. Ensuring the execution of the Convention by the military authorities

2710   Article 45 requires each Party to the conflict 'acting through its Commanders-in-Chief' to ensure the detailed execution of the Convention. The Conventions do not define the notion of 'Commanders-in-Chief'. The reference to the commanders-in-chief in the plural indicates that the term does not denote just the supreme commander of the armed forces, nor is it limited to the highest level of command; it refers the military command generally.[9] This is also how the term is used in the Second Convention.[10] This broad understanding of the notion of 'Commanders-in-Chief' corresponds to the purpose of Article 45, i.e. to commit Parties to effectively ensuring respect for the Convention's provisions through the military chain of command, and to the increasing emphasis on the role played by military commanders at all levels in this respect.[11] Pursuant to Article 13(2) of the First Convention, the obligation to ensure the detailed execution of the Convention extends to commanders of militias and volunteer corps outside the regular command structure of the State armed forces.

2711   Article 45 specifically designates commanders-in-chief as the agents through which the Parties to the conflict must ensure the detailed execution of the

---

[9] See de Mulinen, 1982, p. 35: 'Article 45 of the First Geneva Convention gives a guide-line showing, below the general responsibility of the State, the role to be played by the military command.' See also Weston D. Burnett, 'Command Responsibility and a Case Study of the Criminal Responsibility of Israeli Military Commanders for the Pogrom at Shatila and Sabra', *Military Law Review*, Vol. 107, 1985, pp. 71–189, at 136–137:

> The use of the term 'commander-in-chief' today denotes a very high-level commander who is likely to be far from the scene of actual hostilities and unable to control fast breaking events in the battle-front. The commanders-in-chief contemplated by the Geneva Conventions, however, are those who are responsible for taking '*action on the spot* during the fighting, to ensure respect and protection for the wounded, sick, and shipwrecked...,' including seeing to it that the enemy's sick bays are protected during the fighting. Clearly, the military commander contemplated is the senior officer commanding at or near the battlefront, not a military commander far removed from the scene of the actual fighting.

[10] See Second Convention, Article 37(1).

[11] See e.g. Additional Protocol I, Articles 80(2) and 87. For the criminal responsibility of commanders, see also ICRC Study on Customary International Humanitarian Law (2005), Rules 152 and 153.

Convention and provide for unforeseen cases. This exclusive reference to the military authorities is not surprising as the implementation of the Convention is primarily the responsibility of the armed forces.[12] Military authorities are in fact in a unique position to ensure and enforce compliance with the Conventions by means of orders and instructions to subordinate levels of the military hierarchy, close supervision of their execution, and sanctions in case of breaches.

2712   Although for practical reasons commanders are singled out as the primary agents responsible for ensuring compliance, ultimate responsibility under international law lies with the Parties to the conflict. They must answer for any failure on the part of their military authorities to exercise their duties and must take the necessary measures to ensure that the Conventions are observed. Hence, each Party to the conflict remains fully responsible for the acts and omissions of its commanders-in-chief and is, consequently, bound to ensure that these actually take the necessary measures of execution.[13]

2713   Even though the present provision does not as such create individual obligations for commanders-in-chief, they may also be personally responsible for violations committed pursuant to their orders, as well as for a failure to take all necessary and reasonable measures to prevent war crimes from being committed by their subordinates or, if such crimes have been committed, to punish the perpetrators.[14]

2714   Although Article 45 does not address this, the Parties to the conflict may decide to delegate certain tasks to civilian authorities.[15] In such a case, the Parties to the conflict remain bound by the general rules, in particular common Article 1, to ensure respect for the Conventions by and through such civilian authorities.

c. Absence of a similar provision in the Third and Fourth Conventions

2715   This provision appears only in the first two Conventions (see also Article 46 of the Second Convention), and the possibility of inserting a corresponding article in the Third and Fourth Conventions was apparently never considered. The earlier 1929 Geneva Convention on Prisoners of War similarly did not contain a provision equivalent to Article 26 of the 1929 Geneva Convention on the Wounded and Sick. It seems, therefore, that the current disparity is essentially inherited from the 1929 Conventions.

---

[12] See e.g. Articles 18 ('The military authorities may appeal') and 39 ('Under the direction of the competent military authority').

[13] See also Hague Convention (IV) (1907), Article 3; Additional Protocol I, Article 91; Draft Articles on State Responsibility (2001), Article 4; and ICRC Study on Customary International Humanitarian Law (2005), Rule 149.

[14] See Additional Protocol I, Articles 86(2) and 87, and ICRC Study on Customary International Humanitarian Law (2005), Rules 152 and 153.

[15] See e.g. de Mulinen, 1984, pp. 446–447: 'Whereas the first *Hague* and *Geneva Conventions* were essentially restricted to the military field, modern law of war is addressing more and more also *civilian authorities and individuals*.'

2716   However, the 1929 Geneva Convention on Prisoners of War required that each prisoner-of-war camp 'be placed under the authority of a *responsible officer*',[16] thereby indicating the responsibility of the military to ensure the execution of the provisions relating to such camps. This interpretation is confirmed by the Third Convention, which specifies that a commissioned officer 'shall be responsible, under the direction of his government, for [the Convention's] application'.[17] A similar provision exists in the Fourth Convention for internment camps.[18] More generally, both the Third and Fourth Conventions provide for the responsibility of the High Contracting Parties for the treatment accorded to protected persons by their agents.[19] When read together with common Article 1, this implies an obligation on the State to ensure observance of the Conventions by and through its agents.

2717   Additional Protocol I, meanwhile, provides for the obligation to take measures of execution in a comprehensive manner covering both the Protocol and the four Conventions: 'The High Contracting Parties and the Parties to the conflict shall without delay take all necessary measures for the execution of their obligations under the Conventions and this Protocol.'[20]

2. The obligations flowing from Article 45

a. The obligation to ensure the detailed execution of the Convention

2718   The obligation to ensure the detailed execution of the Convention concerns its application in actual conflict situations. This task falls primarily on the armed forces as the provisions of the Convention concern first and foremost personnel within the military chain of command. This means that military commanders must take the decisions required by the Convention, give orders and instructions to ensure their execution, supervise compliance and ensure, if breaches have been committed, that disciplinary and, if necessary, penal sanctions are imposed.[21] Through their authority to issue orders and instructions, backed up by an effective system of sanctions, military commanders are able to exercise effective command and control over subordinate levels. This authority must be used to ensure the detailed execution of the Convention.

2719   To make this possible, preparatory work on military doctrine is of paramount importance. 'Doctrine' is understood as all standard principles that guide the action of armed forces at the strategic, operational and tactical levels. It therefore encompasses all directives, policies, procedures, codes of conduct and reference manuals, on which the military are educated and trained during their careers, giving them a common vocabulary and shaping the decision-making

---

[16] Geneva Convention on Prisoners of War (1929), Article 18(1) (emphasis added).
[17] Third Convention, Article 39(1); see also Article 56(2) (Labour detachments).
[18] Fourth Convention, Article 99(1); see also Article 96 (Labour detachments).
[19] Third Convention, Article 12(1), and Fourth Convention, Article 29.
[20] Additional Protocol I, Article 80.   [21] See also Article 49.

process, tactics and behaviour in operations.[22] Doctrine offers the 'standard solution' to commanders as they face new challenges and, while it does not contain all the answers, it does provide the frame for military thinking and decision-making. The obligation to ensure the detailed execution of the Convention, read together with common Article 1, implies, therefore, an obligation to ensure that military doctrine is in conformity with the Convention.

2720   Practically every provision of the First Convention requires implementing measures after the outbreak of an armed conflict in order to ensure the Convention's detailed execution. These measures include:

- *Ensuring respect for and protection of protected persons and objects*: For a commander, this entails issuing orders and instructions to respect and protect the wounded and sick pursuant to Article 12(1) and supervising the execution of these orders and instructions during operations. They must do the same for other persons and objects protected under the First Convention.[23]
- *Fixing the proportion of medical personnel and equipment to be left with abandoned wounded or sick persons*: In the case that wounded or sick persons have to be abandoned to the enemy, it is obligatory, pursuant to Article 12(5), to leave with them medical personnel and material to assist in their care.
- *Organizing search and rescue operations*: It is a requirement, pursuant to Article 15(1), to organize, without delay, the search for and collection of the wounded and sick and the search for the dead.
- *Concluding an armistice, suspension of fire or local arrangement*: Whenever circumstances permit, this entails, pursuant to Article 15(2)–(3), concluding an armistice, suspension of fire or local arrangement to permit the removal, exchange and transport of the wounded left on the battlefield, and likewise concluding a local arrangement for the removal or exchange of the wounded and sick from a besieged or encircled area, and for the passage of medical and religious personnel and equipment on their way to that area.
- *Appealing to private persons*: This involves appealing to the charity of the inhabitants voluntarily to collect and care for the wounded and sick, under the direction of the military authorities, pursuant to Article 18(1), or permitting inhabitants and relief societies spontaneously to collect and care for the wounded and sick, pursuant to Article 18(2).
- *Ensuring that inhabitants and personnel of relief societies who collect and care for the wounded and sick are not molested or convicted*: Military commanders must take measures to ensure that, pursuant to Article 18(3),

---

[22] ICRC, *Integrating the Law*, p. 23; *Handbook on International Rules Governing Military Operations*, pp. 30–31.
[23] See Articles 19–23 (medical units, establishments, hospital zones and localities), Articles 24–27 (medical and auxiliary personnel), Articles 33–34 (buildings and material) and Articles 35–37 (medical transports).

such persons are not harmed, harassed, persecuted or convicted for having
nursed the wounded or sick.

– *Regulating the use of weapons by medical personnel and units in case a decision is made to authorize them to be so equipped*: Military medical personnel
and units may be authorized by their commanders to be equipped with light
individual weapons for self-defence or the defence of the wounded and sick
in their charge.[24]

– *Determining the fate of captured medical or religious personnel*: If such personnel fall into their hands, it is the role of military commanders to determine the percentage of medical or religious personnel to be retained pursuant
to Article 28(1), possibly by special agreement, as provided for in Article 31(2).

– *Arranging the return of personnel whose retention is not indispensable*: Military commanders must, pursuant to Article 30(1), ensure that such personnel
are returned as soon as a road is open for their return and military requirements permit.

– *Ensuring the proper use of the emblem and preventing its misuse*: This
entails, pursuant to Articles 38–44 and 53–54, ensuring appropriate marking
of medical personnel, buildings and equipment, regulating the circumstances
in which they will not be marked and taking measures to prevent misuse of
the emblem.

b. The obligation to provide for unforeseen cases

2721   Article 45 also requires each Party to the conflict, acting through its
commanders-in-chief, to provide for unforeseen cases, in conformity with the
general principles of the Convention. This takes account of the fact that the
Convention, even though it contains detailed provisions, cannot provide an
answer for every possible question that may arise in practice. Three examples
illustrate this point.[25]

2722   The first example concerns the interplay between Articles 28 and 29 of the
First Convention. According to Article 28, 'permanent' personnel designated in
Articles 24 and 26 who fall into the hands of the adverse Party may be retained
only 'in so far as the state of health, the spiritual needs and the number of prisoners of war require'. According to Article 29, on the other hand, 'auxiliary'
personnel designated in Article 25 who fall into the hands of the adverse Party

---

[24] For more details on the arming of medical personnel, see the commentary on Article 22, section
C, and on Article 24, paras 2005–2006.

[25] On the meaning of 'unforeseen cases', see also de Mulinen, 1987, p. 172:

[E]ven with a strategic approach, it will not always be possible to solve all problems immediately. Some gaps will remain, particularly for forces fighting under unusual conditions, such as
a hostile natural environment, the possibly very different tactics and means of combat used
by opposing forces, fighting in the enemy's rear or in encircled areas, long and/or difficult
transportation, supply and evacuation routes. It is part of the responsibility of the commanders concerned to fill such remaining gaps by 'providing for unforeseen cases, in conformity
with the general principles of the law of war'.

qualify as prisoners of war 'but shall be employed on their medical duties in so far as the need arises'. It remains to be determined, however, whether the presence of 'auxiliary' personnel in a prisoner-of-war camp should entail a reduction in the number of permanent medical personnel retained. In the absence of any special agreements in the sense of Article 31(2), the matter must be left to the judgment of the Detaining Power, exercised in conformity with the general principles of the Convention.[26]

2723   The second example lies in the fact that the First Convention does not specify the status of 'auxiliary' personnel in enemy hands during the time they are employed on medical duties on the basis of Article 29. In the absence of a detailed regulation on the matter, their situation seems to correspond best to Article 32 of the Third Convention. This provision applies to prisoners who, though not attached to the medical service of their armed forces, are physicians, surgeons, dentists, nurses or medical orderlies. According to this provision, they 'may be required by the Detaining Power to exercise their medical functions in the interests of prisoners of war' but they are 'exempted from any other work under Article 49 [of the Third Convention]'.[27]

2724   The last example concerns the protection of religious objects used by religious personnel, for which no specific regulation exists in the First Convention, unlike the regulation of medical units and establishments under Articles 19 and 33. In the light of the duty to respect and protect religious personnel under Article 24, it seems, however, that religious objects used by such personnel should similarly be respected and protected.[28]

2725   To the extent that these 'unforeseen cases' may be identified before the outbreak of an armed conflict, as is the case for the three examples given above, and to the extent that this is both possible and reasonable, the High Contracting Parties should already in peacetime provide for these cases in a general manner in their military doctrine, education and training. This ensures that in actual conflict situations these cases will be dealt with in a consistent manner and in accordance with the general principles of the Convention.

c. The general principles of the Convention

2726   Article 45 requires the Parties to the conflict to ensure the detailed execution of the preceding articles and to provide for unforeseen cases, 'in conformity with the general principles of the present Convention'. This wording indicates that

---

[26] An arrangement is proposed in Article 7 of the Model Agreement Relating to the Retention of Medical Personnel and Chaplains, drafted by the ICRC in 1955 pursuant to Resolution 3 of the 1949 Diplomatic Conference.

[27] Third Convention, Article 32. See also the commentary on Article 29 of the First Convention, section C.2.

[28] Protection of religious equipment is also implied in Article 15(3), which foresees the conclusion of local arrangements 'for the passage of medical and religious personnel and equipment' to besieged or encircled areas.

the principles of the Convention govern not only unforeseen cases, but also the execution of the treaty more generally.[29] This interpretation is supported by the fact that Article 8 of the 1864 Geneva Convention, as one of the predecessor provisions, referred to the general principles of the Convention, even though it did not yet mention unforeseen cases.[30]

2727   The general principles of the Convention correspond to the fundamental ideas from which the more specific stipulations are derived. They include, in particular:

- *Respect for and protection of the wounded and sick*: The wounded and sick must be respected and protected in all circumstances, treated humanely and cared for by the Party to the conflict in whose power they may be, without any adverse distinction founded on sex, race, nationality, religion, political opinions, or any other similar criteria (see Article 12(1)–(2)). They must be searched for and collected, protected against pillage and ill-treatment (see Article 15(1)). In addition, no one may ever be molested or convicted for having nursed the wounded and sick (see Article 18(3)).
- *Respect for the dead*: The dead must be searched and protected from despoliation (see Article 15(1)). They are entitled to an honorable burial and respect for their graves (see Article 17(3)).
- *Prevention of persons going missing*: Any particulars which may assist in the identification of the wounded, the sick or the dead must be recorded (see Article 16(1)–(2)). Burial of the dead must be preceded by a careful examination with a view to establishing their identity and their graves must be properly marked and their location recorded (see Article 17(1) and (3)).
- *Respect for and protection of medical and religious personnel*: Medical and religious personnel assigned to the armed forces, including auxiliary personnel under certain circumstances, must at all times be respected and protected by the Parties to the conflict (see Articles 24–27).
- *Respect for and protection of medical units and transports*: Medical units and transports may not be attacked but must at all times be respected and protected by the Parties to the conflict (see Articles 19–20 and 35–37).
- *Respect for and control of the use of the emblems and prevention of their misuse at all times* (see Articles 38–44 and 53–54).

2728   These principles should inform decisions of military commanders when they encounter cases not foreseen by the Conventions. This requirement can also be seen as a reflection of the obligation under general international law to apply a treaty in good faith.[31]

---

[29] See also Des Gouttes, p. 192: 'Il faut que l'esprit de la Convention plane sur toute son exécution, même dans les détails.' ('The spirit of the Convention must infuse every aspect of its implementation, even in the details.')

[30] See also Geneva Convention on the Wounded and Sick (1929), Article 26.

[31] Vienna Convention on the Law of Treaties (1969), Article 26.

Select bibliography

de Mulinen, Frédéric, 'Law of War and Armed Forces', *The Military Law and the Law of War Review*, Vol. 21, 1982, pp. 35–48.
– 'Transformation of modern law of war into documents for practical application', in Christophe Swinarski (ed.), *Studies and Essays on International Humanitarian Law and Red Cross Principles in Honour of Jean Pictet*, ICRC/Martinus Nijhoff Publishers, The Hague, 1984, pp. 445–455.
– 'Law of war training within armed forces. Twenty years experience', *International Review of the Red Cross*, Vol. 27, No. 257, April 1987, pp. 168–179.
ICRC, *Integrating the Law*, ICRC, Geneva, 2007.
– *Handbook on International Rules Governing Military Operations*, ICRC, Geneva, 2013.

ARTICLE 46

PROHIBITION OF REPRISALS

❖ Text of the provision

Reprisals against the wounded, sick, personnel, buildings or equipment protected by the Convention are prohibited.

❖ Reservations or declarations

None

Contents

A. Introduction and definition of the concept of reprisal

2729 Traditionally, international law did not contain a centralized enforcement mechanism. It was against this background that injured States resorted to reprisals as a self-help or self-protection measure. Reprisals would be contrary to international law unless they were taken by the injured State in response to an internationally wrongful act committed by a responsible State, in order to induce the latter to comply with its obligations. 'Reprisal' or 'belligerent reprisal' is the term commonly used in the context of international armed conflict, whereas they have become known as 'countermeasures' outside of this context.[1]

2730   A distinction is generally made between reprisals and retorsion. Retorsion is an unfriendly but lawful measure taken in response to another State's unfriendly or unlawful act. Examples of retorsion would be the severance of diplomatic or consular relations, suspension of air, sea, land or other means of transport or the withdrawal of voluntary aid programmes.[2]

---

[1] For more details on the concept of countermeasures, see the commentary on the 2001 Draft Articles on State Responsibility, pp. 128–139.
[2] See the definition of 'retorsion' given by the ILC, *ibid.* p. 128.

2731   Belligerent reprisals are measures taken in the context of an international armed conflict by a Party in reaction to a violation of international humanitarian law by an adversary.[3] Such measures may not be carried out for the purpose of revenge or punishment, but only with the aim of putting an end to such violations and inducing the adversary to comply with the law.[4] Although the acts constituting belligerent reprisals are in principle unlawful, their wrongfulness is precluded because of the particular circumstances in which they are taken, i.e. in response to a violation committed by an adversary.[5]

2732   Furthermore, reprisals may be carried out only as a measure of last resort, when no other lawful measures are available to induce the adversary to respect the law.[6] Reprisals must cease as soon as the adversary again complies with the law.[7] Lastly, it is largely recognized that reprisal action must be proportionate to the violation it aims to stop.[8] Case law from the Second World War and the ICTY rejected the claim that clearly disproportionate actions in response to the original violation could amount to lawful reprisals.[9]

B. Historical background

2733   Belligerent reprisals have constituted the most important means of coercion available to States, in particular in the conduct of hostilities.[10] The availability

---

[3]   In this commentary, the word 'reprisal' is used as a synonym for 'belligerent reprisal'. For the applicability of this concept in non-international armed conflict, see the commentary on common Article 3, section M.6.

[4]   Reprisals should therefore be directed at the adversary who violated international humanitarian law, and may not be directed against allies of the State which committed the violation. See Henckaerts/Doswald-Beck, commentary on Rule 145, p. 513: 'There is limited practice allowing reprisals against allies of the violating State but it dates back to ... 1930 and to the Second World War. Practice since then appears to indicate that resort to such reprisals is no longer valid.'

[5]   See *ibid.* p. 513. For the historical background on the evolution of the concept of reprisals, see Barsalou, pp. 335–347; Kwakwa, pp. 52–58; and Kalshoven.

[6]   See the case law, mainly for the Second World War, in Henckaerts/Doswald-Beck, commentary on Rule 145, p. 516. See also Greenwood, p. 232; Sandoz/Swinarski/Zimmermann (eds), *Commentary on the Additional Protocols*, 1987, para. 3457; and Darcy, pp. 193–194. In *Kupreškić*, the ICTY also stated that reprisals may be carried out only after a warning to the adverse Party requiring cessation of the violation has remained unheeded; see *Kupreškić* Trial Judgment, 2000, para. 535, and *Martić* Trial Judgment, 2007, para. 466.

[7]   This aspect was already included in the 1880 Oxford Manual and appears consistently in military manuals, official statements and State practice. See Henckaerts/Doswald-Beck, commentary on Rule 145, p. 518.

[8]   *Ibid.* p. 517. It has been stated that, '[R]eprisals should exceed neither what is proportionate to the prior violation nor what is necessary if they are to achieve their aims'; Greenwood, pp. 230–231.

[9]   See Italy, Military Tribunal of Rome, *Kappler case*, Judgment, 1948; Military Tribunal of Rome, *Hass and Priebke case*, Judgment in Trial of First Instance, 1997, Section 4; Netherlands, Special Court (War Criminals) at The Hague, *Rauter case*, Judgment, 1948, pp. 129–138; and United States, Military Tribunal at Nuremberg, *Hostages case*, Judgment, 1948, p. 61. See also Special Arbitral Tribunal, *Naulilaa case*, 1928, pp. 1025–1028, as well as ICTY, *Kupreškić* Trial Judgment, 2000, para. 535, and *Martić* Trial Judgment, 2007, paras 466–468.

[10]   Sandoz/Swinarski/Zimmermann (eds), *Commentary on the Additional Protocols*, 1987, para. 3428.

of reprisals may persuade an adversary not to commit violations of the law in the first place, and in general, the threat of reprisal is also seen as an important deterrent in international law.[11]

2734   Various attempts to consolidate and develop the legal regime applicable to reprisals in the context of the international law of armed conflict were undertaken without reaching the stage of adopting treaty rules.[12] Mention should be made of the draft submitted by Russia at the Brussels Conference of 1874,[13] and the Oxford Manual adopted by the Institute of International Law in 1880.[14] The Peace Conferences held in The Hague in 1899 and 1907 adopted the two successive versions of the Convention respecting the Laws and Customs of War on Land, with annexes. However, they did not address the question of reprisals.[15] Belligerent reprisals were then an accepted feature of the law of war, and their regulation or prohibition was not attainable at the time.[16]

2735   During the First World War, reprisals greatly worsened the fate of victims. In 1916, the ICRC put forward the idea of prohibiting all reprisals against prisoners of war.[17] This initiative succeeded in 1929 with the adoption of Article 2 of the 1929 Geneva Convention on Prisoners of War. In contrast, the 1929 Geneva Convention on the Wounded and Sick is silent on the question of reprisals. Article 2 of the 1929 Convention on Prisoners of War was the first treaty-law provision limiting the category of persons against which reprisals can be taken. This provision did not prevent all reprisals against prisoners of war during the Second World War, though most reprisals or alleged reprisals were committed against the civilian population in occupied territories.[18]

2736   A Commission of Experts was convened by the ICRC in 1937 to study the revision of the 1929 Geneva Convention on the Wounded and Sick. The Commission was of the opinion that a revision of that Convention should include a clause prohibiting reprisals, not only against the wounded and sick and medical personnel, but also, by a logical extension, against material and property

---

[11] On these issues, see Kwakwa, pp. 74–75.

[12] See Sandoz/Swinarski/Zimmermann (eds), *Commentary on the Additional Protocols*, 1987, para. 3432.

[13] See the detailed historical account of this issue by Kalshoven, pp. 45–51. The proposal to adopt an article on reprisal was not accepted by the government experts.

[14] *Ibid.* pp. 51–55. See, in particular, Oxford Manual (1880), Articles 85 and 86.

[15] Kalshoven, pp. 56–66. Neither of these conferences made any major contribution to the clarification of the concept of belligerent reprisals. However, they touched upon the concept of collective punishment contained in Article 50 of the 1899 and 1907 Hague Regulations.

[16] Kalshoven, p. 51.

[17] Sandoz/Swinarski/Zimmermann (eds), *Commentary on the Additional Protocols*, 1987, para. 3434. See the ICRC's 1916 appeal in *Report of the International Committee of the Red Cross on its Activities During the Second World War, September 1, 1939–June 30, 1947, Volume I: General Activities*, ICRC, Geneva, 1948, pp. 365–372; see also Kalshoven, pp. 69–73.

[18] For instances of reprisals against prisoners of war, see Kalshoven, pp. 178–200. See also Darcy, p. 198, and United States, Military Commission at Rome, *Dostler case*, Judgment, 1945. For examples of reprisals against the civilian population of occupied territories, see Kalshoven, pp. 200–210.

intimately bound up with the safeguarding of those concerned.[19] In 1947, the Conference of Government Experts reaffirmed the 'impossibility of admitting that unoffending and defenceless men should be held indirectly responsible for acts committed by their home Governments'.[20]

2737   The Conference accepted the ICRC's proposal to include a prohibition of reprisals in all four draft conventions.[21] The 1949 Diplomatic Conference followed that recommendation without much discussion.[22] The Conference decided to outlaw the taking of reprisals against certain categories of persons and property and at the same time to provide for alternative methods of compliance, such as the institution of Protecting Powers,[23] the conciliation procedure,[24] the obligation to punish persons responsible for grave breaches,[25] and the enquiry procedure.[26]

2738   Measures of reprisal often affect persons not involved in the original violation and could be regarded as contrary to the principle that no one may be punished for an act that he or she has not personally committed; belligerent reprisals often amount to a collective punishment.

2739   Since 1949, belligerent reprisals have not been resorted to widely.[27] No recent examples of belligerent reprisals against persons or property protected under the First Convention could be found. Belligerent reprisals against civilians and civilian objects were resorted to during the Iran-Iraq war, but these reprisals were not covered by the prohibition contained in the Geneva Conventions.[28] The reticence of States to resort to reprisals can be explained by the fact that

---

[19] See ICRC, *Report on the Interpretation, Revision and Extension of the Geneva Convention of July 27, 1929*, Report prepared for the 16th International Conference of the Red Cross, London, 1938, pp. 32–33.

[20] See *Report of the Conference of Government Experts of 1947*, p. 118.

[21] *Ibid.* p. 275 and Pictet (ed.) *Commentary on the First Geneva Convention*, ICRC, 1952, pp. 343–344.

[22] See *Final Record of the Diplomatic Conference of Geneva of 1949*, Vol. II-A, pp. 183–184 and 199, and Kalshoven, pp. 263–272.

[23] See Articles 8 and 10.   [24] See Article 11.   [25] See Article 49.

[26] For the enquiry procedure, see Article 52. These mechanisms have so far remained rather ineffective as alternative methods of compliance. See Greenwood, pp. 238–239; Kwakwa, pp. 76–79; and Darcy, pp. 249–250. Under Additional Protocol I, an International Fact-Finding Commission was established, but it too has yet to be invoked by Parties to an armed conflict.

[27] For some illustrations of the use of belligerent reprisals in the Vietnam War, in the DRC in 1964, or during the armed conflict in Israel-occupied Arab territory, see Kalshoven, pp. 289–321.

[28] See Henckaerts/Doswald-Beck, commentary on Rule 145, pp. 513 and 519. During the Iran-Iraq war, numerous attacks on civilian objects were reported. In 1984, in a message addressed to the Presidents of the Islamic Republic of Iran and the Republic of Iraq, the UN Secretary-General stated that he was profoundly distressed on learning of the heavy civilian casualties caused by the aerial attack on the town of Banesh on 5 June 1984, . . . and the retaliatory and counter-retaliatory attacks that followed on towns in Iran and Iraq.

Deliberate military attacks on civilian areas cannot be condoned by the international community. The initiation of such attacks in the past, and the reprisals and counter-reprisals they provoke, have resulted in mounting loss of life and suffering to innocent and defenceless civilian populations. It is imperative that this immediately cease.

UN Secretary-General, Message dated 9 June 1984 addressed to the Presidents of the Islamic Republic of Iran and the Republic of Iraq, UN Doc. S/16611, 11 June 1984.

they are mostly regarded as an ineffective means of enforcement, in particular because reprisals risk leading to an escalation of violence through repeated reprisals and counter-reprisals.[29]

2740   In treaty law, the trend that began in 1929 towards outlawing the use of reprisals against certain persons and property protected under the Geneva Conventions[30] continued by States Party to Additional Protocol I, with the extension of this prohibition to all civilians, civilian objects, cultural objects and places of worship, objects indispensable to the survival of the civilian population, the natural environment, and works and installations containing dangerous forces.[31]

C. Discussion

2741 Article 46 prohibits the taking of belligerent reprisals against the wounded, the sick and personnel, buildings or equipment protected under the First Convention. Recourse to reprisals would expose protected persons on all sides of an armed conflict to the risk of rapid and disastrous increases in the severity of measures taken against them.

2742   The persons protected under the First Convention are listed in Article 13 (the wounded and sick), Article 15 (the dead), Article 24 (medical and religious personnel attached to the armed forces), Article 25 (auxiliary medical personnel), Article 26 (personnel of aid societies) and Article 27 (medical personnel of societies of neutral countries).[32]

2743   Article 46 is innovative in that it also explicitly forbids the taking of reprisals against buildings or equipment protected by the Convention. The First Convention does not define the concept of protected property as such. It contains a list of objects which cannot be attacked, destroyed or appropriated. Such properties are listed in Articles 19, 33 and 34 (fixed medical establishments and mobile medical units), Article 20 (hospital ships) and Articles 35 and 36 (means of medical transport, including medical aircraft). On the basis of Article 46, such property cannot be made the object of reprisals.[33]

---

[29] See Henckaerts/Doswald-Beck, commentary on Rule 145, p. 514, and Sandoz/Swinarski/Zimmermann (eds), *Commentary on the Additional Protocols*, 1987, para. 3433.

[30] See also Second Convention, Article 47; Third Convention, Article 13; and Fourth Convention, Article 33.

[31] See Additional Protocol I, Articles 51(6), 52(1), 53(c), 54(4), 55(2) and 56(4). See also Additional Protocol I, Article 20, which prohibits reprisals against persons and objects protected by Part II of Additional Protocol I.

[32] See the commentaries on these articles. However, if such protected persons committed acts harmful to the enemy, they would lose their protection and could, as a result, be the object of attack; see the commentary on Article 24, section F.

[33] However, if such property were used to commit acts harmful to the enemy, it would lose its protection against attacks for the time that it is so used; see the commentary on Articles 21 and 22.

2744   The prohibition of reprisals against persons or property protected under this Convention is absolute. It applies in all circumstances.[34] The possibility to derogate from this rule by invoking military necessity is excluded.[35]

2745   This prohibition applies to all forms of reprisals against protected persons or property, including those which would be of the same nature as the initial offence to which it responds. A party to the conflict might be tempted to respond to an offence by taking identical or similar action. Article 46 prohibits such recourse to reprisals against protected persons or property.

2746   Furthermore, Article 46 prohibits all forms of reprisals, and does not limit itself to measures which would amount to an attack against protected persons or property. It also includes measures which would consist of omissions by States to perform particular acts, such as omitting to provide medical assistance and care to the wounded or sick,[36] or to ensure proper burial of the dead.[37]

2747   Furthermore, the 1969 Vienna Convention on the Law of Treaties provides that the possibilities for suspension or termination of a treaty in case of material breach[38] of the treaty by a State Party 'do not apply to provisions relating to the protection of the human person contained in treaties of a humanitarian character, in particular to provisions prohibiting any form of reprisals against persons protected by such treaties'.[39] This article does not apply retroactively to Article 46 of the First Convention.[40] However, the object of this provision is a clear reaffirmation of the prohibition of reprisals against protected persons in all circumstances and the non-opposability of the suspension or termination of the treaty in case of a material breach.[41] The prohibition contained in Article 46 being absolute, it is clear that a material breach of the Geneva Conventions might lead a State to denounce them, but does not give them the right to direct reprisals against persons or property protected under the Geneva Conventions.

2748   The prohibition contained in Article 46 is well established and has been largely respected since 1949. States have outlawed the use of belligerent reprisals against certain categories of persons or property in the 1949 Geneva Conventions and Additional Protocol I, but have refrained from banning

---

[34] For the applicability of the concept of reprisals in non-international armed conflict, see the commentary on common Article 3, section M.6.

[35] On this issue, see Albrecht, pp. 611–612, who concludes that: '[T]he history of the provisions also shows that their object was to prevent reprisals against the enumerated categories of persons and property under all conditions. . . . The Conventions of 1949 must be held to admit of no exception by way of reprisals.'

[36] Pursuant to Article 12 of the First Convention.

[37] Pursuant to Article 17 of the First Convention.

[38] A material breach of a treaty is 'the violation of a provision essential to the accomplishment of the object or purpose of the treaty'; Vienna Convention on the Law of Treaties (1969), Article 60(3).

[39] Ibid. Article 60(5).

[40] See ibid. Article 4 on the non-retroactivity of the provisions of that Convention.

[41] See the proposal made by Switzerland and the motivation behind the inclusion of Article 60(5) in Official Records of the United Nations Conference on the Law of Treaties, First Session, UN Doc. A/CONF.39/C.1/SR.61, in particular pp. 354–359.

belligerent reprisals altogether. The provisions of the Geneva Conventions, along with those of Additional Protocol I, have had the effect of substantially reducing the scope for lawful belligerent reprisals. For States party to those instruments, the only potential objects of belligerent reprisals not protected by a specific treaty provision are military objectives and members of the enemy's armed forces who have neither surrendered nor been incapacitated.[42]

Select bibliography

Albrecht, A.R., 'War Reprisals in the War Crimes Trials and in the Geneva Conventions of 1949', *American Journal of International Law*, Vol. 47, No. 4, October 1953, pp. 590–614.

Almond, Harry H., Jr. and Kalshoven, Frits, 'Reprisals: the Global Community is not yet Ready to Abandon Them', *Proceedings of the Annual Meeting of the American Society of International Law*, Vol. 74, April 1980, pp. 196–202.

Barsalou, Olivier, 'The History of Reprisals Up to 1945: Some Lessons Learned and Unlearned for Contemporary International Law', *The Military Law and the Law of War Review*, Vol. 49, Nos 3–4, 2010, pp. 335–371.

Bierzanek, Remiguisz, 'Reprisals in Armed Conflicts', *Syracuse Journal of International and Comparative Law*, Vol. 14, 1988, pp. 829–843.

Darcy, Shane, 'The Evolution of the Law of Belligerent Reprisals', *Military Law Review*, Vol. 175, March 2003, pp. 184–251.

De Hemptinne, Jérôme, 'Prohibition of Reprisals', in Andrew Clapham, Paola Gaeta and Marco Sassòli (eds), *The 1949 Geneva Conventions: A Commentary*, Oxford University Press, 2015, pp. 576–596.

Greenwood, Christopher, 'Reprisals and Reciprocity in the New Law of Armed Conflict', in Michael A. Meyer (ed.), *Armed conflict and the New Law: Aspects of the 1977 Geneva Protocols and the 1981 Weapons Convention*, British Institute of International and Comparative Law, London, 1989, pp. 227–250.

Henckaerts, Jean-Marie and Doswald-Beck, Louise, *Customary International Humanitarian Law, Volume I: Rules*, ICRC/Cambridge University Press, 2005, available at https://www.icrc.org/customary-ihl/eng/docs/v1.

Kalshoven, Frits, *Belligerent Reprisals*, 2nd edition, Martinus Nijhoff Publishers, Leiden, 2005.

Kwakwa, Edward, 'Belligerent Reprisals in the Law of Armed Conflict', *Stanford Journal of International Law*, Vol. 27, No. 1, Fall 1990, pp. 49–81.

Yk, Brian Sang, 'Legal Regulation of Belligerent Reprisals in International Humanitarian Law: Historical Development and Present Status', *African Yearbook on International Humanitarian Law*, 2012, pp. 134–184.

---

[42] This is without prejudice to the small number of States which made reservations and declarations to Articles 51–55 of Additional Protocol I. For a commentary on these reservations and declarations, see Henckaerts/Doswald-Beck, commentary on Rule 146, p. 521.

DISSEMINATION OF THE CONVENTION

❖ Text of the provision

The High Contracting Parties undertake, in time of peace as in time of war, to disseminate the text of the present Convention as widely as possible in their respective countries, and, in particular, to include the study thereof in their programmes of military and, if possible, civil instruction, so that the principles thereof may become known to the entire population, in particular to the armed fighting forces, the medical personnel and the chaplains.

❖ Reservations or declarations

None

Contents

A. Introduction

2749 Article 47 aims to ensure the widest possible dissemination of the First Geneva Convention by the High Contracting Parties within their respective countries. A similar provision on dissemination is included in all four Geneva Conventions.[1]

---

[1] See Second Convention, Article 48; Third Convention, Article 127(1); and Fourth Convention, Article 144(1).

2750   The task of dissemination is a legal obligation under the Geneva Conventions, and its inclusion was based on the conviction of the drafters that knowledge of the law is an essential condition for its effective application. While it is now recognized that knowledge of the law alone will not prevent violations,[2] spreading knowledge of the law is understood to be an 'important element of any strategy aimed at creating an environment conducive to lawful behaviour'.[3]

2751   Dissemination of international humanitarian law by the High Contracting Parties within their respective countries sends an important signal of a State's support for the law and can thus enhance its respect. Specific guidance by a State in the form of doctrine, education and training on how to apply international humanitarian law provisions in practice further enhances their implementation. The adoption of an effective national sanctions regime for violations also contributes to respect for the law.[4]

2752   Even though the responsibility for dissemination primarily rests with States, dissemination of international humanitarian law represents one of the functions of the ICRC,[5] as well as being a responsibility of National Societies, of their own accord or as assistance in cooperation with their respective States.[6] The Statutes of the International Red Cross and Red Crescent Movement also recognize a role for the International Federation of Red Cross and Red Crescent Societies in this respect.[7]

---

[2] For a detailed discussion of the factors influencing compliance with international humanitarian law, see ICRC, *The Roots of Behaviour in War*; see also ICRC, *Integrating the Law*, p. 15.

[3] ICRC, *Integrating the Law*, p. 17.

[4] See e.g. *ibid.* p. 35, on the relevance of effective sanctions for compliance with the law by weapon bearers.

[5] See Diplomatic Conference, Geneva, 1974–1977, Res. 21, Dissemination of knowledge of international humanitarian law applicable in armed conflicts, paras 2 and 4; see also *Official Records of the Diplomatic Conference of Geneva of 1974–1977*, Vol. I, p. 214.

[6] See Statutes of the International Red Cross and Red Crescent Movement (1986), Article 3, which reads in part: '[National Societies] disseminate and assist their governments in disseminating international humanitarian law; they take initiatives in this respect'. See also Diplomatic Conference, Geneva, 1974–1977, Res. 21, 'Dissemination of knowledge of international humanitarian law applicable in armed conflicts', para. 3, and *Official Records of the Diplomatic Conference of Geneva of 1974–1977*, Vol. I, p. 214. The role of National Societies was further addressed in resolutions adopted by International Conferences of the Red Cross and Red Crescent: see e.g. 26th International Conference of the Red Cross and Red Crescent, Geneva, 1995, Res. 1, International humanitarian law: From law to action, Report on the follow-up to the International Conference for the Protection of War Victims, paras 6 and 8. See, further, 30th International Conference of the Red Cross and Red Crescent, Geneva, 2007, Res. 3, Reaffirmation and implementation of international humanitarian law: Preserving human life and dignity in armed conflict, 2007, preambular para. 15 and para. 27. The role of National Societies in the dissemination of international humanitarian law has also been recognized in forums outside the Movement; see e.g. UN General Assembly, Res. 93, 'Status of the Protocols Additional to the Geneva Conventions of 1949 and relating to the protection of victims of armed conflicts', 14 December 2012, preambular para. 13.

[7] See Statutes of the International Red Cross and Red Crescent Movement (1986), Article 6(4)(j).

B. Historical background

2753 While the importance of spreading knowledge of international humanitarian law among both the armed forces and the civilian population had been recognized before,[8] an obligation for States to instruct their troops and inform the civilian population about the provisions contained in the Conventions was first codified in the 1906 Geneva Convention, the 1907 Hague Convention (X) and the 1929 Geneva Convention on the Wounded and Sick.[9]

2754   During the 1947 Conference of Government Experts, there was nevertheless agreement 'that the [1929 Geneva Convention on the Wounded and Sick] was not sufficiently well known, and that knowledge of this document should form part of the instruction of all members of the armed forces'. The draft article adopted by the Conference of Government Experts therefore emphasized the obligation to make the text of the Convention known both in peacetime and in time of war and expressly referred to the instruction of medical personnel and chaplains.[10]

2755   The draft article subsequently submitted by the ICRC to the 1948 International Conference of the Red Cross in Stockholm already largely resembled Article 47.[11]

2756   This draft was adopted without substantive change, with the exception of the inclusion of a qualifier 'if possible' regarding the incorporation of the study of the Convention in programmes of civil instruction.[12] Similar draft articles had been suggested for the revision of the 1929 Geneva Convention on Prisoners of War and for the new Convention relative to the Protection of Civilian Persons in Time of War, and were adopted without substantive change.[13]

2757   At the 1949 Diplomatic Conference, the ICRC pointed out that the draft article on dissemination as adopted by the Stockholm Conference was

introduced to meet the desire expressed in various quarters that the Convention should be more widely disseminated amongst the public and amongst those who had occasion to apply it or to refer to its provisions. The text of this Article varies lightly according to the Conventions. [The ICRC] proposed to adopt the text as worded in Article 38 of the Wounded and Sick Convention in the manner that the words 'if possible' figure in all the Conventions.[14]

---

[8] See e.g. First International Conference of the Red Cross, Paris, 1867, Vœux de la Conférence Internationale, Article 9, and Oxford Manual (1880), preambular para. 5.

[9] See Geneva Convention (1906), Article 26; Hague Convention (X) (1907), Article 20; and Geneva Convention on the Wounded and Sick (1929), Article 27.

[10] See *Report of the Conference of Government Experts of 1947*, pp. 59–60. An identical draft article was adopted for inclusion in the revision of the 1907 Hague Convention (X); see *ibid.* p. 101.

[11] See *Draft Conventions submitted to the 1948 Stockholm Conference*, draft article 38, p. 27. The same draft article was submitted for the revision of the 1907 Hague Convention (X); see *ibid.* p. 49.

[12] See *Draft Conventions adopted by the 1948 Stockholm Conference*, draft article 38, p. 25.

[13] See *ibid.* pp. 99 and 159.

[14] *Final Record of the Diplomatic Conference of Geneva of 1949*, Vol. II-B, p. 24.

The suggestion to include 'if possible' in all four Geneva Conventions was made in reaction to concerns expressed at the Stockholm Conference that constitutional limitations affecting certain governments in federal States restricted their ability to centrally regulate education matters.[15] A proposal to this effect was unanimously adopted by the Diplomatic Conference.[16]

2758   As a result, practically identical wording was adopted for Article 47 of the First Convention, Article 48 of the Second Convention, Article 127(1) of the Third Convention and Article 144(1) of the Fourth Convention, varying only with respect to the groups of persons to whom the principles of the Conventions should become known 'in particular'.[17] Article 127(2) of the Third Convention and Article 144(2) of the Fourth Convention contain additional obligations to disseminate the Conventions among authorities who in time of war assume responsibility for prisoners of war, and '[a]ny civilian, military, police or other authorities, who in time of war assume responsibilities in respect of protected persons', respectively.[18] Dissemination obligations are also included in Additional Protocol I,[19] Additional Protocol II,[20] and Additional Protocol III.[21] Other treaties of relevance in situations of armed conflict also contain dissemination obligations binding the States that are party to them.[22]

C. The obligation to disseminate

1. Legal obligation for States Parties

2759   The dissemination of the text of the First Convention is a legal obligation for the States party to this Convention. The term 'undertake' underlines the commitment of States to embrace this obligation, which is a corollary of the wider commitment made by States to respect and ensure respect for the Geneva Conventions.[23]

---

[15] See *ICRC Remarks and Proposals on the 1948 Stockholm Draft*, pp. 63–64 and 84.

[16] See *Final Record of the Diplomatic Conference of Geneva of 1949*, Vol. II-B, pp. 70 and 112.

[17] First Convention, Article 47, and Second Convention, Article 48 ('the armed fighting forces, the medical personnel and the chaplains'); Third Convention, Article 127(1) ('all their armed forces and to the entire population'); Fourth Convention, Article 144(1) ('the entire population').

[18] See also Third Convention, Article 41, and Fourth Convention, Article 99, for provisions on dissemination inside prisoner-of-war and internment camps.

[19] See Additional Protocol I, Article 83, as well as Article 6 (Qualified persons), Article 82 (Legal advisers in armed forces) and Article 87(2) (Duty of commanders) of Additional Protocol I.

[20] See Additional Protocol II, Article 19.

[21] See Additional Protocol III, Article 7. For a commentary, see Quéguiner, p. 199.

[22] See e.g. Hague Convention for the Protection of Cultural Property (1954), Article 25; Second Protocol to the Hague Convention for the Protection of Cultural Property (1999), Article 30; Convention on Certain Conventional Weapons (1980), Article 6; Amended Protocol II to the Convention on Certain Conventional Weapons (1996), Article 14; Protocol IV to the Convention on Certain Conventional Weapons (1995), Article 2; Convention on the Rights of the Child (1989), Article 42; and Optional Protocol on the Involvement of Children in Armed Conflict (2000), Article 6. See also ICRC Study on Customary International Humanitarian Law (2005), Rules 141–143.

[23] For more details on the obligation to respect and ensure respect for the Conventions, see the commentary on common Article 1.

2760   Article 47 tasks States Parties with spreading knowledge of the Convention in their respective countries. However, a 'State cannot act of itself'; it is an entity with 'full authority to act under international law', but in order to implement its obligations it must ultimately act through human beings.[24] If it wants to comply with its obligations under the Geneva Conventions, a State must therefore make these obligations known to the persons and groups of persons empowered to exercise elements of governmental authority, as well as persons and groups of persons in fact acting on its instructions or under its direction or control.[25] States need to assign the implementation of the dissemination obligation to their organs, in particular the relevant ministries and subordinate public authorities. Concrete measures, means and mechanisms need to be put in place for that purpose, such as the establishment of education and training structures within the armed forces.[26]

2761   While the main responsibility for the dissemination of the Conventions rests with States, it need not always be State organs that in practice carry out the dissemination activities. Other persons and groups can be given a mandate at the national level to assist the State in the fulfilment of this obligation. National Societies, in particular, can play a role in spreading knowledge of the Geneva Conventions and more generally of the principles of international humanitarian law. This has been explicitly recognized in the Statutes of the International Red Cross and Red Crescent Movement,[27] as well as in national legislation and in National Societies' statutory instruments.[28]

2762   In addition, the promotion of international humanitarian law and the spreading of knowledge of the Geneva Conventions represent one of the key roles of the ICRC.[29] This was reiterated by the Diplomatic Conference in 1977, which invited 'the ICRC to participate actively in the effort to disseminate knowledge of international humanitarian law'.[30] For that purpose, the ICRC has, for

---

[24] See Draft Articles on State Responsibility (2001), commentary on Article 2, p. 35, para. 5.

[25] For descriptions of persons or groups of persons acting on behalf of a State, see *ibid.* draft articles 4, 5 and 8. Actions or omissions by such persons or groups of persons will be attributable to the State and will entail its international responsibility if they constitute a breach of the State's international obligations under the Geneva Conventions; see also draft articles 1–2. For all the types of persons and entities or groups of persons whose conduct is attributable to the State, see draft articles 4–11.

[26] See e.g. ICRC, *Integrating the Law*, pp. 12–13.

[27] See Statutes of the International Red Cross and Red Crescent Movement (1986), Article 3. The Statutes also recognize a role for the International Federation of Red Cross and Red Crescent Societies assisting the National Societies in this respect; see Article 6(3) and (4)(j) of the Statutes.

[28] See e.g. Royal Charter of the British Red Cross Society, approved by Her Majesty the Queen in Council on 22 July 1997 with effect from 1 January 1998 and revised by Her Majesty the Queen in Council on 17 July 2003, para. 5.2; Austria, *Red Cross Protection Law*, 2008, Article 3; Germany, *Red Cross Act*, 2008, Section 2(1)(2); and Statutes of the French Red Cross, 2012, Article 2.

[29] See Statutes of the International Red Cross and Red Crescent Movement (1986) Article 5(2)(g) and (4).

[30] Diplomatic Conference, Geneva, 1974–1977, Res. 21, Dissemination of knowledge of international humanitarian law applicable in armed conflicts, para. 4:

example, specialized delegates assigned to dissemination tasks in the various regions of the world. It develops dissemination programmes and teaching material for armed and security forces, the media, academic circles and young people, and runs campaigns to heighten public awareness of the law.[31]

2763   The promotion of the Geneva Conventions and international humanitarian law more generally also figures in the mandates of national committees on international humanitarian law.[32]

2. Dissemination in time of peace and in time of armed conflict

2764   The obligation of the High Contracting Parties to disseminate the text of the Geneva Conventions as widely as possible in their respective countries applies 'in time of peace as in time of war'. This obligation therefore belongs to those provisions of the Geneva Conventions to be implemented in time of peace.[33]

2765   This ensures that a State Party's dissemination efforts do not start only once an armed conflict has erupted, when the principles underlying international humanitarian law may be more difficult to convey.[34] The teaching of international humanitarian law in time of peace allows for the development of education and training programmes and materials adapted to various audiences and needs. Furthermore, it enables audiences to become acquainted with international humanitarian law over extended periods and contributes to building knowledge of the law and internalizing its principles over time.

2766   Equally, Article 47 obliges States to continue their efforts to promote and spread knowledge about the Conventions and underlying principles after an armed conflict has broken out and to recall the importance of the rules of international humanitarian law in the face of the reality of armed conflict.

> Invites the International Committee of the Red Cross to participate actively in the effort to disseminate knowledge of international humanitarian law by, inter alia:
> (a) publishing material that will assist in teaching international humanitarian law, and circulating appropriate information for the dissemination of the Geneva Conventions and the Protocols,
> (b) organizing, on its own initiative or when requested by Governments or National Societies, seminars and courses on international humanitarian law, and co-operating for that purpose with States and appropriate institutions.

[31] See ICRC, Advisory Service on International Humanitarian Law, 'National Committees for the Implementation of International Humanitarian Law', p. 2.

[32] The creation of such national committees, bringing together, for example, the relevant State ministries, representatives of the armed forces, the legislature and the judiciary, as well as of members of academic circles and the National Society, was one of the recommendations adopted by the 1995 Intergovernmental Group of Experts on the Protection of War Victims and endorsed by the 26th International Conference of the Red Cross and Red Crescent in 1995. As at 30 September 2015, national committees for the implementation of international humanitarian law, or similar bodies, existed in 107 countries. A full list of such committees may be found at https://www.icrc.org/eng/resources/documents/misc/table-national-committees.htm.

[33] For more details on 'the provisions which shall be implemented in peacetime', see the commentary on common Article 2, section C.

[34] See e.g. Surbeck, p. 541.

D. Scope of the obligation

1. General

2767 According to the dissemination provisions found in the four Geneva Conventions, the High Contracting Parties are to disseminate the text of the Conventions 'as widely as possible in their respective countries'.[35]

2768 Where the language or languages used in a State are neither English nor French, the two authentic languages of the Geneva Conventions, nor Russian or Spanish, the two languages for which the Swiss Federal Council was entrusted with arranging official translations,[36] proper dissemination of the text of the Conventions will require their translation into the national language or languages.[37]

2769 The obligation to disseminate the 'text' of the Conventions includes common Article 3 applicable in non-international armed conflict, which binds all Parties to the conflict, both States and non-State armed groups. In this respect, the dissemination by the High Contracting Parties of common Article 3 and other international humanitarian law provisions applicable in non-international armed conflict among governmental authorities and the entire population is important in creating an environment conducive to lawful behaviour in the event of a non-international armed conflict.[38]

2770 The obligation to disseminate the text of the Conventions 'as widely as possible in their respective countries' leaves States a certain margin of discretion with respect to the measures to be taken, depending, for example, on the means available.[39] Nevertheless, a State is obliged to reach out 'as widely as possible' according to its capacity and means. Modern information technology and the Internet provide the opportunity to disseminate international humanitarian law to larger audiences at a lesser cost.[40]

2771 The formulation of the dissemination obligation reflected the conviction of the drafters at the time that knowledge of the law is a precondition for compliance and that the spreading of knowledge would generate respect. However, empirical research indicates that '[k]nowledge does not suffice to induce

---

[35] First Convention, Article 47; Second Convention, Article 48; Third Convention, Article 127(1); Fourth Convention, Article 144(1).

[36] On the languages of the Conventions, see First Convention, Article 55; Second Convention, Article 54; Third Convention, Article 133; and Fourth Convention, Article 150.

[37] On the communication between High Contracting Parties of translations of the Conventions, see First Convention, Article 48; Second Convention, Article 49; Third Convention, Article 128; and Fourth Convention, Article 145.

[38] For further details, see the commentary on common Article 3, section M.5.a. See also Additional Protocol II, Article 19, which explicitly requires the dissemination of the Protocol.

[39] See e.g. Junod, p. 360.

[40] See e.g. e-learning modules on 'Basic rules and principles of IHL' designed by the ICRC and available at https://www.icrc.org/en/online-training-centre, and the online version of Marco Sassòli, Antoine Bouvier and Anne Quintin, *How Does Law Protect in War?*, available at https://www.icrc.org/casebook/.

a favourable attitude towards a norm',[41] and that doctrine, education, training and equipment, as well as sanctions, are key factors in shaping the behaviour of weapon bearers during operations.[42]

2772 As a consequence, the scope of Article 47 must not be reduced to an obligation to post and distribute the text of the Convention. The formulation 'disseminate ... so that the principles thereof may become known' has a wider meaning than 'publish the text' or 'make it available'. Dissemination aims at making the spirit of the Geneva Conventions understood by all people and to have their content internalized rather than their text simply publicized. As such, Article 47 obliges States to 'include the study thereof in their programmes of military and, if possible, civil instruction'.

2. Military instruction programmes

2773 The study of international humanitarian law by the military is essential. Members of the armed forces bear the responsibility for applying most of its provisions. At the same time, by virtue of their service, they may likely come into situations in which they benefit from the protection of international humanitarian law, for example when they are wounded or sick. Knowledge of the provisions of international humanitarian law protecting them may help prevent violations of the rights secured to them.[43]

2774 Article 47 does not prescribe how the High Contracting Parties are to comply with their obligation to include the study of the First Convention in their programmes of military instruction. They can do so in a variety of ways.

2775 In practice, States issue military manuals and other standard reference materials on international humanitarian law or, in some cases, integrate the law into their field manuals. Furthermore, they develop materials, courses and movies for the teaching of their armed forces. These learning materials are often adapted in their complexity and detail to the rank and respective roles and responsibilities of the specific target audience. In addition, States not only teach international humanitarian law as a subject of theoretical knowledge, but include it in regular practical training and exercises, in order to ensure that compliance with the rules of international humanitarian law becomes a reflex.[44]

---

[41] ICRC, *Roots of Behaviour in War*, 2004, p. 8, and Spoerri, p. 113.
[42] See ICRC, *Integrating the Law*, pp. 17 and 23–35, and Spoerri, p. 114.
[43] For example, by informing persons protected under the Geneva Conventions of the assurance of the law that they 'may in no circumstances renounce in part or in entirety the rights secured to them by the present Convention'; see common Article 7 (Article 8 in the Fourth Convention).
[44] See e.g. South Africa, *Revised Civic Education Manual*, 2004, Chapter 4: International Humanitarian Law (Law of Armed Conflict), para. 38: 'In the circumstances of combat, soldiers may often not have time to consider the principles of the LOAC [law of armed conflict] before acting. Soldiers must therefore not only know these principles but must be trained so that the proper response to specific situations is second nature.' See also Côte d'Ivoire, *Teaching Manual*, 2007, Book I, p. 7: 'The objective of this instruction is to trigger within the soldier a spontaneous

2776   In order to be effective and to induce behaviour compliant with the law, inter-national humanitarian law must not be taught as an abstract and separate set of legal norms, but must be integrated into all regular military activity, train-ing and instruction.[45] Such integration should aim to inspire and influence the military culture and its underlying values, in order to ensure that legal consid-erations and principles of international humanitarian law are incorporated, as much as possible, into military doctrine and decision-making.[46]

3. Civil instruction programmes

2777   The study of the Conventions in programmes of civil instruction is another important element of the dissemination of international humanitarian law.

2778   Proper dissemination of the rules and principles of the Conventions and a meaningful integration of international humanitarian law into military doc-trine requires political commitment. Such commitment is dependent not only on the 'buy-in' of military commanders but also on that of civilian authorities, in particular members of the executive, legislature and judiciary, as well as law enforcement officers.

2779   In addition, it is a characteristic of the Geneva Conventions that they not only contain obligations directed towards the State and those acting on its behalf, but also provisions addressing persons or groups of persons whose actions are not attributable to the State.[47] Bringing the Geneva Conventions to the knowledge of the general population is therefore a significant element for

---

reaction which is to conform with the principles of that law. The soldier must know that respect for these rules is part of military discipline and that every violation leads to disciplinary and/or penal sanctions.' See also Verri, pp. 614–615.

[45] See e.g. Burkina Faso, *Decree Introducing IHL in the Armed Forces*, 1994: 'The teaching of international humanitarian law (IHL) in the Armed Forces is mandatory. It is disseminated at all levels of military hierarchy and forms an integral part of every programme of ... training or instruction'; Italy, *LOAC Elementary Rules Manual*, 1991, para. 22: 'Law of war training has to be integrated into normal military activity'; Madagascar, *Military Manual*, 1994, para. 22; and Spain, *LOAC Manual*, 1996, para. 10.8.c.(2). See also Philippines, *Joint Circular on Adher-ence to IHL and Human Rights*, 1991, para. 3(d): 'These provisions [among which the relevant provisions of the 1949 Geneva Conventions] shall be integrated into the regular Program of Instruction for AFP [Armed Forces of the Philippines] and PNP [Philippine National Police] troops/police information and education sessions in all levels of command/office'; and Russian Federation, *Regulations on the Application of IHL*, 2001, paras 171–172:

171. International humanitarian law shall be trained [*sic*] both in peacetime and in time of war as part of servicemen's training and education. International humanitarian law training shall be integrated in combat (commanders') training curricula ...

172. The aim of international humanitarian law training is to prepare servicemen to dis-charge their duty in a complex situation in compliance with international humanitarian law.

[46] See further ICRC, *Integrating the Law*, pp. 17 and 23–35.

[47] See e.g. Article 15(1) of the First Convention and Article 18(1) of the Second Convention, which imply a general prohibition of pillage and ill-treatment of the wounded, sick and shipwrecked, and of the despoliation of the dead; Article 18(2) of the First Convention, according to which the 'civilian population shall respect [the] wounded and sick, and in particular abstain from offering them violence'; Article 44 of the First Convention, restricting the use of the emblem; and Article 13(2) of the Third Convention, which, *inter alia*, implies a general prohibition of acts of violence, intimidation or insults against prisoners of war.

attaining full compliance with the Conventions.[48] This is also relevant because the obligation of States Parties to suppress all violations of the Conventions and, in the case of grave breaches, to repress them under domestic criminal law, applies not only to violations committed by persons acting on behalf of a State, but also to violations by private persons. Thus, members of the general population may become subject to prosecution for grave breaches of the Geneva Conventions and their knowledge of the Conventions is therefore important.[49]

2780   Civil instruction programmes can also take the form of specific training courses held for media professionals. Such training helps to ensure that media representatives understand the legal and humanitarian issues in armed conflict and that they correctly report on these.[50]

2781   The obligation to include the study of the Geneva Conventions in programmes of civil instruction is qualified by the insertion of 'if possible', owing to concerns expressed during the negotiations that constitutional limitations in federal States could prevent a State Party from prescribing general public education programmes. Other concerns include overburdened curricula, limited financial means, lack of interest among the target audiences or an apprehension of being misunderstood as preparing for armed conflict.[51] Practice has shown, however, that these concerns can be overcome: the study of the Conventions and international humanitarian law more generally has been included in programmes directed to the civilian population, for example through school or university curricula.[52]

2782   Familiarizing the entire population with international humanitarian law contributes to an environment conducive to respect for the law, in which the principles and rules underlying and forming international humanitarian law are accepted, supported and defended, and, should the need arise, applied to address humanitarian issues specific to each context.

Select bibliography

Bothe, Michael, 'The role of national law in the implementation of international humanitarian law', in Christophe Swinarski (ed.), *Studies and Essays on International Humanitarian Law and Red Cross Principles in Honour of Jean Pictet*, ICRC/Martinus Nijhoff Publishers, The Hague, 1984, pp. 301–312.
Harroff-Tavel, Marion, 'The International Committee of the Red Cross and the promotion of international humanitarian law: Looking back, looking forward',

---

[48] See also common Article 1, according to which the 'High Contracting Parties undertake to respect and to ensure respect for the present Convention in all circumstances'. For further details, see the commentary on this article.

[49] For further details, see the commentary on Article 50, section C.3.

[50] The ICRC has provided training for media professionals in a number of contexts. See also the reference book for journalists: Roy Gutman, David Rieff and Anthony Dworkin (eds), *Crimes of War: What the Public Should Know*, 2nd edition, W.W. Norton & Company, New York, 2007.

[51] See Junod, p. 360.   [52] For examples, see Kadam, pp. 167–169.

International Review of the Red Cross, Vol. 96, Nos 895/896, 2014, pp. 817–857.

ICRC, Advisory Service on International Humanitarian Law, 'National Committees for the Implementation of International Humanitarian Law', 2003.

– Advisory Service on International Humanitarian Law, 'The Obligation to Disseminate International Humanitarian Law', 2003.

– *Integrating the Law*, ICRC, Geneva, 2007.

– *The Roots of Behaviour in War: Understanding and Preventing IHL Violations*, by Daniel Muñoz-Rojas and Jean-Jacques Frésard, ICRC, Geneva, October 2005.

Junod, Sylvie S., 'La diffusion du droit international humanitaire', in Christophe Swinarski (ed.), *Etudes et essais sur le droit international humanitaire et sur les principes de la Croix-Rouge en l'honneur de Jean Pictet*, ICRC/Martinus Nijhoff Publishers, The Hague, 1984, pp. 359–368.

Kadam, Umesh, 'Teaching international humanitarian law in academic institutions in South Asia: An overview of an ICRC dissemination programme', *International Review of the Red Cross*, Vol. 83, No. 841, March 2001, pp. 167–169.

Meyer, Michael A., 'The role of a National Society in the implementation of international humanitarian law – taking up the challenge!', *International Review of the Red Cross*, Vol. 37, No. 317, April 1997, pp. 203–207.

Mikos-Skuza, Elżbieta, 'Dissemination of the Conventions, Including in Time of Armed Conflict', in Andrew Clapham, Paola Gaeta and Marco Sassòli (eds), *The 1949 Geneva Conventions: A Commentary*, Oxford University Press, 2015, pp. 597–614.

Quéguiner, Jean-François, 'Commentary on the Protocol additional to the Geneva Conventions of 12 August 1949, and relating to the Adoption of an Additional Distinctive Emblem (Protocol III)', *International Review of the Red Cross*, Vol. 89, No. 865, March 2007, pp. 175–207.

Spoerri, Philip, 'From Dissemination towards Integration: An ICRC Perspective', *Military Law and the Law of War Review*, Vol. 52, No. 1, 2013, pp. 113–122.

Surbeck, Jean-Jacques, 'La diffusion du droit international humanitaire, condition de son application', in Christophe Swinarski (ed.), *Etudes et essais sur le droit international humanitaire et sur les principes de la Croix-Rouge en l'honneur de Jean Pictet*, ICRC/Martinus Nijhoff Publishers, The Hague, 1984, pp. 537–549.

Verri, Pietro, 'Institutions militaires: le problème de l'enseignement du droit des conflits armés et de l'adaptation des règlements à ses prescriptions humanitaires', in Christophe Swinarski (ed.), *Etudes et essais sur le droit international humanitaire et sur les principes de la Croix-Rouge en l'honneur de Jean Pictet*, ICRC/Martinus Nijhoff Publishers, The Hague, 1984, pp. 603–619.

TRANSLATIONS. IMPLEMENTING LAWS AND REGULATIONS

❖ Text of the provision

The High Contracting Parties shall communicate to one another through the Swiss Federal Council and, during hostilities, through the Protecting Powers, the official translations of the present Convention, as well as the laws and regulations which they may adopt to ensure the application thereof.

❖ Reservations or declarations

None

Contents

A. Introduction

2783 Article 48 requires the High Contracting Parties to communicate to one another the official translations they may have undertaken of the Convention, as well as of laws and regulations they may have adopted to ensure the Convention's application.

2784 This provision is common to the four Geneva Conventions.[1] Additional Protocol I contains an almost identical provision.[2]

2785 The purpose of the communication of official translations of the Geneva Conventions and of laws and regulations ensuring their application is to enable all High Contracting Parties to inform themselves of the way in which other

[1] See Second Convention, Article 49; Third Convention, Article 128; and Fourth Convention, Article 145.
[2] See Additional Protocol I, Article 84.

States understand their obligations under the Conventions and how they have implemented them. Such knowledge may help to avoid or reduce discrepancies and may also encourage States to increase their efforts in the translation and implementation of the Conventions.

2786   The broad reference to the translation and application of 'the present Convention' in Article 48 includes common Article 3. Since the adoption of the Geneva Conventions in 1949, High Contracting Parties have increasingly engaged as Parties to or in support of other States undergoing a non-international armed conflict in their territory. Knowledge of one another's understanding of common Article 3 is therefore of particular importance.

B. Historical background

2787   The 1906 Geneva Convention and the 1907 Hague Convention (X) already required States Parties to communicate to one another, through the depositary, legislative measures for the repression and punishment of certain violations of these Conventions in time of war.[3] The 1929 Geneva Convention on the Wounded and Sick equally obligated them to communicate such measures through the depositary.[4] The time frame provided for communication in these three Conventions was five years after their respective ratification.

2788   For its part, the 1929 Geneva Convention on Prisoners of War contained the obligation for States Parties to communicate official translations of the Convention, as well as of laws and regulations adopted for the application of the Convention, through the depositary but without defining a time frame.[5]

2789   The draft articles submitted by the ICRC to the 1948 International Conference of the Red Cross in Stockholm on the communication of information between High Contracting Parties largely reflected the existing provisions. The draft for the revision of the 1929 Geneva Convention on the Wounded and Sick and the 1907 Hague Convention (X) foresaw a reduction of the time frame for communication from five years to one year after ratification.[6]

2790   The Stockholm Conference adopted the proposed draft articles for the revision of the 1929 Geneva Convention on the Wounded and Sick and the 1907 Hague Convention (X) without a time limit for the communication of legislative measures, but set a maximum period of two years for taking the necessary legislative measures.[7] The draft articles for the revision of the 1929 Geneva

---

[3] See Geneva Convention (1906), Article 28, and Hague Convention (X) (1907), Article 21.
[4] See Geneva Convention on the Wounded and Sick (1929), Article 29.
[5] See Geneva Convention on Prisoners of War (1929), Article 85.
[6] See *Draft Conventions submitted to the 1948 Stockholm Conference*, draft first convention, article 39, p. 28, and draft second convention, article 37, p. 49.
[7] See *Draft Conventions adopted by the 1948 Stockholm Conference*, draft first convention, article 39, p. 25, and draft second convention, article 43, p. 47.

Convention on Prisoners of War and for the new civilians convention were adopted with minor changes.[8]

2791 The 1949 Diplomatic Conference decided to adopt for all four Conventions the text used for the Convention on Prisoners of War, i.e. requiring the communication of translations and of laws and regulations without stipulating a time frame.[9]

C. Discussion

1. Obligation to communicate

2792 Under Article 48, States are required to make available their translations of the First Convention and of the laws and regulations adopted for its implementation to all other States Parties 'through the Swiss Federal Council and, during hostilities, through the Protecting Powers'.

2793 The use of the expression 'shall communicate' indicates that the communication is a legal obligation for States party to the First Convention. As is evident from Article 48's requirement that translations be communicated 'to one another', the obligation exists towards all other High Contracting Parties.

2794 Effective communication implies that the High Contracting Parties inform one another of the existence of translations and of laws and regulations adopted, and that they make their content available to one another.

2795 The 1949 Geneva Conventions, unlike their predecessors,[10] prescribe no time frame for the communication of the measures adopted. In order to be effective, communication should therefore take place as soon as possible after official translations, laws or regulations have been issued or adopted.[11]

2796 In general, States are to communicate their translations, laws and regulations 'through the Swiss Federal Council', which is the depositary of the Conventions.[12] As in other provisions of the Convention,[13] the reference to 'High Contracting Parties' rather than 'Parties to the conflict', makes it clear that the obligation of communication already applies in peacetime.

2797 'During hostilities', the High Contracting Parties are to communicate translations, laws and regulations 'through the Protecting Powers'.[14] The wording of

---

[8] See *ibid.* draft third convention, article 118, p. 99, and draft fourth convention, article 129, p. 159. The phrase 'during hostilities, through the Protecting Powers' was added.

[9] See *Final Record of the Diplomatic Conference of Geneva of 1949*, Vol. II-B, pp. 70, 112 and 354.

[10] For details, see section B.

[11] See in this respect Article 84 of Additional Protocol I regulating the communication of official translations of the Protocol and of laws and regulations adopted for its application, which expressly requires that communication take place 'as soon as possible'.

[12] For further details on the role of the Swiss Federal Council as the depositary, see the commentaries on Articles 55–58, 60–64 and on the testimonium and signature clause.

[13] See e.g. Articles 1, 47, 49 and 54.

[14] This presupposes the appointment of Protecting Powers in a given armed conflict, an option rarely chosen in the decades following the adoption of the 1949 Geneva Conventions; for further details, see the commentary on Article 8. Parties to a conflict may also agree to entrust other

Article 48 seems to indicate that this applies to all High Contracting Parties, and not only to the States party to the conflict. Given the role of Protecting Powers to 'safeguard the interests of the Parties to the conflict',[15] the Protecting Powers are likely to concentrate on the communication of translations, laws and regulations between States party to the conflict, whereas the Swiss Federal Council would continue to transfer communications between States not party to the conflict.

2798   When receiving copies of national laws and regulations relating to the adoption of the Convention from States pursuant to Article 48, the Swiss Federal Council is only obligated to communicate what it receives and is not responsible for translating the documents. The same applies to Protecting Powers when they communicate laws and regulations during hostilities.

2799   Official translations of the Geneva Conventions and of national laws and regulations on their application are today usually made publicly available in the official gazettes of High Contracting Parties or in other publications issued by them. They are also increasingly made available on the internet. This usefully complements communication as provided for in Article 48. However, such availability and accessibility of translations, laws and regulations cannot be fully equated with the active communication of such documents, an obligation that ensures that all States are made aware of them.

2800   In addition to the legal obligation under Article 48, it would be useful for such documents also to be communicated to the ICRC. Even though there exists no obligation in this respect under the Geneva Conventions, the usefulness of sharing such information with the ICRC has been noted.[16]

2. Translations

2801   The Geneva Conventions are authenticated in English and French; in addition, the Swiss Federal Council was entrusted with arranging official translations of

---

intermediaries with the communication of documents between them; for further details, see the commentary on Article 10.

[15] See common Article 8 (Article 9 in the Fourth Convention).

[16] In 1995, the Intergovernmental Group of Experts convened by the Swiss Government requested, *inter alia*, that the ICRC be provided with any information that might be of assistance to other States in their efforts to disseminate and implement IHL and that the ICRC collect, assemble and transmit that information to States and to the Conference. The Intergovernmental Group of Experts further recommended that 'the ICRC, with the assistance of National Societies, the International Federation of Red Cross and Red Crescent Societies... and academic institutions,... strengthen its capacity to provide advisory services to States, with their consent, in their efforts to implement and disseminate IHL'. These recommendations were subsequently endorsed by Resolution 1 of the 26th International Conference of the Red Cross and Red Crescent in 1995. Established in 1995 and fully operational since 1996, the ICRC's Advisory Service on International Humanitarian Law has been systematically collecting national laws, regulations and case law and has been making this information available on the ICRC website (https://www.icrc.org/ihl-nat), as well as through updates on national legislation and case law published in the *International Review of the Red Cross*.

the Conventions into Russian and Spanish to ensure consistent texts in these two languages, without making these texts authentic.[17] For the Additional Protocols of 1977, the Arabic, Chinese, English, French, Russian and Spanish texts are authentic.

2802 The Geneva Conventions contain no explicit legal obligation for High Contracting Parties to translate the Conventions into their national language. However, the requirement to translate treaties to which a State has become party may exist under domestic legislation. Furthermore, it is difficult to see how States could fulfil some of the obligations under the Convention, for example to disseminate the text of the Convention under Article 47, without having such translations available.[18]

2803 Translations of the Conventions may be based on either the English or the French authentic text, although a translation will be most accurate if a comparison is made with both of the authentic texts.[19] States that share a national language may agree on a common translation or harmonize their translations, but have no obligation to do so.[20]

2804 Article 48 refers to 'official translations'. These are translations undertaken by States themselves or by third parties, for example a National Red Cross or Red Crescent Society, and officially endorsed by the State.

2805 Since the entry into force of the 1949 Geneva Conventions, the Swiss Federal Council has received a number of official translations of the Geneva Conventions from High Contracting Parties and has notified the other Parties of the translations received. The procedure under Article 48 does not require any reaction by the other States Parties, and their silence cannot be interpreted as approving the validity of a translation transmitted to them. At the time of writing of this commentary, according to the information available to the

---

[17] See the commentary on Article 55, section C. The official character of the translations into Russian and Spanish resides in the fact that the source from which they are derived is specified in the Convention itself.

[18] See Article 47. See also Article 99(1) of the Fourth Convention, according to which the 'officer in charge of [a] place of internment must have in his possession a copy of the present Convention in the official language, or one of the official languages, of his country'. The availability of translations of the Geneva Conventions into national languages will make it easier for States to comply with their obligations under the Third and Fourth Conventions to make the texts of those Conventions available in prisoner-of-war/internment camps in a language that the prisoners of war/internees understand; see Third Convention, Article 41, and Fourth Convention, Article 99(2).

[19] See Article 33 of the 1969 Vienna Convention on the Law of Treaties on the interpretation of treaties authenticated in one or more languages; see also the commentary on Article 55, section B.2, for details on the resolution of potential divergences between the two authentic language versions of the Conventions.

[20] For example, Germany, Austria, Switzerland and Lichtenstein do not have a uniform official translation of the First Convention into German and differences can be found in the translations of the title, of specific terms (e.g. 'armed forces' is translated as 'Streitkräfte', 'bewaffnete Kräfte' or 'bewaffnete Streitkräfte') and of certain articles (e.g. Article 62). These differences are stylistic rather than substantive, however.

Swiss Federal Council and the ICRC, there are some 60 official translations of the Geneva Conventions into national languages, even though not all of them were necessarily communicated as provided for in Article 48.

3. Implementing laws and regulations

2806 The 'laws and regulations' to be communicated under Article 48 should be understood in the widest possible sense to cover all rules emanating from the executive or legislative authorities relating to the application of the Convention.[21]

2807 Thus, States Parties are expected to communicate any laws or regulations adopted as part of the implementation of specific provisions of the Convention, for example measures adopted under Articles 26 and 27 (recognition and authorization by High Contracting Parties of National Societies and other voluntary aid societies),[22] Article 44 (legislation on the use of the emblem), Article 49 (legislation on penal sanctions for grave breaches and measures for the suppression of other violations) and Article 54 (measures for the prevention and repression of misuse of the emblem).

2808 Since the entry into force of the 1949 Geneva Conventions, the Swiss Federal Council has received from High Contracting Parties a number of laws and regulations on the application of the Geneva Conventions and has officially notified the other Parties of the documents received. At the time of writing of this commentary, however, the majority of such documents seem not to have been communicated by the High Contracting Parties as required by Article 48.

Select bibliography

ICRC, Advisory Service on International Humanitarian Law, Domestic law and IHL, https://www.icrc.org/en/war-and-law/ihl-domestic-law.

---

[21] See Pictet (ed.), *Commentary on the First Geneva Convention*, ICRC, 1952, p. 350.
[22] See the commentaries on Article 26, para. 2067 and on Article 27, para. 2136.

CHAPTER IX

REPRESSION OF ABUSES AND INFRACTIONS

2809 The 1949 Geneva Conventions contain, for the first time in international humanitarian law, a comprehensive set of treaty provisions on the suppression of abuses and on penal sanctions. As a delegate to the 1949 Diplomatic Conference stated, the object of these articles 'is to increase respect for the Conventions, and to strengthen them and the protection they provide by supplying a means of deterring people from violating their provisions and, if necessary, by enforcing obedience to the Conventions.'[1]

2810 This chapter, consisting of six articles, regulates important new issues in addition to provisions which appeared in earlier Conventions. Articles 49 and 50, together with Article 51, are new and have been incorporated in a similar form in all four Geneva Conventions.[2]

2811 The inclusion of Article 49 was thought to provide a watertight mechanism that would ensure the effective prosecution of alleged perpetrators of serious violations of the Conventions. Article 49 obliges States Parties to enact legislation providing effective penal sanctions, and to either prosecute or extradite, regardless of their nationality, alleged offenders who are suspected of having committed one of these grave breaches against persons or property protected by the Convention.

2812 Article 50 is closely linked to Article 49. It contains an exhaustive list of the gravest offences, which States undertake to investigate, and then to either prosecute or extradite alleged offenders.

2813 Article 51 prevents States Parties from absolving themselves or any other State Party of any liability incurred by them or by another State Party in respect of the grave breaches referred to in Article 50. It clarifies the relationship between individual criminal responsibility for grave breaches of the Conventions and State responsibility for acts committed by the armed forces or persons acting under the authority or command of a State in respect of grave breaches.

2814 Article 52 deals with the procedure for enquiries into alleged violations of the Convention; it sets out the legal basis for the establishment of an enquiry

---

[1] See Fourth Report drawn up by the Special Committee of the Joint Committee, Report on Penal Sanctions, *Final Record of the Diplomatic Conference of Geneva of 1949*, Vol. II-B, p. 114.
[2] See Second Convention, Articles 50–52; Third Convention, Articles 129–131; and Fourth Convention, Articles 146–148.

procedure when the Parties have diverging views regarding any alleged violations of the Geneva Conventions. It also seeks to ensure that the Parties put an end to and repress alleged violations, if they are established through the enquiry. Article 52 corresponds to Article 30 of the 1929 Geneva Convention on the Wounded and Sick and is common to all four Geneva Conventions.[3]

2815   Articles 53 and 54 deal with the misuse of the distinctive emblem. Article 53 sets out a very broad prohibition on the use of the emblems, their designations, and imitations thereof, by a range of third parties.

2816   Article 54 requires States Parties to take the necessary measures to prevent and repress abuses of the emblems, their designations and other protected signs, as set out in Article 53.

2817   Both Articles 53 and 54 already figured, in a simpler form, in the 1906 and 1929 Geneva Conventions on the Wounded and Sick and only feature in the first of the 1949 Conventions.[4]

---

[3] See Second Convention, Article 53; Third Convention, Article 132; and Fourth Convention, Article 149.

[4] With the exception of Article 54 of the First Convention, which is also reproduced in Article 45 of the Second Convention.

PENAL SANCTIONS

❖ Text of the provision*

(1) The High Contracting Parties undertake to enact any legislation necessary to provide effective penal sanctions for persons committing, or ordering to be committed, any of the grave breaches of the present Convention defined in the following Article.

(2) Each High Contracting Party shall be under the obligation to search for persons alleged to have committed, or to have ordered to be committed, such grave breaches, and shall bring such persons, regardless of their nationality, before its own courts. It may also, if it prefers, and in accordance with the provisions of its own legislation, hand such persons over for trial to another High Contracting Party concerned, provided such High Contracting Party has made out a 'prima facie' case.

(3) Each High Contracting Party shall take measures necessary for the suppression of all acts contrary to the provisions of the present Convention other than the grave breaches defined in the following Article.

(4) In all circumstances, the accused persons shall benefit by safeguards of proper trial and defence, which shall not be less favourable than those provided by Article 105 and those following of the Geneva Convention relative to the Treatment of Prisoners of War of August 12, 1949.

❖ Reservations or declarations

None

Contents

* Paragraph numbers have been added for ease of reference.

A. Introduction

2818   In 1949, the system of repression contained in the Geneva Conventions (here-inafter referred to as 'the grave breaches regime') was a remarkable innovation in the law regulating international armed conflict. Article 49 is common to the four Conventions.[1]

2819   The obligations to enact legislation providing effective penal sanctions (paragraph 1) and to initiate the investigation and prosecution of alleged offenders suspected of having committed or ordered the commission of grave breaches, regardless of their nationality (paragraph 2) were designed to provide a water-tight mechanism which would ensure the effective prosecution of alleged perpetrators of serious violations of the Conventions. Paragraph 3 complements this regime by calling on all States Parties to take any measures necessary for the suppression of all acts contrary to the Convention other than grave breaches. Paragraph 4 sets out the obligation to grant the accused a fair trial.

2820   In 1977, these common provisions were supplemented and clarified by a series of provisions set out in Additional Protocol I. For States party to that

---

[1] See Second Convention, Article 50; Third Convention, Article 129; and Fourth Convention, Article 146.

instrument, Additional Protocol I expands the list of grave breaches,[2] provides for the responsibility of individuals under other forms of responsibility,[3] and makes it clear that grave breaches form part of the category of war crimes.[4] The grave breaches regime also acted as a 'blueprint for other treaties, ranging from the Torture to the Enforced Disappearances Conventions'.[5]

2821 Grave breaches of the Geneva Conventions today form part of a complex set of crimes under international law, consisting of serious violations of international humanitarian law often referred to as war crimes, as well as gross human rights violations, such as crimes against humanity and genocide. Grave breaches are part of the wider category of serious violations of humanitarian law that States are called upon to suppress in both international and non-international armed conflict.[6] They remain 'segregated from other categories of war crimes',[7] as the list of grave breaches contained in the Geneva Conventions and Additional Protocol I is a limitative one which is only applicable in international armed conflict.[8] Furthermore, the grave breaches regime imposes on States Parties the obligation to either prosecute or extradite alleged offenders, regardless of their nationality, as opposed to a right to do so recognized in international law in connection with alleged perpetrators of war crimes.[9]

B. Historical background

2822 The following overview of the developments which led to the inclusion of Article 49 provides the essential background for understanding the way that the system of penal sanctions is designed in the Geneva Conventions.

1. The system of repression up to 1949

2823 The punishment of individuals for serious violations of the laws and customs of war, often referred to as war crimes, is as old as the rules regulating warfare.[10] Sanctions for such violations have been an integral part of those rules and were

---

[2] See, in particular, Additional Protocol I, Articles 11 and 85.

[3] See, in particular, Additional Protocol I, Article 86(2) on command responsibility and Article 87 (Duty of commanders)

[4] See Additional Protocol I, Article 85(5). For further details, see Sandoz/Swinarski/Zimmermann (eds), *Commentary on the Additional Protocols*, ICRC, 1987, para. 3408.

[5] James G. Stewart, 'Introduction', *Journal of International Criminal Justice*, Vol. 7, No. 4, September 2009, pp. 653–655, at 654.

[6] See ICRC Study on Customary International Humanitarian Law (2005), Rule 158: 'States must investigate war crimes allegedly committed by their nationals or armed forces, or on their territory, and, if appropriate, prosecute the suspects. They must also investigate other war crimes over which they have jurisdiction and, if appropriate, prosecute the suspects.'

[7] Sandoz, 2009, p. 679.

[8] For a discussion of whether serious violations of international humanitarian law committed in non-international armed conflict amount to grave breaches, see section G.

[9] For a full explanation of the obligation contained in Article 49(2), see section D.1.

[10] For an extensive historical background, see Green, 1996b; Cryer; and McCormack, 1997a. See also Draper; Green, 1996a; Wells, especially chapter 6, entitled 'Prosecution for war crimes

seen as essential to ensuring compliance with this body of law by soldiers.[11] Individual responsibility for breaches of the laws and customs of war was recognized by many civilizations.[12] Similar principles formed part of the law of warfare in the European medieval period.[13] Prosecutions could be undertaken by the enemy into whose hands the alleged offender had fallen, or alternatively, by the military authorities of the alleged offender. The 1863 Lieber Code contains an elaborate set of rules on many aspects of the laws and customs of war and highlights the need to maintain discipline and the importance of taking action against violations of these rules.[14]

2824   Early codifications of the laws and customs of war did not, however, contain detailed provisions on the individual criminal responsibility of offenders.[15] The 1906 Geneva Convention was the first international treaty to contain two articles dealing with the repression of violations, such as the abuse of the emblem and other violations of the Convention, for example robbery and ill-treatment of the wounded and sick in the armies.[16] The Hague Conventions of 1899 and 1907 only provide for the responsibility of States Parties to pay damages in case of violations of the Conventions.[17] States were left free to punish, or not, acts committed by their own troops against the enemy, or again, acts committed by enemy troops, in violation of the laws and customs of war.[18]

---

in history', p. 91; Lauterpacht; McCormack, 1997b; Levie; Greppi, p. 531; and La Haye, pp. 104–107.

[11] For more details on this issue, see ICRC, *The Roots of Behaviour in War: A Survey of the Literature*, ICRC, Geneva, October 2004.

[12] Such as in Asia, where, according to the sixteenth-century code of Bushido, for example, 'every soldier must report to the commander about prisoners of war … he shall be guilty of manslaughter if he kills them with his own hands'; see Sumio Adachi, 'The Asian concept', in *International Dimensions of Humanitarian Law*, Henry Dunant Institute, Geneva, 1988, p. 13.

[13] See, in particular, Green, 1996a, p. 278; Keen, p. 3; and Meron, 1998.

[14] On the role and impact of the Lieber Code, see Sandoz. See also Lieber Code (1863), Articles 44, 47 and 71.

[15] Neither the 1864 Geneva Convention nor the 1868 St Petersburg Declaration contains any provisions dealing with the repression of violations. After 1870, the then ICRC President Gustave Moynier, among others, was already calling for the establishment of an international tribunal for the repression of breaches of the 1864 Geneva Convention; see Gustave Moynier, *Considérations sur la sanction pénale à donner à la Convention de Genève*, Imprimerie F. Regamey, Lausanne, 1893. In 1895, the Institute of International Law adopted a resolution on this issue; see http://www.justitiaetpace.org/idiF/resolutionsF/1895_camb_03_fr.pdf. It is also interesting to note that the Oxford Manual adopted by the Institute in 1880 as a model for national military codes provides, in its Article 84, that 'offenders against the laws of war are liable to the punishments specified in the penal law'. For a full review of early instruments dealing with the repression of violations of the laws and customs of war, see Graven p. 241; Bassiouni/Wise, p. 86; Sandoz, 1986, p. 209; Abi-Saab, p. 99; Levie, p. 96; Green, 1984, p. 3; and Wells, p. 68.

[16] See Geneva Convention (1906), Articles 27 and 28, and Hague Convention (X) (1907), Article 21.

[17] See Hague Regulations (1907), Article 3. A similar obligation is contained in Article 91 of Additional Protocol I.

[18] There are several cases where States asserted their right to punish individuals for violations of the laws of war. For example, in 1902 a private commission in the United States investigated the serious violations committed by US troops during the Philippine insurrection of 1899–1902. A number of soldiers were tried by US courts-martial. See McCormack, 1997b, p. 696, and Mettraux, 2003, p. 135.

2825 Widespread atrocities were committed during the First World War, in particular against civilians, such as indiscriminate bombings, rape, and the sinking
of civilian boats and hospital ships, such as the *Llandovery Castle*.[19] These
acts reinforced the belief that it was necessary to pursue justice in response to
atrocities and that the system contained in existing international treaties was
anything but satisfactory.[20] Towards the end of the war, the Allies established
a Commission on the Responsibility of the Authors of the War and on Enforcement of Penalties, whose main task was to list the atrocities committed by
the German forces and to create a coherent inventory of violations of the laws
and customs of war.[21] On the basis of the facts it gathered, the Commission
listed 32 violations of the laws and customs of war that warranted criminal
punishment.[22] It suggested that war criminals should be tried before domestic courts, with the exception of four categories of defendants, who should be
placed before an ad hoc tribunal.[23]

2826 For the first time in a major peace treaty, the 1919 Treaty of Versailles contained three articles establishing individual criminal responsibility under international law for violations of the laws and customs of war. Article 227 of the
Treaty provided for the trial of the former Emperor of Germany, and Articles
228 and 229 recognized the 'right of the Allied and Associated Powers to bring
before military tribunals Germans accused of having committed acts in violation of the laws and customs of war'. Pursuant to Article 228 of this treaty,
the Allies submitted a list of 896 alleged war criminals to the German authorities. The latter refused to turn them over, and in the end, the Supreme Court
of the German Reich in Leipzig tried only 12 individuals. Nine were acquitted
and three were found guilty.[24] Moreover, the German Emperor was never surrendered by the Dutch Government. As a result, only a few Germans accused
of serious violations of the laws and customs of war were tried by the Allies
in Europe during or after the First World War.[25] The Allies, on the other hand,

---

[19] For an overview of this issue during the First World War, see Sandoz, 2009, pp. 665–673, citing
in particular James F. Willis, *Prologue to Nuremberg: The Politics and Diplomacy of Punishing
War Criminals of the First World War*, Greenwood Press, Westport, 1982, pp. 13–19.

[20] Interestingly, Sandoz, 2009, p. 666, notes that, at the beginning of the war, 'there was reluctance
to go too far and too quickly in the direction of international repression for fear that each side
would use prosecutions as a basis for reprisals'.

[21] The Commission's report was reproduced in the *American Journal of International Law*, Vol. 14,
No. 1, 1920, pp. 95–126.

[22] For an analysis of this first list of war crimes, see Sandoz, 2009, pp. 667–669. It is important to
note that this list cannot be considered a serious and systematic inventory of State practice, as
it is driven mainly by facts and also omits numerous crimes committed by the Allies.

[23] *Ibid.* p. 670. The four categories of defendants is clarified in the Commission's report, reproduced in the *American Journal of International Law*, Vol. 14, No. 1, 1920, pp. 121–122. The
Commission's proposal to create an ad hoc tribunal was contested by the US delegation, and
consequently was not adopted in the 1919 Treaty of Versailles.

[24] These trials are referred to as the 'Leipzig Trials'. See La Haye, p. 106, citing McCormack, 1997b,
pp. 705–770; Levie, pp. 97–98; Wells, p. 70; Cryer, pp. 33–35; and Maogoto.

[25] During the conflict, there were also accounts of war crimes trials conducted by individual Allied
States against German soldiers for violations of the laws of war, such as pillage, robbery, and
murder of wounded soldiers on the battlefield. See McCormack, 1997a, p. 44.

were under no obligation under the Treaty of Versailles to try their own soldiers for similar violations. The prosecution of alleged war criminals, or its absence, was therefore characterized by the one-sidedness of a justice invoked by the Allies, which has been described as 'a scandalous failure of justice'.[26]

2827   Noticeable progress was made in the 1929 Geneva Convention on the Wounded and Sick, as a more comprehensive chapter on the suppression of abuses was included, containing for the first time detailed provisions on the enforcement of the Convention. Article 29 of this Convention called on States Parties to propose to their legislatures, should their penal laws be inadequate, the necessary measures for the repression in time of war of *any act* contrary to the provisions of the Convention,[27] including misuse of the emblem.[28] Article 30 provided for the establishment of an enquiry mechanism in case of alleged violation of the Convention.[29]

2828   During the Second World War, numerous statements about the individual responsibility of alleged perpetrators who had violated the laws and customs of war were made by the Allies.[30] In 1942, the Allies decided to set up the UN War Crimes Commission for the investigation of war crimes, affirming that:

[T]he Commission should proceed upon the footing that international law recognises the principle that a war crime is a violation of the laws and customs of war, and that no question can be raised as to the right of the United Nations to put on trial as a war criminal in respect of such violations any hostile offender who may fall into their hands.[31]

2829   At the end of the Second World War, these undertakings were fulfilled at the national level with 2,116 known military tribunal hearings conducted by Australia, Canada, China, France, Greece, the Netherlands, Norway, Poland, the United Kingdom and the United States up to 1949,[32] and at the international level with the creation of two International Military Tribunals. On 8 August 1945, France, the Soviet Union, the United Kingdom and the United States established the International Military Tribunal for Germany (IMT),

---

[26] See Sandoz, 2009, p. 671.

[27] The High Contracting Parties had to notify the Swiss Federal Council of all provisions related to such repression no later than five years from the date of ratification of the Convention. Very few High Contracting Parties actually complied with this obligation.

[28] See Geneva Convention on the Wounded and Sick (1906), Article 28. For more details on the abuse of the emblem, see the commentary on Article 53 of the First Convention.

[29] For further details on the enquiry mechanism, see the commentary on Article 52 of the First Convention.

[30] See the 1942 Declaration of St James establishing the UN War Crimes Commission and the 1943 Moscow Declaration concerning atrocities. On this issue, see Green, 1996a, p. 14; Cryer, pp. 36–37; and Maogoto, pp. 87–97.

[31] UN War Crimes Commission, *The History of the United Nations War Crimes Commission and the Development of the Laws of War*, p. 171.

[32] Wells, p. 74. The details for prosecuting Germans whose offences had taken place in a specific country were set down in the 1945 Allied Control Council Law No. 10. For a study of some of these trials held by the Nuremberg Military Tribunals, see Heller, pp. 203–230.

based in Nuremberg.[33] The IMT tried 24 defendants for crimes against peace, war crimes[34] and crimes against humanity. Furthermore, it recognized a number of principles which came to form the basis of modern international criminal law.[35] In relation to war crimes, the IMT took the view that the laws of war contained in the Hague Conventions of 1907 reflected customary international law,[36] and it considered that it was 'too well settled to admit of argument' that the violations of the Hague Conventions of 1907 'constituted crimes for which the guilty individuals were punishable'.[37] By order of General Douglas MacArthur, the supreme commander for the Allied Powers, the International Military Tribunal for the Far East was established in January 1946 and prosecuted 25 Japanese superior officers, whose crimes had not been limited to a specific location.[38]

2. The 1949 Geneva Conventions and their preparatory work

2830 The events of the Second World War convinced the ICRC that any future international convention on the laws and customs of war must necessarily include effective provisions on the repression of violations. This conviction was strengthened by the numerous appeals which it received to intervene on behalf of prisoners of war who were accused of war crimes and tried under ad hoc national legislation. Also, the ICRC could not remain indifferent to the argument that complete respect for the Conventions must be based on the imposition of effective penalties on those guilty of violating them.[39]

2831   A second Conference of Government Experts in 1947 took as a starting point for the drafting of the chapter on repression of abuses Articles 28, 29 and 30

---

[33] See IMT Charter for Germany (1945), Article 1. Many legal and historical works have been written about this tribunal; see e.g. Eugene Davidson, *The Trial of the Germans: An Account of the 22 Defendants before the International Military Tribunal at Nuremberg*, Macmillan, New York, 1966; Bradley F. Smith, *Reaching Judgment at Nuremberg*, Basic Books, New York, 1977; William J. Bosch, *Judgment on Nuremberg: American Attitudes toward the Major German War-Crime Trials*, University of North Carolina Press, Chapel Hill, 1970; Annette Wieviorka (ed.), *Les procès de Nuremberg et de Tokyo*, Editions Complexes, Brussels, 1996; Maogoto, pp. 98–100; Ann Tusa and John Tusa, *The Nuremberg Trial*, reprinted edition, Cooper Square Press, New York, 2003; and George Ginsburgs and Vladimir N. Kudriavtsev (eds), *The Nuremberg Trial and International Law*, Martinus Nijhoff Publishers, Leiden, 1990. See also Meron, 2006.
[34] For the definition of war crimes, see IMT Charter for Germany (1945), Article 6(b).
[35] See the report of the International Law Commission, which formulated the 1950 Nuremberg Principles, *Yearbook of the International Law Commission*, Vol. II, 1950, p. 374.
[36] See IMT, *Case of the Major War Criminals*, Judgment, 1948, pp. 253–254.
[37] *Ibid.*
[38] Additional trials of persons whose crimes had been carried out in a specific country were conducted at the national level. See Wells, pp. 74–77; Cryer, pp. 42–48; Maogoto, pp. 100–106; Richard H. Minear, *Victors' Justice: The Tokyo War Crimes Trial*, 1st edition, Princeton University Press, 1971; C. Hosoya *et al.* (eds), *The Tokyo War Crimes Trial: An International Symposium*, 1st edition, Kodansha America Inc., New York, 1986; and Yuki Tanaka, Tim McCormack and Gerry Simpson (eds), *Beyond Victor's Justice? The Tokyo War Crimes Trial Revisited*, Martinus Nijhoff Publishers, Leiden, 2011.
[39] See Pictet (ed.), *Commentary on the First Geneva Convention*, ICRC, 1952, p. 357. For a different analysis of the role and views of the ICRC, see Lewis, pp. 229–273.

of the 1929 Convention on the Wounded and Sick. It also included a new article calling for 'any wilful violation of the present Convention, leading to the death of persons protected by its provisions, to grave ill-treatment of the said persons, or serious damage to hospital buildings and equipment' to be 'considered as a war crime' and for '[t]he responsible persons to be liable to appropriate penalties'.[40]

2832   In 1948, the ICRC submitted to the International Conference of the Red Cross in Stockholm a draft article on penal sanctions, which called on States to search for persons charged with breaches of the Convention, and to refer them for trial to their own courts or hand them over for judgment to another State Party. The Conference included these new obligations in the draft text[41] and requested the ICRC to continue its work on the question and to submit proposals to a later Diplomatic Conference. In response, the ICRC invited four governmental experts to meet in Geneva at the beginning of December 1948. The outcome of this work was a set of four draft articles, to be included in each of the four Conventions, on the punishment of persons guilty of violating the provisions of the Conventions.[42]

2833   Since it had not been possible for the draft texts prepared by the ICRC to reach the governments until just before the opening of the Diplomatic Conference in 1949, certain delegations objected to their being taken as a basis for discussion.[43] The Dutch delegation, however, submitted them as its own, so that the draft texts came officially before the Conference.

2834   The four draft articles had a significant impact on the negotiations and the drafting of the common provisions on grave breaches, even if some suggestions were not adopted by the Diplomatic Conference.[44] First, according to

---

[40] See *Report of the Conference of Government Experts of 1947*, pp. 63–64 (Article 33). For a thorough analysis of this meeting, see Lewis, pp. 243–248.

[41] Draft article 40, adopted by the 17th International Red Cross Conference in Stockholm, read as follows:

> The Contracting Parties shall be under the obligation to search for persons charged with breaches of the present Convention, whatever their nationality. They shall further, in accordance with their national legislation or with the Conventions for the repression of acts considered as war crimes, refer them for trial to their own courts, or hand them over for judgment to another Contracting Party.

> See *Draft Conventions adopted by the 1948 Stockholm Conference*, p. 25. The Conference also adopted draft article 39, which read: 'Within a maximum period of two years, the governments of the High Contracting Parties shall, if their penal laws are inadequate, enact or propose to their legislative assemblies the measures required to make unlawful, in time of war, all acts contrary to the provisions of the present Convention.' For an analysis of this meeting, see Lewis, pp. 253–257.

[42] These four draft articles were entitled 'Legislative measures', 'Grave violations', 'Superior orders' and 'Safeguard', respectively. For further details, see Pictet (ed.), *Commentary on the First Geneva Convention*, ICRC, 1952, p. 358; Best, pp. 160–163; and *ICRC Remarks and Proposals on the 1948 Stockholm Draft*. See also Graven, pp. 248–250; Nebout, in particular pp. 17–22; de La Pradelle, pp. 251–255; and Lewis, pp. 257–262.

[43] See *Final Record of the Diplomatic Conference of Geneva of 1949*, Vol. II-B, p. 24.

[44] The text considered by the Diplomatic Conference was the *Draft Conventions adopted by the 1948 Stockholm Conference*. The ICRC's four draft articles and other amendments

Article 49(1) as ultimately adopted by the Conference, States Parties 'undertake to enact legislation necessary to provide effective penal sanctions for persons committing or ordering to be committed any of the grave breaches listed' in the subsequent article. This is clearly an obligation put on States to enact effective penal sanctions and not merely an obligation to *propose* to the legislative assemblies, should their penal law be inadequate, implementing legislation, as it was in the 1929 Convention on the Wounded and Sick or in the Stockholm Draft. However, the suggestion by the ICRC and others that this task should be undertaken within two years, and that this should be communicated to the Swiss Federal Council, was not adopted,[45] with some delegations taking the view that the legislator could not be bound by a time limit.[46]

2835   Second, the adopted version of Article 49 extends the penal responsibility of the person committing a grave breach to whoever ordered the breach to be committed, a welcome improvement on the Stockholm Draft. However, the suggestion that other forms of responsibility should be included, and the concept of superior orders or other defences touched upon, was not followed by the Diplomatic Conference. It was felt that these questions should be left to the judges who would apply national law.[47]

2836   Third, the suggestion contained in the ICRC proposal to give the State holding an alleged perpetrator the option of surrendering the person to an international tribunal for prosecution was not accepted by the Diplomatic Conference. The Conference did not want to take a decision which might hamper the future development of international law. The report on penal sanctions, which was presented to the Joint Committee of the Conference, states: '[T]he Diplomatic Conference is not here to work out international penal law. Bodies far more competent than we are have tried to do it for years.'[48]

2837   Discussion also centred on the name to be given to these violations, with the Soviet Union suggesting that the word 'crimes' be used and not 'grave breaches'.[49] A number of delegations were opposed to the word 'crime', 'firstly because this word had a different meaning in the national laws of different countries and secondly because an act only becomes a crime when this act is

submitted by different delegations were discussed by the Special Committee of the Joint Committee, as well as by the Joint Committee in charge of the common articles of the Conventions. For an analysis of the Conference's deliberations on this issue, see Lewis, pp. 262–269, and de La Pradelle, pp. 255–264.

[45] This proposal was also supported by the Soviet Union. See *Minutes of the Diplomatic Conference of Geneva of 1949*, Mixed Commission, 16 July 1949, pp. 3–13, and de La Pradelle, p. 258.

[46] This view was expressed by the US delegate, who also stated that, 'as far as his country was concerned, such a time limit was not acceptable'; *Minutes of the Diplomatic Conference of Geneva of 1949*, Mixed Commission, 16 July 1949, p. 7.

[47] See *ibid.* p. 6. Among the ICRC draft articles was one dealing with the concept of superior orders. On this point, see also Sandoz, 2009, p. 675.

[48] *Final Record of the Diplomatic Conference of Geneva of 1949*, Vol. II-B, p. 115.

[49] The concept of 'grave breaches' appears for the first time in the ICRC's draft article 40; see *ICRC Remarks and Proposals on the 1948 Stockholm Draft*, p. 18. On the Russian amendments, see de La Pradelle, pp. 258 and 260–261.

made punishable by a penal law'.[50] In the end, the provision on judicial safeguards for the accused suggested by the ICRC was not adopted in its original form, as some safeguards were already included in the Third and Fourth Conventions.[51]

C. Paragraph 1: The obligation to enact implementing legislation

1. Legislation providing effective penal sanctions

2838   According to Article 49(1), States Parties 'undertake to enact any legislation necessary to provide effective penal sanctions for persons committing, or ordering to be committed, any of the grave breaches' listed in Article 50. This is clearly an obligation for all States Parties, and not only for States party to an armed conflict. States Parties should fulfil this obligation without delay.[52] States should strive to have their implementing legislation in place when they deposit their instrument of ratification or accession. As the International Court of Justice noted in the *Obligation to Prosecute or Extradite case*, in relation to a similar obligation contained in the 1984 Convention against Torture:

> This obligation, which has to be implemented by the State concerned as soon as it is bound by the Convention, has in particular a preventive and deterrent character, since by equipping themselves with the necessary legal tools to prosecute this type of offence, the States parties ensure that their legal systems will operate to that effect and commit themselves to co-ordinating their efforts to eliminate any risk of impunity.[53]

2839   The wording of Article 49 ('to undertake to enact any legislation') differs from that of Article 29 of the 1929 Geneva Convention on the Wounded and Sick, which only called on States to 'propose to their legislatures should their penal laws be inadequate, the necessary measures for the repression in time of war of any act contrary to the provisions of the present Convention'.[54] The use of the term 'undertake' in Article 49 means that States Parties are under an unconditional obligation to enact any implementing legislation necessary to provide effective penal sanctions for persons committing or ordering to be committed any of the grave breaches listed in Article 50. There is no doubt that

---

[50] See *Minutes of the Diplomatic Conference of Geneva of 1949*, Mixed Commission, 16 July 1949, p. 8.

[51] *Ibid.* p. 6. Paragraph 4 of Article 49 (judicial safeguards) was, however, included in the final version of the Conventions; see *ibid.* p. 11.

[52] This can also be read together with Article 80 of Additional Protocol I, which more generally requires High Contracting Parties and Parties to an armed conflict to take without delay all necessary measures for the execution of their obligations under the Conventions and the Protocol.

[53] ICJ, *Obligation to Prosecute or Extradite case*, Judgment, 2012, para. 75.

[54] The preparatory work for the 1949 Diplomatic Conference shows that the drafters wanted to move away from the 1929 wording. They borrowed the much stronger wording of Article 5 of the 1948 Genocide Convention, which lays down the obligation to enact legislation 'to provide effective penalties'. See *Final Record of the Diplomatic Conference of Geneva of 1949*, Vol. II-B, p. 115.

this represents a clear and imperative measure for all States Parties, to be acted upon already in peacetime.[55]

2840 National legislation must provide effective penal sanctions in each State Party's national judicial system. What are the characteristics of an effective penal sanction?[56]

2841 The implementing legislation ought to provide for penal sanctions that are appropriate and can be strictly applied. Penal sanctions, as opposed to disciplinary ones, will be issued by judicial institutions, be they military or civilian, and will usually lead to the imprisonment of the perpetrators, or to the imposition of fines. Because of their seriousness, imprisonment is widely recognized as a central element in punishing grave breaches and other serious violations of humanitarian law.[57]

2842 It is widely acknowledged that, to be effective, penal sanctions must be sufficiently dissuasive: they should stop ongoing violations of humanitarian law and prevent their repetition or the occurrence of new violations.[58] Sanctions should be imposed as quickly as possible after the act has been committed in order to have a significant deterrent effect. Another crucial aspect of a dissuasive sanction is that it ought to be foreseeable for persons who are likely to be involved in armed conflicts.[59] In order to play an effective preventive role, criminal provisions sanctioning serious violations of humanitarian law should be made public and disseminated appropriately.[60] Ultimately, the efficacy of sanctions and their dissuasive character depend on the degree to which the rule whose infringement is subject to sanctions has been internalized by the weapon bearers.

2843 Moreover, it is often thought that, to be effective, penal sanctions must also be applicable to all perpetrators without discrimination, irrespective of the Party to which they belong, in order to uphold the principle of equal application of the law and avoid the creation of a feeling of 'victor's justice'.[61] Furthermore, penal sanctions ought to respect the principle of individualization of the sentence and the principle of proportionality between the severity of the punishment and the gravity of the offence.[62]

---

[55] On this point, see Dörmann/Geiss, p. 707. See also the commentary on common Article 1, para. 170, on the use of the term 'undertake'. See further ICJ, *Military and Paramilitary Activities in and against Nicaragua case*, Merits, Judgment, 1986, para. 220, and *Application of the Genocide Convention case*, Merits, Judgment, 2007, para. 162.

[56] The ICRC conducted a process of consultations and exchanges on the role of 'sanctions'. The discussion below summarizes the main findings of this process, which have been included in La Rosa, 2008. See also ICRC Advisory Service on International Humanitarian Law, 2014, *National measures to repress violations of international humanitarian law (Civil law systems)*, Vol. I, pp. 61–66, and Vol. II, pp. 133–141.

[57] La Rosa, 2008, p. 244.   [58] *Ibid.* pp. 222 and 226.   [59] *Ibid.* p. 226.

[60] International humanitarian law needs to be integrated into the training and education of weapon bearers. See the commentary on Article 47.

[61] La Rosa, 2008, p. 227.

[62] For further details, see *ibid.* pp. 227–228 and 245. This is particularly important in order to avoid a general lack of comprehension and resentment among both the victims and the alleged perpetrators.

2844   The choice of penalties rests with each State Party. Even though there will be no uniformity in the penalties applied by States Parties, the grave breaches regime aims for uniformity in sanctioning all grave breaches listed therein. Reliance on domestic criminal law inevitably implies that those crimes will be subject to the specificities of each criminal justice system.

2845   State practice, in particular in the last 20 years, has also shown that, to be able to provide effective penal sanctions for grave breaches and other serious violations of humanitarian law, it is often necessary to include in domestic legislation some general principles of international criminal law, particularly when they are at variance with the general principles of domestic criminal law.[63] For example, a statute of limitations[64] or the defence of superior orders[65] does not apply to grave breaches and other serious violations of humanitarian law. Furthermore, amnesties granted to persons who have participated in an armed conflict shall not extend to those who are suspected of having committed grave breaches or other serious violations of humanitarian law.[66]

2846   Apart from ensuring that the substance of the grave breaches listed in the Geneva Conventions is covered by national criminal legislation, the implementing legislation must also establish a jurisdictional basis for the prosecution of all grave breaches. As prescribed in paragraph 2 of Article 49, States Parties must be able to prosecute all persons who have committed or ordered the

---

[63] On this point, see the comments made by States in ICRC, *Preventing and repressing international crimes*, Vol. I, p. 38. See also ICRC, *National measures to repress violations of international humanitarian law (Civil law systems)*, pp. 150–151.

[64] See, in particular, ICRC Study on Customary International Humanitarian Law (2005), Rule 160 (and supporting practice pp. 614–618), and Article 29 of the 1998 ICC Statute, which provides that 'the crimes within the jurisdiction of the Court shall not be subject to any statute of limitations'. It has been suggested in the literature that a national statute of limitations, which drastically reduces the time span for the institution of criminal proceedings, would preclude a State from effectively complying with its obligations under Article 49 of the Convention; see e.g. Kreß, p. 806.

[65] See in particular, ICRC Study on Customary International Humanitarian Law (2005), Rule 155, which provides that 'obeying a superior order does not relieve a subordinate of criminal responsibility if the subordinate knew that the act ordered was unlawful or should have known because of the manifestly unlawful nature of the act ordered'. This rule is spelled out in the 1993 ICTY Statute, the 1994 ICTR Statute, the 1998 ICC Statute, UNTAET Regulation No. 2000/15 and the 2002 SCSL Statute.

[66] In international armed conflict, the granting of amnesties or any other measures, precluding in effect any genuine investigation and prosecution, cannot extend to those suspected of having committed grave breaches, as this would violate the absolute obligations contained in Article 49 to investigate and, if appropriate, prosecute or extradite alleged offenders. See ECCC, *Ieng Sary* Decision on Ieng Sary's Rule 89 Preliminary Objections, 2011, para. 39, where the Extraordinary Chambers stated: 'As Cambodia is under an absolute obligation to ensure the prosecution or punishment of perpetrators of grave breaches of the 1949 Geneva Conventions, genocide and torture, the 1996 Royal Decree cannot relieve it of the duty to prosecute these crimes or constitute an obstacle thereto.' Another question might arise as to whether an amnesty law adopted in one State Party would prevent other High Contracting Parties from exercising their jurisdiction over the alleged perpetrators and prosecuting them for grave breaches. Furthermore, human rights bodies have stated that amnesties are incompatible with the duty of States to investigate crimes under international law and violations of non-derogable human rights law; for more details, see Henckaerts/Doswald-Beck, commentary on Rule 159, pp. 612–614.

commission of grave breaches, regardless of their nationality. It is commonly accepted, therefore, that alongside the other bases of criminal jurisdiction, universal jurisdiction over grave breaches must be included in the implementing legislation.[67] It is imperative that States Parties implement legislation of universal reach.[68]

2. The practical implementation of the obligation to enact legislation

2847 States Parties must ensure that their legislation prohibits and punishes grave breaches, regardless of the nationality of the perpetrator. The first step for every State Party is therefore to determine whether their legislation requires the specific integration of these crimes. It will be necessary to assess whether national legislation already contains the relevant prohibitions and the jurisdictional basis to extend jurisdiction to grave breaches committed by any perpetrators, regardless of their nationality.[69] This task is certainly a complex one and requires a thorough study of the relevant domestic legal framework. Over the last 60 years, States Parties have chosen to implement these obligations in different ways, based on their respective legal systems, culture and legislative practice. The legislator has a number of available options.[70]

2848 The first option consists of applying the existing military or ordinary national criminal law. States Parties can take the view that their domestic criminal law already provides adequate provisions for the prosecution of grave breaches and therefore it is not necessary to introduce new crimes.[71] However, in many instances, the crimes under domestic law do not fully correspond to the criminal behaviour in armed conflict covered by the grave breaches.[72] Some

---

[67] For a definition of the concept of universal jurisdiction, see section D.1, para. 2860.

[68] See Dörmann/Geiss, p. 709.

[69] In some monist countries, international humanitarian law does not need to be translated into national law and can be directly enforced by domestic courts, as the primacy of international law over national law is provided for in the constitution. See ICRC, *Preventing and repressing international crimes*, Vol. I, pp. 36–37, citing the examples of France and Hungary.

[70] For further details on the methods of incorporating international crimes into domestic law, see ICRC, *The Domestic Implementation of International Humanitarian Law*, chapter 3, and *Preventing and repressing international crimes*, Vol. I, pp. 29–39. See also Dörmann/Geiss, pp. 710–717, and Blazeby.

[71] The participants in the Third Universal Meeting of National Committees for the Implementation of International Humanitarian Law took the view that, in the light of its numerous drawbacks, this method should only be applied for a transitory period. See ICRC, *Preventing and repressing international crimes*, Vol. I, pp. 30–32. On the pros and cons of this option, see also Ferdinandusse, pp. 729–734.

[72] Also note that, under Article 10(2)(a) of the 1993 ICTY Statute and Article 9(2)(a) of the 1994 ICTR Statute, each Tribunal may still prosecute a person who has been tried before a national court for 'acts constituting serious violations of international humanitarian law' if the acts for which the person was tried were 'categorized as an ordinary crime'. For these tribunals, prosecutions of these violations simply as ordinary crimes are not the same as prosecution under the material provisions of the respective Statute. On this point, see Dörmann/Geiss, p. 710. On the ICC's interpretation of Article 20(3) of its Statute in the light of the *ne bis in idem* rule, see *Gaddafi* Judgment on the appeal of Libya against the decision of the Pre-Trial Chamber of

specific grave breaches would not easily form part of domestic criminal law.[73] Furthermore, some objective elements of grave breaches, such as the nexus to the armed conflict or the status of protected persons, may not easily be captured by domestic crimes. Lastly, the penalties in existing law for domestic crimes might not be appropriate in the light of the seriousness of the war crimes or grave breaches in question.[74]

2849   The second option that has been chosen by some States Parties aims at criminalizing all serious violations of international humanitarian law at the national level by making a general reference to the relevant provisions of international humanitarian law, to international law in general, or to the laws and customs of war, and specifying a range of penalties.[75] This option has the advantage of being simple and straightforward: all breaches are made punishable by a simple reference to the relevant instrument or to customary law. No new national legislation is needed when the treaties are amended or new obligations arise for a State which becomes party to a new treaty. The main disadvantage of this method is that criminalization by a generic provision may prove insufficient in view of the principles of legality and specificity.[76] National judges will have the task of clarifying and interpreting the law in the light of the provisions of international law, leaving the judiciary with considerable room for interpretation.[77]

2850   The third option consists in providing in domestic law for specific crimes corresponding to the grave breaches contained in the Geneva Conventions. This can be achieved, for example, by transcribing into national law the full list of

---

31 May 2013 on the Admissibility of the Case, 2014, in particular paras 60–84. See also ECCC, *Ieng Sary* Decision on Ieng Sary's Rule 89 Preliminary Objections, 2011, paras 32–36.

[73] Some grave breaches are rather specific and uniquely related to armed conflict, such as the unlawful deportation or transfer of a protected person (Article 146 of the Fourth Convention) or compelling a protected person or a prisoner of war to serve in the forces of a hostile power (Article 129 of the Third Convention).

[74] On these issues, see also Dörmann/Geiss, pp. 709–710, and the conclusions of the Public Commission to Examine the Maritime Incident of 31 May 2010, Second Report – The Turkel Commission, February 2013. Reflecting on the content of Israeli criminal law, the Commission stated:

> In order to adhere to the requirements of international law to 'enact legislation necessary to provide effective penal sanctions' for those committing war crimes, the Commission is of the opinion that it is satisfactory to 'translate' the behavior amounting to a war crime into an existing offense in the domestic legislation, provided that it reflects the severity of the violation under international law. . . . The Ministry of Justice should initiate legislation wherever there is a deficiency regarding international prohibitions that do not have a 'regular' equivalent in the Israeli Penal Law, and rectify that deficiency through Israeli criminal legislation (p. 365).

[75] For examples of States Parties that have chosen this option, see ICRC, *Preventing and repressing international crimes*, Vol. I, p. 33.

[76] In accordance with the principle of legality, '[n]o one may be accused or convicted of a criminal offence on account of any act or omission which did not constitute a criminal offence under national or international law at the time it was committed; nor may a heavier penalty be imposed than that which was applicable at the time the criminal offence was committed'; ICRC Study on Customary International Humanitarian Law (2005), Rule 101. The principle of specificity requires that the definition of the proscribed act be sufficiently precise.

[77] For further details, see ICRC, *Preventing and repressing international crimes*, Vol. I, p. 33.

grave breaches with identical wording and laying down the range of penalties applying to each offence, or by separately redefining or rewriting in national law the description of the types of conduct constituting each breach.[78] Specific criminalization will better respect the principle of specificity, as the criminal conduct will be clearly defined and the sanction for such conduct made predictable. This option entails a major task for the legislator, as it involves extensive review of existing penal legislation, but lacks the flexibility needed to incorporate future developments in this field of law. This option has often been followed by the common-law countries which have incorporated the full list of grave breaches into their legislation.[79] Some countries have also chosen to adopt a comprehensive approach to the incorporation of international crimes into their national legislation, and to include not only the list of grave breaches, but also the list of war crimes contained in the ICC Statute[80] and other crimes reflected in customary or treaty law.[81]

2851 The fourth option consists in a mixed approach combining criminalization by a general provision with the explicit and specific criminalization of certain serious crimes.[82] This might be the best method in order to respect the principles of legality and specificity without the need to amend the legislation whenever the State becomes party to a new treaty. This method permits treaty obligations to be carried out fully and with due differentiation of the various crimes.

2852 A number of tools are at the disposal of States Parties to help them in their efforts to incorporate grave breaches and other war crimes into their domestic legal systems.[83]

---

[78] For examples of States Parties that have chosen this option, see *ibid.* pp. 33–35.

[79] See e.g. United Kingdom, *Geneva Conventions Act*, 1957, as amended, which served as a model for the legislation of many other common-law countries. See also ICRC, National Implementation of IHL database, available at https://www.icrc.org/ihl-nat.

[80] *Ibid.* See, in particular, the legislation of Burundi, Cyprus, Denmark, Ireland, Kenya, New Zealand and South Africa, to cite but a few examples.

[81] *Ibid.* See e.g. the legislation of Australia, France, Germany, the Netherlands and Spain.

[82] For examples of States Parties that have chosen this option, see ICRC, *Preventing and repressing international crimes*, Vol. I, p. 36.

[83] Helpful starting points include the factsheets, ratification kits and reports on expert meetings produced by the ICRC or other institutions that have looked at the intricacies of implementing war crimes legislation at the domestic level. See e.g. ICRC, *National measures to repress violations of international humanitarian law (Civil law systems)*, and Segall. Also useful are model laws, such as those contained in ICRC, Advisory Service on International Humanitarian Law, *Model Law, Geneva Conventions (Consolidation) Act, Legislation for Common Law States on the 1949 Geneva Conventions and their 1977 and 2005 Additional Protocols*, August 2008; the Revised Commonwealth Model Law on implementing the ICC Statute and related commentary, produced by the Commonwealth Secretariat; and the Arab Model Law Project on Crimes within ICC Jurisdiction. Databases containing the implementing legislation of many States Parties are invaluable tools enabling States to learn from one another's experience. Three databases are particularly relevant. One is produced by the ICRC, at https://www.icrc.org/ihl-nat. Others are the documents compiled on the website of the Coalition for the International Criminal Court, at https://www.iccnow.org/?mod=documents, and a third database on the website of the ICC, at http://www.legal-tools.org/browse. Lastly, universal and regional meetings of national committees on international humanitarian law and similar bodies can also be instrumental in

3. Forms of individual criminal responsibility and available defences

2853   States Parties need to ensure that national implementing legislation provides effective penal sanctions for persons who have committed grave breaches or have ordered their commission.[84] The text of Article 49 establishes the individual criminal responsibility of offenders under international law, but limits it to the person committing the crime and the person who ordered the crime, without mentioning other forms of individual responsibility or available defences. The preparatory work for the Convention makes it clear that the negotiators could not reach general agreement on other forms of individual criminal responsibility, such as complicity and command responsibility, or on certain grounds potentially excluding criminal responsibility, such as duress or the plea of superior orders. The position adopted by the Conference was that '[t]hese should be left to the judges who would apply the national laws'.[85]

2854   Practice has evolved since the adoption of the 1949 Geneva Conventions, and it is generally recognized today that individuals are not only criminally responsible for committing or ordering the commission of grave breaches and other serious violations of humanitarian law, but also for assisting in, facilitating or aiding and abetting the commission of such crimes.[86] They are also criminally responsible for planning or instigating their commission.[87]

2855   Commanders and other superiors can be held criminally responsible for grave breaches and other serious violations of humanitarian law committed pursuant to their orders.[88] They can also be held individually responsible for failing to take proper measures to prevent their subordinates from committing such

---

giving an impetus to States of the same region or legal tradition and encouraging them to implement their obligations under international humanitarian law as quickly as possible. For a full review of all relevant documents, see ICRC, *Preventing and repressing international crimes*, Vol. I, pp. 75–85.

[84]   For an interpretation of the word 'persons' and a discussion of who can commit a grave breach, see the commentary on Article 50, section C.3.

[85]   See *Minutes of the Diplomatic Conference of Geneva of 1949*, Mixed Commission, 16 July 1949, p. 6.

[86]   As to the question of attempt, Article 25(3)(f) of the 1998 ICC Statute includes, among acts engaging individual criminal responsibility, attempts to commit grave breaches or war crimes. However, the 1945 Allied Control Council Law No. 10 did not recognize attempt as an act engaging criminal responsibility for war crimes. Similarly, the 1968 UN Convention on the Non-Applicability of Statutory Limitations to War Crimes and Crimes against Humanity does not apply to attempted war crimes, nor do the Statutes of either the ICTY or the ICTR provide for this form of responsibility. Article 49, however, does not preclude States from subjecting such attempts to penal or disciplinary sanctions.

[87]   On the forms of responsibility, see Henckaerts/Doswald-Beck, commentary on Rule 151, in particular p. 554. See also ICTY Statute (1993), Article 7; ICTR Statute (1994), Article 6; ICC Statute (1998), Article 25; and SCSL Statute (2002), Article 6. Lastly, it may be noted that both the ICTY and the ICTR have extended their jurisdiction to a particular form of criminal responsibility, namely responsibility as part of a joint criminal enterprise or common purpose. See, in particular, ICTY, *Tadić* Appeal Judgment, 1999, paras 195–226; *Krnojelac* Appeal Judgment, 2003, para. 30; and *Vasiljević* Appeal Judgment, 2004, paras 96–99. For more details, see, *inter alia*, Mettraux, 2005, pp. 287–293; Danner/Martinez; Sluiter; and Cassese.

[88]   See Henckaerts/Doswald-Beck, Rule 152 and its commentary.

violations, or, if already committed, for failing to punish the persons responsible.[89] It is essential for national law to provide for the effective sanctioning of commanders or superiors, if the system of repression is to be effective during armed conflict.[90] States Parties should therefore consider extending all those forms of criminal responsibility to grave breaches and other war crimes in their domestic legislation.

2856   At the 1949 Diplomatic Conference, defences available to alleged perpetrators of grave breaches were also omitted and were considered to be best regulated by domestic law. As practice on this issue has developed since 1949, legislators should consider including references to various grounds for excluding criminal responsibility, such as duress, that are open to alleged perpetrators of grave breaches.[91] Furthermore, it is widely accepted that obeying a superior order does not relieve a subordinate of criminal responsibility if the subordinate knew that the act ordered was unlawful or should have known because of the manifestly unlawful nature of the act.[92] A corollary of this rule is that every combatant has a duty to disobey a manifestly unlawful order.[93] The fact that a war crime was committed as a result of superior orders has nevertheless been taken into account as a factor mitigating the punishment.[94]

4. Critical assessment

2857   A first prerequisite for the grave breaches system to be effective is the enactment of penal sanctions under domestic law so that the domestic courts of States Parties can enforce the law. In 1965, the 20th International Conference of the Red Cross adopted a resolution appealing to governments 'which have

---

[89] For the contours of the concept of command responsibility, see *ibid.* Rule 153 and its commentary, pp. 558–563; Additional Protocol I, Articles 86(2) and 87; ICTY Statute (1993), Article 7(3); and ICC Statute (1998), Article 28;. The most important recent judicial decisions on command responsibility were taken by the ICTY: see *Hadžihasanović* Decision on Interlocutory Appeal Challenging Jurisdiction in Relation to Command Responsibility, 2003; *Delalić* Appeal Judgment, 2001, paras 222–241; *Aleksovski* Appeal Judgment, 2000, paras 72 and 76; *Kunarac* Trial Judgment, 2001, paras 394–399; *Blaškić* Appeal Judgment, 2004, paras 53–85; and *Perišić* Appeal Judgment, 2013, paras 86–120. See also ICTR, *Bagilishema* Appeal Judgment, 2002, paras 24–50, and *Kajelijeli* Trial Judgment, 2003, to name but a few. See also Mettraux, 2009.

[90] This is clearly recognized in Article 87 of Additional Protocol I.

[91] See the list of grounds excluding criminal responsibility in Article 31 of the 1998 ICC Statute. For the controversy surrounding the applicability of the ground of self-defence, as set forth in Article 31(1)(c) of the 1998 ICC Statute, to war crimes, see Eric David, *Principes de droit des conflits armés*, 5th edition, Bruylant, Brussels, 2012, paras 4.430–4.431 and 4.352.

[92] Henckaerts/Doswald-Beck, Rule 155 and commentary. This rule was already present in the IMT Charters for Germany and the Far East setting up the Nuremberg and Tokyo tribunals. It follows that a superior order cannot therefore relieve a person from criminal responsibility unless that person was under a legal obligation to obey orders from the government or the superior in question, did not know that the order was unlawful, and the order was not manifestly unlawful (Article 33 of the 1998 ICC Statute). On this issue, see also Article 7(4) of the 1993 ICTY Statute and Article 6(4) of the 1994 ICTR Statute.

[93] See Henckaerts/Doswald-Beck, Rule 154 and commentary.

[94] See e.g. ICTY, *Erdemović* Appeal Judgment, 1997, Joint Separate Opinion of Judge McDonald and Judge Vohrah, para. 34, and *Mrđa* Sentencing Judgment, 2004, paras 65 and 67.

so far not done so to complete their legislation so as to ensure adequate penal sanctions for violations of these Conventions'.[95] By the following International Conference in 1969, the ICRC had received information on national implementing legislation for only 49 out of 122 States Parties.[96] Many common-law States enacted Geneva Conventions Acts, while a number of civil-law countries chose to amend their criminal codes, military manuals or military criminal codes.[97]

2858   The establishment of the ICC has had a profound effect on the approach of many States to national implementing legislation. The ICC Statute leaves the primary role in the effective prosecution of international crimes to national courts and emphasizes that the ICC must be complementary to national criminal jurisdictions. The ICC is only able to exercise jurisdiction when national jurisdictions are unable or unwilling to prosecute alleged perpetrators.[98] A State might not be able to undertake prosecutions effectively if it is not equipped with adequate legislation penalizing the crimes contained in the ICC Statute, including grave breaches of the Geneva Conventions. A significant number of States party to the Geneva Conventions and/or the ICC Statute have therefore looked at the content of their national legislation and often decided to adopt specific provisions to ensure that they are able to prosecute perpetrators of war crimes, including grave breaches of the Geneva Conventions.[99] At the time of writing, information on national implementing legislation can be found for more than 125 out of the 196 States Parties.[100]

D. Paragraph 2: The obligation to search for and prosecute or extradite alleged offenders

2859 The 1949 Geneva Conventions were the first international treaties to put States Parties under an unconditional obligation to search for alleged perpetrators of grave breaches and to either prosecute before their own courts or extradite them, regardless of their nationality. This obligation can be referred to as *primo prosequi, secundo dedere* (first to prosecute, second to extradite). The

---

[95] See ICRC, *Respect of the Geneva Conventions: Measures Taken to Repress Violations*, Report prepared for the 21st International Conference of the Red Cross, Istanbul, 1969, pp. 1–2.

[96] *Ibid.* p. 3.

[97] For examples, see the ICRC's National Implementation of IHL database, available at https://www.icrc.org/ihl-nat. For further details, see section C.2.

[98] See ICC Statute (1998), Articles 13, 14 and 17. For an interpretation of Article 17, see, in particular, ICC, *Katanga* Judgment on the Appeal against the Oral Decision on Admissibility, 2009, paras 58–86.

[99] Ironically, it must also be noted that the creation of international criminal tribunals and the establishment of the ICC represent 'a modern reaction to the failure of States to prosecute'; Dörmann/Geiss, p. 705.

[100] See national legislation available in the ICRC's National Implementation of IHL database, https://www.icrc.org/ihl-nat. See also ICRC, *Preventing and repressing international crimes*, Vol. II, pp. 53–122.

Convention clearly puts the obligations to search, investigate and prosecute first, and this obligation exists independently of any extradition request.[101]

1. The obligation to search for and prosecute alleged offenders regardless of their nationality

a. Search for and trial of alleged offenders

2860 The obligations to search for and prosecute alleged offenders imply that each State Party must provide in its national legislation for the mechanisms and procedures to ensure that it can actively search for alleged offenders, make a preliminary inquiry into the facts and, when so warranted, submit any such cases to the appropriate authorities for prosecution. It is important to note that in paragraphs 2 and 3 of Article 49, the drafters chose to use the words '*each State party*', leaving no doubt that these obligations are not restricted to Parties to armed conflict, but apply to all States party to the Conventions.[102]

2861 The decision whether or not to prosecute an alleged perpetrator should be taken by competent authorities in line with national legal requirements. National laws regarding standards of suspicion or grounds for arrest and detention will apply. The wording of Article 49(2) – 'bring such persons before its own courts' – does not imply an absolute duty to prosecute or to punish. The competent authorities might conclude that there are not sufficient reasons to believe that the alleged perpetrator committed the grave breach or that there is simply not enough evidence available to secure a conviction.[103]

2862 The obligation to bring alleged offenders before national courts does mean, however, that if the competent authorities have collected sufficient evidence to bring a criminal charge, they cannot rely, for example, on national rules of prosecutorial discretion and decide not to press charges. In those circumstances, they must prosecute the case.[104] Any other conclusion would be at

---

[101] See Henzelin, p. 353, as well as Van Elst, p. 819 and Van Steenberghe, p. 1113, who prefers the maxim '*prosequi vel dedere*' (prosecute or surrender), p. 1114. See also the view expressed by the International Court of Justice in the *Obligation to Prosecute or Extradite case*, in relation to the 1984 Convention against Torture: 'Article 7, paragraph 1, requires the State concerned to submit the case to its competent authorities for the purpose of prosecution, irrespective of the existence of a prior request for the extradition of the suspect. . . . Extradition is an option offered to the State by the Convention, whereas prosecution is an international obligation under the Convention, the violation of which is a wrongful act engaging the responsibility of the State'; *Obligation to Prosecute or Extradite case*, Judgment, 2012, paras 94 and 95. An identical reasoning applies to Article 49 of the Geneva Convention, which is phrased in a similar way to Article 7 of the 1984 Convention against Torture.

[102] Debates during the 1949 Diplomatic Conference show that the participants rejected the Italian proposal to limit to Parties to an armed conflict the obligation to search for persons alleged to have committed any of the grave breaches and to bring them before domestic courts. The Dutch delegate stated that 'each Contracting Party should be under this obligation, even if neutral in a conflict'; *Minutes of the Diplomatic Conference of Geneva of 1949*, Mixed Commission, 16 July 1949, p. 7.

[103] On this point, see e.g. Kreß, p. 801, and O'Keefe, p. 816.

[104] On this point, see e.g. Gaeta, p. 631.

odds with the obligations contained in Article 49(2), as well as those contained in common Article 1 to respect and ensure respect for the Convention.

b. Universal jurisdiction

2863 The obligations to search for and prosecute alleged offenders before a State's own courts must be carried out 'regardless of their nationality'. The effective implementation of these obligations requires that each State Party, as mentioned above, has previously extended the universality principle to the list of grave breaches in its national legislation. The universality principle, also referred to as universal jurisdiction, has been defined as 'criminal jurisdiction based solely on the nature of the crime, without regard to where the crime was committed, the nationality of the alleged or convicted perpetrator, the nationality of the victim, or any other connection to the state exercising such jurisdiction'.[105]

2864　Prosecutions for grave breaches could of course be based on other accepted titles of jurisdiction, such as territoriality, active and passive personality or the protective principle. However, universal jurisdiction must also be provided for in national legislation, to ensure that any State Party, and not only States party to an armed conflict,[106] is able to exercise its jurisdiction over alleged offenders regardless of their nationality. The object and purpose of this paragraph is clearly to give all States Parties the means to prevent impunity and to deny safe haven to alleged perpetrators of grave breaches.

2865　The preparatory work for the Conventions makes it clear that the drafters intended to provide all States Parties with an additional basis of jurisdiction so that any State Party would be able to assert its jurisdiction over alleged perpetrators of grave breaches.[107] Subsequent practice has shown that States

---

[105] *The Princeton Principles on Universal Jurisdiction*, Princeton University, 2001, Principle 1. The African Union-European Union Technical Ad hoc Expert Group on the Principle of Universal Jurisdiction used the following definition: 'Universal criminal jurisdiction is the assertion by one state of its jurisdiction over crimes allegedly committed in the territory of another state by nationals of another state against nationals of another state where the crime alleged poses no direct threat to the vital interests of the state asserting jurisdiction.' Council of the European Union, *Report of the AU-EU Technical Ad hoc Expert Group on the Principle of Universal Jurisdiction*, Doc. 8672/09, Brussels, 15 April 2009, p. 3. For a discussion of the concept of universal jurisdiction, see in particular Bassiouni, pp. 81–157.

[106] During the 1949 Diplomatic Conference, the Dutch delegate stated that 'each Contracting Party should be under this obligation, even if neutral in a conflict'. 'The Chairman was of the opinion that a neutral State did not violate its neutrality by trying or handing over an accused, under an international obligation.' *Minutes of the Diplomatic Conference of Geneva of 1949*, Mixed Commission, 16 July 1949, p. 7.

[107] The universality principle was clearly mentioned during the 1949 Diplomatic Conference in the discussion on Article 49(2): '[T]he principle of universality should be applied here. The Contracting Party in whose power the accused is, should either try him or hand him over to another Contracting Party.' *Ibid*. See also *Final Record of the Diplomatic Conference of Geneva of 1949*, Vol. II-B, p. 364, where the UK delegate stated:

　　If the High Contracting Parties carry out their obligations, under the first paragraph of this Article, to enact any legislation necessary to provide effective penal sanctions for persons

Parties undoubtedly understand Article 49 as providing for universal jurisdiction. More than 100 national laws have extended this form of jurisdiction to the list of grave breaches.[108]

2866   The obligation to search for and investigate implies activity on the part of the State authorities. The text of Article 49 does not require any link to the prosecuting State, such as a requirement that the alleged offender be present in the territory of the prosecuting State.[109] A literal interpretation of Article 49(2) could therefore imply that each State Party must search for and prosecute any alleged perpetrators the world over, regardless of their nationality. Such a literal interpretation has not been widely shared by States Parties in the last 60 years. The practice since 1949 shows that some States, while having extended the principle of universal jurisdiction to grave breaches, have made prosecution conditional on the presence, temporary or permanent, of the alleged offender in the territory of the State Party.[110] In practice, States Parties cannot effectively prosecute alleged perpetrators unless they were present in their territory or in places under their jurisdiction at some point in time. Another condition sometimes also found in domestic legislation is that of special prosecutorial discretion.[111] It might manifest itself in the need to obtain approval from the attorney-general or the director of public prosecutions before any proceedings based on universal jurisdiction can be started.[112]

committing..., etc., grave breaches of the Convention, it necessarily follows that they will be able to bring before their Courts any such persons.... [I]t is obvious that the Courts of such a State will have jurisdiction to try any person committing such an offence.

See also de La Pradelle, pp. 258–259.

[108] See the ICRC's National Implementation of IHL database, available at https://www.icrc.org/ihl-nat. See also UN Secretary-General, *Report on the scope and application of the principle of universal jurisdiction*, 2011, para. 134, and ICRC, *Preventing and repressing international crimes*, Vol. II, pp. 53–122.

[109] Some States, faithful to the wording of the Geneva Conventions, do not require the existence of any link between the alleged perpetrator and the prosecuting State, and allow prosecution of an alleged perpetrator who is not present on their territory. See ICRC, *Preventing and repressing international crimes*, Vol. I, p. 60, citing Austria, Canada, Germany, Italy and New Zealand as examples.

[110] The information collected by the ICRC shows that over 40 States require the presence, temporary or permanent, of the alleged offender on the territory of the prosecuting State before they can initiate prosecutions of alleged offenders for war crimes. See *ibid.* pp. 59–60. Examples of these States include Argentina, Bosnia and Herzegovina, Colombia, the Democratic Republic of the Congo, Denmark, Ethiopia, Ireland, the Netherlands, Samoa, Senegal, Spain and the United Kingdom. See also the ICRC's National Implementation of IHL database, available at https://www.icrc.org/ihl-nat, and the ICRC's contribution to the UN General Assembly's debate on the scope of application of universal jurisdiction, in UN Secretary-General, *Report on the scope and application of the principle of universal jurisdiction*, 2011, para. 136; and La Rosa/Chavez Tafur. See also the practice compiled in this regard in Council of the European Union, *Report of the AU-EU Technical Ad hoc Expert Group on the Principle of Universal Jurisdiction*, Doc. 8672/09, Brussels, 16 April 2009, paras 18 and 24. For a discussion of the requirement that the suspect be present before any proceedings can be started, see, in particular Lafontaine, pp. 1277–1286.

[111] See La Rosa/Chavez Tafur, pp. 36–37.

[112] Such a condition is sometimes included in the national legislation of common-law countries such as Australia, Botswana, Canada, Kenya, New Zealand, Samoa, Uganda and the United Kingdom, and has also been included in the Belgian Criminal Code.

2867   These requirements or procedures are helpful in avoiding actions that are not founded in law, but should not be used by States Parties to bring political considerations into play, or as a way of evading their duties to search for and either prosecute or extradite an alleged offender.[113] While States may attach conditions to the application of universal jurisdiction to grave breaches, such conditions must, in each context, be aimed at increasing the effectiveness and predictability of universal jurisdiction and not at unnecessarily restricting the possibility of prosecuting suspected offenders.[114]

c. Time frame for the performance of the obligations

2868   Even if Article 49 does not contain a specific time frame for the performance of the obligations to investigate and either prosecute or extradite, it is implicit in the text that States Parties should act within a reasonable time and in a manner compatible with the object and purpose of the provision.[115] The object and purpose of the obligation to prosecute or extradite contained in Article 49 is to prevent alleged perpetrators from going unpunished by ensuring that they cannot find refuge in any State.[116] Therefore, as soon as a State Party realizes that a person who allegedly committed or ordered the commission of a grave

---

[113] See Segall, pp. 81 and 129. It is interesting to note that, on 17 March 2014, the Spanish National Court refused to apply the new sections of the Organic Law 1/2014 on universal jurisdiction, which require *inter alia* the presence of the perpetrator on Spanish territory before universal jurisdiction can be extended to the case at hand. The High Court found that this new provision was in contradiction with the grave breaches provisions of the Geneva Conventions, obliging Spain as a High Contracting Party to prosecute the crime regardless of the perpetrators' nationalities and wherever they may be. See High Court of Spain, Case No. 27/2007.

[114] See the ICRC's contribution to the UN General Assembly's debate on the scope and application of the principle of universal jurisdiction, in UN Secretary-General, *Report on the scope and application of the principle of universal jurisdiction*, 2011, paras 136–138, as well as 'Information and observations on the scope of application of universal jurisdiction', submitted by the ICRC pursuant to UN General Assembly Res. 65/33, 30 April 2013, p. 4. In this respect, note the decision of 25 July 2012 by the Swiss Federal Criminal Court, which, in relation to the possible extension of universal jurisdiction to a former Algerian minister of defence accused of war crimes, and the requirement under Swiss law that the accused be present on the territory when a criminal investigation is opened, states:

> [T]oo strict an interpretation of the requirement that the accused be present on Swiss territory would amount to letting the accused decide whether the proceedings should go ahead. This is not what the Swiss Parliament had in mind when it decided to change the law so that Switzerland could take part effectively in international efforts to punish human rights violations.
>   Accordingly, it is sufficient that the appellant was present in Switzerland when he was questioned by the Office of the Attorney-General of Switzerland. The fact that he is no longer in Switzerland at present should not by itself hinder the investigation launched by the Office of the Attorney-General. [unofficial English translation]

Switzerland, Federal Criminal Court, *A. v. Ministère Public de la Confédération case*, Judgment, 2012, para. 3.1.

[115] For a similar reasoning, see ICJ, *Obligation to Prosecute or Extradite case*, Judgment, 2012, para. 114.

[116] For a similar reasoning, see *ibid.* para. 120, and ILC, *Report of the Working Group on the Obligation to extradite or prosecute* (aut dedere aut judicare), UN doc. A/CN.4/L.829, 2013, para. 30.

breach is on its territory or under its jurisdiction, its duty is to ensure that such person is found and, when so warranted, either tried by domestic courts or extradited without delay.[117] Article 49(2) puts the onus on States Parties, first, to investigate the facts, and, when so warranted, to prosecute or extradite alleged perpetrators.

2869   It is interesting to note the similarities between Article 49(2) and Articles 6 and 7 of the 1984 Convention against Torture and the interpretation given by the International Court of Justice of the latter provisions in the *Obligation to Prosecute or Extradite case*. On the obligation to investigate, the Court found that Senegal had violated Article 6, as it had not immediately initiated a preliminary inquiry as soon as it had reasons to suspect that the alleged perpetrator, present on its territory, had committed acts of torture.[118]

2870   Similarly, on the obligation to prosecute contained in Article 7 of that Convention, the Court recalled Senegal's duty to take all measures necessary for its implementation as soon as possible, in particular once the first complaint had been filed against the alleged perpetrator.[119]

2871   In addition, the obligations contained in Article 49(2) also imply that a State Party should take action when it is in a position to investigate and collect evidence, anticipating that either it itself at a later time or a third State, through legal assistance, might benefit from this evidence, even if an alleged perpetrator is not present on its territory or under its jurisdiction.[120] Lastly, the wording of Article 49(2) arguably allows for the issuance of an arrest warrant, even if the alleged perpetrator is not present on the territory of the issuing State,[121] and for trials *in absentia*, if permissible under domestic law.[122] This led the ICRC to

---

[117] See the statement made by the ICRC before the UN General Assembly, 67th session, Sixth Committee, 18 October 2012.

[118] See ICJ, *Obligation to Prosecute or Extradite case*, Judgment, 2012, para. 88. According to the ICJ, '[t]he establishment of the facts at issue, which is an essential stage in that process, became imperative in the present case at least since the year 2000, when a complaint was filed in Senegal against Mr. Habré'; *ibid*. para. 86. The same reasoning is applicable to grave breaches under the Geneva Conventions.

[119] ICJ, *ibid*. para. 117.

[120] On this particular point, see Kreß, p. 801. This interpretation is also in line with the views of the Institute of International Law, which in 2005 stated: 'Apart from acts of investigation and requests for extradition, the exercise of universal jurisdiction requires the presence of the alleged offender in the territory of the prosecuting State …'. Institute of International Law, *Universal criminal jurisdiction with regard to the crime of genocide, crimes against humanity and war crimes*, 17th Commission, Krakow, 2005, para. 3(b).

[121] The African Union Model National Law on Universal Jurisdiction over International Crimes is interesting as it makes the exercise of universal jurisdiction conditional only on the presence of the accused on the territory of the State at the time of commencement of the trial, therefore not excluding the possibility that States may launch investigations or pre-trial procedures *in absentia*. African Union Model National Law on Universal Jurisdiction over International Crimes, 2012, AU Doc. EX.CL/731(XXI)c, section 4.

[122] Judge ad hoc Van den Wyngaert stated in the *Arrest Warrant case* that '[t]here is no rule of *conventional international law* to the effect that universal jurisdiction *in absentia* is prohibited'; ICJ, *Arrest Warrant case*, Judgment, 2002, Dissenting Opinion of Judge ad hoc Van den Wyngaert, para. 54. See also the Joint Separate Opinion of Judges Higgins, Kooijmans and Buergenthal, para. 56. For a discussion of this issue, see O'Keefe, who concludes: 'Given that the

conclude that 'States may institute legal enquiries or proceedings even against persons outside their territory'.[123]

d. Potential immunities from jurisdiction and prosecution

2872 The obligation to search for and prosecute alleged offenders applies to any person, whether a national or a foreigner, who is suspected of having committed or ordered the commission of a grave breach. The Convention and its preparatory work do not address the issue of immunities which certain persons, such as heads of State, could enjoy under international law and which could prevent a court from prosecuting or enforcing a sentence against an alleged foreign offender.[124] Official capacity, such as being a head of State or head of government, does not exempt a person from criminal responsibility for grave breaches, but may render such persons immune from proceedings before domestic courts on the basis of the existing state of international law.

2873   The practice of the International Court of Justice has shed some light on the current state of international law regarding immunities for certain public officials.[125] The *Arrest Warrant* case arose out of an international arrest warrant issued by a Belgian investigating magistrate against the then incumbent Minister for Foreign Affairs of the Democratic Republic of the Congo (DRC).[126]

1949 Geneva Conventions mandate, and a fortiori permit, the extension of national criminal jurisdiction over grave breaches on the basis of universality, the exercise of this jurisdiction, by means of the issuance of an arrest warrant or trial, in the absence of the accused is internationally lawful' (p. 830). See also Rabinovitch: '[I]f it is unclear whether custom prohibits the exercise of *in absentia* jurisdiction, it is equally unclear whether or not it permits such an exercise. That said, State practice in recent years has increasingly supported the view that States may exercise universal jurisdiction *in absentia* if they so desire' (p. 511).

[123] See UN Secretary-General, *Report on the scope and application of the principle of universal jurisdiction*, 2011, para. 124. For a critical view on the issue of the legality of trials *in absentia* in the light of human rights, see, for example, Chris Jenks and Eric Talbot Jensen, 'All Human Rights are Equal, But Some are More Equal than Others: The Extraordinary Rendition of a Terror Suspect in Italy, the NATO SOFA, and Human Rights', *Harvard National Security Journal*, Vol. 1, 2010, pp. 172–202. On the importance of respect for the right to a fair trial and on the issue of trials *in absentia*, see European Committee on Crime Problems, Committee of Experts on the Operation of European Conventions in the Penal Field, *Judgments in Absentia, Secretariat Memorandum prepared by the Directorate of Legal Affairs*, PC-OC (98) 7, 3 March 1998, and Elizabeth Herath, 'Trials *in Absentia*: Jurisprudence and Commentary on the Judgment in Chief Prosecutor v. Abul Kalam Azad in the Bangladesh International Crimes Tribunal', *Harvard International Law Journal*, Vol. 55, June 2014, online edition.

[124] It has been stated, in relation to the 1984 Convention against Torture, and referring to the broad immunity *ratione materiae* of potentially all State officials and former State officials, that 'international law could not without absurdity require criminal jurisdiction to be assumed and exercised where the Torture Convention conditions were satisfied and, at the same time, require immunity to be granted to those properly charged'; Statement of Lord Bingham of Cornhill, with reference to the *Pinochet case* (Nos 1 and 3), in United Kingdom, House of Lords, *Jones and others case*, Judgment, 2006, para. 19.

[125] At the time of writing, this issue is also being discussed by the International Law Commission; on the topic of immunity of State officials from foreign criminal jurisdiction, see ILC, *Report of the International Law Commission, Sixty-third session (26 April–3 June and 4 July–12 August 2011)*, UN Doc. A/66/10, 2011, paras 102–203, and *Report of the International Law Commission, Sixty-fourth session (7 May–1 June and 2 July–3 August 2012)*, UN Doc. A/67/10, 2012, paras 82–139.

[126] ICJ, *Arrest Warrant case*, Judgment, 2002.

Mr Yerodia was charged with inciting genocide, crimes against humanity and grave breaches of the Geneva Conventions and Protocols against Tutsi residents in Kinshasa. The DRC submitted that Belgium had violated customary and conventional international law by issuing an international arrest warrant against its official. The ICJ judgment did not touch upon the question of whether there is a right in international law to extend universal jurisdiction to these crimes,[127] but focused instead on the issue of the immunities of a minister for foreign affairs under international law.

2874 The International Court of Justice found that ministers for foreign affairs enjoy inviolability and full immunity from criminal jurisdiction throughout the duration of their tenure in office.[128] According to the Court, there is no exception in customary international law to this rule, even where the minister in question is suspected of having committed war crimes or crimes against humanity.[129] The Court held that:

[A]lthough various international conventions on the prevention and punishment of certain serious crimes impose on States obligations of prosecution or extradition, thereby requiring them to extend their criminal jurisdiction, such extension of jurisdiction in no way affects immunities under customary international law, including those of Ministers for Foreign Affairs.[130]

The Court concluded that the circulation of the arrest warrant failed to respect the immunity of an incumbent minister for foreign affairs, and that in so doing Belgium had violated its international obligations towards the DRC.[131]

2875 The International Court of Justice emphasized that such immunity is not synonymous with impunity, as the territorial State can always prosecute its own foreign minister or choose to waive the latter's immunity. Alternatively, an international court or tribunal which has jurisdiction may prosecute such alleged perpetrators. Lastly, once ministers cease to hold office, the Court found that they could be tried by a court of another State in respect of acts committed prior or subsequent to the period in office, as well as in respect of acts committed in a private capacity during that period.[132] The Court stopped short of establishing whether war crimes or crimes against humanity committed while in office can be considered private or official acts.

2876 Some of these findings have been criticized by academics and commentators for a variety of reasons.[133] Some ICJ judges have taken the view that the

---

[127] Even if the judgment does not touch on the concept of universal jurisdiction, 10 judges commented on this issue in their separate or dissenting opinions. For an analysis of these opinions, see La Haye, pp. 238–241.

[128] ICJ, *Arrest Warrant case*, Judgment, 2002, para. 54.   [129] *Ibid.* para. 58.

[130] *Ibid.* para. 59.   [131] *Ibid.* para. 70.   [132] *Ibid.* para. 61.

[133] Among the many commentaries written about this decision, see: Malcom D. Evans and Chanaka Wickremasinghe, 'Arrest Warrant of 11 April 2000 (*Democratic Republic of the Congo v. Belgium*), Preliminary Objections and Merits, Judgment of 14 February 2002', *International and Comparative Law Quarterly*, Vol. 52, No. 3, July 2003, pp. 775–781; Philippe Sands, 'What is the ICJ for?', *Revue belge de droit international/Belgian Review of International Law*, No. 1–2, 2002, pp. 537–545; Jean-Pierre Cot, 'Éloge de l'indécision. La cour et la

commission of grave breaches and other war crimes cannot be regarded as official acts, and therefore should not benefit from immunities when the person leaves office.[134] Other commentators as well as international and national courts, while recognizing both functional and personal immunities for heads of State in office, have taken the view that, once the person has left office, international law has evolved to recognize an exception to functional immunities for the commission of international crimes, including grave breaches of the Geneva Conventions.[135] In other words, once the person leaves office, he

competence universelle', *Revue belge de droit international/Belgian Review of International Law*, No. 1–2, 2002, pp. 546–553; Jean Salmon, 'Libres propos sur l'arrêt de la C.I.J. du 14 février 2002 dans l'affaire relative au mandat d'arrêt du 11 avril 2000 (R.D.C. C. Belgique)', *Revue belge de droit international/Belgian Review of International Law*, No. 1–2, 2002, pp. 512–517; Alain Winants, 'The *Yerodia* Ruling of the International Court of Justice and the 1993/1999 Belgian Law on Universal Jurisdiction', *Leiden Journal of International Law*, Vol. 16, No. 3, September 2003, pp. 491–509; Maurice Kamto, 'Une troublante "immunité totale" du ministre des affaires étrangères', *Revue belge de droit international/Belgian Review of International Law*, No. 1–2, 2002, pp. 518–530; Sassòli, pp. 785–819; Jan Wouters and Leen De Smet, 'The ICJ's Judgment in the Case Concerning the Arrest Warrant of 11 April 2000: Some Critical Observations', *Yearbook of International Humanitarian Law*, Vol. 4, 2001, pp. 373–388; Brems, pp. 935–939; M. Cherif Bassiouni, 'Universal jurisdiction unrevisited: The International Court of Justice decision in Case concerning the Arrest Warrant of 11 April 2000 (Democratic Republic of the Congo v. Belgium)', *Palestine Yearbook of International Law*, Vol. 12, No. 1, 2002, pp. 27–48; and Darryl Robinson, 'The Impact of the Human Rights Accountability Movement on the International Law of Immunities', *Canadian Yearbook of International Law*, Vol. 40, 2002, pp. 151–191. See also Antonio Cassese, 'When May Senior State Officials Be Tried for International Crimes? Some Comments on the Congo v. Belgium Case', *European Journal of International Law*, Vol. 13, No. 4, 2002, pp. 853–875; Steffen Wirth, 'Immunity for Core Crimes? The ICJ's Judgment in the *Congo* v. *Belgium* Case', *European Journal of International Law*, Vol. 13, No. 4, 2002, pp. 877–893; Salvatore Zappalà, 'Do Heads of State in Office Enjoy Immunity from Jurisdiction for International Crimes? The Ghaddafi Case before the French Cour de Cassation', *European Journal of International Law*, Vol. 12, No. 3, 2001, pp. 595–612; Kreß; Bing Jia, 'The Immunity of State Officials for International Crimes Revisited', *Journal of International Criminal Justice*, Vol. 10, No. 5, December 2012, pp. 1303–1321; and Dapo Akande and Sangeeta Shah, 'Immunities of State Officials, International Crimes, and Foreign Domestic Courts', *European Journal of International Law*, Vol. 21, No. 4, 2011, pp. 815–852.

134 See the Joint Separate Opinion of Judges Higgins, Kooijmans and Buergenthal, who state: '[T]hat immunity prevails only as long as the Minister is in office and continues to shield him or her after that time only for "official acts". It is now increasingly claimed in the literature ... that serious international crimes cannot be regarded as official acts.' ICJ, *Arrest Warrant case*, Judgment, 2002, Joint Separate Opinion of Judges Higgins, Kooijmans and Buergenthal, pp. 63–90. See also the Dissenting Opinion of Judge ad hoc van den Wyngaert, *ibid.* para. 36.

135 In support of this finding, see e.g. Antonio Cassese, 'When May Senior State Officials Be Tried for International Crimes? Some Comments on the Congo v. Belgium Case', *European Journal of International Law*, Vol. 13, No. 4, 2002, pp. 864–874; Steffen Wirth, 'Immunity for Core Crimes? The ICJ's Judgment in the *Congo* v. *Belgium* Case', *European Journal of International Law*, Vol. 13, No. 4, 2002, pp. 877–893; Jan Wouters and Leen De Smet, 'The ICJ's Judgment in the Case Concerning the Arrest Warrant of 11 April 2000: Some Critical Observations', *Yearbook of International Humanitarian Law*, Vol. 4, 2001, pp. 373–388; Maurice Kamto, 'Une troublante "immunité totale" du ministre des affaires étrangères', *Revue belge de droit international/Belgian Review of International Law*, No. 1–2, 2002, pp. 518–530; Salvatore Zappalà, 'Do Heads of State in Office Enjoy Immunity from Jurisdiction for International Crimes? The Ghaddafi Case before the French Cour de Cassation', *European Journal of International Law*, Vol. 12, No. 3, 2001, pp. 595–612; Sassòli, pp. 802–803; and Kreß, pp. 803–805, who concludes that 'there is no right to immunity *ratione materiae* under current international law in cases of crimes under international law. Accordingly, no such legal bar to the prosecution of a grave breach exists' (p. 805).

For an overview of the reasoning on this issue in various sources, see Dapo Akande and Sangeeta Shah, 'Immunities of State Officials, International Crimes, and Foreign Domestic

or she would become liable to prosecution for grave breaches committed before or during the time in office. This approach is in line with the object and purpose of the grave breaches regime contained in the Geneva Conventions.[136] Some national implementing laws specifically provide that immunities do not constitute a bar to the prosecution of State officials.[137]

2877   Immunities under national law, such as constitutional immunities, are not a bar to the prosecution by domestic courts of heads of State or heads of government. As the obligation to prosecute alleged perpetrators of grave breaches flows from an unequivocal international obligation, it would amount to a

Courts', *European Journal of International Law*, Vol. 21, No. 4, 2011, pp. 815–852, especially at 825–846. These authors reach a similar conclusion when they state: '[W]here extra-territorial jurisdiction exists in respect of an international crime and the rule providing for jurisdiction expressly contemplates prosecution of crimes committed in an official capacity, immunity *ratione materiae* cannot logically co-exist with such a conferment of jurisdiction' (p. 843). See also the view of the ICTY Appeals Chamber in the *Blaškić* case: 'Under these norms [of international criminal law prohibiting war crimes, crimes against humanity and genocide], those responsible for such crimes cannot invoke immunity from national or international jurisdiction even if they perpetrated such crimes while acting in their official capacity'; *Blaškić* Decision on the Issuance of the *Subpoena Duces Tecum*, 1997, para. 41. See Switzerland, Federal Criminal Court, *A.* v. *Ministère Public de la Confédération case*, Judgment, 2012, para. 5.4.3, where the Court had to decide whether a former minister of defence enjoyed immunity from prosecution before the Swiss courts for war crimes committed in Algeria. It took the position that:

> It would be both contradictory and meaningless to express, on the one hand, a desire to combat serious violations of fundamental humanitarian principles, while, on the other hand, accepting such a broad interpretation of the rules governing functional immunity (*ratione materiae*) for former dictators or officials that, as a result, no investigation could be launched *ab initio*. If that were the case, it would give rise to the difficult proposition that perpetrators of acts that violate fundamental values of international law could be protected by that very same body of law. Such a situation would be paradoxical and ultimately render Swiss criminal policy unenforceable in the vast majority of cases. That was not what was intended. It therefore follows in this case that the appellant may not invoke any form of *ratione materiae* immunity. [unofficial English translation]

In civil proceedings, US courts have reached the same conclusion based on a reasoning more akin to the Joint Separate Opinion of Judges Higgins, Kooijmans and Buergenthal in the *Arrest Warrant* case, finding that acts committed in violation of *jus cogens* norms cannot constitute official sovereign acts (see United States, US Court of Appeals for the Ninth Circuit, *Siderman de Blake* v. *Republic of Argentina*, Judgment, 1992, para. 718 (holding that '[i]nternational law does not recognize an act that violates *jus cogens* as a sovereign act'); see also United States, Court of Appeals for the Fourth Circuit, *Yousuf* v. *Samantar*, Judgment, 2012, pp. 21–22, in which the Court found that 'under international and domestic law, officials from other countries are not entitled to foreign official immunity for *jus cogens* violations, even if the acts were performed in the defendant's official capacity'.

[136] Some have argued that '[w]hen the Geneva Conventions and customary international law conferred universal jurisdiction in respect of those crimes, it cannot be supposed that immunity *ratione materiae* was left intact as that would have rendered the conferment of such jurisdiction particularly meaningless'; Dapo Akande and Sangeeta Shah, 'Immunities of State Officials, International Crimes, and Foreign Domestic Courts', *European Journal of International Law*, Vol. 21, No. 4, 2011, pp. 815–852, at 844.

[137] In its *ICC Act*, 2002, South Africa chose not to extend immunity to heads of State or government before domestic courts for the crimes falling within the ICC's jurisdiction. Under section 4(2)(a) of the Act, the fact that a person is or was a head of State or government, a member of a government or parliament, an elected representative or a government official 'is neither (i) a defence to crime; nor (ii) a ground for any possible reduction of sentence once a person has been convicted of a crime'. See also Niger, *Penal Code*, 1961, as amended, Article 208(7).

breach of this international treaty obligation if domestic courts were to allow constitutional immunities prevail.[138]

2. The option to extradite alleged offenders

2878   Article 49(2) gives States that receive a request for extradition the option of not prosecuting offenders themselves but rather, if they prefer, handing them over to a requesting State Party for trial, provided that the said State Party has made out a *prima facie* case.

2879   The preparatory work for the Conventions shows that States made a conscious choice to use the term 'handing over' and refused to use the word 'extradition'.[139] That choice was heavily influenced by the discussions that took place during the Second World War, notably during the work of the UN War Crimes Commission. States felt that, in the light of the failure to secure the surrender of war criminals after the First World War, it was essential to adopt an executive or administrative procedure, instead of a judicial one like extradition, to facilitate and expedite the trials of war criminals.[140] The Commission felt that 'the machinery of extradition is a slow and cumbersome business, ill-suited to speedy retribution after a war'.[141] The 1949 Diplomatic Conference was conscious that it was adopting a treaty to regulate armed conflicts in the years to come, and so it settled on the wording 'handing over,' provided that the State Party in question has made out a *prima facie* case. This reflected a feeling that it was surely necessary to protect individuals against excessive or unjustified requests. The choice of the term 'handing over' in Article 49 and its historical significance seem, however, to have been overlooked by States Parties over the years, and the term used in national legislation and in the literature nowadays is 'extradition'.

---

[138] For a discussion of this issue, see Kreß, p. 805.

[139] In response to a proposal by the delegates of Italy and Monaco to replace the words 'handing over' by 'extradition', the Dutch delegate explained that 'the use of the word "extradition" was less practicable because of the large variety of extradition laws and extradition treaties. The notion of "handing over" was a notion of customary international law in so far as it was extensively practised by States after the last war in connection with the activities of the UN War Crimes Commission'. See *Minutes of the Diplomatic Conference of Geneva of 1949*, Mixed Commission, 16 July 1949, p. 9 and *Final Record of the Diplomatic Conference of Geneva of 1949*, Vol. II-B, pp. 116–117.

[140] The UN War Crimes Commission negotiated a draft convention for the surrender of war criminals. The draft explanatory memorandum attached to it stated:

> The purpose in view is to make it certain that the United Nations will reciprocally transfer to one another, persons in their power who are wanted for trial as war criminals or quislings, or have already been convicted on such charges, and to secure this result in the simplest possible way, avoiding the complications and delays of normal extradition procedure, and, in particular, excluding the possibility of refusing surrender on the ground that the acts charged have the character of political offences.

UN War Crimes Commission, *The History of the United Nations War Crimes Commission and the Development of the Laws of War*, p. 396; for a full overview, see pp. 392–399 and 102–104. The draft convention for the surrender of war criminals never came into being; see *ibid.* pp. 397–399.

[141] *Ibid.* p. 103.

2880 Extradition is an option given to States Parties on whose territory the accused are or into whose hands they have fallen.[142] It relieves States Parties of the obligation to submit the case to their appropriate authorities for prosecution. In the absence of a request for extradition, the obligation to investigate and, if warranted, to prosecute alleged perpetrators of grave breaches is absolute.

2881 Extradition can be carried out in accordance with the provisions of each State Party's legislation, provided that the requesting State has 'made out a *prima facie* case'.[143] This obliges the requesting State to produce evidence showing that the charges against the accused are sufficient. It has also been defined as requiring 'actual evidence that must be presented to the authorities that would allow them to form the opinion that the person sought would have been required to stand trial had the alleged conduct of the criminal offence occurred in the requested state'.[144] Most common-law countries apply this condition, requiring that some evidence or reasonable ground for the suspicion of guilt of the alleged offenders be provided by the requesting State before they can be extradited.[145] This is often referred to as the 'probable cause' or '*prima facie*' test.[146] In most civil-law countries, however, judges do not generally require any proof of culpability of the offence charged, but only the establishment of the identity and nationality of the accused and the production of various documents, such as the arrest warrant. Many multilateral treaties that provide for extradition do not define the quantum of proof, but simply refer to the legal

---

[142] For a discussion of the interpretation of the concept of extradition in the Convention against Torture, see ICJ, *Obligation to Prosecute or Extradite case*, Judgment, 2012, paras 89–95, at 95:

> It follows that the choice between extradition or submission for prosecution, pursuant to the Convention, does not mean that the two alternatives are to be given the same weight. Extradition is an option offered to the State by the Convention, whereas prosecution is an international obligation under the Convention, the violation of which is a wrongful act engaging the responsibility of the State.

See also Henzelin, pp. 351–357, at 353; Kreß, pp. 796–800; and ILC, *Final Report of the Working Group on the obligation to extradite or prosecute* (aut dedere aut judicare), UN doc. A/CN.4/L.844, 5 June 2014, para. 25.

[143] The French text of Article 49 reads: 'pour autant que cette Partie contractante ait retenu contre lesdites personnes des charges suffisantes' ('provided such High Contracting Party has made out a "*prima facie*" case'). During the 1949 Diplomatic Conference, the French delegate asked what was meant by a 'prima facie case'. The Dutch and US delegates replied that 'the State asking for the alleged perpetrator to be handed over had to provide statements which would satisfy the ... Detaining Power that a finding of guilty on the charges against the accused was highly probable'. *Minutes of the Diplomatic Conference of Geneva of 1949*, p. 10.

[144] UN Office on Drugs and Crime, *Manual on Mutual Legal Assistance and Extradition*, p. 47.

[145] See Bedi, pp. 177–179, and Godinho, p. 512, where he states:

> Probable cause is a traditional requirement for extradition for common law countries. It is a protection against unjustified extradition, according to which the requested State engages in a review of the evidence provided by the requesting State in order to ascertain whether there are reasonable grounds to believe that the accused whose surrender is requested may have indeed committed the crime charged, thereby justifying the trial.

[146] For some examples of application of the *prima facie* test in common-law countries, see United States, District Court for the Southern District of Texas, *Surrender of Elizaphan Ntakirutimana case*, Order, 1997, and Sixth Circuit Court of Appeals, *Demjanjuk case*, Judgment, 1985. See also United Kingdom, High Court of Justice, *Brown (Bajinja) and others case*, Judgment, 2009.

requirements under the national law of the requested State.[147] Recent practice in extradition treaties, both bilateral and multilateral, appears to apply
less stringent evidentiary requirements in extradition proceedings,[148] leaving
the Geneva Conventions as probably the only multilateral treaty with a strict
prima facie requirement.[149]

2882   The purpose behind the imposition of the *prima face* condition[150] is not
only to protect individuals against excessive or unjustified requests, but also to
ensure that the penal proceedings envisaged will not be frustrated or reduced in
scope as a result of transfer to another State Party.[151] In the light of the object
and purpose of Article 49, as well as the obligations contained in Article 1 to
respect and ensure respect for the Conventions, a request for extradition from
a State whose aim might be to protect its own national, and conduct a sham
trial that will lead to an acquittal, should be refused.

2883   To ensure that grave breaches will be prosecuted, States must make sure that
their national law permits them to extradite and seek extradition of suspected
offenders for these crimes. They must also ensure that the double criminality
requirement[152] and the political offence exception[153] are not used to prevent
extradition for these crimes.[154]

---

[147] See e.g. Hague Convention for the Suppression of Unlawful Seizure of Aircraft (1970), Article
8(2)–(3); Convention for the Suppression of Unlawful Acts against the Safety of Civil Aviation (1971), Article 8(2)–(3); Convention on Crimes against Internationally Protected Persons
(1973), Article 8(1)–(2); International Convention against the Taking of Hostages (1979), Article
10; International Convention for the Suppression of Terrorist Bombings (1997); International
Convention for the Suppression of the Financing of Terrorism (1999), Article 11(2)–(3); Article
9(2)–(3); UN Convention against Transnational Organized Crime (2000), Articles 7, 8 and 11;
and UN Convention against Corruption (2003), Article 44(8)–(9).

[148] As an example of this trend, see the US-UK Extradition Treaty of 2003, where a request from
the United States to the United Kingdom does not need to establish a *prima facie* case, but a
request from the United Kingdom to the United States does. The UK Secretary of State for the
Home Department stated that this new treaty reflects 'best modern practice in extradition'
and 'brings the evidential rules for requests from the United States into line with those for
European countries'. See United Kingdom, House of Commons, Written ministerial statement
by the Secretary of State for the Home Office, *Hansard*, 31 March 2003, Vol. 402, Written
Ministerial Statements, cols 41WS–42WS.

[149] See e.g. ILC, *Survey of multilateral conventions which may be of relevance for the work of
the International Law Commission on the topic 'The obligation to extradite or prosecute* (aut
dedere aut judicare)', *Study by the Secretariat*, UN Doc. A/CN.4/630, particularly para. 141.

[150] The fulfilment of the *prima facie* condition at the extradition stage does not, however, preclude
the possibility that the trial of the alleged perpetrator might lead to an acquittal.

[151] See Sandoz/Swinarski/Zimmermann (eds), *Commentary on the Additional Protocols*, ICRC,
1987, para. 3567.

[152] This requirement, namely that the conduct incriminated shall constitute a crime in both the
requested and the requesting States, is sometimes included in extradition arrangements.

[153] In accordance with this exception, extradition may be refused where the offence is of a political
nature. See Article 1 of the Additional Protocol to the 1957 European Convention on Extradition, which provides that the list of grave breaches contained in common Articles 50, 51, 130
and 147 of the four 1949 Geneva Conventions, respectively, cannot be considered to amount
to political offences, and be exempted from extradition on that basis.

[154] See Segall, p. 131, and ILC, *Final Report of the Working Group on the obligation to extradite or
prosecute* (aut dedere aut judicare), UN doc. A/CN.4/L.844, 5 June 2014, para. 37, which states:
'Whatever the conditions under domestic law or a treaty pertaining to extradition, they must
not be applied in bad faith, with the effect of shielding an alleged offender from prosecution in
or extradition to an appropriate criminal jurisdiction.'

2884   Many national laws preclude the extradition of accused persons who are nationals of the country holding them.[155] In that case and other cases where extradition might be refused, the States detaining alleged perpetrators must bring them before their own courts. It should also be noted that extradition can take place as long as the principle of *non-refoulement* is complied with. For example, States are under an obligation not to extradite persons to another State where there are substantial grounds for believing that they might be subjected to torture.[156]

2885   There do not seem to have been many recorded cases of extradition for grave breaches. In the *Ganić* case, a senior Magistrates' Court judge in the United Kingdom explored the existence of a *prima facie* case against an alleged perpetrator of grave breaches. He rejected this finding as two careful and thorough investigations had previously concluded that there was no sufficient evidence on which to bring charges against the alleged offender.[157] Ultimately his extradition was refused as the proceedings were found to be brought for political purposes and therefore amounted to an abuse of process.[158] In another instance, Cameroon accepted a request from the Government of Belgium to have Théoneste Bagosora extradited to Belgium to face prosecution for serious violations of the Geneva Conventions and Additional Protocols. The domestic court in Cameroon granted the request without requiring Belgium to provide evidence that the charges against Bagosora were sufficient.[159]

2886   The Geneva Conventions are silent as to the criteria that should be applied in the event that a State Party receives competing extradition requests for the same person and for the same conduct amounting to a grave breach. The requested State Party is therefore left to decide which request takes priority according to its national legislation. The Informal Expert Group on Effective Extradition Casework Practice recommends that States use a list of criteria which provide practical guidance to States on handling concurrent or competing requests for extradition.[160]

---

[155] For some examples, see ICRC, Customary International Humanitarian Law, practice relating to Rule 161, section C, available at https://www.icrc.org/customary-ihl/eng/docs/v2_rul.

[156] This is contained for example in the Convention against Torture (1984), Article 3 and is a recognized principle of customary international law. For more details on this point, see the commentary on common Article 3, para. 709.

[157] United Kingdom, City of Westminster Magistrates' Court, *Ganić case*, Judgment, 2010, paras 14–28 and 40.

[158] *Ibid.* paras 39–40.

[159] See Cameroon, Court of Appeal, *Bagosora case*, Judgment, 1996. Bagosora was arrested in Cameroon pursuant to a Belgian international arrest warrant. The offender was not transferred to Belgium for the purpose of prosecution, as Belgium deferred its case against Bagosora to the ICTR.

[160] See UN Office on Drugs and Crime, *Report of the Informal Expert Working Group on Effective Extradition Casework Practice*, Vienna, 2004, paras 122–126. Some of these criteria, to name but a few, are: the jurisdiction where the majority of the criminality occurred, or where the majority of the loss or damage was sustained; in cross-border crimes, the capacity of a jurisdiction to prosecute all offences; the location, attendance and protection of witnesses; the possibility for victims to participate in or follow the proceedings; and, for each jurisdiction, the

2887   Lastly, it is important to stress that the preparatory work for the Conventions does not exclude the possibility of a State Party handing over an accused person to an international criminal court or tribunal. It was a deliberate choice of the 1949 Diplomatic Conference not to preclude this possibility.[161] In the case of competing requests from a State and the ICC, Article 90 of the ICC Statute provides detailed rules.[162]

3. Critical assessment

2888   On paper the grave breaches regime amounts to a watertight mechanism, which should have been an effective means of countering serious violations of the Conventions and the impunity of war criminals throughout the world. Grave breaches can be prosecuted on the basis of various titles of jurisdiction, such as territoriality, active and passive personality, the protective principle or universality.[163] States Parties have, however, made little use of this mechanism, which was ground-breaking at the time.[164] A Danish High Court case in 1994 is reported to be the first instance of national prosecution of perpetrators for grave breaches of the Geneva Conventions on the basis of universal jurisdiction.[165] This led many commentators to admit that, more than 40 years after the adoption of this innovative mechanism, prosecutions of grave breaches, in particular on the basis of universal jurisdiction, were almost unheard of.[166]

extent to which there could be a just and fair trial. See also the similar criteria adopted in *The Princeton Principles on Universal Jurisdiction*, Princeton University, 2001, Principle 8.

[161] See *Final Record of the Diplomatic Conference of Geneva of 1949*, Vol. II-B, p. 115. See also Kreß, who believes that the establishment of the ICC demonstrates that States consider the surrender of a person to the Court as another valid form of freely choosing the appropriate forum under the grave breaches regime. See also ILC, *Final Report of the Working Group on the obligation to extradite or prosecute* (aut dedere aut judicare), UN doc. A/CN.4/L.844, 5 June 2014, para. 20, which states: '[T]he obligation to extradite or prosecute may be satisfied by a "third alternative", which would consist of the State surrendering the alleged offender to a competent international criminal tribunal or a competent court whose jurisdiction the State concerned has recognized.'

[162] For further details on the mechanics of Article 90 of the 1998 ICC Statute, see e.g. Claus Kreß and Kimberly Prost, 'Article 90: Competing Requests', in Otto Triffterer and Kai Ambos (eds), *The Rome Statute of the International Criminal Court: A Commentary*, 3rd edition, Hart Publishing, Oxford, 2016, pp. 2059–2067, and Julien Cazala, 'Article 90 – Demandes concurrentes', in Julian Fernandez and Xavier Pacreau (eds), *Statut de Rome de la Cour pénale internationale, Commentaire article par article*, Éditions A. Pedone, Paris, 2012, pp. 1849–1861.

[163] Domestic prosecutions of war crimes or grave breaches in countries where the crimes were committed have been undertaken in particular in the last 20 years, for example in Bosnia and Herzegovina, Cambodia, Croatia or Iraq. For more details, see the commentary on Article 50, para. 2908; La Haye, pp. 256–270, and Ferdinandusse.

[164] See, for example, the statement by the ICRC delegation to the UN before the Preparatory Committee for the Establishment of an International Criminal Court on 15 August 1997: 'The obligation to prosecute alleged perpetrators of grave breaches of humanitarian law is often either ignored or inadequately fulfilled in practice.'

[165] See Denmark, High Court, *Sarić case*, Judgment, 1994. See also Maison.

[166] See Frits Kalshoven: 'Since the entry into force of the Conventions, in October 1950, little action of this type was undertaken against suspects other than a state's nationals, and even

2889   As to the drafters' stated objective of denying safe haven to alleged perpetrators of grave breaches, State practice shows a tendency to exercise universal jurisdiction over crimes under international law only rarely, priority often being given to States with a direct link to the crime.[167] At the time of writing, there seem to have been only 17 reported cases over the past 60 years where domestic courts or tribunals have exercised universal jurisdiction over alleged perpetrators of war crimes or grave breaches.[168]

2890   As mentioned above, as soon as a State Party realizes that a person alleged to have committed or ordered the commission of a grave breach is on its territory or under its jurisdiction, *its duty* is to ensure that such person is searched for, and, when found and so warranted, prosecuted without delay. The mandatory requirement contained in Article 49 to either prosecute or extradite is not as such well translated into domestic law; universal jurisdiction, along with other bases of jurisdiction, is often extended to grave breaches as a possible tool open to States, but the absolute obligation to either prosecute or extradite, as such, does not seem to be integrated into domestic law. It is not clear whether prosecutors or investigating magistrates know that they are under an obligation to investigate allegations of grave breaches.

2891   Each State Party must implement its obligations under Article 49 and establish within its domestic system the legal basis as well as the various procedures for national prosecutors to start investigating and ultimately prosecuting alleged perpetrators of grave breaches. Adequate domestic law in each country is essential to the effective exercise of universal jurisdiction under the grave breaches regime. States have encountered a number of challenges while implementing these obligations, in particular in relation to the extension of universal jurisdiction to grave breaches. Various legal, technical and practical challenges, as well as political ones, explain the relatively small body of State practice. The distance between the location of an event and the place of

---

this rarely' (*Constraints on the Waging of War*, 2nd edition, ICRC, Geneva, 1991, p. 77); Geoffrey Best: 'This noble innovation has achieved nothing' (Best, p. 396); and the ICRC's report to the 1999 Council of Delegates, which states: '[T]his system of penal repression on the national level has only rarely been applied by States. Sandoz takes the view that 'the reality was disappointing. Many States did not fulfil their obligation to enact the "legislation necessary to provide effective penal sanctions" and the system of universal jurisdiction was never applied in practice' (Sandoz, 2009, p. 675). Dörmann and Geiss also speak of 'the reluctance of domestic criminal justice systems to deal with grave breaches, the absence or insufficiency of national legislation in a considerable number of states and the remarkably modest corpus of domestic jurisprudence governing these offences' (Dörmann/Geiss, pp. 704). See also Bothe, and Ferdinandusse, pp. 738–740.

[167] See the statement by the ICRC before the UN General Assembly, 67th session, Sixth Committee, 18 October 2012, and the statement by the ICRC before the UN General Assembly, 68th session, Sixth Committee, 15 October 2014.

[168] See ICRC, *Preventing and repressing international crimes*, Vol. II, pp. 123–131. The small number of prosecutions can also be explained by the fact that most armed conflicts in the world are of a non-international character, and thus do not trigger the grave breaches regime. See also Ferdinandusse, pp. 738–740, on the various reasons behind the lack of prosecutions for grave breaches.

prosecution, and the difficulties of having access to victims and witnesses and securing a sufficient amount of probative evidence, are among the challenges encountered.

2892   For the system of national repression of grave breaches to function effectively, States must also be able to assist one another in connection with criminal proceedings for these offences.[169] The Geneva Conventions do not contain specific provisions on mutual legal assistance and cooperation. However, in 1973, the UN General Assembly called on States to 'co-operate with each other … with a view to halting and preventing war crimes and crimes against humanity' and to 'assist each other in detecting, arresting and bringing to justice' suspected offenders.[170] Pursuant to Additional Protocol I, '[t]he High Contracting Parties shall afford one another the greatest measure of assistance in connexion with criminal proceedings brought in respect of grave breaches'.[171] The law on international cooperation and assistance in criminal matters also developed greatly through the adoption of the ICTY, ICTR and ICC Statutes, which contain extensive provisions in this regard.[172] Today, the obligation to make every effort to cooperate, to the extent possible, in the investigation of war crimes and the prosecution of the suspects is part of customary international law.[173]

2893   More recently, some States have created special units at the domestic level for the prosecution of international crimes, a strategy which reinforces the efficiency of investigations and the likelihood of success of prosecutions.[174] Many States have also stressed the importance of adopting prosecutorial prioritization strategies in order to establish a strategic order in which war crimes and gross human rights violations are investigated and prosecuted at the domestic level.[175]

E. Paragraph 3: Suppression of violations of the Convention other than grave breaches

2894   Pursuant to Article 49(3), each State Party 'shall take measures necessary for the suppression of all acts contrary to the present Convention other than the grave breaches defined' in Article 50.

---

[169] On these issues, see Segall, pp. 127–135, at 130.

[170] UN General Assembly, Res. 3074, Principles of international co-operation in the detection, arrest, extradition and punishment of persons guilty of war crimes and crimes against humanity, 3 December 1973, paras 3–4.

[171] Additional Protocol I, Article 88(1).

[172] See ICTY Statute (1993), Article 29; ICTR Statute (1994), Article 28; and ICC Statute (1998), Articles 86–102.

[173] ICRC Study on Customary International Humanitarian Law (2005), Rule 161.

[174] See ICRC, *Preventing and repressing international crimes*, Vol. I, pp. 57–58.

[175] See, in particular, on this issue, UN, *Report of the Special Rapporteur on the promotion of truth, justice, reparation and guarantees of non-recurrence, Pablo de Greiff*, UN Doc. A/HRC/27/56, 27 August 2014.

2895   At first sight, it might seem that the French and English texts of Article 49(3) differ slightly, as the English term 'suppression' is translated as 'faire cesser' (put a stop to) in French. However, a closer look at the preparatory work shows that the word 'repression/répression' in both the English and French first drafts was changed to 'suppression' in the English version during the debates in the Joint Committee. The Report of the Joint Committee to the Plenary Assembly explains: 'By using the word "suppression" in the English text, it was intended to signify that all necessary measures would be taken to prevent a recurrence of acts contrary to the Convention.'[176] The word 'suppression' was first translated as 'redressement' ('correction') in French before being changed to 'faire cesser': 'prendra les mesures nécessaires pour faire cesser les actes contraires aux dispositions de la présente Convention' ('take measures necessary to put a stop to acts contrary to the provisions of the present Convention') in the final French version of the paragraph.

2896   It is clear from the genesis of this provision that States Parties are therefore under an obligation to address all other violations of the Conventions, in addition to grave breaches. The use of the formulation 'shall take measures necessary for the suppression of all acts contrary to the Convention' implies that States Parties may take a wide range of measures to ensure that violations of the Conventions are stopped and measures taken to prevent their repetition.[177] It is a far-reaching provision. States Parties will determine the best way to fulfil these obligations, for example by instituting judicial or disciplinary proceedings for violations of the Conventions other than grave breaches, or by taking a range of administrative or other regulatory measures or issuing instructions to subordinates.[178] The measures chosen will depend on the gravity and the circumstances of the violation in question, in accordance with the general principle that every punishment should be proportional to the severity of the breach.[179]

2897   States Parties have implemented these obligations in a variety of ways. At first, most States Parties only extended criminal responsibility to the list of grave breaches as they appear in the Geneva Conventions.[180] Only a few States,

[176] See *Final Record of the Diplomatic Conference of Geneva of 1949*, Vol. II-B, p. 133. For the discussions that took place in the Joint Committee, see *Minutes of the Diplomatic Conference of Geneva of 1949*, pp. 20–21.

[177] The word 'suppress' is generally defined as 'putting a stop to' a thing actually existing and as synonymous to prohibit or put down. See Bryan A. Garner (ed.), *Black's Law Dictionary*, 10th edition, Thomson Reuters, 2014, p. 1669.

[178] Prosecuting alleged perpetrators or taking any other measures aimed at preventing or suppressing violations of the Convention are a way of implementing the obligations contained in Article 1 of the Convention. On this point, see ICTY, *Tadić* Decision on Defence Motion on Jurisdiction, 1995, para. 71.

[179] See Sandoz/Swinarski/Zimmermann (eds), *Commentary on the Additional Protocols*, ICRC, 1987, para. 3402. See also Medlong, pp. 829–856.

[180] Many common law-countries initially chose not to extend individual criminal responsibility beyond the list of grave breaches: see e.g. Canada, *Geneva Conventions Act*, 1985, as amended; India, *Geneva Conventions Act*, 1960; Kenya, *Geneva Conventions Act*, 1968;

such as Ireland, Nigeria and South Africa, chose to implement Article 49(3) by extending responsibility to all violations of the Convention.[181] State practice has evolved, in particular since the adoption of the ICC Statute. Nowadays, many States Parties have enacted criminal legislation punishing the commission of a list of war crimes, which goes well beyond the list of grave breaches.[182]

2898   States have also implemented the obligation to suppress all acts contrary to the Convention by widely disseminating the text of the Conventions, pursuant to Article 47, and adopting military regulations, administrative orders and other regulatory measures sanctioning violations of the Convention, thereby helping to prevent their recurrence. The proper implementation of other obligations under this Convention contributes to the effective implementation of the obligation to take all measures necessary to suppress violations of the Convention.[183] For example, once the occurrence of a violation has been established by an enquiry procedure set up under Article 52, States Parties must, in line with their obligations under Article 49(3), take a series of actions depending on the nature of the violation.[184]

F. Paragraph 4: Safeguards of proper trial and defence

2899   Article 49(4) provides: 'In all circumstances, the accused persons shall benefit by safeguards of proper trial and defence, which shall not be less favourable than those provided by Article 105 and those following of the Geneva Convention relative to the Treatment of Prisoners of War of August 12, 1949.'

Namibia, *Geneva Conventions Act*, 2003; Sri Lanka, *Geneva Conventions Act*, 2006; and United Kingdom, *Geneva Conventions Act*, 1957, as amended. See also the ICRC's National Implementation of IHL database, available at https://www.icrc.org/ihl-nat.

[181] See Ireland, *Geneva Conventions Act*, 1962, as amended, which provides for the punishment of other violations, referred to as minor breaches, when committed in the Republic of Ireland or by an Irish citizen. Nigeria's *Geneva Conventions Act*, 1960, permits the governor-general to provide that other breaches committed in Nigeria or by Nigerian citizens are liable to punishment; see the ICRC's National Implementation of IHL database, available at https://www.icrc.org/ihl-nat. See also South Africa, *Geneva Conventions Act*, 2012, chapter 2, section 5(3), which provides: 'Any person who within the Republic contravenes or fails to comply with a provision of the Conventions not covered by subsection (2), is guilty of an offence.' The ICRC's Model Geneva Conventions Act for common-law States includes a section 4 calling for the punishment of 'any person, whatever his or her nationality, who ... commits, or aids, abets or procures any other persons to commit, a breach of any of the Conventions or Protocols not covered by section 3'; see ICRC, Advisory Service on International Humanitarian Law, *Model Law, Geneva Conventions (Consolidation) Act, Legislation for Common Law States on the 1949 Geneva Conventions and their 1977 and 2005 Additional Protocols*, August 2008, p. 4.

[182] See e.g. Australia, *ICC Act*, 2002; Canada, *Crimes Against Humanity and War Crimes Act*, 2000, as amended; Finland, *Penal Code*, 1889, as amended, chapter 11; France, *Penal Code*, 1992, as amended; Switzerland, *Penal Code*, 1937, as amended, in particular Title Twelve on war crimes; and United Kingdom, *ICC Act*, 2001. All the aforementioned legislation can be found in the ICRC's National Implementation of IHL database, available at https://www.icrc.org/ihl-nat.

[183] See, in particular, Article 52 on the enquiry procedure.

[184] On this issue, see the commentary on Article 52, section F, and Théo Boutruche, 'Good offices, Conciliation and Enquiry', in Andrew Clapham, Paola Gaeta and Marco Sassòli (eds), *The 1949 Geneva Conventions: A Commentary*, Oxford University Press, 2015, pp. 561–574, para. 21.

2900 The experience of the ICRC in the years following the Second World War showed that certain safeguards of proper trial and defence are essential in all cases where persons are accused of war crimes or grave breaches. These safeguards are particularly necessary where the accused person is tried by a foreign court. Accordingly, the ICRC included a special article on the subject in the proposals which it submitted to the 1949 Diplomatic Conference. The Conference did not take up the suggestion, at any rate not at first. The French delegation, however, realizing the desirability of placing all accused persons on the same footing, whatever their individual status, proposed the present paragraph 4 during the discussions in the Joint Committee. The Joint Committee approved the French proposal, and it was adopted by the Conference without being modified in any way.[185]

2901 Grave breaches can be committed by civilians and combatants alike.[186] Both must benefit in all circumstances from the safeguards of proper trial and defence. The expression 'safeguards of proper trial and defence' must be understood to refer to the minimum judicial guarantees of fair trial and due process. Paragraph 4 provides that such safeguards may not be less favourable than those provided for in Article 105 and the following articles of the Third Convention. At a minimum, States Parties must apply the safeguards contained in these articles when conducting war crimes trials.[187]

2902 Since 1949, the list of judicial guarantees has evolved through the development of both humanitarian and human rights law.[188] Article 49(4) must be read in the light of the guarantees listed in Article 75(4) of Additional Protocol I, which are now recognized as part of customary international law.[189] The judicial guarantees which are generally recognized today as indispensable include:

– The obligation to inform the accused without delay of the nature and cause of the offence alleged;[190]

---

[185] For further details on the genesis of this provision, see Pictet (ed.), *Commentary on the First Geneva Convention*, ICRC, 1952, pp. 368–369.

[186] For further details, see the commentary on Article 50, section C.3.

[187] For a detailed discussion of the contents of these safeguards, see the commentaries on Articles 105–108 of the Third Convention.

[188] See, in particular, Additional Protocol I, Article 75(4); see also International Covenant on Civil and Political Rights (1966), Article 14; European Convention on Human Rights (1950), Article 6; American Convention on Human Rights (1969), Article 8; and African Charter on Human and Peoples' Rights (1981), Article 7.

[189] See e.g. United States, Supreme Court, *Hamdan case*, Judgment, 2006, pp. 632–634. The Court looked to Article 75 of Additional Protocol I, noting that, even though the United States had not ratified the Protocol, the US Government had no objections to Article 75, which sets out many of the minimum requirements.

[190] See Third Convention, Article 105, and Additional Protocol I, Article 75(4)(a). See also International Covenant on Civil and Political Rights (1966), Article 14(3)(a); European Convention on Human Rights (1950), Article 6(3)(a); and American Convention on Human Rights (1969), Article 8(2)(b).

- The requirement that an accused have the necessary rights and means of defence;[191]
- The right not to be convicted of an offence except on the basis of individual penal responsibility;[192]
- The principle of *nullum crimen, nulla poena sine lege* ('no crime or punishment without a law') and the prohibition of a heavier penalty than that provided for at the time of the offence;[193]
- The right to be presumed innocent;[194]
- The right to be tried in one's own presence;[195]
- The right not to be compelled to testify against oneself or to confess guilt;[196]
- The right to be advised of one's judicial and other remedies and of the time limits within which they may be exercised;[197]
- The right to present and examine witnesses;[198]

---

[191] See Third Convention, Article 105, and Additional Protocol I, Article 75(4)(a). See also International Covenant on Civil and Political Rights (1966), Article 14(3); European Convention on Human Rights (1950), Article 6(3); American Convention on Human Rights (1969), Article 8(2); and African Charter on Human and Peoples' Rights (1981), Article 7(c).

[192] See Third Convention, Article 99, and Additional Protocol I, Article 75(4)(b).

[193] See Third Convention, Article 99, and Additional Protocol I, Article 75(4)(c). See also International Covenant on Civil and Political Rights (1966), Article 15; European Convention on Human Rights (1950), Article 7; American Convention on Human Rights (1969), Article 9; and African Charter on Human and Peoples' Rights (1981), Article 7(2).

[194] See Additional Protocol I, Article 75(4)(d). See also International Covenant on Civil and Political Rights (1966), Article 14(2); European Convention on Human Rights (1950), Article 6(2); American Convention on Human Rights (1969), Article 8(2); and African Charter on Human and Peoples' Rights (1981), Article 7(1)(b).

[195] See Additional Protocol I, Article 75(4)(e). See also International Covenant on Civil and Political Rights (1966), Article 14(3)(d). Persons can, however, renounce their right to be present during their own trial. For a critical view on the issue of the legality of trials *in absentia* in the light of human rights, see e.g. Chris Jenks and Eric Talbot Jensen, 'All Human Rights are Equal, But Some are More Equal than Others: The Extraordinary Rendition of a Terror Suspect in Italy, the NATO SOFA, and Human Rights', *Harvard National Security Journal*, Vol. 1, 2010, pp. 172–202, and other references provided in para. 2871.

[196] See Additional Protocol I, Article 75(4)(f). See also International Covenant on Civil and Political Rights (1966), Article 14(3)(g); and American Convention on Human Rights (1969), Article 8(2)(g) and (3). This right is not explicitly stipulated in the 1950 European Convention on Human Rights, but it has been interpreted by the European Court of Human Rights as one of the elements of fair trial under Article 6(1); see e.g. *Pishchalnikov* v. *Russia*, Judgment, 2009, para. 71.

[197] See, in particular, Article 106 of the Third Convention, recognizing a right of appeal or petition from any sentence pronounced. See also Additional Protocol I, Article 75(4)(j). Human rights instruments guarantee a right to appeal; see International Covenant on Civil and Political Rights (1966), Article 14(5); Convention on the Rights of the Child (1989), Article 40(2)(b)(v); Protocol 7 to the European Convention on Human Rights (1984), Article 2(1); American Convention on Human Rights (1969), Article 8(2)(h); and African Charter on Human and Peoples' Rights (1981), Article 7(1)(a). 'The influence of human rights law on this issue is such that it can be argued that the right of appeal proper – and not only the right to be informed whether appeal is available – has become a basic component of fair trial rights in the context of armed conflict' (Henckaerts/Doswald-Beck, commentary on Rule 100, pp. 369–370).

[198] See Third Convention, Article 105, and Additional Protocol I, Article 75(4)(g). See also International Covenant on Civil and Political Rights (1966), Article 14(3)(e); European Convention on Human Rights (1950), Article 6(3)(d); and American Convention on Human Rights (1969), Article 8(2)(f).

- The right to have the judgment pronounced publicly;[199]
- The right not to be prosecuted or punished more than once by the same Party for the same act or on the same charge (*non bis in idem*).[200]

G. Applicability of the grave breaches regime in non-international armed conflicts

2903   The grave breaches regime amounts to a major building block in the foundation of international criminal law. Despite being restricted to international armed conflicts and having been largely inoperative for decades, it has acted as a catalyst in creating a more structurally coherent and comprehensive treaty regime governing war crimes. In this respect, the question has been raised as to the possible extension of this regime to non-international armed conflicts.

2904   The preparatory work for the Conventions shows that the issue of individual criminal responsibility for violations of common Article 3 was discussed only superficially.[201] A few States wished for common Article 3 to include the possibility for States to consider violations of this article as war crimes,[202] but most States clearly rejected this proposal. The majority view at the time was that, except for Article 3, the provisions of the four Geneva Conventions, including the grave breaches regime, were not applicable in non-international armed conflicts.[203] The study of the debates in 1949 on the grave breaches provisions shows that their application in non-international armed conflicts was not even envisaged.[204] Similarly, international criminal responsibility for violations of Additional Protocol II was never discussed or recognized as such during the 1974–1977 negotiations.[205]

2905   Even though the extension of the grave breaches regime to non-international armed conflicts was not envisaged in 1949, some authors and judicial

---

[199] See Third Convention, Article 107, and Additional Protocol I, Article 75(4)(i). See also International Covenant on Civil and Political Rights (1966), Article 14(1); European Convention on Human Rights (1950), Article 6(1); and American Convention on Human Rights (1969), Article 8(5).

[200] See Third Convention, Article 86; Fourth Convention, Article 117(3); and Additional Protocol I, Article 75(4)(h). See also International Covenant on Civil and Political Rights (1966), Article 14(7); Protocol 7 to the European Convention on Human Rights (1984), Article 4; and American Convention on Human Rights (1969), Article 8(4).

[201] See the commentary on common Article 3, para. 871.

[202] This was the view expressed by the Italian delegate; see *Final Record of the Diplomatic Conference of Geneva of 1949*, Vol. II-B, p. 49.

[203] See the view expressed by the Rapporteur of the Special Committee: 'The Special Committee voiced a definite opinion that the dispositions of the Conventions were, on principle, not applicable to civil war, and that only certain stipulations expressly mentioned would be applicable to such conflicts.' *Ibid.* pp. 36–37.

[204] See e.g. the Fourth Report drawn up by the Special Committee of the Joint Committee, *Final Record of the Diplomatic Conference of Geneva of 1949*, Vol. II-B, pp. 114–118, where it is made clear that the grave breaches regime is only applicable to the gravest violations in international conflict.

[205] See *Official Records of the Diplomatic Conference of Geneva of 1974–1977*, Vol. VIII, p. 376, and La Haye, p. 133.

pronouncements have argued for it.[206] However, it is difficult to conclude that such extension has materialized in customary international law in the light of the relative dearth of State practice and *opinio juris* supporting such extension.[207] The large majority of national implementing legislation has not extended the regime of grave breaches to non-international armed conflicts[208] and, during the negotiation of the ICC Statute, States, while elaborating the list of war crimes, maintained the dichotomy between international and non-international armed conflicts. In other words, the grave breaches regime, which *obliges* States to either prosecute or extradite accused persons, was not extended to war crimes committed in non-international armed conflicts. In practice, the non-applicability of the grave breaches regime to war crimes committed in non-international armed conflicts should not excessively hamper the enforcement of individual criminal responsibility in such conflicts, as a growing number of States have now equipped themselves with the means to exercise universal jurisdiction over such war crimes.[209] A number of national laws, in particular the ones enacted since the adoption of the ICC Statute, provide evidence for a right established in customary international law to extend universal jurisdiction to serious violations of international humanitarian law in non-international armed conflicts.[210]

---

[206] See ICTY, *Tadić* Decision on Defence Motion for Interlocutory Appeal on Jurisdiction, Separate Opinion of Judge Abi-Saab, 1995, as well as the judgment of the Trial Chamber in *Delalić*, where the Trial Chamber affirmed:

> In his Separate Opinion, however, Judge Abi-Saab opined that 'a strong case can be made for the application of Article 2, even when the incriminated act takes place in an internal conflict'. The majority of the Appeals Chamber did indeed recognise that a change in the customary law scope of the 'grave breaches regime' in this direction may be occurring. This Trial Chamber is also of the view that the possibility that customary law has developed the provisions of the Geneva Conventions since 1949 to constitute an extension of the system of 'grave breaches' to internal armed conflicts should be recognised.

> *Delalić* Trial Judgment, 1998, para. 202. See also the Dissenting Opinion of Judge Rodrigues in *Aleksovski* Trial Judgment, 1999.

[207] See, for an exception, the position taken by the United States in its *amicus curiae* brief in the *Tadić* proceedings in 1995, asserting that grave breaches under Article 2 of the 1993 ICTY Statute could be committed during both international and non-international armed conflicts (cited in ICTY, *Tadić* Decision on the Defence Motion on Jurisdiction, 1995, para. 35). For a recent reaffirmation of this position, see United States, *Law of War Manual*, 2015, para. 18.9.3.2. For a study of this issue, see Moir; Boelaert-Suominen; and La Haye, pp. 253–256.

[208] For a study of national implementing legislation on this question, see La Haye, pp. 227–235.

[209] See the commentary on common Article 3, paras 877–880.

[210] See Henckaerts/Doswald-Beck, commentary on Rule 157, pp. 604–607. For a contrary view on the customary nature of this rule, see John B. Bellinger III and William J. Haynes II, 'A US government response to the International Committee of the Red Cross study *Customary International Humanitarian Law*', *International Review of the Red Cross*, Vol. 89, No. 866, June 2007, pp. 443–471, and United States, *Law of War Manual*, 2015, para. 18.21.1; but see Jean-Marie Henckaerts, '*Customary International Humanitarian Law*: a response to US Comments', *International Review of the Red Cross*, Vol. 89, No. 866, June 2007, pp. 473–488. For a discussion of the customary right to extend universal jurisdiction over war crimes committed in non-international armed conflicts, see La Haye, pp. 216–273.

Select bibliography

Abi-Saab, George, 'The Concept of War Crimes', in Sienho Yee and Wang Tieya (eds), *International Law in the Post-Cold War World: Essays in Memory of Li Haopei*, Routledge, London, 2001, pp. 99–118.

Bassiouni, M. Cherif, 'Universal Jurisdiction for International Crimes: Historical Perspectives and Contemporary Practice', *Virginia Journal of International Law*, Vol. 42, No. 1, Fall 2001, pp. 81–162.

Bassiouni, M. Cherif and Wise, Edward M., *Aut Dedere, Aut Judicare: The Duty to Extradite or Prosecute in International Law*, Martinus Nijhoff Publishers, Dordrecht, 1995.

Bedi, Satya Deva, *Extradition: A Treatise on the Laws Relevant to the Fugitive Offenders Within and With the Commonwealth Countries*, William S. Hein & Company, Getzville, New York, 2001.

Best, Geoffrey, *War and Law Since 1945*, Clarendon Press, Oxford, 1994.

Blazeby, Leonard, 'Implementation of International Humanitarian Law within the Commonwealth', *Commonwealth Law Bulletin*, Vol. 34, No. 4, 2008, pp. 797–806.

Boelaert-Suominen, Sonja, 'Grave Breaches, Universal Jurisdiction and Internal Armed Conflicts: Is Customary Law Moving Towards a Uniform Enforcement Mechanism for all Armed Conflicts?', *Journal of Conflict and Security Law*, Vol. 5, No. 1, June 2000, pp. 63–103.

Bothe, Michael, 'The role of national law in the implementation of international humanitarian law', in Christophe Swinarski (ed.), *Studies and Essays on International Humanitarian Law and Red Cross Principles in Honour of Jean Pictet*, ICRC/Martinus Nijhoff Publishers, The Hague, 1984, pp. 301–312.

Brems, Eva, 'Universal Criminal Jurisdiction for Grave Breaches of International Humanitarian Law: The Belgian Legislation', *Singapore Journal of International and Comparative Law*, Vol. 6, No. 2, 2002, pp. 909–952.

Cassese, Antonio, *International Criminal Law*, 3rd edition, Oxford University Press, 2013, pp. 181–192 and 199–205.

Cohen, Amichai and Shany, Yuval, 'Beyond the Grave Breaches Regime: The Duty to Investigate Alleged Violations of International Law Governing Armed Conflicts', *Yearbook of International Humanitarian Law 2011*, Vol. 14, 2012, pp. 37–84.

Cryer, Robert, *Prosecuting International Crimes: Selectivity and the International Criminal Law Regime*, Cambridge University Press, 2005, pp. 9–48.

Danner, Allison M. and Martinez, Jenny S., 'Guilty Associations: Joint Criminal Enterprise, Command Responsibility, and the Development of International Criminal Law', *California Law Review*, Vol. 93, No. 1, 2005, pp. 75–169.

Darcy, Shane and Powderly, Joseph (eds), *Judicial Creativity at the International Criminal Tribunals*, Oxford University Press, 2010.

de La Pradelle, Paul, *La Conférence diplomatique et les nouvelles Conventions de Genève du 12 août 1949*, Les Éditions internationales, Paris, 1951.

Dörmann, Knut and Geiss, Robin, 'The Implementation of Grave Breaches into Domestic Legal Orders', *Journal of International Criminal Justice*, Vol. 7, No. 4, September 2009, pp. 703–721.

Draper, Gerald I.A.D., 'The Modern Pattern of War Criminality', *Israel Yearbook on Human Rights*, Vol. 6, 1976, pp. 9–48.

Ferdinandusse, Ward, 'The Prosecution of Grave Breaches in National Courts', *Journal of International Criminal Justice*, Vol. 7, No. 4, September 2009, pp. 723–741.

Fleck, Dieter, 'Shortcomings of the Grave Breaches Regime', *Journal of International Criminal Justice*, Vol. 7, No. 4, September 2009, pp. 833–854.

Gaeta, Paola, 'Grave Breaches of the Geneva Conventions', in Andrew Clapham, Paola Gaeta and Marco Sassòli (eds), *The 1949 Geneva Conventions: A Commentary*, Oxford University Press, 2015, pp. 615–646.

Godinho, Jorge A.F., 'The Surrender Agreements between the US and the ICTY and ICTR: A Critical View', *Journal of International Criminal Justice*, Vol. 1, No. 2, August 2003, pp. 502–516.

Graven, Jean, 'La répression pénale des infractions aux Conventions de Genève', *Revue internationale de criminologie et de police technique*, Vol. 10, 1956, pp. 241–263.

Green, Leslie C., 'The Law of Armed Conflict and the Enforcement of International Criminal Law', *Canadian Yearbook of International Law*, Vol. 22, 1984, pp. 3–25.

– *The Contemporary Law of Armed Conflict*, Manchester University Press, 1996. (1996a)

– 'Enforcement of the Law in International and Non-International Conflicts – The Way Ahead', *Denver Journal of International Law and Policy*, Vol. 24, 1996, pp. 285–320. (1996b)

Greppi, Edoardo, 'The evolution of individual criminal responsibility under international law', *International Review of the Red Cross*, Vol. 81, No. 835, September 1999, pp. 531–553.

Heller, Kevin Jon, *The Nuremberg Military Tribunals and the Origins of International Criminal Law*, Oxford University Press, 2011, pp. 203–230.

Henckaerts, Jean-Marie and Doswald-Beck, Louise, *Customary International Humanitarian Law, Volume I: Rules*, ICRC/Cambridge University Press, 2005, available at https://www.icrc.org/customary-ihl/eng/docs/v1.

Henzelin, Marc, *Le principe de l'universalité en droit pénal international : Droit et obligation pour les états de poursuivre et juger selon le principe de l'universalité*, Bruylant, Geneva, 2000.

ICRC, National Implementation of IHL database, https://www.icrc.org/ihl-nat.

– Advisory Service on International Humanitarian Law, *National measures to repress violations of international humanitarian law (Civil law systems)*, Report on the Meeting of Experts, Geneva, 23–25 September 1997, ICRC, Geneva, September 2000.

– Advisory Service on International Humanitarian Law, *The Domestic Implementation of International Humanitarian law: A Manual*, ICRC, Geneva, 1st edition 2011, updated edition 2015.

– Advisory Service on International Humanitarian Law, *Preventing and repressing international crimes: Towards an 'integrated' approach based on domestic practice*, Report of the Third Universal Meeting of National Committees for the Implementation of International Humanitarian Law, prepared by Anne-Marie La Rosa, Vols I–II, ICRC, Geneva, February 2014.

Keen, Maurice H., *The Laws of War in the Late Middle Ages*, Routledge & Kegan Paul, London, 1965.

Kreß, Claus, 'Reflections on the Judicare Limb of the Grave Breaches Regime', *Journal of International Criminal Justice*, Vol. 7, No. 4, September 2009, pp. 789–809.

Lafontaine, Fannie, 'Universal Jurisdiction – the Realistic Utopia', *Journal of International Criminal Justice*, Vol. 10, No. 5, December 2012, pp. 1277–1302.

La Haye, Eve, *War Crimes in Internal Armed Conflicts*, Cambridge University Press, 2008.

La Rosa, Anne-Marie, 'Sanctions as a means of obtaining greater respect for humanitarian law: a review of their effectiveness', *International Review of the Red Cross*, Vol. 90, No. 870, June 2008, pp. 221–247.

La Rosa, Anne-Marie and Chavez Tafur, Gabriel, 'Where do we stand on universal jurisdiction? Proposed points for further reflection and debate', *Politorbis – Revue de politique étrangère*, No. 54, No. 2, 2012, pp. 31–40.

Lauterpacht, Hersch, 'The Law of Nations and the Punishment of War Crimes', *British Yearbook of International Law*, Vol. 21, 1944, pp. 58–95.

Levie, Howard S., 'War Crimes', in Michael N. Schmitt (ed.), *The Law of Military Operations: Liber Amicorum Professor Jack Grunawalt*, International Law Studies, U.S. Naval War College, Vol. 72, 1998, pp. 95–112.

Lewis, Mark, *The Birth of the New Justice: The Internationalization of Crime and Punishment, 1919–1950*, Oxford University Press, 2014.

Maison, Raffaëlle, 'Les premiers cas d'application des dispositions pénales des Conventions de Genève par les juridictions internes', *European Journal of International Law*, Vol. 6, No. 1, 1995, pp. 260–273.

Maogoto, Jackson N., *War crimes and Realpolitik: International Justice from World War I to the 21st Century*, Lynne Rienner Publishers, Boulder, Colorado, March 2004, pp. 37–64.

McCormack, Timothy L.H., 'From Sun Tzu to the Sixth Committee: the Evolution of an International Criminal Law Regime', in Timothy L.H. McCormack and Gerry J. Simpson (eds), *The Law of War Crimes: International and National Approaches*, Kluwer Law International, 1997, pp. 31–64. (1997a)

– 'Selective Reaction to Atrocity: War Crimes and the Development of International Criminal Law', *Albany Law Review*, Vol. 60, No. 3, Spring 1997, pp. 681–731. (1997b)

Medlong, Jesse, 'All Others Breaches: State Practice and the Geneva Conventions' Nebulous Class of Less Discussed Prohibitions', *Michigan Journal of International Law*, Vol. 34, No. 4, 2013, pp. 829–856.

Meron, Theodor, 'Crimes and Accountability in Shakespeare', *American Journal of International Law*, Vol. 92, No. 1, January 1998, pp. 1–40.

– 'Reflections on the Prosecutions of War Crimes by International Tribunals', *American Journal of International Law*, Vol. 100, No. 3, July 2006, pp. 551–579.

Mettraux, Guénaël, 'US Courts-Martial and the Armed Conflict in the Philippines (1899–1902): Their Contribution to National Case Law on War Crimes', *Journal of International Criminal Justice*, Vol. 1, No. 1, April 2003, pp. 135–150.

– *International Crimes and the Ad Hoc Tribunals*, Oxford University Press, 2005.

– *The Law of Command Responsibility*, Oxford University Press, 2009.

Moir, Lindsay, 'Grave Breaches and Internal Armed Conflicts', *Journal of International Criminal Justice*, Vol. 7, No. 4, September 2009, pp. 763–787.

Nebout, Guy, *Le problème des sanctions à appliquer en cas d'infractions graves aux Conventions de Genève du 12 août 1949*, Pierre Moulin, Lyon, 1954.

O'Keefe, Roger, 'The Grave Breaches Regime and Universal Jurisdiction', *Journal of International Criminal Justice*, Vol. 7, No. 4, September 2009, pp. 811–831.

Rabinovitch, Ryan, 'Universal Jurisdiction in Absentia', *Fordham International Law Journal*, Vol. 28, No. 2, 2004, pp. 500–530.

Roberts, Ken, 'The Contribution of the ICTY to the Grave Breaches Regime', *Journal of International Criminal Justice*, Vol. 7, No. 4, September 2009, pp. 743–761.

Sandoz, Yves, 'Penal Aspects of International Humanitarian Law', in M. Cherif Bassiouni (ed.), *International Criminal Law*, Vol. 1, Transnational Publishers, Ardsley, New York, 1986, pp. 209–232.

– 'The History of the Grave Breaches Regime', *Journal of International Criminal Justice*, Vol. 7, No. 4, September 2009, pp. 657–682.

Sassòli, Marco, 'L'arrêt Yerodia: quelques remarques sur une affaire au point de collision entre les deux couches du droit international', *Revue générale de droit international public*, Vol. 106, No. 4, 2002, pp. 791–817.

Segall, Anna, *Punishing Violations of International Humanitarian Law at the National Level: A Guide for Common Law States – Drawing on the proceedings of a meeting of experts (Geneva, 11–13 November 1998)*, ICRC, Geneva, 2001.

Sluiter, Göran (ed.), 'Symposium', *Journal of International Criminal Justice*, Vol. 5, No. 1, March 2007, pp. 67–226.

UN Office on Drugs and Crime, *Manual on Mutual Legal Assistance and Extradition*, United Nations, New York, 2012.

UN Secretary-General, *Report on the scope and application of the principle of universal jurisdiction*, UN Doc. A/66/93, 20 June 2011.

UN War Crimes Commission, *The History of the United Nations War Crimes Commission and the Development of the Laws of War*, His Majesty's Stationery Office, London, 1948.

van Elst, Richard, 'Implementing Universal Jurisdiction over Grave Breaches of the Geneva Conventions', *Leiden Journal of International Law*, Vol. 13, No. 4, December 2000, pp. 815–854.

van Steenberghe, Raphaël, 'The Obligation to Extradite or Prosecute: Clarifying its Nature', *Journal of International Criminal Justice*, Vol. 9, No. 5, 2011, pp. 1089–1116.

Wagner, Natalie, 'The development of the grave breaches regime and of individual criminal responsibility by the International Criminal Tribunal for the former Yugoslavia', *International Review of the Red Cross*, Vol. 85, No. 850, June 2003, pp. 351–383.

Wells, Donald A., *War Crimes and Laws of War*, 2nd edition, University Press of America, 1991.

GRAVE BREACHES

❖ Text of the provision

Grave breaches to which the preceding Article relates shall be those involving any of the following acts, if committed against persons or property protected by the Convention: wilful killing, torture or inhuman treatment, including biological experiments, wilfully causing great suffering or serious injury to body or health, and extensive destruction and appropriation of property, not justified by military necessity and carried out unlawfully and wantonly.

❖ Reservations or declarations

None

Contents

A. Introduction

2906 Article 50 is closely linked to Article 49. It contains an exhaustive list of offences bearing the most gravity, for which States undertake to provide effective penal sanctions and to either prosecute or extradite, regardless of their nationality, alleged offenders who are suspected of having committed one of these grave breaches against persons or property protected by the Convention.[1] Article 50 is common to the four Conventions. It is reproduced in identical terms in the Second Convention and contains additional grave breaches in the Third and Fourth Conventions.[2]

2907 As mentioned in the commentary on Article 49, grave breaches of the Geneva Conventions today form part of a complex set of crimes under international law, consisting of serious violations of international humanitarian law often referred to as war crimes, as well as gross violations of human rights such as crimes against humanity and genocide. Grave breaches are part of the wider category of serious violations of international humanitarian law that States are called upon to suppress in both international and non-international armed conflicts.[3] They remain 'segregated from other categories of war

---

[1] For a full explanation of these obligations, see the commentary on Article 49.

[2] See Second Convention, Article 51; Third Convention, Article 130; and Fourth Convention, Article 147.

[3] See ICRC Study on Customary International Humanitarian Law (2005), Rule 158: 'States must investigate war crimes allegedly committed by their nationals or armed forces, or on their territory, and, if appropriate, prosecute the suspects. They must also investigate other war crimes over which they have jurisdiction and, if appropriate, prosecute the suspects.'

crimes',[4] as the list of grave breaches contained in the Geneva Conventions and Additional Protocol I is a limitative one which is only applicable in international armed conflicts.[5]

2908 States Parties have largely complied with the obligation contained in Article 49(1) to enact implementing legislation. However, they have not often followed through on the obligation to either prosecute or extradite perpetrators of the grave breaches listed in Article 50.[6]

2909 The first reported cases of national prosecutions for grave breaches took place in the 1990s, following the break-up of the former Yugoslavia, when German, Danish and Swiss courts prosecuted individuals mainly for grave breaches of the Third and Fourth Conventions.[7] Domestic prosecutions of grave breaches in countries where the crimes were committed have also been undertaken, for example in Bosnia and Herzegovina,[8] Cambodia,[9] Croatia[10] and Iraq.[11]

2910 The end of the Cold War, the creation of international courts and tribunals mandated to prosecute alleged perpetrators of war crimes, including grave breaches, and in particular the establishment in 1998 of the ICC, all acted as catalysts in the enforcement of the grave breaches regime.[12] The list of grave breaches of the 1949 Geneva Conventions was included in the Statutes of the ICTY, the ICC, the Special Panels for Serious Crimes in East Timor, the Supreme Iraqi Criminal Tribunal, the Extraordinary Chambers in the Courts of Cambodia (ECCC) and the Extraordinary African Chambers within the Courts of Senegal.[13] These international criminal courts have prosecuted a

---

[4] Yves Sandoz, 'The History of the Grave Breaches Regime', *Journal of International Criminal Justice*, Vol. 7, No. 4, September 2009, pp. 657–682, at 679.

[5] For a discussion of whether serious violations of international humanitarian law committed in non-international armed conflicts amount to grave breaches, see the commentary on Article 49, section G.

[6] Addressing the Sixth Committee of the UN General Assembly in 1993, the ICRC stated that it was regrettable that the system of universal penal jurisdiction had not been fully implemented by States and that, as a result, effective repression of war crimes had not become a reality.

[7] For examples of cases, see Denmark, *Sarić case*; Germany, *Sokolović case*; and Switzerland, *Grabež case*. On this point, see, in particular, James G. Stewart, 'Introduction', *Journal of International Criminal Justice*, Vol. 7, No. 4, September 2009, pp. 653–654, at 654, and La Haye, 2008, pp. 243–253.

[8] See the work of the Human Rights Chamber of the Court of Bosnia and Herzegovina, http://www.sudbih.gov.ba/?jezik=e.

[9] See the work of the Extraordinary Chambers in the Courts of Cambodia (ECCC), http://www.eccc.gov.kh/en.

[10] For examples of domestic prosecutions in Croatia, see the ICRC's National Implementation of IHL database, available at https://www.icrc.org/ihl-nat.

[11] For an overview of the work of the Supreme Iraqi Criminal Tribunal, see Michael A. Newton, 'The Iraqi High Court: controversy and contributions', *International Review of the Red Cross*, Vol. 88, No. 862, June 2006, pp. 399–425.

[12] The work of international human right bodies is also relevant and has been referred to in the commentaries below on certain grave breaches. It has not been possible, however, to include exhaustive references to all relevant human rights decisions or judgments.

[13] See ICTY Statute (1993), Article 2; ICC Statute (1998), Article 8(2)(b); UNTAET Regulation No. 2000/15, Section 6.1(a); Cambodia, *Law on the Establishment of the ECCC*, 2001, as amended, Article 6; Iraq, *Law Establishing the Supreme Iraqi Criminal Tribunal*, 2005, Article 13(a); and Statute of the Extraordinary African Chambers within the Courts of Senegal (2013), Article 7.1.

wide range of acts constituting grave breaches, creating a valuable body of case law interpreting these crimes.[14] The ICTY has breathed life into the grave breaches regime and brought clarity to many of its different aspects, ranging from the general requirements for its application to the specific underlying crimes.[15]

2911   After a long period of neglect, the need to prosecute grave breaches, among other international crimes, has taken on renewed importance today.[16]

B. Historical background

2912   Early international instruments codifying the laws and customs of war did not contain detailed provisions on the individual criminal responsibility of alleged perpetrators or a list of war crimes.[17] The 1906 Geneva Convention was the first international treaty to deal with the repression of violations of the Convention, such as abuse of the emblem and acts of robbery and ill-treatment of the wounded and sick of the armed forces.[18] The Hague Regulations (1907) only provide for the responsibility of States to pay compensation in case of violations of the Conventions.[19]

---

[14] On this issue, see, in particular, Roberts, pp. 743–761; Natalie Wagner, 'The development of the grave breaches regime and of individual criminal responsibility by the International Criminal Tribunal for the former Yugoslavia', *International Review of the Red Cross*, Vol. 85, No. 850, June 2003, pp. 351–383; Shane Darcy and Joseph Powderly (eds), *Judicial Creativity at the International Criminal Tribunals*, Oxford University Press, 2010. There has, however, been a tendency, in particular for prosecutors at the ICTY, to charge alleged perpetrators with war crimes rather than grave breaches, thereby dispensing with the need to first establish the existence of an international armed conflict, as well as the protected status of the person or property in question.

[15] See Roberts, p. 744:

> In particular, in affirming the requirement that grave breaches must be committed in an international armed conflict, the Tribunal has examined the conditions under which a conflict may be established to be international, has articulated the contours of a necessary nexus between this international armed conflict and the grave breaches and has offered a new definition of a 'protected person' that ensures that the grave breaches regime remains relevant in modern warfare.

[16] See, in particular, the initiative to end sexual violence in armed conflict led by the United Kingdom. In paragraph 4, the Declaration on Preventing Sexual Violence in Conflict, adopted in London on 11 April 2013, states:

> Ministers recalled that rape and other forms of serious sexual violence in armed conflict are war crimes and also constitute grave breaches of the Geneva Conventions and their first Protocol. States have an obligation to search for and prosecute (or hand over for trial) any individual alleged to have committed or ordered a grave breach regardless of nationality.

> See also Theo Rycroft, 'Criminalization and Prosecution of Sexual Violence in Armed Conflict at the Domestic Level: Grave Breaches and Universal Jurisdiction', in *Vulnerabilities in Armed Conflicts: Selected Issues*, Proceedings of the 14th Bruges Colloquium, 17–18 October 2013, College of Europe/ICRC, Collegium No. 44, Autumn 2014, pp. 73–82.

[17] For more details, see the commentary on Article 49, section B.1.

[18] See Geneva Convention (1906), Articles 27 and 28. See also Hague Convention (X) (1907), Article 21.

[19] See Hague Regulations (1907), Article 3, which contains a general provision dealing with the responsibility of States. A similar obligation is contained in Article 91 of Additional Protocol I.

2913 Noticeable progress was made in the 1929 Geneva Convention on the Wounded and Sick, with the inclusion of a more comprehensive chapter on the suppression of abuses, containing for the first time detailed provisions on the enforcement of the Convention. It called on States Parties to 'propose to their legislatures should their penal laws be inadequate, the necessary measures for the repression in time of war of *any act* contrary to the provisions of the present Convention' (emphasis added),[20] including misuse of the emblem.[21] Article 30 provided for the establishment of an enquiry procedure in case of alleged violations of the Convention.[22]

2914 The 1947 Conference of Government Experts took as a starting point for the drafting of the chapter on repression of abuses Articles 28, 29 and 30 of the 1929 Convention. It also included a new draft article calling for '[a]ny wilful violation of the present Convention, leading to the death of persons protected by its provisions, to grave ill-treatment of the said persons, or serious damage to hospital buildings and equipment' to be 'considered as a war crime' and called for '[t]he responsible persons [to] be liable to appropriate penalties'.[23]

2915 The 1948 International Conference of the Red Cross in Stockholm adopted two draft articles on penal sanctions, but they did not contain a list of offences to be punished.[24] The ICRC, having been requested to submit further proposals on this issue to the 1949 Diplomatic Conference, suggested an open-ended list of grave breaches, including 'in particular those which cause death, great human suffering, or serious injury to body or health, those which constitute a grave denial of personal liberty or a derogation from the dignity due to the person, or involve extensive destruction of property, also breaches which by reason of their nature or persistence show a deliberate disregard of this Convention'.[25]

2916 The preparatory work does not reveal much of the content of the discussions which led to the elaboration of the list of grave breaches. Only a few points can be noted, beyond the fact that the list of grave breaches builds on

---

[20] Geneva Convention on the Wounded and Sick (1929), Article 29(1). According to Article 29(2), the High Contracting Parties had to notify the Swiss Federal Council of all provisions related to such repression no later than five years from the date of ratification of the Convention. Very few High Contracting Parties actually complied with this obligation.

[21] See Geneva Convention on the Wounded and Sick (1929), Article 28. For more details on abuse of the emblem, see the commentary on Article 53.

[22] For further details on the enquiry procedure, see the commentary on Article 52.

[23] See *Report of the Conference of Government Experts of 1947*, pp. 63–64 (Article 33).

[24] See *Draft Conventions adopted by the 1948 Stockholm Conference*, draft article 40, p. 25, which reads:

> The Contracting Parties shall be under the obligation to apprehend persons charged with acts contrary to the present Convention, regardless of their nationality. They shall furthermore, in obedience to their national legislation or to the conventions for the repression of acts that may be defined as war crimes, refer such persons for trial by their own courts, or if they so prefer, hand them over for trial to another Contracting Party'.

[25] See *ICRC Remarks and Proposals on the 1948 Stockholm Draft*, draft article 119(a), entitled 'Grave violations'.

the list of war crimes contained in Article 6(b) of the 1945 IMT Charter for Germany. The report on penal sanctions to the Joint Committee indicates that: 'This category has been carefully defined, so as to avoid including acts which allow for various degrees of gravity and could not therefore be considered to be grave breaches if only committed in their less serious forms.'[26] States felt it necessary to establish what these grave breaches were to be able to ensure universality of treatment in their repression.[27] Furthermore, the list of grave breaches was meant to be a warning to possible offenders and to draw public attention to the crimes, the perpetrators of which were to be searched for in all States.[28] Subsequent practice by States Parties has shown that this list is considered an exhaustive enumeration of grave breaches under the Geneva Conventions,[29] even if nothing prevents States from widening the category of war crimes to include other serious violations of international humanitarian law in their national legislation.[30]

2917   During the 1949 Diplomatic Conference, there were a few proposals which were not accepted. First, there were lengthy discussions following two amendments proposed by the USSR to use the term 'war crimes' or 'serious violations' instead of 'grave breaches'.[31] The Soviet proposals were rejected by the majority of delegations because 'the word "crimes" had a different meaning in the national laws of different countries and because an act only becomes a crime when this act is made punishable by a penal law'.[32] Second, the Italian delegation suggested including in the list of grave breaches the imposition of collective penalties. The proposal was rejected because the collective penalties thus imposed could be of varying degrees of severity and 'offences should not be inserted when they could be of varying degrees of gravity and would not be considered a grave breach if committed in their less serious form'.[33]

2918   The list of grave breaches is part of customary international law, particularly in the light of the universal ratification of the Geneva Conventions and the extensive State practice reflecting the definition of grave breaches.[34]

---

[26] *Final Record of the Diplomatic Conference of Geneva of 1949*, Vol. II-B, p. 115.
[27] Pictet (ed.), *Commentary on the First Geneva Convention*, ICRC, 1952, p. 370.
[28] *Ibid.* p. 371.
[29] For more details, see the commentary on Article 49, paras 2821 and 2857–2858. Furthermore, the doctrine usually holds that the list of grave breaches is exhaustive; see Gross, p. 820, and Gerald I.A.D. Draper, 'The Modern Pattern of War Criminality', *Israel Yearbook on Human Rights*, Vol. 6, 1976, p. 28.
[30] Until the early 2000s, most States Parties implemented their obligations under Articles 49 and 50 of the First Convention by providing penal sanctions for the list of grave breaches contained in the four Geneva Conventions. Parties to the ICC have, since 1998, often enlarged the inventory of war crimes in their national legislation beyond the list of grave breaches.
[31] See *Final Record of the Diplomatic Conference of Geneva of 1949*, Vol. II-B, pp. 116–117.
[32] *Ibid.* p. 116. Article 85(5) of Additional Protocol I adds the clarification that 'grave breaches shall be regarded as war crimes'.
[33] *Final Record of the Diplomatic Conference of Geneva of 1949*, Vol. II-B, p. 118.
[34] See Henckaerts, p. 690.

C. General clarifications on the scope of grave breaches

2919 At the time of the adoption of Article 50, States did not pay much attention to the constitutive elements of grave breaches, leaving these issues to national legislators and prosecutors.[35] In the meantime, national case law and the judgments of international criminal courts and tribunals have shed light on these issues. They can serve as useful guidelines with regard to the standards States could apply when implementing Article 50 in their domestic legal system and prosecuting alleged offenders.

1. Grave breaches are committed in the context of an international armed conflict

2920 For an act to amount to a grave breach of the Geneva Conventions, it must be committed in the context of an international armed conflict.[36] It is not enough for an international armed conflict to have existed when the crime was committed; there must also be a sufficient link or nexus between the criminal act and the international armed conflict. The assessment of whether the acts of the alleged perpetrator were sufficiently connected with the armed conflict will be made *a posteriori*, but it must be made in an objective manner.[37]

2921 The existence of a nexus between the crime and the international armed conflict is central to the distinction between a grave breach and an ordinary crime. For example, a murder committed for purely personal reasons while an international armed conflict is occurring on the territory of a State cannot be said to have been committed in the context of or associated with the conflict, and therefore does not amount to the grave breach of wilful killing.[38]

2922 The nexus has been found to be established if proof of a close connection between the criminal act and the armed conflict as a whole can be shown. This connection does not necessarily imply a strict geographical or temporal coincidence between the acts of the accused and the armed conflict.[39] For example, the acts of the perpetrator need not be committed in the course of fighting or the takeover of a town.[40] A close connection between the acts of the perpetrator and the armed conflict can be shown even if substantial clashes were not

---

[35] See the commentary on Article 49, paras 2835–2837.

[36] For a discussion of whether the regime of grave breaches has been extended to non-international armed conflicts, see the commentary on Article 49, section G. For a discussion of the definition of an international armed conflict, see the commentary on common Article 2.

[37] For a study of the concept of the nexus between the acts of the accused and the armed conflict, see Mettraux, pp. 38–51.

[38] See *ibid.* pp. 38–39.   [39] See *ibid.* p. 40.

[40] ICTY, *Delalić* Trial Judgment, 1998, para. 193. In *Brđanin*, the ICTY Appeals Chamber found that 'the Trial Chamber clearly established the existence of an international armed conflict and furthermore reasonably concluded that the rapes in Teslić, committed as they were during weapons searches, were committed in the context of an armed conflict and were not "individual domestic crimes" as suggested by Brđanin'; *Brđanin* Appeal Judgment, 2007, para. 256. See also ICTY, *Prlić* Trial Judgment, 2013, para. 109.

occurring in the region at the time and in the place where the crimes were allegedly committed.[41] It is sufficient for the acts of the perpetrator to be closely related to the hostilities occurring in other parts of the territories controlled by the Parties to the conflict.[42]

2923   The ICTY Appeals Chamber took the view that the nexus requirement would be met if the grave breach was committed in 'furtherance of or under the guise of the armed conflict'. It also held that:

> The armed conflict need not have been causal to the commission of the crime, but the existence of an armed conflict must, at a minimum, have played a substantial part in the perpetrator's ability to commit it, his decision to commit it, the manner in which it was committed or the purpose for which it was committed.[43]

2924   Various factors have been taken into account by international courts and tribunals to establish that the acts of the accused were closely related to the armed conflict such as:

- the fact that the perpetrator was a combatant;
- the fact that the victim was a person protected under the Geneva Conventions or Additional Protocol I;
- the fact that the victim was a member of the armed forces of the opposing Party;
- the circumstances in which the crime was committed;
- the fact that the act may be said to serve the ultimate goal of a military campaign;
- the fact that the crime was committed with the assistance or with the connivance of the Parties to the conflict; and
- the fact that the crime was committed as part of or in the context of the perpetrator's official duties.[44]

2925   There is no presumption that because an act is committed in time of international armed conflict, it necessarily constitutes a grave breach. International courts and tribunals have used the above factors in order to establish beyond a reasonable doubt that the perpetrators' acts were closely related to an armed

---

[41] See ICTY, *Delalić* Trial Judgment, 1998, para. 194, where the Trial Chamber takes the view that 'there need not have been any actual armed hostilities', and *Tadić* Trial Judgment, 1997, para. 573.

[42] See ICTY, *Tadić* Trial Judgment, 1997, para. 573; *Kunarac* Trial Judgment, 2001, para. 568; *Prlić* Trial Judgment, 2013, para. 109; and *Stakić* Appeal Judgment, 2006, para. 342.

[43] ICTY, *Kunarac* Appeal Judgment, 2002, para. 58. In this case, the Appeals Chamber was actually looking at a war crime under Article 3 of the 1993 ICTY Statute, and not at a grave breach of the Geneva Conventions. However, the same definition of the nexus is used by the ICTY under both Article 3 (war crimes) and Article 2 (grave breaches) of its Statute.

[44] See Mettraux, p. 46, referring to a number of cases, including ICTY, *Kunarac* Appeal Judgment, 2002, paras 58–59, and ICTR, *Rutaganda* Appeal Judgment, 2003, para. 577. For an application of the nexus requirement by national courts, see the *Mpambara case* in the Netherlands, where both the District Court and the Court of Appeal of The Hague discussed at length the existence of the nexus between the armed conflict and the acts of the accused.

conflict. The elements of crimes for grave breaches adopted by the Preparatory Commission for the ICC contains a contextual element, which reads: 'the conduct took place *in the context of* and *was associated with* an international armed conflict' (emphasis added).[45] The drafters chose to use these two expressions cumulatively, on the understanding that 'in the context of' refers to the existence of an armed conflict in the country or area where the act was committed, and that 'was associated with' refers to the necessary nexus between the armed conflict and the perpetrator's conduct.[46] The words 'associated with' also indicate that conduct which takes place after the cessation of active hostilities, but which is still associated with the conflict, can amount to a grave breach.[47]

2. *Grave breaches are committed against protected persons or property*

2926 To fall within the category of grave breaches, the prohibited acts must be committed against persons or property protected under the relevant Geneva Convention.[48]

2927 Under the First Convention, persons protected are listed in Article 13 (the wounded and sick), Article 15 (the dead), Article 24 (military medical and religious personnel), Article 25 (auxiliary medical personnel), Article 26 (personnel of aid societies) and Article 27 (medical personnel of societies of neutral countries).[49] However, if such persons commit acts harmful to the enemy, they lose their protection, at least for as long as they commit such acts.[50]

2928 The Geneva Conventions do not define the concept of protected property as such. They contain a list of objects which cannot be attacked, destroyed or appropriated, and which are therefore property protected under the Geneva Conventions. Under the First Convention, such property is listed in Articles 19, 33 and 34 (fixed medical establishments and mobile medical units), Article 20 (hospital ships) and Articles 35 and 36 (means of medical transport,

---

[45] See ICC Elements of Crimes (2002), Article 8 (War crimes). For an application of these criteria, see ICC, *Katanga* Trial Judgment, 2014, para. 1176, and *Bemba* Trial Judgment, 2016, paras 142–144 and 664–666.

[46] For more details on these negotiations, see Dörmann, pp. 17–28; La Haye, 2004, pp. 310–311; and Kreß, pp. 125–127.

[47] This will be the case as long as international humanitarian law applies, for example in the case of a civilian internee or a prisoner of war who might be detained even after the cessation of active hostilities and who could be the victim of torture. The perpetrator could still be prosecuted for the grave breach of torture, as his or her behaviour can still be said to be associated with the armed conflict.

[48] For States party to this instrument, Additional Protocol I expands the list of protected persons who can be the subject of grave breaches under the Protocol, in particular in Articles 8, 11 and 85.

[49] See the commentaries on Articles 13, 15, 24, 25, 26 and 27.

[50] For details on the concept of 'acts harmful to the enemy' and a discussion of the conditions under which protection might be regained, see the commentary on Article 24, section F.

including medical aircraft). If such property is used to commit acts harmful to the enemy,[51] it loses its protection for as long as it is so used.

3. Potential perpetrators of grave breaches

2929 It is not necessary to be a member of the armed forces to commit grave breaches of the Geneva Conventions. Members of the armed forces and civilians alike can commit grave breaches in the context of an international armed conflict.

2930 In addition to members of the armed forces, other categories of persons, including civilian leaders and subordinate executives,[52] have been found guilty of committing grave breaches or other war crimes: members of government, including heads of State,[53] party officials and administrators,[54] industrialists and businessmen,[55] judges and prosecutors,[56] doctors and nurses,[57] and concentration-camp inmates with civilian status.[58]

4. General comments on the mental element of grave breaches

2931 In all modern criminal-law systems, alleged perpetrators must fulfil two conditions to be held criminally responsible: (1) through their behaviour, they must have caused a certain event or state of affairs forbidden by criminal law (referred to as the material element, or *actus reus*); and (2) they must have had a defined

---

[51] For an interpretation of this concept, see the commentary on Article 21, section C.1 and in general the commentary on Article 22.

[52] Ordinary civilians have also been found guilty of war crimes, such as in United Kingdom, Military Court at Essen, *Essen Lynching case*, Judgment, 1945, in which civilians were convicted of killing or participating in the killing of three British prisoners of war.

[53] See e.g. the 2012 proceedings against Charles Taylor before the SCSL, arguably for acts committed during a non-international armed conflict, and the proceedings against Japanese members of government before the International Military Tribunal for the Far East, as reported in B.V.A. Röling and C.F. Rüter (eds), *The Tokyo Judgement*, Vol. I, APA University Press, Amsterdam, 1977, pp. 29–31.

[54] See e.g. the *Wagner case* in 1946 before the French Permanent Military Tribunal at Strasbourg, where the chief defendant was the head of the civil government of Alsace, and the others were high administrative officers of the Nazi Party and judicial officers; see also the *Boškoski and Tarčulovski case* before the ICTY, where Boškoski was at the time of the event minister of the interior of the former Yugoslav Republic of Macedonia, or the *Šešelj case*, where the accused was the president of the Serbian Radical Party.

[55] See, in particular, the *Zyklon B case* in 1946 before the UK Military Court in Hamburg, where two German industrialists were sentenced to death for having supplied Zyklon B poison gas to concentration camps. Other trials of industrialists include the 1947 *Flick case*, the 1947–48 *I.G. Farben Trial* and the 1948 *Krupp case* before the US Military Tribunal at Nuremberg.

[56] See e.g. the *Altstötter case* in 1947 before the US Military Tribunal at Nuremberg, in which Altstötter and the other defendants were former German judges, prosecutors or officials in the Reich Ministry of Justice, and the *Wagner case* in 1946 before the French Permanent Military Tribunal at Strasbourg, where the accused Huber was found guilty of complicity in the murder of 14 people on whom he had passed unjustified death sentences. See also Dörmann, p. 37.

[57] See, in particular, United States, Military Commission in Wiesbaden, *Hadamar Trial*, 1945.

[58] See, in particular, United Kingdom, Military Court at Lüneburg, *Kramer case*, Judgment, 1945.

state of mind in relation to causing the event or state of affairs (referred to as the mental element, or *mens rea*).[59]

2932 The Geneva Conventions are silent as to the requisite degree of *mens rea* attached to most grave breaches.[60] The Conventions oblige States to prosecute grave breaches domestically, but leave it to States Parties to determine the requisite mental element attached to them, unless specifically defined in Article 50. As those grave breaches have been integrated into domestic law, the standard mental element applicable in each legal system will apply to grave breaches when they are prosecuted at the national level. Depending on the legal system to which they belong, domestic courts place their own interpretation on notions such as intent, fault or negligence.[61]

2933 From the wording of Article 50 itself, two important points can be noted and should be implemented in national legislation. The use of the term 'wilful' indicates, at least for the crimes of killing and causing great suffering or serious injury to body or health, that either intentional or reckless conduct will engage the responsibility of the perpetrator.[62]

2934 Furthermore, any element of specific intent forming part of the crime in international humanitarian law must be proven before an accused person is found guilty of a grave breach in a national court. For instance, the grave breach of torture is a specific-intent crime. The prosecutor will have to prove that the alleged perpetrator not only intended to inflict severe pain or suffering on the victim, but that he specifically intended to inflict this for such purposes as obtaining information or a confession, punishing, intimidating or coercing the victim or a third person, or discriminating on any ground against the victim or a third person.[63]

2935 International criminal law provides guidance to domestic courts and prosecutors when they prosecute individuals for grave breaches pursuant to Articles 49 and 50 of the First Convention and have to decide on the mental element applicable to grave breaches. The following remarks on mental elements are meant to highlight the general state of international criminal law as applied thus far

---

[59] See 'Paper prepared by the International Committee of the Red Cross relating to the mental element in the common law and civil law systems and to the concepts of mistake of fact and mistake of law in national and international law', in Preparatory Commission for the International Criminal Court, Working Group on Elements of Crimes, UN Doc. PCNICC/1999/WGEC/INF/2/Add.4, 15 December 1999, p. 3.

[60] For some grave breaches, the *mens rea* is specified in Article 50, when it lists 'wilful' killing, 'wilfully' causing great suffering, or extensive destruction carried out 'wantonly'.

[61] See Cassese, pp. 39–40.

[62] See Sandoz/Swinarski/Zimmermann (eds), *Commentary on the Additional Protocols*, ICRC, 1987, para. 3474. The French version of the commentary uses the term 'dol éventuel' for 'recklessness'. See the definition of this concept below.

[63] In the words of Cassese, p. 44:

International rules may require a special intent (*dolus specialis*) for particular classes of crime. Such rules, in addition to providing for the intent to bring about a certain result by undertaking certain conduct (for example death by killing), may also require that the agent pursue a *specific goal* that goes beyond the result of his conduct.

by international courts and tribunals. However, it is not easy to identify the various forms of mental element in international criminal law, and differences of interpretation or approach between international jurisdictions are also noted below.

a. The mental element applicable to the material elements of the crimes

2936 In international criminal law, it is generally accepted that the material elements of an act and a mental element related to the perpetrator's state of mind must coincide before a perpetrator can be convicted of a crime.[64] Perpetrators must intend to commit the relevant material elements of a particular offence before they can be found guilty of that offence. Cases of negligence do not usually support the conviction of alleged perpetrators in international criminal law.

2937 International courts and tribunals have not developed a uniform rule on the mental element applicable to all war crimes or grave breaches, but have tended instead to define the mental element for each crime on a case-by-case basis.[65] In a number of cases, the tribunals have found alleged offenders responsible for having committed a grave breach if they intended to commit the relevant material elements of the offence. They have used the words 'intentionally', 'deliberately' or 'intentional' interchangeably and applied them to the material element of the crime (in contrast to the elements of a crime expressing a circumstance or a consequence).[66] Furthermore international courts and tribunals have made a distinction between general intent and specific intent, recognizing that for certain grave breaches, such as torture, a specific intent or purpose must be proven before the perpetrator can be found guilty of the crime in question. Third, another form of culpability used by the international tribunals is the concept of indirect intent, also referred to as recklessness, or *dolus eventualis*.[67] This concept refers to a state of mind where 'the person foresees that his action is likely to produce its prohibited consequences and nevertheless takes the risk of so acting'.[68] Under this form of culpability, the tribunals found that, for the grave breach of wilful killing, the perpetrator must intend to kill or to inflict serious injury, in reckless disregard of human life, or in the reasonable knowledge that such act or omission was likely to lead to death.[69] In other cases, the tribunals defined the concept of indirect intent in

---

[64] See Werle/Jessberger, para. 460.

[65] *Ibid.* para. 462. For a study of this issue, see Badar, 2006, pp. 313–348, and Badar, 2013.

[66] See, in particular, Badar, 2006, p. 347.

[67] *Ibid.* It should be noted that recklessness and *dolus eventualis* do not overlap entirely. Recklessness covers both *dolus eventualis* and certain cases of gross negligence under some civil-law systems.

[68] Cassese, pp. 45–46.

[69] See Werle/Jessberger, paras 464–465, as well as further details on the grave breach of wilful killing, paras 2956–2958.

a slightly different way, seemingly raising the threshold necessary to fulfil the mental element when it required the perpetrator to be aware of the substantial likelihood that the result would occur.[70]

2938 The mental element attached to all international crimes has been defined in a uniform manner in Article 30 of the 1998 ICC Statute:

1. Unless otherwise provided, a person shall be criminally responsible and liable for punishment for a crime within the jurisdiction of the Court only if the material elements are committed with intent and knowledge. . . .
2. For the purposes of this article, a person has intent where:
   A. In relation to conduct, that person means to engage in the conduct;
   B. In relation to a consequence, that person means to cause that consequence or is aware that it will occur in the ordinary course of events.
3. For the purposes of this article, 'knowledge' means awareness that a circumstance exists or a consequence will occur in the ordinary course of events.[71]

2939 Intent and knowledge therefore apply to the material elements of each crime under the ICC Statute, both in terms of the conduct of the perpetrator and its consequences, unless otherwise provided elsewhere, such as in the definitions of the crimes themselves or in the ICC Elements of Crimes.[72] The drafting history of Article 30 suggests that the concept of recklessness was considered as a basis of international criminal responsibility but rejected by the drafters.[73] Most commentators agree that it is difficult to read the concept of recklessness into the definition of intent or knowledge in Article 30.[74] This position therefore contrasts with the interpretation of the mental element adopted by the international criminal tribunals. Article 30 appears to be stricter than international and domestic case law or domestic legislation, which often accept the concept of recklessness as regards the consequences of a perpetrator's

---

[70] See e.g. ICTY, *Kvočka* Trial Judgment, 2001, para. 251; *Blaškić* Appeal Judgment, 2004, para. 42; *Kordić and Čerkez* Appeal Judgment, 2004, para. 30; and *Galić* Appeal Judgment, 2006, para. 152. See also Werle/Jessberger, para. 465, and ICTY, *Prlić* Trial Judgment, 2013, Vol. 5, Separate Opinion of Judge Trechsel: Recklessness, *dolus eventualis*, indirect intent, pp. 107–111.

[71] For a commentary on Article 30, see e.g. Werle/Jessberger, paras 467–497.

[72] This could be the case if, for example, the crimes in question include a certain threshold of *mens rea* in their definition, such as the words 'wilful' or 'wanton'.

[73] See Preparatory Committee on the Establishment of an International Criminal Court, Working Group on General Principles of Criminal Law and Penalties, UN Doc. A/AC.249/1997/WG.2/CRP.4, 20 February 1997, as well as UN Doc A/CONF.183/DC/R.76.

[74] See Donald K. Piragoff and Darryl Robinson, 'Article 30: Mental Element', in Otto Triffterer and Kai Ambos (eds), *The Rome Statute of the International Criminal Court: A Commentary*, 3rd edition, Hart Publishing, Oxford, 2016, pp. 1111–1124; Jens David Ohlin, 'Searching for the Hinterman: In Praise of Subjective Theories of Imputation', *Journal of International Criminal Justice*, Vol. 12, No. 2, 2014, pp. 325–343, at 333; William A. Schabas, *The International Criminal Court: A Commentary on the Rome Statute*, Oxford University Press, 2010, p. 473; and Roger S. Clark, 'Drafting a General Part to a Penal Code: Some Thoughts Inspired by the Negotiations on the Rome Statute of the International Criminal Court and by the Court's First Substantive Law Discussion in the *Lubanga Dyilo* Confirmation Proceedings', *Criminal Law Forum*, Vol. 19, No. 3–4, 2008, pp. 519–552.

conduct.[75] The first judgment of the ICC affirms that the concepts of reckless-ness and *dolus eventualis* were deliberately excluded from the framework of the ICC Statute,[76] but it clarifies the content of the mental element that the Prosecutor must establish: perpetrators must mean to engage in a form of con-duct, or be aware that if they engage in such conduct, a consequence will occur in the ordinary course of events.[77]

2940   Domestic and international courts routinely infer from the facts of the case and all circumstantial evidence whether or not perpetrators intended to com-mit the crime or were aware that their conduct was going to bring about a cer-tain result.[78] The ICTY took the view that, while the necessary intent might be inferred from all the circumstances surrounding the infliction of harm to the protected person or property, it must be the only reasonable inference to be drawn from the evidence.[79]

b. The mental element applicable to the existence and character of the armed conflict

2941   The question arises whether there is any mental element required for the other three distinct elements of grave breaches: the existence and character of an armed conflict, the nexus between the conflict and the conduct of the perpe-trator, and the fact that the victim was a protected person or the property was protected under the Geneva Conventions.

2942   The Conventions are silent as to which mental element, if any, is attached to the existence and character of the armed conflict. The existence of an armed conflict, together with the nexus between the act of the accused and the armed conflict, are the factors distinguishing an ordinary crime from a grave breach. There is no requirement for the perpetrator to make a legal evaluation as to the character of the armed conflict, or to legally assess the existence of an armed conflict. Similarly, there is no requirement to prove that the per-petrator is aware of the facts that established the character of the conflict as international or non-international. Such a requirement would come close

---

[75] See Werle/Jessberger, para. 476.   [76] ICC, *Lubanga* Trial Judgment, 2012, para. 1011.

[77] For an illustration of this *mens rea*, see e.g. ICC, *Lubanga* Trial Judgment, 2012, para. 1013, in relation to the crime of conscripting, enlisting or using children under the age of 15 to participate actively in hostilities:

> The Chamber is of the view that the prosecution must establish, as regards the mental ele-ment, that:
> (i) the accused and at least one other perpetrator meant to conscript, enlist or use children under the age of 15 to participate actively in hostilities or they were aware that in imple-menting their common plan this consequence 'will occur in the ordinary course of events'; and
> (ii) the accused was aware that he provided an essential contribution to the implementation of the common plan.

> This interpretation has been suggested by the majority of authors; see Werle/Jessberger, paras 476–479.

[78] See Cassese, p. 57.

[79] See Mettraux, p. 72, referring in particular to ICTY, *Krnojelac* Trial Judgment, 2002, para. 67, for the general standard of proof applied by the international criminal tribunals.

to asking the perpetrator to make a legal evaluation of the character of the conflict.

2943 It is important, however, that the perpetrator be aware of some factual circumstances establishing the existence of an armed conflict. In most instances, it would be so obvious that there was an armed conflict going on, and that the perpetrator knew it, that no particular proof as to such knowledge would be required. It is understood that if the prosecutor provides the necessary proof to establish the existence of the armed conflict and the nexus between the armed conflict and the acts of the perpetrator, he or she would not normally have to provide additional proof of the perpetrator's knowledge of factual circumstances that establish the existence of an armed conflict. The latter will generally be a 'by-product' of the evidence required to prove the former. In the context of an international armed conflict, some factual circumstances establishing the existence of an armed conflict could be identified, such as the presence of foreign uniforms and foreign troops on the territory.

2944 One might think of certain forms of conduct, such as the use of certain weapons or ammunition, which could be illegal during an armed conflict but legal in other situations not amounting to an armed conflict. In those circumstances, it is important to require proof that the perpetrator was aware of the existence of the armed conflict before he or she is found guilty of a war crime.

2945 For a long time, the international criminal tribunals did not require proof of any knowledge by perpetrators of the existence and character of the conflict or the existence of a nexus between their acts and the armed conflict. They were treated as purely jurisdictional elements. In 2006, the ICTY Appeals Chamber reversed these findings in *Naletilić and Martinović* where it found that:

> 116. . . . the existence and international character of an armed conflict are both jurisdictional prerequisites . . . and substantive elements of crimes . . .
>
> . . .
>
> 118. . . . the Prosecution has to show 'that the accused *knew* that his crimes' had a nexus to an international armed conflict, or at least that he had knowledge of the factual circumstances later bringing the Judges to the conclusion that the armed conflict was an international one.[80]

2946 It is interesting to note that some national courts have defined the common elements of grave breaches or war crimes in a manner similar to the ICTY.[81]

---

[80] ICTY, *Naletilić and Martinović* Appeal Judgment, 2006, paras 116 and 118. The Chamber went on to say: 'The perpetrator only needs to be aware of factual circumstances on which the judge finally determines the existence of the armed conflict and the international (or internal) character thereof' (para. 119). See also *Prlić* Trial Judgment, 2013, para. 109.

[81] See the case law of the Court of Bosnia and Herzegovina, for example *Andrun case*, Verdict, 2008, p. 14:

> The following general elements of the criminal offense of War Crimes against Civilians, which needed to be established, follow from the cited legal definition:
> • The act of the perpetrator must be committed in violation of the rules of international law,
> • The violation must take place in time of war, armed conflict or occupation,
> • The act of the perpetrator must be related to war, armed conflict or occupation,
> • The perpetrator must order or perpetrate the act.

Some courts have then proceeded to see whether those common elements were fulfilled in the case at hand, without requiring proof that the perpetrator was aware of the existence of the armed conflict, the nexus or the protected status of the victim.[82]

2947   When similar questions were discussed by the Preparatory Commission in charge of drafting the ICC Elements of Crimes, there were diverging views among delegations.[83] Under the ICC Statute, the following mental element was adopted for each crime: 'The accused was aware of factual circumstances that established the existence of an armed conflict.'[84] The introduction to the section on Article 8 (War Crimes) in the Elements of Crimes attempts to clarify this mental element. First, the introduction makes it clear that perpetrators are not required to make a legal evaluation as to the existence of an armed conflict or its character as international or non-international. Second, the mental element must not be understood as requiring perpetrators to be aware of the facts that established the character of the conflict as international or non-international.[85] Third, it is not necessary for perpetrators to be aware of the full complexity of the facts determining the existence of an armed conflict. Perpetrators must simply know sufficient facts to be aware of the existence of an armed conflict.[86]

c. The mental element applicable to the status of protected person or property

2948   The grave breaches listed in Article 50 are committed against persons or property protected under the First Geneva Convention. The question arises whether the alleged perpetrator needs to know that the person or property was protected under the Convention. The case law of the ICTY requires the prosecution to prove that the victims were protected persons or that the property was protected under the relevant Geneva Convention. However, the ICTY has not required any proof that the alleged perpetrator was aware of the protected status of the victim or the property.[87]

---

[82] See *ibid*. pp. 14–18.

[83] For the historical background and a commentary on this issue as it pertains to the Elements of Crimes, see Dörmann, pp. 20–22; Dörmann/La Haye/von Hebel, pp. 120–124; and La Haye, 2008, pp. 111–115.

[84] The direct article ('the') before the term 'factual circumstances', was dropped in order to indicate that the perpetrator needs only to be aware of some factual circumstances and not all factual circumstances. See Dörmann, p. 21.

[85] This issue was discussed in a general way for all war crimes, including grave breaches. No particular requirement was adopted for grave breaches, e.g. that the accused should be aware of factual circumstances establishing the character of the armed conflict.

[86] The third clarification in the introduction states: 'There is only a requirement for the awareness of the factual circumstances that established the existence of an armed conflict that is implicit in the terms "took place in the context of and was associated with"'; ICC Elements of Crimes (2002), p. 18. For an illustration of this requirement, see ICC, *Bemba* Trial Judgment, 2016, paras 145–147 and 667.

[87] See the following cases, where the ICTY Chambers concluded that the armed conflict amounted to an international armed conflict, and where the status of protected person or protected property was discussed: *Tadić* Trial Judgment, 1997, para. 578, and Appeal Judgment, 1999,

2949 Under the ICC Elements of Crimes, the alleged perpetrator needs to have been aware of the factual circumstances that established the status of protected person.[88] It is not necessary for the perpetrator to have known of the protected status of the person or property under the Geneva Conventions in legal terms, which would be a question of law; knowledge of the factual circumstances establishing such status is sufficient.[89]

D. List of grave breaches

1. Wilful killing

2950 The prohibition of 'murder' first appears in Article 12 of the First Convention, as well as in common Article 3. There is no difference between the notion of 'wilful killing' and the notion of 'murder' as prohibited under Article 12 and common Article 3.[90] The elements of the crime of murder or wilful killing have been defined in the same way by international courts and tribunals, whether the events amount to a grave breach, a war crime or a crime against humanity.[91]

a. Material element

2951 The material element of this grave breach is that the alleged perpetrator killed or caused the death of a protected person.

paras 163–166; *Kordić and Čerkez* Trial Judgment, 2001, paras 147–160, and Appeal Judgment, 2004, paras 322–331; *Delalić* Trial Judgment, 1998, paras 244–277, and Appeal Judgment, 2001, paras 52–106; *Blaškić* Trial Judgment, 2000, paras 125–133, and Appeal Judgment, 2004, paras 167–182; *Aleksovski* Appeal Judgment, 2000, para. 151; *Naletilić and Martinović* Trial Judgment, 2003, paras 203–208; and *Brđanin* Trial Judgment, 2004, paras 125, 155 and 585. Badar believes that an accused charged for example with the 'crime of wilful killing must be proved to have been aware of the fact that the victim was a protected person . . . in addition to the mental state required with regard to the result element', p. 338.

[88] For an illustration of this requirement, see ICC, *Katanga* Trial Judgment, 2014, para. 900.

[89] It is also interesting to note that, in the 2002 ICC Elements of Crimes, footnotes were appended to the mental elements attached to certain war crimes involving protected status, pointing out that these elements recognized the interplay between Articles 30 and 32 of the 1998 ICC Statute. This emphasized the general rule that ignorance of the facts, if it negates the mental element required by the crime, may be an excuse, but that ignorance of the law, such as the definition of protected persons or property, is not a ground for excluding criminal responsibility. See ICC Elements of Crimes (2002), fns 32, 39, 40, 41 and 43.

[90] The ICTY took the view that 'there can be no line drawn between "wilful killing" and "murder" which affects their content'; see ICTY, *Delalić* Trial Judgment, 1998, para. 422. For examples of convictions for the war crime of murder following the Second World War, see e.g. United Kingdom, Military Court at Almelo, *Almelo Trial*, Judgment, 1945; Military Court at Brunswick, *Gerike case*, Trial, 1946; Military Court at Lüneburg, *Krammer* case, Judgment, 1945, p. 126; and Military Court at Wuppertal, *Rohde case*, Judgment, 1946.

[91] For murder and wilful killing as a grave breach, see, in particular, ICTY, *Orić* Trial Judgment, 2006, para. 345, and *Brđanin* Trial Judgment, 2004, para. 380; and ICC, *Katanga* Trial Judgment, 2014, para. 789. For examples of murder as a war crime and murder as a crime against humanity, see ICTY, *Delalić* Trial Judgment, 1998, para. 422, and Appeal Judgment, 2001, para. 423; *Stanišić and Župljanin* Trial Judgment, 2013, para. 42; *Tolimir* Trial Judgment, 2012, para. 714; *Popović* Trial Judgment, 2010, para. 787; *Lukić and Lukić* Trial Judgment, 2009, para. 903; *Milutinović* Trial Judgment, 2009, para. 136; *Martić* Trial Judgment, 2007, para. 58; *Blagojević and Jokić* Trial Judgment, 2005, para. 556; ICC, *Katanga* Trial Judgment, 2014, paras 765–767; *Bemba* Trial Judgment, 2016, paras 91–97; and ECCC, *Nuon and Khieu* Trial Judgment, 2014, paras 412–413.

2952   The perpetrator's conduct does not have to be the sole cause of the death of the protected person, but it must at minimum have contributed substantially thereto.[92]

2953   The notion of killing has been used interchangeably with causing death. Thus, this grave breach covers not only such acts as shooting a protected person to death, but also such conduct as reducing the food rations of protected persons, resulting in their starvation and ultimately their death.[93] Wilful killing is prohibited and amounts to a grave breach, irrespective of the motivation behind the act. 'Mercy killings' intended to put wounded combatants 'out of their misery' are prohibited.[94]

2954   The judgments of international courts and tribunals also make it clear that not only acts but also omissions which cause the death of protected persons, such as the wounded and sick or medical personnel, amount to the grave breach of wilful killing.[95] An example would be failing to take action by wilfully leaving the wounded and sick without medical assistance, which ultimately leads to their death.[96]

2955   In the case law of international courts and tribunals, there is no requirement that the body of the victim be recovered in order to prove death beyond a reasonable doubt.[97] The death of the victim may be established by circumstantial

---

[92] For examples, see ICTY, *Delalić* Trial Judgment, 1998, para. 424; *Kordić and Čerkez* Trial Judgment, 2001, para. 229; *Tolimir* Trial Judgment, 2012, para. 715; *Haradinaj* Retrial Judgment, 2012, para. 427; *Đorđević* Trial Judgment, 2011, para. 1708; *Popović* Trial Judgment, 2010, para. 788; *Lukić and Lukić* Trial Judgment, 2009, para. 903; *Milutinović* Trial Judgment, 2009, para. 137; *Orić* Trial Judgment, 2006, para. 347; SCSL, *Brima* Trial Judgment, 2007, para. 689; and ECCC, *Kaing* Trial Judgment, 2010, para. 331. This principle was also applied by national courts, such as in the *Andrun case*, where the Court of Bosnia and Herzegovina found Andrun guilty of the crime of murder for having participated substantially in the murder of persons protected under the Geneva Conventions; see *Andrun case*, Verdict, 2008, pp. 23–26.

[93] See Silja Vöneky, 'Implementation and Enforcement of International Humanitarian Law', in Dieter Fleck (ed.) *The Handbook of International Humanitarian Law*, 3rd edition, Oxford University Press, 2013, pp. 647–700, at 671–672.

[94] See also the commentary on Article 12, para. 1404.

[95] For a discussion of the material element of the crime of murder or wilful killing, see e.g. ICTY, *Delić* Trial Judgment, 2008, para. 46; *Kordić and Čerkez* Appeal Judgment, 2004, para. 36; *Hadžihasanović* Trial Judgment, 2006, para. 31; *Galić* Appeal Judgment, 2006, para. 147; *Kvočka* Appeal Judgment, 2005, para. 261; *Halilović* Trial Judgment, 2005, para. 35; *Brđanin* Trial Judgment, 2004, para. 381; *Dragomir Milošević* Appeal Judgment, 2009, para. 108; *Mrkšić* Trial Judgment, 2007, para. 486; *Krajišnik* Trial Judgment, 2006, para. 715; *Limaj* Trial Judgment, 2005, para. 241; *Blagojević and Jokić* Trial Judgment, 2005, para. 556; *Perišić* Trial Judgment, 2011, para. 102; *Gotovina* Trial Judgment, 2011, para. 1725; *Đorđević* Trial Judgment, 2011, para. 1708; *Milutinović* Trial Judgment, 2009, para. 137; *Prlić* Trial Judgment, 2013, paras 110–111; ICTR, *Ndindiliyimana* Trial Judgment, 2011, para. 6165; *Nyiramasuhuko* Trial Judgment, 2011, para. 6165; *Nizeyimana* Trial Judgment, 2012, para. 1552; *Zigiranyirazo* Trial Judgment, 2008, para. 442; ECCC, *Kaing* Trial Judgment, 2010, para. 331; SCSL, *Sesay* Trial Judgment, 2009, para. 142; *Taylor* Trial Judgment, 2012, para. 412; *Brima* Trial Judgment, 2007, para. 688; and *Fofana and Kondewa* Trial Judgment, 2007, para. 146.

[96] The ECCC found an accused guilty of the grave breach of wilful killing as detainees died 'as the result of omissions known to be likely to lead to death and as a consequence of the conditions of detention imposed upon them'; *Kaing* Trial Judgment, 2010, para. 437.

[97] For examples, see ICTY, *Krnojelac* Trial Judgment, 2002, para. 326; *Kvočka* Appeal Judgment, 2005, para. 260; *Đorđević* Trial Judgment, 2011, para. 1708; *Boškoski and Tarčulovski* Trial Judgment, 2008, para. 305; *Mrkšić* Trial Judgment, 2007, para. 486; *Limaj* Trial Judgment, 2005, para. 241; and *Brđanin* Trial Judgment, 2004, para. 383.

evidence, provided that the only reasonable inference that can be drawn from such evidence is that the victim is dead.[98] The circumstantial evidence used by international courts and tribunals has included such factors as proof of incidents of mistreatment directed against the individual; patterns of mistreatment, and disappearance of other individuals in the location at question; the time elapsed since the person disappeared; and the fact that there has been no contact by that person with others whom he or she would have been expected to contact, such as family members.[99]

b. Mental element

2956 The 1949 Diplomatic Conference chose to indicate in Article 50 the state of mind required for the perpetrator to be found guilty of the grave breach of killing, namely, that it be 'wilful'. As mentioned above in the general comments on the mental element, the traditional understanding of the word 'wilful' is that it covers both 'intent' and 'recklessness'.[100]

2957 International courts and tribunals have found perpetrators guilty of the grave breach of wilful killing if they intended to kill or inflict serious bodily harm, knowing that such bodily harm is likely to cause the protected person's death.[101] Some chambers have chosen to define the concept of 'recklessness' in

---

[98] See, in particular, ICTY, *Kvočka* Appeal Judgment, 2005, para. 260; *Lukić and Lukić* Appeal Judgment, 2012, para. 149; *Krnojelac* Trial Judgment, 2002, paras 326–327; *Tadić* Trial Judgment, 1997, para. 240; *Brđanin* Trial Judgment, 2004, para. 385; *Stanišić and Župljanin*, Trial Judgment, 2013, para. 40; *Tolimir* Trial Judgment, 2012, para. 715; *Perišić* Trial Judgment, 2011, para. 103; *Popović* Trial Judgment, 2010, para. 789; *Delić* Trial Judgment, 2008, para. 47; *Martić* Trial Judgment, 2007, para. 59; *Orić* Trial Judgment, 2006, para. 347; *Halilović* Trial Judgment, 2005, para. 37; SCSL, *Brima* Trial Judgment, 2007, para. 689; ICC, *Katanga* Trial Judgment, 2014, para. 768; and ECCC, *Nuon and Khieu* Trial Judgment, 2014, para. 413.

[99] See ICTY, *Krnojelac* Trial Judgment, 2002, para. 327, citing, in fn. 857, a large number of human rights cases in the European Court of Human Rights, the Inter-American Court of Human Rights and national legal systems which use the same factors to infer that the victim is dead. See also SCSL, *Brima* Trial Judgment, 2007, para. 689, and ECCC, *Kaing* Trial Judgment, 2010, para. 332. Other factors have also been used, such as 'the coincident or near-coincident time of death of other victims, the fact that the victims were present in an area where an armed attack was carried out … and the circumstances in which the victim was last seen, and the behaviour of soldiers in the vicinity, as well as towards other civilians, at the relevant time'; ICTY, *Halilović* Trial Judgment, 2005, para. 37. These factors were also referred to in ICTY, *Martić* Trial Judgment, 2007, fn. 112; *Delić* Trial Judgment, 2008, fn. 87; and *Lukić and Lukić* Trial Judgment, 2009, para. 904.

[100] See Sandoz/Swinarski/Zimmermann (eds), *Commentary on the Additional Protocols*, ICRC, 1987, para. 3474. The French version of the commentary uses the term 'dol éventuel' for 'recklessness'. See also ICTY, *Blaškić* Trial Judgment, 2000, para. 152, which affirms that 'the *mens rea* constituting all the violations of Article 2 of the Statute includes both guilty intent and recklessness which may be likened to serious criminal negligence'. This view is also supported by various decisions emerging from the war crimes trials after the Second World War, such as United Kingdom, Military Court at Brunswick, *Gerike case*, Trial, 1946, p. 78, and Military Court at Helmstedt, *Tyrolt case*, Trial, 1946.

[101] See e.g. ICTY, *Delalić* Appeal Judgment, 2001, para. 422; *Kordić and Čerkez* Trial Judgment, 2001, paras 235–236, and Appeal Judgment, 2004, para. 36; *Krnojelac* Trial Judgment, 2002, para. 324; *Blaškić* Trial Judgment, 2000, para. 217; *Vasiljević* Trial Judgment, 2002, para. 205; *Naletilić and Martinović* Trial Judgment, 2003, para. 248; *Tolimir* Trial Judgment, 2012, para. 716; *Perišić* Trial Judgment, 2011, para. 102; *Blagojević and Jokić* Trial Judgment, 2005, para. 556; *Brđanin* Trial Judgment, 2004, para. 381; SCSL, *Taylor* Trial Judgment, 2012,

a slightly different way by requiring that the act be committed 'with the intent to kill the victim or wilfully causing serious bodily harm which the perpetrator should reasonably have known might lead to death'.[102] Other chambers have spoken of 'indirect intent', which 'comprises the perpetrator's knowledge that the death of the victim was the probable or likely consequence of his act or omission'.[103] Despite some variations in the way this mental element has been phrased, they have consistently understood 'wilful' to cover the concepts both of intent and of recklessness, or *dolus eventualis*.

2958   These jurisdictions have also consistently found that it is not sufficient to prove that the alleged perpetrator knew that his or her act might possibly cause death.[104] Furthermore, ordinary negligence has not been found to constitute 'indirect intent'.[105]

2959   Lastly, as a separate matter, premeditation is not required as the *mens rea* for the grave breach of wilful killing.[106]

para. 412; *Sesay* Trial Judgment, 2009, para. 142; *Brima* Trial Judgment, 2007, para. 688; *Fofana and Kondewa* Trial Judgment, 2007, para. 146; and ECCC, *Kaing* Trial Judgment, 2010, para. 333. In *Galić*, the ICTY Appeals Chamber held that the *mens rea* was fulfilled if the alleged perpetrator had the intent '(i) to kill, or (ii) to inflict serious injury, in reckless disregard of human life' (Appeal Judgment, 2006, para. 147). For a similar definition, see also *Kupreškić* Trial Judgment, 2000, paras 560–561.

[102] ICTY, *Kvočka* Appeal Judgment, 2005, para. 261; *Krstić* Trial Judgment, 2001, para. 485; *Stanišić and Župljanin* Trial Judgment, 2013, para. 39; *Gotovina* Trial Judgment, 2011, para. 1725; *Dragomir Milošević* Appeal Judgment, 2009, para. 108; *Krajišnik* Trial Judgment, 2006, para. 715; *Hadžihasanović* Trial Judgment, 2006, para. 31; *Halilović* Trial Judgment, 2005, para. 35; *Stanišić and Simatović* Trial Judgment, 2013, para. 974; ICTR, *Setako* Appeal Judgment, 2011, para. 257; *Nizeyimana* Trial Judgment, 2012, para. 1552; and *Karemera* Appeal Judgment, 2014, para. 670. A similar reasoning emerges from the Second World War cases, where the responsibility of perpetrators was found to be engaged if, owing to their position or skills, they must have been aware of the facts and the likelihood of death; see e.g. United Kingdom, Military Court at Hamburg, *Zyklon B case*, Trial, 1947, and United States, Military Tribunal at Nuremberg, *Von Leeb case*, Trial, 1949.

[103] See e.g. ICTY, *Mucić* Trial Judgment, 1998, para. 435; *Perišić* Trial Judgment, 2011, para. 104; *Delić* Trial Judgment, 2008, para. 48; and *Strugar* Trial Judgment, 2005, para. 235.

[104] See e.g. ICTY, *Martić* Trial Judgment, 2007, para. 60: 'The *mens rea* of murder is the intent to kill, including indirect intent, that is the knowledge that the death of the victim was a probable consequence of the act or omission. This Trial Chamber does not consider it to be sufficient that the perpetrator knew that death would be a *possible* consequence of his act or omission.' See also *Strugar* Trial Judgment, 2005, para. 235:

It is now settled that the *mens rea* is not confined to cases where the accused has a direct intent to kill or to cause serious bodily harm, but also extends to cases where the accused has what is often referred to as an indirect intent. While the precise expression of the appropriate indirect intent has varied between decisions, it has been confirmed by the Appeals Chamber that the awareness of a mere possibility that a crime will occur is not sufficient in the context of ordering under Article 7(1) of the Statute.

For further examples, see ICTY, *Limaj* Trial Judgment, 2005, para. 241; *Mrkšić* Trial Judgment, 2007, para. 486; *Boškoski and Tarčulovski* Trial Judgment, 2008, para. 305; and ICTR, *Zigiranyirazo* Trial Judgment, 2008, para. 442.

[105] See ICTY, *Tolimir* Trial Judgment, 2012, para. 715; *Perišić* Trial Judgment, 2011, para. 104; *Đorđević* Trial Judgment, 2011, para. 1708; *Delić* Trial Judgment, 2008, para. 48; *Orić* Trial Judgment, 2006, para. 348; and ICTR, *Rukundo* Trial Judgment, 2009, para. 579.

[106] See e.g. ICTY, *Orić* Trial Judgment, 2006, para. 348; *Brđanin* Trial Judgment, 2004, para. 386; *Đorđević* Appeal Judgment, 2014, paras 546–551; ICTR, *Ndindiliyimana* Trial Judgment, 2011, para. 2143; and SCSL, *Brima* Trial Judgment, 2007, para. 690.

2. Torture

2960 The prohibition of torture is contained in Article 12 of the First Convention, as well as in common Article 3.[107] Although the prohibition is well established in international humanitarian law, there is no definition of torture in the Geneva Conventions. The case law of international courts and tribunals and the elaboration of the ICC Elements of Crimes have clarified the constitutive elements of the grave breach of torture under international criminal law.[108]

a. Material element

2961 The alleged perpetrator inflicted severe pain or suffering, whether physical or mental, upon one or more protected persons.

2962 The threshold of severe pain or suffering, be it physical or mental, is reflected consistently in the case law of international courts and tribunals.[109] Existing case law has not determined the absolute degree of pain required for an act to amount to torture.[110] It is difficult to articulate the exact threshold of suffering between lesser forms of inhuman treatment and an act amounting to torture. They have considered that only acts of substantial gravity may amount to torture, and lesser forms of mistreatment may constitute cruel or inhuman

---

[107] See the commentary on the prohibition of torture contained in Article 12, section F.2.c, and in common Article 3, section G.2.e. A violation of the prohibition of torture under common Article 3 does not, however, amount to the grave breach of torture.

[108] It is interesting to note that some national courts, while prosecuting individuals for the war crime or the grave breach of torture, have adopted a similar definition of torture. See Court of Bosnia and Herzegovina, *Andrun case*, Verdict, 2008, pp. 26–35, at 26:

> Based on the above-mentioned definition of 'torture' in times of armed conflict, the following elements stem:
> – torture must consist of the infliction, by act or commission, of severe pain, whether physical or mental;
> – this act or omission must be intentional;
> – it must aim at obtaining information or a confession, or at punishing, intimidating, humiliating or coercing the victim or a third person, or at discriminating, on any ground, against the victim or a third person;
> – it must be linked to an armed conflict;
> – at least one of the persons involved in the torture must be a public official or must at any rate act in a non-private capacity, e.g. as a de facto organ of a State or any other authority-wielding entity.

[109] At first, the International Criminal Tribunals took the view that the definition of torture in the 1984 Convention against Torture reflected customary international law for the purposes of international humanitarian law, and they defined the elements of the crime of torture accordingly; see ICTY, *Delalić* Trial Judgment, 1998, para. 494, and *Furundžija* Trial Judgment, 1998, para. 162. For the evolution of the position of the Tribunals, see below. See also the commentary on common Article 3, section G.2.e. For an academic commentary on this evolution, see Christoph Burchard, 'Torture in the Jurisprudence of the Ad Hoc Tribunals: A Critical Assessment', *Journal of International Criminal Justice*, Vol. 6, No. 2, 2008, pp. 159–182, or Elizabeth Santalla Vargas, 'La múltiple faceta de la tortura y los "otros tratos" en la jurisprudencia de la Corte Interamericana de Derechos Humanos y de los Tribunales Penales Internacionales', in Eduardo Ferrer Mac-Gregor and Alfonso Herrera García, *Diálogo Jurisprudencial en Derechos Humanos: Entre Tribunales Constitucionales y Cortes Internacionales*, Tirant lo Blanch, Mexico D.F., 2013, pp. 1317–1320.

[110] See ICTY, *Naletilić and Martinović* Appeal Judgment, 2006, para. 299.

treatment.[111] Torture has been defined by those tribunals as severe pain or suffering, while cruel or inhuman treatment is generally defined as serious pain or suffering.[112] The other factor distinguishing torture from the grave breaches of inhuman treatment or wilfully causing great suffering or serious injury to body or health is that torture must be inflicted for a specific purpose.[113]

2963   In making the severity assessment, courts and tribunals have considered a whole series of factors, both objective – relating to the severity of the conduct – and subjective, relating to the particular situation of the victim.[114]

2964   The following objective factors, among others, have been taken into account: the nature and context of the infliction of pain, the premeditation and institutionalization of the ill-treatment, whether the mistreatment occurred over a prolonged period,[115] and the manner and method used.[116]

2965   The following subjective factors relating to the particular victim have been used by courts and tribunals when assessing the severity of the conduct: the physical condition of the victim, the physical or mental effect of the treatment on the victim, the victim's state of health,[117] the position of inferiority of the victim, the victim's age, the victim's sex, and the social, cultural and religious background of the victim.[118]

2966   Some conduct which at first sight might not appear sufficiently serious to amount to torture could, because of its intensity, its duration or the manner in which it is implemented, amount to torture.[119] While in general allegations of torture must be considered on a case-by-case basis so as to determine whether, in the light of the acts committed and their context, severe physical or mental

---

[111] In contrast, under the 2002 ICC Elements of Crimes, the grave breaches of torture and inhuman treatment are defined in the same way, as the infliction of 'severe physical or mental pain or suffering upon one or more persons'. The distinction between the two offences was found to be the specific purpose for which torture is inflicted on a protected person. ICC Elements of Crimes (2002), Article 8(2)(a)(ii)-1 and 8(2)(a)(ii)-2.

[112] Some authors have challenged the need to establish a hierarchy of suffering for torture and inhuman treatment; see the commentary on common Article 3, para. 630.

[113] On the mental element of the crime of torture, see paras 2972–2975.

[114] See ICTY, *Kvočka* Trial Judgment, 2001, para. 143.

[115] The ICTY Chambers have noted that, although the duration over which suffering is inflicted may affect the determination of whether it amounts to torture or to wilfully causing great suffering, no rigid time requirement is built into the definition of either crime. See *Naletilić and Martinović* Appeal Judgment, 2006, para. 300.

[116] See e.g. ICTY, *Kvočka* Trial Judgment, 2001, para. 143; *Mrkšić* Trial Judgment, 2007, para. 514; *Krnojelac* Trial Judgment, 2002, para. 182; *Limaj* Trial Judgment, 2005, para. 237; *Haradinaj* Retrial Judgment, 2012, para. 417; *Naletilić and Martinović* Appeal Judgment, 2006, para. 300; *Brđanin* Trial Judgment, 2004, para. 484; and *Martić* Trial Judgment, 2007, para. 75.

[117] *Ibid.*

[118] See, in particular, ICTY, *Limaj* Trial Judgment, 2005, para. 237; *Martić* Trial Judgment, 2007, para. 75; *Mrkšić* Trial Judgment, 2007, para. 514; and *Brđanin* Trial Judgment, 2004, para. 484.

[119] This could be the case for solitary confinement or the deliberate deprivation of food. See e.g. ICTY, *Krnojelac* Trial Judgment, 2002, para. 183: 'Solitary confinement is not, in and of itself, a form of torture. However, in view of its strictness, its duration, and the object pursued, solitary confinement could cause great physical or mental suffering of the sort envisaged by this offence.'

pain or suffering was inflicted,[120] there are some acts that may amount *per se* to torture, such as rape, if it is inflicted for one of the prohibited purposes.[121]

2967   The ICTY has also highlighted the fact that the act of torture does not need to cause a permanent injury[122] or a physical injury, as mental harm is a recognized form of torture.[123] Evidence of suffering need not even be visible after the commission of the crime.[124] Examples of mental suffering recognized by the international criminal tribunals as amounting to torture include being forced to watch severe mistreatment inflicted on a relative,[125] threats of death causing severe mental suffering,[126] and obliging victims to collect the dead bodies of other members of their ethnic group, in particular those of their neighbours and friends, in very difficult circumstances.[127]

2968   Examples of acts of torture can be found in the case law of the Second World War, where the International Military Tribunal for the Far East found that the most prevalent forms of torture systematically inflicted by Japanese soldiers upon Allied forces or civilians in occupied territories included 'water treatment, burning, electric shocks, the knee spread, suspension, kneeling on sharp instruments and flogging'.[128] Numerous practices were prosecuted by the international criminal courts and tribunals and found to amount to the war crime or grave breach of torture, such as severe beatings, threats to shoot or kill, rape, deprivation of medical treatment, locking victims in isolation cells for a long period, interrogation of a victim under threat to his or her life, causing burn injuries, forcing victims to watch executions of others, forcing victims to bury the bodies of their neighbours and friends, and administering electric shocks.[129] It is important to note that not only an act but also an omission which

---

[120] See ICTY, *Naletilić and Martinović* Appeal Judgment, 2006, para. 299; *Brđanin* Appeal Judgment, 2007, para. 251; and *Martić* Trial Judgment, 2007, para. 75.

[121] For more details, see the commentary on common Article 3, para. 703.

[122] See ICTY, *Kvočka* Trial Judgment, 2001, paras 148–149; *Limaj* Trial Judgment, 2005, para. 236; *Haradinaj* Retrial Judgment, 2012, para. 417; *Mrkšić* Trial Judgment, 2007, para. 514; and *Brđanin* Trial Judgment, 2004, para. 484.

[123] See e.g. ICTY, *Kvočka* Trial Judgment, 2001, paras 148–149; *Limaj* Trial Judgment, 2005, para. 236; *Haradinaj* Retrial Judgment, 2012, para. 417; and *Mrkšić* Trial Judgment, 2007, para. 514.

[124] For examples, see ICTY, *Kunarac* Appeal Judgment, 2002, para. 150; *Brđanin* Trial Judgment, 2004, para. 484; and *Stanišić and Župljanin* Trial Judgment, 2013, para. 48.

[125] See ICTY, *Kvočka* Trial Judgment, 2001, para. 149.

[126] See ICTY, *Naletilić and Martinović* Trial Judgment, 2003, paras 294–295.

[127] ICTY, *Brđanin* Trial Judgment, 2004, paras 508–511. The Tribunal found that the coercing of these Bosnian Muslim non-combatants to collect the bodies of other members of the ethnic group who had been unlawfully killed, particularly those of their neighbours and friends, and bury them, in the circumstances in which this took place, could not but cause severe pain and suffering. The Trial Chamber, by majority, also found that this was done in order to intimidate the victims.

[128] International Military Tribunal for the Far East, *Case of the Major War Criminals*, Judgment, 1948, para. 406.

[129] See e.g. *Mucić* Trial Judgment, 1998, paras 495–496 and 971–977; *Naletilić and Martinović* Trial Judgment, 2003, paras 350–352; *Brđanin* Trial Judgment, 2004, paras 492, 503–511 and 524; *Martić* Trial Judgment, 2007, para. 76.

inflicts severe pain or suffering on a victim can amount to the grave breach of torture.

2969   The ICTY has taken the view that, in case of doubt whether the act is sufficiently severe to amount to torture, this doubt should be interpreted in favour of the accused, who should be acquitted of torture, and, if the conditions of a lesser offence are met, be convicted of it.[130]

2970   Under international humanitarian law, the official status of the perpetrator does not constitute an element of the definition of the crime of torture or the grave breach of torture.[131] Even if some ICTY Chambers have held that 'at least one of the persons involved in the torture process must be a public official or must at any rate act in a non-private capacity, e.g. as a de facto organ of a State or any other authority-wielding entity',[132] later case law by the Appeals Chamber has found that 'the public official requirement is not a requirement under customary international law in relation to the criminal responsibility of an individual for torture outside of the framework of the Torture Convention'.[133] The official status of a perpetrator may constitute an aggravating factor in sentencing.[134]

2971   Lastly, it is important to note that the pain or suffering arising only from, inherent in or incidental to lawful sanctions falls neither within the primary prohibition of torture nor within the grave breach of torture.[135]

b. Mental element

i. Torture is a specific intent crime

2972   The alleged perpetrator inflicted the pain or suffering for such purposes as obtaining information or a confession, punishing, intimidating or coercing the victim or a third person, or discriminating, on any ground, against the victim or a third person.

2973   Severe pain or suffering inflicted on a protected person amounts to torture only if the perpetrator aims to attain a certain purpose. In the absence of such purpose, even severe infliction of pain would not amount to the grave breach

---

[130] On these issues, see Mettraux, pp. 110–116, at 114, citing ICTY, *Krnojelac* Trial Judgment, 2002, para. 219.

[131] This is the case under Article 1 of the 1984 Convention against Torture.

[132] ICTY, *Furundžija* Appeal Judgment, 2000, para. 111, citing *Furundžija* Trial Judgment, 1998, para. 162.

[133] ICTY, *Kunarac* Appeal Judgment, 2002, para. 148. This finding was upheld in ICTY, *Kvočka* Appeal Judgment, 2005, para. 284; *Limaj* Trial Judgment, 2005, para. 240; *Haradinaj* Retrial Judgment, 2012, para. 419; *Mrkšić* Trial Judgment, 2007, para. 514; *Brđanin* Trial Judgment, 2004, para. 488; and *Stanišić and Župljanin* Trial Judgment, 2013, para. 49.

[134] Mettraux, p. 111, citing ICTY, *Delalić* Trial Judgment, 1998, para. 495.

[135] This issue has not been dealt with by the international criminal tribunals, but is included in the definition of torture in Article 1 of the 1984 Convention against Torture, Article 2(2) of the 1985 Inter-American Convention against Torture and Article 7(2)(e) of the 1998 ICC Statute. The last defines torture as a crime against humanity.

of torture.[136] The severity of the suffering and the purpose element are the two factors that enable a distinction to be made between torture and inhuman treatment, or between torture and wilfully causing great suffering or serious injury to body or health.

2974 The use of the words 'for such purposes as' in this mental element indicates that the 'listed purposes do not constitute an exhaustive list and should be regarded as merely representative'.[137] Those purposes form part of the definition of torture under Article 1 of the 1984 Convention against Torture, and have been used both in the ICC Elements of Crimes for the grave breach and the war crime of torture and, consistently, by the ICTY,[138] which took the view that this part of the definition of torture was reflected in customary international law.[139] This non-exhaustive list shows that the notion of purpose is quite broad.[140] Some trial chambers have found that 'humiliation', which they considered quite close to the concept of intimidation, was also one possible purpose of torture.[141]

2975 There is no requirement that severe pain or suffering be inflicted exclusively for one or more of the purposes mentioned. The prohibited purpose need not be the sole or the main purpose of the act or omission in question.[142] In the specific case of rape, the ICTY Appeals Chamber found it irrelevant that the perpetrator may have had a different motivation, if he acted with the requisite intent and for one of the prohibited purposes.[143] The Appeals Chamber held that:

[E]ven if the perpetrator's motivation is entirely sexual, it does not follow that the perpetrator does not have the intent to commit an act of torture or that his conduct does not cause severe pain or suffering, whether physical or mental, since such pain or suffering is a likely and logical consequence of his conduct.... [T]he Appellants did intend to act in such a way as to cause severe pain or suffering... to their victims, in pursuance of one of the purposes prohibited by the definition of the crime of torture, in particular the purpose of discrimination.[144]

---

[136] See e.g. ICTY, *Krnojelac* Trial Judgment, 2002, para. 180; *Haradinaj* Retrial Judgment, 2012, para. 418; and *Brđanin* Trial Judgment, 2004, para. 486.

[137] ICTY, *Delalić* Trial Judgment, 1998, para. 470.

[138] For examples, see ICTY, *Limaj* Trial Judgment, 2005, para. 239; *Mrkšić* Trial Judgment, 2007, para. 515; *Haradinaj* Retrial Judgment, 2012, para. 418; *Martić* Trial Judgment, 2007, para. 77; and *Brđanin* Trial Judgment, 2004, para. 486.

[139] See ICTY, *Kunarac* Trial Judgment, 2001, para. 485; *Delalić* Trial Judgment, 1998, paras 470–472; and *Krnojelac* Trial Judgment, 2002, para. 185.

[140] See the commentary on common Article 3, paras 640–644.

[141] See ICTY, *Furundžija* Trial Judgment, 1998, para. 162, and *Kvočka* Trial Judgment, 2001, paras 131, 152 and 157. Other trial chambers did not follow suit in this regard; see e.g. ICTY, *Krnojelac* Trial Judgment, 2002, para. 186. See also Mettraux, p. 114.

[142] See, in particular, ICTY, *Kvočka* Trial Judgment, 2001, para. 153; *Krnojelac* Trial Judgment, 2002, para. 184; *Kunarac* Appeal Judgment, 2002, para. 155; *Haradinaj* Trial Judgment, 2008, para. 128, and Retrial Judgment, 2012, para. 418; *Limaj* Trial Judgment, 2005, para. 239; *Martić* Trial Judgment, 2007, para. 77; *Mrkšić* Trial Judgment, 2007, para. 515; and *Brđanin* Trial Judgment, 2004, para. 484.

[143] See ICTY, *Kunarac* Appeal Judgment, 2002, para. 153, reaffirmed in *Limaj* Trial Judgment, 2005, para. 238; see also *Mrkšić* Trial Judgment, 2007, para. 515.

[144] ICTY, *Kunarac* Appeal Judgment, 2002, para. 153.

ii. Other remarks on the mental element

2976   The infliction of severe pain or suffering must be intentional or deliberate. The case law from international courts and tribunals shows that negligent or reckless behaviour cannot form the basis for responsibility for torture.[145] Perpetrators must have intended to act in a way which, in the normal course of events, would cause severe pain or suffering, whether mental or physical, to their victims.[146] Furthermore, torture is considered to be a specific intent crime, as it must not only be committed deliberately but also for a specific purpose such as one of the prohibited purposes listed above.

3. Inhuman treatment

a. Definition

2977   Inhuman treatment has been defined as 'intentional treatment which does not conform with the fundamental principle of humanity, and forms the umbrella under which the remainder of the listed "grave breaches" in the Conventions fall'.[147] The obligation to treat persons protected under the Conventions humanely is apparent throughout the Geneva Conventions.[148] Therefore, humane treatment has been said to constitute the 'cornerstone of all four Conventions'.[149]

2978   The Geneva Conventions do not specifically define inhuman treatment. The term covers treatment which ceases to be humane and therefore encompasses acts which violate the basic principle of humane treatment.[150] The term 'inhuman' is defined as 'lacking positive human qualities; cruel and barbaric; without compassion for suffering'.[151] The word 'treatment' must be understood in its most general sense, as applying to all aspects of a person's life. The requirement of humane treatment and the prohibition of certain acts incompatible with it have been found to be general and absolute in character. They are valid in all circumstances and at all times.[152]

---

[145] See e.g. ICTY, *Krnojelac* Trial Judgment, 2002, para. 184; *Kunarac* Trial Judgment, 2001, para. 497; *Furundžija* Trial Judgment, 1998, para. 162; and ICTR, *Akayesu* Trial Judgment, 1998, para. 594.

[146] See e.g. ICTY, *Kunarac* Appeal Judgment, 2002, para. 153; *Mrkšić* Trial Judgment, 2007, para. 515; *Haradinaj* Retrial Judgment, 2012, para. 418; and *Limaj* Trial Judgment, 2005, para. 238.

[147] ICTY, *Delalić* Trial Judgment, 1998, para. 543.

[148] See First Convention, Article 12; Second Convention, Article 12; Third Convention, Articles 13, 20 and 46; Fourth Convention, Articles 27 and 32; common Article 3; Additional Protocol I, Articles 10 and 75; and Additional Protocol II, Articles 4(1) and 7(2).

[149] ICTY, *Delalić* Trial Judgment, 1998, para. 532.

[150] In the First Convention, this principle is contained in Article 12. The obligation to treat people humanely is also included in common Article 3, but its violation does not amount to the grave breach of inhuman treatment as defined in Article 50.

[151] *Concise Oxford English Dictionary*, 12th edition, Oxford University Press, 2011, p. 731.

[152] See also the commentary on humane treatment in common Article 3, section F.1.b, and in Article 12, section F.1.a.

b. Material element

2979   The material element of this grave breach is that the perpetrator caused serious mental harm or physical injury to a protected person or carried out a serious attack on such person's human dignity.

2980   The grave breach of inhuman treatment covers more than an attack on the physical integrity or health of the protected person. In so far as the aim of the First Convention is to grant protection to the wounded and sick or to medical personnel and to preserve their human dignity, it can be argued that 'inhuman treatment' also includes the infliction of serious mental harm, as well as measures that seriously violate the human dignity of persons protected. The ICTY has consistently applied this material element to the grave breach of inhuman treatment.[153] However, when negotiating the ICC Elements of Crimes, States decided not to include conduct that constitutes 'a serious attack on human dignity'. It was felt that the war crime of 'outrages upon personal dignity in particular humiliating and degrading treatment' would better cover a serious attack on human dignity.[154]

2981   Furthermore, as mentioned during the discussion of the grave breach of torture, inhuman treatment also covers serious mental or physical suffering which falls short of the threshold of severe mental or physical suffering required for the grave breach of torture.[155] To determine the seriousness of an act, and whether a particular act or omission amounts to inhuman treatment or torture, all the factual circumstances must be taken into account on a case-by-case basis.[156]

2982   There is no difference between the notion of 'inhuman treatment' committed in an international armed conflict and the notion of 'cruel treatment' prohibited under common Article 3. The elements of the crimes of inhuman and cruel treatment have been defined in the same way by international courts and tribunals. The sole distinction between these two offences stems from the nature of the victim in question: 'cruel treatment' is committed against persons protected under common Article 3, whereas 'inhuman treatment' is committed

---

[153] See, in particular, ICTY, *Delalić* Trial Judgment, 1998, paras 516–544, and Appeal Judgment, 2001, para. 446; *Naletilić and Martinović* Trial Judgment, 2003, para. 236; *Kordić and Čerkez* Trial Judgment, 2001, para. 256, and Appeal Judgment, 2004, para. 39; *Blaškić* Trial Judgment, 2000, paras 154–155; and *Prlić* Trial Judgment, 2013, para. 113.

[154] See Dörmann, pp. 63–64.

[155] Under the ICC Elements of Crimes, inhuman treatment is defined as the infliction of 'severe physical or mental pain or suffering upon one or more persons'. The main distinction between torture and inhuman treatment under the ICC Statute consists in the requirement that the pain or suffering be inflicted for a purpose if it is to amount to the grave breach of torture. ICC Elements of Crimes (2002), Article 8(2)(a)(ii)-1 and 8(2)(a)(ii)-2.

[156] As with respect to torture, similar objective and subjective factors have been used to determine the level of seriousness of the conduct and whether it amounts to inhuman treatment. For more details, see the discussion of the grave breach of torture in paras 2963–2966 and the commentary on cruel treatment in common Article 3, section G.2.d.

against persons protected under the Geneva Conventions during an international armed conflict.[157]

2983   Moreover, the grave breaches of inhuman treatment and wilfully causing great suffering or serious injury to body or health have also been defined in a very similar manner by those same bodies. There is a certain overlap between these two concepts. The main difference between them is that the grave breach of inhuman treatment also extends to acts constituting an attack on human dignity, which are not covered by the grave breach of wilfully causing great suffering or serious injury to body or health.

2984   Criminal tribunals have found that the following examples amounted to inhuman treatment: the forcible digging of trenches under dangerous conditions, or the use of prisoners of war or detainees as human shields,[158] beatings, inhuman living conditions in a detention centre,[159] attempted murder[160] sexual violence[161] or deliberately hiding the existence of detainees from ICRC representatives in order to cause severe mental suffering to the detainees.[162]

c. Mental element

2985   Perpetrators must intend to commit the relevant material elements of the offence of inhumane treatment before they can be found guilty of that offence.[163] The general remarks on the mental element highlighted in section C.4.a apply here.

4. Biological experiments

a. Definition

2986   The Geneva Conventions do not contain a definition of biological experiments. Article 12 of the First and Second Conventions prohibits 'biological experiments', whereas Article 13 of the Third Convention and Article 32 of the

---

[157] See e.g. ICTY, *Delalić* Appeal Judgment, 2001, para. 426, and Trial Judgment, 1998, para. 442.
[158] See, in particular, ICTY *Blaškić* Trial Judgment, 2000, paras 713–716 and 738, and *Prlić*, Trial Judgment, 2013, para. 115.
[159] See e.g. ICTY *Prlić* Trial Judgment, 2013, paras 117–119.
[160] See e.g. ICTY, *Orić* Trial Judgment, 2006, para. 352. For other examples stemming from human rights case law, see ICTY, *Delalić* Trial Judgment, 1998, paras 534–541, and Dörmann, pp. 66–69.
[161] See ICTY, *Prlić* Trial Judgment, 2013, para. 116.
[162] See Court of Bosnia and Herzegovina, *Andrun case*, Verdict, 2008, p. 36:

> [T]he Accused deliberately and intentionally prevented the International Red Cross in its humanitarian mission in order to cause severe mental suffering to the detainees. The witness Enver Bojčić said that it was psychologically devastating for them and that they saw the act concerned as they were outside the law and that they could be killed by anyone.

> The perpetrator was found guilty of inhumane treatment.

[163] See e.g. ICTY *Aleksovski* Trial Judgment, 1999, para. 56, and *Prlić* Trial Judgment, 2013, para. 120.

Fourth Convention prohibit 'medical or scientific experiments'. The common provisions enumerating grave breaches in the four Conventions list 'biological experiments' as a grave breach. It is understood, however, that there is considerable overlap between these concepts.[164]

2987　Carrying out biological experiments on protected persons violates the injunction to treat those persons humanely. Not only did the 1949 Diplomatic Conference make torture and inhuman treatment grave breaches, but it decided to highlight biological experiments as one particularly serious kind of inhuman treatment or torture.[165] The Diplomatic Conference explicitly prohibited biological experiments 'with a view to preventing a recurrence of the cruel experiments which had been made in concentration camps during the last war'.[166]

2988　During the Second World War, prisoners of war and other detainees were subjected by Nazi Germany to all kinds of inhuman medical procedures, which included testing the effect of high altitude on human beings, freezing experiments, seawater experiments, infections, surgical procedures, poison experiments, incendiary-bomb experiments, and forced sterilization.[167] Chinese, Korean and Russian prisoners of war were also used as subjects for medical research by the Imperial Japanese Army, which infected them with plague, cholera, epidemic haemorrhagic fever, tuberculosis, typhoid, tetanus, anthrax, typhus and dysentery, and used them for vivisections[168] and demonstrations of surgery techniques.[169]

2989　After the Second World War, 23 doctors and administrators were accused of war crimes involving medical experiments on prisoners of war and civilians before a US military tribunal at Nuremberg.[170] Seven of them were convicted and sentenced to death, nine were convicted and sentenced to prison terms, and seven were acquitted. The judgment outlined 10 basic principles to be observed while performing medical or biological experiments, in order to satisfy moral, ethical and legal principles.[171]

---

[164] See *Final Record of the Diplomatic Conference of Geneva of 1949*, Vol. II-A, p. 381, where delegates discussed the choice of terms, and p. 191.

[165] Hence the text of Article 50, which reads: '...wilful killing, torture or inhuman treatment, including biological experiments'.

[166] *Final Record of the Diplomatic Conference of Geneva of 1949*, Vol. II-A, p. 248.

[167] See United States, Military Tribunal at Nuremberg, *The Medical Trial*, Judgment, 1947.

[168] See Takashi Tsuchiya, 'Why Japanese doctors performed human experiments in China in 1933–1945', *Eubios Journal of Asian and International Bioethics*, Vol. 10, No. 6, November, 2000, pp. 179–180. See also *The Economist*, 'Digging up Japan's past: Deafening silence – An investigation into wartime atrocities, but the media keeps strangely quiet', 24 February 2011.

[169] See Sheldon H. Harris, 'Medical Experiments on POWs', in Roy Gutman, David Rieff and Anthony Dworkin (eds), *Crimes of War: What the Public Should Know*, 2nd edition, W.W. Norton & Company, New York, 2007, pp. 287–288.

[170] See United States, Military Tribunal at Nuremberg, *The Medical Trial*, Judgment, 1947. There were also other trials dealing with this war crime; see e.g. Poland, Supreme National Tribunal, *Hoess case*, Trial Judgment, 1947, and United States, Military Tribunal at Nuremberg, *Milch case*, Trial, 1947.

[171] For a review of these principles, see Dörmann, pp. 73–74.

b. Material elements

2990 The grave breach of biological experiments requires the cumulative presence of three material elements, namely:

i. The perpetrator subjected one or more protected persons to a particular biological experiment

2991 With respect to Article 50 of the First Convention, the prohibition of biological experiments prevents the wounded and sick, particularly when held in detention, from being used as 'guinea pigs' for biological experiments in any circumstances. In its ordinary meaning, the term 'biological experiment' refers to conduct the primary purpose of which is to study the effects, at that time unknown, of a product or situation (e.g. extreme cold or altitude) on the human body.

2992 *The Medical Trial*, subsequent legal developments[172] and State practice have made it clear that this prohibition is absolute, as a detained person cannot validly give consent to a particular biological experiment.[173] Consent is not a defence to this crime.[174]

ii. The experiment seriously endangered the physical or mental health or integrity of such persons

2993 Article 12 of the First Convention prohibits any attempts upon the lives of protected persons, or violence to their persons, including biological experiments. As for the closely related prohibition of medical or scientific experiments, Article 13 of the Third Convention specifies that 'any unlawful act or omission by the Detaining Power causing death or seriously endangering the health of a prisoner of war in its custody is prohibited, and will be regarded as a serious breach of the present Convention'. There was therefore a clear willingness of States Parties to criminalize this offence when it caused the death or seriously endangered the health of protected persons. Article 11(4) of Additional Protocol I prohibits any medical or scientific experiments, but defines a grave breach as '[a]ny wilful act or omission which seriously endangers the physical or mental health or integrity of any person who is in the power of the Party other than the one on which he depends'. Under the ICC Elements of Crimes, the elements adopted for the grave breach of biological experiments follow the standard set

---

[172] See Article 11(2) of Additional Protocol I: 'It is, in particular, prohibited to carry out on such persons, even with their consent ... medical or scientific experiments.'

[173] See Henckaerts/Doswald-Beck, commentary on Rule 92, making reference to many international instruments and official statements, as well as case law, which refer to this prohibition without specifically mentioning a possible exception if the detained person consents to the procedure.

[174] This point is also made in footnote 46 to the 2002 ICC Elements of Crimes concerning the war crime of medical or scientific experiments under Article 8(2)(b)(x)-2 of the 1998 ICC Statute, which reads: 'Consent is not a defence to this crime.'

out in Article 11(4) of Additional Protocol I and require, for the crime to be completed, that the experiment seriously endanger the physical or mental health or integrity of such persons.[175]

2994   In terms of the prohibition under international humanitarian law, a biological experiment is outlawed even if it does not cause the death or seriously endanger the health of the victim. However, for such an experiment to reach the threshold of a grave breach under Article 50, it must seriously endanger the health or integrity of the protected person. In this respect, the scope of the criminal responsibility for conducting biological experiments is more restricted than the scope of the prohibition on carrying out such experiments under international humanitarian law.

iii. The experiment was neither justified by the medical, dental or hospital treatment of, nor carried out in, such person's or persons' interest

2995   This requirement makes it clear that only those biological experiments conducted on protected persons that are justified by their medical, dental or hospital treatment and, more broadly, carried out in their interest, are not prohibited and therefore do not amount to a grave breach. Accordingly, this provision prohibits any medical procedure which is not indicated by the state of health of the protected person and which is not consistent with generally accepted medical standards which would be applied under similar medical circumstances to persons who are nationals of the Party conducting the procedure and who are in no way deprived of liberty.[176] In order to determine the generally accepted medical standards in this area, two documents prepared by the Council for International Organizations of Medical Sciences are of particular relevance: the International Ethical Guidelines for Epidemiological Studies and the International Ethical Guidelines for Biomedical Research Involving Human Subjects.[177]

2996   The prohibition of biological experiments does not prevent doctors in charge of wounded and sick persons from trying new therapeutic methods that are justified on medical grounds and dictated solely by a desire to improve the patients' condition. Accordingly, patients can freely consent to drug trials aimed at improving their health, provided that they are offered in the same manner and under the same conditions as to ordinary citizens, including the armed forces of the Detaining Power. The drugs to be tested must be part of a therapeutic treatment for the protected person's illness. The prohibition of

---

[175] It is important to note that in the 2002 ICC Elements of Crimes as they pertain to the *war crime* of medical or scientific experiments, States used the threshold of Article 13 of the Third Convention, and required that the experiment should either cause death or seriously endanger the physical or mental health or integrity of a person or persons.

[176] This is borrowed from the wording of Article 11(1) of Additional Protocol I and fn. 46 to the 2002 ICC Elements of Crimes regarding the war crime of medical or scientific experiments.

[177] See Council for International Organizations of Medical Sciences, *International Ethical Guidelines for Epidemiological Studies*, Geneva, February 2008, and *International Ethical Guidelines for Biomedical Research Involving Human Subjects*, Geneva, 2002.

biological experiments should not be understood as outlawing therapeutic or clinical research.[178] No negative consequences can arise for a protected person who refuses to participate in a trial. A recent formulation of medical ethics for the specific problem of biomedical research can be found in the World Medical Association's Recommendations Guiding Physicians in Biomedical Research Involving Human Subjects.[179]

c. Mental element

2997   Perpetrators must intend to commit the relevant material elements of the offence of biological experiments before they can be found guilty of that offence. The general remarks on the mental element highlighted in section C.4.a apply here.

5. Wilfully causing great suffering or serious injury to body or health

2998   The grave breach of 'causing great suffering or serious injury to body or health' is meant to cover acts and omissions which, while not amounting to torture, affect the body or health of protected persons, including the wounded and sick, medical personnel and religious personnel. The prohibition on causing great suffering or serious injury to body or health is not found *per se* in any particular article of the Geneva Conventions, but it expresses the obligation to treat protected persons humanely and to respect their physical and mental integrity at all times. A great variety of forms of conduct can fall under this grave breach, which, unlike the grave breach of torture, need not be committed for any particular purpose.[180] To distinguish this grave breach from the grave breach of inhuman treatment, the ICTY explained that wilfully causing great suffering would not cover harm relating solely to the victim's human dignity.[181] Examples of causing great suffering or serious injury to body or health could be the mutilation of the wounded,[182] their exposure to useless and unnecessary

---

[178] See *Final Record of the Diplomatic Conference of Geneva of 1949*, Vol. II-A, p. 191:

> Biological experiments. The Committee discussed at great length whether these words required definition, and more particularly whether their scope ought not to be restricted by adding, for example: 'not necessary for their medical treatment'. In reality, however, the world [*sic*] biological, in its generally accepted sense, does not apply to therapeutic treatment, whether medical or surgical.

[179] See Dörmann, pp. 236–239.

[180] See ICTY, *Naletilić and Martinović* Trial Judgment, 2003, para. 341; *Delalić* Trial Judgment, 1998, paras 442 and 508; *Kordić and Čerkez* Trial Judgment, 2001, para. 244; *Blaškić* Trial Judgment, 2000, para. 156; and ECCC, *Kaing* Trial Judgment, 2010, para. 453.

[181] See ICTY, *Kordić and Čerkez* Trial Judgment, 2001, para. 245. For the differences and similarities between inhuman treatment and wilfully causing great suffering, see para. 2983. There is a great deal of overlap between these two offences. The ICTY has held that "... all acts or omissions found to constitute torture or wilfully causing great suffering or serious injury to body or health would also constitute inhuman treatment"; *Delalić* Trial Judgment, 1998, para. 442.

[182] For more details on mutilation, see the commentary on common Article 3, section G.2.c.

suffering,[183] or severe beatings or other severe forms of mistreatment of detainees.[184]

a. Material element

2999 The material element of this grave breach is that the perpetrator caused great physical or mental suffering or serious injury to body or health, including the mental health, of a protected person.

3000 The conduct of the perpetrator, be it an act or an omission, must have caused great suffering *or* serious injury to body or health. The case law of international courts and tribunals has consistently reaffirmed that suffering, the first alternative of this grave breach, could be either physical or mental.[185] With regard to the second alternative, the causing of serious injury to body or health, some ICTY Trial Chambers, as well as the ICTY Appeals Chamber, have found that the term 'health' could include mental health.[186] States negotiating the ICC Elements of Crimes took the view, however, that it would be difficult to conceive of mental injury.[187] Under the ICC Elements of Crimes, the elements adopted for this grave breach therefore include the phrase 'mental or physical' only in relation to the suffering caused.

3001 The requisite level of suffering is defined as 'great' or 'serious'. The ICTY Trial Chambers have used the ordinary meaning of these words to determine the requisite level of suffering:

> The Oxford English Dictionary defines this word ['serious'] as 'not slight or negligible'. Similarly, the term 'great' is defined as 'much above average in size, amount or intensity'. The Trial chamber therefore views these quantitative expressions as providing for the basic requirement that a particular act of mistreatment results in a requisite level of serious suffering or injury.[188]

3002 As mentioned earlier, for the grave breaches of torture and inhuman treatment, the assessment of the seriousness of the pain or suffering is relative and must take into account all relevant circumstances, including the nature of the act or omission, the context in which the crime occurred, its duration and repetition, the physical, mental and moral effects of the act on the victim, and the

---

[183] See Pictet (ed.), *Commentary on the First Geneva Convention*, ICRC, 1952, p. 372.

[184] See e.g. ICTY, *Delalić* Trial Judgment, 1998, paras 1012–1018, where the accused was found guilty of the grave breach of causing great suffering or serious injury to body or health for having tied a victim to a roof beam, beaten him, struck him with a baseball bat, and poured gasoline on his trousers, setting them on fire and burning his legs.

[185] See *ibid.* paras 506–511, in particular para. 509. See also ECCC, *Kaing* Trial Judgment, 2010, paras 450–455.

[186] See ICTY, *Blaškić* Trial Judgment, 2000, para. 156; *Delalić* Appeal Judgment, 2001, para. 424; *Kordić and Čerkez* Trial Judgment, 2001, para. 245; and *Naletilić and Martinović* Trial Judgment, 2003, para. 339.

[187] See Dörmann, p. 76.   [188] ICTY, *Delalić* Trial Judgment, 1998, para. 510.

personal circumstances of the victim, including, age, sex and health.[189] Various international courts and tribunals have taken the view that 'causing serious bodily or mental harm does not necessarily mean that the harm is permanent and irremediable',[190] but it 'must go beyond temporary unhappiness, embarrassment or humiliation. It must be harm that results in a grave and long-term disadvantage to a person's ability to lead a normal and constructive life.'[191]

b. Mental element

3003   The grave breach set out in Article 50 reads: 'wilfully causing great suffering or serious injury to body or health'. As mentioned earlier, the traditional understanding of the word 'wilful' in Article 50 is that it covers both 'intent' and 'recklessness'.[192]

3004   The international courts and tribunals have taken this approach while determining the requisite mental element for this grave breach.[193] They have found that it is not sufficient to prove that the alleged perpetrator knew that his or her act might possibly cause such suffering or injury.[194] Ordinary negligence has not been found to be included in the understanding of the word 'wilful'.[195]

6. Extensive destruction and appropriation of property, not justified by military necessity and carried out unlawfully and wantonly

a. Protected property

3005   The Geneva Conventions do not define the concept of protected property *per se*. They contain a list of objects which cannot be attacked, destroyed or

---

[189] Mettraux, p. 76. See ICTY, *Krnojelac* Trial Judgment, 2002, para. 131, and *Delalić* Trial Judgment, 1998, para. 536, citing European Court of Human Rights, *A v. UK*, Judgment, 1998, para. 20.

[190] ICTR, *Akayesu* Trial Judgment, 1998, para. 502. This statement was made in relation to the crime of genocide by causing serious bodily or mental harm to members of the group.

[191] ECCC, *Kaing* Trial Judgment, 2010, para. 454. See also ICTY, *Krstić* Trial Judgment, 2001, paras 511–513.

[192] See Sandoz/Swinarski/Zimmermann (eds), *Commentary on the Additional Protocols*, ICRC, 1987, para. 3474. The French version of the commentary uses the term 'dol éventuel' for 'recklessness'. See e.g. ICTY, *Blaškić* Trial Judgment, 2000, para. 152, which affirms that: '[T]he *mens rea* constituting all the violations of Article 2 of the Statute includes both guilty intent and recklessness which may be likened to serious criminal negligence.' This view is also supported by various decisions emerging from the war crimes trials after the Second World War, such as the 1946 *Gerike* case before the UK Military Court at Brunswick and the 1946 *Tyrolt* case before the UK Military Court at Helmstedt.

[193] See ECCC, *Kaing* Trial Judgment, 2010, para. 454, and ICTY, *Blaškić* Trial Judgment, 2000, para. 152.

[194] See e.g. ICTY, *Martić* Trial Judgment, 2007, para. 60, and *Strugar* Trial Judgment, 2005, para. 235. For further details, see the commentary on wilful killing, para. 2958.

[195] For examples, see ICTY, *Tolimir* Trial Judgment, 2012, para. 716; *Perišić* Trial Judgment, 2011, para. 104; *Đorđević* Trial Judgment, 2011, para. 1708; *Delić* Trial Judgment, 2008, para. 48; *Orić* Trial Judgment, 2006, para. 348; and ICTR, *Rukundo* Trial Judgment, 2009, para. 579, mostly in relation to the interpretation of the word 'wilful' for the crime of wilful killing or murder.

appropriated. Under the First Convention, such property is listed in Articles 19, 33 and 34 (fixed medical establishments and mobile medical units), Article 20 (hospital ships) and Articles 35 and 36 (medical transports, including medical aircraft).

3006   The regime governing the destruction and appropriation of other public or private property is generally dealt with in provisions of the Hague Regulations and in Additional Protocol I.[196] Such acts do not amount to a grave breach under the First Convention.

b. Material elements

3007 This grave breach requires the cumulative presence of three material elements.

i. The alleged perpetrator unlawfully destroyed or appropriated certain protected property

3008 The material element is phrased in the alternative form 'the perpetrator destroyed or appropriated certain property'. The preparatory work for the Convention makes it clear that 'appropriation of protected property' was added as an additional and distinct grave breach, next to the destruction of 'certain property'.[197]

3009   The destruction of protected property can take various forms: setting fire to it, attacking it or otherwise seriously damaging it. Examples of this grave breach under the First Convention would be the destruction of material and stores of mobile or fixed medical units[198] and the destruction of ambulances or fixed establishments and mobile medical units of the armed forces.[199] A partial destruction of property could fall within this grave breach if the partial destruction could be qualified as extensive destruction.

3010   The destruction of such protected property amounts to a grave breach if the destruction is unlawful under the specific standards pertaining to the primary obligations of international humanitarian law. For example, in the case of the destruction of material and stores of mobile or fixed medical units, any intentional destruction would be unlawful. The Convention provides for no exceptions.[200] In the case of the destruction of fixed medical establishments or mobile medical units, they may not be destroyed unless they are used to commit, outside their humanitarian duties, acts harmful to the enemy.[201] In those circumstances, their destruction would not be unlawful and would not

---

[196] See, in particular, Hague Regulations (1907), Articles 23(g), 28, 46, 47 and 52–56, and Additional Protocol I, Articles 52–56.

[197] See *Final Record of the Diplomatic Conference of Geneva of 1949*, Vol. II-B, p. 117.

[198] See the commentary on Article 33, section B.3. The obligation not to destroy the material of fixed and mobile medical establishments applies to the property of the enemy as well as to each Party's own property.

[199] See Articles 19 and 35.   [200] See Article 33(3).

[201] See the commentary on Article 21, section C.1 and Article 22.

amount to a grave breach under Article 50, assuming that other conditions on lawful attacks are complied with.

3011   The appropriation of protected property can take various forms, such as the taking, obtaining or withholding of property, theft, requisition, plunder, spoliation and pillage. There does not need to be a definite transfer of title of the property appropriated. Examples of this grave breach would be the unlawful appropriation of the real and personal property of aid societies pursuant to Article 34 of the First Convention.

3012   The appropriation would be unlawful if, pursuant to Article 34(2), there is no urgent necessity to take the property and if the welfare of the wounded and sick has not been ensured. Similarly, cases where the material of medical units is taken in disregard of the conditions laid down in Article 33(1)–(2) would amount to the grave breach of unlawful appropriation of protected property. Another example of unlawful appropriation would be the taking of medical transports, such as medical aircraft or ambulances, without complying with the requirements of Article 35 of the First Convention, i.e. without ensuring the care of the wounded and sick contained therein.

ii. The destruction or appropriation was not justified by military necessity

3013   As seen in the examples above, the fact that the destruction or appropriation might be justified by military necessity is built into most articles dealing with protected property under the First Convention.[202] A rule of armed conflict cannot be derogated from by invoking military necessity, unless this possibility is explicitly provided for in the rule in question and to the extent it is provided for. This, it may be said, also applies to the grave breach in question. Therefore, if a prohibition on destroying or appropriating a type of protected property does not provide for the exception of military necessity, its destruction or appropriation cannot be justified on the ground of military necessity.[203] For example, pursuant to Article 33(3) of the First Convention, the intentional destruction of material and stores of fixed and mobile medical units cannot be justified by military necessity.

---

[202] For a study of the concept of military necessity, see Jean de Preux, 'Article 35', in Sandoz/Swinarski/Zimmermann (eds), *Commentary on the Additional Protocols*, ICRC, 1987, paras 1389–1397, and ICRC, *Interpretive Guidance on the Notion of Direct Participation in Hostilities under International Humanitarian Law*, by Nils Melzer, ICRC, Geneva, 2009, pp. 78–82. The ICTY has used the definition of military necessity contained in Article 14 of the 1863 Lieber Code as 'the necessity of those measures which are indispensable for securing the ends of the war, and which are lawful according to the modern law and usages of war.' See *Kordić and Čerkez* Appeal Judgment, 2004, para. 686, and *Prlić* Trial Judgment, 2013, para. 168. The ICC also used Article 14 of the 1863 Lieber Code and noted that 'only "imperative" reasons of military necessity, where the perpetrator has no other option in this regard, could justify acts of destruction which would otherwise be proscribed by this provision'; *Katanga* Trial Judgment, 2014, para. 894.

[203] See Jean de Preux, 'Article 35', in Sandoz/Swinarski/Zimmermann (eds), *Commentary on the Additional Protocols*, ICRC, 1987, para. 1389.

iii. The destruction or appropriation was extensive

3014 Unlawful destruction or appropriation must be extensive for it to amount to a grave breach. An isolated act would not normally be enough to constitute a grave breach; however, in the light of the destructive power of certain weapons, the requirement that the destruction be extensive could possibly be met by a single act of destruction, such as the intentional bombing of a hospital.[204] The notion of 'extensive' will be evaluated in accordance with the facts of the case.[205]

3015 A partial destruction which might not qualify as an 'extensive' destruction or appropriation will not amount to this grave breach but can still be a serious violation of international humanitarian law.

c. Mental element

3016 Article 50 requires that the destruction or appropriation be carried out wantonly. A wanton act means that the perpetrator acted 'unreasonably or maliciously risking harm while being utterly indifferent to the consequences'.[206] The case law of the international criminal tribunals has not defined the term 'wanton' further. The tribunals have, however, taken the view that the perpetrator must have acted with intent or in reckless disregard of the likelihood of the property's destruction or its appropriation.[207]

Select bibliography

Badar, Mohamed Elewa, 'Drawing the Boundaries of Mens Rea in the Jurisprudence of the International Criminal Tribunal for the Former Yugoslavia', *International Criminal Law Review*, Vol. 6, No. 3, 2006, pp. 313–348.
– *The Concept of Mens Rea in International Criminal Law: The Case for a Unified Approach*, Bloomsbury Publishing, 2013.
Cassese, Antonio, *International Criminal Law*, 3rd edition, Oxford University Press, 2013.

---

[204] See ICTY, *Brđanin* Trial Judgment, 2004, para. 587; *Naletilić and Martinović* Trial Judgment, 2003, para. 576; and *Prlić* Trial Judgment, 2013, para. 126. See also *Blaškić* Trial Judgment, 2000, para. 157.

[205] See ICTY, *Blaškić* Trial Judgment, 2000, para. 157. It might be noted that the French translation of 'extensive' in Article 50 is 'executées sur grande échelle' ('on a large scale').

[206] Bryan A. Garner (ed.), *Black's Law Dictionary*, 10th edition, Thomson Reuters, 2014, p. 1815. It goes on to say that 'one acting wantonly may be creating no greater risk of harm, but he is not trying to avoid it and is indifferent to whether harm results or not. Wanton conduct has properly been characterized as "vicious" and rates extreme in the degree of culpability'; *Black's Law Dictionary* citing Rollin M. Perkins and Ronald N. Boyce, *Criminal Law*, 3rd edition, 1982, pp. 879–880.

[207] See ICTY, *Brđanin* Trial Judgment, 2004, para. 589; *Naletilić and Martinović* Trial Judgment, 2003, para. 577(iv) and fn. 1440; *Kordić and Čerkez* Trial Judgment, 2001, para. 341(iii); and *Prlić*, Trial Judgment, 2013, paras 127 and 131. See also Badar, 2006, pp. 343–346.

Dautricourt, Joseph, 'La protection pénale des conventions internationales human-itaires – La définition des infractions graves', *Revue de Droit Pénal et de Crim-inologie*, 1955, pp. 1–55.

Dörmann, Knut, *Elements of War Crimes under the Rome Statute of the International Criminal Court: Sources and Commentary*, Cambridge University Press, 2003.

Dörmann, Knut, La Haye, Eve and von Hebel, Herman, 'The Context of War Crimes', in Roy S. Lee and Hakan Friman (eds), *The International Criminal Court: Elements of Crimes and Rules of Procedure and Evidence*, Transnational Publishers, 2001, pp. 112–123.

Gross, Oren, 'The Grave Breaches System and the Armed Conflict in the Former Yugoslavia', *Michigan Journal of International Law*, Vol. 16, Spring 1995, pp. 783–829.

Henckaerts, Jean-Marie, 'The Grave Breaches Regime as Customary International Law', *Journal of International Criminal Justice*, Vol. 7, No. 4, Spring 2009, pp. 683–701.

Henckaerts, Jean-Marie and Doswald-Beck, Louise, *Customary International Humanitarian Law, Volume I: Rules*, ICRC/Cambridge University Press, 2005, available at https://www.icrc.org/customary-ihl/eng/docs/v1.

Knuckey, Sarah, 'Murder in Common Article 3', in Andrew Clapham, Paola Gaeta and Marco Sassòli (eds), *The 1949 Geneva Conventions: A Commentary*, Oxford University Press, 2015, pp. 449–467.

Kreß, Claus, 'War Crimes Committed in Non-International Armed Conflict and the Emerging System of International Criminal Justice', *Israel Yearbook on Human Rights*, Vol. 30, 2000, pp. 103–178.

La Haye, Eve, 'The elaboration of elements for war crimes', in Flavia Lattanzi and William A. Schabas (eds), *Essays on the Rome Statute of the International Criminal Court*, Vol. II, Il Sirente Publishers, Ripa di Fagnano Alto, 2004, pp. 305–331.

– *War Crimes in Internal Armed Conflicts*, Cambridge University Press, 2008.

Mettraux, Guénaël, *International Crimes and the* Ad Hoc *Tribunals*, Oxford University Press, 2005.

Roberts, Ken, 'The Contribution of the ICTY to the Grave Breaches Regime', *Journal of International Criminal Justice*, Vol. 7, No. 4, September 2009, pp. 743–761.

Werle, Gerhard and Jessberger, Florian, *Principles of International Criminal Law*, 3rd edition, Oxford University Press, 2014.

RESPONSIBILITIES OF THE CONTRACTING PARTIES

❖ Text of the provision

No High Contracting Party shall be allowed to absolve itself or any other High Contracting Party of any liability incurred by itself or by another High Contracting Party in respect of breaches referred to in the preceding Article.

❖ Reservations or declarations

None

Contents

A. Introduction and historical background

3017 Article 51 clarifies the relationship between individual criminal responsibility for grave breaches of the Conventions and State responsibility for acts committed by the armed forces or persons acting under the authority or command of a State in respect of grave breaches. This article is common to the four Conventions.[1]

3018 It was an entirely new article which formed part neither of earlier conventions nor of draft versions of the 1949 Conventions discussed prior to the Diplomatic Conference.[2] It was inserted in all four Geneva Conventions on the proposal of the Italian delegation, which had previously endeavoured unsuccessfully to introduce the idea in Article 6 on special agreements. During the Diplomatic Conference, the Italian representative stated: 'The State must be held responsible for offences committed by its nationals, and it would be illogical for individuals to be prosecuted while the State was able to evade its liability by

---

[1] See Second Convention, Article 52; Third Convention, Article 131; and Fourth Convention, Article 148.

[2] See *Final Record of the Diplomatic Conference of Geneva of 1949*, Vol. II-B, pp. 91 and 133, *Minutes of the Diplomatic Conference of Geneva of 1949*, Mixed Commission, 20 July 1949, pp. 1–15 and Paul de La Pradelle, *La Conférence Diplomatique et les nouvelles Conventions de Genève du 12 août 1949*, Les Éditions internationales, Paris, 1951, p. 259.

means of agreements with another State.'[3] A number of delegations opposed the Italian proposal, such as the UK representative, who stated that 'this amendment is going much too far in the direction of attempting to bind States in their future relations with one another, and particularly in their liberty to conclude a treaty of peace at the end of the war'.[4] The Joint Commission ultimately approved it by 18 votes to 16, with 3 abstentions.[5]

B. Discussion

3019   Article 51 prevents States Parties from absolving themselves or any other State Party of *any liability* incurred by them or by another State Party in respect of the breaches referred to in Article 50. This sentence needs to be understood in the context of its adoption and its placement in the Geneva Conventions, in Chapter IX, entitled 'Repression of abuses and infractions'. It is closely linked to Article 50, which spells out the grave breaches of the Conventions.

3020   First, the expression 'any liability'[6] contained in Article 51 includes the responsibility of States Parties to search for, bring to trial or extradite alleged perpetrators of grave breaches contained in Article 49. Article 51 therefore aims to prevent a situation whereby States Parties, in future peace treaties or armistices, would absolve themselves or another State Party of this responsibility. The obligations under Article 49 being absolute, Article 51 means that any agreements negotiated by States Parties cannot affect the fulfilment of the obligations under Article 49.[7]

3021   Furthermore, Article 51 aims to prevent an alleged perpetrator of grave breaches from relying, at trial, on a provision of a peace treaty which, as part of war settlements, exonerates the State from its responsibility for violations under the Convention.[8] War reparations[9] are generally negotiated in peace

---

[3] *Final Record of the Diplomatic Conference of Geneva of 1949*, Vol. II-B, p. 91.
[4] See *Minutes of the Diplomatic Conference of Geneva of 1949*, Mixed Commission, 20 July 1949, p. 12.
[5] See *Final Record of the Diplomatic Conference of Geneva of 1949*, Vol. II-B, p. 133.
[6] The term 'liability' means 'the quality, state or condition of being legally obliged or accountable; legal responsibility to another or to society, enforceable by civil remedy or criminal punishment'. It can be used interchangeably with 'responsibility' in this context. Bryan A. Garner (ed.), *Black's Law Dictionary*, 10th edition, Thomson Reuters, 2014, p. 1053.
[7] See the report of the Joint Committee to the Plenary Assembly of the 1949 Diplomatic Conference, which states: 'This provision was the only means of ensuring that the compulsory character of the prosecution, as proclaimed in the preceding Article, should continue in force.' *Final Record of the Diplomatic Conference of Geneva of 1949*, Vol. II-B, p. 133.
[8] It has been common practice in peace treaties for the victors to demand reparation from the vanquished without reciprocity. Peace treaties negotiated at the end of the Second World War between the Allies and Bulgaria, Finland, Hungary, Italy, Japan and Romania provide for the vanquished to waive any claims against the Allied or Associated Powers arising directly out of the war or out of actions taken because of the existence of a state of war in Europe after 1 September 1939. See e.g. Treaty of Peace between the Allied and Associated Powers and Bulgaria (1947), Article 28, or Treaty of Peace between the Allied and Associated Powers and Italy (1947), Article 76.
[9] Nowadays the concept of reparations has evolved and is understood broadly as covering 'measures that seek to eliminate all the harmful consequences of a violation of rules of international

settlements and must neither render impossible nor hinder the proper prosecution of alleged perpetrators.[10] Subsequent State practice shows that the adoption of detailed peace treaties did not prevent the prosecution of certain grave breaches or other war crimes,[11] and in that respect, one of the aims of Article 51 has therefore been achieved since 1949.

3022   Second, the expression 'any liability' contained in Article 51 recalls the responsibility of States Parties for grave breaches committed by their armed forces or persons acting under their authority or command, and the requirement for the responsible State to make full reparation for the loss or injury caused by grave breaches. This principle is also recognized in a number of treaties, including Article 3 of the 1907 Hague Convention (IV), Article 91 of Additional Protocol I and Article 38 of the 1999 Second Protocol to the Hague Convention for the Protection of Cultural Property.[12] In addition, it is contained in other texts, such as the 2005 Basic Principles and Guidelines on the Right

law applicable in armed conflict and to re-establish the situation that would have existed if the violation had not occurred'. See e.g. the ILA's Declaration of International Law Principles on Reparation for Victims of Armed Conflict, Resolution 2/2010, Article 1(1).

[10]   In support of this interpretation, see the letter from the Dutch Minister for Foreign Affairs to the Parliament, dated 24 May 1991, reproduced in the *Netherlands Yearbook of International Law*, Vol. 23, 1992, pp. 379–382, at 381:

> The relevant waivers [i.e. contained in Articles 14(b) and 16 of the 1951 Peace Treaty for Japan] are not incompatible with Articles 51, 52, 131 and 138 of the First, Second, Third and Fourth Geneva Conventions of 1949. These articles determine that no Member State may discharge itself or any other Member State from any liability based on serious breaches of the Conventions, as defined in other Articles of the Geneva Conventions. Yet it appears from the legislative history of the four Articles mentioned above, that these Articles of the Geneva Conventions have only limited application, namely to prevent the criminal prosecution of persons who had committed war crimes from being hindered or even made impossible if the State of those persons were to be exonerated from responsibility for those crimes. Financial arrangements with global effects (so called 'lump sums') are not prohibited by all this, and moreover could be seen as constituting a way of expressing liability. Similarly, no prohibition can be inferred from other treaties of from public international law in general.

[11]   The 1995 Dayton Accords, which ended the armed conflict in Bosnia and Herzegovina, provides amnesty for all crimes other than serious violations of international humanitarian law: 'Any returning refugee or displaced person charged with a crime, other than a serious violation of international humanitarian law as defined in the Statute of the International Tribunal for the Former Yugoslavia since January 1, 1991 or a common crime unrelated to the conflict, shall upon return enjoy an amnesty.' Agreement on Refugees and Displaced Persons annexed to the Dayton Accords (1995), Article VI. See also Article 7(3) of the Agreement on Normalization of Relations between Croatia and the Federal Republic of Yugoslavia (1996), which states: 'The Contracting Parties shall declare general amnesty for all acts committed in connection with the armed conflicts, except for the gravest violations of humanitarian law having the nature of war crimes.'

[12]   Article 3 of the 1907 Hague Convention (IV) reads: 'A belligerent party which violates the provisions of the said Regulations shall, if the case demands, be liable to pay compensation. It shall be responsible for all acts committed by persons forming part of its armed forces.' See the commentary on Article 91 of Additional Protocol I in Sandoz/Swinarski/Zimmermann (eds), *Commentary on the Additional Protocols*, ICRC, 1987, paras 3645–3661, for a detailed discussion on the principle of State responsibility for acts committed by its armed forces and the forms of compensation available. Article 38 of the 1999 Second Protocol to the Hague Convention for the Protection of Cultural Property states: 'No provision in this Protocol relating to individual criminal responsibility shall affect the responsibility of States under international law, including the duty to provide reparation.'

to a Remedy and Reparation for Victims of Gross Violations of International Human Rights Law and Serious Violations of IHL and has been recognized as part of customary international law.[13] This principle applies to all Parties to armed conflicts, vanquished and victors alike. Article 51 therefore aims to prevent the defeated Party from being compelled, in an armistice agreement or peace treaty, to abandon all claims due in respect of grave breaches committed by persons in the service of the victor. The preparatory work recalls that most States were of the view that Article 51 does not 'cover special financial arrangements under which a State can finally liquidate a claim to damages by an agreed lump sum payment or a settlement in compensation'.[14] States are free to negotiate between themselves any financial settlements relating to the end of the armed conflict. However, Article 51 prevents a situation in which the vanquished would agree to waive claims against the victors in relation to the right to receive reparation in respect of the commission of grave breaches.[15]

3023   War reparations between belligerents have often been settled in peace treaties. It has been common practice for the victors to demand reparation from the vanquished without reciprocity.[16] Practice following the Second World War does not reveal that States carved out an exception for the commission of grave breaches;[17] in some instances the vanquished waived all claims to damages against the victors arising out of the armed conflict.[18]

---

[13] See ICRC Study on Customary International Humanitarian Law (2005), Rules 149 and 150, as well as Basic Principles and Guidelines on the Right to a Remedy and Reparation for Victims of Gross Violations of International Human Rights Law and Serious Violations of IHL (2005), Articles 2 and 3. See also Draft Articles on State Responsibility (2001), Article 31 (Reparation), which states: 'The responsible State is under an obligation to make full reparation for the injury caused by the internationally wrongful act.'

[14] See *Final Record of the Diplomatic Conference of Geneva of 1949*, Vol. II-B, p. 133.

[15] See also ICRC, Report on the Protection of War Victims, reproduced in *International Review of the Red Cross*, Vol. 75, No. 803, October 1993, pp. 391–445, section 4.3(3): 'This provision [Article 51]...also implies that, irrespective of the outcome of an armed conflict, no decision or agreement can dispense a State from the responsibility to make reparation for damages caused to the victims of breaches of international humanitarian law.'

[16] See e.g. the following peace treaties, all of 10 February 1947: Treaty of Peace between the Allied and Associated Powers and Bulgaria (1947), Article 28; Treaty of Peace between the Allied and Associated Powers and Finland (1947), Article 29; Treaty of Peace between the Allied and Associated Powers and Hungary (1947), Article 32; Treaty of Peace between the Allied and Associated Powers and Italy (1947), Article 76; and Treaty of Peace between the Allied and Associated Powers and Romania (1947), Article 30. See also Peace Treaty for Japan (1951), Article 19, and Joint Declaration on Soviet-Japanese Relations (1956), Article 6. See also Sandoz/Swinarski/Zimmermann (eds), *Commentary on the Additional Protocols*, ICRC, 1987, para. 3647.

[17] See, in this regard, d'Argent, p. 772, who states, in connection with claims arising out of the commission of grave breaches: 'Nulle part, dans la pratique des renonciations, on ne trouve d'exceptions, expresse ou tacite, à leur portée s'agissant de ce type de créances.' ('Nowhere in the practice of waivers of claims of this type do we find exceptions, explicit or implicit, to their scope.')

[18] See, in particular, Peace Treaty for Japan (1951), Article 19, and Joint Declaration on Soviet-Japanese Relations (1956), Article 6, whereby the Soviet Union and Japan agreed 'to renounce all claims by either State, its institutions or citizens, against the other State, its institutions or citizens, which have arisen as a result of the war since 9 August 1945'. In 1956, both the Soviet Union and Japan were party to the 1949 Geneva Conventions and therefore bound to respect Article 51. However, the question arises whether Article 51 can be seen as applying

3024 The practice in the last 50 years, however, has revealed a tendency for States party to an armed conflict not to absolve themselves of their liability in respect of the commission of grave breaches, particularly by establishing means or mechanisms for individuals to receive reparation arising out of violations of international law committed during armed conflict. They have taken the form of mixed claims commissions and quasi-judicial bodies established by the UN Security Council or by peace treaties.[19] The peace agreement of December 2000 between Ethiopia and Eritrea, for example, establishes an impartial claims commission charged with deciding all claims between the two governments and between private entities for loss, damages or injury related to the armed conflict and resulting from violations of international humanitarian law or other violations of international law.[20] An example of a quasi-judicial body established by the Security Council is the United Nations Compensation Commission, which is entrusted with adjudicating claims against Iraq for any direct loss, damage, including environmental damage, or injury to foreign governments, nationals and corporations as a result of Iraq's invasion and occupation of Kuwait.[21]

3025 Article 51 recalls the responsibility of States for grave breaches committed by their armed forces or persons acting under their authority or command, a responsibility which leads to a duty to pay compensation, as spelled out in Article 3 of the 1907 Hague Regulations and Article 91 of Additional Protocol I. These articles are silent, however, as to who are the ultimate beneficiaries of reparations for violations of international humanitarian law. They do not

retroactively to the events of the Second World War. Also note the position of Germany's Federal Constitutional Court in the *East German Expropriation case* in 2004, in which the Court held that:

> In the Two-Plus-Four Talks, the Federal Republic of Germany impliedly waived any claims under the Hague Land Warfare Convention. ...
>
> It is not in contradiction to this that each of the four Geneva Conventions of the year 1949 contains a provision depriving the states that are parties the right to release themselves or another from the responsibility for 'serious violations' of public international law .... In the practice of the law of war, however, this principle has not yet succeeded in establishing itself.

Contrary to Article 51, the Court held that: 'It cannot be concluded from the provisions of the Geneva Convention that the states are forbidden to waive claims under the Hague Land Warfare Convention in connection with entering into a peace treaty.' Germany, Federal Constitutional Court, *East German Expropriation case*, Order, 2004, paras 110–114.

[19] For other examples, see the Agreement on Refugees and Displaced Persons annexed to the Dayton Peace Accords (1995), Articles I, VII, XI and XII, which established the Commission for Displaced Persons and Refugees to resolve real-property claims in Bosnia and Herzegovina. See also Article 24 of the 1994 Treaty of Peace between the State of Israel and the Hashemite Kingdom of Jordan, which provides for the establishment of a claims commission for the mutual settlement of all financial claims. A similar provision is contained in the 1978 Framework for Peace in the Middle East, Article C(4), and the 1979 Peace Treaty between Egypt and Israel, Article VIII. See also Gillard, pp. 539–540.

[20] Peace Agreement between Eritrea and Ethiopia (2000), Article 5.

[21] See UN Security Council, Res. 687, 3 April 1991, paras 16–19. The UN Compensation Commission has dealt with violations of international humanitarian law, as well as violations of the *jus ad bellum* principle and general public international law. For more details, see Christophe S. Gibson, Trevor M. Rajah and Timothy J. Feighery, *War Reparations and the UN Compensation Commission: Designing Compensation After Conflict*, Oxford University Press, 2015.

indicate whether only States are recipients or also individuals, nor do they specify the means of enforcing this right. Much has been written about the existence of a right for individuals in international humanitarian law to receive reparation and the ways and means of enforcing such a right before domestic or international forums.[22] This debate, however, goes beyond a commentary on Article 51 of the First Convention, and is addressed in the commentary on Article 91 of Additional Protocol I, where it most directly fits.

Select bibliography

Cameron, Lindsey and Chetail, Vincent, *Privatizing War: Private Military and Security Companies under Public International Law*, Cambridge University Press, 2013, pp. 539–570.

d'Argent, Pierre, *Les réparations de guerre en droit international public. La responsabilité internationale des États à l'épreuve de la guerre*, Bruylant, Brussels, 2002.

David, Eric, *Principes de droit des conflits armés*, 5th edition, Bruylant, Brussels, 2012.

Gillard, Emanuela-Chiara, 'Reparation for violations of international humanitarian law', *International Review of the Red Cross*, Vol. 85, No. 851, September 2003, pp. 529–553.

Kalshoven, Frits, 'State Responsibility for Warlike Acts of The Armed Forces', *International and Comparative Law Quarterly*, Vol. 40, 1991, pp. 827–848.

– expert opinion, 'Article 3 of the Convention [IV] Respecting the Laws and Customs of War on Land, signed at The Hague, 18 October 1907', in Hisakazu Fujita, Isomi Suzuki and Kantaro Nagano (eds), *War and the Rights of Individuals: Renaissance of Individual Compensation*, Nippon Hyoron-sha, Tokyo, 1999, p. 37.

Sassòli, Marco, 'State responsibility for violations of international humanitarian law', *International Review of the Red Cross*, Vol. 84, No. 846, June 2002, pp. 401–434.

---

[22] For a summary of the various views, see Cameron, pp. 546–566; Gillard, pp. 536–545; d'Argent, pp. 774–808; and David, paras 4.41–4.56. See also ICJ, *Jurisdictional Immunities of the State case*, Judgment, 2012, and in particular the Dissenting Opinion of Judge Cançado Trindade, paras 63–72 and 240–287.

ARTICLE 52

ENQUIRY PROCEDURE

❖ Text of the provision*

  (1) At the request of a Party to the conflict, an enquiry shall be instituted, in a manner to be decided between the interested Parties, concerning any alleged violation of the Convention.

  (2) If agreement has not been reached concerning the procedure for the enquiry, the Parties should agree on the choice of an umpire who will decide upon the procedure to be followed.

  (3) Once the violation has been established, the Parties to the conflict shall put an end to it and shall repress it with the least possible delay.

❖ Reservations or declarations

None

Contents

A. Introduction

3026   Article 52 is part of the system elaborated by the four Geneva Conventions of 1949, and subsequently by Additional Protocol I, to ensure that Parties to international armed conflicts comply with their obligations under these

---

* Paragraph numbers have been added for ease of reference.

instruments. The article is common to the four Conventions.[1] It appears under the heading 'Repression of abuses and infractions' in the First and Second Conventions, and 'Execution of the Convention' in the Third and Fourth Conventions.

3027   Article 52 sets out the legal basis for the establishment of an enquiry procedure when the Parties have diverging views regarding any alleged violations of the Geneva Conventions (paragraphs 1 and 2). Establishing whether a violation of international humanitarian law has occurred in a particular case may help to prevent doubts or inaccurate accusations from undermining the Parties' willingness to respect this legal framework. Article 52 also seeks to ensure that the Parties put an end to and repress alleged violations, if they are established through the enquiry (paragraph 3).

3028   This article is not the only one that requires a verification of facts by means of the compliance mechanisms established under the Geneva Conventions and Additional Protocol I. Other provisions entail, to a certain extent, the need for as-yet unproven facts to be assessed, whether by the Parties to the conflict themselves, the Protecting Powers or their substitutes, the ICRC or the International Fact-Finding Commission established pursuant to Article 90 of Additional Protocol I. These mechanisms all have specific characteristics corresponding to different ways of promoting greater respect for international humanitarian law, and offer complementary tools to ensure respect for the relevant instruments. Some may be tasked to undertake an 'enquiry' in its formal meaning, while others, like the ICRC, need to clarify facts and situations within the more general framework of protection activities.

3029   Parties to international armed conflicts have the primary responsibility to take appropriate measures, including investigative measures, to redress violations of international humanitarian law. An investigation is, for example, inherent to the grave breaches system established under the Conventions and where applicable, Additional Protocol I.[2] It is a preliminary step in fulfilling the obligation to prosecute persons alleged to have committed or ordered the commission of grave breaches or to hand them over for trial to another Party to these instruments. It is also a prerequisite of the obligation to take measures necessary for the suppression of other violations of the Conventions or Additional Protocol I, i.e. violations which are not characterized as 'grave breaches'. The obligation to suppress all violations of the Conventions and to ensure the prosecution of those responsible for 'grave breaches' will make the formal enquiry procedure unnecessary in most cases. If a State finds that persons depending on it have violated the Convention, it must take measures to redress the situation, whether or not an enquiry has been requested by the adverse Party.

[1] See Second Convention, Article 53; Third Convention, Article 132; and Fourth Convention, Article 149.
[2] See the commentaries on Article 49 of this Convention and on Article 85 of Additional Protocol I.

The institution of a formal enquiry procedure is therefore only necessary if the existence of the violation is contested. Enquiring into alleged violations of international humanitarian law is also one of the functions that may be exercised by the Protecting Powers (or their substitutes).[3] This function may be part of their duty 'to safeguard the interests of the Parties to the conflict'[4] or of their role in the 'conciliation procedure'.[5] Protecting Powers may therefore be used as an alternative to the enquiry procedure.[6] Parties to an international armed conflict may indeed wish to solicit the support of their peers to help them settle disputes related to alleged violations of international humanitarian law. This option has, however, been theoretical so far. Protecting Powers have been appointed on only five occasions since the adoption of the Geneva Conventions in 1949[7] and have never been requested to undertake investigations into alleged violations of international humanitarian law.

3030   The ICRC is also entitled to exercise monitoring activities in times of both international and non-international armed conflict.[8] This role, however, is of a different nature than the enquiry procedure. The ICRC usually does not seek to resolve disputes among Parties to an armed conflict concerning alleged violations of international humanitarian law or to make public statements regarding its findings. Except in strictly defined circumstances,[9] the organization focuses on confidential dialogue with each side. The ICRC has also been invited to participate in formal enquiry procedures on a number of occasions. In 1998, for instance, it was asked by the authorities of the Republic of Serbia to open an ad hoc investigation into events in Kosovo.[10] The organization, however, has always declined such proposals, considering that involvement in an enquiry procedure might jeopardize its humanitarian activities in favour of the victims of armed conflict.[11]

---

[3] See Gasser, p. 348: '[T]he Protecting Power may open a formal investigation, if commissioned to do so, only with the consent of the Party to which it is accredited.'

[4] Common Article 8 (Article 9 in the Fourth Convention); see also common Article 10 (Article 11 in the Fourth Convention) and Additional Protocol, Article 5(1).

[5] Common Article 11 (Article 12 in the Fourth Convention).

[6] The Parties to a conflict establishing an enquiry procedure pursuant to Article 52 could, of course, also decide to use the Protecting Powers to conduct this procedure.

[7] See the commentary on Article 8, para. 1115; Bugnion, p. 864.

[8] In times of international armed conflict, the ICRC is recognized as having the same supervisory function as the Protecting Powers (Article 126(4) of the Third Convention and Article 143(5) of the Fourth Convention). The ICRC (or any other impartial humanitarian organization) is also entitled to undertake any humanitarian activities that it may deem necessary, subject to the consent of the Parties to the conflict (see common Article 9 (Article 10 in the Fourth Convention) and Additional Protocol I, Article 81(1)). In times of non-international armed conflict, common Article 3(2) provides that the ICRC (or any other impartial humanitarian organization) 'may offer its services to the Parties to the conflict'.

[9] See ICRC, 'Action by the International Committee of the Red Cross in the event of violations of international humanitarian law'.

[10] See ICRC, 'Kosovo: ICRC position on invitation to head investigation', News Release No. 98/10 of 20 March 1998. For other examples, see section E, para. 3052.

[11] The ICRC explains its position as follows:

3031   Lastly, for States Parties to Additional Protocol I, the enquiry function is at the heart of Article 90 of the Protocol, which provides for the creation of a permanent body, the International Fact-Finding Commission.[12] Although it is also related to enquiries into alleged violations of international humanitarian law, Article 90 is not intended to replace Article 52 (Articles 53, 132 and 149 respectively in the other three Conventions). On the contrary, it explicitly states that the enquiry procedure under the Geneva Conventions 'shall continue to apply to any alleged violation of the Conventions and shall extend to any alleged violation of this Protocol'.[13] This is especially important as Article 52 and its parallel provisions in the other three Conventions have a broader material scope of application. While it allows for enquiries into 'any alleged violation of the Convention', Article 90 circumscribes the competence of the International Fact-Finding Commission to violations of a particular seriousness, namely grave breaches or other serious violations of the Geneva Conventions or Additional Protocol I.[14]

B. Historical background[15]

3032   The concept of an enquiry procedure as a means to resolve diverging views among States was not new in 1949. It was introduced into a multilateral treaty for the first time with the adoption of the 1899 Hague Convention (I).[16] The procedure was later considerably developed when this Convention was amended in 1907.[17] In its 1907 version, the Hague Convention recommends the establishment of an 'International Commission of Enquiry' to facilitate the solution of disputes of an international nature that may arise from 'a difference of opinion on points of facts'.[18] Such Commission must be instituted by special agreement between the States concerned[19] and its conclusions must be limited to a

---

> The ICRC will not act as a commission of inquiry and, as a general rule, it will not take part in an inquiry procedure. However, if solicited by one or more parties to a conflict, the ICRC may encourage them to appeal to the International Fact-Finding Commission or, at the request of all the parties to the conflict, it may offer its good offices to help set up a commission of inquiry, limiting itself to proposing non-ICRC persons who are qualified to be part of such a commission.
>
> However, the ICRC will only offer its limited services providing this will not in any way undermine its traditional activities or its reputation for impartiality and neutrality. It will also endeavour to ensure that the inquiry procedure provides every guarantee of impartiality and gives all parties the means to put their point of view across. (italics in original)

ICRC, 'Action by the International Committee of the Red Cross in the event of violations of international humanitarian law', pp. 398–399.

[12] For further details on the International Fact-Finding Commission, see the commentary on Article 90 of Additional Protocol I.

[13] Additional Protocol I, Article 90(2)(e).   [14] *Ibid.* Article 90(2)(c).

[15] For a detailed account of the drafting process of Article 52, see de La Pradelle, pp. 265–286.

[16] Hague Convention (I) (1899), Articles 9–14.   [17] Hague Convention (I) (1907), Articles 9–36.

[18] *Ibid.* Article 9.   [19] *Ibid.* Article 10.

statement of facts, leaving to these States 'entire freedom as to the effect to be given to the statement'.[20]

3033   In the field of international humanitarian law, a similar procedure, although described in far less detail, was laid down for the first time in the 1929 Geneva Convention on the Wounded and Sick, Article 30 of which provides that: 'On the request of a belligerent, an enquiry shall be instituted, in a manner to be decided between the interested parties, concerning any alleged violation of the Convention; when such violation has been established the belligerents shall put an end to and repress it as promptly as possible'. At the time of its adoption, this new provision was perceived as a significant step forward in the application of the Convention.[21]

3034   Very soon, however, the weakness of the procedure became apparent. It was pointed out that application of the article would be difficult, as it presupposed agreement between the Parties to the conflict on the practical details of the procedure.[22] As early as 1937, the ICRC undertook consultations to discuss the problem and a possible revision of the Geneva Conventions to ensure the effective use of the enquiry in practice.[23]

3035   On the basis of these consultations, the ICRC submitted to the 1949 Diplomatic Conference a draft article that had been approved the previous year by the International Conference of the Red Cross in Stockholm. This draft provision was common to the draft First and Second Conventions.[24] It proposed a new 'investigation procedure' allowing 'any High Contracting Party' to 'demand the institution of an inquiry' on alleged violations of the relevant Convention. The draft article provided that the commission of enquiry would be composed of three members selected from a list of persons that would have been prepared in time of peace by the High Contracting Parties. Two members of the Commission would have been appointed by each Party to the procedure and these two

---

[20] *Ibid.* Article 35.

[21] See Des Gouttes, *Commentaire de la Convention de Genève de 1929 sur les blessés et malades*, ICRC, 1930, commentary on Article 30, pp. 212–220.

[22] In a circular sent to National Societies in 1936, the ICRC stressed that 'la procédure de l'article 30, qui ne constituait d'ailleurs qu'une ébauche, est insuffisante' ('the Article 30 procedure, which was no more than a rough draft anyway, is insufficient') (ICRC, *Révision et extension de la Convention de Genève et Projets de Conventions nouvelles* (Revision and Extension of the Geneva Convention and New Draft Conventions), 328th Circular, Geneva, 31 July 1936, p. 6). This problem had already been highlighted during the drafting of Article 30. The President of the First Committee of the Diplomatic Conference had expressed concern that the need to reach agreement on the procedure might 'paralyse' the obligation to set up an enquiry (see *Proceedings of the Geneva Diplomatic Conference of 1929*, Geneva, 1930, p. 406).

[23] These consultations took place within the framework of a Commission of International Experts in 1937, the 16th International Conference of the Red Cross in London in 1938, the Preliminary Conference of National Societies in 1946, the Conference of Government Experts in 1947, and the 17th International Conference of the Red Cross in Stockholm in 1948. For further details on this process, see Pictet (ed.), *Commentary on the First Geneva Convention*, ICRC, 1952, pp. 374–376.

[24] See *Draft Conventions adopted by the 1948 Stockholm Conference*, pp. 25–26 and 47–48; see also *Final Record of the Diplomatic Conference of Geneva of 1949*, Vol. I, pp. 55–56 and 70.

members would then together have chosen the third one. Failing an agreement between the first two members, the third one would have been appointed 'by the President of the Court of International Justice or, if the latter is a national of a belligerent State *or incapacitated, by his substitute, or failing the latter*, by the President of the International Committee of the Red Cross'. The draft article also provided that the Commission would have been entitled not only to provide conclusions on the disputed facts, but also to make appropriate recommendations.

3036   Discussions during the Diplomatic Conference did not, however, reveal support for the ICRC's proposal. It was felt, rather, that the Stockholm drafts 'set up a procedure for recruitment which was too complicated, and that it would be appropriate to revert once more to the provision contained in Article 30 of the Wounded and Sick Convention of 1929, while defining its terms more clearly'.[25] The Diplomatic Conference decided therefore to keep the 1929 provision as it was, with the exception of a new paragraph recommending the appointment of an umpire in case of disagreement between the Parties concerning the institution of the procedure.

C. Scope of application

3037 Article 52 applies to alleged violations of the Conventions in international armed conflicts. However, according to the first paragraph, the scope of the enquiry procedure may extend to 'any' alleged violation of the Conventions. Thus, nothing would appear to prevent an enquiry procedure being set up to look into alleged violations of common Article 3. In 1949, however, the drafters placed Article 52 in Chapter IX of the Convention and did not intend to extend this procedure to non-international conflicts.[26] In addition, neither common Article 3 nor Additional Protocol II, both of which apply to non-international armed conflicts, makes any mention of an enquiry procedure. It would seem, therefore, that the procedure contained in Article 52 applies only to alleged violations committed in international armed conflicts. The absence of practice makes it difficult to clarify this issue further. However, Parties to non-international armed conflicts are free – and should be encouraged – to conclude special agreements under common Article 3(3), whereby they could agree to set up an enquiry procedure.[27]

---

[25] See *Final Record of the Diplomatic Conference of Geneva of 1949*, Vol. II-B, pp. 119–120.

[26] Common Article 3 was seen in 1949 as the only article applicable in non-international armed conflicts.

[27] For an example of an enquiry procedure having been considered by the Parties to what was, at the time, a non-international armed conflict, see Memorandum of Understanding on the Application of IHL between Croatia and the Socialist Federal Republic of Yugoslavia (1991), Article 12, which states:

> 12. Request for an enquiry.
> 1. Should the ICRC be asked to institute an enquiry, it may use its good offices to set up a commission of enquiry outside the institution and in accordance with its principles.

3038   As the scope of the enquiry procedure may extend to 'any alleged violations of the Convention', it means first that the procedure is not limited to
specific categories of violations, such as those reaching a minimum threshold of seriousness. Other provisions on investigation into violations of international humanitarian law do include limitations in their material scope of
application. For instance, the Geneva Conventions (and Additional Protocol
I) have elaborated a specific system governing individual criminal responsibility, which applies only to the 'grave breaches' expressly listed in these
instruments.[28]

3039   The reference to a 'violation' of the Convention in paragraph 1 implies that
the work of the investigative body must consist in verifying the existence of
unproven or disputed facts and providing a legal assessment of such facts.[29]
The notion of 'violation' of a legal norm entails both factual and legal aspects.
This is further confirmed by paragraph 3 of Article 52. The obligation to put
an end to and repress the established violation with the least possible delay
presupposes both that the conduct at issue has been verified and that it has
been classified in the light of the relevant legal rules.

3040   A 'violation' in this framework may be perpetrated not only by the armed
forces and other persons or groups acting on behalf of the Parties to the conflict,
but also by private persons whose conduct is not attributable to the State.[30]

3041   An enquiry may be requested concerning any 'alleged' violation of the Conventions. Under the procedure envisaged in Article 52, this assumes that there
are doubts or diverging views among the Parties to the conflict as to whether a
violation of these instruments actually occurred. The purpose of this provision
suggests that an enquiry becomes necessary and obligatory once the allegation
is contested by the Party whose conduct is questioned. The preparatory work
on the Geneva Conventions shows that the procedure was discussed as a means
of settling 'disputes which might arise in connection with the interpretation
or the application of the Conventions'.[31]

> 2. The ICRC will take part in the establishment of such a commission only by virtue of a
> general agreement or an ad hoc agreement with all the parties concerned.

> Reproduced in Marco Sassòli, Antoine A. Bouvier and Anne Quintin, *How Does Law Protect
> in War?*, Vol. III, 3rd edition, ICRC, Geneva, 2011, pp. 1713–1717.

[28] See Articles 49–51 of the First Convention and Additional Protocol I, Articles 85–86. Another
example may be found in Article 90(2)(c) of Additional Protocol I, which limits the competence of the International Fact-Finding Commission to alleged grave breaches or other serious
violations of the Geneva Conventions or Additional Protocol I. See also Article 90(2)(e) of the
Protocol.

[29] See Ihraï, p. 159.

[30] See Article 52(1), 'any alleged violation of the Convention'; see also the commentary on common Article 1 insofar as it relates to the High Contracting Parties' obligation to 'ensure respect'
for the Convention also by private persons.

[31] See the Sixth Report drawn up by the Special Committee of the Joint Committee, *Final Record
of the Diplomatic Conference of Geneva of 1949*, Vol. II-B, p. 119. This was also clear during
the drafting of Article 30 of the 1929 Geneva Convention on the Wounded and Sick; see, in
particular, *Proceedings of the Geneva Diplomatic Conference of 1929*, Geneva, 1930, p. 402.

3042   Lastly, with respect to the temporal scope of Article 52, the enquiry procedure may be activated, at any time, either during or after the end of an armed
conflict, as long as it relates to violations of the Convention.

D. Paragraph 1: Conditions for the institution of the enquiry

3043   The wording used in Article 52(1) makes it clear that the holding of the enquiry
is compulsory once one of the belligerents has asked for it: the procedure 'shall
be instituted' ('devra être ouverte'). The unique condition for this obligation
is 'the request of a Party to the conflict'. In theory, the mechanism provided
by Article 52 may therefore be activated unilaterally, meaning that it may be
imposed on the adverse Party.

3044   While the draft article submitted to the Diplomatic Conference in 1949 provided that 'any High Contracting Party' would be entitled to ask for the establishment of the procedure, paragraph 1 of Article 52 makes it clear that only a
'Party to the conflict' may address such a request. Other Parties to the Geneva
Conventions are not allowed to formally launch the procedure. They are, however, entitled to encourage the belligerents to make use of Article 52. This
is a means for them to fulfil their duty to 'ensure respect' for the Geneva
Conventions.[32] In such a case, however, neither of the belligerents is legally
bound to accept the enquiry.

3045   As provided in paragraph 1, the enquiry must be instituted 'in a manner to be
decided between the interested Parties'. This condition, emphasized on many
occasions since the adoption of the article,[33] constitutes a major obstacle to its
effective implementation. It is indeed extremely difficult to secure agreement
between opposing States in an armed conflict, especially when it is a matter
of investigating an alleged offence by one of them and when this may require
giving investigators access to the areas or persons concerned.

3046   The 'interested Parties' which must decide how the procedure is to be carried
out include the State requesting the institution of the enquiry and the Party or
Parties to the conflict whose conduct is to be investigated. It would be possible
that different Parties to the conflict affected by the same pattern of violations
(ill-treatment of wounded or sick soldiers belonging to different Parties to the
conflict) may decide to jointly request the enquiry.

3047   The Parties determining the 'manner' in which the procedure is to be carried
out are not bound to stick to a particular framework, because Article 52 is silent
in this regard. This issue was already discussed during the preparatory work on
Article 30 of the 1929 Geneva Convention on the Wounded and Sick. Some
delegations insisted that the details of the procedure could not be determined

---

[32] See common Article 1 and Additional Protocol I, Article 1(1).
[33] See e.g. Pictet (ed.), *Commentary on the First Geneva Convention*, ICRC, 1952, p. 377; Gasser,
p. 352; and ICRC, *Strengthening Legal Protection for Victims of Armed Conflict*, p. 14.

in advance and therefore suggested that procedural rules for the enquiry should not be introduced in the provision. It was therefore decided that this question would be left to the appreciation of the Parties to the conflict based on the circumstances of each case.[34]

3048   Defining the procedural framework of the enquiry is a crucial phase. It determines the precise scope of the procedure and helps to ensure that the investigations are carried out in an efficient and credible manner.[35] The Parties could draw inspiration in this regard from existing model rules for the establishment and conduct of international enquiry procedures, such as the relevant chapter of the 1907 Hague Convention (I).[36] They should at the very least agree on the composition and powers of the body undertaking the enquiry and on the identification of the facts allegedly amounting to a violation of the Convention(s).[37] Further guidance may be agreed upon by the Parties themselves or left to the appreciation of the investigative body.[38] Decisions to be taken in this regard should address the time frame, methodology and outcome of the procedure, as well as expenses incurred by the procedure.

3049   The request for an enquiry may be communicated directly by one of the belligerents or through its Protecting Power, where it exists. The second option should be the normal channel for such communications in time of armed conflict. As mentioned previously, however, this option has never been used in practice. Alternative ways of transmitting the request for an enquiry on behalf of a Party to the conflict may also include resorting to the services of the substitutes of the Protecting Powers, such as a neutral State, the ICRC or any other impartial organization.[39]

E. Paragraph 2: Procedure if the Parties do not reach agreement on the institution of the enquiry

3050 Paragraph 2 of Article 52 was new in 1949. It was added to strengthen the existing enquiry mechanism under Article 30 of the 1929 Geneva Convention on the Wounded and Sick. That provision had never been applied in practice and, when the interested Parties could not reach agreement on the procedure to be followed, it was felt that an alternative solution had to be proposed.[40] Paragraph 2 provides that, in such situations, the Parties should designate an umpire who would be tasked with determining how the enquiry would be carried out.

3051   This new paragraph is not much help, however, in facilitating the actual launching of the procedure. First, it does not create a strict legal obligation,

---

[34] See *Proceedings of the Geneva Diplomatic Conference of 1929*, Geneva, 1930, p. 399, and Ihraï, p. 158.
[35] Franck/Scott, p. 310.   [36] See Hague Convention (I) (1907), Articles 9–36.
[37] *Ibid.* Article 10.   [38] *Ibid.* Article 18.
[39] See common Article 10 (Article 11 in the Fourth Convention).
[40] See *Final Record of the Diplomatic Conference of Geneva of 1949*, Voll. II-B, p. 52.

as it only suggests that the Parties to the conflict 'should' make use of the services of the umpire. Second, it provides that this decision must be based on an 'agreement'; this merely reproduces, but does not resolve, the weakness of the existing provision in paragraph 1. If the Parties are unable to reach agreement on the organization of the procedure, it is hardly conceivable that they might agree on the appointment of an umpire. Therefore, in spite of the insertion of paragraph 2, the adoption of Article 52 and its parallel provisions in the other three Conventions in 1949 has not brought any progress with regard to the activation of the enquiry procedure.

3052   In practice, very few attempts have been made to resort to the enquiry mechanism of the Geneva Conventions, and none have resulted in the actual launching of the procedure. Even when the ICRC endeavoured to encourage the Parties to the conflict to use this mechanism, they never actually set up an enquiry for lack of consent. The procedure was proposed on only four occasions, twice before the adoption of the 1949 Geneva Conventions and twice thereafter:

(a) During the war between Italy and Ethiopia (1935–36), both sides addressed complaints of violations of international humanitarian law to the ICRC. The organization offered its services to help set up an international commission of enquiry. The Parties, however, never reached agreement on the formation of the commission.

(b) Following the Katyn Massacre (1943), the ICRC was asked by the German Red Cross to participate in the exhumation of the victims and by the Polish Government in Exile to conduct an independent investigation. The ICRC replied that it would be ready to lend assistance in appointing neutral experts to carry out the enquiry on condition that all the Parties concerned asked it to do so. The Soviet Government never addressed such a request and the Polish Government withdrew its proposal.

(c) During the Korean War (1952), the Democratic People's Republic of Korea accused the United States of America of using bacteriological weapons. The US Government asked the ICRC to conduct an independent enquiry into this allegation. The ICRC replied that it would set up an enquiry commission if all Parties agreed. This was not possible, however, as the Democratic People's Republic of Korea never responded to this proposal.

(d) During the war between Israel and Arab States (1973–74), the belligerents alleged serious violations of international humanitarian law against each other and asked the ICRC to investigate. The ICRC proposed the constitution of two bipartite enquiry commissions,[41] but no agreement was reached between the Parties on this procedure.[42]

---

[41] See 'ICRC proposes commissions of enquiry', in *International Review of the Red Cross*, Vol. 14, No. 154, January 1974, p. 49.
[42] For further details on these cases, see Bugnion, pp. 935–939.

F. Paragraph 3: Follow-up of the enquiry

3053   The third paragraph of Article 52 deals with the responsibilities of the Parties to the conflict once it has been established through the enquiry that a violation of the Geneva Conventions has been committed. The same applies to procedures concerning alleged violations of Additional Protocol I, where applicable.[43] This paragraph provides that the Parties 'shall put an end to [the violation] and shall repress it with the least possible delay'. The conclusions of the investigative body, although limited to the assessment and characterization of past events, is therefore not devoid of factual and legal consequences, and can be of relevance during an ongoing armed conflict. These conclusions entail the duty for the Parties to adopt concrete measures to redress the situation. While the enquiry is a mechanism of an international character, its follow-up involves measures that must be taken at the domestic level.

3054   These measures are not optional. Paragraph 3, as indicated by the use of the word 'shall', creates a legally binding obligation for the Party whose conduct was found to be unlawful. The mechanism in Article 52 differs in this regard from the classic enquiry procedure, as enshrined in the 1907 Hague Convention (I), according to which the Parties are entirely free to decide what the follow-up to the procedure should be.[44]

3055   The measures mentioned in paragraph 3 are rooted in the duty to respect and ensure respect for the Geneva Conventions (and Additional Protocol I, where applicable) in all circumstances. They are also in line with Article 49, which confirms that each High Contracting Party is bound to ensure criminal repression of those responsible for 'grave breaches' of the Convention[45] and to take measures necessary for the suppression of other violations.[46] The obligation to terminate an ongoing violation of the Convention is also based on the rules on State responsibility.[47]

3056   Two kinds of follow-up measures are mentioned in Article 52. First, the Parties to the conflict must 'put an end' to the violation(s). If the violation is still ongoing, for example where Parties to the conflict do not take all possible measures to search for the wounded, sick and dead on the battlefield,[48] the obligation to 'put an end' means that the concerned authorities must stop the unlawful conduct. If the violation has already occurred, for example murder of a protected person,[49] the obligation implies that the authorities must ensure that the unlawful conduct will not be repeated. States Parties may determine the best way to comply with this obligation, including, for example, by taking administrative measures, issuing instructions to combatants in conformity with the Convention, or providing relevant training to their armed forces.

---

[43] See Additional Protocol I, Article 90(2)(e).   [44] See Hague Convention (I)(1907), Article 35.
[45] See Article 49(2).   [46] See Article 49(3).
[47] See Draft Articles on State Responsibility (2001), Article 30.
[48] See Article 15(1).   [49] See Article 12(2).

3057   Second, the Parties to the conflict must 'repress' the violation, i.e. search for and apply a sanction to those responsible. This may include penal prosecution and punishment. If the established violation constitutes a grave breach of the Convention(s) or, as applicable, Additional Protocol I, repression must be in accordance with the legislation that each High Contracting Party must enact to ensure 'effective penal sanctions for persons committing, or ordering to be committed, any of the grave breaches' listed in the Geneva Conventions and Additional Protocol I, where applicable.[50] This also means that further investigation must be carried out in accordance with domestic criminal procedures. While the enquiry conducted on the basis of Article 52 must seek to establish whether a Party to an international armed conflict has violated one of the provisions of the Convention(s), or Additional Protocol I, where applicable, it is not aimed at reaching conclusions regarding individual criminal responsibility. The same consideration applies for acts contrary to the Convention(s) or Additional Protocol I other than grave breaches,[51] for which a Party may also have adopted penal sanctions. Concerning such acts, disciplinary sanctions or other measures may also be applied, depending on domestic law and regulations.

3058   A third obligation incumbent on the Party whose conduct was found to be unlawful is not mentioned in Article 52, but derives from customary international law. State practice and *opinio juris* confirm that a State responsible for violations of international humanitarian law is required to make full reparation for the loss or injury caused.[52] Reparation does not necessarily consist of awarding compensation, as provided under other humanitarian law treaties,[53] but can also take other forms, such as restitution, rehabilitation, satisfaction or the guarantee that the violations will not be repeated.[54]

G. Developments since 1949

3059   The main reason why the mechanism established under Article 52 has so far never been used is related to the conditions for its practical application.[55] The actual opening of the enquiry requires that all interested Parties agree either

---

[50] See Article 49(1) and Additional Protocol I, Article 85(1).

[51] See Article 49(3) and Additional Protocol I, Article 85(1).

[52] See Henckaerts/Doswald-Beck, commentary on Rule 150, pp. 537–545. The Geneva Conventions of 1949 also address the issue of State responsibility in case of 'grave breaches' (see First Convention, Article 51; Second Convention, Article 52; Third Convention, Article 131; and Fourth Convention, Article 148). More generally, the obligation to make full reparation is also part of State responsibility for internationally wrongful acts; see Draft Articles on State Responsibility (2001), Articles 31 and 34–38.

[53] See Hague Convention (IV) (1907), Article 3, and Additional Protocol I, Article 91.

[54] See Basic Principles and Guidelines on the Right to a Remedy and Reparation for Victims of Gross Violations of International Human Rights Law and Serious Violations of IHL (2005).

[55] This problem was foreseen as early as the preparatory work on Article 30 of the 1929 Geneva Convention on the Wounded and Sick (see *Proceedings of the Geneva Diplomatic Conference of 1929*, Geneva, 1930, p. 406) and has been highlighted on numerous occasions since then. See e.g. *60 ans des Conventions de Genève et les décennies à venir – 60 Years of the Geneva*

on the procedure to be followed or on the choice of the umpire. Article 52 does not ensure the automatic activation of the enquiry upon the request of one Party only. In practice, it appears that it is not realistic to expect that Parties between whom relationships have already broken down, and who are involved in an armed conflict with each other, are able to reach agreement on setting up an enquiry, particularly one aimed at addressing an issue as sensitive as violations of international humanitarian law. Where fact-finding missions have been set up in the recent past to investigate such violations, they have invariably involved mechanisms that do not require the ad hoc consent of the Parties. Thus, the ineffectiveness of the enquiry mechanism established under the 1949 Geneva Conventions is due mainly to lack of political will.

3060   Another perceived weakness of the enquiry mechanism is its lack of institutionalization.[56] In the absence of a pre-existing permanent body and standard procedure, Article 52 requires lengthy negotiations and preparatory work before investigations can actually start. This may discourage the Parties to the conflict from resorting to this mechanism, especially in situations where the risks of losing essential pieces of evidence and the protection of the victims necessitate a rapid response. If the institutionalization of the enquiry is part of the solution, however, it is not a guarantee of success. The International Fact-Finding Commission, which came into existence in 1991 pursuant to Article 90 of Additional Protocol I, has never been called upon to act. In this case, too, the lack of consent by the Parties to the conflict remains a major obstacle.

3061   Despite the failure of the enquiry procedure under the 1949 Geneva Conventions, some experts still support it as a potentially attractive option. This was confirmed through a series of regional expert seminars organized by the ICRC in 2003 on improving compliance with international humanitarian law.[57] The experts stressed that the bilateral nature of the procedure was an advantage that might still be of interest to Parties to the conflict willing to solve disputes over compliance with international humanitarian law without external interference. Proposals were made during the 2003 consultations to overcome obstacles that might be hindering actual resort to the procedure. It was suggested that a draft model enquiry procedure should be developed and made available to Parties to a conflict in order to facilitate their reliance on the mechanism. It was proposed that the formal enquiry procedure established for international armed conflicts could also be used in non-international armed conflicts.[58]

Conventions and the Decades Ahead, Report of a conference held on 9–10 November 2009, Swiss Confederation/ICRC, Bern, 2010, p. 39.

[56] This weakness of Article 52 is usually mentioned in comparison with the advantage of Article 90 of Additional Protocol I, which creates a permanent fact-finding commission and establishes minimal procedural rules.

[57] See ICRC, 'Improving Compliance with International Humanitarian Law', p. 53.

[58] *Ibid.* p. 68.

3062   To this day, however, the concrete application of Article 52 has remained hypothetical. This does not mean that alleged violations of international humanitarian law are not investigated in practice. On the contrary, such investigations take place regularly. However, instead of enquiries requested by Parties to an armed conflict, which are dependent on their consent, as provided by international humanitarian law, formal investigations often take place on the initiative and under the aegis of the international community, either at the United Nations or at the regional level. This has been possible for both international and non-international armed conflicts.

3063   Within the UN system, investigation procedures have been established mainly by the Security Council[59] and the Human Rights Council (formerly the Commission on Human Rights),[60] although other UN bodies have also used such mechanisms within the framework of their respective mandates.[61] At the regional level, fact-finding procedures concerning the conduct of Parties to armed conflicts have been initiated by various organizations, such as the African Union,[62] the Council of Europe,[63] the European Union[64] and the Organization of American States.[65] In some cases, investigative bodies were set up to ensure that the monitoring of the Parties to an armed conflict and their activities was pursued over long periods of time and that reports were released at regular intervals. In other cases, procedures were initiated to investigate a specific past event or series of events which had occurred over a relatively short period of time.

---

[59] See e.g. UN Security Council, Final Report of the Commission of Experts established pursuant to Security Council Resolution 780 (1992), UN Doc. S/1994/674, 27 May 1994, and Report of the International Commission of Inquiry on Darfur to the United Nations Secretary-General Pursuant to Security Council Resolution 1564 of 18 September 2004, Geneva, 25 January 2005.

[60] See e.g. UN Commission on Human Rights, *Report on the situation of human rights in Kuwait under Iraqi occupation*, prepared by Mr. Walter Kälin, Special Rapporteur of the Commission on Human Rights, in accordance with Commission resolution 1991/67, UN Doc. E/CN.4/1992/26, 16 January 1992; UN Human Rights Council, *Report of the United Nations Fact-Finding Mission on the Gaza Conflict*, UN Doc. A/HRC/12/48, 15 September 2009; UN Human Rights Council, *Report of the International Commission of Inquiry to investigate all alleged violations of international human rights law in the Libyan Arab Jamahiriya*, UN Doc. A/HRC/17/44, 1 June 2011; and UN Human Rights Council, *Report of the independent international commission of inquiry on the Syrian Arab Republic*, UN Doc. A/HRC/S-17/2/Add.1, 23 November 2011.

[61] See e.g. UN Secretary-General, *Report of the Mission to Inspect Civilian Areas in Iran and Iraq Which Have Been Subject to Military Attack*, Un Doc. S/15834, 20 June 1983.

[62] See e.g. *Report of the African Commission on Human and Peoples' Rights' Fact-Finding Mission to the Republic of Sudan in the Darfur Region*, 8–18 July 2004, EX.CL/364 (XI), Annex III, 20 September 2004.

[63] See e.g. *Human Rights in Areas Affected by the South Ossetia Conflict. Special Mission to Georgia and Russian Federation*, report by Thomas Hammarberg, Council of Europe Commissioner for Human Rights, COE Doc. CommDH(2008)22, 8 September 2008.

[64] See *Report of the Independent International Fact-Finding Mission on the Conflict in Georgia*, mandated by Council of Europe decision 2008/901/CFSP of 2 December 2008.

[65] See Inter-American Commission on Human Rights, *Third report on the human rights situation in Colombia*, OAS Doc. OEA/Ser.L/V/II.102, Doc. 9 rev. 1, 26 February 1999.

3064 Recent decades have also witnessed a considerable development of fact-finding related to international humanitarian law. Investigation has been a necessary and central part of the work undertaken by ad hoc international criminal tribunals, such as the ICTY and the ICTR, mixed national and international criminal tribunals, such as the Special Court for Sierra Leone, and, lastly, the ICC.

Select bibliography

Bassiouni, M. Cherif, 'The United Nations Commission of Experts Established Pursuant to Security Council Resolution 780 (1992)', *American Journal of International Law*, Vol. 88, No. 4, October 1994, pp. 784–805.

Bothe, Michael, 'Fact-finding as a means of ensuring respect for international humanitarian law', in Wolff Heintschel von Heinegg and Volker Epping (eds), *International Humanitarian Law Facing New Challenges: Symposium in Honour of Knut Ipsen*, Berlin, Springer, 2007, pp. 249–267.

Boutruche, Théo, 'Credible Fact-Finding and Allegations of International Humanitarian Law Violations: Challenges in Theory and Practice', *Journal of Conflict and Security Law*, Vol. 16, No. 1, Spring 2011, pp. 105–140.

– 'Good offices, Conciliation and Enquiry', in Andrew Clapham, Paola Gaeta and Marco Sassòli (eds), *The 1949 Geneva Conventions: A Commentary*, Oxford University Press, 2015, pp. 561–574.

Buergenthal, Thomas, 'The United Nations Truth Commission for El Salvador', *Vanderbilt Journal of Transnational Law*, Vol. 27, No. 3, 1994, pp. 498–544.

Bugnion, François, *The International Committee of the Red Cross and the Protection of War Victims*, ICRC/Macmillan, Oxford, 2003, pp. 935–939.

Cerna, Christina M., 'Human rights in armed conflict: Implementation of international humanitarian law norms by regional intergovernmental human rights bodies', in Fritz Kalshoven and Yves Sandoz (eds), *Implementation of International Humanitarian Law/Mise en œuvre du droit international humanitaire*, Martinus Nijhoff Publishers, Dordrecht, 1989, pp. 31–67.

Cohen, Amichai and Shany, Yuval, 'Beyond the Grave Breaches Regime: The Duty to Investigate Alleged Violations of International Law Governing Armed Conflicts', *Yearbook of International Humanitarian Law 2011*, Vol. 14, 2012, pp. 37–84.

de La Pradelle, Paul, *La Conférence diplomatique et les nouvelles Conventions de Genève du 12 août 1949*, Les Éditions internationales, Paris, 1951.

Franck, Thomas M. and Scott, Fairley H., 'Procedural Due Process in Human Rights Fact-Finding by International Agencies', *American Journal of International Law*, Vol. 74, No. 2, April 1980, pp. 308–345.

Gasser, Hans-Peter, 'Scrutiny', *Australian Year Book of International Law*, Vol. 9, 1985, pp. 345–358.

Henckaerts, Jean-Marie and Doswald-Beck, Louise, *Customary International Humanitarian Law, Volume I: Rules*, ICRC/Cambridge University Press, 2005, available at https://www.icrc.org/customary-ihl/eng/docs/v1.

HPCR Advanced Practitioner's Handbook on Commissions of Inquiry: Monitoring, Reporting and Fact-Finding, Program on Humanitarian Policy and Conflict Resolution, Harvard Humanitarian Initiative, March 2015.

ICRC, 'Improving Compliance with International Humanitarian Law', ICRC Expert Seminars, summary report to the 28th International Conference of the Red Cross and Red Crescent, Geneva, 2–6 December 2003, Annex III.
- 'Action by the International Committee of the Red Cross in the event of violations of international humanitarian law or of other fundamental rules protecting persons in situations of violence', *International Review of the Red Cross*, Vol. 87, No. 858, June 2005, pp. 393–400.
- *Strengthening Legal Protection for Victims of Armed Conflict*, Report prepared for the 31st International Conference of the Red Cross and Red Crescent, ICRC, Geneva, 2011, pp. 10–14.
Ihraï, Saïd, 'Les mécanismes d'établissement des faits dans les Conventions de Genève de 1949 et dans le Protocole I de 1977', in Fritz Kalshoven and Yves Sandoz (eds), *Implementation of International Humanitarian Law/Mise en œuvre du droit international humanitaire*, Martinus Nijhoff Publishers, Dordrecht, 1989, pp. 153–168.
Orentlicher, Diane F., 'Bearing Witness: The Art and Science of Human Rights Fact-Finding', *Harvard Human Rights Journal*, Vol. 3, Spring 1990, pp. 83–135.
Stewart, James G., 'The UN Commission of Inquiry on Lebanon: A Legal Appraisal', *Journal of International Criminal Justice*, Vol. 5, No. 5, 2007, pp. 1039–1059.
Vité, Sylvain, *Les procédures internationales d'établissement des faits dans la mise en œuvre du droit international humanitaire*, Bruylant, Brussels, 1999.
Waldman, Adir, *Arbitrating Armed Conflict: Decisions of the Israel-Lebanon Monitoring Group*, JurisNet, Huntington, 2003.
Zegveld, Liesbeth, 'The importance of fact-finding missions under international humanitarian law', in Chantal Meloni and Gianni Tognoni (eds), *Is There a Court for Gaza? A Test Bench for International Justice*, T.M.C. Asser Press, The Hague, 2012, pp. 161–167.

ARTICLE 53

MISUSE OF THE EMBLEM

❖ Text of the provision*

(1) The use by individuals, societies, firms or companies either public or private, other than those entitled thereto under the present Convention, of the emblem or the designation "Red Cross" or "Geneva Cross", or any sign or designation constituting an imitation thereof, whatever the object of such use, and irrespective of the date of its adoption, shall be prohibited at all times.

(2) By reason of the tribute paid to Switzerland by the adoption of the reversed Federal colours, and of the confusion which may arise between the arms of Switzerland and the distinctive emblem of the Convention, the use by private individuals, societies or firms, of the arms of the Swiss Confederation, or of marks constituting an imitation thereof, whether as trademarks or commercial marks, or as parts of such marks, or for a purpose contrary to commercial honesty, or in circumstances capable of wounding Swiss national sentiment, shall be prohibited at all times.

(3) Nevertheless, such High Contracting Parties as were not party to the Geneva Convention of July 27, 1929, may grant to prior users of the emblems, designations, signs or marks designated in the first paragraph, a time limit not to exceed three years from the coming into force of the present Convention to discontinue such use, provided that the said use shall not be such as would appear, in time of war, to confer the protection of the Convention.

(4) The prohibition laid down in the first paragraph of the present Article shall also apply, without effect on any rights acquired through prior use, to the emblems and marks mentioned in the second paragraph of Article 38.

❖ Reservations or declarations

United States of America: Reservation made on ratification[1]

---

* Paragraph numbers have been added for ease of reference.
[1] United Nations *Treaty Series*, Vol. 213, 1955, pp. 378–381. See fn. 51 below for the text of the reservation.

Contents

A. Introduction

3065   Article 53 sets out a very broad prohibition on the use of the distinctive emblems, their designations, and imitations thereof, by a range of third parties.[2] The article also covers the arms of the Swiss Confederation and designs that may constitute imitations thereof. Such uses are prohibited regardless of their purpose and, in many cases, irrespective of their date of adoption.

3066   The prohibition set out under Article 53 applies at all times, that is, both in situations of armed conflict and in times of peace. Article 53 encompasses both misuse of the emblem in its protective sense and when used as an indicative sign,[3] even though no explicit distinction is drawn between these two types of use in the article. Although the gravity of misuse of the emblem in times of war cannot be doubted, it is recognized that misuse of the indicative sign in peacetime, such as for commercial purposes, serves to undermine its particular meaning and purpose.[4]

3067   In setting out such a strict prohibition on third-party use, Article 53 serves to reaffirm the special nature and status of the distinctive emblems. This status may be regarded as genuinely unique under international law.

3068   The terms of Article 53 vary from paragraph to paragraph, and, on a strict reading, may appear to be complex. However, national practice (in particular, available domestic legislation) shows that, generally, States afford similar levels of protection to all of the distinctive emblems set out in Article 53 and their designations, as well as, in many cases, to the Swiss emblem. Imitations of these signs are equally prohibited.

3069   Where instances of misuse of the emblems, designations and imitations by third parties occur, it is the responsibility of States, supported by National

---

[2] These 'third parties' include 'individuals, societies, firms or companies either public or private, other than those entitled thereto under the present Convention', as set out under the first paragraph of the article.

[3] See the commentary on Article 44, sections C and D, in regard to protective and indicative uses.

[4] Pictet (ed.), *Commentary on the First Geneva Convention*, ICRC, 1952, p. 385.

Red Cross and Red Crescent Societies (hereinafter 'National Societies') and the ICRC, to ensure that such abuses are appropriately addressed, in accordance with the present article and existing national legislation.

B. Historical background

3070 The original Geneva Convention of 1864 had no provision dealing with the repression of infractions, and was also silent on the subject of abuses and misuses of the distinctive emblem. However, abuses of the red cross emblem, both in peacetime and during armed conflict, were apparent as early as 1866.[5] Partly owing to concerted efforts by the ICRC and National Societies to tackle such misuse,[6] the revised Geneva Convention of 1906 required States to 'take or recommend to their legislatures' measures necessary to prevent abuses of the emblem, in relation to both commercial use by third parties and wrongful use in times of war.[7]

3071   In 1929, the relevant provision was revised to form Article 28, which was new, of the updated Convention. The new article also prohibited use of the arms of the Swiss Confederation[8] and covered imitations of the red cross emblem and its designation, and those of the Swiss arms. The intention of the latter was to capture signs or names (primarily those used for commercial undertakings) that, while not exactly replicating the emblem or designation, would be so close in design as inevitably to create an association with them.[9] However, although the red crescent and red lion and sun emblems were newly recognized under the 1929 Convention, they were not included in Article 28,

---

[5] For specific examples of such abuses, see *ibid.* p. 381.

[6] For example, the 3rd International Conference of the Red Cross (Geneva, 1884) recommended that 'energetic legislative or similar measures be taken, in all countries, to prevent abuse of the emblem of the Convention, the red cross on a white ground, in time of peace as in time of war'. A similar resolution was adopted by the 4th International Conference (Karlsruhe, 1887). See Pictet (ed.), *Commentary on the First Geneva Convention*, ICRC, 1952, p. 381. Such efforts by the components of the International Red Cross and Red Crescent Movement, in cooperation with States, continue today.

[7] Geneva Convention (1906), Articles 27 and 28. The 1906 Convention forbade misuse of the emblem for both protective and indicative purposes, although at the time no conscious distinction had yet been drawn between the two uses. It should be noted that efforts to address abuses of the emblem in wartime had been made as early as 1899, through the forbidding of 'improper use of . . . the distinctive badges of the Geneva Convention' in Article 23 of the 1899 Hague Regulations, and in the same article of the revised 1907 Hague Regulations. See Pictet (ed.), *Commentary on the First Geneva Convention*, ICRC, 1952, p. 382.

[8] It is reported that, in order to circumvent the prohibition on the use of the red cross emblem in the 1906 Geneva Convention, the white cross on a red ground was increasingly used for commercial purposes, in an attempt to take advantage of the similarity between it and the red cross emblem. See Pictet (ed.), *Commentary on the First Geneva Convention*, ICRC, 1952, pp. 382–383.

[9] Commercial undertakings, prevented after 1906 from making use of the emblem without risk of prosecution, devised signs which could not be said to be the red cross, but gave the impression that they were. This enabled them to claim for their products, with impunity, at least some of the prestige attaching to the emblem. Examples included a red cross with a figure or another cross superimposed; a cross which had only the outline or part of it in red; backgrounds of different colours; a cross half red and half white on a ground in which the two colours were reversed; and a red star which from a distance looked like a cross. Such practices, harmful to the emblem and to the organization, had to be eliminated.

meaning that States were under no international obligation to prohibit their improper use. Those States that used one of these alternate signs could ensure their protection in their territories under domestic laws. In addition, a separate article covering misuse in wartime was not retained in the 1929 Convention, leading to a misperception that Article 28 applied to commercial abuses only.[10]

3072   In 1949, the text of Article 28 was revised and incorporated into two separate provisions, Articles 53 and 54 of the First Convention. While Article 53 retained and developed the various abuses mentioned in Article 28, the requirement to take necessary measures to prevent and repress these acts was moved to Article 54.[11]

C. Unique nature of protection

3073   In proscribing, in very broad terms, the use of the distinctive emblems (as well as use of the arms of the Swiss Confederation, relevant designations, and imitations) by any, other than those entitled to use them, Article 53 serves to reinforce the special purpose and unique status of these signs. There are some other internationally recognized symbols that enjoy a certain level of protection under specific international agreements or resolutions. For example, under international humanitarian law, there are other signs designated for specific purposes (such as to protect cultural property in armed conflict),[12] the use of which may also be restricted by national legislation. In addition, use of the emblem and flag of the United Nations is restricted,[13] and the UN General Assembly has recommended the implementation of national measures to prevent its unauthorized use.[14] However, the very wide prohibition on the use of the distinctive emblems by third parties set out under Article 53, coupled with the positive obligation of States, established in Article 54, to take appropriate national measures to repress instances of abuse and misuse, constitutes

---

[10] Although Article 28 of the 1929 Geneva Convention on the Wounded and Sick stipulated that States were to prevent such abuses 'at all times', confusion arose from the explicit mention of commercial purposes in the article (even though the provision also referred generally to 'any other purposes'). It was reported in 1952 that, where national legislation had been introduced to give effect to the 1929 obligations, 'it generally covers commercial abuses only'. See Pictet, (ed.), *Commentary on the First Geneva Convention*, ICRC, 1952, p. 381.

[11] See the commentary on Article 54.

[12] The cultural property emblem, adopted by the 1954 Hague Convention for the Protection of Cultural Property, consists of 'a shield, pointed below, per saltire blue and white' (Article 16(1)).

[13] Use of the emblem of the United Nations is restricted by UN General Assembly resolution 92(1) of 7 December 1946, as well as by internal regulations issued by the UN Secretariat. Use of the UN flag is regulated by the UN Flag Code and Regulations, issued by the UN Secretary-General. Article 38(2) of Additional Protocol I prohibits the use of the 'distinctive emblem of the United Nations, except as authorized by that Organization'.

[14] Paragraph 2(a) of UN General Assembly resolution 92(1) of 7 December 1946 recommends that Members of the UN take such legislative or other appropriate measures as are necessary to prevent unauthorized use of the emblem, the official seal and the name or initials of the UN, in particular for commercial purposes. Unauthorized use of the UN emblem is also prohibited under the domestic law of some States, e.g. Sweden and Switzerland.

a level of protection over and above that afforded to other internationally recognized signs.[15] The prohibition is wide enough to cover such use wherever it may occur and in whatever form. For example, while this could not have been foreseen at the time of drafting, the prohibition extends to unauthorized use of the distinctive emblems, their designations, and imitations thereof in the digital sphere and on the internet. It is the responsibility of States to ensure that private and/or commercial organizations uphold the restrictions set out in Article 53.

D. Discussion

1. *Paragraph 1: Red cross emblem, related designations, and imitations*

3074 Article 53(1) covers the use of the red cross emblem and the designations 'Red Cross' and 'Geneva Cross', as well as imitations of these. While many national laws refer both to the red cross emblem and to the designation 'Red Cross' in conformity with this paragraph, it does not appear that a great number explicitly prohibit the use of the designation 'Geneva Cross'.[16] Many national laws also prohibit the use of imitations of the red cross emblem, as well as imitations of the designation 'Red Cross'. It is for each individual State to determine those signs that may constitute an imitation of the emblem or of related designations. Particular formulations may be included in the national legislation itself.[17] In addition, in some countries the question of which designs or wording may constitute an imitation in their territory has arisen in their national

---

[15] For example, Article 53 not only prohibits the use of the red cross emblem and related designations, but also the use of imitations thereof. In addition, parts of Article 53 have, in effect, retroactive application (see para. 3078).

[16] Some of the countries that do explicitly refer to the designation 'Geneva Cross' in their relevant legislation are Belgium, Canada, Nigeria, Sweden, Switzerland, the United Kingdom, the United States and Uruguay. While the term 'Geneva Cross' is a synonym of the designation 'Red Cross', its use in practice is less common than the latter term (in addition, there are no recorded cases concerning improper use of 'Geneva Cross').

[17] For example, a number of countries with a Geneva Conventions Act, including Australia, Barbados, India and the United Kingdom, define imitations of the distinctive emblems or designations as being designs or wording 'so nearly resembling [any of the emblems or designations] as to be capable of being mistaken for ... or understood as referring to, one of those emblems'. Other countries use wording such as a 'colourable imitation' or similar (Malaysia, United States), or refer to use of the emblems or designations that is intended to 'generate confusion or a deception' (Italy). In its *Study on the Use of the Emblems*, p. 309, the ICRC sets out the following recommendations regarding imitations:

  1. Imitation is a form of misuse of the emblem or the name, that is, the use of a sign or designation that, owing to its shape and/or colour or title, may be confused with the emblem or its name.
  2. The criterion for deciding if a given mark constitutes an imitation should be whether there is a risk of confusion in the public mind between that mark and the emblem or its name. This test should be interpreted in the manner most favourable to the [Geneva Conventions] and the emblem (and/or name).

  The Study also helpfully sets out various examples both of signs and of wording that would constitute such an imitation. See ICRC, *Study on the Use of the Emblems: Operational and Commercial and Other Non-Operational Issues*, Geneva, 2011, p. 312.

case law.[18] The observance of these rules in practice is further considered in section E below.

3075   The prohibition set out in the first paragraph also applies to the red crescent and red lion and sun emblems (by virtue of Article 53(4)) and to the red crystal emblem (by virtue of Article 6 of Additional Protocol III). However, there are some important differences in application, in particular concerning the issue of prior use of the latter emblems, which are addressed below in section D.4.

3076   This paragraph also sets out categories of third parties for whom the use of the emblem and related designations is prohibited, namely 'individuals, societies, firms or companies either public or private, other than those entitled thereto under the present Convention'. These categories are intended to be exhaustive, rather than restrictive: in effect, the use of the emblem is forbidden to everyone not authorized by the Convention.[19] This view was confirmed by delegates to the 1949 Diplomatic Conference, who considered that the prohibition on use set out in Article 53 was 'rendered absolute'.[20] In general, national laws giving effect to Article 53 follow this interpretation: rather than identifying the specific persons or bodies unable to use the emblem, designations and related signs, the prohibition extends to all individuals and entities not explicitly entitled to do so under Article 44.[21]

---

[18] For example, in 1994 the German Federal Court of Justice ruled that a commercial ambulance service may not use a design of a red/brown emblem on an ivory or darker ground, for the following reasons: the contested sign would usually bring to mind the red cross emblem; similarities between the sign and the red cross emblem would largely outweigh differences; the impression would be of a stylized and modernized emblem. Germany, Federal Court of Justice, *German Red Cross case*, Judgment, 1994. See also Switzerland, Federal Tribunal, *A. SA v. Swiss Red Cross*, Judgment, 2014.

[19] Those persons and entities entitled to such use are set out under Article 44 of the First Convention, and include, first and foremost, authorized medical establishments, units, personnel and material, as well as National Red Cross or Red Crescent Societies (within certain limits) and the international Red Cross organizations. The international Red Cross organizations are the ICRC and the International Federation of Red Cross and Red Crescent Societies. Article 44 also allows the emblem to be used, as an exceptional measure, to identify a third-party aid post or ambulance exclusively assigned to the purpose of giving free treatment to the wounded and sick, with the express permission of the relevant National Red Cross or Red Crescent Society. For further discussion of the persons and entities authorized to use the distinctive emblems, see the commentary on Article 44. Other Geneva Conventions and the Additional Protocols also contain provisions on emblem use. For example, Article 8 of Additional Protocol I extends such use to authorized civilian medical personnel, hospitals and units.

[20] *Final Record of the Diplomatic Conference of Geneva of 1949*, Vol. II-A, p. 199.

[21] A number of national laws use text formulations that refer broadly to 'all' or 'any' persons and/or entities being subject to the prohibition under Article 53, with those entitled to use the emblem under Article 44 listed as exceptions. See e.g. Germany, *Code of Administrative Offences*, 1968, Article 125 (Use of the Red Cross or the Swiss heraldic bearing); Namibia, *Red Cross Act*, 1991, Article 3; Poland, *Penal Code*, 1997, Article 126; and United States, *Geneva Distinctive Emblems Protection Act*, 2006 section 706a. Additionally, in practice it appears to be immaterial as to whether a reported misuser is able to be identified as belonging to one of the categories of third parties set out under Article 53(1). If the individual or entity is not an authorized user as set out under Article 44, they are generally regarded as unable to use the red cross emblem, related designations, or imitations thereof.

3077 Article 53(1) prohibits the use of the red cross emblem and related designations 'whatever the object of such use'. This means that the emblem or related designations cannot be used, except as provided for in the Convention,[22] for any reason, however commendable, including for any other humanitarian purpose. The phrase effectively prevents any arguments being brought by unauthorized users that their use of the emblem or designations is justified, either because there was no intention to represent the true purpose of the emblem[23] or because the use is for a purpose similar to that of the emblem.[24]

3078 The prohibition set out in the first paragraph of Article 53 applies irrespective of when the sign in question was adopted. This means that the provision must be given effect, even where the use of the red cross emblem, the related designations, or an imitation of these by an individual or entity preceded the coming into force of the Convention. Similar wording was included in the 1906 and 1929 Geneva Conventions. Indeed, the retroactive application of this and other earlier provisions has consistently been considered important in ensuring that the emblem and designations maintain their special meaning and unique status. The application of Article 53 to prior existing signs is tempered by the exception set out in Article 53(3), discussed in section D.3.

3079 Lastly, Article 53(1) stipulates that the prohibition applies 'at all times'. This includes all instances of use of the emblem, whether in peacetime or in situations of armed conflict.[25] Many, although not all, national laws on the use of the emblem distinguish between peacetime and situations of armed conflict,[26] and may provide for different penalties depending on whether the misuse occurred in one or the other context.[27] While the consequences of

---

[22] Although Article 53(1) refers to the present Convention, in effect the emblem may only be used as provided for in the four Geneva Conventions and their Additional Protocols.

[23] For example, in 1979, the Supreme Court of the Netherlands rejected an argument by the accused that he had not 'made use' of the protected emblem, since it had not been 'used in such way that it has some significance or fulfils some function'. The Court ruled that the use of the red cross emblem by the accused, regardless of intent, was sufficient to violate the relevant national law. The Netherlands, Supreme Court (Minor Offences Division), *In re Ernest case*, Judgment, 1979.

[24] For example, a number of agencies or organizations involved in humanitarian pursuits or the delivery of aid have in practice made improper use of the red cross emblem or an imitation thereof, normally because of a misunderstanding that the emblem constitutes a symbol of general humanitarian assistance or perhaps in an effort to benefit from the protection the emblem represents.

[25] The prohibition in Article 53 applies to all uses of the emblem and related designations, whether as a protective sign or in an indicative sense, both in strict form (i.e. a red cross of arms of equal length on a white ground) and as an imitation.

[26] For example, abuses of the distinctive emblems, their designations or other protected signs occurring in situations of armed conflict (whether by military personnel or by civilians) should normally be included in relevant legislation covering violations of the laws and customs of war. Unauthorized use in peacetime may be dealt with under a country's criminal code or similar legislation. Some countries, in particular those protecting the emblem through the laws establishing the National Red Cross or Red Crescent Society, e.g. Antigua and Barbuda, Belize, Brunei Darussalam, Jamaica and Lesotho, do not distinguish between peacetime and situations of armed conflict.

[27] See the commentary on Article 54, section C.3.

improper use of the emblem in situations of armed conflict may be particularly serious,[28] protection of the emblem in peacetime is also important, in order to ensure that its special meaning and purpose is well understood, respected and not undermined.[29]

2. Paragraph 2: The arms of the Swiss Confederation

3080   Article 53(2) prohibits use of the arms of the Swiss Confederation (hereinafter 'the Swiss emblem'), as well as imitations of the Swiss emblem.[30] First added in 1929, the provision makes it clear that such protection is warranted owing to the reversal of the colours of the Swiss emblem in the red cross emblem, and in order to avoid any adverse consequences for the respect owed to the red cross emblem that might result from misuse of the Swiss emblem. Confusion between the red cross emblem and the Swiss emblem can, in particular, arise where companies or individuals seek to exploit the resemblance between the two emblems in order to mislead the public.[31] Consequently, the paragraph both reinforces the 'compliment to Switzerland' set out under Article 38 of the Convention, and, in providing an additional, albeit indirect, means of protection for the red cross emblem, adds to the special status of the red cross emblem. Use of the Swiss emblem is explicitly prohibited by a great number of countries, often as part of their national legislation on the use of the distinctive emblems.[32]

3081   When compared with other national flags or armorial bearings, the protection afforded to the Swiss emblem under Article 53 may be regarded as unique in international law. Other treaties provide some measure of protection for

---

[28] For example, Article 85(3)(f) of Additional Protocol I identifies the perfidious use of the distinctive emblem as a grave breach of the Protocol (when committed wilfully and causing death or serious injury). In addition, under Article 8(2)(b)(vii) of the 1998 ICC Statute, '[m]aking improper use . . . of the distinctive emblems of the Geneva Conventions' constitutes a war crime in international armed conflict, where such use results in death or serious personal injury. For those countries that are party to the ICC Statute, such improper use is therefore punishable as a war crime in their territories.

[29] In 2007, the Oslo District Court in Norway ruled that a dental clinic using an imitation of the red cross emblem to mark its offices had violated the prohibition in the Norwegian Criminal Code on the unlawful use of any sign or name designed to be used in connection with aiding the wounded and sick in time of armed conflict. In reaching its decision, the Court recalled that the purpose of the red cross emblem was to provide protection in armed conflict, and that its misuse in peacetime could undermine respect for it in wartime. Norway, District Court of Oslo, *Bogstadveien tannlegevakt case*, Judgment, 2007.

[30] The Swiss emblem consists of a white cross, with arms of equal length, on a red ground.

[31] Prior to this prohibition being introduced in 1929, the Swiss emblem or imitations thereof were increasingly used by third parties to create an association with the red cross emblem (the use of which was already regulated), in particular for commercial purposes. In practical terms, there are many modern examples of third parties, who are normally unaware of the relevant legal provisions, attempting to use the Swiss arms or imitations for the same effect.

[32] Examples of countries explicitly prohibiting use of the Swiss emblem in their legislation on emblem use include Australia, Austria, Belgium, Bolivia, Cambodia, France, Germany, India, Mauritius, Sri Lanka, the United Kingdom and the United States.

countries' national flags or symbols: for example, to protect their unauthorized use for commercial purposes[33] or, indirectly, to prevent their desecration.[34] In addition, States may prevent unauthorized use of their flags or national symbols and/or prohibit their desecration (as well as that of foreign flags) under national legislation.[35] However, the Swiss emblem is the only national marking to be protected specifically under international humanitarian law.[36]

3082   Article 53 prohibits use of the Swiss emblem or imitations thereof as trademarks or commercial marks (or parts of such marks),[37] as well as for purposes 'contrary to commercial honesty'. While there is no commonly agreed interpretation of this phrase, in general, it may be understood as referring to misleading or deceptive practices in a commercial context aimed at creating a false impression or belief about an entity, product or service.[38] Aside from its use in commercial contexts, the provision also prevents use of the Swiss emblem in circumstances 'capable of wounding Swiss national sentiment'. There is little evidence as to how this aspect of Article 53 may be interpreted in practice, although somewhat similar provisions under recently amended Swiss national laws refer to use that is 'contrary to morality or convention or against current law': this notion may arguably also encompass the wounding of national sentiment.[39]

---

[33] Article 6*ter*(a) of the 1883 Paris Convention for the Protection of Industrial Property prohibits the commercial use, not authorized by the competent authorities, of State flags and emblems.

[34] Article 22(2) of the 1961 Vienna Convention on Diplomatic Relations places a State under a special duty to protect the premises of foreign missions on its territory against intrusion or damage and to prevent disturbances of the peace or impairment of the dignity of such missions. This could include measures to prevent or repress the desecration of foreign States' flags or other symbols.

[35] For example, and of most relevance here, Switzerland has federal legislation regulating the use of its flag and coat of arms for commercial purposes (a number of Swiss brands use the Swiss emblem on their products as a guarantee of quality and an indication of source). See fn. 39.

[36] It may be noted that Additional Protocol I also prohibits making use of the emblem of the United Nations and, more generally, of the flags of neutral or other States that are not Parties to the conflict (Articles 37–39).

[37] While the provision refers to both 'trademarks' and 'commercial marks' (and parts of such marks), the relative meaning of these terms, if any, will in practice depend on the relevant national laws. For example, under French law, a trademark refers to the mark of the manufacturer or producer of the product, while a 'commercial mark' refers to the mark of the distributor of the product. They should also be protected under copyright law.

[38] In general, it will be for individual States to determine which acts or practices are undertaken for purposes contrary to commercial honesty. Such practices may include those aimed at misleading consumers, as well as those generating unfair competition with other commercial entities. Practical examples might include, for instance, wrongful use of the Swiss emblem on foodstuffs or other products with the intention of showing that they have been medically tested or are otherwise related to health. Some national laws prohibiting use of the Swiss emblem (in particular those taking the form of a Geneva Conventions Act) do not identify the specific purposes of such use.

[39] In explaining this aspect of the amendment, the Swiss Government states that the use of the Swiss cross may be considered offensive if it is capable of wounding large portions of the Swiss population or when it lacks respect for the population as a whole. However, these interests need to be balanced against freedom of expression and artistic freedom. See Switzerland, Federal Council, 'Message relatif à la modification de la loi sur la protection des marques et à la loi fédérale sur la protection des armoiries de la Suisse et autres signes publics (Projet "Swissness")

3083   Read strictly, Article 53 does not provide for as wide a prohibition on the use of the Swiss emblem as that afforded the red cross emblem.[40] The second paragraph refers for the most part to commercial use of the Swiss emblem (except as set out above). Despite the somewhat restrictive language of this provision, in practice a number of States that explicitly prohibit the use of the Swiss emblem in their national legislation do so on a basis similar to that which applies to the distinctive emblems.[41] In addition, it would seem that, in practice, where misuse of the Swiss emblem occurs in contravention of Article 53, it is often in a commercial context.[42]

3084   In practice, National Societies may work with the Swiss Embassy in their respective countries, where relevant, to address reported misuses of the Swiss emblem in their territories.[43] In the case of companies registered in Switzerland, the use of Swiss national markings on products and for services is regulated by Swiss federal law.[44] The Swiss Government has indicated that, even where such use is not contrary to this legislation, it may still be prohibited where it would constitute a violation of Article 53.[45]

---

du 18 novembre 2009' ('Message concerning the amendment of the Trademark Protection Act and the Federal Act on the Protection of Swiss Coats of Arms and Other Public Insignia ('Swissness' Project) of 18 November 2009'), *Feuille fédéral*, No. 50, December 2009, pp. 7711–7846, at 7806.

[40] It would not have been possible to impose a general prohibition on use, in part because Swiss citizens and entities are permitted to use the Swiss emblem for a variety of purposes. In addition, it is interesting to note that, unlike the first paragraph of Article 53, which refers to the use of the red cross emblem, related designations, and imitations by 'individuals, societies, firms or companies either public or private', the second paragraph appears to focus primarily, or perhaps wholly, on use by 'private individuals, societies or firms'. The reason for the lack of an explicit reference to public entities in the second paragraph is unclear: one possibility may be that the drafters were primarily concerned with private, commercial misuse of the Swiss arms (of which there was much practical evidence), and did not envisage similar misuse by entities of a public nature.

[41] This appears to be more likely in those countries that have a Geneva Conventions Act, such as Australia, India, Malaysia and the United Kingdom.

[42] Commercial misuse of the Swiss emblem by third parties often occurs in a context similar to that of misuse of the red cross emblem (e.g. primarily for medical, first-aid or health-related products, as well as a variety of other circumstances). However, some charities and other non-commercial entities may also misuse the Swiss emblem, often as an indirect reference to the red cross emblem.

[43] For example, in the United Kingdom, where a misuse of the Swiss emblem or an imitation arises, the British Red Cross Society often consults the Swiss Embassy to obtain its view as to whether the user should be approached. If the individual or company is not authorized to use the Swiss emblem under relevant Swiss federal provisions, the misuse will normally be taken up by the British Red Cross.

[44] The Federal Law on the Protection of Coats of Arms and Other Public Insignia was revised in 2013 (Switzerland, *Public Insignia Law*, 1931, as amended). Previously, the Law did not allow for the use of the 'Swiss cross' (to be differentiated from the 'Swiss coat of arms' – a Swiss cross in a triangular shield – which is subject to much stricter control) on products, but only in relation to services, although this provision was not widely enforced. The revised Law permits the use of the Swiss cross on products as well as services, although such use is subject to strict conditions set out in the 2008 Federal Law on the Protection of Trademarks and Indications of Source.

[45] That is, where such use would be abusive or offensive or create confusion with the red cross emblem. See Switzerland, Federal Council, 'Message', fn. 39, pp. 7820–7821. The Swiss Federal Institute of Intellectual Property regularly addresses instances of misuse of the Swiss arms by virtue of Article 53.

3. Paragraph 3: Prior users

3085 Article 53(3) sets out an exception to the prohibition on the use of the red cross emblem, related designations, and imitations established in paragraph 1. At the time of adoption of the 1949 Geneva Conventions, it was agreed that, for those States that were already party to the 1929 Geneva Convention, the provisions prohibiting the misuse of the red cross emblem and the Swiss emblem would take effect immediately (given that the 1929 Convention had already prohibited such use).[46] For countries that were not party to the 1929 Convention, a grace period of three years could be granted to prior users of the red cross, related designations, or imitations thereof.[47] This would allow sufficient time for these States to enact and enforce national measures to prevent use of the red cross emblem, and for prior users to make the changes necessary to discontinue such use. The exception applies from the date that the Convention enters into force for a particular State.[48] Importantly, however, the three-year grace period cannot be granted where the use of the red cross emblem would appear to confer the protection of the Convention in situations of armed conflict.[49]

3086 It is not possible to determine the extent to which the exception for prior use of the red cross emblem, related designations, and imitations thereof has been utilized by States in practice. However, an examination of national legislation suggests that few countries make special provision for prior use of these signs.[50] One notable exception is the United States, which made a reservation on ratification of the 1949 Geneva Conventions concerning Article 53, to the effect that any use of the red cross emblem within its jurisdiction prior to 1905

---

[46] That is, the provision would take effect on the date that the Convention entered into force for each country.

[47] No such exception was granted to prior users of the Swiss emblem: the improper use of national flags and markings was already prohibited under other treaties (e.g. the 1883 Paris Convention for the Protection of Industrial Property) and, in many countries, national legislation.

[48] As written, the provision is unclear as to whether it was intended that the three-year grace period would begin from the original entry into force of the Convention (i.e. six months after the first two instruments of ratification had been adopted, in accordance with Article 58(1) – which occurred on 21 October 1950), or from the date that the Convention entered into force for each individual ratifying State (in accordance with Article 58(2)). Practicality and State sovereignty would suggest that the grace period should run from the time that the Convention enters into force for an individual State, in order to allow sufficient time for national measures to be imposed and for prior users to bring their products or services into line with the provision.

[49] For example, the grace period could not be granted to a doctor's surgery using a large red cross emblem to identify its premises, as this could easily be confused with the protective sign used in armed conflicts. In contrast, a small company using the red cross emblem as part of its logo could, depending on the particular circumstances, be granted a grace period to make necessary changes to the design.

[50] One exception is the Syrian Arab Republic, which prohibits the use of the red cross and red crescent emblems by unauthorized parties. Article 8 of its 2005 Emblem Law stipulates the following for prior users: 'Persons having breached provisions of this law shall be given an interim period of six (6) months to adjust their situation, starting from the date of the issuance of the law. If this period expires, penalties provided for in this law shall be applicable to persons having committed the breaches.' The six-month interim period applies to users of either the red cross or the red crescent emblem.

would not be made unlawful within its territory, provided that such use 'does not extend to the placing of the Red Cross emblem, sign, or insignia upon aircraft, vessels, vehicles, buildings or other structures, or upon the ground'.[51]

3087   Consequently, rather than granting a grace period to prior users, third parties in the United States using the red cross emblem or related designations prior to 1905 would be able to continue such use, provided that such use would not lead to confusion with the emblem or designations as a protective device.[52] It is estimated that, of approximately 20 companies or other entities in the United States considered to be 'approved users' of the red cross emblem prior to 1905, half of these continue to use the red cross emblem today.[53] In general, while the use of the red cross emblem or designations by those not entitled to do so under Article 44 cannot be considered as helpful, it would appear that such third-party use is sufficiently limited in the United States so as not to have had a generally negative impact on matters of emblem protection in that territory.[54]

---

[51] The full text of the relevant paragraph of the reservation reads:

> The United States in ratifying the Geneva Convention for the amelioration of the condition of the wounded and sick in armed forces in the field does so with the reservation that irrespective of any provision or provisions in said convention to the contrary, nothing contained therein shall make unlawful, or obligate the United States of America to make unlawful, any use or right of use within the United States of America and its territories and possessions of the Red Cross emblem, sign, insignia, or words as was lawful by reason of domestic law and a use begun prior to January 5, 1905, provided such use by pre-1905 users does not extend to the placing of the Red Cross emblem, sign, or insignia upon aircraft, vessels, vehicles, buildings or other structures, or upon the ground.

> The reservation refers to pre-1905 use because in that year the American Red Cross received a revised official charter from Congress, strengthening the rules relating to the use of the red cross emblem by entities other than the National Society (in 1948 this section of the Charter was removed, and a revised version was placed in the US Criminal Code). See http://www.redcross.org/about-us/history/federal-charter.

[52] The 'placing of the Red Cross emblem, sign, or insignia upon aircraft, vessels, vehicles, buildings or other structures, or upon the ground', as set out in the US reservation, is an action normally associated with the use of the emblem as a protective device in situations of armed conflict. See fn. 53 regarding the request for prior users (such as the Red Cross Shoe brand) to cease using the emblem or name for commercial purposes during the Second World War.

[53] One such prior user is the shoe company Nine West, which acquired the United States Shoe Corporation, the maker of the 'Red Cross shoe', in 1995. By 1939, the Red Cross Shoe brand had become the most popular shoe brand in the United States. At the request of President Roosevelt, in the 1940s the brand replaced the words 'Red Cross' with 'Gold Cross', owing to the potential for confusion with the red cross emblem (in the context of the widespread use of the emblem as a protective device during the Second World War) and with the wartime activities of the American Red Cross. It resumed its use of the name 'Red Cross Shoes' in 1948. Other companies considered to be approved pre-1905 prior users include Cargill, Inc. (Red Cross salt, dating from 1895), Gonzo products (Red Cross Nurse Disinfectant, dating from 1902) and several pharmacies. When a company acquires a brand that is considered a prior user, the right to use the emblem is transferred to the new owner. However, the use is restricted to the product or brand that originally owned the right.

[54] While an outcome of historical circumstances in the United States, any such use of the emblem or designations by third parties is far from ideal. This was demonstrated in 2008 when Johnson & Johnson, a pre-1905 user of the red cross emblem on some of its products, filed a complaint against the American Red Cross concerning the licensing by the American Red Cross of its brand (including its name and the red cross emblem) to four third-party companies for use on certain products. The basis of the claim was unfair commercial competition. While the Court eventually found in favour of the American Red Cross, it is regrettable that the circumstances

4. Paragraph 4: Other distinctive emblems

3088 Article 53(4) stipulates that the 'emblems and marks mentioned in the second paragraph of Article 38' are prohibited from use, along the same lines as those set out in paragraph 1. In spite of the mention of 'marks', as well as 'emblems', it is clear that this paragraph refers to the emblems of the red crescent and the red lion and sun, as set out in Article 38(2).

3089 This paragraph was a new insertion in the 1949 text of the present Convention. Prior to 1949, the red crescent and red lion and sun were protected under national law in the countries which used them instead of the red cross. However, there was no obligation for other States to do the same. By virtue of this paragraph, the unlawful use of these two alternative emblems is now prohibited in all States party to the Convention.[55]

3090 As paragraph 4 refers back to paragraph 1, the prohibition on the use of the red crescent and red lion and sun emblems also includes imitations of these signs. However, paragraph 4 differs from paragraph 1 in one essential respect. That is, the prohibition concerning the two alternative emblems does not affect any rights acquired through prior use; it applies only to those who claim the right to use the emblems after the Convention has come into force.[56]

3091 An examination of relevant national legislation suggests that a great number of domestic laws extend protection to the red crescent and red lion and sun emblems (in spite of the latter no longer being in use)[57] similar to that

---

leading to this case, i.e. the use of the emblem in a commercial context by both Johnson & Johnson and the American Red Cross, occurred at all. See United States, *Johnson & Johnson case*, Opinion and Order, 2008.

[55] In countries that are predominantly Muslim but which make use of the red cross as the emblem of their armed forces medical service and as the indicative sign of their National Society, the issue has arisen of other organizations, businesses or other third parties wishing to display or use a red crescent. The unlawful use of the red crescent emblem by any third-party or humanitarian organization in such contexts should be duly addressed, mindful of the confusion such use is liable to cause. This is in particular the case where there is a risk of confusion with the National Society in the country, which could undermine the Movement's Fundamental Principle of unity, which prescribes that there 'can only be one Red Cross or one Red Crescent Society in any one country'.

[56] The question of whether the prohibition on the use of the red crescent and red lion and sun emblems should apply to prior users proved to be particularly controversial during the negotiations on this provision. In order for consensus to be reached, the Turkish delegation suggested the caveat on prior use, which it said must be understood 'in the widest possible sense'. See *Final Record of the Diplomatic Conference of Geneva of 1949*, Vol. II-B, p. 240.

This exception for prior use of the red crescent and red lion and sun emblems is reflected in a number of States' domestic laws on emblem use. For example, for those countries with a Geneva Conventions Act, there is normally a provision stipulating that persons who used the red crescent or red lion and sun emblem as a registered trademark or on commercial products prior to the Act's coming into force are exempt from the prohibition on use. See e.g. Australia, *Geneva Conventions Act*, 1957, as amended, section 15(5), and Kiribati, *Geneva Conventions Act*, 1993, section 9(4).

[57] That said, some national laws on emblem use extend such protection to the red cross and red crescent emblems only, and do not include reference to the red lion and sun emblem. See e.g. Cambodia, *Red Cross or Red Crescent Emblem Law*, 2002; Morocco, *Emblem Law*, 1958; Poland, *Penal Code*, 1997; South Africa, *Emblem Act*, 2007; and Turkmenistan, *Emblem Law*, 2001. Many of these laws (although not all) were promulgated after the date by which the red lion and sun emblem ceased to be used in practice.

afforded the red cross emblem.[58] This means that not only are imitations of these emblems covered, but in many cases also the designations 'Red Crescent' and 'Red Lion and Sun', as well as imitations of these. Given that Article 53(4) is in fact silent as to whether it is also prohibited to use these designations, such national practice shows that, in many cases, States have adopted an expansive interpretation of this provision.[59] By the time Additional Protocol III was adopted in 2005, the designations 'red crescent' and 'red lion and sun' were understood as having the same protection as the other designations set out in Article 53(1).[60]

E. National implementation of Article 53

3092   Available national practice on Article 53 suggests that, although implementation varies greatly from country to country, the provision is generally applied in practice. As indicated above, a great number of States have enacted legislation giving effect to Article 53, often in more expansive terms than those of the provision itself. As mentioned previously, national legislation normally prohibits both commercial misuse of the emblems and wartime abuses. Where misuse of the emblem occurs, it is often perpetrated by entities and individuals within the medical, health and first-aid sectors, suggesting that a great many instances stem from a wrong understanding of the true meaning of the distinctive emblems.[61] There is also a particular risk of misuse of the indicative sign or National Society logo, name, or imitation thereof, for fraudulent purposes.

---

[58] Examples of States extending similar protection to all of the distinctive emblems include Australia, Canada, Germany, Estonia, Indonesia, Israel (which also extends protection to its own emblem, the Red Shield of David), Singapore, Sri Lanka and the United Kingdom.

[59] For those States that have ratified Additional Protocol III, their national legislation should also prohibit use of the red crystal emblem, the designations 'red crystal' and 'third Protocol emblem', and imitations thereof, in accordance with Article 6(1) of that Protocol. Article 6(2) allows an exception to be granted to prior users of the red crystal emblem or related designations, similar to the exception provided for prior users of the red crescent and red lion and sun emblems in Article 53(4) of the present Convention. It should be noted that, while Article 2(1) of Additional Protocol III designated the additional emblem as the 'third Protocol emblem', the 29th International Conference of the Red Cross and Red Crescent decided that the additional emblem would be designated as the 'red crystal' (29th International Conference of the Red Cross and Red Crescent, Geneva, 2006, Res. 1, para. 2). This somewhat unusual procedure is an illustration of the fact that States attend the International Conference in their capacity as States party to the 1949 Geneva Conventions, and also demonstrates the close links between the International Conference and international humanitarian law.

[60] Article 6(1) of Additional Protocol III requires States Parties to take measures necessary to prevent and repress any misuse of the emblems mentioned in Articles 1 and 2 of the Protocol, as well as their designations.

[61] On this point, Meyer comments that '[i]n countries like the United Kingdom which for the most part have been spared armed conflict for the past 40 years, the red cross emblem has frequently become closely identified with first aid and with general health or medical care, its primary and unique meaning during armed conflict often being forgotten or unknown. For this reason it is perhaps particularly important for National Societies in such countries to help the authorities monitor unauthorized uses or misuses of the emblems' (Meyer, p. 459). In recent years, considerable efforts have been undertaken in a number of countries to encourage the use of specific symbols for first-aid activities (in many cases, a white cross on a green background)

This may be the case, for instance, in attempts to divert funds intended for Movement components in support of their humanitarian activities.

3093   Many National Societies play a key role in supporting their governments' implementation of Article 53.[62] The ICRC may also assist in these efforts, where required, in order to build national capacity.[63] The International Federation of Red Cross and Red Crescent Societies may assist too, when requested. Such a role is normally carried out by instigating a dialogue with each alleged misuser. The experience of a number of countries indicates that the implementation of Article 53 through legal action is a rarity;[64] most of the time, on being contacted by the National Society, the misuser will agree to cease use of the emblem, designation or imitation thereof.[65] While this outcome is positive and preferable, from the perspective of emblem protection, it may in fact be useful for court proceedings to be initiated, where required, in order to raise awareness of the significance of the emblems and of the legal restrictions on their use. Such actions would also demonstrate publicly the will of States to give effect to their international and domestic legal obligations.

and for a variety of medical services (such as the blue star of life for ambulance services). For further information about such alternative signs, see the commentary on Article 44, para. 2695.

[62] See Statutes of the International Red Cross and Red Crescent Movement (1986), Article 3(2), third paragraph. It should also be noted that third parties normally unable to use the distinctive emblems or their designations in accordance with Article 53 may, in some cases, be permitted to do so within certain limits, owing to the existence of a partnership with a National Red Cross or Red Crescent Society. According to the terms of the partnership, for example, the third party may be authorized to include the logo of the National Society (which normally includes the red cross emblem or the red crescent emblem, accompanied by the name of the National Society) on materials it produces about the partnership, subject to certain conditions. However, use of the emblem on third-party items for sale is prohibited. This type of third-party use is provided for in the 1991 Emblem Regulations. See also the commentary on Article 44, paras 2683–2684.

[63] This forms an integral part of the ICRC's mandate as a guardian of international humanitarian law and of its cooperation with National Societies; see Statutes of the International Red Cross and Red Crescent Movement (1986), Article 5(2)(c) and (g) and (4)(a).

[64] One such rare case in the United Kingdom in 1988 concerned the public distribution by the Labour Party (at that time the leading opposition political party) of a leaflet bearing a design of a pound sterling sign superimposed on a red cross, against a yellow background. The aim of the leaflet was to support a campaign against cuts to health care. Despite being approached repeatedly by both the British Red Cross Society and the Ministry of Defence, the Labour Party refused to withdraw the design. Aside from being wrongfully used to represent health care, of particular concern in this instance was the fact that a design similar to the red cross emblem was being used on a wide scale for a political purpose, thereby serving to undermine the emblem's neutrality. In a case brought by the UK Government, the Labour Party's general secretary was found guilty of contravening section 6 of the 1957 Geneva Conventions Act (referring to unauthorized use of the distinctive emblems, designations and similar designs). A separate case was also brought against a newspaper editor who had published the design in support of the Labour Party's campaign; he was also convicted. The process of resolving this matter through the courts was not without difficulty (Meyer, pp. 463–464).

[65] This is the experience of the Swiss Red Cross Society and of the British Red Cross Society, and appears to be the case in a number of countries. Frequently, misusers will be unaware of the restrictions on the use of the distinctive emblems, related designations, and imitations thereof; simply bringing these to the attention of misusers may be sufficient to compel them to cease such use. The approach of the British Red Cross is elaborated in Meyer, p. 461.

3094   National Societies may also encourage adherence to Article 53 by conducting awareness-raising campaigns on the true meaning of the distinctive emblems and the restrictions on their use within their territories.[66]

Select bibliography

ICRC, *Study on the Use of the Emblems: Operational and Commercial and Other Non-Operational Issues*, ICRC, Geneva, 2011.

Leach, Leslie, 'Nepal Red Cross Society: Emblem Protection Campaign Review', report produced by the Nepal Red Cross Society and the ICRC, February 2007.

Meyer, Michael A., 'Protecting the emblems in peacetime: The experiences of the British Red Cross Society', *International Review of the Red Cross*, Vol. 29, No. 272, October 1989, pp. 459–464.

---

[66] One such campaign was implemented by the Nepal Red Cross Society in 2001. The national campaign aimed to address the widespread misuse of the red cross emblem across Nepal. It is reported that by 2006, 73 out of 75 districts had been declared 'emblem-misuse-free' and the majority of former misusers, including hospitals, clinics, pharmacies, ambulances and others, had begun to use their own logos (Leach, p. 4).

PREVENTION OF MISUSE OF THE EMBLEM

❖ Text of the provision

The High Contracting Parties shall, if their legislation is not already adequate, take measures necessary for the prevention and repression, at all times, of the abuses referred to under Article 53.

❖ Reservations or declarations

None

Contents

A. Introduction

3095 Article 54 places a positive obligation on States Parties to take the necessary measures to prevent and repress abuses of the distinctive emblems, their designations and other protected signs, as set out under Article 53. States are required to prevent and repress such abuses at all times. Consequently, the measures taken must address abuses both in time of peace and in time of armed conflict. Failure to regulate use of the emblems in peacetime may contribute to abuse in situations of armed conflict.[1]

3096 Article 54 requires States to take the necessary measures in the event that their legislation is not already adequate. This means that, apart from the

---

[1] ICRC, *Study on the Use of the Emblems*, p. 281.

administrative measures incumbent on the competent authorities, each country must enact legislation to prohibit and punish misuse of the emblems at all times.

B. Historical background

3097   As early as 1864, proposals were made to include in the original Geneva Convention a provision on the punishment of persons using the brassard displaying the red cross emblem as a cover for spying.[2] A provision worded similarly to Article 54 was first included in the 1906 Geneva Convention.[3] The provision was later expanded upon in the 1929 Geneva Convention on the Wounded and Sick.[4] Neither of these earlier articles made it mandatory for States to adopt the measures necessary to prevent and repress abuses of the emblem: for example, under Article 28 of the 1929 Convention, the governments of the High Contracting Parties were simply required to 'adopt or propose to their legislatures' such measures.[5] By the time of the adoption of the 1949 Geneva Conventions, most domestic legislation was still considered to be inadequate with respect to this provision.[6]

3098   In 1949, the text of Article 28 was revised and incorporated into two separate provisions: Articles 53 and 54 of the First Convention.[7] Importantly, the language of Article 54 was strengthened so that the provision could no longer be interpreted as discretionary, as is evident from the use of the word 'shall'. The obligation was reiterated with regard to all of the distinctive emblems of the Geneva Conventions in Article 6(1) of Additional Protocol III (entitled 'Prevention and repression of misuse').

C. Discussion

3099   Under Article 54, States must introduce specific domestic legislation to regulate use of the distinctive emblems, their designations and other protected signs, where existing provisions are deemed inadequate.[8] Consequently, wherever domestic legislation is deemed to be inadequate, it must be amended.[9] To

---

[2] Perruchoud, p. 210.   [3] Geneva Convention (1906), Article 27(1).
[4] Geneva Convention on the Wounded and Sick (1929), Article 28(1).   [5] *Ibid.*
[6] In his commentary on Article 54, Pictet noted that: 'In most cases, however, national legislation is still most inadequate, even in regard to the 1929 stipulations.' Pictet (ed.), *Commentary on the First Geneva Convention*, ICRC, 1952, p. 393.
[7] See the commentary on Article 53, para. 3072.
[8] These are not the only national measures required under the 1949 Geneva Conventions and their Additional Protocols. For example, States must also ensure that their domestic legislation provides for the punishment of grave breaches of the Geneva Conventions and, where applicable, Additional Protocol I, as well as for the protection of the fundamental guarantees provided for in these instruments. Segall, p. 71.
[9] The provision is so broad that it necessarily encompasses the obligation to enact legislation dealing with challenges that emerge long after its adoption. For example, it applies to all potential misuse of the emblems in the digital sphere.

date, over 130 countries are recorded as having introduced one or more forms of domestic legislation to prevent and repress misuse of one or more of the distinctive emblems, their designations and other protected signs.[10]

1. Form and placement of legislation

3100   Article 54 does not specify where in a State's domestic legal framework such measures should be incorporated, nor the exact form they should take. In practice, these aspects will depend on the State's particular legal system and national traditions.[11] In States with monist systems,[12] specific provisions to give effect to Article 54 will normally need to be introduced into the legislation, over and above the general 'ratification law' adopted as part of the treaty accession procedure.[13] In States with dualist systems, separate implementing legislation is usually required to give domestic effect to major treaty obligations, including those arising from the 1949 Geneva Conventions. This implementing legislation may include provisions on the regulation of the use of the distinctive emblems, their designations and other protected signs. Regardless of a State's legal system, comprehensive implementation of Article 54 normally requires stand-alone legislation and/or the incorporation of relevant provisions into a variety of domestic laws and regulations, including one or more of the following:

– Geneva Conventions Act[14]

---

[10] As recorded in the ICRC's National Implementation of IHL database, available at https://www
.icrc.org/ihl-nat. Not all of these countries will have comprehensive legislation protecting all
of the distinctive emblems, their designations and related signs. For example, some may only
include protection of the specific emblem and designation used in their own territory.

[11] For example, the ICRC's Advisory Service on International Humanitarian Law, when advising
governments on the implementation of Article 54, takes an individual, State-by-State approach
to such matters.

[12] In a monist system, treaties normally take direct effect in domestic law. States with civil-law
traditions are usually monist, while common-law States are normally dualist. Some countries
may use a mixture of both systems. In some States, treaties may be 'self-executing' and may
not necessarily require implementing legislation; see Anthony Aust, *Modern Treaty Law and
Practice*, 3rd edition, Cambridge University Press, 2013, pp. 163–167, and David Sloss, 'Domestic Application of Treaties', in Duncan B. Hollis (ed.), *The Oxford Guide to Treaties*, Oxford
University Press, 2012, pp. 367–395, at 373–376.

[13] The 'ratification law' is normally adopted by parliament and published in the official gazette.
Many provisions in international humanitarian law treaties require the adoption of more than
what a typical ratification law contains (e.g. emblem protection measures, the establishment
of a national information bureau, etc.). ICRC, *The Domestic Implementation of International
Humanitarian Law*, p. 24 (a summary of provisions of the Geneva Conventions and their Additional Protocols requiring national implementation measures is set out at p. 60).

[14] States with common-law systems will often (but not always) have a Geneva Conventions Act
that includes provisions on regulation of the distinctive emblems, their designations and other
protected signs. It is estimated that approximately 28 countries have adopted a Geneva Conventions Act. These include, among others, Australia, Botswana, Canada, Ghana, India, Ireland,
Malawi, Malaysia, New Zealand, Nigeria, Papua New Guinea, Singapore, the United Kingdom
and Vanuatu. In Kenya and Uganda, where the legal systems of both countries are a mix of
English common law and African customary law, the emblem is protected in laws other than a
Geneva Conventions Act, although both countries also have such Acts.

- Criminal Code[15]
- Code of Military Justice[16]
- Civil Code[17]
- Law on the use and protection of the distinctive emblems[18]
- Law establishing the National Red Cross or Red Crescent Society[19]
- Law on war crimes (including those implementing the 1998 ICC Statute)[20]
- Emergency Act[21]
- Trade Marks Act[22]

3101   Penalties for abuses of the distinctive emblems, their designations or other protected signs (whether by military personnel or by civilians) occurring in situations of armed conflict should normally be included in relevant legislation covering violations of the laws and customs of war. This would include, for example, a Geneva Conventions Act or other specific law addressing serious violations of humanitarian law, as well as the Code of Military Justice. Additionally, in practice such abuses may be dealt with in other pieces of legislation, including the Criminal Code (in particular for civil-law countries), law on the distinctive emblems, or the law establishing the National Red Cross or Red Crescent Society.

---

[15] States with civil-law systems may include relevant provisions in their criminal/penal codes: e.g. Azerbaijan, Croatia, Denmark, Ethiopia, France, Georgia, Indonesia, Norway, Poland, the Russian Federation and Venezuela. This is less usual in countries with a common-law system, where criminal offences are often included in the relevant implementing legislation (e.g. the Geneva Conventions Act). One exception is the United States, which, while having a legal system based on common law, includes relevant offences in its Criminal Code (*Geneva Distinctive Emblems Code*, 1948, as amended by the *Geneva Distinctive Emblems Protection Act*, 2006).

[16] For example, Algeria, France, Mali, Mexico, Niger, Spain, Switzerland and Tunisia.

[17] For example, Germany includes relevant provisions in its Civil Code (as well as in other legislation).

[18] States with stand-alone legislation protecting the distinctive emblems include Belarus, Bolivia, Guatemala, Montenegro, Nicaragua, the Philippines, Serbia and Tajikistan.

[19] Some countries include emblem provisions only in the law establishing or recognizing the National Red Cross or Red Crescent Society (sometimes referred to as the Red Cross or Red Crescent Act). Examples include Antigua and Barbuda, Belize, the People's Republic of China, Haiti, Jordan, Malta, the Republic of Korea, Thailand and Zambia. Other countries, such as Austria, Lithuania and South Africa, have incorporated emblem provisions in the law establishing the National Society and in other instruments. While perhaps understandable, such practice may not be ideal. This is because National Red Cross and Red Crescent Societies are not primarily responsible for regulation of the distinctive emblems: States bear this responsibility in line with their obligations under humanitarian law.

[20] For example, Chile includes unauthorized use of the red cross emblem as an offence in its *Law on Crimes against Humanity, Genocide and War Crimes*, 2009, Article 34. This legislation is in addition to Chile's *Emblem Law*, 1939, as amended.

[21] One such example is Brunei Darussalam's *National Society Incorporation Act*, 1990.

[22] A number of countries, such as Canada, Japan and Malaysia, include relevant provisions under trademark legislation (whether primary or secondary legislation), as well as in other instruments (such as a Geneva Conventions Act or other law). Some others, such as Qatar, only include relevant provisions in trademark legislation. See also Article 13 of the ICRC's Model Law on the Use of the Emblem, which commits national trademark offices to refuse the 'registration of associations and trade names, and the filing of trademarks, commercial marks and industrial models and designs making use of the emblem of the red cross, the red crescent or the red crystal or the designation "red cross", "red crescent" or "red crystal" in violation of the present law'.

2. Non-legislative measures

3102 The measures referred to in Article 54 may include those of a non-legislative nature. Perhaps chief among these is raising awareness of the significance of the distinctive emblems and of the consequent legal restrictions on their use. Such dissemination may take the form of, for example, military manuals and guidance issued by national trademark registries.[23] Another practical measure is the monitoring role that many National Red Cross and Red Crescent Societies (hereinafter 'National Societies') can play with respect to misuse of the distinctive emblems within their national territories. Further, private organizations may take administrative measures to help protect the emblems and designations.[24]

3. Preventive and repressive measures

3103 Article 54 stipulates the need for measures to be aimed at both the prevention and repression of abuses. Prevention refers to measures designed to counteract misuse of the distinctive emblems and their designations before they occur, for example:

- The adoption of national legislation and regulations, including sufficiently strong sanctions, to deter misuse;
- Promoting awareness of the significance of the distinctive emblems and of the consequent legal restrictions on their use among the armed forces, the police forces, the concerned authorities, the civilian population, and other relevant groups such as health professionals, non-governmental organizations and commercial entities;
- The adoption in peacetime of measures to regulate use of the distinctive emblems in armed conflict.[25]

3104　Repressive measures are normally those designed to stop or punish misuse, such as unauthorized use of the distinctive emblems by third parties.

---

[23] National Red Cross and Red Crescent Societies have a formally recognized role in supporting their respective governments in relation to dissemination. See section C.5.

[24] One example of relevant measures taken by a private (non-profit) organization are those instigated by the Internet Corporation for Assigned Names and Numbers (ICANN) to help prevent registration of the protected designations as new top- or second-level domain names. Such measures include a temporary reservation on registration of the designations as top-level domain names, as approved by ICANN's Board on 20 June 2011. Components of the International Red Cross and Red Crescent Movement are at present working with ICANN's various constituency bodies to encourage a confirmation of the permanent protection of the designations. Another example is the inclusion of items bearing the distinctive emblems and/or designations as part of the Prohibited Items Policy of the online marketplace eBay, applicable across a number of countries in Europe.

[25] This should include identification of the competent authority empowered to authorize use of the emblems in the event of an armed conflict. It could also include the measures to be taken by a National Red Cross or Red Crescent Society at the beginning of an armed conflict, to avoid any confusion with the indicative use of the emblem (Article 7 of the 1991 Emblem Regulations).

They may include fines, forfeiture of goods connected with the offence, and/or imprisonment.[26] Many laws provide for a minimum and a maximum penalty without establishing the criteria for determining the level of severity of the penalty. In some cases, the amount of the fine or the length of imprisonment may vary depending on the circumstances in which the offence was committed, such as during armed conflict.[27] A higher penalty may also apply to repeat offenders.[28]

3105   Over the years, there has been a relatively small number of court actions regarding unauthorized use of the distinctive emblems, including in Austria, Canada, France, Germany, the Netherlands, Norway, Switzerland and the United Kingdom.[29] States are responsible for repressing violations regardless of whether the National Society has expressed concern to relevant public authorities or objected to an unlawful use of the emblem. In practice, it would seem that the most effective means of preventing unauthorized use is through enhanced public awareness and understanding of the meaning of the distinctive emblems. That said, for legislation to have an appropriate deterrent effect, it is essential that prosecutions are instituted, where necessary.

4. Red crystal emblem

3106   The 2005 Additional Protocol III to the 1949 Geneva Conventions extends the obligation to prevent and repress misuse of the distinctive emblems, their designations and other protected signs to the red crystal emblem and designation.[30] To this end, States party to Additional Protocol III should make suitable

---

[26] In some countries, interim relief, such as injunctions, may be available. For example, the French Red Cross Society was able to take swift action in seeking such a measure regarding the misuse of the emblem in the James Bond film 'The Living Daylights' (see Meyer, p. 463). Civil servants may additionally risk disciplinary sanctions under some national laws; see e.g. Colombia, *Emblem Law*, 2004, Article 13.

[27] For example, Belgium has differing penalties for misuse of the distinctive emblems or their designations in peacetime and in armed conflict; see Belgium, *Law on Protection of the Emblem*, 1956, Articles 1 and 2. In armed conflict there may also be so-called perfidious use of a distinctive emblem. The First Convention did not identify such use as a 'grave breach' of the Convention. This was rectified by Article 85(3)(f) of Additional Protocol I and means that, for States party to that Protocol, the penalty for perfidious use is very likely to be more severe.

[28] See e.g. Guinea, *Emblem Law*, 1995, Article 11.

[29] It should be noted that, while some of these were criminal prosecutions, others took the form of civil court actions. For further information about relevant UK cases, see Meyer, pp. 459–464, and Sassòli/Bouvier/Quintin, p. 621. Other cases may be found in the ICRC's National Implementation of IHL database, available at https://www.icrc.org/ihl-nat.

[30] Additional Protocol III, Article 6(1). It should be noted that, while Article 2(1) of the Protocol designated the additional emblem as the 'third Protocol emblem', the 29th International Conference of the Red Cross and Red Crescent decided that the additional emblem would be designated as the 'red crystal' (29th International Conference of the Red Cross and Red Crescent, Geneva, 2006, Res. 1, para. 2). This somewhat unusual procedure is an illustration of the fact that States attend the International Conference in their capacity as States party to the 1949 Geneva Conventions, and also demonstrates the close links between the International Conference and international humanitarian law. It would be helpful for States to enact legislation regulating use of both designations, i.e. 'third Protocol emblem' and 'red crystal'.

amendments to their emblem protection legislation, and take any additional measures deemed necessary. Provisions protecting the red crystal emblem and designation have been introduced in a number of countries.[31]

5. Assisting bodies

3107 There are various bodies that may assist States in adopting and/or implementing the measures necessary to give effect to Article 54. For example, a number of countries have established national committees on international humanitarian law.[32] While these are not legally required, they have proven effective in supporting States in relation to national implementation of humanitarian law treaties. Such support includes assistance in developing national measures to address misuse of the distinctive emblems, their designations and other signs protected under humanitarian law.

3108 The specific role of national committees will depend on their mandate and composition, as well as on governmental practices in the individual State. Committees comprising relevant government officials may have a role in drafting national legislation to incorporate humanitarian law, including provisions on emblem use, at the domestic level. Other committees may not have such a direct role, but may still fulfil a useful function by encouraging the government departments directly concerned to draw up and adopt the necessary legislation.[33]

3109 In addition, the ICRC runs an Advisory Service on International Humanitarian Law, created on the recommendation of the Intergovernmental Group of Experts for the Protection of War Victims, which was endorsed by the 26th International Conference of the Red Cross and Red Crescent in 1995. The purpose of the service is to assist States in enacting domestic legislation, through the provision of technical assistance and relevant publications, such as ratification kits and model laws. The Advisory Service has drafted a model law on protection of the emblem,[34] as well as a model Geneva Conventions

---

[31] See e.g. Belgium, Canada, Cyprus, Lithuania, the Philippines, Singapore, the United Kingdom and the United States.

[32] The ICRC reported that, as at 30 September 2015, national committees for the implementation of international humanitarian law, or similar bodies, existed in 107 countries. A full list of such committees may be found at https://www.icrc.org/eng/resources/documents/misc/table-national-committees.htm. By region, at present Africa and Europe have the largest number of national committees (29 each), followed by the Americas (19).

[33] Third Universal Meeting of National Committees for the Implementation of International Humanitarian Law, Geneva, 27–29 October 2010, Responses of the United Kingdom Interdepartmental Committee on International Humanitarian Law to the Working Group Questions.

[34] Model Law on the Emblems: National Legislation on the Use and Protection of the Emblem of the Red Cross, Red Crescent and the Red Crystal. Designed primarily for use by States with civil-law systems, the model law may also be useful for those States with common-law systems which require additional provisions to those contained in their Geneva Conventions Acts.

Act.[35] As part of its mandate under the Statutes of the International Red Cross and Red Crescent Movement to work for the faithful application of international humanitarian law, the ICRC has a role in ensuring that the normative framework regulating the use and protection of the emblems is known, understood and properly applied, including in situations of armed conflict.

3110   Lastly, National Red Cross and Red Crescent Societies have a formal responsibility to cooperate with their governments to ensure respect for humanitarian law and to protect the distinctive emblems.[36] Many National Societies carry out monitoring and dissemination activities in this regard.[37] In addition, National Societies may assist in promoting the true meaning and special purpose of the emblem in their respective territories by ensuring that their own use is in conformity with the Geneva Conventions and other established rules.[38]

D. National implementation of Article 54

3111   Article 54 makes it mandatory for States to take the measures necessary to prevent and repress, at all times, abuses of the distinctive emblems, their designations and other protected signs. Many States have taken steps to give effect to this obligation. These may be found in both domestic legislation and in non-legislative measures. There is no one form of legislative or practical measures used by States to give effect to Article 54. Rather, the nature of such measures will depend on the legal tradition of each State.

3112   Although there have been some prosecutions for unauthorized use, in practice the most effective means of deterring abuses is by promoting public awareness and understanding of the meaning of the distinctive emblems and of the need to restrict their use in order to preserve their protective value. For this to be effective, each State must take a continuing interest in ensuring that

---

[35] Model Law Geneva Conventions (Consolidation) Act: Legislation for Common Law States on the 1949 Geneva Conventions and their 1977 and 2005 Additional Protocols. Part IV of the Model Law deals with the emblem.

[36] Such activities form part of National Societies' permanent status and role as auxiliaries to their respective public authorities in the humanitarian field. See Statutes of the International Red Cross and Red Crescent Movement (1986), Article 3(2)(3). See also Meyer, pp. 459–464, and ICRC, Study on the Use of the Emblems, pp. 290–293.

[37] Such monitoring and dissemination can include a range of activities, such as contacting third parties reported to have misused the emblem, designation or an imitation thereof, as and when required, and publishing and circulating materials on the meaning and purpose of the emblems. Some National Societies have also undertaken large-scale campaigns throughout their territory aimed at preventing such abuse: for example, in 2001 the Nepal Red Cross Society undertook such a campaign at a time of armed conflict within Nepal. The campaign was reportedly highly successful, with a majority of hospitals, clinics, pharmacies, ambulances and other former misusers reverting to other identifying signs or designs. For further information, see Leslie Leach, 'Nepal Red Cross Society: Emblem Protection Campaign Review', report produced by the Nepal Red Cross Society and the ICRC, February 2007.

[38] Use of the emblem by National Societies is governed by, in particular, Article 44 of the First Convention and by the 1991 Emblem Regulations. For further information on the use of the emblem by National Societies, see the commentary on Article 44.

the integrity of the emblems is upheld. This may need to include prosecutions where these are required. Without such steadfast governmental interest, there is a real risk that, in practice, the emblems will lose their unique status and protective functions when they are required most.

3113   Different bodies, including National Societies, have a recognized role in working with State authorities to protect the emblems, their designations and other protected signs.

Select bibliography

ICRC, *Study on the Use of the Emblems: Operational and Commercial and Other Non-Operational Issues*, ICRC, Geneva, 2011.
– *The Domestic Implementation of International Humanitarian Law: A Manual*, ICRC, Geneva, 1st edition 2011, updated edition 2015.
Meyer, Michael A., 'Protecting the emblems in peacetime: The experiences of the British Red Cross Society', *International Review of the Red Cross*, Vol. 29, No. 272, October 1989, pp. 459–464.
Perruchoud, Richard, *Les résolutions des Conférences internationales de la Croix-Rouge*, Henry Dunant Institute, Geneva, 1979.
Sassòli, Marco, Bouvier, Antoine A. and Quintin, Anne, *How Does Law Protect in War?*, Vol. II, 3rd edition, ICRC, Geneva, 2011.
Segall, Anna, *Punishing Violations of International Humanitarian Law at the National Level: A Guide for Common Law States – Drawing on the proceedings of a meeting of experts (Geneva, 11–13 November 1998)*, ICRC, Geneva, 2001.

FINAL PROVISIONS

3114 The procedural, formal and diplomatic provisions which it is customary to place at the end of any treaty are grouped under this heading. The final provisions, except for Article 55 (Languages), correspond largely to the provisions of the 1929 Conventions.[1] The final provisions are nearly identical in all four 1949 Geneva Conventions.[2]

1. Purpose and content

3115 Under this heading are grouped the technical clauses common to all treaties, which, in the Conventions, are very similar to those of all multilateral treaties. They concern the procedure for becoming a Party to the Conventions, entry into force, languages and depositary functions such as notification and registration. Like many other treaties, the Conventions are silent with regard to reservations; thus, these follow the rules of general international law.[3]

3116 Some special features in the final clauses are justified by the humanitarian aim of the Conventions. Examples would be the small number of Parties necessary for their entry into force, the immediate effect given to ratifications and accessions in certain circumstances, and the restrictions that apply to the effects of denunciation.[4]

2. Depositary

3117 A treaty's depositary is normally designated by the treaty. Before the establishment of the League of Nations and later of the United Nations, only States

---

[1] See the commentaries on the respective articles, the section on the historical background.

[2] Owing to differences in the treaties preceding the four individual Geneva Conventions, the two exceptions are the provision on signature (Article 56 of the First Convention, Article 55 of the Second Convention, Article 136 of the Third Convention and Article 151 of the Fourth Convention) and the provision on the Convention's relation to previous Conventions (Article 59 of the First Convention, Article 58 of the Second Convention, Articles 134–135 of the Third Convention and Article 154 of the Fourth Convention).

[3] On the subject of reservations, see the commentary on Article 57, section C.2.

[4] See Articles 58, 62 and 63.

were depositaries. Since then, international organizations have increasingly been entrusted with depositary functions.[5]

3118   The Geneva Conventions designate Switzerland as the depositary.[6] To be more precise, the provisions under this heading, as well as the testimonium and signature clause, refer to the depositary by the name given to the government of Switzerland, the 'Swiss Federal Council'.[7] The Swiss Federal Council has delegated the task of depositary to the Directorate of International Law of the Federal Department of Foreign Affairs.[8]

3. Vienna Convention on the Law of Treaties

3119   The Vienna Convention on the Law of Treaties was adopted 20 years after the Geneva Conventions and therefore does not apply to the Geneva Conventions qua treaty law.[9] However, because the Vienna Convention generally reflects customary international law, it can be relied upon in relation to the Geneva Conventions. Further details are provided in the references to the Vienna Convention in the commentaries in this chapter.

---

[5] See United Nations, Office of Legal Affairs, Treaty Section, *Summary of practice of the Secretary-General as depositary of multilateral treaties*, UN Doc. ST/LEG/7/Rev.1, United Nations, New York, 1999, p. 3, para. 2.

[6] Switzerland has always been appointed as depositary of the Geneva Conventions, though not explicitly in the 1864 Geneva Convention; see, nevertheless, Article 15(1) of the Additional Articles to the 1864 Geneva Convention (1868) that never entered into force. See also Geneva Convention (1906), Articles 28(2), 32(2), 33(1) and the testimonium; Geneva Convention on the Wounded and Sick (1929), Articles 29(2), 32, 36, 37, 38(1), 39 and the testimonium; and Geneva Convention on Prisoners of War (1929), Articles 85, 91, 94, 95, 96(1), 97 and the testimonium.

[7] See Article 55 (Languages), Article 57 (Ratification), Article 61 (Notification of Accessions), Article 62 (Immediate Effect), Article 63 (Denunciation) and Article 64 (Registration with the United Nations), as well as the testimonium and signature clause.

[8] See Switzerland, Conseil fédéral et administration fédérale, *Ordonnance sur l'organisation du Département fédéral des affaires étrangères*, RS 172.211.1, 20 April 2011, Article 8(3)(d) *in fine* (the Directorate of Public International Law 'assume la fonction de dépositaire').

[9] See Vienna Convention on the Law of Treaties (1969), Article 4.

ARTICLE 55

LANGUAGES

❖ Text of the provision*

(1) The present Convention is established in English and in French. Both texts are equally authentic.

(2) The Swiss Federal Council shall arrange for official translations of the Convention to be made in the Russian and Spanish languages.

❖ Reservations or declarations

None

Contents

A. Introduction and historical background

3120 Until the early twentieth century, most multilateral treaties were written in only one or two languages. The 1929 Geneva Conventions, for example, were concluded only in French, which was still the leading diplomatic language at that time.

3121 Since the emergence of the League of Nations, and later of the United Nations, most treaties have been written in several languages. A treaty may be authenticated, i.e. recognized as a true original, in one or several languages, depending on the decision of the body which adopts it. By means of authentication, the negotiators declare that the text corresponds to their intention and is

---

* Paragraph numbers have been added for ease of reference.

definitive.[1] The languages that are declared authentic will in general be those in which the body concerned conducted its work, or at least in which it adopted the treaty.

3122   The 1949 Conventions were drafted simultaneously in English and French. Throughout the Diplomatic Conference of 1949, as well as during the preparatory work, two versions of each Convention were drawn up simultaneously. French and English were both recognized on an equal footing as official languages for the purpose of discussion, as well as for the publication of all documents.[2]

3123   However many authentic language versions there are, the principle of a single treaty has to be guaranteed.[3] This is recognized in Article 55(1) of the First Convention which declares both the English and French texts as 'equally authentic'.

3124   This paragraph, providing for two equally authentic language versions, was already contained in the draft prepared by the ICRC for the 1948 International Conference of the Red Cross in Stockholm (Stockholm draft), which adopted it without change.[4] The changes introduced at the Diplomatic Conference in 1949, including the addition of the second paragraph mandating the depositary to arrange for official translations in Russian and Spanish, are discussed below.

3125   This provision is common to the four Conventions.[5] The equally authentic nature of the English and French versions therefore applies to the four Conventions. Similarly, official translations in Russian and Spanish of all Conventions have been arranged.

B. Paragraph 1: Languages of the Convention

1. Authentic texts

3126   The first paragraph begins by noting that the Convention has been drawn up in English and in French. It then determines that the two texts are 'equally authentic'. Therefore, each text carries the same weight and is as valid as the other. It was to the English version just as much as to the French that the Plenipotentiaries appended their signatures in 1949–1950. In the same way, ratifications and accessions are valid for the two versions and cannot be limited to one version only. States which are party to the Convention are equally bound by both language versions.

---

[1] See Vienna Convention on the Law of Treaties (1969), Article 10, which is declaratory of customary international law (Villiger, p. 171).

[2] See Rule 38 of the Rules of Procedure, *Final Record of the Diplomatic Conference of Geneva of 1949*, Vol. I, pp. 187–188.

[3] See Sinclair, p. 148; Villiger, p. 458; and Papaux and Samson, pp. 869–870, paras 11–12.

[4] See *Draft Conventions submitted to the 1948 Stockholm Conference*, Article 43, p. 31, and *Draft Conventions adopted by the 1948 Stockholm Conference*, Article 43, p. 27.

[5] See Second Convention, Article 54; Third Convention, Article 133; and Fourth Convention, Article 150.

3127   The solution thus adopted was consistent with the most recent international practice at the time. It may help to make interpretation of the Convention easier: when the different versions are compared, one sheds light on the other. But a problem might arise when the texts are divergent or contradictory. It can sometimes be difficult to give exact expression to the same idea in different languages.

2. Divergence

3128   A treaty may provide that, in case of divergence between the authentic versions, a particular text shall prevail as the authoritative text.[6] To overcome the potential divergence between the French and the English text, the Stockholm draft provided that, where doubt existed as to the interpretation of a provision, the French version should be taken as the authoritative one.[7] But this proposal was not adopted by the Diplomatic Conference of 1949.[8]

3129   The approach chosen instead, namely that both languages are 'equally authentic' without one of them prevailing in case of divergence, means that both versions are 'equally authoritative'.[9] It may therefore be presumed that both versions have exactly the same meaning and that each of them faithfully represents the provisions as adopted by the Diplomatic Conference.[10] It is therefore possible, in principle, to consult a single language version on the presumption that it correctly reflects the common will of the Parties, and that the provisions are expressed in the same way in the other version.[11] A careful effort was made throughout the Conference to make sure that the draft provisions in each language matched precisely, although the Conference had little possibility just before the opening for signature to ensure that the two versions of the text corresponded exactly. A comparison of the authentic texts may therefore reveal a difference in meaning or obvious errors. Examples are discussed in the commentaries on the provisions concerned.[12]

3130   When a comparison of the authentic texts discloses a difference in meaning, and the treaty does not provide for a particular version to prevail, as is the case for the Geneva Conventions, the 1969 Vienna Convention on the Law of Treaties provides for the application first of the general rules of interpretation

---

[6] This possibility is now provided for in Article 33(1) of the 1969 Vienna Convention on the Law of Treaties.

[7] See *Draft Conventions submitted to the 1948 Stockholm Conference*, Article 43, p. 31, and *Draft Conventions adopted by the 1948 Stockholm Conference*, Article 43, p. 27.

[8] See *Final Record of the Diplomatic Conference of Geneva of 1949*, Vol. I, p. 56, and Vol. II-B, pp. 25, 30, 70–71 and 112–113.

[9] See Vienna Convention on the Law of Treaties (1969), Article 33(1).

[10] See *ibid.* Article 33(3): 'The terms of the treaty are presumed to have the same meaning in each authentic text.' See also ICJ, *Kasikili/Sedudu Island case*, Judgment, 1999, para. 25.

[11] Villiger, p. 458.

[12] See the commentary on common Article 3, para. 625 and Article 25, para. 2027, fn. 21.

and then of the supplementary means.[13] If the difference in meaning cannot be removed in this manner, the meaning which best reconciles the texts, having regard to the object and purpose of the treaty, must be adopted.[14]

3131   Obvious errors in typing, printing, spelling or punctuation can also be corrected when the signatory and contracting States agree that this should be done. In 1949, a list of errata, for both the English and the French version, was added to each of the original texts of the four Conventions. These errata were incorporated in the certified true copies delivered by the Swiss Federal Council to the signatory and acceding States, pursuant to the testimonium at the end of the Convention.[15] Pursuant to the Vienna Convention on the Law of Treaties, the depositary now follows a specific procedure,[16] which may also apply to points of substance if there is no dispute as to the existence of the error.[17]

C. Paragraph 2: Official translations

1. Purpose

3132   This provision, entrusting the preparation of official translations into Russian and Spanish to the Swiss Federal Council, is based on a proposal by some Latin American countries and the USSR at the Diplomatic Conference.[18] Its purpose is to avoid the production of different versions in the numerous Spanish-speaking countries, as well as to promote dissemination and understanding of the Convention.

3133   The Swiss Federal Council has established such translations and informed the States Parties accordingly.[19]

---

[13] Article 33 of the 1969 Vienna Convention on the Law of Treaties may be used even though the Geneva Conventions were concluded prior to the entry into force of that Convention because this provision is generally viewed today as reflecting a rule of customary international law (Villiger, p. 461).

[14] Vienna Convention on the Law of Treaties (1969), Article 33(4). The two preceding articles of the Convention, Articles 31 and 32, provide for the general and supplementary rules on interpretation.

[15] See the commentary on the testimonium and signature clause, section B.2.

[16] Vienna Convention on the Law of Treaties (1969), Article 79, which can be assumed to reflect customary law (Villiger, p. 969). The depositary, on its own initiative or upon request, notifies the States which participated in the negotiations, as well as the signatory and contracting States, of the error and the proposal to correct it. If, within a specified appropriate time limit (frequently 90 days following notification), no objection is raised by a signatory or contracting State, the depositary makes and initials the correction in the original text, executes a *procès-verbal* (record) of the rectification of the text, and sends a copy of it to the signatory and contracting States for their information. Sandoz/Swinarski/Zimmermann (eds), *Commentary on the Additional Protocols*, ICRC, 1987, para. 3861, mention two corrections the depositary made to Additional Protocol I.

[17] Aust, pp. 293–295. For a discussion of the types of errors addressed by Article 79 of the Vienna Convention, see Kolb, pp. 1784–1785, and Villiger, pp. 961–963 and 967–968; Villiger also addresses the relationship between Articles 33(3) and 79(3) of the Vienna Convention (see pp. 459 and 967–968).

[18] See *Final Record of the Diplomatic Conference of Geneva of 1949*, Vol. II-B, p. 371.

[19] For the Spanish version, for example, the notification was done on 10 February 1950.

2. *Legal effects of the translations*

3134   According to paragraph 1, only the English and French texts of the Convention are authentic. The translations into Spanish and Russian have the legal status of official translations. The official character of these translations resides in the fact that the source from which they are derived is specified in the Convention itself. But the Russian and Spanish texts, unlike the French and English, are not authentic.[20] Should they vary from the French and English versions, it is the latter which will be regarded as correct.[21]

3135   These official translations must be distinguished from translations undertaken by individual Parties for their own purposes. Such translations may be established in all languages, but although, pursuant to Article 48, they must be transmitted to the other Parties through the depositary, they remain translations by the Parties and do not become official translations under the present article.[22] If such translations diverge from one of the authentic languages, this has no effect on the international obligations. The Parties remain bound by the authentic versions and may not claim that the translated version prevails, even for domestic purposes. Today, the Conventions have been translated into some 55 languages.[23]

Select bibliography

Aust, Anthony, *Modern Treaty Law and Practice*, 3rd edition, Cambridge University Press, 2013, pp. 222–226 (Interpretation of treaties in more than one language) and 293–295 (Correction of errors).

Distefano, Giovanni and Henry, Etienne, 'Final Provisions, Including the Martens Clause', in Andrew Clapham, Paola Gaeta and Marco Sassòli (eds), *The 1949 Geneva Conventions: A Commentary*, Oxford University Press, 2015, pp. 155–188.

Kolb, Robert, 'Article 79: Correction of error in texts or in certified copies of treaties', in Olivier Corten and Pierre Klein (eds), *The Vienna Conventions on the Law of Treaties: A Commentary*, Vol. II, Oxford University Press, 2011, pp. 1770–1796.

Ouguergouz, Fatsah, Villalpando, Santiago and Morgan-Foster, Jason, 'Article 77: Functions of depositaries', in Olivier Corten and Pierre Klein (eds), *The Vienna Conventions on the Law of Treaties: A Commentary*, Vol. II, Oxford University Press, 2011, pp. 1715–1753.

Papaux, Alain and Samson, Rémi, 'Article 33: Interpretation of treaties authenticated in two or more languages', in Olivier Corten and Pierre Klein (eds), *The*

---

[20] See Vienna Convention on the Law of Treaties (1969), Article 33(2).

[21] Examples of such divergences include the Russian translation of 'ensure respect' in common Article 1 as 'заставлять соблюдать' ('force respect') and the Spanish translation of 'the necessary protection and facilities' in Article 18(1) as 'la protección y las facilidades oportunas' ('the appropriate protection and facilities').

[22] See the commentary on Article 48 of the First Convention.   [23] See also *ibid*.

Vienna Conventions on the Law of Treaties: A Commentary, Vol. I, Oxford University Press, 2011, pp. 866–884.

Schenker, Claude, *Practice Guide to International Treaties*, Federal Department of Foreign Affairs, Bern, 2015, pp. 16–17, available at https://www.fdfa.admin.ch/treaties.

Sinclair, Ian, *The Vienna Convention on the Law of Treaties*, 2nd edition, Manchester University Press, 1984, pp. 147–152 (Plurilingual treaties).

United Nations, Office of Legal Affairs, Treaty Section, *Summary of practice of the Secretary-General as depositary of multilateral treaties*, UN Doc. ST/LEG/7/Rev.l, United Nations, New York, 1999, paras 38–62 (Original text).

Villiger, Mark E., *Commentary on the 1969 Vienna Convention on the Law of Treaties*, Martinus Nijhoff Publishers, Leiden, 2009, pp. 450–462 (Article 33) and pp. 955–969 (Article 79).

ARTICLE 56

SIGNATURE

❖ Text of the provision

The present Convention, which bears the date of this day, is open to signature until February 12, 1950, in the name of the Powers represented at
the Conference which opened at Geneva on April 21, 1949; furthermore,
by Powers not represented at that Conference but which are parties to the
Geneva Conventions of 1864, 1906 or 1929 for the Relief of the Wounded
and Sick in Armies in the Field.

❖ Reservations or declarations

None

Contents

A. Introduction

3136 Article 56 establishes the period during which the Convention is open for signature and indicates who is entitled to sign it. The other three Conventions
contain a similar provision.[1]

3137 Signature does not bind States to the Conventions. For States signatory to
the Conventions, this is achieved by ratification, dealt with in the subsequent
article.[2] For non-signatory States, this can be achieved through accession.[3]

---

[1] See Second Convention, Article 55; Third Convention, Article 136; and Fourth Convention, Article 151. These provisions differ in respect of the additional Powers that may sign the Convention.
[2] On ratification, see First Convention, Article 57; Second Convention, Article 56; Third Convention, Article 137; and Fourth Convention, Article 152.
[3] On accession, see First Convention, Article 60; Second Convention, Article 59; Third Convention, Article 139; and Fourth Convention, Article 155.

3138   By signing the Conventions, States undertake not to defeat the object and purpose of the treaty they have signed, even if it has not yet entered into force.[4] Even though the subsequent article provides that '[t]he present Convention shall be ratified', there is no obligation to proceed to ratification.

3139   As regards the signature of the Final Act of the Conference, this merely amounted to authentication of the instruments drawn up by the Conference.[5]

B. Historical background

3140   The wording of the provision is identical to that of the draft adopted by the 1948 International Conference of the Red Cross in Stockholm.[6] It was adopted by the plenary of the Diplomatic Conference without much discussion.[7]

3141   The provision is nearly identical to provisions in the 1929 Geneva Conventions.[8] However, whereas the 1929 Conventions used the word 'countries', the draft as well as the text finally adopted by the Conference uses the term 'Powers'. The documents do not indicate whether this difference was meant to be substantive. However, in the follow-up practice of the depositary and the Parties to the Conventions, 'Powers' was used to mean 'States'. The only substantive difference with the two 1929 Conventions is that the latter were open to signature only by States represented at the Diplomatic Conference, whereas the present provision opens the possibility for a larger number of States to sign, in addition to those attending the Conference.[9] States which did not attend the Conference but which were Parties to the 1864, 1906 or 1929 Conventions could also sign the Conventions within a period of six months.

3142   Whereas for the first three Conventions the possibility of signing was extended to States which were not attending the Conference but which were Parties to the 1864, 1906 or 1929 Conventions, this was not the case for the Fourth Convention, because no convention on the protection of civilians existed before 1949.[10]

---

[4] Vienna Convention on the Law of Treaties (1969), Article 18(a), which may be considered declaratory of customary international law (Villiger, p. 252).

[5] See Vienna Convention on the Law of Treaties (1969), Article 10, which is declaratory of customary international law (Villiger, p. 171).

[6] *Draft Conventions adopted by the 1948 Stockholm Conference*, draft article 44, p. 27.

[7] See *Final Record of the Diplomatic Conference of Geneva of 1949*, Vol. II-B, pp. 25, 30, 71, 113 and 373.

[8] See Geneva Convention on the Wounded and Sick (1929), Article 31, and Geneva Convention on Prisoners of War (1929), Article 90.

[9] A list of the 'Powers represented at the Diplomatic Conference which opened at Geneva on April 21, 1949' can be found in *Final Record of the Diplomatic Conference of Geneva of 1949*, Vol. I, pp. 158–170.

[10] There were, however, the 1934 Tokyo Draft Convention on the Protection of Civilians and the 1938 ILA Draft Convention for the Protection of Civilian Populations against New Engines of War. The Tokyo Draft Convention in particular served as an important basis for the discussions which led to the adoption of the Fourth Geneva Convention of 1949.

C. Discussion

1. Date of the Convention

3143 Article 56 states that the Convention bears the date of the day mentioned in the final clause, namely 12 August 1949. The other three Geneva Conventions adopted by the Diplomatic Conference of 1949 also bear this date. The final vote on the Convention by a plenary meeting of the Conference was held one day earlier, on 11 August 1949.[11] On 12 August, the closing session of the Conference was held, during which the delegations signed the Final Act as a means of authenticating the text.[12] Those delegations that were mandated to do so by their governments could also sign the Convention.[13]

3144 The Swiss Federal Council assumed its responsibilities as depositary of the Geneva Conventions as from the time of the adoption of their texts on 12 August 1949.[14]

3145 The article gives States an opportunity to sign the Convention up to 12 February 1950 and 61 States signed the Convention during this period. This opportunity is extended not only to Powers represented at the Conference, but also to those which, although absent from Geneva, were Parties to the 1864, 1906 or 1929 Conventions.[15] States which have not signed the Convention may become Parties to the Convention by acceding to it.[16]

3146 As several States at the Conference had asked for a delay to enable them to subject the adopted texts to a final examination before signing, it was decided to hold a second signing ceremony on 8 December 1949.[17]

---

[11] See *Final Record of the Diplomatic Conference of Geneva of 1949*, Vol. II-B, p. 519. On the adoption of a treaty, see Vienna Convention on the Law of Treaties (1969), Article 9. On the customary status of Article 9, see Villiger, p. 163.

[12] See *Final Record of the Diplomatic Conference of Geneva of 1949*, Vol. II-B, pp. 527–528. On the authentication of a treaty text, see Vienna Convention on the Law of Treaties (1969), Article 10, which is declaratory of customary international law (Villiger, p. 171).

[13] On that day, the four Conventions were signed by 16 countries. One country signed the first three Conventions, another one the First, Third and Fourth Conventions. See *Final Record of the Diplomatic Conference of Geneva of 1949*, Vol. II-B, p. 528.

[14] Vienna Convention on the Law of Treaties (1969), Article 24(4), which is declaratory of customary international law (Villiger, p. 348).

[15] This option was used by the Philippines and Poland, which were not present at the Conference, but which, as Parties to the 1929 Conventions, exercised their right to sign the 1949 Conventions on 8 December 1949. Furthermore, Paraguay, as a Party to the 1906 and 1864 Conventions, also made use of this option on 10 December 1949. Sri Lanka (then Ceylon) is not listed as having sent a delegation to the Conference, but it signed the Final Act and, on 8 December 1949, also signed the Conventions, without having been a Party to the earlier Conventions. This seems to indicate that partial attendance at the Conference was considered to be sufficient to fulfil the conditions for signature.

[16] See Articles 60 and 61 of the Convention. On accession to treaties in general, see Vienna Convention on the Law of Treaties (1969), Article 15.

[17] See *Final Record of the Diplomatic Conference of Geneva of 1949*, Vol. II-B, pp. 526–527 and 532–537. On this occasion, the Convention was signed by 27 States.

2. Effects of signature

3147   As stipulated in the subsequent Article 57, signatory States are not bound by the Convention until they have ratified it. By providing for ratification in this subsequent article, the Convention implicitly excludes the possibility for a State to express its consent to be bound solely by signature. Therefore, it was not necessary for the signatories to explicitly sign 'subject to ratification'.

3148   Even though signature was therefore not the final expression of the consent to be bound, it was nevertheless not without legal effect. The act of signature marks the agreement of the signatories to a text which cannot thereafter be altered in substance.

3149   Moreover, pursuant to customary international law and the 1969 Vienna Convention on the Law of Treaties, signatories have an obligation not to defeat the object and purpose of the treaty they have signed, even if it has not yet entered into force.[18] The importance of this act cannot therefore be disregarded.

3150   Certain delegations made reservations at the time of signature.[19] These reservations did not remain in force, however, unless they were confirmed when the instrument of ratification was deposited.[20]

3. Authorization to sign

3151   For a treaty signature to be valid, it must be made by a duly authorized representative of the State. Heads of State, heads of government and ministers for foreign affairs are considered as representing their State without having to produce full powers for the purpose of performing all acts relating to the conclusion of a treaty.[21] All other representatives have to produce full powers emanating from the competent authority of the State.[22] The Diplomatic Conference of 1949 elected a Credentials Committee, consisting of the representatives of seven States, which had to verify the credentials of the delegations wishing

---

[18] Vienna Convention on the Law of Treaties (1969), Article 18(a), which may be considered as declaratory of customary international law (Villiger, p. 252). This rule applies until a State 'shall have made its intention clear not to become a party to the treaty'. For further commentary, see Boisson de Chazournes/La Rosa/Mbengue and Villiger, pp. 242–253 (Article 18).

[19] Reservations were made to: First Geneva Convention, Articles 3, 10, 11, 13, 66 and 68; Second Geneva Convention, Articles 3, 10 and 11; Third Geneva Convention, Articles 3, 4, 10, 11, 12, 60, 66 and 85; and the Fourth Geneva Convention, Articles 11, 12, 44, 45, 46, 60 and 68. For the text of these reservations, see *Final Record of the Diplomatic Conference of Geneva of 1949*, Vol. I, pp. 342–357. A substantive discussion of the reservations appears in the commentaries on the articles concerned.

[20] See, in general, Vienna Convention on the Law of Treaties (1969), Article 23(2), which appears well established as customary international law (Villiger, p. 325). For a further discussion of reservations to the Geneva Conventions, see the commentary on Article 57, section C.2. The text of the reservations is available on the websites of the depositary (https://www.fdfa.admin.ch/depositary) and the ICRC (https://www.icrc.org/ihl).

[21] Vienna Convention on the Law of Treaties (1969), Article 7(2), which reflects customary international law (Villiger, p. 146).

[22] For a definition of the term 'full powers', see Vienna Convention on the Law of Treaties (1969), Article 2(1)(c).

to sign the Conventions. This committee was unable to accomplish its task during the Conference, but did so in time for the signing ceremony held on 8 December 1949.[23]

3152   For States which signed the Conventions after the second signing ceremony, the credentials were verified by the Swiss Federal Council in its capacity as depositary.

Select bibliography

Aust, Anthony, *Modern Treaty Law and Practice*, 3rd edition, Cambridge University Press, 2013, pp. 89–92 (Signature) and 107–109 (Obligation not to defeat the object and purpose of a treaty prior to its entry into force).

Boisson de Chazournes, Laurence, La Rosa, Anne-Marie and Mbengue, Makane Moïse, 'Article 18: Obligation not to defeat the object and purpose of a treaty prior to its entry into force', in Olivier Corten and Pierre Klein (eds), *The Vienna Conventions on the Law of Treaties: A Commentary*, Vol. I, Oxford University Press, 2011, pp. 369–403.

Bradley, Curtis A., 'Treaty Signature', in Duncan B. Hollis (ed.), *The Oxford Guide to Treaties*, Oxford University Press, 2012, pp. 208–219.

Distefano, Giovanni and Henry, Etienne, 'Final Provisions, Including the Martens Clause', in Andrew Clapham, Paola Gaeta and Marco Sassòli (eds), *The 1949 Geneva Conventions: A Commentary*, Oxford University Press, 2015, pp. 155–188.

Rosenne, Shabtai, 'Participation in the Geneva Conventions (1864–1949) and the Additional Protocols of 1977', in Christophe Swinarski (ed.), *Studies and Essays on International Humanitarian Law and Red Cross Principles in Honour of Jean Pictet*, ICRC/Martinus Nijhoff, The Hague, 1984, pp. 803–812.

Schenker, Claude, *Practice Guide to International Treaties*, Federal Department of Foreign Affairs, Bern, 2015, pp. 22–24, available at https://www.fdfa.admin.ch/treaties.

Sinclair, Ian, *The Vienna Convention on the Law of Treaties*, 2nd edition, Manchester University Press, 1984, pp. 29–44 (The conclusion and entry into force of treaties).

United Nations, Office of Legal Affairs, Treaty Section, *Summary of practice of the Secretary-General as depositary of multilateral treaties*, UN Doc. ST/LEG/7/Rev.l, United Nations, New York, 1999, paras 101–119 (Full powers and signatures).

Villiger, Mark E., *Commentary on the 1969 Vienna Convention on the Law of Treaties*, Martinus Nijhoff Publishers, Leiden, 2009, pp. 132–146 (Article 7) and 242–253 (Article 18).

---

[23] *Final Record of the Diplomatic Conference of Geneva of 1949*, Vol. II-B, pp. 518 and 532–533.

ARTICLE 57

RATIFICATION

❖ Text of the provision*

(1) The present Convention shall be ratified as soon as possible and the ratifications shall be deposited at Berne.

(2) A record shall be drawn up of the deposit of each instrument of ratification and certified copies of this record shall be transmitted by the Swiss
Federal Council to all the Powers in whose name the Convention has
been signed, or whose accession has been notified.

❖ Reservations or declarations
None

Contents

A. Introduction

3153 Only a State's consent to be bound by a treaty can give it obligatory force and
make it binding on that State. A State can express its consent to be bound by a
treaty by different means, depending on the specific provisions of the treaty in
question.[1]

---

* Paragraph numbers have been added for ease of reference.
[1] See Vienna Convention on the Law of Treaties (1969), Articles 11–15. Although the Vienna Convention is dated 20 years after the Geneva Conventions and does not as such apply to treaties
concluded before its entry into force (see Article 4), it is generally considered to codify customary
international law.

1142

3154 As used in Article 57, ratification is the formal act by which a State accepts a Convention it has signed previously, thereby establishing 'on the international plane its consent to be bound'.[2]

3155 Article 57, which is a provision that is common to the four Conventions,[3] therefore complements the preceding article on signature.[4]

3156 For States not having previously signed the Convention, Article 60 provides for accession as the means of expressing consent to be bound.[5]

3157 Ratification becomes effective when the instrument of ratification is deposited with the depositary, which shows the will of the State concerned to be bound vis-à-vis the other States. Only the deposit of the instrument of ratification and not the authorization to ratify – which, under the law of most countries, must be given to the government by the parliament – has force under international law.

3158 As signature does not bind a State definitively, its internal procedures are usually simpler, and the signature can be appended more easily. On the other hand, ratification commits the State, which must henceforth comply with all the obligations contained in the treaty once it enters into force. Ratification therefore requires a thorough examination of the treaty on its merits, and means that specific approval procedures laid down in a State's domestic law must be followed.[6]

3159 However, the provisions of a treaty do not become legal obligations until it has entered into force in general and for the State concerned, pursuant to its provisions.[7] Nevertheless, the minimum obligation of every State, during the period between the deposit of its instrument of ratification and the entry into force of the treaty in general (and entry into force for that particular

---

[2] *Ibid.* Article 2(1)(b).
[3] See Second Convention, Article 56; Third Convention, Article 137; and Fourth Convention, Article 152.
[4] For further details on signature, see the commentary on Article 56.
[5] For further details on accession, see the commentary on Article 60. States coming into being following a separation from another State or the dissolution of a State can also, instead of acceding, declare their succession to the preceding State with respect to an international treaty. The main difference between the two forms is that, with accession, the treaty obligations enter into force pursuant to the provisions of the treaty, whereas with succession, the obligations continue to be applicable to the new State as from the date of its coming into being, even if succession is declared at a later stage. This possibility, as a general principle, is not explicitly mentioned in the Convention, as is the case with most international treaties. For further information on succession, see also the commentary on Article 60. For the current status of the Conventions, see: https://www.icrc.org/ihl.
[6] According to Article 46 of the 1969 Vienna Convention on the Law of Treaties, '[a] State may not invoke the fact that its consent to be bound by a treaty has been expressed in violation of a provision of its internal law regarding competence to conclude treaties as invalidating its consent unless that violation was manifest and concerned a rule of its internal law of fundamental importance'. This article can be assumed to be declaratory of customary international law (Villiger, p. 594).
[7] For details on the coming into force of the Convention, see the commentary on Article 58.

State) is to refrain from acts which would defeat the object and purpose of the treaty.[8]

3160   The provision contains two paragraphs addressed to different Parties. The first paragraph is addressed to the signatory States, whereas the second paragraph sets out procedural obligations for the depositary.

B. Historical background

3161   The wording of the provision is identical to that of the draft adopted by the 1948 International Conference of the Red Cross in Stockholm.[9] It was adopted by the Diplomatic Conference without much discussion.[10] The French term *'procès-verbal'* was changed to 'record' in the final English version of the provision.[11] The provision is substantially identical to provisions in the 1929 Conventions.[12]

C. Paragraph 1: Ratification

1. General

3162   This paragraph contains, by means of the formulation 'shall be ratified as soon as possible', a pressing recommendation to each signatory to hasten the ratification procedure and not to intentionally delay its national approval procedures. However, notwithstanding the wording of the provision ('shall be ratified'), the signature of a treaty subject to ratification, under general international law, does not legally obligate the signatory to ratify the treaty. It remains each State's sovereign decision whether and when to ratify a treaty it has previously signed. The ratification process for the four Conventions was concluded in 1976, when the last signatory State deposited its instrument of ratification. Thereafter, States became party through accession or succession.[13]

3163   The provision also indicates where the instruments of ratification must be deposited. However, the formulation 'at Berne' is not very precise and is understandable only in conjunction with the second paragraph, the other final provisions and the final clause, by which the Swiss Federal Council is identified as the depositary of the Conventions.

---

[8] On the effects of signature, see the commentary on Article 56, as well as Vienna Convention on the Law of Treaties (1969), Article 18, which may be considered as declaratory of customary international law (Villiger, p. 252).
[9] See *Draft Conventions adopted by the 1948 Stockholm Conference*, draft article 45, p. 27.
[10] See *Final Record of the Diplomatic Conference of Geneva of 1949*, Vol. II-B, pp. 25, 30, 71, 113 and 373.
[11] *Ibid.* pp. 162–163.
[12] See Geneva Convention on the Wounded and Sick (1929), Article 32, and Geneva Convention on Prisoners of War (1929), Article 91.
[13] On accession, see Article 60.

3164 The deposit can either be made in person by a representative of the State concerned, or the instrument can be transmitted to the depositary in writing through diplomatic channels. The current practice of the depositary, however, does not require these specific forms of transmittal. The instrument can also be sent by regular mail or other informal means.[14] The means of transmittal has no influence on the validity of the instrument.

3165 The instrument of ratification must be signed on behalf of the State by a person authorized to represent the State for this purpose. Pursuant to international law and practice, heads of State, heads of government and ministers for foreign affairs are considered as representing their State in virtue of their functions and without having to produce full powers.[15] In line with the practice of the depositary of the Conventions and the Additional Protocols, as well as of other depositaries, instruments signed by other persons, e.g. a minister other than the foreign minister, or a deputy minister, must be accompanied by full powers.[16]

3166 The instrument of ratification must specify the treaty in question and clearly express the will of the State to be bound by the treaty and to comply with its obligations. If the signatory wishes to formulate one or more reservations, or has already done so at the time of signature, the instrument must also contain these reservations.

2. Reservations

3167 At the time of the adoption of the Geneva Conventions, the international law on reservations was subject to controversy.[17] Based on the 1951 advisory opinion of the International Court of Justice in *Reservations to the Genocide Convention*, the 1969 Vienna Convention on the Law of Treaties provides that, when a State signs, ratifies or accedes to a treaty, it may formulate a reservation unless 'the reservation is incompatible with the object and purpose of the treaty' or the treaty contains specific provisions on the possibility of formulating reservations.[18] The Conventions contain no such provisions.

---

[14] It can, for example, be deposited at the depositary's office by an employee of the embassy of the State concerned, by private courier service, or by other means. It can also be deposited through an ICRC delegation. However, as with every other method of transmittal, the deposit will only be considered effective once the instrument reaches the depositary.

[15] See Vienna Convention on the Law of Treaties (1969), Article 7(2), which reflects customary international law (Villiger, p. 146).

[16] For a description of the form and content of instruments of ratification, see Aust, pp. 99–100.

[17] See Pictet (ed.), *Commentary on the First Geneva Convention*, ICRC, 1952, p. 404, and Villiger, pp. 262–264.

[18] Vienna Convention on the Law of Treaties (1969), Article 19. Although the Vienna Convention is dated 20 years after the Geneva Conventions and does not as such apply to treaties concluded before its entry into force (see Article 4), it is generally considered to codify customary international law. The articles on reservations, Articles 19–22 in particular, appear meanwhile to be well established as customary international law (Villiger, p. 325). For a more

3168   Reservations must be made in writing and sent to the contracting States and other States entitled to become Parties to the treaty.[19] A reservation made at the time that a treaty is signed subject to ratification must, in order to be valid, be formally confirmed when the treaty is ratified by the State which formulated the reservation.[20] On the other hand, it is not possible to formulate reservations later than upon ratification or accession.

3169   It is the responsibility of every State concerned to determine whether any particular statement by another State constitutes a reservation.[21] In addition, every State also determines individually whether a reservation formulated by another State is compatible with the object and purpose of the treaty and, consequently, whether it wants to formulate an objection to that reservation.[22]

3170   A State may enter an objection to a reservation made by another State. Unless the State which formulates the objection clearly expresses its intention to the contrary, an objection by a contracting State does not prevent the treaty from entering into force between the State formulating the objection and the State which made the reservation, provided that at least one other contracting State has accepted the reservation.[23] However, 'the provisions to which the reservation relates do not apply as between the two States to the extent of the reservation'.[24]

3171   States which do not raise objections to a reservation are considered to have accepted it after a period of 12 months.[25] This is intended to give States enough time, once they have expressed their consent to be bound by a treaty – or, if they are already party to it, once they are notified of a reservation by another State – to examine the admissibility of reservations and to decide on a possible objection.

3172   A reservation only applies as between the State making it and other States bound by the treaty that have accepted it. It therefore modifies the provisions to which it refers only in the relations between the Parties concerned.[26] The

---

detailed description of the law on reservations and further references, see Aust, pp. 114–144; Reuter, pp. 77–84; Sinclair, pp. 51–82; and Swaine.

[19] Vienna Convention on the Law of Treaties (1969), Article 23(1). Usually, a State sends its reservations, as well as any objections or withdrawals of reservations and objections, to the depositary, which then informs the other contracting States and signatories in accordance with the duties entrusted to it by the specific treaty or by general international law.

[20] *Ibid.* Article 23(2).

[21] The 1969 Vienna Convention on the Law of Treaties defines a reservation as 'a unilateral statement, however phrased or named, made by a State, when signing, ratifying, accepting, approving or acceding to a treaty, whereby it purports to exclude or to modify the legal effect of certain provisions of the treaty in their application to that State' (Article 2(1)(d)).

[22] This does not preclude collective steps, in particular to obtain clarification of the meaning of a reservation. For an example of such a step through the intermediary of the depositary, see Pilloud, pp. 171–173; see also Pictet (ed.), *Commentary on the Third Geneva Convention*, ICRC, 1960, pp. 423–425 (in relation to Article 85 of the Third Convention). Nor does it preclude a court or tribunal from deciding on the admissibility of a reservation in a specific case, if it has jurisdiction.

[23] Vienna Convention on the Law of Treaties (1969), Article 20(4).

[24] *Ibid.* Article 21(3).   [25] *Ibid.* Article 20(5).   [26] *Ibid.* Article 21(1)

reservation does not modify the treaty provisions for the other Parties to the treaty *inter se*.[27]

3173   A reservation or an objection to a reservation may be withdrawn in writing at any time.[28] The withdrawal of a reservation becomes operative in relation to all other contracting States when they have received notice thereof.[29] The withdrawal of an objection becomes operative when notice thereof has been received by the State which formulated the reservation.[30]

For a more detailed discussion of the reservations to the Geneva Conventions, see the commentaries on the specific provisions. In the case of the First Convention, reservations have been made with respect to Articles 3, 10, 11, 13, 38, 44 and 53.

D. Paragraph 2: Record and communication

3174 This paragraph provides instructions to the depositary on the procedures to be followed when a signatory deposits its instrument of ratification. The intention is to ensure that all signatories and acceding States are informed of the ratifications the depositary receives.

3175   Pursuant to this provision, whenever an instrument of ratification was deposited, the depositary established a record signed by the head of the Treaty Section of the Swiss Ministry of Foreign Affairs, confirming the receipt of an instrument of ratification that was found to be in good and due form, and the date on which it was received. The original of this record was deposited, together with the instrument, in the depositary's archives. Certified copies were transmitted to all signatories and acceding States, pursuant to the provision.[31]

3176   More recent conventions generally no longer require a record to be drawn up for every deposit of an instrument of ratification, which means that no formal document certifying the deposit of the instrument is established. Instead, simple notification to the States Parties by the depositary is considered to be sufficient. Such notification is usually provided in the form of a diplomatic note, informing the Parties to the treaty of the action that has taken place.[32] This is also the case for the Additional Protocols.[33]

---

[27] *Ibid.* Article 21(2).   [28] *Ibid.* Article 23(4).

[29] *Ibid.* Article 22(3)(a). For example, Switzerland withdrew its reservations with regard to Articles 57 and 58 of Additional Protocol I on 17 June 2005, and Ukraine withdrew its reservations with regard to several articles of the Conventions on 30 June 2006.

[30] *Ibid.* Article 22(3)(b).

[31] On the procedure followed for accessions or successions, see the commentary on Articles 60 and 61. Article 61 does not specify, as Article 57 does in the case of ratifications, that the Swiss Federal Council is to draw up a record of each accession, nor that it must transmit a copy of the record to other States. The depositary of the Geneva Conventions observes this distinction between ratification and accession in its practice.

[32] The depositary of the Geneva Conventions, like most depositaries nowadays, sends its notifications by electronic means. The depositary notifications since 1977 are available on https://www.fdfa.admin.ch/treaties.

[33] See Additional Protocol I, Article 100; Additional Protocol II, Article 26; and Additional Protocol III, Article 15.

3177   Lastly, Article 64 of the Convention requires the depositary to inform the United Nations Secretariat of all ratifications, accessions and denunciations received.

Select bibliography

Aust, Anthony, *Modern Treaty Law and Practice*, 3rd edition, Cambridge University Press, 2013, pp. 95–100 (Ratification), 114–144 (Reservations) and 283–296 (The depositary).

Boudreault, Lise S., 'Les réserves apportées au Protocole additionnel I aux Conventions de Genève sur le droit humanitaire', *Revue québécoise de droit international*, Vol. 6, No. 2, 1989–90, pp. 105–119, at 108–112.

Distefano, Giovanni and Henry, Etienne, 'Final Provisions, Including the Martens Clause', in Andrew Clapham, Paola Gaeta and Marco Sassòli (eds), *The 1949 Geneva Conventions: A Commentary*, Oxford University Press, 2015, pp. 155–188.

Pilloud, Claude, 'Reservations to the Geneva Conventions of 1949', *International Review of the Red Cross*, Vol. 16, No. 180, March 1976, pp. 107–124.

– 'Reservations to the Geneva Conventions of 1949 (II)', *International Review of the Red Cross*, Vol. 16, No. 181, April 1976, pp. 163–187.

Reuter, Paul, *Introduction to the Law of Treaties*, 2nd edition, Graduate Institute of International Studies, Geneva, 1995, pp. 77–84 (Reservations).

Schenker, Claude, *Practice Guide to International Treaties*, Federal Department of Foreign Affairs, Bern, 2015, pp. 29–30, available at https://www.fdfa.admin.ch/.

Sinclair, Ian, *The Vienna Convention on the Law of Treaties*, 2nd edition, Manchester University Press, 1984, pp. 39–42 (Expression of consent to be bound by a treaty) and 51–82 (Reservations).

Swaine, Edward T., 'Treaty Reservations', in Duncan B. Hollis (ed.), *The Oxford Guide to Treaties*, Oxford University Press, 2012, pp. 277–301.

United Nations, Office of Legal Affairs, Treaty Section, *Summary of practice of the Secretary-General as depositary of multilateral treaties*, UN Doc. ST/LEG/7/Rev.l, United Nations, New York, 1999, paras 120–133 (Deposit of binding instruments).

Villiger, Mark E., *Commentary on the 1969 Vienna Convention on the Law of Treaties*, Martinus Nijhoff Publishers, Leiden, 2009.

COMING INTO FORCE

❖ Text of the provision*

(1) The present Convention shall come into force six months after not less than two instruments of ratification have been deposited.

(2) Thereafter, it shall come into force for each High Contracting Party six months after the deposit of the instrument of ratification.

❖ Reservations or declarations

None

Contents

A. Introduction

3178 Article 58 determines the moment at which the Convention, by its entry into force, formally becomes part of international law. It also settles the date on which the full legal effects of the Convention begin for the signatory States ratifying it.[1]

3179 A certain period must elapse between the date on which the required number of instruments is deposited and the entry into force. This period allows ratifying States to take implementing measures and the depositary to notify other contracting States of the new ratification. Verification that the conditions set

---

* Paragraph numbers have been added for ease of reference.

[1] See the commentary on Article 57 on ratification; see also the commentary on Article 61 on notification of accessions, which provides the same six-month rule in the case of accession.

forth by the Convention have been met and the determination of the date of entry into force are a matter for the depositary. The provisions relating to the entry into force of a treaty and to certain functions of the depositary are applicable from the time of the adoption of its text.[2]

3180   Paragraph 1 of Article 58 addresses the coming into force of the Convention, after the first two States have deposited their instruments of ratification, while paragraph 2 addresses the coming into force of the Convention for signatory States depositing their instruments of ratification after the first two States.

3181   This provision is common to the four Conventions.[3] The process for entry into force after ratification and the date of that entry into force for a State have been the same for the four Conventions.

B. Historical background

3182   This provision reproduces the text of the 1929 Geneva Conventions in virtually identical terms.[4] In the draft adopted by the 1948 International Conference of the Red Cross in Stockholm, the duration between ratification and entry into force was left open.[5] A proposal made in the Joint Committee that 'the period for coming into force should be six months, similar to the Conventions of 1929' met with no objections.[6] The provision thus completed was adopted unanimously.[7]

C. Paragraph 1: Entry into force of the Convention following the deposit of the first two instruments of ratification

3183   Generally, a 'treaty enters into force in such manner and upon such date as it may provide or as the negotiating States may agree'.[8] The Convention provides for an entry into force six months after the date on which the second instrument of ratification is deposited. The words 'not less than two' aimed to provide for the possibility of several States ratifying on the same day. The number of ratifications required before the Convention would enter into force was reduced to a minimum, namely two, which reflects the humanitarian nature of the Convention and the openness of the Conventions to acceding States. It allowed its entry into force as soon as possible, even if, initially, the Convention

---

[2] See Vienna Convention on the Law of Treaties (1969), Article 24(4), which is declaratory of customary international law (Villiger, p. 348).
[3] See Second Convention, Article 57; Third Convention, Article 138; and Fourth Convention, Article 153.
[4] Geneva Convention on the Wounded and Sick (1929), Article 33; Geneva Convention on Prisoners of War (1929), Article 92.
[5] *Draft Conventions adopted by the 1948 Stockholm Conference*, draft article 46, p. 28.
[6] See *Final Record of the Diplomatic Conference of Geneva of 1949*, Vol. II-B, p. 25 (Canada).
[7] See *ibid.* pp. 30, 71 and 113.
[8] Vienna Convention on the Law of Treaties (1969), Article 24(1), which is declaratory of customary international law (Villiger, p. 348).

had legal effects only between the first two States that ratified it. This initial phase was in fact very short, since the third State, Monaco, ratified the Conventions only 75 days after the second State, Yugoslavia. At all times, however, States not party to the Convention were still bound by the rules of customary international law.

3184 The interval of six months between the deposit of the second instrument of ratification and the Convention's entry into force for the first two contracting Parties was designed to allow the States involved to initiate preparatory measures of a legislative, regulatory or practical nature for implementing their new obligations.[9] Although the Parties had previously signed the Conventions and had already had time between signature and ratification to prepare for their implementation, the provisions of the Conventions are complex and needed time to be implemented, for instance, at every level of the armed forces. In practice, the waiting period was longer only for the first State to ratify the Convention, i.e. six months following the date of deposit of the second instrument of ratification. It also allowed the depositary to notify the contracting States of the Convention's forthcoming entry into force.

3185 When a waiting period is prescribed for the general entry into force of a treaty, the depositary has to calculate the date of entry into force. As the interval is formulated in months in this provision, the time runs from the date of the deposit of the instrument in question. Thus, the Convention entered into force on the six-month anniversary of the date on which the second instrument of ratification was deposited, i.e. on 21 October 1950, Switzerland having ratified it on 31 March 1950 and Yugoslavia on 21 April 1950. The same calculation applied afterwards for each State ratifying it in accordance with the second paragraph or acceding to it.[10]

D. Paragraph 2: Entry into force of the Convention for States depositing their instrument of ratification after the initial two States

3186 Generally, '[w]hen the consent of a State to be bound by a treaty is established on a date after the treaty has come into force, the treaty enters into force for that State on that date, unless the treaty otherwise provides'.[11] Article 58(2) provides that, after the Convention has come into force in accordance with the

---

[9] For further details on these preparatory measures, see the commentary on common Article 2, section C.

[10] Exceptionally, if an instrument is deposited, for example on 31 March, since there is no corresponding date in September, the treaty would enter into force on the last day of September, i.e. 30 September. Similarly, for a deposit made on 30 or 31 August, the treaty would enter into force on 28 or 29 February of the following year. See United Nations, *Summary of practice of the Secretary-General as depositary of multilateral treaties*, p. 70.

[11] Vienna Convention on the Law of Treaties (1969), Article 24(3), which is declaratory of customary international law (Villiger, p. 348).

first paragraph, it 'shall come into force for each High Contracting Party six months after the deposit of the instrument of ratification'.

3187   The interval of six months between the deposit by a signatory State of its instrument of ratification and the entry into force of the Convention between that State and the other contracting Parties is identical to that in paragraph 1, for the reasons described above. After the six-month period, the State in question is bound by the Convention in its relations with all States which have ratified it not less than six months before. Thereafter, it is bound in its relations with other signatory States six months after each of them ratifies the Convention and, in its relations with acceding States, six months after their accession.[12]

3188   The only exception to this waiting period is contained in Article 62 of the Convention, under which 'the situations provided for in Articles 2 and 3 shall give immediate effect to ratifications deposited and accessions notified by the Parties to the conflict before or after the beginning of hostilities or occupation'. For obvious humanitarian reasons, the six-month interval which normally separates the ratification or accession by a State from the entry into force of the Convention for that State is therefore dispensed with. This situation has never arisen in the case of ratification; it has, however, arisen in the case of accession.[13]

3189   When the Convention enters into force for a High Contracting Party, it does not follow that all its provisions must be applied immediately. The majority of its provisions, as indicated in Articles 2 and 3, only apply in the event of armed conflict, although most of them require preparatory measures.[14] In addition, in accordance with Article 2(1), certain provisions must be implemented immediately, i.e. in peacetime.[15]

3190   At the time of writing, the Conventions are in force for more than 190 States.[16]

Select bibliography

Aust, Anthony, 'Article 24: Entry into force', in Olivier Corten and Pierre Klein (eds), *The Vienna Conventions on the Law of Treaties: A Commentary*, Vol. I, Oxford University Press, 2011, pp. 628–637.
  – *Modern Treaty Law and Practice*, 3rd edition, Cambridge University Press, 2013, pp. 145–158 (Entry into force) and 289–291 (Functions of the depositary).

Distefano, Giovanni and Henry, Etienne, 'Final Provisions, Including the Martens Clause', in Andrew Clapham, Paola Gaeta and Marco Sassòli (eds), *The 1949*

---

[12] On accession to the Convention and its effect, see Articles 60–61.
[13] See the commentary on Article 62, para. 3249.
[14] On preparatory measures, see the commentary on common Article 2, section C.
[15] See the commentary on common Article 2, section C.
[16] For the current status of the Conventions, see: https://www.icrc.org/ihl.

Geneva Conventions: A Commentary, Oxford University Press, 2015, pp. 155–188.

Reuter, Paul, *Introduction to the Law of Treaties*, 2nd edition, Graduate Institute of International Studies, Geneva, 1995, pp. 66–68 (Entry into force).

Schenker, Claude, *Practice Guide to International Treaties*, Federal Department of Foreign Affairs, Bern, 2015, pp. 13–14, available at https://www.fdfa.admin.ch/.

Sinclair, Ian, *The Vienna Convention on the Law of Treaties*, 2nd edition, Manchester University Press, 1984, pp. 44–47 (Entry into force).

United Nations, Office of Legal Affairs, Treaty Section, *Summary of practice of the Secretary-General as depositary of multilateral treaties*, UN Doc. ST/LEG/7/Rev.l, United Nations, New York, 1999, paras 221–247 (Entry into force).

Villiger, Mark E., *Commentary on the 1969 Vienna Convention on the Law of Treaties*, Martinus Nijhoff Publishers, Leiden, 2009, pp. 339–348 (Article 24).

RELATION TO PREVIOUS CONVENTIONS

❖ Text of the provision

The present Convention replaces the Conventions of August 22, 1864, July 6, 1906, and July 27, 1929, in relations between the High Contracting Parties.

❖ Reservations or declarations

None

Contents

A. Introduction

3191 Article 59 governs the relation of the First Convention to the 1864 Geneva Convention, the 1906 Geneva Convention and the 1929 Geneva Convention on the Wounded and Sick by providing that the First Convention 'replaces' these earlier Conventions in relations between States party to it.

3192 The Second, Third and Fourth Conventions contain similar provisions regulating the relation of these Conventions to previous treaties or parts of treaties with similar subject matter.[1]

3193 Additional Protocols I, II and III also include provisions clarifying the relation between them and the Geneva Conventions.[2]

B. Historical background

3194 Beginning with the 1906 Geneva Convention, the earlier Conventions listed in Article 59 themselves contained provisions comparable to Article 59, governing the relation of these Conventions to their respective precursors.[3]

---

[1] See Second Convention, Article 58; Third Convention, Articles 134–135; and Fourth Convention, Article 154.

[2] See Additional Protocol I, Article 1(3); Additional Protocol II, Article 1(1); Additional Protocol III, Article 1(2).

[3] See Article 31 of the 1906 Geneva Convention and Article 34 of the 1929 Geneva Convention on the Wounded and Sick. For a similar provision, see also Article 4 of the 1907 Hague Convention IV, regulating the relation of that Convention to the 1899 Hague Convention II.

3195   The draft article that ultimately became Article 59 was submitted by the ICRC to the 1948 International Conference of the Red Cross in Stockholm. It reproduced the wording of the 1929 Geneva Convention on the Wounded and Sick, while adding the 1929 Convention to the list of earlier Conventions referenced.[4] The draft article was adopted by the Stockholm Conference and subsequently by the 1949 Diplomatic Conference without substantive changes.[5]

C. Discussion

3196   Unlike the Additional Protocols,[6] none of the successive Geneva Conventions on the Wounded and Sick contains a provision prescribing a process for its amendment. If a treaty does not lay down a specific procedure for its amendment, it may be amended by agreement between its Parties.[7] Amendment is understood to refer not only to the partial, but also to the complete amendment of a treaty, a process sometimes referred to as 'revision' of the treaty.[8] The amendment of a treaty needs to be distinguished from the modification of a treaty.[9] Amendments are in principle meant to be applicable 'as between all the Parties' to the original treaty and all the Parties to the original treaty are entitled to become a Party to the amended treaty, even though not all of them may decide to do so. Modifications, in contrast, are agreements concluded by some Parties to a treaty with the intention to change the treaty 'as between themselves alone' (*inter se*).[10]

3197   Since the adoption of the very first Geneva Convention in 1864, the regulation of its subject matter, the 'Amelioration of the Condition of the Wounded in Armies in the Field',[11] was successively amended (or revised) by the 1906 Geneva Convention, the 1929 Geneva Convention on the Wounded and Sick and the 1949 First Convention. The First Convention's purpose of 'revising' the earlier ones is specifically mentioned in the preamble.[12]

---

[4]   See *Draft Conventions submitted to the 1948 Stockholm Conference*, draft article 47, p. 31.
[5]   See *Draft Conventions adopted by the 1948 Stockholm Conference*, draft article 47, p. 28, and *Final Record of the Diplomatic Conference of Geneva of 1949*, Vol. I, p. 217.
[6]   See Article 97 of Additional Protocol I and Article 24 of Additional Protocol II, regulating the procedure for the amendment of the Protocols.
[7]   A principle codified in Articles 39 and 40 of the 1969 Vienna Convention on the Law of Treaties; for a discussion, see e.g. Ardault/Dormoy; Aust, pp. 232–244; and Brunnée.
[8]   See International Law Commission, p. 232, para. 3.
[9]   See Vienna Convention on the Law of Treaties (1969), Article 41.
[10]   For further details, see Rigaux/Simon, pp. 989–990, and Aust, p. 242. The successive Geneva Conventions on the Wounded and Sick were adopted with a view to the possible ratification or accession by all States party to earlier Conventions, as well as by other States; they are therefore not mere *inter se* modifications of the earlier Conventions.
[11]   See the title of the 1864 Geneva Convention.
[12]   See the commentary on the Preamble, section C. See also the documents sent to the States party to the 1929 Geneva Conventions and the 1907 Hague Convention (X) in preparation for the 1949 Diplomatic Conference, notifying them of the intention to convene a Diplomatic Conference

3198   When a treaty is amended, the consequences for the States party to the earlier treaty need to be considered. This is especially important with respect to multilateral treaties, such as the Geneva Conventions, where, at least initially, not all States party to the earlier treaty may decide to become party to the later treaty.[13]

3199   For that purpose, Article 59 provides that the First Convention 'replaces' the previous Conventions dealing with its subject matter 'in relations between the High Contracting Parties'. Thus, between States party to the First Convention, that Convention prevails over the previous Conventions mentioned in Article 59 to which they may also be party, superseding those previous Conventions in their mutual relations.[14]

3200   At the time of writing of this commentary, Article 59 has fulfilled its purpose. With the 1949 Geneva Conventions having achieved universal ratification, the First Convention has become applicable in relations between all States, whether as the first convention on the wounded and sick to which a State has become party or in replacement of earlier conventions by virtue of Article 59. Potential new States which in the future may become party to the 1949 Geneva Conventions will normally not have been party to their precursors, so that a situation requiring governance by Article 59 will not arise.

3201   The universal ratification of the 1949 Geneva Conventions also means that earlier Conventions cannot be revived if a State party decides to denounce any of the 1949 Conventions, as these earlier conventions have been effectively replaced.[15] Rather, upon denunciation, a State, whether a Party to earlier conventions or not, would remain bound by customary international humanitarian law.[16]

Select bibliography

Ardault, Karine and Dormoy, Daniel, 'Article 40: Amendment of multilateral treaties', in Olivier Corten and Pierre Klein (eds), *The Vienna Conventions on the Law of Treaties: A Commentary*, Vol. II, Oxford University Press, 2011, pp. 978–984.

Aust, Anthony, *Modern Treaty Law and Practice*, 3rd edition, Cambridge University Press, 2013, pp. 192–204 (successive treaties) and 232–244 (amendment).

---

on, *inter alia*, the revision of these Conventions; see *Final Record of the Diplomatic Conference of Geneva of 1949*, Vol. I, pp. 145–151.

[13] See ILC, *Draft Articles on the Law of Treaties with Commentaries*, p. 232, para. 1 (expressly referring to the amendment of the 1864 Geneva Convention).

[14] See *ibid.* p. 215, para. 6, with fn. 112, expressly referring to Article 59 of the First Convention.

[15] For details on the denunciation of the Geneva Conventions, see the commentary on Article 63. The conditions for an implied termination of a treaty by conclusion of a later treaty on the same subject matter between all States party to the earlier treaty are now codified in Article 59 of the 1969 Vienna Convention on the Law of Treaties; for a detailed discussion, see e.g. Dubuisson.

[16] See also Article 63(4).

Benvenuti, Paolo, 'Relationship with Prior and Subsequent Treaties and Conventions', in Andrew Clapham, Paola Gaeta and Marco Sassòli (eds), *The 1949 Geneva Conventions: A Commentary*, Oxford University Press, 2015, pp. 689–700.

Brunnée, Jutta, 'Treaty Amendments', in Duncan B. Hollis (ed.), *The Oxford Guide to Treaties*, Oxford University Press, 2012, pp. 347–366.

Distefano, Giovanni and Henry, Etienne, 'Final Provisions, Including the Martens Clause', in Andrew Clapham, Paola Gaeta and Marco Sassòli (eds), *The 1949 Geneva Conventions: A Commentary*, Oxford University Press, 2015, pp. 155–188.

Dubuisson, François, 'Article 59: Termination or suspension of the operation of a treaty implied by conclusion of a later treaty', in Olivier Corten and Pierre Klein (eds), *The Vienna Conventions on the Law of Treaties: A Commentary*, Vol. II, Oxford University Press, 2011, pp. 1325–1347.

ILC, *Draft Articles on the Law of Treaties with Commentaries*, text adopted by the International Law Commission at its eighteenth session, in 1966, and submitted to the General Assembly as a part of the Commission's report covering the work of that session (at para. 38); see also *Yearbook of the International Law Commission, 1966*, Vol. II, pp. 187–274.

Rigaux, Anne and Simon, Denys, 'Article 41: Agreement to modify multilateral treaties between certain parties only', in Olivier Corten and Pierre Klein (eds), *The Vienna Conventions on the Law of Treaties: A Commentary*, Vol. II, Oxford University Press, 2011, pp. 986–1008.

ACCESSION

❖ Text of the provision

From the date of its coming into force, it shall be open to any Power in whose name the present Convention has not been signed, to accede to this Convention.

❖ Reservations or declarations

None

Contents

A. Introduction

3202 Under general international law, a State can express its consent to be bound by a treaty in a variety of ways.[1] Among these, the Geneva Conventions retain two alternatives: signature followed by ratification, or accession. Accession gives States the possibility of binding themselves to the Conventions in a single act, instead of the two-stage process (signature then ratification) laid down in Articles 56 and 57. Accession is also the only means for a State that has not signed the Convention to become a Party to it. The procedure for accession provided in Article 60 is common to the four Conventions.[2]

---

[1] A principle today codified in the Article 11 of the 1969 Vienna Convention on the Law of Treaties, which mentions 'signature, exchange of instruments constituting a treaty, ratification, acceptance, approval or accession, or by any other means if so agreed'.

[2] See also Second Convention, Article 59; Third Convention, Article 139; and Fourth Convention, Article 155.

B. Historical background

3203 The draft provision adopted by the 1948 International Conference of the Red Cross in Stockholm was largely identical to the final text adopted, but contained in addition the condition that the accession had to be 'duly notified'.[3] This wording reflected that of the corresponding provisions in the 1929 Conventions.[4] The Drafting Committee of the Conference changed the text to the current wording and thus left the notification requirement addressed entirely in a separate provision (Article 61), which prompted no discussion at the Conference.[5]

C. Discussion

1. Conditions of accession

3204 Ratification is only possible for States fulfilling the conditions for signature set out in Article 56, whereas any State which has not signed the Convention may accede to it.[6]

3205　No limitation or condition on accession is imposed other than that the Convention must have already entered into force. The invitation is addressed to 'any Power', whether or not it is a Party to one of the earlier Conventions.[7] The Geneva Conventions, which draw their strength and reach from their traditional universality, are, as in 1929, treaties open to all. However, entities wishing to accede to the Conventions have to be a 'State', i.e. they have to fulfil the criteria of statehood defined by international law.[8] The existence of a State is not only a legal but also a political question. Recognition is not enough to create a State, nor does its absence negate it. However, when statehood is a condition for accession to a treaty, it is of importance whether or not the depositary and the other States Parties are convinced that an acceding entity fulfils the criteria for statehood. If the depositary cannot clearly determine whether an

---

[3] *Draft Conventions adopted by the 1948 Stockholm Conference*, p. 28: 'From the date of its coming into force, the present Convention shall be open to accession, duly notified, by any Power in whose name this Convention has not been signed.'

[4] Geneva Convention on the Wounded and Sick (1929), Article 35; Geneva Convention on Prisoners of War (1929), Article 93.

[5] *Final Record of the Diplomatic Conference of Geneva of 1949*, Vol. II-B, p. 163.

[6] On conditions for accession in general, see Vienna Convention on the Law of Treaties (1969), Article 15, and Aust, pp. 101–103.

[7] For the meaning of the term 'Power' as equivalent to 'State', see the commentary on Article 56, para. 3141.

[8] The most cited qualifications necessary for a State are (a) a permanent population, (b) a defined territory, (c) government and (d) capacity to enter into relations with the other States. This definition is part of customary international law as codified in the 1933 Montevideo Convention on the Rights and Duties of States. For a detailed discussion of the legal criteria of statehood, see Crawford, pp. 127–142 (adding as criteria to 'produce a working definition': (e) a degree of permanence, (f) willingness to observe international law, (g) sovereignty, and (h) function as a State), and *The Creation of States in International Law*, 2nd edition, Oxford University Press, 2006.

entity wishing to accede to a treaty is a State, it has to leave this determination to the States Parties in order to maintain its impartiality in the performance of its functions.[9]

3206   Like other depositaries,[10] the depositary of the Geneva Conventions does not consider itself in a position to determine the often political question of whether an entity whose status is unclear is a State. Therefore, if the depositary is not in a position to determine whether or not an entity wishing to accede to the Convention is a State, it informs the States Parties of the deposit of the instrument of accession, without determining the validity of such accession and without formally listing the entity wishing to accede as a State Party to the Convention.[11]

3207   In this context, the functions of the depositary and its role as a State Party to the treaty have to remain clearly distinct and separate. The depositary has to assess the situation in an objective way, according to the applicable legal conditions. In the course of this assessment, political considerations the State may have as a State Party, for example with regard to its recognition of the acceding entity, must not be taken into account.

3208   In the practice of the depositary of the Geneva Conventions and their Additional Protocols, there are cases of accessions of entities which were, at the time of accession, not (yet) recognized as States by Switzerland. The depositary did not always deal with these cases in entirely the same way, not because Switzerland did not recognize the entities in question, but because of their differing statuses within the international community.

3209   In 1960 and 1974, the depositary notified the States Parties of the accessions of the Provisional Government of the Algerian Republic and of the Republic of Guinea-Bissau, respectively, without, however, confirming a date of entry into force. In parallel, the Swiss Confederation addressed a diplomatic note to the States Parties indicating that Switzerland, as a State Party to the Conventions, did not recognize the entity in question, in the case of Algeria, and did not, by taking note of its accession, make a statement on the international status of Guinea-Bissau.

3210   Also in 1974, the depositary notified the States Parties of the accession of the Revolutionary Provisional Government of the Republic of South Vietnam, confirming the immediate applicability of the Conventions. In parallel, Switzerland, as a State Party to the Conventions, addressed a diplomatic note to the States Parties identical to that sent in relation to the accession of Guinea-Bissau.

---

[9] See Vienna Convention on the Law of Treaties (1969), Article 76(2), which is an established rule of customary international law (Villiger, p. 932).

[10] For the practice of the UN secretary-general, see United Nations, *Summary of practice of the Secretary-General as depositary of multilateral treaties*, paras 82–97.

[11] The depositary notifications since 1977 are available on https://www.fdfa.admin.ch/treaties.

3211 In 1983, the depositary notified the States Parties of the accession of the United Nations Council for Namibia, confirming the entry into force of the Conventions. Although Switzerland had not recognized Namibia at the time, it did not in this case address a parallel note of non-recognition to the other States Parties.

3212 In 1989, 1990 and 1991, the depositary informed the States Parties that Palestine had deposited an instrument of accession but that owing to the uncertain status of this entity within the international community, it was not in a position to determine whether this act constituted a valid accession.[12] Subsequently, the depositary notified the States Parties that the State of Palestine had acceded to the four Geneva Conventions and Additional Protocol I on 2 April 2014 and to Additional Protocols II and III on 4 January 2015.

2. *Nature and effect of accession*

3213 Accession is a single act expressing the consent of a State to be bound by the Convention and making it applicable to that State's relations with the other contracting Parties. Thus, like ratification, it requires a thorough examination by the acceding State of the merits of the treaty in question, and means that specific approval and implementation procedures laid down in the domestic law of that State must be followed.[13]

3214 Accession has the same effect as ratification, namely that the acceding State is bound by the treaty in question. As in the case of ratification, the Convention enters into force for the acceding State six months after the deposit of the instrument of accession.[14]

3215 Accession to the Conventions can, according to the text of the provision, only take place after their entry into force, i.e. six months after the first two instruments of ratification have been deposited. However, with the accession of Jordan on 29 May 1951 and entry into force of the Conventions for this State on 29 November 1951, the depositary accepted, and the signatories did not object to, the deposit of an instrument of accession before the entry into force of the Conventions, which took place on 21 October 1951. This was possible because at the time of the deposit of Jordan's instrument of accession, the date of entry into force of the Conventions pursuant to Article 58 (and its parallel provisions in the other three Conventions) was already determined.[15] Therefore, it

---

[12] See also Caflisch/Gamma. For a critique, see David, para. 1.212.

[13] According to Article 46 of the 1969 Vienna Convention on the Law of Treaties, '[a] State may not invoke the fact that its consent to be bound by a treaty has been expressed in violation of a provision of its internal law regarding competence to conclude treaties as invalidating its consent unless that violation was manifest and concerned a rule of its internal law of fundamental importance'. This article can be assumed to be declaratory of customary international law (Villiger, p. 594).

[14] See Article 61(1).

[15] Switzerland having ratified it on 31 March 1950 and Yugoslavia on 21 April 1950.

was clear that the accession would only take effect after the coming into force of the Conventions. To stick to the letter of the provision would have led to the rather peculiar situation that from the date of the end of the period of signature (12 February 1950) up to the date of entry into force (21 October 1951), States that had not signed the Conventions would have been unable to express their consent to be bound by them. More recent international treaties no longer contain such restrictions and are usually open for accession to all States that have not signed them, either without temporal limitation or after the end of the deadline for signature.[16]

3. Reservations

3216   The formulation of reservations and declarations is possible for an acceding State to the same extent and under the same rules and conditions as for a signatory State at the time of ratification.[17]

4. Succession

3217   The subject of succession is covered neither by the final provisions of the Conventions nor by the 1969 Vienna Convention on the Law of Treaties.[18] It is governed by the 1978 Vienna Convention on Succession of States in respect of Treaties, which at March 2016 had only 22 Parties. It has been argued that the 1978 Vienna Convention is largely a progressive development of international law rather than a codification of customary law and that it is, therefore, 'not a reliable guide to the customary law rules on treaty succession'.[19] However, the UN secretary-general is of the opinion that 'the Convention in many of its aspects codifies established customary law on the matter'.[20]

3218   The 1978 Vienna Convention posits the principle of 'tabula rasa' ('clean slate'), whereby a new State is not bound by the treaties of the predecessor State.[21] This is without prejudice, however, to the new State being bound by customary international law.[22] The Vienna Convention also makes an exception for treaties relating to boundary and other territorial regimes as not being affected by a succession of States.[23] However, under the Convention automatic

---

[16]   See e.g. Additional Protocol I, Article 94; Additional Protocol II, Article 22; Additional Protocol III, Article 10; Anti-Personnel Mine Ban Convention (1997), Article 16; and Convention on Cluster Munitions (2008), Article 16.

[17]   On reservations, see the commentary on Article 57, section C.2.

[18]   On the subject of State succession in treaties, see Aust, pp. 320–340; Crawford, pp. 423–444; Andreas Zimmermann; and Zimmermann/Devaney.

[19]   Aust, p. 321.

[20]   United Nations, *Summary of practice of the Secretary-General as depositary of multilateral treaties*, para. 287.

[21]   Vienna Convention on Succession of States in respect of Treaties (1978), Article 16.

[22]   See *ibid.* Article 5.

[23]   *Ibid.* Articles 11–12; see also Aust, pp. 322–323, and Crawford, p. 439.

succession is set forth as the default rule in the case of a uniting of States or the separation of parts of a State, i.e. the creation of a new State outside the context of decolonization.[24] But it is not clear to what extent the distinction drawn in the Vienna Convention reflects the practice of States.[25]

3219   Another possible exception is treaties which reflect generally accepted rules of international law, in particular those concerned with human rights or international humanitarian law.[26] Already in the 1960s, in the context of decolonization, the ICRC defended the position that there was automatic succession with regard to the Geneva Conventions, unless the State made an explicit declaration to the contrary.[27] The UN Security Council implicitly followed this position in at least one situation.[28] Following the adoption of the Vienna Convention on Succession of States in respect of Treaties in 1978, the ICRC and the Standing Commission of the Red Cross and Red Crescent concluded that the 'tabula rasa' principle had to be accepted. Thus they adapted their interpretation of the definition of membership of the International Conference of the Red Cross and Red Crescent to the effect that only those new States which had made a formal démarche in relation to the Conventions could be members of the Conference.[29]

3220   Even so, in 2001 the ICTY Appeals Chamber took the position that the Geneva Conventions are subject to automatic succession because of their object and purpose and their customary nature.[30] This position avoids any gap in the protection afforded by the Conventions to any victims of armed conflict that might otherwise result from a succession of States. The Eritrea-Ethiopia

---

[24] Vienna Convention on Succession of States in respect of Treaties (1978), Articles 31 and 34.

[25] For a discussion, see Aust, p. 321; Crawford, pp. 438–439; and David, paras 1.162–1.168.

[26] Aust, pp. 323–324; Hafner/Novak, pp. 421–423. Automatic succession to human rights treaties is supported by the UN Commission on Human Rights: see Res. 1993/23, Succession of States in respect of international human rights treaties, 5 March 1993; Res. 1994/16, Succession of States in respect of international human rights treaties, 25 February 1994; Res. 1995/18, Succession of States in respect of international human rights treaties, 24 February 1995; UN Human Rights Committee, *General Comment No. 26, Continuity of Obligations*, UN Doc. CCPR/C/21/Rev.1/Add.8/Rev.1, 8 December 1997; and UN Secretary-General, *Succession of States in respect of international human rights treaties*, UN Doc. E/CN.4/1995/80, 28 November 1994, para. 10. See also ICJ, *Application of the Genocide Convention case*, Preliminary Objections, Judgment, 1996, Separate Opinion of Judge Shahabuddeen, pp. 634–639, and Separate Opinion of Judge Weeramantry, pp. 640–655. For an overview of State practice with regard to succession to human rights treaties, see UN Secretary-General, *Succession and accession of States to international human rights treaties*, UN Doc. E/CN.4/1994/68, 26 November 1993. See also Kamminga.

[27] See Henri Coursier, 'L'accession des nouveaux Etats africains aux Conventions de Genève', *Annuaire français de droit international*, Vol. 7, 1961, pp. 760–761; 'The Universality of the Geneva Conventions', *International Review of the Red Cross*, Vol. 6, No. 64, July 1966, p. 386.

[28] UN Security Council, Res. 307 (The India/Pakistan Subcontinent), 21 December 1971, para. 3.

[29] Bruno Zimmermann, pp. 118–119.

[30] ICTY, *Mucić* Appeal Judgment, 2001, paras 107–115, particularly para. 111 ('It may be now considered in international law that there is automatic State succession to multilateral humanitarian treaties in the broad sense, *i.e.*, treaties of universal character which express fundamental human rights.'). See also ICTY, *Blaškić* Decision on Defence Motion, 1997, para. 12. For a critical appraisal, see Stern, pp. 176–190, and Rasulov.

Claims Commission on the other hand found that although '[t]reaty succession may happen automatically for certain types of treaties', it had 'not been shown evidence that would permit it to find that such automatic succession to the Geneva Conventions occurred in the exceptional circumstances here, desirable though such succession would be as a general matter'.[31]

3221   But a gap can also be avoided by a declaration of succession. The practice of the depositary of the Conventions, in accordance with the practice of the UN secretary-general as depositary in the case of treaties which do not contain a specific provision on succession, has been to accept instruments of succession from newly existing States on the condition that the Convention was applicable, through the predecessor State, on the territory of the new State prior to succession.[32]

3222   The general condition for being a State Party to the Convention as contained in the article on accession, which is statehood, also has to be fulfilled in the case of succession.

3223   There is no clear rule in international law on the question of the legal effects of succession on the possible reservations and declarations of the predecessor State. If the instrument of succession or any accompanying declarations of the successor State do not make clear the will of the State in this respect, the depositary would invite the successor State to specify whether or not it intends to maintain the reservations and declarations of the predecessor State. It may also be admissible for the successor State to make new reservations or declarations, according to the same rules as acceding States.[33]

3224   If successor States are not bound by the treaty obligations of their predecessors, they are free to choose whether they want to declare their succession to all or some of the treaties applicable to the predecessor. Consequently, they also have the possibility of becoming a Party to the Convention by accession, like any other State, instead of by depositing an instrument of succession.

---

[31] Eritrea-Ethiopia Claims Commission, *Prisoners of War, Ethiopia's Claim*, Partial Award, 2003, paras 24–25. The Commission noted that senior Eritrean officials had made clear that Eritrea did not consider itself bound by the Geneva Conventions; that Ethiopia had consistently maintained that Eritrea was not a Party; and that the ICRC had not regarded Eritrea as a Party either.

[32] Vienna Convention on Succession of States in respect of Treaties (1978), Article 17. See, for example, the declarations of succession of the States emerging from the former Yugoslavia: Slovenia on 25 June 1991 and Croatia on 8 October 1991 (depositary's notifications of 7 July 1992), Bosnia and Herzegovina on 6 March 1992 (notification of 17 February 1993), the Former Yugoslav Republic of Macedonia on 8 September 1991 (notification of 13 December 1993) and the Federal Republic of Yugoslavia on 27 April 1992 (notification of 30 November 2001). See also the notifications of 12 June 1978 relating to the declaration of succession by Tonga, of 8 May 1981 relating to the succession of Tuvalu and of Grenada, and of 27 September 1984 relating to the declaration of succession by Samoa. For the wording of the declarations, see the depositary notifications, available at https://www.fdfa.admin.ch/treaties.

[33] Crawford, p. 442, calling these issues 'as yet unsettled'; see also Bruno Zimmermann, pp. 122–123.

3225   Alongside political considerations, which may influence States in their choice of succession or accession,[34] there are differences between the two in their legal effects. One important difference is that by depositing an instrument of succession, the State consents to be bound by the treaty from the date of the State's coming into existence.[35] Hence, successions lead to a continued application of a treaty, whereas entry into force after an accession depends on the provisions of the treaty and is in most cases delayed after the deposit of the instrument.[36]

3226   At the time of writing, of the 196 States party to the Convention, 55 have become party by way of succession, mostly out of decolonization processes.[37] Although in not all of these cases did the instruments deposited use the term 'succession', in substance they were succession and were dealt with by the depositary accordingly.

3227   Article 64 entrusts the depositary with the task of informing the UN Secretariat of ratifications, accessions and denunciations of the Convention. The same would obviously also apply to successions.[38]

Select bibliography

Aust, Anthony, *Modern Treaty Law and Practice*, 3rd edition, Cambridge University Press, 2013, pp. 101–103 (Accession) and 320–340 (Succession to treaties).

Caflisch, Lucius and Gamma, Serge, 'La Suisse, dépositaire des Conventions de Genève', *Allgemeine schweizerische Militärzeitschrift*, Vol. 165, No. 3, 1999, pp. 7–9.

Crawford, James R., *Brownlie's Principles of Public International Law*, 8th edition, Oxford University Press, 2012, pp. 423–444 (Succession to rights and duties).

Daillier, Patrick, Forteau, Mathias, Pellet, Alain, Müller, Daniel and Nguyen, Quoc Dinh, *Droit international public*, 8th edition, Librairie générale de droit et de jurisprudence (LGDJ), Paris, 2009, pp. 599–619 (State succession).

David, Eric, *Principes de droit des conflits armés*, 5th edition, Bruylant, Brussels, 2012.

Distefano, Giovanni and Henry, Etienne, 'Final Provisions, Including the Martens Clause', in Andrew Clapham, Paola Gaeta and Marco Sassòli (eds), *The 1949 Geneva Conventions: A Commentary*, Oxford University Press, 2015, pp. 155–188.

---

[34] A newly existing State may wish to explicitly demonstrate the continuity of its legal obligations by choosing succession or to highlight its new independence by opting for accession.

[35] This seems logical given that 'the essence of succession to treaty rights and obligations being that the notification of succession is merely formal confirmation of what has already happened by operation of law' (Aust, p. 335).

[36] With respect to the First Convention, see Article 61. If a State chooses accession instead of succession and is, at that time, involved in an armed conflict, Article 62 on immediate effect applies.

[37] For the current status of the Conventions, see: https://www.icrc.org/ihl.

[38] See also the commentary on Article 64, para. 3312.

Hafner, Gerhard and Novak, Gregor, 'State Succession in Respect of Treaties', in Duncan B. Hollis (ed.), *The Oxford Guide to Treaties*, Oxford University Press, 2012, pp. 396–427.

Kamminga, Menno T., 'State Succession in Respect of Human Rights Treaties', *European Journal of International Law*, Vol. 7, No. 4, 1996, pp. 469–484.

Rasulov, Akbar, 'Revisiting State Succession to Humanitarian Treaties: Is There a Case for Automaticity?', *European Journal of International Law*, Vol. 14, No. 1, 2003, pp. 141–170.

Rosenne, Shabtai, 'Participation in the Geneva Conventions (1864–1949) and the Additional Protocols of 1977', in Christophe Swinarski (ed.), *Studies and Essays on International Humanitarian Law and Red Cross Principles in Honour of Jean Pictet*, ICRC/Martinus Nijhoff Publishers, The Hague, 1984, pp. 803–812.

Schenker, Claude, *Practice Guide to International Treaties*, Federal Department of Foreign Affairs, Bern, 2015, p. 30, available at https://www.fdfa.admin.ch/treaties.

Sinclair, Ian, *The Vienna Convention on the Law of Treaties*, 2nd edition, Manchester University Press, 1984, p. 42 (Accession).

Stern, Brigitte, 'La succession d'États', *Recueil des cours de l'Académie de droit international de La Haye*, Vol. 262, 1996, pp. 9–438, at 176–190.

United Nations, Office of Legal Affairs, Treaty Section, *Summary of practice of the Secretary-General as depositary of multilateral treaties*, UN Doc. ST/LEG/7/Rev.l, United Nations, New York, 1999.

Zimmermann, Andreas, 'State Succession in Treaties', version of November 2006, in Rüdiger Wolfrum (ed.), *Max Planck Encyclopedia of Public International Law*, Oxford University Press, http://opil.ouplaw.com/home/EPIL.

Zimmermann, Andreas and Devaney, James G., 'Succession to treaties and the inherent limits of international law', in Christian J. Tams, Antonios Tzanakopoulos and Andreas Zimmermann (eds), *Research Handbook on the Law of Treaties*, Edward Elgar, Cheltenham, 2014, pp. 505–540.

Zimmermann, Bruno, 'La succession d'états et les Conventions de Genève', in Christophe Swinarski (ed.), *Etudes et essais sur le droit international humanitaire et sur les principes de la Croix-Rouge en l'honneur de Jean Pictet*, ICRC/Martinus Nijhoff Publishers, The Hague, 1984, pp. 113–123.

NOTIFICATION OF ACCESSIONS

❖ Text of the provision*

(1) Accessions shall be notified in writing to the Swiss Federal Council, and shall take effect six months after the date on which they are received.

(2) The Swiss Federal Council shall communicate the accessions to all the Powers in whose name the Convention has been signed, or whose accession has been notified.

❖ Reservations or declarations

None

Contents

A. Introduction

3228 This article determines the time of entry into force of the Convention for an acceding State and contains two elements of a procedural nature: the form of accession and the tasks of the depositary in the context of accessions.[1]

3229 Since declarations of succession follow the same procedural rules as accessions,[2] the legal principles and practice described in the commentary on this article are also applicable to successions.

---

* Paragraph numbers have been added for ease of reference.

[1] On the nature and effect of accession, see the commentary on Article 60, section C.2.

[2] On succession, see the commentary on Article 60, section C.4.

3230   This provision is common to the four Conventions.[3] The process for accession and the date of entry into force of the Conventions after accession by a State have been the same for the four Conventions.

B. Historical background

3231   This provision is substantively the same as the corresponding provisions in the 1929 Geneva Conventions.[4] The ICRC draft adopted by the 1948 International Conference of the Red Cross in Stockholm submitted to the Diplomatic Conference used identical language but did not specify the six-month timeline.[5] This was added, as in Article 58 on entry into force after ratification, during the discussions in the Joint Committee of the Conference.[6] The provision thus completed was adopted unanimously.[7]

C. Paragraph 1: Formal requirements for and effect of accession

1. Formal requirements for accession

3232   According to Article 61(1), accessions 'shall be notified in writing'. This formulation is different from that in Article 57 on ratification, which requires instruments of ratification to be 'deposited'.[8] This raises the question of whether the formal requirements for a valid accession are different from those for ratification.

3233   The term 'notified' might suggest that the document by which a State declares its accession to the Convention does not need to be as formal as an instrument of ratification. However, to express a State's consent to be bound in a legally valid manner, the instrument has to contain the same basic elements as an instrument of ratification, irrespective of its form: a clear denomination of the treaty to which the State wishes to accede; the expression of its consent to be bound; possible reservations or declarations; and the original signature of a person authorized to represent the State for that purpose.[9]

3234   As the requirements for a valid accession are the same as for ratification, the depositary does not differentiate between instruments of ratification and instruments of accession when specifying the form or mode of transmission.

---

[3] See also Second Convention, Article 60; Third Convention, Article 140; and Fourth Convention, Article 156.

[4] Geneva Convention on the Wounded and Sick (1929), Article 36; Geneva Convention on Prisoners of War (1929), Article 94.

[5] *Draft Conventions adopted by the 1948 Stockholm Conference*, draft article 49, p. 28.

[6] *Final Record of the Diplomatic Conference of Geneva of 1949*, Vol. II-B, p. 71 (United States).

[7] See *ibid*. pp. 30, 113 and 373.

[8] The wording used in Article 57 is 'ratifications shall be deposited' (paragraph 1) and 'the deposit of each instrument of ratification' (paragraph 2).

[9] See also the commentary on Article 57, section C.1.

In 1976, the ratification process for the Convention was concluded with the last signatory State depositing its instrument of ratification.[10]

2. Effect of accession

3235 Like ratifications, an accession takes effect six months after it has been received by the depositary. Indeed, since a State becomes bound by the Conventions through an accession in the same way as a signatory through ratification, there would be no reason to stipulate a different timeline.

D. Paragraph 2: Communication by the depositary

3236 Article 61 does not specify, as Article 57 does in the case of ratification, that the Swiss Federal Council is to draw up a record of each accession, nor that it must transmit a copy of the record to other States.[11] The depositary applies this differentiation between ratification and accession in its practice: while it draws up records of ratifications and sends them to States Parties, it does not follow this procedure for accessions. Besides the fact that establishing such records of accessions is not foreseen by the Convention, it is neither a task of depositaries under Article 77 of the 1969 Vienna Convention on the Law of Treaties or under customary international law, nor a common feature of other depositaries' practice in this regard.

3237 Usually, the depositary confirms the receipt of an instrument of accession, the date of the deposit and the date of the entry into force of the Convention for the acceding State by means of a diplomatic note sent to that State.

3238 In addition, Article 61(2) requires that the depositary communicate an accession 'to all the Powers in whose name the Convention has been signed, or whose accession has been notified'. In practice today, the depositary transmits a notification of the deposit of the instrument of accession to all States party to the Conventions through diplomatic channels. This notification contains information about the acceding State, the date of deposit, the date of entry into force of the Convention for the State in question and, if applicable, reservations and declarations of the acceding State. Nowadays, more and more depositaries, including the depositary of the Geneva Conventions, are using electronic means to make such notifications to States agreeing to this mode of transmission.

---

[10] This was the ratification by Bolivia, which had signed the Conventions on 8 December 1949, on 10 December 1976.

[11] On the content of such a record, see the commentary on Article 57, para. 3175.

3239   According to Article 64 of the Convention, the depositary must inform the Secretariat of the United Nations of all ratifications, accessions and denunciations received.[12]

Select bibliography

Aust, Anthony, *Modern Treaty Law and Practice*, 3rd edition, Cambridge University Press, 2013, pp. 101–103 (Accession) and 289–293 (Functions of the depositary).

Daillier, Patrick, Forteau, Mathias, Pellet, Alain, Müller, Daniel and Nguyen, Quoc Dinh, *Droit international public*, 8th edition, Librairie générale de droit et de jurisprudence (LGDJ), Paris, 2009, pp. 599–619 (State succession).

Schenker, Claude, *Practice Guide to International Treaties*, Federal Department of Foreign Affairs, Bern, 2015, pp. 18–19, available at https://www.fdfa.admin.ch/treaties.

United Nations, Office of Legal Affairs, Treaty Section, *Summary of practice of the Secretary-General as depositary of multilateral treaties*, UN Doc. ST/LEG/7/Rev.1, United Nations, New York, 1999.

Villiger, Mark E., *Commentary on the 1969 Vienna Convention on the Law of Treaties*, Martinus Nijhoff Publishers, Leiden, 2009, pp. 934–954 (Article 77).

---

[12] This obligation of the depositary stems from the fact that the Convention is registered with the Secretariat of the United Nations pursuant to Article 64 and to Article 102(1) of the 1945 UN Charter, according to which '[e]very treaty and every international agreement entered into by any Member of the United Nations ... shall as soon as possible be registered with the Secretariat and published by it'.

IMMEDIATE EFFECT

❖ Text of the provision

The situations provided for in Articles 2 and 3 shall give immediate effect to ratifications deposited and accessions notified by the Parties to the conflict before or after the beginning of hostilities or occupation. The Swiss Federal Council shall communicate by the quickest method any ratifications or accessions received from Parties to the conflict.

❖ Reservations or declarations

None

Contents

A. Introduction

3240 According to common Articles 2 and 3, the Convention is applicable in the following cases:

(a) declared war or any other armed conflict between two or more of the High Contracting Parties, even if the state of war is not recognized by one of them (Article 2(1));[1]

(b) partial or total occupation of the territory of a High Contracting Party, even if the occupation meets with no armed resistance (Article 2(2));

(c) armed conflict not of an international character occurring in the territory of one of the High Contracting Parties (Article 3(1)).

---

[1] Article 2(1) also explicitly provides that the applicability of the Conventions in case of war, other armed conflict between High Contracting Parties or occupation is '[i]n addition to the provisions which shall be implemented in peacetime'.

Should one of these situations arise, Article 62 provides that the six-month interval which normally separates the ratification or accession of a State from the entry into force of the Convention[2] is dispensed with for any State party to that conflict.

3241   This provision is common to the four Conventions.[3] The rule of immediate effect therefore applies to all four Conventions.

3242   It should be noted that the Additional Protocols do not contain a corresponding provision. The question therefore arises as to whether the immediate effect principle would apply also to the Protocols and, in the affirmative, under which conditions.[4]

B. Historical background

3243   Both of the 1929 Geneva Conventions contained similar provisions, but they referred only to 'a state of war'.[5] The draft conventions adopted by the 1948 International Conference of the Red Cross in Stockholm expanded on the idea by referring to the situations defined in draft common article 2, which had not yet been divided into the current common Articles 2 and 3.[6]

3244   The Conference's decision to divide draft common article 2 into two separate provisions raised the question of whether the provision regarding immediate effect should be modified to encompass situations of 'civil war' too.[7] The Conference voted on the issue and the decision was taken to make the provision also applicable to situations of armed conflict not of an international character.[8]

C. Discussion

1. Immediate effect

3245   When a State is a Party to one of the situations provided for in common Articles 2 and 3, its ratification of or accession to the Convention takes effect

---

[2] See Article 58(2) (Coming into force) and Article 61(1) (Notification and communication of accessions).

[3] See also Second Convention, Article 61; Third Convention, Article 141; and Fourth Convention, Article 157.

[4] See the commentaries on Article 95 of Additional Protocol I and Article 23 of Additional Protocol II.

[5] Geneva Convention on the Wounded and Sick (1929), Article 37; Geneva Convention on Prisoners of War (1929), Article 95.

[6] See Draft Conventions adopted by the 1948 Stockholm Conference, draft article 50, p. 28.

[7] Final Record of the Diplomatic Conference of Geneva of 1949, Vol. II-B, p. 373 (Romania).

[8] After some doubts were expressed (ibid. pp. 374–375 (Canada)), the vote on the issue was deferred to the Plenary Meeting. The decision of the Conference to include non-international armed conflict in the scope of the provision was passed by 28 votes to 2 with 10 abstentions and the article as a whole was adopted by 38 votes to none, with 2 abstentions (ibid. p. 386).

immediately. Accordingly, the Convention enters into force for that State on the day of receipt by the depositary of the instrument of ratification or accession,[9] without the usual six-month delay.[10]

3246 If a State has already deposited its instrument of ratification or accession, and hostilities are breaking out or an occupation is under way before the expiry of the six-month waiting period, the Convention enters into force from the outbreak of hostilities or the beginning of the occupation.[11]

3247 Moreover, the wording of this provision does not seem to exclude the possibility of a ratification or accession taking immediate effect in a situation of 'declared war' in which no hostilities or occupation have yet taken place.[12]

3248 In line with the principle set forth in common Article 2, a ratification or accession takes effect immediately, even when another Party to the conflict is not party to the Conventions, regardless of whether or not that Party accepts to apply the Conventions on an ad hoc basis in accordance with Article 2(3). Even if no other Party to the conflict is party to the Conventions, the ratifying or acceding State becomes bound by the obligations incumbent on all High Contracting Parties.[13]

3249 The 'immediate effect' provided in the Geneva Conventions was applied by the depositary in the following cases:

- accession to the four Geneva Conventions by the Republic of Korea on 16 August 1966;
- accession to the four Geneva Conventions by the State of Eritrea on 14 August 2000;
- accession to the four Geneva Conventions and to the three Additional Protocols[14] by the Republic of South Sudan on 25 January 2013;[15]
- accession to the four Geneva Conventions and Additional Protocol I by the State of Palestine on 2 April 2014, as well as to Additional Protocol III on 4 January 2015.

---

[9] Despite what the formulation of Article 62 might suggest, there is no difference between 'deposit' (of a ratification) and 'notification' (of an accession). The terms used merely reflect the wording of Articles 57 (Ratification) and 61 (Notification and communication of accessions); see the commentary on the latter, section C.1.

[10] For a discussion of this delay, see the commentaries on Article 58, section D, and Article 61, section C.2.

[11] For a discussion of these conditions, see the commentaries on common Article 2, sections D and E and common Article 3, section C. Hostilities amounting to a non-international armed conflict in the sense of common Article 3 would trigger the immediate applicability of the Convention as a whole, even though not all provisions are applicable to non-international armed conflicts.

[12] On the concept of 'declared war', see the commentary on common Article 2, section D.1.

[13] See Articles 1, 6, 23, 26, 40–43, 47–49 and 54.

[14] Regarding the Protocols, see the commentaries on Article 95 of Additional Protocol I and on Article 23 of Additional Protocol II.

[15] In addition, the Republic of South Sudan had already accepted the application of the Conventions on the basis of Article 2(3) (de facto application of the Conventions by a State not party); for further details see the commentary on that article, section F.2.

2. The quality of 'Party to the conflict'

3250   Under general international law, one of the tasks of the depositary of a treaty is to determine not only the initial date of entry into force of the treaty, but also the date at which the treaty enters into force for States becoming Parties at a later time.[16] Therefore, in view of Article 62, the depositary, while staying impartial,[17] also has to make a preliminary assessment of whether a State is a Party to a conflict at the time of the deposit of its instrument of ratification or accession in order to set the date of entry into force of the Convention for that Party.

3251   This task can be easy if the ratifying or acceding State declares itself to be a Party to a conflict; in that case, the depositary will probably take the same view.

3252   However, the depositary has no competence to make a final determination either of the quality of a State as a Party to a conflict or, in consequence, on the date of entry into force of the Conventions for that State, which would be binding upon the State concerned as well as on the other States Parties. Therefore, the depositary's assessment may be challenged by another State, or even by the ratifying or acceding State itself if it had not publicly expressed its legal reading of the situation. At the time of writing, this has never arisen, but in such a case the depositary would have to 'bring the question to the attention of the signatory States and the contracting States', pursuant to Article 77(2) of the 1969 Vienna Convention on the Law of Treaties.[18]

3253   As regards the accession of the Republic of Korea on 16 August 1966, the depositary received a note verbale from the Korean embassy in Switzerland on 21 September 1966 stating that 'the Republic of Korea, in view of the actual participation of its Armed Forces in the Vietnamese war, comes under the category of "the Parties to [the] conflict" prescribed in the respective provisions of Article 62 [of the First Convention, of Article 61 of the Second Convention, of Article 141 of the Third Convention, and of Article 157 of the Fourth Convention]'. The acceding State itself 'therefore requested that the accession . . . shall take immediate effect, invoking the respective provisions of the said Articles'.[19]

---

[16] See Vienna Convention on the Law of Treaties (1969), Article 77(f), which appears generally to reflect a codification of customary international law (Villiger, p. 945), and Ouguergouz/Villalpando/Morgan-Foster, pp. 1747–1748. On entry into force of the Conventions, see also the commentary on Article 58.

[17] See Vienna Convention on the Law of Treaties (1969), Article 76(2), which is an established rule of customary international law (Villiger, p. 932).

[18] See also Ouguergouz/Villalpando/Morgan-Foster, p. 1745.

[19] In its subsequent communication of 23 September 1966 to the States Parties, the depositary stated that the accession of the Republic of Korea took effect immediately following the request of the Korean Government, by note of its embassy of 21 September 1966 and pursuant to Articles 62, respectively 61, 141 and 157 of the four Conventions, and attached a copy of the instrument of accession and of the note verbale.

3254　When depositing its instrument of accession on 14 August 2000, the State of Eritrea did not publicly express its position regarding its immediate effect. Nevertheless, on 4 September 2000 the depositary notified States Parties of this accession as follows:

> On 14 August 2000, the State of Eritrea deposited with the Swiss Federal Council its instrument of accession to the Geneva Conventions of 12 August 1949 for the protection of war victims. According to Articles 62, respectively 61, 141 and 157 of the four Conventions, the situations provided for in Articles 2 and 3 shall give immediate effect to ratifications deposited and accessions notified by the parties to the conflict before or after the beginning of hostilities or occupation.

> It is interesting to note that the depositary cited the provision on immediate effect without mentioning the actual date of entry into force of the Convention for the State of Eritrea.

3255　In its notification of 7 February 2013 following the accession of the Republic of South Sudan, the depositary set the date of entry into force of the Convention for that State as follows:

> On 25 January 2013, the Republic of South Sudan deposited with the Swiss Federal Council its instrument of accession to the four Geneva Conventions and to their three Additional Protocols. Pursuant to Articles 62, respectively 61, 141 and 157 of the four Conventions, the accession by the Republic of South Sudan to the four Conventions and to their three Additional Protocols took effect on 25 January 2013.

3256　Similarly, the notification of the accession of the State of Palestine made on 10 April 2014 stated:

> On 2 April 2014, the State of Palestine deposited with the Swiss Federal Council its instrument of accession to the four Geneva Conventions . . . and to their Additional Protocol [I]. Pursuant to Articles 62, respectively 61, 141 and 157 of the four Conventions, the accession of the State of Palestine to the four Conventions and to the Protocol I took effect on 2 April 2014.

3. Communication by the quickest method

3257　As depositary, the Swiss Federal Council is to 'communicate by the quickest method any ratifications or accessions' to which immediate effect is given. This communication is made to all governments of the States party to the Conventions. Formerly, the depositary would transmit a draft text to the Swiss diplomatic representations to be communicated by them via note verbale to the governments concerned. Since the end of the 1960s, the depositary has prepared the final document itself, entitled 'Notification', dated and stamped, which is then transmitted to governments as is by the Swiss diplomatic representations.

3258　In the case of the immediate effect of a ratification or accession, the depositary deals with the instrument as quickly as possible and informs the Swiss representations of the urgency of its transmission. The representations should use the quickest method available.

3259   The 'quickest method' has evolved along with technological progress, as has the practice of depositaries; while at one time the quickest method would have been the telegram, nowadays it is email.

3260   In the four above examples in which accessions took immediate effect, the depositary notified the States Parties within a period ranging from a couple of days to a couple of weeks.[20]

Select bibliography

Distefano, Giovanni and Henry, Etienne, 'Final Provisions, Including the Martens Clause', in Andrew Clapham, Paola Gaeta and Marco Sassòli (eds), *The 1949 Geneva Conventions: A Commentary*, Oxford University Press, 2015, pp. 155–188.

Ouguergouz, Fatsah, Villalpando, Santiago and Morgan-Foster, Jason, 'Article 77: Functions of depositaries', in Olivier Corten and Pierre Klein (eds), *The Vienna Conventions on the Law of Treaties: A Commentary*, Vol. II, Oxford University Press, 2011, pp. 1715–1753.

Villiger, Mark E., *Commentary on the 1969 Vienna Convention on the Law of Treaties*, Martinus Nijhoff Publishers, Leiden, 2009, pp. 934–946 (Article 77).

---

[20] Communication to the Swiss representations two days after receiving the note verbale of 21 September 1966 from the Republic of South Korea making clear its position; and notifications 21 days after the deposit of the instrument of accession by the State of Eritrea on 14 August 2000, 13 days after the deposit of the instrument of accession by the Republic of South Sudan on 25 January 2013, and 8 days after the deposit of the instrument of accession by the State of Palestine on 2 April 2014. Some more days might then be necessary for the information to reach the governments of the States Parties.

ARTICLE 63

DENUNCIATION

❖ Text of the provision*
   (1) Each of the High Contracting Parties shall be at liberty to denounce the present Convention.
   (2) The denunciation shall be notified in writing to the Swiss Federal Council, which shall transmit it to the Governments of all the High Contracting Parties.
   (3) The denunciation shall take effect one year after the notification thereof has been made to the Swiss Federal Council. However, a denunciation of which notification has been made at a time when the denouncing Power is involved in a conflict shall not take effect until peace has been concluded, and until after operations connected with the release and repatriation of the persons protected by the present Convention have been terminated.
   (4) The denunciation shall have effect only in respect of the denouncing Power. It shall in no way impair the obligations which the Parties to the conflict shall remain bound to fulfil by virtue of the principles of the law of nations, as they result from the usages established among civilized peoples, from the laws of humanity and the dictates of the public conscience.
❖ Reservations or declarations
   None

Contents

* Paragraph numbers have been added for ease of reference.

A. Introduction

3261 Denunciation refers to a unilateral act by which a State Party seeks to terminate its participation in a treaty.[1] According to international law, treaties are subject to denunciation only if they contain a provision allowing for such.[2] Absent such a provision, denunciation is possible if it is established that the Parties intended to admit the possibility of denunciation or if a right of denunciation may be implied by the nature of the treaty.[3]

3262 Article 63, which is a provision common to the four Conventions,[4] provides clarity on this issue with respect to each of the Geneva Conventions by confirming the admissibility of denunciation, by defining the procedure to be followed and by indicating the effect of a denunciation.

B. Historical background

3263 Both of the 1929 Geneva Conventions contained similar provisions enabling States Parties to denounce the treaties, with the denunciation taking effect one year after its notification to the Swiss Federal Council.[5] They specified, however, that denunciations would 'not take effect during a war in which the denouncing Power is involved', but that in such cases the Conventions remained applicable 'beyond the period of one year, until the conclusion of peace'. The 1929 Geneva Convention on Prisoners of War provided, moreover, that the Convention continued to be binding 'in any case, until operations of repatriation shall have terminated'.

3264 The draft conventions adopted by the 1948 International Conference of the Red Cross in Stockholm maintained that denunciations 'shall not take effect

---

[1] See Anthony Aust, 'Treaties, Termination', version of June 2006, para. 1, in Rüdiger Wolfrum (ed.), *Max Planck Encyclopedia of Public International Law*, Oxford University Press, http://opil.ouplaw.com/home/EPIL.

[2] See Vienna Convention on the Law of Treaties (1969), Article 54.

[3] See *ibid.* Article 56.

[4] See also Second Convention, Article 62; Third Convention, Article 142; and Fourth Convention, Article 158. The text of these articles is identical in the four Conventions, with the exception of paragraph 4, which in the first three Conventions refers to 'release and repatriation' and in the Fourth Convention refers to 'release, repatriation and reestablishment'.

[5] See Geneva Convention on the Wounded and Sick (1929), Article 38, and Geneva Convention on Prisoners of War (1929), Article 96.

during a conflict in which the denouncing Power is involved'.[6] The drafts further specified that in such cases the 'Convention shall continue [to be] binding beyond the period of one year, until the conclusion of peace, and in any case until the operations connected' with the release, repatriation or reestablishment of the persons protected by the respective Convention 'are terminated'.

3265   During the discussions on the article at the 1949 Diplomatic Conference, the Special Committee decided that its chairman should provide a 'better wording', without substantive modification.[7] In the course of this redrafting, the express specification that 'denunciation shall not take effect during a conflict in which the denouncing Power is involved' was deleted, together with the clarification that in such cases the Convention would continue to be binding beyond the period of one year after which denunciation would normally take effect. Instead, the provision as finally adopted states that 'a denunciation of which notification has been made at a time when the denouncing Power is involved in a conflict shall not take effect until peace has been concluded, and until after operations connected with the release and repatriation of the persons protected by the present Convention have been terminated'. In so far as this provision links the extension of the waiting period to the fact that a 'notification has been made at a time when the denouncing Power is involved in a conflict', there is a notable difference to the 1929 Conventions and the drafts adopted by the Stockholm Conference in 1948. These provisions had simply stated that 'the denunciation shall not take effect' during a conflict, irrespective of when the denunciation was notified, before or after the outbreak of conflict.[8]

C. Paragraph 1: Right of denunciation

3266 Article 63(1) expressly gives any High Contracting Party the right to withdraw from the Convention unilaterally. The legal effect of the denunciation is that the denouncing State is no longer bound by the provisions of the Convention denounced. Conversely, the denouncing State can no longer derive any rights from the Convention either.

3267   Whether or not a treaty can be denounced may be relevant to the internal approval procedures of States when considering ratification or accession to the treaty.

3268   Under international treaty law, even treaties that do not contain a denunciation clause can be terminated or suspended by all Parties or one Party if there is a material breach by one of the Parties.[9] This rule does not apply,

---

[6] See *Draft Conventions adopted by the 1948 Stockholm Conference*, draft article 51, p. 29.
[7] *Final Record of the Diplomatic Conference of Geneva of 1949*, Vol. II-B, p. 72.
[8] For the legal effects of this change, see section E.
[9] See Vienna Convention on the Law of Treaties (1969), Article 60(2).

however, to treaties of a 'humanitarian character'.[10] Therefore, even if there was a material breach of a Convention by one of the High Contracting Parties, the only way of terminating the application of that Convention would be through the procedure provided for in this article.

3269   Since their entry into force in 1950, no State has denounced any of the Geneva Conventions. Even if a State were to denounce a Convention, it would still be bound by customary international humanitarian law in this sphere.[11]

D. Paragraph 2: Notification of a denunciation

3270 Paragraph 63(2) determines the formal requirements for a denunciation and the tasks of the depositary following receipt of notification of the denunciation. It deals with the same issues and uses the same wording as Article 61 on accession.

3271   Like accessions, denunciations must be notified in writing to the Swiss Federal Council, in its capacity as depositary of the Geneva Conventions. A document of denunciation has to contain the clear expression of the State's will, the denomination of the treaty to which it refers and the original signature of a person authorized to represent the State for that purpose.[12]

3272   While Article 61 requires that the depositary 'communicate' accessions, Article 63 requires that denunciations be 'transmitted' to the Parties. This difference in wording did not feature in the ICRC drafts, both of which used 'communicate'. It arose during the redrafting of the provision on denunciation at the Conference. There is no indication in the preparatory work that it was intended to impose on the depositary different ways of informing High Contracting Parties of denunciations and accessions. Therefore, the depositary would inform the Parties of a denunciation in the same way as it does an accession.[13] However, as there have been no denunciations of any of the Geneva Conventions to date, there is no practice of the depositary in this regard.

3273   Another difference in the description of the procedure for the depositary is that only 'High Contracting Parties' have to be informed of denunciations, whereas accessions must be communicated to 'all the Powers in whose name the Convention has been signed, or whose accession has been notified'. According to this wording, information on denunciation is potentially addressed to a smaller group of States, since in theory there could be signatories who are not High Contracting Parties and who are therefore not encompassed by this provision.[14] However, this difference is no longer of any practical

---

[10] See *ibid.* Article 60(5).

[11] See section F.2.c.

[12] For the requirements for accession, see the commentary on Article 61, section C.1.

[13] For the practice of the depositary with regard to communication of accessions, see the commentary on Article 61, section D.

[14] This differentiation was already present in the 1929 Conventions and was reproduced in the ICRC drafts. The negotiators at the Diplomatic Conference obviously did not see the necessity of unifying the procedures in this regard. See Geneva Convention on the Wounded and Sick

consequence, since all signatories have become High Contracting Parties to the Convention.

3274   The depositary would also have to determine the time at which the denunciation takes effect pursuant to paragraph 3 of the provision, and communicate this date to the High Contracting Parties.

3275   According to Article 64 of the Convention, the depositary must also inform the Secretariat of the United Nations of all ratifications, accessions and denunciations received.[15]

E. Paragraph 3: Temporal effect of a denunciation

3276   A denunciation will not take effect immediately. Under peacetime conditions, it will only take effect one year after its notification to the Swiss Federal Council. The one-year period was already specified in the 1929 Geneva Conventions and is in conformity with the notice period for denunciation provided for in the 1969 Vienna Convention on the Law of Treaties.[16]

3277   Should the denouncing Power be involved in an armed conflict or an occupation,[17] the denunciation does not take effect 'until peace has been concluded',[18] or, even where peace has been concluded, until the release and repatriation of protected persons is complete.[19] This clause is the counterpart of Article 62 on immediate effect of ratifications deposited and accessions notified by Parties to the conflict. Both provisions are dictated by the best interests of the victims of armed conflict and aim at ensuring the application of the Convention as long as there is an armed conflict, or as long as persons affected by an armed conflict need the Convention's protection. In the case of denunciation, prolonging the time until the notification of a denunciation takes effect is intended to prevent a Party from reneging on its contractual obligations in a situation where their fulfilment is most needed.

3278   According to the wording of Article 63(3), the involvement of a Power in an armed conflict only affects denunciations it notifies 'at a time when the denouncing Power is involved in a conflict' and not those notified before the conflict began, the latter being subject to the regular waiting period of one year.

(1929), Articles 36 and 38, and Geneva Convention on Prisoners of War (1929), Articles 94 and 96.

[15] This obligation of the depositary arises because the Convention is registered with the Secretariat of the United Nations pursuant to Article 64 of the First Convention, as well as to Article 102(1) of the 1945 UN Charter, according to which '[e]very treaty and every international agreement entered into by any Member of the United Nations...shall as soon as possible be registered with the Secretariat and published by it'.

[16] See Vienna Convention on the Law of Treaties (1969), Article 56(2).

[17] For a discussion of these notions, see the commentaries on common Article 2, sections D and E and common Article 3, section C.

[18] For a discussion of this notion, see the commentaries on common Article 2, section D.2.c and common Article 3, section C.4.c.

[19] For the notion of release (and return), see Articles 30–32. For the notion of repatriation, see Article 5.

As mentioned earlier, this wording is a consequence of the redrafting of the provision during the 1949 Diplomatic Conference. The 1929 Conventions and the drafts adopted by the Stockholm Conference simply stated that a 'denunciation shall not take effect during a conflict', making it clear that even if a conflict started after the notification of denunciation, i.e. during the waiting period, the denunciation would not take effect until the conclusion of peace and the termination of, for example, repatriations. The object and purpose of the present article, like that of Article 62 on immediate effect, calls for the interpretation that a denunciation notified less than a year before a conflict breaks out also has its effect suspended until the end of that conflict. There is no indication in their drafting history that the 1949 Conventions should contain a narrower rule on the issue than the one in the corresponding Article 38(3) of the 1929 Geneva Convention on the Wounded and Sick. The ambiguity of the wording of Article 63 was avoided in the drafting of the corresponding articles in the 1977 Additional Protocols, which clearly state that the effect of denunciation is suspended if the State concerned is engaged in a conflict at the time the denunciation would normally take effect.[20]

F. Paragraph 4: Effect of denunciation

1. First sentence: Effect limited to the denouncing Power

3279   The principle that 'denunciation shall have effect only in respect of the denouncing Power' was already laid down in earlier humanitarian law treaties.[21] It was also included in the draft adopted by the 1948 International Conference of the Red Cross in Stockholm.[22] It was adopted, without any substantive change, by the 1949 Diplomatic Conference.

3280   The content of this provision might be regarded as self-evident. It expressly clarifies that the fact that a State – once its denunciation of a Geneva Convention has become effective – is no longer bound by that Convention has consequences only on the treaty obligations of and vis-à-vis that State, and not on the treaty obligations of and between other States party to the Convention.[23] In this respect, this provision is complementary to common Article 2(3), whose first sentence underlines that the 'si omnes' requirement contained in a number of earlier humanitarian law treaties does not apply to the Geneva Conventions.[24]

---

[20] See Article 99 of Additional Protocol I, as applicable, and Article 25 of Additional Protocol II, as applicable. For details, see the commentaries on these articles.

[21] See Geneva Convention (1906), Article 33(2); Hague Convention (X) (1907), Article 27(2); Geneva Convention on the Wounded and Sick (1929), Article 38(2); and Geneva Convention on Prisoners of War (1929), Article 96(2).

[22] See *Draft Conventions adopted by the 1948 Stockholm Conference*, draft article 51, p. 29.

[23] See Abi-Saab, pp. 267–268, with further references.

[24] Article 24 of the 1906 Geneva Convention and Article 18 of the 1907 Hague Convention (X) still contained the 'si omnes' condition. It was renounced in Article 25(2) of the 1929 Geneva

3281 Article 99 of Additional Protocol I, which regulates the denunciation of the Protocol, contains a similar provision.[25]

2. Second sentence: Remaining obligations of the denouncing Power

3282 This sentence was not included in the draft article on denunciation submitted by the ICRC to the 1948 Stockholm Conference.[26] However, the Stockholm Conference added the following: 'Lastly, the denunciation shall in no way affect the other obligations, even if similar, by which the denouncing Party is bound by virtue of any other rules of international law.'[27]

3283 During the 1949 Diplomatic Conference, the necessity of including this sentence was questioned.[28] In the course of the negotiations, one delegation suggested replacing the sentence 'by a provision similar to that in the so-called de Martens clause figuring in the Preamble of the IVth Hague Convention of 1907, which reserves the application of the principles of the law of nations'.[29] Despite the doubts expressed by some delegations,[30] the provision was ultimately adopted.[31]

Convention on the Wounded and Sick and in Article 82(2) of the 1929 Geneva Convention on Prisoners of War. For further details, see the commentary on common Article 2, section F.1.

[25] See the commentary on Article 99(3) of Additional Protocol I. Article 25 of Additional Protocol II, regulating the denunciation of that Protocol, contains no express provision limiting the effect of denunciation to the High Contracting Party concerned; for further details, see the commentary on Article 25 of Additional Protocol II. For the effect of denunciation by a Party to a multilateral treaty under general international law, see today also Vienna Convention on the Law of Treaties (1969), Article 70(2).

[26] See *Draft Conventions submitted to the 1948 Stockholm Conference*, pp. 32, 136, 213 and 241–242.

[27] In the case of draft article 129 of the future Third Convention and draft article 139 of the future Fourth Convention, the wording was: 'Lastly, the denunciation shall in no way impair the other obligations, even if similar, by which the denouncing Party is bound under any other rules of international law.' See *Draft Conventions adopted by the 1948 Stockholm Conference*, pp. 29, 50, 102 and 162; see also *Final Record of the Diplomatic Conference of Geneva of 1949*, Vol. I, pp. 57, 71, 101 and 139.

[28] See *Final Record of the Diplomatic Conference of Geneva of 1949*, Vol. II-B, p. 25: 'Mr. Castrén (Finland) felt that the last sentence of the last paragraph was redundant, for it was obvious that denunciation of an international treaty had no effect on the other international obligations of the denouncing party.'

[29] For this suggestion by the delegation of Monaco, see *ibid.* p. 72.

[30] See *ibid.* (France, United States and United Kingdom).

[31] For further details, see Schircks, pp. 25–26. The second sentence of the fourth paragraph of Article 63 can also be read in relation with the Diplomatic Conference's decision, after intense debate, not to include a detailed preamble in the Conventions. See Pictet (ed.), *Commentary on the First Geneva Convention*, ICRC, 1952, p. 413; *Commentary on the Second Geneva Convention*, ICRC, 1960, p. 282; *Commentary on the Third Geneva Convention*, ICRC, 1960, pp. 16 and 648; and *Commentary on the Fourth Geneva Convention*, ICRC, 1958, p. 625. See also Schircks, p. 25. An ICRC draft for a preamble to the Conventions began with words similar to the idea laid down in Article 63: 'Respect for the personality and dignity of human beings constitutes a universal principle which is binding even in the absence of any contractual undertaking.' See *ICRC Remarks and Proposals on the 1948 Stockholm Draft*, pp. 8, 26, 36 and 66–67. See also the commentary on the Preamble.

a. The relation to the Martens Clause

3284   As noted above, to date no High Contracting Party has denounced a Geneva Convention. Hence, there is no State practice on the effect of a denunciation and the remaining obligations by virtue of the principles of the law of nations.

3285   The formula used in Article 63 was inspired by the so-called 'Martens Clause'. Guidance on the meaning of the final sentence of Article 63 can therefore be found in an analysis of this clause.

3286   The Martens Clause first appeared in the preamble to the 1899 Hague Convention (II). Its adoption was the result of debates in the Second Sub-commission of the Second Commission of the 1899 Hague Peace Conference, which was entrusted with finding ways to give the rules contained in the 1874 Brussels Declaration legally binding force.[32] When the discussion turned to Articles 9 and 10 of the Declaration, laying down the conditions for combatant status and for *levées en masse*, the Belgian delegate reminded the Sub-commission that it had been, in particular, controversies on the scope of the rights of Occupying Powers and on the right of populations to forceful resistance that had led to the failure of the Brussels Conference. So that the Hague Peace Conference might avoid similar difficulties, the delegate suggested these questions remain unregulated by treaty law, underlining the need especially of smaller States to defend themselves by using all their resources, including their populations, a possibility that should not be limited by a treaty.[33] Fyodor Fyodorovich Martens, delegate of Russia to the Peace Conference and chair of the Second Commission and Second Sub-commission, submitted that it had not been the intention of the Brussels Conference to abolish a right of populations to defend their countries or to regulate acts not fulfilling the conditions laid down in Articles 9 and 10: the aim had rather been to give to populations acting in accordance with the conditions more guarantees than they had had before.[34] Martens proceeded by reading a declaration to be inserted into the procès-verbal, intended to avoid misunderstandings in particular of Articles 9 and 10. Part of that declaration was a paragraph whose content would become known as the Martens Clause.[35] On this basis, the Second Sub-commission unanimously adopted Articles 9 and 10, which became Articles 1 and 2 of the 1899 Hague Regulations.

---

[32] On the proceedings at the 1899 Hague Peace Conference, see also e.g. Cassese, pp. 193–198, and Schircks, pp. 17–22.

[33] See *Conférence internationale de la paix*, Troisième partie, pp. 111–113; see also Schircks, pp. 18–19.

[34] See *Conférence internationale de la paix*, Troisième partie, p. 152. Martens had already been involved in the preparation of the 1874 Brussels Conference, which had been initiated by Tsar Alexander II of Russia; on the degree of Martens' contribution, see Schircks, p. 18, with fn. 29, with further references.

[35] For the full text of the declaration, see *Conférence internationale de la paix*, Troisième partie, p. 152. On the origin of the clause, see Graditsky.

3287   After further discussion on whether or not to place Martens' declaration in an operative article,[36] it was adopted as part of the preamble to the 1899 Hague Convention (II).[37] Paragraph 9 of the preamble reflects the part of Martens' declaration that is today understood as the Martens Clause; in the official English translation it reads:

> Until a more complete code of the laws of war is issued, the High Contracting Parties think it right to declare that in cases not included in the Regulations adopted by them, populations and belligerents remain under the protection and empire of the principles of international law, as they result from the usages established between civilized nations, from the laws of humanity, and the requirements of the public conscience.[38]

The preambular paragraphs surrounding paragraph 9 incorporated further elements of Martens' declaration, indicating its relation to the question of combatant status and the right of populations to forceful resistance.

3288   Wording identical to paragraph 9 of the preamble to the 1899 Hague Convention (II) was subsequently included in the preamble to the 1907 Hague Convention (IV).[39]

3289   Today, versions of the Martens Clause have found entry in many international treaties, leaving behind its original link to the question of combatant status and the right of populations to forceful resistance.[40] Besides Article 63 and its parallel provisions in the other Conventions,[41] versions of it are

---

[36] See *Conférence internationale de la paix*, Troisième partie, pp. 154–159; see also Schircks, pp. 20–21.

[37] See *Conférence internationale de la paix*, Première partie, pp. 195–197; see also Schircks, pp. 21–22.

[38] The authentic French text of paragraph 9 of the Preamble reads:

> En attendant qu'un code plus complet des lois de la guerre puisse être édicté, les Hautes Parties Contractantes jugent opportun de constater que, dans les cas non compris dans les dispositions réglementaires adoptées par Elles, les populations et les belligérants restent sous la sauvegarde et sous l'empire des principes du droit des gens, tels qu'ils résultent des usages établis entre nations civilisées, des lois de l'humanité et des exigences de la conscience publique.

> There is only one substantive difference between paragraph 9 of the Preamble and Martens' original declaration. The formulation 'un code tout-à-fait complet' (a fully complete code) was replaced by 'un code plus complet' ('a more complete code'), probably owing to the realization that a complete regulation is impossible (Schircks, p. 22).

[39] The authentic French text of paragraph 8 of the preamble to the 1907 Hague Convention (IV) is identical to the 1899 version; the non-authentic, official English translation differs slightly. The preambular paragraphs surrounding the Martens Clause were also retained.

[40] See Convention on Certain Conventional Weapons (1980), Preamble, para. 5, and Convention on Cluster Munitions (2008), Preamble, para. 11. Elements of the Martens Clause can also be found in other treaties; see Geneva Gas Protocol (1925), Preamble, paras 1–3; Biological Weapons Convention (1972), Preamble, para. 9; Anti-Personnel Mine Ban Convention (1997), Preamble, para. 8; and ICC Statute (1998), Preamble, para. 2.

[41] See Second Convention, Article 62; Third Convention, Article 142; Fourth Convention, Article 158.

contained in Additional Protocols I and II.[42] The clause has also been found to be a rule of customary international law.[43]

b. The meaning of the Martens Clause

3290 Despite recognition of the Martens Clause in treaty law and as customary law,[44] its meaning has remained subject to discussion. Various readings have been offered.[45]

3291   It has been contended that the Martens Clause and especially the terms 'laws of humanity' and the 'requirements of the public conscience',[46] either individually or combined, have an autonomous normative value under international law.[47] As regards their meaning, the term 'laws of humanity' has been associated with the notion of 'elementary considerations of humanity',[48] while the term 'requirements of the public conscience' has been suggested as being identifiable in the motivation of States, organizations or individuals that has led to the adoption of treaties in the area of humanitarian law.[49]

3292   In contrast to the view that sees the 'laws of humanity' and the 'requirements of the public conscience' as potentially autonomous sources of international law, it has been held that the Martens Clause has no influence on the system of the sources of international law, but functions within the triad of sources (treaties, customary law, general principles of law) as it is commonly understood to be expressed in Article 38(1)(a)-(c) of the 1945 ICJ Statute.[50]

3293   In that context, it has been suggested that the clause might accelerate the creation of customary international humanitarian law, reducing the need for State practice when a potential customary rule is supported by the 'laws of

---

[42] See Additional Protocol I, Article 1(2), and Additional Protocol II, Preamble, para. 4.

[43] See ICJ, *Legality of the Threat or Use of Nuclear Weapons*, Advisory Opinion, 1996, para. 84.

[44] See *ibid.* para. 87, according to which the 'continuing existence and applicability' of the clause 'is not to be doubted'. See, furthermore, e.g. Meron, p. 85, and Schircks, p. 31.

[45] For an overview, see e.g. Bernstorff, paras 8–13; Cassese, pp. 189–215; Crawford, pp. 14–22; Empell, pp. 147–153; Nishimura Hayashi, pp. 146–150; Meron, pp. 80–82 and 85–89; Pustogarov, pp. 129–131; Salter, pp. 407–436; Schircks, p. 15; Thürer, pp. 398–401; and Ticehurst, pp. 125–134.

[46] The wording of the elements of the Martens Clause used here is that of the official English translation of the original version in the preamble to the 1899 Hague Convention (II).

[47] See the statements submitted to the ICJ by a number of States in the context of the 1996 *Nuclear weapons case* available at http://www.icj-cij.org/, which to a greater or lesser degree attribute a certain legally binding force to the clause.

[48] For that term, see ICJ, *Corfu Channel case*, Merits, Judgment, 1949, p. 22, and *Military and Paramilitary Activities in and against Nicaragua case*, Merits, Judgment, 1986, paras 215 and 218. For a detailed discussion on the meaning of 'laws of humanity', see e.g. Meron, p. 82; Thürer, p. 401; and Schircks, pp. 96–121.

[49] For a detailed discussion, see Schircks, pp. 122–133, and Veuthey. See also e.g. Meron, pp. 83–85, and Thürer, pp. 401–402.

[50] See ICTY, *Kupreškić* Trial Judgment, 2000, para. 525; Meyrowitz, pp. 422–424; Miyazaki, p. 437; and Spieker, p. 46. For more details on the triad of sources of international law, including the question of whether the enumeration in Article 38(1)(a)-(c) is exhaustive outside the delimitation of the ICJ's competence, see Schircks, pp. 147– 167, and Brownlie, pp. 4–5.

humanity' or the 'requirements of the public conscience', as expressions of especially imperative *opinio juris*.[51]

3294   Furthermore, the Martens Clause and, in particular, the 'laws of humanity' and the 'requirements of the public conscience' have been proposed as guidelines in the interpretation of international humanitarian law.[52]

3295   It has also been argued that the clause could serve to clarify that, in the context of humanitarian law, 'general principles of law recognized by civilized nations' in the sense of Article 38(1)(c) of the ICJ Statute can arise from the 'usages established between civilized nations, from the laws of humanity, and the requirements of the public conscience'. The 'principles of international law' noted in the Martens Clause as resulting from these elements would consequently be read as similar to the 'general principles of law'.[53]

3296   As a minimum, the Martens Clause can be seen as a reminder of the continued validity of customary international law beside treaty law.[54] The expression 'usages established between civilized nations' in the Martens Clause is generally understood as equivalent to customary international law.[55]

3297   Bearing in mind that, despite the number of subjects today regulated in considerable detail under humanitarian treaty law, no codification can be complete, the Martens Clause should also be regarded as expressly preventing the *argumentum e contrario* that what is not explicitly prohibited by treaty law is necessarily permitted.[56] For a further reminder that Parties to an armed conflict

---

[51]   See ICTY, *Kupreškić* Trial Judgment, 2000, para. 527; see also Cassese, pp. 213–215; see further Rensmann, pp. 114–115. For a discussion of this view, see Schircks, pp. 168–169.

[52]   See ICTY, *Kupreškić* Trial Judgment, 2000, para. 525; see also Cassese, pp. 212–213, and Schircks, pp. 58–62, with further examples in case law.

[53]   See Bothe/Partsch/Solf, p. 44, commenting on Article 1(2) of Additional Protocol I; Meyrowitz, pp. 424–425; Spieker, p. 46; and Thürer, pp. 399 and 402–406. For a discussion of this view, see Schircks, pp. 169–171. For an overview of how 'general principles of law' in the sense of Article 38(1)(c) of the 1945 ICJ Statute are more commonly understood under international law, see Schircks, pp. 161–167, and Brownlie, pp. 16–18.

[54]   In this sense, see the statements submitted to the ICJ by a number of States in the context of the *Nuclear Weapons case*, available at http://www.icj-cij.org/, in particular the letter dated 16 June 1995 from the Legal Adviser to the Foreign and Commonwealth Office of the United Kingdom of Great Britain and Northern Ireland, together with Written Comments of the United Kingdom, p. 48, and the oral statement of the United States, CR 1995/34, Public sitting held on Wednesday 15 November 1995, p. 78. See also Greenwood, p. 35, noting: 'The Martens Clause should be treated as a reminder that customary international law continues to apply even after the adoption of a treaty on humanitarian law and as a statement of the factors which are likely to lead states to adopt a ban on a particular weapon or means of warfare'. See further Manual on International Law Applicable to Air and Missile Warfare (2009), commentary on Rule 2(c).

[55]   See Schircks, p. 81, with further references.

[56]   In this sense, see *Official Records of the Diplomatic Conference of Geneva of 1974–1977*, Vol. VIII, p. 18, para. 11 (Belgium); see also the letter dated 16 June 1995 from the Legal Advisor to the Foreign and Commonwealth Office of the United Kingdom of Great Britain and Northern Ireland, together with Written Comments of the United Kingdom, p. 48, and the oral statement of the United States, CR 1995/34, Public sitting held on Wednesday 15 November 1995, p. 78, in the context of the *Nuclear Weapons case*, available at http://www.icj-cij.org/. See also Bothe/Partsch/Solf, p. 44, commenting on Article 1(2) of Additional Protocol I. For a discussion and further references, see Cassese, pp. 189 and 192–193. At first sight, this aspect of the Martens Clause could be regarded as a rejection under international humanitarian law of the

are not unlimited in their actions, reference should also be made to Article 35(1) of Additional Protocol I.

3298   Lastly, the Martens Clause should be seen as underlining the dynamic factor of international humanitarian law, confirming the application of the principles and rules of humanitarian law to new situations or to developments in technology, also when those are not, or not specifically, addressed in treaty law.[57]

c. The impact of the Martens Clause in case of a denunciation

3299   As can be seen from the foregoing, the point of departure is not the same for the Martens Clause as it is for the principle affirmed in the denunciation provision of the Geneva Conventions. As one commentator has noted,

[t]he problem envisaged [in Article 63] is not exactly that to which the Martens clause was addressed... The purpose of this common article is not to safeguard the continued validity and applicability in relations between the parties of pre-existing rules on which agreement proved impossible and which consequently did not figure in the codification treaty. The purpose is rather to safeguard the continued application of the whole body of non-conventional or customary rules outside the conventional community, *i.e.* the community of States bound by the codification *Convention*. In both cases, however, the final aim is to surround pre-existing law with ample recognition and safeguards.[58]

3300   Thus, if a High Contracting Party were to denounce one of the Geneva Conventions, it would continue to be bound not only by other treaties to which it remains a Party, but also by other rules of international law, such as customary law. An *argumentum e contrario*, suggesting a legal void following the denunciation of a Convention, is therefore impossible. Today, however, the validity of international law beyond treaty law also follows from the system of international law in general.[59] Since the customary law character of 'the great majority' of the provisions contained in the Geneva Conventions is recognized,[60] the effects of a denunciation of a Convention would therefore, at least with respect to the overall substance of the law, be relatively limited.

---

so-called 'Lotus principle', according to which international law permits States to do what it does not explicitly prohibit them from doing. However, in the *Lotus case* the PCIJ did not consider treaty law ('conventions') alone as containing the rules of international law binding on States, but equally customary law ('usages generally accepted as expressing principles of law'), both being expressions of the will of States; see *Lotus case*, Judgment, 1927, p. 18. At least insofar as the Martens Clause's main purpose is seen as a reminder of the applicability of customary law beside treaty law, the clause and the 'Lotus principle' are therefore not opposites. On the relation between the 'Martens Clause' and the 'Lotus principle', see Schircks, p. 15.

[57] See ICJ, *Legality of the Threat or Use of Nuclear Weapons*, Advisory Opinion, 1996, para. 87: 'Finally, the Court points to the Martens Clause, whose continuing existence and applicability is not to be doubted,' as an affirmation that the principles and rules of humanitarian law apply to nuclear weapons.'

[58] See Abi-Saab, p. 275, footnote omitted.

[59] See ICJ Statute (1945), Article 38(1)(a)–(c), and Vienna Convention on the Law of Treaties (1969), Article 43. For a commentary on Article 43, see Bannelier.

[60] See ICJ, *Legality of the Threat or Use of Nuclear Weapons*, Advisory Opinion, 1996, para. 82.

3301 The above considerations are to be taken into account also in relation to non-international armed conflicts. A High Contracting Party's denunciation of a Geneva Convention comprises common Article 3. However, the denouncing State would continue to be bound by other humanitarian law treaties to which it is a Party, as well as by customary law applicable to non-international armed conflicts. Since the provisions of common Article 3 have been found to be binding outside the context of treaty law,[61] the effects of a denunciation of a Convention would have no substantive influence on the rules binding on the Parties to a non-international armed conflict.

Select bibliography

Abi-Saab, Georges, 'The specificities of humanitarian law', in Christophe Swinarski (ed.), *Studies and Essays on International Humanitarian Law and Red Cross Principles in Honour of Jean Pictet*, ICRC/Martinus Nijhoff Publishers, Geneva/The Hague, 1984, pp. 265–280.

Aust, Anthony, *Modern Treaty Law and Practice*, 3rd edition, Cambridge University Press, 2013, pp. 245–272 (Duration and termination).

Bannelier, Karine, 'Article 43: Obligations imposed by international law independently of a treaty', in Olivier Corten and Pierre Klein (eds), *The Vienna Conventions on the Law of Treaties: A Commentary*, Vol. II, Oxford University Press, 2011, pp. 1031–1043.

Bernstorff, Jochen von, 'Martens Clause', version of December 2009, in Rüdiger Wolfrum (ed.), *Max Planck Encyclopedia of Public International Law*, Oxford University Press, http://opil.ouplaw.com/home/EPIL.

Bothe, Michael, Partsch, Karl Josef and Solf, Waldemar A., *New Rules for Victims of Armed Conflicts: Commentary on the Two 1977 Protocols Additional to the Geneva Conventions of 1949*, Martinus Nijhoff Publishers, The Hague, 1982, p. 44.

Brownlie, Ian, *Principles of Public International Law*, 7th edition, Oxford University Press, 2008, pp. 3–5.

Cassese, Antonio, 'The Martens Clause: Half a Loaf or Simply Pie in the Sky?', *European Journal of International Law*, Vol. 11, No. 1, 2000, pp. 187–216.

Conférence internationale de la paix, The Hague, 18 May–29 July 1899, Ministry of Foreign Affairs, The Hague, Imprimerie nationale, 1899, Sommaire général, – Première partie, – Troisième partie (Deuxième Commission).

Crawford, Emily, 'The Modern Relevance of the Martens Clause', *Sydney Law School Legal Studies Research Paper*, No. 11/27, 2011, pp. 1–23.

Distefano, Giovanni and Henry, Etienne, 'Final Provisions, Including the Martens Clause', in Andrew Clapham, Paola Gaeta and Marco Sassòli (eds), *The 1949 Geneva Conventions: A Commentary*, Oxford University Press, 2015, pp. 155–188.

Empell, Hans-Michael, 'Die Martens'sche Klausel – grundlegende Norm des humanitären Völkerrechts oder Vorschrift ohne Wert?', *Humanitäres Völkerrecht – Informationsschriften*, Vol. 22, 2009, pp. 145–153.

---

[61] See ICJ, *Military and Paramilitary Activities in and against Nicaragua case*, Merits, Judgment, 1986, para. 218; see also ICTY, *Tadić* Decision on the Defence Motion for Interlocutory Appeal on Jurisdiction, 1995, para. 98, and ICTR, *Akayesu* Trial Judgment, 1998, para. 608.

Graditsky, Thomas, 'Bref retour sur l'origine de la clause de Martens : Une contribution belge méconnue', in Julia Grignon (ed.), *Hommage à Jean Pictet par le Concours de droit international humanitaire Jean-Pictet*, Editions Yvon Blais, Cowansville and Schulthess Editions Romandes, Geneva, 2016.

Greenwood, Christopher, 'Historical Development and Legal Basis', in Dieter Fleck (ed.), *The Handbook of International Humanitarian Law*, 2nd edition, Oxford University Press, 2008, pp. 1–43.

Kolb, Robert, *La bonne foi en droit international public*, Publications de l'Institut universitaire de hautes études internationales, Geneva, 2000, pp. 1770–1796.

Meron, Theodor, 'The Martens Clause, Principles of Humanity, and Dictates of Public Conscience', *American Journal of International Law*, Vol. 94, No. 1, January 2000, pp. 78–89.

Meyrowitz, Henry, 'Réflexions sur le fondement du droit de la guerre', in Christophe Swinarski (ed.), *Etudes et essais sur le droit international humanitaire et sur les principes de la Croix-Rouge en l'honneur de Jean Pictet*, ICRC/Martinus Nijhoff Publishers, Geneva/The Hague, 1984, pp. 419–431.

Miyazaki, Shigeki, 'The Martens Clause and International Humanitarian Law', in Christophe Swinarski (ed.), *Studies and Essays on International Humanitarian Law and Red Cross Principles in Honour of Jean Pictet*, ICRC/Martinus Nijhoff Publishers, Geneva/The Hague, 1984, pp. 433–444.

Münch, Fritz, 'Die Martens'sche Klausel und die Grundlagen des Völkerrechts', *Zeitschrift für ausländisches öffentliches Recht und Völkerrecht*, Vol. 36, 1976, pp. 347–373.

Nishimura Hayashi, Mika, 'The Martens Clause and Military Necessity', in Howard M. Hensel (ed.) *The Legitimate Use of Military Force – The Just War Tradition and the Customary Law of Armed Conflict*, Ashgate, Aldershot, 2008, pp. 135–159.

Pustogarov, Vladimir V., 'The Martens Clause in International Law', *Journal of the History of International Law*, Vol. 1, No. 2, 1999, pp. 125–135.

Rensmann, Thilo, 'Die Humanisierung des Völkerrechts durch das ius in bello – Von der Martens'schen Klausel zur "Responsibility to Protect"', *Zeitschrift für ausländisches öffentliches Recht und Völkerrecht*, Vol. 68, No. 1, 2008, pp. 111–128.

Salter, Michael, 'Reinterpreting Competing Interpretations of the Scope and Potential of the Martens Clause', *Journal of Conflict and Security Law*, Vol. 17, No. 3, 2012, pp. 403–437.

Schenker, Claude, *Practice Guide to International Treaties*, Federal Department of Foreign Affairs, Bern, 2015, p. 14, available at https://www.fdfa.admin.ch/treaties.

Schircks, Rhea, *Die Martens'sche Klausel, Rezeption und Rechtsqualität*, Dissertation, University of Zurich, Nomos , Baden-Baden, 2002.

Sinclair, Ian, *The Vienna Convention on the Law of Treaties*, 2nd edition, Manchester University Press, 1984, pp. 181–194 (Termination and suspension of operation of treaties).

Sperduti, Giuseppe, *Lezioni di diritto internazionale*, Giuffrè, Milan, 1958, pp. 68–74.

Spieker, Heike, 'Martens Klausel', *Humanitäres Völkerrecht – Informationsschriften*, Vol. 1, 1988, p. 46.

Thürer, Daniel, *International Humanitarian Law: Theory, Practice, Context*, Pocketbooks of the Hague Academy of International Law, 2011, pp. 398–402.

Ticehurst, Rupert, 'The Martens Clause and the Laws of Armed Conflict', *International Review of the Red Cross*, Vol. 37, No. 317, April 1997, pp. 125–134.

United Nations, Office of Legal Affairs, Treaty Section, *Summary of practice of the Secretary-General as depositary of multilateral treaties*, UN Doc. ST/LEG/7/Rev.l, United Nations, New York, 1999, paras 259–262 (Suspension, termination).

Veuthey, Michel, 'Public Conscience in International Humanitarian Law Today', in Horst Fischer, Ulrike Froissart, Wolff Heintschel von Heinegg and Christian Raap (eds), *Krisensicherung und Humanitärer Schutz – Crisis Management and Humanitarian Protection, Festschrift für Dieter Fleck*, Berliner Wissenschafts-Verlag, 2004, pp. 611–642.

Villiger, Mark E., *Commentary on the 1969 Vienna Convention on the Law of Treaties*, Martinus Nijhoff Publishers, Leiden, 2009, pp. 681–689 (Article 54).

ARTICLE 64

REGISTRATION WITH THE UNITED NATIONS

❖ Text of the provision

The Swiss Federal Council shall register the present Convention with the Secretariat of the United Nations. The Swiss Federal Council shall also inform the Secretariat of the United Nations of all ratifications, accessions and denunciations received by it with respect to the present Convention.

❖ Reservations or declarations

None

Contents

A. Introduction

3302 According to Article 102(1) of the 1945 UN Charter, '[e]very treaty and every international agreement entered into by any Member of the United Nations after the present Charter comes into force [24 October 1945] shall as soon as possible be registered with the Secretariat and published by it'.

3303   Article 64, which is common to the four Conventions,[1] entrusts the Swiss Federal Council, as depositary of the Conventions, with the task of arranging for their registration with the UN Secretariat and of informing it of any ratifications, accessions and denunciations which it receives with respect to the Conventions.[2]

---

[1] See Second Convention, Article 63; Third Convention, Article 143; and Fourth Convention, Article 159.

[2] A parallel provision exists for the Additional Protocols; see Additional Protocol I, Article 101; Additional Protocol II, Article 27; and Additional Protocol III, Article 16.

B. Historical background

3304 This provision can be traced back to the 1929 Geneva Conventions.[3] At that time, Article 18 of the 1919 Covenant of the League of Nations already provided that '[e]very treaty or international engagement entered into hereafter by any Member of the League shall be forthwith registered with the Secretariat and shall as soon as possible be published by it'.

3305 The draft conventions adopted by the 1948 International Conference of the Red Cross in Stockholm reproduced the obligation of registration with the UN Secretariat, as required by Article 102(1) of the UN Charter. According to the draft, '[t]he present Convention shall be transmitted by the Swiss Federal Council to the United Nations Organization, for the purpose of registration.'[4] This wording prompted the observation during the Joint Committee that it was 'assumed that the Swiss Federal Council would forward to the United Nations Organization, for the purpose of registration, a copy and not the original document of the present Convention'.[5] A brief discussion about the necessity of introducing this provision in the Convention confirmed that the formality of registration would in no way affect the validity of the Convention.[6] The Special Committee therefore amended the Stockholm Draft to its current wording.[7] This amendment was then adopted unanimously by the Joint Committee and later in the Plenary Meeting of the Conference.[8]

C. Discussion

1. First sentence: Registration

3306 The first sentence of Article 64 deals with the registration of the Convention with the UN Secretariat. It corresponds to the obligation under Article 102(1) of the 1945 UN Charter for all treaties entered into by a UN Member State to be registered as soon as possible with the UN Secretariat.[9] In the case of this

---

[3] Geneva Convention on the Wounded and Sick (1929), Article 39; Geneva Convention on Prisoners of War (1929), Article 97. Both articles provided for a certified copy of the Convention to be deposited by the Swiss Federal Council in the archives of the League of Nations and for the Swiss Federal Council to communicate to the League of Nations any ratifications, accessions and denunciations which it received.

[4] See *Draft Conventions adopted by the 1948 Stockholm Conference*, Article 52, p. 29.

[5] *Final Record of the Diplomatic Conference of Geneva of 1949*, Vol. II-B, p. 25.

[6] *Ibid.* pp. 72–73 and 95. On the issue of validity, see also section C.1.

[7] Adopted by 6 votes for, 1 against with 1 abstention; see *Final Record of the Diplomatic Conference of Geneva of 1949*, Vol. II-B, pp. 113–114.

[8] See *ibid.* p. 30. The Drafting Committee reached the current wording of this provision after slightly redrafting it from 'Government of the Swiss Confederation' to 'Swiss Federal Council' and from 'notices of termination' to 'denunciations' (*ibid.* p. 163).

[9] By Resolution 97 (I) of 14 December 1946 on Registration and Publication of Treaties and International Agreements, the UN General Assembly adopted the 'Regulations to give effect to Article 102 of the Charter of the United Nations'. These Regulations have been amended several times (Resolution 364B (IV) of 1 December 1949, Resolution 482 (V) of 12 December 1950, and Resolution 33/141 of 19 December 1978, and Resolution 52/153 of 15 December 1997). The

Convention, the task of registration with the UN Secretariat is entrusted to the Swiss Federal Council.[10]

3307   Registration with the United Nations helps to make treaties more widely known, ensuring transparency and security in international relations. However, the obligation to register is not a condition for the entry into force of the Convention or for the entry into force of the Convention with respect to a State that has ratified or acceded to it. The binding force of the Convention results solely from the procedures of ratification, accession and entry into force laid down in Articles 57–61.

3308   According to Article 102(2) of the UN Charter, no Party to any treaty entered into by a UN Member which has not been registered with the UN Secretariat may invoke it before any organ of the United Nations.[11] As the Conventions have been registered, they may be invoked before UN organs, including its principal judicial organ, the International Court of Justice. Resolution I of the 1949 Diplomatic Conference recommends 'in the case of a dispute relating to the interpretation or application of the present Conventions which cannot be settled by other means, the High Contracting Parties concerned endeavour to agree between themselves to refer such dispute to the International Court of Justice'.[12]

3309   The Convention entered into force on 21 October 1950, six months after the second ratification, by Yugoslavia on 21 April 1950, pursuant to Article 58 of the Convention. Shortly after its entry into force, a certified true copy of the Convention was duly transmitted on 2 November 1950 by the depositary to the UN Secretariat for registration and publication. The Secretariat then

---

Regulations define the scope of the obligation of UN Members and the procedure to be followed by the Secretariat to execute this function. Essentially, registration needs the transmission to the Secretariat of a certified true and complete copy of the treaty, with its attachments in all its authentic languages, together with the text of all reservations and declarations and the names of the signatories, as well as the date and method of entry into force (see also an annually updated note verbale of the legal counsel of the UN with an attached checklist, available at http://treaties.un.org).

[10] While the registration of bilateral agreements and of multilateral treaties which do not specify a depositary is, when not agreed upon between the Parties, left to each Party's initiative, multilateral treaties which provide for a depositary usually entrust that depositary with the task of arranging for their registration. Even in the absence of such a clause, the depositary must carry out this duty. See Article 77(1)(g) of the 1969 Vienna Convention on the Law of Treaties, which lists the registration of a treaty among the functions of the depositary, and which appears generally to codify customary international law (Villiger, p. 945). Once a treaty is registered, all Parties to it are relieved of the obligation to register. The designation of the depositary also constitutes an authorization for it to perform the registration; see Vienna Convention on the Law of Treaties (1969), Article 80(2). This authorization for all depositaries was necessary since, until 1969, the UN Secretariat accepted registration by the depositary only when the latter had been expressly authorized to that effect (see Villiger, p. 975, and Martens, p. 2098).

[11] The consequences of non-registration remain uncertain and controversial; see, in particular, Aust, pp. 301–303, and Martens, pp. 2107–2109. It is also doubtful whether an international humanitarian law treaty could be ignored by an organ of the UN merely because it had not been registered.

[12] *Final Record of the Diplomatic Conference of Geneva of 1949*, Vol. I, p. 361.

provided the depositary with a certificate of registration, which is deposited in the archives of the Swiss Confederation.[13]

3310 After their registration, treaties are published in the United Nations *Treaty Series*, which is available on the internet.[14] The UN Secretariat is responsible for their publication, which is made in the authentic languages of the treaty and, if these do not include English and French, with translations into those languages.

3311 The four Geneva Conventions are published in their two authentic languages, English and French,[15] in the United Nations *Treaty Series*.[16]

2. Second sentence: Subsequent treaty actions

3312 The second sentence of Article 64 entrusts the depositary also with the task of informing the UN Secretariat of ratifications, accessions and denunciations of the Convention.[17] The same would obviously also apply to successions.[18]

3313 In addition, the depositary is required to inform the UN Secretariat of all subsequent treaty actions affecting the Convention. This obligation is not directly provided for in the Convention or in the UN Charter. It ensues from Article 2 of the Regulations to give effect to Article 102 of the Charter of the United Nations, which provides:

When a treaty or international agreement has been registered with the Secretariat, a certified statement regarding any subsequent action which effects a change in the parties thereto, or the terms, scope or application thereof, shall also be registered with the Secretariat.[19]

3314 Pursuant to this provision of the Regulations, the depositary should also inform the UN Secretariat of every subsequent reservation, objection and declaration, including of a territorial nature. Any potential amendment of the Convention, on the other hand, would constitute a new treaty in itself.

---

[13] This certificate, numbered 2425 for the First Convention, and 2426, 2427 and 2428 respectively for the other three Conventions, bears the following wording: 'The Secretary-General of the United Nations Hereby certifies that the Government of the Swiss Confederation has registered with the Secretariat in accordance with Article 102 of the Charter of the United Nations the [Convention]. Signed at Geneva, on 12 August 1949. The registration took place on 2 November 1950 under No. 970 [respectively 971, 972 and 973]. Done at New York, on 23 January 1951. To the Government of the Swiss Confederation. The Secretary-General [signature]'.

[14] See http://treaties.un.org.

[15] See First Convention, Article 55; Second Convention, Article 54; Third Convention, Article 133; and Fourth Convention, Article 150.

[16] See United Nations *Treaty Series*, Vol. 75, 1950, pp. 3–474, under Nos 970–973 for the four Conventions respectively.

[17] On ratification, see Article 57; on accession and notification thereof, see Articles 60–61; on denunciation, see Article 63. The information will include any reservations and declarations contained in the respective instruments.

[18] On succession, see the commentary on Article 60, section C.4.

[19] On the Regulations, see fn. 9.

3315   In order to fulfil the task of registering subsequent treaty actions affecting the Convention, the depositary in practice transmits to the UN Secretariat a copy of every notification it sends to the States party to that Convention.[20] Such a notification is regarded as the 'certified statement' required by Article 2 of the aforementioned Regulations.

3316   All subsequent treaty actions are also published in the United Nations *Treaty Series*.[21]

Select bibliography

Aust, Anthony, *Modern Treaty Law and Practice*, 3rd edition, Cambridge University Press, 2013, pp. 297–307 (Registration and publication).

Hinojal-Oyarbide, Arancha and Rosenboom, Annebeth, 'Managing the Process of Treaty Formation – Depositaries and Registration', in Duncan B. Hollis (ed.), *The Oxford Guide to Treaties*, Oxford University Press, 2012, pp. 248–276.

Jacqué, Jean-Paul, in Jean-Pierre Cot and Alain Pellet (eds), *La Charte des Nations Unies. Commentaire article par article*, Article 102, Vol. II, Economica, Paris, 2005, pp. 2117–2132.

Klein, Pierre, 'Article 80: Registration and publication of treaties', in Olivier Corten and Pierre Klein (eds), *The Vienna Conventions on the Law of Treaties: A Commentary*, Vol. II, Oxford University Press, 2011, pp. 1797–1805.

Martens, Ernst, 'Article 102', in Bruno Simma, Daniel-Erasmus Khan, Georg Nolte and Andreas Paulus (eds), *The Charter of the United Nations: A Commentary*, Vol. II, 3rd edition, Oxford University Press, 2011, pp. 2089–2109.

Ouguergouz, Fatsah, Villalpando, Santiago and Morgan-Foster, Jason, 'Article 77: Functions of depositaries', in Olivier Corten and Pierre Klein (eds), *The Vienna Conventions on the Law of Treaties: A Commentary*, Vol. II, Oxford University Press, 2011, pp. 1715–1753, at 1748–1750.

Reuter, Paul, *Introduction to the Law of Treaties*, 2nd edition, Graduate Institute of International Studies, Geneva, 1995, pp. 70–71 (Registration and publication).

Schenker, Claude, *Practice Guide to International Treaties*, Federal Department of Foreign Affairs, Bern, 2015, pp. 37–40, available at https://www.fdfa.admin.ch/treaties.

United Nations, Office of Legal Affairs, *Treaty Handbook*, Revised edition, 2012, pp. 29–38.

Villiger, Mark E., *Commentary on the 1969 Vienna Convention on the Law of Treaties*, Martinus Nijhoff Publishers, Leiden, 2009, pp. 944 (Article 77) and 970–976 (Article 80).

---

[20] See e.g. Articles 57(2), 61(2), 62, second sentence, and Article 63(2).
[21] See http://treaties.un.org.

TESTIMONIUM AND SIGNATURE CLAUSE

❖ Text of the testimonium and signature clause

IN WITNESS WHEREOF the undersigned, having deposited their respective full powers, have signed the present Convention.

DONE at Geneva this twelfth day of August 1949, in the English and French languages. The original shall be deposited in the Archives of the Swiss Confederation. The Swiss Federal Council shall transmit certified copies thereof to each of the signatory and acceding States.

❖ Reservations or declarations

None

Contents

A. Introduction

3317 The Convention's 'testimonium', beginning by the specific formulation 'in witness whereof', provides that, in order to sign the Convention in the name of a State, the representative of that State has to have deposited full powers.[1]

3318   The signature clause contains the place and date of the adoption of the Convention and recalls its authentic languages.[2] It furthermore specifies the tasks of the depositary relating to the conservation of the original of the Convention and the delivery of the certified true copies.

3319   Both sentences, placed at the very end of the Convention after the last article and before the signatures, were adopted by the Plenary of the 1949 Diplomatic

---

[1] For the authorization to sign and the effect of such signature, see the commentary on Article 56, sections C.2 and C.3.
[2] On authentic languages, see Article 55.

Conference after only minor wording changes implemented during the Joint, Special and Drafting committees.[3]

B. Testimonium and signature clause

1. Full powers

3320   According to customary international law, as codified by the 1969 Vienna Convention on the Law of Treaties, only heads of State, heads of government and ministers for foreign affairs are *ex officio* considered as representing their State for the purpose of performing all acts relating to the conclusion of a treaty, including signature.[4] All other representatives desiring to sign a treaty in the name of a State normally have to produce full powers.[5] The Convention's testimonium reflects this. The original of the full powers deposited by the State's representative and collected by the depositary at the occasion of every signature is kept with the original of the Convention in the Swiss Federal Archives. At the time, it was usual to specify the very place of filing of the original treaties. Therefore, as did other treaties at that time, the 1949 Conventions mention the Swiss Federal Archives, where all treaties deposited with the Swiss Federal Council are in principle to be found.

2. Certified copies

3321   The original of the Convention, as happens with multilateral treaties in general, is established in just one signed document grouping all its authentic language versions. Thus, the depositary has to deliver a certified copy of the said original to each of the 'signatory and acceding States'. The main purpose of the certified copy is to allow these States to submit the treaty to their competent internal authorities for approval before the treaty is ratified or its accession notified.

3322   A certified copy has to reproduce faithfully and in full the provisions of the original. Usually, at the end of the text of the copy, a representative of the depositary signs a dated statement certifying that the foregoing text is a true copy of the Convention. At the time of the adoption of the 1949 Conventions,

---

[3] *Final Record of the Diplomatic Conference of Geneva of 1949*, Vol. II-B, pp. 30 (Joint Committee), 73, 114 (Special Committee), 163, 170, 186 (Drafting Committee) and 373 (23rd Plenary Meeting of the Conference).

[4] See Vienna Convention on the Law of Treaties (1969), Article 7(2), which accurately reflects customary international law (Villiger, p. 146).

[5] See Vienna Convention on the Law of Treaties (1969), Article 7(1), which accurately reflects customary international law (Villiger, p. 146). Article 2(1)(c) of the Vienna Convention defines 'full powers' as: 'a document emanating from the competent authority of a State designating a person or persons to represent the State for negotiating, adopting or authenticating the text of a treaty, for expressing the consent of the State to be bound by a treaty, or for accomplishing any other act with respect to a treaty'.

the certified copy used to include the Final Act of the conference that adopted the treaty. Consequently, the Swiss Federal Council formally delivered certified copies of the Final Act of the Diplomatic Conference of Geneva, to which the texts of the Conventions were attached. According to the more recent practice of depositaries, only the text of a convention, with or without the signatures, is nowadays reproduced in the certified copy.[6]

Select bibliography

Aust, Anthony, *Modern Treaty Law and Practice*, 3rd edition, Cambridge University Press, 2013, pp. 381–383 (Testimonium).

United Nations, Office of Legal Affairs, Treaty Section, *Summary of practice of the Secretary-General as depositary of multilateral treaties*, UN Doc. ST/LEG/7/Rev.l, United Nations, New York, 1999, paras 63–72 (Certified copies).

Villiger, Mark E., *Commentary on the 1969 Vienna Convention on the Law of Treaties*, Martinus Nijhoff Publishers, Leiden, 2009.

---

[6] United Nations, *Summary of practice of the Secretary-General as depositary of multilateral treaties*, paras 63–64.

SOURCES

Contents

I. Preparatory work

Proceedings of the Geneva Diplomatic Conference of 1906
Convention de Genève : Actes de la Conférence de révision réunie à Genève du 11 juin au 6 juillet 1906, Imprimerie Henri Jarrys, Geneva, 1906, available at https://library.icrc.org/library/Direct.aspx?noticenr=2228.

Proceedings of the Geneva Diplomatic Conference of 1929
Actes de la Conférence diplomatique convoquée par le Conseil fédéral suisse pour la révision de la Convention du 6 juillet 1906 pour l'amélioration du sort des blessés et malades dans les armées en campagne et pour l'élaboration d'une Convention relative au traitement des prisonniers de guerre et réunie à Genève du 1er au 27 juillet 1929, Imprimerie du Journal de Genève, 1930, available at https://library.icrc.org/library/Direct .aspx?noticenr=2234.

Draft revision of the 1929 Geneva Convention submitted by the ICRC to National Societies in 1937
Projet de révision de la Convention de Genève du 27 juillet 1929 présenté aux Sociétés nationales de la Croix-Rouge par le Comité international de la Croix-Rouge, ICRC, Geneva, May 1937, available at https://library.icrc .org/library/Direct.aspx?noticenr=9503.

Reports and Documents for the Preliminary Conference of National Societies of 1946

Conférence préliminaire des Sociétés nationales de la Croix-Rouge pour l'étude des Conventions et de divers problèmes ayant trait à la Croix-Rouge, Genève, 26 juillet au 3 août 1946 : documentation fournie par le Comité international de la Croix-Rouge, Vol. I: Révision de la Convention de Genève et dispositions connexes, ICRC, Geneva, 1946, available at https://library.icrc.org/library/Direct.aspx?noticenr=37685.

Minutes of the Preliminary Conference of National Societies of 1946

Procès-verbaux de la Conférence préliminaire des Sociétés nationales de la Croix-Rouge pour l'étude des Conventions et de divers problèmes ayant trait à la Croix-Rouge (Genève, 26 juillet–3 août 1946), ICRC, Geneva, 1947, 7 volumes, available at https://library.icrc.org/library/Direct.aspx?searchfield=t&searchterm=%25proc%C3%A8s-verbaux%251946.

Report of the Preliminary Conference of National Societies of 1946

Report on the Work of the Preliminary Conference of National Red Cross Societies for the study of the Conventions and of various Problems relative to the Red Cross (Geneva, 26 July–3 August 1946), ICRC, Geneva, 1947, available at https://library.icrc.org/library/Direct.aspx?noticenr=6876.

Report of the Commission on the Religious and Intellectual Needs of Prisoners of War and Civilian Internees of 1947

Rapport sur les travaux de la Commission constituée pour étudier les dispositions conventionnelles relatives aux besoins religieux et intellectuels des prisonniers de guerre et des civils internés (Genève, 3 et 4 mars 1947), ICRC, Geneva, May 1947, available at https://library.icrc.org/library/Direct.aspx?noticenr=6911.

Minutes of the Conference of Government Experts of 1947

Procès-verbaux de la Conférence d'experts gouvernementaux pour l'étude des Conventions protégeant les victimes de la guerre (Genève, 14–26 avril 1947), ICRC, Geneva, 1947, available at https://library.icrc.org/library/Direct.aspx?searchfield=t&searchterm=Conf%C3%A9rence%20d%27experts%251947.

Report of the Conference of Government Experts of 1947

Report on the Work of the Conference of Government Experts for the Study of the Conventions for the Protection of War Victims (Geneva, 14–26 April 1947), ICRC, Geneva, 1947, available at https://library.icrc.org/library/Direct.aspx?noticenr=6929.

Draft Conventions submitted to the 1948 Stockholm Conference

Draft Revised or New Conventions for the Protection of War Victims, established by the International Committee of the Red Cross with the assistance of government experts, National Red Cross Societies and other humanitarian associations, texts submitted to the XVIIth International Red Cross Conference (Stockholm, August 1948), ICRC, Geneva, May 1948, available at https://library.icrc.org/library/Direct .aspx?noticenr=6933.

Minutes of the Legal Commission at the 1948 Stockholm Conference
Sténogramme des séances de la Commission juridique, XVIIe Conférence internationale de la Croix-Rouge (Stockholm, août 1948), ICRC, Geneva, January 1949, available at https://library.icrc.org/library/Direct .aspx?noticenr=18382.

Addenda to the Draft Conventions submitted to the 1948 Stockholm Conference
Addenda aux projets de Conventions révisées ou nouvelles protégeant les victimes de la guerre, Rapport du Comité international de la Croix-Rouge (Sous point III de l'ordre du jour de la Commission juridique), XVIIe Conférence internationale de la Croix-Rouge (Stockholm, août 1948), No. 4*bis*, ICRC, Geneva, August 1948, available at https://library.icrc.org/library/ Direct.aspx?noticenr=6931.

Draft Conventions adopted by the 1948 Stockholm Conference
Revised and New Draft Conventions for the Protection of War Victims: Texts Approved and Amended by the XVIIth International Red Cross Conference (Stockholm, August 1948), ICRC, Geneva, 1948, available at https://library.icrc.org/library/Direct.aspx?noticenr=6979.

ICRC Remarks and Proposals on the 1948 Stockholm Draft
Revised and New Draft Conventions for the Protection of War Victims: Remarks and Proposals Submitted by the International Committee of the Red Cross, Document for the consideration of Governments invited by the Swiss Federal Council to attend the Diplomatic Conference at Geneva (21 April 1949), ICRC, Geneva, February 1949, available at https://library .icrc.org/library/Direct.aspx?noticenr=6981.

Minutes of the Diplomatic Conference of Geneva of 1949
Sténogrammes de la Conférence diplomatique de Genève 1949, available at https://library.icrc.org/library/Direct.aspx?searchfield=t&searchterm= Conférence%20diplomatique%201949%20:%20sténogrammes.

Final Record of the Diplomatic Conference of Geneva of 1949
Final Record of the Diplomatic Conference of Geneva of 1949, convened by the Swiss Federal Council for the establishment of international conventions for the protection of war Victims and held at Geneva from 21 April to 12 August 1949, 4 volumes (Vol. I: Final and draft texts, resolutions, texts of other Geneva and Hague Conventions, Vol. IIA: Minutes of

plenary meetings, summary records of meetings, reports, Vol. IIB: Summary records of meetings, reports to the plenary assembly, Vol. III: Annexes for all of the Geneva Conventions, index of speakers), Federal Political Department, Bern, 1950, available at https://library.icrc.org/library/Direct.aspx?noticenr=2253.

Report of the Conference of Government Experts of 1971
Report on the Work of the Conference of Government Experts on the Reaffirmation and Development of International Humanitarian Law Applicable in Armed Conflicts, First Session (Geneva, 24 May–12 June 1971), 8 volumes, ICRC, Geneva, August 1971, available at https://library.icrc.org/library/Direct.aspx?noticenr=9173.

Report of the Conference of Government Experts of 1972
Report on the Work of the Conference of Government Experts on the Reaffirmation and Development of International Humanitarian Law Applicable in Armed Conflicts, Second Session (Geneva, 3 May–3 June 1972), 2 volumes, ICRC, Geneva, July 1972, available at https://library.icrc.org/library/Direct.aspx?noticenr=9297.

Official Records of the Diplomatic Conference of Geneva of 1974–1977
Official Records of the Diplomatic Conference on the Reaffirmation and Development of International Humanitarian Law Applicable in Armed Conflicts (Geneva, 1974–1977), 17 volumes, Federal Political Department, Bern, 1978, available at https://library.icrc.org/library/Direct.aspx?noticenr=2374.

II. Treaties

1864

Geneva Convention
Convention for the Amelioration of the Condition of the Wounded in Armies in the Field, Geneva, 22 August 1864.

1868

St Petersburg Declaration
Declaration Renouncing the Use, in Time of War, of Explosive Projectiles Under 400 Grammes Weight, St Petersburg, 29 November–11 December 1868.

Additional Articles relating to the Condition of the Wounded in War
Additional Articles relating to the Condition of the Wounded in War, Geneva, 20 October 1868.

1899

Hague Convention (I)
  Convention (I) for the Pacific Settlement of International Disputes, The Hague, 29 July 1899.

Hague Convention (II)
  Convention (II) with Respect to the Laws and Customs of War on Land, The Hague, 29 July 1899.

Hague Regulations
  Regulations concerning the Laws and Customs of War on Land, annexed to Convention (II) with Respect to the Laws and Customs of War on Land, The Hague, 29 July 1899.

Hague Convention (III)
  Convention (III) for the Adaptation to Maritime Warfare of the Principles of the Geneva Convention of 22 August 1864, The Hague, 29 July 1899.

1906

Geneva Convention
  Convention for the Amelioration of the Condition of the Wounded and Sick in Armies in the Field, Geneva, 6 July 1906.

1907

Hague Convention (I)
  Convention (I) for the Pacific Settlement of International Disputes, The Hague, 18 October 1907.

Hague Convention (III)
  Convention (III) relative to the Opening of Hostilities. The Hague, 18 October 1907.

Hague Convention (IV)
  Convention (IV) respecting the Laws and Customs of War on Land, The Hague, 18 October 1907.

Hague Regulations
  Regulations concerning the Laws and Customs of War on Land, annexed to Convention (IV) respecting the Laws and Customs of War on Land, The Hague, 18 October 1907.

Hague Convention (V)
  Convention (V) respecting the Rights and Duties of Neutral Powers and Persons in Case of War on Land, The Hague, 18 October 1907.

Hague Convention (VI)
   Convention (VI) relating to the Status of Enemy Merchant Ships at the Outbreak of Hostilities, The Hague, 18 October 1907.

Hague Convention (VII)
   Convention (VII) relating to the Conversion of Merchant Ships into War-Ships, The Hague, 18 October 1907.

Hague Convention (VIII)
   Convention (VIII) relative to the Laying of Automatic Submarine Contact Mines, The Hague, 18 October 1907.

Hague Convention (IX)
   Hague Convention (IX) concerning Bombardment by Naval Forces in Time of War, The Hague, 18 October 1907.

Hague Convention (X)
   Hague Convention (X) for the Adaptation to Maritime Warfare of the Principles of the Geneva Convention, The Hague, 18 October 1907.

Hague Convention (XI)
   Hague Convention (XI) relative to Certain Restrictions with regard to the Exercise of the Right of Capture in Naval War, The Hague, 18 October 1907.

Hague Convention (XII)
   Hague Convention (XII) relative to the Creation of an International Prize Court, The Hague, 18 October 1907.

Hague Convention (XIII)
   Hague Convention (XIII) concerning the Rights and Duties of Neutral Powers in Naval War, The Hague, 18 October 1907.

1909

London Declaration concerning the Laws of Naval War
   Declaration concerning the Laws of Naval War, London, 26 February 1909.

1918

Agreement between France and Germany concerning Prisoners of War
   Agreement between France and Germany concerning Prisoners of War, Bern, 15 March 1918, *Bulletin international des Sociétés de la Croix-Rouge*, Vol. 49, No. 194, April 1918, pp. 265–279.

Second Agreement between France and Germany concerning Prisoners of War and Civilians
   Second Agreement between France and Germany concerning Prisoners of War and Civilians, Bern, 26 April 1918, *Bulletin international des Sociétés de la Croix-Rouge*, Vol. 49, No. 195, July 1918, pp. 396–418.

1919

Treaty of Versailles
    Treaty of Versailles, Versailles, 28 June 1919.

1925

Geneva Gas Protocol
    Protocol for the Prohibition of the Use in War of Asphyxiating, Poisonous
    or Other Gases, and of Bacteriological Methods of Warfare, Geneva, 17 June
    1925.

1929

Geneva Convention on the Wounded and Sick
    Convention for the Amelioration of the Condition of the Wounded and
    Sick in Armies in the Field, Geneva, 27 July 1929.

Geneva Convention on Prisoners of War
    Convention relative to the Treatment of Prisoners of War, Geneva, 27 July
    1929.

1933

Montevideo Convention on the Rights and Duties of States
    Convention on the Rights and Duties of States, Montevideo, 26 December
    1933.

1944

Chicago Convention on International Civil Aviation
    Convention on International Civil Aviation, Chicago, 7 December 1944,
    as amended by the Protocol relating to an Amendment to the Convention
    on International Civil Aviation, Montreal, 10 May 1984.

1945

IMT Charter for Germany
    Charter of the International Military Tribunal for Germany, concluded by
    the Government of the United States of America, the Provisional Govern-
    ment of the French Republic, the Government of the United Kingdom of
    Great Britain and Northern Ireland, and the Government of the Union of
    Soviet Socialist Republics, acting in the interests of all the United Nations
    and by their representatives duly authorized thereto, annexed to the Lon-
    don Agreement, London, 8 August 1945.

UN Charter
> Charter of the United Nations, adopted by the Conference on International Organizations, San Francisco, 26 June 1945.

ICJ Statute
> Statute of the International Court of Justice, San Francisco, 26 June 1945.

1947

Treaty of Peace between the Allied and Associated Powers and Bulgaria
> Treaty of Peace between the Allied and Associated Powers on the one part and Bulgaria on the other part, Paris, 10 February 1947, United Nations *Treaty Series*, Vol. 41, No. 643, 1949.

Treaty of Peace between the Allied and Associated Powers and Finland
> Treaty of Peace between the Allied and Associated Powers on the one part and Finland on the other part, Paris, 10 February 1947, United Nations *Treaty Series*, Vol. 48, No. 746, 1950.

Treaty of Peace between the Allied and Associated Powers and Hungary
> Treaty of Peace between the Allied and Associated Powers on the one part and Hungary on the other part, Paris, 10 February 1947, United Nations *Treaty Series*, Vol. 41, No. 644, 1949.

Treaty of Peace between the Allied and Associated Powers and Italy
> Treaty of Peace between the Allied and Associated Powers on the one part and Italy on the other part, Paris, 10 February 1947, United Nations *Treaty Series*, Vol. 49, No. 747, 1950.

Treaty of Peace between the Allied and Associated Powers and Romania
> Treaty of Peace between the Allied and Associated Powers on the one part and Romania on the other part, Paris, 10 February 1947, United Nations *Treaty Series*, Vol. 42, No. 645, 1949.

1948

Genocide Convention
> Convention on the Prevention and Punishment of the Crime of Genocide, adopted by the UN General Assembly, Res. 260 A (III), 9 December 1948.

1949

First Geneva Convention
> Convention (I) for the Amelioration of the Condition of the Wounded and Sick in Armed Forces in the Field, Geneva, 12 August 1949.

Second Geneva Convention
> Convention (II) for the Amelioration of the Condition of the Wounded, Sick and Shipwrecked Members of Armed Forces at Sea, Geneva, 12 August 1949.

Third Geneva Convention
> Convention (III) relative to the Treatment of Prisoners of War, Geneva, 12 August 1949.

Fourth Geneva Convention
> Convention (IV) relative to the Protection of Civilian Persons in Time of War, Geneva, 12 August 1949.

1950

European Convention on Human Rights
> European Convention for the Protection of Human Rights and Fundamental Freedoms, Rome, 4 November 1950, as amended by Protocol No. 11, Strasbourg, 11 May 1994.

1951

Peace Treaty for Japan
> Treaty of Peace signed between the Allied Powers and Japan, San Francisco, 8 September 1951.

Refugee Convention
> Convention relating to the Status of Refugees, adopted by the UN Conference of Plenipotentiaries on the Status of Refugees and Stateless Persons convened pursuant to UN General Assembly Res. 429 (V), Geneva, 28 July 1951, as amended by the 1967 Protocol relating to the Status of Refugees, approved by the UN Economic and Social Council, Res. 1186 (XLI), 18 November 1966, and taken note of by the UN General Assembly, Res. 2198 (XXI), 16 December 1966.

1954

Hague Convention for the Protection of Cultural Property
> Convention for the Protection of Cultural Property in the Event of Armed Conflict, The Hague, 14 May 1954.

1956

Joint Declaration on Soviet-Japanese Relations
> Joint Declaration by the Union of Soviet Socialist Republics and Japan concerning the restoration of diplomatic relations between the two countries, Moscow, 19 October 1956.

1961

Vienna Convention on Diplomatic Relations
Vienna Convention on Diplomatic Relations, adopted by the UN Conference on Diplomatic Intercourse and Immunities, Vienna, 18 April 1961.

1963

Vienna Convention on Consular Relations
Vienna Convention on Consular Relations, Vienna, 24 April 1963.

1965

Convention on the Elimination of Racial Discrimination
International Convention on the Elimination of All Forms of Racial Discrimination, adopted by the UN General Assembly, Res. 2106 A (XX), 21 December 1965.

1966

International Covenant on Civil and Political Rights
International Covenant on Civil and Political Rights, adopted by the UN General Assembly, Res. 2200 A (XXI), 16 December 1966.

International Covenant on Economic, Social and Cultural Rights
International Covenant on Economic, Social and Cultural Rights, adopted by the UN General Assembly, Res. 2200 A (XXI), 16 December 1966.

1968

UN Convention on the Non-Applicability of Statutory Limitations to War Crimes and Crimes against Humanity
Convention on the Non-Applicability of Statutory Limitations to War Crimes and Crimes against Humanity, adopted by the UN General Assembly, Res. 2391 (XXIII), 26 November 1968.

1969

American Convention on Human Rights
American Convention on Human Rights (also known as Pact of San José), adopted by the OAS Inter-American Specialized Conference on Human Rights, San José, 22 November 1969, United Nations *Treaty Series*, No. I 17955.

OAU Convention Governing Refugee Problems in Africa
OAU Convention Governing the Specific Aspects of Refugee Problems in Africa, adopted by the Sixth Ordinary Session of the OAU Assembly of Heads of State and Government, Addis Ababa, 10 September 1969.

Vienna Convention on the Law of Treaties
Convention on the Law of Treaties, Vienna, 23 May 1969.

1970

Hague Convention for the Suppression of Unlawful Seizure of Aircraft
Convention for the Suppression of Unlawful Seizure of Aircraft, The Hague, 16 December 1970.

1971

Convention for the Suppression of Unlawful Acts against the Safety of Civil Aviation
Convention for the Suppression of Unlawful Acts against the Safety of Civil Aviation, Montreal, 23 September 1971.

1972

Biological Weapons Convention
Convention on the Prohibition of the Development, Production and Stockpiling of Bacteriological (Biological) and Toxin Weapons and on Their Destruction, opened for signature at London, Moscow and Washington, D.C., 10 April 1972.

1973

Convention on Crimes against Internationally Protected Persons
Convention on Punishment of Crimes against Internationally Protected Persons, including Diplomatic Agents, adopted by the UN General Assembly, Res. 3166 (XVIII), 14 December 1973.

1977

Additional Protocol I
Protocol additional to the Geneva Conventions of 12 August 1949, and relating to the Protection of Victims of International Armed Conflicts (Protocol I), Geneva, 8 June 1977.

Additional Protocol II
Protocol additional to the Geneva Conventions of 12 August 1949, and relating to the Protection of Victims of Non-International Armed Conflicts (Protocol II), Geneva, 8 June 1977.

1978

Framework for Peace in the Middle East
Framework for Peace in the Middle East agreed at Camp David, Washington D.C., 17 September 1978, United Nations *Treaty Series*, Vol. 1138, No. 17853, 1979.

Vienna Convention on Succession of States in respect of Treaties
Vienna Convention on Succession of States in respect of Treaties, Vienna, 23 August 1978.

1979

International Convention against the Taking of Hostages
International Convention against the Taking of Hostages, adopted by the UN General Assembly, Res. 34/146, 17 December 1979.

Peace Treaty between Egypt and Israel
Treaty of Peace between the Arab Republic of Egypt and the State of Israel, Washington, D.C., 26 March 1979, United Nations *Treaty Series*, Vol. 1136, No. 17813, 1979.

1980

Convention on Certain Conventional Weapons
Convention on Prohibitions or Restrictions on the Use of Certain Conventional Weapons Which May Be Deemed to Be Excessively Injurious or to Have Indiscriminate Effects, Geneva, 10 October 1980.

1981

African Charter on Human and Peoples' Rights
African Charter on Human and Peoples' Rights, adopted by the 18th Ordinary Session of the OAU Assembly of Heads of State and Government, Nairobi, 27 June 1981, OAU Doc. CAB/LEG/67/3 rev.5.

1982

UN Convention on the Law of the Sea
United Nations Convention on the Law of the Sea, Montego Bay, 10 December 1982, UN Doc. A/CONF.62/122.

1983

Protocol 6 to the European Convention on Human Rights
Protocol No. 6 to the European Convention for the Protection of Human Rights and Fundamental Freedoms concerning the Abolition of the Death Penalty, Strasbourg, 28 April 1983.

1984

Convention against Torture
Convention against Torture and Other Cruel, Inhuman or Degrading Treatment or Punishment, adopted by the UN General Assembly, Res. 39/46, 10 December 1984.

1985

Inter-American Convention against Torture
Inter-American Convention to Prevent and Punish Torture, adopted by the 15th Regular Session of the OAS General Assembly, Res. 783 (XV-O/85), Cartagena de Indias, 9 December 1985.

1986

Vienna Convention on the Law of Treaties between States and International Organizations
Convention on the Law of Treaties between States and International Organizations or between International Organizations, Vienna, 21 March 1986.

1987

European Convention for the Prevention of Torture
European Convention for the Prevention of Torture and Inhuman or Degrading Treatment or Punishment, Strasbourg, 26 November 1987.

Agreement concerning the Treatment of War Graves of Members of the UK Armed Forces in the German Democratic Republic
Agreement between the Government of the United Kingdom of Great Britain and Northern Ireland and the Government of the German Democratic Republic concerning the treatment of war graves of members of the armed Forces of the United Kingdom of Great Britain and Northern Ireland in the German Democratic Republic, Berlin, 27 April 1987, United Nations *Treaty Series*, Vol. 1656, No. 28493, 1999.

1989

Second Optional Protocol to the International Covenant on Civil and Political Rights
Second Optional Protocol to the International Covenant on Civil and Political Rights aiming at the Abolition of the Death Penalty, adopted by the UN General Assembly, Res. 44/128, 15 December 1989.

1990

Protocol to the American Convention on Human Rights to Abolish the Death Penalty
Protocol to the American Convention on Human Rights to Abolish the Death Penalty, adopted by the 20th Regular Session of the OAS General Assembly at Asunción, 8 June 1990, OAS *Treaty Series*, No. 73, 1990.

1994

Treaty of Peace between the State of Israel and the Hashemite Kingdom of Jordan
Treaty of peace between the State of Israel and the Hashemite Kingdom of Jordan, Arava/Araba Crossing Point, 26 October 1994, United Nations *Treaty Series*, Vol. 2042, No. 35325, 2002.

1995

Agreement on Refugees and Displaced Persons annexed to the Dayton Accords
General Framework Agreement for Peace in Bosnia and Herzegovina, Annex 7, Agreement on Refugees and Displaced Persons, signed by the Republic of Bosnia and Herzegovina, the Federation of Bosnia and Herzegovina and the Republika Srpska, Dayton, 22 November 1995.

Dayton Accords
General Framework Agreement for Peace in Bosnia and Herzegovina, initialled at Dayton, 21 November 1995, signed at Paris, 14 December 1995.

Protocol IV to the Convention on Certain Conventional Weapons
Protocol on Blinding Laser Weapons to the Convention on Prohibitions or Restrictions on the Use of Certain Conventional Weapons Which May Be Deemed to Be Excessively Injurious or to Have Indiscriminate Effects, Vienna, 13 October 1995.

1996

Agreement on Normalization of Relations between Croatia and the Federal Republic of Yugoslavia
Agreement on Normalization of Relations between the Republic of Croatia and the Federal Republic of Yugoslavia, Belgrade, 23 August 1996.

Amended Protocol II to the Convention on Certain Conventional Weapons
Protocol on Prohibitions or Restrictions on the Use of Mines, Booby-Traps and Other Devices, as amended, to the Convention on Prohibitions or Restrictions on the Use of Certain Conventional Weapons Which May Be Deemed to Be Excessively Injurious or to Have Indiscriminate Effects, Geneva, 3 May 1996.

1997

International Convention for the Suppression of Terrorist Bombings
International Convention for the Suppression of Terrorist Bombings, New York, 15 December 1997, United Nations *Treaty Series*, Vol. 2149, No. 37517, 2003.

Anti-Personnel Mine Ban Convention
Convention on the Prohibition of the Use, Stockpiling, Production and Transfer of Anti-Personnel Mines and on their Destruction, Ottawa, 18 September 1997.

1998

ICC Statute
Rome Statute of the International Criminal Court, adopted by the UN Diplomatic Conference of Plenipotentiaries on the Establishment of an International Criminal Court, Rome, 17 July 1998, UN Doc. A/CONF.183/9.

NATO Standardization Agreement 2931
Standardization Agreement 2931, Orders for the Camouflage of the Red Cross and the Red Crescent on Land in Tactical Operations, adopted by the North Atlantic Treaty Organization, Brussels, 4 March 1998.

1999

International Convention for the Suppression of the Financing of Terrorism
International Convention for the Suppression of the Financing of Terrorism, New York, 9 December 1999, adopted by the UN General Assembly, Res. 54/109, Annex, United Nations *Treaty Series*, Vol. 2178, No. 38349, 2004.

Second Protocol to the Hague Convention for the Protection of Cultural Property
Second Protocol for the Protection of Cultural Property in the Event of Armed Conflict, The Hague, 26 March 1999.

2000

Optional Protocol on the Involvement of Children in Armed Conflict
Optional Protocol to the Convention on the Rights of the Child on the Involvement of Children in Armed Conflict, adopted by the UN General Assembly, Res. 54/263, 25 May 2000, Annex I.

Peace Agreement between Eritrea and Ethiopia
Agreement between the Government of the State of Eritrea and the Government of the Federal Democratic Republic of Ethiopia for the resettlement of displaced persons, as well as rehabilitation and peacebuilding in both countries (also known as Algiers Agreement), Algiers, 12 December 2000, United Nations *Treaty Series*, Vol. 2138, No. I-37274.

UN Convention against Transnational Organized Crime
United Nations Convention against Transnational Organized Crime, New York, 15 November 2000, adopted by the UN General Assembly, Res. 54/263, Annex I, United Nations *Treaty Series*, Vol. 2225, No. 39574, 2007.

2001

Amendment to Article 1 of the 1980 Convention on Certain Conventional Weapons
Amendment to Article 1 of the Convention on Prohibitions or Restrictions on the Use of Certain Conventional Weapons Which May Be Deemed to Be Excessively Injurious or to Have Indiscriminate Effects, Geneva, 21 December 2001.

2002

Protocol 13 to the European Convention on Human Rights
Protocol No. 13 to the European Convention for the Protection of Human Rights and Fundamental Freedoms concerning the Abolition of the Death Penalty in All Circumstances, Vilnius, 3 May 2002.

SCSL Statute
Statute of the Special Court for Sierra Leone, annexed to the Agreement between the United Nations and the Government of Sierra Leone on the Establishment of a Special Court for Sierra Leone, Freetown, 16 January 2002, annexed to Letter dated 6 March 2002 from the UN Secretary-General to the President of the UN Security Council, UN Doc. S/2002/246, 8 March 2002, p. 29.

2003

UN Convention against Corruption
United Nations Convention against Corruption, New York, 31 October 2003, adopted by the UN General Assembly, Res. 58/4, Annex, United Nations *Treaty Series*, Vol. 2349, No. 42146, 2007.

Protocol V to the Convention on Certain Conventional Weapons
 Protocol on Explosive Remnants of War to the Convention on Prohibitions
 or Restrictions on the Use of Certain Conventional Weapons Which May
 Be deemed to Be Excessively Injurious or to Have Indiscriminate Effects,
 Geneva, 28 November 2003.

2005

Additional Protocol III
 Protocol additional to the Geneva Conventions of 12 August 1949, and
 relating to the Adoption of an Additional Distinctive Emblem (Protocol
 III), Geneva, 8 December 2005.

2006

Convention on Enforced Disappearance
 International Convention for the Protection of all Persons from Enforced
 Disappearance, adopted by the UN General Assembly, Res. 61/177, 20
 December 2006, Annex.

Convention on the Rights of Persons with Disabilities
 Convention on the Rights of Persons with Disabilities, adopted by the UN
 General Assembly, Res. 61/106, 13 December 2006, Annex I.

2008

Agreement between the UN and the AU and the Government of Sudan concerning the Status of the AU/UN Hybrid Operation in Darfur
 Agreement between the United Nations and the African Union and the
 Government of Sudan concerning the Status of the African Union/United
 Nations Hybrid Operation in Darfur, Khartoum, 9 February 2008.

Convention on Cluster Munitions
 Convention on Cluster Munitions, Dublin, 30 May 2008.

2013

Arms Trade Treaty
 Arms Trade Treaty, New York, 2 April 2013.

Statute of the Extraordinary African Chambers within the Courts of Senegal
 Statute of the Extraordinary African Chambers within the courts of Senegal created to prosecute international crimes committed in Chad between
 7 June 1982 and 1 December 1990, annexed to the Agreement between

the Government of the Republic of Senegal and the African Union on the Establishment of Extraordinary African Chambers within the Senegalese Judicial System, Dakar, 22 August 2012.

III. Other documents

1863

Lieber Code
Instructions for the Government of Armies of the United States in the Field, prepared by Francis Lieber, promulgated as General Orders No. 100 by President Abraham Lincoln, Washington D.C., 24 April 1863.

1874

Brussels Declaration
Project of an International Declaration concerning the Laws and Customs of War, Brussels, 27 August 1874.

1880

Oxford Manual
The Laws of War on Land, Manual adopted by the Institute of International Law, Oxford, 9 September 1880.

1942

Declaration of St James
Inter-Allied Declaration on Punishment for War Crimes, establishing the United Nations War Crimes Commission, London, 13 January 1942.

1943

Moscow Declaration
Declaration concerning Atrocities, made at the Moscow Conference, signed by the United States of America, the United Kingdom of Great Britain and Northern Ireland, the Union of Soviet Socialist Republics and China, Moscow, 30 October 1943.

1950

Nuremberg Principles
Principles of International Law Recognized in the Charter of the Nuremberg Tribunal and in the Judgment of the Tribunal, adopted by the International Law Commission, UN Doc. A/1316, New York, 29 July 1950.

1985

Basic Principles on the Independence of the Judiciary
Basic Principles on the Independence of the Judiciary, adopted by the Seventh United Nations Congress on the Prevention of Crime and the Treatment of Offenders, Milan, 26 August–6 September 1985, UN Doc. A/CONF.121/22/Rev.1, 1985, p. 59, endorsed by UN General Assembly Res. 40/32, 29 November 1985, and Res. 40/146, 13 December 1985.

1986

Statutes of the International Red Cross and Red Crescent Movement
Statutes of the International Red Cross and Red Crescent Movement, adopted by the 25th International Conference of the Red Cross, Geneva, 23–31 October 1986, as amended in 1995 and 2006.

1991

Emblem Regulations
Regulations on the Use of the Emblem of the Red Cross or the Red Crescent by the National Societies, adopted by the 20th International Conference of the Red Cross, Vienna, 1965, and revised by the Council of Delegates, Budapest, 1991.

Agreement between Croatia and the Socialist Federal Republic of Yugoslavia on a Protected Zone around the Hospital of Osijek
Agreement Relating to the Establishment of a Protected Zone around the Hospital of Osijek between Croatia and the Socialist Federal Republic of Yugoslavia, Pécs, 27 December 1991.

Memorandum of Understanding on the Application of IHL between Croatia and the Socialist Federal Republic of Yugoslavia
Memorandum of Understanding on the Application of International Humanitarian Law between Croatia and the Socialist Federal Republic of Yugoslavia, Geneva, 27 November 1991, reproduced in Michèle Mercier, *Crimes without Punishment: Humanitarian Action in Former Yugoslavia*, East Haven, London, 1996, Appendix: Document IV, pp. 196–198.

1993

Cotonou Agreement on Liberia
Cotonou Peace Agreement on Liberia between the Interim Government of National Unity of Liberia (IGNU) of the first part and the National Patriotic Front of Liberia (NPFL) of the second part and the United Liberation Movement of Liberia for Democracy (ULIMO) of the third part, Cotonou,

25 July 1993, annexed to Letter dated 6 August 1993 from the Chargé d'affaires a.i. of the Permanent Mission of Benin to the United Nations addressed to the Secretary-General, UN Doc. S/26272, 9 August 1993.

ICTY Statute
Statute of the International Tribunal for the Prosecution of Persons Responsible for Serious Violations of International Humanitarian Law Committed in the Territory of the Former Yugoslavia since 1991, adopted by UN Security Council Res. 827, 25 May 1993, as amended by Res. 1166, 13 May 1998, and Res. 1329, 30 November 2000.

1994

Comprehensive Agreement on Human Rights in Guatemala
Comprehensive Agreement on Human Rights between the Government of the Republic of Guatemala and the Unidad Revolucionaria Nacional Guatemalteca, Mexico City, 29 March 1994, annexed to Letter dated 8 April 1994 from the UN Secretary-General to the President of the UN General Assembly and to the President of the UN Security Council, UN Doc. A/48/928-S/1994/448, 19 April 1994, Annex I.

ICTR Statute
Statute of the International Criminal Tribunal for the Prosecution of Persons Responsible for Genocide and Other Serious Violations of International Humanitarian Law in the Territory of Rwanda and Rwandan citizens responsible for genocide and other such violations committed in the territory of neighbouring States between 1 January 1994 and 31 December 1994, adopted by UN Security Council Res. 955, 8 November 1994, as amended by Res. 1165, 30 April 1998, Res. 1329, 30 November 2000, Res. 1411, 17 May 2002 and 1431, 14 August 2002.

San Remo Manual on International Law Applicable to Armed Conflicts at Sea
San Remo Manual on International Law Applicable to Armed Conflicts at Sea, Louise Doswald-Beck (ed.), 12 June 1994, Prepared by international lawyers and naval experts convened by the International Institute of Humanitarian Law, Cambridge University Press, 1995.

1996

ILC Draft Code of Crimes against the Peace and Security of Mankind
Draft Code of Crimes against the Peace and Security of Mankind, adopted by the International Law Commission, 5 July 1996, reprinted in *Report of the International Law Commission on the work of its forty-eighth session*, 6 May–26 July 1996, UN Doc. A/51/10, 1996.

1997

Seville Agreement
Agreement on the organization of the international activities of the components of the International Red Cross and Red Crescent Movement (the Seville Agreement), adopted by the Council of Delegates, Seville, 25–27 November 1997, reprinted in ICRC/International Federation of Red Cross and Red Crescent Societies, *Handbook of the International Red Cross and Red Crescent Movement*, 14th edition, Geneva, 2008, pp. 639–654.

1998

Comprehensive Agreement on Respect for Human Rights and IHL in the Philippines
Comprehensive Agreement on Respect for Human Rights and International Humanitarian Law between the Government of the Republic of the Philippines and the National Democratic Front of the Philippines, The Hague, 16 March 1998.

Guiding Principles on Internal Displacement
Guiding Principles on Internal Displacement, presented to the UN Commission on Human Rights by the Special Representative of the UN Secretary-General on Internally Displaced Persons, UN Doc. E/CN.4/1998/53/Add.2, 11 February 1998.

1999

UN Secretary-General's Bulletin
Observance by United Nations Forces of International Humanitarian Law, Secretary-General's Bulletin, UN Secretariat, UN Doc. ST/SGB/1999/13, 6 August 1999.

2000

UNTAET Regulation No. 2000/15
Regulation on the Establishment of Panels with Exclusive Jurisdiction over Serious Criminal Offences, UN Doc. UNTAET/REG/2000/15, Dili, 6 June 2000.

2001

Bangkok Principles on Status and Treatment of Refugees
Final Text of the AALCO's 1966 Bangkok Principles on Status and Treatment of Refugees, as adopted at the 40th session of the Asian-African Legal Consultative Organization (AALCO), New Delhi, 24 June 2001.

Draft Articles on State Responsibility
  Draft articles on Responsibility of States for Internationally Wrongful Acts, adopted by the International Law Commission at its fifty-third session, 23 April–1 June and 2 July–10 August 2001, reprinted in *Report of the International Law Commission on the work of its fifty-third session*, UN Doc. A/56/10, 2001, para. 76 (text of the draft articles) and para. 77 (text of the draft articles with commentaries thereto).

2002

ICC Elements of Crimes
  Finalized draft text of the Elements of Crimes, adopted by the 23rd Meeting of the Preparatory Commission for the International Criminal Court, New York, 30 June 2000, Report of the Preparatory Commission for the International Criminal Court, UN Doc. PCNICC/2000/INF/3/Add.2, Addendum, 6 July 2000, as adopted by the Assembly of States Parties to the Rome Statute of the International Criminal Court, First Session, 3–10 September 2002, *Official Records*, UN Doc. ICC-ASP/1/3, 25 September 2002, and ICC-ASP/1/3/Corr.1, 31 October 2002.

2004

N'Djamena Humanitarian Ceasefire Agreement on the Conflict in Darfur
  Humanitarian Ceasefire Agreement on the Conflict in Darfur, signed by the Government of Sudan, the Sudan Liberation Movement/Army, the Sudan Justice and Equality Movement, the African Union and the Chadian Mediation, N'Djamena, 8 April 2004.

N'Djamena Protocol on the Establishment of Humanitarian Assistance in Darfur
  Protocol on the Establishment of Humanitarian Assistance in Darfur, signed by the Government of Sudan, the Sudan Liberation Movement/Army, the Sudan Justice and Equality Movement, the African Union and the Chadian Mediation, N'Djamena, 8 April 2004, annexed to the N'Djamena Humanitarian Ceasefire Agreement, 8 April 2004.

2005

Basic Principles and Guidelines on the Right to a Remedy and Reparation for Victims of Gross Violations of International Human Rights Law and Serious Violations of IHL
  Basic Principles and Guidelines on the Right to a Remedy and Reparation for Victims of Gross Violations of International Human Rights Law and Serious Violations of International Humanitarian Law, adopted by UN General Assembly Res. 60/147 of 16 December 2005.

ICRC Study on Customary International Humanitarian Law
ICRC Study on Customary International Humanitarian Law, published as Jean-Marie Henckaerts and Louise Doswald-Beck (eds), *Customary International Humanitarian Law, Volume I: Rules*, ICRC/Cambridge University Press, 2005, available at www.icrc.org/customary-ihl.

Supplementary Measures to the Seville Agreement
Supplementary measures to enhance the implementation of the Seville Agreement, Annex to Resolution 8, adopted by the Council of Delegates, Seoul, 16–18 November 2005, reprinted in ICRC/International Federation of Red Cross and Red Crescent Societies, *Handbook of the International Red Cross and Red Crescent Movement*, 14th edition, Geneva, 2008, pp. 655–664.

2006

Draft Articles on Diplomatic Protection
Draft Articles on Diplomatic Protection, with commentary, adopted by the International Law Commission at its fifty-eight session, 1 May–9 June and 3 July–11 August 2006, reprinted in Report of the International Law Commission on the work of its fifty-eight session, UN Doc. A/61/10, 2006.

Sanremo Manual on the Law of Non-International Armed Conflict
The Manual on the Law of Non-International Armed Conflict, With Commentary, Professor Michael N. Schmitt, Professor Charles H.B. Garraway and Professor Yoram Dinstein, International Institute of Humanitarian Law, Sanremo, 2006, reprinted in *Israel Yearbook on Human Rights*, Vol. 36, 2006, p. 333.

2008

Montreux Document on Private Military and Security Companies
The Montreux Document on pertinent international legal obligations and good practices for States related to operations of private military and security companies during armed conflict, adopted at Montreux, 17 September 2008, ICRC/Swiss Federal Department of Foreign Affairs, August 2009.

2009

Manual on International Law Applicable to Air and Missile Warfare
HPCR Manual on International Law Applicable to Air and Missile Warfare, Program on Humanitarian Policy and Conflict Research (HPCR) at Harvard University, Bern, 15 May 2009, and HPCR Manual on International Law Applicable to Air and Missile Warfare: Commentary, Massachusetts, March 2010, Cambridge University Press, 2013.

Updated EU Guidelines on Compliance with International Humanitarian Law
> Updated European Union Guidelines on promoting compliance with international humanitarian law (IHL), Council of the European Union, *Official Journal of the European Union* 2009/C 303/12, 15 December 2009 (the original version dates from 2005, see *Official Journal* 2005/C 327/04).

2011

Draft Articles on the Responsibility of International Organizations
> Draft Articles on the Responsibility of International Organizations, with commentary, adopted by the International Law Commission at its sixty-third session, 26 April–3 June and 4 July–12 August 2011, reprinted in Report of the International Law Commission on the work of its sixty-third session, UN Doc. A/66/10, 2011.

2012

Copenhagen Process: Principles and Guidelines
> The Copenhagen Process: Principles and Guidelines, The Copenhagen Process on the Handling of Detainees in International Military Operations, Copenhagen, 19 October 2012.

2013

Tallinn Manual on the International Law Applicable to Cyber Warfare
> Tallinn Manual on the International Law Applicable to Cyber Warfare, Cambridge University Press, 2013.

IV. Military manuals

Argentina

Law of War Manual
> Leyes de Guerra (Law of War), RC-46–1, Público, II Edición 1969, Ejército Argentino, edición original aprobado por el Comandante en Jefe del Ejército, Impreso en el Instituto Geográfica Militar, Buenos Aires, 9 May 1967, 2nd edition, 1969.

Australia

Manual of the Law of Armed Conflict
> Law of Armed Conflict, Australian Defence Doctrine Publication, Executive Series ADDP 06.4, Headquarters, Australian Defence Force, Defence Publishing Service, Canberra, 11 May 2006.

Belgium

Specific Procedure on the Prisoners of War Information Bureau
Procédure spécifique : Structure et fonctionnement du Bureau de Renseignements sur les prisonniers de guerre (Specific Procedure: Structure and Functioning of the Prisoners of War Information Bureau), Ministère de la Défense, 2007.

Law of Armed Conflict Training Manual
Droit des conflits armés: manuel du cours pour conseillers en droit des conflits armés (Law of Armed Conflict: Course Manual for Advisers on the Law of Armed Conflict), Publication CDCA-DCA, Ecole royale militaire, Direction de la formation continue, edition of April 2009.

Benin

Law of Armed Conflict Manual
Le Droit de la Guerre (The Law of Armed Conflict), III fascicules, Ministère de la Défense Nationale, Forces Armées du Bénin, 1995.

Burundi

Regulation on International Humanitarian Law
Règlement n° 98 sur le droit international humanitaire (Regulation on International Humanitarian Law), Ministère de la Défense Nationale et des Anciens Combattants, Projet 'Moralisation' (BDI/B-05), Bujumbura, August 2007.

Cameroon

Instructor's Manual
Droit international humanitaire et droit de la guerre, Manuel de l'instructeur en vigueur dans les Forces Armées (International Humanitarian Law and the Law of War: Instructor's Manual for the Armed Forces), Présidence de la République, Ministère de la Défense, Etat-major des Armées, edition of 1992.

Instructor's Manual
Droit des conflits armés et droit international humanitaire, Manuel de l'instructeur en vigueur dans les forces de défense (Law of Armed Conflict and International Humanitarian Law: Instructor's Manual for the Defence Forces), Présidence de la République, Ministère de la Défense, Etat-major des Armées, edition of 2006.

Disciplinary Regulations
Règlement de discipline générale dans les forces de défense (General Disciplinary Regulations in the Defence Forces), Décret n° 2007/199, Président de la République, 7 July 2007.

Canada

LOAC Manual
The Law of Armed Conflict at the Operational and Tactical Levels, B-GJ-005–104/FP-021, Office of the Judge Advocate General, 13 August 2001.

Prisoner of War Handling Manual
Prisoner of War Handling: Detainees and Interrogation & Tactical Questioning in International Operations, Joint Doctrine Manual, B-GJ-005–110/FP-020, National Defence Headquarters, 1 August 2004.

Code of Conduct
Code of Conduct for CF Personnel, B-GG-005–027/AF-023, Office of the Judge Advocate General, February 2007.

Use of Force for CF Operations
Use of Force for CF Operations, Canadian Forces Joint Publication, B-GJ-005–501/FP-001, Chief of the Defence Staff, August 2008.

Chad

IHL Manual
Le droit international humanitaire adapté au contexte des opérations de maintien de l'ordre (International Humanitarian Law in Law-Enforcement Operations), Ministère des Armées, edition of 1996.

Instructor's Manual
Droit international humanitaire : Manuel de l'instructeur en vigueur dans les forces armées et de sécurité (International Humanitarian Law: Instructor's Manual for the Armed and Security Forces), Présidence de la République, Ministère de la Défense Nationale, Etat-major général des Armées, edition of 2006.

Colombia

Operational Law Manual
Manual de Derecho Operacional (Operational Law Manual), Manual FF.MM 3–41 Público, Ministerio de Defensa Nacional, Comando General de las Fuerzas Militares, Santafé de Bogotá, 2009.

Côte d'Ivoire

Teaching Manual
> Droit de la guerre, Manuel d'instruction (Law of War, Teaching Manual),
> Ministère de la Défense, Forces Armées Nationales, November 2007.
> > Livre I: Instruction de base
> > Livre II: Instruction du gradé et du cadre, Manuel de l'instructeur
> > Livre III, Tome 1: Instruction de l'élève officier d'active de 1ère année,
> > Manuel de l'élève
> > Livre III, Tome 2: Instruction de l'élève officier d'active de 2ème année,
> > Manuel de l'instructeur
> > Livre IV: Instruction du chef de section et du commandant de compagnie, Manuel de l'élève
> > Livre V: Instruction de l'officier d'état-major

Croatia

LOAC Compendium
> Compendium 'Law of Armed Conflicts', Ministry of Defence, 1991.

Commanders' Manual
> Basic Rules of the Law of Armed Conflict – Commanders' Manual, Ministry of Defence, 1992.

Djibouti

Manual on International Humanitarian Law
> Manuel sur le droit international humanitaire et les droits de l'homme applicables au travail du policier (Manual on International Humanitarian Law and Human Rights Applicable to Policing), Ministère de l'Intérieur, Direction Générale de la Police, June 2004.

France

LOAC Teaching Note
> Fiche didactique relative au droit des conflits armés (Teaching Note on the Law of Armed Conflict), annexée à Directive n° 147 de la Ministère de la Défense, 4 January 2000.

Germany

Military Manual
> Humanitarian Law in Armed Conflicts – Manual, Joint Service Regulation (ZDv) 15/2, DSK VV207320067, official English translation of 'Humanitäres Völkerrecht in bewaffneten Konflikten – Handbuch', Federal Ministry of Defence, Bonn, August 1992.

Military Manual
> Law of Armed Conflict – Manual, Joint Service Regulation (ZDv) 15/2, DSK AV230100262, official English translation of 'Humanitäres Völkerrecht in bewaffneten Konflikten – Handbuch', Federal Ministry of Defence, Berlin, May 2013.

Hungary

Military Manual
> A Hadijog, Jegyzet a katonai, föiskolák hallgatói részére (Textbook of Military Martial Law: Notes for Students at the Military College), Magyar Honvédség Szolnoki Repülötiszti Föiskola (Hungarian National Defence College, Szolnok), 1992.

Israel

Manual on the Rules of Warfare
> Rules of Warfare on the Battlefield, Military Advocate-General's Corps Command, IDF School of Military Law, Department of International Law, 2nd edition, 2006.

Italy

LOAC Elementary Rules Manual
> Regole elementari di diritto di guerra (Law of War Elementary Rules), SMD-G-012, Stato Maggiore della Difesa, I Reparto, Ufficio Addestramento e Regolamenti, Rome, 1991.

Kenya

LOAC Manual
> Law of Armed Conflict, Military Police Basic Course (ORS), 4 précis, The School of Military Police, 1997.

Madagascar

Military Manual
> Le droit des conflits armés (The Law of Armed Conflict), Ministère des Forces Armées, August 1994.

Mali

Army Service Regulations
> Règlement du service dans l'armée, 1ère Partie: Discipline générale (Army Service Regulations, Part I: General Discipline), Ministère de la Défense Nationale, 1979.

Morocco

Disciplinary Regulations

Règlement de discipline général dans les Forces Armées Royales (General Disciplinary Regulations in the Royal Armed Forces), Dahir n° 1–74–383 du 15 rejeb 1394, 5 August 1974, published in *Bulletin Officiel*, 9 December 1974.

Nepal

Army Handbook

Nepal Army Handbook on Law of Armed Conflict, Fighting by the Rules, Chief of the Army Staff, Nirendra Pd. Aryal, Brig. Gen. (JAG), 2011.

Netherlands

Military Handbook

Handboek KL-Militair (Military Handbook), Voorschrift VS 2–1352, Koninklijke Landmacht (Royal Army), Druk 1, 3 October 2003.

Military Manual

Humanitair Oorlogsrecht: Handleiding (The Humanitarian Law of War: A Manual), Voorschift No. 27–412, Koninklijke Landmacht, Militair Juridische Dienst, September 2005.

New Zealand

Military Manual

Interim Law of Armed Conflict Manual, DM 112, New Zealand Defence Force, Directorate of Legal Services, 26 November 1992.

Nigeria

IHL Manual

International Humanitarian Law (IHL), Directorate of Legal Services, Nigerian Army, 1994.

Peru

IHL Manual

Manual de Derecho Internacional Humanitario para las Fuerzas Armadas (Manual of International Humanitarian Law for the Armed Forces),

Resolución Ministerial N° 1394–2004-DE/CCFFAA/CDIH-FFAA, Centro del Derecho Internacional Humanitario de las Fuerzas Armadas, Lima, 1 December 2004, published in *Diario Oficial 'El Peruano'*, 8 December 2004, p. 281904.

IHL and Human Rights Manual
Manual de Derecho Internacional Humanitario y Derechos Humanos para las Fuerzas Armadas (Manual of International Humanitarian Law and Human Rights for the Armed Forces), Resolución Viceministerial N° 049–2010/DE/VPD, Ministerio de Defensa, Dirección de Educación y Doctrina, Centro del Derecho Internacional Humanitario y Derechos Humanos de las Fuerzas Armadas, Lima, 21 May 2010.

Philippines

Joint Circular on Adherence to IHL and Human Rights
Implementation Guidelines for Presidential Memorandum Order No. 393 dated 9 September 1991, Directing the Armed Forces of the Philippines and the Philippine National Police to Reaffirm their Adherence to the Principles of Humanitarian Law and Human Rights in the Conduct of Security/Police Operations, Joint Circular Number 2–91, Department of National Defense and Department of Interior and Local Government, 1991.

Air Power Manual
Air Power Manual, Philippine Air Force, Headquarters, Office of Special Studies, May 2000.

LOAC Teaching File
The Law of Armed Conflict, Teaching File for Instructors, Armed Forces of the Philippines, Quezon City, 2006.

Russian Federation

Military Manual
Instructions on the Application of the Rules of International Humanitarian Law by the Armed Forces of the USSR, Appendix to Order No. 75 of the Defence Minister, 1990.

Regulations on the Application of IHL
Application of IHL Rules, Regulations for the Armed Forces of the Russian Federation) (Nastavlenie po mezhdunarodnomu gumanitarnomu pravu dlya Vooruzhennyh Sil Rossiiskoi Federatsii), Ministry of Defence, Moscow, 8 August 2001.

Senegal

IHL Manual
Le Droit international humanitaire adapté au contexte des opérations de maintien de l'ordre (International Humanitarian Law in Law-Enforcement Operations), Ministère des Forces Armées, Haut Commandement de la Gendarmerie et Direction de la Justice Militaire, Cabinet, 1999.

Sierra Leone

Instructor Manual
The Law of Armed Conflict. Instructor Manual for the Republic of Sierra Leone Armed Forces (RSLAF), Armed Forces Education Centre, September 2007.

Sri Lanka

Military Manual

A Soldier's Guide to the Law of Armed Conflict, Sri Lanka Army Headquarters, Colombo, 20 November 2003.

South Africa

LOAC Manual
Presentation on the South African Approach to International Humanitarian Law, Appendix A, Chapter 4: International Humanitarian Law (The Law of Armed Conflict), National Defence Force, 1996. This manual is also included in Chapter 4 of the Draft Civic Education Manual of 1997.

Revised Civic Education Manual
Revised Civic Education Manual, South African National Defence Force, 2004.

Spain

LOAC Manual
Orientaciones: el derecho de los conflictos armados (Guidelines on the Law of Armed Conflict), Publicación OR7–004, 2 tomos, Estado Mayor del Ejército, División de Operaciones, 18 March 1996.

LOAC Manual
Orientaciones: el derecho de los conflictos armados (Guidelines on the Law of Armed Conflict), Tomo 1, Publicación OR7–004 (2a edición),

Ministerio de Defensa, Ejército de Tierra, Mando de Adiestramiento y Doctrina, Dirección de Doctrina, Orgánica y Materiales, 2 November 2007.

Sweden

IHL Manual
International Humanitarian Law in Armed Conflict, with reference to the Swedish Total Defence System, Swedish Ministry of Defence, January 1991.

Switzerland

Military Manual
Lois et coutumes de la guerre (Laws and Customs of War), Manuel 51.7/III dfi, Armée suisse, 1 January 1984.

Basic Military Manual
Lois et coutumes de la guerre (Extrait et commentaire) (Laws and Customs of War (Extracts and Commentary)), Règlement 51.7/II f, Armée suisse, 1 September 1987.

Togo

Military Manual
Le Droit de la Guerre (The Law of War), III fascicules, Etat-major Général des Forces Armées Togolaises, Ministère de la Défense Nationale, 1996.

Turkey

LOAC Manual
Guide to the Law of Armed Conflict of Armed Forces, Partnership for Peace Training Center Command, Turkish General Staff, Ankara, July 2001.

Ukraine

Manual on the Application of IHL Rules
Manual on the Application of the Rules of International Humanitarian Law in the Armed Forces of Ukraine, Order No. 400, Ministry of Defence, Kyiv, 11 September 2004.

United Kingdom of Great Britain and Northern Ireland

Military Manual
The Law of War on Land, being Part III of the Manual of Military Law, The War Office, Her Majesty's Stationery Office, London 1958.

Manual of the Law of Armed Conflict
    The Manual of the Law of Armed Conflict, Joint Service Publication 383, UK Ministry of Defence, 1 July 2004, published by Oxford University Press, 2005.

Joint Medical Doctrine
    Joint Medical Doctrine, Joint Doctrine Publication 4–03 (JDP 4–03), 3rd edition, promulgated as directed by the Chiefs of Staff, May 2011.

Joint Doctrine Captured Persons
    Captured Persons (CPERS), Joint Doctrine Publication 1–10 (JDP 1–10), 3rd edition, promulgated as directed by the Chiefs of Staff, January 2015.

Allied Joint Doctrine for Medical Support, with UK National Elements
    Allied Joint Doctrine for Medical Support, with UK National Elements, Ministry of Defence, NATO Standard Allied Joint Publication-4.10(B), published by NATO Standardization Office, May 2015.

United States of America

Field Manual
    The Law of Land Warfare, Field Manual 27–10, Department of the Army, Washington D.C., 18 July 1956, as modified by Change No. 1, 15 July 1976.

Air Force Pamphlet
    Air Force Pamphlet 110–31, International Law – The Conduct of Armed Conflict and Air Operations, US Department of the Air Force, 1976.

Air Force Commander's Handbook
    Commander's Handbook on the Law of Armed Conflict, Air Force Pamphlet 110–34, Judge Advocate General, Department of the Air Force, Judge Advocate General, Washington D.C., 25 July 1980.

Navy Regulations
    United States Navy Regulations, Department of the Navy, Washington D.C., 14 September 1990.

Operational Law Handbook
    Operational Law Handbook, JA 422, Center for Law and Military Operations and International Law Division, The Judge Advocate General's School, United States Army, Charlottesville, Virginia, 1993.

Army Regulation on Enemy Prisoners, Retained Personnel, Civilian Internees and Other Detainees
    Military Police: Enemy Prisoners of War, Retained Personnel, Civilian Internees and Other Detainees, Army Regulation 190–8/OPNAVINST 3461.6/AFJI 31–304/MCO 3461.1, Headquarters, Departments of the

Army, the Navy, the Air Force, and the Marine Corps, Washington D.C., 1 October 1997.

Medical Evacuation in a Theater of Operations
Medical Evacuation in a Theater of Operations: Tactics, Techniques, and Procedures, Field Manual 8–10–6, Department of the Army, Washington D.C., 14 April 2000.

Veterinary Service Manual
Veterinary Service: Tactics, Techniques, and Procedures, Headquarters, Department of the Army, Field Manual 4–02.18, Washington, DC, 30 December 2004.

Army Uniforms and Insignia
Wear and Appearance of Army Uniforms and Insignia, Army Regulation 670–1, Headquarters, Department of the Army, Washington, D.C., 3 February 2005.

Human Intelligence Collector Operations
Human Intelligence Collector Operations, Field Manual 2–22.3, Headquarters, Department of the Army, Washington, D.C., 6 September 2006.

Medical Evacuation Manual
Medical Evacuation, Field Manual 4–02.2, Headquarters, Department of the Army, Washington D.C., 8 May 2007.

Naval Handbook
The Commander's Handbook on the Law of Naval Operations, NWP 1–14M/MCWP 5–12.1/COMDTPUB P5800.7A, Department of the Navy, Office of the Chief of Naval Operations and Headquarters, US Marine Corps, Department of Homeland Security and US Coast Guard, Washington D.C., edition of July 2007.

Law of War Deskbook
Law of War Deskbook, International and Operational Law Department, The United States Army Judge Advocate General's Legal Center and School, Charlottesville, Virginia, January 2010.

Manual for Military Commissions
Manual for Military Commissions, Department of Defense, Office of the Secretary of Defense, published in implementation of Chapter 47A of Title 10, United States Code, as amended by the Military Commissions Act of 2009, 10 U.S.C, sections 948a, *et seq.*, edition of April 2010.

Law of Armed Conflict Deskbook
Law of Armed Conflict Deskbook, International and Operational Law Department, The United States Army Judge Advocate General's Legal Center and School, Charlottesville, Virginia, 2012.

Army Health System
    Army Health System, Field Manual 4–02, Headquarters, Department of the Army, Washington, D.C., August 2013 (supersedes Army Tactics, Techniques, and Procedures 4–02, October 2011).

Religious Affairs in Joint Operations
    Religious Affairs in Joint Operations, Joint Publication 1–05, Joint Chiefs of Staff, 20 November 2013.

Manual on Detainee Operations
    Detainee Operations, Joint Publication 3–63, Joint Chiefs of Staff, Washington D.C., 13 November 2014.

Law of War Manual
    Department of Defense Law of War Manual, Office of General Counsel, Department of Defense, Washington D.C., June 2015.

V. National legislation

Australia

ICC Act
    International Criminal Court Act 2002, an Act to facilitate compliance by Australia with obligations under the Rome Statute of the International Criminal Court, and for related purposes, Act No. 41 of 2002, 27 June 2002.

Geneva Conventions Act, as amended
    Geneva Conventions Act 1957, Act No. 103 of 1957 as amended, an Act to enable effect to be given to certain Conventions done at Geneva on 12 August 1949 and to a Protocol additional to those Conventions done at Geneva on 10 June 1977, and for related purposes, adopted on 18 December 1957, published in *Gazette*, 1959;
    as amended by an Act to amend the Geneva Conventions Act 1957, Act No. 27 of 1991, adopted on 4 March 1991 and published in *Acts of the Parliament of the Commonwealth 1991*, Vol. I, Australian Government Publishing Service, Canberra, 1992, pp. 929–1006, and an Act to amend the Criminal Code Act 1995 and certain other Acts in consequence of the enactment of the International Criminal Court Act 2002, and for other purposes, Act No. 42 of 2002, assented to on 27 June 2002.

Austria

Red Cross Protection Law
    Bundesgesetz über die Anerkennung des Österreichischen Roten Kreuzes und den Schutz des Zeichens des Roten Kreuzes (Rotkreuzgesetz – RKG)

(Federal Law on the Recognition of the Austrian Red Cross and the Protection of the Red Cross Emblem (Red Cross Law)), 6 December 2007, published in *Bundesgesetzblatt für die Republik Österreich* (BGBl.), Part I, No. 33, 11 January 2008.

Azerbaijan

Emblem Law
Law of the Republic of Azerbaijan on the use and protection of the red cross and red crescent emblems, No. 128-IIQ, 8 May 2001, published in *Collection of Legislative Acts of the Republic of Azerbaijan*, No. 6, 30 June 2001, Article 382, pp. 1060–1064.

Belarus

Law on the Emblem
Law on the use and protection of the emblem of the Red Cross and the Red Crescent in the Republic of Belarus, Law No. 382–3, 12 May 2000, National Registry of the Legal Acts of the Republic of Belarus, 3 May 2000, 4/1168, published in *Vedomosti of the National Assembly of the Republic of Belarus*, 2000, N13, p. 121.

Belgium

Law on Protection of the Emblem
Loi du 4 juillet 1956 relative à la protection des dénominations, signes et emblèmes de la Croix-Rouge (Law relating to the protection of the names, signs and emblems of the Red Cross), 4 July 1956, published in *Moniteur belge*, No. 193, 11 July 1956, p. 4616.

Bosnia and Herzegovina

Emblem Law
Law on the use and protection of the red cross emblem and the title of the Red Cross Society of Bosnia and Herzegovina, 29 April 2002, published in the *Official Gazette of Bosnia and Herzegovina*, No. 11/02, 30 May 2002, pp. 274–276.

Brunei Darussalam

National Society Incorporation Act
Persatuan Bulan Sabit Merah Negara Brunei Darussalam (Incorporation) Act, An Act to incorporate the Red Cross Society by the name of Persuatan Bulan Sabit Merah Negara Brunei Darussalam, 28 November 1990.

Burkina Faso

Decree Introducing IHL in the Armed Forces
  Arrêté n° 94–0125/DEF/CAB portant institution du Droit International
  Humanitaire (D.I.H.) au sein des Forces Armées (Decree introducing Inter-
  national Humanitarian Law (IHL) in the Armed Forces), 26 December 1994.

Emblem Law
  Décret   n°   2003–621/PRES   promulguant   la   loi
  n° 059–2003/AN du 23 octobre 2003 portant utilisation et protection
  des emblèmes de la croix rouge et du croissant rouge au Burkina Faso (Law
  on the use and protection of the red cross and red crescent emblems in
  Burkina Faso), 23 October 2003, published in *Journal officiel du Burkina
  Faso*, No. 52, 25 December 2003, pp. 1831–1833.

Cambodia

Law on the Establishment of the ECCC, as amended
  Law on the Establishment of the Extraordinary Chambers in the Courts
  of Cambodia for the Prosecution of Crimes Committed during the Period
  of Democratic Kampuchea, 10 August 2001, published in *Royal Gazette*,
  Vol. 9, No. 30, 15 August 2001, pp. 2149–2170; as amended on 27 October 2004, published in *Royal Gazette*, Vol. 4, No. 40, 31 October 2004,
  pp. 2149–2170.

Red Cross or Red Crescent Emblem Law
  Royal Decree on the Use and Protection of the Red Cross or Red Crescent
  Emblem, 6 May 2002.

Cameroon

Emblem Law
  Law No. 97–2 on the protection of the red cross emblem and name, 10
  January 1997, published in *Official Gazette of the Republic of Cameroon*,
  7th Year, No. 2, 1 February 1997, pp. 63–66.

Canada

Geneva Conventions Act, as amended
  Geneva Conventions Act, An Act respecting the Geneva Conventions,
  1949, 1985, published in *Revised Statutes of Canada*, 1985, Vol. V, 1985,
  chapter G-3;
  as amended by An Act to amend the Geneva Conventions Act, the
  National Defence Act and the Trade-marks Act, 12 June 1990, published
  in *Canada Gazette*, Part III, Vol. 13, 14 September 1990, chapter 14;

as amended by An Act to amend the Geneva Conventions Act, an Act to incorporate the Canadian Red Cross Society and the Trade-marks Act, 22 June 2007, published in *Canada Gazette*, Part III, Vol. 30, No. 2, 31 July 2007, chapter 26.

Crimes Against Humanity and War Crimes Act, as amended
Crimes Against Humanity and War Crimes Act, An Act respecting genocide, crimes against humanity and war crimes and to implement the Rome Statute of the International Criminal Court, and to make consequential amendments to other Acts, 29 June 2000, published in *Canada Gazette*, Part III, Vol. 23, No. 3, 9 August 2000, chapter 24;
as amended by An Act to amend the Criminal Code (organized crime and law enforcement) and to make consequential amendments to other Acts, assented to on 18 December 2001, published in *Canada Gazette*, Part III, Vol. 24, No. 5, 13 February 2002, chapter 32.

Central African Republic

Emblem Law
Loi n° 09.006 portant protection de l'emblème et du nom Croix-Rouge en République centrafricaine (Law protecting the emblem and name of the Red Cross in the Central African Republic), 8 June 2009.

Chile

Emblem Law, as amended
Ley núm. 6.371, de 1939, que protege el Emblema de la Cruz Roja (Law protecting the Red Cross Emblem), 8 August 1939;
as amended by Ley núm. 19.511, Modifica la Ley núm. 6.371, de 1939, que protege el Emblema de la Cruz Roja (Law amending the Law protecting the Red Cross Emblem), 31 July 1997, published in *Diario Oficial de la República de Chile*, No. 35.858, 3 September 1997, p. 2.

Law on Crimes against Humanity, Genocide and War Crimes
Ley núm. 20.357, que tipifica crímenes de lesa humanidad y genocidio y crímenes y delitos de guerra (Law repressing crimes against humanity, genocide and war crimes), 26 June 2009, published in *Diario Oficial de la República de Chile*, 18 July 2009.

Colombia

Emblem Law
Ley 875 del 2 de enero de 2004 por la cual se regula el uso del emblema de la Cruz Roja y de la Media Luna Roja y otros emblemas protegidos por los Convenios de Ginebra del 12 de agosto de 1949 y sus protocolos adicionales

(Law regulating use of the emblem of the Red Cross and the Red Crescent and other emblems protected by the Geneva Conventions of 12 August 1949 and their Additional Protocols), 2 January 2004, published in *Diario Oficial*, No. 45.418, 2 January 2004.

Decree No. 138

Decreto No. 138 por el cual se reglamentan los artículos 5, 6, 14 y 18 de la Ley 875 de 2004 y se dictan otras disposiciones (Decree regulating Articles 5, 6, 14 and 18 of Law No. 875 of 2004 and establishing other provisions), adopted by the President on 25 January 2005, published in *Diario Oficial*, No. 45.804, 27 January 2005.

Finland

Penal Code, as amended

Penal Code, Act No. 39/1889, 19 December 1889; as amended by Act No. 212/2008, Chapter 11, War crimes and crimes against humanity (Laki rikoslain muuttamisesta), 11 April 2008, published in *Suomen säädöskokoelma*, 17 April 2008, pp. 525–530.

France

Penal Code, as amended

Loi n° 92–683 du 22 juillet 1992 portant réforme des dispositions générales du code pénal (Law reforming the general provisions of the Penal Code), 22 July 1992, published in *Journal officiel de la République française*, No. 169, 23 July 1992 p. 9864, NOR: JUSX8900136L;

as further amended in 1992 and 1993 and amended by Loi n° 2010–930 du 9 août 2010 portant adaptation du droit pénal à l'institution de la Cour pénale internationale (Law adapting criminal law to the establishment of the International Criminal Court), 9 August 2010, published in *Journal officiel de la République française*, No. 183, 10 August 2010, p. 14678, NOR: JUSX0500268L.

Georgia

Emblem Law

Law No. 902 on the Red Cross and Red Crescent emblem and designation, 2 October 1997, published in *Parlamentis Utskebani*, No. 43, 30 October 1997, pp. 8–10.

Germany

Code of Administrative Offences

Gesetz über Ordnungswidrigkeiten (OWiG) (Code of Administrative Offences), 24 May 1968, published in *Bundesgesetzblatt* (BGBl.), Part I, No. 33, 30 May 1968, pp. 481–502.

Red Cross Act

Gesetz über das Deutsche Rote Kreuz und andere freiwillige Hilfsgesellschaften im Sinne der Genfer Rotkreuz-Abkommen (DRK-Gesetz – DRKG) (Act on the German Red Cross and other voluntary societies as defined in the Geneva Conventions), 5 December 2008, published in *Bundesgesetzblatt* (BGBl.), Part I, No. 56, 10 December 2008, p. 2346.

Guatemala

Emblem Law, as amended

Ley de protección y uso del Emblema de la Cruz Roja (Law on protection and use of the Red Cross Emblem), 4 November 1997, Decreto número 102–97 del Congreso de la República, published in *Diario de Centro América*, No. 78, 18 November 1997, pp. 2562–2566;

as amended by Decreto número 27–2011 : reformas al Decreto número 102–97 del Congreso de la República, Ley de protección y uso del emblema de la Cruz Roja (Decree amending Decree No. 102–97 on protection and use of the Red Cross Emblem), 8 December 2011, published in *Diario de Centro América*, No. 40, 8 December 2011, pp. 1–2.

Guinea

Emblem Law

Loi L/95010/CTRN portant usage et protection de l'emblème et du nom de la Croix-Rouge guinéenne (Law on the use and protection of the emblem and name of the Guinean Red Cross), 9 May 1995, published in *Journal Officiel*, No. 10, 25 May 1995, pp. 494–660.

India

Geneva Conventions Act

Geneva Conventions Act, 1960, An Act to enable effect to be given to certain international Conventions done at Geneva on the twelfth day of August, 1949, to which India is a party, and for purposes connected therewith, Act No. 6 of 1960, 12 March 1960, published in *Gazette of India*, No. 7, 12 March 1960, pp. 208–215.

Iraq

Law Establishing the Supreme Iraqi Criminal Tribunal

Law No. 10/2005 establishing the Supreme Iraqi Criminal Tribunal, 9 October 2005, published in *Al-Waqa'i Al-Iraqiya*, No. 4006, Year 47, 18 October 2005. Further to the promulgation of this law, the Elements of Crimes for the Supreme Iraqi Criminal Tribunal were adopted.

Ireland

Geneva Conventions Act, as amended
Geneva Conventions Act, 1962, An Act to enable effect to be given so far as Ireland is concerned to certain provisions of the Conventions done at Geneva on the 12th day of August, 1949, relative to the amelioration of the condition of the wounded and sick in armed forces in the field, the amelioration of the condition of wounded and shipwrecked members of armed forces at sea, the treatment of prisoners of war, and the protection of civilian persons in time of war, Act No. 11 of 21 April 1962, published in *The Acts of the Oireachtas* passed in the year 1962, pp. 114–487;

as amended by an Act to enable effect to be given to the Protocols additional to the Geneva Conventions of 1949 adopted at Geneva on 8 June 1977 and for that purpose to amend the Geneva Conventions Act, 1962, the Red Cross Acts, 1938 to 1954, and section 1 of the Prisoners of War and Enemy Aliens Act, 1956, and to provide for connected matters, Act No. 35 of 13 July 1998, published in *The Acts of the Oireachtas* passed in the year 1998, pp. 827–908.

Kazakhstan

Emblem Instruction
Instruction No. 455 on procedure for the usage of the heraldic emblem of the red crescent on a white background, Order of the Minister of Defence of the Republic of Kazakhstan, 26 November 2002.

Kenya

Geneva Conventions Act
The Geneva Conventions Act, An Act of Parliament to enable effect to be given to certain International Conventions done at Geneva on the 12th August 1949, and for purposes incidental thereto, Act No. 51 of 19 November 1968, published in *The Acts 1968*, No. 51 of 1968.

Kiribati

Geneva Conventions Act
Geneva Conventions Act 1993, An Act to enable continued effect to be given to the Geneva Conventions relating to the wounded, prisoners of war and civilians in time of war, done on 12th August 1949; and for connected purposes, 16 June 1993.

Kyrgyzstan

Emblem Law

Law on the use and protection of the emblem of the red crescent and red cross, 8 September 2000, published in *Vedomosti Zakonodatel'nogo Sobraniya Zhogorku Kenesha Kyrgyzskoy Respubliki*, 2000.

Lithuania

Law on the Red Cross Society and Emblems

Lietuvos Raudonojo Kryžiaus draugijos, Raudonojo Kryžiaus ir Raudonojo Pusmenulio emblemos ir pavadinimo istatymas (Law on the Lithuanian Red Cross Society, the Red Cross and Red Crescent emblems and name), No. VIII-1978, 10 October 2000, published in *Valstybės žinios*, No. 89–2744, 2000.

Mali

Emblem Law

Loi nº 9/018 relative à l'utilisation et à la protection de l'emblème et du nom de la Croix-Rouge et du Croissant-Rouge au Mali (Law on the use and protection of the emblem and name of the Red Cross and the Red Crescent in Mali), 26 June 2009.

Morocco

Emblem Law

Dahir nº 1–58–256 du 15 rebia II 1378 (29 octobre 1958) relatif à l'emploi de l'emblème du Croissant-Rouge (Decree on use of the Red Crescent emblem), 29 October 1958, published in *Bulletin officiel*, No. 2406, 5 December 1958, p. 1968.

Namibia

Red Cross Act

Namibia Red Cross Act, 1991, Act to accord recognition to the Namibia Red Cross Society as the only Red Cross Society in Namibia; to prohibit the unauthorised use of the name or emblem of the Red Cross or Red Crescent; and to provide for matters incidental thereto, 28 November 1991, published in *Government Gazette of the Republic of Namibia*, No. 313, 7 December 1991.

Geneva Conventions Act

Geneva Conventions Act, 2003, Act to give effect to certain Conventions done at Geneva on 12 August 1949 and to certain Protocols additional to those Conventions done at Geneva on 10 June 1977; and to provide for matters relating thereto, Act No. 15, 28 November 2003, published in *Government Gazette of the Republic of Namibia*, No. 3109, 18 December 2003.

Niger

Penal Code, as amended

Loi n° 61–27 du 15 juillet 1961, portant institution du Code pénal (Law instituting the Penal Code), 15 July 1961, published in *Journal officiel*, 15 November 1961;

as amended in 2003 by Loi n° 2003–25 du 13 juin 2003 modifiant la loi n° 61–27 du 15 juillet 1961, portant institution du Code pénal (Law amending Law No. 61–27 instituting the Penal Code), published in *Journal officiel spécial*, No. 4, 7 April 2004.

Nigeria

Geneva Conventions Act

Geneva Conventions Act, 1960, An Act to enable effect to be given in the Federal Republic of Nigeria to certain international conventions done at Geneva on the twelfth day of August, nineteen hundred and forty-nine and for purposes connected therewith, Act No. 54 of 30 September 1960, published in *Laws of the Federation of Nigeria*, Revised edition, Vol. IX, CAP. 162, 1990, pp. 6265–6280.

Panama

Emblem Law

Ley núm. 32 de 4 de julio de 2001 que dicta disposiciones para la protección y el uso del emblema de la Cruz Roja y el de la Media Luna Roja (Law providing for the protection and use of the Red Cross and Red Crescent emblems), 4 July 2001, published in *Gaceta Oficial*, Year XCVII, No. 24339, 6 July 2001, pp. 21–26.

Philippines

Emblem Act

Red Cross and Other Emblems Act of 2013, An Act defining the use and protection of the red cross, red crescent, and red crystal emblems, providing penalties for violations thereof and for other purposes, Republic Act No. 10530, 7 May 2013.

Poland

Penal Code
> Penal Code, 6 June 1997, published in *Journal of Laws of the Republic of Poland*, No. 88, 2 August 1997, item No. 553, pp. 2677–2716.

South Africa

ICC Act
> Implementation of the Rome Statute of the International Criminal Court, Act No. 27 of 2002, Act to provide for a framework to ensure the effective implementation of the Rome Statute of the International Criminal Court in South Africa; to ensure that South Africa conforms with its obligations set out in the Statute; to provide for the crime of genocide, crimes against humanity and war crimes; to provide for the prosecution in South African courts of persons accused of having committed the said crimes in South Africa and beyond the borders of South Africa in certain circumstances; to provide for the arrest of persons accused of having committed the said crimes and their surrender to the said Court in certain circumstances; to provide for cooperation by South Africa with the said Court; and to provide for matters connected therewith, 12 July 2002, published in *Government Gazette*, Vol. 445, No. 23642, 18 July 2002.

Emblem Act
> South African Red Cross Society and Legal Protection of Certain Emblems Act, Act No. 10 of 2007, Act to provide statutory recognition for the South African Red Cross Society; and to provide statutory protection for certain emblems; and to provide for matters connected therewith, 9 August 2007, published in *Government Gazette*, Vol. 506, No. 30178, 16 August 2007.

Geneva Conventions Act
> Implementation of the Geneva Conventions Act, Act No. 8 of 2012, Act to enact the Geneva Conventions and Protocols additional to those Conventions into law; to ensure prevention and punishment of grave breaches and other breaches of the Conventions and Protocols; and to provide for matters connected therewith, 11 July 2012, published in *Government Gazette*, Vol. 565, No. 35513, 12 July 2012.

Sri Lanka

Geneva Conventions Act
> Geneva Conventions Act, Act No. 4 of 2006, An Act to give effect to the First, Second, Third and Fourth Geneva Conventions on Armed Conflict and Humanitarian Law; and to provide for matters connected therewith or incidental thereto, 26 February 2006, published as a Supplement to Part II

of the *Gazette of the Democratic Socialist Republic of Sri Lanka*, 3 March 2006.

Switzerland

Public Insignia Law, as amended
Loi fédérale pour la protection des armoiries publiques et autres signes publics (Federal law on the protection of coats of arms and other public insignia), Loi n° 232.21, 5 June 1931;
as amended by Loi du 21 juin 2013 sur la protection des armoiries de la Suisse et des autres signes publics (Law on the protection of the coats of arms of Switzerland and other public insignia), 21 June 2013 entry into force on 1 January 2017, published in *Recueil officiel des lois fédérales*, 2015, pp. 3679–3696.

Penal Code, as amended
Code pénal suisse (Swiss Penal Code), RS 311.0, 21 December 1937, published in *Recueil officiel des lois fédérales*, 1938, pp. 781–876;
taking into account amendments up to Ordonnance du 12 décembre 2008 sur l'adaptation des dispositions légales suite au transfert des unités de renseignements du Service d'analyse et de prévention au DDPS (Département fédéral de la défense, de la protection de la population et des sports) (Ordinance of 12 December 2008 on the Adaptation of Legal Provisions Following the Transfer of Instruction Units of the Analysis and Prevention Service of the DDPS (Federal Department of Defence, Civil Protection and Sport)), published in *Recueil officiel des lois fédérales*, 2008, pp. 6261–6268.

Tajikistan

Emblem Law
Law on the use and protection of the Red Cross and Red Crescent emblems and appellations in the Republic of Tajikistan, Law No. 26, 12 May 2001.

Thailand

Red Cross Act
The Red Cross Act, B.E. 2499, 1 August 1956, published in *Government Gazette*, Vol. 63, No. 73, 14 August 1956, pp. 924–929.

Turkmenistan

Emblem Law
Law of Turkmenistan on the use and protection of the red crescent and red cross symbols, 7 July 2001, published in *XXI Asyr – Türkmenin Altyn Asyry*, No. 186 (23169), 27 July 2001, p. 2.

United Kingdom of Great Britain and Northern Ireland

Geneva Conventions Act, as amended

Geneva Conventions Act, 1957, an Act to enable effect to be given to certain international conventions done at Geneva on the twelfth day of August, nineteen hundred and forty-nine, and for purposes connected therewith (Chapter 52), 31 July 1957, published in *The Public General Acts and Church Assembly Measures of 1957*, pp. 543–682 (also applicable to Fiji, Gambia, Kiribati, Solomon Islands, Trinidad and Tobago, and Tuvalu); amended by the Geneva Conventions (Amendments) Act, 1995, an Act to make provision for the amendment of the Geneva Conventions Act 1957 to enable effect to be given to the Protocols additional to the Geneva Conventions of 1949 done at Geneva on 10 June 1977; and for connected purposes (Chapter 27), 19 July 1995, published in *The Public General Acts and General Synod Measures 1995*, 1997, pp. 1854–1920;

as amended by the Geneva Conventions and United Nations Personnel (Protocols) Act, 2009, an Act to amend the Geneva Conventions Act 1957 so as to give effect to the Protocol additional to the Geneva Conventions of 12 August 1949 done on 8 December 2005; and to amend the United Nations Personnel Act 1997 so as to give effect to the Optional Protocol to the Convention on the Safety of United Nations and Associated Personnel adopted by the General Assembly of the United Nations on 8 December 2005 (Chapter 6), 2 July 2009.

ICC Act

International Criminal Court Act, 2001, an Act to give effect to the Statute of the International Criminal Court; to provide for offences under the law of England and Wales and Northern Ireland corresponding to offences within the jurisdiction of that Court; and for connected purposes (Chapter 17), 11 May 2001, published in *The Public General Acts and General Synod Measures 2001*, 2001, pp. 1261–1340;

as amended by the International Criminal Court Act (Overseas Territories) Order 2009, 8 July 2009;

as amended by the Coroners and Justice Act, 2009, an Act to amend the law relating to coroners, to investigation of deaths and to certification and registration of deaths; to amend the criminal law; to make provision about criminal justice and about dealing with offenders; to make provision about the Commissioner for Victims and Witnesses; to make provision relating to the security of court and other buildings; to make provision about legal aid and about payments for legal services provided in connection with employment matters; to make provision for payments to be made by offenders in respect of benefits derived from the exploitation of material pertaining to offences; to amend the Data Protection Act 1998; and for connected purposes (Chapter 25), 12 November 2009.

United States of America

Geneva Distinctive Emblems Code
> Geneva Distinctive Emblems, United States Code, Title 18 – Crimes and Criminal Procedure, Part I – Crimes, Chapter 33 – Emblems, Insignia, and Names, section 706a, 25 June 1948.

Uniform Code of Military Justice, as amended
> Uniform Code of Military Justice, United States Code, Title 10 – Armed Forces, Subtitle A – General Military Law, Part II – Personnel, Chapter 47, sections 801–946, adopted 5 May 1950;
> as amended by the John Warner National Defense Authorization Act for Fiscal Year 2007, an Act to authorize appropriations for fiscal year 2007 for military activities of the Department of Defense, for military construction, and for defense activities of the Department of Energy, to prescribe military personnel strengths for such fiscal year, and for other purposes, Public Law 109–364, 120 Stat. 2083, 17 October 2006, section 552.

Geneva Distinctive Emblems Protection Act
> Geneva Distinctive Emblems Protection Act of 2006, an Act to amend title 18, United States Code, to prevent and repress the misuse of the Red Crescent distinctive emblem and the Third Protocol (Red Crystal) distinctive emblem, Public Law 109–481, 12 January 2007.

Uruguay

Emblem Decree
> Decreto núm. 679/992, Emblemas: Díctanse normas para el uso de los emblemas de la cruz roja y de la media luna roja, así como los vocablos 'Cruz Roja', 'Cruz de Ginebra' y 'Media Luna Roja' (Decree on the use of the emblems of the red cross and the red crescent, and of the names 'Red Cross', 'Geneva Cross' and 'Red Crescent'), 24 November 1992, published in *Diario Oficial*, 1 March 1993, pp. 499–500.

Uzbekistan

Law on Use and Protection of the Red Crescent and Red Cross Emblems
> Law No. 615-II on use and protection of the emblems of the Red Crescent and the Red Cross, 29 April 2004, published in *Sobranie zakonodatelstva Respubliki Uzbekistan*, No. 20, 2004, p. 234.

Yemen

Emblem Law
> Law No. 43/1999 on the organization and use of the emblems of the Red Cross and Red Crescent and on the prohibition of their misuse,

20 September 1999, published in *Official Gazette of the Republic of Yemen*, No. 18, 30 September 1999, pp. 1–4.

VI. National case law

Australia

Ohashi case

Military Court at Rabaul, In re Ohashi and others, Judgment, 23 March 1946, summarized in *Annual Digest and Reports of Public International Law Cases*, Vol. 13, 1946, p. 383.

Bosnia and Herzegovina

Andrun case

Court of Bosnia and Herzegovina, Section I for War crimes, No. X-KRŽ-05/32, Verdict, 19 August 2008.

Cameroon

Bagosora case

Cour d'Appel du Centre (Court of Appeals of the Centre Region), Ministère Public contre Théoneste Bagosora (Public Prosecutor *v.* Théoneste Bagosora), Case No. 433/COR, Judgment, 15 March 1996.

Canada

Ell case

Supreme Court, Ell *v.* Alberta, Judgment, 26 June 2003, [2003] 1 *S.C.R. (Supreme Court Reports)* 857.

Munyaneza case

Quebec Superior Court, Criminal Division, Province of Quebec, Her Majesty the Queen *v.* Désiré Munyaneza, Case No. 500–73–002500–052, Judgment, 22 May 2009, *R.J.Q. (Recueil de jurisprudence du Québec)* 1432.

Colombia

Constitutional Case No. C-225/95

Constitutional Court, Sentencia C-225/95, Expediente No. L.A.T.-40, Constitutional revision of Additional Protocol II and the Law 171 of 16 December 1994 implementing this protocol, Judgment, 18 May 1995.

Constitutional Case No. C-291/07

Constitutional Court, Plenary Chamber, Sentencia C-291/07 Judgment, 25 April 2007.

Denmark

Sarić case
>High Court (Ostre Landsrets), Prosecutor *v.* Refik Sarić, Case No. S-3396–94, Judgment, 25 November 1994, published in *Ugeskrift for Retsvaesen*, 1995, p. 838.

France

Bommer case
>Permanent Military Tribunal at Metz, Trial of Alois and Anna Bommer and their daughters, Judgment, 19 February 1947, summarized in *Law Reports of Trials of War Criminals*, Vol. IX, 1949, p. 62.

Wagner case
>Permanent Military Tribunal at Strasbourg, In re Wagner and others, Judgment, 3 May 1946, summarized in *Annual Digest and Reports of Public International Law Cases*, Vol. 13, 1946, p. 385.

Germany

East German Expropriation case
>Federal Constitutional Court (Bundesverfassungsgericht), Order of the Second Senate (Zweiter Senat), 26 October 2004, 2 BvR 955/00, 1038/01.

Fuel Tankers case
>Federal Prosecutor General at the Federal Court of Justice (Generalbundesanwalt beim Bundesgerichtshof), Investigation proceedings against Colonel (Oberst) Klein and Company Sergeant Major (Hauptfeldwebel) Wilhem because of suspected offences under the International Crimes Code and other offences (Ermittlungsverfahren gegen Oberst Klein und Hauptfeldwebel Wilhelm wegen des Verdachts einer Strafbarkeit nach dem VStGB und anderer Delikte), Case No. 3 BJs 6/10–4, Decision to Terminate Proceedings pursuant to section 170 para. 2 sentence 1 of the Penal Procedure Code (Einstellung des Verfahrens gemäß § 170 Abs. 2 Satz 1 StPO), 16 April 2010.

German Red Cross case
>Federal Court of Justice (Bundesgerichtshof), Deutsches Rotes Kreuz *v.* Rettungsdienst Süd/Nord GmbH, Judgment, 23 June 1994, I ZR 15/92.

Sokolović case
>– Higher Regional Court of Düsseldorf (Oberlandesgericht Düsseldorf), Prosecution *v.* Maksim Sokolović, Case No. 2 StE 6/97, Judgment, 29 November 1999.

– Federal Court of Justice (Bundesgerichtshof), Prosecution *v.* Maksim Sokolović, Case No. 3 StR 372/00, Judgment, 21 February 2001, published in *Neue Juristische Wochenschrift*, 2001, Vol. 37, p. 2728.

Targeted Killing in Pakistan case
Federal Prosecutor General at the Federal Court of Justice, Aerial Drone Deployment on 4 October 2010 in Mir Ali, Pakistan, Case No. 3 BJs 7/12–4, Decision to Terminate Proceedings, 23 July 2013, published in *International Law Reports*, No. 157, pp. 722–761.

Israel

Bassiouni case
Supreme Court sitting as High Court of Justice, Jaber al Bassiouni al Ahmed and others *v.* Prime Minister and Minister of Defence of Israel, HCJ 9132/07, Judgment, 27 January 2008.

Physicians for Human Rights v. Prime Minister of Israel and others
Supreme Court sitting as High Court of Justice, Physicians for Human Rights and others *v.* Prime Minister of Israel and others & Gisha Legal Centre for Freedom of Movement and others *v.* Minister of Defence, HCJ 201/09 & HCJ 248/09, Judgment, 19 January 2009.

Public Committee against Torture in Israel case
Supreme Court, The Public Committee against Torture in Israel and others *v.* Government of Israel and others, HCJ 769/02, Judgment, 14 December 2006.

Tzemel case
Supreme Court sitting as High Court of Justice, Leah Tzemel, Attorney, and others *v.* The Minister of Defence and Commander of the Antzar Camp, HCJ 593/82, Judgment, 13 July 1983, summarized in *Israel Yearbook on Human Rights*, Vol. 13, 1983, pp. 360–364.

Italy

Hass and Priebke case

– Military Tribunal of Rome, In re Hass and Priebke, Judgment in Trial of First Instance, No. 322, 22 July 1997, published in *Rassegna della Giustizia Militare*, Nos 1–2-3, 1999, p. 103.
– Military Appeals Court, In re Hass and Priebke, Judgment on Appeal, No. 24, 7 March 1998, published in *Rassegna della Giustizia Militare*, Nos 4–5-6, 1999, p. 25.

- Supreme Court of Cassation, In re Hass and Priebke, Judgment in Trial of Third Instance, No. 1295, 16 November 1998, published in *Rassegna della Giustizia Militare*, Nos 4–5-6, 1999, p. 145.

Kappler case

Military Tribunal of Rome, In re Kappler, Judgment, 20 July 1948, summarized in *Annual Digest and Reports of Public International Law Cases*, Vol. 15, 1948, p. 471.

Netherlands

In re Ernest case

Supreme Court (Minor Offences Division), In re Ernest Andreas Josephus Maria van A., Case No. 484, Judgment, 15 May 1979, published in *Nederlandse Jurisprudentie*, 1979, p. 1543.

Mpambara case

- District Court (Rechtbank), The Hague, Mpambara case, Judgment, 23 March 2009, LJ number BK0520.
- Court of Appeal (Gerechtshof), The Hague, Mpambara case, Judgment, 7 July 2011, LJ Number BR0686.

Rauter case

- Special Court (War Criminals) at The Hague, In re Rauter, Judgment, 4 May 1948, published in *Law Reports of Trials of War Criminals*, Vol. XIV, 1949, p. 88.
- Special Court of Cassation, In re Rauter, Judgment, 12 January 1949, summarized in *Annual Digest and Reports of Public International Law Cases*, Vol. 16, 1949, p. 526.

Norway

Bogstadveien tannlegevakt case

District Court of Oslo (Oslo Tingsrätt), Case No. 07–002291MED-OTIR/02, Public Prosecutor (den offentilga patalemyndigheten) *v.* Bogstadveien tannlegevakt, Judgment, 9 February 2007.

Poland

Hoess case

Supreme National Tribunal of Poland, Trial of Obersturmbannfürher Rudolf Franz Ferdinand Hoess, Judgment, 11–29 March 1947, summarized in *Law Reports of Trials of War Criminals*, Vol. VII, 1948, p. 11.

Switzerland

A.v. Ministère Public de la Confédération case
Federal Criminal Court, A. *v.* Ministère Public de la Confédération, B. and C., Judgment, 25 July 2012.

A. SA v. Swiss Red Cross
Federal Tribunal, First Civil Court, Case A. ___ SA *v.* Swiss Red Cross, Judgment, 20 May 2014.

Grabež case
Military Tribunal at Lausanne, Prosecutor *v.* Goran Grabež, Judgment, 18 April 1997, published in *American Journal of International Law*, Vol. 92, 1998, p. 78.

United Kingdom of Great Britain and Northern Ireland

Almelo Trial
Military Court at Almelo, Trial of Otto Sandrock and three others (aka 'Almelo Trial'), Judgment, 24–26 November 1945, published in *Law Reports of Trials of War Criminals*, Vol. I, 1947, p. 35.

Brown (Bajinja) and others case
High Court of Justice Divisional Court, Vincent Brown aka Vincent Bajinja and others *v.* The Government of Rwanda and the Secretary of State for the Home Department, Case No. CO/6247/2008, Judgment, 8 April 2009.

Essen Lynching case
Military Court at Essen, The Essen Lynching Case, Judgment, 21–22 December 1945, summarized in *Law Reports of Trials of War Criminals*, Vol. I, 1947, p. 88.

Ganić case
City of Westminster Magistrates' Court, The Government of the Republic of Serbia v. Ejup Ganić, Judgment, 27 July 2010, *[2010] EW Misc 11 (MC)*.

Gerike case
Military Court at Brunswick, Trial of Heinrich Gerike and seven others (aka 'The Velpke Children's Home case'), Trial, 20 March–3 April 1946, summarized in *Law Reports of Trials of War Criminals*, Vol. VII, 1948, pp. 76–81.

Jones and others case
House of Lords, Opinions of the Lords of Appeal for Judgment in the Cause, Jones (Respondent) *v.* Ministry of Interior Al-Mamlaka Al-Arabiya AS Saudiya (the Kingdom of Saudi Arabia) (Appellants); Mitchell and others (Respondents) *v.* Al-Dali and others and Ministry of Interior Al-Mamlaka

Al-Arabiya AS Saudiya (the Kingdom of Saudi Arabia) (Appellants); Jones (Appellant) *v.* Ministry of Interior Al-Mamlaka Al-Arabiya AS Saudiya (the Kingdom of Saudi Arabia) (Respondents) (Conjoined Appeals), Judgment, 14 June 2006, [2006] UKHL 26.

Kramer case

Military Court at Lüneburg, In re Kramer and others (aka 'Auschwitz and Belsen concentration camps case'), Judgment, 17 November 1945, summarized in *Law Reports of Trials of War Criminals*, Vol. II, 1947, p. 1.

R (on the application of Maya Evans) v. Secretary of State for Defence

High Court of Justice, Queen's Bench Division, Divisional Court, The Queen (on the application of Maya Evans) *v.* Secretary of State for Defence, Case No. CO/11949/2008, Judgment, 25 June 2010.

Rohde case

Military Court at Wuppertal, Trial of Werner Rohde and eight others, Judgment, 29 May–1 June 1946, summarized in *Law Reports of Trials of War Criminals*, Vol. V, 1948, p. 54.

Serdar Mohammed and others v. Ministry of Defence

– Judgment

High Court of Justice Queen's Bench Division, Royal Courts of Justice, Serdar Mohammed and others *v.* Ministry of Defence, Case No. HQ12X03367, Judgment, 2 May 2014.

– Appeal Judgment

England and Wales Court of Appeal (Civil Division), Serdar Mohammed and others *v.* Ministry of Defence, Case Nos A2/2014/1862, A2/2014/4084 and A2/2014/4086, Judgment, 30 July 2015.

Stalag Luft III case

Military Court at Hamburg, Trial of Max Wielen and 17 others (aka 'Stalag Luft III Case'), Trial of 1 July–3 September 1947, summarized in *Law Reports of Trials of War Criminals*, Vol. XI, 1949, pp. 31–52.

Tyrolt case

Military Court at Helmstedt, Trial of Georg Tyrolt and others, Trial, 20 May–24 June 1946, referenced in *Law Reports of Trials of War Criminals*, Vol. VII, p. 81.

Zyklon B case

Military Court at Hamburg, Trial of Bruno Tesch and two others (aka 'The Zyklon B case'), 1–8 March 1946, summarized in *Law Reports of Trials of War Criminals*, Vol. I, 1947, p. 93.

United States of America

Altstötter case
>Military Tribunal at Nuremberg, In re Altstötter and others (aka 'The Justice Trial'), Judgment, 4 December 1947, summarized in *Annual Digest and Reports of Public International Law Cases*, Vol. 14, 1947, p. 278.

Al Warafi case
>US Court of Appeals for the DC Circuit, Mukhtar Yahia Naji Al Warafi v. Barack Obama, Case No. 11–5276, Judgment, 24 May 2013.

Demjanjuk case
>US Court of Appeals for the Sixth Circuit, John Demjanjuk v. Joseph Petrovsky and others, Case No. 85–3435, Judgment, 31 October 1985, published in *Federal Reporter*, Vol. 776, 1985, p. 571.

Dostler case
>Military Commission at Rome, Trial of General Anton Dostler, Commander of the 75th German Army Corps, Judgment, 8–12 October 1945, summarized in *Law Reports of Trials of War Criminals*, Vol. I, 1947, p. 22.

Flick case
>Military Tribunal at Nuremberg, In re Flick and others (aka 'The Flick case'), Judgment, 22 December 1947, summarized in *Annual Digest and Reports of Public International Law Cases*, Vol. 14, 1947, p. 266.

Hadamar Trial
>Military Commission in Wiesbaden, Trial of Alfons Klein and six others (aka 'The Hadamar Trial'), 8–15 October 1945, summarized in *Law Reports of Trials of War Criminals*, Vol. I, 1947, p. 46.

Hamdan case

>- Government Brief on the Merits, Brief for Respondents, submitted 23 February 2006.
>- Supreme Court, Salim Ahmed Hamdan, Petitioner v. Donald H. Rumsfeld, Secretary of Defense, and others, Judgment, 29 June 2006, 548 US 557, 126 S. Ct. 2749.
>- Guantanamo Military Commission, United States of America v. Salim Ahmed Hamdan, Ruling on Defence Motion for Article 5 Status Determination, 17 December 2007.

Hostages case
>Military Tribunal at Nuremberg, Military Tribunal V, The United States of America v. Wilhelm List and eleven others, Judgment, 19 February 1948, published in *Trials of War Criminals Before the Nuernberg Military Tribunals Under Control Council Law No. 10, Nuernberg, October 1946–*

April 1949, Volume XI, United States Printing Office, Washington, 1950, pp. 757–1319, aka 'The Hostages Trial', Trial of 8 July 1947–19 February 1948, summarized in *Law Reports of Trials of War Criminals*, Vol. VIII, 1949, pp. 34–92.

I.G. Farben Trial

Military Tribunal at Nuremberg, Trial of Carl Krauch and twenty-two others (aka 'The I.G. Farben Trial'), Trial of 14 August 1947–29 July 1948, summarized in *Law Reports of Trials of War Criminals*, Vol. X, 1949, p. 1.

Johnson & Johnson case

US District Court for the Southern District of New York, Johnson & Johnson *v.* the American National Red Cross, Opinion and Order, 14 May 2008, 552 *Federal Supplement* 2d 434 (S.D.N.Y. 2008).

Krupp case

Military Tribunal at Nuremberg, Military Tribunal III, The United States of America *v.* Alfried Felix Alwyn Krupp von Bohlen und Halbach and eleven others, Judgment, 31 July 1948, published in *Trials of War Criminals before the Nuernberg Military Tribunals under Control Council Law No. 10, Nuernberg, October 1946–April 1949*, Volume IX, United States Printing Office, Washington, 1950, pp. 1327–1484; aka 'The Krupp Trial', Trial of 17 November 1947–30 June 1948, summarized in *Law Reports of Trials of War Criminals*, Vol. X, 1949, p. 69.

Milch case

Military Tribunal at Nuremberg, Trial of Erhard Milch, 20 December 1946–17 April 1947, summarized in *Law Reports of Trials of War Criminals*, Vol. VII, 1948, p. 27.

Pohl case

Military Tribunal at Nuremberg, United States *v.* Oswald Pohl and others, Judgment, 3 November 1947, reprinted in *Trials of War Criminals before the Nuremberg Military Tribunals under Control Council Law No. 10*, Vol. V, 1997, p. 958.

Siderman de Blake v. Republic of Argentina

US Court of Appeals for the Ninth Circuit, Siderman de Blake *v.* Republic of Argentina, Case No. 85–5773, Judgment, 22 May 1992, published in *Federal Reporter*, Vol. 965, 1992, p. 699.

Surrender of Elizaphan Ntakirutimana case

US District Court for the Southern District of Texas – Laredo Division, In the Matter of the Surrender of Elizaphan Ntakirutimana, Memorandum and Order, 17 December 1997, published in *International Law Materials*, Vol. 37, 1998, p. 398.

The Medical Trial

Military Tribunal at Nuremberg, In re Brandt and others (aka 'The Medical Trial'), Judgment, 20 August 1947, summarized in *Annual Digest and Reports of Public International Law Cases*, Vol. 14, 1947, p. 296.

Von Leeb case

Military Tribunal at Nuremberg, Trial of Wilhelm von Leeb and thirteen others (aka 'The German High Command Trial'), Trial of 30 December 1947–28 October 1948, summarized in *Law Reports of Trials of War Criminals*, Vol. XII, 1949, p. 1.

Yochio and others case

Military Commission at the Mariana Islands, Trial of Tachibana Yochio and thirteen others, Trial of 2–15 August 1946, summarized in *Law Reports of Trials of War Criminals*, Vol. XIII, 1949, p. 152.

Yousuf v. Samantar

US Court of Appeals for the Fourth Circuit, Yousuf *v.* Samantar, Case No. 08–1555, Judgment, 2 November 2012, published in *Federal Reporter*, Vol. 699, 2012, p. 763.

VII. Decisions and judgments of international and mixed judicial and quasi-judicial bodies

African Commission on Human and Peoples' Rights

Association of Victims of Post Electoral Violence & INTERIGHTS v. Cameroon

Association of Victims of Post Electoral Violence & INTERIGHTS *v.* Cameroon, Communication No. 272/03, Decision, 46th Session, Banjul, 11–25 November 2009.

Centre for Free Speech v. Nigeria

Centre for Free Speech *v.* Nigeria, Communication No. 206/97, Decision, 26th Session, Kigali, 15 November 1999.

Civil Liberties Organisation and others v. Nigeria

Civil Liberties Organisation, Legal Defence Centre, Legal Defence and Assistance Project *v.* Nigeria, Communication No. 218/98, Decision, 29th Session, Tripoli, 23 April–7 May 2001.

Constitutional Rights Project v. Nigeria

Constitutional Rights Project (in respect of Wahab Akamu, G. Adega and others) *v.* Nigeria, Communication No. 60/91, Decision, 17th Session, Lomé, 13–22 March 1995.

Doebbler v. Sudan
Curtis Francis Doebbler *v.* Sudan, Communication No. 236/2000, Decision, 33rd Session, Niamey, 15–29 May 2003.

Malawi African Association and others v. Mauritania
Malawi African Association *v.* Mauritania, Communication No. 54/91 (combined with Amnesty International *v.* Mauritania (Communication No. 61/91); Ms Sarr Diop and others *v.* Mauritania (Communication No. 98/93); Collectif des Veuves et Ayants-droit *v.* Mauritania (Communication Nos 164/97–196/97; and Association Mauritanienne des Droits de l'Homme *v.* Mauritania (Communication No. 210/98)), Decision, 27th Session, Algiers, 11 May 2000.

Arbitral tribunals

Naulilaa case
Special Arbitral Tribunal, The Naulilaa Case (Portugal *v.* Germany), Judgment, 31 July 1928, *United Nations Reports of International Arbitral Awards*, Vol. II, p. 1012.

Eritrea-Ethiopia Claims Commission

Prisoners of War, Eritrea's Claim
Partial Award, Prisoners of War, Eritrea's Claim 17, The Hague, 1 July 2003.

Prisoners of War, Ethiopia's Claim
Partial Award, Prisoners of War, Ethiopia's Claim 4, The Hague, 1 July 2003.

Jus Ad Bellum, Ethiopia's Claim
Partial Award, Jus Ad Bellum, Ethiopia's Claims 1–8, The Hague, 19 December 2005.

Central Front, Eritrea's Claim
Partial Award, Central Front, Eritrea's Claims 2, 4, 6, 7, 8 & 22, The Hague, 28 April 2004.

Central Front, Ethiopia's Claim
Partial Award, Central Front, Ethiopia's Claim 2, The Hague, 28 April 2004.

Diplomatic Claim, Eritrea's Claim
Partial Award, Diplomatic Claim, Eritrea's Claim 20, The Hague, 19 December 2005.

European Commission of Human Rights

Corsacov v. Moldova
Corsacov *v.* Moldova, Application No. 18944/02, Judgment, 4 April 2006.

Greek case
Denmark, Norway, Sweden and Netherlands *v.* Greece, Application Nos 3321/67, 3322/67, 3323/67 and 3344/67, Report adopted on 5 November 1969, *Yearbook of the European Convention on Human Rights*, Vol. 12 A (1969), Martinus Nijhoff, The Hague, 1972.

Kismir v. Turkey
Kismir *v.* Turkey, Application No. 27306/95, Judgment, 31 May 2005.

Menesheva v. Russia
Menesheva *v.* Russia, Application No. 59261/00, Judgment, 9 March 2006.

European Court of Human Rights

A v. UK
A *v.* the United Kingdom, Application No. 100/1997/884/1096, Judgment, 23 September 1998, *Reports of Judgments and Decisions* 1998-VI.

Aksoy v. Turkey
Aksoy *v.* Turkey, Application No. 100/1995/606/694, Judgment, 18 December 1996, *Reports of Judgments and Decisions* 1996-VI.

Al-Saadoon and Mufdhi v. UK
Al-Saadoon and Mufdhi *v.* the United Kingdom, Application No. 61498/08, Judgment, 2 March 2010, *Reports of Judgments and Decisions* 2010.

Al-Skeini and others v. UK
Al-Skeini and others *v.* the United Kingdom, Application No. 55721/07, Judgment, 7 July 2011.

Aydin v. Turkey
Aydin *v.* Turkey, Application No. 57/1996/676/866, Judgment, 25 September 1997, *Reports of Judgments and Decisions* 1997-VI.

Belilos case
Belilos *v.* Switzerland, Application No. 10328/83, Judgment, 29 April 1988, Series A No. 132.

Çakici v. Turkey
Çakici *v.* Turkey, Application No. 23657/94, Judgment, 8 July 1999.

Catan and others v. Moldova and Russia
Catan and others *v.* the Republic of Moldova and Russia, Application Nos. 43370/04, 8252/05 and 18454/06, Grand Chamber, Judgment, 19 October 2012.

Çiraklar v. Turkey
Çiraklar *v.* Turkey, Application No. 70/1997/854/1061, Judgment, 28 October 1998.

Chahal v. UK
Chahal *v.* the United Kingdom, Application No. 70/1995/576/662, Judgment, 15 November 1996.

Chiragov and others v. Armenia
Chiragov and others *v.* Armenia, Application No. 13216/05, Grand Chamber, Judgment, 16 June 2015.

Cyprus v. Turkey
Cyprus *v.* Turkey (Merits), Application No. 25781/94, Judgment, 10 May 2001, *Reports of Judgments and Decisions* 2001-IV.

De Cubber case
De Cubber *v.* Belgium, Application No. 9186/80, Judgment, 26 October 1984, Series A No. 86.

Dougoz v. Greece
Dougoz *v.* Greece (Merits and Just Satisfaction), Application No. 40907/98, Judgment, 6 March 2001.

El Masri v. the former Yugoslav Republic of Macedonia
El-Masri *v.* the former Yugoslav Republic of Macedonia, Application No. 39630/09, Judgment, 13 December, 2012.

Findlay v. UK
Findlay *v.* the United Kingdom, Application No. 110/1995/616/706, Judgment, 25 February 1997, *Reports of Judgments and Decisions* 1997-I.

Hirsi Jamaa and others v. Italy
Hirsi Jamaa and others *v.* Italy, Application No. 27765/09, Judgment, 23 February 2012.

Hüsniye Tekin v. Turkey
Hüsniye Tekin *v.* Turkey, Application No. 50971/99, Judgment, 25 October 2005.

Hurtado v. Switzerland
Hurtado *v.* Switzerland, Application No. 17549/90, Judgment, 28 January 1994.

Ilaşcu and others v. Moldova and Russia
Ilaşcu and others *v.* Moldova and Russia, Application No. 48787/99, Judgment, 8 July 2004.

Incal v. Turkey
Incal *v.* Turkey, Application No. 41/1997/825/1031, Judgment, 9 June 1998.

Iovchev v. Bulgaria
Iovchev *v.* Bulgaria, Application No. 41211/98, Judgment, 2 February 2006.

Ireland v. UK
Ireland *v.* the United Kingdom, Application No. 5310/71, Judgment, 18 January 1978, Series A No. 25.

Jaloud v. The Netherlands
Jaloud *v.* The Netherlands, Application No. 47708/08, Judgment, 20 November 2014.

Koval v. Ukraine
Koval *v.* Ukraine, Application No. 65550/01, Judgment, 19 October 2006.

Loizidou v. Turkey
Loizidou *v.* Turkey (Merits and Just Satisfaction), Application No. 40/1993/435/514, Judgment, 18 December 1996, *Reports of Judgments and Decisions* 1996-VI.

Mehdi Zana v. Turkey
Mehdi Zana *v.* Turkey, Application No. 29851/96, Judgment, 6 March 2001.

Mamatkulov and Askarov v. Turkey
Mamatkulov and Askarov *v.* Turkey, Application Nos. 46827/99 and 46951/99, Judgment, 4 February 2005, *Reports of Judgments and Decisions* 2005-I.

Öcalan v. Turkey
Öcalan *v.* Turkey, Application No. 46221/99, Judgment, 12 May 2005.

Osman v. UK
Osman *v.* the United Kingdom, Application No. 23452/94, Judgment, 28 October 1998.

Piersack v. Belgium
Piersack *v.* Belgium, Application No. 8692/79, Judgment, 1 October 1982, Series A No. 53.

Pishchalnikov v. Russia
Pishchalnikov *v.* Russia, Application No. 7025/04, Judgment, 24 September 2009.

Şahiner v. Turkey
Şahiner *v.* Turkey, Application No. 29279/95, Judgment, 25 September 2001.

Salman v. Turkey
Salman *v.* Turkey (Merits and Just Satisfaction), Application No. 21986/93, Judgment, 27 June 2000.

Selmouni v. France
Selmouni *v.* France, Application No. 25803/94, Judgment, 28 July 1999.

Soering v. UK
Soering *v.* the United Kingdom, Application No. 14038/88, Judgment, 7 July 1989.

Thlimmenos v. Greece
Thlimmenos *v.* Greece, Application No. 34369/97, Judgment, 6 April 2000, *Reports of Judgments and Decisions* 2000-IV.

Yankov v. Bulgaria
Yankov *v.* Bulgaria, Application No. 39084/97, Judgment, 11 December 2003.

Extraordinary Chambers in the Courts of Cambodia (ECCC)

Ieng Sary case
Decision on Ieng Sary's Rule 89 Preliminary Objections (*Ne bis in idem* and Amnesty and Pardon), Case No. 002/19–09–2007/ECCC/TC, Decision, 3 November 2011.

Kaing case
The Prosecutor *v.* Kaing Guek Eav (alias: Duch), Case No. 001/18–07–2007/ECCC/TC, Judgment, 26 July 2010.

Nuon and Khieu case
The Prosecutor *v.* Nuon Chea and Khieu Samphan, Case No. 002/19–09–2007/ECCC/TC, Judgment, 7 August 2014.

Inter-American Commission on Human Rights

Case 7823 (Bolivia)
Bolivia, Case 7823, Juan Antonio Solano, Resolution No. 32/82, 8 March 1982, *Annual Report of the Inter-American Commission on Human Rights 1981–1982*, OAS Doc. OAS/Ser.L/V/II.57 doc. 6 rev. 1, 20 September 1982, p. 42.

Case 10.480 (El Salvador)
El Salvador, Case 10.480, Lucio Parada Cea and others, Report No. 1/99, 27 January 1999, *Annual Report of the Inter-American Commission on Human Rights 1998*, OAS Doc. OEA/Ser.L/V/II.102 doc. 6 rev., 16 April 1999.

Case 10.548 (Peru)
Peru, Case 10.548, Hugo Bustíos Saavedra, Report No. 38/97, 16 October 1997, *Annual Report of the Inter-American Commission on Human Rights 1997*, OAS Doc. OEA/Ser.L/V/II.98 doc. 6 rev., 13 April 1998.

Case 10.970 (Peru)

Peru, Case 10.970, Raquel Martí de Mejía, Report No. 5/96, 1 March 1996, *Annual Report of the Inter-American Commission on Human Rights 1995*, OAS Doc. OEA/Ser.L/V/II.91 doc. 7 rev., 28 February 1996, p. 157.

Case 11.006 (Peru)

Peru, Case 11.006, Alan García, Report No. 1/95, 7 February 1995, *Annual Report of the Inter-American Commission on Human Rights 1994*, OAS Doc. OEA/Ser.L/V.88 doc. 9 rev. 1, 17 February 1995, p. 71.

Case 11.084 (Peru)

Peru, Case 11.084, Jaime Salinas, Report No. 27/94, 30 November 1994, *Annual Report of the Inter-American Commission on Human Rights 1994*, OAS Doc. OEA/Ser.L/V.88 doc. 9 rev.1, 17 February 1995, p. 113.

Case 11.137 (Argentina)

Argentina, Case 11.137, Juan Carlos Abella (aka 'La Tablada case'), Report No. 55/97, 18 November 1997, *Annual Report of the Inter-American Commission on Human Rights 1997*, OAS Doc. OEA/Ser.L/V/II.98 doc. 6 rev., 13 April 1998, p. 271.

Case 11.142 (Colombia)

Colombia, Case 11.142, Arturo Ribón Avilán, Report No. 26/97, 30 September 1997, *Annual Report of the Inter-American Commission on Human Rights 1997*, OAS Doc. OEA/Ser.L/V/II.98 doc. 6 rev., 13 April 1998.

Case 11.520 (Mexico)

Mexico, Case 11.520, Tomás Porfirio Rondin (aka 'Aguas Blancas case'), Report No. 49/97, 18 February 1998, *Annual Report of the Inter-American Commission on Human Rights 1997*, OAS Doc. OEA/Ser.L/V/II.98 doc. 6 rev., 13 April 1998.

Case 11.565 (Mexico)

Mexico, Case 11.565, Ana, Beatriz, and Celia González Pérez *v.* Mexico, Report No. 129/99, 19 November 1999, *Annual Report of the Inter-American Commission on Human Rights 1999*, OAS Doc. OEA/Ser.L/V/II.106 doc. 6 rev., 13 April 2000.

Case 11.710 (Colombia)

Colombia, Case 11.710, Prada González y Bolaño Castro, Report No. 63/01, 6 April 2001, *Annual Report of the Inter-American Commission on Human Rights 2000*, OAS Doc. OEA/Ser.L/V/II.111 doc. 20 rev., 16 April 2001, p. 781.

Inter-American Court of Human Rights

Caesar v. Trinidad and Tobago
> Caesar *v.* Trinidad and Tobago, Merits, Reparations and Costs, Judgment, 11 March 2005, Series C No. 123 (2005).

Castillo Petruzzi and others v. Peru
> Castillo Petruzzi and others *v.* Peru, Merits, Reparations and Costs, Judgment, 30 May 1999, Series C No. 52 (1999).

Judicial Guarantees case
> Judicial Guarantees in States of Emergency (Articles 27(2), 25 and 8 American Convention on Human Rights), Advisory Opinion OC-9/87, 6 October 1987, Series A No. 9 (1987), *Annual Report of the Inter-American Court of Human Rights 1988*, OAS Doc. OEA/Ser.L/V/III.19 doc. 13, 31 August 1988, p. 13.

'Juvenile Reeducation Institute' v. Paraguay
> 'Juvenile Reeducation Institute' *v.* Paraguay, Preliminary Objections, Merits, Reparations and Costs, Judgment, 2 September 2004, Series C No. 112 (2004).

Loayza Tamayo v. Peru
> Loayza Tamayo *v.* Peru, Merits, Judgment, 17 September 1997, Series C No. 33 (1997).

Mapiripán Massacre case
> The 'Mapiripán Massacre' *v.* Colombia, Merits, Reparations and Costs, Judgment, 15 September 2005, Series C No. 134 (2005).

Maritza Urrutia v. Guatemala
> Maritza Urrutia *v.* Guatemala, Merits, Reparations and Costs, Judgment, 27 November 2003, Series C No. 103 (2003).

Pueblo Bello Massacre case
> The Pueblo Bello Massacre *v.* Colombia, Merits, Reparations and Costs, Judgment, 31 January 2006, Series C No. 140 (2006).

Tibi case
> Tibi *v.* Ecuador, Preliminary Objections, Merits, Reparations and Costs, Judgment, 7 September 2004, Series C No. 114 (2004).

Velásquez Rodríguez case
> Velásquez Rodríguez *v.* Honduras, Merits, Judgment, 29 July 1988, Series C No. 4 (1988), *Annual Report of the Inter-American Court of Human Rights 1988*, OAS Doc. OEA/Ser.L/V/III.19 doc. 13, 31 August 1988, p. 35.

Villagrán Morales and others v. Guatemala
Villagrán Morales and others *v.* Guatemala (aka the 'Street Children case'), Merits, Judgment, 19 November 1999, Series C No. 63 (1999).

International Court of Justice (ICJ)

Aegean Sea Continental Shelf case

– Aegean Sea Continental Shelf case (Greece *v.* Turkey), Judgment, 19 December 1978, *ICJ Reports 1978*, p. 3.

Application of the Genocide Convention case

– Preliminary Objections, Judgment
  Case Concerning Application of the Convention on the Prevention and Punishment of the Crime of Genocide (Bosnia and Herzegovina *v.* Yugoslavia (Serbia and Montenegro)), Preliminary Objections, Judgment, 11 July 1996, *ICJ Reports 1996*, p. 595.
– Merits, Judgment
  Case Concerning Application of the Convention on the Prevention and Punishment of the Crime of Genocide (Bosnia and Herzegovina *v.* Serbia and Montenegro), Merits, Judgment, 26 February 2007, *ICJ Reports 2007*, p. 43.

Armed Activities on the Territory of the Congo case
  Case concerning Armed Activities on the Territory of the Congo (Democratic Republic of the Congo *v.* Uganda), Judgment, 19 December 2005, *ICJ Reports 2005*, General List No. 116.

Arrest Warrant case
  Case concerning the Arrest Warrant of 11 April 2000 issued against the Minister for Foreign Affairs of the Democratic Republic of the Congo by a Belgian Court (Democratic Republic of the Congo *v.* Belgium), Judgment, 14 February 2002, *ICJ Reports 2002*, p. 3.

Corfu Channel case
  The Corfu Channel case (United Kingdom *v.* Albania), Merits, Judgment, 9 April 1949, *ICJ Reports 1949*, p. 4.

Fisheries Jurisdiction case
  Fisheries Jurisdiction case (Spain *v.* Canada), Jurisdiction of the Court, Judgment, 4 December 1998, *ICJ Reports 1998*, p. 432.

Interpretation of the Agreement of 25 March 1951 between the WHO and Egypt
  Interpretation of the Agreement of 25 March 1951 between the WHO and Egypt, Advisory Opinion, 20 December 1980, *ICJ Reports 1980*, p. 73.

Jurisdictional Immunities of the State case
>   Jurisdictional Immunities of the State (Germany *v.* Italy: Greece intervening), Judgment, 3 February 2012, *ICJ Reports 2012*, p. 99.

Kasikili/Sedudu Island case
>   Case concerning Kasikili/Sedudu Island (Botswana *v.* Namibia), Judgment, 13 December 1999, *ICJ Reports 1999*, p. 1045.

Legal Consequences of the Construction of a Wall in the Occupied Palestinian Territory
>   Legal Consequences of the Construction of a Wall in the Occupied Palestinian Territory (aka 'Wall case'), Advisory Opinion, 9 July 2004, *ICJ Reports 2004*, p. 136.

Legality of the Threat or Use of Nuclear Weapons
>   Legality of the Threat or Use of Nuclear Weapons (aka 'Nuclear Weapons case'), Advisory Opinion, 8 July 1996, *ICJ Reports 1996*, p. 226.

Legality of the Use by a State of Nuclear Weapons in Armed Conflict (WHO)
>   Legality of the Use by a State of Nuclear Weapons in Armed Conflict, Advisory Opinion, 8 July 1996, *ICJ Reports 1996*, p. 66.

Military and Paramilitary Activities in and against Nicaragua case
>   Case concerning the Military and Paramilitary Activities in and against Nicaragua (Nicaragua *v.* United States of America) (aka 'Nicaragua case'), Merits, Judgment, 27 June 1986, *ICJ Reports 1986*, p. 14.

Morocco case
>   Case concerning rights of nationals of the United States of America in Morocco (France *v.* United States of America), Merits, Judgment, 27 August 1952, *ICJ Reports 1952*, p. 176.

Namibia case
>   Legal Consequences for States of the Continued Presence of South Africa in Namibia (South West Africa) notwithstanding Security Council Resolution 276 (1970), Advisory Opinion, 21 June 1971, *ICJ Reports 1971*, p. 16.

Nuclear Tests case

– Nuclear tests (Australia *v.* France), Judgment, 20 December 1974, *ICJ Reports 1974*, p. 253.
– Nuclear tests (New Zealand *v.* France), Judgment, 20 December 1974, *ICJ Reports 1974*, p. 457.

Obligation to Prosecute or Extradite case
>   Questions relating to the Obligation to Prosecute or Extradite (Belgium *v.* Senegal), Judgment, 20 July 2012, *ICJ Reports 2012*, p. 422.

Reparation for Injuries Suffered in the Service of the United Nations
  Reparation for Injuries Suffered in the Service of the United Nations, Advisory Opinion, 11 April 1949, *ICJ Reports 1949*, p. 174.

Reservations to the Genocide Convention
  Reservations to the Convention on the Prevention and Punishment of the Crime of Genocide, Advisory Opinion, 28 May 1951, *ICJ Reports 1951*, p. 15.

Territorial Dispute case (Libya v. Chad)
  Case concerning the Territorial Dispute (Libyan Arab Jamahiriya v. Chad), Judgment, 3 February 1994, *ICJ Reports 1994*, p. 6.

International Criminal Court (ICC)

Bemba case

– Decision on the Confirmation of Charges
  The Prosecutor *v.* Jean-Pierre Bemba Gombo, Case No. ICC-01/05–01/08, Pre-Trial Chamber II, Decision pursuant to article 61(7)(a) and (b) of the Rome Statute on the Charges of the Prosecutor against Jean-Pierre Bemba Gombo, 15 June 2009.

– Trial Judgment
  The Prosecutor *v.* Jean-Pierre Bemba Gombo, Case No. ICC-01/05–01/08, Trial Chamber III, Judgment Pursuant to Article 74 of the Statute, 21 March 2016.

Gaddafi case
  The Prosecutor *v.* Saif Al-Islam Gaddafi and Abdullah Al-Senussi, Case No. ICC-01/11–01/11 OA 4, Judgment on the appeal of Libya against the decision of the Pre-Trial Chamber of 31 May 2013 on the Admissibility of the Case, 21 May 2014.

Katanga case

– Decision on the Confirmation of Charges
  The Prosecutor *v.* Germain Katanga, Case No. ICC-01/04–01/07, Pre-Trial Chamber I, Decision on the Confirmation of Charges, 26 September 2008.

– Judgment on the Appeal against the Oral Decision on Admissibility
  The Prosecutor *v.* Germain Katanga and Mathieu Ngudjolo Chui, Case No. ICC-01/04–01/07 OA, Judgment on the Appeal of Mr Germain Katanga against the Oral Decision of Trial Chamber II of 12 June 2009 on the Admissibility of the Case, 25 September 2009.

- Trial Judgment
  The Prosecutor *v.* Germain Katanga, Case No. ICC-01/04–01/07, Trial Chamber II, Judgment pursuant to Article 74 of the Rome Statute, 7 March 2014.

Lubanga case

- Decision on the Confirmation of Charges
  The Prosecutor *v.* Thomas Lubanga Dyilo, Case No. ICC-01/04–01/06, Pre-Trial Chamber I, Decision on the Confirmation of Charges, 29 January 2007.
- Trial Judgment
  The Prosecutor *v.* Thomas Lubanga Dyilo, Case No. ICC-01/04–01/06, Judgment pursuant to Article 74 of the Rome Statute, Trial Chamber I, 14 March 2012.

Ntaganda case

  The Prosecutor *v.* Bosco Ntaganda, Case No. ICC-01/04–02/06, Pre-Trial Chamber II, Decision on the Confirmation of Charges (Decision pursuant to Article 61(7)(a) and (b) of the Rome Statute on the Charges of the Prosecutor against Bosco Ntaganda), 9 June 2014.

International Criminal Tribunal for Rwanda (ICTR)

Akayesu case

- Trial Judgment
  The Prosecutor *v.* Jean-Paul Akayesu, Case No. ICTR-96–4-T, Trial Chamber I, Judgment, 2 September 1998.
- Appeal Judgment
  The Prosecutor *v.* Jean-Paul Akayesu, Case No. ICTR-96–4-A, Appeals Chamber, Judgment, 1 June 2001.

Bagilishema case

- Trial Judgment
  The Prosecutor *v.* Ignace Bagilishema, Case No. ICTR-95–1A-T, Trial Chamber I, Judgment, 7 June 2001.
- Appeal Judgment (Reasons)
  The Prosecutor *v.* Ignace Bagilishema, Case No. ICTR-95–1A-A, Appeals Chamber, Judgment (Reasons), 3 July 2002.

Bagosora case

  The Prosecutor *v.* Théoneste Bagosora, Gratien Kabiligi, Aloys Ntabakuze & Anatole Nsengiyumva, Case No. ICTR-98–41-T, Trial Chamber I, Judgment and Sentence, 18 December 2008.

Bisengimana case
   The Prosecutor *v.* Paul Bisengimana, Case No. ICTR-00–60-T, Trial Chamber II, Judgment and Sentence, 13 April 2006.

Gacumbitsi case
   The Prosecutor *v.* Sylvestre Gacumbitsi, Case No. ICTR-01–64-T, Trial Chamber III, Judgment, 17 June 2004.

Kajelijeli case
   The Prosecutor *v.* Juvénal Kajelijeli, Case No. ICTR-98–44A-T, Trial Chamber II, Judgment, 1 December 2003.

Kamuhanda case
   The Prosecutor *v.* Jean de Dieu Kamuhanda, Case No. ICTR-99–54A-T, Trial Chamber II, Judgment, 22 January 2004.

Karemera case
   Edouard Karemera and Mathieu Ngirumpatse *v.* the Prosecutor, Case No. ICTR-98–44-A, Appeals Chamber, Judgment, 29 September 2014.

Kayishema and Ruzindana case
   The Prosecutor *v.* Clément Kayishema and Obed Ruzindana, Case No. ICTR-95–1-T, Trial Chamber II, Judgment, 21 May 1999.

Musema case
   The Prosecutor *v.* Alfred Musema, Case No. ICTR-96–13-T, Trial Chamber I, Judgment and Sentence, 27 January 2000.

Muvunyi case
   The Prosecutor *v.* Tharcisse Muvunyi, Case No. ICTR-2000–55A-T, Trial Chamber II, Judgment and Sentence, 12 September 2006.

Nahimana case

– Trial Judgment
   The Prosecutor *v.* Ferdinand Nahimana, Jean-Bosco Barayagwiza and Hassan Ngeze, Case No. ICTR-99–52-T, Trial Chamber I, Judgment, 3 December 2003.

– Appeal Judgment
   Ferdinand Nahimana, Jean-Bosco Barayagwiza and Hassan Ngeze *v.* the Prosecutor, Case No. ICTR-99–52-A, Appeals Chamber, Judgment, 28 November 2007.

Ndindiliyimana case
   The Prosecutor *v.* Augustin Ndindiliyimana, Augustin Bizimungu, François-Xavier Nzuwonemeye and Innocent Sagahutu, Case No. ICTR-00–56-T, Trial Chamber II, Judgment and Sentence, 17 May 2011.

Niyitegeka case

The Prosecutor *v.* Eliézer Niyitegeka, Case No. ICTR-96–14-T, Trial Chamber I, Judgment and Sentence, 16 May 2003.

Nizeyimana case

The Prosecutor *v.* Ildéphonse Nizeyimana, Case No. ICTR-2000–55C-T, Trial Chamber III, Judgment and Sentence, 19 June 2012.

Ntagerura case

Prosecutor *v.* André Ntagerura and others, Case No. ICTR-99–46-T, Trial Chamber III, Judgment and Sentence, 24 February 2004.

Ntakirutimana case

The Prosecutor *v.* Elizaphan Ntakirutimana and Gérard Ntakirutimana, Case Nos. ICTR-96–10-A & ICTR-96–17-A, Appeals Chamber, Judgment, 13 December 2004.

Nyiramasuhuko case

The Prosecutor *v.* Pauline Nyiramasuhuko, Arsène Shalom Ntahobali, Sylvain Nsabimana, Alphonse Nteziryayo, Joseph Kanyabashi and Élie Ndayambaje, Case No. ICTR-98–42-T, Trial Chamber II, Judgment and Sentence, 24 June 2011.

Renzaho case

The Prosecutor *v.* Tharcisse Renzaho, Case No. ICTR-97–31-T, Trial Chamber I, Judgment and Sentence, 14 July 2009.

Rukundo case

The Prosecutor *v.* Emmanuel Rukundo, Case No. ICTR-2001–70-T, Trial Chamber II, Judgment, 27 February 2009.

Rutaganda case

– Trial Judgment

The Prosecutor *v.* Georges Anderson Nderubumwe Rutaganda, Case No. ICTR-96–3-T,
Trial Chamber I, Judgment, 6 December 1999.
– Appeal Judgment

Georges Anderson Nderubumwe Rutaganda *v.* the Prosecutor, Case No. ICTR-96–3-A, Appeals Chamber, Judgment, 26 May 2003.

Rutaganira case

The Prosecutor *v.* Vincent Rutaganira, Case No. ICTR-95–1C-T, Trial Chamber III, Judgment and Sentence, 14 March 2005.

Setako case

Ephrem Setako *v.* the Prosecutor, Case No. ICTR-04–81-A, Appeals Chamber, Judgment, 28 September 2011.

Zigiranyirazo case

> The Prosecutor *v.* Protais Zigiranyirazo, Case No. ICTR-01–73-T, Trial Chamber III, Judgment, 18 December 2008.

International Criminal Tribunal for the Former Yugoslavia (ICTY)

Aleksovski case

– Trial Judgment

> The Prosecutor *v.* Zlatko Aleksovski, Case No. IT-95–14/1-T, Trial Chamber I, Judgment, 25 June 1999.

– Appeal Judgment

> The Prosecutor *v.* Zlatko Aleksovski, Case No. IT-95–14/1-A, Appeals Chamber, Judgment, 24 March 2000.

Blagojević and Jokić case

> The Prosecutor *v.* Vidoje Blagojević and Dragan Jokić, Case No. IT-02–60-T, Trial Chamber I, Section A, Judgment, 17 January 2005.

Blaškić case

– Decision on Defence Motion

> The Prosecutor *v.* Tihomir Blaškić, Case No. IT-95–14-PT, Decision on the Defence Motion to Strike Portions of the Amended Indictment Alleging 'Failure to Punish' Liability, Trial Chamber, 4 April 1997.

– Decision on the Issuance of the *Subpoena Duces Tecum*

> The Prosecutor *v.* Tihomir Blaškić, Case No. IT-95–14, Appeals Chamber, Judgment on the Request of the Republic of Croatia for Review of the Decision of Trial Chamber II of 18 July 1997, 29 October 1997.

– Trial Judgment

> The Prosecutor *v.* Tihomir Blaškić, Case No. IT-95–14-T, Trial Chamber I, Judgment, 3 March 2000.

– Appeal Judgment

> The Prosecutor *v.* Tihomir Blaškić, Case No. IT-95–14-A, Appeals Chamber, Judgment, 29 July 2004.

Boškoski and Tarčulovski case

> The Prosecutor *v.* Ljube Boškoski and Johan Tarčulovski, Case No. IT-04–82-T, Trial Chamber II, Judgment, 10 July 2008.

Brđanin case

– Trial Judgment

> The Prosecutor *v.* Radoslav Brđanin, Case No. IT-99–36-T, Trial Chamber II, Judgment, 1 September 2004.

– Appeal Judgment

    The Prosecutor *v.* Radoslav Brđanin, Case No. IT-99–36-A, Appeals Chamber, Judgment, 3 April 2007.

Delalić case

– Trial Judgment

    The Prosecutor *v.* Zejnil Delalić, Zdravko Mucić (aka 'Pavo'), Hazim Delić and Esad Landžo (aka 'Zenga'), Case No. IT-96–21-T, Trial Chamber II, Judgment, 16 November 1998.

– Appeal Judgment

    The Prosecutor *v.* Zejnil Delalić, Zdravko Mucić (aka 'Pavo'), Hazim Delić and Esad Landžo (aka 'Zenga'), Case No. IT-96–21-A, Appeals Chamber, Judgment, 20 February 2001.

Delić case

    The Prosecutor *v.* Rasim Delić, Case No. IT-04–83-T, Trial Chamber I, Judgment, 15 September 2008.

Đorđević case

    The Prosecutor *v.* Vlastimir Đorđević, Case No. IT-05–87/1-T, Trial Chamber II, Judgment, 23 February 2011.

Dragomir Milošević case

    Prosecutor *v.* Dragomir Milošević, Case No. IT-98–29/1-A, Appeals Chamber, Judgment, 12 November 2009.

Erdemović case

    The Prosecutor *v.* Dražen Erdemović, Case No. IT-96–22-A, Appeals Chamber, Judgment, 7 October 1997.

Furundžija case

– Trial Judgment

    The Prosecutor *v.* Anto Furundžija, Case No. IT-95–17/1-T, Trial Chamber II, Judgment, 10 December 1998.

– Appeal Judgment

    The Prosecutor *v.* Anto Furundžija, Case No. IT-95–17/1-A, Appeals Chamber, Judgment, 21 July 2000.

Galić case

– Trial Judgment

    The Prosecutor *v.* Stanislav Galić, Case No. IT-98–29-T, Trial Chamber I, Judgment, 5 December 2003.

– Appeal Judgment

    The Prosecutor *v.* Stanislav Galić, Case No. 98–29-A, Appeals Chamber, Judgment, 30 November 2006.

Gotovina case

The Prosecutor *v.* Ante Gotovina, Ivan Čermak and Mladen Markač, Case No. IT-06–90-T, Trial Chamber I, Judgment, 15 April 2011.

Hadžihasanović case

– Decision on Interlocutory Appeal Challenging Jurisdiction in Relation to Command Responsibility

The Prosecutor *v.* Enver Hadžihasanović, Mehmed Alagić and Amir Kubura, Case No. IT-01–47-AR72, Appeals Chamber, Decision on Interlocutory Appeal Challenging Jurisdiction in Relation to Command Responsibility, 16 July 2003.

– Trial Judgment

The Prosecutor *v.* Enver Hadžihasanović and Amir Kubura, Case No. IT-01–47-T, Trial Chamber II, Judgment, 15 March 2006.

Halilović case

Prosecutor *v.* Sefer Halilović, Case No. IT-01–48-T, Trial Chamber I, Section A, Judgment, 16 November 2005.

Haradinaj case

– Trial Judgment

The Prosecutor *v.* Ramush Haradinaj, Idriz Balaj and Lahi Brahimaj, Case No. IT-04–84-T, Trial Chamber I, Judgment, 3 April 2008.

– Retrial Judgment

The Prosecutor *v.* Ramush Haradinaj, Idriz Balaj and Lahi Brahimaj, Case No. IT-04–84*bis*-T, Trial Chamber II, Judgment, 29 November 2012.

Jelisić case

The Prosecutor *v.* Goran Jelisić, Case No. IT-95–10-T, Trial Chamber I, Judgment, 14 December 1999.

Kordić and Čerkez case

– Trial Judgment

The Prosecutor *v.* Dario Kordić and Mario Čerkez, Case No. IT-95–14/2-T, Trial Chamber III, Judgment, 26 February 2001.

– Appeal Judgment

The Prosecutor *v.* Dario Kordić and Mario Čerkez, Case No. IT-95–14/2-A, Appeals Chamber, Judgment, 17 December 2004.

Krajišnik case

The Prosecutor *v.* Momčilo Krajišnik, Case No. IT-00–39-T, Trial Chamber I, Judgment, 27 September 2006.

Krnojelac case

– Trial Judgment

The Prosecutor *v.* Milorad Krnojelac, Case No. IT-97–25 T, Trial Chamber II, Judgment, 15 March 2002.

– Appeal Judgment

The Prosecutor *v.* Milorad Krnojelac, Case No. IT-97–25-A, Appeals Chamber, Judgment, 17 September 2003.

Krstić case

The Prosecutor *v.* Radislav Krstić, Case No. IT-98–33-T, Trial Chamber I, Judgment, 2 August 2001.

Kunarac case

– Trial Judgment

The Prosecutor *v.* Dragoljub Kunarac, Radomir Kovač and Zoran Vuković, Case Nos. IT-96–23-T and IT-96–23/1-T, Trial Chamber II, Judgment, 22 February 2001.

– Appeal Judgment

The Prosecutor *v.* Dragoljub Kunarac, Radomir Kovač and Zoran Vuković, Case Nos. IT-96–23 and IT-96–23/1-A, Appeals Chamber, Judgment, 12 June 2002.

Kupreškić case

The Prosecutor *v.* Zoran Kupreškić, Mirjan Kupreškić, Vlatko Kupreškić, Drago Josipović, Dragan Papić and Vladimir Šantić (aka 'Vlado'), Case No. IT-95–16-T, Trial Chamber II, Judgment, 14 January 2000.

Kvočka case

– Trial Judgment

The Prosecutor *v.* Miroslav Kvočka, Milojica Kos, Mlado Radić, Zoran Žigić and Dragoljub Prcać, Case No. IT-98–30/1-T, Trial Chamber I, Judgment, 2 November 2001.

– Appeal Judgment

The Prosecutor *v.* Miroslav Kvočka, Mlado Radić, Zoran Žigić and Dragoljub Prcać, Case No. IT-98–30/1-A, Appeals Chamber, Judgment, 28 February 2005.

Limaj case

The Prosecutor *v.* Fatmir Limaj, Haradin Bala and Isak Musliu, Case No. IT-03–66-T, Trial Chamber II, Judgment, 30 November 2005.

Lukić and Lukić case

– Trial Judgment

The Prosecutor *v.* Milan Lukić and Sredoje Lukić, Case No. IT-98–32/1-T, Trial Chamber III, Judgment, 20 July 2009.

– Appeal Judgment
  The Prosecutor *v.* Milan Lukić and Sredoje Lukić, Case No. IT-98–32/1-A, Appeals Chamber, Judgment, 4 December 2012.

Martić case

– Rule 61 Decision
  The Prosecutor *v.* Milan Martić, Case No. IT-95–11-R61, Trial Chamber I, Decision, 8 March 1996.
– Trial Judgment
  The Prosecutor *v.* Milan Martić, Case No. IT-95–11-T, Trial Chamber I, Judgment, 12 June 2007.

Milutinović case

  The Prosecutor *v.* Milan Milutinović, Nikola Šainović, Dragoljub Ojdanić, Nebojša Pavković, Vladimir Lazarević and Sreten Lukić, Case No. IT-05–87-T, Vol. 1, Trial Chamber, Judgment, 26 February 2009.

Mrđa case

  The Prosecutor *v.* Darko Mrđa, Case No. IT-02–59-S, Trial Chamber I, Sentencing Judgment, 31 March 2004.

Mrkšić case

– Trial Judgment
  The Prosecutor *v.* Mile Mrkšić, Miroslav Radić and Veselin Šljivančanin, Case No. IT-95–13/1-T, Trial Chamber II, Judgment, 27 September 2007.
– Appeal Judgment
  The Prosecutor *v.* Mile Mrkšić and Veselin Šljivančanin, Case No. IT-95–13/1-A, Appeals Chamber, Judgment, 5 May 2009.

Mucić case

– Trial Judgment
  The Prosecutor *v.* Zejnil Delalić, Zdravko Mucić (aka 'Pavo'), Hazim Delić and Esad Landžo (aka 'Zenga'), Case No. IT-96–21-T, Trial Chamber II, Judgment, 16 November 1998.
– Appeal Judgment
  The Prosecutor *v.* Zejnil Delalić, Zdravko Mucić (aka 'Pavo'), Hazim Delić and Esad Landžo (aka 'Zenga'), Case No. IT-96–21-A, Appeals Chamber, Judgment, 20 February 2001.

Naletilić and Martinović case

– Trial Judgment
  The Prosecutor *v.* Mladen Naletilić (aka 'Tuta') and Vinko Martinović (aka 'Stela'), Case No. IT-98–34-T, Trial Chamber, Judgment, 31 March 2003.

- Appeal Judgment

  The Prosecutor *v.* Mladen Naletilić (aka 'Tuta') and Vinko Martinović (aka 'Stela'), Case No. IT-98–34-A, Appeals Chamber, Judgement, 3 May 2006.

Orić case

The Prosecutor *v.* Naser Orić, Case No. IT-03–68-T, Trial Chamber II, Judgment, 30 June 2006.

Perišić case

- Trial Judgment

  The Prosecutor *v.* Momčilo Perišić, Case No. IT-04–81-T, Trial Chamber I, Judgment, 6 September 2011.

- Appeal Judgment

  The Prosecutor *v.* Momčilo Perišić, Case No. IT-04–81-A, Appeals Chamber, Judgment, 28 February 2013.

Popović case

The Prosecutor *v.* Vujadin Popović, Ljubiša Beara, Drago Nikolić, Ljubomir Borovčanin, Radivoje Miletić, Milan Gvero and Vinko Pandurević, Case No. IT-05–88-T, Trial Chamber II, Judgment, 10 June 2010.

Prlić case

The Prosecutor *v.* Jadranko Prlić, Bruno Stojić, Slobodan Praljak, Milivoj Petković, Valentin Ćorić and Berislav Pušić, Case No. IT-04–74-T, Trial Chamber III, Judgment, 29 May 2013.

Šešelj case

The Prosecutor *v.* Vojislav Šešelj, Case No. IT-03–67, Second Amended Indictment, 25 June 2007.

Stanišić and Simatović case

The Prosecutor *v.* Jovica Stanišić and Franko Simatović, Case No. IT-03–69-T, Trial Chamber I, Judgment, 30 May 2013.

Simić case

The Prosecutor *v.* Blagoje Simić, Miroslav Tadić and Simo Zarić, Case No. IT-95–9-T, Trial Chamber II, Judgment, 17 October 2003.

Slobodan Milošević case

The Prosecutor *v.* Slobodan Milošević, Case No. IT-02–54-T, Trial Chamber, Decision on Motion for Judgment of Acquittal, 16 June 2004.

Stakić case

- Trial Judgment

  The Prosecutor *v.* Milomir Stakić, Case No. IT-97–24, Trial Chamber II, Judgment, 31 July 2003.

– Appeal Judgment
   The Prosecutor *v.* Milomir Stakić, Case No. IT-97–24-A, Appeals Chamber, Judgment, 22 March 2006.

Stanišić and Župljanin case
   Prosecutor *v.* Mićo Stanišić & Stojan Župljanin, Case No. IT-08–91-T, Trial Chamber II, Judgment, 27 March 2013.

Strugar case
   The Prosecutor *v.* Pavle Strugar, Case No. IT-01–42-T, Trial Chamber II, Judgment, 31 January 2005.

Tadić case

– Decision on the Defence Motion on Jurisdiction
   The Prosecutor *v.* Duško Tadić (aka 'Dule'), Case No. IT-94–1-T, Trial Chamber, Decision on the Defence Motion on Jurisdiction, 10 August 1995.
– Decision on the Defence Motion for Interlocutory Appeal on Jurisdiction
   The Prosecutor *v.* Duško Tadić (aka 'Dule'), Case No. IT-94–1-AR72, Appeals Chamber, Decision on the Defence Motion for Interlocutory Appeal on Jurisdiction, 2 October 1995.
– Trial Judgment
   The Prosecutor *v.* Duško Tadić (aka 'Dule'), Case No. IT-94–1-T, Trial Chamber II, Judgment, 7 May 1997.
– Appeal Judgment
   The Prosecutor *v.* Duško Tadić (aka 'Dule'), Case No. IT-94–1-A, Appeals Chamber, Judgment, 15 July 1999.

Tolimir case
   The Prosecutor *v.* Zdravko Tolimir, Case No. IT-05–88/2-T, Trial Chamber II, Judgment, 12 December 2012.

Vasiljević case

– Trial Judgment
   The Prosecutor *v.* Mitar Vasiljević, Case No. IT-98–32-T, Trial Chamber II, Judgment, 29 November 2002.
– Appeal Judgment
   The Prosecutor *v.* Mitar Vasiljević, Case No. IT-98–32-A, Appeals Chamber, Judgment, 25 February 2004.

International Military Tribunal for Germany

Case of the Major War Criminals
   Trial of the Major War Criminals before the International Military Tribunal, Nuremberg, Judgment, 1 October 1946, *Official Documents*, Vol. I,

pp. 171–341, reprinted in *American Journal of International Law*, Vol. 41, 1947, pp. 172–331.

International Military Tribunal for the Far East

Case of the Major War Criminals
Trial of the Major War Criminals before the International Military Tribunal, Tokyo, Judgment, 4–12 November 1948, reprinted in *International Law Documents, 1948–1949*, International Law Studies, U.S. Naval War College, Vol. 46, 1950, pp. 76–106.

Permanent Court of International Justice (PCIJ)

Lotus case
The case of the S.S. 'Lotus' (France v. Turkey), Judgment, 7 September 1927, *Collection of Judgments*, Series A., No. 10.

Special Court for Sierra Leone (SCSL)

Brima case

– Trial Judgment
The Prosecutor v. Alex Tamba Brima, Brima Bazzy Kamara and Santigie Borbor Kanu, Case No. SCSL-04–16-T, Trial Chamber II, Judgment, 20 June 2007.
– Appeal Judgment
The Prosecutor v. Alex Tamba Brima, Brima Bazzy Kamara and Santigie Borbor Kanu, Case No. SCSL-2004–16-A, Appeals Chamber, Judgment, 22 February 2008.

Fofana and Kondewa case
The Prosecutor v. Moinina Fofana and Allieu Kondewa, Case No. SCSL-04–14-T, Trial Chamber I, Judgment, 2 August 2007.

Kallon and Kamara case
The Prosecutor v. Morris Kallon and Brima Bazzy Kamara, Case No. SCSL-2004–15-AR72(E), Appeals Chamber, Decision on Challenge to Jurisdiction: Lomé Accord Amnesty, 13 March 2004.

Koroma case
The Prosecutor v. Johnny Paul Koroma (aka 'JPK'), Case No. SCSL-03-I, Indictment, 3 March 2003.

Sesay case

– Corrected Amended Consolidated Indictment
The Prosecutor v. Issa Hassan Sesay (aka 'Issa Sesay'), Morris Kallon (aka 'Bilai Karim') and Augustine Gbao (aka 'Augustine Bao'), Case

No. SCSL-04–15-PT, Corrected Amended Consolidated Indictment, 2 August 2006.

– Trial Judgment

The Prosecutor *v.* Issa Hassan Sesay (aka 'Issa Sesay'), Morris Kallon (aka 'Bilai Karim') and Augustine Gbao (aka 'Augustine Bao'), Case No. SCSL-04–15-T, Trial Chamber I, Judgment, 2 March 2009.

– Appeal Judgment

The Prosecutor *v.* Issa Hassan Sesay (aka 'Issa Sesay'), Morris Kallon (aka 'Bilai Karim') and Augustine Gbao (aka 'Augustine Bao'), Case No. SCSL-04–15-A, Appeals Chamber, Judgment, 26 October 2009.

Taylor case

The Prosecutor *v.* Charles Ghankay Taylor (aka 'Dankpannah Charles Ghankay Taylor', aka 'Dankpannah Charles Ghankay Macarthur Taylor'), Case No. SCSL-03–01-T, Trial Chamber II, Judgment, 18 May 2012.

UN Committee against Torture

Danilo Dimitrijević v. Serbia and Montenegro

Danilo Dimitrijević *v.* Serbia and Montenegro, Communication No. 172/2000, Decisions of the Committee against Torture under article 22 of the Convention against Torture and Other Cruel, Inhuman or Degrading Treatment or Punishment, adopted on 16 November 2005, UN Doc. CAT/C/35/D/172/2000, 29 November 2005.

T.A. v. Sweden

T.A. *v.* Sweden, Communication No. 226/2003, Decisions of the Committee against Torture under article 22 of the Convention against Torture and Other Cruel, Inhuman or Degrading Treatment or Punishment, adopted on 6 May 2005, UN Doc. CAT/C/34/D/226/2003, 27 May 2005.

UN Human Rights Committee

Bahamonde v. Equatorial Guinea

Angel N. Oló Bahamonde *v.* Equatorial Guinea, Communication No. 468/1991, Views under Article 5(4) of the Optional Protocol to the International Covenant on Civil and Political Rights, adopted on 20 October 1993, reproduced in *Annual Report of the Human Rights Committee to the UN General Assembly*, UN Doc. CCPR/C/49/D/468/1991 (1993).

Eduardo Bleier v. Uruguay

Eduardo Bleier *v.* Uruguay, Communication No. R.7/30, Views under Article 5(4) of the Optional Protocol to the International Covenant on Civil and Political Rights, adopted on 24 March 1980, UN Doc. Supp. No. 40 (A/37/40) (1982), p. 130.

Espinoza de Polay v. Peru

Rosa Espinoza de Polay (on behalf of her husband Victor Alfredo Polay Campos) *v.* Peru, Communication No. 577/1994, Views under Article 5(4) of the Optional Protocol to the International Covenant on Civil and Political Rights, adopted on 6 November 1997, UN Doc. CCPR/C/61/D/577/1994 (1998).

Karttunen v. Finland

Arvo O. Karttunen *v.* Finland, Communication No. 387/1989, Views under Article 5(4) of the Optional Protocol to the International Covenant on Civil and Political Rights, adopted on 23 October 1992, UN Doc. CCPR/C/46/D/387/1989 (1992).

Osbourne v. Jamaica

George Osbourne *v.* Jamaica, Communication No. 759/1997, Views of the Human Rights Committee under Article 5(4) of the Optional Protocol to the International Covenant on Civil and Political Rights, adopted on 13 April 2000, UN Doc. CCPR/C/68/D/759/1997 (2000).

Rodríguez v. Uruguay

Rodríguez *v.* Uruguay, Communication No. 322/1988, Views under Article 5(4) of the Optional Protocol to the International Covenant on Civil and Political Rights, adopted on 19 July 1994, UN Doc. CCPR/C/51/D/322/1988 (1994).

Torres Ramírez v. Uruguay

William Torres Ramírez *v.* Uruguay, Communication No. 4/1977, Views under Article 5(4) of the Optional Protocol to the International Covenant on Civil and Political Rights, adopted on 23 July 1980, UN Doc. A/35/40 (1980), p. 121.

Tshitenge Muteba v. Zaire

Tshitenge Muteba *v.* Zaire, Communication No. 124/1982, Views under Article 5(4) of the Optional Protocol to the International Covenant on Civil and Political Rights, adopted on 24 July 1984, UN Doc. A/39/40 (1984), p. 182.

Yin Fong v. Australia

Kwok Yin Fong *v.* Australia, Communication No. 1442/2005, Views under Article 5(4) of the Optional Protocol to the International Covenant on Civil and Political Rights, adopted on 23 October 2009, UN Doc. CCPR/C/97/D/1442/2005 (2009).

VIII. Commentaries on the Geneva Conventions and their Additional Protocols published by the ICRC

Des Gouttes, Commentaire de la Convention de Genève de 1929 sur les blessés et malades, ICRC, 1930
Paul Des Gouttes, La Convention de Genève pour l'amélioration du sort des blessés et des malades dans les armées en campagne du 27 juillet 1929: Commentaire, ICRC, Geneva, 1930.

Pictet (ed.), Commentary on the First Geneva Convention, ICRC, 1952
Jean S. Pictet (ed.), The Geneva Conventions of 12 August 1949: Commentary, Vol. I: Geneva Convention for the Amelioration of the Condition of the Wounded and Sick in Armed Forces in the Field, ICRC, Geneva, 1952.

Pictet (ed.), Commentary on the Second Geneva Convention, ICRC, 1960
Jean S. Pictet (ed.), The Geneva Conventions of 12 August 1949: Commentary, Vol. II: Geneva Convention for the Amelioration of the Condition of Wounded, Sick and Shipwrecked Members of Armed Forces at Sea, ICRC, Geneva, 1960.

Pictet (ed.), Commentary on the Third Geneva Convention, ICRC, 1960
Jean S. Pictet (ed.), The Geneva Conventions of 12 August 1949: Commentary, Vol. III: Geneva Convention relative to the Treatment of Prisoners of War, ICRC, Geneva, 1960.

Pictet (ed.), Commentary on the Fourth Geneva Convention, ICRC, 1958
Jean S. Pictet (ed.), The Geneva Conventions of 12 August 1949: Commentary, Vol. IV: Geneva Convention relative to the Protection of Civilian Persons in Time of War, ICRC, Geneva, 1958.

Sandoz/Swinarski/Zimmermann (eds), Commentary on the Additional Protocols, ICRC, 1987
Yves Sandoz, Christophe Swinarski and Bruno Zimmermann (eds), Commentary on the Additional Protocols of 8 June 1977 to the Geneva Conventions of 12 August 1949, ICRC/Martinus Nijhoff Publishers, Geneva, 1987.

INDEX[1]

Notes

Except where otherwise indicated 'Conventions' refers to the Geneva Conventions and 'Protocols' to the Additional Protocols to the Geneva Conventions

Locators are usually paragraph numbers. On occasion, where there are no relevant paragraph numbers, emboldened page numbers are used, sorted to the beginning of the list.

Abbreviations used in the index

AP I (Additional Protocol relating to international armed conflicts (1977))
AP II (Additional Protocol relating to non-international armed conflicts (1977))
AP III (Additional Protocol III relating to the adoption of an additional distinctive emblem (2005))
CAT (Convention against Torture (1984))
Chicago Convention (Chicago Convention on International Civil Aviation (1944))
CRPD (Convention on the Rights of Persons with Disabilities (2006))
ECHR (European Convention on Human Rights (1950))
Emblem Regulations (Regulations concerning identification as amended 30 November 1993 (AP I, Annex I))
Fundamental Principles (Fundamental Principles of the International Red Cross and Red Crescent Movement, incorporated in the preamble of the ICRC Statute)
GC (Geneva Convention)
HC V (1907) (Hague Convention V (Rights and Duties of Neutral Powers) (1907))
HC X (1907) (Hague Convention on the Laws and Customs of War on Land)
HR (Hague Regulations (1907))
HRC (UN Human Rights Committee)
ICANN (Internet Corporation for Assigned Names and Numbers)
ICC (International Criminal Court/ICC Statute)
ICRC (International Committee of the Red Cross)
ICRC Statutes (Statutes of the Movement/ICRC Statutes)
ICTR (International Criminal Tribunal for Rwanda/ICTR Statute)
ICTY (International Criminal Tribunal for the Former Yugoslavia/ICTY Statute)
IHFFC (International Humanitarian Fact-Finding Commission)
IHL (international humanitarian law)
ILC (ILC Articles on State Responsibility (2001))
The Movement (International Red Cross and Red Crescent Movement)
National Societies (National Red Cross and Red Crescent Societies)
R2P (responsibility to protect)
SCSL (Special Court for Sierra Leone/SCSL Statute)

---

[1] This index was prepared by Cambridge University Press.